THE ROUTLEDGE HANDBOOK
OF TERRORISM RESEARCH

This major new Handbook synthesizes more than two decades of scholarly research, and provides a comprehensive overview of the field of terrorism studies.

The content of the Handbook is based on the responses to a questionnaire by nearly 100 experts from more than 20 countries as well as the specific expertise and experience of the volume editor and the various contributors. Together, they guide the reader through the voluminous literature on terrorism and propose a new consensus definition of the term, based on an extensive review of existing conceptualizations. The work also features a large collection of typologies and surveys a wide range of theories of terrorism. Additional chapters survey terrorist databases and provide a guide to available resources on terrorism in libraries and on the internet. The Handbook also includes the most comprehensive world directory of extremist, terrorist and other organizations associated with guerrilla warfare, political violence, protest, organized crime and cyber-crime.

The Routledge Handbook of Terrorism Research will be an essential work of reference for students and researchers of terrorism and political violence, security studies, criminology, political science and international relations, and of great interest to policy makers and professionals in the field of counter-terrorism.

Alex P. Schmid is Director of the Terrorism Research Initiative (TRI), an international network of scholars who seek to enhance human security through collaborative research; he is also Editor of TRI's online journal *Perspectives on Terrorism*. Until 2009, he was Director of the Centre for the Study of Terrorism and Political Violence (CSTPV) at the University of St Andrews, UK, where he held a chair in International Relations and, until 2005, Officer-in-Charge of the Terrorism Prevention Branch at the UN Office on Drugs and Crime (UNODC) in Vienna. Currently he is Fellow-in-Residence at the Netherlands Institute for Advanced Study in the Humanities and Social Sciences (NIAS).

THE ROUTLEDGE
HANDBOOK OF
TERRORISM RESEARCH

Edited by Alex P. Schmid

Routledge
Taylor & Francis Group

LONDON AND NEW YORK

First published in paperback 2013

First published 2011
by Routledge
2 Park Square, Milton Park, Abingdon, Oxon, OX14 4RN

Simultaneously published in the USA and Canada
by Routledge
711 Third Avenue, New York, NY 10017

Routledge is an imprint of the Taylor & Francis Group, an informa business

Typeset in Bembo
by Keystroke, Station Road, Codsall, Wolverhampton

British Library Cataloguing in Publication Data
A catalogue record for this book is available from the British Library

Library of Congress Cataloging-in-Publication Data
The Routledge handbook of terrorism research / edited by Alex P. Schmid.
    p. cm.
    Includes bibliographical references.
    1. Terrorism.   2. Terrorism—Research.   I. Schmid, Alex Peter.   II. Title: Handbook of terrorism research.
HV6431.R685 2011
363.325—dc22   2010039024

ISBN13: 978-0-415-41157-8 (hbk)
ISBN13: 978-0-415-52099-7 (pbk)
ISBN13: 978-0-203-82873-1 (ebk)

MIX
Paper from
responsible sources
FSC
www.fsc.org   FSC® C013604

Printed and bound by CPI Group (UK) Ltd, Croydon, CR0 4YY

FOR SHANTU

CONTENTS

FIGURES

TABLES

ABOUT THE AUTHORS

Alex P. Schmid is Director of the Terrorism Research Initiative (TRI), an international network of scholars who seek to enhance human security through collaborative research; he is also Editor of TRI's online journal *Perspectives on Terrorism*. Until 2009, he was Director of the Centre for the Study of Terrorism and Political Violence (CSTPV) and held a chair in International Relations at the University of St Andrews. Between 1999 and 2005, he was Officer-in-Charge of the Terrorism Prevention Branch of the United Nations, where he held the position of Senior Crime Prevention and Criminal Justice Officer at the United Nations Office on Drugs and Crime (UNODC) in Vienna. Before joining the United Nations, Dr. Schmid held the Synthesis Chair on Conflict Resolution at the Erasmus University in Rotterdam. Between 1988 and 1999 he served as Research Coordinator of the Interdisciplinary Research Programme on Causes of Human Rights Violations (PIOOM) at Leiden University, the Netherlands. Earlier in his career, Professor Schmid was an Einstein Fellow at the Center for International Affairs, Harvard University. In the 1990s, he also served as an elected member on the Executive Board of the International Scientific and Professional Advisory Council (ISPAC) of the United Nations Crime Prevention and Criminal Justice Program. Alex Schmid became a Member of the Royal Netherlands Academy of Arts and Sciences in 2004 and an Advisor to Europol's TE-SAT in 2010. He has authored and edited more than 150 reports and publications, including the award-winning *Political Terrorism*, last reissued in 2005. Currently, he is coordinating a research project on 'Terrorists on Trial' at the Netherlands Institute for Advanced Studies in the Humanities and Social Sciences (NIAS).

Neil G. Bowie holds an MA (Hons) in Politics and International Relations from the University of Aberdeen, a postgraduate diploma in Systems Analysis and Design from Edinburgh Napier University (1987–1988) and a PGCE from the University of Strathclyde. For 20 years, he lectured in Computer Science in further education, in Edinburgh. Currently he is a doctoral candidate within the Centre for the Study of Terrorism and Political Violence, School of International Relations, at the University of St Andrews. His particular interest centres on the use of database technologies in the field of terrorism research.

Gillian Duncan has worked at the Centre for the Study of Terrorism and Political Violence (CSTPV) at the University of St Andrews since 2002. Before that, she was Project Administrator for a DFID (Department for International Development)-sponsored project on International Water Law at the University of Dundee and was part of the Economic Development, Arts and Tourism Department of Belfast City Council, where she assisted in the formation of the Belfast Economic

Development Strategy from 1992 to 1999. Ms Duncan is a Member of the Institute of Administrative Management and a Member of the Association of University Administrators. She also acts as secretary to the journal *Terrorism and Political Violence*.

Joseph J. Easson has been the Data Manager of the Centre for the Study of Terrorism and Political Violence (CSTPV) at the University of St Andrews since September 2006. After completing an MA General (Hons) in Classics and History at the University of Edinburgh, he completed a Postgraduate Diploma in Information Systems at Edinburgh Napier University. Prior to his present position, he was the Registry Manager at Edinburgh College of Art and before that an Application Developer in the commercial sector. His primary responsibility at the CSPTV is the systematization of the electronic resources held within the CSTPV and developing its e-learning platform.

Benjamin J.E. Freedman is Editorial Assistant of *Perspectives on Terrorism*. He served as a Research Intern for the Stein Program on Counter-terrorism and Intelligence at the Washington Institute for Near East Policy and as a Consular Intern for the US Department of State in Marseille, France. He graduated *magna cum laude* from Bowdoin College with a degree in government and legal studies, focusing on comparative and Middle East politics.

Donald Holbrook holds a BA in Political Science (with Distinction) from the University of Iceland, an MPhil in International Relations from the University of Cambridge, and an MLitt (with Distinction) in International Security Studies from the University of St Andrews. Prior to his postgraduate studies, he worked as Research Assistant at the University of Iceland, analysing European Union Treaty Reform and the position of small states within the European Union – a topic on which he has also co-authored papers. He was appointed Research Fellow at the Centre for the Study of Terrorism and Political Violence, University of St Andrews, in October 2008, investigating extremist Islamist ideologies and the linkage with UK national security concerns, and has written reports and presentations on this topic. He is also a PhD candidate at the University of St Andrews, focusing on the communication strategy of Al-Qaeda's leadership.

Albert J. Jongman has worked since February 2002 as an analyst with the Ministry of Defense of the Netherlands. He studied at the University of Groningen (the Netherlands) and at Stockholm University (Sweden). He holds a Master's degree in Western Sociology. He specialized in War and Peace Studies and from 1981 to 1987 worked at the Polemological Institute of Groningen University, before joining the Center for the Study of Social Conflicts (COMT) at Leiden University, where he worked from 1988 to 2001. During this period, he was Data Manager of the Project on Interdisciplinary Research on the Root Causes of Gross Human Rights Violations (PIOOM) and participated in several projects, including the World Conflict and Human Rights Map. He has published and lectured on war, political violence and terrorism. His publications include *Contemporary Genocides: Causes, Cases, Consequences* (Leiden: PIOOM, 1996). In his current position, he participates in several Advanced Research Working Groups of NATO and in several activities of the Dutch National Coordinator for Counterterrorism.

Brynjar Lia is a historian and Research Professor at the Norwegian Defence Research Establishment (FFI) where he heads its research programme on international terrorism and global jihadism. He was a Visiting Fulbright Scholar at Harvard. He has authored highly acclaimed works such as a biography of the Al-Qaeda strategist Abu Musab al-Suri (Columbia University Press, 2008) and *Globalisation and the Future of Terrorism: Patterns and Predictions* (Routledge, 2005).

Bradley McAllister is a Lecturer at the University of Georgia's School of Public and International Affairs. Until 2009, he was a Research Fellow with the Centre for the Study of Terrorism and

Political Violence (CSTPV) at the University of St Andrews, where he specialized in the study of the internal organizing dynamics of terrorist networks. Prior to taking a position with the CSTPV, he worked for the Center for International Trade and Security of the University of Georgia as a Research Fellow, looking at the nexus between terrorism and proliferation issues. He has published numerous peer-reviewed articles on the subject of terrorism – specifically, terrorist networks and the role of non-proliferation in broader counter-terror strategies. He holds an MA in Conflict, Development and Security from the University of Leeds and is completing his doctoral degree in Political Science at the University of Georgia's School of Public and International Affairs. He also serves as Assistant Editor of *Perspectives on Terrorism*.

Sarah V. Marsden is currently a Research Assistant at the University of St Andrews' Centre for the Study of Terrorism and Political Violence (CSTPV). For her PhD, she is developing an empirically founded typology of terrorist groups. Previously, she worked at Middlesex University, where she carried out research and evaluation work in the field of Forensic Psychology. As part of this, Ms Marsden led research on radicalization and community-based efforts to counter violent extremism. Her research interests focus on terrorism and political violence – in particular, the evolution and characteristics of different terrorist groups, the process of radicalization, and the concept of success in terrorism and counterterrorism. On the last-named topic, she is co-authoring a major study for START (University of Maryland).

Eric Price is a member of the Chartered Institute of Library and Information Professionals (CILIP), the leading professional body for librarians, information specialists and knowledge managers in the United Kingdom. He worked for the International Atomic Energy Agency (IAEA) in Vienna from 1980 to 2007. As an IAEA librarian he also provided, until 2002, services to the staff of various units of the UN system in Vienna, included UNODC's Terrorism Prevention Branch. He has also contributed to various UN publications, including *Global Terrorism*, by Paul Medhurst (New York: UNITAR, 2000).

FOREWORD

Professor Alex Schmid produced his first handbooks on terrorism research a quarter of a century ago. They have stood the test of time. The escalating human and societal costs inflicted by the expanding use of the tactic of terrorism since then has led to an even greater need for dispassionate research and objective analysis of the key concepts surrounding terrorism and counterterrorism.

Like the economy before it, terrorism has gone global, even if it remains predominantly a national phenomenon. Terrorism is a tactic employed by many different groups in many different parts of the world in pursuit of many different objectives. Given the heterogeneous nature of the subject, it is especially important to have some shared understanding of the key assumptions and an appreciation of the qualities of key data sets on which analysts rely for evidence.

The threat posed by terrorism to the sense of security of democratic citizens encourages politicians of all hues to search for easy answers, rapid analysis and quick fixes. The detailed, careful, and dispassionate evaluation of prevailing theories, familiar concepts, popular typologies, and familiar databases suggests that easy answers are unlikely to lead to lasting solutions to the problem of terrorism.

This book by Professor Schmid and his colleagues represents a prodigious effort to bring together the collective wisdom of experts from around the world. Just as Schmid's earlier handbooks provided an invaluable resource to students, scholars and policy makers, this new volume should be the starting point of every serious student of the subject.

In Social Science, as in other realms, knowledge is advanced by building on the work of one's predecessors. One of the difficulties of the field of terrorism is that scholars are racing to catch up with the perpetrators. The impact of the 9/11 attack and the American government's reaction to that attack has transformed concepts of international security. They also transformed the field of terrorism studies and led to an exponential growth in scholarship. Schmid and his colleagues have done an enormous service by stepping back from the rush for instant analysis and instead served the profession by providing compilations of available data. A scholar wishing to make a contribution to the discipline can turn to this handbook for guidance on where the literature stands on a range of issues from definitions and theories of terrorism, to patterns of escalation and causes of terrorism. The raw materials for further analysis are also provided in the extensive appendices providing directories of terrorism groups, communiqués by the leadership of Al-Qaeda and a bibliography of terrorism.

The work on this *Handbook of Terrorism Research* took place at the St Andrews' Centre for the Study of Terrorism and Political Violence. The CSTPV, located in one of Europe's oldest universities, is Europe's oldest centre for the study of political violence. Much work remains to be done in understanding and preventing further outbreaks of political violence but this handbook will facilitate the work of those committed to doing so.

Professor Louise Richardson FRSE
Principal and Vice Chancellor, University of St Andrews

ACKNOWLEDGEMENTS

Alex P. Schmid

This *Handbook of Terrorism Research* was largely written between 2006 and 2009 while I was Director of the Centre for the Study of Terrorism and Political Violence (CSTPV) at the School of International Relations at the University of St Andrews, UK. The volume is a successor volume to my previous handbooks: *Political Terrorism: A Research Guide to Concepts, Theories, Databases and Literature* (Amsterdam: North-Holland, 1984. [585 pp.]) and *Political Terrorism: A New Guide to Actors, Authors, Concepts, Data Bases, Theories, and Literature* (revised, expanded and updated edition prepared under the auspices of the Center for International Affairs, Harvard University, 1988 [700 pp.]). The latter volume was re-issued unchanged by Transaction Books (New Jersey) in 2005.

Those previous volumes were well received. Walter Laqueur, author of standard works in the field of Terrorism Studies, called the Research Guide in 1999 'the most comprehensive handbook on terrorism',[1] while I.L. Horowitz, in his Foreword to the 1984 and 1988 volumes, characterized it as one 'that will stand for many years as quintessential effort to gather the facts, theories and histories of terrorism as event and ideology'. In 2001, Andrews Silke (University of East London) called the handbook 'seminal' and 'the most important review of research and researchers into terrorism to date'.[2] The 1984 edition also won the 'Best Book in Political Science' award from the Association of Political Scientists in the Netherlands.

The current volume, while similar in structure to these previous Research Guides, is different in content, reflecting the evolution of the field of Terrorism Studies. There is, however, the same focus on analysing and evaluating concepts, typologies, theories, databases and literature as in the original volumes. The bibliography at the end of this volume includes mainly books issued since the 1988 edition was published. However, it is smaller – about 4,600 items as compared to nearly 5,900 items in the 1988 edition. This is not due to a smaller output of writings – on the contrary. However, with the advent of electronic online bibliographies, paper-based bibliographies have to a large extent become obsolete – except for the unfortunate few who do not yet have online access to major collections like the one in the US Library of Congress. The 1988 volume described some 1,200 armed groups in more than 200 small-print pages in its 'World Directory of Terrorist and Other Organizations associated with Guerrilla Warfare, Political Violence, and Protest'. The current volume contains a smaller number of group descriptions in its Glossary. More than 6,400 terrorist and other non-state groups linked to armed violence and conflict are listed – but not described – in a catalogue compiled by Albert J. Jongman, who was responsible for the 1984 and 1988 *World Directories*. The Handbook also contains several appendices, including a chronology of definitions of terrorism and one of Al-Qaeda communiqués.

A volume of this size on a topic that is so much in flux is bound to have shortcomings. The major one is that it has been difficult to update all information received and processed since 2006, especially when it comes to the latest status of extremist and terrorist groups. This is particularly evident in the Glossary. To a much lesser extent, it is also true in the discussion of the literature on terrorism, which continues to evolve at great speed. These and other shortcomings of this volume are my responsibility as editor and, to a lesser extent, those of my co-authors, who, like me, worked on this volume alongside many other obligations. What merit this Handbook has is to a considerable extent due to the input of more than 90 experts from academia and counter-terrorism agencies, who completed a long questionnaire in 2006.

In compiling the present volume, I had the support of colleagues from the CSTPV – in particular Gillian Duncan, Joseph Easson, Brad McAllister, Sarah Marsden, Neil Bowie and Donald Holbrook who (co-)authored sections of the present volume. Beyond my colleagues from CSTPV, a major section is the work of Albert J. Jongman. A new section on the use of library and internet resources is from the hand of Eric Price, former librarian at the International Atomic Energy Agency (IAEA) in Vienna. Earlier, he assisted me when I was Officer-in-Charge of the Terrorism Prevention Branch at the United Nations in Vienna between 1999 and 2005. Brynjar Lia from the Norwegian Defence Research Establishment (FFI) contributed an appendix on causal factors of terrorism to this volume, while Benjamin Freedman compiled a list of officially blacklisted extremist and terrorist (support) groups. I wish to thank them all for their assistance. I also wish to thank the respondents to the questionnaire. Because of their professional positions, some of them did not want to be identified by name. I wish to express my gratitude to those 27 respondents who chose to remain anonymous as well as those I can mention here: James Albrecht, Daniel Arce, Donna Artz, Joost Augusteijn, Anis Bajrektarevic, Navin Bapat, Richard Barrett, Richard Chasdi, Ronald Clark, Roger Davies, Chris Dishman, Walter Enders, Christine Fair, Peter Flemming, James Forest, Boaz Ganor, Mayurdhwajasinh J. Gohel, B. Gokool, Avishag Gordon, Daniel Gressang, John Horgan, Michael Intriligator, Shanaka Jayasekara, Jeffrey Kaplan, Kiran Krishan, Robert Lieber, James and Brenda Lutz, Stefan Malthaner, Gus Martin, Edward Marks, Ariel Merari, Edward Mickolus, Lyubov Mincheva, Magnus Norell, Manya Omelicheva, Nick Pratt, Anders Romarheim, Nick Ross, Ajai Sahni, Peter St John, Harjit Sandhu, Todd Sandler, Yoram Schweitzer, Frank Shanty, Samuel Shapira, Jeffrey Simon, Joshua Sinai, Matenia Sirseloudi, Stephen Sloan, Martha and Tim Smith, Friedrich Steinhäusler, Ekaterina Stepanova, Chris Stout, Andrew Tan, Valery Tishkov, Bram van Liere, Peter Waldmann, Michael Whine, Robert Whyte, Paul Wilkinson, Clive Williams, Gordon Woo and Michael Whine. They all allowed me and my colleagues to quote them, and their rich contributions undoubtedly make this a more authoritative volume. We also wish to thank those publishers who allowed us to quote from the work of their authors as well as the authors themselves whose work we considered worth citing. In particular, I would like to thank the RAND Corporation, ITERATE, the US NCTC (WITS), the Armed Forces of Austria and the International Institute for Strategic Studies. In a number of cases, it was not possible to establish who the current copyright holders of certain tables, graphs or quotes cited are. We offer them our apologies and invite them to approach us so that we can make appropriate arrangements to compensate them for the use of their intellectual property.

My final and greatest thanks go to my wife, Dr Shantu Watt, who has stood by my side through all these years and gracefully accepted that my work too often took precedence over family life. This Handbook is dedicated to her.

Alex P. Schmid
Wassenaar, December 2010

Notes

1 Walter Laqueur, *The New Terrorism*. Oxford: Oxford University Press, 1999, p. 283.
2 Andrew Silke, 'The Devil You Know: Continuing Problems with Research on Terrorism'. *Terrorism and Political Violence,* 13(4), Winter 2001, p. 3.

1
INTRODUCTION

Alex P. Schmid

Essentially, terrorism is nothing more than a method that may be adopted by a wide range of ideologies and for an equally wide range of objectives. It is not integrally linked to any ideology. It will be adopted as long as it is calculated to have significant potential for success. Such success, within the terrorist paradigm, may not be defined on the same criteria that are held by stable societies and state systems. Within the paradigm of a protracted war of terrorist attrition, apparent failures are conceived of as way stations to success. . . . Essential to the potential for the 'success' of terrorism is the legitimacy that terrorism has in the eyes not only of the terrorists themselves, but of a substantial public – including many in the victim societies who accept or propagate the 'false sociologies'. The de-legitimisation of terrorism – at the level of the de-legitimisation of genocide – would, consequently, have to precede coherent international and national policy responses. For such a process of de-legitimisation to occur, it is essential to take up each of the 'false sociologies' that have been advanced in support of terrorism and demonstrate that they derive from questionable or fallacious reasoning.

Ajai Sahni, Director, Institute for Conflict Management, New Delhi[1]

It has been said that good political science ought to start by asking two questions and, once these are answered, proceed to the third: (1) What do we know? (2) What are we going to learn? And (3) how can we learn?[2] This Handbook tries to address all three of these questions. Its main purpose is to synthesize existing knowledge regarding the concept of terrorism – its typologies, theories, data as well as the literature on terrorism so that we know better what we know (1). In addition, the reader is provided with an opportunity to learn about certain types of 'fallacious reasoning' as alluded to in the quote above. This should allow him or her to see further in the field of Terrorism Studies, providing him or her[3] with a learning moment in the sense of (2). As to the 'how': by comparing the insights gained from those who contributed to this handbook with his or her own, the reader is provided with an opportunity to learn (3).

In this introduction, I will, mainly on the basis of some 90 responses to a questionnaire,[4] outline some of the developments in the field of Terrorism Studies. Some have questioned whether one can speak of Terrorism Studies as a single field. The study of terrorism can indeed be approached from different disciplines such as criminology, political science, war and peace studies, communication studies or religious studies; as a consequence, one can interpret terrorism in different frameworks:

1   acts of terrorism as/and crime;
2   acts of terrorism as/and politics;
3   acts of terrorism as/and warfare;
4   acts of terrorism as/and communication;
5   acts of terrorism as/and religious crusade/jihad.[5]

These are, as it were, five conceptual lenses through which we can look at terrorism. All of these 'frames' are useful to understand better some aspects of some forms of terrorism. Yet it would be wrong to single out any one of these frameworks and claim that it is the 'right' one. They are not mutually exclusive, either.[6] An act of terrorist violence can be criminal and political at the same time, making it a political crime or a criminal offence with political repercussions. An act of terrorism can be committed in the context of warfare and constitute a grave breach of the laws of war – a war crime. An act of terrorism can primarily be a propagandistic communication stunt to impress one audience or to reach other audiences which otherwise might not 'listen' to less violent protest. An act of terrorist violence can also be interpreted as a sacrifice with religious connotations, whereby the terrorist offers innocent lives for the sacred cause or views himself as a martyr. As trends in the use of terrorism change, one type of interpretation can become more appropriate than another. Terrorism changes as the instruments of violence and communication change and as contexts evolve.

Every student of terrorism tends to approach the subject with a certain ideological baggage and/or has a preferred interpretation framework. My original approach, as outlined in *Violence as Communication* (1982),[7] was based on the fourth of the five approaches listed above. In brief, I viewed – and continue to view – terrorism primarily as a certain combination of violence and communication whereby the immediate victims are often civilians and the main addressee of the 'language of blood' is often a government or its citizens – or, in the case of state terrorism, a section of the public.[8] The communication study approach was a marginal approach in the early 1980s but has become more accepted as the communication revolution brought about by 24/7 television news and the internet has sharpened its contours. However, the impact of the revolution in worldwide instant bi-directional communications is but one of several recent trends.

Before we explore some trends with the help of our experts, we should, however, stand still for a moment and look at the core concept behind terrorism: terror.

Terror

The literature on terrorism has, strangely enough, not focused very much on an analysis of 'terror' as a state of mind.[9] With the exception of some of the writings on kidnapping and hostage taking, the experience of being terrorized has not stood at the centre of attention in Terrorism Studies. This near-absence can perhaps be explained by the fact that terrorism does not only produce terror – that terror is perhaps not even the main result for the majority of the members of target audiences of an act or campaign of terror, certainly when they watch terror from the relative safety of a chair, watching television. Terrorists play on our fear of sudden violent death and try to maximize uncertainty and hence anxiety to manipulate actual and prospective victims and those who have reason to identify with them. When, following a terrorist atrocity, the question 'will I be next?' looms large in a target audience, one of the intended psychological impacts has been achieved. Depending on the setting, prospective victims can be shocked by numbing fear (as in a hostage situation when the deadline for an ultimatum approaches) or they can panic and flee, having witnessed one atrocity and being anxious to avoid becoming a victim of the next. Chronic anxiety about being victimized without warning can be caused by natural as well as human action. To live under the shadow of a volcano, on the fault line of an earthquake zone or behind a fragile dam against the sea can also cause a pervasive atmosphere of anxiety, a horror bordering on terror in the minds of those exposed to constant danger to their lives. Yet such nature-induced horror resonates differently among witnessing audiences as compared with man-made terror.

'Terror' is, first of all, a state of mind characterized by intense fear of a threatening danger on an individual level and by a climate of fear on the collective level.[10] 'Terrorism', on the other hand, is an activity, method or tactic which, as a psychological outcome, aims to produce 'terror'.[11] As one study commissioned in the mid-1970s by the US Department of Justice put it:

> Terror is a natural phenomenon; terrorism is the conscious exploitation of it. Terrorism is coercive, designed to manipulate the will of its victims and its larger audience. The great degree of fear is generated by the crime's very nature, by the manner of its perpetration, or by its senselessness, wantonness, or callous indifference to human life. This terrible fear is the source of the terrorist's power and communicates his challenge to society.[12]

In psychological terms, 'terror' can be seen as a strongly felt emotional reaction to certain acts of violence, a special type of extreme fear or profound anxiety paralysing a person ('chilled by terror') because he or she cannot escape an impending threat of violence. Typical solutions to such a psychic state of fear are escape or hiding. While the second is possible to some extent in cases of terror (avoiding situations where chances of victimization are higher), the first is not in situations of being kidnapped, hijacked or otherwise taken hostage. In other than these situations of direct, stark victimization, terrorism often creates a level of anxiety (uncertainty, tension and fear)[13] that is over and above what is realistically necessary given the actual level of threat. M.E. Silberstein, a physician, described the feeling of 'terror' in these terms:

> Terror is a state of intense fear induced by the systematic threat of imprisonment, mutilation, or death. It is intensified when the victim is helpless in the hands of another human being. We are all afraid of being hurt or killed. The terrorist manipulates persons and governments by making the threat of bodily harm manifest. The terrorist threatens the most fundamental human drive – the will to survive intact. He or she strips from the defences of human courage that most important element of antifear, the real or supposed ability to fight back to defend one's person. Because the terrorist's victims are unarmed, non-combatant, and random and because they are totally helpless, the victim's fear is experienced by all observers of the victim's plight, who are equally vulnerable and who desire to live their lives unmolested. These secondary victims of terrorism, all who think by association that their lives are in equal danger, fear equally for their persons.[14]

The relative paucity of research on 'terror' itself by students of terrorism is not without parallels. Few psychology books focus on what supposedly should be the central concept: the psyche, the human soul. However, while the existence of a soul is disputed,[15] nobody denies the existence of extreme fear – terror – the feeling which terrorists evoke through perpetrating atrocities in the public's view and which they then utilize to play politics with. Those who play on the political nervous system of a nation by calculated use of atrocities sometimes sit in government. However, when referring to terrorism, most of the experts we consulted use the term predominantly for referring to certain violent acts of armed non-state actors. This focus is reflected in most of the answers in the following pages.

Contemporary trends in non-state terrorism

Let us begin by looking at some recent changes. In the 1990s, Bruce Hoffman and others have, for instance, observed a substantial rise of religiously motivated terrorism, especially after clerics managed to seize power in Iran in the 1979:[16]

- 1968: no international terrorist group could be classified as non-secular;
- 1980: 2 out of 64 international groups could be classified as non-secular;
- 1992: 11 out of 48 international terrorist groups were religious;
- 1994: 16 out of 49 international terrorist groups were religious;
- 1995: 25 out of 58 active groups in international terrorist organizations were predominantly religious in character or motivation.

This brings us to the question of what trends the respondents to our questionnaire discerned more recently (2006).[17] The following three lists identify three clusters of such trends as our respondents saw them.[18]

I first list six trends in the ideology and structure of terrorist groups:

1 proliferation of extremist religious doctrines, which have replaced Marxist secularism as the primary alternative discourse (Sinai);
2 the rise of Islamist-inspired political ideologies that justify the use of terrorism, and their appeal throughout the Islamic world (Gurr, Malthaner);
3 a shift from hierarchically organized terrorist groups to networks of loosely aligned groups and individuals sharing a common ideological framework (leaderless networks) (Gressang, Kaplan);
4 signs of convergence of terrorist and criminal networks (narco-terrorism) (Kaplan, Shanty);
5 increased significance of the internet and communication technologies for diffusion of radical and militant ideologies, indoctrination and training (Stepanova, Barrett, Gressang Tishkov, Davies);
6 diaspora support for terrorism (homegrown terrorism) (Jayasekara, Forest).

Along with these perceived changes, our respondents noted a number of operational developments:

1 a trend towards maritime and cross-border terrorism (Shanty);
2 a trend towards increased lethality and maximum devastation (Chasdi, M.J. Gohel);
3 the spread of suicide tactics to places previously unimagined (Fair);
4 attempts at chemical, biological, radiological and nuclear (CBRN) terrorism;
5 selection of ever more illegitimate targets such as children and medical personnel;
6 an increase in attacks on critical national infrastructures and transport systems (M.J. Gohel);
7 a trend towards cyber-terrorism (Steinhäusler);
8 the use of innovation or new technologies by terrorist groups (Simon, Stepanova);
9 proliferation of tactical experiences from Iraq, such as the use of improvised explosive devices (Davies);
10 increasing capacity on the part of political movements using terror tactics to secure territorial bases from which to mount violent campaigns (Gurr);
11 kidnapping and taking of hostages without serious negotiations, rather for videotaped killing (beheadings);
12 emerging low-tech operations based on migrant or slum population;
13 the development of strategic thought in jihadi-Salafi theory.

These trends, in turn, have brought about changes in governmental responses to non-state terrorism:

1 militarization of counter-terrorism;
2 governmental overreaction to terrorism;
3 growth of repression in Western and other countries due to counter-terrorism;
4 re-examination of the rules of war and its modification to counter terrorism and insurgencies (Ganor);

5 growth of public and private security agencies that feed on public insecurity (Gurr);
6 increased international cooperation to combat terrorism (Kalis).

Each of these observations contains varying degrees of truth, but it would be wrong to generalize such 'trends'. What is true for some terrorist groups and some regions strongly affected by terrorist campaigns is less true for others (although, owing to globalization, there is a fast distance learning process taking place). For instance, take the observed trend towards convergence (or confluence) of terrorist and organized crime groups.[19] This is true in some countries (e.g. Colombia) but less so in others (e.g. Sri Lanka). What can be observed is that many terrorist groups (e.g. the Kurdistan Workers' Party, PKK) have developed in-house fund-raising capabilities along the same lines as organized crime groups. At the same time, a number of organized crime syndicates (e.g. in Mexico) use tactics of terrorism. That is not the same as a convergence between political terrorists and organized crime groups. One reason why there is hesitancy among the majority of terrorist groups to ally with organized crime figures is that it would seriously compromise their security.

Another phenomenon we are frequently warned about is a trend towards 'cyber-terrorism'. While there has been plenty of cyber-crime (e.g. identity theft on the internet, fraud, hacking) and even an occasional case of cyber-murder (like changing, via the internet, a hospital pharmacy's prescription for a patient, who, as a consequence, died from an overdose), cyber-terrorism has, to my knowledge, not yet occurred (depending, of course, on how one wishes to define 'cyber' and 'terrorism').[20] This raises the issue of how narrow or broad the definition of terrorism should be.

Terrorism and political violence other than terrorism

Using broad (and changing) definitions of 'terrorism' has been a constant problem in the field of Terrorism Studies.[21] The broader the concept of terrorism is made, the greater the chance that different people will be talking about different things when they use the term 'terrorism' – which is one reason why the United Nations has not yet managed to reach consensus on terrorism. Especially dangerous is the facile equation of terrorism with 'political violence'. There are very many manifestations, forms and types of political violence, and to see them as more or less the same as terrorism or simply as a sub-category of terrorism (rather than the other way round: terrorism as a sub-category of political violence) is misleading and confusing. The following are some categories, forms and manifestations of political violence other than terrorism on different levels of analysis, though the list is not an exhaustive or systematic one:

- hunger strike/self-burning (political suicide);
- blockade/public property damage/looting/arson/sabotage;
- internment/concentration camps;
- violent repression of peaceful demonstrations;
- hate crimes/lynching/vigilantism;
- violent demonstration/mob violence/rioting;
- raids/brigandry/warlordism;
- political justice/show trials;
- *razzia* (pillage)/arbitrary arrests/mass eviction/unlawful deportation;
- torture/mutilation/mass rape;
- assassination/political murder/liquidation/*attentat* (murder attempt)/targeted killing/tyrannicide;
- summary extra-judicial execution/massacre;
- disappearances (= kidnapping + torture/maiming + murder);
- ethnic cleansing/purge/pogrom;
- rebellion/revolt/banditry/peasant uprising/urban insurrection/national liberation struggle/ guerrilla warfare/low-intensity conflict due to insurgency;

- military intervention/invasion/interstate aggression (war);
- resistance to invasion/occupation/irregular/partisan warfare;
- (elite) *coup d'état*/(mass) revolution;
- civil war/armed intrastate conflict, with or without foreign participation;
- ethnocide/politicide/genocide/democide.

While some of these manifestations play a role in terrorism,[22] the equation of acts of terrorism with many other manifestations from the much broader field of 'political violence' by many politicians and some writers on terrorism has not been helpful to the study of terrorism proper. It would be wiser to restrict the use of the term 'terrorism' to a type of political violence that deliberately (i.e. not incidentally or as collateral damage) targets civilians and non-combatants rather than use it indiscriminately no matter who or what is the target.

As a tactic, method or form of direct action, terrorism can be used by a very diverse group of actors. While we will discuss types of terrorists in a later chapter, it is useful to be reminded here of some of the diversity of terrorist actors.[23] A basic typology of terrorism is as follows:

- religious and millenarian groups;
- ethno-nationalist, separatist and irredentist groups;
- racist and right-wing groups;
- revolutionary left-wing and anarchist groups;
- vigilante and paramilitary death squads;
- state or state-sponsored terrorists;
- criminal organizations employing terrorist tactics;
- single-issue groups;
- psychologically disturbed individuals and copycat terrorists;
- 'lone wolf' and 'leaderless resistance' terrorists.

Add to this diversity of actors the diversity of motives and combine them, and one begins to realize the complexity of the terrorist phenomenon that calls for explanations.[24] Some of the principal motivations of terrorists are as follows:

- revenge: historically, retaliation has been a powerful motive for terrorists;
- intimidation and disorientation: wearing down the morale of an opponent;
- demands: political blackmail to obtain concessions ('fulfil our demands, or else . . .');
- propaganda/attention- or recognition-seeking: propaganda of the deed;
- provocation of counter-measures/overreaction;
- disruption, e.g. of a peace process or of a regime's economic sources of income;
- seeking martyrdom: performing suicide operations as an example for others to emulate;
- morale building: demonstrating to terrorists' constituency an image of strength;
- elimination of opposing forces (e.g. by a surgical strike 'at the heart of the state');
- extortion of money to finance a campaign of violence.

If one adds to these (non-exhaustive) lists of perpetrator types and underlying motives some of the instruments in the terrorist toolbox, the task of explaining terrorism becomes even more challenging. The following are some major tactics from the terrorists' toolkit:

- distribution of death lists of persons to be killed;
- punishment, e.g. through mutilation such as cutting off hands;
- mass rape for the humiliation of males in the opposite camp;
- kidnapping of people for ransom or political concessions;

- hostage taking in combination with site occupation for coercive bargaining;
- hijacking or skyjacking for political blackmail;
- assassination of high-level public figures to terrorize other public figures;
- arson or firebombing of iconic objects in the opponent's camp;
- focused or indiscriminate assaults on people in public spaces;
- bombings, e.g. car or truck bombings;
- disappearances (kidnapping + torture + murder);
- beheadings in front of a rolling camcorder for broadcasting;
- torture for intimidation;
- suicide- or kamikaze-type human bomb attacks;
- large-scale massacres;
- mass poisoning;
- use of unconventional weapons (CBRN).

In short: terrorism is complex and wide enough which is why it is often treated as a field of studies in its own right.[25]

Let us now turn our attention to terrorism and how our 91 experts think about terrorism.

What to study in the field of terrorism?

How can one study terrorism when it often accompanies other forms of political violence, including insurgencies and war – not to mention other, less violent or not violent forms of political communications, both persuasive and coercive?[26] Clearly, it should not be studied in isolation. The answers of our expert respondents might give us some clues. In the following, they provide us with a long research agenda, with much less overlap than one would expect. In the following two lists, I divide their answers into items related to terrorism and counter-terrorism respectively. The following are their responses to the question 'Where do you see the main research priorities in the field of political terrorism?'

- in explaining terrorism as violence vis-à-vis other forms of violence;
- in creating a comprehensive database that covers all violent incidents by country;
- the definition of terrorism as a basic tool of international cooperation (Ganor);
- understanding the fundamental causes of terrorism;
- determination of the factors leading individuals or groups to become terrorists (Enders, Malthaner);
- identifying the genesis of terrorist campaigns;
- group emergence and decline database, cross-national, longitudinal database;
- identifying (early-warning) indicators for the emergence of radicalization processes (Malthaner, Gressang);
- finding out how and why terrorism ends (Arzt, Horgan);
- de-radicalization – under what circumstances and through what set of actions by authorities, affected communities, etc. do terrorist campaigns end? (Kaplan);
- research, preferably comparative, into the justification and legitimization of terrorism in various conflicts, ideologies, religions and communities;
- the problem of political transformation of armed movements that have used terrorist means and their integration in the context of stabilization or the peace process (Stepanova);
- ideologies and structures of terrorist groups (Stepanova);
- analysing and critiquing the ideologies and doctrines that are used to recruit and issue articulated and well-researched counter-arguments (M.J. Gohel);
- analysis of terrorist social networks;

- understanding how individuals make the decision to leave terrorism (Horgan);
- understanding innovation in terrorist tactics, targets, strategies and weapons (Kaplan);
- examining the reasons why there is a seemingly endless supply of suicide terrorists (Kaplan);
- the roots of popular support to terrorist groups (Bajrektarevic, Fair, Malthaner);
- factors influencing terrorist groups' willingness to escalate the level and scope of violence;
- better understanding of connections between terrorism and the media;
- better understanding of the role of the internet in the development of terrorism;
- the link between terrorism and insurgency;
- linkages and similarities between transnational organized crime and terrorist groups (Bajrektarevic);
- discovering how real is the threat of cyberterrorism (Arzt);
- terrorism and failed, failing or transitional/developing states (Shanty);
- outside sponsoring or support (Tishkov);
- funding and financing of terrorism by using NGOs or charities;
- measuring the costs of terrorism (Enders).

This list is long but, despite partial overlap, it is useful to present a broad range of suggestions for further research on terrorism. The second list, focusing on counter-terrorism, is just as long. It summarizes responses to the question 'Where do you see the main research priorities in the field of political terrorism, its prevention and counter-measures against terrorism?':

- prevention policy-oriented research;
- understanding the interactive relationship between state policies and sub-state terrorism: the circumstances under which state counter-measures increase or decrease terrorism;
- the optimal balance in counter-terrorism between counter-terrorism tasks performed by intelligence, by law enforcement and by the military (Stepanova);
- the generation of a comprehensive cross-national, longitudinal database of counter-terrorism measures undertaken by states to combat both domestic and international terrorism;
- analyses of the sort of governmental response terrorist groups expect – and even take account of in their planning – following their attacks;
- how to address or talk to 'terrorist' movements and individuals; how to carry on the public debate;
- determining the proper balance between protecting society from terrorist attacks and protecting the public's civil liberties (Kaplan);
- measures of effectiveness for counter-terrorism policy and operations;
- the effects of counter-measures on democracy and the rule of law;
- the long-term impact of foreign policy and humanitarian double standards;
- the relationship between authorities and the public in increasingly risk-averse societies that are attacked by terrorists;
- how to improve or change governance in a given situation to 'defeat' or alleviate or manage insurgency or terrorism;
- whether it is possible to deter terrorism; the factors that influence terrorist groups' and individuals' deterrability (Merari);
- comparative analysis of the success of different strategies used for counter-terrorism;
- the diplomacy of counter-terrorism: lessons learned, ignored and disputed (Arzt);
- options for prosecuting international terrorists (Arzt);
- whether abusive interrogative techniques are necessary and effective in questioning terrorism's supporters and actors (Albrecht);
- the rhetoric of terrorism and counter-terrorism;
- the conflict between freedom of speech and incitement to terrorism, especially with regard to terrorist use of the internet (Barrett);

- developing strategies to counter the ideologies of terrorism;
- measuring the effectiveness of efforts to counter terrorist ideologies (Pratt);
- the effectiveness of rehabilitation and reconciliation programmes (Barrett);
- assessment of the successes and failures of peace measures and dialogues (Sahni);
- countering ideological support to Islamic-inspired terrorism (Pratt);
- Islamic counter-arguments to those who claim a religious justification for terrorism (Barrett);
- factors affecting policy makers' perceptions of the threat of terrorism and responses to it;
- the effectiveness of restrictions on civil and political liberties in the fight against terrorism;
- public resilience in times of crisis;
- understanding the role of public perception in influencing public policy;
- information about terrorism – how to inform the public;
- how states and non-state actors construct notions of legitimacy (Horgan);
- the role of civil society in the development of counter-terrorism strategies (Horgan);
- factors influencing popular support for resort to insurgent violence (Merari);
- preventing terrorists' acquisition or development of WMD (Forest);
- intelligence development in insurgent theatres, and globally, particularly with regard to indigenous sources of information where there are cultural and language barriers (Davies);
- information operations to counter terrorism (Davies);
- factors influencing terrorist groups' willingness to escalate the level and scope of violence (Merari);
- empirical study of personality factors (Merari);
- ways to end insurgent violence (Merari).

What is interesting is that the suggestions focus very much on non-state terrorism, as if state (or regime) terrorism were a thing of the past. Also strange is the absence of concern for victim issues. Yet despite such limitations and a predominantly Western focus, these are very useful suggestions. However, many of these topics will be hard to investigate, especially if the researcher has access only to open sources. This brings us to the question of how to study clandestine actors working from the underground or secret government locations.

How to study terrorism?

As in the case of research on organized crime or torture, some methods of study are clearly inappropriate (e.g. a preferred approach of anthropologists: participatory observation), and others are very risky (such as interviewing terrorists in the field). In recent years, the data situation has greatly improved, thanks to well-funded government efforts like WITS or GTD (see the following list). However, the creation of computer-based databases increases the temptation to work, by preference, with quantitative data and neglect qualitative research (e.g. comparative case studies). We find this tendency, to some extent, reflected in the answers we received to the question 'Which data collections on terrorism do you find most useful for your research?' The following were the most frequently mentioned resources (many of them will be discussed in more detail later in this volume):

- the Global Terrorism Database (based on Pinkerton's Global Intelligence Services) (www.start. umd.edu);
- WITS (Worldwide Incident Tracking System) (http://wits.nctc.gov);
- RAND (www.rand.org);
- ITERATE (International Terrorism: Attributes of Terrorism Events) by Ed Mickolus *et al.* (Institute for Quantitative Social Science at Harvard University http://dvn.iq.harvard. edu/dvn/);
- the US State Department (Patterns of Global Terrorism; Terrorism Country Reports) (www. state.gov/s/ct/rls/);

- TWEED (www.nsd.uib.no/macrodataguide/set.html?id=39&sub=1);
- ISVG (Institute for the Study of Violent Groups) (www.isvg.org/about.html);
- the Terrorism Knowledge Base/MIPT (National Memorial Institute for the Prevention of Terrorism (until March 2008);
- the Terrorism Research Center (www.terrorism.com);
- the ICT (Institute for Counter-Terrorism, Herzliya, Israel) (www.ict.org.il);
- the Center for Non-proliferation Studies (CNS) at the Monterey Institute, California (cns.miis.edu/research/terror.htm);
- Jane's Terrorism and Insurgency Centre data on terrorist events and group profiles (www.jtic. janes.com);
- the Open Source Center (formerly the Foreign Broadcasting Information Service – FBIS) (www.opensource.gov);
- Militarized Interstate Dispute Data (www.correlatesofwar.org/COW2%20Data/MIDs/MID 310.html);
- the International Crisis Behavior Project data (www.cidcm.umd.edu/icb/);
- the Digital National Security Archive (www/gwo.edu/~nsarchiv/);
- the International Policy Institute for Counter-Terrorism (www.ict.org.il);
- the EPIC Counter-Terrorism Proposal Page (http://epic.org/privacy/terrorism);
- SATP (South Asia Terrorism Portal, Institute for Conflict Management (New Delhi)) (http://www.satp.org);
- the Interpol and Europol databases (www.interpol.int and www.europol.net);
- the ICTY's (International Criminal Tribunal for the former Yugoslavia) internal database (www.icty.org);
- the FAS (Federation of American Scientists) Intelligence Resource Program. List of Liberation Movements, Terrorist Organizations . . . and other parastate entities (www.fas.org/irp/world/para/index/html);
- INSCR (Integrated Network for Societal Conflict Research) (www.systemicpeace.org/inscr/inscr.htm);
- the Minorities at Risk (MAR) and Minorities at Risk Organizational Behavior (MAROB) databases at the Center for International Development and Conflict Management, University of Maryland at College Park (www.cidcm.umd.edu/inscr/mar);
- the Uppsala Conflict Data Project's Global Conflict Database, Department of Peace and Conflict Research, Uppsala University (www.pcr.uu.se/database/index.khk);
- the ADL (Anti-Defamation League) database (www.adl.org/about.asp);
- the FBI database on counter-terrorism (www.fbi.gov/terrorinfo/counterrorism/faqs.htm);
- the NCTC (US National Counterterrorism Center) (www.nctc.gov);
- the United Nations Security Council Resolution 1267 Committee List of individuals and entities belonging to, or associated with, the Taliban and Al-Qaeda (www.un.or/doc/sc/committees/1267/1267ListEng.htm);
- TRITON (www.hazmansol.com);
- the SFPS State Failure Problem Set (George Mason University) (http://globalpolicy.gmu.edu/pitf/pitfpset.htm);
- statements by terrorists in primary documents at CSTPV (www.st-andrews.ac.uk/~cstpv);
- court transcripts of American terrorist trials (www.icpsr.umich.edu/icpsrweb/ICPSR/studies/4639;jsessionid=8517D56F82B201DD1763EC33AA29CE87?keyword=terrorists).

The preponderance of quantitative and US-generated data is quite marked. Only a few (such as the last two) datasets are predominantly qualitative in nature. We will present 20 databases in more detail in Chapter 5.

As important as data, and linked to them, is methodology. Respondents to the questionnaire were also asked which research methods they had personally used for the study of terrorism. The answers – shown here in declining order of frequency of being mentioned – reveal great variety but also indicate that the use of quantitative data is not as dominant as suggested by the previous list. The following are the main methods:

- study of documents originating from terrorists/sympathizers;
- study of scholarly books and articles on terrorism;
- study of newspapers and other media outputs on terrorism;
- interviews with government officials dealing with terrorism;
- study of open government documents;
- study of court documents relating to trials of terrorists;
- statistical analysis of terrorist incidents;
- study of classified government documents;
- study of terrorist interrogation transcripts;
- terrorist and sleeper communication intercepts;
- interviews with imprisoned terrorists.

These responses suggested a broad array of approaches to the study of terrorism. Using them, some respondents studied jihadist websites and internet video recordings; others, open-source media. Yet others interviewed victims and supporters of terrorism, (expert) witnesses, other researchers, journalists and members of the general public. Some indicated that they use game theory, mathematical modelling and matrices, and have developed theoretical methods and models. What was encouraging was that, compared to much research some decades ago,[27] more researchers actually turn to primary sources. On the other hand, interviewing terrorists directly, even in prison, appears to be difficult, as so few have managed (or cared?) to do so.

Which theory to use to study terrorism?

If we look at the theories used by our respondents to study terrorism, it becomes clear that there is again great variety. More than half of the researchers had their own 'theory': 45 respondents out of 83 who answered this question said they use their own theory.[28] Here is an example from a US-based Muslim scholar, who summarized his theory of political violence in Islamic movements (not terrorism in general), as follows:

> Islamist violence emerges when authoritarian political systems grant Islamists social or cultural space, but deny them meaningful access to the political process. This created the precondition for violence because Islamists are able to build networks and legitimacy, but are blocked politically. The proximate cause of Islamist violence breaks out when Islamists encounter reactive and indiscriminate repression by the states that seek to roll back the challenge to their legitimacy by popular Islamist movements. As these Islamists are repressed at home, they externalize the violence (i.e. global jihad) in the hope of undermining the international support for authoritarian regimes that repress them.

Thirty-eight respondents indicated that they use someone else's theory. Among the latter group, references were, inter alia, made to the following theories and approaches:

- W. Laqueur's historical analysis (G. Martin);
- B. Hoffman's ideas on New Terrorism;
- C. Tilly's relational approach (V. Tishkov);

- D. Rapoport's 'four waves' theory;
- Schmid and J. De Graaf's communication perspective;
- M. Crenshaw's theory of terrorism as a strategic choice;
- M. Crenshaw's instrumental/organizational theories of terrorism (J. Simon, S. Malthaner);
- P. Waldmann's theory of terrorism as provocation (S. Malthaner);
- J.B. Bell's notions of the 'rebel ecosystem' (D. Gressang);
- P. Merkl's emphasis on small group dynamics (J. Augusteijn);
- R. Crelinsten's theory of controllers and the controlled;
- M. Sageman's psycho-sociological theory of social networks;
- M. Bloom's work on suicide terrorism;
- Nacos's work on terrorism's portrayal in the media;
- Silke's ideas on the psychology of terrorists (B. Van Liere);
- T.R. Gurr's psycho-sociological relative deprivation theory (E. Stepanova);
- P. Waldmann, B. Liam, A. Hansen *et al.*'s theory of asymmetric conflict (E. Stepanova);
- T. Ellingsen and N.P. Gleditsch's theory on the ambiguous (U-shaped) relationship between terrorism and democracy (E. Stepanova);
- D. Ronfeldt and J. Arquilla's theory of terrorism as network warfare;
- A. Moghadam's multicausal approach to suicide terrorism;
- J.M. Post's psychodynamic theory of terrorist behaviour;
- D. Della Porta's use of social movement theory;
- A.P. Schmid's theory of terrorism as psychological warfare (M.J. Gohel);
- A. Dershowitz's discussion on pre-emption as a counter-terrorism measure (B. Ganor);
- M. Taylor's psychological and rational choice theories (J. Horgan).

We find, underlying such responses, different views as to what constitutes a 'theory' as opposed to a 'framework' or a 'perspective' – the latter being less ambitious concepts for understanding the phenomenon, at least when it comes to forecasting. There were also a number of respondents who felt that there are no well-established theories. One prominent researcher wrote, 'There really is no theory of terrorism, which is the biggest conceptual problem in the field.' There were more who said they did not know what 'a theory of terrorism' is, with one of them suggesting perceptively that such a theory would have to be derived from a more general theory of the processes of violent political conflict.

One of the characteristics of a very good theory is its ability to anticipate what comes next. We therefore asked our experts, 'What, in your view, are the most powerful indicators of escalation and de-escalation of terrorist campaigns?' We got a wealth of very diverse suggestions on different levels of analysis which I will try to summarize in two lists, one on escalation and the other on the opposite, leaving out most of those responses where the response regarding escalation is the opposite of its counterparts in the de-escalation table.

The following are indicators that a terrorist campaign is escalating or likely to escalate:

- failing governance;
- government suppression (Horgan);
- government overreaction (Kaplan, Gressang);
- grievances that cannot be remedied through normal political channels (Enders);
- declining alternatives to terrorism (Williams);
- advocates of greater violence winning an internal leadership struggle;
- growing animosity towards a state or subsection of society (Forest);
- increasing level of support by the constituency of a terrorist group for use of terrorist means (Stepanova);
- radicalization of a constituency, with terrorist groups becoming the only viable form of political expression (Kaplan);

- adoption of the cause into (more) mainstream politics; growth of a political wing (Barrett);
- a group receiving ideological, moral, propaganda, financial, weapons, logistics and training support from abroad;
- increasing frequency or severity or sophistication of tactics and weapon technology;
- increased complexity and geographic spread of attacks (Davies, M.J. Gohel);
- increased use of the media, including terrorists' own outlets;
- increased ability to control territory; decline in state functioning in area of terrorist operation (Sahni).

And here are some indicators that a terrorist campaign is likely to de-escalate:

- decreasing civilian and security personnel fatalities;
- increasing terrorist fatalities (Sahni);
- arrest, death or loss of a charismatic leader;
- attrition (ageing leadership, more defections, surrenders, lack of recruits) (Weinberg, Khalis, Sahni);
- loss of funding, weapons, a safe haven, etc. by the group;
- internal strife within the group (Chenoweth);
- former supporters turning against the group's cause (Wright);
- diminishing community support (Beyoghlow);
- success in countering the propaganda of extremist ideologies (Mincheva);
- change of rhetoric away from extreme antagonism; a decrease in propaganda (Smith);
- conciliatory statements by resistance leaders (Krishan);
- unilateral concessions from terrorists;
- political contacts, ceasefire, (back-channel) negotiations (Hafez, Chasdi, Augusteijn);
- progressive restoration of the functioning of government machinery, particularly in hinterland areas;
- trust in the security forces by the general population, increasing confidence among non-combatants as regards their own safety (Forest).

These lists are very heterogeneous and based more on practical observations than on any theoretical framework. But then, forecasting is difficult, especially when individual initiatives and clandestine small group dynamics are involved. In political science, few theories (except perhaps in the field of voting behaviour in democracies) are very successful at prognosis.

In order to look into the future, one has to know the past – what's past is prologue' (Shakespeare). When it comes to terrorism, this involves attention to the (root) causes. Here we find a bewildering array of explanations (see also the lists at the end of Chapter 4 (pp. 272–279)).

Root causes of terrorism

In order to illustrate the existing perplexity (or confusion?) about (root) causes of terrorism, we only have to look at various reactions to the events of 11 September 2001. In the United Nations, member states debated these events for a whole week. The explanations given in October 2001 in the General Assembly on 9/11 diverged widely. Here is a sample from the interventions by some 170 speakers:[29]

- communities struck by poverty, disease, illiteracy, bitter hopelessness (Armenia);
- social inequality, marginalization and exclusion (Benin);
- political oppression, extreme poverty and the violation of basic rights (Costa Rica);
- injustices, misery, starvation, drugs, exclusion, prejudices, despair for lack of perspectives (Dominican Republic);

- inequality and oppression (Finland);
- oppression of peoples in several parts of the world, particularly in Palestine (Malaysia);
- alienation of the young in situations of economic deprivation and political tension and uncertainty, a sense of injustice and lack of hope (New Zealand);
- rejection of the West with all its cultural dimensions (Palestine);
- hunger, poverty, deprivation, fear, despair, absence of a sense of belonging to the human family (Namibia);
- situations that lead to misery, exclusion, reclusion, and the injustices which lead to growing frustration, desperation and exasperation (Senegal).

Let us compare such official UN member state explanations concerning the causes for Al-Qaeda's attack on the United States with some from our respondents. Our questionnaire included the question 'What are, in your view, the main causes of the terrorist attacks of 11 September 2001 against the United States?' One would expect all the respondents to have a more or less theoretical explanation. In fact, only 57 (out of 91) answered this particular question. In other words, more than one-third of the experts either felt they had no good answer or that the answer was too difficult – or perhaps that it was too obvious. When one analyses the answers, no clear pattern emerges. There were almost as many different responses as there were respondents, although there was some overlap. Table 1.1 shows a sample of them. Usually respondents provided about three 'causal factors'.

One of the most perceptive responses came from respondent G. Ajai Sahni, executive director of the Institute for Conflict Management in New Delhi:

1   The principal cause of the 9/11 attacks was a consolidation of the Islamist extremist constituency in the form of a permanent establishment of Al-Qaeda in the Pakistan–Afghanistan region, and the calculation that those carrying out the attacks could engineer a progressive escalation of Islamist terrorism directed against the various 'enemies of Islam' through demonstrative catastrophic terrorist strikes.
2   Within this context, the 9/11 strikes were intended to attract retaliatory violence; they were expected to result in the consolidation of the extremist Islamist forces, to undermine US prestige and that country's sense of invulnerability, and to catalyse a chain of events that would destabilize the emerging unipolar world order in unpredictable ways, in order to create a space for political uncertainty in which the Islamists could make a focused bid for power.
3   To take the war to American soil, to make the United States seem vulnerable and weak.
4   The attack was to act as a catalyst, to be a model for future actions.
5   For the Islamist terrorists, the present world order is not only irrevocably unjust but utterly debased, a challenge and an insult to God's will on earth. The system cannot, in other words, be 'improved'; it must be swept aside, destroyed, whatever the costs.
6   The apparent stability of the world order, in this view, is a stagnant pool; the act of terror, a rock, or even a pebble, thrown into it. What matters is not the immediate or direct impact, but the ripples it will create. And with a thousand little pebbles, the wasted, crumbling, degenerate walls and structures of this system will collapse, and a deluge will wash away the 'evil of the world'.

Let us compare our respondents' specific answers to this unique terrorist incident with more general findings from the Terrorism Studies literature on the causes of terrorism. In a volume edited by Tore Bjørgo, *Root Causes of Terrorism: Myths, Reality and Ways Forward*, the editor and his colleagues identify 14 preconditions and precipitants of (non-state) terrorism:[30]

1   lack of democracy, civil liberties and the rule of law;
2   failed or weak states;

3 rapid modernization;
4 extremist ideologies;
5 historical antecedents of political violence, civil wars, revolutions, dictatorship or occupation;
6 hegemony and inequality of power;
7 illegitimate or corrupt governments;
8 powerful external actors upholding illegitimate governments;
9 repression by foreign occupation or by colonial powers;
10 the experience of discrimination on the basis of ethnic or religious origin;
11 failure or unwillingness by the state to integrate dissident groups or emerging social classes;
12 the experience of social injustice;
13 the presence of charismatic ideological leaders;
14 triggering events.

The longer terrorist campaigns last, the more the original factors that led to much violence in the first place tend to be replaced with other factors that sustain terrorism – factors such as (1) cycles of

Table 1.1 Sample answers to the question 'What are, in your view, the main causes of the terrorist attacks of 11 September 2001 against the United States?'

Respondent A
1 Nineteen unremarkable men, motivated by a fanatical ideology; goaded by base prejudice; recruited from a failing culture overtaken by the West; trained for years in remote locations and subsequently living covertly in the targeted countries; and controlled by an organization modelled on successful Fortune 500 companies;
2 no others.

Respondent B:
1 US foreign policy;
2 weakness of American intelligence;
3 shortcomings of the US preventive measures (particularly airport security, etc.).

Respondent C:
1 An extended period of political unrest in Middle East;
2 an international culture accepting of political violence as a problem-solving tool;
3 growth of religious extremism and polarization of extremist views.

Respondent D:
1 An attempt to deter the United States (the government and especially the public, using a psychological campaign) from supporting Muslim states which are not Islamic radical oriented, threatening the United States and seeking to force the American military out of 'any Muslim soil'; an attempt to stop US monetary support for non-radical Arab countries such as Egypt and Jordan and the support for Israel in order to create circumstances that will make it possible for local Islamic radical movements to revolt against the regimes in their respective countries;
2 an attempt to fulfil what the planners and the perpetrators believe is a divine command: fighting the main superpower in the world, which threatens their aspiration to spread their radical version of Islam all over the world and create an Islamic caliphate state governed by Shari'ah law;
3 leading their potential constituency to believe that they are fighting against the evil forces of the world, and hence getting their appreciation and support.

Respondent E:
1 Propaganda of the deed (proving one's capabilities and the adversary's weakness);
2 declaration of war against the most salient representative of the 'West's' spirit and might;
3 recruiting purposes;
4 'watch me and do the same'.

---

revenge; (2) the need of the group to provide for its members and the survival of the group itself; and (3) the rationale of not giving up profitable criminal activities originally initiated to sustain the group. Together, these factors often mean that bridges for a return to normal politics have been burned; there is no exit strategy.[31]

It is a challenge to arrive at a theory that can apply to several types of terrorism, ideally to state as well as non-state terrorism. Such a theory of terrorist campaigns is likely to be on a high level of abstraction. It would have to include:

- root causes (such as the weight of an unresolved historical experience of violent conflict);
- proximate causes (such as expectations of political gain from the use of terrorist tactics);
- precipitants (such as a polarizing public event);
- preponderance of conflict 'accelerators' over 'decelerators'.[32]

A general explanatory theory of terrorism might well remain elusive unless it is embedded in a broader theory of violent conflict. Yet perhaps we should strive to narrow, rather than broaden, the analysis. One of our respondents, Ariel Merari, has pointed out that 'because of the diversity of terrorism and its multi-faceted nature, no single theoretical framework can meaningfully encompass the multiple phenomena that are usually referred to as "terrorism". At best, we can hope to generate theories which are limited to specific aspects of terrorism.'

In our questionnaire, we also asked our experts, 'Which of the currently circulating theories on terrorism do you find particularly ill-founded and misleading?' Here are some of the answers:

- The 'new terrorism' motivated by religious imperatives is fundamentally different from terrorism 20–30 years ago (Gressang).
- Terrorism is war, and countermeasures must be kept out of the legal sphere to the greatest extent possible.
- Terrorism is caused by the underdog, by discriminated populations (A. Gordon).
- Poverty and ignorance breed terrorism.
- Suicide terrorism is mainly a response to foreign occupation (as R. Pape claimed).
- Theories that suggest personality disorder or emotional or psychological strain as the cause of terrorism are unfounded.
- Modern international terrorism is primarily a manifestation of a 'clash of civilizations' or a by-product of North–South confrontation (Stepanova).
- Theories of 'state terrorism', artificially extending the definition of terrorism to repressive actions by states, are misleading (Stepanova).
- The 'long war' theory of terrorism propagated by the Pentagon.
- The 'carrot and stick' theory, which holds that terrorists should be provided with incentives (i.e. carrots) to behave well (Enders).
- The view that democracy is the antidote to terrorism (Chenoweth).
- The view that the EU approach to terrorism is 'milder' in terms of safeguarding main civil liberties while countering terrorism than the US approach (Omelicheva).
- Any theory that either is (1) US-centric and/or (2) ignores local conditions and/or (3) provides one simple answer (Marks).
- The view that terrorism is the greatest problem facing international society (Flemming).
- Conspiracy theories (e.g. that 9/11 was a Jewish conspiracy (Mincheva).
- Terrorism can be eliminated provided root causes are addressed (Shanty).
- Attacking terrorists causes more terrorism (Shanty).
- Terrorist networks are closely linked with organized criminal groups (Shanty).
- The creation of a Palestinian state will end terrorist attacks against Israel (Shanty).

To test theories, even 'ill-founded and misleading' ones, is never easy. Take the 'long war' theory: assuming that Rapoport's insightful 'four-wave theory' of terrorism (see Chapter 5) is correct and an average terrorist campaign wave lasts some 30 years, where should we put the starting point? If we place it, for the current wave of religious terrorism, in 1979, when the Iranian Revolution was successful, the current Salafist-jihadist terrorist wave should be on its last legs by now. If we take 1988 when Al-Qaeda was founded, it has still ten or more years to go. Or take the 'democracy is an antidote to terrorism' theory. While there is considerable empirical confirmation for the theory that democracies do not make war on each other, and while there is good logic underlying the assumption that where people can have their grievances addressed by elected governments, there is no need to resort to political violence, including terrorism, the situation is in fact more complicated. Just as states are not all the same, democracies too come in various forms, and their age matters too. There are, for instance, democracies where 'the winner takes all' after an election victory (the United Kingdom is an example), and there are democracies that do not follow this 'Westminster model' but have a proportional distribution of ministers in the government, depending on their party's relative electoral strength (as in Switzerland). The former type of democracy contributed, in Northern Ireland, to a quasi-tyranny of the Protestant majority over the Catholic minority, which was discriminated against and marginalized for a long time. In other words, it all depends how you define 'democracy' and how you define 'terrorism' – and how other factors impact on both.

Myths and fallacies about terrorism

The absence of consensus on a definition of terrorism has had a negative impact on serious theory building. Beyond social science theories there are many 'conspiracy theories'. There has been an abundance of those, though more among the Arab public and press than among scholars. There was such an abundance of purported 'facts' and 'half-truths' circulated after 9/11 that it was not difficult to construct seemingly plausible enough theories, convincing all those who have a vested interest in foregone conclusions and, even more so, guilt attribution (blame it on the CIA, the Jews, etc.).

With such dubious 'theories' in mind, a related question was addressed to our experts: 'What are, in your view, the most common (other) myths, misinterpretations and popular fallacies on terrorism?' Here are some of the answers:

- The 9/11 attacks were an American and/or Zionist conspiracy (Martin).
- There is a tendency to use terrorism as a synonym for almost all existing forms of violence in the world (Stepanova).
- There is a tendency to degrade terrorism to banal criminal activity and to overestimate the level of its integration with organized crime ((Stepanova).
- There is a tendency to equate Islamism (Islamic radicalism) with terrorism (Stepanova).
- There is gross exaggeration of terrorists' alleged drive to acquire unconventional materials, including weapons of mass destruction (WMD) (Stepanova).
- Terrorist use of WMD is inevitable.
- There is overestimation of the volume and scope of terrorism financing (Stepanova).
- Counter-terrorism is mistaken for the 'war on terrorism' (Stepanova).
- Terrorists are wild-eyed, mentally deficient religious maniacs (Smith and Smith).
- Terrorists are not rational (Lutz and Lutz).
- Terrorism does not work (Lutz and Lutz).
- The United States and Israel don't negotiate with terrorists.
- A terrorist personality can be narrowly profiled.
- Groups like Al-Qaeda can be appeased by making concessions to them.
- Democracy solves terrorism; if terrorists only knew how great democracy was, they would want it.

- Terrorism is a response to the world's efforts to prevent terrorism (Pratt).
- Terrorism can be resolved through concessions.
- Terrorism is a result of the Israeli–Palestinian conflict (Pratt).
- Terrorism is a result of hostility to US government policy in Iraq (Pratt).
- Terrorism is the inevitable by-product of poverty (Pratt).
- Using deadly force and military might is the only, or the most effective way, to combat terrorism.
- Chemical, biological, radiological and nuclear weapons (weapons of mass destruction) are easy to obtain and use in terrorist attacks.
- Sunni and Shi'ah terrorist groups would never work together (Forest).
- A 'global war on terror' can be won (Forest).
- 'They hate us for our values and our freedoms' (Forest).
- Terrorists act out of desperation.
- There is a standard profile of terrorists.
- Terrorism is largely state sponsored (Barrett).
- Terrorists can be won over by exposure to alternative value systems (Barrett).
- That terrorism is the product of social deprivation and lack of opportunity (Whine).
- Killing the current core operators and leaders will solve the problem (Marks).
- Combatting terrorism is a 'war' in any traditional sense of the term 'war' (Marks).
- Terrorism, at least in the short run, can be defeated, i.e. eliminated, rather than 'managed' (Marks).
- Terrorism is the legitimate result of state terror (Sirseloudi).
- Terrorists are freedom fighters (Sirseloudi).
- There is a legitimation for terrorist acts (state and non-state).
- International terrorism is somehow a mortal threat to most nation-states (Romarheim).
- Terrorism can be countered by increasing welfare schemes and focusing on development (Sahni).
- Terrorists have genuine grievances (Sahni).
- Use of force against terrorism will only contribute to a further escalation of terrorism (Sahni).
- Terrorism can be resolved through negotiations with terrorist groups, and through conciliation of terrorist leaders and their sponsors (Sahni).
- Terrorism is random and lacks specific direction. In reality, terrorism is purposeful and it invariably involves selectivity in its execution.
- One man's terrorist is another man's freedom fighter (Gordon).
- Societies that support terrorism are amendable to accretions of reform that can help eliminate the ideological and recruitment base of terrorism without radical structural transformation of such host societies (Sahni).
- If you invest enough money and economic aid in countries that support terrorism, this will certainly stop terrorist activities (Gordon).

Are these propositions all myths, or half-truths at best? As long as they are not properly tested, the jury is still out. Take, for instance, the 'theory' that there is a clearly identifiable 'terrorist personality' which can be profiled. Much has been speculated about the personality of 'the terrorist'. Among scholars the majority opinion is that such a search is probably futile. In psychological terms, there is no single profile of the archetypal terrorist. Since terrorism is a technique – basically boiling down to killing civilians to influence (impress, provoke, shock, coerce, harm) relevant third parties – it can be used by many different 'players'. All you need is plenty of explosives and no scruples and the conviction that terrorism 'works'. Terrorist can be believers or atheists, left- or right-wingers, opponents or supporters of the state. The terrorist can be a dictator, a director of a secret police service, or the leader of a vigilante death squad loosely connected to the security forces of the government. Alternatively, the terrorist can be a local rebel who has gone underground, or a foreign 'sleeper' who waits for the signal to strike terror in the heart of a host society. The 'terrorists' themselves rarely accept the label and prefer to call themselves 'freedom fighters', 'holy warriors', 'soldiers of God', or 'jihadists', or use some other term with heroic connotations. The self-labelling usually stands in stark contrast to the criminal violence terrorists practise against unprepared and defenceless civilians. In many cases, we do not even know who carried out a terrorist bombing. Almost two-thirds of terrorist acts are no longer claimed – which was not the case when terrorism was 'young'. That makes identification of the perpetrators difficult. Many people use violence, but some uses of violence (as for self-defence) are more legitimate and/or legal than others.

So far, no terrorist personality has been found. In fact, most terrorists have been found to be clinically quite normal, despite their decidedly extra-normal violence.[33] However, there is as yet no proof that there is no such thing as a terrorist personality. The question 'Is there, in your view, something like a "terrorist personality" that can be profiled?' was answered by 52 of the 91 respondents. The majority (36 respondents) thought there was no such personality, but 16 thought there was. A balanced assessment of the state of the current debate has been given by one of our respondents, Ariel Merari. He wrote:

> There is no scientific basis for either an unequivocal 'yes' or 'no'. At present, the only scientifically correct answer is: so far, no empirical evidence has been found for the existence of universal terrorist personality traits (i.e. across nationalities, cultures, political contexts, and roles). However, no serious attempt has been made thus far to find out whether such commonalities exist. Such an attempt must include systematic interviews and standard psychological tests administered by trained psychologists. All that we can say for now is that it is unlikely that there are common universal personality traits for terrorists. However, the following points should be borne in mind:
>
> The likelihood that some common personality traits are shared by terrorists within the same culture, nationality, political context and role (e.g. hijackers, suicide bombers, etc.) is, presumably, greater than the likelihood that common traits can be found universally (across nationality, culture, political contexts and roles). There is no reason to assume that terrorists are characterized by a single personality pattern; it is hypothetically more reasonable to assume that several different personality patterns are associated with involvement in terrorism. It would be a mistake to expect a perfect correlation between any personality pattern and involvement in terrorism.

As in the case of the 'terrorist personality', a number of other myths, misinterpretations and fallacies listed above contain elements of truth that apply at least in part to some sub-populations of terrorists.

Terrorists and freedom fighters

One of the most widespread assumptions is that 'one man's terrorist is another man's freedom fighter'. (Incidentally, while there have been many attempts to find a 'terrorist personality', the 'freedom fighter' has escaped such profiling.)

One of our respondents, Jeffrey Simon, observed:

> The familiar phrase 'one person's terrorist is another person's freedom fighter' really goes to the heart of the terrorist phenomenon. What one observer views as terrorism, another can view as freedom-fighting. The major difference between terrorism and guerrilla warfare is that guerrilla wars usually include concerted efforts by medium-sized or large groups of armed combatants to topple a government or to gain control over a section of a country

through a campaign of rural (and sometimes urban) attacks, including (at times) direct engagements with the national military forces. And while terrorism (such as assassination of government officials) is a tactic of guerrilla insurgents, it is not the primary tactic or means for achieving their goals, whereas for terrorist groups it is.

Here are ten more, largely overlapping, responses from our experts to the question 'What is, in your view, the relationship between "terrorism" and "national liberation struggles"/"freedom-fighting"/ "resistance against foreign occupation"?'

1 Legally speaking, there is none, as these are distinct concepts. International humanitarian law prohibits attacks against civilians and civilian objects regardless of the cause – or its justness – underlying a situation of armed conflict and therefore already prohibits most acts that would be considered 'terrorist' if committed in peacetime (the response from an international lawyer linked to the ICRC).
2 Terrorism is always violent (it involves the use of force or the threat of force), whereas national liberation struggles, freedom-fighting and resistance against foreign occupation can also occur (and frequently do occur) non-violently (Chenoweth).
3 'Terrorism' is a tactic, while 'freedom-fighting' is the motivation and the justification.
4 That depends on the target; freedom fighters who attack only combatants are not terrorists (Enders).
5 Terrorism is a tactic that violates the norms of warfare. Not all freedom fighters choose to use terrorism.
6 An individual can be both a terrorist and a freedom fighter at the same time, as a result of the same action. It is also possible to be one or neither of the two (Van Liere).
7 Terrorism is primarily directed against non-combatants, whereas the other categories are directed against minority domination or occupation forces.
8 Freedom-fighting is what you favour, and terrorism is what you disfavour.
9 The important thing is how the uncommitted public views the objectives of the groups operating on their behalf or in their name. . . . Is an act of violence sanctioned because the groups seem less 'violent' or 'evil' than the state forces? At what point does this calculus begin to change? (Fair).
10 The dilemma of 'terrorists or freedom fighters' has been misleading, at best, from the very beginning and best reflects the highly politicized nature of all discussions on terrorism. There are no terrorist goals; there are terrorist means. Attempts to define these groups as either purely insurgent ('freedom fighters') or purely terrorist are misleading, as these groups are both insurgent and terrorist at the same time. Thus, the dilemma 'terrorists versus freedom fighters' does not make any sense and should not be applied to insurgent movements that combine terrorist tactics with other means. . . . Governments faced with insurgencies may often try to de-legitimize the entire armed resistance movements (and their goals) by labelling opponents as terrorists, regardless of whether a certain group or part of the movement actually uses terrorist means or not (Stepanova).

The freedom fighter versus terrorist controversy is especially pronounced when it comes to the Israeli–Palestinian conflict. Here we notice that the position of some scholars appears to be (co-) determined by their background. Let us therefore contrast here the views of a Muslim and an Israeli scholar. According to a US-based Muslim scholar,

Terrorism is different from national liberation struggles, freedom-fighting, and resistance against occupation, but groups that engage in national liberation and resistance often engage in terrorism. Terrorism entails the intentional targeting of civilians, even if that is for the purpose of ending oppression or occupation. National liberation and resistance to occupation entail targeting personnel or infrastructure that is directly responsible for the maintaining political oppression or occupation or provides the repressive regimes or occupiers direct material support and political legitimacy.

If occupation involves establishing settlements, as the French have done in Algeria or Israel in Palestine, then attacking those settlers is part of the national liberation struggle (not terrorism) because these settlers are creating territorial and demographic realities based on domination and aggression, not free choice and collective will. Moreover, historically, settlers, while they appear to act like civilians, are often armed and hostile to the indigenous populations of the occupied lands. Finally, settlers are often a voice against ending occupations and a voting bloc that gives legitimacy to the occupation, hence constituting direct material support for occupiers.

An Israeli scholar (Ganor) says:

> The concepts of 'terrorist' and 'freedom fighter' do not contradict one another. . . . One of the most widespread efforts to forestall a definition of terrorism and to empty it of any meaning is the attempt to compare terrorist activity with actions aimed at national liberation. This is being done by intentionally mixing between illegitimate mean and justified goal.

As an example of someone who manages 'to jump over the shadow' of origin, here is the response of a US-based scholar with a Middle Eastern background. Richard Chasdi observed:

> Terrorism is a 'means' to an end and hence, to compare 'terrorism' as a means, to 'freedom', which is a goal or 'end', is thereby in effect logically flawed. When 'freedom' is the goal pursued over the political landscape, what that essentially means . . . is freedom to pursue 'self-determination' as mentioned in the Charter of the United Nations in Chapter I article 2. . . . To be sure, 'resistance against foreign occupation' meets the *jus ad bellum* ('justice to go to war') component of a 'post-attack' condition, but that does not address *jus in bello* ('justice in war') concerns that revolve around (1) 'discrimination', (2) 'military necessity' [and] (3) 'proportionality'. If one or more of these elements of the jurisprudential standard of *jus in bello* is violated, the person(s) or group that commits those infractions may fall into the sphere of terrorism, *inter alia* if *mens rea* ('criminal intent') can be proven.

The controversy on this issue is also very much alive on the Indian subcontinent, owing to the Kashmir issue. While we had no Pakistani respondent to this question, we have three insightful replies from scholars from India or of Indian descent. An Indian respondent, Harjit Sandhu, said:

> Freedom fighters target tyrants and their agents. By contrast, a terrorist spreads fear among masses and kills indiscriminately to threaten all. Terrorists usually aren't fighting for anyone's freedom. Instead, they're usually fighting for their own chance to be tyrants, hence their disregard even for the lives of the people they may claim to be 'liberating'.

Another Indian, Ajai Sahni, commented:

> The justifications of terrorism in terms of liberation struggle, freedom fighting, etc. derive from questionable or fallacious reasoning. Take, for instance, the 'one man's terrorist'

argument. This is clearly based on contra-factual demand for the uniqueness of identity. The fact is a man has multiple identities. . . . He may . . . be freedom fighter and terrorist; the first identity defines what he fights for, the second, the method he employs. . . . 'Freedom fighters' . . . cannot reconcile an act of random and wanton violence that terminates the very possibility of freedom for innocent others within any consistent ethical paradigm. The murder of innocents would be unacceptable within virtually any concept of 'just war'. Even as there can be no 'just genocide', 'just terrorism' can or should make no real sense in legitimate political discourse. It is only because these arguments have not been widely articulated or debated that the confusion, and hence the ambivalence, over terrorism has persisted in both public and policy circles.

M.J. Gohel, a UK-based scholar of Indian descent, said:

Surprisingly, many in the Western world have accepted the mistaken assumption that terrorism and national liberation are two extremes in the scale of legitimate use of violence. The struggle for 'national liberation' would appear to be the positive and justified end of this sequence, whereas terrorism is the negative and odious one. It is impossible, according to this approach, for any organization to be both a terrorist group and a movement for national liberation at the same time. In failing to understand the difference between these two concepts, many have, in effect, been caught in a semantic trap laid by the terrorist organizations and their allies.

The confusion of 'terrorists' with 'freedom fighters' is one of the main 'false sociologies' (Sahni) in the discourse on terrorism. At the risk of repetition, it is worth pointing out the current position of international humanitarian law in this matter. These are the four requirements for 'freedom fighters' (or 'resistance fighters') to meet to be considered 'lawful belligerents' (or 'combatants') under international occupation law:

1   The combatants must comply with the rules of international law applicable in armed conflicts.
2   They must carry arms openly during each engagement and also, though the terms are complicated, before it.
3   Combatants are obliged, wherever possible, to distinguish themselves from the civilian population while they are engaged in an attack or in a military operation preparatory to an attack.
4   Members of regular, uniformed armed units are of course expected to wear uniform.[34]

To judge by this list, it would appear that a good number of today's 'freedom fighters' might not quite make it into the category of 'lawful belligerents'. While in a few 'freedom fighters' a future statesman might 'slumber',[35] many are more likely to degenerate to little more than bandits. Even worse, many of those who have been successful have become lifelong leaders of *de facto* one-party states, often ruling their country by methods similar to those that brought them to power. Adherence to international law is a prerequisite – a necessary but perhaps not a sufficient condition – for becoming a legitimate freedom fighter.[36] The same standards distinguish a soldier from a war criminal.

The discussion on terrorism can profit from the distinction made in the discussion on the ethics of war. For centuries, just war theorists have made a distinction between *jus ad bellum* (the right to conduct a [just] war) and *jus in bello* (the legality of certain techniques in warfare). Certain forms of warfare are more just than others, notably wars of self-defence when attacked, warfare in support of a coalition partner who has come under attack, and wars legitimized by the Security Council of the United Nations.[37] In warfare, certain weapons (e.g. chemical weapons, dum-dum projectiles) and certain techniques (the taking of hostages, the use of civilians as human shields) are forbidden.

Terrorism is, in my view, about methods and techniques (e.g. the use of civilian victims to wage psychological warfare against an opponent). The motives of terrorists might be legitimate and just, but that alone does not make them lawful belligerents. The dilemma of many insurgents rebelling against the forces of state power is that they rarely have a chance of success if they attack the security forces of the state head-on. They therefore often portray their choice of terrorism as their modus operandi as 'necessary' because of the asymmetry of forces between themselves and their opponents. Yet that does not make these methods legitimate, let alone legal. Nor are such illicit methods necessarily more effective than alternative forms of political struggle. One study that examined 42 terrorist campaigns waged by 28 terrorist groups of different backgrounds over a five-year period found that they failed to achieve their limited policy goals no less than 93 per cent of the time. [38]

A terrorist, on the other hand, is usually not uniformed (unless he wears the uniform of his opponent as a ruse) and hides his weapons. Guerrilla fighters and soldiers act in situations of armed conflict. Terrorists, on the other hand, often act in peacetime, outside zones of conflict although they might also act in a situation of (quasi-)occupation. All three – soldiers, guerrillas and terrorists – use violence, but the first two groups target only armed security forces, although they might hit civilians by mistake or, under military necessity, are prepared to risk considerable 'collateral damage' among civilian facilities and populations. Terrorists, on the other hand, target unarmed civilians and non-combatants deliberately to produce shock and awe. In war, much of their behaviour would constitute war crimes. In peacetime, it constitutes gross violations of human rights and serious crimes. However, this does not exclude the possibility that terrorists also occasionally (if they are not suicidal or when the odds are not overwhelmingly against them) attack armed forces in ambushes and hit-and-run operations. On those occasions, they are, however, not 'terrorists' but 'guerrilla fighters', 'partisans', 'insurgents', 'rebels', 'enemy combatants', etc. Yet when the basic distinction between attacks on armed and unarmed people is dropped, a group that disregards it is likely to be qualified as terrorist only. Al-Qaeda's leader, Osama bin Laden, has taken such a position when he said, 'We do not have to differentiate between military or civilian. As far as we are concerned, they [the Americans] are all targets.'[39] We will come back to this crucial distinction in Chapter 2, on definition.

Terrorism and religion

In our questionnaire, we also asked our experts, 'What, if any, is, in your view, the relationship between "terrorism" and "religion"?' Again they were divided, but then the definitions of religion vary almost as much as those of terrorism.[40] Here are some of the answers:

- There is no relationship whatsoever (Kaplan, Whine).
- There is no necessary connection (Enders).
- Religion often provides a script for what an individual or group wants to do for non-religious reasons. Religion is perhaps more the 'rules of engagement' than the cause of political violence. Conversely, terrorism can create fear that brings people to religion.
- Terrorism is a method to achieve some further goal. This further goal can be described in terms of religion. Religious beliefs can be a motivating force for terrorists (Van Liere).
- Some groups cloak their use of terrorism with religious and quasi-religious reasons (Mickolus).
- Religion can provide a motivation to sacrifice much, including one's own life.
- Terrorism can be religiously, ideologically or socially motivated – and sometimes a combination of these.
- Many perpetrators rationalize and justify terrorism by invoking religion.
- Believing that God is on one's side is a powerful incentive to action. A second link between terrorism and religion is the concept of 'martyrdom'. The belief that one will be rewarded in the afterlife motivates some followers to perpetrate suicide terrorist attacks. Third, religious (sacred) terrorists believe that their ends and means are sanctioned by divine authority, which

humans have no right to alter. Therefore, religious terrorist conflicts are more difficult to resolve than secular terrorist conflicts (Simon).

- The enculturing in religious discourses is by now one of the most important processes of recruitment for Salafi-jihadi movements.
- Religion provides an additional operating and motivational space for violence that other secular ideologies cannot provide. On the margin, the benefits of religion-sanctioned violence can be argued to prove that divine benefits that will always exceed secular costs for those committed to religious violence. For instance, the perpetrator's personal utility derived from 'eternal salvation' will always trump the risk of imprisonment or even actual imprisonment to an adherent of an organization that uses religiously motivated violence. . . . By dancing around this subject of religion and violence, analysts deprive themselves of this insight that in a fundamental way, religious [ideologies] can motivate different kinds of violence as compared with secular ideologies (Fair).
- Religious terrorists are the most lethal because a belief that their actions are guided by a higher power that translates into stronger moral disengagement. As a result, no matter who is killed or injured by the terrorist acts, it's viewed as serving God's will (Forest).
- The nexus between religion and nationalism is even more deadly!
- Humans who behave violently prefer to have some kind of relieving justification for this conduct (Romarheim).
- Those who believe they will reach paradise as martyrs, or believe the world is about to end and all disbelievers are doomed (messianic), will often lack moral bindings as regards methods applied and destruction and havoc inflicted on their surroundings and fellow citizens (Romarheim).

It is worthwhile to quote some of the respondents at greater length. Here are three insightful replies. The first is from a US-based Muslim scholar:

> I am an instrumentalist when it comes to the relationship between religion and terrorism. Religion is a cultural 'toolkit' that contains within it texts, traditions, symbols, rituals, and myths that could be manipulated or selectively exploited by political contenders to mobilize people for collective action.
>
> The phenomenon of terrorism in religious movements is not a new one. Historically, all three Abrahamic traditions have experienced the rise of radical offshoots that promote extreme interpretations of religion and engage in 'holy' violence to promote worldly political objectives. The same can be said for nearly all non-Abrahamic traditions such as Hinduism, Buddhism, and so on. Those who want to promote a peaceful agenda that includes compromise with former enemies and accommodation with extant political elites will find in their religious tradition the requisite verses and symbols for peace. Those who want to promote a militant agenda that includes anti-civilian violence and rebellion against incumbent governments will find in their religion the required verses and symbols for war. Thus, the best way to proceed analytically is by looking at the political agendas of religious groups, the conditions that may encourage them to turn to violence, and the dynamics of contention that facilitate their growth or decline. There is hardly any evidence to suggest that the content of religion is sufficient to give rise to political extremism and terrorism. All world religions have featured periods of peace and periods of extreme violence.

In a similar vein, another scholar, Assaf Moghadam, held:

> Religion has an ambiguous relationship with violence in general. Although religion is often associated with positive values such as compassion and peace, the mythology of most world religions is filled with violent images and bloody histories.

The main problem in studying the role played by religious radicalism (extremism) in motivating, supporting, justifying and guiding a certain group's terrorist activity can be most evidently demonstrated by the case of Islamist terrorism. The problem is that while religious extremism may serve as a powerful driving force and/or be effectively instrumentalized to guide/justify terrorist activity, it does not necessarily or automatically lead to terrorism or indeed, to violence(!) It should also be stressed that groups using terrorist means in the name of religion do not necessarily represent some 'deviant sects', but are often guided by a radical interpretation of religion's basic tenets, concepts and notions, such as the radical militant interpretation of a traditional and essential Islamic concept of jihad. Still, while Islamist jihadi terrorism has become the main form of transnational (in fact, supra-national) terrorism over the recent decade, it does not mean that all Islamist (radical Islamic) movements include jihad in a set of their first priorities and are ready to use violence, particularly against civilians (e. g. the strongly extremist Hizb-ut-Tahrir movement in Central Asia has consciously opted not just for abstaining from the use of terrorist means, but for non-violence in general) [a view that is not uncontested; A.S.].

Ekaterina Stepanova, a Russian scholar, warned that generalizations should be applied only with extreme care; she nevertheless identified some general features shared by most terrorist groups with a distinct religious imperative:

- Terrorist activities are usually dependent on the blessing by 'spiritual authorities/guides' (not necessarily people of the most solid theological credentials).
- They are justified by direct references to sacred texts (which usually may also be used by more moderate forces to justify exactly the opposite point).
- The main audience of terrorist acts tends to be of a much higher order ('Allah is sufficient as a witness!'), etc.

She also noted that many groups operating in places like Kashmir, Chechnya, Iraq or Mindanao effectively combine religious extremism with radical nationalism. Further, she noted that it is possible to distinguish at least two theoretical approaches to the role of religious extremism vis-à-vis terrorist activities:

1   the manipulative/instrumentalist approach, which argues that religious beliefs are simply utilized by terrorist groups as an effective means of communication, a powerful propaganda strategy and a way to transnationalize a group's agenda and broaden its constituency, in the absence of any equally powerful secular ideology;
2   a more socio-ideological approach that views the role of religious radicalism as that of a reaction of parts of disillusioned elites and societies at large to painful processes of economic, socio-political and cultural modernization, secularization and (for Muslims in particular) Westernization perceived as threatening their identity or even physical survival and building on real grievances based on past and present injustices committed by 'modernists', 'aliens' or 'non-believers' against a religious community in whose name the group claims to speak (such as US-led interventions in Iraq or Afghanistan).

She further observed that

[t]he very lack of immediate progress towards their ideological goals makes these movements particularly dependent on the support of at least parts of the local population, which they need to survive while, as they believe, they slowly advance towards the future

'ideal Islamic government' (which partly explains Islamist groups' extensive social and humanitarian activities). It is the imperative to keep pace with the prevailing popular mood that leads many of them to turn to armed struggle in the first place. In sum, the relationship between terrorism and religious radicalism/extremism does exist and the latter may become a very powerful and effective ideological basis for the former, but the link is not necessarily a binding one.

Her views were, in part, echoed by a number of other respondents, including former US ambassador Edward Marks, who wrote:

Terrorism is not a discrete human activity; it arises from and remains embedded in the complicated human socio-political environment. Insofar as a given human being or group is motivated by religious perspectives which have a political purpose or objective requiring or mandating the use of violence, then religion can be aids to be a precursor or enhancer of terrorism. . . . 'Kill them all, God will know his own' and other formulations which place the 'Other' outside conventional religious restrictions to the use of violence provide a religious (and moral) counterargument enabling the use of violence against usually prohibited targets such as civilians. Religion can also be used to stiffen the morale of the weaker side, showing that the temporary power imbalance is temporary, as God will reverse it. In other words, to overcome the presumption of failure. In today's world there is a clear connection between some terrorism and some strains of fundamentalist religion in every region of the world: Islam, of course, but also Judaism, Protestant and Catholic Christianity, Buddhism, and even Hinduism. Something in the modern world, perhaps globalization, is unsettling many people, and their search for security leads some to religiously founded rejection of the modern world and beyond that to violence.

To illustrate a similar point, Ajai Sahni from India pointed out that

[r]eligious beliefs can be used to justify any possible perversion. Thus, a faith system based on the teachings of a man who advocated complete non-violence and exhorted his followers to 'turn the other cheek' was at one time in history used to justify the tortures and abuses of the Inquisition, and the conquering rampages of the Crusades. . . . All religious texts contain a sufficient measure of ambiguity to lend themselves to virtually any ethical scheme.

Dr. Sahni also made another valid point, reminding us that Islamophobia is not the only problem:

It needs to be emphasized in the strongest terms possible that moderate Islam is, today, under deep, penetrating and sustained attack in every concentration of Muslim populations, and there is a 'hardening' of beliefs that may lend itself to an extension of the extremist jihad in an uncertain future. The demonization of Islam is loudly protested, both by neutral scholars and by the apologists for extremist Islam. But there is a neglect of an even more vicious process of the demonization of all other faiths and nations among the people of Islam – and this goes beyond the 'great Satan', America, or the 'brahminical conspiracy' of 'Hindustan', or the visceral anti-Semitism of the Arabs, to embrace all *kafirs* or non-Muslims, and also all Muslims who do not conform to the perverse vision of extremist Islam. There is a profound ideology of hatred that is being fervently propagated through Islamist institutions, particularly the madrassas or religious schools and seminaries that are proliferating rapidly across South Asia, and it is winning many ardent converts. As stated before, these are still a minority among Muslims; but this is a vocal, armed, well-supported, extremely violent and growing minority. The majority, by contrast, has tended to passivity and conciliation, and there is little present evidence of the courage of conviction or the will for any moderate Islamic resistance to the rampage of extremist Islam.

M.J. Gohel, a UK-based scholar of Indian origin, remarked:

> In order to rally support for a political programme seeking to replace the secular and democratic world, Islamists have camouflaged, with surprisingly considerable success amongst some, their real intentions under a cloak of perceived religious persecution and their desire to seek justice, and assert that agenda through violence and which, in order to make it more palatable, is promoted as defensive action by a religion under threat from the immoral and infidel West, and interpreting religious text as providing legitimacy for such militant action.
>
> Thus terrorists, as also extremist clerics and radical elements, have labelled terrorism as jihad, suicide bombers as martyrs, transforming criminal violent action into a desirable holy religious duty or endeavour for the devout, and who will be rewarded in paradise for their sacrifice.
>
> Using the protection of religion as the motivational factor has enabled the terrorists to provide a reason, a gloss, for their indiscriminate violence, which excuse has unfortunately received a hearing amongst significant numbers across the world, which would not have been the case if religion had not been brought into the equation, and the terrorists were exposed for what is in reality their political agenda: to destroy freedom and impose a fundamentalist lifestyle, similar to the Taliban rule in Afghanistan.

Boaz Ganor, from Israel, in turn, held:

> There is no direct relationship between terrorism and religion. But religious extremists are commonly using incitement and brainwashing messages in order to provoke their followers to use terrorism in order to fulfil the so-called divine command. Religion is also used to challenge the internationally widely accepted laws of war, and permit in the name of God deliberate attacks against civilians and civilian targets. Religious extremists are sometimes trying to justify their wrongdoing as a defensive war that is designed to protect their religion from malicious intent of other religions with the cooperation of the 'infidels' from their own religion. In many cases the religious extremist provocateurs have concrete political goals which they are trying to achieve – revolting against regimes, demolishing 'infidel' states, or creating a new religious political entity.

Marxists tried to divide human societies by 'class' and propagated class war. Fascists used the equally fuzzy concept of 'race' to identify their public enemy. Salifist Islamists now use religion, dividing humankind into true Muslims on the one hand and unbelievers (*kafir*) and heretics (*takfir*) on the other hand and they alone arrogate who belongs to which group. In each generation, it seems, fanatics come up with a new justification for killing fellow human beings and find adherents among the uneducated and as well their well-educated ideological entrepreneurs who see a chance to instrumentalize class, race or religion to achieve political power for themselves.

Other conceptual questions

To return to our questionnaire and the answers we received from our expert respondents: another question we asked was 'Which (other) conceptual questions on terrorism are, in your view, not yet adequately solved?' Here are some of the answers we received:

- The challenge to research on terrorism lies in the strong political influences on the conceptualization of terrorism, through official or legal definitions of terrorism by governments, states or international organizations, definitions that are not aimed at guiding research (Scandinavian researcher).
- The increasing inadequacy of the basic and most commonly used typologies of terrorism (domestic (= internal) versus international terrorism; distinctions based on motivation, as most groups are driven by more than one motivation (e.g. national + religious + socio-political goals) (Stepanova).
- [If terrorism is seen as a form of asymmetric conflict waging]: The problem of fitting the role of so-called loyalist, vigilante, self-defence and other similar types of pro-government/anti-insurgent paramilitary violence (Stepanova).
- The distinction between terrorism and (guerrilla) war(fare) still seems murky (Weinberg).
- Further conceptualization and refinement of a 'continuum of combat escalation' ranging from terrorism posited at one axis, to full-blown and sustained war at the other axis is needed (Chasdi).
- Insurgency and terrorism have become mixed up. Is there a need to differentiate between the two, and, if so, what norms need to be applied? (Krishan).
- Given the lacuna in international law, how do you deal with a non-state international terrorist? Humanitarian law is not sufficiently developed (Pratt).
- Who are legitimate targets for those who are engaged in 'national liberation struggles'/'freedom fighting'/'resistance against foreign occupation?' (Pratt).
- A clearer distinction between 'terrorist groups' and groups that deploy terrorism as one of many insurgent and political strategies is needed.
- The state/non-state actor question is one of the most controversial and divisive conceptual aspects. The issue is extremely politicized since it decides whether states such as Israel, Iran, Syria and Russia (to only mention a few) can in fact exercise acts of terrorism (Romarheim).
- Defining the meaning of state terrorism, and distinguishing this from state-sponsored terrorism.
- Theoretical conceptualizations delving deeper into the interconnections and relationships between (1) oppression, (2) 'repression', (3) counterterror, and (4) state terror is needed (Chasdi).
- The 'effectiveness' of terrorism as an insurgent tactic – that is, does it actually work in terms of the objectives of its practitioners (Marks).
- Measuring counter-terrorism's success and failures (Ganor).
- Drawing a distinction between 'good terrorists' (those who are against imperial nations) and 'bad terrorists' (who are against democratic rule and values) (Tishkov).
- Determining right and wrong in counterterrorism measures, especially in reference to the 'democratic dilemma' – efficiency versus liberal democratic values (Ganor).

If we compare this list with the answers we received when we put the same question, 'Which conceptual questions on terrorism are, in your view, not yet adequately solved?', to experts in 1986, we find that some of the problems have remained more or less the same – unresolved or still disputed despite a quarter-century of thinking on these issues.[41] To varying degrees, this refers to conceptual issues such as:

- the boundaries between terrorism and other forms of political violence;
- whether government terrorism and resistance terrorism are part of the same phenomenon;
- the relationship between guerrilla warfare and terrorism;
- the problem of value judgements in determining which acts of political violence are legitimate or patriotic and which are terroristic;
- the relationship between terrorism as a concept and terrorism as a phenomenon;
- the relationship between crime and terrorism.

We will return to some of these questions in the next chapter. In the remainder of this chapter we will look at the issue of countering terrorism and what our respondents had to say about that. While in the previous section we did not quantify how many respondents shared one view or another, in this section we will look how many of the 91 respondents supported certain positions. However, it should be kept in mind that not all respondents answered all questions. On the other hand, respondents sometimes provided more than one answer, so that the number of answers is sometimes less than and sometimes greater than the total number of respondents.

Countering terrorism

While some critical theorists blame Terrorism Studies for the 'problem-solving approach',[42] mainstream researchers have no problems with that, arguing that this is entirely legitimate, just as the medical profession studies diseases in order to be able to cure them. In our questionnaire, we asked our experts a number of questions on how to counter terrorism. The first of these questions was 'What are, in your view, the most effective countermeasures against international terrorism?' Some of our respondents provided more than one answer. The following are the ten most frequently mentioned countermeasures, in declining order of perceived effectiveness, with the number of experts mentioning each measure in parentheses:

1 intelligence (47);
2 inter-agency and international information sharing and cooperative action (44);
3 cutting off many of the sources of funding of terrorists (24);
4 a prudent foreign policy (16);
5 international consensus over the definition and scope of terrorism (13);
6 limiting the spread of terrorist ideology through propaganda and the internet (11);
7 educating the public about what do if an attack is suspected, and after an attack (10);
8 providing counter-terrorism assistance to countries lacking expertise (10);
9 military cooperation (9);
10 improved border, airport and maritime security (8).

From this list, it becomes clear that the single dominant element for effective counter-terrorism is judged to be 'intelligence', followed by the related category of 'inter-agency and international information sharing and cooperative action' based on it. Even the third item, relating to the funding of terrorists, has a strong intelligence component. Following the money trail of the terrorists has probably brought with it more successes in terms of intelligence gained in the process than in terms of actual assets frozen or terrorist attacks prevented for lack of money.

The intelligence failures and shortcomings that led to the catastrophic terrorism of 11 September 2001 formed the background to the importance given to intelligence. We only have to recall that the 9/11 Report of the National Commission on Terrorist Attacks upon the United States and other investigations[43] revealed major gaps and shortcomings such as:

•   over-reliance on SIGINT (signals intelligence: intelligence obtained through the interception of signals) over HUMINT (human intelligence: intelligence obtained through interpersonal contact);
•   lack of coordination and collaboration between the 15 US intelligence agencies;
•   unwillingness of adequate information sharing, especially between the CIA and the FBI;
•   lack of imagination to interpret information that fell 'outside the box';
•   inability to process suspicious passport and visa information in time;
•   near-failure to penetrate the Al-Qaeda network;
•   lack of sufficient linguistic and analytical skills to exploit relevant information in real time.[44]

While intelligence is the key to selective counter-terrorism not targeting broad segments of the public, intelligence gathering on underground conspiracies in open societies faces human rights and privacy concerns. Intelligence efforts are also hampered by the increasing use of encryption by terrorists, their use of unfamiliar foreign languages and the sheer volume of intelligence gathered automatically from intercepted phone calls, emails and other electromagnetically transmitted communications, which have to be read and interpreted in actionable time to be of operational use.

In the framework of this chapter, I cannot present, let alone discuss, each of the counter-measures listed by our experts who answered the questionnaire. Some of the results came as a surprise. I was, for instance, amazed how few experts pleaded for the so-called root causes of terrorism to be addressed. Perhaps this is due to a sense of desperation about the multitude of issues that can 'cause' terrorism. It might also have to do with the fear that understanding the causes might create (more) sympathy for the terrorists in some quarters, excusing their behaviour.

Let us look at some other countermeasures mentioned by a smaller number of our experts:

11 deterrence (8);
12 public support and involvement (7);
13 remedying root causes (7);
14 international peace building and state building in failed or weak states (7);
15 arrests of key members of groups (7);
16 solid alliances – no seams between states which terrorists can exploit (7);
17 Sorting out politics and ethics: support for democracy or for anti-fundamentalist non-democratic regimes (6);
18 making the International Criminal Court (ICC) more proactive (6);
19 strengthening anti-proliferation measures (6);
20 targeted killings of terrorists and increasing manhunt capability (6).

Among these less frequently mentioned countermeasures, there were some that I thought would score much higher, such as 'winning hearts and minds'. That approach only figures among the minority suggestions in the following list. An interesting suggestion is the last one: it is well known that martial arts schools tend to attract organized crime figures. Some of the same fascination with fighting (and weapons!) is also likely to be found among people who are on the path to terrorism. The following are countermeasures against international terrorism that received from one to three mentions from our experts, again in declining order of perceived effectiveness:

21 maintaining strong legitimacy among the public for fairness of the system;
22 sustained universal efforts towards improvements in human development;
23 winning hearts and minds;
24 changing ideologies;
25 enforcement of Security Council Resolution 1373 and others by states;
26 biometric identity recognition;
27 scientific community R&D, e.g. on early warning/detection;
28 decoupling from religion;
29 isolation of radicals;
30 networking of Martial Arts clubs as reliable sources of information on violence-prone individuals.

There was other valuable advice in suggestions made by some of the experts, including these three 'do nots': (1) do not overreact; (2) do not use military force, except in exceptional cases (e.g. hostage taking); and (3) do not follow the extra-legal practices of certain countries in the war on terrorism.

The views listed so far reflected countermeasures deemed effective against international terrorism. The question is whether or not the same measures apply to domestic terrorism. As far as 'intelligence' is concerned, it indeed appears again as the most frequently mentioned category by our respondents. The following are the ten most frequently mentioned measures seen as being effective against domestic terrorism, with the number of mentions in parentheses:

1 intelligence (41);
2 visible counter-terrorism police capabilities (24);
3 preventive detention (16);
4 financial tracking of suspected terrorists and sympathizers (15);
5 inter-agency information sharing and cooperative action (14);
6 media compliance with information policy (10);
7 government cooperation with civic groups, religious institutions, etc. (9);
8 prohibiting external actors to define spiritual and political life of local communities (9);
9 adequate anti-terrorism legislation (8);
10 law enforcement and assurance of human security for all (8).

Here 'intelligence' as a category is immediately followed by 'police capabilities', which did not rank high on the list for international terrorism. The police, especially in the case of community policing, can be an excellent source of intelligence, as they can detect changes in the environment early on. Assumed links between organized crime and preparatory acts to launch terrorist campaigns is another reason why the police component probably scores high when it comes to domestic terrorism in some countries. However, the application of situational crime prevention to terrorism is something that is still underutilized.[45]

Among other countermeasures for domestic terrorism, our experts mentioned the following with some frequency. Again the number of mentions is given in parentheses:

11 development of inclusive institutions that provide alternative methods of political change (8);
12 protection of major targets (7);
13 an understanding of the issues (7);
14 public support and involvement (7);
15 border controls (7);
16 regulation of religious schools and meeting places (5);
17 demonstration of good governance, fairness, stability, determination (5);
18 liberal democracy (5);
19 neutralizing extreme indoctrination (5);
20 strengthening of the state (5).

If we go further down the frequency scale, here are a few of the less often mentioned countermeasures against domestic terrorism. It is a mixed, and even contradictory, bag of proposals, as we find among them pleas for both amnesty and for the death penalty for terrorists:

• regulating religious clergy;
• situational crime prevention;
• assimilation of immigrants;
• maintaining a strong sense of legitimacy among the public regarding the fairness of the system;
• targeted assassinations;
• addressing root causes;
• the death penalty for terrorist activities;
• an amnesty for terrorists;

- profiling;
- easing of restrictions on rules of evidence in court.

It is amazing that some countermeasures, in particular 'legitimacy', scored so low. In my view, legitimacy is of crucial importance – even more important in the long run than intelligence. The key question in a state faced with serious terrorist attacks is: who holds the moral high ground – not only in our own eyes but in the eyes of the world, including the diasporas in our midst and the 'man in the street' at home and abroad? If people think that what the terrorists want and do is more legitimate than what liberal democratic governments want and do, there will be a continuing supply of recruits to their ranks. To take the current concern with Al-Qaeda and other Salafist terrorists: if a revival of the caliphate offers a more desirable perspective to their followers than the Western vision of one world of good governance, democracy, rule of law and social justice, the world is likely to continue to be plagued by jihadi terrorism.

If we compare the five top measures against international terrorism proposed by our experts (p. 29) with those they proposed as effective against domestic terrorism (p. 31), there is much less overlap than might have been expected: only 'intelligence' and 'inter-agency information sharing and cooperative action' are among the top five. Given the fact that the distinction between domestic and international terrorism has become increasingly meaningless in a world of instant tele-communication and large-scale cross-border mobility across porous borders, this is a somewhat surprising finding.

Lessons learned

So far, we have addressed assumed best practices. Let us now turn to the lessons learned, both negative and positive, on the basis of the experts' experience of their own countries' encounters with terrorism.[46] The question I posed was 'What (both positive and negative) lessons can, in your view, be learned from your country's experience with terrorism?' Again, on the positive side, intelligence scores high, although it was not in first place, a place taken by international cooperation. The number of mentions for each proposed lesson is given in parentheses:

1   Build international cooperation/coalitions/regimes/norms for counter-terrorism (19).
2. Intelligence, above all, is what it takes to defeat terrorism (16).
3   Common understanding of the problem is needed (12).
4   Protect civil liberties while ensuring security (12).
5   Effective preparations (training) are needed to enhance capability to cope with terror (10).
6   There is a need to improve communication between law enforcement and intelligence (10).
7   Sufficient political culture (tolerance) is needed to encourage potential terrorists to refrain from hostile or revenge acts (10).
8   Terrorism should be treated as a law enforcement issue; stronger counter-terrorism laws need to be designed (9).
9   There is no local support for terror group agitation (7).
10 Terrorists cannot destroy the soul of a nation (7).

Among the less frequently mentioned positive lessons learned, one stands out very clearly: 'Avoid Abu Ghraib-type atrocities'. Nothing has done more harm to the United States claim of moral leadership than the revelations of Abu Ghraib and their subsequent mishandling, *de facto* exculpating high-ranking officials. Here is a list of selected minority views on lessons to be learned.

1   Avoid Abu Ghraib-type atrocities.
2   Never make unilateral concessions to a terrorist (group).

3 Do not allow extremist religious propaganda by outsiders.
4 Transparent government and law enforcement are needed.
5 Terrorism is real, not just a scare tactic.
6 Ex-combatants need to be reintegrated into society.
7 Terrorists should be arrested rather than killed to avoid the creation of martyrs.
8 Dialogue with immigrants is necessary.
9 Recognize when your opponent is prepared to concede (as with the Provisional Irish Republican Army).
10 Law enforcement is important.

We also asked our respondents about 'negative lessons learned'. Here are some of the most frequent answers with the number of mentions given in parentheses:

1 US experiences in Iraq suggest that military interventions are not necessarily effective (15).
2 There tends to be a loss of human rights (12).
3 There have been failures of intelligence (10).
4 Arrogance in foreign policy decision making can breed terrorism (9).
5 There is always a danger of repeat attacks (8).
6 Re-examine barriers between law enforcement and intelligence (8).
7 Training frontline troops is useless unless command elements have matching training (7).
8 The connection between Iraq and terrorism was weak (6).
9 Military measures without political solutions are likely to increase violence (6).
10 It is a mistake to define efforts to defeat terrorism as a 'war' in the first place (5).

Among the remaining, less frequently mentioned, 'negative lessons learned', there is also the sobering advice that 'Being "nice" to terrorists does not help'. Some of the lessons learned mentioned by only a few experts are extremely pertinent, some debatable. The following negative lessons learned from respondents' country experience are a selection of minority views, each having received fewer than five mentions:

• Terrorists can be as innovative and smart as us.
• Do not give terrorists free publicity.
• Without the most emphatic pressure, troops will misbehave and make things worse.
• Being 'nice' to terrorists does not help.
• Perception of regional imperialism must be avoided.
• Collective punishments do not work.
• Statistics on terrorism and definitions can be very misleading.
• Language and its use matter in profound ways with respect to counter-terrorism efforts. (An example is President Bush's remark about engaging in a 'crusade').
• There tends to be a continued growth and expansion of conspiracy theories, which further feeds and fuels those prone to be recruited. The problem is further aggravated by the total non-existence of any counter-argument or attempt to dispel these dangerous and inflammatory urban legends.
• The current Islamic threat is transnational, involving myriad groups, and there is no specific grievance that can be addressed, nor any specific leadership with whom one can seek a compromise.

Where do all these expert opinions leave us? What is needed is, to the extent possible, rigorous empirical testing of the hypotheses contained in many of the countermeasures referred to by experts. This also applies to the positive and negative 'lessons learned'. What we need are evidence-based findings, devoid of politics, 'political correctness' and bowing to special interest considerations. This is not to deny the value of insights of experts such as the ones we presented. These are in general based on intuitive knowledge, gained from experience. Often this is the only thing we have to go by until rigorous testing becomes possible for a given situation.

My own list of measures to prevent and combat non-state terrorism is also based on such intuitive knowledge gained while interacting with counter-terrorism officials in UN member states in the period 1999–2005.[47] It is attached as an appendix to this chapter.

In the following chapters, we will explore in more depth some of the issues raised in this introduction, addressing issues of definition, typology, theory, data and literature respectively.

Notes

1 In response to a questionnaire mailed out by A.P. Schmid in 2006.
2 Asbjørn S. Nørgaard, 'Political Science: Witchcraft or Craftmanship? Standards for Good Research'. *World Political Science Review*, 4(1), 2008, Article 5.
3 For female readers: I will not in all possible instances in this volume add 'her' to 'him' (or vice versa) where both genders can be meant, since this makes for tedious reading. For compensation, I will not use the term 'woman-made disaster' for 'man-made disaster'.
4 The questionnaire contained questions on definitions and other conceptual issues, research, databases and statistics, theoretical issues, resources, websites/bibliography/literature, and authors and their contribution to the field, as well as questions on the prevention of terrorism and counter-terrorist measures. It was answered by 91 experts (although not all questions were answered by all of them). A few remarks on the composition of the group of experts who were kind enough to answer the questionnaire in 2006 are in place. The professional background of the respondents (some had filled in more than one category, producing 136 entries) was as follows (several entered more than one category):

Academic	77
Intelligence analyst	15
Government official/civil servant	12
Law enforcement	9
Military	8
Media	8
Official of an international organization	5
Consultant	4
Victimology	3
Deviance	2
Non-governmental organization	3
Other (humanities, medicine, the insurance industry, etc.)	8

Fifty-three of the respondents had a political science background, 12 had a background in law, 7 one in psychology, 9 came from the military, another 7 listed as background law enforcement, yet another 6 sociology. Five had a background in history, 4 one in economy, 3 in philosophy, another 3 in journalism and media studies, 2 in biology and another 2 in international relations. Others (1 in each case) had backgrounds in anthropology, business studies, criminology, education, humanities, intelligence, mathematics, medicine, narcotics, oriental studies, physics, policy analysis, risk assessment and security studies. Curiously, none had a background in religious studies. In terms of gender, 80 per cent of the respondents were male and 20 per cent female. In terms of nationality, 43 of 85 respondents were from in the United States, 6 respondents were from Israel, 8 from the United Kingdom, 4 from Germany, 4 from Russia, 3 from Canada, 3 from Norway, 2 from Australia and 2 from the Netherlands. The remaining respondents were (1 for each country) from India, France, Egypt, Ireland, Bulgaria, Greece, Sri Lanka, Serbia, Switzerland, Sweden, Bosnia-Herzegovina and Mauritius. Non-Western countries are only weakly represented, with 4 respondents. Only 3 respondents were from countries with a strong Muslim presence.
5 Alex P. Schmid, 'Frameworks for Conceptualizing Terrorism'. *Terrorism and Political Violence*, 16(2), 2004, pp. 197–221.
6 These five frameworks are not exhaustive; there are other conceptual lenses. One can, for instance, also explore terrorism in a framework of (social) psychology. This is especially appropriate when one is dealing with 'lone wolf' terrorists. This approach is also germane when it comes to the study of victims of terrorism. The psychological dimension – which overlaps with the communication dimension but also touches on the religious dimension – might bring us closer to a better understanding of some of the root causes of terrorism (e.g. humiliation resulting in revenge).

7 A.P. Schmid and J. de Graaf, *Violence as Communication: Insurgent Terrorism and the Western News Media*. London: Sage, 1982.

8 An indication that terrorists view their attacks as forms of communication can, for instance, be gained from a statement of Osama Bin Laden in late January 2009, referring to Al-Qaeda's use of planes as means of attacking the United States: "'If it was possible to carry our messages to you by words we wouldn't have carried them to you by planes. The message sent to you with the attempt by the hero Nigerian Umar Farouk Abdulmutallab is a confirmation of our previous message conveyed by the heroes of September 11.'" (BBC New Channel, 24 January 2010).

9 Fear is the most powerful of emotions. As one authority put it, 'Terror appears to fit into the category of instinct-response which humans share with most animals. For example, most humans and animals fear the sight of mutilated bodies. Experiments with chimpanzees during which the animals were shown pictures of chimpanzees with their heads or limbs cut off elicited instinct-responses of extreme trepidation. This fear of violence done to the body is at the basis of the terror process' (Richard L. Gregory (ed.), *The Oxford Companion to the Mind*. Oxford: Oxford University Press, 1987, p. 770).

10 A study by Jean Decety (University of Chicago) found that '[w]hen children see others in pain, their brains respond as if it were happening to them'. This response has also been shown in adults. Dr Decety concluded, 'What it shows us is that we have this inborn capacity to resonate with the pain of others.' The study appeared in the journal *Neuropsychologia* and the quotations here are from Reuters: 'Empathy comes naturally to children: study', 11 July 2008, 12:34 a.m. EDT, at www.reuters.com/article/health/News/idUSN 1031553520080 (accessed 11 July 2008).

11 Alex P. Schmid, *Political Terrorism: A Research Guide to Concepts, Theories, Databases and Literature*. Amsterdam: North-Holland, 1984, pp. 64–72..

12 U.S. National Advisory Committee on Criminal Justice Standards and Goals, *Report of the Task Force on Disorders and Terrorism*. Washington, DC: GPO, 1976, p. 3.

13 J. Wolpe, 'Furcht'. In Wilhelm Arnold, Hans Jürgen Eysenck and Richard Meili, *Lexikon der Psychologie*, vol. 1. Augsburg, Germany: Bechtermünz Verlag 1996, p. 102.

14 Martin Eliott Silverstein, 'Emergency Medical Preparedness'. *Terrorism*, 1(1), 1977, pp. 51–52.

15 Cf. Rosalie Osmond, *Imagining the Soul: A History*. Stroud, UK: Sutton Publishing, 2003.

16 Adapted from Bruce Hoffman, 'Terrorism and WMD: Some Preliminary Hypotheses'. *Nonproliferation Review*, 4(3), Spring–Summer 1997, p. 48.

17 Most of the questionnaires were answered in the second half of 2006, some in early 2007.

18 Where no name is listed after a statement, it means that the respondent(s) preferred to remain anonymous. The exact wording of a response has sometimes been changed or shortened, as very similar responses by several respondents have been combined. The names after a statement are often illustrative and not exhaustive, as it would have made for cumbersome reading to provide longer lists in each case.

19 For a recent study, see John Rollins and Liana Sun Wyler, *International Terrorism and Transnational Crime: Security Threats, U.S. Policy, and Considerations for Congress*. Washington, DC: Congressional Research Service, 5 January 2010.

20 Threat (or rather, vulnerability) analysts have also raised the spectre of other forms of terrorism that have also not yet occurred to the terrorists themselves. An example is 'agro-terrorism' – attacks on the human food chain at source.

21 More than 30 years ago, Anthony Arblaster observed, 'There is an evident tendency to equate political violence with a single form of such violence – terrorism; and then to imply, or to assume, that all terrorism is "revolutionary" or "aimed at the overthrow of governments". Neither of these assumptions is valid. Although terrorism is so clearly a political phenomenon, and one which evokes strongly political responses, there is a curious way in which so much writing about terrorism evades the political, preferring to concentrate on the moral, or tactical or psychological dimensions of the subject.' Arblaster, 'Terrorism: Myths, Meaning and Morals'. *Political Studies*, 25(3), September 1977, pp. 414, 421.

22 Where the dominant goal of a perpetrator is to victimize civilians (in peacetime) and non-combatants (in wartime) so as to intimidate, coerce or impress and thereby influence (related) third parties, certain acts of political violence become 'terrorist'. An assassination of a tyrant is not terrorism, as victim and target are the same. Yet other political murders might be terrorist; a hijacking for escape, while criminal, is not terrorist, while a hijacking involving demands to third parties (e.g. to release prisoners) and not to the direct victims (who cannot capitulate and thereby escape the threat of being killed) is 'terrorist'.

23 Adapted from A.P. Schmid, *Political Terrorism*. Amsterdam: North-Holland, 1988, p. 48.

24 Adapted from Schmid, *Political Terrorism*, pp. 97–99, where 20 motives were identified from the literature.

25 Another reason for the emergence of Terrorism Studies as a field is the marginal attention given to terrorism by many who study crime and conflict. This is, for instance, reflected in the minimal coverage of terrorism in handbooks on crime and conflict such as Mike Maguire, Rod Morgan and Robert Reiner (eds), *The*

Oxford Handbook of Crime, 2nd edn. Oxford: Oxford University Press, 1997, and in Charles Webel and Johan Galtung (eds), *Handbook of Peace and Conflict Studies*. London: Routledge, 2007.

26 There is a distinction between 'not violent' and 'non-violent'. The latter refers to a specific form of persuasive and coercive influencing of an opponent and third parties to a conflict as practised by Mahatma Gandhi, Martin Luther King and others. The former merely refers to an absence of overt violence in political activities.

27 Cf. Andrew Silke (ed.), *Research on Terrorism: Trends, Achievements and Failures*. London: Frank Cass, 2004.

28 While there are many theories around, there are few rigorous theories that meet a number of requirements such as those identified by Earl Conteh-Morgan in his book *Collective Political Violence: An Introduction to the Theories and Cases of Violent Conflicts*. New York: Routledge, 2004, p. 8 (reproduced in chapter 5).

29 Defining Terrorism & its Root Causes. References to the definition of terrorism and the root causes as discussed in the United Nations General Assembly debate 'Measures to eliminate international terrorism', October 1–5, 2001, United Nations, New York; at www.reachingcriticalwill.org/political/1com/terror.html (accessed 10 August 2005).

30 On pp. 258–260. There are many such lists. Dean and Yonah Alexander, for instance, list ten factors and conditions likely to encourage future terrorism: (i) the absence of a universal definition of terrorism; (ii) disagreement as to the root causes of terrorism; (iii) religionization of politics; (iv) exploitation of the media; (v) double standards of morality; (vi) loss of resolve by governments to take effective action against terrorism; (vii) weak punishment of terrorists; (viii) violation of international law by, and promotion of, terrorism by some nations; (ix) complexities of modern societies; and (x) high costs of security in democracies. Dean C. Alexander and Yonah Alexander, *Terrorism and Business: The Impact of September 11, 2001*. Ardsley, NY: Transnational, 2003, p. 195.

31 T. Bjørgo (ed.), *Root Causes of Terrorism: Myths, Reality and Ways Forward*. London: Routledge, 2005, pp. 260–261.

32 For an attempt to explain terrorist campaigns along these lines, see Matenia P. Sirseloudi, 'Early Detection of Terrorist Campaigns'. *Forum on Crime and Society*, 4(1–2), December 2004, pp. 71–92. (Special issue on terrorism, edited by A.P. Schmid.)

33 Among those who tried to suggest a profile of a terrorist, we find that they describe the 'terrorist personality' in terms of characteristics such as young (20–40), alienated, impressionable, with low self-esteem, imbued with a belief in the efficacy of violence, with a desire for publicity and attention, with delusions of immortality, living in the future, with a resistance to compromise, but intelligent, with organizational skills and well educated. For a discussion of 'the terrorist', see the critique of Jeff Victoroff, 'The Mind of the Terrorist: A Review and Critique of Psychological Approaches'. *Journal of Conflict Resolution*, 49(1), February 2005, and Rex A. Hudson, *The Sociology and Psychology of Terrorism: Who Becomes a Terrorist and Why?* Washington, DC: Library of Congress, Federal Research Division, September 1999; see also Rex Hudson, *The Other (Veiled) Face of Suicide Bombing: Who Becomes a Shahida and Why?* Washington, DC: Federal Research Division, Library of Congress, November 2005; for the suicide terrorist, one of the best overviews of psychological theories can be found in Diego Gambetta (ed.), *Making Sense of Suicide Missions*. Oxford: Oxford University Press, 2005. See also Anne Marie Oliver and Paul Steinberg, *The Road to Martyrs' Square: A Journey into the World of the Suicide Bomber*. Oxford: Oxford University Press, 2005.

34 Adam Roberts, *Occupation, Resistance and Law: International Law on Military Occupations and on Resistance*. Stockholm: FOA ([Swedish] National Defense Research Institute), 1980, p. 170.

35 In this context, Josef Joffe writes, 'Almost never is the new terrorist simply a freedom fighter inside whom a statesman slumbers. States created by terror do not tend to transform themselves into friendly members of the world community'. Joffe, 'The Trap of Understanding – Western World Deceives Itself: Terrorism Is Not Weapon of the Weak'. *Die Zeit* (Hamburg), 9 September 2004.

36 This is also recognized by various regional organizations, including the Arab League (1998), the Islamic Conference (1999) and the African Union (1999). See United Nations, Office of Legal Affairs *International Instruments Related to the Prevention and Suppression of International Terrorism*. New York: United Nations, 2001, pp. 153–154, 189–190, 210. The concept of 'freedom' requires some more scrutiny: 'Whose freedom?' '"Freedom from" or "freedom to"?', etc. Yet that is beyond the scope of this chapter.

37 Traditionally, there are six just war criteria (*jus ad bellum*):

1   a just cause;
2   an honest intention;
3   proportionality vis-à-vis the threat;
4   authorization by legitimate authority;
5   *ultima ratio* – exhaustion of all other means;
6   adherence to international law.

Hans Küng, Gespräch, 'Rechtswidrig und unmoralisch'. *Der Spiegel* (Hamburg), 17 March 2003, pp. 61–66.

38 Special Report, *Dying to Lose: Explaining the Decline in Global Terrorism*. Vancouver: Simon Fraser University, 2008; *Human Security Brief 2007*, p. 4. In his article 'Why Terrorism Does Not Work', Max Abrahms found that 'contrary to the prevailing view that terrorism is an effective means of political coercion, the universe of cases suggests that, first, contemporary terrorist groups rarely achieve their policy objectives and, second, the poor success rate is inherent to the tactic of terrorism itself'. Abrahms, 'Why Terrorism Does Not Work'. *International Security*, 31(2), October 2006, p. 42 (abstract).

39 Osama bin Laden (1998), quoted in The National Commission on Terrorist Attacks upon the United States, *9/11 Report*. New York: the NYT edition, 2004, p. 72.

40 Cf. John Bowker, *Concise Dictionary of World Religions*. Oxford: Oxford University Press, 2006, pp. xviii.

41 Cf. A.P. Schmid *et al.*, *Political Terrorism*. Amsterdam: North-Holland, 1988, pp. 29–31 (Appendix A: 'Unsolved Conceptual Problems of Terrorism').

42 Richard Jackson, 'Research for Counterterrorism: Terrorism Studies and the Reproduction of State Hegemony'. Paper presented at the annual meeting of the International Studies Association 48th Annual Convention. Available at http://convention3.allacademic.com/meta/p_mla_apa_research (accessed 28 December 2009).

43 Cf. Statement of Representative Saxby Chambliss, chairman, House Intelligence Subcommittee on Terrorism and Homeland Security before the House Armed Services Committee Special Oversight Panel on Terrorism, 2 September 2002. Available at www.fas.org/irp/congress/2002_090502chambliss.html (accessed 19 June 2006).

44 Thomas H. Kean and Lee H. Hamilton, *The 9/11 Reports: The National Commission on Terrorist Attacks Upon the United States*. New York: New York Times, 2004; Statement of Representative Saxby Chambliss, chairman, House Intelligence Subcommittee on Terrorism and Homeland Security before the House Armed Services Committee Special Oversight Panel on Terrorism, 2 September 2002. Available at www.fas.org/irp/congress/2002_090502chambliss.html (accessed 19 June 2006).

45 Regarding demotivation through situational prevention, Tore Bjørgo has suggested increasing the difficulties, costs and risk, and reducing the rewards and excuses, for carrying out terrorist attacks by:

  • increasing the effort: target hardening, controlling access to facilities, deflecting the offenders, controlling weapons and other tools of terror;
  • increasing the risks: assisting natural surveillance and increasing formal surveillance, reducing anonymity, extending guardianship and placing managers at facilities;
  • reducing the rewards: reducing access to attractive targets, not giving in to blackmail, reducing publicity, denying benefits;
  • reducing provocations: avoiding excessive use of force, humiliation and other unnecessary provocations that may cause anger, resentment and calls for revenge; discouraging imitation;
  • removing excuses: making clear that terrorist violence is unacceptable, countering depersonalization of victims, alerting consciences and avoiding provocative acts.

  T. Bjørgo, 'Strategies for Preventing Terrorism', unpublished text, 2006.

46 For a broad and systematic compilation of lessons learned, see the inventories of 'lessons learned' maintained by the Memorial Institute for the Prevention of Terrorism at www.mipt.org/Lessons-Learned.asp.

47 For the official UN counter-terrorism strategy, as unanimously adopted by the United Nations General Assembly on 8 September 2006, see: http://daccess-dds-ny.un.org/doc/UNDOC/GEN/N05/504/88/PDF/N0550488.pdf?OpenElement.

Appendix 1.1

Twelve Rules for Preventing and Combatting Terrorism

Alex P. Schmid

1 Try to address the underlying conflict issues exploited by the terrorists and work towards a peaceful solution while not making substantive concessions to the terrorists themselves.

2 Prevent alienated individuals and radical groups from becoming terrorist extremists by confronting them with a mix of 'carrot' and 'stick' tactics and searching for effective counter-motivation measures.

3 Stimulate and encourage defection and conversion of free and imprisoned terrorists and find ways to reduce the tacit or open support of aggrieved constituencies for terrorist organizations.

4 Deny terrorists access to arms, explosives, false identification documents, safe communication, and safe travel and sanctuaries; disrupt and incapacitate their preparations and operations through infiltration, communications intercepts and espionage, and by limiting their criminal and other fund-raising capabilities.

5 Reduce low-risk/high-gain opportunities for terrorists to strike by enhancing communications security, energy security and transportation security, by hardening critical infrastructures and potential sites where mass casualties could occur, and by applying principles of situational crime prevention to the countering of terrorism.

6 Keep in mind that terrorists seek publicity and exploit the media and the internet to gain recognition, propagate their cause, glorify their attacks, win recruits, solicit donations, gather intelligence, disseminate terrorist know-how and communicate with their target audiences. Try to devise communication strategies to counter them in each of these areas.

7 Prepare for crisis and consequence management for both 'regular' and 'catastrophic' acts of terrorism in coordinated simulation exercises and educate first responders and the public on how best to cope.

8 Establish an all-sources early detection and early warning intelligence system against terrorism and other violent crimes on the interface between organized crime and political conflict.

9 Strengthen coordination of efforts against terrorism both within and between states; enhance international police and intelligence cooperation, and offer technical assistance to those countries that lack the know-how and means to upgrade their counter-terrorism instruments.

10 Show solidarity with, and offer support to, victims of terrorism at home and abroad.

11 Maintain the moral high ground in the struggle with terrorists by defending and strengthening the rule of law, good governance, democracy and social justice and by matching your deeds with your words.

12 Last but not least: counter the ideologies, indoctrination and propaganda of secular and non-secular terrorists and try to get the upper hand in the war of ideas – the battle for the hearts and minds of those the terrorists claim to speak and fight for.

2

THE DEFINITION
OF TERRORISM

Alex P. Schmid

Increasingly, questions are being raised about the problem of the definition of a terrorist. Let us be wise and focused about this: terrorism is terrorism. . . . What looks smells and kills like terrorism is terrorism.

> *Sir Jeremy Greenstock, British Ambassador to the United Nations,*
> *in post-September 11, 2001 speech*[1]

It is not enough to declare war on what one deems terrorism without giving a precise and exact definition.

> *President Emile Lahoud, Lebanon (2004)*[2]

An objective definition of terrorism is not only possible; it is also indispensable to any serious attempt to combat terrorism.

> *Boaz Ganor, Director of the International Policy Institute for Counter-Terrorism*[3]

Definition power

More than 70 years after the League of Nations first proposed (in 1937) a legal definition of terrorism, such an agreement is still elusive. 'There is', in the words of Britain's independent reviewer of terrorism legislation, Lord Carlile of Berriew, 'no single definition of terrorism that commands full international approval'.[4] There are hundreds of definitions of terrorism in use; 250 of them can be found in Appendix 2.1 at the end of this chapter. They emphasize a variety of attributes of terrorism such as its often symbolic character, its often indiscriminate nature, its typical focus on civilian and non-combatant targets of violence, its sometimes provocative and sometimes retributive aims, the disruption of public order and the putting in danger of public security, the creation of a climate of fear to influence audiences wider than the direct victims, its disregard for the rules of war and the rules of punishment, and its asymmetric character (armed versus unarmed; weak versus strong). Some key elements of many definitions also refer to the fact that terrorism is usually an instrument for the attempted realization of a political or religious project that perpetrators lacking mass support are seeking, that it generally involves a series of punctuated acts of demonstrative public violence, followed by threats of more in order to impress, intimidate and/or coerce target audiences.[5] Yet such a listing of frequent and similar elements of terrorism is in itself not a definition.

In science, a definition is basically an equation: a new, unknown or ill-understood term (the definiendum) is described (defined) by a combination of at least two known, understandable terms (the definiens).[6] A simple example would be: terrorism equals political violence or violence for political purposes[7] (but note: to define a narrow concept like terrorism with a broad concept like 'political violence' is not very useful[8]). Unlike a mathematical equation, a definition is a conceptualization not with numbers and algebraic symbols but using mostly everyday language. A definition says what a word is meant to mean. Usually, users of new words achieve some agreement as to the meaning soon after their introduction. (However, this meaning is not fixed for all time.)

In most situations, the adoption of a standard meaning is simply a matter of convenience. Not so with the 'loaded' term 'terrorism', which not only refers to a special form of (political) violence or special type of criminal offence, but is also used as a 'pejorative political term of stigmatization' to express moral condemnation in official and public discourse.[9] Despite considerable efforts by lawyers, we still lack an internationally agreed legal definition of terrorism.[10]

'Terrorism' may well be the most politicized term in the political vocabulary these days. Used as a label for a certain form of political violence, it reflects, if it 'sticks', negatively on a political opponent, demonizing him and de-legitimizing his conduct. In its pejorative dimension, the fate of the term 'terrorist' is comparable to the use and abuse of other terms in political vocabulary – terms like 'racist', 'fascist' or 'imperialist'. As one author, Philip Herbst, put it,

> Carrying enormous emotional freight, *terrorism* is often used to define reality in order to place one's own group on a high moral plane, condemn the enemy, rally members around a cause, silence or shape policy debate, and achieve a wide variety of agendas. . . . *Terrorist* became the mantra of our time, carrying a similar negative charge as *communist* once did. Like that word, it tends to divide the world simplistically into those who are assigned the stigma and those who believe themselves above it. Conveying criminality, illegitimacy, and even madness, the application of *terrorist* shuts the door to discussion *about* the stigmatized group or *with* them, while reinforcing the righteousness of the labellers, justifying their agendas and mobilizing their responses.[11]

Used as a rhetorical device, the term 'terrorism' threatens to become a mere invective in political debates, where charges and counter-charges compete for the moral indignation or approval of relevant audiences. Those involved in the definition debate have often tried to mould definitions in a way that suits their needs.[12] In other words, definitions generally tend to reflect the political interests and the moral judgement (or lack thereof) of those who do the defining.[13]

As a consequence, terrorism is a 'contested concept'[14] in the sense that people find it difficult to agree on its meaning or the scope of that meaning. Like a number of other '-isms', terrorism has, owing to the bloody historical record of the phenomena associated with the term, become a term of stigma. Only few terrorists use the term for self-description. Usually they opt for terms like 'revolutionary', 'freedom fighter', 'martyr', 'urban guerrilla', 'resistance fighter' or even 'soldier'. As a consequence, 'one man's terrorist is another man's freedom fighter' (a statement attributed to US president Ronald Reagan but one that he himself actually called 'misleading').[15] While such a statement undoubtedly reflects widespread political praxis, its relativism is highly unsatisfactory from an ethical and intellectual point of view. It is an open invitation to maintain and perpetuate double standards. Academics in pursuit of logic and truth cannot accept that. Nor should citizens accept it from their political leaders or from self-proclaimed champions claiming to speak in the name of an adopted constituency.

Few will, in principle, contest the view that it is desirable to have a common understanding of the problem of terrorism. Yet how can consensus on the meaning of terrorism be reached? First of all, we have to realize that there is no intrinsic essence to the concept of terrorism – it is a man-made construct and as such tends to reflect the interests of those who do the defining. A successful definition sets the parameters for the public debate and can shape the agenda of the community. To be called a 'terrorist' can, like being called a 'witch', have dire consequences.

In many conflicts, the government is the principal 'defining agency' and holds 'definition power'.[16] Terms critical for the exercise of power and for possessing legitimacy are therefore often contested.[17] In politics, key terms are often value laden, and formulas – such as 'axis of evil' – signal disapproval, appeal to emotions, but can also serve as mobilization tools. When groups or individuals have different interests in a situation, the labelling of one and the same situation has – given the (de-)legitimizing function of some words – implications for the situation itself and its permanence. Therefore, a crucial question in the definition debate is: who should have defining power? Should this task be left to the terrorists themselves, their victims or to the media? Should it be left to national governments (parliaments, the executive branch, or the judiciary) or to regional organizations or to the United Nations? Or should it be left to religious leaders who claim to be in possession of 'Truth'? In my view, there is a role for academics here. In the following, we shall try to approach the subject from a detached academic point of view.

From terror to terrorism: the etymology of two terms

While terrorism is, as we have already noted, an 'essentially contested concept', at least from the etymological point of view the original historical meanings of both 'terror' and 'terrorism' are relatively straightforward. The word 'terror' derives from the Latin verb *terrere*, which means 'bring someone to tremble through great fear'.[18] It refers to an individual psychological state of mind and has been around for centuries. It received some of its present heavily political load only during the French Revolution (which, incidentally, also applies to the term 'revolution'). It was first signalled in the French language in the fourteenth century and entered the English language in the sixteenth. Jean Bodin, the French political writer, used the concept 'terror' in his *Les six livres de la République* (1577) when referring to fear caused by excessive violence: 'Cruelty keeps men in fear, and inactive, inspiring the subject with terror of the prince.'[19] Thomas Hobbes, the author of *Leviathan*, in turn referred to terror as the fear of (violent) death.[20] Jean-Jacques Rousseau, in his *Discours sur l'économie politique* (1755), perceptively referred to terror as a (despotic) substitute for the spontaneous respect for the law, calling its 'harshness of punishment . . . nothing but a vain expedient thought up by small minds to substitute terror for this respect which they are unable to achieve'.[21] Mikkel Thorup credits Montesquieu, the author of *De l'ésprit des lois* (1757), with laying the groundwork for the subsequent 'politicization of the concept', opening up the way for 'terror' to refer to a specific form of brutal and unpredictable government.[22] Thorup described the change brought about by the revolutionary events in late-eighteenth-century France in these words:

> The French Revolution signals a shift in conceptual meaning in two tempi. First, we have the 'Robespierran moment', meaning here giving the concept of terror a futuristic element, separating the concept from its unqualified meaning of fear and its quasi-political meaning of policing, ordinary or extraordinary, and merging it with ideas of virtue and creation. Second, we have the 'anti-Robespierran moment' separating the concept from the (regular or legitimate) state and monopolizing it among illegitimate states (despotisms) and private actors (terrorists).[23]

Regarding the first shift in meaning, on 5 September 1793 the National Convention, led by the Jacobins, had declared terror the order of the day, thereby giving legal status to a number of emergency measures. The *Courier de l'égalité* of that day wrote approvingly, 'It is necessary that the terror caused by the guillotine spreads in all of France and brings to justice all the traitors. There is no other means to inspire the necessary terror which will consolidate the Revolution.'[24]

The suffix '-ism' that is added to 'terror' is sometimes held to refer to terrorism's systematic character, either on the theoretical level where the suffix refers to a political philosophy (as in liberal – liberalism, social – socialism, etc.), or on the practical level, where it refers to a manner of acting or an attitude (as in fanatic – fanaticism). While some attribute to terrorism a doctrinal quality ('the philosophy of the bomb'), it also refers to a type of action, a systematic method of violent action. However, the historical root of the suffix as it emerged during and after the reign of terror of 1793–1794 does not refer directly to either of these possibilities.[25]

As mentioned above, after 5 September 1793, 'terror' was declared a legal instrument of state violence. By late June 1794, those delegates in the French National Convention who had previously backed Maximilien Robespierre feared for their own lives after Robespierre had announced that he was in possession of a new list of traitors. Therefore, they decided to overthrow Robespierre and his accomplices on the Committee of Public Safety on 27 June 1794. They could not accuse him of 'terror' without implicating themselves, as most of them had voted to make terror the order of the day. Therefore, they accused him of '*terrorisme*', a term that had an illegitimate and repulsive flavour of despotic, arbitrary and excessive violence – a criminal abuse of power. For this aberration, Robespierre and his associates were sent to the guillotine on 9 and 10 Thermidor of year II in the revolutionary calendar (27 and 28 July 1794).

In subsequent years, in the 'anti-Robespierran moment' (Thorup), terrorism came increasingly to be seen as a despotic instrument of rule against society, and – a century – later, during the heyday of anarchism – against representatives of the state.

While the historical origins of the concepts of 'terror' and 'terrorism' are relatively uncontroversial, their contemporary moral and substantive load and scope are matters of continuing debate. This debate has, however, focused mainly on 'terrorism' and less on 'terror'.[26] In the following, we will look mainly at the scholarly debate, basing ourselves largely on the responses to a questionnaire mailed to academic and other experts on terrorism.

Definitions of terrorism: an analysis of the responses to the questionnaire

Whole dissertations have been written about the definition of terrorism.[27] Many scholars are sick and tired of discussing the definition issue.[28] One author, Omar Malik, titled his contribution to the debate 'Enough of a Definition of Terrorism'.[29] Some people consider the quest for a more perfect definition of 'terrorism' as 'no more than a futile polemical exercise, chasing a chimera', to quote Kiran Krishan, one of our respondents to a questionnaire mailed out in 2006 to scholars and other experts in the field of terrorism. Walter Laqueur held as early as 1977 that '[a]ny definition of political terrorism venturing beyond noting the systematic use of murder, injury and destruction or the threats of such acts toward achieving political ends is bound to lead to endless controversies'.[30] More recently, he wrote, 'After thirty years of hard labour there is still no generally agreed definition of terrorism.'[31] Brian Jenkins (of the RAND Corporation) has called the definition problem the 'Bermuda Triangle of terrorism'. Philip Schlesinger, a British sociologist, even argued that 'no commonly agreed definition can in principle be reached, because the very process of definition is in itself part of a wider contestation over ideologies or political objectives'.[32] Following this logic, the late J. Bowyer Bell (MIT, Cambridge, Massachusetts), in turn, proclaimed, 'Tell me what you think about terrorism, and I will tell you who you are.'[33] Is it impossible to find an objective and watertight definition that satisfies both legal and scientific criteria? So far, this goal has been elusive.

However, giving up on the scholarly debate would leave the field to those who simply hold that '[t]errorism is what bad guys do' (B.M. Jenkins), or '[o]ne man's terrorist is the other man's freedom fighter.'[34] There are many who take this defeatist position. J.V. Witbeck suggested, 'Perhaps the only honest and globally workable definition of terrorism is an explicitly subjective one – violence I don't support.' In my view, this is neither honest nor workable. While a 'perfect' definition might be beyond reach, there is plenty of room for improvement of many widely used existing definitions. We should try to reach at least a 'good enough' definition. At the end of this chapter, we shall attempt to do so with an academic consensus definition (ACD), revising the previous ACD of 1988.

Some of our respondents questioned, given the controversial nature of the term, whether 'a comprehensive and well thought out definition remove[s] this controversy and facilitate[s] research'. 'Would we be better served by moving toward a less controversial term such as "political violence", "dissident violence", or "anti-civilian violence?"', asked one of them (Hafez). Yet any of these three alternatives would miss an essential feature of terrorism, namely the application of criminal violence against civilians and non-combatants to intimidate and manipulate others as well as the actual victim.

There are good reasons to be clear about the definition of terrorism. Roberta Senechal de la Roche has pointed out that '[w]ithout a useful definition of terrorism, a theory of the subject is not even possible.'[35] Jenny Teichman, in turn, has pointed out that moral judgements can only be made when the question of definition has been adequately answered.[36] Therefore we will, in this chapter, make another attempt to sort things out with the help of 91 respondents to our questionnaire and with the help of some other writers who have tried to tackle the thorny problem of defining terrorism.

In our questionnaire, four questions referred to definitions:

1 'Whose "definition of terrorism" do you utilize?'
2 'What is your comment/criticism on the 1988 *academic consensus definition of terrorism?*'
3 'What is your comment/criticism on the *UN draft definition of terrorism?*'
4 'What is your comment/criticism on the *United States of America's State Department definition of terrorism?*'

I will, in the following, present and discuss responses to these questions, though not necessarily in the above order. From the answers of the respondents (some of whom preferred to remain anonymous) I will select those elements that are likely to carry the definitional debate further. I will, at times, make ample use of quotations while on other occasions I shall try to summarize the contributions of respondents. Occasionally, I will also contextualize the discussion, especially the one conducted in the framework of the United Nations.

Let us begin with a recapitulation of all the reasons why terrorism is difficult to define. Boaz Ganor has given us a long list:

1 because terrorism is a 'contested concept' and political, legal, social science and popular notions of it often diverge;
2 because the definition question is linked to (de-)legitimization and criminalization;
3 because there are many ' terrorisms' with different forms and manifestations;
4 because the term has undergone changes of meaning in the more than 200 years of its existence;
5 because terrorist organizations are (semi-)clandestine and the secrecy surrounding them makes objective analysis difficult;
6 because the definition question is linked to whether or not terrorists work for or against one's own (national) interests, and, consequently, double standards tend to be applied;
7 because the boundaries with other forms of political violence (e.g. assassination, [guerrilla] warfare) are hazy or unclear;
8 because the state, with its (claimed) monopoly of the use of force and its legal definition power, can exclude any of its own activities (e.g. indiscriminate repression) from the definition;
9 because it is linked to a discussion of primary responsibility for initiating a downward spiral of action–reaction violence and a discussion of root causes;
10 because some authors use two different vocabularies (force vs. violence; terror vs. terrorism) for state- and non-state actors;
11 because the conceptual and normative frameworks of the users of the term differ (e.g. criminal justice model, war model);
12 because the discussion on terrorism has been linked to issues regarding self-determination, and armed resistance against foreign occupation and racist regimes;

13 because those who engage in acts of terrorism often also engage in other, more legitimate forms of armed conflict and/or engage in party politics;

14 because the violence perpetrated by the terrorists' opponent might be as indiscriminate as, or worse than, that perpetrated by those who are deemed to be 'terrorists';

15 because the assessment of the terrorist act is intertwined with the discussion concerning the actor's goals and the status of the actor him- or herself.[37]

An important point on this list is point 7. There has been a tendency to expand the meaning of the term 'terrorism' to cover other forms of political violence, of which there are many. There is also a certain multifunctionality of certain types of violence. A militant group using coercive methods might combine tactics. A movement like the African National Congress, led by Nelson Mandela, engaged in non-violent action, sabotage, guerrilla warfare and terrorism. Yet overall, the number of ANC attacks on civilians was small, and so was the number of casualties. Does this make the ANC a 'terrorist organization'? Certainly it was an organization that made use of terrorist tactics. So did, on a much larger scale, the South African government. Yet, as the saying goes, two wrongs do not make a right. There are also overlapping 'grey' zones; it is not all black and white, criminal or legitimate. Context matters.[38]

As one of our respondents, Jeffrey Simon, has pointed out,

> The quest for a definition of terrorism is basically an attempt to describe in clear, black-and-white terms a complex and diverse phenomenon that defies clear-cut descriptions. Definitions of terrorism attempt to answer the question, 'What is terrorism and who qualifies as a terrorist?' Different governments, institutions, scholars and others all have their own criteria when it comes to deciding how to label violence that is linked to political, religious, social, and other causes. . . . Organizational and bureaucratic perspectives and responsibilities also influence the definitions. That is why many governments have different definitions of terrorism among various agencies and departments within that government.

This is a valid point, and to illustrate it let us now discuss three definitions:

1 the one put forward by the US State Department;
2 the draft definition of the United Nations;
3 the Academic Consensus Definition developed in the 1980s.

Problems with the US State Department definition

The US government maintains more than 20 definitions of 'domestic' or 'international' terrorism, 'terrorist activity', 'acts of terrorism' or 'federal crime of terrorism', some partly changing and overlapping, some radically different.[39] The definition of the United States of America's Department of State in 2006, when we sent out our questionnaire, was as follows:

> The term 'terrorism' means: premeditated, politically motivated violence perpetrated against noncombatant targets by subnational groups or clandestine agents [usually intended to influence an audience'].[40]

Between 1982 and 2004, the State Department's definition has changed no fewer than seven times.[41] These changes have, on the whole, been minor but not insignificant. The last element of the definition quoted above ('usually intended to influence an audience') had been dropped by 2006.[42]

Several respondents have used the State Department's definition, and its advantages have been pointed out by a number of them. For instance, one of them, working for the Pentagon, noted that it captures some essential points of terrorism:

- Premeditation – Terrorism is not an accident or a crime of passion. It takes time, resources and planning.
- Political motivation – To me, this element is key. The motivation is what makes murder 'terrorism' instead a general crime.
- Non-combatants (which includes military who are not on duty at the time of the attack) – Like political motivation, this element separates 'terrorism' from an act of war or general crime.
- Sub-national groups and clandestine agents – Allows for independent actors and state-sponsored groups.
- Influence – The act of violence is a message. This element returns to the political motivation behind terrorism.

Some respondents felt, however, that this definition does not cover all of the issues related to terrorism. While it covers 'political terrorism', it does not explicitly refer to other motives behind terrorism. Chris Dishman pointed out that terrorism is not always 'politically motivated'; 'it could be for revenge, for God or for other reasons'. Another respondent had 'serious objections to how the State Department actually applies this definition to various groups, namely in a somewhat arbitrary manner' (N. Bapat). Yet another took issue with the element of 'clandestine agents' in the definition, pointing out, 'Not all spies are terrorists.' Another respondent pointed out, correctly, that the reference to 'clandestine agents' serves to cover 'state-sponsored groups'.

One respondent, while praising 'the advantage of remarkable simplicity and yet cover[ing] all the salient points', commented that a possible disadvantage is that it is a definition which would unfairly be exploited by authoritarian regimes to apply to genuine resistance movements fighting subjugation in their own countries' (M.J. Gohel). Yet another respondent (D. Gressang) held that it could be argued that the State Department's definition 'is a bit too narrow in that it focuses attention on actual or presumed *political* motivations. A strict interpretation would seem to exclude terrorism motivated [by] religion . . . and issue-specific terrorism (such as the Earth Liberation Front)'.

One respondent (S. Jayasekara) noted that the US State Department's definition 'lacks the "indiscriminate" nature of the violence perpetrated in acts of terrorism'. Bruce Hoffman, on the other hand, has argued that it is deficient in that it 'fail[s] to consider the psychological dimension of terrorism'.[43] Another respondent noticed that it leaves out the crucial element of 'intimidation'. Other respondents criticized the definition's original coda, 'usually intended to influence an audience', as too vague (B. van der Liere). John Horgan held that '[t]his . . . descriptive term should not be included in the definition. In any case, the definition should not include terms that are "usually" true, suggesting that there are exceptions to the rule'. One can take issue with this point: few laws in *social* science are without exception.[44]

Another respondent noted, correctly, that '[t]he influence the audience is subjected to is achieved through fear. The word "fear", or the expression "to spread fear", is an element that [is] lack[ing] in this definition. . . . A final shortcoming of this definition is the failure to include *threats* of killing and destruction' – a point also noted by others.

Yet others criticized the State Department's definition for excluding attacks directed against property – something that is included in the FBI definition.[45] Stephan Malthaner noted that '[w]hile the definition does to some degree specify types of actors and motives, it is rather vague about types of actions included, that is, the terrorist strategy itself. Particularly it does not specify how terrorists aim to influence an audience (intimidation)'.

Some of these 'problems' are minor. In the following, we turn to a few major problems with the US State Department's definition.

Non-combatant targets

The main point of contention with the State Department's definition is arguably the interpretation of 'non-combatant'. For many years, the State Department issued explanations as to how it interprets the term 'non-combatant'. In its 2005 report (published in 2006) the State Department noted:

> For the purposes of this report, . . . the term 'non-combatant', which is referred to but not defined in 22 USC.2656f(d)(2), is interpreted to mean, in addition to civilians, military personnel (whether or not armed or on duty) who are not deployed in a war zone or a war-like setting.

A footnote to the State Department's definition in its report for 2003 had similar language:

> For the purposes of this definition, the term 'non-combatant' is interpreted to include, in addition to civilians, military personnel who at the time of the incident are unarmed and/or not on duty. . . . We also consider as acts of terrorism attacks on military installations or on armed military personnel when a state of military hostilities does not exist at the site, such as bombings against US bases in Europe, the Philippines, or elsewhere.[46]

The words 'not deployed in a war zone or a war-like setting' were specifically added in 2006, whereas in previous years the phrasing was 'when a state of military hostilities does not exist at the site'. Other changes included rephrasing the term 'military personnel who at the time of the incident are unarmed and/or not on duty' (2004 and previous years) to 'whether or not armed or on duty' (2005, published in 2006). This implies that not only civilians but also military personnel are considered 'non-combatants' even if they are 'armed' as long as they are not 'deployed in a war zone or a war-like setting' (such as Iraq). In other words, the State Department interprets 'non-combatant' very flexibly. Recently, it even expanded the definition to include any combatants attacked outside of war zones.[47]

These changes in the wording reflect the 'need' to cover changing situations in US foreign military policy. Yet they also reflect changes of tactics by militants referred to as 'terrorists'. As Hudson has pointed out, 'The Islamist terrorists do not distinguish between combatants and non-combatants; both are equally legitimate targets in their view.' One respondent even went so far as to say that '[t]errorism may be aimed at military (i.e. combatant) targets'. He probably had in mind incidents like the attack on the USS *Cole* in the port of Aden (Yemen) on 12 October 2002 in an Al-Qaeda suicide mission using an explosives-laden rubber boat.

One of our respondents also found the focus on non-combatant 'outdated', given the fact that in Iraq and Afghanistan terrorists are aiming at US military personnel, not 'non-combatant targets'. Yet the elastic way 'non-combatant target' is defined in some US circles makes it controversial. Al-Qaeda's attack on the Pentagon was interpreted as a terrorist attack because the Pentagon is the 'world's largest office building' (Christine Fair). The same respondent asked, '[A]re intelligence operatives "non-combatants" or political officials non-combatants? What if they are deeply involved in the conflict at hand? While innocuous enough, this is hard to operationalize and [it is] even harder to build a consensus on what this means.' The focus on non-combatant targets (as opposed to civilian targets) creates, as one respondent (D. Gressang) pointed out, ambiguity:

> What, exactly, is a non-combatant? Some would argue that any individual trained and employed in the use of arms (i.e. soldiers, police) are, by definition, combatants. Others would argue that those not engaged in hostile activities, even if in the uniformed military (i.e. medics, military chaplains), are not combatants. Not having a clear distinction makes the State Department's definition difficult to work with in considering acts of violence.

One of the best examples is the bombing of Khobar Towers [a residential building in Saudi Arabia housing foreign military personnel]. Those who say service members are automatically combatants because of their profession would, using this definition, say it was *not* an act of terror. Those who classify combatants and non-combatants by activities would say, using State's definition, that the Khobar bombing *was* an act of terror. Effective analysis seems to demand one answer, not answers contingent on sub-definitions and interpretation.

Some respondents find the use of the term 'non-combatant' problematic as it blurs the distinction between armed conflict and terrorism: 'Acts against "non-combatant targets" committed in armed conflict are war crimes; there is no need to superimpose a "terrorist" label.' D. Artz holds that 'non-combatant' is an ambiguous term: 'Does it include off-duty soldiers, i.e. Israeli soldiers standing at a bus stop, awaiting a weekend leave?' An Israeli respondent held that 'the term "non-combatant" should be defined so as to include members of security forces, except when the assailants are recognized as a legitimate fighting force by the Fourth Geneva Convention and the violent act is committed in the context of a declared war'. However, few wars are 'declared' these days.

John Horgan concluded:

> The State Department's definition of terrorism cannot serve as a sufficiently broad common denominator for international agreement on the definition of terrorism. Only the narrower definition of deliberate injury to civilians solves this problem and enables us to set a clear moral threshold that must not be crossed. This ethical norm is likely to be accepted by both Western countries and Third World countries, and perhaps even by some terrorist organizations.

In this, he comes close to the position of Boaz Ganor, the director of the International Institute for Counter-Terrorism (ICT) in Herzliya, Israel, who defined terrorism concisely and unequivocally as 'a form of violent struggle in which violence is deliberately used against civilians in order to achieve political goals (nationalistic, socioeconomic, ideological, religious, etc.)'.[48] While Ganor has a very valid point, and his thinking on issues of definition and typology is among the most sophisticated, the focus on 'civilians' rather than 'non-combatants' takes away some ambiguity but creates new problems. It also overlooks the fact that there is widespread use of terrorism in war.[49]

What terrorism shares with genocide is the unilateral attack of the armed against the unarmed and defenceless. It is this asymmetry, in combination with the fact that capitulation of the direct victim is not possible because it is not accepted and respected, that creates terror. In a situation where both sides are armed – even if one side is not ready for battle – many will hesitate to use the term 'terrorism'. Otherwise, it will be difficult to achieve moral clarity when it comes to the distinction between terrorism and more legitimate acts of organized violence as in war.

In concrete situations, the issues can become complicated. Was, in the 9/11 attacks, the Pentagon a more legitimate target than the World Trade Center because it was headquarters of a military power with global reach that was comfortable with helping to stabilize repressive regimes like those of Egypt and Saudi Arabia? Both attacks were terroristic because civilians had been hijacked and murdered when the aircraft in which they were trapped were used like cruise missiles and because the intended effect was clearly directed not at the victims themselves. Yet suppose that real unmanned cruise missiles had been utilized in peacetime in both attacks: would it then be wrong to call the attack on the Pentagon 'terrorist' while calling the simultaneous attack on the World Trade Center 'terrorist'? To complicate matters: some of those killed in the Pentagon were uniformed members of the armed forces (albeit mostly unarmed at the moment of the attack), while others were civilians. The attack was, of course, a crime. Yet the attacks on the Pentagon (2001), on the USS *Cole* (2000), on Khobar Towers (1996) or on the US and French army barracks in Lebanon (1983) differ in some ways, morally if not legally, from similar suicide attacks where civilians are deliberately targeted.

Yet not everybody agrees in declaring attacks on civilians to be a moral line that cannot legitimately be crossed. Virginia Held, for instance, wrote:

> It is voting publics that often put in power the governmental leaders, and support the policies, that terrorists oppose. *If* other means have failed and *if* violence against the members of a state's armed services is justified, it is unclear why those who bring about that state's policies and give its armed services their orders should be exempt.[50]

This point has been made even more forcefully by Hugo Slim in his book *Killing Civilians: Method, Madness and Morality in War*. As one reviewer summarized it:

> [M]arking out a special category of people called 'civilians' from the wider enemy group in war 'is a distinction that is not, and never has been, either clear, meaningful or right' for many perpetrators of war – not even for many civilians themselves. . . .
> But who qualifies as a civilian? International law provides only a negative description: someone who is not a member of the armed forces, who does not carry a weapon, who does not take part in hostilities. This is clearly inadequate. An estimated 60% of the world's weapons-bearers are civilians (hunters, for example). On the other hand, many of those who do not carry arms (or wear uniforms) may be very much part of the war effort – ammunition workers, porters, victuallers and the like. And what of the ideologues whose hate-filled doctrines fuel the conflict, the newspaper editors who disseminate the propaganda or the taxpayers who pay for the war? Should they be afforded special protection when the unwilling teenage conscript is not'?[51]

Clearly, the issue is complicated. While attacks on non-combatants might be too narrow for a definition of terrorism, attacks on civilians might be too broad. We will return to this issue again below.

Terrorism: a non-state activity only?

Most states use the term 'terrorism' for non-state actors only but, somewhat inconsequentially, some of them, notably the United States, make an exception when that non-state actor is 'sponsored' by a foreign state. One of our respondents (C. Fair) took issue with the fact that the US State Department's definition implies that 'terrorism is the purview of non-state actors'. She adds:

> It also absolves states of any responsibility for their role in terrorist developments within their borders and beyond. . . . It also decreases space for the international community to hold repressive states accountable even while one also holds militant groups to the same accountability. I would argue that when states use terrorism the moral challenge is even greater because of their obligation to protect their citizens. This definition also appears patently to serve US interests specifically.

Several other respondents shared Fair's views, in one form or another. Richard Chasdi, for instance, held that the US State Department definition of terrorism was 'crafted with geopolitical considerations in mind'. He noted that the term 'clandestine agents' might obliquely refer to 'state terrorism' but concluded that if an attack were to be perpetrated by non-clandestine agents, it could fall outside the definition. Others (e.g. Frank Shanty) also deplored the fact that the definition precludes state terrorism. One respondent pointed out that '[i]t does not include terrorism by states, e.g. Saddam's brutality against the Kurds and Shiites in Iraq – or a state's assassination of its critics abroad (e.g. Iran's activities prior to 1993)'. Another respondent noted:

This definition has the disadvantage of excluding by definition from the group of possible perpetrators other than non-state agents, thereby excluding by definition terrorism by the state. While it is legitimate to develop typologies of different types of terrorism, one should be careful not to use a definition of a sub-type of terrorism as defining the phenomenon as a whole.

In sum, the US Department of State definition of terrorism, while concise, can hardly serve as a model for a social science definition of terrorism, for the following reasons:

- Its wording has changed several times with changing circumstances.
- The interpretation of the word 'non-combatant' has changed over time.
- Its focus on 'political violence' is on the one hand too narrow (regarding 'political') and on the other hand too broad (regarding 'violence').
- Its exclusion of the psychological element of excessive 'fear' has, especially after the dropping of the reference to 'intended to influence an audience', washed out the core of the concept of terrorism.
- The absence of the elements of 'threat' and 'intimidation' must also be seen as shortcomings.
- It excludes state terrorism but, somewhat stealthily, brings it in through the back door with the reference to 'clandestine agents', which can be and has been used to include the foreign activities of certain governments, but not all those that employ 'clandestine agents' for acts of terrorism.
- Domestic terrorism by organs of the state under repressive regimes is not acknowledged in the State Department definition.

After a public debate about the changing and sometimes opaque criteria used by the State Department for including or excluding incidents in an annually published database, the collection of data on terrorist incidents worldwide was passed to the US National Counterterrorism Center (NCTC), which has shown a greater awareness of some of the difficulties in defining terrorism. In a note on the methodology utilized to compile the NCTC's database of terrorist incidents from 22 November 2005, it stated:

> The data provided on the website consists of incidents in which sub-national or clandestine groups or individuals deliberately or recklessly attacked civilians or non-combatants (including military personnel and assets outside war zones and war-like settings). Determination of what constitutes a terrorist act, however, can be more art than science; information is often incomplete, fact patterns may be open to interpretation, and perpetrators' intent is rarely clear. Moreover, information may become available over time, changing initial judgments about incidents. Users of this database should therefore recognize that reasonable people may differ on whether a particular incident actually constitutes terrorism or some other form of political violence. NCTC has made every effort to limit the degree of subjectivity involved in the judgments. . . . The very definition of terrorism relative to all other forms of political violence is open to debate; interaction with academics and outside terrorism experts convinces us that there will never be a 'bright red line.' We will continue to refine our counting rules as the study of terrorism evolves. In sum, tracking attacks against civilians and non-combatants can help us understand important trends related to the nature of the attacks, where they're occurring.[52]

The NCTC approach clearly demonstrates a greater sensitivity regarding the definition issue than that of the State Department. In its interaction with academics, the NCTC manifests a healthy desire to improve standards, yet it continues to reflect, in many ways unavoidably, a US-centric worldview.[53]

We next turn to the perspective of the United Nations.

Critique of the UN draft definition for the Comprehensive Convention on International Terrorism

The United Nations and the definition issue

How does the United Nations, with its more than 192 member states, come to terms with the definition issue? To understand this, some contextual background information is necessary. When the United Nations was established after the Second World War, it could, in principle, build on the work of the League of Nations, which in 1937 had tried to define acts of terrorism as '[a]ll criminal acts directed against a State and intended or calculated to create a state of terror in the minds of particular persons, or a group of persons or the general public'.[54]

However, the League of Nations Convention against Terrorism never received sufficient support to enter into force (it was signed by 24 states but ratified only by 1 – colonial India),[55] and responsibility for the treaty was not passed on to the United Nations in 1945. The United Nations started its debate on terrorism as late as 1972, when terrorist attacks at the Munich Olympic Games (killing 11 Israeli athletes) and Lod Airport (28 people killed) served as a wake-up call to the international community. In 1972, the General Assembly (GA) passed a resolution with the unusually long title of 'Measures to prevent international terrorism which endangers or takes innocent human lives or jeopardises fundamental freedoms, and study of the underlying causes of those forms of terrorism and acts of violence which lie in misery, frustration, grievance and despair, and which cause some people to sacrifice human lives, including their own, in an attempt to effect radical changes'.[56] The title itself already indicates how divided the United Nations was on the issue. In the 1970s, many non-aligned states, some of them having only recently gained independence themselves, considered certain acts of terrorism (such as hostage taking) as legitimate in struggles of national liberation. It would take years before the right to self-determination and terrorism became decoupled – a process still not completed.[57]

An Ad Hoc Committee on International Terrorism, consisting of 35 state representatives, was established by GA resolution 3034 (in 1972). It consisted of three subcommittees, one of them dealing with the problem of defining terrorism, while a second dealt with root causes and a third with the prevention of terrorism. While seven draft proposals were submitted by different groups of nations, no consensus could be reached on a definition of terrorism. The Non-Aligned Group defined international terrorism as 'acts of violence committed by a group of individuals which endanger human lives and jeopardise fundamental freedoms, the effects of which are not confined to one state'. The proposal stressed that this definition should not affect the inalienable right to self-determination of people subjected to colonial and racist regimes. Other states made similar distinctions. Greece, for instance, proposed that one should distinguish between terrorism and freedom-fighting, and defined, in its proposal, international terrorism as criminal acts of violence against innocent persons committed in the territory of a third state with the aim of putting pressure on any disputant or for personal satisfaction. Haiti stressed, in its proposal, the political purpose of the violence, while Iran wanted to label violence against freedom movements acts of terrorism too. France, on the other hand, in its proposal, described international terrorism as a heinous act of barbarism committed on foreign territory. As a result of such diverging views, no resolution on the definition of terrorism could be adopted. After six years, the committee was phased out, after already having been suspended between 1973 and 1976. The attempt to reach a UN consensus definition remained shelved until the end of the Cold War.[58] In 1994, the General Assembly reached, without defining the phenomenon under consideration, at least some consensus on the nature of terrorism:

> The United Nations Member States solemnly reaffirm their unequivocal condemnation of all acts, methods and practices of terrorism, as criminal and unjustifiable, wherever and by whoever committed, including those which jeopardize the friendly relations among States and people and threaten the territorial integrity and security of States.[59]

General Assembly resolutions, however, do not in themselves constitute international law,[60] although they can carry greater moral authority than Security Council resolutions.

The Ad Hoc Committee on Terrorism in the post-Cold War period

The definition discussion was resumed in December 1996, when an Ad Hoc Committee on Terrorism was established (by GA resolution 51/210). It was charged with drafting a number of conventions against various aspects of terrorism, including a Comprehensive Convention, which would supplement or replace the existing 'sectoral' conventions,[61] which contain some notable gaps.[62] This Ad Hoc Committee on Terrorism has been discussing a draft Comprehensive Convention on International Terrorism for more than ten years. While most articles of the drafts have been completed, finalization is held up by, *inter alia*, the question of definition. At the present stage (autumn 2010), the following informal text of article 2 exists with regard to the definition:

> Any person commits an offence within the meaning of this [the present] Convention if that person, by any means, unlawfully and intentionally, causes:
>
> (a) Death or serious bodily injury to any person; or
> (b) Serious damage to public or private property, including a place of public use, a State or government facility, a public transportation system, an infrastructure facility or to the environment; or
> (c) Damage to property, places, facilities or systems referred to in paragraph 1 (b) of this [the present] article, resulting or likely to result in major economic loss; when the purpose of the conduct, by its nature or context, is to intimidate a population, or to compel a Government or an international organization to do or to abstain from doing any act.[63]

In November 2001, in the wake of the terrorist attacks of September 11, 2001, the United Nations came very close to a definition from the Ad Hoc Committee on Terrorism's discussion on a Comprehensive Convention against International Terrorism. The spirit of compromise, which could be found in many negotiators, did, however, stumble in the light of resistance by the 56-member Organization of the Islamic Conference, which rejected an Australian compromise definition because it would not exempt national liberation movements fighting foreign occupation such as the Israeli occupation of Palestinian land.[64]

Another issue that gave rise to discussion in the General Assembly and the Ad Hoc Committee on Terrorism was whether or not only the violent acts carried out by 'any person' (individuals) could be labelled terrorism or whether certain activities of states, executed by their governments, should also be covered by the term. It turned out that the majority of states prefer to limit the application of the term 'terrorism' to individuals and groups. At the same time, however, a number of states and observers regard themselves or some non-state groups as victims of state or state-sponsored terrorism.[65] In order to bridge the gap, UN language often uses the elastic formula 'terrorism in all its forms and manifestations', to which member states can give different interpretations.[66]

The main controversial issues regarding the definition of terrorism in the UN Ad Hoc Committee on Terrorism related to the following issues:

- whether or not the term 'terrorism' should apply to the actions of governments or states in the same way that it applies to the actions of non-state groups;
- whether or not one should differentiate between terrorism and the rights of peoples to self-determination and to combat foreign occupation;

- whether or not to include activities of national armed forces in the exercise of their official duties and during armed conflicts if these are 'governed' by or 'in conformity with' international law;
- whether or not to include the activities of national armed forces related to their potential use of nuclear weapons (since atomic weapons are almost by definition terrifying).[67]

In addition, the issue of the relationship of the Comprehensive Convention to existing and future counter-terrorism treaties was a bone of contention. When by March 2008 the Ad Hoc Committee could not reach a consensus, it recommended that the Sixth [legal] Committee of the General Assembly establish a working group with a view to finalizing the draft comprehensive convention on international terrorism. The deadlock can only be broken by political goodwill, as the concerns expressed by different delegates are primarily political (rather than legal) in nature.[68]

Problems with the UN draft definition of terrorism

In recent years, the main stumbling block has been article 18, which refers to the type of actors to which the Convention should apply[69] (armed forces, parties, groups?). Draft article 2 (on definitions) has been left largely untouched, although the discussion might be reopened once article 18 has been settled. This is indeed a crucial point, as one of our respondents pointed out:

> Read together, article 2 and the coordinator's version of article 18(2) suggest that only the activities of state armed forces in armed conflicts would not be considered terrorist acts, whereas the acts of non-state armed groups would be captured by the Convention. This risks seriously undermining respect for international humanitarian law [IHL] by non-state actors because certain acts committed in war, including by non-state actors, such as attacks against military objectives, are not crimes under IHL, but would be criminalized under the draft Convention.

Our respondents' comments on article 2 (definition) of this UN draft Convention ranged from 'a useful contribution to international law' and 'admirably vague' (J. Kaplan) to 'too legalistic'. One respondent thought that terrorism has moved on while the draft Convention has not, and he called it 'out of fashion'. He argued, 'We are facing System (Global) Terrorism, not unlawful or crazy 'persons' who *caused* 'death or serious bodily injury to any person; or serious damage to public or private property . . . etc.' In a similar vein, Avishag Gordon noted 'there should be more emphasis on loss of human lives rather than on loss of public or private property. It seems that the lethal and indiscriminate characteristics of suicide terrorism were not considered in the UN definition.'

Another respondent noted 'the underlying problem of inferring motives, or intentions, from action – cf. the fuzzy phrase "when the purpose of the conduct, *by its nature or context*, is to intimidate a population, or to compel . . .".' Yet another saw in this UN draft definition 'the risk here that a genuine resistance movement involved in a struggle for freedom could be labelled as a terrorist outfit' (M.J. Gohel). This is a valid point: when a definition serves to deny public legitimacy to one violent actor while allowing another violent actor engaging in the same sort of conduct to escape being caught in the definition, the door is open for double standards, which, in turn, will erode support for it. L. Mincheva also was concerned 'it does not clearly identify terrorist actors speaking instead of "persons" alone. Simultaneously my reading of it tends to blends terrorist activities with those of "regular" insurgencies'.

In this connection, another respondent (D. Gressang) raised the question 'Who determines the legality/illegality of an act?' Another respondent also stressed this point:

> There is a lack of clarity about what 'unlawfully' means. Is it unlawful if it breaks the Geneva Conventions, or if it breaks the principles in the UN Charter, or the Universal

Declaration of Human Rights, etc.? Or is it unlawful relative to each sovereign state's domestic standards?

That question has also been touched on by the Ad Hoc Committee on Terrorism, and the prevailing opinion there appears to be that not domestic (national) law but international law should determine the legality.[70]

Another problem perceived by some respondents was that the draft Convention's definition was 'overly broad'. Stefan Malthaner thought that the range of acts ('damage to property', etc.) as well as the range of actors ('any person') included is too broad.[71] Another respondent thought that the current text could even include acts of 'criminal extortion'. A criminologist among the respondents held that '[t]his definition doesn't clearly distinguish terrorism from ordinary crime', a point made by several other respondents. Nick Ross, for instance, noted that the text is so widely drawn that it covers 'all homicide . . . as well as major arson or large-scale vandalism'. Harjit Sandhu commented that it is a 'wide definition and lacks precision'. The current text includes, as Donna Artz notes, death or serious bodily injury to persons even if it does *not* have intimidation as its purpose. That problem could be solved, as Christine Fair pointed out, if 'or' were to be replaced by 'and' between sub-paragraphs (b) and (c) (see below).

A major problem was raised by another respondent:

> Is 'when the purpose of the conduct, by its nature or context, is to intimidate a population, or to compel a Government or an international organization to do or abstain from doing any act', referring to (a) and (b)? As the text now reads, it appears to refer only to (b), which would make (a) a stand-alone sub-paragraph, extending the meaning of an act of terrorism to 'Death or serious bodily injury' caused 'to any person' committed by 'any person' acting 'unlawfully and intentionally', without a qualification based on 'intimidation'.[72]

The chairman of the Ad Hoc Committee, however, has contested such a reading.[73]

One respondent, Christine Fair, noted that

> this definition does not provide any means to distinguish criminality (which may not have a specific intent other than personal or corporate benefit of the perpetrator) and terrorism. Using this definition to collect data on terrorist events would simply produce an event log of widely ranging violence. By this excerpt of the UN definition, conceivably rapists, gangs, petty criminals and others would be defined as terrorists. This could be somewhat mitigated if the 'or' was removed from the first criterion and substituted with an 'and'.

Several respondents have made this point. One of them remarked:

> I find it to be is flawed and insufficient. It does not even clearly separate terrorism from plain murder. It also does not separate terrorism from sabotage. You don't sabotage someone's life. Terrorism is foremost about killing – or threatening to kill – non-combatants.

Another respondent (J. Augusteijn) held that '[t]he introduction of the subjective concepts of "serious" and "major" do not contribute to the building of a consensus over what qualifies as an act of terrorism' – a view shared by others.[74] Jeffrey Simon noted, 'Among the problems with this definition are the phrases "serious bodily injury" and "major economic loss." That implies that a car bombing that only causes minor injuries and minor property damage is not an act of terrorism.'

Bram Van der Liere noted, 'According to this definition, a national organisation cannot be the victim of terrorism. Perhaps this is useful in an international legalistic environment, but it is not an essential characteristic of terrorism that it is never directed at national organisations.' He also observed that 'a specification of "purpose . . . by its nature and context"' might be useful, while questioning 'the requirement of unlawfulness', arguing:

> Conceptually, terrorism is possible in a society that lacks a law or even a legal tradition. Moreover, this requirement may make it too easy for governments to evade the charge of terrorism by changing laws or allowing for exceptions in their legal system.

The fact that states are deciding about the text of the Comprehensive Convention facilitates the inclination to exclude state actions from its scope. As Richard Chasdi pointed out,

> First, is that this definition essentially fails to account for state terrorism, either conducted within the spheres of 'oppression' and 'repression' as Stohl and Lopez suggest, or as a function of counterterror offensives. In essence, that definition dovetails to the actions what some writers call 'insurgent terrorism' or 'oppositional terrorism.'

Another respondent held that '[i]t is a state-biased definition. It lacks meaningful description of state-sponsored terror'.[75]

Several respondents (e.g. J. Forest) noted that the draft convention misses the reasons behind an act of terrorism, focusing instead on purpose or effect. Ekaterina Stepanova again put this issue in its proper context (see note[76]).

Some other respondents (e.g. B. Ganor, J. Horgan) thought the UN draft definition was too broad, general or generic. One of them wrote, 'Far too general and of little practical use – by this definition anyone who commits a violent offence, engages in extortion, causes criminal damage etc. is a terrorist!!'

Yet another group of respondents, however, thought that the definition was too narrow. To quote F. Shanty:

> I think this definition is too narrow and falls somewhat short. For example, while the definition includes 'death or bodily injury', there is no mention of the taking of hostages, which has been a common practice in many past and current terrorist operations. The taking of hostages is a violent act, which is intended to 'to intimidate a population, or to compel a Government or an international organization to do or abstain from doing any act'.

Indeed, neither is kidnapping mentioned in the draft comprehensive definition (but, like hostage taking, it is outlawed, at least with regard to 'diplo-nappings', in the 'sectoral' Convention on the Prevention and Punishment of Crimes against Internationally Protected Persons, including Diplomatic Agents (1973)[77]).

Kiran Krishan's criticism covers some of the same ground when he writes:

(a) It is too tame a definition, aimed only at individuals. We know from experience that often national governments and large non-governmental organisations are involved.
(b) The emphasis is on 'physical' acts resulting in death, serious damage to property, etc. The holding out of a serious threat, say use of a WMD, ought to fall within the purview of the definition.
(c) Acts such as collection of funds, propaganda, providing safe haven, and such similar acts, all constitute acts of terror or [acts] abetting terror, and should find mention.

Navin Bapat also held that 'the definition does not necessarily maintain that the act is taken for political purposes. So, under this could well apply to gang activity as well as to groups with a political agenda'. This point was also stressed by another respondent, who held that '[p]oints (a) and (b) do not distinguish terrorism from ordinary crime. Terrorism is an act of *political* violence, not any violence.'

Among other elements missing is the communicative dimension of terrorism. While the draft UN Convention text refers to intimidation and coercion, there is nothing in it that takes into account the element of propaganda. In the words of one respondent, 'I think that it is lacking elements such as communicating a message and terrorizing a specific population.' This element was arguably central in the 9/11 attacks. One respondent also referred to this 'propaganda of the deed' element, writing, 'I think the motive needs to be elaborated on. In religious terrorism, another objective would be to unite the constituency (the Ummah) through large-scale, awesome attacks which often ignite fervour in certain circles rather than intimidate.'

Joshua Sinai complained, 'The definition fails, once again, to give centrality to civilian or non-combatant targets.' This point is shared and elaborated by Hafez, who writes:

1   I take issue with the use of 'any person' in (a). This means that violence can never be used against armed personnel of illegitimate occupying powers or oppressive regimes. It should make explicit the targeting of civilians.
2   A distinction has to be made between violence that intentionally targets civilians and legitimate armed resistance to occupation, oppression or war that does not target civilians.

Nick Pratt echoed this: 'It overlooks the idea of "non-combatants" or civilians as targets. "Any person" is too general. We could be speaking of a soldier, an LEA [law-enforcing agency] official, or a security guard.'

Another respondent, in turn, noted:

> The scope of these provisions is problematic from a human rights point of view. These are against the principle of legal certainty, which is protected in Article 7 of the European Convention on Human Rights. How will this definition apply to situations like anti-globalisation protesters, or environmental activists taking direct action? How can individuals identify when they fall within the definition of terrorism, and how can the political application of the definition be avoided? Such a broad definition of terrorism will create potential difficulties with freedom of expression, freedom of association, fair trial rights and private life.

Ekaterina Stepanova perceptively noted with regard to the target of terrorist violence:

> The formula 'death or serious body injury to *any person*' [my italics, E.S.] is found both in this earlier version and in the more recent drafts of the UN comprehensive convention against terrorism, such as A/59/894 of 12 August 2005 (Art. 2, Para. 1a, p. 9). While aimed to stress 'indiscriminate' nature of terrorism, this wording does not fully and accurately reflect this meaning and may in fact be interpreted as extending to cover, for instance, rebel attacks against armed governmental personnel or against soldiers of the occupying army. Nor did the UNSC Resolution 1566 clearly define the immediate target of terrorist attacks (referring instead to 'criminal acts, including against civilians').[78] Against this background, the UN High-level Panel on Threats, Challenges and Change Report, in its special section on terrorism, has found, in my view, a more accurate wording, referring to 'any action intended to cause death or serious bodily harm to *civilians or non-combatants*' [my italics].[79] This wording is close to the one used in the International Convention for the Suppression of the Financing of Terrorism (1999), which refers to acts intended to

cause death or injury 'to a civilian or any other person not taking an active part in the hostilities in a situation of armed conflict'.[80]

A US respondent commented:

The failure of the United Nations to agree on a basic definition of terrorism after so many decades epitomizes the problem of having to fashion a consensus definition. Agreement on a definition of terrorism is essential for combating terrorism on a multilateral, global basis, but the reform summit of the United Nations General Assembly, which met in mid-September 2005, failed to agree on a definition. Perhaps the above, homogenized definition is the result. Although the United States and other Western nations were able to expunge language favoured by developing countries that would have exempted 'national liberation movements,' the Western countries were forced to abandon their basic definition, which would have condemned as terrorism any violence against civilians for political purposes, regardless of the cause. The last four words, 'regardless of the cause,' were the hang-up because this would have categorized Palestinian suicide bombings as terrorism. The definitional impasse once again demonstrated the difficulty of reaching international agreement on a definition of the term.

Frustration with the slow progress in the Ad Hoc Committee on Terrorism (part of the Sixth (legal) Committee of the UN General Assembly) has led others in the United Nations, such as the Security Council, the Secretary-General and the Policy Working Group on the United Nations and Terrorism, to offer their suggestions. The Policy Working Group, for instance, wrote in 2002:

13. Without attempting a comprehensive definition of terrorism, it would be useful to delineate some broad characteristics of the phenomenon. Terrorism is, in most cases, essentially a political act. It is meant to inflict dramatic and deadly injury on civilians and to create an atmosphere of fear, generally for a political or ideological (whether secular or religious) purpose. Terrorism is a criminal act, but it is more than mere criminality. To overcome the problem of terrorism it is necessary to understand its political nature as well as its basic criminality and psychology. . . .

14. While terrorist acts are usually perpetrated by subnational or transnational groups, terror has also been adopted by rulers at various times as an instrument of control. The rubric of counter-terrorism can be used to justify acts in support of political agendas, such as the consolidation of political power, elimination of political opponents, inhibition of legitimate dissent and/or suppression of resistance to military occupation. Labelling opponents or adversaries as terrorists offers a time-tested technique to de-legitimize and demonize them. The United Nations should beware of offering, or being perceived to be offering, a blanket or automatic endorsement of all measures taken in the name of counter-terrorism.

15. The phenomenon of terrorism is complex. This does not, however, imply that it is impossible to adopt moral clarity regarding attacks on civilians. Terrorism deserves universal condemnation, and the struggle against terrorism requires intellectual and moral clarity and a carefully differentiated implementation plan.[81]

One respondent from the US policy-making counter-terrorist camp had this to say about the UN draft Comprehensive Convention:

This looks like a legal definition to a political problem. I don't think a legal definition can contain/describe this political problem. It's like trying to pin Jell-O to the wall. Because

I see terrorism as a political problem, I accept that the definition of what constitutes terrorism and who is a terrorist can change. As someone involved in defense and security, I see value in a flexible – even vague – definition that, importantly, allows one to exclude some acts and include others while still being able to build cooperation around the problem. One man's freedom fighter being another's terrorist has political implications that can benefit a state's interests. I know this is not good science. Nor is it good policy to say that we should use the term 'terrorist' as a weapon; however, I think it's true and essential to both terrorism and counterterrorism.

From a political science point of view, the draft criminal law focus of the comprehensive definition is unsatisfactory, as several respondents have pointed out. Boaz Ganor, for instance, noted:

- Causes: The definition of terrorism should refer to the intention of the perpetrator and not to the consequences of the attack, which in many cases are coincidental.
- The spectrum of the definition: This is an example of a too wide definition that actually contains almost all forms of violence and therefore it is useless for operational and for international cooperation needs.
- Specifying the consequences of the terrorist act as an integral part of the definition itself is counterproductive since probably it will be impossible to include all possible ramifications of terrorism in the definition. Including, for example, *causing serious damage to public transportation* in the definition but excluding the serious damage to the commercial life in the targeted state has no merit.

And a Scandinavian researcher noted:

At first sight, this does not appear to be a definition of terrorism at all, though there are elements of definition in it. In my view it is a cumbersome attempt at definition that does not emphasize the characteristics of terrorism in a way that makes it possible to distinguish terrorist activities from other kinds of violence, political or not. This is a bit surprising given the political setting from which the definition has emerged and one wonders whether it will make international or diplomatic consensus on what constitutes terrorism easier to achieve. A clearer definition was to be expected.

Shortcomings of the UN draft definition of terrorism

To sum up this discussion: the definition contained in article 2 of the draft UN Comprehensive Convention on International Terrorism is problematic in a number of ways, in particular:

- It does not distinguish an act of terrorism from an ordinary criminal offence such as a plain murder or sabotage ('public or private property').
- It excludes certain typical terrorist crimes such as kidnapping, hostage taking and hijacking when these cause no death or serious bodily injury.
- It fails to identify civilians and non-combatants as main targets ('any person' can mean a soldier, a policeman, a security guard, a criminal or a terrorist, among others).
- The linkage between sub-paragraph (a) and sub-paragraphs (b) and (c) is not explicit, and the linkage of sub-paragraph (c) appears to be only to (b), not to (a).
- The motivational aspects of terrorist acts, including the overwhelmingly political nature of terrorist attacks, are not addressed.
- While this draft text correctly identifies intimidation of the public and bringing pressure to bear on state authorities to accede to political demands as key purposes of terrorism, it does not address

a major objective of non-state terrorism, namely to bring, or keep, a particular issue in the forefront of public consciousness by means of perpetrating acts of violence that the news media cannot ignore. The idea of 'propaganda of the deed' is central to much of non-state terrorism and often prevails over the elements of 'intimidation' and 'compulsion' in terrorist motivation.

- Given its vagueness, the definition cannot serve as a scientific yardstick for the collection of data on acts of terrorism.
- Owing to its vagueness, the definition can be abused to criminalize legitimate resistance movements and attacks on military infrastructure.
- Owing to its vagueness, it is a doubtful legal basis for international cooperation.
- Terroristic repression of citizens and residents of a state by the regime's security forces are not covered, as the convention text only speaks about 'any person' (pending the outcome of article 18 negotiations).
- Subjective terms like 'serious damage to public or private property', 'serious bodily injury' and 'major economic loss' can hamper international cooperation against terrorism, for example when it comes to extradition requests.
- By focusing on the act rather than the intention or motivation, the definition 'catches' too wide a group of militant persons.
- Because it outlaws only 'unlawfully' caused acts without clarifying explicitly in the text itself whether this refers to national or international law, agents of the state can be exempted from the reach of the convention.

Taken as a whole, these points of criticism are strong and valid. It makes one wonder why certain of the obvious weaknesses in article 2 of the draft UN Comprehensive Convention against Terrorism, over which seasoned international lawyers from many countries deliberated for years, were not removed long ago.

In its session in March 2008, the Ad Hoc Committee, while dealing with issues related to the Preamble and article 18 of the draft Convention, did not review the definitional article 2. This might be an indication that no attempt will be made to address some of the weaknesses in the present draft text. This is an unfortunate situation and continues at the time of this writing (autumn 2010).

The inability of the General Assembly (to which the Ad Hoc Committee responds through the Sixth [legal] Committee to produce a satisfactory definition brought the Security Council to come up with an implicit definition in its resolution 1566 (2004), where terrorist acts are defined as

> criminal acts, including against civilians, committed with the intent to cause death or serious bodily injury, or taking of hostages, with the purpose to provoke a state of terror in the general public or in a group of persons or particular persons, intimidate a population or compel a government or an international organization to do or to abstain from doing any act, and all other acts which constitute offences within the scope of and as defined in the international conventions and protocols related to terrorism, are under no circumstances justifiable by considerations of a political, philosophical, ideological, racial, ethnic, religious or other similar nature.[82]

The following is a list of universal legal instruments: international conventions and protocols related to international terrorism. The source is Electronic Legal Resources on International Terrorism, https://www.unodc.org/tldb/, Terrorism Prevention Branch, United Nations Office on Drugs and Crime (accessed 17 August 2010):

1 Convention on Offences and Certain Other Acts Committed On Board Aircraft. Signed in Tokyo on September 14, 1963. Convention entered into force on 4 December 1969. Status: 185 parties.

2 Convention for the Suppression of Unlawful Seizure of Aircraft. Signed in The Hague on 16 December 1970. Convention entered into force on 14 October 1971. Status: 185 parties.

3 Convention for the Suppression of Unlawful Acts against the Safety of Civil Aviation. Signed in Montreal on 23 September 1971. Convention entered into force on 26 January 1973. Status: 188 parties.

4 Protocol for the Suppression of Unlawful Acts of Violence at Airports Serving International Civil Aviation, Supplementary to the Convention for the Suppression of Unlawful Acts against the Safety of Civil Aviation. Signed in Montreal on 24 February 1988. Protocol entered into force on 6 August 1989. Status: 171 parties.

5 Convention on the Prevention and Punishment of Crimes against Internationally Protected Persons, including Diplomatic Agents. Adopted in New York on 14 December 1973. Convention entered into force on 20 February 1977. Status: 173 parties.

6 International Convention against the Taking of Hostages. Adopted in New York on 17 December 1979. Convention entered into force on June 3, 1983. Status: 167 parties.

7 Convention on the Physical Protection of Nuclear Material. Signed in Vienna on 26 October 1979. Convention entered into force on 8 February 1987. Status: 143 parties.

8 2005 Amendment to the Convention on the Physical Protection of Nuclear Material. Status: 41 states have deposited instruments of ratification, acceptance or approval with the depositary.

9 Convention for the Suppression of Unlawful Acts against the Safety of Maritime Navigation. Done in Rome on 10 March 1988. Convention entered into force on 1 March 1992. Status: 156 parties.

10 Protocol of 2005 to the Convention for the Suppression of Unlawful Acts against the Safety of Maritime Navigation. Status: 16 states have deposited instruments of ratification, acceptance or approval with the depositary.

11 Protocol for the Suppression of Unlawful Acts against the Safety of Fixed Platforms Located on the Continental Shelf. Done in Rome on 10 March 1988. Protocol entered into force on 1 March 1992. Status: 145 parties.

12 Protocol of 2005 to the Protocol for the Suppression of Unlawful Acts against the Safety of Fixed Platforms Located on the Continental Shelf. Not yet entered into force. Status: 12 states have deposited instruments of ratification, acceptance or approval with the depositary.

13 Convention on the Marking of Plastic Explosives for the Purpose of Detection. Done in Montreal on 1 March 1991. Convention entered into force on 21 June 1998. Status: 144 parties.

14 International Convention for the Suppression of Terrorist Bombings. Adopted in New York on 15 December 1997. Convention entered into force on 23 May 2001. Status: 164 parties.

15 International Convention for the Suppression of the Financing of Terrorism. Adopted in New York on 9 December 1999. Convention entered into force on 10 April 2002. Status: 173 parties.

16 International Convention for the Suppression of Acts of Nuclear Terrorism. Adopted in New York on 13 April 2005. Convention entered into force on 7 July 2007. Status: 67 parties.

Only one of these international instrument contains – and then only implicitly – a definition of terrorism. Article 2 of the International Convention for the Suppression of the Financing of Terrorism contains language in 2(b) which can be viewed as defining:

1 Any person commits an offence . . . if that person by any means, directly or indirectly, unlawfully and wilfully, provides or collects funds with the intention that they are to be used, in full or in part, in order to carry out:
    (A) An act which constitutes an offence within the scope of and as defined in one of the treaties listed in the annex; or
    (B) Any other act intended to cause death or serious bodily injury to a civilian, or to any other person not taking an active part in the hostilities in a situation of armed

conflict, when the purpose of such act, by its nature or context, is to intimidate a population, or to compel a government or an international organization to do or to abstain from doing any act'.[83]

Given the fact that the Financing of Terrorism Convention has been ratified by more than four out of five states, the acceptance of article 2(b) would appear to imply a high degree of consensus on a key element of the definition of terrorism, namely to cause bodily harm to civilians for the intimidation of a population or the coercion of a government. Beyond that, these international instruments relating to the prevention and punishment of terrorist and related crimes cover, *inter alia*, the following offences which states ratifying them are obliged to introduce in their national legislation:

- physical attacks on internationally protected persons and their (and their government's property);
- the seizure of hostages to compel third parties to act in a certain way;
- the use of explosive or other lethal devices against public targets with the intention to cause death, serious injury, or major economic loss;
- the unlawful possession of radioactive material with the intention to cause death or serious injury or the unlawful use of such material with the intention to cause death, serious bodily injury, substantial property or environmental damage, or to compel a person, organization, or state to do or not to do something;
- jeopardizing the safety of a civil aviation aircraft by the use or threat of force or intimidation;
- doing things that endanger the safety of a civil aviation aircraft;
- acts of violence that cause serious injury or death of nuclear material that causes, or is likely to cause serious injury, death, or property damage; and
- gaining control over a vessel or fixed maritime platform by threat, force, or intimidation or endangering the safe navigation of the vessel or fixed maritime platform.[84]

Reuven Young has observed that

[g]iven the broad support, considerable overlap in obligations, recurring themes in conventions, and the endorsement of the definition of terrorism in Resolution 1566 by the Security Council, a powerful definitional jurisprudence exists in international law sufficient for states to draw on in forming their own definition of terrorism in domestic law.[85]

The emerging consensus about a UN definition – while it has not yet materialized in the work of the Ad Hoc Committee on Terrorism – has perhaps best been expressed by the recommended 'description' of terrorism in the report of the High-Level Panel on Threats, Challenges and Change in December 2004:

An[y] action, in addition to actions already specified by the existing conventions on aspects of terrorism, the Geneva Conventions and Security Council resolution 1566 (2004), that is intended to cause death or serious bodily harm to civilians and non-combatants, when the purpose of such act, by its nature or context, is to intimidate a population, or to compel a Government or an international organization to do or to abstain from doing any act.[86]

Slowly, the United Nations is moving towards a legal definition of terrorism. This definition, however, is, as we have seen in our discussion of the article 2 of the draft Comprehensive Convention, far from satisfactory in terms of social science. It is to this field we turn next.

Critique of, and comments on, the academic consensus definition (1988)

One question we asked our experts was 'What is your comment/criticism on the 1988 *academic consensus definition* of terrorism?' To recall: this definition had been arrived at on the basis of two rounds of questionnaire responses, and two versions were published in the 1984 and 1988 editions respectively of A.P. Schmid *et al.*'s research guide *Political Terrorism*.

The first round led to the following formulation in 1984:

> Terrorism is a method of combat in which random or symbolic victims serve as an instrumental *target of violence*. These instrumental victims share group or class characteristics, which form the basis for their selection for victimization. Through previous use of violence or the credible threat of violence other members of that group or class are put in a *state of chronic fear (terror)*. This group or class, whose members' sense of security is purposefully undermined, is the *target of terror*. The victimization of the target of violence is considered extra-normal by most observers from the witnessing audience on the basis of its atrocity, the time (e.g., peacetime) or place (not a battlefield) of victimization, or the disregard for rules of combat accepted in conventional warfare. The norm violation creates an attentive audience beyond the target of terror; sectors of this audience might in turn form the main object of manipulation. The purpose of this indirect method of combat is either to immobilize the target of terror in order to produce disorientation and/or compliance, or to mobilize secondary *targets of demands* (e.g., a government), or *targets of attention* (e.g., public opinion) to changes of attitudes or behaviour favouring the short or long-term interests of the users of this method of combat.[87]

In the second (1988) round, on the basis of some 50 responses to a questionnaire soliciting comments on the first version, the following text emerged:

> Terrorism is an anxiety-inspiring method of repeated violent action, employed by (semi-) clandestine individual, group or state actors, for idiosyncratic, criminal, or political reasons, whereby – in contrast to assassination – the direct targets of violence are not the main targets. The immediate human victims of violence are generally chosen randomly (targets of opportunity) or selectively (representative or symbolic targets) from a target population, and serve as message generators. Threat- and violence-based communication processes between terrorist (organization), (imperilled) victims, and main targets are used to manipulate the main target (audience(s)), turning it into a *target of terror*, a *target of demands*, or a *target of attention*, depending on whether intimidation, coercion, or propaganda is primarily sought.[88]

This definition has received considerable acceptance both inside and outside academia. In the words of Lord Carlile of Berriew, the British independent reviewer of terrorism legislation, it 'has found wide respect'.[89] Jane's Intelligence, for instance, has used it. Adrian Guelke called it 'probably the most rigorous effort there has been to define terrorism'.[90] It also received a number of favourable comments from respondents to the questionnaire, one calling it 'better than most' (Wallace) and another 'the most comprehensive and the most widely accepted among scholars' (Shanty). However, this 'academic consensus definition' has also received a fair share of deserved criticism. Several of our respondents called it 'too long'. One respondent, while qualifying it as 'an impressive attempt to define a specific human activity' called it 'very academic', reminding us that terrorism 'exists within the wider socio-political context of society as a whole' (E. Marks). Yet another respondent (Vladimir Lukov) called it 'excellent and extremely unclear to non-academic people'. Van der Liere held that '[t]he definition is rather a description than a definition', but conceded, 'That being said, I think this "definition" is the most accurate description of the phenomenon of terrorism in the literature.'

One respondent, Chasdi, himself the author of a very carefully crafted definition (to be quoted later), wrote: 'The underlying strength of the "1988 academic consensus definition of terrorism" revolves around its notion of a "duality of effect" with respect to dynamics between "victim" and "perpetrator"'.

At the same time, he noted that

> in its attempt to be comprehensive in nature, that definition seems rather cumbersome, which detracts from its potential to be more parsimonious. For example, the terms 'target of demands' and 'target of attention' are redundancies insofar as those dynamics are inherent to the act itself. The amorphous term 'idiosyncratic' is not only another example of this inelegant and all too wordy endeavour, but it seems to work to open the door to overlap between 'political terrorism,' which should be the focus here, and common criminal activity.' . . . Another criticism here is that some of the categories used in the '1988 academic consensus definition' such as 'targets of opportunity' and 'representative or symbolic targets' may overlap in the larger world of action.

Let us look at some of the major objections and problems.

Terrorism and assassination

Several respondents noted as one of the more serious shortcomings of the academic consensus definition its stance vis-à-vis assassination. Adrian Guelke had already noticed this in 1995:

> A striking aspect of Schmid's definition of terrorism . . . is its general exclusion of assassination. Schmid argues that 'while assassination aims at having the victim dead, terrorism does not care about the victim itself'. This is an attempt by Schmid to meet the point that there is often no reasonable basis for inferring intent to cause terror to others in the case of an assassination. In particular, the political purpose behind an assassination may be achieved directly by the death of the targeted individual. Where that is the case, it may not seem appropriate to label the act one of terrorism. None the less, that has not prevented assassination along with bombings from being seen by the media and the public as typical of terrorism.[91]

One respondent (Christine Fair) pointed out that 'assassination is very much in the pantheon of terrorist tactics . . . and I don't understand its exclusion here'. M.J. Gohel replied, 'The inclusion of the words "in contrast to assassination – the direct targets of the violence (terrorism) are not the main targets" should, arguably, be re-evaluated.'[92]

Clearly, qualification and clarification are needed. When I referred to assassinations, I thought primarily of stand-alone events like the assassination of US president John F. Kennedy (1963) or that of Martin Luther King (1968). In such isolated assassinations, victim and target do coincide. This is not indiscriminate violence but focused use of lethal force. Since the sole, or main, purpose of such targeted assassinations was arguably the elimination of unique personalities, I judged them to be not terroristic.[93] This is also in line with the conceptualization of Iviansky (1977):

> 'Individual terror' may be defined as a system of modern revolutionary violence aimed at leading personalities in the government or the Establishment (or any other human targets). The motivation is not necessarily personal but rather ideological and strategic. This method differs from traditional political conspiracy assassination, in that it is, in essence, not directed at individuals who are considered stumbling-blocks to the seizure of power or sworn enemies of the organization, but rather against the foreign conqueror, the social order, or

the Establishment embodied in these individuals. Infliction of personal injury is intended to weaken or destroy regimes, but, paradoxically, *one of the clearest manifestations of modern 'individual terror' is its impersonal character.* It seeks to sow discord and panic, to undermine and jeopardize the security of rulers and regimes, and to serve as the spearhead of revolution by stirring up the masses with exemplary deeds and the creation of revolutionary cadres trained to further the struggle.[94]

However, when a terrorist group uses serial assassinations, the effect of a political murder can certainly be terroristic, as was the case in the 1890s and the pre- First World War period, when several heads of state and government were murdered by gunfire or bombing at the hand of anarchist revolutionaries. Let us illustrate this with a historical example, the assassination of Tsar Alexander II of Russia in 1881. This relatively liberal ruler (he had liberated the serfs and introduced reforms) was killed because he had, in the eyes of the revolutionaries of the People's Will, not done enough. By killing him, they wanted to punish him (the direct target). However, they also wanted to send a signal to 'the people' of Russia (the ultimate target) that the tsar was not almighty and the monarchy not a God-given form of government. (Looking at democracy emerging in more and more countries in Western Europe, the members of the People's Will thought that terrorism had no place in democracies, where peaceful change was possible.) In line with the new doctrine of 'propaganda of the deed', the assassination of the tsar was meant to signal to the Russian masses that revolt was possible. In other words, the ultimate targets of the assassination were the Russian masses, to be awakened from their lethargy and fear of authorities. The tsar was only the instrumental victim.

This victim–target differentiation is characteristic of much of modern non-state terrorism. However, this does not mean that the victim cannot be part of the target population. When Léon Jules Léauthier used his shoemaker's knife on a rich man in a café in Paris on 12 November 1893, he said, 'I shall not strike an innocent if I strike the first bourgeois I meet.'[95] An individual presumed 'bourgeois' was his victim (it happened to be the Serbian ambassador to France, Georgewitch); the bourgeoisie as a class was his target. In other cases, the ultimate audience targeted might be the government, international public opinion, or both, or more than just these two audiences. Terrorism is violence for communication whereby the direct victim serves as message generator. One of its practitioners, the Harvard-educated 'Unabomber', Theodore Kaczynski, said in 1995, 'In order to get our message before the public with some chance of making a lasting impression, we've had to kill people.'[96]

However, it is a fact that even a single assassination when perpetrated by a terrorist group or guerrilla organization, as in the case of the killing of the former Pakistani prime minister Benazir Bhutto in January 2008, is likely to create fear and demoralization beyond the immediate target – a characteristic of terrorism – because of the strong identification of parts of the population with the victim. Boaz Ganor commented:

> Although I tend to agree that in most cases terrorism is meant to create anxiety within a larger audience then the immediate victims, the proposed definition excludes 'personal terrorism' – targeted assassination of political leaders and other key figures from the spectrum of the terrorism phenomenon.

Jeffrey Simon also held that the academic consensus definition

> makes a faulty distinction between 'terrorism' and 'assassination'. Assassination is one type of terrorist tactic. It does not matter if a terrorist tactic involving assassination is directed at a wider audience or at the main target; it is still an act of terrorism. . . . The phrase 'The immediate human victims of violence are generally chosen randomly (targets of oppor-tunity) or selectively (representative or symbolic targets) from a target population' ignores

terrorist acts aimed at eliminating key individuals (heads of states, rival faction leaders, etc.). Those targets are not chosen randomly, nor are they always 'representative or symbolic' targets. They could be chosen to eliminate the particular individual who may have had the power to influence events that the terrorists were opposed to.

My inclination still goes in the direction of Thomas P. Thornton's suggestion that as 'a general rule, assassination and sabotage are non-symbolic acts directed against persons and things respectively. Terror is a symbolic act that may be directed against things or people'.[97]

However, while some strong arguments can be brought forward in defence of my initial choice to exclude 'assassination', clearly the critics have a strong point. In this regard, the 'academic consensus definition' needs to be clarified – revised. It cannot be contested that militants who engage in terrorism also often engage not only in impersonal killing but also in personal assassination. They kill high-profile leaders and other prominent public figures, and not just more or less anonymous civilians. Yet this brings us back to the question: should all violence perpetrated by terrorists be labelled 'terroristic'? If terrorism is a tactic, those who engage in it can also engage in other tactics, for example of guerrilla warfare (targeting the security forces of the state). They can also engage in party politics (through front organizations) or even in tactics used by non-violent actors like hunger strikes (where victim and target also do not coincide). Implicit in some of the criticism is that terrorism is what terrorists do; once a group has been designated 'terrorist', all acts of violence by members of that group are ' terrorist' – faulty circular reasoning.

One of the conceptual problems implicit in the inclusion or exclusion of the classical type of assassination is that a killing by a terrorist group might be – as one of our respondents rightly put it – a 'multiple function assault' (C. Fair). By this, she referred to the fact that it is meant to 'degrade confidence in the state, increase confidence in the lethality of the organization, instil fear in attending public rallies and events where notable figures are present [and] increase pressure of non-combatant[s] . . . upon the government for settlement, etc.'.

From the above discussion, I conclude that a revision regarding the role of assassination in the academic consensus definition is called for. An assassination of a political leader, even if it does not terrorize others directly, has certain political repercussions that might be (a major part of) the motive for the killing, and both the elimination of the victim and the influencing of one or several audiences might have been intended even in a stand-alone political murder. Where such killings of high-level personalities gain a serial character, there can be little doubt left that future victims on the targeting list are terrorized. On the other hand, few would call a classical tyrannicide 'terrorism'. Assassinations, like hijackings, can be terroristic or not, depending on context, intent and outcome. From the terrorists' point of view, an assassination can be dual-purpose: eliminate an opponent and scare other members of the opponent's camp.

Terrorism and (organized) crime

Some respondents also suggested changes in the academic consensus definition regarding the inclusion or exclusion of criminal activities in the definition. One respondent (D. Gressang) thought that '[w]hile comprehensive . . . [the academic consensus] definition is not exclusive enough in that it would appear to include ordinary criminal activities such as extortion. . . . The main intent of terrorism is persuasion, not financial gain, and this definition has a difficult time drawing that distinction'. Boaz Ganor raised a similar criticism:

> This is one of the worst problems of the proposed definition. By including criminal motivation as one possible reason of terrorism, the definition includes so many acts that have nothing to do with the phenomenon of terrorism such as criminal Mafia activity, or criminal extortion, etc. Terrorism differs from other violent acts since political reasoning

and not criminal motivation are motivating it. (Even the Islamic radical terrorist organisations such as Al Qaeda that are being motivated by divine command, at the end of the day, have political goals, such as creating an Islamic [caliphate] state governed by Shari'ah law).

Another respondent (J. Sinai) blamed the academic consensus definition for 'fail[ing] to provide a workable criterion to distinguish between organized criminal intimidation, which often does involve a component of manipulation through random violence or demonstrative terror intended to manipulate a wider audience into compliance or submission with other criminal objectives. Yet at the same time, he admitted that '[s]uch conduct is also shared with terrorist organizations engaged in widespread extortion and other systems of revenue harvesting through campaigns of random intimidation'.

Kiran Krishan also felt uneasy about the inclusion of the category of crime, noticing that

> terrorism in its most virulent form is essentially political. By making terrorism inclusive of criminal activity, the bitterness and heinousness of this hideous and noxious form of political activity gets somewhat mitigated. The criminals act for private gains, and, therefore, their venality is understandable even if not acceptable. The perfidy of political beings that kill and maim innocents in the name of people is harder to accept. If there be an order of such people, criminals certainly rank higher. The definition is too long, and by that, purports to be all-inclusive.

One can take issue with these objections. In fact, another respondent complained that one of the major deficiencies in definitions of terrorism is the exclusion of criminal behaviour:

> Criminals who utilize terrorist tactics can often have the same effect on governments and societies as the more 'traditional' terrorists. History is filled with many cases of individual criminals and lone operators who have perpetrated acts of violence, including hijackings, airport bombings, and threats to release weapons of mass destruction. To exclude these acts of violence from definitions of terrorism weakens our understanding of the terrorism phenomenon.

A key common element in both political and criminal persuasive coercion is 'intimidation'. Organized crime groups use violence against 'non-cooperative' shopkeepers or restaurant owners in order to intimidate the owners of other businesses on their territory and persuade them to pay 'protection money' to avoid being victimized as well. Terrorists often engage in similar extortion by acts of coercive intimidation in order to collect 'revolutionary taxes'. In both cases, an instrumental victim serves to manipulate a wider target group. Once a few who have refused to pay have been killed, other will think twice about playing hero. While there are clear differences between ordinary criminals and political terrorists – a common criminal, for instance, would never engage in a suicide bombing – there are also similarities:

- Both operate secretly and usually from an underground.
- Both use 'muscle' and ruthlessness, and their victims are mainly 'civilians'.
- Intimidation is characteristic of both groups.
- Both use similar (though not entirely overlapping) tactics: kidnappings, assassination, extortion for 'protection money', 'revolutionary taxes'.
- In both cases, the control of the 'greedy group' over the individual member is strong.
- Both use front organizations such as legitimate businesses or charities.

It cannot be denied that there are also significant differences:

- Terrorist groups are usually ideologically or politically motivated, while organized crime groups are profit oriented.
- Terrorist groups often wish to compete with governments for legitimacy; organized crime groups do not.
- Terrorist groups usually relish media attention; organized crime groups do not.
- Terrorist victimization is generally less discriminate than the violence used by organized crime groups.

In reality, there are hybrid organizations and dual purposes to acts of violence. A kidnapping might serve both to extort political concessions and to collect criminal ransom money. Ted Gurr, in his response to the questionnaire, also noted this dilemma:

> I currently am puzzling about the connections between political and economic motives for violent political action. Most academics analyze terrorism as a tactic used in pursuit of political objectives, though often it also is used for material gain, not only to support the movement's political agenda but – in an agenda shift – for the personal benefit of the actors. If a movement or network has BOTH economic and political objectives, and uses terror/ exercises influence in both the economic and political spheres, how do we disentangle the relative importance of the two different objectives?

The answer to this question can only be given in concrete cases, e.g. with regard to narco-terrorism in Colombia. When the Colombian government sought to extradite a number of cocaine kingpins to the United States in the 1980s, the drug cartels declared, in their own words, 'total and absolute war on the government' and began to utilize tactics usually associated with terrorists. The number of assassinations and bombings generated by the cartels was very substantial. The following illustrates the extent of terroristic attacks by drug lords in Colombia during a ten-year period (1984–1993):

- Assassinations were carried out, as in the case of the Minister of Justice, Rodrigo Lara Bonilla, on 30 April 1984.
- The Supreme Court was stormed in 1984 by M-19 and drug traffickers, leading to 115 people being killed, including 11 Supreme Court judges.
- Between 1988 and 1990, assassins hired by the Medellín cartel killed 290 policemen for $1,000 each.
- Over 400 bombings were carried out between August 1989 and July 1990 alone.
- A mid-air explosion was caused to the Colombian Avianca B-727 flight no. 203 on 27 November 1989 en route from Bogotá to Cali, killing 111 people (allegedly because there were five police informers on board).
- The Medellín drug baron Pablo Escobar conducted 60 car bombings in 1993 in an attempt to persuade the government not to bring him to trial.

In the light of such manifestations, a categorical exclusion of the criminal motivation from a definition of terrorism does not seem to be warranted. There are similarities in the modus operandi of organized crime groups and terrorist groups and in some of their targeting practices, even though terrorist violence aims to affect the political process in a way organized crime often does only indirectly.

Based on the principle that 'whatever exists, is possible' and looking at the examples of FARC (Fuerzas Armadas Revolucionarias de Colombia, or Revolutionary Armed Forces of Colombia) and AUC (Autodefensas Unidas de Colombia, or United Self-Defence Forces of Colombia) in

Colombia. This suggests that a strict exclusion of the criminal element from a definition of terrorism does not seem to be warranted.[98]

A related underlying problem is that it is often unclear, in specific cases, what the intentions of actors are. The motivation might be 'political', 'criminal, 'idiosyncratic' or (as Khalis, Simon, Kaplan and Lieber) noted, 'tribal', 'ethnic', 'gender-based', 'religious', 'apocalyptic', 'social' or 'ideological'[99] – including motives that are currently not part of the academic consensus definition.

Terrorism and civilian victims

Perhaps most serious is the criticism the academic consensus definition received regarding the civilian status of the victims. One of the respondents (Sinai) argued that the academic consensus definition 'seeks to over-define the act, but leaves out the critical principle of intentional targeting of civilians or non-combatants'. Ekaterina Stepanova also stresses this important point: 'The definition does not clearly state that the main victims of terrorism are civilians and non-combatants either (although it somewhat hints at that by referring to random-choice or symbolic victims from a "target population")'. Equally, Boaz Ganor emphasizes:

> The most important factor of the definition of terrorism, in my view, is missing in the proposed definition – the deliberate attack aimed against civilians. By the proposed definition, an attack aimed against military personal, and even some kind of military acts in regular war, might be regarded as terrorism.

Yet on the other hand, another respondent (Ross) pointed out that '[t]argets are often military (look at al Qaeda's attacks, e.g. on US warships').[100] Ross also stressed, 'The aim of instilling terror is not unique. Threat- and violence-based messages are part of conventional warfare (think of . . . direct intimidation as with sirens on dive bombers)'. Yet other respondents begged to differ. Kiran Krishan, for instance, writes, 'Deliberate induction of dread is what sets terrorism apart from simple murder or assault. To that extent, the above definition is absolutely on target.'

We have discussed the issue of the nature of terrorist targets already in the section on the US State Department definition of terrorism. Not much can be added here. The question is: should the term 'terrorism' be applied only when it deliberately targets victims who are:

- non-combatants
- civilians
- harmless civilians
- any person who is not a party to the conflict
- unarmed or defenceless persons
- innocent people.

These are overlapping categories, but the overlap is only partial and varies from situation to situation on the ground. For instance: an Israeli settler on the West Bank is likely to be armed but might be a civilian at the time of victimization. He is certainly a party to the conflict, as he occupies land taken away from Palestinians in 1967. The category of innocence is also problematic and it might be better to settle for 'harmless civilians' as a halfway station between 'innocent' and 'non-combatant'. However, that would place the burden of proof that they are 'harmless' on the civilian victims rather than on the terrorists. Given the emerging international legal consensus, it might be wiser to settle for 'civilians and non-combatants' – whereby the term ' non-combatant' would apply to terrorism in the context of armed conflict and 'civilians' to war- and peacetime terrorism.

When armed forces conduct military operations in areas inhabited by civilians, human error and inaccurate weapons not infrequently cause 'collateral damage'. For the victims, it makes little difference whether their death is due to a targeting error by the military or is the result of a suicide bomber targeting civilians deliberately who argues that he has no other choice when trying to make an impact in asymmetrical warfare against a foreign military apparatus which bombs with its airforce. Yet can there be also moral equivalence for the non-partisan observer? The militant in a confrontation like those in Iraq or Afghanistan might argue that a terrorist is simply a bomber without an airforce. However, there is a moral difference: a military pilot is bound to adhere to the laws of war and risks punishment if he violates these laws. A terrorist, on the other hand, seeks out civilian targets deliberately, as he sees benefits in not adhering to the rules of warfare. Terrorism is for him a means to his end. In that, he resembles a war criminal who has no sense of honour, no sense of mercy, no sense of fairness, no sense of moral restraint and possibly not even a sense of his acts' illegality. In that mental framework, the end justifies all means. It is true that there are even worse crimes than terrorism, genocide being the most obvious case.[101] Yet that too involves the one-sided, deliberate killing of civilians. It is the wanton assault on civilians and non-combatants that provides much of the terror to terrorism.[102] In this sense, a revised academic consensus definition needs to be made more explicit.

What distinguishes a soldier from a war criminal is that the soldier makes this crucial distinction between combatants and non-combatants (such as prisoners of war and wounded enemy soldiers) and civilians. What distinguishes an insurgent freedom fighter from a terrorist should be no different.

The dispute regarding 'terrorism' as against 'freedom-fighting' does not really address a legal issue; it is a political debate, and it has already been discussed in the Introduction (Chapter 1). Ariel Merari summarizes the legal distinctions between conventional war, guerrilla warfare and terrorism as in Table 2.1. However, some observers fear that this classification, sound though it is, describes a vanishing situation. The term 'fourth-generation warfare' has been introduced to describe a new situation where hostilities are 'widely dispersed and largely undefined', where 'the distinction between war and peace' is blurred to the vanishing point', where there are 'no definable battlefields or fronts' and where 'the distinction between "civilian" and "military" may disappear' and actions occur concurrently 'throughout all participants' depth, including their society as a cultural, not just physical, entity'. Since military targets are usually hardened and non-state terrorists weak, the latter will, owing to their operational limitations, generally focus their attacks on soft, civilian targets.

Terrorism and the state

Some respondents criticized the academic consensus definition also for 'not explicitly restricting the notion of terrorism to apply to "genuine" non-state actors that have to use violence or threat of violence in an asymmetric way against a much "stronger" opponent "enjoying a higher formal status"' (E. Stepanova).[103] One respondent (Enders) said that he was 'uncomfortable with the inclusion of state actors in the definition'. Richard Barrett shared this point of view: 'While I agree that a state actor may, to all intents and purposes, commit an act which is indistinguishable from terrorism, I believe it should be called something else.' This opinion is shared by several others (Moghadam, Chenoweth, Bapat) and reflects international legal developments as summarized by Reuven Young, who concluded an 80-page analysis on the evolution of terrorism as a legal concept in international law by observing: '"Terrorism" no longer describes state conduct. It now refers to the acts of sub-state actors.'[104] Yet here we face a major problem. To restrict the use of the term 'terrorism' to non-state actors can lead to paradoxical outcomes. When the Nazi Brownshirts of the 1920s beat up and killed socialist and communist political opponents in the streets and places of assembly to terrorize foes and impress friends, they were terrorists. When the National Socialist Party came to power in Germany in 1933 and used the same methods on a much larger scale – should we stop calling them terrorists? By reserving the term 'terrorism' for non-state actors only, we neglect the multiple uses of terrorism by governments since the French Revolution and create, in effect, a double standard. It is true that the measured use of force by the state, when controlled

Table 2.1 Characteristics of terrorism, guerrilla warfare and conventional war as modes of violent struggle (according to Merari)

Characteristics	Conventional war	Guerrilla warfare	Terrorism
Unit size in battle	Large (armies, corps, division)	Medium (platoons, companies, battalions)	Small (usually fewer than 10 persons)
Weapons	Full range of military hardware (air force, armour, artillery, etc.)	Mostly infantry-type light weapons but sometimes artillery pieces as well	Hand guns, hand grenades, assault rifles and specialized weapons, e.g. car bombs, remote-controlled bombs, barometric pressure bombs
Tactics	Usually joint operations involving several military branches	Commando-type tactics	Specialized tactics: kidnapping, assassinations, car-bombing, hijacking, barricade-hostages, etc.
Targets	Mostly military units, industrial and transportation infrastructure	Mostly military, police, and administration staff, as well as political opponents	State symbols, political opponents, and the public at large
Intended impact	Physical destruction	Mainly physical attrition of the enemy	Psychological coercion
Control of territory	Yes	Yes	No
Uniform	Wear uniform	Often wear uniform	Do not wear uniform
Recognition of war zones	War limited to recognized geographical zones	War limited to the country in strife	No recognized war zones. Operations carried out worldwide
International legality	Yes, if conducted by rules	Yes, if conducted by rules	No
Domestic legality	Yes	No	No

by the constitution, the rule of law and the judiciary, and proportional to the actual threat, must be judged differently from vigilante or revolutionary 'justice' which is not rule-based. However, when a regime steps outside the legal principles while demanding adherence to them by its opponents, we are in a different situation. If a regime can conduct 'terrorism' abroad, either directly or as a state sponsor, why should its domestic use not be called state or regime terrorism? Frankly, I see no good reason to exclude terrorism conducted by organs of a state from the conceptual reach of the term 'terrorism'. The state might have a monopoly of legitimate force but it has to use it defensively and minimally in the framework of a social contract, a constitution and the rule of law. While the state makes laws, its organs and agents cannot stand above or outside the law – certainly not when it comes to international law. Table 2.2 lists government and opposition politics as mirror images.

The premise on which this table is built is that the use of persuasion and coercion in the political process occurs on three levels, which I have labelled 'persuasive politics', 'pressure politics' and 'violent politics' respectively.[105] Often, the main opposition party is not in a position to 'play in the same league' as those holding state power. The power asymmetry can 'force' it to respond on a

Table 2.2 The spectrum of political action

State of peace	
State actor	*Non-regime actor*
Persuasive politics	
I. Rule of law (routinized rule, legitimated by tradition, customs, constitutional procedures, compromise politics of give and take)	I. Constitutional opposition politics (formation of opposition press and parties, rallies, electoral contests, litigation [use of courts for political struggle])
Pressure politics	
II. Oppression (manipulation of competitive electoral process, censorship, surveillance, harassment, discrimination, infiltration of opposition, misuse of emergency legislation)	II. Extra-parliamentary action (incl. non-violent action (social protest for political persuasion of rulers and masses; demonstrations to show strength of public support; strikes, boycotts, non-cooperation, civil disobedience, and other forms of pressure politics short of violence)
Violent politics	
III. Violent repression for control of state power	III. Use of violence for challenging state power
III.1 Political justice; mass arrests, banning,deportation	III.1 Material destruction, sabotage, arson
III.2 Assassination	III.2 Assassination (individuated political murder)
III.3 State terrorism (torture, death squads, disappearances, concentration camps)	III.3 Terrorism (de-individuated political murder)
III.4 Massacres	III.4 Indiscriminate massacres
III.5 Counter-insurgency	III.5 Insurgency
State of civil war	

Source: Adapted from Alex P. Schmid *et al.*, *Political Terrorism*. Amsterdam: North-Holland, 1988, pp. 58–59.

different level. Violence by a state actor can be countered by non-violent campaigns for pragmatic reasons (no weapons are available) as well as for reasons of principle (the desire to hold the moral high ground in a conflict in order to attract international support). On the other hand, there are situations where the state holds the moral high ground and where terrorists use provocations from the repertoire of violent politics to upset a democratic government. The fact that terrorism is more frequent in democracies than in non-democracies is a testimony to the widespread use of this strategy. Table 2.2 refers to domestic terrorism; the situation is even more complicated in the case of transnational terrorism.

Yet the underlying logic is the same. In order to understand terrorism, we should not lose sight of the fact that acts of political terrorism occur alongside a multitude of other political and criminal acts, some violent, some not; some conventional, some not; some committed by the terrorists themselves, some by like-minded but less violent people who share their goals without approving of their methods. These are all part of the general repertoire of persuasive political communications and coercive actions available to participants in the political process. To isolate terrorist acts and terrorist organizations from this wider interplay of actors in political conflicts does not contribute to a better understanding of the phenomenon of terrorism.

Terrorist targeting: should attacks on property be included?

One of our respondents, while calling the academic consensus definition 'a very strong and useful definition', criticized, inter alia, the fact that 'in the 1988 definition only humans are considered to be the immediate targets of violence. I think that attacks on individuals' property, livestock, etc. can inspire anxiety, threaten population, and can be used for manipulation of the main target (e.g. government)'. The 'failure' to address attacks on 'property' was also raised by others, such as Khalis. Indeed, many definitions, especially legal ones, include attacks on property and critical infrastructure under the listing of criminal terrorist offences. Clearly, there are borderline cases, as when people are in an office (property). An attack on uninhabited (but highly symbolic) property (icons like the Statue of Liberty or the Eiffel Tower at night) has an intimidating effect. Yet the inclusion of property as such would open the door to labelling all kinds of acts of vandalism, arson and sabotage as terrorism, which would further expand an already broad concept, making it analytically less useful. The Boston Tea Party of 1773, in which a group of white settlers disguised as Native Americans, threw 342 chests of tea into the sea to protest against British taxation – an attack in which nobody was hurt – could qualify as terrorism if attacks on property were to be included. Admittedly, attacks on critical infrastructure that is vital to civilian survival constitute a borderline case. Legal definitions often include such targeting under the heading of terrorism. Social science definitions, however, probably should be more restrictive if the concept of terrorism is to retain some analytical rigour. After all, there are a plethora of other, related concepts covering various aspects of political aspects and violent conflict (e.g. sabotage).

Other points of criticism and concern

Respondents to the questionnaire took issue with several other elements of the academic consensus definition. Here are the main remaining points made:

Targets

The nature of the target, the intent behind the targeting and the process of targeting are subject to debate when it comes to terrorism. One of the respondents, for instance, finds it 'somewhat superfluous to state that targets are chosen "randomly" or "selectively"', adding, 'Such an either/or relationship does not decrease the universe of terrorism the description defines, and is thus not strictly a defining criterion separating terrorism from other forms of political violence.' Lutz made the valid point that '[t]argets are NOT chosen randomly, they are random representatives of a particular group (which can include an entire national population)'. However, the opportunistic targeting practices of some terrorists often come close to randomness.

Threat

Some respondents thought that the element of 'threat' was insufficiently covered by the academic consensus definition. Chris Dishman, for instance, wrote, 'I would highlight that it's violent action or the threat of violent action.' However, one can argue that 'threat' is contained in the element of 'intimidation'. The 'threat' aspect of terrorism is also, to some extent, contained in the triangular communication process triggered by a terrorist attack: perpetrator hits victim and the fear of repetition is communicated to other potential targets and constitutes a threat.

Anxiety

Donna Artz held that 'anxiety-producing' in the academic consensus definition was 'too subjective'. She asked, 'What about acts of terror that fail to produce anxiety? Better would be, "intended to cause anxiety".' This is a point also made by Simon, who noted that the phrase 'anxiety-inspiring method of repeated violent action' excludes many incidents of terrorism.[106] Boaz Ganor also noted:

The *anxiety* is one of the main and common outcomes of the phenomenon of terrorism but not a critical factor of the definition of this phenomenon since there could be terrorist attacks which were not meant to inspire fear and anxiety but just killings. One example is the killing of the Israeli Prime Minister Rabin in 1995 by an Israeli extremist. When creating a definition we should avoid using factors that have exceptions.

Again a valid point, but the assassination of Yitzhak Rabin was meant to stop a statesman willing to make peace, and this can be construed as a warning to other peacemakers. However, it is questionable whether this was terroristic.

Paradoxically, the main outcome of terrorism might not be terror in some target populations but anger, even rage and/or feelings of impotence, despondency or panic.

Serial character

Other criticism of the academic consensus definition (by D. Artz and S. Jayasekara) referred to the observation that, to be terrorism, violent action does not have to be 'repeated'; it can consist of only one act (such as the bombing of the Oklahoma Federal Building in 1995), a view supported by Whine. Yet while there is no doubt that a single act can create 'terror', I would still argue that 'terrorism' usually refers to a campaign-type series of punctuated hit-and-run or hit-and-die attacks. Again we are facing the issue of whether or not we should allow 'exceptions' in a definition.

Terrorist identity

Sinai observed:

> The issue of continuity or persistence of terrorist identity is . . . not addressed by this or other dominant definitions. Does a single act of terrorism identify a terrorist or a terrorist organization in perpetuity, at the time of incidence, or till such time as a 'political' or judicial resolution of the act has been arrived at?

It is evident that militant political activists often engage, simultaneously or consecutively, in a broad spectrum of violent and non-violent, legal and illegal, legitimate and illegitimate acts. Terrorists like Menachem Begin have ended up as winners of the Nobel Prize for Peace. Yet I do not see why such metamorphosis should be part of a definition.

Clandestinity

Artz thought that 'clandestine' seems 'unduly narrowing an element' – a notion shared by Stepanova. The fact is, however, that terrorists usually act from an underground, or, in the case of state terrorism, under a mantle of (semi-)clandestinity allowing for plausible denial. It is not an open fight, as in war, and it is usually a one-sided attack. To secure surprise, cover is necessary.

These are all points to be kept in mind when reformulating the academic consensus definition, as I shall try to do at the end of this chapter.

Let us, at this stage, however, recapitulate some of the perceived weaknesses and actual shortcomings of the 1988 academic consensus definition:

- The definition is too long, too academic and rather cumbersome.
- It excludes 'assassination', which should be included.
- It talks about randomly chosen targets, whereas it is the victims who are random rather than the choice of target.
- There are redundancies and overlaps in the description of targets (targets of demand, targets of attention, targets of opportunity, representative and symbolic targets).

- It does not confine the reach of the concept to politically motivated terrorism but includes criminally motivated (and idiosyncratic) terrorism as well.
- It is not explicit enough in stressing that the victims are civilians and non-combatants.
- It includes state terrorism, which according to some respondents should be excluded.
- The element of 'threat' is only indirectly alluded to via 'intimidation'.
- The element 'anxiety-producing' is seen as problematic, as other outcomes are possible, or the intention to produce anxiety may not be realized.
- A single incident can be 'terroristic'; the violent action does not have to be 'repeated'.
- It excludes attacks on property.

One problem is that not all respondents agree on certain problematic elements. Some are in favour of including state or regime terrorism, others are not. Some want to exclude criminally motivated terrorism, others not. The same is true when it comes to attacks on property. In this situation, I will have to make a choice when repairing/reformulating/upgrading the academic consensus definition based on the strength of arguments on each side as I see it. The outcome is reflected in the revised academic consensus definition 2011 presented at the end of this chapter. An appendix (Appendix 2.1) listing more than 250 academic, governmental, intergovernmental and other definitions follows this.[107] While many of these definitions cover familiar ground, occasionally some new elements turn up, such as the aspect of punishment in Rapoport's definition (see Appendix 2.1). I will, when formulating a new academic consensus definition, also draw from these definitions.

The definition question is one that many respondents would like to leave behind, but it comes back to haunt many of us in one way or another. Typical is a comment by Christine Fair:

> I find it very frustrating from a data collection point of view that there is no consensus across organizations and across countries (and among organizations within countries!) on what should be listed as a 'terrorist' event or what organization should be listed as a 'terrorist organization'. I care less about the nuances of the varied definitions than I do about having a definition that is systematically applied and . . . [is] universal in its acceptance. I simply don't have a dog in the definitional fight but I am deeply affected by this battle over definitions.

How to proceed in the 'battle of definitions'? The most sensible way appears to be to disaggregate existing definitions and dissect and discuss the individual attributes, elements and dimensions that go into definitions and search for common ground. It is to this task we turn next.

Elements to be considered for inclusion in a revised academic consensus definition

The art of making a good definition is to include as few elements as possible but also as many as necessary. The first academic consensus definition, of 1984, which derived *inter alia* from some 50 responses to a questionnaire, contained 22 elements (Table 2.3).

The second academic consensus definition, based on the comments of 50 academics on the first, was published in 1988 and contained 16 elements – 6 fewer than the 1984 definition. In 'Terrorism: The Definitional Problem' (2004), I tried to compare how frequent just 10 attributes of terrorism were in academic definitions on the one hand and (inter)governmental ones on the other (more on this below). In the same year, Leonard Weinberg, Ami Pedahzur and Sivan Hirsch-Loeffler analysed 73 definitions of terrorism from four leading journals in the field of terrorism. They then offered a minimalist consensus definition based on the lowest common denominator, which contained only 5 elements: 'Terrorism is a (1) politically motivated (2) tactic involving the (3) threat or use of force or (4) violence in which the pursuit of (5) publicity plays a significant role'.[108] This minimalist definition has, mainly because of its generality, several shortcomings. There is:

Table 2.3 Frequencies of definitional elements in 109 definitions of 'terrorism'

Element		Frequency (%)
1	Violence, force	83.5
2	Political	65
3	Fear, terror emphasized	51
4	Threat	47
5	(Psychological) effects and (anticipated) reactions	41.5
6	Victim–target differentiation	37.5
7	Purposive, planned, systematic tactic	32
8	Method of combat, strategy, tactic	30.5
9	Extra-normality, in breach of accepted rules, without humanitarian constraints	30
10	Coercion, extortion, induction of compliance	28
11	Publicity aspect	21.5
12	Arbitrariness; impersonal, random character, indiscrimination	21
13	Civilians, non-combatants, neutrals, outsiders as victims	17.5
14	Intimidation	17
15	Innocence of victims emphasized	15.5
16	Group, movement, organization as perpetrator	14
17	Symbolic aspect, demonstration to others	13.5
18	Incalculability, unpredictability, unexpectedness of occurrence of violence	9
19	Clandestine, covert nature	9
20	Repetitiveness; serial or campaign character of violence	7
21	Criminal	6
22	Demands made on third parties	4

Source: Alex P. Schmid *et al.*, *Political Terrorism: A Research Guide to Concepts, Theories, Data Bases and Literature*. Amsterdam: North-Holland, 1984, pp. 76–77.

- no reference to perpetrators or victims;
- no mention of fear or terror;
- no mention of motive or goal;
- no mention of non-combatant targets;
- no mention of criminal and immoral tactics (hostage taking, kidnapping, focused or indiscriminate murder).

In other words, the price for consensus on terrorism has, in this case, been a (too) thorough-going reduction of complexity and a high level of abstraction. The new academic consensus definition will not be as parsimonious.

In 'Terrorism – The Definitional Problem' (2004),[109] I compared academic definitions with more legalistic (inter)governmental definitions. I took ten elements which in my view covered core features of terrorism:

1. the demonstrative use of violence against human beings;
2. the (conditional) threat of (more) violence;
3. the deliberate production of terror or fear in a target group;
4. the targeting of civilians, non-combatants and innocents;
5. the purpose of intimidation, coercion and/or propaganda;
6. the fact that it is a method, tactic or strategy of waging conflict;
7. the importance of communicating the act(s) of violence to larger audiences;
8. the illegal, criminal and immoral nature of the act(s) of violence;
9. the predominantly political character of the act;
10. its use as a tool of psychological warfare to mobilize or immobilize sectors of the public.[110]

I argued that these elements might not be present in all acts of violence we call 'terrorist'. One incident might have five of the ten component elements, another might have fewer or more, and a third might show yet another combination of elements. Theoretically, it is possible that the various component elements of two incidents might not overlap at all (one might contain elements 1–5, the other, 6–10). Yet within the universe of a larger sample of violent incidents that seem to qualify as terroristic, there should be frequent overlap. Even when there is no common core, they resemble each other as do members of a family, as a number of characteristics can be found in different combinations, so that one can talk about a 'family resemblance' between them.[111]

Figure 2.1 includes ten elements which were found in 88 definitions from national government sources (such as the penal laws) and from international organizations. Since international organizations are set up by states, their definitional elements tend not to stray too far from national definitional elements.

Three elements clearly stand out: the element of terror, the element of opprobrium (illegal, criminal) and the element of coercion. What is notable is that there are almost no references to psychological warfare[112] or tactics[113] or strategy in these (inter)governmental definitions, and the category of communication[114] is also barely utilized by this non-academic set of definitions.

I contrasted this finding with findings based on a sample of academic and some other non-governmental definitions – a sample twice as large as the one taken from countries and international organizations. The distribution of definitional elements that emerges is shown in Figure 2.2.

What emerges from this comparison is that the illegal, criminal character of terrorism, which scores high in (inter)governmental definitions (85 per cent), scores much lower in academic definitions (30 per cent). On the other hand, the political character of terrorism, which is mentioned in 85 per cent of the academic definitions, can be found in only 25 per cent of governmental definitions and those of international organizations. The categories 'psychological warfare', 'communication' and 'strategy or tactic' score 12 per cent, 27 per cent and 35 per cent respectively in academic and NGO definitions while being virtually absent in governmental definitions and those of international organizations. The element of 'terror' and the element of 'coercion', on the other

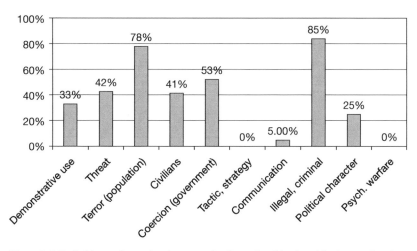

Figure 2.1 Definitions of terrorism by countries (in national law) and by international organizations (in conventions and international law) according to ten selected categories.

Source: Alex Schmid, 'Terrorism – The Definitional Problem'. *Case Western Reserve Journal of International Law*, 36(2–3), 2004, p. 407.

Note: *n* = 75 (countries) + 13 (international organizations) = 88 in total. Coding was done by K. Trompeter and K. Hecht, two interns from the United Nations Office on Drugs and Crime's Terrorism Prevention Branch.

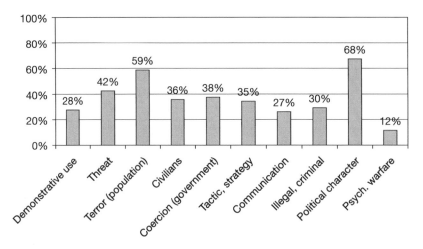

Figure 2.2 Definitions of terrorism by academics (and related).

Source: Alex Schmid, 'Terrorism – The Definitional Problem'. *Case Western Reserve Journal of International Law*, 36(2–3), 2004, p. 407.

Note: *n* = 75 (countries) + 13 (international organizations) = 88 in total. Coding was done by K. Trompeter and K. Hecht, two interns from the United Nations Office on Drugs and Crime's Terrorism Prevention Branch.

hand, score much higher with governments than with academia (78 per cent versus 59 per cent respectively and 53 per cent versus 38 per cent).

This comparison between academic and (inter-) governmental definitions demonstrates that there is less common ground between a social science and a legal definition than one would expect.

Towards a revised academic consensus definition of terrorism

In the following, we will discuss a dozen elements which, in my view, have stood the test of expert scrutiny or have emerged from the previous discussion as worth being including in a revised academic consensus definition. Then I shall reorder those elements about which I feel that most of the respondents can agree[115] – elements that together provide a fair and good enough description of what, in the common academic view, can be said to constitute 'terrorism'. I do this largely, but not exclusively, on the basis of the discussion so far, occasionally adding missing elements from elsewhere.

Element no. 1: Dual character of the term 'terrorism'

Some people assume that terrorism is an ideology ('the philosophy of the bomb'). However, this goes too far, given the very diverse population of practitioners. Yet one can view terrorism as a *doctrine* about the presumed strategic effectiveness of a special form of political violence where the primary victims of violence – typically civilians and non-combatants – are not the primary targets. The doctrine postulates the efficacy of the use of this special form of violence to generate power in political conflict. On the other hand, however, and at the same time, terrorism refers to a *practice*, tactic or method of [(de-)personalized] murder, (suicide) bombings, massacres, kidnappings and acts of hostage taking as well as composite tactics (disappearances, concentration camps, death squads, etc.) to influence and manipulate the political process, either nationally or internationally.[116] As a 'direct action' practice, terrorism involves deliberately planned, punctuated, publicity- or rumour-generating acts of shocking violence against others than armed forces. In that sense, the term has a dual character, which might be acknowledged in a revised academic consensus definition.[117]

Element no. 2: Threefold context

In the course of its history since 1793, terrorism has been practised in a variety of contexts. While it has always been a violent and criminal means to an end (positive power outcome, the achievement of a short- or long-term goal), it has been used in three quite different (though sometimes over-lapping) contexts:

1   as a form of rule by fear, for example when a repressive and illegitimate political regime wants to enforce conformity, obedience and non-resistance through extra-legal terror;
2   as a continuation of protest and propaganda by other means, for example when a group wants to draw the attention of the public to a real or alleged injustice or to disrupt the public order, or when it uses armed agitation in an attempt to provoke a revolutionary situation while not yet capable of much more than occasional acts of 'exemplary violence'; or
3   as a form of irregular warfare where indiscriminate atrocities against civilians and non-combatants are conducted either as a form of punishment against the civilian population, which might be hosting members of an armed resistance group, or in the framework of asymmetric and psychological warfare, often next to guerrilla warfare or regular warfare, in order to create deterrence and compliance.[118]

To limit the use of the term only to the second or third context and exclude the first does not do justice to the phenomenology of terrorism. A reference to context should therefore be included in a consensus definition.

Element no. 3: Perpetrator as source or agent of violence

Few would dispute that it takes a terrorist to terrorize and that the panic and fear caused by natural disasters (such as an earthquake and its aftershocks) or unintentional man-made disasters (such as the explosion of an ammunition factory in an urban neighbourhood) are different from terrorism. Such events can produce temporary terror but it is 'epiphenomenal terror' – extreme fear as a by-product – as Paul Wilkinson first noted. It takes a human agent to produce terrorism. However, there is some dispute about the type of agent that can produce terrorism. Some confine the use to agents who are non-state actors – from 'lone wolf'-type individuals to small cells of underground organizations to diffuse transnational network embedded in violence-prone ideological movements. Others perpetrators include secret agents of a political party linked to the state bureaucracy acting at home or abroad. Yet other perpetrators also include figures from organized crime, while some also attribute the capacity to engage in terrorism to mentally disturbed individuals and idiosyncratic individuals bent on revenge or conducting some personal crusade against one or another perceived evil in society. Most analysts agree that the agent is usually acting from an underground, in anonymity or, when in government, under the veil of secrecy. To summarize: few will dispute that for a definition of terrorism, a reference to human perpetrators and/or their superiors is called for; there can be no terrorism without a terrorist.

Element no. 4: Political

There is a widespread assumption that terrorism is 'political', not merely 'criminal' or 'psychotic' violence. Yet what is really meant by 'political'? When the term was first created, in ancient Greece, it referred to the common concerns of the free male citizens of the city of Athens (the *polis*) and was linked to their invention of democracy. In early modern, post-medieval France, the *politiques* were those lawyers who pleaded for a neutral and sovereign state power above the parties of the confessional powers. In political science, 'politics' is usually defined in terms of one or several of the following concepts: policy, power, authority, state, resource allocation and/or conflict.[119] The

New Oxford Handbook of Political Science (1996), for instance, defines 'politics' as 'constrained use of social power'.[120] That definition already gets us into problems when it comes to terrorism, since terrorism is widely considered to be a form of violence without moral (including social) restraint: terrorism would fall outside politics by that particular definition. Yet clearly, most non-state terrorists want to influence the state government's politics and/or the party politics of society.

In fact, quite frequently political parties have links to terrorists: they are sometimes acting as a front for a terrorist organization or are split into a legal parliamentary and a violent and illegal extra-parliamentary faction.[121] Terrorism, then, is often a special form of violent politics, next to milder forms such as violent protests, political hunger strikes and protest suicides, storming of government buildings, etc. 'Political violence' is, as I pointed out earlier (pp. 5–6) a broad concept. It can include 'collective violent action', 'civil strife', 'mass political violence' and 'internal war' – all overlapping concepts.[122]

The question remains: do some forms of violence have to be necessarily 'political' to be labelled 'terrorist'? Perhaps paradoxically, the strongest defence of the classification of terrorism as 'political' has been offered by Ben Golder and George Williams when they noted that '[t]he lack of consensus on what constitutes terrorism points to its inescapably political nature'.[123] In short, 'political' is an element that ought to be included in a definition of terrorism, but non-political terrorism should not be totally ruled out either.

Element no. 5: Violent act

Few will dispute that terrorism is a special form of use of (political) violence without moral restraints. In addition, some might want to qualify this by specifying that terrorist violence entails the demonstrative, deliberate, unilateral, illegal or illegitimate application of extreme force to inflict death or serious injury, either indiscriminate or selective, usually in peacetime or outside zones of combat by means of (suicide)bombing – the most typical terrorist method, ranging from letter bombs and firebombing, from improvised explosive devices to heavy vehicle-based bombs using fertilizers or military explosives, armed assault, massacre, summary executions and other acts of murder, as well as kidnapping and (barricade) hostage taking for coercive bargaining, endangering people's physical integrity, freedom, health and right to life. The destructive acts themselves are criminal offences outside the context of war and tend to qualify as war crimes in a context of war if civilians and non-combatants are deliberately targeted. The violent act is generally meant to be 'exemplary' and serves the aim of intimidating, impressing or coercing third parties linked, directly or indirectly, to the victims. As one author noted,

> One of the most obvious and blatant benefits of atrocity is that it quite simply scares the hell out of people. The raw horror and savagery of those who murder and abuse cause people to flee, hide, and defend themselves feebly, and often their victims respond with mute passivity.[124]

While in genocide the goal of violence is extermination, terrorism seeks to bring about compliance in a target population.[125]

Compliance as a terrorist goal can generally be achieved better by discriminate selective violence, as state or regime terrorists generally realize. Indiscriminate terrorism is a more dangerous weapon but, lacking intelligence and operational skills to engage in selective violence, insurgent terrorists often resort, at least initially, to indiscriminate violence, which is cheaper and therefore tempting in a situation of great asymmetry between the parties for the weaker side.[126] Violence (or the threat thereof) is the one thing a terrorist non-state group cannot give up since it is often its only political bargaining instrument. State terrorists, on the other hand, can do without the violence, once the regime has shown what it can do with terrorism. It will only have to refresh the memory of people from time to time – either with real acts of terror or propagandistic reminders of the terror it meted out in the past.[127] For this reason, among others, a mere inclusion of the element of violence in a definition of terrorism – while essential – is not enough. There also has to be a reference to the element of threat, which creates the so characteristic sense of intimidation typical of both political and criminal bullying.

Element no. 6: Threat-based communication

It is doubtful whether a single act of violence can create a climate of fear. At the very least, a fear of repetition, if not a full campaign of terrorist attacks, is need to bring home the intended (but erroneous because highly exaggerated) message that terrorists can strike anyone, anywhere, at any time. The threat of terrorist violence can take several forms: the most basic one is a form of conditional killing ('do this or . . .').[128] We find this in the case of kidnapping victims or hostages taken as in a hijacking (dual-phase incidents), or it can take the form of some threatened future violence in the case of single-phase incidents such as assassinations (e.g. through the publication of 'death lists' of persons to be targeted for killing). The threat or use of sudden, sometimes selective but often indiscriminate, life-threatening violence has an intimidating character and as such can cause existential terror among members of a wider public who identify with recent victims or fear that they will be in the near future themselves victims. The target audience which the terrorist aims to reach has some sort of relationship with the victims, a relationship which is (re-)activated by the victimization, for example in the form of identification by the target population with the victim population based on common characteristics so that many among the audience ask themselves: 'Am I also threatened? Will I be next'?

A feeling of threat is usually created by one or several acts of violence (often an 'exemplary deed'). Threats gain credibility from precedents, so that many people are put in fear of bodily injury or death. The apparent main purpose of the terrorist victimization is often expressive, namely to convey a message to people other than the victims themselves. In a sense, the violence is triangular: a perpetrator harms a victim in order to influence an ultimate target indirectly. However, the elimination of the victim might also be a concomitant goal – serving as a warning to others who share characteristics with the victim. In that sense, a terrorist assassination is often dual-purpose.

There is a similarity between threats and intimidation from terrorists and those of ordinary bullies, and especially figures belonging to organized crime. It is well known that mafia-type organizations visit business premises (e.g. restaurants) and offer 'protection'. What they imply is that they will burn down a shop or shoot at customers or kidnap the children of the owner if he does not pay regularly to those who offer 'protection' (allegedly against other criminal organizations who also 'offer' their 'services'). In a similar way, terrorists may visit local business and ask for 'revolutionary taxes'. If these are not paid, the consequences can range from arson to murder. If they are paid, nothing happens to those who have given in to the extortion – except that they will be revisited periodically for further extortion. In other words, a form of blackmail takes place. In order to show that they 'mean business', mafia clans and terrorist groups stage one or two exemplary punishments of non-payers or late payers of 'protection money' or 'revolutionary taxes' in order to intimidate others who might consider not paying or might be bold enough to report the blackmail attempt to the police. The threat of violence, based on a proven or credible record of actual violence, serves to intimidate the wavering. There is victim–target differentiation: 'punishing' one or a few non-compliant victims sends a message to many other targets in the same situation.

It has been frequently observed that the 'threat' emanating from terrorists is highly disproportional to the actual amount of violence they can apply (state terrorists excluded). Because of the unexpectedness and apparent randomness of some of the terrorist targeting, it is often difficult to make proper threat assessments. As a consequence, vulnerability assessments often replace threat and risk assessments. A consequence is that the danger or threat of terrorism is often grossly exaggerated – helped by terrorist propaganda and announcements of further strikes. The mass media, whose news values offer greater coverage to life-threatening events than to normal situations, tend to show great eagerness to give prominence to acts of terrorism. This increases threat perceptions way beyond the reality of the actual danger. Terrorists play with the threat of future violence and use the conditional suspension of the threat of violence (e.g. in the form of cease-fires) as a bargaining tool. The simple issuing of threats (which sometimes turn out to be mere boasts or hoaxes) influences public behaviour and forces the authorities to increase threat levels and provide commensurate additional security for critical infrastructure and public meeting places, which can be very costly, while the cost for the terrorists might be only that of a phone call or email.

Element no. 7: Differentiation between direct civilian victims and the ultimate target audience

Here we come to the very core of terrorism that sets it apart from most other forms of violence. The direct victim of violence (or threat thereof) is different from the ultimate target (audience). For this reason, anyone can, in principle, become a victim of terrorism. In the dominant understanding among experts, the victims are predominantly not members of an armed force. Some authors on terrorism only allow certain victim groups to classify the violence as terrorist. The range of 'terrorist' victims can stretch from human beings who are (1) innocent (e.g. children), (2) harmless civilians (e.g. women), (3) unarmed civilians, (4) civilians in general, (5) the defenceless in general, (6) those who are neutral or not a party to the conflict, (7) indiscriminately chosen (random) victims, (8) non-military targets, (9) genuine non-combatants (e.g. prisoners of war), (10) non-civilian non-combatants (e.g. military personnel in peacetime or outside zones of combat), or (11) unarmed police not on duty. There is considerable disagreement among authors as to how wide the circle should be drawn, but a majority label deliberate attacks on civilians and non-combatants terrorism when such assaults serve to put pressure on third parties. Many governments also include attacks on infrastructure and property under the terrorism label, although it is difficult to see how such acts can, by themselves, 'terrorize' anyone in most circumstances.

The direct victims are often impersonally targeted, like the arbitrarily killed persons hit by a hidden bomb in a crowd. Their specific identity – except in (serial) assassinations – is of no major concern or of particular importance to the terrorist as long as even random victimization generates enough attention and publicity to send a political message to the ultimate target audience(s). In the case of a martyrdom operation, such as a suicide bombing, the perpetrator is also among the victims (although one hesitates to place him or her in the same category of victims). Unlike a belligerent in war, the victim of terrorism cannot, through a change of attitude or behaviour, save his or her life, for example by capitulation. Direct victims are generally only passive tools for the realization of terrorist goals. In this sense, most victims of terrorism, while chosen as representative or symbolic targets of direct violence, are only secondary targets, mere props for the staging of a violent spectacle meant to influence the perception and behaviour of one or several other audiences – the ultimate targets in the macabre spectacle of terror.

Earlier, we saw that the defencelessness and helplessness of the victim in the face of unprovoked and unexpected violence creates the feeling of terror. A soldier in battle might fear for his life, but he is armed and often has a chance to defend himself (and others) against an enemy's armed force or against irregular fighters who might or might not be lawful belligerents (in the sense of the Geneva Convention and its protocols). A civilian or a non-combatant, on the other hand, has no fair chance to neutralize the threat posed by a terrorist attack. It is true that a soldier in battle might also feel extreme fear – terror – especially if the superiority of the adversary is overwhelming or when he has reason to fear that the adversary will not adhere to the rules of war if and when he becomes a prisoner of war. However, many acts of terrorism occur in peacetime and primarily victimize civilians who cannot defend themselves. They, and third parties, often feel that they are outsiders, neutrals, innocent civilians or, in the terminology of international humanitarian law, non-combatants.

Terrorists often do not make a distinction between lawful combatants and innocent non-combatants; all are seen as part of the enemy camp, as they generally see people as either part of their problem or part of the solution to their problem. At times, terrorists appear to target certain types of civilians – e.g. a school class of children – precisely because of their innocence. That increases the despair (but also the outrage) among the ultimate target group. The terrorist tendency to see the world only in terms of supporters or opponents tends to eradiate the categories of neutrals and innocents. In other words, innocence is either irrelevant or even a special incentive for targeting, owing to the extra shock value produced by the extra-normal violence of the terrorist. On the other hand, it is true that members of armed groups labelled terrorists do occasionally target military objects and security forces personnel as well. Civilians are targeted more often than soldiers because they are easier to target, but some terrorists do not accept a difference between belligerents and non-belligerents. In the words of Bin Laden, 'We do not have to differentiate between military or civilian. As far as we are concerned, they [Americans] are all targets'.[129]

If those opposing terrorism want to maintain the moral high ground, they will have to continue to observe this distinction between the unarmed civilian population and regular or irregular armed forces. However, they should only label as 'terrorism' attacks that deliberately target civilians and non-combatants. There is an unfortunate tendency to call all armed attacks 'terroristic' even if they are directed at the security forces. Such attacks might be criminal or legitimate, depending on context – but they are usually not terroristic even when performed by terrorists. The armed forces might, however, be one of the many possible audiences that non-state terrorists might wish to reach by killing civilians and non-combatants.

There are, as the following list of ten terrorist audiences makes clear, multiple audiences, some deliberately targeted, some not. The list is not exhaustive.

1   the adversary/-ies of the terrorist organization (often a government);
2   the constituency/ society of the adversary/-ies;
3   the targeted direct victims and their families and friends;
4   others who have reason to fear that they might be the next targets;
5   'neutral', distant publics;
6   the constituency the terrorist organization belongs to, or wants to belong to;
7   potential sympathetic sectors of domestic and foreign (diaspora) publics;
8   other terrorist groups that are rivals for prominence;
9   the terrorist and his organization; and, last but not least,
10 the media.

Some audiences are targeted because they are likely to identify with the direct victims or because they can be held responsible for them. The addressees of the terrorist threat communication can be multiple: they usually include (for non-state terrorism) an enemy government opposed by the terrorist, that state's population or some regime-linked sections thereof, the actual or imaginary constituency of the terrorist group, the mass media, and sometimes also rival or friendly terrorist groups. In some situations, the primary target audience that the terrorists had in mind when engaging in an act of demonstrative violence might not have a direct relationship with the victim group but might instead identify with the perpetrators and feel elated rather than despondent as a consequence of the terrorist attack. In those situations, the primary target audience is often the terrorists' intended constituency to whom the exemplary deed of terrorist violence is offered or 'dedicated', perhaps as a demonstration that rebellion or resistance is possible or that revenge has been taken.

However, typically an attack by a non-state terrorist group is directed at a soft public target and has as primary addressee the government, which, in turn, is often reproached by the public or sections thereof for not having protected them well enough. When citizens are successfully attacked by an underground terrorist group, the demonstrated inability of the government to protect all members of society all the time against terrorist attacks tends to weaken the social contract between government and citizens. Rather than blaming the terrorists for the attack, sectors of the public tend to blame their own government for not protecting them well enough. Paradoxically, some of the very same people blame the government for reducing their civil liberties when trying to prevent acts of terrorism by increasing security measures.

Element no. 8: Terror/fear/dread

The deliberate act of violence (or series of such acts) is designed to produce a psychological effect – extreme fear or terror – out of proportion to its physical result. To achieve such dread or fear, or at least widespread anxiety in audiences beyond the direct victims and witnesses, the terrorist tries to impress the public by his ruthlessness, his cruelty, the excessive destructiveness of the act of violence, the element of surprise, the presence of many onlookers, or a combination of these or similar elements meant to create – and then coercively exploit – shock, exaggerated fear and, if repeated, a climate of terror. To achieve this, the terrorist cleverly exploits the inherent bias of the news value system of the mass media in countries where there is no censorship, which offers free publicity to acts of violence full of drama and conflict.

The degree of fear experienced by secondary victims depends on spatial and emotional distance from the primary victim and can range from fright to anxiety to despair. However, that applies only to those who identify with the victim of terrorist violence. Those who identify positively with the perpetrator of an act of terrorism and/or have good reason to hate the victim might have opposite feelings ranging from satisfaction ('they deserved it') to enthusiasm ('revenge has finally been exacted').

Element no. 9: Intent

Terrorist acts appear to be intended to 'terrorize' a target group and, secondarily, to exploit insecurity created by the fact that, (sections of) the public have been put in fear. They also utilize to good effect the publicity created by the violent deed (or threats thereof, once 'credibility' for violence has been established). With their deed, terrorists claim for themselves a place in the political arena and want to affect the political agenda. They want to impress, intimidate and – in extreme cases – subjugate or expel target populations or coerce political authorities into considering their demands and appeasing them by granting concessions (e.g. in the case of hostage negotiations). The primary purpose of a daring terrorist attack might even be to impress favourably the (potential) constituency of a terrorist group rather than to traumatize segments of the public in the opponent's camp. Related purposes associated with terrorist acts are the search for attention, publicity and, ultimately, recognition, but they can also include destabilization, disruption of election campaigns, spoiling of peace processes, ethnic cleansing, etc. The range of alleged, claimed, reported or proven intents is wide. Other purposes cited in the literature on terrorism include provocation of repression; the mobilization of supporters; affecting public opinion in one way or another; causing polarization in society; breaking resistance; punishing, disciplining, controlling, dissuade or deterring target groups; enforcing obedience, allegiance and conformity; disorienting and demoralize target audiences; creating alarm, insecurity, a climate of panic; causing disorder; injuring or eliminating opponents; disrupting or discrediting the process of government; eroding public institutions; destroying public confidence in government or disrupting the normal functioning of society; projecting an image of strength and determination; advertising the goals of the terrorist organization; immobilizing the security forces; winning recruits for the terrorist cause; morale building within the terrorist group itself or among its sympathizers; punishing errant members of and traitors to the organization; winning concessions through coercive bargaining; punishing persons held responsible for attacks on members of the group; blackmailing; subjugating; and intimidating.

Intent is often difficult to establish, and the extent to which results match intent is also difficult to measure. The immediate outcome of an act of violence or series of such acts might be terror but the degree to which such terror can be instrumentalized towards achieving a political goal is what ultimately counts. Terror is a blunt instrument of rule and anti-rule, and hard to orchestrate. Sometimes the principal outcome is, as we observed before, not terror but outrage and feelings of revenge resulting in massive mobilization against the perpetrators who might, as a consequence, be 'terrorized' themselves.

The *primary* aim of a terrorist act is often to threaten, intimidate and demoralize a third party or the populace which on the basis of existing ties or situational characteristics identifies with the immediate, sometimes symbolic, victims – the threat being: you might very well be the next victim. A *secondary* aim of the terrorist act is often coercion: the threat of new acts of terrorism is used as a compelling or deterring bargaining tool. Terrorists sometimes 'promise' (temporary) discontinuation of further victimization – subject to compliance with terrorist demands. They threaten with repetition of acts of terrorism in case of non-compliance – from which they expect a deterrent effect. In other words, extortion and blackmail based on intimidation take place. The act of coercion involved goes beyond the boundaries that define the acceptable use of coercion in social relations. Terrorist groups often claim responsibility (e.g. by means of a video message) and link this claim to public demands for a redress of grievances, release of prisoners, political concessions (e.g. the end of foreign occupation), ransom monies, publication of a manifesto, etc. A *tertiary* aim of a terrorist act is to impress others who are not directly a target of violence, a target of terror or a target of demands but a mere target of attention. Some targeted audiences are not threatened themselves, but the threat against others comes to their attention and might give satisfaction to some members of that audience. This target of attention can be the terrorists' own constituency or a (segment of the) domestic public. Sometimes international visibility, recognition and support are sought and the primary and secondary aims are less apparent.

To summarize: intent is often difficult to proof in acts of terrorism. For one thing, many acts of terrorism are no longer claimed, or are claimed by several groups. The real intent might also differ from the purported intent. At times, an act of terrorism is intended to have diverse effects with different audiences – terrorizing one and stimulating another. Yet to dismiss intent as an element of definition is nevertheless not advisable.

Element no. 10: Campaign

While a single act can strike temporary terror in a target population, more often than not terrorist acts come in series and have the character of a campaign that is pursued until a certain political result has been achieved or, more likely in the case of non-state terrorism, until the group has been weakened so much that it tries to gain some political leverage by declaring a conditional cease-fire. The campaign might involve multiple simultaneous attacks, dual- or multi-phase acts of terrorism (kidnappings, hijackings, other forms of hostage taking) or single-phase attacks (bombings, shootings, arson, etc.). It might also be coordinated with activities of a political front organization or a rural guerrilla group, or linked to events such as peace processes or elections, which the perpetrators try to disrupt. While some groups engaging in terrorism use terrorism as a stand-alone technique in which they engage on a part-time or full-time basis, others mix it with street violence, electoral politics (and violence surrounding elections) and/or tactics from the repertoire of guerrilla warfare. Yet except for a *coup d'état* or in a blitzkrieg (lightning war), political violence rarely achieves decisive results with one stroke. That is certainly true for terrorism as a weapon of the weak. To have some chance of becoming effective, it requires a campaign of terrorist attacks, just as guerrilla warfare requires a protracted conflict.

These ten attributes/elements or dimensions are, in my view, major building blocks for the reformulation of an academic consensus definition of the concept of terrorism.

Defining what terrorism is not: the negative approach

Before I try to reformulate the academic consensus definition on the basis of the discussion so far, it might be worthwhile to look at the definition problem from the other side – listing elements which should be excluded – following the advice of Thomas H. Mitchell who, given the heterogeneous nature of the terrorist phenomenon, suggested that 'a definition of terrorism must clearly establish what terrorism is not'.[130] While this advice, taken literally, would lead to a very long and clumsy formulation, the underlying idea is sound. In my view, such a list could contain the following ten elements, which reflect situations that should not be labelled 'terrorist'. Thus, 'terrorism' should exclude:

1   mere acts of property damage, as well as acts of sabotage such as interrupting the flow of an oil pipeline, even when the saboteurs are engaging in acts of terrorism on other occasions;
2   attacks on military installations, aircraft, navy vessels, barracks, and the like, which are guarded, even when those who attack military installations or personnel are otherwise also engaging in acts of terrorism;
3   attacks on police stations and armed police on patrol during armed conflict in zones of combat;
4   cases of collateral damage where the targeting of civilians was not deliberate (e.g. when an attack on a police station misfires and civilians are (also) victims);
5   cases of attacks on secular or religious symbols unless such an attack is combined with the victimization of people (an attack on a church known to be empty would not qualify; an attack on a church, mosque or synagogue where people are sheltering would);
6   certain types of assassinations, for example when the direct victim is the only target, as opposed to de-individuated murder where the victim serves only as message generator to reach a wider audience;
7   acts which if a situation of war existed would not qualify as war crimes, nor be crimes against humanity or grave breaches of the laws of war;
8   guerrilla warfare activities that are not war crimes, crimes against humanity or grave breaches of humanitarian law;
9   acts of legal use of force by legitimate authorities to impose public order when acting with restraint and in proportion to the threat and within the boundaries of the rule of law;
10   acts of (collective) political violence which are spontaneous, as in riots, demonstrations and other forms of public protest and dissent; industrial action (strikes) and revolts.

Contested elements and the necessity of consensus

What has emerged from our discussion so far is that a number of respondents find it difficult to agree with certain elements from the ten 'positive' elements and/or the ten 'negative' attributes, dimensions or elements listed above. The main contested elements of the definition of terrorism appear to be the following ten:

1   Some authors stretch the concept of terrorism to include attacks on the military, while at the same time excluding certain activities by the military.
2   Some authors include attacks on the military outside zones of combat and outside wartime as terrorism, while others do not.
3   Some authors are also prepared to label the destruction of property terrorism.
4   Some authors are prepared to label certain harmful acts (such as computer hacking) terrorism even when no direct violence is involved or no terror results (as, so far, in the so-called cyber-terrorism).
5   Some authors and authorities tend to label all forms of militancy and violence by militant group terrorism, once a group has been designated a terrorist organization.
6   Some authors exclude acts of a state or government and their agents from their understanding of terrorism.
7   Some exclude certain intimidating violent activities by (organized) crime groups from being labelled terrorism.

8　Some authors and authorities exclude freedom fighters (struggling for national liberation) and the activities of those who are trying to rid a territory of foreign occupation, no matter what the nature of these acts of popular (or unpopular) resistance and 'fighting' is and despite the fact that there is no definition of 'nation' or 'people' in international law.

9　Some authors include (all) assassinations in the concept of terrorism; a few do not.

10　Some authors argue that terrorism has nothing to do with religion (in particular, Islam), while others see a link between religions that claim to be in possession of absolute truth and terrorists, whom Marx once labelled 'dangerous dreamers of the absolute'.

In the face of such opposing views, how can greater consensus be reached? Full consensus would imply that all respondents to our questionnaire and academic colleagues beyond them agreed on the elements to be included and excluded in a definition of terrorism. Such a full consensus will never be reached. Yet what we can hope for is that a majority of academic analysts can agree on the core elements. There will always be borderline cases where honest people can disagree.

The definition problem is not just an 'academic' problem. The absence of a common definition encourages the continuation of double standards and stands in the way of international co-operation.[131] Anthony Quainton, a former director of the Office for Combating Terrorism at the US State Department, has said that '[t]his problem of definition has bedevilled the development of an effective counter-terrorist strategy at both the national and international level'.[132] There is a need for a consensus definition. There are, according to Boaz Ganor, the director of the International Institute for Counter-Terrorism, no fewer than eight reasons why it is important to have a common international understanding as to what constitutes terrorism:

1　Developing an effective international strategy requires agreement on what it is we are dealing with; in other words, we need a definition of terrorism.

2　International mobilization against terrorism . . . cannot lead to operational results as long as the participants cannot agree on a definition.

3　Without a definition, it is impossible to formulate or enforce international agreements against terrorism.

4　Although many countries have signed bilateral and multilateral agreements concerning a variety of crimes, extradition for political offences is often explicitly excluded, and the background of terrorism is always political.

5　The definition of terrorism will be the basis and the operational tool for expanding the international community's ability to combat terrorism.

6　It will enable legislation and specific punishments against those perpetrating, involved in, or supporting terrorism, and will allow the formulation of a codex of laws and international conventions against terrorism, terrorist organizations, states sponsoring terrorism, and economic firms trading with them.

7　At the same time, the definition of terrorism will hamper the attempts of terrorist organizations to obtain public legitimacy, and will erode support among those segments of the population willing to assist them (as opposed to guerrilla activities).

8　Finally, the operational use of the definition of terrorism could motivate terrorist organizations, as a result of moral and utilitarian considerations, to shift from terrorist activities to alternative courses (such as guerrilla warfare) in order to attain their aims, thus reducing the scope of international terrorism.[133]

When reformulating our academic consensus definition on the basis of comments and criticism received, we should try not to step too far away from the emerging international political and legal consensus of what constitutes terrorism as it manifested itself in early December 2004, when the broad-based international High-level Panel on Threats, Challenges and Change tried to cut through the Gordian knot of defining terrorism and proposed a description of terrorism as

> any action, in addition to actions already specified by the existing conventions on aspects of terrorism, the Geneva Conventions and Security Council resolution 1566 (2004), that is intended to cause death or serious bodily harm to civilians or non-combatants, when the purpose of such act, by its nature or context, is to intimidate a population, or to compel a Government or an international organization to do or to abstain from doing any act.[134]

By emphasizing that 'attacks that specifically target innocents and non-combatants must be condemned clearly and unequivocally by all', the High-level Panel set the bottom line, making clear that 'terrorism is never an acceptable tactic, even for the most defensible of causes'.[135]

In the following, we shall try to arrive at an explanatory definition of terrorism with the help of ten attributes that appear central and which we discussed above. I hope that the resulting definition holds the middle ground between concreteness and abstraction, the first demanding many descriptors and the latter few. In doing so, I hope to catch not just the core of the concept of terrorism but also some attributes that reflect – if not fully represent – its mechanism and the complexity of empirical reality.

The revised academic consensus definition (2011) tries to capture the core dimension of terrorism in its first paragraph (below in *italics*), with the remainder (points 2–12) serving an explanatory purpose. It is, in my view, a distillation of the best current thinking available on the subject. The reader can determine its quality for him- or herself by comparing it with a selection of more than 250 other definitions listed in the Appendix concluding this chapter.

The revised academic consensus definition of terrorism (Rev. ACDT 2011)

1 *Terrorism refers on the one hand to a **doctrine** about the presumed effectiveness of a special form or tactic of fear-generating, coercive political violence and, on the other hand, to a conspiratorial **practice** of calculated, demonstrative, direct violent action without legal or moral restraints, targeting mainly civilians and non-combatants, performed for its propagandistic and psychological effects on various audiences and conflict parties.*

2 Terrorism as a tactic is employed in *three main contexts*: (i) illegal state repression; (ii) propagandistic agitation by non-state actors in times of peace or outside zones of conflict and; (iii) as an illicit tactic of irregular warfare employed by state and non-state actors.

3 The physical *violence* or threat thereof employed by terrorist actors involves single-phase acts of lethal violence (such as bombings and armed assaults), dual-phase life-threatening incidents (like kidnapping, hijacking and other forms of hostage taking for coercive bargaining), as well as multi-phase sequences of actions (such as in 'disappearances' involving kidnapping, secret detention, torture and murder).

4 Public(-ized) terrorist victimization initiates *threat-based communication processes* whereby, on the one hand, conditional demands are made to individuals, groups, governments, societies or sections thereof, and, on the other hand, the support of specific constituencies (based on ties of ethnicity, religion, political affiliation and the like) is sought by the terrorist perpetrators.

5 At the origin of terrorism stands *terror* – instilled fear, dread, panic or mere anxiety – spread among those identifying, or sharing similarities, with the direct victims, generated by some of the modalities of the terrorist act – its shocking brutality, lack of discrimination, dramatic or symbolic quality and disregard of the rules of warfare and the rules of punishment.

6 The main direct *victims* of terrorist attacks are in general not any armed forces but are *usually civilians, non-combatants or other innocent and defenceless persons* who bear no direct responsibility for the conflict that gave rise to acts of terrorism.

7   The *direct victims are not the ultimate target* (as in a classical assassination, where victim and target coincide) but serve as message generators, more or less unwittingly helped by the news values of the mass media, to reach various audiences and conflict parties that identify either with the victims' plight or the terrorists' professed cause.

8   Sources of terrorist violence can be individual *perpetrators*, small groups, diffuse transnational networks as well as state actors or state-sponsored clandestine agents (such as death squads and hit teams).

9   While showing similarities with methods employed by organized crime, as well as those found in war crimes, terrorist violence is *predominantly political* – usually in its motivation but nearly always in its societal repercussions.

10 The immediate *intent* of acts of terrorism is to terrorize, intimidate, antagonize, disorientate, destabilize, coerce, compel, demoralize or provoke a target population or conflict party in the hope of achieving from the resulting insecurity a favourable power outcome, for example obtaining publicity, extorting ransom money, obtaining submission to terrorist demands and/or mobilizing or immobilizing sectors of the public.

11 The *motivations* to engage in terrorism cover a broad range, including redress for alleged grievances, personal or vicarious revenge, collective punishment, revolution, national liberation and the promotion of diverse ideological, political, social, national or religious causes and objectives.

12 Acts of terrorism rarely stand alone, but rather form part of a *campaign* of violence which alone can, owing to the serial character of acts of violence and threats of more to come, create a pervasive climate of fear that enables the terrorists to manipulate the political process.

Conclusion

This has brought us to the end of our journey into the treacherous territory of definitions. It is sad that there appears to be such a large chasm between the proposed revised academic consensus definition of terrorism (which can be abbreviated to Rev. ACDT 2011) and the legal draft definition emerging (in article 2) from the Ad Hoc Committee on Terrorism of the Sixth (legal) Committee of the General Assembly of the United Nations in its negotiations on a Comprehensive Convention on International Terrorism. The absence of consensus on a legal definition on a global (i.e. United Nations) level is a serious matter, as it impedes international cooperation against an inhumane practice of waging conflict.

Yet the presence of international legal consensus is, in itself, no guarantee that the international community can effectively ban such a violent phenomenon as terrorism. If international legal consensus were enough, there would be no torture, war crimes and genocide in the contemporary world, as these are concepts on which there is international legal agreement. With this in mind one could question whether it is important to have an academic consensus definition. The social sciences and the humanities do not have mathematics as their common language, as do the natural sciences. They are constantly under assault from both popular and political discourses as they share a common language with these forces that express social preferences and political power. While the rise of universities in the past thousand years and the rise of the exact sciences within them have led to technical discoveries that have changed the face of the world and our understanding of it, the academic contributions of the social sciences have been much more modest. It can be argued that this is partly due to a certain deficit in precision in the social sciences which has caused our academic knowledge to be much less cumulative than it could have been were there greater consensus on its objects under investigation. In that sense, striving for academic consensus does matter, and our search for an academic consensus definition of terrorism has not been a useless exercise.

Notes

1 John Collins, 'Terrorism', in J. Collins and R. Glover (eds), *Collateral Language: A User's Guide to America's New War*. New York: New York University Press, 2002, pp.167–168.

2 Al Jazeera, 'Beirut Wants "Terrorism" Defined', 13 January 2004. Available at http://english.aljazeera.net/ NR/exeres/854F5DE3-FC2D-4059-8907-7954937F4B6C.htm.

3 Boaz Ganor, 'Terrorism: No Prohibition without definition' (7 October 2001). Available at http://www. ict.org.il/articles/articledet.cfm?articleid=393.

4 *The Definition of Terrorism: A Report by Lord Carlile of Berriew QC, Independent Reviewer of Terrorism Legislation.* Cm 7052. London, Home Department, March, p. 47.

5 Alex P. Schmid, 'Terrorism: The Definitional Problem', *Case Western Reserve Journal of International Law*, 36(2 & 3), 2004, pp. 375–419.

6 If the right side of the equation contains less than two terms, the equation is not a definition but a synonym, a translation or a tautology.

7 The 1974 British Prevention of Terrorism (Temporary Provisions) Act defined terrorism as 'the use of violence for political ends, and includes any use of violence for the purpose of putting the public or any section of the public in fear'. *The Definition of Terrorism: A Report by Lord Carlile of Berriew Q.C., Independent Reviewer of Terrorism Legislation.* Cm7052. London: House Department, March 2007.

8 In the words of Anthony Arblaster, 'There is an evident tendency to equate political violence with a single form of such violence – terrorism; and then to imply, or to assume, that all terrorism is "revolutionary" or "aimed at the overthrow of governments". Neither of these assumptions is valid. Although terrorism is so clearly a political phenomenon, and one which evokes strongly political responses, there is a curious way in which so much writing about terrorism evades the political, preferring to concentrate on the moral, or tactical or psychological dimensions of the subject.' Arblaster, 'Terrorism: Myths, Meaning and Morals'. *Political Studies,* 25(3), September 1977, pp. 414, 421.

9 Reuven Young, 'Defining Terrorism: The Evolution of Terrorism as a Legal Concept in International Law and Its Influence on Definitions in Domestic Legislation'. *Boston College International and Comparative Law Review*, 29, 2006, p. 30.

10 As Professor Jeffrey Addicott, Director of the Center for Terrorism Law at St. Mary's University School of Law in San Antonio, Texas, pointed out, 'There is no internationally agreed legal definition. In one modern definition of terrorism . . . it is violence against civilians to achieve political or ideological objectives by creating fear. Most common definitions of terrorism include only those acts which are intended to create fear [and] are perpetrated for an ideological goal and deliberately target or disregard the safety of non-combatants. Some definitions also include acts of unlawful violence and war.' Summary of speech before the Kuwait Bar Association, as quoted in *Arab Times*, quoted 26 June 2008 in a press release by the Center for Terrorism Law. Addicott himself was also quoted as saying, 'Defining terrorism . . . it is the systematic use of terror especially as a means of coercion.' For attempts to define terrorism in international law, see B. Saul, 'Attempts to Define "Terrorism" in International Law'. *Netherlands International Law Review*, 52, 2005, pp. 57–83.

11 Philip Herbst, *Talking Terrorism: A Dictionary of the Loaded Language of Political Violence*. Westport, CT: Greenwood Press, 2003, pp. 163–164.

12 The Non-Aligned Movement, meeting in 2006 in Havana, for instance, tried to redefine terrorism. As an Associated Press writer reported, 'Iran, Syria, North Korea and more than 100 other nations are pushing to broaden the world's definition of "terrorism" to include the U.S. occupation of Iraq and the Israeli invasion of Lebanon. Converging on Fidel Castro's communist Cuba for a summit this week, members of the Nonaligned Movement complain of a double standard: powerful nations like the United States and Israel decide for the world who the terrorists are, but face no punishment for their own acts of aggression. A draft of the group's joint declaration condemns "terrorism in all its forms", especially violence that targets civilians. . . . Cuba says the U.S. is particularly hypocritical in the case of a former CIA operative and Castro foe wanted in Venezuela in the 1976 bombing of a Cuban jetliner from Caracas that killed 73 people. . . . Many Arab officials say al-Qaida is in a different category, one representing true terrorists. Al-Akwa [Kalid A. al-Akwa, a Yemeni Foreign Ministry official] agreed. "They target civilians, they lack the cause and the justification, they don't distinguish among anyone – they're even attacking us Muslims", he said. "And they have a different political agenda, to extend an Islamist system that doesn't really have anything to do with our religion".' Vanessa Arrington (AP), 'Defining terror: rest of the world want "real-world" definition'. Associated Press, 12 September 2006.

13 Alex P. Schmid, 'Terrorism: The Definitional Problem'. *Case Western Reserve Journal of International Law*, 36(2–3), 2004, p. 384.

14 W.B. Gallie, 'Essentially Contested Concepts'. *Proceedings of the Aristotelian Society*, 56, 1956, pp. 167–198; William Connelly, *The Terms of Political Discourse*. Princeton, NJ: Princeton University Press, 1993, p. 10.

15 In his radio address of 13 May 1986, President Reagan said, 'Effective antiterrorist action has also been thwarted by the claim that – as the quip goes – "One man's terrorist is another man's freedom fighter." That is a catchy phrase, but also misleading. Freedom fighters do not need to terrorize a population into submission. Freedom fighters target the military forces and the organized instruments of repression keeping dictatorial regimes in power'. *U.S. Department of State Bulletin*, September 1986 (President Reagan's address to the nation on 31 May 1986); available at: http://findarticles.com/p/articles/mi_m1079/is_v86/ai_4517358 (accessed 23 March 2008).

16 In the words of Peter Sederberg, 'The definition of terms, like other human actions, reflects the interests of those doing the defining. Those who successfully define the terms of a political debate set the agenda for the community. . . . Definition therefore involves the exercise of power'. Peter Sederberg, *Terrorist Myths, Illusion, Rhetoric, and Reality* (1989), p. 3, quoted in *A Review of U.S. Counterterrorism Police: American Muslim Critique and Recommendations*. Los Angeles: Muslim Public Affairs Council, September 2003, p. 15.

17 Andreas Musloff, *Krieg gegen die Öffentlichkeit: Terrorismus und Politischer Sprachgebrauch*. Opladen, Germany: Westdeutscher Verlag, 1997. Jeff Lewis introduced the concept of 'language wars', which he defines as 'disputes over meaning that are more or less systematic and historically constituted. In contemporary culture language wars are frequently conducted through the mass media and may involve groups with markedly uneven access to the resources of culture and expressivity. At their most critical, these language wars may erupt into actual physical violence'. Lewis, *The Role of the Media and Culture in Global Terror and Political Violence*. London: Pluto, 2005, p. 19.

18 Michael Petschenig, *Der kleine Stowasser: Lateinisch–deutsches Schulwörterbuch*. Leipzig: G. Freytag, 1944, p. 492.

19 Jean Bodin, *Six Books of the Commonwealth*. Oxford: Basil Blackwell, 1955, ch. 1, quoted in Mikkel Thorup, '"A Terror to Evil Doers": Elements to the History of the Concept of Terror'. Quoted from manuscript, January 2008, p. 3.

20 Leo Strauss, *The Political Philosophy of Thomas Hobbes: Its Basis and Genesis*. Chicago: University of Chicago Press, 1992, quoted in Mikkel Thorup, '"A Terror to Evil Doers"', p. 3.

21 Jean-Jacques Rousseau, *Oeuvres complètes*. Paris: Galimard, 1964, vol. 3, p. 249, quoted in Mikkel Thorup, '"A Terror to Evil Doers"', p. 7.

22 Mikkel Thorup, '"A Terror to Evil Doers"', p. 7.

23 Ibid., p. 12. Robespierre himself had given a rather peculiar definition of 'terror': 'Terror is nothing other than justice, prompt, severe, inflexible; it is therefore an emanation of virtue; it is not so much a special principle as it is a consequence of the general principle of democracy applied to our country's most urgent needs'. Quoted in *Modern History Sourcebook: Maximilien Robespierre: Justification of the Use of Terror*. Available at: www.fordham.edu/halsall/mod/robespierre-terror.html. For a selection of texts of Robespierre, see: *Maximilien Robespierre: Virtue and Terror*. Introduction by Slavoj Žižek. Texts selected and annotated by Jean Ducange. London, Verso, 2007.

24 Quoted in Paul Wurth, *La répression internationale du terrorisme*. Lausanne: La Concorde, 1941, p. 11.

25 For a more detailed discussion of the two terms and their etymology, see: Alex P. Schmid, *Political Terrorism*. Amsterdam: North-Holland, 1984, pp. 64–67.

26 Some authors use the term 'terrorism' for a certain type of political violence employed by non-state actors while reserving the term 'terror' for a certain type of arbitrary and excessive violence by the state against groups or individuals in a target population. See, for instance, Richard M. Pearlstein, *Fatal Future? Transnational Terrorism and the New Global Disorder*. Austin: University of Texas, 2004, p. 2. *The Oxford Companion to the Mind*, on the other hand, defines 'terror' as 'the specific fear that some evil event or action is going to occur. Its origins go back to the notion of trembling. . . . Terror appears to fit into the category of instinct-response which humans share with most animals. For example, most humans and animals fear the sight of mutilated bodies. . . . The fear of violence done to the body is at the basis of the terror process. In the ancient world terror was the basis of tyranny, as in Rome under Marius and Sulla. Historically many political leaders have chosen rule by terror tactics rather than by customary, legal means – that is, by the systematic use of violence to inhibit political opposition'. Richard L. Gregory (ed.), *The Oxford Companion to the Mind*. Oxford: Oxford University Press, 1987, p. 770.

27 E.g. R.P. Hoffman, 'Terrorism: A Universal Definition'. PhD thesis, Claremont Graduate School, Claremont, CA, 1984. The author arrived, at the end of his work, at this definition: 'Terrorism is a purposeful human activity which is directed towards the creation of a general climate of fear, and is designed to influence, in ways desired by the protagonist, other human beings and, through them, some course of events' (ibid., p. 181). Remarkable (and odd) is the absence of any direct reference to violence or the threat thereof.

28 In an ISA paper from 2007, Olga Bogatyrenko noted that '[g]iven the exceptional salience and policy relevance of this concept [terrorism], it is surprising to see that over 77% of scholars in leading political science journals who focus on terrorism fail to define it, and many of the remaining 23% offer definitions of their own without paying due consideration to the implications of their conceptual choices'. Olga Bogatyrenko, 'Definitional Analysis of Terrorism: Constructing Concepts and Populations for Social Science Research'. Paper prepared by Olga Bogatyrenko for the 2007 meeting of the International Studies Association, February–March 2007, p. 2.

29 Omar Malik, *Enough of a Definition of Terrorism*. London: Royal Institute of International Affairs, 2000. Malik himself defined terrorism as 'the deliberate creation and exploitation of fear through violence or the threat of violence in the pursuit of political change. All terrorist acts involve violence or the threat of violence. Terrorism is specifically designed to have far-reaching psychological effects beyond the immediate victim(s) or object of the terrorist attack' (ibid., p. 11). This definition is biased in favour of the status quo; it excludes vigilante violence in the pursuit of stabilizing an existing political order.

30 W. Laqueur, *Terrorism*. London: Weidenfeld & Nicolson, 1977, p. 79. Even that definition is not uncontroversial, as it would also include genocide and go way beyond the creation and manipulation of fear to influence target groups.

31 Walter Laqueur, *No End to War: Terrorism in the Twenty-First Century*. New York: Continuum, 2004, p. 232.

32 Quoted in Alex P. Schmid, *Political Terrorism: A Research Guide to Concepts, Theories, Data Bases and Literature*. Amsterdam: North-Holland, 1984, p. 7.

33 Quoted in Alex P. Schmid, 'Introduction to Terrorism'. Lecture delivered on 16 March 1989 during the AEGEE/COMT conference 'Towards a European Response to Terrorism: National Experiences and Lessons for the Europe of 1992', p. 1.

34 The term 'freedom fighter' was popularized by Menachem Begin, leader of the Jewish underground organization Irgun Zvai Leumi (National Military Organization), which used terror tactics, including the blowing up of the King David Hotel, to drive the British (whom Begin labelled 'terrorists') out of Palestine. He later became Israeli prime minister and winner of the Nobel Prize for Peace. See Menachem Begin, *The Revolt*. London: W.H. Allen, 1983 (preface, rev. ed.). However, the term was coined in 1850 by Karl Heinzen, author of *Murder and Liberty*. Cf. Daniel Bessner and Michael Stauch, 'Karl Heinzen and the Intellectual Origins of Modern Terror'. *Terrorism and Political Violence*, 22(2), 2010, pp. 143–176, which contains a full translation from German into English of *Mord und Freiheit* (pp. 153–176).

35 Roberta Senechal de la Roche, 'Toward a Scientific Theory of Terrorism'. *Sociological Theory*, 22(1), March 2004, pp. 1–4 (quoted from MS). She adds, 'That others may use the term terrorism pejoratively – or that violent actors or their opponents may like or dislike the word – is irrelevant to a scientific definition of the phenomenon. A definition is not a value judgment and cannot be evaluated from a moral or ideological point of view. And because it is a conceptual rather than a factual or explanatory statement, a definition cannot be evaluated as right or wrong. Instead we evaluate a scientific definition solely by its usefulness in the ordering of facts.'

36 Jenny Teichmann, 'How to Define Terrorism'. *Philosophy*, 64, 1989, p. 505.

37 Boaz Ganor, 'Defining Terrorism: Is One Man's Terrorist Another Man's Freedom Fighter?' *ICT Papers*, 4, August 1998, pp. 22–23, 29; quoted with the permission of the author and the International Policy Institute for Counter-Terrorism.

38 That is not undisputed: Richard Perle, former chairman of the US Defense Policy Board, declared in 2002 that 'terrorism must be de-contextualised'. Quoted in Gwynne Dyer, 'Two Takes on Terrorism'. *Trinidad News*, 7 May 2008.

39 W. Seth Carus, *Defining Terrorism*. Washington, DC: Center for the Study of Weapons of Mass Destruction, National Defense University, 2008 (MS), pp. 1–2, 19, 22.

40 United States Code 22, Section 2656 (d). Quoted in United States Department of State, *Patterns of Global Terrorism, 1999*. Washington, DC: Department of State, April 2000, p. viii. See www.state.gov/s/ct/rls/pgtrpt/ for the various versions.

41 W. Seth Carus, *Defining Terrorism*, p. 29. The State Department warned, in its report for 2005, that '[i]t should be noted that 22 USC 2656f(d) is one of many US statutes and international legal instruments that concern terrorism and acts of violence, many of which use definitions of terrorism and related terms that are different from those used in this report.' Quoted ibid., p. 44, n. 125.

42 US Department of State, *Country Reports on Terrorism*, 2006, April 2007, pp. 317–319. For a complete collection of the State Department's reports on terrorism, see www.terrorisminfo.mipt.org/Patterns-of-Global-Terrorism.asp on the Website of the Memorial Institute for the Prevention of Terrorism (MIPT) in Oklahoma.

43 Bruce Hoffman, *Inside Terrorism*. New York: Columbia University Press, 2006: p. 32.

44 A.J.F. Köbben, 'Why Exceptions? The Logic of Cross-Cultural Analysis'. *Current Anthropology*, 8(1–2), 1967, pp. 3–34.

45 The FBI definition: 'Terrorism includes the unlawful use of force or violence against persons or property to intimidate or coerce a Government, the civilian population, or any segment thereof, in furtherance of political or social objectives'. Code of Federal Regulations, 28 CFR 0.85 (1) – cf. www.fbi.gov.

46 US Department of State, Office of the Coordinator for Counter-terrorism, *Patterns of Global Terrorism 2003*. Washington, DC: US Department of State, publication 11124, April 2004, p. xii, quoted in Bruce Hoffman, *Inside Terrorism* (2006), p. 31.

47 W. Seth Carus, *Defining Terrorism*. Washington, DC: Center for the Study of Weapons of Mass Destruction, National Defense University, 2008, p. 45, n. 127.

48 Boaz Ganor, *The Counter-Terrorism Puzzle: A Guide for Decision Makers*. New Brunswick, NJ: Transaction, 2005, p. 17. Boaz Ganor, 'Terrorism: No Prohibition without Definition', (7 October 2001). Available at www.ict.org.il/articles/articledet.cfm?articleid=393. Ganor added, 'Lacking such a definition, no coordinated fight against international terrorism can ever really get anywhere.' In contrast, he defines 'guerrilla warfare' as 'the deliberate use of violence against military and security personnel in order to attain political, ideological and religious goals.' He adds, 'The aims of terrorism and guerrilla warfare may well be identical; but they are distinguished from each other by the means used – or more precisely, by the targets of their operations. The guerrilla fighter's targets are military ones, while the terrorist deliberately targets civilians.'

49 See Howard S. Levie, *Terrorism in War: The Law of War Crimes*. New York: Oceana, 1993. Levie notes in his preface, 'Apart from the battlefield war crimes, and to a certain extent even there (denial of quarter and shooting of recently captured prisoners of war and wounded soldiers), many categories of war crimes committed by the Nazis during World War II were intended to establish a reign of terror among various elements of the enemy. The inmates of the concentration camps were terrorized (for example, by gruesome, drawn-out hangings in the presence of individuals who could look forward to the same end); the civilian inhabitants of occupied territories were terrorized (for example by the execution of innocent hostages chosen at random and by such procedures as that of the "Night and Fog Decree" and the "Terrorist and Sabotage Decree"); members of the resistance movements were terrorized (for example, by the summary executions of persons merely suspected of being parties having knowledge of such organizations or of being relatives of such parties); attempts were made to terrorize Allied flyers by encouraging the German public to lynch the members of crews of downed aircraft (the "Terror Flyer Order"); attempts were made to terrorize merchant seamen by a program of slaughtering the members of shipwrecked crews in order to discourage experienced personnel from agreeing to make the Atlantic crossing; etc.' (pp. i–ii). See also Stathis N. Kalyvas, 'The Paradox of Terrorism in Civil War'. *Journal of Ethics*, 8, 2004, pp. 97–138. Kalyvas argues that '[a] great deal of violence in civil wars is informed by the logic of terrorism: violence tends to be used by political actors against civilians in order to shape their political behaviour' and that 'indiscriminate violence emerges because it is much cheaper than its main alternative – selective violence. It is more likely under a steep imbalance of power between the competing actors, and where and when resources and information are low; however, most political actors eventually switch to selective violence' (abstract, p. 97).

50 Virginia Held, 'Terrorism and War'. *Journal of Ethics*, 9, 2004, pp. 59–75 at p. 60. She adds, ' A frequently used argument of states engaged in what they call "countering terrorism" but which the recipients of their violence often consider terrorism, is that they do not "target" civilians; if civilians are killed it is by accident, even though foreseeable. But such states' possession of weapons of precision capable of attacking, when they choose to, targeted persons intentionally and civilians only unintentionally is just another way in which their superior power allows them to be dominant. It may be that such domination is what a group engaging in terrorism is resisting' (ibid., p. 61).

51 Quoted from summary of anonymous reviewer on Hugo Slim, 'Killing Civilians: Method, Madness and Morality in War'. New York, Columbia University Press, 2008; quoted in *The Economist,* 16 February 2008, p. 96.

52 Cf. http://wits.nctc.gov/Methodology.do (accessed 25 May 2008).

53 For a critique and discussion, see the Human Security Report 2007, released in May 2008, which devotes a whole chapter on the metrics of terrorism, discussing WITS, next to MIPT and GTD in a comparative way. See www.humansecuritybrief.info/access.html (chapter 1).

54 Article 1, para. 2, Convention for the Prevention and Repression of Terrorism; 16 November 1937, League of Nations Doc. C546M.383 (1937), quoted in Paul Wurth, *La répression internationale du terrorisme*. Lausanne: Imprimérie la Concorde, 1941, p. 50. The convention was drafted in response to the assassination of King Alexander I of Yugoslavia by Croatian separatists and the French foreign minister in 1934 and Italy's refusal to extradite the perpetrator, citing the political crime exception.

55 Reuven Young, 'Defining Terrorism: The Evolution of Terrorism as a Legal Concept in International Law and Its Influence on Definitions in Domestic Legislation'. *Boston College International and Comparative Law Review*, 29, 2006, p. 36.

56 On 8 December 1972, the first Ad Hoc Committee on Terrorism was established (A/Res. 3034 (XXVII)) by the UN General Assembly; a second Ad Hoc Committee on the issue was established on 17 December 1996 (G.A Res. 51/210). G. Doucet, 'Terrorism: Search for a Definition or Liberticidal Drifting'. In G. Doucet (ed.), *Terrorism, Victims, and International Criminal Responsibility*. Paris: SOS Attentats, 2003, p. 280n.

57 Reuven Young, 'Defining Terrorism', pp. 38–39. In the discussion of the Draft Comprehensive Terrorism Convention, the Organization of the Islamic Conference argued for the 'exclusion of acts done in the pursuance of liberation struggles and proposed the following paragraphs to be included in the Draft Convention: "Peoples' struggle including armed struggle against foreign occupation, aggression, colonialism, and hegemony, aimed at liberation and self-determination in accordance with the principles of international law shall not be considered a terrorist crime".' Quoted ibid., p. 589, n. 199.

58 Dr Kshitij Prabha, Associate Fellow, IDSA, 'Defining Terrorism'. Available at: www.idsa-india.org/an-apr-08.html (accessed 10 July 2001).

59 In the same declaration, it is noted that '[c]riminal acts intended or calculated to provoke a state of terror in the general public are in any circumstance unjustifiable, whatever the considerations of a political, philosophical, ideological, racial, ethnic, religious or any other nature that may be invoked to justify them'. Quoted in Annex Declaration on Measures to Eliminate International Terrorism. General Assembly resolution 49/60 of 9 December 1994, Annex; repr. in United Nations, Office of Legal Affairs, *International Instruments Related to the Prevention and Suppression of International Terrorism*. New York: United Nations, 2001, p. 231. General Assembly resolution 49/60 of 9 December 1994. Israel and the United States voted against this resolution as it implied an exception for those fighting for the right to self-determination against foreign and racist regimes.

60 Security Council resolutions, passed under chapter VII of the UN Charter, on the other hand, are binding for all member states. An example is SC Res. 1373 (28 September 2001), which established the Counter-Terrorism Committee but did not define terrorism itself on that occasion, providing room for states to engage in opportunistic and bad-faith implementation of the many provisions mandated by the Security Council. Only in October 2004, with SC Res. 1566, was the definitional gap to some extent narrowed, when, in paragraph 3, the Security Council '*Recalls* that criminal acts, including against civilians, committed with the intent to cause death or serious bodily injury, or taking of hostages, with the purpose to provoke a state of terror in the general public or in a group of persons or particular persons, intimidate a population or compel a government or an international organization to do or to abstain from doing any act, which constitute offences within the scope of and as defined in the international conventions and protocols relating to terrorism, are under no circumstances justifiable by considerations of a political, philosophical, ideological, racial, ethnic, religious or other similar nature'. SC Res. 1566 (2004), para. 4. However, the Security Council did not explicitly identify this text in terms of a definition; rather it was a compromise formulation meant to sent a clear political message in response to the Beslan event. Quoted in Reuven Young, 'Defining Terrorism', p. 45.

61 The official title of the committee is 'Ad Hoc Committee established by General Assembly resolution 51/210 of 17 December 1996'. The understanding which its current chairman brings to terrorism can be gauged from the following statement: '[T]he common element in all acts of terrorism is the toll extracted in terms of innocent human lives by the systematic use of tactics of shock, physical intimidation and terror'. Amrith Rohan Perera, *International Terrorism*. New Delhi: Vikas, 1997, p. 1. 'Sectoral' refers here to the different manifestations of terrorism, such as 'hijackings' and 'hostage taking'.

62 The gaps in the existing international anti-terrorist conventions and protocols include, in the words of Michael Scharf, the fact that 'assassinations of businessmen, engineers, journalists and educators are not covered, while similar attacks against diplomats and public officials are prohibited. Attacks or acts of sabotage by means of other than explosives against a passenger train or bus, or a water supply or electric power plant, are not covered; while similar attacks against an aeroplane or an ocean liner would be. And most forms of cyber-terrorism are not covered by the anti-terrorism conventions'. Scharf, 'Defining Terrorism by Reference to the Laws of War: Problems and Prospects'. In International Scientific and Professional Advisory Council, *Countering Terrorism through International Cooperation*. Milan: ISPAC, 2001, p. 135.

63 The text continues by outlawing threats of terrorism and attempts of terrorist attacks: '2. Any person also commits an offence if that person makes a credible and serious threat to commit an offence as set forth in paragraph 1 of the present article. 3. Any person also commits an offence if that person attempts to commit an offence as set forth in paragraph 1 of the present article.' Furthermore the text outlaws 'participation',

'organization', and 'contribution' to the commission of one or more offences as set forth in paragraph 1, 2, or 3 of the present article. Source: Informal text of articles 2 and 2 bis of the draft comprehensive convention, prepared by the Coordinator. Reproduced from document A/57/37, Annex II, Article 2. United Nations. Report of the Ad Hoc Committee established by General Assembly resolution 51/210 of 17 December 1996. Sixth session (28 January – 1 February 2002). General Assembly, Official Records, 57th Session, Supplement no. 37 (A/57/37). This text has remained basically unaltered since 2002! (NB: Article 2.2. refers to the threat of the offence described in article 2.1, while article 2.3 refers to the attempt to commit such an offence. See also: http://daccessdds.un.org/doc/UNODC/GEN/N05/460/57/PDF/N0546057.pdf? OpenElement for the text of draft convention as of August 2005 (access is password protected).

64 The Organization of the Islamic Conference demanded in October 2004 the exclusion of 'activities of the parties during an armed conflict, including in situations of foreign occupation'. UN Information Service, 2 July 2004, 'Annan hopes U.N. will approve comprehensive treaty against terrorism in the next month.' United Nations Information Service press release, 24 January 2002.

65 Andreas Zumach, 'Definitionsstreit bei der UN-Generalversammlung: Was ist eigentlich Terrorismus?' *Die Presse* (Vienna), 6 October 2001, p. 5.

66 Typical is this statement: 'Pakistan condemns terrorism in all its forms and manifestations. Pakistan also condemns state terrorism which is the most ignoble form of terrorism.' Pakistan Mission to the United Nations, New York. Available at: www.un.int/pakistan/terrorism.html (10 July 2001).

67 Hans Corell, 'International Instruments against Terrorism: The Record So Far and Strengthening the Existing Regime'. In: United Nations, *Combating International Terrorism: The Contribution of the United Nations*. New York: United Nations, 2003, p. 23.

68 Private communication by a UN official who followed the negotiations, 7 March 2008.

69 The General Assembly's Department of Public Information noted in 2005: [F]inalizing the comprehensive convention has been elusive. A major point of difference has been the lack of agreement on whether the activities of "armed forces" proper should be exempted from the scope of application of the convention since those are governed by international humanitarian law, and whether the exemption should also cover armed resistance groups involved in struggles against colonial domination and foreign occupation. There is also disagreement regarding activities of a State's military forces and whether there should be any circumstance in which official actions could be considered acts of terrorism.' 'Ad Hoc Body Elaborating Comprehensive Convention on Terrorism to Reconvene Early Next Near, Sixth Committee Decides', General Assembly GA/L/3292, Department of Information press release, 29 November 2005, p. 1.

70 Cf. UN Ad Hoc Committee on Terrorism, 'Measures to Eliminate International Terrorism'. Oral report of the chairman of the Working Group, 26 October 2007, 62nd Session, 6th Committee, Agenda item 108. New York: United Nations, 2007, para. 19.

71 Richard Barrett, on the other hand, said that 'this definition . . . allows for a state employee to commit a terrorist act but avoids the state itself being labeled as terrorist'.

72 The chairman of the UN Ad Hoc Committee on the Elimination of International Terrorism, Ambassador A. Rohan Perera of Sri Lanka, however, holds that the last paragraph, beginning with 'when . . .', does not refer only to (b). Personal communication, March 2008.

73 Personal communication, Ambassador R. Perera, March 2008.

74 In international treaty making, e.g. the Convention against Organized Crime (Palermo Convention, 2000), 'serious' is often defined in terms of length of a minimum prison sentence due for a crime; for example, crimes that have mandatory sentences of at least five years are 'serious'.

75 E. Stepanova's comments are, in this regard, very pertinent: '[W]hile Art. 2 of the UN draft comprehensive convention does not touch specifically upon the problem of "state terrorism" and Art. 20 (Para 2) of A/59-894 explicitly states that "the activities of armed forces during an armed conflict, as those terms are understood under IHL, which are governed by that law, are not governed by the present Convention", this . . . key definitional problem has to be mentioned, as the calls by some governments, international organizations and NGOs, particularly human rights advocacy groups, to extend the notion of terrorism to apply to repressive violent actions against civilians exercised by the state itself persist. Recognizing that the use of force by the state against civilians does not fall under the definition of terrorism as such, the [UN] High-level Panel [convened by K. Annan] called for recognition, in the preamble, that "[s]tate use of force against civilians is regulated by the Geneva Conventions and other instruments, and, if of sufficient scale, constitutes a war crime by the persons concerned or a crime against humanity". While these clarifications on the draft Comprehensive Convention may provide an optimal solution, the draft may still face persistent objections on human rights grounds. It has been argued, for instance, that while reference to the international legal ban on the use of force by states against civilians is limited by the Geneva Convention and Protocols that regulate the situation of the open armed conflict only (including both

international and non-international conflicts), terrorist violence could be employed in the absence of an open armed conflict as such. In response to these concerns, the High-level Panel suggested . . . extend[ing] the notion of terrorism to cover such cases, having defined it as "any action, *in addition to actions* [my italics, E.S.] already specified by the existing conventions on various aspects of terrorism, the Geneva Conventions and UNS_R 1566 (2004)", which employs or threatens violence against civilians to achieve the purposes typical for terrorist attacks (as they are defined by the draft convention, i.e. to pressure the government by intimidating the population).'

76 '[T]here are almost no variations in UN documents, as far as the goals of terrorist violence, or threat to use violence, are concerned. While the UN GA definition refers to the conduct that, by its nature or context, seeks "to intimidate a population, or to compel a Government or an international organization to do or abstain from doing any act", the UNSCR 1566, for instance, elaborates a bit by adding that the purpose of terrorists is *"to provoke a state of terror in the general public or in a group of persons or particular persons,* intimidate a population or compel a government or an international organization to do or abstain from doing any act" [my italics]. The High Panel's conclusion is the same: a certain action is viewed as an act of terrorism "when the purpose of such act, by its nature or context, is to intimidate a population, or to compel a Government or an international organization to do or to abstain from doing any act". The main advantage of this wording is that it reflects the asymmetrical nature of terrorism, i.e. the use of, or threat to use, violence as a way to exercise pressure on a national government or the international community.

But this generalized interpretation of terrorists' objectives is subject to criticism. Intimidating a population is not so much the terrorists' goal in and of itself as the means to achieve their real final objectives *which always have a political dimension.* In contrast, the UN wording does not refer to the overwhelmingly *political nature* of terrorists' ultimate goals (sometimes also formulated in ideological and religious categories). A number of national anti-terrorism laws, including the US anti-terrorism legislation, define terrorism as criminal tactics employed to achieve political goals, and many academic definition of terrorism also emphasize its political motivation. This idea has not, however, been reflected in the UN documents, which may partly be explained by pragmatic concerns: the drafters of the convention may realize that any clearer and more specific definition of terrorists' goals is bound to cause new objections from member states and would have further delayed the adoption of the convention, perhaps for an indefinite period of time. Plus, the dominant "law-enforcement" approach dictates the practical need to "criminalize" terrorist violence as much as possible, at the expense of overlooking the profoundly political and politicized nature of this type of violence (see, for instance, Art. 15 of A/59/894, stressing that "none of the offences set forth in art. 2 of the present Convention, shall be regarded, for the purposes of extradition or mutual legal assistance, as a political offence . . . or as *an offence inspired by political motives*" [my italics]). While the UN's very broad wording in respect to terrorists' motivations is, perhaps, inevitable, it is hardly permissible for any serious academic definition.'

77 Cf. the International Convention against the Taking of Hostages (1979) and the Convention on the Prevention and Punishment of Crimes against Internationally Protected Persons, including Diplomatic Agents (1973); for texts, see United Nations, *International Instruments Related to the Prevention and Suppression of International Terrorism.* New York: United Nations, 2001, pp. 30–47.

78 UN document S/RES/1566 (2004).

79 *A More Secure World: Our Shared Responsibility.* Report of the Secretary-General's High-level Panel on Threats, Challenges and Change. New York: United Nations, 2004, p. 52, para. 164d.

80 International Convention for the Suppression of the Financing of Terrorism, article 2, para. 1b.

81 Report of the Policy Working Group on the United Nations and Terrorism (S/2002/875), paras 13–15, as quoted by H. Sandhu, one of the respondents.

82 UN Security Council resolution 1566 (2004).

83 *United Nations International Instruments Related to the Prevention and Suppression of International Terrorism.* New York: United Nations, 2001, pp. 115–116.

84 Summary of these treaties by Reuven Young, 'Defining Terrorism', pp. 47–48.

85 Ibid., p. 65.

86 Report of the Secretary-General's High-level Panel on Threats, Challenges and Change. UN Doc. A/59/565, 2 December 2004, para. 44.

87 Alex P. Schmid, *Political Terrorism: A Research Guide to Concepts, Theories, Data Bases and Literature.* Amsterdam: North-Holland, 1984, p. 111.

88 Alex P. Schmid, Albert J. Jongman *et al., Political Terrorism: A New Guide to Actors, Authors, Concepts, Data Bases, Theories, and Literature.* Revised edition prepared under the auspices of the Center for International Affairs, Harvard University. Amsterdam: North-Holland, 1988, p. 28.

89 *The Definition of Terrorism: A Report by Lord Carlile of Berriew Q.C., Independent Reviewer of Terrorism Legislation.* Cm7052. London: Home Department, March 2007, p. 7.

90 Adrian Guelke, *The Age of Terrorism and the International Political System*. London: I.B. Tauris, 1995, p. 18.

91 Guelke added, 'However, from Schmid's reservations about including assassination in a definition of terrorism, a more general implication about the characteristics of terrorism may be inferred. This is that terrorism tends to be seen as a method of violence where the connection between means and ends is indirect rather than direct.' Ibid., p. 29.

92 M.J. Gohel illustrated this by pointing out that '[f]or instance, the IRA bombing of a hotel in Brighton on 12 October 1984, where some of the British Government Cabinet Ministers were staying, together with Conservative Party members, was an act of both assassination and terrorism; the direct targets of violence were indeed the main targets. Similarly, the IRA mortar bomb attack on Downing Street in February 1991 was an attempt to assassinate, as also an act of terrorism.'

93 However, even as regards the Kennedy assassination there are other interpretations. One respondent, Chasdi, held: 'Plainly, the assassination of US President John F. Kennedy in 1963 was an act of terror or state terror insofar as that terrorist assault did, I think, have what amounts to primary, secondary, and perhaps tertiary audiences even though exactly who those audiences were, whether or not they were those who supported "peaceful coexistence" with the Soviets, or the Civil Rights movement, or something else, remains shrouded in mystery. Another criticism of the "assassination" conceptualization here is that in an overwhelming number of cases of terrorist assaults, "the direct targets of violence are not the main targets." Why exclude assassination, a term that is inextricably bound up with an inherent political dimension, by contrast to the terms "murder" or "killing," which are open-ended politically neutral terms?'

94 Z. Iviansky, 'Individual Terror: Concept and Typology'. *Journal of Contemporary History*, 12(1), 1977, p. 50 (emphasis added).

95 Quoted in M. Fleming, 'Propaganda by the Deed: Terrorism and Anarchist Theory in Late Nineteenth-Century Europe'. *Terrorism*, 4(1–4), 1980, p. 14.

96 *New York Times*, June 1995; quoted in Thomas J. Badley, 'Defining International Terrorism: A Pragmatic Approach'. *Terrorism and Political Violence*, 10(1) Spring 1998, p. 98.

97 Thomas Perry Thornton 'Terror as Weapon of Political Agitation'. In H. Eckstein (ed.), *Internal War: Problems and Approaches*. New York: The Free Press of Glencoe, 1964, pp. 77–78.

98 For a discussion of the similarities and differences, see A.P. Schmid, 'The Links between Transnational Organized Crime and Terrorist Crimes'. *Transnational Organized Crime*, 2(4), Winter 1996, pp. 40–82. Another issue is where we draw a line around 'political'. If we follow the French philosopher Foucault, 'politics is everything and everywhere', the crime aspect is included. Quoted in Jeff Lewis, *Language Wars*. London: Pluto, 2005, p. 27. We will discuss the meaning of 'political' and 'political violence' later in this chapter.

99 Such an extended list of motives would, Kaplan wrote, 'more properly weighing the motivational factors in the order of their importance in contemporary terrorism. It gives proper respect to the sincerity of the religiously motivated, and brings in some of the key factors in motivating modern terrorism by acknowledging tribal grievances . . . and introducing the new factor of gender as a motivation for terrorism. Here I have in mind the emergence of mass rape both as a terrorist tool and as a way of achieving "genocide on the cheap" by sub-state actors. Both motivate women to undertake terrorist actions. I'm thinking too of the deaths of male kinsmen and husbands (Chechnya and Sri Lanka) and the humiliation of females in a conservative culture (Palestine) as motivations for terrorism based on gender issues. Finally, in gender terms, I'm thinking of more feminist considerations ("If men can become suicide bombers, women can too"), which again is a factor in Palestine and Sri Lanka.'

100 A case can be made that some acts of violence by military personnel and on military personnel can constitute terrorism. As Ben Saul argued, 'a prohibited act committed *in peacetime* may amount to terrorism. Second, a prohibited act committed *by* a military member in peacetime may amount to terrorism'. He also noted that '[a]cts of terror or terrorism committed in armed conflict are already specifically prohibited and criminalized in armed conflict under IHL [international humanitarian law]'. Saul, 'Attempts to Define "Terrorism" in International Law'. *Netherlands International Law Review*, 52, 2005, pp. 69, 81.

101 This leads to intriguing moral questions such as: is terrorism allowed in case of genocide? If one considers taking the family of a genocidal dictator hostage to force him to stop the mass victimization, it could be argued that terrorism would be the lesser evil.

102 However, soldiers too can be terrorized if the enemy possesses a weapon far superior to their own and kills them from a distance that allows no fair symmetric fight. The disparity in firepower can, in such cases, be as great as the one between soldiers with semi-automatic weapons and unarmed civilians.

103 Stepanova added that she would also exclude 'clandestine' state actors' covert and other secret activities from the definition of terrorism.

104 Reuven Young, 'Defining Terrorism', p. 101.

105 Table 2.2 conveys the various types of interaction between government and opposition. It opens the eyes of the observer to variations, e.g. the asymmetry caused when a democratic state under the rule of law (I in the diagram) is faced with an adversary using instruments from the repertoires II and/or III.

106 Simon illustrated this by adding, 'The assassination of a terrorist by another terrorist (factional fighting, rivalry among groups, revenge, etc.) would not cause anxiety among the general public. The assassination of government officials and business people in some cases would also have little effect on the anxiety level of the public in that country. We also have the case of people becoming desensitized to terrorism where a car bombing, an assassination, a hijacking, etc. does not cause the same reaction as when it was first introduced. That is why terrorists always either seek to perpetrate acts with larger numbers of casualties or depart from previous tactics to do something different (e.g. a hijacking–suicide mission like 9/11) to ensure that there would be anxiety, reaction, etc. Therefore, we can't have anxiety as a condition for a definition of terrorism since it does not apply to many cases.

107 For older definition catalogues, see A.P. Schmid, *Political Terrorism*, pp. 119–158; and A.P. Schmid and A.J. Jongman, *Political Terrorism A New Guide*. pp. 32–38.

108 Leonard Weinberg, Ami Pedahzur and Shivan Hirsch-Hoefler, 'The Challenges of Conceptualizing Terrorism'. *Terrorism and Political Violence*, 16(4), Winter 2004, pp. 777–794. The journals surveyed were *Terrorism* (Crane Russak & Co., 1978–1991), *Terrorism* (Minneapolis, MN: John Scherer, 1982, 1986–1989), *Terrorism and Political Violence* (1990–2001), and *Studies in Conflict and Terrorism* (London: Taylor & Francis, 1992–2002). In addition, Weinberg, Pedahzur and Hirsch-Hoeffler incorporated the elements of Schmid's 1988 analysis of 109 definitions into the construction of the new acadcemic (minimal) consensus definition. A short definition along these lines had already been suggested by Edward S. Herman in 1986: 'Terrorism may . . . be defined by the use of violence in conjunction with a search for media publicity'. Herman, 'Power and the Semantics of Terrorism'. In Ellen Ray and William H. Schaap (eds), *Covert Action: The Roots of Terrorism*. New York: Ocean Press, 2003, p. 44.

109 Alex P. Schmid, 'Terrorism – The Definitional Problem'. *Case Western Reserve Journal of International Law*, 36(2–3), 2004, pp. 375–419. The following list and Figure 2.1 are reproduced with the permission of CWRJIL.

110 Martha Crenshaw offered, in 2003, a similar list, identifying 13 elements:

1 a specialized form of political violence;
2 conspiratorial and deceptive;
3 requires few numbers and few resources;
4 symbolic targets, most often civilian and undefended;
5 performed for psychological effect on key audiences, including those who identify with the victims and those who identify with the perpetrators;
6 key element of surprise and shock, as well as fear in targeted audiences;
7 does not directly engage the armed forces of the enemy;
8 primarily seeks publicity and recognition for a cause;
9 usually performed in an urban environment, bombings being the preferred method;
10 strategy can serve different ideologies and goals (e.g. revolutionary, nationalist, reactionary or vigilante, single–issue);
11 can become an end in itself, although rarely successful in the long term if not combined with other methods;
12 usually associated with non-state organizations but can be used by state or state bureaucracies as a clandestine tool of foreign policy or against dissidents living abroad;
13 a 'contested' concept because of its pejorative connotations and use as a political label to condemn or delegitimize an opponent.'

Crenshaw, 'Characteristics of Terrorism'. Paper prepared for the North and West Africa Counter-Terrorism Topical Seminar, 12–17 October 2003, Bamako, Mali, pp. 1–2.

111 The concept of 'family resemblances' comes from Ludwig Wittgenstein (*Philosophische Untersuchungen*, in L. Wittgenstein. *Schriften*, vol. 1. Frankfurt am Main: Suhrkamp, 1980, pp. 279–544) and its use for finding a solution to the definition problem of terrorism has been suggested by Christopher Daase, 'Terrorismus: Begriffe, Theorien und Gegenstrategien'. *Ergebnisse und Prozesse sozialwissenschaftlicher Forschung*, 76, 2001, p. 1. *Die Friedens-Warte*, p. 66. Christopher Daase, following Wittgenstein, holds that 'two cases of "terrorism" can therefore have a family similarity (and rightfully carry the same term), if they share no common characteristic at all, but can be connected with each other via a developmental line of related cases' (Daase, op. cit., p. 66). Following Wittgenstein, Daase argues that the use of the concept of family

similarity allows the creation of rules for concept utilization where there is no strict demarcation of concepts (ibid.).

112 The psychological warfare dimension of terrorism has been neglected by many governments, while some of the most knowledgeable analysts see it as central. The Israeli expert Boas Ganor, for instance, holds that 'terrorism is a form of psychological warfare against the public morale, whereby terrorist organizations, through indiscriminate attacks, attempt to change the political agenda of the targeted population. . . . By convincing the target population that terrorist attacks can be stopped only by appeasement of the terrorist organizations, the terrorists hope to win concessions to their demands. The greatest danger presented by terrorism is thus not necessarily the direct physical damage that it inflicts, but the impact on the way policymakers feel, think, and respond'. Ganor, 'Israel's Counter-Terrorism Policy: Efficacy versus Liberal-Democratic Values, 1983–1999', unpublished MS, p. 1. See also Alex P. Schmid, 'Terrorism as Psychological Warfare'. *Democracy and Terrorism*, 1(2), 2005, pp. 137–146.

113 While some see terrorism, like fascism, imperialism or racism, as an ideology, there is much to be said for seeing it as a tactic that is not linked to any specific ideology. Zbigniew Brzezinski, US national security adviser under President Jimmy Carter, said in 2003 that 'war on terrorism' was a poor and misleading formulation because of its abstraction. 'Terrorism', he said, 'is a technique for killing people. That doesn't tell us who the enemy is. It's as if we said that World War II was not against the Nazis but against blitzkrieg [lightning war]'. For the text of Brzezinski's speech of 28 October 2003 on new American strategies for security and peace, see www.prospect.org/webfeatures/2003/10/brzezinski-z-10-31.html (accessed 18 November 2003).

114 Paradoxically, this communication element is one of the few common elements in academic definitions, as demonstrated by Leonhard Weinberg *et al.* quoted above.

115 Wittgenstein wrote, 'If language is to be a means of communication, there must be agreement not only in definitions, but also . . . in judgments'. Ludwig Wittgenstein, *Philosophical Investigations*. Oxford: Basil Blackwell, 1968, vol. 31, p. 75, as quoted in Garrett O'Boyle, 'The "I know it when I see it" approach to definition: a conceptual basis?' Trinity College, Dublin, March 2008 paper, p. 31.

116 Based on Thomas Perry Thornton, 'Terror as Weapon of Political Agitation', in H. Eckstein (ed.), *Internal War: Problems and Approaches*. New York: The Free Press of Glencoe, 1964, pp. 73–78.

117 For a discussion on the relationship between the concept of 'terrorism', the term terrorism, the object these describe and the definition, see Alex P. Schmid, 'Terrorism – The Definitional Problem', pp. 400–401; and, in more depth, George Löckinger, *Terrorismus, Terrorismusabwehr, Terrorismusbekämpfung*. Vienna: Ministry of Defence, 2005, p. 29.

118 Based on M.G. Marshall, 'Global Terrorism: An Overview and Analysis', draft manuscript, 9 November 2002, p. 3. An updated and shortened version of this study is contained in Monty G. Marshall and Ted Robert Gurr, *Peace and Conflict 2005*. College Park: Center for International Development and Conflict Management, University of Maryland, 2005, pp. 62–76.

119 A. Hoogerwerf, *Politicologie: begrippen en problemen*. Alphen aan den Rijn: Samsom, 1979, p. 39.

120 Robert E. Goodin and H.-D. Klingemann, *A New Handbook of Political Science*. Oxford: Oxford University Press, 1996, p. 7.

121 Leonard Weinberg and Ami Pedahzur, *Political Parties and Terrorist Groups*. London: Routledge, 2003. The authors found that of almost 400 terrorist groups, almost one-third had some kind of links with political parties. In more than half of those cases, terrorist groups were actually created by political parties. On the basis of their statistical material, the authors concluded that 'we are not dealing with historical or political curiosities, far from it. Terrorism and party politics often go hand-in-hand' (ibid., p. 35).

122 Das Gupta Kasturi, 'A Typological Analysis of Collective Political Violence'. PhD thesis, Louisiana State University, 1979, p. 1.

123 Ben Golder and George Williams, 'What is "Terrorism"? Problems of Legal Definition'. *University of New South Wales Law Journal*, 27(2), 2004, p. 272.

124 Dave Grossman, *On Killing: The Psychological Costs of Learning to Kill in War and Society*. Boston: Little, Brown, 1995, p. 207; quoted in Stathis N. Kalyvas, 'The Paradox of Terrorism in Civil War'. *Journal of Ethics*, 8, 2004, p. 100.

125 Stathis N. Kalyvas has elaborated this distinction: 'The logic of terrorism informs the use of violence in civil wars in a fundamental way: violence tends to be used by political actors to induce civilians into compliance. . . . I focus on *indiscriminate violence* in the context of civil war: this is the type of violence whereby the victims are selected on the basis of their membership in some group and irrespective of their individual actions.' Making a distinction between two key aims of violence – extermination and compliance – Kalyvas notes that '[s]ometimes violence is used to exterminate an entire group, rather than place it under control. When, however, the finality of violence is not exhausted in the mass killing of a group of people, violence becomes "instrumental to the attainment of some other goal" – namely the

establishment of control through compliance. Although the methods used to achieve compliance and extermination may be similar, these objectives are fundamentally different, both in terms of content and implications. A way to distinguish between the two is to ask whether a political actor intends to govern the population it targets for violence; an empirical indicator of this intention is whether the targets of violence (as opposed to its victims) have the option to surrender. In most civil wars, political actors promote amnesty programs to encourage insurgent defection and spare or even reward civilians who defect and collaborate with them – whereas in genocides the surrender of victims does not prevent their murder but expedites it. Resorting to violence in the context of civil war in order to achieve compliance is generally referred to as "*terrorism*". Although this is different from the term's everyday use, its underlying logic is not; it encompasses two analytically distinct, though often overlapping, functions: elimination and deterrence. The victim of violence may be targeted to eliminate a particular risk (e.g. information leaks) and, also, to deter others from engaging in similar behaviour; in other words, victims and targets of violence are distinct'. Kalyvas, 'The Paradox of Terrorism in Civil War', pp. 97–99.

126 Ibid., p. 138.
127 To quote from a Soviet NKVD 'Document of Terror' from the early 1950s:' 'The only tool which general terror knows and uses is force. . . . [The] tool used by enlightened terror is any means which is able to produce the planned psychological effect. . . . It consists of executing a typical, planned action in classic form. Subsequently this action is brought home to the resonant mass [of people] through printed statements, the radio, the motion picture, the press – in short, through all the means of propaganda available. Naturally such propaganda cannot be dry and factual reports. Its propaganda must be lively, colourful, dramatic – that is, dynamic. But it is not important that it follows the truth in details.' Quoted in Alex P. Schmid, 'Repression, State Terrorism, and Genocide: Conceptual Clarifications'. In P. Timothy Bushnell, Vladimir Shlapentokh, Christopher K. Vanderpool and Jeyaratnam Sundram (eds), *State Organized Terror: The Case of Violent Repression*. Boulder, CO. Westview Press, 1991.
128 In the case of Al-Qaeda, this element was stressed after the Madrid bombings of 11 March 2004 when Al-Qaeda sent this message: 'Stop targeting us, release our prisoners and leave our land, we will stop attacking you. The people of US allied countries have to put pressure on their governments to immediately end their alliance with the US in the war on terror (Islam). If you persist we will continue.' Quoted in Mike Whitney, 'War or Shabby PR Ploy? Rejecting the Language of Terrorism'. Axis of Logic, 30 March 2004, at www.axisoflogic.com/artman/publish/article_6027.shtml.
129 Osama bin Laden (1998), quoted in 'National Commission on Terrorist Attacks upon the United States, 9/11 Report'. New York: New York Times, 2004, p. 72.
130 Thomas H. Mitchell, 'Defining the Problem'. In David Charters (ed.), *Democratic Responses to International Terrorism*. Ardsley, NY: Transnational, 1991, quoted in Jeffrey Jan Ross, 'Defining Terrorism: An International Consensus, a Critical Issue after 9/11'. In Frank Shanty and Raymond Picquet (eds), *Encyclopedia of World Terrorism: 1996–2002*. Armonk, NY: M.E. Sharpe, 2003, p. 12.
131 Double standards exist on both sides. Bin Laden said in a video after 9/11, 'There are two types of terror. Good and bad. What we are practising is good terror.' Quoted in *Sunday Telegraph* (London), 11 November 2001, cited by Roberto Toscano, 'Defining Terrorism', unpublished paper, n.d., n.p., p. 2.
132 Anthony C.E. Quainton, 'Moral and Ethical Considerations in Defining a Counter-terrorist Policy'. In David C. Rapoport and Yonah Alexander (eds), *The Rationalization of Terrorism*. Frederick, MD: University Publications of America, 1982, p. 40.
133 Boaz Ganor, 'Defining Terrorism: Is One Man's Terrorist Another Man's Freedom Fighter?' *ICT Papers*, vol. 4, August 1998, pp. 22–23, 29. Reproduced with the permission of the author and the International Policy Institute for Counter-Terrorism.
134 Report of the High-level Panel on Threats, Challenges and Change. *A More Secure World: Our Shared Responsibility*. New York: United Nations, 2004. Available at: www.un.org/secureworld/report2.pdf (accessed 19 August 2010).
135 Ibid., p. 51.

Appendix 2.1

250-plus Academic, Governmental and Intergovernmental Definitions of Terrorism

Compiled by Joseph J. Easson and Alex P. Schmid

Year not known   Anonymous
Kill one, frighten ten thousand.[1]

1794   Robespierre
Terror is nothing else than immediate justice, severe, inflexible; it is therefore an outflow of virtue, it is not so much a specific principle than a consequence of the general principle of democracy applied to the most pressing needs of the motherland.[2]

1879   Russian Narodnaya Volya Party, in *The People's Will*
Terroristic activity consists of the destruction of the most harmful persons in the government, the protection of the Party from spies, and the punishment of official lawlessness and violence in all the more prominent and important cases where it is manifested. The aim of such activity is to break down the prestige of government, to furnish continuous proof of the possibility of pursuing a contest with the government, to raise in that way the revolutionary spirit in the people, and finally, to form a body suited and accustomed to warfare.[3]

1880   Mozorov
[T]erroristic struggle has exactly this advantage that it can act unexpectedly and find means and ways which no one anticipates. All that the terroristic struggle really needs is a small number of people and large material means. This represents really a new form of struggle. It replaces by a series of individual political assassinations, which always hit their target, the massive revolutionary movements, where people often rise against each other because of misunderstanding and where a nation kills off its own children, while the enemy of the people watches from a secure shelter and sees to it that the people of the organization are destroyed. The movement punishes only those who are really responsible for the evil deed. Because of this the terroristic revolution is the only just form of revolution. At the same time it is the most convenient form of revolution. Using insignificant forces it had an opportunity to restrain all the efforts of tyranny, which seemed to be undefeated up to this time. 'Do not be afraid of the Tsar, do not be afraid of despotic rulers because all of them are weak and helpless against secret, sudden assassination', it says to mankind.[4]

1909   Chernov

Terror is a form of military combat, a form of war, and as in war, any state whose military tactics are outdated exposes itself to failure. So too in internal war . . . in the war of terror, we must master modern techniques of warfare. Terror will be terror in the true sense of the word only if it represents the revolutionary implementation of the achievements of the most advanced technical sciences at any given moment.[5]

1936   Hardman

Terrorism is a term used to describe the method or the theory behind the method whereby an organized group or party seeks to achieve its avowed aims chiefly through the systematic use of violence. Terroristic acts are directed against persons who as individuals, agents or representatives of authority interfere with the consumption of the objectives of such a group. . . . The terrorist does not threaten; death or destruction is part of his program of action, and if he is caught his behaviour during trials is generally directed primarily not toward winning his freedom but toward spreading a knowledge of his doctrines. . . . Terrorism is a method of combat in the struggle between social groups and forces rather than individuals, and it may take place in any social order. Terrorism as a method is always characterized by the fact that it seeks to arouse not only the reigning government or the nation in control but also the mass of people to a realization that constituted authority is no longer safely entrenched and unchallenged. The publicity value of the terroristic act is a cardinal point in the strategy of terrorism.[6]

1937   League of Nations Convention for the Prevention and Repression of Terrorism

In the present Convention, the expression 'acts of terrorism' means criminal acts directed against a State and *intended or calculated* to create a state of terror in the minds of particular persons, or a group of persons or the general public.[7]

1939   Waciorsky

Terrorism is a method of action by which an agent tends to produce terror in order to impose his domination.[8]

1948   Chisholm

Political terror is the planned use of violence or threat of violence against an individual or social group in order to eradicate resistance to the aims of the terrorist. Political terror differs from fear in its organization and aims. Terror is a comparatively commonplace social phenomenon. The lynching of a Negro by a white mob is an act of terror. However, unlike political terror it is a generally unplanned act with limited aims . . . the political terrorist, on the other hand, engages in planned acts designed to reduce [the terrorist's] opponents to a plastic state of mind wherein they surrender all opposition to the wielder of the sword, and passively agree to support his projects blindly, unquestioningly. . . . Political terror is a type of fear, or more accurately, a combination of fear and dread. Dread is the awareness of an imminent, but unknown danger. It is a paralysing, isolating emotion that renders impossible any constructive action. Fear either serves as a powerful inhibiting factor that deters us from acting because of unpleasant consequences or as an energizing agent that drives us to act in an effort to escape an unpleasant situation. . . .The first task of the mass terrorist is to destroy group solidarity. . . . A second element of political terrorism is ruthlessness. . . . Political terror is not a secret device. Indeed, it is really a publicity campaign. The political terrorist does not desire to kill off his opponents (who may number the vast majority of the population) but to subjugate them. Therefore the actual instances of violence are merely examples of the treatment given to obstructionists. . . . Through propaganda the terrorist spreads the word that violence rules the land.[9]

1951 Arendt

A fundamental difference between modern dictatorship and all other tyrannies of the past is that terror is no longer used as a means to exterminate and frighten opponents, but as an instrument to rule masses of people who are perfectly obedient. Terror as we know it today strikes without any preliminary provocation, its victims are innocent even from the point of view of the prosecutor. This was the case in Nazi Germany when full terror was directed against Jews, i.e. against people with certain common characteristics which were independent of their specific behaviour . . . Russian practice, on the other hand, is even more 'advanced' than the German in one respect: arbitrariness of terror is not even limited by racial differentiation, while the old class categories have long since been disregarded, so that anybody in Russia may suddenly become a victim of the police terror. We are not concerned here with the ultimate consequence of rule of terror – namely, that nobody, not even the executors, can ever be free of fear; in our context we are dealing merely with the arbitrariness by which victims are chosen, and for this it is decisive that they are objectively innocent, that they are chosen regardless of what they may or may not have done.[10]

1960   Crozier

I define terrorism, provisionally, as the threat or the use of violence for political ends. As a weapon, it may be wielded by rebels or by their opponents; in the second case, however, it becomes counter-terrorism . . . It comes in several varieties: it may be indiscriminate or selective; it may be used against the enemy or against members of one's own side. If people in the terrorists' own camps are the victims, they are labelled traitors. . . . The enforcement of conformity and obedience through fear: that is one aspect of terrorism.[11]

1964   Thornton

[I]n an internal war situation, terror is a symbolic act designed to influence political behaviour by extra normal means, entailing the use or threat of violence. . . . Terrorism may gain political ends in one of two ways – either by mobilizing forces or by immobilizing forces and reserves sympathetic to the cause of the insurgents or by immobilizing forces and reserves that would normally be available to the incumbents. . . . The political function or terror must also be emphasized, in contrast to the military role that is often ascribed to it. The military function of terror is negligible. . . . Definition of terror as a symbolic act does not mean that a person, say, is assassinated only symbolically and not in fact; rather, it means that the terroristic act is intended and perceived as a symbol. . . . If the terrorist comprehends that he is seeking a demonstration effect, he will attack targets with a maximum symbolic value. . . . The symbolic concept of the terrorist act enables us to make two crucial distinctions: between terror and sabotage and between terror and assassination. . . . If the objective is primarily the removal of a specific thing (or person) with a view towards depriving the enemy of its usefulness, then the act is one of sabotage. If, on the other hand, the objective is symbolic, we are dealing with terror. . . . As a general rule, assassination and sabotage are non-symbolic acts directed against persons and things, respectively. Terror is a symbolic act that may be directed against things or people.[12]

1964   Walter

The word 'terrorism' conventionally means a type of violent action, such as murder, designed to make people afraid. In ordinary language, however, the word 'terror' is ambiguous, often suggesting any kind of extreme apprehension, without regard to the cause. Moreover, it can mean, on the one hand, the psychic state – extreme fear – and, on the other hand, the thing that terrifies – the violent event that produces the psychic state. I shall try to avoid confusion by maintaining a precise usage, employing terms such as 'terrorism' and 'organized terror' consistently as equivalents to *process of terror*, by which I mean a compound with three elements: the act or threat of violence, the emotional reaction, and the social effects. . . . A *system of terror* may be defined broadly to include certain states of war as well as certain political communities, as long as the term refers to a sphere of relationships controlled by the terror process. . . . Systems of terror fall into two major categories, depending on whether they work against or coincide with the dominant power structure. . . . The [first] type may be referred to as a *siege of terror*. . . . The [second] form may be called a *regime of terror*. . . . Violence, the principal element of the terror process, should be distinguished from 'force', 'coercion', and 'power', for it is important to understand how terrorism differs from the ordinary political practice of coercion. . . . The term 'violence' will be restricted to the sense of *destructive harm*; hence, a destructive kind of force. . . . In contrast [to punishment], the terror process begins with violence, which is followed by intense fear and irrational reactive behaviour patterns. . . . In the terror process, no one can be secure, for the category of transgression is, in reality, abolished. Anyone may be a victim, no matter what action he chooses. Innocence is irrelevant.[13]

1965   Gaucher

Le terrorisme est une méthode de lutte. . . . Il constitue un système de lutte ouvertement déclarée, élaboré par un état-major, mis à l'épreuve par une petite armée secrété, sélectionnée et disciplinée. Il multiplie les coups, les ordonne, en calcule et en dose les effets, en escompte tel ou tel résultat, en corrige l'exercice. . . . Bref, le terrorisme est – ou veut être – une stratégie. L'exercice de la terreur, conçue comme telle, choisie delibrément d'après controverses, et méthodiquement mise au point, commence ainsi véritablement en Russie vers 1879.[14]

1966   Aron

An action of violence is labelled 'terrorist' when the psychological effects are out of proportion to its purely physical result. In this sense, the so-called indiscriminate acts of revolutionaries are terrorist, as were the Anglo-American zone bombings. The lack of discrimination helps to spread fear, for if no one in particular is a target, no one can be safe.[15]

1969   *The Shorter Oxford English Dictionary*

Terror: . . . 1. The state of being terrified or greatly frightened; intense fear, fright, or dread. Also, with and pl., an instance of this. 2. *trans.* The action or quality of causing dread; terrific quality, terribleness; also conc. a thing or person that excites terror or awe; something terrifying, awe-inspiring. . . . Terrorism: . . . A system of terror. 1. Government by intimidation; the system of the Terror (1793–4); . . . 2. *gen.* A policy intended to strike with terror those against whom it is adopted; the fact of terrorizing or condition of being terrorized. . . . Terrorist: . . . a. Applied to the Jacobins and their agents and partisans in the French Revolution. b. Any one who attempts to further his views by a system of coercive intimidation; *spec.* applied to members of one of the extreme revolutionary societies in Russia. . . . Terrorize: 1. *trans.* To fill or inspire with terror, reduce to a state of terror. 2. *intrans.* To rule, or maintain power, by terrorism; to practice intimidation.[16]

1970   Dallin and Breslauer

By 'political terror' we mean the arbitrary use, by organs of political authority, of severe coercion against individuals or groups, the credible threat of such use, or the arbitrary extermination of such individuals or groups. [T]error, in our usage, does not necessarily include violence: just as some violence involves no terror, some terror (e.g. intimidation) requires no violence. . . . We distinguish between 'purposive terror', which is instituted and intended by the policy-makers, and 'situational terror', which is generally a product of uncontrolled and undisciplined behaviour by low-level cadres. . . . Purposive terror at this stage was essentially limited to the selective elimination of active political opponents and representatives of pre-revolutionary elites with the 'demonstration effect' aimed at broader strata of the population as yet distinctly subordinate. . . . Our definition of terror stresses the element of arbitrariness both in the decision-maker's ability to disregard any binding legal norms and in the calculability of the application of terror as perceived by the citizen. The second characteristic must not be confused, however, with capriciousness in the identification of victims. Whereas terror may come to affect any member of society either as victim or as target, it appears that in Communist systems neither the entire society is the primary target of terror campaigns, nor is terror randomly applied. And where the prophylactic removal of entire categories is involved, such groups – though not necessarily the individual victims within them – tend to be chosen for selective and total elimination by a rational, albeit peculiar, process.[17]

1970   Silverman and Jackson

Terrorism as element in this process of violent change can be defined as the use of physical violence, however indirect, for political-psychological effect through fear for one's own person. . . . Terrorism however is not a distinct stage in revolutionary development, but a contemporary tactic to both guerrilla and conventional warfare. . . . In addition terrorism differs from guerrilla in as much as its purpose is to influence the opponent and any third parties rather than to annihilate him. . . . The purpose of the act, not the nature of the act, not the nature of the act itself is the essential characteristics which distinguishes terrorism . . . The target, therefore, is often someone other than the victim of a terrorism act. Consequently the psychological consequences of the act are more important than the act itself. . . . Whether a specific act of torture, murder, arson or kidnapping can be defined as terrorism will depend on how that particular act is perceived by the international audience. . . . In order for it to be considered terrorism, the intended audience must identify with the victim, be associated with what he represents and experience feelings of fear and insecurity for their own well-being. The intended audience must be aware that it is the target at which the influence or intimidation is directed.[18]

1971   Mallin

A barroom brawl is violence; so is nuclear warfare. Terror tactics occupy a portion of the overall spectrum. Obviously the threat of a nuclear war – or the threat of a physical beating to an individual – can be viewed as forms of terror; but these lie within the broad, semantic meaning of the word. In the context of internal political struggle, terror has two basic applications. Dictatorial regimes often maintain themselves in power through the use of terror tactics. These tactics characteristically include arbitrary arrests, tortures, murders, kangaroo courts, lengthy imprisonments, and close vigilance over the words, thoughts, and activities of citizens. This is one side of the coin. The other side is the commission by revolutionary organizations of acts of violence whose psychological effects are expected to further the causes pursued by those groups, the desired end result almost invariably being the overthrow of the existing government. . . . The basis of terror tactics is the threat –

threat to a government that it must abandon power or face continued trouble and danger for its officials; threat to a population that they face constant disruption unless they help overthrow the government. . . . Terrorism is a form of guerrilla warfare. The basic tactic for guerrillas is to hit and run and hide, hit, run, hide. Guerrillas conceal themselves in mountains or rural areas. Terror tactics are employed in urban areas as well . . . they are often aptly referred to as 'urban guerrilla warfare'. [19]

1971   Marighela

By terrorism I mean the use of bomb attacks.[20]

1971   Moss

Terrorism could be defined as the systematic use of intimidation for political ends. . . . It can be employed as a defensive or an offensive weapon, to preserve the status quo. . . . It can be used to erode democratic institutions and clear the way for the seizure of power by an authoritarian movement (like Nazis) as well as to resist an absolutist invader. . . . Terrorism is only one form of urban militancy. Unlike riots, political strikes, student demonstrations and ghetto revolts, terrorism is a minority technique, and the deed to ensure security under urban conditions dictates a fairly standard form of organization: members of the terrorist groups are divided into cells or 'firing groups' of from three to five men, with a link man in each.[21]

1972   Moss

Terrorism might be defined as the systematic use of intimidation for political purposes. That formula is broad enough to cover all sort of varying situations. Terrorists can be classified according to their beliefs, or their targets, but it is probably more useful to single out three tactical varieties of terrorism. Repressive terror is used by a government to keep its grip over the population or by the rebel movement as a means of eliminating rivals, coercing popular support, or maintaining conformity inside the organization (in other words, bumping off 'traitors' and silencing criticism). Defensive terror can be used by private groups like the American vigilantes to keep order or uphold the status quo; by patriots against a foreign invader; or by a community defending its traditional rights. Offensive terror . . . is used against a regime or a political system.[22]

1972   Crenshaw Hutchinson

Revolutionary terrorism is a part of insurgent strategy in the context of internal warfare or revolution: the attempt to seize political power from the established regime of a state, if successful causing fundamental political and social change. . . . Summarizing the basic components of a definition of the concepts of terrorism produces the following list of essential properties which empirical examination of data must reveal: (1) Terrorism is part of a revolutionary strategy – a method used by insurgents to seize political power from an existing government. (2) Terrorism is manifested in acts of socially and politically unacceptable violence. (3) There is a consistent pattern of symbolic or representative selection of the victims or objects of acts of terrorism. (4) The revolutionary movement deliberately intends these actions to create a psychological effect on specific groups and thereby to change their political behaviour and attitudes.[23]

1972   Gross

During the second half of the 19th century, a theory of individual terror developed among revolutionary Russians in their struggle against autocracy. Unlike political assassinations as an isolated act, individual terror . . . is a systematic, tactical course of action with political objectives. Individual terror attacked directly, above all, key decision makers and administrators or acted in lieu of punishment against persons responsible for cruelties and oppression. One of its functions was redistribution and deterrence. The leaders of the organization expected that assassination of an oppressive administrator would deter his successor from inhuman, oppressive acts. . . . The major function of individual terror was, however, weakening of the government and of the autocratic institutions of the Tsarist Empire. . . . It did not hurt innocent people; it was discriminating. In a sense – in their view – it was tactics and punishment at the same time. Individual terror was to a large extent a tool of those who were 'outs' and stormed the autocratic institutions. . . . Mass terror is apolitical tactic of the 'ins', of those in the saddle, in an effort to consolidate power, and usually to eliminate groups of innocent people defined as class, race or nation. Thus, objectives of mass terror are broader than solely a rule by fear. . . . The rule of mass terror was usually in the past and still is a government of a minority, which maintains its power primarily by manipulation of fear, not by consensus.[24]

1972 Günther

If terror (dread) alone is a neutral word belonging to the natural context, the verb and the adjective terrorize and terroristic refer to people only who bring about dread with other people. Terrorism is therefore ultimately a systematization that operates with dread as an element of action. . . . The terrorism of impotence is the one that now produces dread in the contemporary world. . . . A war . . . is already placed at some distance for the majority of the people by the spatial element. The terrorism of impotence, on the other hand, cannot be territorially confined. While it claims comparatively few victims, it nevertheless resembles those mythical beasts that can at random pick out and devour one or the other human being.[25]

1972 Morrison *et al.*

Terrorism is defined as events involving relatively highly organized and planned activity, on the part of small but cohesive groups, in which the aim of the activity is to damage, injure, or eliminate governments' property or personnel. These activities include bomb plants, sabotage of electrical and transportation facilities, assassinations (attempted and successful), and isolated guerrilla activities.[26]

1973 Hacker

Terror is the use of the intimidation instrument of rule by the powerful, terrorism the imitation and practice of terror methods by the (at least until now) powerless, despised and desperate who believe there is no other way than terrorism to be taken seriously and to be reckoned with. . . . Terror and terrorism are not the same but they show their clear relationship in their dependence on propaganda and publicity, in their ruthless use of violence which is brutally simplifying and concretizing, and, above all, in their clearly demonstrated display of indifference towards human life. The same word, 'terror' refers both to the rule of fear of the powerful, which serves to preserve power, and to the punctuated or organized rule of fear by the impotent, the wannabee powerful or not yet powerful that is directed against the powerful. Terror and terrorism imitate each other and condition each other, overlap and flow into each other; common to both of them is the predominant or exclusive focus on the anticipated effect of an as general as possible insecurity and rule of fear. . . . Terrorist acts are demonstrations of a readiness and capacity to act which, intended as threats, are meant to bring about intimidation. . . . Even the mad deeds of disturbed people and the misdeeds of criminal lone wolves or cliques can bring about a terroristic effect through the danger of repetition and imitation . . . however, 'real' terror is only present when the intimidation is not an accidental result but the intention and goal of the exercise. . . . Terrorism in its purest form is determined and justified by its calculated and anticipated effects. Terrorism wants, above all, to impress; the effect on the general public is the purpose and meaning of the terrorist enterprise; compared to that, the fate of the randomly chosen or selected victims is unimportant; they are only means to achieve intimidation. . . . Terror is a social invention, the elaboration and application of methods of rule and control over human beings by exploiting their fear and their partly manipulated docile passivity and willing irresponsibility. From the spectrum of possibilities, the choice to apply terror is always taken when other alternatives have allegedly or really failed.[27]

1973   Horowitz

The definition of someone as a terrorist is a labelling device. . . . [W]hat is usually referred to as terrorism is un-sponsored and unsanctioned violence against the body or bodies of others. However, whether or not violence performed with official sanction, against the leadership or the membership of other groups and institutions is non-terrorist in character, it is part of a continuous process of definition and redefinition in political life. And in the current ambiguous and even ubiquitous conditions, performing a terrorist act does not uniquely make one a terrorist, any more than random non-violence alone defines the pacifist.[28]

1973   Neale

Symbolic act entailing the use or threat of violence and designed to influence political behaviour by producing a psychological reaction in the recipient that is also known as terror. Terrorism is sometimes known as 'politics by violence' and anarchist followers of Michael Bakunin called it 'the propaganda by the deed'.[29]

1974   Crozier

'[T]errorism' means 'motivated violence for political ends' (a definition that distinguishes terrorism from both vandalism and non-political crime). Measures of extreme repression, including torture, used by States to oppress the population or to repress political dissenters, who may or may not be terrorists or guerrillas, are termed 'terror' (the converse of terrorism).[30]

1974   Fairbairn

Terrorism is a mode of behaviour that is not of course confined to revolutionary guerrilla wars. As a means of dissuading people from supporting the enemy and to punish those who have supported the enemy it has been found in most traditional guerrilla wars. To give the impression that the guerrillas are more to be feared than the enemy is an old aim in such struggles. . . . Terrorism is a form of violence that has, at any rate until recently, been regarded with peculiar horror by most people. It had normally seemed to be a cowardly form of activity – the murder of an unarmed person or persons by a man (or woman) likely to escape in the confusion – or, where escape was unlikely, the action of someone with a deranged mind. If explosives were used, terrorist acts were likely also to kill innocent bystanders.[31]

1974   Paust

Terrorism is thus viewed as the purposive use of violence or the threat of violence by the precipitator(s) against an instrumental target in order to communicate to a primary target a threat of future violence so as to coerce the primary target into behaviour or attitudes through intense fear or anxiety in connection with a demanded power (political) outcome.[32]

1974   United Kingdom. Prevention of Terrorism Act (1974)

For the purposes of this legislation, terrorism is the use of violence for political ends and includes any use of violence for the purpose of putting the public or any section of the public in fear.[33]

1974   Wilkinson

Our main concern is with political terror: that is to say with the use of coercive intimidation by revolutionary movements, regimes or individuals. . . . We have thus identified some of the key characteristics common to all forms of political terror: indiscriminateness, unpredictability, arbitrariness, ruthless destructiveness and the implicitly amoral and antinomian nature of a terrorist's challenge. . . . Political terrorism, properly speaking, is a sustained policy involving the waging of organized terror either on the part of the state, a movement or faction, or by a small group of individuals. Systematic terrorism invariably entails some organizational structure, however rudimentary, and some kind of theory or ideology of terror.[34]

1975   Bite

International terrorism may be defined as politically and socially motivated violence conducted outside the territories of parties to a conflict or directed against the citizens or properties of a third party. It is effective because of the fear it generates and thrives on publicity. Forms of terrorism include aircraft hijackings, kidnappings, and seizure of hostages for ransom, assassinations and bombings. The victims of these attacks are usually civilians.[35]

1975   Bouthoul

Certain specific qualities of terrorism thus begin to appear. They are:

1   Its clandestine nature: terrorist actions are the work of small and very secret groups.
    . . .
2   Terrorist action is not a battle: terrorists do not restrict themselves to attacks upon an overt enemy, but also strike at the innocent in order to create fear and insecurity. . . .
3   Terrorism attempts to act in secrecy: the anonymous, unidentifiable threat creates huge anxiety, and the terrorist tries to spread fear by contagion, to immobilize and subjugate those living under this threat. . . .
4   Extreme terrorism exhibits two other traits: the first is psychological: it is a tendency toward obsession, single-minded fanaticism, the logic of paranoia taken to its ultimate.
    . . .
5   Terrorism is much influenced by intellectual and doctrinal fashions. . . . At the same time, it often presents itself as a form of propaganda action, aiming to promote a certain doctrine or set of demands, using the modern techniques of publicity. . . .
6   There is also noticeable in terrorism an element of imitation in the techniques employed. . . .
7   Among terrorists there is the power of suggestion: there are, for example, solitary men who are controlled by an idée fixe. . . . When terrorism involves groups, romanticism predominates, its variety reflecting the character of the struggle, hatred or fervour, a territorial demand or love of a cause. Such romanticism and the idée fixe are sustained by constant repetition, propaganda and autosuggestion.[36]

1975 Fromkin

Terrorism is violence used to create fear; but it is aimed at creating fear in order that the fear, in turn, will lead somebody else – not the terrorist – to embark on some quite different programme of action that will accomplish whatever it is that the terrorist really desires. . . . Other strategies sometimes kill the innocent by mistake. Terrorism kills the innocent deliberately; for not even the terrorist necessarily believes that the particular person who happens to become his victim deserves to be killed or injured. . . . Terrorism is the indirect strategy that wins or loses only in terms of how uncompromising you should be in response to it. The decision as to how accommodating or how uncompromising you should be in your response to it involves questions that fall primarily within the domain of political philosophy. . . . The important point is that the choice is yours. That is the ultimate weakness of terrorism as a strategy. It means that, though terrorism cannot always be prevented, it can always be defeated. You can always refuse to do what they want you to do. . . . But the price of doing so is constantly rising, as technology increases the range and magnitude of horrible possibilities.[37]

1975 Jenkins

Without attempting to define terrorism in a way that will satisfy all lawyers and scholars, we may for the moment satisfy ourselves with the following description: The threat of violence, individual acts of violence, or a campaign of violence designed primarily to instil fear – to terrorize – may be called terrorism. Terrorism is violence for effect: not only, and sometimes not at all, for the effect on the actual victims of the terrorists' cause. Terrorism is violence aimed at the people watching. Fear is the intended effect, not the by-product of terrorism. That, at least, distinguishes terrorist tactics from mugging and other common forms of violent crime that may terrify but are not terrorism. Those we call terrorists may include revolutionaries and other political extremists, criminals professing political aims, and a few authentic lunatics. Terrorists may operate alone or may be members of a large and well-organized group. Terrorists may even be government agents. Their cause may have extreme goals – the destruction of all government, in itself not a new idea. Or their cause may be one that is comparatively reasonable and understandable – self-rule for a particular ethnic group. Or their motive may be purely personal – money or revenge. The ambition of terrorists may be limited and local – the overthrow of a particular regime – or it may be global – a simultaneous worldwide revolution. . . . Terrorism may properly refer to a specific set of actions the primarily intent of which is to produce fear and alarm that may serve a variety of purposes. But terrorism in general usage frequently is also applied to similar acts of violence – all ransom kidnappings, all hijackings, thrill-killings – which are not intended by their perpetrators to be primarily terror-producing. Once a group carried out a terrorist act, it acquires the label terrorist, a label that tends to stick; and from that point on, everything this group does, whether intended to produce terror or not, is also henceforth called terrorism. If it robs a bank or steals arms from an arsenal, not necessarily acts of terrorism but common urban guerrilla tactics, these too are often described as terrorism. At some point in this expanding use of the term, terrorism can mean just what those who use the term (not the terrorists) want it to mean – almost any violent act by any opponent.[38]

1975 Jenkins and Johnson

Common characteristics do emerge from the list of incidents included in the chronology. . . .These characteristics suggest the following description: International terrorism can be a single incident or a campaign of violence waged outside the presently accepted rules and procedures of international diplomacy and war; it is often designed to attract worldwide attention to the existence and cause of the terrorists and to inspire fear. Often the violence is carried out for effect. The actual victim or victims of terrorist attacks and the target audience may not be the same; the victims may be totally unrelated to the struggle.[39]

1975   Sobel

The word terrorism is employed to specify acts of violence for political coercion. But there seems to be no definition that will satisfactorily cover all uses of the term. . . . In general, the word terrorism is used to define almost all illegal acts of violence committed for political purposes by clandestine groups. The lawyer William A. Hannay, writing in the April 1974 issue of *International Lawyer* about [a] United Nations debate on terrorism, asserted that 'recent contemporary usage tends to curb its [the term's] meaning to either random or extortionate violence, aimed ultimately at the target state of a guerrilla, resistance or liberation movement but which strikes at unarmed civilians, diplomats or non-combatants.[40]

1976   US FBI

However, the task force concluded that 'terrorism is a technique, a way of engaging in certain types of criminal activity, so as to attain particular ends'. Terrorism is defined as the unlawful use of force or violence against persons or property to intimidate or coerce a government, the civilian population, or any segment thereof, in furtherance of political or social objectives.[41]

1976   Fearey

What precisely is 'international terrorism'? . . . First, as with other forms of terrorism, it embodies an act which is essentially criminal. It takes the form of assassination or murder, kidnapping, extortion, arson, maiming or an assortment of other acts which are commonly regarded by all nations as criminal. Second, international terrorism is politically motivated. An extremist political group, convinced of the rightness of its cause, resorts to violent means to advance that cause – means incorporating one of the acts I have just cited. Often the violence is directed against innocents, persons having no personal connection with the grievance motivating the terrorist act. And third, international terrorism transcends national boundaries, through the choice of a foreign victim or target, commission of the terrorist act in a foreign country, or effort to influence the policies of a foreign government. The international terrorist strikes abroad, or at a diplomat or other foreigner at home, because he believes he can thereby exert the greatest possible pressure on his own or another government or on world opinion. The international terrorist may or may not wish to kill his victim or victims. In abduction or hostage-barricade cases he usually does not wish to kill – though he often will find occasion to do so at the outset to enhance the credibility of his threats. In other types of attacks innocent deaths are his specific, calculated, pressure-shock objective. Through brutality and fear he seeks to impress his existence and his cause on the minds of those who can, through action or terror induced inaction, help him to achieve that cause.[42]

1976   Kossoy

Terrorism is intimidation by actual or threatened use of violence as a method of governing or securing political or other ends.[43]

1976   Pierre

There is nothing new about terrorism per se. The term first came into modern usage during the Reign of Terror in revolutionary France. It commonly refers to the threat of violence and the use of fear to coerce, persuade or gain public attention. Terror has been used by ideologies of both the Right and the Left, by the former to repress a population and by the latter to win self-determination and independence. Governments have used terror as an instrument of state as well as by guerrillas or insurgents as an instrument of subversion. The conception of international terrorism is more difficult to endow with a universally accepted definition. In this analysis it will refer to acts of violence across national boundaries, or with clear international repercussions, often within the territory or involving the citizens of a third party to a dispute. Thus it is to be distinguished from domestic terrorism of the sort that has taken place in Ulster, the Soviet Union or South Africa. Admittedly, the line is often thin between terror which is essentially domestic, and that possessing a clear international character. International terrorism is usually, though not exclusively, political in intent and carried out by non-governmental groups, although they may receive financial and moral support from nation-states.[44]

1976   US Central Intelligence Agency
The threat or use of violence for political purposes when (1) such action is intended to influence the attitudes and behaviour of a target group wider than its immediate victims, and (2) its ramifications transcend national boundaries (as a result, for example, of the nationality or foreign ties of its perpetrators, its locale, the identity of its institutional or human victims, its declared objectives or the mechanics of its resolution).

Political terrorism is, then, the above sort of violence employed in pursuit of political objective. It is calculated violence aimed at influencing the attitude and behavior of one or more target audiences. Another refinement has been made between International Terrorism, defined as 'Such action when carried out by individuals or groups controlled by a sovereign state', and Transnational Terrorism, 'such action when carried out by basically autonomous non-state actors, whether or not they enjoy some degree of support by sympathetic states'.[45]

1976   US Task Force (1976)
In fact, terrorism is a technique, a way of engaging in certain types of criminal activity, so as to attain particular ends. For the perpetrator of terroristic crimes, terror – or the sensation of massive, overwhelming fear induced in victims – transcends in importance the criminal activity itself, which is merely the vehicle or instrumentality. Terror is a natural phenomenon; terrorism is the conscious exploitation of it. Terrorism is coercive, designed to manipulate the will of its victims and its larger audience. The great degree of fear is generated by the crime's very nature, by the manner of its perpetration, or by its senselessness, wantonness, or callous indifference to human life. This terrible fear is the source of the terrorist's power and communicates his challenge to society. . . .

Thus, terrorism, although it has its individual victims, is really an onslaught upon society itself. Any definition of terrorism for the purpose of constructing effective responses to it must bear these considerations in mind.

It is not useful, therefore, merely to enumerate a series of violent, criminal acts or threats that would constitute terroristic behaviour; such a definition misses, altogether, the terrorist's true objective. Any law intended to strike at terrorism must address the purpose as well as the instrumentality. Because they have failed to do so, international attempts at definition have substantially failed: Viewed in terms of motivation and ends, 'what is terrorism to some is heroism to others' (Per M. Cherif Bassiouni, cited in International Terrorism and Political Crimes). Although it is presently an effective bar to any concerted response to international or transnational terrorism, this lack of agreement about terms and criminal policy ought not to frustrate those responsible for this society's responses to acts of terrorism. For the purpose of the present report, no such universality of consensus is needed in order to arrive at working definitions.

Terrorism is a tactic or technique by means of which a violent act or the threat thereof is used for the prime purpose of coercive purposes. . . .

Political terrorism is characterized by: (1) its violent, criminal nature; (2) its impersonal frame of reference; and (3) the primacy of its ulterior objective, which is the dissemination of fear throughout the community for political ends or purposes. Political terrorism may be defined, therefore, as violent, criminal behaviour designed primarily to generate fear in the community, or a substantial segment of it, for political purpose. Excluded from this definition are acts or threats of a purely personal character and those, which are psycho-pathological and have no intended socio-political significance.[46]

1976   Watson

Political terrorism can be defined as a strategy, a method by which an organized group or party tries to get attention for its aims, or force concessions toward its goals, through the systematic use of deliberate violence. Typical terrorists are individuals trained and disciplined to carry out the violence decided upon by their organizations. And, if caught, true terrorists can be expected to speak and act during their trials not primarily to win personal freedom, but to try to spread their organization's political ideas. n: Not a new definition. It was based on a more detailed one in the *Encyclopedia of the Social Sciences* published in 1934.[47]

1976   Weisband and Roguly

Violence in order to be terrorism must be political. Since terrorist violence tries to create the framework for political interactions, terrorists are forced to locate their actions in some political or moral context. . . . Terrorism is different from criminal violence in that its purpose is symbolic, its means psychological, and its ends political. Terrorism often serves as the cutting edge of a revolutionary movement, but, precisely because it is the vehicle of organized insurgency, it must point the way to a political resolution. It must negate its nihilism. . . . An act of terrorist violence uninformed by discipline or politics stops dead without achieving its aims. For violence to have impact it can never be its own reward; when effective, terrorism pulls violence out of the realm of war and into the world of politics. But politics has rules, patterns of normative interaction, do's and don'ts of legitimate conduct. In the beginning it is the terrorist's task to violate norms of civilized conduct. Yet terrorism is fundamentally a psychological strategy and must point to a way of resolving the conflict. If terrorist violence appears wanton, it threatens to lose the support, or at least the respect, it is seeking to gain. Thus the terrorist irrevocably comes face to face with a torturous self-contradiction: as he becomes more successful, he must become more responsible. He is left to live with the painful tension of responsible violence, that is, calculated, disciplined, and permeated with politics. As he wins recognition through violence, he must place limitations on the use of violence. . . . Every resistance movement struggles for recognition. Attention is the lifeblood of its existence. For the terrorist the path to legitimacy is through one's reputation for resilience, for self-sacrifice and daring, for brutality, and, above all, for effective discipline over words and actions. The terrorist is his own torch and bomb; he ignites the flames of national passion and, if possible, of political sympathy, and he does it by violating universal human sensibilities. It is the credibility that violence produces whenever it appals that renders terrorism horrifying yet powerful and, if successful, self-legitimating.[48]

1976   Wilkinson

Political terrorism may be briefly defined as a special form of clandestine, undeclared and unconventional warfare waged without any humanitarian restraints or rules. . . . It is a common but elementary mistake to equate terrorism with guerrilla warfare in general. Political terrorism proper through the use of bombing, assassinations, massacres, kidnaps and hijacks can and does occur without benefit of guerrilla war. This has been so throughout history. Historically rural war was largely waged without resort to terrorist tactics, although today urban and rural guerrilla movements in Africa and Latin America do employ terrorism. . . . Terrorism is employed as a weapon of psychological warfare to help create a climate of panic, or collapse, to destroy public confidence in government and security agencies, and to coerce communities and movement activists into obeying the terrorist leadership.[49]

1976   Wolf

Political terrorism may be defined as the threat or use of deliberate violence, indis-criminately or selectively, against either enemies or allies to achieve a political end. The intent is to register a calculated impact on a target population and on other groups for the purpose of altering the political balance in favour of the terrorists. . . . Phrased another way the terrorist's strategic intent is to destroy the confidence a particular minority group has in its government by causing that government to act outside the law. Always, terrorist strategy aims not to defeat the forces of the incumbent regime militarily – for the terrorist this is an impossible task – but to bring about the moral alienation of the masses from the government until its isolation has become total and irreversible.[50]

1977   Anonymous

Political terrorism is a continuation of public protest by different means.[51]

1977   Clutterbuck

[T]errorism – the attack on an individual to frighten and coerce a large number of others – is as old as civilization itself. It is the recourse of a minority or even of a single dissident frustrated by the inability to make society shift in the desired direction by what that society regards as 'legitimate' means. It is primarily an attack on the rule of law, aimed either to destroy it or (as in more recent times) to change it radically to conform to the terrorist's idea of society. . . . Terrorism is not precisely the same as violence. Terrorism aims, by the use of violence or the threat of violence, to coerce governments, authorities or populations by inducing fear. Television has enormously expanded their ability to do so.[52]

1977   Finger and Alexander

However, 'terrorism' in its public or ideological senses has a completely different meaning in terms of its nature and implications. It is clearly illustrated by the following cases selected at random from world-wide press-coverage in 1976 and 1977. [There follows a summary by A.S.]: – The pro-independence Puerto Rican group FALN start small fires in three Manhattan department stores; – 14 South Moluccans in the Netherlands seize a Dutch train and a school; . . . in Karlsruhe, Siegfried Buback, West Germany's Chief Prosecutor, is killed at a stop light when fired at from a motorcycle; – members of the Zimbabwe African National Union (ZANU) in Rhodesia kill seven Roman Catholic missionaries; – in Lebanon four unidentified gunmen kill a Druze leader driving on a mountain road. [end of summary]. The foregoing acts of violent behaviour – characterized by a technique of perpetrating random and brutal intimidation, coercion or destruction of human lives and property, and used intentionally by sub-national groups, operating under varying degrees of stress, to obtain realistic or illusory goals – are symptomatic of what we consider 'terrorism' to be. Indeed, we seem to have entered an 'age of terrorism', the pattern of which is unlike any other period in history when ideological and political violence occurred.[53]

1977   Funke

Political terrorism can be generally described as systematic, planned threatening with, or application of, violence organized to strike by surprise.[54]

1977   Greisman

For the purposes of this paper, it is necessary to shortcut the definitional debate and focus on the one quality that gives terrorism its unique place in the catalogue of organized violence. Terrorist acts require an audience, the target is of secondary importance, i.e. those that see the target attacked will become terrorized and this is the real goal of terrorism.[55]

1977   Holton

According to one widely accepted definition, terrorism is a method of coercing a population or its leadership by means of fear or traumatization.[56]

1977   Horowitz

The definition of terrorism I employ is this: the selective use of fear, subjugation, and intimidation to disrupt the normal operations of a society. The power to inflict such injury is a bargaining power, which in its very nature bypasses due process of law. It seeks an outcome by means other than democratic or consensus formula. The act of terror – whoever performs it – in some sense, violates civil liberties. [57]

1977   Iviansky

'[I]ndividual terror' may be defined as a system of modern revolutionary violence aimed at leading personalities in the government or the Establishment (or any other human targets). The motivation is not necessarily personal but rather ideological or strategic. This method differs from traditional political conspiracy assassination, in that it is, in essence, not directed at individuals who are considered stumbling blocks to the seizure of power or sworn enemies of the organization, but rather against the foreign conqueror, the social order, or the Establishment embodied in these individuals. Infliction of personal injury is intended to weaken or destroy regimes, but, paradoxically, one of the clearest mani-festations of modern 'individual terror' is its impersonal character. It seeks to sow disorder and panic, to undermine and jeopardize the security of rulers and regimes, and to serve as the spearhead of revolution by stirring up the masses with exemplary deeds and the creation of revolutionary cadres trained to further the struggle.[58]

1977   Jenkins

Terrorism can be described as the use of actual or threatened violence to gain attention and to create fear and alarm, which in turn will cause people to exaggerate the strength of the terrorists and the importance of their cause. Since groups that use terrorist tactics are typically small and weak, the violence they practice must be deliberately shocking. . . . The fundamental issue is fear. Perhaps the biggest danger posed by terrorists lies not in the physical damage they do, but in the atmosphere of alarm they create, which corrodes democracy and breeds repression.[59]

1977 Jenkins

The threat of violence, individual acts of violence, or a campaign of violence designed primarily to instil fear – to terrorize – may be called terrorism. Terrorism is violence for effect; not only, and sometimes not at all, for the effect on the actual victims of the terrorist. In fact, the victim may be totally unrelated to the terrorists' cause. Terrorism is violence aimed at the people watching. Fear is the intended effect, not the by-product, of terrorism. That at least distinguishes terrorist tactics from mugging and other forms of violent crime that may terrify but are not terrorism.[60]

1977 Laqueur

Terrorism, interpreted here as the use of covert violence by a group for political ends, is usually directed against a government, less frequently against another group, class or party. The ends may vary from the redress of specific 'grievances' to the overthrow of a government and the taking of power, or to the liberation of a country from foreign rule. Terrorists seek to cause political, social and economic disruption, and for this purpose frequently engage in planned or indiscriminate murder. . . . Note: Any definition of political terrorism venturing beyond noting the systematic use of murder, injury and destruction or the threats of such acts toward achieving political ends is bound to lead to endless controversies.[61]

1977 Leiser

Terrorism is any organized set of acts of violence designed to create an atmosphere of despair or fear, to shake the faith of ordinary citizens in their government and its representatives, to destroy the structure of authority which normally stands for security, or to reinforce and perpetuate a governmental regime whose popular support is shaky. It is a policy of seemingly senseless, irrational, and arbitrary murder, assassination, sabotage, subversion, robbery, and other forms of violence, all committed with dedicated indifference to existing legal and moral codes or with claims to special exemption from conventional social norms. The politics of terrorists are pursued with the conviction that the death and suffering of innocent persons who have little or no direct connection with the causes to which the terrorists are dedicated are fully justified by whatever success terrorists may enjoy in achieving their political ends.[62]

1977 Mallin

Therefore, in this article the following working definition is offered: Political terrorism is the threat of violence or an act or series of acts of violence effected through surreptitious means by an individual, an organization, or a people to further his or their political goals. Under this definition sabotage committed for political purposes is indeed a form of terrorism. . . . Terrorism as a military arm is a weapon of psychological warfare.[63]

1977 Mickolus

Although we may disagree on definitions of terrorism, transnational terrorism will be defined as: The use, or threatened use, of anxiety-inducing, extra-normal violence for political purposes by any individual or group, whether acting for or in opposition to established governmental authority, when such action is intended to influence the attitudes and behaviour of a target group wider than the immediate victims and when, through the nationality or foreign ties of its perpetrators, its location, the nature of its institutional or human victims, or the mechanics of its resolution, its ramifications transcend national boundaries.[64]

1977   Milbank

Political terrorism is, then, the above sort of violence employed in pursuit of political objective. It is calculated violence aimed at influencing the attitude and behaviour of one or more target audiences. Another refinement has been made between International Terrorism, defined as, 'Such action when carried out by individuals or groups controlled by a sovereign state' and Transnational Terrorism, 'such action when carried out by basically autonomous non-state actors whether or not they enjoy some degree of support by sympathetic states'.[65]

1977   Paust

I offer a definitional approach that is objective. . . . Much of the reasoning behind the need for this approach has already been publicized (and published); however, in any comprehensive focus upon the terroristic process, the following factors should be carefully considered:

1   Precipitators,
2   Perspectives,
3   Acts involving the threat or use of violence,
4   Instrumental targets (human and non-human)
5   Primary targets and secondary targets,
6   Incidental or spill-over victims and
7   The result of such terror which coerces the primary target into a given behaviour or attitude.

Terrorism is therefore viewed as a form of violent strategy, a form of coercion utilized to alter the freedom of choice of others. Terrorism, thus defined, involves the intentional use of violence or the threat of violence by the precipitator(s) against an instrumental target in order to communicate to a primary target a threat of future violence. The object is to use intense fear or anxiety to coerce the primary target into behaviour or to mould its attitudes in connection with a demanded power (political) outcome. . . . In a specific context the instrumental and primary targets could well be the same person or group. . . . Additionally, the instrumental target need not be a person; attacks on power stations, for example, can produce a terror outcome in the civilian population of the community dependent upon the station for electricity. There must be a terror outcome, or the process could hardly be labelled as terrorism. . . . Terrorism can also be precipitated by governments, groups, or individuals; consequently, any exclusion of one or more sets of precipitators from the definitional framework is highly unrealistic. Equally unrealistic are definitional criteria which refer to 'systematic' uses of violence; terrorism can occur at an instant and by one act.[66]

1977   Price

The standard definition is that it is planned violence intended to have psychological influence on politically relevant behaviour (Hutchinson, 1971: 383–385). To clarify this, it is noted that the multiple targets of a terrorist act include the victim of terror, who may be too dead to be influenced psychologically, and the group who identify with the victim, and therefore receive the implicit message, 'You may be next.' All others aware of the act form the resonant mass, which may react emotionally in a positive or negative fashion; depending on which side they sympathize with in the conflict (Thornton, 1964: 78–79).[67]

1977   Silverstein
Terror is a state of intense fear induced by the systematic threat of imprisonment, mutilation or death. It is intensified when the victim is helpless in the hands of another human being. We are all afraid of being hurt or killed. The terrorist manipulates persons and governments by making the threat of bodily harm dramatically manifest. The terrorist threatens the more fundamental human drive – the will to survive intact. He strips from the defences of human courage the most important element of anti-terror, the real or supposed ability to fight back, to defend one's person. Because his victims are unarmed, non–combatant, and random, and because they are totally helpless, the victim's fear is experienced by all observers of the victim's plight, who are equally vulnerable and who desire to live their lives unmolested. The secondary victims of terrorism, all those who think by association that their lives are in equal danger, fear equally for their persons. Because they fear bodily harm, they are as manipulable as though the hand grenades were actually strapped to their bodies.[68]

1977   Singh
Political terrorism comprises only one type of violent activity subsumed under the general heading of unconventional warfare. . . . Terror incorporates two facets: 1. A state of fear or anxiety within an individual or a group, and 2. the tool that induces the state of fear. Thus, terror entails the threat or use of symbolic violent acts aimed at influencing political behaviour.[69]

1977   Smith
Terrorism involves both the use and the threat of violence. The threat of the terrorist derives not from his words but from his deeds, from a resort to violence that conveys a threat of further violence. This initial violence must therefore be symbolic. The victim must represent a whole class of persons who are identified as possible targets. However, while the particular class of persons to be terrorized may be carefully selected, the actual identity of those attacked is arbitrary. It is this lack of discrimination that is the source of terror. . . . Resort to terrorism – and especially reliance on terrorism – in order to promote political objectives is an indication of weakness. Lacking sufficient popular support to challenge a government through constitutional channels or even through full-scale civil war, a dissident group may see in terrorism the only chance of success.[70]

1977   Waldmann
[S]ince terroristic methods are employed neither in the service of power maintenance alone nor exclusively with the aim to bring down a system of power, they are rather in principle useful for both purposes. The notion of terror hints less at the goal perspective than at the mode and degree of intensity of violence. Most authors see it, following the classical treatment of H. Arendt, as a form of power exercise which is based on the systematic production of dread and fear. In doing this they attribute special weight to the social-psychological element of [its] effect. . . . Among the general features of terroristic strategy figure incalculability and lacking prognostic ability; terror, as it were, overfloods its victims. The arbitrariness in the selection of objects of violence, which is heightened by the disregard for all juridical and humanitarian principles, is not based on a cult of spontaneity by the terrorist actors or on their inability to plan and direct the violence but is elevated into a principle by them. In accordance to this principle they victimize primarily innocent

people like children and old people who are not in the slightest manner involved in the conflict issue. . . . The measures of terrorist groups are furthermore not exclusively directed against their real or perceived enemies, but can be targeted with equal severity on their own members and supporters. . . . A further generally recognizable trait is the attempts of justification and explanation, which accompany acts of terror. . . . Here the close interrelatedness of violence and ideology or propaganda noted earlier finds a confirmation.[71]

1977 Wilkinson

Political terrorism may be briefly defined as coercive intimidation. It is the systematic use of murder and destruction, and the threat of murder and destruction in order to terrorize individuals, groups, communities or governments into conceding to the terrorists' political demands. . . . Terroristic violence has the following salient characteristics:

1   It is inherently indiscriminate in its effects. . . . No one can be certain that they will not be the next victims. . . .
2   Terrorism is essentially arbitrary and unpredictable, both in the minds of its victims and audience and in its effects upon individuals and society. . . .
3   Terrorism implicitly denies recognition of all rules and conventions of war. It refuses to distinguish between combatants and non-combatants and recognizes no humanitarian constraints or obligations to prisoners or to the wounded. . . . No one is innocent. . . .
4   The terrorists' rejection of all moral constraints is also reflected in particularly hideous and barbarous cruelties and weapons. . . .
5   Politically motivated terrorism is generally justified by its perpetrators on one or more of the following grounds: (i) any means are justified to realize an allegedly transcendental end (in Weber's terms, 'value-rational' grounds); (ii) closely linked to (i) is the claim that extreme violence is an intrinsically beneficial, regenerative, cathartic and ennobling deed regardless of other consequences; (iii) terrorism can be shown to have 'worked' in the past, and is held to be either the 'sole remaining' or 'best available' method of achieving success (in Weber's terms 'instrumental-rational' grounds); (iv) the morality of the just vengeance or 'an eye for an eye and a tooth for a tooth'; and (v) the theory of the lesser evil: greater evils will befall us or our nation if we do not adopt terror against our enemies.[72]

1977 Wördemann

Terror, understood in the sense of Hannah Arendt . . . is an institution intrinsic to established totalitarian power, but also of an established power which is totalitarian in its aspirations and direction of development, even when the aimed for totalitarian situation has not yet been reached. Terror is the inevitable inner force of totalitarian power, occasionally the desperate and senseless mode of fighting of democratic power, but always an expression of established power. Terrorism is the use of force by a small and isolated group which does not have the force to attack the established power of terror or the generally accepted power of the [rule of,] law and the laws by means of a broad-based mass uprising or conventional methods.[73]

1978 Bell

Today terror, a form of political violence that falls between war and peace and offers a model to madmen and criminals appears all but endemic in open, liberal societies. . . . For terror, however defined, has most assuredly now become a serious Western preoccupation. . . . Almost without exception the public's perception of the terrorist is of someone associated with a revolutionary organization. There may be state terror or criminals and madmen, vigilantes and authorized assassins; but for the many the real terrorist belongs to a revolutionary organization. . . . At the very beginning we face the definitional problem: one man's terrorist is another man's patriot. Like love, terrorism is easy to recognize but difficult to define. . . . In the nineteenth century the word terrorism had a relatively clear meaning. People called themselves 'terrorists' . . . and held to a particular revolutionary strategy – personal terror, propaganda of the deed. Today the word is often used as a pejorative, so that there is no agreeable common definition of the word.[74]

1978 Crenshaw Hutchinson

The concept of terrorism is both historically and theoretically an inexact one. . . . Since there is no commonly accepted definition of terrorism, this analysis begins by proposing one that both corresponds to the reality of the Algerian case and potentially applies to other examples of revolutionary terrorism. . . . The essential components of a definition can be summarized as follows:

1 Terrorism is a systematic and purposeful method used by a revolutionary organization to seize political power from the incumbent government of a state.
2 Terrorism is manifested in a series of individual acts of extraordinary and intolerable violence.
3 Terrorism involves a consistent pattern of symbolic or representative selection of its physical victims or objects.
4 Terrorism is deliberately intended to create a psychological effect on specific groups of people (with the nature of the effect varying according to the identity of the group) in order to change political behaviour and attitudes in a manner consonant with the achievement of revolutionary objectives. . . . In its most extreme form, terrorism creates 'terror', an emotional state of extreme fear and anxiety. It differs from other instruments of violence because it 'lies beyond the norms of violent political agitation that are accepted by a given society. . . . Its victims are usually civilians, although they may include the military or the police, and the scene is normally a peaceful one – in which such violence is surprising. . . . The relationship between terrorist and victim distinguishes terrorism from simple sabotage or assassination.[75]

1978 Evans and Murphy

The threat or use of violence by private persons for political ends, where the conduct itself or its political objectives, or both, are international in scope.[76]

1978 Franck

It has been argued, on the one hand, that terrorism arises in response to governmental injustice and, on the other, that it is essentially a response to perceived governmental weakness. Some psychologists have argued that terrorism is an extreme search for 'meaning' and, consequently, is a subjective experience responsive to the psyche of the terrorist rather than being directly related to external variables.[77]

1978 Hamilton

For the purposes of this study, the following definition will be used: Terrorism consists of (1) planned acts of violence, employed for (2) explicitly political purposes, ultimately directed against (3) an established state or organizational power, and involving (4) a relatively small number of conspirators. Additional characteristics include a typically sporadic pattern of activity and, frequently, an emphasis on civilian rather than purely military targets. The definition is intended to distinguish terrorism from apolitical criminal violence, mass turmoil such as demonstrations, riots, or strikes, and from larger political violence phenomena involving large-scale or continuous fighting or widespread popular revolts. It would also be desirable to make a clear distinction between terrorism and small-scale guerrilla war, but here the line (drawn between two types of small-scale insurgent conspiracies) becomes less clear. A theoretical distinction based on dissimilar tactics on rural vs. urban bases will encounter a number of exceptions when put into practice. It seems better, for present purposes, to emphasize the similarities rather than force a problematic separation. The definition above excludes conservative, pro-government violence as well, whether in the form of covertly authorized vigilantism or of undisguised police power. With this exclusion, the definition in effect corresponds to the most general Western use of the word.[78]

1978   Holton

Terrorism is a method of coercion of a population or its leadership through fear or traumatization. What usually catches our attention is an act that attempts to impose terror by individuals or small groups on other individuals or groups and through them indirectly on their governments. . . . Type I terrorism consists of acts that attempt to impose terror by individuals or small groups on other individuals and groups and through them indirectly on their governments. Type II terrorism is the imposition by governments on individuals or on groups of local or foreign populations, e.g. the use of atomic weapons, poison gas, Nazi camps for genocide. The new type of terrorism – Type III – has all the components for success. Type III terrorism results from states disseminating high-level technology. Target nations will not have opened to them the conventional responses and will have to devise new methods.[79]

1978   Jenkins

At some point in this expanding use of the term, terrorism can mean just what those who use the term (not the terrorist) want it to mean – almost any violent act by an opponent. The difficulty of defining terrorism has led to the cliché that one man's terrorist is another man's freedom fighter. The phrase implies that there can be no objective definition of terrorism, that there is no universal standard of conduct in peace or war. That is not true. . . . The rules of war grant civilian non-combatants at least theoretical immunity from deliberate attack. They prohibit taking civilian hostages and actions against those held captive. The rules of war recognize neutral territory. Terrorists recognize no neutral territory, no non-combatants, no bystanders. . . . One man's terrorist is everyone's terrorist. Terrorism, in the Rand chronology, is defined by the nature of the act, not by the identity of the perpetrators or the nature of their cause. All terrorist acts are crimes – murder, kidnappings, and arson. Many would also be violations of the rules of war, if a state of war existed. All involve violence or the threat of violence, often coupled with specific demands. The violence is directed mainly against civilian targets. The motives are political. The actions generally are carried out in a way that will achieve maximum publicity. The perpetrators are usually members of an organized group, and unlike other criminals, they often claim credit for the act. And finally the act is intended to produce effects beyond the immediate physical damage. The fear created by terrorists may be intended to cause people to exaggerate the strength of the terrorists and the importance of their cause, to provoke extreme reactions, to discourage dissent, or to enforce compliance. This definition of terrorism would not limit the application of term solely to nongovernmental groups. Governments, their armies, their secret police may also be terrorists. Certainly the threat of torture is a form of terrorism designed to inspire dread of obedience to authorities.[80]

1978 Kaplan

What is terror? The term functions as a political symbol, as well as a category of political science. . . . I mean by terror the use of force primarily to produce a certain fearful state of mind – terror in fact. Some element of fear is evoked by every exercise of power; in terror this element looms large, whether as cause or as reason. Moreover, the fear is to be evoked in someone other than those to whom the force is applied. Terror is the use of force in a context which differentiates the victim of the violence employed from the target of the action. Since victim and target may be related in various ways, the distinction between them may be unclear or debatable. Machine-gunning school children or bombing a civilian airliner are unmistakable acts of terror, since the victims are not involved in whatever motivated the acts, and so cannot be the targets. . . . The killing of an isolated soldier in a barroom may be an act of terror even though he is not only victim but also part of the target. Related to the distinction between target and victim is that between demands made by the terrorists and the aim of his act of terror. . . . Terror appears to be lacking a moral when it is only demands that are lacking; the aim – to terrorize – may be apparent just because the victims cannot in any way be mistaken for targets.[81]

1978 Karanović

In conclusion, terrorism may be defined as systematic and organized violence against non-resisting persons to create fear in them for the purpose of retaining or gaining governmental authority, or for the purpose of using that authority for exploitation or oppression or to extract political concessions.[82]

1978 Lösche

In general, terrorism can be understood as a form of exercise of power based on the systematic production of fear and fright. This definition encompasses also the utilization of terror by institutions of the state for the maintenance of [the regime's] own rule, as is, for instance, known in the case of fascist and Stalinist regimes. However, if one excludes the use of force on the part of the state or social and political classes, e.g. groups during a revolution, then one can define terrorism in a narrow sense as a method by which an organized group tries to realize its goals by the systematic threat or application of violence (usually in the form of a surprise coup) which, as a rule, is directed against such persons and objects as represent or symbolize state or public authority One can identify three characteristics for this type of terrorism:

1 The direct, immediate and present threat or use of violence against objects or persons.
2 The organized and systematic cooperation of several perpetrators in a group. . . .
3 The reference to a political goal. . . . [83]

1978 Mickolus

The use, or threat of use, of anxiety-inducing extra-normal violence for political purposes by an individual or group, whether acting for or in opposition to established governmental authority, when such action is intended to influence the attitudes and behaviour of a target group wider than the immediate victims and when, through the nationality or foreign ties of its perpetrators, its location, the nature of its institutional or human victims, or the mechanics of its resolution, its ramifications transcend national boundaries.[84]

1978 Schreiber

Definitions are important, since the rhetoric of political denunciation brands with the term 'terrorist' those people whom others may call 'revolutionaries', 'freedom fighters', or 'founding fathers', and since, on the other side, small-time criminals or unhinged fanatics have dignified their images with pretended political motives. In what follows we will not go far wrong if we define terrorism as a political act, ordinarily committed by an organized group, involving death or the threat of death to non-combatants. This definition excludes private kidnappings designed to extort money, and it excludes both gangland killings prompted by revenge motives or power struggles and well-publicized but essentially non-political acts of murder, even mass murder, committed by deranged individuals or fanatical groups. What makes the terrorist act political is its motive and its direction: It must be the intent of the perpetrators to harm or radically alter the state.[85]

1978   Schwind

Following former attempts to reach a definition, terrorism could perhaps be described more precisely also as:

- a (primarily) politically motivated behaviour;
- of a non-state group without electoral prospects in a democratic context which aims;
- by means of violent acts against persons and/or property;
- to coerce people (especially the political leadership of democratic states) in order to obtain its will thereby.[86]

1978   Shultz

Political terrorism may be defined as the threat and/or use of extra-normal forms of political violence, in varying degrees, with the objective of achieving certain political objectives/goals. Such goals constitute the long-range and short-term objectives that the group or movement seeks to obtain. These will differ from group to group. Such action generally is intended to influence the behaviour and attitudes of certain targeted groups much wider than its immediate victims. However, influencing behaviour is not necessarily the only aim of terrorist acts. The ramifications of political terrorism may or may not extend beyond national boundaries.[87]

1978   Zawodny

Political terrorism is the weapon of the impatient and/or the disparate used in order to change values and institutions through extralegal means. Whether the terrorist is a 'bandit' or a hero will depend on the observer's own order of values. Terrorism is a weapon that has dynamics of its own. It is a weapon that can and does get out of hand among those who use it, especially in urban settings.[88]

1978   Zinam

Though it has been stated that is useless to argue about conflicting classifications, the use of terms and their definitions is not neutral. This is especially true if the term conveys a pejorative connotation, like violence. . . . Force is morally neutral like power, its source. It can be used for both good and bad ends. Violence is defined here as an illegitimate use of force. . . . Terrorism is the apex of violence. Once violence is defined, the definition of terrorism is a comparatively easy task. It is important to note that 'violence may occur without terror, but not terror without violence'. . . . In this study, terrorism is broadly defined as the use or threat of violence by individuals or by organized groups to evoke fear and submission to attain some economic, political, socio-psychological, ideological, or other objective.[89]

1979 Bassiouni

[A] consensus definition proposed by this author has achieved a significant degree of international acceptance. It generally defines 'terrorism' as: A strategy of unlawful violence calculated to inspire terror in the general public or a significant segment thereof in order to achieve a power-outcome or to propagandize a particular claim or grievance. Using this general definition, it was possible to draft a more specific definition of international terrorism in this manner: International terrorism consists of acts of terrorism containing an international element or directed against an international target. Such conduct contains an international element when:

1   The perpetrator and victim are citizens of different states; or
2   The conduct is performed in whole or in part in more than one state. Internationally protected targets are:
    • innocent civilians;
    • duly accredited diplomats and personnel of international organizations acting in their official capacities;
    • international civil aviations;
    • the mail and other means of international communications;
    • members of non-belligerent armed forces.

Under the above-stated consensus definition of terrorism, it is distinguished from other forms of violence in that it employs a strategy calculated to inspire terror whereas in other acts of violence, terror is of incidental importance. In common crimes of violence, terror (other than the victim's) is totally unintended. Moreover, common criminals shun publicity for obvious reasons whereas ideologically motivated offenders seek to instil terror in the general public in order to achieve their power-outcome. Thus, whereas all acts of violence are capable of producing some terror, 'terroristic' acts are those calculated to produce terror as part of a coercive strategy to achieve an essentially political outcome. By an elaboration of this concept, acts of terrorism may be more readily contrasted with other forms of violence and consequently other sub-categories of terror violence may emerge.[90]

1979 Karanovič

[T]errorism may be defined as systematic and organized violence against non-resistant persons to create fear in them for the purpose of retaining or gaining governmental authority, or for the purpose of using that authority for exploitation or oppression or to extract political concessions.[91]

1980 Allemann

[I]t seems of the utmost importance to draw a clear line between 'unconventional' warfare used in civil strife such as guerrilla or partisan activities on the one hand, and terrorist campaigns on the other. The claim of the terrorists to constitute a type of 'urban guerrilla' has to be recognized as a semantic trick aimed not only at being recognized as a belligerent party but also at masking the essentially criminal nature of their methods. On the other hand, it would be equally misleading to subsume every politically motivated crime under the heading of 'terrorism'. As far as actions such as murder attempts upon political opponents pursue precise and limited aims and are directed against exactly defined individual targets, they belong to a different category altogether – which, of course, is not a matter of moral judgement but simply of phenomenological exactitude. It would be commendable, therefore, to restrict the concept of terrorism to what the word implies: to those actions and series of actions that are designed to create an atmosphere of terror, to spread a more or less generalized feeling of utter insecurity and panic either in the ranks of the administration, its security forces, and the ruling social strata or in the public at large. This does not exclude, of course, that a campaign of this kind may be combined with some limited and strictly practical aims such as the pressing for the release of arrested underground activists. Such aims are, however, integrated in and subordinated to a more far-reaching purpose: to provoke and foster a previously non-existing 'revolutionary situation', to convince larger masses of the possibilities of an 'armed struggle', and to discredit and humiliate the constituted state authorities. Under this perspective, the practice of taking hostages is proving more and more a classical weapon of modern terrorism because it serves both purposes equally well: the purpose of exacting specific concessions from the state and the purpose of demonstrating the helplessness of its organs, thereby alienating the masses from the institutions of a political and social system incapable of protecting itself and its servants against the onslaught of a tiny but militant minority.[92]

1980   Hacker

Terror and terrorism very rarely represent senseless, explosive outbursts, symptomatically signifying loss of control, but are predominantly instances of strategic, deliberate purposeful aggression, carefully timed and figured out to produce optimal results, that is, maximal audience reaction and participation. Terror, which is inflicted from above, is the manufacture and spread of fear by dictators, governments, and bosses. It is the attempt of the powerful to exert control through intimidation. Terrorism, which is imposed from below, is the manufacture and spread of fear by rebels, revolutionaries and protesters. It is the attempt of the so far powerless, the would-be powerful, to exert control through intimidation. Terror and terrorism are not the same, but they belong together, indissolubly linked by the shared belief that fear is the strongest, if not the only, effective human motivation and that violence is the best if not the only method to produce and maintain fear. On the terrorists (not definition): Terrorists can be roughly divided into three groups according to their main motivations: the crazy, the criminal, and the crusading (the most typical variety). Crusading terrorists are idealistically inspired. They seek, not personal gain, but prestige and power for a collective goal; they believe that they act in the service of a higher cause.[93]

1980   Mickolus

The working definition of international/transnational terrorism used by the ITERATE project is the use, or threat of use, of anxiety-inducing, extra-normal violence for political purposes by any individual or group, whether acting for or in opposition to established governmental authority, when such action is intended to influence the attitudes and behaviour of a target group wider than the immediate victims and when, through the nationality or foreign ties of its perpetrators, its location, the nature of its institutional or human victims, or the mechanics of its resolution, its ramifications transcend national boundaries.[94]

1980   Schmid and de Graaf

Terrorism is the deliberate and systematic use or threat of violence against instrumental (human) targets (C) in a conflict between two (A, B) or more parties, whereby the immediate victims C – who might not even be part of the conflicting parties – cannot, through a change of attitude or behaviour, dissociate themselves from the conflict.[95]

1981   Green

Terrorist and terrorism refers to anyone who attempts to further his views of coercive intimidation.[96]

1981 Hess

By terrorism, I wish to understand

1   a series of deliberate acts of direct, physical violence, which is applied
2   intermittently and unpredictably, yet systematically
3   with the goal of psychic effectiveness
4   in the framework of a political strategy.[97]

1981 Hess

. . . the threat or use of violence for political purposes by individuals or groups, whether acting for, or in opposition to, established governmental authority, when such actions are intended to shock or intimidate a large group wider than the immediate victims.[98]

1981 Lodge

. . . the resort to violence for political ends by unauthorized, non-governmental actors in breach of accepted codes of behaviour regarding the expression of dissatisfaction with, dissent from or opposition to the pursuit of political goals by the legitimate government authorities of the state whom they regard as unresponsive to the needs of certain groups of people.[99]

1981 Sederberg

[T]errorism may be usefully defined as severe acts of violence directed at non-combatants by the contending sides of a political struggle.[100]

1982 Devine and Rafalko

We define terrorism as violence directed, as a matter of political strategy, against innocent persons.[101]

1982 Quainton

(International) Terrorism = 'the threat or use of violence for political purposes when such action is intended to influence the attitudes and behaviour of a group wider than its immediate victims; its ramifications transcend national boundaries'.[102]

1983 Army Regulation 310-25 U.S. Army, Dictionary of United States Army Terms

The use or threat of violence in furtherance of a political aim.[103]

1983 Wilkins

Terrorism is the attempt to achieve political, social, economic, or religious change by the actual or threatened use of violence against persons or property; the violence employed in terrorism is aimed partly at destabilizing the existing political or social order, but mainly at publicizing the goals or cause espoused by the terrorists; often, though not always, terrorism is aimed at provoking extreme counter-measures which will win public support for the terrorists and their cause.[104]

1984 Anand

[T]errorism is described as the art of compelling an individual, group, or authority to adopt a particular disposition or accept the imposed demands under conditions of fear created by passive action or violence – demonstrated, threatened or implied.[105]

1984   German Federal Republic, Ministry of the Interior

Terrorism is the enduringly conducted struggle for political goals, which are intended to be achieved by means of assaults on the life and property of other persons, especially by means of severe crimes as detailed in art. 129a, sect. 1 of the penal law book (above all: murder, homicide, extortionist kidnapping, arson, setting off a blast by explosives) or by means of other acts of violence, which serve as preparation of such criminal acts.[106]

1984   Hoffmann

Terrorism is a purposeful human political activity, which is directed toward the creation of a general climate of fear, and is designed to influence, in ways desired by the protagonist, other human beings and, through them, some course of events.[107]

1984   Nanes

Terrorism is a violent act or an act dangerous to human life in violation of the criminal laws of any state to intimidate or coerce a government, the civilian population, or any segment thereof in furtherance of political or social objectives.[108]

1984   Nutter

In terrorism studies the basic issue is usually called the 'definitional problem', the delineation of explicit criteria by which one may judge an event or group to be either terrorist or not (see Jenkins, 1978: 1). The absence of well-defined and operationalized limits on the behaviour labelled 'terrorism' is a critical lacuna. It is difficult to research terrorism for two reasons. First, the term is often applied 'promiscuously' to include nearly the entire spectrum of socio-political violence and conflict. Second, more rigorous scholarly specifications are often produced and then ignored. The end result is confusion. . . . Yet the problem goes beyond that of simple definition. The basic epistemological assumption is that terrorism is a discrete behaviour, conceptually and operationally isolable from 'legitimate' political violence, guerrilla warfare, banditry, civil war, criminal violence, etc. This view may be termed the 'box' approach to terrorism (and conflict), or in Bell's language, the 'terrorist pigeonhole'. The box view implies that there are some criteria by which events may be classified – all events within a box meet same criteria. Less than rigorous specification and application of the criteria is what is commonly meant by the 'definitional problem', which has led to inappropriate comparisons. But terrorism is not a unitary concept, nor even necessarily a class of homogeneous acts. It is labelled a tactic, as indeed it is, considered against the broader background of social conflict (see Gurr for one classification scheme). However, terrorism is actually several tactics lumped together. Commonly, one thinks of skyjacking, kidnapping, bombing, assassination, and hostage taking as acts of terrorism. That they are categorized together implies some underlying basis of identity, presumably tapped by common characteristics. . . . Categories are merely simplifications. Perhaps terrorism, or small-scale violence, is not amenable to this kind of simplification. Surely the measurement of its characteristics is not truly dichotomous. There are innumerable degrees of violence. The continuum of violence stretches from a few dollars worth of property damage to the massacre of hundreds of people. The coerciveness of violence can at least be divided into three categories – non-coercive, indirect or implied coercion (making an example of someone), and direct coercion. There are many degrees of 'politicalness' and target discrimination and legitimacy . . . . We should not be dealing with boxes at all.[109]

1984   Schmid

Terrorism is a method of combat in which random or symbolic victims serve as an instrumental target of violence. These instrumental victims share group characteristics, which form the basis for their selection for victimization. Through previous use of violence or the credible threat of violence other members of that group or class are put in a state of chronic fear (terror). This group or class, whose members' sense of security is purposefully undermined, is the target of terror. The victimization of the target of violence is considered extra-normal by most observers from the witnessing audience on the basis of its atrocity, the time (e.g. peacetime) or place (not a battlefield) of victimization, or the disregard for rules of combat accepted in conventional warfare. The norm violation creates an attentive audience beyond the target of terror; sectors of this audience might in turn form the main object of manipulation. The purpose of this indirect method of combat is either to immobilize the target of terror in order to produce disorientation and/or compliance, or to mobilize secondary targets of demands (e.g. a government) or targets of attention (e.g. public opinion) to changes of attitude or behaviour favouring the short or long-term interests of the users of this method of combat.[110]

1984   Schmid
Act of Terrorism = Peacetime Equivalent of War Crime

1   Deliberate attacks on civilians;
2   Taking of hostages;
3   Killing of Prisoners/Kidnapped Persons.[111]

1984   Smith
California, one of the few states to provide a definition of terrorism in its criminal code, specifies that terrorize as used in its statute means: to create a climate of fear and intimidation by means of threats or violent action causing sustained fear for personal safety in order to achieve social or political goals.[112]

1984   US Federal Bureau of Investigation
Terrorism is defined as the unlawful use of force or violence against persons or property to intimidate or coerce a government, the civilian population, or any segment thereof, in furtherance of political or social objectives.

On the Terrorist Incident (not definition): a terrorist incident is defined as a violent act or an act dangerous to human life in violation of the criminal laws of the US or of any state to intimidate or coerce a government, the civilian population, or any segment thereof, in furtherance of political or social objectives.[113]

1984   Wellman
A terrifying act which is used to coerce with the threat of great harm of one or more persons if the threat is not heeded.[114]

1985   Coady
A political act, ordinarily committed by an organized group, which involves the intentional killing or other severe harming of non-combatants or the threat of the same or intentional severe damage to the property of non-combatants or the threat of the same.[115]

1985   Gordon
Terrorism: the systematic use of violence and intimidation to achieve an end. International terrorism: events of terrorism which extend across the boundaries of two or more nations, involving actions such as skyjacking and the bombing of targets in international offices and airports.[116]

1986   Ahmad
Let us begin with the dictionary definition of terror – 'intense, overpowering fear' – and

of terrorism – 'the use of terrorizing methods of governing or resisting a government'. The simple definition has the virtue of fairness; it focuses on the use of coercive violence and its effects on the victims of terror without regard to the status of the perpetrator. Terrorism does not refer to the mutual fear of armed adversaries, but only to acts of intimidating and injuring unarmed, presumably innocent civilians. Therein lies the revulsion over terrorist acts. This definition leaves out the question of motivation. Motives have varied, and so have methods. Many terrorists in our time have no identifiable goals. There are five sources of terrorism – state, religion, protest/revolution, crime and pathology. Only the first three have political motivation.[117]

1986   Gunter

Terrorism is a phenomenon that usually stems from the failure of its perpetrators to develop sufficient political and military strength to present their case in a more conventional manner.[118]

1986   Gurr

I accept the essential accuracy and utility of Thornton's classic definition of the subject matter: 'terror is a symbolic act designed to influence political behaviour by extraordinary means, entailing the use or threat of violence' (Thornton, 1964: 73). It is consistent with this conception to regard terrorist incidents as tactics used in political conflicts within countries and among them. . . . I also assume that terror as a tactic is not inherently or uniquely revolutionary and is in fact used in the pursuit of a great many different kinds of political and other objectives. . . . 'Terrorism' is a doctrine about the efficacy of unexpected, dramatic, and life-threatening violence for inducing political change, and a strategy of political action which embodies that doctrine. Particular opposition groups may rely exclusively on terror tactics – i.e. a strategy of terrorism – or use them occasionally along with other tactics, as many guerrilla movements do, or use them not at all.[119]

1986   Mitchell *et al.*

[T]errorism by the state (or non-state actors) involves deliberate coercion and violence (or the threat thereof) directed at some victim, with the intention of inducing extreme fear in some target observers who identify with that victims in such a way that they perceive themselves as potential future victims. In this way, they are forced to consider altering their behaviour in some manner desired by the actor.[120]

1986   Kaufman

Terrorism is a word coined by society to deplore a particular kind of political violence that lies wholly outside of accepted conventions of warfare. . . . Since medieval times, philosophers have recognized the distinction between jus ad bellum, the justice of war, and jus in bello, justice in war. Terrorism is more a civilian strategy than what we commonly call war, but the distinction remains meaningful in this area as well. The moral reality of war is divided into two logically independent parts. We make judgements about the broader issues of aggression and self-defence; but, employing a separate calculus, we make judgements about the observance or violation of the customary and positive rules of engagement. By the same token, we must keep distinct our feelings about the terrorist's cause, on the one hand, and the illegitimate means that he uses to advance that cause, on the other. Simply put, the random murder of innocent people is always terrorism, even when representatives of the most oppressed people on the face of the earth perpetrate it.[121]

1986   Netanyahu

Terrorism is the deliberate and systematic murder, maiming, and menacing of the innocent to inspire fear for political ends.[122]

1986 Wilkinson

Terrorism is the systematic use of murder and destruction in order to terrorize individuals, groups, communities or governments into conceding to the terrorists' political demands. Terrorism is a specific method of struggle rather than a synonym for political violence or insurgency.[123]

1986 Wilkinson

Political terrorism may be briefly defined as a special form of clandestine, undeclared and unconventional warfare, waged without any humanitarian restraints or rules.[124]

1987 *Encyclopaedia Britannica*

The systematic use of terror or unpredictable violence against governments, publics, individuals to attain a political objective. Terrorism has been used by political organizations with both rightist and leftist objectives, by nationalistic and ethnic groups, by revolutionaries, and by the arms and secret police of governments themselves.[125]

1987 Ezeldin

Terrorism is a systematic and persistent strategy of violence practised by a state or political group against another state or political group through a campaign of acts of violence, such as murder, assassination, hijacking, and the use of explosives or the like, with the intent of creating a state of terror and public intimidation to achieve political ends.[126]

1987 Laqueur

Most authors agree that terrorism is the use or the threat of use of violence, a method of combat, or a strategy to achieve certain targets, that it aims to induce a state of fear in the victim, that it is ruthless and does not conform with humanitarian rules, and that publicity is an essential factor in the terrorist strategy.[127]

1987 Lynch

Terrorism is commonly defined as the use of violence and threats to use violence as a political weapon to achieve control, to influence government policy, and/or to destabilize and even overthrow government.[128]

1987 South Asian Association for Region Cooperation (SAARC)
Art. 1:
Subject to the overall requirements of the law of extradition, conduct constituting any of the following offences, according to the law of the Contracting State, shall be regarded as terroristic and for the purpose of extradition shall not be regarded as a political offence or as an offence connected with a political offence or as an offence inspired by political motives:

(a) An offence within the scope of the Convention for the Suppression of Unlawful Seizure of Aircraft, signed at The Hague on December 16, 1970;

(b) An offence within the scope of the Convention for the Suppression of Unlawful Acts against the Safety of Civil Aviation, signed at Montreal on September 23, 1971;

(c) An offence within the scope of the Convention on the Prevention and Punishment of Crimes against Internationally Protected Persons, including Diplomatic Agents, signed at New York on December 14, 1973;

(d) An offence within the scope of any Convention to which the SAARC member States concerned are parties and which obliges the parties to prosecute or grant extradition;

(e) Murder, manslaughter, assault causing bodily harm, kidnapping, hostage-taking and offences relating to firearms, weapons, explosives and dangerous substances when used as a means to perpetrate indiscriminate violence involving death or serious bodily injury to persons or serious damage to property;

(f) An attempt or conspiracy to commit an offence described in sub-paragraphs (a) to (e), aiding, abetting or counselling the commission of such an offence or participating as an accomplice in the offences so described].[129]

1987   Thackrah

Terrorism is an organized system of extreme and violent intimidation to create instability within democracies. International terrorists seek to launch indiscriminate and unpredictable attacks on groups (police, army, multinational business, etc.) or nations to change the politico economic balance of the world.[130]

1987   Wardlaw

The threat or use of violence by an individual or a group, whether acting for or in opposition to established authority, when such action is designed to create extreme anxiety and/or fear-inducing effects in a target population larger than the immediate victims with the purpose of coercing that group into acceding to the political demands of the perpetrators.[131]

1987   Wilkinson

Terrorism can briefly be defined as coercive intimidation, or more fully as the systematic use of murder, injury and destruction, or threat of same, to create a climate of terror, to publicize a cause and to coerce a wider target into submitting to the terrorists' aims.[132]

1988   Della Porta

Terrorism is the action of clandestine political organizations, of small dimensions, which try to reach political aims through a continuous and almost exclusive use of violent forms of action.[133]

1988   Linn

At an international conference in Jerusalem (1979), terrorism was defined as 'the deliberate and systematic murder, maiming, and menacing of the innocent to inspire fear for political ends'.[134]

1988   Mozaffari

Political terrorism is use of violence or the threat thereof to achieve a political end by means of creating fear, frustration and insecurity. Political terrorism always carries a political message.[135]

1988   Ross

Terrorism is a method of combat in which random or symbolic victims are targets of violence. Through previous use of violence or the credible threat of violence other members of that group or class are put in a state of chronic fear. The victimization of the target is considered extra-normal by most observers, which creates an audience beyond the target of terror. The purpose of terrorism is either to immobilize secondary targets of demands or targets of attention.[136]

1988   Schmid

Academic Consensus Definition: 'Terrorism is an anxiety-inspiring method of repeated violent action, employed by (semi-) clandestine individual, group, or state actors, for idiosyncratic, criminal, or political reasons, whereby – in contrast to assassination – the direct targets of violence are not the main targets. The immediate human victims of violence are generally chosen randomly (targets of opportunity) or selectively (representative or symbolic targets) from a target population, and serve as message generators. Threat- and violence-based communication processes between terrorist (organization), (imperilled) victims, and main targets are used to manipulate the main target (audience(s)), turning it into a target of terror, a target of demands, or a target of attention, depending on whether intimidation, coercion, or propaganda is primarily sought.[137]

1988 Townsend

The use of force by the armed (meaning not merely 'weaponed' but also psychologically prepared) against the unarmed.[138]

1989 Alexander and Sinai

Terrorism is the deliberate employment of violence or the threat of the use of violence by sovereign states or the sub-national groups encouraged or assisted by sovereign states, to attain strategic and political objectives by acts of violation of law. These criminal acts are intended to create overwhelming fear in a target population larger than the civilian or military victims attacked or threatened.[139]

1989 Crelinsten

I define terrorism as the combined use of threat and violence against one set of targets (victims) to compel compliance or allegiance from another set of targets (the object of explicit or implied demands) and to impress a wider audience.[140]

1989 Hudson

[Terrorism is] the sudden, unexpected act of shocking, calculated, and unlawful violence, or the plausible threat of such violence, by an illegal, sub-national, clandestine group – usually carried out in a peaceful, civilian environment – be it urban, rural, in the air or on a body of water – against certain non-combatants or targets that represent or symbolize a certain country, but sometimes indiscriminately against bystanders or passers by at a particular location, with the intention of garnering publicity, propagandizing a cause, and intimidating as many people as possible in order to attain social, political, or strategic objectives.[141]

1989 Lackey

(Wartime) terrorism is the threat or use of violence against non-combatants for political purposes. In ordinary war, the deaths of civilians are side effects of military operations directed against military targets. In terrorist operations, the civilian is the direct and intentional target of attack.[142]

1989 Murphy

Acts of international terrorism include but are not limited to atrocities, wanton killing, hostage taking, hijacking, extortion, or torture committed or threatened to be committed whether in peacetime or in wartime for political purposes provided that an international element is involved. An act of terrorism is deemed to have an international element when the offence is committed within the jurisdiction of one country, a) against any foreign government or international organization, or any representative thereof; or b) against any national of a foreign country because he is a national of a foreign country; or c) by a person who crosses an international frontier into another country from which his extradition is requested.[143]

1989   Rimanelli
Terrorism is commonly defined as a violent form of political struggle employed by revolutionary groups to maximize their meagre forces and topple domestic regimes through a strategy of terror.[144]

1989   USSR Ministry of the Interior
International terrorism represents the sum total of the following activities:

a)   illegal and premeditated acts of violence committed by people (or by a group of people) on the territory of a state directed toward foreign nationals or international organs or institutions, or toward personnel, means of international transportation or communication, and other foreign or international objects;

b)   illegal or premeditated acts of violence committed by people (or groups of people) organized or supported by a foreign state on a given state's territory directed toward national state organs or public institutions, national political or public figures, populations or other objects.

(Addition in the Soviet version: 'The goal of terrorism is to obtain privileges or advantages illegally from a larger group of people against whom the terrorism is immediately directed'.) [Definition proposed by a participant from the Soviet Ministry of Interior and accepted by members of a joint conference of Soviet and American experts on terrorism in January 1989].[145]

1989   Wardlaw
Political terrorism is the use, or threat of use, of violence by an individual or group, whether acting for or in opposition to established authority, when such action is designed to create extreme anxiety and/or fear-inducing effects in a target group larger than the immediate victims with the purpose of coercing that group into acceding to the political demands of the perpetrators.[146]

1990   Allan
State terrorism – Terrorism as a governing instrument in an effort to preserve the state order.[147]

1990   Gal-Or
Terrorism is a kind of mini-warfare without a conventional military front. Its method of operation differs from one organization to another. Terrorism kills innocent citizens, but with regard to the security of the state.[148]

1990   Hewitt
The goal of insurgent terrorism is to alter the political situation by changing public opinion which purpose is to draw attention to some cause of grievance.[149]

1990   Hughes
By terrorists I mean those who take and threaten hostages, using their hostages' lives as a bargaining counter. By anti-terrorists those who try to oppose them by some equivalent threat if necessary in disregard of legal restrictions.[150]

1990 Weinberg

Terrorism is a type of politically motivated violence threatened or committed by private individuals for the purpose of influencing the behaviour of an audience wider than its immediate victims.[151]

1991 Bunzl

Terrorism is . . . a method to spread fear through repreated application of violence; this method is used conspiratively for political reasons by individuals, groups or states; the immediate victims are chosen either by chance or for symbolic reasons; the deed is accompanied by a message; the panic so created is meant to move whoever is the main addressee to certain actions desired by the terrorists.[152]

1991 George-Abeyie

Terror involves the use of force/violence or threat of force/violence for a political purpose. However, this threat, or actuality, of violence/force is utilized under the cloak of legality and can be the actions of state agents or non-state agents acting within the scope of the law. Terror is legitimate (i.e. legal). It is the legal, sanctioned, legitimate use of force/violence, or the threat thereof. It is this legal utilization of force/violence or threat with the multifaceted purpose noted previously (i.e. the instillation of a fear that 'paralyses then vanishes the will to resist' but does not necessarily physically destroy the opposition) that is unique. The essence of political terror is fear, not destruction. It is the reality of threatened legal force within recognized jure gentium nation-states that often leads to what the outside world views as a strange complacency or fatalism on the part of the oppressed.[153]

1991 Jackson

a) Terrorism is any organized set of acts of violence designed to create an atmosphere of despair or fear to shake the faith of ordinary citizens in their government and its representatives to destroy the structure of authority which normally stands for security or to reinforce and perpetuate a governmental regime whose popular support is shaky. b) Terrorism is a method of combat in which random or symbolic victims serve as an instrumental target of violence. These instrumental victims share group or class characteristics, which form the basis for their selection for victimization.[154]

1991 Narveson

A political action or sequence of actions . . . to inspire the 'target' population with terror, by means of random acts of violence.[155]

1991 Rabbie

Terrorism is a form of psychological warfare using violence, or the threat of it, and extreme fear aimed at modifying the attitudes and behaviour of a target audience in an attempt to achieve political objectives.[156]

1992 Crelinsten

Terrorism is the combined threat and use of violence, planned in secret and executed without warning, that is directed against one set of targets (the direct victims) in order to coerce compliance or to compel allegiance from a second set of targets (targets of demands) and to intimidate or to impress a wider audience (target of terror or target of attention).[157]

1992 Taylor Wilkins

Terrorism is the attempt to achieve political, social, economic, or religious change by the actual or threatened use of violence against persons or property; the violence employed in terrorism is aimed partly at destabilizing the existing political or social order, but mainly at publicizing the goals or cause espoused by the terrorists; often, though not always, terrorism is aimed at provoking extreme counter-measures which will win public support for the terrorists and their cause.[158]

1992   Walker

Terrorism is the use of violence for political ends and includes any use of violence for the purpose of putting the public or any section of the public in fear.[159]

1992   Wilkinson

There are a set of conditions or criteria accepted by all serious workers in the field, most of which were studied by Schmid and Jongman in their systematic review of the literature on terrorism. . . . It is, first of all, the systematic and premeditated use of violence to create a climate of extreme fear for political purposes. Second, it is violence directed at a wider audience – a wider target – than the immediate victim of the violence. Third, as a consequence of this wider targeting, it inevitably involves random and symbolic targets that include civilians. Fourth, it involves extra-normal means in a quite literal sense, which is to say, a deliberate violation of the norms of society regarding conflicts and disputes and political behaviour to create the impact of fear and exploitation of that fear for the terrorists' ends.[160]

1994   Freeman

Terrorism = the use of violence against non-combatants, civilians or other persons normally considered to be illegitimate targets of military action for the purpose of attracting attention to a political cause, forcing those aloof from the struggle to join in, or intimidating opponents into concessions.[161]

1994   Reilly

Terrorism is the use of intentional violence against non-combatants for political ends.[162]

1994   Reisman and Antoniou

Terrorism has come to mean the intentional use of violence against civilian and military targets generally outside of an acknowledged war zone by private groups or groups that appear to be private but have some measure of covert state sponsorship.[163]

1994   Schneider

Political terrorism can be understood as the use of violence or the threat of violence against persons or objects for political reasons, applied by individual persons or a group, acting on behalf or against a government. The terrorists want to hit, by their damaging impact on their direct victims, the target group (their immediate and real victim), which they want to coerce to actions which lie in their interest and which they want to realize.[164]

1995   Houghton

Terrorism is a political crime: an attack on the legitimacy of a specific government, ideology or policy.[165]

1997   Collin

Information terrorism is definition of terrorism through the exploitation of computerized systems deployed by the target.[166]

1997   Hoffman

Religious terrorism tends to be more lethal than secular terrorism because of the radically different value systems, mechanisms of legitimization and justification concepts of morality. For religious terrorist violence first and foremost is a sacramental act of divine duty: executed in direct response to some theological demands or imperative and justified by scripture.[167]

1997   Mullins

Left-wing terrorism is that terrorism intended to change a government to socialism, communism, or anarchism.[168]

1997   Mullins

Right-wing terrorism is terrorism based upon ideologies of racial . . . supremacy.[169]

1998   Anderson

Terrorism differs from ordinary criminal violence not merely because it involves politically motivated violence but mainly in its targeting and intended effects. Terrorism seeks deliberately to target largely non–combatants as its victims and to cultivate terror among both victims and spectators.[170]

1998   Arab League Convention on the Suppression of Terrorism

Article 1 (Definition and General Provisions) states:

Terrorism: Any act or threat of violence, whatever its motives or purposes, that occurs for the advancement of an individual or collective criminal agenda, causing terror among people, causing fear by harming them, or placing their lives, liberty or security in danger, or aiming to cause damage to the environment or to public or private installations or property or to occupy or seize them, or aiming to jeopardize a national resource.

Terrorist offence: Any offence or attempted offence committed in furtherance of a terrorist objective in any of the Contracting States, or against their nationals, property or interests, that is punishable by their domestic law. The offences stipulated in the following conventions, except where conventions have not been ratified by Contracting States or where offences have been excluded by their legislation, shall also be regarded as terrorist offences:

a)   The Tokyo Convention on Offences and Certain Other Acts Committed on Board Aircraft, of 14 September 1963;
b)   The Hague Convention for the Suppression of Unlawful Seizure of Aircraft, of 16 December 1970;
c)   The Montreal Convention for the Suppression of Unlawful Acts against the Safety of Civil Aviation, of 23 September 1971, and the Protocol thereto of 10 May 1984;
d)   The Convention on the Prevention and Punishment of Crimes against Internationally Protected Persons, including Diplomatic Agents, of 14 December 1973;
e)   The International Convention against the Taking of Hostages, of 17 December 1979;
f)   The provisions of the United Nations Convention on the Law of the Sea, of 1982, relating to piracy on the high seas.

Article 2 (Definition and General Provisions) states:
a)   All cases of struggle by whatever means, including armed struggle, against foreign occupation and aggression for liberation and self-determination, in accordance with

the principles of international law, shall not be regarded as an offence. This provision shall not apply to any act prejudicing the territorial integrity of any Arab State.[171]

1998   Chalk

Terrorism is an inexpensive method of warfare that can achieve relatively effective results, giving it a low cost. By utilizing the psychology of fear terrorism can artificially inflate the perceived strength and power projection of a group among a wide number of people. Terrorist acts involve comparatively little personal risk to the perpetrators and far less than more conventional forms of organized violence.[172]

1998   Davidson Smith

Single issue or issue-motivated terrorism can be understood as a form of anti-state terrorism that manifests itself as an extreme, illegitimate, and often violent response to a controversial issue within a given society. Generally, three principal issues are regarded to fall under that definition: animal rights, environmentalism, and abortion.[173]

1998   Ganor

Terrorism is the intentional use of, or threat to use violence against civilians or against civilian targets in order to attain political aims.[174]

1998   Hoffman

Terrorism: '. . . the deliberate creation and exploitation of fear through violence or the threat of violence in the pursuit of political change'.[175]

1998   Khatchadourian

Terrorism is distinguished from all other kinds of violence by its 'bifocal' character; namely, by the fact that the immediate acts of terrorist violence, such as shooting, bombings, kidnappings, and hostage taking, are intended as means to certain goals. In the case of political or political/moralistic/religious terrorism in particular, the acts are intended as means to certain intermediate or long-range or ultimate goals, which vary with the particular terrorist acts or series of such acts. In its bifocal character, terrorism is distinguished from straightforward, mono-focal acts of murder, sabotage, kidnappings, and hostage-taking as well as uprisings, rebellions, and revolutions, coup d'état, and civil war, and war. . . . The major types of terrorism are: predatory, retaliatory, political, and political-moralistic/religious. The terrorism may be domestic or international, 'from above' – i.e. state or state-sponsored terrorism – or from 'below'. Finally terrorism may occur in times of peace and times of war.[176]

1999   Advisory Panel to Assess Domestic Response Capabilities for Terrorism Involving Weapons of Mass Destruction

State-sponsored terrorism is defined . . . as the active involvement of a foreign government in training, arming, and providing other logistical and intelligence assistance as well as sanctuary to an otherwise autonomous terrorist group for the purpose of carrying out violent acts on behalf of that government against its enemies.[177]

1999   Byman

Ethnic terrorism: deliberate violence by a sub-national ethnic group to advance its cause. Such violence focuses either on the creation of a separate state or on the elevation of the status of the communal group over others.[178]

1999   Ganor

[T]errorism is a form of psychological warfare against the public morale, whereby terrorist organizations, through indiscriminate attacks, attempt to change the political agenda of the targeted population. The objective is to lead the civilian population to see the cessation of terrorist attacks as the single most important goal, outweighing any other national, social, economic, or other objectives. By convincing the target population that terrorist attacks can be stopped only by the appeasement of the terrorist organizations, the terrorists hope to win concessions to their demands. The greatest danger presented by terrorism is thus not necessarily the direct physical damage that it inflicts, but rather the injury to public morale and the impact on the way policymakers feel, think, and respond.[179]

1999   Medd and Goldstein

a. Terrorism is premeditated, politically motivated violence perpetrated against non-combatant targets by sub-national groups or clandestine agents, usually intended to influence an audience. b. International terrorism involving citizens or territory of more than one country. c. Terrorist group – any group practising, or that has any significant subgroups that practise, international terrorism. [180]

1999   Merari

Terrorism is a means, not a goal. Because it is the simplest form of armed struggle, it appears wherever and whenever there is a conflict that is sufficiently acute to generate the will of some people to resort to violence. . . . Personal motivation for resorting to terrorism may be different from the declared ideological goal. In itself, ideology is not enough to convince a person to engage in terrorism.[181]

1999   Organization of African Unity (OAU) Convention on the Prevention and Combating of Terrorism

Article 1(3) (Scope of Application) states:

'Terrorist act' means:

(a) any act which is a violation of the criminal laws of a State Party and which may endanger the life, physical integrity or freedom of, or cause serious injury or death to, any person, any number or group of persons or causes or may cause damage to public or private property, natural resources, environmental or cultural heritage and is calculated or intended to:

    (i) intimidate, put in fear, coerce or induce any government, body, institution, the general public or any segment thereof, to do or abstain from doing any act, or to adopt or abandon a particular standpoint, or to act according to certain principles; or

    (ii) disrupt any public service, the delivery of any essential service to the public or to create a public emergency; or

    (iii) create general insurrection in a State.

(b) any promotion, sponsoring, contribution to, command, aid, incitement, encouragement, attempt, threat, conspiracy, organizing, or procurement of any person, with the intent to commit any act referred to in paragraph (a) (i)–(iii).[182]

1999   Organization of the Islamic Conference

Article 1(2) (Definition and General Provisions) states:

'Terrorism' means any act of violence or threat thereof notwithstanding its motives or intentions perpetrated to carry out an individual or collective criminal plan with the aim of terrorizing people or threatening to harm them or imperilling their lives, honour, freedoms, security or rights or exposing the environment or any facility or public or private property to hazards or occupying or seizing them, or endangering a national resource, or international facilities, or threatening the stability, territorial integrity, political unity or sovereignty of independent States.

Article 1(3) (Definition and General Provisions) states:
'Terrorist Crime' means any crime executed, started or participated in to realize a terrorist objective in any of the Contracting States or against its nationals, assets or interests or foreign facilities and nationals residing in its territory punishable by its internal law.

Article 2 (Definition and General Provisions) states:
a) People's struggle including armed struggle against foreign occupation, aggression, colonialism, and hegemony, aimed at liberation and self-determination in accordance with the principles of international law shall not be considered a terrorist crime.
b) None of the terrorist crimes mentioned in the previous Article shall be considered political crimes.
c) In the implementation of the provisions of this Convention the following crimes shall not be considered political crimes even when politically motivated:
    1) Aggression against kings and heads of state of Contracting States or against their spouses, the ascendants or descendants.
    2) Aggression against crown princes or vice-presidents or deputy heads of government or ministers in any of the Contracting States.
    3) Aggression against persons enjoying international immunity including Ambassadors and diplomats in Contracting States or in countries of accreditation.
    4) Murder or robbery by force against individuals or authorities or means of transport and communications.
    5) Acts of sabotage and destruction of public properties and properties geared for public services, even if belonging to another Contracting State.
    6) Crimes of manufacturing, smuggling or possessing arms and ammunition or explosives or other materials prepared for committing terrorist crimes.
d) All forms of international crimes, including illegal trafficking in narcotics and human beings and money laundering aimed at financing terrorist objectives shall be considered terrorist crimes.[183]

1999   Richardson

Terrorism is politically motivated violence directed against non-combatant or symbolic targets which is designed to communicate a message to a broader audience. The critical feature of terrorism is the deliberate targeting of innocents in an effort to convey a message to another party.[184]

1999   Treaty on Cooperation among States Members of the Commonwealth of Independent States in Combating Terrorism

'Terrorism' – an illegal act punishable under criminal law committed for the purpose of undermining public safety, influencing decision-making by the authorities or terrorizing the population, and taking the form of:

*   Violence or the threat of violence against natural or juridical persons;
*   Destroying (damaging) or threatening to destroy (damage) property and other material objects so as to endanger people's lives;
*   Causing substantial harm to property or the occurrence of other consequences dangerous to society;

- Threatening the life of a statesman or public figure for the purpose of putting an end to his State or other public activity or in revenge for such activity;
- Attacking a representative of a foreign State or an internationally protected staff member of an international organization, as well as the business premises or vehicles of internationally protected persons;
- Other acts classified as terrorist under the national legislation of the Parties or under universally recognized international legal instruments aimed at combating terrorism;

'Technological terrorism' – the use or threat of the use of nuclear, radiological, chemical or bacteriological (biological) weapons or their components, pathogenic micro-organisms, radioactive substances or other substances harmful to human health, including the seizure, putting out of operation or destruction of nuclear, chemical or other facilities posing an increased technological and environmental danger and the utility systems of towns and other inhabited localities, if these acts are committed for the purpose of undermining public safety, terrorizing the population or influencing the decisions of the authorities in order to achieve political, mercenary or any other ends, as well as attempts to commit one of the crimes listed above for the same purposes and leading, financing or acting as the instigator, accessory or accomplice of a person who commits or attempts to commit such a crime.[185]

1999   US Department of State (Title 22 of the US Code, Section 2656 (d))
The term 'terrorism' means premeditated, politically motivated violence perpetrated against non-combatant targets by subnational groups or clandestine agents, usually intended to influence an audience. The term 'international terrorism' means terrorism involving citizens or the territory of more than one country. The term 'terrorist group' means any group practising, or that has significant subgroups that practice, international terrorism.[186]

2000   Collins and Horowitz
CBRN terrorism is . . . terrorism where a chemical, biological, radiological, or nuclear device is used or those elements are brought into play by other means, such as a conventional attack on a nuclear power plant.[187]

2000   Combs
[Terrorism is] a synthesis of war and theatre, a dramatization of the most proscribed kind of violence – that which is perpetrated on innocent victims – played before an audience in the hope of creating a mood of fear, for political purposes.[188]

2000   de Mesquita
Terrorism = any act of violence undertaken for the purpose of altering a government's political policies or actions that targets those who do not actually have the personal authority to alter governmental policy.[189]

2000   Laos
A functional definition of terrorism should include the following elements:

(i)   The existence of non-combatant casualties or the indiscriminate use of violence,
(ii) The purpose is to create a public danger or a state of terror,
(iii) The ultimate is to influence an audience and serve ideological, social, philosophical or other ends,
(iv) Those actively committing the criminal offences are non-state or state-sponsored groups agents.[190]

2000 Malik

We may therefore now attempt to define terrorism as the deliberate creation and exploitation of fear through violence or the threat of violence in the pursuit of political change. All terrorist acts involve violence or the threat of violence. Terrorism is specifically designed to have far-reaching psychological effects beyond the immediate victim(s) or object of the terrorist attack.[191]

2001 Coady

Intentionally targeting non-combatants with lethal or severe violence for political purposes.[192]

2001 Cooper

Terrorism is the intentional generation of massive fear by human beings for the purpose of securing or maintaining control over other human beings.[193]

2001 EU Definition of Terrorism

Offences intentionally committed by an individual or a group against one or more countries, their institutions or people, with the aim of intimidating them and seriously altering or destroying the political, economic, or social structures of a country.[194]

2001 The Mitchell Commission report on the Palestinian–Israeli violence (accepted by both sides)

Terrorism involves the deliberate killing of randomly selected non-combatants for political ends. It seeks to promote a political outcome by spreading terror and demoralization throughout a population.[195]

2001 UN Ad Hoc Committee on Terrorism (draft)

UN Ad Hoc Committee on Terrorism: Informal Texts of Art. 2 of the draft Comprehensive Convention on International Terrorism, prepared by the Coordinator:

1. Any person commits an offence within the meaning of this Convention if that person, by any means, unlawfully and intentionally, causes:

- Death or serious bodily injury to any person; or
- Serious damage to public or private property, including a place of public use, a State or government facility, a public transportation system, an infrastructure facility or the environment; or
- Damage to property, places, facilities, or systems referred to in paragraph 1(b) of this article, resulting or likely to result in major economic loss, when the purpose of the conduct, by its nature or context, is to intimidate a population, or to compel a Government or an international organization to do or abstain from doing any act.[196]

2002 Chasdi

The threat, practice, or promotion of force for political objectives by organizations or a person(s) whose actions are designed to influence the political attitudes or policy dispositions of a third party, provided that the threat, practice or promotion of force is directed against (1) non-combatants; (2) military personnel in non-combatant or peacekeeping roles; (3) combatants, of the aforementioned [and that it] violates juridical principles of proportionality, military necessity, and discrimination; or (4) regimes which have not committed egregious violations of the human rights regime that approach Nuremberg category crimes. Moreover, the act itself elicits a set of images that serve to denigrate the target population while strengthening the individual or group simultaneously.[197]

2002 Inter-American Convention against Terrorism (draft)

For the purposes of this Convention, 'act of terrorism' is defined as any unlawful threat of or use of violence, regardless of motive, means, or scope, that is intended to generate widespread terror or alarm in all or part of the population and that seriously jeopardizes the life, the physical, material, or moral well-being, or the freedom of individuals. The following, inter alia, shall be considered acts of terrorism:

a.   A serious attack on the life, the physical, material, or moral well-being, or the freedom of individuals, in particular those who enjoy special international protection, such as heads of state, heads of government, ministers, diplomatic agents, and members of their families;
b.   The use of explosive devices of any type, such as bombs, grenades, rockets, letter-bombs or exploding packages, and destructive weapons, among others;
c.   Kidnapping and the taking of hostages;
d.   The destruction, seizure, or control of an aircraft, vessel, or means of mass transportation that is in operation, or any other act jeopardizing the safety and security thereof;
e.   Any act of violence that jeopardizes the safety and security of airports, ports, or terminals of any type serving air, maritime, or ground traffic;
f.   The unlawful use of nuclear material.

This Convention shall also apply to any attempt at, complicity in, direct or indirect participation in, or extortion related to the acts described in this article.[198]

2002 European Union

An intentional act which may seriously damage a country or an international organization, committed with the aim of seriously intimidating a population, unduly compelling a Government or an international organization to perform or abstain from performing any act, seriously destabilizing or destroying fundamental political, constitutional, economic or social structures by means of attacks upon a person's life, attacks upon the physical integrity of a person, kidnapping, hostage-taking, seizure of aircraft or ships, or the manufacture, possession or transport of weapons or explosives.[199]

2002 Honderich

Violence with a political and social intention, whether or not intended to put people in general in fear, and raising a question of its moral justification – either illegal violence within a society of smaller-scale violence than war between states or societies and not according to international law.[200]

2002 Knobler *et al.*

Bioterrorism – Terrorism using biological agents. . . . the agents that might be used . . . comprise viruses, bacteria, rickettsiae, fungi, and biological toxins.[201]

2002 Schmid

Nuclear terrorism – the use, or credible threat of use, of destructive force against non-combatant/civilian targets for purposes of propaganda, blackmail/extortion or intimidation of a target audience, whereby a) the perpetrator has managed to trigger a fission (or fission/fusion) of nuclear material, b) is credibly held to be in possession of weapon-grade nuclear (U, Pu) material and signals intent of first use; or c) is attacking or sabotaging nuclear reactors or vital support systems (e.g. cooling system) at power stations or nuclear materials (e.g. reactor rods or high-radiation level waste) in transport or at storage sites in order to produce, then or later, an accident or a controlled release/explosion of radioactive substances, or d) disperses in water, soil or air radioactive waste or isotopes, etc. by conventional explosion or dispersion/diffusion.[202]

2003   Boyle

Violent acts intended to influence decisions. . . . Terrorist actions are undertaken to cause fear and demoralization, and thereby to lead to changes in policy on the part of the terrorized party. . . . Terrorist actions are wrong because those who do them seek to affect others' behaviours and decisions by directly or indirectly harming people whom they have no right to harm. The bad means whose use defines actions as terrorist are the intentional harms inflicted on some people to cause fear (often on the part of others than those armed). Those harms are wrongs because the targets of the terrorist harms are in the relevant sense 'innocent'. . . . Terrorist acts are 'indiscriminate' in a strong sense: anyone who can be harmed and whose harming will cause the hoped-for fear is a reasonable target, and so those who might be harmed only as a side effect of other actions are harmed intentionally in terrorist actions. . . . Terrorist actions . . . can be performed by individuals or groups and their targets can be individual or groups.[203]

2003   Card

Mass killing of unarmed civilians targeted deliberately as such and without warning.[204]

2003   Chomsky

Terrorism is the calculated use of violence or threat of violence to attain goals that are political, religious, or ideological in nature . . . through intimidation, coercion, or instilling fear.[205]

2003   Combs and Slann

Terrorism = a synthesis of war and theatre, a dramatization of the most proscribed kind of violence – that which is perpetrated on innocent victims – played before an audience in the hope of creating a mood of fear for political purposes.[206]

2003   Corlett

Terrorism is the attempt to achieve (or prevent) political, social, economic, or religious change by the actual or threatened use of violence against persons or property; the violence (or the threat thereof) employed in terrorism is aimed partly at destabilizing (or maintaining) the existing political or social order, but mainly at publicizing the goals or cause espoused by the agents or by those on whose behalf the agents act; often, though not always, terrorism is aimed at provoking extreme counter-measures which will win public support for the terrorists and their cause.[207]

2003   Dolnik

Suicide terrorism – premeditated acts of ideologically or religiously motivated violence, in which the success of the operation is contingent on self-inflicted death by the perpetrator(s) during the attack.[208]

2003 Elshtain

Terrorism is the random murder of innocent people. The reference is not to moral innocence, for none among us are innocent in that way, but our inability to defend ourselves from murderous attacks as we go to work, take a trip, shop, or ride a bus. In other words, civilians are not combatants.[209]

2003 Kapitan

Terrorism is the deliberate use of violence, or the threat of such, directed upon civilians in order to achieve political objectives.[210]

2003 NATO Standardization Agency

The unlawful use or threatened use of force or violence against individuals or property in an attempt to coerce or intimidate governments or societies to achieve political, religious or ideological objectives.[211]

2003 Weinberg and Pedahzur (New Academic (Minimal) Consensus Definition)

Terrorism is a politically motivated tactic involving the threat or use of force or violence in which the pursuit of publicity plays a significant role.[212]

2003 Sterba

Terrorism is the use or threat of violence against innocent people to elicit terror in them, or in some other group of people, in order to further a political objective.[213]

2004 Best and Nocella

Terrorism is the intentional use of physical violence directed against innocent persons – human and/or non-human animals – to advance the religious, ideological, political, or economic purposes of an individual, organization, corporation, or state government.[214]

2004 Cicovacki

Terrorism essentially consists in the willingness to terrorize, if necessary kill, innocent civilians. Terrorism is thus intolerable because it directly and openly targets innocent people.[215]

2004 Coady

The organized use of violence to attack non-combatants ('innocents') in a special sense or their property for political purposes.[216]

2004 Derrida and Borradori

When one refers to current or explicitly legal definitions of terrorism, what does one find? A reference to a crime against human life and violation of laws (national or international) and implied in it, on the one hand, a distinction between civilian and military (the victims of terrorism are supposed to be civilian) and [on the other hand], the political goal (influence or change the politics of a country by means of terrorizing its civilian population). These definitions therefore do not exclude terrorism by the state.[217]

2004 *Encyclopaedia Britannica*

The systematic use of terror or unpredictable violence against governments, publics, or individuals to attain a political objective. Terrorism has been used by political organizations with both rightist and leftist objectives, by nationalistic and ethnic groups, by revolutionaries, and by the arms and secret police of governments themselves.[218]

2004 Fotion

Terrorism is a policy of coercive intimidation designed to achieve some political end.[219]

2004 Held

When either the intention to spread fear or the intention to harm non-combatants is primary, this is sufficient for terrorism.[220]

2004 International Counter-Terrorism Academic Community

Terrorism is the deliberate use of violence against civilians in order to achieve political goals (ideological, nationalist, social, religious, etc.).[221]

2004 International Law Dictionary and Directory

Terrorism: (From Latin terrere: 'to frighten'.) The sustained clandestine use of violence for a political purpose.[222]

2004 Kapitan

Terrorism is politically motivated violence directed against non-combatants.[223]

2004 Kaplan

Cyberterrorism is typically defined as the use of the internet as a vehicle through which to launch an attack.[224]

2004 Margolis

Terrorism is (i) an aggression, or the perceived threat of an aggression, employing weapons of mass destruction, potential even if not actual or imminent, involving conventional states, now advanced as grounds for a pre-emptive strike under cover of self-defence; (ii) an aggression, or the perceived threat of an aggression, employing unusual or heterodox means of war that override or repudiate all conventional distinctions between combatants and non-combatants, admissible and inadmissible forms of warfare (including but not restricted to weapons of mass destruction), pursued independently by non-state bodies or in collusion with states that favour terrorism themselves; (iii) a figurative transformation, constituting a new form of war, of all forms of political and economic penetration and control exercised by states, blocs of states, or populations however distributed worldwide, whose activities are perceived to be causally responsible for intolerable disparities, inequities of power, cultural indignities and affronts, and injustices regarding the freedom, political self-determination, and quality of life of peoples of the world; and (iv) the figurative transformation of all measures designed to combat manifestation of (i), (ii), or (iii) in any form or combination.[225]

2004 McKenna

Terrorism is a policy committed to the random use or threat of violence directed against innocent members of a community with the intention of eliciting terror in the wider community in order to influence or address the practices or beliefs of that community by way of the terror elicited.[226]

2004 McMahan

Terrorism ought to be defined as intentional attacks, for political or ideological purposes, on those who are in no way morally responsible for an unjust threat or other grievance that provides a just cause for war.[227]

2004 McPherson

I will define terrorism roughly as the deliberate use of force against non-combatants, which can reasonably be expected to cause wider and warranted fear among them, for political ends. My definition focuses on the aspect of terrorism – namely, deliberate use of force against non-combatants – that typically is thought to characterize its distinctive wrongness as compared to war whereby only combatants can be attacked. Left out of the definition, for instance, is the claim that non-combatants are 'innocent'. The relevant understanding of innocence in war is a contested matter, and my argument here will not depend on how this is settled. Provisionally, I will accept that non-combatants in general are relevantly innocent.[228]

2004 Primoratz

The deliberate use of violence, or threat of its use, against innocent people, with the aim of intimidating some other people into a course of action that they otherwise would not take.[229]

2004 Rodin

Terrorism is the deliberate, negligent, or reckless use of force against non-combatants, by state or non-state actors for ideological ends and in the absence of a substantively just legal process.[230]

2004 Simpson

Terrorism consists of acts of indiscriminate violence directed at civilians or non-hostile personnel, in order to terrorize them, or their governments, into carrying out or submitting to the demands of the terrorists.[231]

2004 Smilansky

The intentional targeting of non-combatants with lethal or severe violence for political purposes by members of small or weak groups that lack the capacity to field an army and engage in warfare.[232]

2004 University of Princeton: WordNet 2.0 A Lexical Database for the English Language

Terrorism, act of terrorism, terrorist act – (the calculated use of violence (or threat of violence) against civilians in order to attain goals that are political or religious or ideological in nature; this is done through intimidation or coercion or instilling fear).[233]

2004 Walzer

Terrorism is the deliberate killing of innocent people, at random, in order to spread fear through a whole population and force the hand of its political leaders.[234]

2004 Walzer

War terrorism: the effort to kill civilians in such large numbers that their government is forced to surrender.[235]

2004 Walzer

State terrorism is commonly used by authoritarian and totalitarian government against their own people, to spread fear and make political opposition impossible.[236]

2004 Young

Terrorist actions (whether in the form of one-off attacks or as part of an ongoing campaign) are political actions that involve either the use, or the threat of the use, of violence. The violence may be directed towards persons or property – witness many of the terrorist actions of the African National Congress in South Africa or the destruction by the Tamil 'Tigers' of much of the fleet of Sri Lankan Airways. Typically, the violence will take a physical form, but it may also be psychological.[237]

2004 Zohar

The moral condemnation of terrorism as such is founded upon the central tenet of the 'war ethic' – the principle that war allows only the killing of enemy soldiers, whereas intentional killing of non-combatants remains murder.[238]

2005 Jaggar

Terrorism is the use of extreme threats or violence designed to intimidate or subjugate governments, groups or individuals. It is a tactic of coercion intended to promote further ends that in themselves may be good, bad or indifferent. Terrorism may be practised by governments or international bodies or forces, sub-state groups or even individuals. Its threats or violence are aimed directly or immediately at the bodies or belongings of innocent civilians but these are typically terrorists' secondary targets; the primary targets of terrorists are the governments, groups or individuals that they wish to intimidate.[239]

2005 Lewis

Terrorism is a form of violent assault which targets civilians and civilian infrastructure in order to create fear and insecurity in enemy populations and governments. Terrorism is politically motivated and is designed to communicate the cause of the perpetrators to their enemies and potential affiliates. It is a form of political violence which may be exercised by governments, government agents, sub-national and transnational organizations. As a cultural conduit and bearer of information, the global networked media is profoundly implicated in modern terrorism.[240]

2005 Palmer-Fernandez

Terrorism is the organized use of violence against civilians or their property, the political leadership of a nation, or soldiers (who are not combatants in a war) for political purposes.[241]

2005 Annan

Any action constitutes terrorism if it is intended to cause death or serious bodily harm to civilians and non-combatants, with the purpose of intimidating a population or compelling a Government or an international organization to do or abstain from doing any act. [242]

2006 Horgan

Terrorism is most usefully thought of as a strategy which due to the qualities of the violence associated with it, tends to set in motion a chain of events and counter-events that raise what at the outset might be a manageable problem into something altogether more dangerous and complex, and (as a result of onlookers' responses to it) seems to make the problem increasingly more difficult to understand and address. Indeed, perhaps an alternative definition of terrorism is that terrorism is something that people do as part of a process, with political, social and psychological qualities and dimensions that people engage in, and emerge from anew, with constantly changing (and constantly refining and focusing) perceptions about the nature of what they do and have done at all stages, including ever-changeable perceptions about their motivations for doing so (again, at all stages). The specific qualities, features, arenas and outcomes of the engagement differ from place to place, time to time, and 'offender' to 'victim', back to 'offender'. One increasingly obvious pattern in this symbiotic relationship is that the State continues to engage the terrorist threat with the same dogged persistency (and knowledge that it is fighting a war it cannot win in terms of a clear victory, yet this is not seen as a valid reason for discontinuing the struggle) that the terrorists use to fight a war that paradoxically will lead to the state engaging it in ways that only serve to sustain this cycle of mutual animosity and victimization. As suggested above, the terrorist and his victim are in this sense two aspects of the same thing, and perhaps it is the case that stressing their similarities may lead us to identifying more clearly the adaptive aspects of both how terrorists and their audiences make decisions that affect themselves and each other.[243]

2006 Hudson

Terrorism is the premeditated and planned use of (or attempt to use) sudden, shocking, and unlawful violence against civilians and other non-combatants – a category that may include off-duty (non-uniformed) military and security personnel or peacekeeping forces in peaceful situations – or other symbolic targets perpetrated by a clandestine member(s) or agent(s) of a sub-national and covertly operating group for the purpose of publicizing, in some cases as a state surrogate, a nationalistic, political, religious, or social cause and terrifying a civilian population and coercing a government into changing a policy or accepting a demand as a result of the psychological and/or economic impact of the attack(s).[244]

2006 Mincheva

Criminal tactics, employed by extremist movements [mostly, though not exclusively, identity driven] which target civilians [as well as political and religious leaders] and resort to mass fear produced by the media coverage of its attacks.[245]

2006 Moghadam

Premeditated violence, or the threat of violence, in the pursuit of a political aim, perpetrated by groups against non-combatant targets, and aimed at influencing a wider audience through the creation of fear.[246]

2006 Romansheim

Terrorism is a non-state actor's systematic use – or threat of use – of violence and destruction towards illegitimate targets such as non-combatants to create fear and/or generate attention and to make someone other than the direct target of the violent crime respond in a manner that would enhance the terrorist's political goals.[247]

2006 Sandler

Terrorism is the premeditated use or thereat to use violence by individuals or sub-national groups in order to obtain a political or social objective through the intimidation of a large audience beyond that of the immediate victim.[248]

2006 Schweitzer

[A terrorist act is] a violent politically motivated activity that is non-selective with respect to its victims, and which deliberately and maliciously injures non-combatant individuals going about their daily routines in obviously civilian surroundings. A continuous sequence of such acts would constitute a significant element in defining their perpetrators as a terrorist organization. [249]

2006   Stepanova

. . . the intentional use or threat of violence against civilians and non-combatants by a non-state (sub-national or transnational) actor in an asymmetrical confrontation, in order to achieve political goals.[250]

2006   Tishkov

. . . planned use of lethal violence against civilians in order to cause fear and disorder to reach political goals.[251]

2006   Richardson

Terrorism simply means deliberately and violently targeting civilians for political purposes. It has seven crucial characteristics. . . . [F]irst, a terrorist act is politically inspired. . . . Second, if an act does not involve violence or the threat of violence, it is not terrorism. . . . Third, the point of terrorism is not to defeat the enemy but to send a message. . . . Fourth, the act and the victim usually have symbolic significance. . . . Fifth – and this is a controversial point – terrorism is the act of sub-state groups, not states. . . . A sixth characteristic of terrorism is that the victim of the violence and the audiences the terrorists are trying to reach are not the same. . . . The final and most important defining characteristic of terrorism is the deliberate targeting of civilians.[252]

2008   O'Boyle

A tactic of armed struggle that is lesser in impact than and more or less distinct from war and guerrilla war and is greater in impact than and more or less distinct from riot and sabotage, that involves the use of violence (in the sense of physical force) or the threat of violence directly or indirectly against either primarily military, paramilitary, or state security combatants (T1); against primarily non-combatant civilians (T2); or primarily against property (T3) in an attempt to antagonize, coerce, or intimidate (through the use of or the threat of that violence) a government, population (or sections thereof), society, or alliance of states in the furtherance of a particular ideology or system of ideas (either political, religious or otherwise).[253]

2008   Rapoport

'Terror' is violence with distinctive properties used for political purposes both by private parties and states. That violence is unregulated by publicly accepted norms to contain violence, the rules of war, and the rules of punishment. Private groups using terror most often disregard the rules of war, while state terror generally disregards rules of punishment, i.e. those enabling us to distinguish guilt from innocence. But both states and non-state groups can ignore either set of rules.[254]

2008   Sinai

Terrorism is a tactic of warfare involving premeditated, politically motivated violence perpetrated by sub-national groups or clandestine agents against any citizen of a state, whether civilian or military, to influence, coerce, and, if possible, cause mass casualties and physical destruction upon their targets. Unlike guerrilla forces, terrorist groups are less capable of overthrowing their adversaries' governments than on inflicting discriminate or indiscriminate destruction that they hope will coerce them to change policy.[255]

2008   Deobandi Scholars

Any action that targets innocents, whether by an individual or by any government, or by a private organization, anywhere in the world constitutes, according to Islam, an act of terrorism.[256]

2009   Gianola

[Terrorism is] the strategic activity, be it of an individual or an organized group, of a bearer of collective interests not, or insufficiently, safeguarded by a national or the international order. It is exercised by means of acts of extreme violence against people and property. Its targets are not necessarily part of the audience that is to be influenced by such violence. Its influence is effectuated by attracting the attention of the media or of the general public.[257]

2009   Neumann

[Terrorism is] the deliberate creation of fear, usually through the use (or threat of use) of symbolic acts of violence, to influence the political behaviour of a target audience.[258]

2009   Addicott

If a universal definition is not practicable, one can at least list four key characteristics of terrorism that better reflect the activity:

1   The illegal use of violence directed at civilians to produce fear in a target group.
2   The continuing threat of additional future acts of violence.
3   A predominantly political or ideological character of the act.
4   The desire to mobilize or immobilize a given target group.[259]

2010   NACOS

Terrorism is political violence or the threat of violence by groups or individuals who deliberately target civilians or non-combatants in order to influence the behaviour and actions of targeted publics and governments.[260]

2009   English

Terrorism involves heterogeneous violence used or threatened with a political aim; it can involve a variety of acts, of targets, and of actors; it possesses an important psychological dimension, producing terror or fear among a directly threatened group and also a wider implied audience in the hope of maximizing political communication and achievement; it embodies the exerting and implementing of power, and the attempted redressing of power relations; it represents a subspecies of warfare, and as such it can form part of a wider campaign of violent and non-violent attempts at political leverage.[261]

2010   Tinnes

Terrorism is a communication strategy of sub-state actors that, by its asymmetrical, systematically planned, unpredictable violence against targets selected arbitrarily or for their symbolic value (including civilians), is meant to create a mood of extreme fear or insecurity in the civilian population. By means of psychological manipulation, maximum pressure is meant to be created in order to bring about a desired reaction. Terrorist violence, which transgresses traditional military and social norms of waging conflict and conducting opposition, is meant to assure for itself the largest possible receptive audience to which, by its spectacular effect as a means of communication, messages are meant to be transmitted on the basis of its psychological signalling effect.[262]

Notes

1 Old Chinese saying, cited by R. Clutterbuck in unpublished talk; quoted in P. Wilkinson, *Terrorism and the Liberal State*. London: Macmillan, p. 48.

2 Maximilien Robespierre (February 1794), quoted in Paul Wurth, *La Répression internationale du terrorisme*. Lausanne: Imprimerie la Concorde, 1941, p. 12.

3 Paragraph 2, section d of the programme of the executive committee of the Russian Narodnaya Volya Party, in *The People's Will* (1879), quoted in Ze'ev Iviansky, 'Individual Terror: Concept and Typology', *Journal of Contemporary History*, vol. 12, 1977, p. 46.

4 Nicholas Morozov, 'Terroristic Struggle' (London 1880), in Feliks Gross, *Violence in Politics: Terror and Political Assassination in Eastern Europe and Russia*. The Hague: Mouton, 1972, p. 106.

5 Source: V.M. Chernov (leader of one wing of the Russian Socialist Revolutionary Party), 1909, quoted in Ze'ev Ivianski, 'Individual Terror', p. 49.

6 J.B.S. Hardman, 'Terrorism'. In *Encyclopedia of the Social Sciences*, vol. 14. New York: Macmillan, 1936, pp. 575–576.

7 Art. 1, para. 2, Convention for the Prevention and Repression of Terrorism (1937), quoted in Paul Wurth, *La répression internationale du terrorisme*, Lausanne: p. 50. The convention never came into force, as only colonial India signed up to it.

8 J. Waciorsky, *Le terrorisme politique*. Paris: Pedone, 1939, p. 98.

9 H.J. Chisholm, 'The Function of Terror and Violence in Revolution'. MA thesis, Georgetown University, Washington, DC, 1948, pp.11–12, 18–19, 21–22.

10 H. Arendt, *The Origins of Totalitarianism*. New York: Harcourt Brace Jovanovich, 1951, pp. 6, 331–332.

11 B. Crozier, *The Rebels: A Study of Post-war Insurrections*. London: Chatto & Windus, 1960, pp. 159–160, 173.

12 Thomas Perry Thornton, 'Terror as a Weapon of Political Agitation'. In H. Eckstein (ed.), *Internal War: Problems and Approaches*. New York: The Free Press of Glencoe, 1964, pp. 73–74, 77–78.

13 E.V. Walter, 'Violence and the Process of Terror'. *American Sociological Review*, 29(2), Spring 1964, pp. 248–250, 256.

14 R. Gaucher, *Les terroristes*. Paris: Editions Albin Michel, 1965, pp. 235, 10–11.

15 R. Aron, *Peace and War*. London: Weidenfeld & Nicolson, 1966, p. 170.

16 *The Shorter Oxford English Dictionary*, 3rd edn, vol. 2. Oxford: Clarendon Press, 1969, pp. 2154–2156.

17 A. Dallin and G.W. Breslauer, *Political Terror in Communist Systems*. Stanford: Stanford University Press, 1970, pp. 1, 2, 12, 19, 26.

18 J.M. Silverman and P.M. Jackson, 'Terror in insurgent warfare'. *Military Review*, 50, October 1970, pp. 61–63.

19 J. Mallin (ed.), *Terror and Urban Guerrillas: A Study of Tactics and Documents*. Miami: University of Miami Press, 1971, pp. 3–5.

20 Carlos Marighela, *For the Liberation of Brazil*. Harmondsworth, UK: Penguin Books, 1971, p. 89.

21 R. Moss, 'Urban Guerrilla Warfare'. Adelphi Papers no. 79. London: Institute of Strategic Studies, 1971, pp. 1, 3.

22 R. Moss, *Urban Guerrillas: The New Face of Political Violence*. London: Temple Smith, 1972, p. 32.

23 M. Crenshaw Hutchinson, 'The Concept of Revolutionary Terrorism'. *Journal of Conflict Resolution*, 16(3), 1972, pp. 383–396.

24 F. Gross, *Violence in Politics: Terror and Political Assassination in Eastern Europe and Russia*. The Hague: Mouton, 1972, pp. 9–12.

25 J. Günther, 'Terror und Terrorismus'. *Neue Deutsche Hefte*, 19(4), 1972, p. 33 (translated A.S.).

26 D.G. Morrison, R.C. Mitchell, J.N. Paden and H.M. Stevenson, *Black Africa: A Comparative Handbook*. New York: Free Press, 1972, p. 130n.

27 F. Hacker, *Terror: Mythos, Realität, Analyse*. Reinbek bei Hamburg: Rowohlt, 1975, 1973, pp. 17, 19, 20, 183 (translated by A.S.).

28 I.L. Horowitz, 'Political Terrorism and State Power', *Journal of Political and Military Sociology*, 1, 1973, p. 150.

29 W.D. Neale, 'Terror – Oldest Weapon in the Arsenal', *Army*, August 1973, p. 11.

30 B. Crozier, 'Aid for Terrorism'. In *Annual of Power and Conflict, 1973–1974: A Survey of Political Violence and International Influence*. London: Institute for the Study of Conflict, 1974, p. 4.

31 G. Fairbairn, *Revolutionary Guerrilla Warfare: The Countryside Version*. Harmondsworth, UK: Penguin Books, 1974, pp. 348–349.

32 J.J. Paust, 'Some Thoughts on "Preliminary Thoughts on Terrorism"'. *American Journal of International Law*, 68(3), 1974, p. 502.

33 United Kingdom, Prevention of Terrorism Act 1974, quoted in Catherine Scorer, *The Prevention of Terrorism Acts, 1974 and 1976: A Report on the Operation of the Law*. London: National Council for Civil Liberties, 1976, p. 36.

34 P. Wilkinson, *Political Terrorism*. London: Macmillan, 1974, p. 11.

35 V. Bite, Foreign Affairs Division, Library of Congress, International Terrorism – Issue Brief no. IB 74042, Appendix of US Congress, Senate, Committee on the Judiciary, Subcommittee to Investigate the Administration of the Internal Security Act and Other Internal Security Laws. Part IV, May 14, 1975, 94th Cong., 1st. Sess. Washington, DC: GPO, 1975, p. 253.

36 G. Bouthoul, 'Definitions of Terrorism'. In D. Carlton and C. Schaerf (eds), *International Terrorism and World Security*. London: Croom Helm, 1975, pp. 50–59.

37 D. Fromkin, 'The Strategy of Terrorism'. *Foreign Affairs*, 53(4), 1975, pp. 693, 694, 697.

38 B. Jenkins, *International Terrorism: A New Mode of Conflict*. Los Angeles: Crescent, 1975, pp. 1–2.

39 B.M. Jenkins and J. Johnson, International Terrorism: A Chronology, 1968–1974. Santa Monica, CA: RAND, 1975, p. 3.

40 L.A. Sobel (ed.), *Political Terrorism*. Oxford: Clio Press, 1975.

41 FBI. LEAA, National Advisory Committee on Criminal Justice Standards and Goals, 1976. Disorders and Terrorism: Report of the Task on Disorders and Terrorism. Washington, DC: Department of Justice, as quoted in M. Wilson and J. Lynxwiler, *Abortion Clinic Violence as Terrorism*. Birmingham: University of Alabama at Birmingham, 1988, pp. 264–265.

42 Remarks by R.A. Fearey, US Coordinator for Combating Terrorism, 19 February 1976, in J. Wolf, *Fear of Fear: A Survey of Terrorist Operations and Controls in Open Societies*. New York: Plenum Press, 1981, p. 201.

43 Edward Kossoy, *Living with Guerrillas*. Geneva: Libraire Droz, 1976, p. 328; quoted in Makram Haluani, 'Gewaltpolitik: Eine politikwissenschaftliche Makroanalyse eines politischen Kampfmittels und seine Problematik im heutigen Latein-Amerika'. University of Münster, PhD thesis, 1982, p. 85.

44 A.J. Pierre, 'The Politics of International Terrorism'. Reprinted in J.D. Elliott and K. Gibson (eds), *Contemporary Terrorism*. Gaithersburg, MD: International Academy of Collaborative Professionals, 1978, p. 36.

45 US Central Intelligence Agency, in D.L. Milbank, 'Research Study'. *International and Transnational Terrorism: Diagnosis and Prognosis*. Washington, DC: CIA Political Research Department, 1976, pp. 1, 8.

46 US National Advisory Committee on Criminal Justice, Standards and Goals, *Report of the Task Force on Disorders and Terrorism*. Washington, DC: GPO, 1976, p. 3.

47 F.M. Watson, *Political Terrorism: The Threat and the Response*. Washington, DC: Robert B. Luce, 1976, p. 1.

48 E. Weisband and D. Roguly, 'Palestinian Terrorism: Violence, Verbal Strategy, and Legitimacy'. In Y. Alexander (ed.), *International National, Regional and Global Perspectives*. New York: Praeger, 1976, pp. 258–259, 278–279.

49 P. Wilkinson, *Terrorism versus Liberal Democracy: The Problem of Response*. London: Institute for the Study of Conflict, 1976, pp. 1–3.

50 J.B. Wolf, 'Controlling Political Terrorism in a Free Society'. *Orbis – A Journal of World Affairs*, 19(34), 1976, pp. 1289–1290.

51 Quoted by F. McClintock, in R.D. Crelinsten (ed.), *Research Strategies for the Study of International Political Terrorism*. Montreal, International Centre for Comparative Criminology: 1977, p. 162.

52 R. Clutterbuck, *Guerrillas and Terrorism*. London: Faber & Faber, 1977, pp. 11, 21.

53 Y. Alexander and S.M. Finger (eds), *Terrorism: Interdisciplinary Perspectives*. New York: John Jay Press, 1977, pp. ix–xi.

54 M. Funke, 'Terrorismus – Ermittlungsversuch zu einer Herausforderung'. In M. Funke (ed.), *Terrorismus: Untersuchungen zur Strategie und Struktur revolutionäerer Gewaltpolitik*. Bonn: Schriftenreihe der Bundeszentrale für politische Bildung, 1977, p. 13 (translated by A.S.).

55 H.C. Greisman, 'Social Meaning of Terrorism: Reification, Violence and Social Control'. *Contemporary Crises*, no. 1, July 1977, p. 305.

56 Gerald Holton, 'Reflections on Modern Terrorism'. *Jerusalem Journal of International Relations*, 3(1), Fall 1977, p. 96.

57 I.L. Horowitz, 'Can Democracy Cope with Terrorism?' *Civil Liberties Review*, 4(1), May–June 1977, p. 30.

58 Ze'ev Iviansky, 'Individual Terror: Concept and Typology'. *Journal of Contemporary History*, 12(1), 1977, p. 50.

59 B.M. Jenkins, *Combating International Terrorism: The Role of Congress*. Santa Monica, CA: RAND, 1977, pp. 1, 5.

60 Brian M. Jenkins, 'International Terrorism: A New Mode of Conflict', Research Paper no. 48, California Seminar on Arms Control and Foreign Policy. Los Angeles: Crescent Publications, 1975. Quoted in:

Conrad V. Hassel, Terror: The crime of the Privileged – An Examination and Prognosis'. *Studies in Conflict and Terrorism*, 1(1), 1977, p. 1.

61 W. Laqueur, *Terrorism*. London: Weidenfeld & Nicolson, 1977, pp. 79, 79n.

62 B.M. Leiser, 'Terrorism, Guerrilla Warfare and International Morality'. *Stanford Journal of International Studies*, 12, Spring 1977, pp. 39, 61n.

63 J. Mallin, 'Terrorism as a Military Weapon'. *Air University Review*, 28(2), 1977, p. 60.

64 E.F. Mickolus, 'Statistical Approaches to the Study of Terrorism'. In Y. Alexander and S.M. Finger (eds), *Terrorism: Interdisciplinary Perspectives*. New York: John Jay Press, 1977, pp. 210–246.

65 D. Milbank, quoted in C.V. Hassel, 'Terror: The Crime of the Privileged', p. 8.

66 J.J. Paust, 'A Definitional Focus'. In Y. Alexander and S.M. Finger (eds), *Terrorism: Interdisciplinary Perspectives*. New York: John Jay Press, 1977, pp. 20–21.

67 H.E. Price, 'The Strategy and Tactics of Revolutionary Terrorism'. *Comparative Studies in Society and History*, January 1977, p. 52.

68 M.E. Silverstein, 'Medical Rescue as an Antiterrorist Measure: A Strategist's Cookbook'. In R.D. Crelinsten (ed.), *Research Strategies for the Study of International Political Terrorism*. Montreal: International Centre for Comparative Criminology, 1977, p. 91.

69 B. Singh, 'An Overview'. In Y. Alexander and S.M. Finger (eds), *Terrorism: Interdisciplinary Perspectives*. New York: John Jay Press, 1977, pp. 5–6.

70 W.H. Smith, 'International Terrorism: A Political Analysis'. In *The Year Book of World Affairs*, 1977, vol. 31 London: Stevens, 1977, pp. 138–139, 153.

71 P. Waldmann, *Strategien politischer Gewalt*. Stuttgart: Kohlhammer, 1977, p. 70 (translated by A.S.).

72 P. Wilkinson, *Terrorism and the Liberal State*. London: Macmillan, 1977, pp. 48, 51, 52–53.

73 F. Wördemann, *Terrorismus, Motive, Strategien*. Munich: Piper, 1977, p. 24.

74 J.B. Bell, *A Time of Terror: How Democratic Societies Respond to Revolutionary Violence*. New York: Basic Books, 1978, pp. 3, 49, 95–96.

75 M. Crenshaw Hutchinson, *Revolutionary Terrorism: The FLN in Algeria, 1945–1962*. Stanford, CA: Hoover Institution, 1978, pp. 18, 21, 77–78.

76 A.E. Evans and J.F. Murphy (eds), *Legal Aspects of International Terrorism*. Lexington, MA: D.C. Heath, 1978. Quoted in R.A. Friedlander's book review in the *American Journal of Comparative Law*, 28, 1980, p. 355.

77 T. M. Franck, 'International legal action concerning terrorism'. *Terrorism*, 1(2), 1978, p. 187.

78 L.C. Hamilton, *Ecology of Terrorism: A Historical and Statistical Study*. Boulder, CO: University of Colorado, 1978, pp. 23–24.

79 Gerald Holton, 'Reflections on Modern Terrorism'. *Jerusalem Journal of International Relations*, 3(1), 1978, pp. 265–266.

80 B.M. Jenkins, 'The Study of Terrorism: Definitional Problems', 1978, in Y. Alexander and J.M. Gleason (eds), *Behavioral and Quantitative Perspectives on Terrorism*. New York: Pergamon Press, 1981, pp. 4–5.

81 A. Kaplan, 'The Psychodynamics of Terrorism'. In Y. Alexander and J.M. Gleason (eds), *Behavioral and Quantitative Perspectives on Terrorism*. New York: Pergamon Press, 1981, pp. 36–37.

82 M. Karanović, 'Pojam terorizma' (The concept of terrorism). *Jugoslavenska Revija za Kriminologiju i Krivično Pravo*, no. 14, 1978, p. 88.

83 P. Lösche, 'Terrorismus and Anarchismus: Internationale und historische Aspekte'. In M. Funke (ed.), *Extremismus im demokratischen Rechtsstaat*. Bonn: Bundeszentrale für Politische Bildung, 1978, pp. 82–83 (translated by A.S.).

84 E.F. Mickolus 'Trends in Transnational Terrorism'. In M. Livingston (ed.), *International Terrorism in the Contemporary World*. Westport, CT: Greenwood Press, 1978, p. 44.

85 J. Schreiber, *The Ultimate Weapon: Terrorists and World Order*. New York: William Marrow, 1978, p. 20.

86 H.-D. Schwind, 'Zur Entwicklung des Terrorismus' . In H.-D. Schwind (ed.), *Ursachen des Terrorismus der Bundesrepublik*. Berlin: Walter de Gruyter, 1978, p. 26 (translated by A.S.).

87 R. Shultz, 'Conceptualizing Political Terrorism: A Typology'. *Journal of International Affairs*, 32(1), 1978, pp. 8–9.

88 J.K. Zawodny, 'Internal Organizational Problems and the Sources of Tensions of Terrorist Movements as Catalysts of Violence'. *Studies in Conflict and Terrorism*, 1(3–4), 1978, p. 285.

89 O. Zinam, 'Terrorism and Violence in the Light of a Theory of Discontent and Frustration'. In M.H. Livingston (ed.), *International Terrorism in the Contemporary World*. Westport, CT: Greenwood Press, 1978, pp. 241, 244–245.

90 M.Ch. Bassiouni, 'Prolegomenon to Terror Violence'. *Creighton Law Review*, 12(13), 1979, p. 752.

91 Milivoje Karanović, 'The Concept of Terrorism'. In US National Criminal Justice Reference Service, *International Summaries*, 3. Washington, DC: Department of Justice, 1979, p. 88.

92 Fritz Rene Allemann, 'Terrorism: Definitional Aspects', *Terrorism: An International Journal*, 3(3–4), 1980, pp. 185–186.

93 Frederick J. Hacker, 'Terror and Terrorism: Modern Growth Industry and Mass Entertainment'. Los Angeles: Hacker Clinic, 1980.

94 E.F. Mickolus, *Transnational Terrorism: A Chronology of Events, 1968–1979*. London: Aldwych Press, 1980, pp. xiii–xiv.

95 A.P. Schmid & J. de Graaf, *Insurgent Terrorism and the Western News Media*. Leiden: COMT, 1980, p. 8.

96 L.C. Green, 'Aspects of terrorism'. *Terrorism*, 5(4), 1981, pp. 373–374.

97 Henner Hess, 'Terrorismus und Terrorismus-Diskurs'. *Tijdschrift voor Criminologie*, 14, 1981, p. 174.

98 US Central Intelligence Agency, *Patterns of International Terrorism*. Washington, DC: CIA, 1980, p. ii.

99 Juliet Lodge (ed.), *Terrorism: A Challenge to the State*. New York: St. Martin's Press, 1981, p. 5.

100 P.C. Sederberg, *Defining Terrorism*. Colombia: University of South Carolina, 1981, p. 3.

101 Philip E. Devine and Robert J. Rafalko, 'On Terror'. *Annals of the American Academy*, no. 463, September 1982, p. 40.

102 Anthony C.E. Quainton, 'Moral and Ethical Considerations in Defining a Counter-terrorist Policy'. In David C. Rapoport and Yonah Alexander (eds), *The Rationalization of Terrorism*. Frederick, MD: University Publications of America, 1982, p. 39.

103 Army Regulation 310-25, U.S. Army, *Dictionary of United States Army Terms*. Washington, DC: Department of the Army, 1983, p. 260.

104 Burleigh Taylor Wilkins, *Terrorism and Collective Responsibility*. London: Routledge, 1992, p. 6.

105 V.K. Anand, *Terrorism and Security*. New Delhi: Deep & Deep Publications, 1984, p. 19.

106 German Federal Republic, Ministry of the Interior. *Verfassungsschutzbericht 1984*. Bonn: Bundesministerium des Inneren, 1985, p. 17n (translated by A.S.).

107 R.P. Hoffman, 'Terrorism: A Universal Definition'. PhD thesis, Claremont, CA: Claremont Graduate School, 1984, p. 181.

108 Allan S. Nanes, Congressional Developments (1984), p. 72.

109 J.J. Nutter, 'Terrorism: A Problem of Definition or Epistemology?' *Cocta News*, no. 3, 1984, p. 167.

110 A.P. Schmid, *Political Terrorism, A Research Guide to Concepts, Theories, Data Bases and Literature*. Amsterdam: North-Holland, 1984, p. 111.

111 Adapted from A.P. Schmid, ibid., pp. 109–110; for later elaboration, see A.P. Schmid, 'Force or Conciliation? An Overview of Some Problems Associated with Current Anti-terrorist Response Strategies'. *Violence, Aggression and Terrorism*, 2(2), 1988, p. 153.

112 US antiterrorism legislation as quoted by Brent L. Smith, Department of Criminal Justice, University of Alabama in Birmingham, Alabama, 1984, p. 217.

113 *FBI Analysis of Terrorist Incidents in the United States* (1984), p. 87.

114 Carl Wellman, 'On Terrorism Itself'. In Joe P. White (ed.), *Assent/Dissent*. Dubuque, IA: Kendall/Hunt, 1984, pp. 254–255.

115 Anthony Coady, 'The Morality of Terrorism'. *Philosophy*, 60, 1985, p. 52.

116 *American Heritage Dictionary*. Boston: Houghton Mifflin, 1985, p. 671.

117 Eqbal Ahmad, 'Comprehending Terror'. *Middle East Report*, May–June 1986, p. 3.

118 Michael Gunter, 'Contemporary Armenian Terrorism'. *Terrorism*, 8(3), 1985, p. 216.

119 T.R. Gurr, Empirical Research on Political Terrorism: The State of the Art and How It Might Be Improved'. MS, Boulder, CO, 1986, pp. 2–3.

120 Christopher Mitchell, Michael Stohl, David Carleton and George A. Lopez, 'State Terrorism: Issues of Concept and Measurement'. In M. Stohl and G. Lopez (eds), *Government Violence and Repression: An Agenda for Research*. Westport, CT: Greenwood Press, 1986, p. 5.

121 Irving R. Kaufman, 'Cold-Blooded Killers, Not Freedom Fighters', *New York Times,* 22 August 1986, p. A23.

122 Benjamin B. Netanyahu (ed.), *Terrorism: How the West Can Win*. New York: Farrar, Straus & Giroux, 1986, p. 9.

123 Paul Wilkinson, *Terrorism and the Liberal State*, 2nd edn. London: Macmillan, 1986, p. 14.

124 Paul Wilkinson, quoted in W. Gutteridge (ed.), *The New Terrorism*. London: Institute for the Study of Conflict, 1986.

125 Quoted in Mark S. Watson, 'Rogue States and State Sponsored Terrorism'. Available at http://mark swatson.com/WebSite/terrorFrame2Source1_1.htm.

126 Ahmed Galal Ezeldin, *Terrorism and Political Violence: An Egyptian Perspective*. Chicago: University of Illinois, 1987, pp. 39–40.

127 Walter Laqueur, *The Age of Terrorism*. Boston: Little, Brown, 1987, p. 9.

128 Edward A. Lynch, 'International Terrorism: The Search for a Policy'. *Terrorism: An International Journal,* 9(1), 1987, p. 310.

129 UN Office of Legal Affairs, *International Instruments related to the Prevention and Suppression of International Terrorism.* New York: United Nations, 2001, p. 148.

130 R. Thackrah, 'Terrorism: A Definitional Problem'. In P. Wilkinson and A.M. Stewart (eds), *Contemporary Research on Terrorism.* Aberdeen: Aberdeen University Press, 1987, p. 38.

131 Grant Wardlaw, quoted in George Rosie, *The Directory of International Terrorism.* New York: Paragon House, 1987, p. 18.

132 P. Wilkinson, 'Pathways out of Terrorism for Democratic Societies'. In P. Wilkinson and A.M. Stewart (eds), *Contemporary Research on Terrorism.* Aberdeen: Aberdeen University Press, 1987, p. 453.

133 D. Della Porta, in answer to questionnaire, quoted in A.P. Schmid and A.J. Jongman, *Political Terrorism.* Amsterdam: North-Holland, 1988, p. 37.

134 Ruth Linn, 'Terrorism, Morality and Soldiers' Motivation to Fight: An Example from the Israeli Experience in Lebanon'. *Studies in Conflict and Terrorism,* 11(2), 1988, p. 139.

135 Mehdi Mozaffari, 'The New Era of Terrorism: Approaches and Typologies'. *Cooperation and Conflict,* 23(4), 1988.

136 Jeffrey Ian Ross, 'Attributes of Domestic Political Terrorism'. *Studies in Conflic and Terrorism,* 11(3), 1988; based on A.P. Schmid *Political Terrorism: A Research Guide,* 1984.

137 Alex P. Schmid *et al., Political Terrorism,* p. 28.

138 Charles Townsend, in answer to questionnaire, quoted in: A.P. Schmid *et al., Political Terrorism,* p. 38.

139 Y. Alexander and J. Sinai, *Terrorism: The PLO Connection.* New York: Crane Russak, 1989, p. 1.

140 Ronald D. Crelinsten, 'Images of Terrorism in the Media (1966–1985)'. Department of Criminology, University of Ottawa, 1989, p. 167.

141 R.A. Hudson, 'Dealing with International Hostage-Taking: Alternatives to Reactive Counterterrorist Assaults', *Terrorism,* 12(5), 1989, pp. 321 ff.

142 Douglas Lackey, *The Ethics of War and Peace.* Englewood Cliffs, NJ: Prentice Hall, 1989, p. 85.

143 John F. Murphy, before the International Law Association; quoted in J.F. Murphy, *State Support of International Terrorism. Legal, Political, and Economic Dimensions.* Boulder, CO: Westview Press, 1989, pp. 19–20.

144 Marco Rimanelli, 'Italian Terrorism and Society, 1940s–1980s: Roots, Ideologies, Evolution, and International Connections'. In *US–European Relations and International Law.* Washington, DC: Public Affairs Department, George Mason University, 1989.

145 USSR Ministry of Interior (1989), quoted in 'Galia Golan. Gorbachev's "New Thinking" on Terrorism'. *The Washington Papers,* 16(141), 1990, pp. 57–59.

146 Grant Wardlaw, *Political Terrorism: Theory, Tactics, and Counter-measures,* 2nd edn. Cambridge: Cambridge University Press, 1989, p. 16.

147 Richard Allan, *Terrorism: Pragmatic International Deterrence and Cooperation.* Occasional Paper Series 19. New York: Institute for East–West Security Studies, 1990, p. 85.

148 Noemi Gal-Or, 'The Israeli Defense Forces and Unconventional Warfare: The Palestinian Factor and Israeli National Security Doctrine'. *Terrorism and Political Violence,* 2(2), Summer 1990, p. 221.

149 Christopher Hewitt, 'Terrorism and Public Opinion: A Five Country Comparison'. *Terrorism and Political Violence,* 2(2), Summer, 1990, p. 145.

150 Martin Hughes, 'Terror and Negotiation'. *Terrorism and Political Violence,* 2(1), Spring, 1990, p. 73.

151 Leonard Weinberg and William Lee Eubank, 'Political Parties and the Formation of Terrorist Groups'. *Terrorism and Political Violence,* 2(1), Spring, 1990, p. 128.

152 John Bunzl, *Gewalt ohne Grenzen: Nahost-Terror und Österreich.* Vienna: Österreichisches Institutfür Internationale Politik, 1991, p. 3 (translated by A.S.).

153 D.E. Georges-Abeyie, 'Political Criminogenesis of Democracy in the Colonial Settler-State: Terror, Terrorism, and Guerilla Warfare'. *Studies in Conflict and Terrorism,* 14(1), 1991, p. 5.

154 M.W. Jackson, 'Terrorism, "Pure Justice" and Pure "Ethics"'. *Terrorism and Political Violence,* 2(3), Autumn, 1990.

155 Jan Narveson, 'Terrorism and Morality'. In R.G. Frey and Christopher Morris (eds), *Violence, Terrorism and Justice.* Cambridge: Cambridge University Press, 1991, p. 119.

156 Jacob Rabbie, 'A Behavioural Interaction Model: Toward a Social-Psychological Framework for Studying Terrorism'. MS (1991).

157 Ronald D. Crelinsten, 'Victims' Perspectives'. In David L. Paletz and Alex P. Schmid (eds), *Terrorism and the Media: How Researcher, Terrorists, Government, Press, Public and Victims View and Use the Media.* London: Sage, 1992, p. 212.

158 Burleigh Taylor Wilkins, *Terrorism and Collective Responsibility.* London: Routledge, 1992, p. 6.

159 Clive Walker, *The Prevention of Terrorism in British Law*. Manchester: Manchester University Press, 1992, p. 8.

160 P. Wilkinson, 'Observations on the Relationship of Freedom and Terrorism'. In Lawrence Howard (ed.), *Terrorism: Roots, Impact, Responses*. New York: Praeger, 1992, p. 156.

161 C.W. Freeman, *The Diplomat's Dictionary*. Washington, DC: National Defense University Press, 1994, p. 379, quoted in Jamal R. Nassar, *Globalization and Terrorism: The Migration of Dreams and Nightmares*. Lanham, MD: Rowman & Littlefield, 2004, p. 16.

162 Wayne G. Reilly, 'The Management of Political Violence in Quebec and Northern Ireland'. *Terrorism and Political Violence*, 6(1), Spring 1994, p. 45.

163 W. Michael Reisman and Chris T. Antoniou (eds), *The Laws of War: A Comprehensive Collection of Primary Documents on International Law Governing Armed Conflict*. New York: Vintage Books, 1994, p.293.

164 Joachim Schneider, *Kriminologie der Gewalt*. Stuttgart: Hirzel, 1994, p. 175 (translated by A.S.).

165 Matthew G. Devost, Brian Houghton and Neal Allen Pollard, 'Information Terrorism: Political Violence in the Information Age'. *Terrorism and Political Violence*, 9(1), Spring 1997, p. 77.

166 B. Collin, *Convergence of the Physical and Virtual Worlds*. San Jose, CA: Institute for Security and Intelligence, 1997, p. 99.

167 Bruce Hoffman, 'The Confluence of International and Domestic Trends in Terrorism'. *Terrorism and Political Violence*, 9(2), Summer 1997, p. 4.

168 Wayman C. Mullins, *A Sourcebook on Domestic and International Terrorism: An Analysis of Issues, Organizations, Tactics and Responses*. Springfield, IL: Charles C. Thomas, 1997, p. 33.

169 Ibid.

170 Sean K. Anderson, 'Warnings versus Alarms: Terrorist Threat Analysis Applied to the Iranian State-run Media'. *Studies in Conflict and Terrorism*, 21(3), p. 281.

171 Quoted in UN Office of Legal Affairs, *International Instruments related to the Prevention and Suppression of International Terrorism*. New York: United Nations, 2001, pp. 153–154.

172 Peter Chalk, 'Political Terrorism in South-East Asia'. *Terrorism and Political Violence*, 10(2), Summer 1998, p. 97.

173 G. Davidson Smith, *Single Issue Terrorism* (1998), Online available at www.fas.org/irp/threat/com74e.htm as of 13 February 2004. (Commentary, No. 74).

174 Boaz Ganor, 'Defining Terrorism: Is One Man's Terrorist Another Man's Freedom Fighter?' Herzliya, Israel: The Interdisciplinary Center, International Institute for Counter-Terrorism, 1998, p. 12.

175 Bruce Hoffman, *Inside Terrorism*. New York: Columbia University Press, 1998, p. 32.

176 Haig Khatchadourian, *The Morality of Terrorism*. New York: Peter Lang, 1998, p. 11.

177 Advisory Panel to Assess Domestic Response Capabilities for Terrorism Involving Weapons of Mass Destruction, *First Annual Report to the President and the Congress: I. Assessing the Threat*. Arlington, VA: Advisory Panel to Assess Domestic Response Capabilities for Terrorism Involving Weapons of Mass Destruction, 1999, p. iv.

178 Daniel Byman, 'The Logic of Ethnic Terrorism'. *Studies in Conflict and Terrorism*, 21(2), 1998, p. 151.

179 Boaz Ganor, 'Counter-terrorism Policy: Efficacy versus Liberal-Democratic Values, 1983–1999'. PhD dissertation, Hebrew University, Jerusalem, 2002. Quoted from English abstract (13 September 2002) p. 2.

180 US Department of State, *Patterns of Global Terrorism*, 1994, p. 6.

181 Ariel Merari, 'Terrorism as a Strategy of Struggle: Past and Future. *Terrorism and Political Violence*, 11(4), 1999.

182 UN Office of Legal Affairs, *International Instruments related to the Prevention and Suppression of International Terrorism*. New York: United Nations, 2001, p. 212.

183 Quoted ibid., pp. 189–191.

184 Louise Richardson, 'Terrorists as Transnational Actors'. In Max Taylor and John Horgan (eds), *The Future of Terrorism*. London: Frank Class, 1999, p. 2.

185 Quoted in UN Office of Legal Affairs, *International Instruments Related to the Prevention and Suppression of International Terrorism*, pp. 174–175.

186 22 United States Code, Section 2656 (d), quoted in US Department of State, *Patterns of Global Terrorism 1999*. Washington, DC: Deptartment of State, April 2000, p. viii.

187 Joseph J. Collins and Michael Horowitz, *Homeland Defense: A Strategic Approach*. Washington, DC: Center for Strategic and International Studies, 2000, p. 13.

188 Cindy C. Combs, *Terrorism in the Twenty-First Century*. Upper Saddle Rivver, NJ: Prentice Hall, 2000, p. 8.

189 Quoted in Michael Clark, 'China's "War on Terror" in Xinjiang: Human Security and the Causes of Violent Uighur Separatism'. *Terrorism and Political Violence*, 20(20), 2000, quoted from proofs.

190 Nicolas K. Laos, 'Fighting Terrorism: What Can International Law Do?' *Perceptions*, 5(1), March–May 2000, p. 191.

191 Omar Malik, 'Terrorism: Method or Madness. Paper 1. Enough of the Definition of Terrorism'. London: Royal Institute of International Affairs, 2000, p. 11.

192 C.A.J. Coady, 'Terrorism'. In Lawrence C. Becker and Charlotte B. Becker (eds), *Encyclopedia of Ethics*, 2nd edn. New York: Routledge, 2001.

193 H.H.A. Cooper, 'Terrorism: The Problem of Terrorism Revisited'. *American Behavioral Scientist*, 44(6), February 2001, pp. 881–893.

194 Quoted in Jeffrey Benner, 'Who EU Calling a Terrorist?' *Wired News*, at www.wired.com/news/print/0,1294,48807,00.html.

195 Quoted in Michael J. Jordan, 'Terrorism's Slippery Definition Eludes UN Diplomats'. *Christian Science Monitor*, 4 February 2002.

196 UN Doc. A/C.6/56/L.9, Annex I.B, 2001.

197 Richard J. Chasdi, the author of *Tapestry of Terror: A Portrait of Middle East Terrorism, 1994–1999*. Lanham, MD: Lexington Books, 2002, in response to questionnaire.

198 OAS document CP/CAJP1891/02 corr. 1. of 25 March 2002. For the final version of 3 June 2002 (which is less specific), see www.oas.org/xxxiiga/english/docs_en/docs_items/AGres1840_02.htm (accessed 22 July 2010).

199 Quoted in Ignacio Pelaez Marqués (Eurojust), 'Regional and Subregional Efforts Complementing Global Efforts in the Fight against Terrorism. Part 6: The Contribution of the European Union'. In United Nations, Office on Drugs and Crime, *Combating International Terrorism: The Contribution of the United Nations*. New York: United Nations, 2003, p. 108.

200 Ted Honderich, *After the Terror*. Edinburgh: Edinburgh University Press, 2002, pp. 98–99.

201 Stacey L. Knobler, Adel A.F. Mahmoud and Leslie A. Pray (eds), *Biological Threats and Terrorism: Assessing the Science and Response Capabilities: Workshop Summary*, Institute of Medicine, Board on Global Health. Washington, DC: National Academy Press, 2002. Based on a Workshop of the Forum on Emerging Infections, ISBN 0-309-08253-6, S. 276. Online, available at: books.nap.edu/books/0309082536/html/index.html (accessed 11 March 2004).

202 Alex P. Schmid, 'Nuclear Terrorism: How Real is the Threat? Keynote Address', in International Atomic Energy Agency, Office of Physical Protection and Material Security, *Measures to Prevent, Intercept and Respond to Illicit Uses of Nuclear Material and Radioactive Sources*. Vienna: IAEA, 2002, p. 16.

203 Joseph Boyle, 'Just War Doctrine and the Military Response to Terrorism'. *Journal of Political Philosophy*, 11(2), 2003, pp. 155–157.

204 Claudia Card, 'Questions Regarding a War on Terrorism', *Hypatia*, 18(1), Winter 2003.

205 Noam Chomsky, 'Terror and Just Response'. In J.P. Sterba (ed.), *Terrorism and International Justice*. Oxford: Oxford: University Press, 2003, p. 69.

206 Cindy C. Combs, Martin Slann *et al.*, *Encyclopedia of Terrorism*. New York: Checkmark Books, 2003, p. 209.

207 J. Angelo Corlett, *Terrorism: A Philosophical Analysis*. Dordrecht: Kluwer Academic Publishers, 2003, p. 119.

208 Adam Dolnik, 'Die and Let Die: Exploring Links between Suicide Terrorism and Terrorist Use of Chemical, Biological, Radiological, and Nuclear Weapons'. *Studies in Conflict and Terrorism*, 26(1), 2003, p. 20.

209 Jean Bethke Elshtain, *Just War against Terror*. New York: Basic Books, 2003, pp. 18–19.

210 Tomis Kapitan. 'The Terrorism of "Terrorism"'. In J.P. Sterba (ed.), *Terrorism and International Justice*. Oxford: Oxford University Press, 2003, p. 48.

211 NATO Standardization Agency, *NATO Glossary of Terms and Definitions* (English and French). AAP-6 (2004). Brussels: NATO, 2004 (Allied Administrative Publications).

212 Leonard Weinberg and Ami Pedahzur, 'The Challenges of Conceptualizing Terrorism'. Paper prepared for presentation at the annual meeting of the American Political Science Association, Panel 21fl14, Empirical Analyses of Terrorism, Philadelphia, 27–31 August 2003, pp. 10–11. The journals surveyed were *Terrorism* (New York: Crane, Russak, 1978–1991), *Terrorism* (Minneapolis: John Scherer, 1982– 89), *Terrorism and Political Violence* (1990–2001), and *Studies in Conflict and Terrorism* (London: Taylor & Francis, 1992–2002). In addition, Weinberg and Pedahzur incorporated the elements of Schmid's 1988 analysis of 109 definitions into the construction of a new (minimal) consensus definition.

213 J.P. Sterba, 'Terrorism and International Justice'. In J.P. Sterba (ed.), *Terrorism and International Justice*. Oxford: Oxford University Press, 2003, p. 206.

214 Steven Best and Anthony Nocella (eds), *Terrorists or Freedom Fighters: Reflections on the Liberation of Animals*. New York: Lantern Books, 2004, p. 370.

215 Predrag Cicovacki, 'Terrorism and War'. *Acorn: Journal of the Gandhi-King Society*, 12(2), Spring–Summer 2004, pp. 5–17.

216 C.A.J. Coady, 'Defining Terrorism'. In Igor Primoratz (ed.), *Terrorism: The Philosophical Issues*. New York: Palgrave Macmillan, 2004, p. 5.

217 Jacques Derrida, 'Auto-immunités, suicides réels et symboliques entretien réalisé par Giovana Borradori'. In Jacques Derrida and Jürgen Habermas, *Le 'concept' du 11 septembre: dialogues à New York (octobre–décembre 2001*. Paris: Éditions Galilée, 2004, pp. 155–156 (translated by A.S.).

218 'Terrorism'. In *Encyclopaedia Britannica*, 2004, *Encyclopaedia Britannica Online*, 9 June 2004, http://search.eb.com/eb/article?eu=73664 .

219 Nick Fotion, 'The Burdens of Terrorism'. In I. Primoratz (ed.), *Terrorism: The Philosophical Issues*. New York: Palgrave Macmillan, 2004, p. 44.

220 Virginia Held, 'Terrorism, Rights, and Political Goals'. In I. Primoratz (ed.), *Terrorism: The Philosophical Issues*, p. 65.

221 International Counter-Terrorism Academic Community (ICTAC), 2004, quoted in International Policy Institute for Counter-Terrorism, *ICT Newsletter*, no. 4, Spring 2004, p. 11.

222 http://august1.com/pubs/dict/t.htmh (accessed 17 August 2004).

223 Tomis Kapitan, 'Terrorism in the Arab–Israeli Conflict'. In I. Primoratz (ed.), *Terrorism: The Philosophical Issues*, p. 175.

224 Eban Kaplan, 'Terrorists and the internet'. Council Foreign Relations, 8 January 2004, at www.cfr.org/publication/100005/terrorists_and_the_internet.html.

225 Joseph Margolis, 'Terrorism and the New Forms of War'. *Metaphilosophy*, 35(3), April 2004, p. 411.

226 Michael McKenna, 'Understanding Terrorism and the Limits of Just War Theory'. Quoted from unpublished MS.

227 Jeff McMahan, 'The Ethics of Killing in War'. *Ethics*, 114(4), July 2004.

228 Lionel McPherson, quoted from unpublished MS.

229 Igor Primoratz, 'What Is Terrorism?' In I. Primoratz (ed.), *Terrorism: The Philosophical Issues*, p. 24.

230 David Rodin, 'Terrorism without Intent'. *Ethics*, 114, July 2004, p. 755.

231 Peter Simpson, 'Violence and Terrorism in Northern Ireland'. In Igor Primoratz (ed.), *Terrorism: The Philosophical Issues*, p. 161.

232 Saul Smilansky, 'Terrorism, Justification, and Illusion'. *Ethics*, 114, July 2004, p. 790.

233 www.cogsci.princeton.edu/cgi-bin/webwn?stage=1&word=terrorism (accessed 17 August 2004).

234 Michael Walzer, 'After 9/11: Five Questions about Terrorism'. In Walzer, *Arguing about War*. New Haven, CT: Yale University Press, 2004, p. 130.

235 Ibid.

236 Ibid.

237 Robert Young, 'Political Terrorism as a Weapon of the Politically Powerless'. In Igor Primoratz (ed.), *Terrorism: The Philosophical Issues*, p. 56.

238 Noam Zohar, 'Innocence and Complex Threats: Upholding the War Ethic and the Condemnation of Terrorism'. *Ethics*, 114, July 2004, p. 734.

239 Alison M. Jaggar, 'What Is Terrorism, Why Is It Wrong, and Could It Ever Be Morally Permissible?' *Journal of Social Philosophy*, 36(2), 2005, p. 209.

240 Jeff Lewis, *Language Wars: The Role of Media and Culture in Global Terror and Political Violence*. London: Pluto Press, 2005, p. 53.

241 Gabriel Palmer-Fernandez, 'Terrorism, Innocence and Justice'. *Philosophy and Public Quarterly*, 25(3), Summer 2005, p. 24.

242 UN Secretary-General Kofi Annan, quoted in Jeffrey F. Addicott, *Terrorism Law: Materials, Cases, Comments*, 5th edn. Tucson, AZ: Lawyers & Judges Publishing Company, Inc., 2009, p. 4.

243 In response to questionnaire mailed by A.P. Schmid.

244 In response to questionnaire mailed by A.P. Schmid.

245 In response to questionnaire mailed by A.P. Schmid.

226 In response to questionnaire mailed by A.P. Schmid.

247 In response to questionnaire mailed by A.P. Schmid.

248 In response to questionnaire mailed by A.P. Schmid.

249 In response to questionnaire mailed by A.P. Schmid.

250 In response to questionnaire mailed by A.P. Schmid.

251 In response to questionnaire mailed by A.P. Schmid.

252 Louise Richardson, *What Terrorists Want: Understanding the Enemy, Containing the Threat*. New York: Random House, 2006, pp. 4–6.

253 In response to questionnaire mailed by A.P. Schmid.

254 David Rapoport, 'Before the Bombs There Were the Mobs: American Experiences with Terror'. *Terrorism and Political Violence*, 20(2), at note 12 (quoted from MS).

255 In response to questionnaire mailed by A.P. Schmid.

256 Y. Sikand, 'Deoband's Anti-Terrorism Convention: Some Reflections', 11 March 2009, at TwoCircles.net (accessed 7 June 2008).

257 Danica Gianola, *Il volto del terrorismo*. Florence: MEF Firenze Atheneum, 2009, p. 195 (translation from Italian by D.G.).

258 Peter Neumann, *Old and New Terrorism*. Cambridge: Polity Press, 2009, p. 8.

259 Jeffrey F. Addicott, *Terrorism Law: Materials, Cases, Comments*, 5th edn. Tucson, AZ: Lawyers & Judges Publishing Company, 2009, p. 4.

260 Brigitte L. Nacos, *Terrorism and Counterterrorism*, 3rd edn. Boston: Longman, 2010, p. 31.

261 Richard English, *Terrorism: How to Respond*. Oxford: Oxford University Press, 2009.

262 Judith Tinnes, 'Internetbenutzung islamistischer Terror- und Insurgentengruppen unter besonderer Berücksichtigung von medialen Geiselnahmen in Irak, Afghanistan, Pakistan und Saudi-Arabien'. PhD dissertation, Universität des Saarlandes, Saerbrücken, 2010, p. 28 (translated by A.S.).

3

TYPOLOGIES OF TERRORISM AND POLITICAL VIOLENCE

Sarah V. Marsden and Alex P. Schmid

As the previous chapter must have made clear, the conceptualisation of terrorism is fraught with challenges – not least of which is the issue of categorisation, such as:

- Are there theoretical or practical distinctions between terrorist groups?
- What is the utility of trying to identify such differences? and
- What is the best way to approach classification?

Typologies have been repeatedly discussed in the literature on terrorism but have, on the whole, been neglected concerns for most counter-terrorist practitioners.

Here, an attempt will be made to survey the past and present state of knowledge with regard to typologies of terrorism and, to a lesser extent, other forms of political violence. The aim is to provide an overview of some of the most prominent typologies developed in the field. Our survey is a representative rather than an exhaustive catalogue of efforts. The approach taken is primarily descriptive, with analytical consideration of the typologies focusing on broad methodological questions and their usefulness in addressing terrorist phenomena.

To begin with, the utility of typologies in the social sciences and, in particular, in the field of Terrorism Studies is discussed. Comparable efforts to introduce classificatory rigour to some other forms of political violence are then reviewed, to provide a broader canvas on which to position efforts in the field of Terrorism Studies. A short summary of the comprehensive discussion on terrorism typologies presented in the 1988 edition of Schmid *et al.*'s *Political Terrorism* is then given.[1] This is followed by a review of more recent proposals. Finally, consideration of the progress made in the past 20 years of typology work is given, with a view to outlining some fruitful lines of future enquiry.

The utility of typology

Typologies have been used throughout the natural and social sciences as a means of classifying apparently related phenomena.[2] From the eighteenth-century Linnaean classification of the natural world of plants[3] and the nineteenth-century Mendeleev periodic table of the chemical elements,[4] to the twentieth-century classification of personality types in the social sciences,[5] their value has been widely recognised.[6]

Typology has been defined as 'a purposive, planned selection, abstraction, combination and (sometimes) accentuation of a set of criteria with empirical references'.[7] Typologies vary along a number of axes: from the relationship between the type and real-life experience; the degree of abstraction applied; the purpose of the type; the time-span to which it applies; its spatial scope; and the function required of it.[8] Their role has been characterised as descriptive, classificatory and explanatory.[9] A number of arguments have been made for their utility. These include the clarification they bring to inquiry; the parsimony they promote; their application to social action and policy; and their central relationship to theory.

One of the primary benefits of typology is the greater conceptual clarity they allow.[10] This is particularly important when it comes to terrorism and political violence, as it 'frequently involves the interaction and effects of the actions of many persons and collectives involving a multiplicity of motivations, psychological effects and subjective evaluations'.[11] Typologies therefore provide discipline, and enable inaccuracies in a conceptual approach to surface – above and beyond the basic purpose of allowing for the ordering of data.[12]

Arguably, all knowledge is based on constructs, described as idealised representations of phenomena in the social world.[13] Their classification provides a storage system for evidence[14] – a kind of 'data-container'.[15] These break down broad types of phenomena into more convenient units of analysis,[16] which is particularly useful in furthering the understanding of – in our case – terrorism and political violence.[17] Described as especially helpful in young research domains,[18] their ultimate utility with respect to conceptual clarity is said to be due to the fact that 'concept formation stands prior to quantification', since 'we cannot know what to measure unless we know first what we are measuring'.[19]

Associated with this is the parsimonious way in which typologies order complex data.[20] The more straightforward a typology is, the greater is its utility[21] – although too much simplicity has its price. However, we have to keep in mind that – unlike in the natural sciences – exact recurrences of social phenomena are rare.[22] Therefore, the aim of constructing a typology – to reduce such events to ideal-types, without oversimplifying them – is highly valuable.[23]

A further advantage of typologies can be seen in their practical application to the social and political realm. Described as heuristics,[24] typologies should provide the most salient information related to compounds of attributes[25] considered important in the phenomena under scrutiny. This is especially pertinent in the realm of policy since increasingly nuanced explanations, in particular of new or developing situations, are facilitated by typologies.[26] Even simple binary dichotomies such as 'new' and 'old' terrorism have been described as useful to some decision makers.[27] Generally, application to practical policy problems is often considered the mark of quality of a useful typology.[28]

There is also a coherent relationship between typology and theory.[29] This is manifest in a variety of ways: in their foundation and development;[30] in the development of theory based on the typology;[31] and through the criteria of testing and falsifiability.[32] Some argue further, saying that typologies constitute theory in their own right,[33] with some noting an iterative relationship between theory and typology.[34]

A number of reasons have been given for typology to be considered theory; specifically, that they identify constructs and their interrelationships, and that these can be falsifiable and testable.[35] This last point is a particularly useful attribute of rigorously developed typologies.[36] The multiple constructs identified in typologies invite a number of routes for testing hypotheses, for example through comparing phenomena of the same type and across types, as well as through applying instances that are outside the initially established framework.[37] The latter might actually encourage the development of a new theory capable of incorporating the 'outlier'. The utility of typology building has been usefully summarized by G.K. Roberts,[38] who noted that typology should aim 'to discover new relationships among things so ordered, to generate hypotheses, to lead on to the development of theories, and to identify areas for investigation'.[39]

However, it should be borne in mind that the utility of the typology is dependent upon the needs of the user.[40] In the terrorism field, these are many, and include social scientists, counter-terrorism experts, politicians, lawyers and policy makers, all of whom may have different specifi-cations of what makes a useful typology of terrorist groups. With this in mind, and against the criteria for utility identified above, a wide variety of typologies will now be considered, beginning by outlining some of those developed in other spheres of political violence, in order to position the endeavour of typological development in the field of Terrorism Studies in its wider context.

'Typologising' political violence

Political violence is a heterogeneous term covering a wide variety of phenomena.[41] The multiplicity of behaviours considered under its rubric make its classification a demanding task. The issue of definition and the wide, sometimes contrasting, characterisations of political violence employed are particularly problematic.[42] In response, a number of routes have been followed in the development of typologies of political violence.

Where data are of sufficiently high quality, the analysis of political violence as an aggregate category has been advocated.[43] However, where this is not possible, and bearing in mind the variety of types of political violence perpetrated by state and non-state actors, focus on specific forms of violence has been recommended.[44] This is considered likely to enhance the explanatory power of the conceptualisation, and often results in deconstruction, creating sub-types of political violence.[45]

Given the complexity of the phenomena, a simplistic, unitary conceptualisation of political violence is described as more likely to lie 'in the eye of the beholder than in empirical reality'.[46] Therefore, any typology of political violence may be considered a simplification, or exaggeration of reality.[47] As discussed above, the utility of any such attempt should be seen, at the broadest level, in its ability to contribute to knowledge growth[48] and its facilitation of new findings.[49] This can include theory development,[50] as well as serving as a basis for data collection.[51]

In the field of political violence, typologies are thought to be a prerequisite for generalising beyond single cases.[52] This may be considered particularly helpful with respect to the analysis and prevention of conflict.[53] Hence, typologies of political violence are more than research tools, and can be used in the context of defence.[54] For example, where a relationship is posited between a group type and its choice of warfare, the forecasting of likely behaviour may be possible.[55] Further, typologies of political violence are considered useful in policy making[56] – specifically, in the way they can identify what is causally significant and downplay that which is not.[57]

Given these benefits, it is perhaps not surprising that the application of typology in the field of political violence is widespread. Typological efforts have focused on assassination,[58] civil war,[59] *coups d'état*,[60] ethnic conflict,[61] genocide and politicide,[62] hostage taking,[63] insurgency,[64] looting,[65] resistance,[66] revolution,[67] riots,[68] suicide bombers,[69] vigilantism,[70] violent non-state actors,[71] war[72] and warlordism.[73]

In order to systematise these efforts and provide clarity to that which follows, an updated version of the typology of political violence developed by Schmid [74] is now presented. This is illustrated in Table 3.1, and resembles the work of Crelinsten[75]. (It appeared in Chapter 2 as Table 2.2, but is worth repeating here, for clarity.) It aims to position the forms of political violence in a wider classificatory system, and provide a broader context in which to position typologies of political violence and terrorism.

This spectrum of political action reflects the interplay between the forces of order and the forces of change in violent and non-violent opposition modes. It focuses on actors and forms of political violence. In this context, forms of violence may be considered tactics, strategies of action or outcomes. In circumstances where the rule of law is upheld, confrontation is seen through opposition politics, and is classified as free persuasive politics. In the second stage of the escalation, pressure politics are applied by one or both sides, which might or might not be legal and/or legitimate. Some forms of government repression might be legitimate; others might constitute 'crimes of repression'.[76] Some of the tactics available to those opposing an oppressive status quo can be qualified as sedition and subversion.[77] On the other hand, the conceptualisation of forms of illegitimate behaviour by a ruling power against its constituents can be described as oppression and repression.[78] However, in practice there is overlap between these concepts.[79]

Violent politics incorporates a variety of actions available, to varying degrees, to both sides of the conflict dyad, with the list of potential types of behaviour described as nearly endless.[80] For those in power, a greater range of repressive tactics is available, differentiated by the scale of the response to the forces of change. In it most extreme form, national political conflict results in civil war and, where the opposition is victorious, revolution.

In the framework outlined in Table 3.1, the action and reaction of either party are positioned to correspond roughly in line with the strategies available to them. This enables the examination of the tactics in both sides' repertoire, and the potential symmetries and asymmetries of particular conflict scenarios. Such a conceptualisation is useful, for it can reveal asymmetries in conflict waging, for example when a democratic regime is attacked by tactics from the repertoire of violent politics from the side of a non-state violent actor. Ekaterina Stepanova has also used the concept of asymmetry.[81] She delineates terrorist groups in line with two criteria: (1) the scope of a group's aims with respect to global or local concerns; and (2) the position of terroristic action in relation to other forms of violent confrontation, and the extent to which they are used alongside alternative forms of violence. Using these criteria, three functional types of terrorism are identified. The first is 'classic terrorism of peacetime'. Terrorism of this type is separate from any wider armed conflict, and includes

Table 3.1 The spectrum of political action

State of peace	
State actor	Non-regime actor
Persuasive politics	
I. Rule of law (routinised rule, legitimated by tradition, customs, constitutional procedures, compromise politics of give and take)	I. Constitutional opposition politics (formation of opposition press and parties, rallies, electoral contests, litigation [use of courts for political struggle])
Pressure politics	
II. Oppression (manipulation of competitive electoral process, censorship, surveillance, harassment, discrimination, infiltration of opposition, misuse of emergency legislation)	II. Extra-parliamentary action (incl. non-violent action (social protest for political persuasion of rulers and masses; demonstrations to show strength of public support; strikes, boycotts, non-cooperation, civil disobedience, and other forms of pressure politics short of violence)
Violent politics	
III. Violent repression for control of state power	III. Use of violence for challenging state power
III.1 Political justice; mass arrests, banning,deportation	III.1 Material destruction, sabotage, arson
III.2 Assassination	III.2 Assassination (individuated political murder)
III.3 State terrorism (torture, death squads, disappearances, concentration camps)	III.3 Terrorism (de-individuated political murder)
III.4 Massacres	III.4 Indiscriminate massacres
III.5 Counter-insurgency	III.5 Insurgency
State of civil war	

Source: Adapted from Alex P. Schmid *et al.*, *Political Terrorism*. Amsterdam: North-Holland, 1988, pp. 58–59.

'stand-alone' left- and right-wing terrorism. Second, 'conflict-related terrorism' is defined as an 'embedded' tactic incorporated into asymmetric armed conflict. Here, those using terrorism are motivated by a particular cause, and their fight is usually confined to a particular region. They use terrorism as one tactic among others, such as guerrilla-type attacks targeting security forces and critical infrastructures. The third type identified by Stepanova, 'superterrorism', is described as global in scope, and is seen as a relatively new phenomenon. The aims of those falling in this category are said to be existential and non-negotiable. The term is applicable to Al-Qaeda and some other parts of the wider Salafist-jihadist movement. Characteristics of these three types of terrorism are said to be interactive and connected, with the possibility of types combining with one another, dependent upon circumstances. This fluidity, while disturbing on the one hand, is useful on the other, given the interaction of uses and users of terrorism in a dynamic real-world context. It also highlights the problem of static and strictly delineated conceptualisations of political violence, and the need for typologies to be able to incorporate multiple tactics and forms of political action.

One attempt to do this through the presentation of a spectrum of types of political violence has been developed by R. Dekmejian, and is reproduced in Table 3.2.[82] The scale is defined by the magnitude of the violence, and the direction of the violence, which is described as anti-state or state. In the broad category of anti-state political violence, individual terrorism encompasses people acting in isolation against the state and includes terrorist acts by 'lone wolves'. Subnational terrorist actors whose target is the state are delineated by the author by cause. There are therefore three categories of subnational terrorist group: ethnic nationalists who are acting as a result of affiliation with a particular ethnic group; religious militants, a category that can include cults and fundamentalist zealots; and ideological radicals, including groups that hold extreme left- and right-wing ideologies. Transnational terrorism against states is defined by the location of its operation: where violence is enacted away from the group's domestic base, or those with a constituency spread across nations, for example Al-Qaeda. State terrorism is said to outweigh the violence perpetrated by non-state actors, and includes state-sponsored terrorism attacking domestic and transnational targets. The most extreme form of political violence described in the spectrum is that of genocide and politicide, and is defined as being carried out by state actors.

Table 3.2 The spectrum of (terrorist) political violence, according to R. Dekmejian

Direction of violence	Anti state				State
Magnitude	Micro				Macro
Type	Individual terrorism	Subnational terrorism	Transnational terrorism	State terrorism against domestic and transnational opponents	Politicide and genocide
Perpetrators	Assassins	Ethnic nationalists	Transnational terrorist organisations and states	Secret police	Secret police
	Bombers	Religious militants Ideological radicals Hybrid organisations		Special forces Military Paramilitaries Other state-sponsored groups	Special forces Military Paramilitaries Other state-sponsored groups

Source: R.H. Dekmejian, *Spectrum of Terror*. Washington, DC: CQ Press, 2007, p. 10.

While the use of such a spectrum of political violence is helpful, this proposal is limited by its heavy emphasis on terrorism. Of the five types of political violence described, four of these are terroristic, with the fifth being politicide and genocide. This therefore leaves out a considerable number of types of political violence. In addition, the conflation of tactics, motivations, areas of operations and forms of organisation identified in the perpetrators aspect of the design makes comparison across groups less straightforward, and arguably reduces its analytical utility.

The conceptualisation presented in Table 3.1 resembles an approach proposed by Parmentier and Weitekamp,[83] which also incorporates political crimes and serious violations of human rights. While issues of definition remain unresolved, political crimes are considered to be in line with the subjective and objective criteria identified in the Norgaard Principles.[84] These describe six characteristics used to ascertain whether a crime is political: (1) the motive of the offender; (2) the context in which the act is committed; (3) the legal and factual nature of the act, including its gravity; (4) the political objective of the act: at whom it was directed; (5) whether it was carried out following an order from a group of which the actor was a member; and (6) the relationship between the act and the political objective – specifically, the proximity of the relationship and its proportionality.

Parmentier and Weitekamp[85] describe a number of typologies of political crime, which could be superimposed, on the spectrum of political action outlined in Table 3.1. One typology defines two forms of political crime; purely political and related political offences,[86] the second of which is said to incorporate elements of 'common crime' or non-political criminality. A second typology contrasts crimes in defiance of political authority, and those used to defend it.[87] This was developed into crimes committed against the state, aiming to damage the establishment, and those committed by the state against those considered to threaten it.[88] Similarly, Ross[89] proposes crimes by the state (non-oppositional crimes) and those against the state (oppositional crimes). Some of these are also reflected in the behaviours listed in the violent regime and violent action elements of the spectrum of political violence described in Table 3.1.

However, according to Parmentier and Weitekamp,[90] these various conceptualisations presented by different authors,[91] neglect two features of modern political violence: (1) the indistinct division between state and non-state actors, which can result in groups of the same type in conflict with one another; and (2) the international nature of much political crime. This is represented in Figure 3.1. In this conceptualisation, societies are considered pyramids of at least three layers: state apparatus, society organised in non-state groups and associations, and individuals. It is hypothesised that the international community is made up of many such pyramids. Political crimes are all criminal activities undertaken by people in any of these layers against people, institutions or organisation in any other of these layers, national and international, where the intentions, context and consequences are political.

While useful in its consideration of multiple actors and their interrelations, this typology may be more accurately characterised as a typology of political actors, rather than political crimes. Its authors

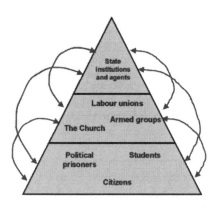

Figure 3.1 Types of political crimes, according to S. Parmentier and E. Weitekamp.

Source: S. Parmentier and E.G.M. Weitekamp, 'Political crimes and serious violations of human rights: towards a criminology of international crimes'. In S. Parmentier and E.G.M. Weitekamp (eds), *Crime and Human Rights: Sociology of Crime, Law and Deviance*, vol. 9. Oxford: Elsevier, 2007.

claim that it is more extensive than existing conceptualisations. This may be accurate with respect to the level of analysis applied, but it is not clear whether this is the case with respect to political violence itself. Since it fails to provide details of types of political violence, its explanatory and descriptive power is limited in this regard.

Typologies of crime, political crime and political violence

The scope of political violence is considerable, and involves a complex array of levels of analysis and overlapping classificatory systems. Thus, what is presented here provides a flavour of work in the field of typologies of crime and political violence. We will consider typologies of violent crime to position the forms of political crime against 'common crime'; attention will also be paid to various forms of non-violent protest. Then, the focus will shift to types of political violence – specifically, typologies of assassination – to give an overview of a specific type of violent behaviour. With respect to the actors responsible for the various kinds of violence, typologies of violent non-state actors will be considered; particular attention will be given to warlordism. A number of conceptualisations of war will also be presented, to offer a wider context against which to consider terrorism. Alongside this, the various types of war crime and human rights violations carried out by states will be discussed to provide a balance to the behaviours of non-state actors.

In addressing 'common crime' or non-political criminality, the focus will remain on violent and serious crime to provide a broad comparator of conceptualisations in each type of behaviour. In the United States, serious violent crime includes rape, robbery, aggravated assault and homicide.[92] In terms of the British classificatory system, violent crime includes robbery, sexual offences, assault and murder.[93] A basic typology proposed in the British Crime Survey (a social survey of victimisation) is based on the relationship between the victim and offender. There are therefore crimes described as domestic violence, involving members of the same household, including partners and ex-partners; mugging, or robbery/attempted robbery; stranger violence, where the victim and offender were not known to one another; and acquaintance violence, when the victim and perpetrator know one another at least by sight.[94]

Typologies of crime have been developed around a number of criteria.[95] These include legalistic ones, where crime is most commonly classified by the degree of punishment it incurs; person centred ones, where criminal classification is on the basis of the personality of the offender; and social typologies, which consider the social context of the offender and the act.[96] A comprehensive typology of criminality has been developed by Clinard and Quinney,[97] and incorporates nine forms of crime. These include violent personal, occasional property, public order, conventional criminal, political criminal, occupational criminal, corporate criminal, organised criminal and professional criminal.

An adaptation of this[98] describes the various types of crime as follows: violent crime, which causes bodily injury or death; property crime, involving the intentional deprivation of the right to property; public order crimes, which disrupt socially acceptable behaviour; occupational crimes, carried out during the course of employment; corporate crime, conducted while carrying out business or deriving from inappropriate business practices; organised crime, perpetrated on an ongoing basis by a group dedicated to its commission; professional crime, which provides the main source of financial support for the offender; and finally, political crimes, which violate the laws of government. In the original iteration, political crimes are described as often committed by those who receive support from a particular constituency, and depend for their acceptance on the degree of (il-)legitimacy ascribed to the government's policies.[99]

To enable a contrast to be drawn between violent and non-violent political action, attention will briefly be given to forms of non-violent protest and sanctions. In 2005, Sharp and Paulson[100] identified 198 manifestations, which are broken down into three groups. The first is non-violent protest and persuasion; this includes petitioning, picketing, holding vigils and participating in marches. The second form is non-cooperation and can encompass activities in the political, economic or social spheres. This is considered more disruptive, and in the social realm can include social boycott and excommunication. In the economic environment, two forms of activity are identified: economic boycotts and labour strikes. The largest class of political non-cooperation can include boycotting elections, civil disobedience and the breaking of diplomatic relations. The most disruptive form of non-violent action is non-violent intervention. This involves deliberately disturbing the status quo using psychological, social, economic or political means, and can involve such activities as sit-ins, non-violent obstruction and the activation of alternative social or economic institutions. It can be coercive but remains non-violent.[101]

Where non-violence as moral and principled action is rejected, a considerable number of tactics become available. Some of these are identified in Table 3.1, including assassination. We discuss assassination here as an exemplar form of political violence to which the techniques of typology construction have been applied. Ben-Yehuda[102] approaches the issue from a temporal and strategic perspective, and utilises the definition of assassination originally proposed by Kirkham, Levy and Crotty:[103] 'an act that consists of a plotted, attempted or actual, murder of a prominent political figure (elite) by an individual (assassin) who performs this act in other than a governmental role'.[104] It differentiates assassination from terrorism through the importance placed on the targeted character of the act, in contrast to the more random nature of terrorism. Neglecting motivation, the typology developed describes four categories: pre-planning, centring on the decision to carry out an assassination attempt; planning, where a decision to go ahead with the killing is made, but is not followed through; unsuccessful, meaning that an attack was attempted but no injury was incurred by the intended target; and successful, resulting in either partial success, seen in the injury of the victim, or full success, which sees the target killed. The author goes on to examine political assassinations by Jews in Palestine–Israel and delineates the motivation for the acts as revenge, or acting against traitors. Assassinations are described as an alternative form of social justice,[105] and may therefore be considered as being on the opposite side of a continuum of political action with principled non-violent political action that might ostracise (ban, exclude) but not kill a political opponent at the other end.

Crotty proposed an alternative conceptualisation.[106] This is built on five types of assassination: anomic, where private reasons motivate the killing of a political figure; elite substitution, an attempt to replace the victim with someone from an opposing group; tyrannicide, or the killing of a despot with the aim of installing a more acceptable leader; propaganda of the deed, which, via the killing, focuses attention on a wider problem; and finally, terroristic assassination. According to Crotty, terroristic assassination can exhibit a variety of forms and be driven by a number of motivations. These include random assassinations hoping to undermine belief in the government, or 'targeted killing' aimed at eliminating particular individuals or groups. This form of assassination can also be perpetrated against a larger number of people. In this case, it serves to demonstrate that the government is incapable of dealing with a rebel or insurgent threat, or is meant to undermine the support for the government through fear. It might also serve to try to gain support for the terrorists' group or cause, or might be used as an instrument employed by a small group to intimidate and hold down a wider population.

Consideration will now be given to those who perpetrate acts of political violence. These are becoming increasingly diverse, and some of the perpetrators have been described as privatised violent actors,[107] or violent non-state actors (VNSAs).[108] These have been the focus of a number of authors; the interpretation of two will be presented here. This will aim to give an overview of those groups that may be considered most likely to act against the controlling power and use some of the forms of political violence outlined in Table 3.1. VNSAs are considered to flourish where there is an absence of capacity or legitimacy in the state. VNSAs are diverse in motivation, purpose and function, strength, financing, structure and in their relationship to the state.[109] A number of key groups have been identified by Williams[110] and include warlords, militias, paramilitary forces, terrorist organisations and criminal groups. Many of these types of group are also catalogued by Sullivan,[111] who expands on Mair's[112] original four types of privatised violent actor: terrorists, organised criminals, rebels or insurgents and warlords, adding private military companies, as well as pirates. Differences in objectives, motivation, strategy and ability are recognised between these groups; yet their common denominator is the instrumental use of violence.[113]

In order to explore one category of VNSAs and provide a group-level comparison for the ensuing discussion of terrorism, some of the contributions to the literature on typologies of warlordism will now be presented. Warlords have been described as differing along a number of dimensions: the size and type of their military force, the degree of legitimacy they hold in a given local area, their sources of finance, and the relationship to their constituency, links to global networks and their relationship to the government.[114] One conceptualisation of warlords positions them along a continuum of armed factions based on the motivation and behaviour of the group.[115] It places ideological movements that wish to change society at one end of the spectrum, and absolute warlords at the other. Between these are groups claiming 'their' ethnic rights, whose objective is the promotion of the interests of a particular group, constituting a 'lesser degree of warlordism'; and ethnic ideological 'entrepreneur' factions, where a higher level of violence is exhibited, and warlordism is a marked feature.[116]

A further characterisation builds on the work of Hill,[117] who described three types of militia: freelance – most often small groups with little local loyalty; clan, which relates to a particular identity; and personal militias, which act at the behest of a particular leader, often based on ideology or ethnic group membership. Jackson[118] suggests that each type of militia typically has a different kind of leader: freelance militias have a gang leader; clan militias have a 'traditional' leader or 'chief'; while personal militias have warlords at their head.

So far, consideration has been given to typologies of 'common crime', forms of non-violent political action, violent political crime, and the various actors who may carry out these forms of crime. We now turn to war, which can be found at the most extreme end of the spectrum of political violence.

To begin with, on the broadest level of analysis, differentiation between 'new wars' and 'old wars' has been suggested.[119] The change from old to new is supposed to have taken place in the 1980s and 1990s, and incorporates a number of emerging themes in the analysis of war and political violence. It specifies that a new form of conflict can be waged with different actors, tactics and goals. Here, combatants and non-combatants are difficult to define, and aims revolve around ideological cleavage, rather than the traditional focus on conquest of territory.[120] This temporal dimension to conflict development is utilised by Pfetsch and Rohloff,[121] who propose three types of conflict. First, they distinguish international conflicts between states, enacted primarily from 1945 to the late 1960s; second, there is violence perpetrated because of ethnic, religious, regional and national power positions, manifest predominantly until the 1990s; and third, there is what is described as the reprivatisation of violence carried out at a subnational level by gangs and organised criminals.

The actor as the predominant focus of analysis can be found in a number of typologies. One long-established example is offered by the Correlates of War Project (CoW) of David Singer. Recently amended to reflect the changing nature of war,[122] the CoW project now classifies three types – interstate war, extra-state war and intra-state war – as opposed to the two types of international war and civil war in Singer's previous conceptualisation. An alternative approach to an actor-led characterisation is that developed by Vasquez,[123] which proposes to distinguish between 'wars of inequality' and 'wars of rivalry'. The first of these are between unequal parties, and the second between more evenly matched opponents. A typology that combines the type of actor and the purpose of the conflict identifies four types of war:[124] (1) interstate or non-interstate; (2) revolution and/or ideology that aim to change the nature of the state; (3) identity or secession, working to change a particular group's relation to the state; and (4) factional, which includes *coups d'état* and warlordism.

Rather than simply distinguishing between old and news wars, and following a temporal approach to the classification of war and conflict, Reed[125] proposes five generations of warfare. The last of these purports to describe the type of violence practised by Al-Qaeda, thus positioning one of the most recent manifestations of terrorism on a continuum of war mutations (see Figure 3.2). This is an evolving model of conflict, incorporating changing domains, adversaries, force and objectives in a multidimensional representation of war. Five generations are posited, the difference between them being attested to via the question of whether an army from one generation, without significantly larger forces, can defeat an army from a subsequent generation. If not, there has been a 'dialectically qualitative shift', and the arrival of a new generation of warfare is implied.[126]

Beginning with the Peace of Westphalia in 1648 following the end of the Thirty Years War between Catholic and Protestant rulers in Europe, the generations move through the industrial revolution (second generation); the Second World War (third generation); and asymmetrical warfare as used by Mao Zedong and the North Vietnamese in the Vietnam War among others (fourth generation). This is considered to evolve into fifth-generation warfare as practised by actors such as Al-Qaeda, the arrival of which is held to be marked by 11 September 2001. Characteristics of the proposed fifth generation are the almost virtual presence of (often networked) actors in what is described as an 'omnipresent battlefield'; and second, the fact that fifth-generation actors do not necessarily use military force, but use both multiple-kinetic and non-kinetic types of force.

This conceptualisation boldly positions political terrorism in its manifestation as irregular warfare in a wider historical sweep. By incorporating objectives, domains of conflict, the nature of the actors

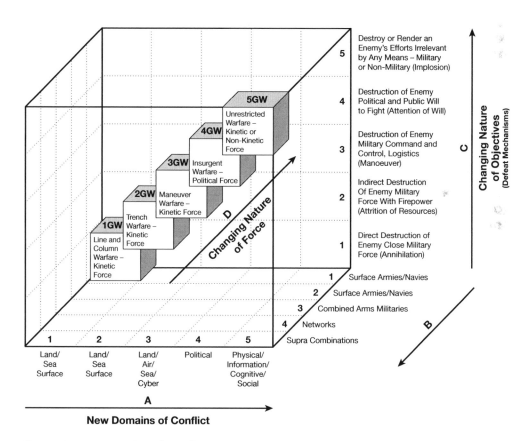

Figure 3.2 A generational typology of war and conflict, according to Reed.

Source: D.J. Reed, 'Beyond the war on terror: into the fifth generation of war and conflict'. *Studies in Conflict and Terrorism*, 31(8), 2008, pp. 684–722.

and the force they apply, it boldly incorporates elements that are separate or excluded in some other typologies. Two common methods of delineating types of war seen in Reed's typology are through the actors and their objectives. One typology that utilises both has been developed by Holsti,[127] who outlines four categories of war: state against state; decolonising wars of national liberation; internal wars fought for ideological reasons; and state–nation conflicts, including wars carried out by particular ethnic, linguistic and religious groups.

Interstate war as described through these typologies has, historically, been one of the most extreme forms of political violence, although it is, in principle, governed by the rules or customs of war codified in the Hague and Geneva Conventions.[128] Broadly speaking, international humanitarian law covers two avenues of managing the violence enacted in war:[129] rules regarding behaviour during hostilities (*jus in bello*), covering the means by which warfare is carried out, especially with regard to non-combatants and soldiers incapable of fighting; and the right to declare and go to war, for example as (collective) self-defence (*jus ad bellum*).[130]

Where the laws of war are not adhered to, war crimes or other breaches of the laws of war, including crimes against humanity, may have been committed.[131] According to the 1945 International Military Tribunal of Nuremberg Charter,[132] these may include

> murder, ill-treatment or deportation to slave labour or for any other purpose of civilian population of or in occupied territory, murder or ill-treatment of prisoners of war or persons on the seas, killing of hostages, plunder of public or private property, wanton destruction of cities, towns or villages, or devastation not justified by military necessity.[133]

There are three types of breaches;[134] first, non-serious breaches or common violations, the sanction for which is administrative. Then, there are serious breaches, which come in two forms: war crimes, which states are at their discretion as to whether to prosecute; and grave breaches, or serious war crimes, committed against people protected under the Geneva Conventions, for which prosecution is mandatory.[135]

Political crimes carried out by the ruling power can be described alternatively as violations of international humanitarian law or human rights violations, depending on the context – whether they are committed in a time of war or in peace time.[136] Human rights violations have been conceptualised in a number of ways. One legalistic approach posits three generations of human rights.[137] The first generation, based on the Magna Carta, the American Bill of Rights and the Rights of Man of the French Revolution, includes freedom of expression, conscience and religion, freedom of the press, freedom of assembly, free correspondence and freedom from arbitrary detention. The second generation, said to have emerged from the nineteenth-century class struggles, incorporates economic, social and certain cultural rights, including the right to work, health care, education and participation in cultural life. Finally, the third generation includes 'candidate' rights for groups based on the 'equal rights of peoples'.[138] These include the right of peoples to existence, the rights of minorities to their own culture, religion and language, and the rights of people to humanitarian assistance.

An alternative typology of serious human rights violations is that proposed by Parmentier and Weitekamp.[139] This is displayed in Figure 3.3 and uses the quantitative measure of frequency of the act, and the qualitative measure of gravity. This may be considered useful for conceptualising degrees of human rights violations. However, the classificatory device of gravity and frequency would require more detailed explanation to maximise its utility. This may lead to a more fully developed typology that delineates types of human rights violations, rather than the less specified spectrum of seriousness.

In considering only a sample of typologies of crime, non-violent protest and political violence other than terrorism, the variety in levels of analysis, and the differences in the features of particular oppositional phenomena considered important by analysts, are indeed wide-ranging. War, for instance, is 'typologised' by some authors along multiple dimensions such as purpose, adversary, force and domain, while other authors focus on the types of actors and the objective of their violence.

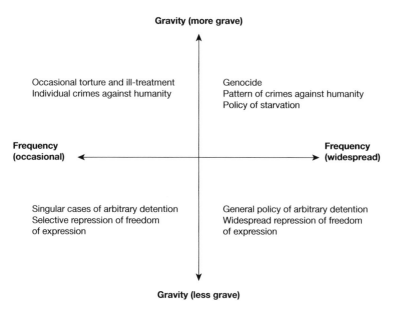

Gravity (more grave)

Occasional torture and ill-treatment
Individual crimes against humanity

Genocide
Pattern of crimes against humanity
Policy of starvation

**Frequency
(occasional)**

**Frequency
(widespread)**

Singular cases of arbitrary detention
Selective repression of freedom
of expression

General policy of arbitrary detention
Widespread repression of freedom
of expression

Gravity (less grave)

Figure 3.3 A (non-exhaustive) typology of serious human rights violations.

Source: S. Parmentier and E.G.M. Weitekamp, 'Political crimes and serious violations of human rights: towards a criminology of international crimes'. In S. Parmentier and E.G.M. Weitekamp (eds), *Crime and Human Rights: Sociology of Crime, Law and Deviance*, vol. 9. Oxford: Elsevier, 2007.

In moving the discussion on to non-state actors, the multiplicity of types operating that have force or violence in their behavioural repertoire was illustrated. This was further highlighted by a more detailed examination of warlords, of which a number of types were presented. Finally, consideration was given to war crimes and human rights violations, to balance the discussion by focusing on the illegitimate or illegal actions of those in power.

Against this background of violence other than terrorism, we now turn to terrorism itself. In the previous discussion, terrorists were represented either as a fifth generation of virtual networked players utilising new forms of force[140] or as one of a variety of regime and violent non-state actors.[141] Given the potential consequences of terroristic behaviour, and the complexity of the inter-relationships between types of political violence, the conceptualisation of terrorism is arguably one of considerable importance. This is illustrated in the numerous attempts made to address this question over the years. The contested state of the definition of terrorism (as illustrated in Chapter 2) makes the relationship to other forms of political violence a complex one. With this in mind, a review of typologies of terrorism will now presented. What follows is an outline of efforts to develop a typology of terrorism as represented in the chapter by Schmid, Stohl and Flemming in the second (1988) edition of *Political Terrorism: A New Guide to Actors, Authors, Concepts, Databases, Theories and Literature*[142] This serves to position the typology debate in its historical context before we move on to more recent typological work.

Pre-1988 typologies of terrorism

The typologies identified by Schmid, Stohl and Flemming were delineated into a number of classes, based respectively on the type of international terrorism, the type of actor and the type of political orientation, together with multidimensional and purpose-based typologies. An outline of those considered most useful by the authors of the 1988 review is given, alongside their proposals for typology.

Demarcations of international terrorism through a legislative lens were described by two authors, and focused on the relationship between the actor, the state where they were based, and the victim. Dror[143] divided international terrorism into three kinds: imported terrorism, transient terrorism and extra-territorial terrorism. The first was terrorism enacted 'by and on behalf of aliens'; the second described violence 'by and against aliens'; while the third considered terrorism targeting 'external representatives and the symbols of the democracy'. From a prosecutorial point of view, these are useful distinctions. A similar legalistic description was provided by Waugh,[144] who distinguished between spill-over terrorism of foreign nationals against foreign individuals or property; integrated internal terrorism, where either the target or the terrorist is indigenous; and external terrorism, where the terrorist act takes place outside the boundary of the target government. However, while these are useful for legal purposes, their utility for social science is less obvious, as these categories are unable to contribute to our understanding of terrorism or explain the behaviour of terrorists. Enhancing understanding and explanation of the phenomenon under consideration, however, are key attributes of a useful typology. Yet the difference in approach, illustrated by two legalistic attempts of typologising, highlights the problem of developing a universally helpful, inclusive typology of terrorism and terrorists.

A number of typologies categorised as actor-based were summarized in the Schmid, Stohl and Flemming chapter of 1988, partly based on the difference between state and non-state actors. This allowed differentiation between establishment regime (state or governmental) terror, and non-state, insurrectional agitational terror,[145] and the parallel differentiation between regime terror and an anti-regime siege of terror.[146] These two classifications were considered unproblematic, but were juxtaposed with categorisations that implied judgements about the legitimacy of the actors, probably an insufficient criterion of classification. As we saw in Chapter 2, on definitions, some authors also use the concept of 'terror' for a certain type of state violence, and 'terrorism' for the non-state variant.

In consideration of typologies based on the political orientation of the group, a number of proposals were outlined. These included one differentiating between national or anti-colonial liberation movements, regional or separatist movements, social-revolutionary movements in industrialised countries, defensive associations to protect group privileges, and opposition movements in dictatorial systems where non-violent political change is blocked.[147] Another, built on the difference between left- and right-wing terrorists whose target is the state, incorporated the following categories: ethnic, religious and nationalist groups; Marxist-Leninsts; anarchists; pathological groups or individuals; neo-fascist groups or individuals; and ideological mercenaries.[148] At a broader level, delineation between nationalist-separatist (including ethnic); issue; ideological; exile; state and state-sponsored; and religious terrorism was proposed by G. Davidson Smith.[149]

To try to overcome ambiguity regarding the assignment of groups to types, as may be the problem with some of those identified above,[150] Schmid, Stohl and Flemming[151] proposed categorising actors that target the state and actors that do not. This last category included paramilitary vigilante groups. It was proposed that where vigilantism, described as an understudied phenomenon, fulfils key criteria of terrorism (violence against civilians, or intended to intimidate or otherwise influence third parties), it should be included in typologies. Vigilantes come in three main forms: crime-control vigilantes; social-group-control vigilantism; and regime-control vigilantes.[152]

A further type of violent actor, who the authors argued should be incorporated into typologies of terrorism, is that of the 'lone-wolf' terrorist.[153] Wilkinson[154] subsumed this type under 'sub-revolutionary' terrorism, which includes manifestations of terrorism whose aim is less ambitious than state change. This was built upon by Shultz[155] to produce a categorisation of revolutionary terrorism. Depicted as violence or threat of violence aiming to effect change, it incorporates the following categories: revolutionary terrorism, aiming for fundamental revolutionary change of the political-social process; sub-revolutionary terrorism, which hopes to change parts of the political system; and establishment terrorism carried out by those in power against opposition to their rule.[156]

A number of authors have proposed multidimensional typologies. Merari[157] considers a group's target population and operational base, producing a 2 × 2 matrix of potential types of terrorism. Schmid and de Graaf developed a more comprehensive multidimensional typology in the early 1980s.[158] They proposed a typology incorporating political orientation, motives and actors, as represented in Figure 3.4. Widely used in the literature,[159] it introduced the category 'single–issue terrorism', which has since been applied to non-state actors with a narrow political agenda, such as those who bomb abortion clinics. In subsequent publications, Schmid added the category 'religious terrorism', which was absent in his original 'basic typology of terrorism' from 1982.

A final category of typologies reviewed in Schmid *et al.*'s *Political Terrorism* (1988) is that of purpose-based categorisations. Using a division into types of purpose, but not into a formal typology, Thornton[160] split terrorist aims into morale building, advertising, disorientation, elimination of opposing forces and provocation of countermeasures by incumbents. This was subsequently expanded by J. Bowyer Bell,[161] who considered four types of revolutionary terror – organisational, allegiance, functional and symbolic – and two forms of manipulative terror – that which exploits and escalates the impact of the violence, and that which is used in a bargaining situation. Crenshaw[162] also builds on Thornton's seminal work and presents a typology incorporating tactical considerations and proximate objectives. This is represented in Table 3.3.

The category of degree of discrimination was first proposed in Karber's[163] typology, which interprets terrorism as a symbolic use of violence as well as a means of communication. Here, the message changes in line with the level of discrimination, hence 'the more general the target group, the more diffuse the message'.[164] The degree of discrimination is juxtaposed with the influence of the terrorist act. This is categorised as 'instrumental influence', where there is an immediate impact on behaviour because of fear, and 'affective influence', which produces a long-term behavioural impact because of identification with the actor. The result is four types of terrorism: coercive bargaining, advertising and recruiting, social paralysis, and social conscience. Three of these were produced in a different effort,[165] with the last category of social conscience being described as 'mass casualties', illustrating a considerable diversion from Karber.[166]

Shultz has developed one typology that incorporates many of the variables identified in the literature.[167] It utilises causes, environment, goals, strategy, means, organisation and participation, and contrasts them with categories of terrorist group ideology: revolutionary, sub-revolutionary and establishment terrorism. This is a comprehensive approach, and produces an array of potentially useful features of the terrorist group's origins, purpose and organisation. It is reproduced in Table 3.4. As can be seen, the variables identified are largely the same for (sub-)revolutionary and establishment, which makes it more of a mechanical classification than a content-rich typology.

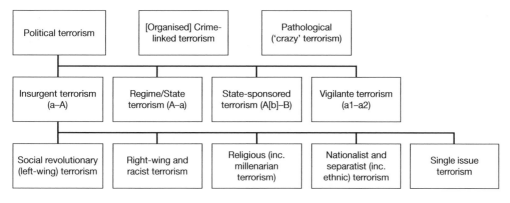

Figure 3.4 A basic typology of terrorism, by A. P. Schmid (1982).
A = state actor; a1, a2 = non-state actors; [b] = proxy actors; B = other state actor.

Table 3.3 Typology of acts of terrorism, according to Crenshaw (1979)

Proximate objectives	Tactical considerations		
	Target	Response	Discrimination
Morale building	Sympathisers	Enthusiasm	Irrelevant
Advertising	Mass	Curiosity	High
Disorientation	Mass	Anxiety	Low
Elimination	Victim and identification group	Despair and immobility	High
Provocation	Identification group	Fear	High

Source: Adapted from A.P. Schmid, M. Stohl and P. Flemming, 'Typologies'. In A.P. Schmid *et al.*, *Political Terrorism*. Amsterdam: North-Holland, 1988.

Table 3.4 Shultz's multi-dimensional typology

General categories	Causes	Environment	Goals	Strategy	Means	Organisation	Participation
Revolutionary and Sub-revolutionary	Economic, political, social, psycho-logical	Internal (urban/revolu-tionary groups) External (autono-mous, non-state revolu-tionary actors)	Long range/strategic objectives Short term/tactical objectives	Primary/secondary role in overall strategy	Various capabilities/techniques	Nature & degrees of organisa-tional structures	Participant profiles leadership style/attitude
Establishment	Economic, political, social, psycho-logical	Internal (repression of urban/rural population) External (other states/non-state actors)	Long range/strategic objectives Short term/tactical objectives	Primary/secondary role in overall strategy	Various capabilities/techniques	Nature & degrees of organisa-tional structures	Participant profiles Leadership style/attitude

Source: Adapted from A.P. Schmid, M. Stohl and P. Flemming, 'Typologies'. In A.P. Schmid *et al.*, *Political Terrorism*. Amsterdam: North-Holland, 1988.

Through this presentation of the state of the art around 1990, the variety of approaches, levels of analysis and degrees of methodological rigour employed is clear. As already observed, the utility of a typology is in large part dependent on the user and the question being asked of it. Goldaber proposed one illuminating typology that explicitly recognises this[168] – a typology of hostage takers, presented in Table 3.5. Goldaber's typology is structured around a number of questions such as: who is the hostage taker? What is the distinguishing characteristic or situation? These questions are tabulated against those whose motivation is described as psychological, criminal or political. These three categories are broken down into sub-categories; for example, 'political' includes social protestor, ideological zealot and terrorist extremist. Each type is then described in response to the questions posed. This allows the user to identify the question they need answering and to produce an outline response in line with the specifications of the typology. In our view, this is one of the very best typologies available, offering great usefulness to practising hostage negotiators.

A number of ways of presenting typologies has so far been proposed. A young Austrian scholar under the supervision of Schmid portrays one new endeavour in Figure 3.5.[169] Löckinger's typological tree organises the various forms of terrorism into four categories: actors, means and methods, motives, and, finally, by geographic range. These various types are further broken down

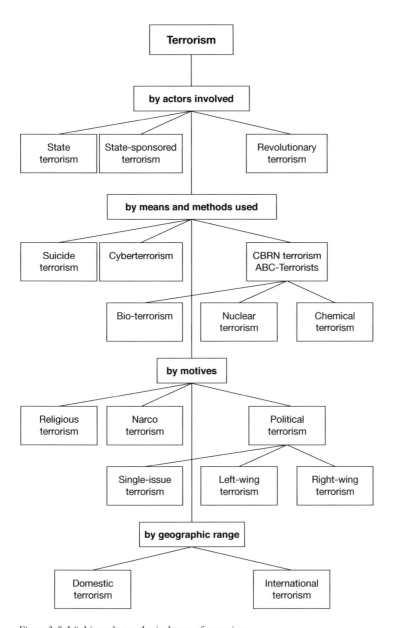

Figure 3.5 Löckinger's typological tree of terrorism.

Source: G. Löckinger, *Terrorismus, Terrorismusabwehr, Terrorismusbekampfung.* Vienna: Ministry of Defence.

Table 3.5 Typology of hostage takers, adapted from Goldaber (1979)

	PSYCHOLOGICAL			CRIMINAL			POLITICAL		
	Suicidal personality	Vengeance seekers	Disturbed individual	Cornered perpetrator	Aggrieved inmate	Felonious extortionist	Social protestor	Ideological zealot	Terrorist extremist
Who's the hostage taker	An unstable, hopeless, depressed individual in crisis	An otherwise ordinary person who is a disaffected former associate	An acutely or chronically unbalanced individual	Potentially any criminal	A frustrated, desperate leader who can organise other inmates	An unemotional, cunning, professional criminal	An idealistic, educated young person	A fanatic, programmed cultist	An individual willing to sacrifice himself for his political philosophy
What is his distinguishing characteristic or situation?	Doesn't care if he is killed	Is driven by an irrational single purpose	Manifest lack of judgement leading to an unsound assessment of reality	Is caught unaware with no prior plan for handling predicament	Is familiar with the setting, prison authority, adversaries, and his victims	Is knowledgeable about, and respectful of police power	Is an exuberant celebrant in an uplifting group experience	Is willing to sacrifice himself for his beliefs	Has realistic assessment of impact of act
When does he take the hostage?	In a severe emotional, decompensating states	After meticulous planning	When his aberrant mind seizes on the idea as a solution to his problem	In desperation, when victims are available	After considerable planning, or spontaneously when pushed beyond endurance	While executing a carefully prepared plot	When he identifies the need to eliminate a social injustice	After he has sustained a wrong	When publicity potential is greatest

Where does he commit the act?	In any place when his defences fall	In a spot that brings him maximum satisfaction	In any setting	In the area in which he is trapped	In his own environment	In location of his selection	At the site of the unwanted entity or event or where the protest is most visible	Anywhere	Where his victim is off guard
Why does he do it?	To cause someone else to fulfil his deathwish	To gain revenge	To achieve mastery and to solve his problem	To effectuate escape	To bring about situational change or to obtain freedom	To obtain money	To create social change or social justice	To redress a grievance	To attain political change
How does he take the hostage?	With irrational taunts	Through overt action or furtive behaviour	In an improvised, illogical manner	With weapon and as a reflexive response	With planned, overpowering force	With a weapon in a calculated manner	In a group by massing a human thrust or blockade	With robot-like violence or non-violent conduct	With emotional and violent execution of a crafty plot

Source: I. Goldaber, 'Typology of hostage-takers', cited in A.P. Schmid, M. Stohl and P. Flemming, 'Typologies'. In A.P. Schmid *et al.*, *Political Terrorism*. Amsterdam: North-Holland, 1988, p. 54.

into sub-types, which describe the major dimensions of terrorism and how they have been conceptualised. This typology helpfully provides a graphic illustration of the different ways in which terrorism may be considered, and allows the positioning of new work into the meta-framework, generating a dynamic representation of the manifestations of terrorism.

A similar outline of ways in which terrorism and its characteristics can be displayed has been developed by Boaz Ganor[170] and is depicted in Figure 3.6. Ganor aims to combine categories utilised in terrorism typologies, and uses multiple dyadic juxtapositions as an organising principle. This is a combination of typologies, rather than a typology for the organisation of terrorist groups. As Ganor recognises, its explanatory power is reduced by the scope of the criteria it considers, as the more features of a group considered in any conceptualisation, the less helpful it is to the analyst. This leads to Ganor's development of the 'limiting variable' typology represented in Figure 3.8.

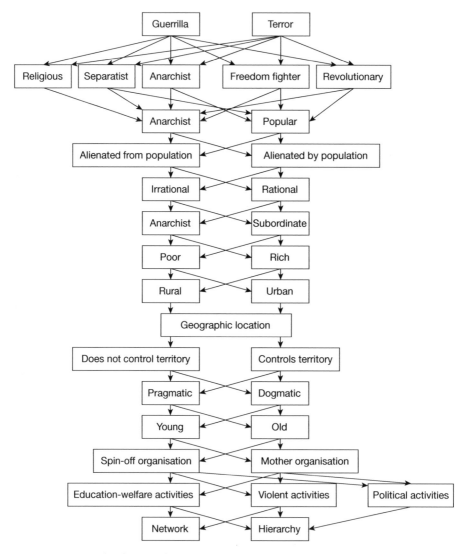

Figure 3.6 Ganor's classification of terrorist organisations by their characteristics.

Source: B. Ganor, 'Terrorist organisation typologies and the probability of a boomerang effect'. *Studies in Conflict and Terrorism*, 31(4), 2008, pp. 269–283.

Applying Goldaber's approach to typology development, what follows is an overview of typologies of terrorism developed in recent years, based on key questions like: who are the terrorists? Why do they utilise terrorism? Where do they stage their acts? When does it change? And how do they do it? If described in single terms and related to more traditional descriptions of typologies, this might be defined as the actor, motivation or purpose, location, time-frame, and organisation of terrorist groups. A number of multidimensional typologies have been developed; these will be allocated to the question deemed to be of greatest relevance to the typology. Thus, while this approach does not make it possible to draw absolutely neat boundaries between types of typology, the hope is that researchers will be directed to the most useful conceptualisations for their needs. We also hope that through this categorisation of the field, gaps in knowledge may be more easily identified.

Who are the terrorists?

As may be observed from the number of typologies outlined in the preceding discussion, actor-based categorisations are a favourite way of classifying terrorism. This is still the case, with a number of the more recent typologies also applying this level of analysis. A key variable is the relationship of the terrorist (group) to the state. Thus, Chakravorti[171] divides terrorism into three types: establishment, anti-establishment and criminal professional. The first identifies the rulers – those holding state power utilising the weapon of terror to enforce social cohesion through forced compliance based on the threat of violence. Anti-establishment terrorism, on the other hand, is directed against the government controlling authority, with criminal-professional terrorism included in this typology because of the often-claimed (and less often found) links between criminal groups and both establishment and anti-establishment terrorism. The very high level of abstraction and the inclusion of actors who may not use terrorism as a sole or primary route to goal attainment mean that its analytical usefulness is somewhat limited.

Looking at the broader global stage, Lizardo and Bergesen[172] consider the position of the terrorist group in relation to the world system. Thus, groups are either embedded in the structural core, on its periphery, or in between, in the semi-periphery.[173] This identifies three actor–target dyads: (1) core actors against governments; (2) peripheral or semi-peripheral actors against peripheral or semi-peripheral governments; and (3) peripheral or semi-peripheral actors against core states. These categories are utilised alongside ideological justification to outline three types of terrorism. Ideology is delineated according to historical period, and echoes Rapoport's[174] theory of four waves of terrorism. The outcome is a typology of three types. The first of these is described as 'terror in the core', where terrorist violence is carried out in core states as a sign of revolt. The second is 'struggling against oppression' and, according to Lizardo and Bergesen, is held to constitute most terrorist activity. Type 1 groups often grow from this type of violence, which tends to be located in the semi-periphery or periphery of the global system and targets local governments. The third type refers to 'the transnational turn', when groups in the semi-periphery attack core targets across international borders. First seen in the 1960s, when transnational terrorism was used against European countries in the framework of the Palestinian–Israeli confrontation, the current wave of religious terrorism is also assigned to this category. This has increasingly diffuse targets but aims to destroy some features of the implied world system.

The degree of political alienation of the terrorist group from the political process has also been used as a way of classifying such groups.[175] In this conceptualisation, there is a continuum from activists via militants to terrorists, with each sub-type evincing different levels of alienation, termed medium, high and extreme. Rhetoric and action are used as measures for positioning the group on the spectrum. This use of a continuum is helpful in considering radicalisation processes, allowing phased movement through the scale. It allows the possibility of tracing groups in their progress towards or away from political alienation. If the measures of rhetoric and action were defined more concretely, this would allow the formulation of testable hypotheses as to when and how groups move from one category to another. This, in turn, might have very practical benefits for governments when they are deciding the threshold beyond which an organisation is judged to have become extremist, and likely to engage in terrorism.

The case of narco-terrorism is one that straddles two of the forms of terrorism identified in the typology exhibited in Figure 3.4.[176] Some groups identified as carrying out terrorism linked to organised crime and others engaged in political terrorism are said to be working together, in particular with respect to narcotics.[177] This 'grey area phenomenon'[178] or crime–terror nexus[179] describes the alleged – and in some cases real – logistical or operational links between ideologically motivated terrorist groups and organised criminal enterprises driven more by profit than by power, and is exemplified in the politicised concept of narco-terrorism. The utility of combining conceptual and operational responses to codify the concept of narco-terrorism has been discussed by Schmid.[180] The view taken was that there are forms of cooperation between criminal organisations and between different terrorist organisations – and further, that some terrorist groups profit from engaging in criminal activities, while there is also some evidence of organised criminal groups using terrorist tactics. Finally, cooperation is seen between terrorist groups and organised criminal groups. However, these links are, in most cases, insufficiently strong to justify a category of narco-terrorism. Furthermore, the legal and conceptual ramifications are likely to result in an unhelpful stretching of the terrorism concept.[181]

The category of narco-terrorism has been used especially by political operators in the field of counter-terrorism who sought an opportunity to infuse new life into the 'war on drugs' by linking it to the 'war on terror'. Attempts to link Al-Qaeda's core to drug trafficking, while numerous, stand on very shaky empirical grounds.[182] However, in the case of the FARC in Colombia, for instance, the evidence is more solid. In reality, terrorists often use criminal methods to keep their groups alive, and criminal gangs sometimes have recourse to terrorist methods to intimidate sectors of the state or the public. In most instances, however, terrorist groups use organised crime methods as an in-house money-making mechanism rather than risk endangering their security by entering dangerous liaisons with drug traffickers and the like.[183]

A number of typologies dealing with state or regime terrorism have been proposed, and most often represent the relationship between those carrying out acts of terrorism and sectors of the government. Thus, Pillar[184] describes state sponsors of terrorism as identified in US law; enablers of terrorism; and cooperators in counter-terrorism efforts. The use of terrorism by states as a foreign policy tool has been described as consisting of five forms.[185] These include coercive terrorist diplomacy, where overt but often implicit threats are made to demand compliance with a particular goal. Clandestine state terrorism, on the other hand, is covert and involves agents of the state perpetrating acts of terrorism against another state. A proxy group on behalf of the state carries out state-sponsored terrorism; surrogate terrorism is a more remote form of sponsorship involving the enabling of a group leading to an enhanced capacity to carry out terrorism. Finally, there is state acquiescence in the execution of terrorism which, subsequently, is not condemned or opposed by the state because of the existence of mutually shared interests between state and terrorist actors (for more details, see Chapter 4 on theories of terrorism).

This spectrum of support has also been described in the form and degree of assistance a state provides to terroristic behaviour. Richardson[186] describes this spectrum as moving from complete state control, discussed in terms of state repression rather than terrorism, through the recruitment and training of actors who will act internationally; close control, where the state provides direction to a group; provision of training, finance and a safe haven to an autonomous group; and financial support alone, where the aims of the group and the state coincide.

Why do terrorists act?

The question of why terrorists act is possibly the broadest question, and incorporates typologies previously considered under the rubrics of motivation, cause, purpose, objective and aim. While these are not synonymous, their ability to inform understanding of the reasons underlying terrorist behaviour, and the need for parsimony of presentation, warrant their consideration as a group. There are a plethora of potential purposes and functions that have been attributed to, and claimed by, terrorist groups. An early catalogue of these found at least 20 factors discussed by authors,[187] ranging from enforcement to obedience, projection of strength, acquisition of popular support and to win recruits, as well as provocation and to terrorise a particular audience. The first two pieces of work presented below are not strictly typologies but are noted here because they are considered to feed into the potential development of terrorist group types by identifying structural causes for group development.

At the broadest level, Ross[188] looks at structural causes of political terrorism. Other potential causes are recognised as being psychological, and rational-choice-based drivers. However, the empirical focus here is structural. Through examination of the literature, case studies on the causes of terrorism and terrorist organisation development, the author identified, using terminology originally introduced by Martha Crenshaw, a number of permissive and precipitant causes.[189] Permissive, or 'deeper systemic conditions that pre-structure and facilitate the presence of the precipitant [causes]', were found to be in a number of forms. First, geographical location in urban environments tends to facilitate terrorism more than rural settings. Second, the type of political system has an effect, with wealthy democracies being at greater risk of harbouring terrorists. Finally, and most importantly, the level of modernisation of a country was identified as significant. Precipitant causes were found to be social, cultural and historical facilitation of norms allowing terrorism's development; organisational split and development between more and less extreme elements of a group; the presence of other forms of unrest acting as catalysts; support for the group; failure by counter-terrorist organisations; availability of weapons; and grievances (real and perceived). This last is considered the most important factor. The cumulative picture produced by these causal factors is displayed in Figure 3.7. This acknowledges the centrality of feedback mechanisms, and considers the context of the terrorist group, including supporters and opponents. It may also be considered to fulfil Roberts'[190] criteria of being able to identify new relationships among phenomena, having the potential for hypothesis generation and theory development, and being able to identify new areas for investigation. It also has the considerable advantage of being empirically based, giving it a solid foundation.

An alternative attempt to Martha Crenshaw's mapping of the various causes of terrorism is that of Post *et al.*[191] Through consultation with experts in the field, they identify four broad categories of causes. These are historical, cultural and contextual features; key actors such as the regime, and opponents and supporters of the group; group and organisational characteristics, for example group processes and structures; and features of the immediate situation, or triggering events. These are deconstructed into 32 variables with key indicators of risk of group radicalisation subsumed within them. This comprehensive approach outlines a plethora of potentially important circumstances in the development of group violence. However, this thoroughness may make it unwieldy for analysts and, while it fulfils many of the criteria for being a useful framework of analysis, it may not be as helpful as more parsimonious conceptualisations. The authors did, however, apply the framework to types of terrorist groups as identified by Schmid and de Graaf,[192] with the addition of a category for new religions. This produced an overview of those factors considered important in radical group development per type of terrorist group, thus providing a base for empirical testing, and highlighting gaps of knowledge in the field.

A similar attempt to identify key variables was made by Sirseloudi and Schmid, and is represented in Table 3.6.

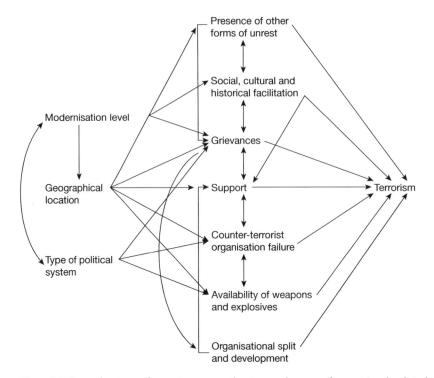

Figure 3.7 General pattern of causation among the structural causes of oppositional political terrorism.

Source: J. Ross, 'Structural causes of oppositional political terrorism: towards a causal model'. *Journal of Peace Research*, 30(3), 1993, pp. 317–329.

One concept that recurs in the typological literature is the role of ideology. Paul Wilkinson,[193] for instance, categorised terrorist groups by political motivation or ideological orientation, listing them under the headings of nationalism, separatism, racism, vigilantism, ultra-left ideology, religious fundamentalism, millennialism and single-issue campaigns. In addition to these, the author proposed that state terrorism and state-sponsored terrorism be added to the list. Similar conceptualisations have been presented by Bruce Hoffman,[194] who details ethno-nationalist, left- and right-wing, and religious terrorism. Vasilenko,[195] in turn, distinguishes between political, separatists, nationalist, religious and criminal terrorism. Cronin[196] identifies leftist, rightist, ethno-nationalist/separatist and sacred terrorism. These are all considered to have had prominence in particular time periods, with sacred terrorism being the most recent phase. Cronin highlights the difficulty of allocating groups to concrete categories, as they may have a number of motivating ideologies. However, the domination of one is not unusual, and is argued to be related to terrorist group behaviour, violence and development. This allows the possibility of hypothesis testing, and subsequent theory development, as well as directing potential interventions. The treatment of sacred or religious terrorism as a sub-category of ideological terrorism raises a new set of questions, the answer to which is dependent upon on how one defines religion – a concept almost as contested as terrorism, as the following list[197] illustrates.

- A religion is a unified system of beliefs and practices relative to sacred things, that is to say, things set apart and forbidden – beliefs and practices which unite into one single moral community called a Church, all those who adhere to them (Emile Durkheim).
- Religion is (1) a system of symbols which acts to (2) establish powerful, pervasive and long-lasting moods and motivations in human beings by (3) formulating conceptions of a general

Table 3.6 Indicators pointing towards the formation of terrorist groups and the occurrence of terrorist campaigns

Root causes		*Accelerators*	
1	Lack of democracy	1	Counter-terrorist campaign causing many
2	Lack of rule of law		victims 'calling' for revenge and retaliation
3	Lack of good governance	2	Humiliation of the group or its supporters
4	Lack of social justice	3	Threat
5	The backing of illegitimate regimes	4	Peace talks
6	High/rising distributive inequality	5	Elections
7	Historical experience of violent conflict waging	6	Symbolic dates
8	Support for groups using terrorist means		*Decelerators*
9	Vulnerability of modern democracies	1	Moderate counter-campaign using legitimate
10	Failed states / safe havens outside state control		means
		2	Loss of charismatic leaders/key resources/
			territory for retreat
		3	Essential concessions towards the terrorist
			constituencies' political demands
		4	Responsible media coverage
Proximate causes		*Precipitants*	
1	Escalatory counter strategy	1	Risk assessments of attacks
2	Expectations of support group (esp. regarding diaspora)	2	Logistical preparations
		3	De-legitimation of the enemy
3	Declining support/rising support	4	Disappearance of key persons
4	Declining media coverage	5	Rising interest in potential targets
5	'Successful' rival groups	6	Increase of internal violence
6	Problems of internal group cohesion		
7	Group's leader's personal image-strategy		
8	De-escalating low-intensity conflict		
9	Escalating violent political conflict		
10	Entrance of new actor in existing conflict situation		

Source: Adapted from M.P. Sirseloudi, 'Early detection of terrorist campaigns'. *Forum on Crime and Society*, 4(1–2), 2004–2005, pp. 71–92. (Special Issue on Terrorism, edited by A.P. Schmid); partly based on PIOOM Checklists for Country Dispute and Tension Profiles; PIOOM Checklist for Country Conflict Escalation Profiles. In A.P. Schmid, *Thesaurus and Glossary of Early Warning and Conflict Prevention Terms*. London: FEWER, 2000, pp. A2–A43.

order of existence and (4) clothing these conceptions with such an aura of factuality that (5) the moods and motivations seem uniquely realistic (Clifford Geertz).

- Religion is the sigh of the oppressed creature, the heart of a heartless world, just as it is the spirit of a spiritless situation. It is the opiate of the people (Karl Marx).
- Religion is the daughter of Hope and Fear, explaining to Ignorance the nature of the Unknowable (Ambrose Bierce).
- Religion is what the individual does with his own solitariness (A.N. Whitehead).
- Religions are organised systems that hold people together (John Bowker).
- Religion is the human attitude towards a sacred order that includes within it all being – human or otherwise – i.e. belief in cosmos, the meaning of which both includes and transcends man (Peter Berger).

If religion is defined with John Bowker as 'organised systems that hold people together', then the same can be said of nationalism. In that sense, some more chauvinistic forms of patriotism can be considered as secular religions – sharing with most religion a similar obscure core (the core concept 'nation' is undefined in international law, nor is there a legal definition of what constitutes a 'people'). Fettweis[198] identifies two types: nationalist terrorists and ideological terrorists. The first claim to represent a particular ethnic group and desire territorial gain, whereas ideological terrorists are motivated by political, religious or other ideas, aiming to change society. A number of hypotheses are outlined as a consequence of this, including the identification of strategies, tactics and terrorist group development, as well as potentially successful counter-terrorism approaches. Again, the level of analysis makes it amenable to empirical testing, and allows the generation and testing of hypotheses, although the potential multiple political ideologies subsumed within the ideological terrorist type may limit potential conclusions and their utility. Fettweis's distinction, however, stands and falls with the definition of nationalism. If it is also seen as an ideology, it becomes problematic. On the other hand, some nationalism is, as indicated above, almost indistinguishable from religious cults. In those cases, aggressive nationalism is, *de facto*, the secular equivalent of religion, requiring people to sacrifice themselves for their country if necessary.

A typology that combines ideology, goals and recruitment is that developed by Chasdi.[199] The product is a three-dimensional 'typology cube' outlining 36 types of Middle Eastern terrorist groups. These describe the various interrelations between three types of ideology: Marxist-Leninist, religious and Palestinian nationalist; four types of goal: an Islamic state in Palestine and/or other areas in the Middle East, a secular Palestinian state, a Marxist-Leninist state in Palestine and/or other areas of the Middle East, and a religious Jewish state in Israel; and three types of recruitment style: a clan and/or disenfranchised person; followers of a charismatic leader; and Palestinians, Palestinian refugees and/or disenfranchised Palestinians. Eight types of actual group from the possible 36 were identified by the author and were given appropriate designations. This is a strong example of reducing the level of analysis to a region in order to enhance its practical utility. By identifying specific forms of violent actor in the Middle East, considerable gains are made in understanding and explanatory power, providing insight for social scientists and policy makers alike.

Another typology that takes as its subject a specific geographical area is that developed by Leman-Langlois and Broduer.[200] It is described as an 'operational typology' based on an analysis of all terrorist incidents, included failed attempts and hoaxes, linked to Canada in the period 1973–2003. It is reproduced as Table 3.7. By using two variables – the scope of desired impact and the time-frame the terrorists have in mind for justifying their violence – four types of terrorism are derived. Demand-based terrorists are generally small groups making specific demands for action. Private justice terror often wants retribution for an act previously carried out. Revolutionary terror demands change at

Table 3.7 Fundamental terrorist rationales

Justification of action[b]	Scope of desired impact[a]	
	Narrow	Wide
Forward-looking	Demand-based terror	Revolutionary terror
Backward-looking	Private-justice terror	Restoration terror

Notes

[a] Likelihood of success or reasonableness of expectations and desires is not considered.

[b] Internal moral justification only, with no attempt at determining whether others would consider it legitimate.

Source: S. Leman-Langlois and J.-P. Broduer, 'Terrorism old and new: counterterrorism in Canada'. *Police Practice and Research*, 6(2), 2005, pp. 121–140.

a structural state level, normally directed at states outside Canada but enacted by diasporas within its borders, and restoration terror wishes to re-establish a particular historical period.

The utility of the time-directional category for the justification of action is not clear; and the degree to which this enhances conceptual clarity with respect to terrorist group behaviour is also not immediately obvious. In practice, whether one takes a past Golden Age or a future Utopia as reference point for contemporary action might make little difference. However, the category of desired impact is a helpful one. This conceptualisation also allows the inclusion of hoaxes, as these may be reasonably assumed to have an (albeit short-lasting) intended consequence, just as do fully fledged attacks.

Also responding to the question of why terrorist groups act, a 'limiting variable' typology has been proposed.[201] Arguably one of the most innovative of the recent typologies, this one, developed by Boaz Ganor, classifies organisations by the variable that limits their terror activities. It includes four groups of organisation, and is displayed in Figure 3.8. The types of groups are delineated by the level of motivation and operational capability they have at any given time. Where these variables both exceed the terror-level threshold, terrorism will occur.

The underlying idea of this model is explained through the 'terror equation' and the 'counter-terror equation'. The terror equation posits that an organisation's activities are dependent on motivation levels to execute attacks, multiplied by the extent of the organisation's operational capability to realise that motivation. Motivation is dependent upon a variety of factors, including an organisation's goals and interests, internal pressures on its leadership, external pressures, morale considerations, the counter-terrorism policies of the states dealing with it, the results of a rational cost–benefit consideration of paths of action, and desire for vengeance. The extent of the organisation's operational capability is influenced by a separate group of factors, including the offensive and defensive actions taken by its opponent, policy changes by a supportive state, a reduction in supporter assistance, financial difficulties, shortage of weapons, lack of infrastructure and problems with recruitment. Therefore, the counter-terror equation requires the implementation of offensive and defensive measures that will change the cost–benefit outcome of the decision makers in the terrorist organisation by impacting on its operational capabilities and the leaders' motivations to attack.

These are useful and relatively underdeveloped aspects of typological inquiry, in particular due to the addition of the oppositional actors' behaviour and its effects. However, the 'limiting variable', defined as level of operational capability and extent of motivation, hypothesised to impact on the likelihood of a group committing an act of terrorism, requires further specification as it is a conflation of many other variables rather than a single causal feature. Similarly, the terror and counter-terror equations need fuller explanation. Compressing the various interacting influences on terrorist groups is a valuable exercise. However, it remains to be seen whether these can be supported empirically, and whether it is possible to condense them in the manner implied through the equation metaphor.

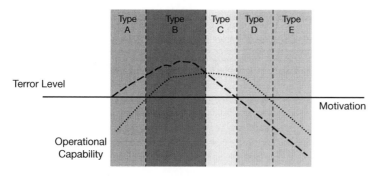

Figure 3.8 Ganor's typology of terrorist organisations.

Source: B. Ganor, 'Terrorist organisation typologies and the probability of a boomerang effect'. *Studies in Conflict and Terrorism*, 31(4), 2008, pp. 269–283.

Where do terrorists operate?

With respect to the location of terrorist activity, two points of reference recur in the literature: terrorists' base, and their target. This is seen in the work of Dror[202] and Waugh[203] referred to earlier, consideration of which appears not to have moved on significantly since their work. The only exception may be the emergence of 'transnational terrorism', increasingly incorporated into typological work after it had, in the 1970s, been pushed aside by 'international terrorism' – a formula that served well those who wanted to link it to 'international communism'.

The concept of transnational terrorism is one considered by a number of authors. Reinares[204] highlights the considerable ambiguity over the delineation between international and transnational terrorism. International terrorism is said to encapsulate two aims: first, demands for changes to the structure and power nexus in whole regions of the world; and second, that the terrorist actors and/or their victims and/or ultimate targets are located in a number of different countries. According to one conceptualisation, transnational terrorism involves those who both originate and operate in more than one country over which the target state has no direct jurisdiction. The aims of transnational terrorists are of a lesser scale, aiming to impact upon only a small number of states. Thus, in this conceptualisation all international terrorism is transnational terrorism, while the converse is not true. Since former president George W. Bush vowed to stop all terrorism with a global reach (i.e. able to reach the US mainland), the term 'global terrorism' has become popular for describing Al-Qaeda and some of its affiliates. One of its drawbacks is that it implies for this particular organisation a far greater reach than it is capable of. On the other hand, it suggests, correctly, a link to the concept of globalisation.

That transnational terrorism is a new phenomenon is the thesis of Hough's[205] typology of terrorism. He identifies three levels of terrorism, differentiated by objectives, targeting and geography, generating domestic, international and transnational types of terrorism. International terrorism is then divided into four types: first, 'pure' international terrorism, including its use as part of a domestic insurgency; second, that carried out by independent non-state groups or individuals; third, state-sponsored terrorism enacted by those other than the state; and finally, terroristic violence by state agents on the state's behalf. The author concludes that transnational terrorism is qualitatively different from international terrorism, and constitutes a new type of violence. He uses it with particular reference to Al-Qaeda, and differentiates it from international terrorism because it does not necessarily link objectives to a particular geographic entity.

A similar approach is adopted by Wilkinson,[206] who distinguishes between international terrorism (between individuals or groups from nation-states) and domestic or internal terrorism (carried out by those from within a country). However, Wilkinson points out that where a terrorist group has a reasonably long life, this is a less useful dichotomy, as international backing is often implicated in domestic struggles in the form of financial and other support. This again illustrates the complexity of allocating terrorist groups to particular types, and fulfilling the criteria of exclusivity posited to identify a valid typology.[207] With the spread of ethnic, religious and linguistic diasporas, and the enhanced mobility of people in general, due to cheaper cross-border transportation, distinctions between domestic (national) and inter- or transnational terrorism have arguably lost much of their relevance.

The categories of international and domestic terrorism are expanded by Seger,[208] who also lists regional groups, special interest extremists, and lone terrorists practising leaderless warfare. These classifications are applied to deterrence. For example, Seger argues that special interest groups are deemed more predictable as they have a limited set of specific targets. In contrast, the lone (lone-wolf) terrorist is considered the least predictable and therefore the hardest to identify and potentially deter. The practical application of terrorist group type to potential deterrence is, however, problematic for transnational groups without identifiable territorial bases (which could be hit in retaliation, the fear of such retaliation potentially acting as a deterrent). It is also problematical for those suicide terrorists who welcome a martyr's death as a route to paradise.

Charles Tilly[209] identifies two criteria by which to partition terrorist groups: whether or not they are specialists in the use of violent coercion; and whether they carry out acts of violence in their own territory or outside of it. This is represented in Figure 3.9 and illustrates four types of 'terror-wielding groups': militias, conspirators, autonomists and zealots.

Militias may be acting on behalf, or in support of, government or, alternatively, be of the non-government variety, but in both cases will be specialists in coercive violence operating within their own country. Conspirators tend to carry out operations outside their home territory; autonomists are allied more closely to political groups, but sometimes use terroristic violence in their own areas; and zealots are similar to autonomists but, according to Tilly, tend to operate outside their territory.

A synthesis of the typologies just outlined is presented in Figure 3.10 and aims to provide a formulaic representation of actors and their potential targets. This utilises the concept of violent non-state actors (VSNAs)[210] and juxtaposes them with state actors and other VSNAs. While this dichotomy is not clear-cut, it contributes to conceptual clarity and enables an outline of possible interactions to be identified. It views possible actor–target relations across three potential groups across various geographical boundaries. It assumes that terrorism can be carried out against other VNSAs as well as states, and requires a complete specification of terms. However, it may help frame potential routes for investigation in an inclusive and systematic way, assisting with future research and identifying undertheorised areas, or potential threats, once the role of diasporas and cross-border operations are also taken into account.

When does terrorism change?

Time-span-based or periodical approaches to terrorism have seen a number of proposals evinced. Perhaps the best known of these is Rapoport's[211] 'four waves of terrorism' theory. As will be discussed in more depth in the theory chapter in this volume (Chapter 4), Rapoport identified four qualitatively different types of terrorism. First there was an anarchist wave beginning in the 1880s and lasting for almost 40 years, then an anti-colonial wave lasting for a similar length of time. This was superseded in the 1960s by the New Left wave, a shorter period that ended in the 1990s, with only a few older groups still remaining active. Most recently, a new, religious wave, which began in 1979 with the Iranian Revolution, is posited. The aim of all four types of terrorism is revolution, with a number of audiences implicated in the violence of the groups: foreign terrorist organisations, diaspora groups, liberal sympathisers and foreign governments.

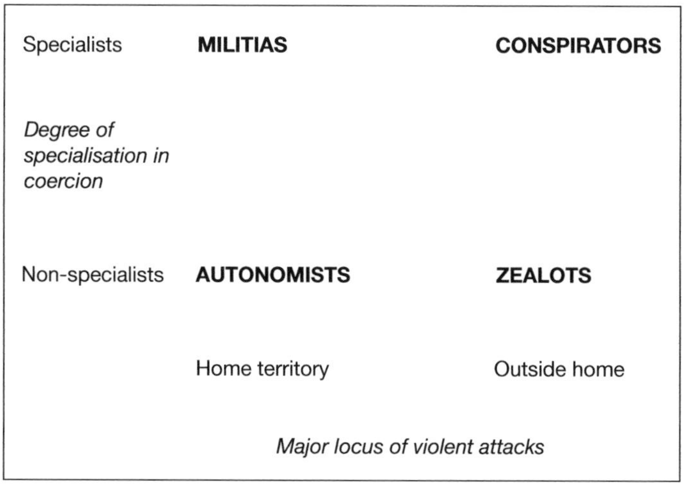

Specialists	**MILITIAS**	**CONSPIRATORS**
Degree of specialisation in coercion		
Non-specialists	**AUTONOMISTS**	**ZEALOTS**
	Home territory	Outside home
	Major locus of violent attacks	

Figure 3.9 A typology of terror-wielding groups and networks.

Source: C. Tilly, 'Terror, terrorism and terrorists'. *Sociological Theory*, 22(1), 2004, pp. 5–13.

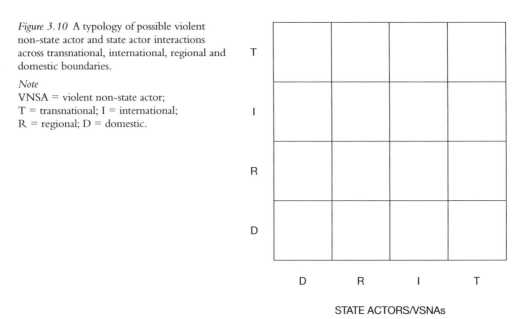

Figure 3.10 A typology of possible violent non-state actor and state actor interactions across transnational, international, regional and domestic boundaries.

Note
VNSA = violent non-state actor;
T = transnational; I = international;
R = regional; D = domestic.

Rapoport's typology has been widely used and has already undergone partial empirical testing.[212] However, the potential for overlap between categories is acknowledged by the author,[213] and highlights the complexity of terroristic phenomena and the associated problems with its characterisation. Also, the potentially static nature of the four-wave thesis has been highlighted, and it is said not to account for the context in which terrorist groups develop.[214] As elaborated in Chapter 4, there has also been an attempt to identify a fifth, 'tribal' wave.[215] This has its origins in the fourth wave, and is 'identifiable as a wave of millenarian violence contemporaneous with the ongoing religious wave of terrorism'.[216] Characteristics of fifth-wave groups include the extreme nature of the violence they commit. In particular, it is posited that should they manage to grasp state power, the result would – as in Cambodia under the Khmer Rouge – be genocide, the ultimate form of anti-civilian violence. However, the identification of such a fifth wave rests, for now, on shaky grounds.

How do terrorists operate?

As with all the questions posed which structure the typologies presented thus far, the area of how terrorists operate offers broad scope for interpretation. Here, it will be approached from two perspectives. First, we shall consider the organisational make-up of terrorist groups; and second, we will look at it from a tactical point of view, looking at the methods and means utilised by terrorists. It is worth noting that the organisational style of analysis was absent from the review of typologies in the 1988 edition of Schmid *et al.*'s *Political Terrorism*. This indicates the evolving nature of investigation into terrorist organisations, and the increasing importance of understanding the internal dynamics of groups.[217] The classification of terrorist groups by organisational structure has seen a noticeable evolution, arguably reflecting the changing nature of terrorist group make-up. From hierarchical organisations such as the Irish Republican Army (IRA), there has been increasing commentary on networks as appropriate organisational characterisation. An outline of recent efforts will be given here.

Arquilla and Ronfeldt[218] first applied the concept of networks to terrorist groups. Crucially facilitated by the increasing availability and sophistication of technology, small groups are able to communicate and coordinate activities without a central command. Decision making and operations are decentralised and depend on constitutive consensus building, allowing for local autonomy. There are different forms, including the chain or line network, where information is passed along a chain;

the hub or star network, where groups or individuals are linked into a central point; and the all-channel network, where all nodes are linked to one another. These are illustrated in Figure 3.11.

Jackson takes a broadly similar approach.[219] The genesis of this characterisation is the command and control authority relationships operating in terrorist groups. The premise is that organisations are held together by the links between constituent units, or nodes: individuals at a low level, and components of an organisation at a higher level. These enable the organisation to communicate, exchange information, convey authority and shape the behaviours of others in the organisation. Each node may refer to an individual, group, part of a group, organisation or even a state.[220] Three different kinds of authority are said to be exerted among group members: strategic, operational and tactical control. Three types of groups are thereby specified: tightly controlled groups, coupled networks and loosely coupled ones. Tightly controlled groups' commanders exert strategic, operational and tactical control, and can plan complex operations. This is most often found in hierarchies. Coupled networks have looser relationships among units and less direct modes of communication. Loosely coupled movements exhibit a pursuit of general goals based on a common ideology. Described as 'leaderless resistance', their operations are characterised by an absence of control at the tactical level, weak influence at the operational level but a strategic embedding by opinion leaders in the social, religious or political movement.

Many authors, in the fields of both criminal organisations and terrorist groups, have embraced the network model rather uncritically. Various definitions of network exist and are inconsistently applied; it is also far from clear what constitutes, for an entity working in the underground, a resilient, functional and efficient network in organisational terms. Mishal and Rosenthal[221] reject the network approach in consideration of Al-Qaeda and propose one based on a metaphor linked to drifting sandbanks: the dune organisation. This is based on time perception, chain of command and control, communication lines, and level of division of labour, and is dependent upon a 'process of vacillation between territorial presence and mode of disappearance'. Inspired by the de-territorialisation brought about by globalisation processes, the dune organisation is almost random as it moves from one territory to another, changing its characteristics as it goes. While the dune metaphor has some explanatory power for the nebulous waxing and waning of underground formations between heartlands and diasporas, it does not reflect an organisational model.

A further typology is built on the analogy of business organisations.[222] Here, terrorist groups are based on respective levels of centralisation of resources and centralisation of operations. These two axes result in four types of group, which correspond to business models: (1) hierarchy, (2) franchise, (3) venture capital, and (4) brand. Hierarchy uses centralised operations and resources and is characterised by tight lines of command. Venture capital has decentralised operations and centralised resources, often with isolated and insulated cells. Franchise groups combine centralised operations with decentralised resources. Brand groups have the lowest degree of centralisation, with decentralised resources and operations. They rely mainly on 'ideological self-identification and ad hoc cooperation'. While underground terrorist organisations are hardly comparable to international business corporations, this typology is actually one of the better ones for explaining the spread of Al-Qaeda.

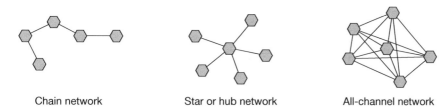

Chain network   Star or hub network   All-channel network

Figure 3.11 Basic types of networks (Arquilla and Ronfeldt).

Kaplan developed a further typology, which combines a variety of features related to the manner in which terrorist groups operate.[223] This considers a number of features of terrorist action including tactics, degree of force, agency and geographic context. A graphical representation is found in Figure 3.12. Kaplan's typology explicitly aims at developing a conceptualisation allowing 'meaningful normative evaluations of terrorist acts or types of terrorism'.[224] It therefore includes a number of features considered most important for such judgements to be made. First, the typology raises the question of whether groups discriminate in line with judgements on legitimate and illegitimate targets, with legitimate targets considered those relating to the military, social infrastructure or symbolically important property. The typology then distinguishes lethal from non-lethal attacks, before moving on to consider whether the actor is a state or non-state entity. The normative relevance of the actor is argued to be an indirect measure, as it brings into focus the different ways in which state and non-state actors are judged in terms of their rights and responsibilities in relation to the use of force. Finally, the typology distinguishes between the geographic context of the acts as to whether they are within or across international boundaries. These four sets of criteria generate 16 types of terrorism. This is argued to provide a normative framework against which the various forms of terrorism may be considered justified to a greater or a lesser degree. While this does not imply that there are justified acts of terrorism, it is claimed that it allows an assessment of the severity of the act, facilitating a more organised approach to the normative question of justification and harm. In this regard, Kaplan's typology is unique in relation to the various typologies considered here, as no other approach considers the normative dimension so explicitly. However, whether acts of terrorism are lethal or non-lethal is often a matter not of terrorist intent but of the bad or good luck of prospective victims. Arguably, non-lethal terrorism cannot terrorise – which undermines support for this typology.

To narrow the focus of analysis a little more, a number of emerging threats and 'modalities of terror' have been identified.[225] These include eco-terrorism, narco-terrorism, agro-terrorism, biological, chemical and nuclear terrorism, cyber-terrorism, as well as suicide terrorism. Most of these concepts are subject to considerable debate over definition and characterisation. Often they emerge not from academic research but are propagated by think tanks and the security and consultancy industry. A brief overview of some of these will be given here to provide a flavour of the debate. In particular, consideration will be given to environmental terrorism and cyber-terrorism.

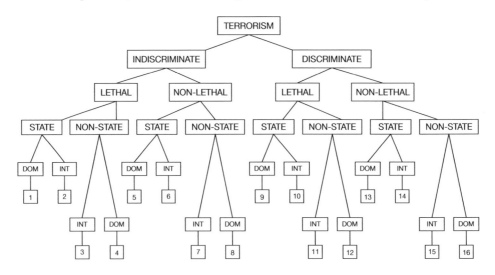

ABBREVIATION KEY: DOM = DOMESTIC   INT = INTERNATIONAL

Figure 3.12 Kaplan's typology of terrorism.

Source: S. Kaplan, 'A typology of terrorism'. *Journal of Political Philosophy*, 6(1), 2008, pp. 1–38.

A distinction should be made between eco-terrorism, which has been described as the extreme element of the environmental movement, and environmental terrorism. Eco-terrorism is better described as a single-issue form of terrorism,[226] and will not be considered further here. The concept of environmental terrorism has been explained, in one conceptualisation, as the threat of environmental destruction, in peace or wartime, designed to create fear over the ecological consequences of the act.[227] This definition is identified alongside the development of a taxonomy of environmental destruction based on whether an act is deliberate or unintentional, whether it is undertaken during peacetime or in war, and whether the act has a symbolic quality or not. Symbolism is considered in two ways: primary symbolism, where environmental destruction is carried out in order to instil fear over the impact on the environment; and secondary symbolism, involving the generation of fear, but not necessarily specific to environmental consequences. Through combining these elements, eight types of environmental destruction are described, two of which are considered to constitute environmental terrorism: 'deliberate, primary symbolism in peacetime' and 'deliberate, primary symbolism in wartime'.[228]

This is a potentially useful framework under which to consider two other forms of political violence that are emerging in the public and academic discourse on terrorism: 'forest jihad' and 'agro-terrorism'. The first refers to the potential threat of arson in the forests of the United States, Europe, Russia and Australia made on jihadist websites.[229] The stated aim of such an attack lies in the economic impact, but it would also serve to engender fear in the population. This would therefore fit into the deliberate, secondary symbolism in peacetime category of Schwartz's[230] taxonomy, as the primary aim is not to create concern over the impact on the environment, but to impact more broadly on the states where it is carried out. So far, however, more forest fires are the work of unscrupulous real-estate developers than of rural terrorists.

Agro-terrorism may be considered to be poised between so-called bio-terrorism and environmental terrorism. It has been described as deliberately introducing a disease agent into the food chain, including directly into livestock.[231] These are considered 'soft' targets[232] that have the potential for infiltration at many stages of the food preparation process. Again, if one applies the taxonomy developed by Schwartz,[233] this would come under the same category as forest jihad, in that the primary aim is not destruction of the environment but to instil fear and inflict casualties. So far, terrorists have shown little interest in 'agro-terrorism', and the rise of the concept has perhaps more to do with post-9/11 scaremongering about the whole gamut of potential vulnerabilities of the US economy than with a close reading of terrorists' writings regarding their targeting priorities. It sometimes appears as though the counter-terrorism lobby, looking for new 'business', appears to work unintentionally in parallel with some terrorists, exaggerating vulnerabilities to generate government programmes against such new threats – threats that the terrorist themselves had, until then, perhaps not considered making. With the media providing a platform for such lobbyists, political momentum is built up that can create additional funding for specific 'terror fighters'.

A different kind of tactic is seen in the use of technology. Termed 'cyber-terrorism', the term is used (and abused) to describe a wide variety of computer- and internet-related hazards. The authors of this chapter have yet to see a single incident of cyber-terrorism where (1) civilians have deliberately been killed by cyber-attacks, and (2) the explicit purpose was to influence (impress, intimidate, coerce) third parties. There have been a few cases of cyber-murder (e.g. by changing, via computer, the strength of a medical prescription in a hospital pharmacy for a particular patient who consequently died from an overdose), but not, to our knowledge, cyber-terrorism. We find that the conceptual enterprise in this area is replete with competing approaches.[234] However, one attempt at a typology of cyber-terrorism is provided by Ballard, Hornik and McKenzie,[235] and is proposed to guide future research efforts. It incorporates four types of what are described as cyber-incidents, and is useful in addressing the various forms of behaviour considered part of the repertoire of 'cyber-terrorism'. The first type of attack is information attacks, where electronically stored information, or computer systems, are damaged, altered or destroyed. Such attacks are considered the most common, and are the subject of most analysis. The second type is described as infrastructure attacks which aim to impact upon computer hardware or programming. Technological facilitation refers to the use of information technology to plan or incite terrorism and acts to facilitate 'traditional' terrorism or cyber-terrorism. Finally, the use of cyber-communications can assist fundraising and the promotion of terrorism as a mode of waging conflict. This use of the internet is well documented in this regard.

It is doubtful whether cyber-terrorism and environmental terrorism as described above constitute 'true' terrorism. Most incidents of cyber-crime, hacking, etc. have nothing to do with terrorism, and while these activities may create economic loss and disruption, there are, so far, few if any signs that the generation and exploitation of life-threatening fear is the intent of those engaging in cyber-attacks. The application of the 'terrorism' description to increasingly diverse forms of behaviour has been called 'conceptual stretching'.[236] The result of this is, among other things, a threat inflation that makes the concept of terrorism fuzzier than it already is. This can, in the end, only serve the true terrorists, who can then argue that terrorism is just a label or, as the critical theorists argue, a 'social construct'. The victims of real terrorism deserve better than that, and gain nothing from such conceptual stretching.[237]

A review of typologies of terrorism requires a balance with respect to forms of counter-terrorism. There are a considerable number of approaches to engaging with terrorism. These have been divided into categories such as anti-terrorism, counter-terrorism, terrorism consequence management[238] and, the most neutral, responding to terrorism.[239] Other conceptualisations include conciliatory or coercive counter-terrorism,[240] or, more broadly, 'discouraging' terrorism.[241] Anti-terrorism is sometimes conceptualised as more reactive, while counter-terrorism is seen by many as more proactive and pre-emptive. However, since the US government reaction to the 9/11 attacks, the label counter-terrorism has 'won' over anti-terrorism; it is now used to include a broad variety of responses to terrorism, both proactive/offensive and reactive/defensive.

The ways in which terrorism is engaged include the categories politics and governance, economic and social, psychological–communication–educational, military, judicial and legal, the police and prison system, intelligence and secret services, and others. Schmid has elaborated these in a 'toolbox of counterterrorism measures'. Within these broad groups, more detailed measures have been outlined.[242] Schmid's toolbox has been described as useful for identifying counter-terrorism approaches,[243] broadening the response repertoire beyond narrow kinetic military approaches.

With respect to typologies of counter-terrorism, one approach based on an analysis of the counter-terrorism policies of EU members has been proposed.[244] It is described as a representation of the various policies in operation rather than an exhaustive classification. It is based on the four elements of EU counter-terrorism strategy: to prevent, protect, pursue, and respond. The outcome is four types of counter-terrorism policy measured against these four strategic aims. These are, first, the *maximalist response*, which engages with all four aims equally; and second, the *human agent approach*, involving a greater focus on the individuals who carry out terrorism, which concentrates more heavily on the protect and pursue aspects of policy. The *confrontational approach* is the most aggressive and weights policy towards measures designed to pursue terrorists. Finally, the *antagonistic approach* balances all but the 'prevent' strategies, with equal focus on protect, pursue and response policy options.

There is agreement that the form of counter-terrorism applied should be dependent on the type of terrorist group a state or society faces.[245] In addition, the dynamic nature of the terrorist threat necessitates a flexible approach to the management and control of non-state terrorism.[246] It is argued that countermeasures should incorporate, *inter alia*, defence and intelligence, and not exclude compromise and conciliation – at least with the constituency the terrorists claim to speak for.[247] The utility of a good typology is clearly seen in the counter-terrorism domain, as exemplified in Goldaber's typology of hostage takers.[248] Terrorism is context-specific and, as a result, the decision as to which policy to adopt to counter it should be built on a firm conceptual understanding of the range of options available. Typology can serve as an auxiliary instrument for this, and, where rigorously constructed, can be applied to match types of terrorist group and types of counterterrorism response. This would provide a firmer conceptual underpinning to terrorist engagement, currently often thought to be lacking in some countries.[249]

Conclusion

This review of typological work in terrorism has shown that there is great variety in both the approaches and the conceptual lenses utilised. Arguably, this is because of the range of contexts in which terrorism occurs. From those whose state support affords them impunity, to those who have too few reservations about victimising the innocent, and those 'true fanatics' who believe their apparently noble ends justify the use of generally ignoble means – the range of motivations and circumstances in which terrorism is used is considerable. Further complexities arise, as terrorism is sometimes used as the sole instrument to further a group's aims, while other groups use it as one instrument among several tactics that can vary in their legality, justification and impact. Since there is no typical psychological terrorist profile and since most terrorists are normal in a clinical sense (albeit not in a moral one), typologies of terrorism that take the terrorist actor as their main criterion for classification are bound to be of limited value.

The various typologies considering the motivation and purpose of terrorist groups incorporate, *inter alia*, structural causes, and political and ideological motivation. They respond to the question of why groups resort to terrorism, either with respect to their own internal justifications, or through the wider influences present in the environment. The debate on 'root causes' and terrorist group justifications is one, and it necessitates multiple levels of analysis, implicating historical, social, political, ideology, group and individual psychology. What would be most helpful is a layered approach allowing the exploration of different levels of analysis within a unified framework of hypothesised causes and justifications for terrorism. The difficulties in this endeavour are numerous and implicate a plethora of variables, making a parsimonious aetiological typology particularly challenging. However, the explanatory weight, and the possibility for theory generation, make it an aspiration worth pursuing in future typological efforts.

The typologies outlining the conflict zone from and in which terrorists operate broadly identify similar features: that terrorists can operate both within and outside their home territory, and that they can potentially do so at a number of levels ranging from domestic, through regional, to international and transnational terrorism and, finally, global terrorism. Lately, the resurgence of piracy off the coast of Somalia has led to the use of the term 'maritime terrorism'. To the extent that civilian sailors are taken hostage and held for ransom, there are indeed similarities, but this is basically piracy, which is robbery of ships, not terrorism. Lately, it has been mainly extortionist and criminal, with hardly any traces of political demands. There is no doubt that location matters, especially when it comes to issues of jurisdiction and for determining who should take the lead in dealing with terrorist and other militant activists who transgress both geographical and moral boundaries. The increasingly high profile of cross-border terrorism makes this particular aspect of terrorist investigation one of considerable pertinence, with these typologies providing a platform on which to position debate.

The broad historical canon of those typologies focusing on when the phenomenon of terrorism changes may be considered useful for analysts looking at how terrorism evolves, and for the knowledge that may be gleaned from comparative analyses. However, the extent to which this uncovers new relationships among those items under consideration is not as clear, although the application of empirical testing to Rapoport's thesis[250] indicates that it is well suited to the development and testing of hypotheses and highlighting areas for investigation.

The various attempts to devise new typologies looking at how terrorists operate may be of some use to counter-terrorists, as they enable them to identify potential organisational weaknesses. They might also sensitise them to the evolving nature of terrorist groups. However, given the level of specificity required to verify empirically these typological conceptualisations, sufficient information may be hard to gather, reducing their practical and theoretical utility.

In comparing the work of the 1970s and 1980s with more recent typological attempts, and with typologies of political violence other than terrorism, a number of features come to the fore. Similarities in the categorisation styles employed can be seen in conceptualisations using actors, purposes, political motivation, ideology and geographical reach as principal units of typology building. The terrorist–state relationship is seen in both new and old typologies, with establishment (government) and anti-establishment (by insurgents and other non-state actors) terrorism considered important differentiating criteria in a number of typologies. Similar categories are seen regarding the 'why' of political motivation, with social-revolutionary, nationalist, left, right, ethnic and religious drivers seen in most new and old categorisations. Comparisons can also be found in classifications by geographical base and target, with international and domestic terrorism, and their permutations seen across typologies developed from the 1980s to the present. Despite being at least seven times less frequent than national terrorism, transnational terrorism has, however, experienced a raised profile. Financial, political and other support is being drawn from a wider geographical pool by currently operative terrorist groups, reflected in the term 'global terrorism' (it might, however, be more appropriate to use the term 'cross-border' or 'inter-regional', since not even Al-Qaeda operates worldwide).

A number of developments have been seen in the review of more contemporary typological attempts, with an increased focus on root causes, temporal dimensions and organisational make-up. Some conceptualisations[251] considered structural causes of terrorism, including historical and cultural factors as well as other actors' influence, and those of supporters and opponents. Distinguishing between different periods of terrorism has also emerged as a useful approach, with Rapoport's[252] four waves of terrorism gaining considerable credence. A similar debate is emerging over the genesis of a 'new' type of terrorism. Finally, a new development has been seen in the analysis of the organisational make-up of the terrorist group, with a number of conceptualisations presented including networks, dune organisations, and analogies to company structures aiming to inform analysis.

In comparison to the brief review of typologies of political violence other than terrorism, similarities in style of categorisation may be observed. Considering the purpose of conflict, similar reasons were posited to terrorist motivations, including revolution, secession, factionalism, and ideological justifications. Actor-based constructs focused at a similar level of abstraction to terrorist groups, with the relationship between combatants described along interstate, extra-state, and intra-state lines, and a variety of other violent non-state actors (VNSAs) categorised, including terrorist actors, militias, criminal groups and warlords.

Finally, the debate about 'new wars' and 'old wars' in the security studies literature has its equivalent in Terrorism Studies. Interestingly, there appears to be some convergence of conceptualisation between war and terrorism. For example, the fifth-generation warfare posited by Reed[253] incorporates terrorist actors. Further, the concept of new warfare presented by Kaldor[254] includes characteristics familiar to terrorism scholars, including ideological rather than territorial drivers of violence, the targeting of civilians as a tactic, and the increasingly unclear line between combatants and non-combatants.

On examination of the ways in which typologies have been developed, the predominance of deductive approaches is evident. Of those reviewed, only a minority applied an inductive, empirical route; most often, they used secondary sources as material and drew conclusions based on their interpretation. Thus, the deductive approach has a dominant presence in the typological literature, although some conceptualisations have been supported by empirical work.[255] It is in this way, through the development of typologies, followed by comprehensive testing and further investigation, that the typological literature is likely to fulfil its potential to successfully describe, classify and explain terrorist behaviour. The inductive route may be considered particularly useful in this, as it allows a building-block approach, where further data may be applied to typologies in order to enhance or challenge them, thereby countering the possible reification of the subject.[256]

The aspirational outcome of an inductive approach to typology construction might be a contribution to a cross-type typology, which includes all possible types in its field of reference.[257]

It is this that has been described as typological theory.[258] At least one researcher has described the achievement of such a grand typology as 'virtually impossible'.[259] The plethora of factors implicated in terrorist group development, operation and aetiology make a comprehensive typology indeed a complex challenge. However, if the goals of discovering relationships, generating hypotheses, developing theory and identifying new areas for investigation[260] are maintained, an iterative, developmental process, crucially informed by empirical testing, can and will provide valuable insights into useful categorisations of terrorist groups and their behaviour in broader contexts of multi-party violence and conflict. However, even as typology-building on terrorism reaches greater maturity, we cannot hope that it will ever achieve the interpretative and predictive power of the periodic table that Dmitri Mendeleev establishes for the chemical elements in 1869. However, in the absence of a universally accepted definition of terrorism and with the lack of a general theory of terrorism, typology construction can nevertheless be a useful instrument to advance our understanding of terrorism – provided it is embedded in a framework that looks at the conflict behaviour of the opponents of the terrorists as well and takes into account additional contextual factors. Theoretical progress in the field of Terrorism Studies will have to be based on typological progress, which, in turn, is based on conceptual progress.

Notes

1 A.P. Schmid, M. Stohl and P. Flemming, 'Typologies'. In A.P. Schmid *et al.*, *Political Terrorism: A New Guide to Actors, Authors, Concepts, Data Bases, Theories, and Literature*. Amsterdam: North-Holland, 1988, pp. 39–59.

2 E.A. Thracian, 'Typologies'. In D.L. Sills (ed.), *International Encyclopedia of the Social Sciences*. New York: Free Press, 1979, pp. 177–185.

3 C. Linnaeus, *Systema naturae*. London: British Museum, 1956.

4 E.R. Scerri, *The Periodic Table: Its Story and Significance*. Oxford: Oxford University Press, 2006.

5 I.B. Myers, M.H. McCaulley, N.L. Quenk and A.L. Hammer, *MBTI Manual: A Guide to the Development and Use of the Myers–Briggs Type Indicator*, 3rd edn. Palo Alto, CA: Consulting Psychologists Press, 1998.

6 J.C. McKinney, 'Typification, typologies, and sociological theory'. *Social Forces*, 48(1), 1969, pp. 1–12.

7 J.C. McKinney, *Constructive Typology and Social Theory*. New York: Appleton-Century-Crofts, 1966.

8 Ibid.

9 C. Elman, 'Explanatory typologies in qualitative studies of international politics'. *International Organization*, 59, Spring 2005, pp. 293–326.

10 O. Behling, 'Some problems in the philosophy of science of organisations'. *Academy of Management Review*, 3(2), 1978, pp. 193–201.

11 P. Wilkinson, *Terrorism and the Liberal State*. Hong Kong: Macmillan, 1977, p. 31.

12 C. Tilly, 'Observations of social processes and their formal representations'. *Sociological Theory*, 22(4), 2004, pp. 595–602.

13 J.C. McKinney, 'Typification, typologies, and sociological theory'.

14 P. Rich, 'The organizational taxonomy: definition and design'. *Academy of Management Review*, 17(4), 1992, pp. 758–784.

15 G. Sartori, 'Concept misformation in comparative politics'. *American Political Science Review*, 64(4), 1970, pp. 1033–1053.

16 P. Wilkinson, 'Current and future trends in domestic and international terrorism: implications for democratic government and the international community'. *Strategic Review for Southern Africa*, 23(2), 2001, p. 106.

17 J.W. Clarke, 'American assassins: an alternative typology. *British Journal of Political Science*, 11(1), 1981, pp. 81–104.

18 A.L. George, 'Integrating comparative and within-case analysis: typological theory'. In A.L. George and A. Bennett (eds), *Case Studies and Theory Development in the Social Sciences*. Cambridge, MA: MIT Press, 2005, pp. 233–263.

19 G. Sartori, 'Concept misformation in comparative politics', p. 1038.

20 D.H. Doty and W.H. Glick, 'Typologies as a unique form of theory building: toward improved understanding and modeling'. *Academy of Management Review*, 19(2), 1994, pp. 230–252.

21 C. Fettweis, 'Propaganda of the deed, 21st century style'. Paper presented at the annual meeting of the International Studies Association 48th Annual Convention, Chicago, 28 February 2007. Retrieved 27 October 2008, from: www.allacademic.com/meta/p181419_index.html.

22 J.C. McKinney, 'Typification, typologies, and sociological theory'.

23 A.L. George, 'Integrating comparative and within-case analysis'.

24 J.W. Clarke, 'American assassins: an alternative typology'.

25 P.F. Lazarsfeld, 'Some remarks on the typological procedures in social research'. *Zeitschrift für Sozialforschung*, 6, 1937, pp. 119–139.

26 A.L. George, 'Integrating comparative and within-case analysis'.

27 R. Propst, '*New terrorists, new attack means? Categorizing terrorist challenges for the early 21st century*, 2002. Retrieved 28 October 2008, from: http://homelandsecurity.org/journal/Articles/propstnewterroristprint.htm.

28 F. Ferracuti, 'A sociopsychiatric interpretation of terrorism'. *Annals of the American Academy of Political and Social Science*, 463, 1982, pp. 129–140.

29 P. Rich, 'The organizational taxonomy'.

30 C. Elman, 'Explanatory typologies in qualitative studies of international politics'.

31 A.L. George, 'Integrating comparative and within-case analysis'.

32 C. Tilly, 'Observations of social processes and their formal representations'.

33 D.H. Doty and W.H. Glick, 'Typologies as a unique form of theory building'.

34 A.L. George, 'Integrating comparative and within-case analysis'.

35 D.H. Doty and W.H. Glick, 'Typologies as a unique form of theory building'; R. Shultz, 'Conceptualising political terrorism: a typology'. *Journal of International Affairs*, 21(1), 1978, pp. 7–15.

36 C. Tilly, 'Observations of social processes and their formal representations'.

37 S. Goldenberg, 'Analytic induction revisited'. *Canadian Journal of Sociology*, 18(2), 1993, pp. 161–176.

38 G.K. Roberts, *A Dictionary of Political Analysis*. London: Longman, 1971.

39 Quoted in A.P. Schmid, M. Stohl and P. Flemming, 'Typologies', p. 40.

40 Ibid.

41 F. Gross, *Violence in Politics: Terror and Political Assassination in Eastern Europe and Russia*. The Hague: Mouton, 1972.

42 N. Ben-Yehuda, 'Political assassination events as a cross-cultural form of alternative justice'. *International Journal of Comparative Sociology*, 38(1–2), 1997, pp. 25–47.

43 N. Sambanis, 'Using case studies to expand economic models of civil war'. *Perspectives on Politics*, 2, 2004, pp. 59–279.

44 S.R. David, 'Internal war: causes and cures'. *World Politics*, 49(4), 1997, pp. 552–576.

45 J. Angstrom, 'Towards a typology of internal armed conflict: synthesising a decade of conceptual turmoil'. *Civil Wars*, 4(3), 2001, pp. 93–116; N. Sambanis, 'Using case studies to expand economic models of civil war'.

46 T.R. Gurr and V.F. Bishop, 'Violent nations, and others'. *Journal of Conflict Resolution*, 20(1), 1976, pp.79–110 at p. 101.

47 H.J. Rosenbaum and P.C. Sederberg, 'Vigilantism: an analysis of establishment violence'. *Comparative Politics*, 6(4), 1974, pp. 541–570; H.O. Dahlke, 'Race and minority riots: a study in the typology of violence'. *Social Forces*, 30(4), 1952, pp. 419–425.

48 J. Angstrom, 'Towards a typology of internal armed conflict'.

49 J.A. Vasquez, 'Capability, types of war, peace'. *Western Political Quarterly*, 39(2), 1986, pp. 313–327.

50 T.R. Gurr and V.F. Bishop, 'Violent nations, and others', p. 46.

51 I.K. Feierabend, R.L. Feierabend and B.A. Nesvold, 'The comparative study of revolution and violence'. *Comparative Politics*, 5(3), 1973, pp. 393–424.

52 L. Cliffe and R. Luckham, 'Complex political emergencies and the state: failure and the fate of the state'. *Third World Quarterly*, 20(1), 1999, pp. 27–50.

53 J. Lider, *Military Theory*. Aldershot, UK: Gower, 1983.

54 Ibid.

55 J. Sinai, 'New trends in terrorism studies'. In M. Ranstorp (ed.), *Mapping Terrorism Research: State of the Art, Gaps and Future Direction*. London: Routledge, 2007, pp. 31–50.

56 N. Sambanis, 'Using case studies to expand economic models of civil war'.

57 J.A. Vasquez, 'Capability, types of war, peace'.

58 N. Ben-Yehuda, 'Political assassination events as a cross-cultural form of alternative justice'; W.S. Crotty, 'Presidential assassinations'. *Society*, 35(2), 1998, pp. 99–107.

59 J. Angstrom, 'Towards a typology of internal armed conflict'; N. Chazan, R. Mortimer, J. Ravenhill and D. Rothchild, *Politics and Society in Contemporary Africa*. Boulder, CO: Lynne Rienner, 1992, pp. 189–210; H. Eckstein, 'On the etiology of internal wars', *History and Theory*, 4(2), 1965, pp. 133–163.

60 D. Lane, 'The Orange Revolution: "people's revolution" or revolutionary coup?' *British Journal of Politics and International Relations*, 10(4), 2008, pp. 525–549.

61 D. Carment, 'The international dimensions of ethnic conflict: concepts, indicators, and theory'. *Journal of*

Peace Research, 30(2), 1993, pp. 137–151; T.R. Gurr and V.F. Bishop, 'Violent nations, and others'; G. Krell, H. Nicklas and A. Ostermann, 'Immigration, asylum, and anti-foreigner violence in Germany'. *Journal of Peace Research*, 33(2), 1996, pp. 153–170; V. Tishkov, 'Ethnic conflicts in the former USSR: the use and misuse of typologies and data'. *Journal of Peace Research*, 36(5), 1999, pp. 571–591; M. Weiner, 'Peoples and state in a new ethnic order?' *Third World Quarterly*, 13(2), 1992, pp. 317–333.

62 B. Harff and T.R. Gurr, 'Toward empirical theory of genocides and politicides: identification and measurement of cases since 1945'. *International Studies Quarterly*, 3(2), 1988, pp. 359–371.

63 R.A. Bell, F.J. Lanceley, T.B. Feldmann, T.H. Worley, C.R. Lewis, W. Cheek and J.J. Stephenson, *Hostage Takers: An Empirical Study of Aircraft Hijackers* (abstract, 1991). Retrieved 30 December 2008 from: www.ncjrs.gov/App/Publications/abstract.aspx?ID=139202; H.H.A. Cooper, *Hostage-Takers*. Geneva, IL: Paladin House, 1981. Retrieved 30 December 2008 from: www.ncjrs.gov/App/Publications/abstract.aspx?ID=75936; I. Goldaber, 'Typology of hostage-takers'. *Police Chief*, 46(6), 1979, pp. 21–23; M.F. Welch, 'Applied typology and victimology in the hostage negotiation process'. *Journal of Crime and Justice*, 7, 1984, pp. 63–86.

64 K. Cobb, 'Organization, insurgency and strategy'. Paper presented at the annual meeting of the International Studies Association 48th Annual Convention, Chicago, 28 February 2007. Retrieved 30 December 2008 from: www.allacademic.com/meta/p178668_index.html.

65 R. Mac Ginty, 'Looting in the Context of violent conflict: a conceptualisation and typology'. *Third World Quarterly*, 25(5), 2004, pp. 857–870.

66 J.A. Hollander and R.L. Einwohner, 'Conceptualizing resistance'. *Sociological Forum*, 19(4), 2004, pp. 533–554; W.E. Lipsky, 'Comparative approaches to the study of revolution: a historiographic essay'. *Review of Politics*, 38(4), 1976, pp. 494–509.

67 I.K. Feierabend *et al.*, 'The comparative study of revolution and violence'; C.A. Johnson, *Revolution and the Social System*. Berkeley, CA: Stanford University Press, 1964.

68 H.O. Dahlke, 'Race and minority riots'; G.T. Marx, 'Issueless riots'. *Annals of the American Academy of Political and Social Science*, 391, 1970, pp. 21–33; J.J. Wanderer, '1967 riots: a test of the congruity of events'. *Social Problems*, 16(2), 1968, pp. 193–198.

69 S. Kimhi and S. Even, 'Who Are the Palestinian Suicide Bombers?' *Terrorism and Political Violence*, 16(4), 2004, pp. 815–840.

70 H.J. Rosenbaum and P.C. Sederberg, 'Vigilantism'; P.C. Sederberg, 'The phenomenology of vigilantism in contemporary America: an interpretation'. *Studies in Conflict and Terrorism*, 1(3–4), 1978, pp. 287–305.

71 J.P. Sullivan, 'Terrorism, crime and private armies'. *Low Intensity Conflict and Law Enforcement*, 11(2), 2002, pp. 239–253; P. Williams, 'Violent non-state actors and national and international security'. International Relations and Security Network, 2008. Retrieved 8 December 2008 from: http://se2.isn.ch/service engine/FileContent?serviceID=ISFPub&fileid=8EEBA9FE–478E-EA2C-AA15–32FC9A59434A &lng=en.

72 R. Beaumont, 'Small wars: definitions and dimensions'. *Annals of the American Academy of Political and Social Science*, 54(1), 1995, pp. 20–35; L. Cliffe and R. Luckham, 'Complex political emergencies and the state'; M. Deutsch, *The Resolution of Conflict: Constructive and Destructive Processes*. New Haven, CT: Yale University Press, 1973; T. Diez, S. Stetter and M. Albert, 'The European Union and the transformation of border conflicts: theorising the impact of integration and association'. EU Border Conf. Working Paper 1, 2004. Retrieved 3 November 2008 from: http://euborderconf.bham.ac.uk/publications/files/WP1Conceptual fwork.pdf, O. Furley, *Conflict in Africa*. London: I.B. Taurus, 1995, pp. 3–4; K. Holsti, *The State, War, and the State of War*. Cambridge: Cambridge University Press, 1966; M. Kaldor, *New and Old Wars: Organized Violence in a Global Era*. Stanford, CA: Stanford University Press, 1999; R.J. Leng and D. Singer, 'Militarized interstate crises: the BCOW typology and its applications'. *International Studies Quarterly*, 32(2), 1988, pp. 155–173; J.S. Levy, *War in the Modern Great Power System, 1495–1975*. Lexington: University Press of Kentucky, 1983; J. Lider, *Military Theory*; H. Miall, O. Ramsbotham and T. Woodhouse, 'Introduction'. In H. Miall, O. Ramsbotham and T. Woodhouse (eds), *Contemporary Conflict Resolution*. Aldershot, UK: Polity Press, 1999, pp. 1–38; F.R. Pfetsch and C. Rohloff, *National and International Conflicts, 1945–1995: New Empirical and Theoretical Approaches*. London: Routledge, 2000; M. Sarkees, F.W. Wayman and P. Singer, 'Inter-state, intra-state, and extra-state wars: a comprehensive look at their distribution over time, 1816–1997'. *International Studies Quarterly*, 47(1), pp. 49–70; B.G. Valeriano and J.A. Vasquez, 'A classification of interstate war'. Paper presented at the annual meeting of the International Studies Association, Centre Sheraton Hotel, Montreal, Quebec, Canada. 2004. Retrieved 3 November, 2008, from: http://www.all academic.com/meta/p74279_index.html; J. A. Vasquez. *The war puzzle*. Cambridge: University Press, 1993.

73 A. Giustozzi. *The debate on warlordism: the importance of military legitimacy*. LSE Crisis States Development Research Centre: Discussion paper no. 13, 2005. Retrieved 2 January, 2008, from: http://www.research4development.info/PDF/Outputs/CrisisStates/dp13.pdf (accessed 2 January 2008); P. Jackson.

'Warlords as alternative forms of Governance'. *Small Wars & Insurgencies*, 14(2), 2003, pp. 131–150; S. Lezhnev. *Crafting peace: strategies to deal with warlords in collapsing states*. Lexington Books, 2005; A. Pejcinova. 'Post-modernizing Afghanistan'. *CEU Political Science Journal: The Graduate Student Review*, 1(5), 2006, pp. 34–55.

74 A. P. Schmid, and A. J. Jongman et al. *Political Terrorism: a new guide to actors, authors, concepts, data bases, theories, and literature*. Amsterdam, North Holland Publ. Company, 1988.

75 R. D. Crelinsten. 'Terrorism as political communication: the relationship between the controller and the controlled'. In P. Wilkinson and A.M. Stewart (eds), *Contemporary research on terrorism*. Aberdeen: University of Aberdeen Press, 1987, pp. 3–23; R. D. Crelinsten. Terrorism, counter-terrorism and democracy: the assessment of national security threats. *Terrorism and Political Violence*, 1(2), 1989, pp. 242–269; R. D. Crelinsten, 'Analysing terrorism and counter-terrorism: a communication model'. *Terrorism and Political Violence*, 14(2), 2002, pp. 77–122.

76 A.P. Schmid, 'Repression, state terrorism, and genocide'. In P.T. Bushnell, V. Shlapentokh, C.K. Vanderpool and J. Sundram (eds), *State Organized Terror: The Case of Violent Internal Repression*. Boulder, CO: Westview Press, 1991, pp. 23–37.

77 J.I. Ross, *The Dynamics of Political Crime*. New York: Sage, 2003; J.I. Ross, 'Political crimes against the state'. In R. Wright and J.M. Miller (eds), *Encyclopedia of Criminology*. New York: Routledge, 2005, pp. 1225–1230.

78 M. Stohl and G.A. Lopez, 'Introduction'. In M. Stohl and G. A. Lopez, *The State as Terrorist*. Westport, CT: Aldwych Press, 1984, pp. 3–10.

79 A.P. Schmid, 'Repression, state terrorism, and genocide'.

80 S. Parmentier and E.G.M. Weitekamp, 'Political crimes and serious violations of human rights: towards a criminology of international crimes'. In S. Parmentier and E.G.M. Weitekamp (eds), *Crime and Human Rights: Sociology of Crime, Law and Deviance*, vol. 9. Oxford: Elsevier, 2007, pp. 109–146.

81 E. Stepanova, *Terrorism in Asymmetrical Conflict: Ideological and Structural Aspects*. SIPRI Research report no. 23. Oxford: Oxford University Press, 2008. The qualifiers 'stand-alone', 'embedded' and 'global' are ours, not Stepanova's.

82 R.H. Dekmejian, *Spectrum of Terror*. Washington, DC: CQ Press, 2007, p. 10.

83 S. Parmentier and E.G.M. Weitekamp, 'Political crimes and serious violations of human rights'.

84 A. Bhargava, 'Defining political crimes: a case study of the South African Truth and Reconciliation Commission'. *Columbia Law Review*, 102(5), 2002, pp. 1304–1339.

85 S. Parmentier and E. Weitekamp, 'Political crimes and serious violations of human rights'.

86 C. van den Wyngaert, *The Political Offence Exception to Extradition*. Antwerp: Kluwer, 1980.

87 A. Turk, *Political Criminality: The Defiance and Defense of Authority*. Beverly Hills, CA: Sage, 1982; J. Roebuck and S. Weeber, *Political Crime in the U.S.* New York: Praeger, 1978.

88 S. Brown, F.-A. Ebensen and G. Geis, *Reconciliation after Violent Conflict: A Handbook*. Stockholm: International Idea, 2003.

89 J.I. Ross, *The Dynamics of Political Crime*; J.I. Ross, 'Political crimes against the state'.

90 S. Parmentier and E. Weitekamp, 'Political crimes and serious violations of human rights'.

91 C. van den Wyngaert, *The Political Offence Exception to Extradition*; A. Turk, *Political Criminality*; J. Roebuck and S. Weeber, *Political Crime in the U.S.*; S. Brown, F.-A. Ebensen and G. Geis, *Reconciliation after Violent Conflict*; J. Ross, *The Dynamics of Political Crime*.

92 Bureau of Justice Statistics, 'Four measures of serious violent crime', 2006. Retrieved 11 March 2009 from www.ojp.usdoj.gov/bjs/glance/tables/4meastab.htm.

93 Home Office (UK), 'Violent crime'. Retrieved 11 March 2009 from: www.homeoffice.gov.uk/crime-victims/reducing-crime/violent-crime/.

94 C. Smith and J. Allen, *Violent Crime in England and Wales*. Home Office Online Report 18/04, 2004. Retrieved 19 March 2009, from: www.homeoffice.gov.uk/rds/pdfs04/rdsolr1804.pdf.

95 M.B. Clinard and R. Quinney, *Criminal Behavior Systems: A Typology*, 2nd edn. New York: Holt, Rinehart & Winston, 1973.

96 Ibid.

97 Ibid.

98 R.D. Hunter and M.L. Dantzker, *Crime and Criminality: Causes and Consequences*. Monsey, NY: Criminal Justice Press, 2005.

99 M.B. Clinard and R. Quinney, *Criminal Behavior Systems*.

100 G. Sharp and J. Paulson, *Waging Nonviolent Struggle*. Boston: Extending Horizon Books, 2005.

101 Strictly speaking, there is a moral difference between *non-violent action* based on a desire to hold the moral high ground in a confrontation by deliberately abstaining from inflicting physical harm on the political opponent, and *not-violent* political action short of using violence, which might involve all sorts of political

manoeuvring and arm-twisting to make the opponent do what he would not do and reserves the right to escalate to coercive violence and bodily harm to the opponent. For a discussion of the difference between 'non-violent' and 'not-violent', see P. Ackerman and J. Duvall, *A Force More Powerful: A Century of Nonviolent Conflict.* New York: Palgrave, 2000.

102 N. Ben-Yehuda, 'Political assassination events as a cross-cultural form of alternative justice'.
103 J.F. Kirkham, S.G. Levy and W.J. Crotty, *Assassination and Political Violence.* New York: Praeger, 1970.
104 Ibid., quoted in N. Ben-Yehuda, 'Political assassination events as a cross-cultural form of alternative justice', p. 28.
105 N. Ben-Yehuda, 'Political assassination events as a cross-cultural form of alternative justice'.
106 W.J. Crotty, 'Presidential assassinations'.
107 S. Mair, 'The new world of privatized violence'. *Internationale Politik und Gesellschaft* (International Politics and Society), 2, 2003, pp. 11–28; Sullivan, 'Terrorism, crime and private armies'.
108 P. Williams, 'Violent non-state actors and national and international security'.
109 Ibid.
110 Ibid.
111 J.P. Sullivan, 'Terrorism, crime and private armies'.
112 S. Mair, 'The new world of privatized violence', p. 118.
113 J.P. Sullivan, 'Terrorism, crime and private armies'; S. Mair, 'The new world of privatized violence'.
114 A. Pejcinova, 'Post-modernizing Afghanistan'.
115 S. Lezhnev, *Crafting Peace.*
116 Ibid.
117 A. Hill, 'Warlords, militia and conflict in contemporary Africa: a re-examination of terms'. *Small Wars and Insurgencies*, 8(1) 1997, pp. 35–51.
118 P. Jackson, 'Warlords as alternative forms of governance'.
119 M. Kaldor, *New and Old Wars.*
120 Ibid.
121 F.R. Pfetsch and C. Rohloff, *National and International Conflicts, 1945–1995.*
122 M. Sarkees *et al.*, 'Inter-state, intra-state, and extra-state wars'.
123 J.A. Vasquez, 'Capability, types of war, peace'; J.A. Vasquez, *The War Puzzle.*
124 H. Miall *et al.*, 'Introduction'.
125 D.J. Reed, 'Beyond the war on terror: into the fifth generation of war and conflict'. *Studies in Conflict and Terrorism*, 31(8), 2008 pp. 684–722.
126 W.S. Lind, 'Fifth generation warfare?' Center for Cultural Conservatism. 2004. Retrieved 25 January 2009, from: www.d-n-i.net/lind/lind_2_03_04.htm.
127 K. Holsti, *The State, War, and the State of War.*
128 R. Arnold, *The ICC as a New Instrument for Repressing Terrorism.* Ardsley, NY: Transnational, 2004.
129 F. Bugnion, 'Just wars, wars of aggression and international humanitarian law'. *International Review of the Red Cross*, 847(84), 2002, pp. 523–546.
130 Ibid.; see also F. de Mulinen, *Handbook on the Law of War for Armed Forces.* Geneva: International Committee of the Red Cross, 1987.
131 R. Arnold, *The ICC as a New Instrument for Repressing Terrorism.*
132 United Nations (1945), Charter of the International Military Tribunal – Annex to the Agreement for the prosecution and punishment of the major war criminals of the European Axis ('London Agreement'). UNHCR Refworld. Retrieved 10 March 2009 from: www.unhcr.org/refworld/docid/3ae6b39614.html.
133 Ibid., article 6.
134 R. Arnold, *The ICC as a New Instrument for Repressing Terrorism.*
135 Ibid.
136 S. Parmentier and E. Weitekamp, 'Political crimes and serious violations of human rights'.
137 N. Schrijver and P. Wijinga, 'Collective rights: towards a new generation of human rights? IPSA Seminar Paper, 1987. The Hague: Institute of Social Studies.
138 United Nations (1945). *Charter.* Retrieved 10 March 2009 from: www.un.org/aboutun/charter/index.shtml.
139 S. Parmentier and E. Weitekamp, 'Political crimes and serious violations of human rights'.
140 D.J. Reed, 'Beyond the war on terror'.
141 P. Williams, 'Violent non-state actors and national and international security'; J.P. Sullivan, 'Terrorism, crime and private armies'.
142 A.P. Schmid *et al.*, 'Typologies', pp. 39–60.
143 Y. Dror, 'Terrorism as a challenge to the democratic capacity to govern'. In M. Crenshaw (ed.), *Terrorism, Legitimacy and Power: The Consequences of Political Violence.* Middletown, CT: Wesleyan University Press, 1983, pp. 69–90.

144 W.L. Waugh Jr *International Terrorism: How Nations Respond to Terrorists*. Salisbury, NC: Documentary Publications, 1982.

145 T.P. Thornton, 'Terror as a weapon of political agitation'. In H. Eckstein (ed.), *Internal War: Problems and Approaches*. New York: Free Press of Glencoe, 1964, pp. 82–88.

146 E.V. Walter, *Terror and Resistance*. London: Oxford University Press, 1969.

147 P. Loesche, 'Terrorismus und Anarchismus'. In M. Funke (ed.), *Extremisten im demokratischen Rechtsstaat*. Bonn: Bundeszentrale für Politische Bildung, 1978, pp. 83–84.

148 B. Crozier, Testimony before the U.S. Senate Subcommittee on Internal Security.

149 G. Davidson Smith, 1988, cited in Schmid *et al.*, 'Typologies', p. 45.

150 A.P. Schmid *et al.*, 'Typologies'.

151 Ibid.

152 H.J. Rosenbaum and P.C. Sederberg, 'Vigilantism'.

153 COT Institute for Safety, Security and Crisis Management, *Lone-Wolf Terrorism: A Study on the Nature, Motivations, Modus Operandi and Prospects of Lone-Wolf Terrorism*. The Hague: COT, 2009.

154 P. Wilkinson, *Terrorism and the Liberal State*, op. cit.

155 R. Shultz, 'Conceptualising political terrorism: a typology'.

156 Ibid.

157 A. Merari, 'Classification of terrorist groups'. *Terrorism: An International Journal*, 1(3–4), 1978, pp. 331–346.

158 A.P. Schmid and J. de Graaf, *Violence as Communication*. London: Sage, 1982, p. 60.

159 For example, Schmid's typology has been used by J.M. Post, K.G. Ruby and E.D. Shaw, 'The radical group in context: 2. Identification of critical elements in the analysis of risk for terrorism by radical group type'. *Studies in Conflict and Terrorism*, 25, 2002, pp. 101–126.

160 T.P. Thornton, 'Terror as a weapon of political agitation'.

161 J. Bowyer Bell, *Transnational Terror*. Washington, DC: American Enterprise Institute, 1975.

162 M. Crenshaw, *Revolutionary Terrorism*. Stanford, CA: Hoover Institution, 1979.

163 P.A. Karber, 'Urban terrorism: baseline data and a conceptual framework'. *Social Science Quarterly*, 52, 1971, pp. 528–529.

164 Ibid., p. 258.

165 U.S. National Advisory Committee on Criminal Justice Standards and Goals, *Disorders and Terrorism: Report of the Task Force on Disorders and Terrorism*. Washington, DC: GPO, 1976.

166 P.A. Karber, 'Urban terrorism'.

167 R. Shultz, 'Conceptualising political terrorism'.

168 I. Goldaber, 'Typology of hostage-takers', cited in Schmid *et al.*, 'Typologies', p. 54.

169 G. Löckinger, *Terrorismus, Terrorismusabwehr, Terrorismusbekampfung*. Vienna: Ministry of Defence, 2005; retrieved 1 March 2009 from: www.bmlv.gv.at/pdf_pool/publikationen/05_ttt_01_ttt.pdf.

170 B. Ganor, 'Terrorist organization typologies and the probability of a boomerang effect'. *Studies in Conflict and Terrorism*, 31(4), 2008, pp. 269–283.

171 R. Chakravorti, 'Terrorism: past present and future'. *Economic and Political Weekly*, 29(36), 1994, pp. 2340–2343.

172 O.A. Lizardo and A.J. Bergesen, 'International terrorism and the world system'. *Sociological Theory*, 22(1), 2004, pp. 38–52.

173 C.K. Chase-Dunn, *Global Formation: Structures of the World-Economy*. Lanham, MD: Rowman & Littlefield, 1998.

174 D.C. Rapoport, 'The four waves of rebel terror and September 11'. *Anthropoetics*, 8(1), 2001. Retrieved 2 November 2008 from: www.anthropoetics.ucla.edu/ap0801/terror.htm.

175 D. Wright-Neville, 'Dangerous dynamics: activists, militants and terrorists in Southeast Asia'. *Pacific Review*, 17(1), 2004, pp. 27–46.

176 A.P. Schmid and A.J. Jongman, *Political Terrorism*, p. 57.

177 R.H. Dekmejian, *Spectrum of Terror*, op. cit.

178 Raufer, 1991, cited in B. Hoffman, *Inside Terrorism*. New York: Columbia University Press, 2006.

179 T. Makarenko, 'The crime–terror continuum: tracing the interplay between transnational organised crime and terrorism'. *Global Crime*, 6(1), 2004, pp. 129–145.

180 A.P. Schmid 'Links between terrorism and other forms of crime: the case of narcoterrorism'. Paper presented at Expert Group Meeting on the Nature of the Links between Terrorism and Other Forms of Crime, Cape Town, 24–27 February 2004.

181 M. Crenshaw, 'The psychology of terrorism: an agenda for the 21st century'. *Political Psychology*, 21(2), 2000, pp. 405–420.

182 F. Shanty, '*The nexus between international terrorism and drug trafficking from Afghanistan (1979–2006)*. University of Southern Australia, Mawson Lakes, unpublished dissertation, 2009.

183 A.P. Schmid, 'The links between transnational organized crime and terrorist crimes'. *Transnational Organized Crime*, 2(4), 1996, pp. 40–82.

184 P.R. Pillar, *Terrorism and U.S. Foreign Policy*. Washington, DC: Brookings Institution, 2001, pp 157–198.

185 M. Stohl, 'Expected utility and state terrorism'. In T. Bjorgo (ed.), *Root Causes of Terrorism*. London: Routledge, 2005, pp. 198–214; M. Stohl and G.A. Lopez, 'Introduction'. In M. Stohl and G.A. Lopez, *Terrible beyond Endurance? The Foreign Policy of State Terrorism*. Westport, CT: Greenwood Press, 1988.

186 L. Richardson, 'Terrorists as transnational actors'. In M. Taylor and J. Horgan (eds), *The Future of Terrorism*. London: Frank Cass, 2000, pp. 209–219.

187 A.P. Schmid, 'Purposes of terrorism'. In A.P. Schmid, *Political Terrorism*, 1984, pp. 96–99.

188 J. Ross, 'Structural causes of oppositional political terrorism: towards a causal model'. *Journal of Peace Research*, 30(3), 1993, pp. 317–329.

189 M. Crenshaw, 'The causes of terrorism'. *Comparative Politics*, 13(4), 1981, pp. 379–399.

190 G.K. Roberts, *A Dictionary of Political Analysis*.

191 J.M. Post, K.G. Ruby and E.D. Shaw, 'The radical group in context: 1. An integrated framework for the analysis of group risk of terrorism'. *Studies in Conflict and Terrorism*, 25, 2002, pp. 73–100.

192 A.P. Schmid and J. de Graaf, *Violence as Communication: Insurgent Terrorism and the Western News Media*. London: Sage, 1982.

193 P. Wilkinson, 'Current and future trends in domestic and international terrorism'.

194 B. Hoffman, 'Terrorism trends and prospects'. In I.O. Lesser, B. Hoffman, J. Arquilla *et al.*, *Countering the New Terrorism*. Santa Monica, CA: RAND, 1999.

195 V.I. Vasilenko, 'The concept and typology of terrorism'. *Statutes and Decisions: The Laws of the USSR and Its Successor States*, 40(5), 2004, pp. 46–56.

196 A.K. Cronin, 'Behind the curve: globalization and international terrorism'. *International Security*, 27(3), 2003, pp. 30–58.

197 Compilation adapted from J. Bowker (ed.), *The Concise Oxford Dictionary of Religions*. Oxford: Oxford University Press, 2006, pp. xviii–xix.

198 C. Fettweis, 'Propaganda of the deed, 21st century style'.

199 R.J. Chasdi, *Serenade of Suffering: A Portrait of Middle East Terrorism, 1968–1993*. Lanham, MA: Lexington Books, 1999; R.J. Chasdi, *Tapestry of Terror: A Portrait of Middle East Terrorism, 1994–1999*. Lanham, MA: Lexington Books, 2002.

200 S. Leman-Langlois and J.-P. Broduer, 'Terrorism old and new: counterterrorism in Canada'. *Police Practice and Research*, 6(2), 2005, pp. 121–140.

201 B. Ganor, 'Terrorist organization typologies and the probability of a boomerang effect'.

202 Y. Dror, 'Terrorism as a challenge to the democratic capacity to govern'.

203 L. Waugh Jr, *International Terrorism*.

204 F. Reinares, 'Conceptualising international terrorism'. *ARI*, no. 82, 2005. Retrieved 3 February 2009 from: www.realinstitutoelcano.org:9081/wps/wcm/connect/resources/file/eb60174d5721d99/Reinares 802.pdf?MOD=AJPERES.

205 M. Hough, 'Domestic, international and transnational terror after 2001: towards a new typology?' *Strategic Review for Southern Africa*, 29(2), 2007, pp. 39–49.

206 P. Wilkinson, 'Current and future trends in domestic and international terrorism'.

207 D.H. Doty and W.H. Glick, 'Typologies as a unique form of theory building'.

208 K.A. Seger, 'Deterring terrorists'. In A. Silke (ed.), *Terrorists, Victims and Society: Psychological Perspectives on Terrorism and Its Consequences*. Chichester, UK: Wiley, 2003, pp. 257–270.

209 C. Tilly, 'Terror, terrorism and terrorists'. *Sociological Theory*, 22(1), 2004, pp. 5–13.

210 P. Williams, 'Violent non-state actors and national and international security'.

211 D. Rapoport, 'The four waves of rebel terror and September 11'.

212 K. Rasler and W.R. Thompson, 'Looking for waves of terrorism'. *Terrorism and Political Violence*, 21(1), 2009, pp. 28–41.

213 D. Rapoport, 'The four waves of rebel terror and September 11'.

214 J. Kaplan, 'The fifth wave: the new tribalism?' *Terrorism and Political Violence*, 19(4), 2007, pp. 545–570.

215 Ibid.

216 Ibid, p. 546.

217 M. Crenshaw, 'An organisational approach to the analysis of political terrorism'. *Orbis*, 29(3), 1985, pp. 465–489.

218 J. Arquilla and D. Ronfeldt, *Networks and Netwars: The Future of Terror, Crime, and Militancy*. Santa Monica, CA: RAND, 2001.

219 B.A. Jackson, 'Groups, networks or movements: a command-and-control-driven approach to classifying terrorist organizations and its application to Al Qaeda'. *Studies in Conflict and Terrorism*, 29(3), 2006, pp. 241–262.

220 J. Arquilla and D. Ronfeldt, 'Networks and netwars'.
221 S. Mishal and M. Rosenthal, 'Al Qaeda as a dune organisation: toward a typology of Islamic terrorist organisations'. *Studies in Conflict and Terrorism*, 28, 2005, pp. 275–293.
222 A. Zelinsky and M. Shubik, 'Terrorist groups as business firms: a new typological framework', 2006. Retrieved 28 October 2008 from: http://papers.ssrn.com/sol3/papers.cfm?abstract_id=959258.
223 S. Kaplan, 'A typology of terrorism'. *Review Journal of Political Philosophy*, 6(1), 2008, pp. 1–38.
224 Ibid, p. 19.
225 R.H. Dekmejian, *Spectrum of Terror*.
226 A.P. Schmid and A.J. Jongman, *Political Terrorism* (1988), op. cit., p. 57.
227 D.M. Schwartz, 'Environmental terrorism: analyzing the concept'. *Journal of Peace Research*, 35(4), 1998, pp. 483–496.
228 Ibid.
229 J. Fighel, 'The "forest jihad" ', International Institute for Counter-Terrorism, 2008. Retrieved 11 February 2009, from www.ict.org.il/Articles/tabid/66/Articlsid/506/Default.aspx.
230 D.M. Schwartz, 'Environmental terrorism'.
231 P. Chalk, 'Terrorism, infrastructure, protection, and the U.S. food and agricultural sector'. RAND testimony, 2001. Retrieved 13 March 2009 from: http://wwwcgi.rand.org/pubs/testimonies/2005/CT184.pdf.
232 G.R. Schmitt, 'Agroterrorism – why we're not ready: a look at the role of law enforcement'. *National Institute of Justice Journal*, 256, 2006, pp. 36–39.
233 D.M. Schwartz, 'Environmental terrorism'.
234 M. Stohl, 'Cyber terrorism: a clear and present danger, the sum of all fears, breaking point or patriot games?'. *Crime, Law and Social Change*, 46, 2006, pp. 223–238.
235 J.D. Ballard, J.G. Hornik and D. McKenzie, 'Technological facilitation of terrorism: definitional, legal and policy issues'. *American Behavioral Scientist*, 45(6), 2002, pp. 989–1016.
236 L. Weinberg, A. Pedahzur and S.Hirsch-Hoefler, 'The challenges of conceptualising terrorism'. *Terrorism and Political Violence*, 16(4), 2004, pp. 777–794.
237 Ibid.; D. Collier and J. Mahon, 'Conceptual stretching revisited: adapting categories in comparative analysis'. *American Political Science Review*, 87(4), 1993, pp. 845–855.
238 K.A. Seger, 'Deterring terrorists'.
239 G. Martin, *Understanding Terrorism*, 2nd edn. Thousand Oaks, CA: Sage, 2006, pp. 475–525.
240 J. Sinai, 'New trends in terrorism studies'.
241 N.J. Smelser, *The Faces of Terrorism: Social and Psychological Dimensions*. Princeton, NJ: Princeton University Press, 2007, pp. 160–169.
242 A.P. Schmid, 'Towards joint political strategies for de-legitimising the use of terrorism'. In A.P. Schmid (ed.), *Countering Terrorism through International Cooperation*, Milan: ISPAC, 2002 appendix A, pp. 266–273.
243 M. Ranstorp, 'Introduction: mapping terrorism research – challenges and priorities'. In M. Ranstorp (ed.), *Mapping Terrorism Research: State of the Art, Gaps and Future Direction*. London: Routledge, 2007, pp. 1–28.
244 COT, *Theoretical Treatise on counter-Terrorism Approaches*. The Hague: COT, 2009, p. 31. Available from www.transnationalterrorism.eu.
245 P.K. Davis and B.M. Jenkins, *Deterrence and Influence in Counterterrorism: A Component in the War on Al Qaeda*. Santa Monica, CA: RAND, 2002.
246 P.C. Sederberg, 'Global terrorism: problems of challenge and response'. In C.W. Kegley Jr (ed.), *The New Global Terrorism: Characteristics, Causes and Controls*. Upper Saddle River, NJ: Prentice Hall, 2003, pp. 267–283.
247 Ibid.
248 I. Goldaber, 'Typology of hostage takers'.
249 P.K. Davis and B.M. Jenkins, *Deterrence and Influence in Counterterrorism*.
250 K. Rasler and W.R. Thompson, 'Looking for waves of terrorism'.
251 J. Ross, 'Structural causes of oppositional political terrorism'. For example: J.M. Post *et al.*, 'The radical group in context'.
252 D. Rapoport, 'The four waves of rebel terror and September 11'.
253 D.J. Reed, 'Beyond the war on terror'.
254 M. Kaldor, *New and Old Wars*.
255 For example, K. Rasler and W.R. Thompson, 'Looking for waves of terrorism'.
256 A.L. George, 'Integrating comparative and within-case analysis'.
257 Ibid.
258 Ibid.
259 T. van Dongen, 'Mapping counterterrorism: a categorisation of policies and the promise of empirically based, systematic comparisons', *Critical Studies on Terrorism*, 3(2), 2010, 227–241.
260 G.K. Roberts, *A Dictionary of Political Analysis*.

4

THEORIES OF TERRORISM

Bradley McAllister and Alex P. Schmid

Introduction

While terrorism is a practice, it is also a doctrine, and as such has abstract underpinnings reflecting a theory about its presumed effectiveness. Terrorists, however, are not the only ones who have theories of terrorism. Counter-terrorists and academic scholars who reflect on the origins, workings and outcomes of terrorist campaigns also have their own theories. With the proliferation of explanations about terrorism, the body of theories has grown considerably since the 1980s, when Schmid first summarized existing theories.[1] In the following, we shall try to offer a new compendium of theories of terrorism. Before doing so, let us look at what constitutes a theory. Theory, to begin with, is, in the social scientific sense, a heuristic procedure used to determine broad lines of cause–effect relationships. It is, in effect, a simplification of reality that illustrates the dynamics of a relationship with certain inputs and outcomes. More often than not, we do not have fully fledged theories, only some empirical generalizations that are the lowest form of theory.

A good theory, however, should, as Earl Conteh-Morgan reminds us, meet a number of requirements, including these:

1 It must be comprehensive or applicable to various situations, and must include relevant variables.
2 It must be cohesive, with all its segments strongly linked to each other with identical variables in its separate paths.
3 It must be empirical and applicable to concrete situations.
4 As a result of the third requirement, a theory must have the greatest validity or empirical evidence to support it or enhance its explanatory power.
5 It must be parsimonious, or be able to explain the problem or event with as little complexity as possible.
6 It must be open to verification.
7 Finally, it must be clear and causal in the relationship between and among variables, and in terms of considering and linking units or factors at multiple levels of analysis.[2]

It has to be said from the outset that not many theories in the social sciences meet all or even most of these criteria. That is also true of most of the theories discussed below – which, however, does not make them useless.

Attempting to evaluate the theoretical contributions to any academic discipline is problematic. Evaluating terrorism studies is especially so. Few subjects are as plagued by normative questions and infested by politics as is terrorism. The definitional debate has ramifications for the discourse in its entirety, and covers every conceivable aspect of the study, including who is a 'terrorist', what acts qualify as 'terrorism', etc. Further, the complexity of terrorism in all its forms and manifestations sets it apart from many other political phenomena. It is a category of action that includes a wide array of tactics and is undertaken by a broad range of actors in pursuit of a great diversity of goals. Theories of terrorism should, on the one hand, be general enough to address the range of terrorisms, broadly conceived, and narrow enough to usefully analyse a specific aspect of the subject. This complexity is directly related to the need for a multidisciplinary approach to the study of terrorism. Terrorism Studies therefore ought to be – and sometimes is – interdisciplinary. Theories of terrorism therefore come from a variety of backgrounds: international relations, political science, history, psychology, criminology and criminal justice, law, sociology, victimology, military science and communication studies, to name the most prolific disciplines. Each of these academic disciplines draws on a particular research tradition with its own goals and scholarly criteria. For a political scientist or historian to evaluate the theoretical work of a psychologist or lawyer can pose certain problems.

Nevertheless, a meta-disciplinary evaluation of the state of theory in terrorism research is desirable for a number of reasons. Social science theory at its root is an explanatory framework for socio-political phenomena and it is the main tool of academics in their quest for understanding the conditions underlying social and political conflict and cooperation. Illustrating the strengths and weaknesses of what has been achieved in Terrorism Studies not only can serve as a roadmap for surveying the existing discourse, but also – by identifying omissions – can point out lacunae in the subject. Filling gaps in our knowledge is a particularly useful way of advancing knowledge; it also offers opportunities for opening new avenues of scholarship. Identifying gaps in our knowledge also paves the way for a more strategic collection of theory-relevant data. All too often, students of terrorism have tended to formulate hypotheses that are testable with available data, rather than generating new data dictated by hypotheses to be tested. The result has often been trivial findings.

As indicated earlier, theoretical progress in Terrorism Studies has historically been retarded by a lack of definitional consensus on the subject. The attempts to reach an academic consensus definition have somewhat diminished this problem, without eradicating it. However, it has enabled researchers to move forward, though cautiously, in conducting more precise research according to a definition that was widely recognized, though not universally accepted. Hopefully, the newly revised academic consensus definition proposed in this volume will further smooth the path towards a universally accepted social science definition.

It is important to state clearly right from the beginning that there exists no general theory of terrorism. One reason for this is the great variety of types of terrorism. As Krumwiede put it in 2004,

> In the light of the diversity of the phenomenon 'terrorism' and the multiplicity, and differential weight, of relevant conditions for concrete cases, it is impossible to formulate substantial general hypotheses with broad validity, that is, hypotheses which are valid for all cases or at least most cases.[3]

Most theorizing on terrorism addresses only one type of terrorism, often without the theorist being fully aware of that fact.

Chapter outline

We will divide our discussion into two parts. The first section deals with theories addressing various manifestations of state or regime terrorism, which ranges from repressive violence of the terrorist kind in times of peace, to sponsorship of international terrorist movements. The second section will look at the much larger category (in terms of research volume) of insurgent or non-state terrorism.

In order to manage the latter, we will subdivide the second part into sections organized by level of analysis:

- the agent or individual level;
- the middle-range or organizational level;
- the systemic or structural level of analysis; and
- the dyadic level of analysis (including theories of counter-terrorism).

State or regime terrorism

State or regime terrorism not only has a longer history than insurgent terrorism but also has been much more costly in terms of human lives. Nevertheless, it is decidedly the less well researched of the two major categories of terrorism.[4] A number of reasons come together to make this the case, among them political, academic and practical considerations. In part, this is due to the fact that as politicized a process as defining insurgent terrorism is, defining what qualifies as state terrorism is even more difficult. During the early Cold War period, there was a considerable amount of research and theorizing on the terrorism emanating from totalitarian regimes, generally written by scholars in liberal democratic societies. Since the late 1970s, there has also been a certain amount of writing on terrorism practised by authoritarian polities which were – and are – often allies of Western democracies in the Cold War period and beyond. Many of these writings have pointed at Western double standards and accused ex-colonial powers and the United States of neo-imperial expansion in the by then largely decolonized developing countries. More often than not, such scholarship has been tainted by ideology, although it has tried to make a legitimate point.

Studies of regime terrorism have to come to terms with the problem of differentiating between legitimate use of force by those claiming a monopoly of violence, and illegitimate state violence. The Weberian definition of statehood assumes a monopoly on the legitimate use of force, but the threshold between a legitimate display of proportionate force for dissuasion and the use of disproportionate, indiscriminate terror for deterrence is often a precarious one to establish. Many young scholars new to the field tended to be attracted by a high-profile topic with ample media coverage and the availability of government research funds. Research into regime terrorism has proven much harder to fund than anti-state violence. Local scholars living in oppressive societies or under highly repressive regimes are, for obvious reasons, less likely to pursue studies of internal regime terror. Scholars from the outside, with the exception of some anthropologists, are generally not exposed to the consequences of repression. They have often lacked linguistic skills, cultural affinity and access to relevant data for the study of highly repressive regimes, except when the regime terror was part of a recently overthrown regime or dated back to a more distant historical past.

However, there have been a number of outstanding comparative studies, especially of communist regimes in the sphere of influence of the Soviet Union. The Soviet system itself, particularly under Stalin,[5] has received much attention, both during the Cold War and thereafter.

Conceptualizing state or regime terrorism

Because of the large-scale potential for violence in the hands of the state, many scholars consider state terrorism as something *sui generis*, not comparable to the small-scale terrorism of revolutionary cells acting from the underground. They certainly have a point: the terrorism and political violence of one single regime like the one in Guatemala produced in the country's 36-year civil conflict more casualties (some 45,000 disappearances and 200,000 killed[6]) than all non-state terrorism worldwide in the same period. Its traumatic experience has not been unique, as the following list makes clear. It estimates the number of fatalities from political violence in seven countries:[7]

East Timor (1975–1993)	>200,000
Guatemala (1965–1995)	200,000
El Salvador (1979–1992)	70,000
Iraq (1980–1990)	200,000
Algeria (1992–)	100,000
(Former) Yugoslavia (1991–1995)	110,000
Chechnya (1994–2004)	100,000

The list is far from complete. State terrorism and repression in Chile in the period 1973–1985 killed more than 20,000 people, while in Argentina some 11,000 people, and quite possibly more, disappeared in the period 1976–1982.[8] Roughly in the same period, the German Red Army Faction (RAF) killed 31 persons and the Italian Red Brigades killed 334 people in the 1970s and 1980s.[9] In other words, state and non-state terrorism are of very different magnitudes, so much so that some analysts consider them to be different phenomena.

Let us look at the conceptual underpinnings of state or regime terrorism. David Claridge, in his award-winning St Andrews dissertation, begins with the assertion that when regime use of force moves from legitimate to illegitimate, it becomes a means of coercion rather than a means of protection.[10] He elaborates by drawing from existing studies on the psychological impact of fear as a mechanism for social control. According to Claridge, the psychological strategy of state terrorism is not so different from that pursued by insurgent groups. It is mainly the far greater material capability at the disposal of the state that differentiates regime from insurgent terrorism.[11] Claridge's definition of regime terrorism is composed of seven parts and is formulated to take into account only actions strictly determined to be terrorism, rather than more commonplace displays of force:[12]

1   The violence is systematic. That is to say, it is a concerted campaign of violence and not a mosaic of random and unrelated events.
2   It either threatens violence, or is actually violent.
3   The violence is political and not meant to address personal needs or desires.
4   The violence is committed either by agents of the state or by state proxies who carry out their campaigns by using materials provided by the state.
5   The violence is not merely geared towards the liquidation of enemies of the regime, but meant to generate fear.
6   Like insurgent terrorism, the ultimate target is not necessarily the actual victim of aggression, but a wider audience of potential victims.
7   The victims of state terrorism are not armed or organized for aggression at the time the state initiates its campaign of intimidating violence (this rules out cases of civil conflict where the state is acting in self-defence).

Regime or state terrorism is not uniform. There are several, sometimes coexisting, types of regime terrorism:

• Direct domestic state terrorism: the killing of unarmed civilians at home in an overt 'dirty war' by organs of the state (regime of terror, state (controlled) terrorism, repressive terrorism, government or enforcement terrorism, terrorism from above);
• domestic state-supported terrorism: the encouragement or condoning of pro-regime death squads and pro-state vigilante groups;
• direct state terrorism abroad: carrying out clandestine acts of terrorism in foreign countries;
• coercive terrorist diplomacy as in Cold War nuclear threats (balance of terror);
• sponsorship or support of foreign terrorist groups operating abroad;

- the sponsorship of, or acquiescence with, regimes employing terrorism (surrogate or proxy terrorism);
- domestic or foreign false flag operations to place blame for terrorist acts on political opponents.[13]

In a similar vein, Michael S. Stohl holds that terrorism can be either international or domestic, employ agents of the state or like-minded proxies, and be either overt or covert in its execution.[14] Despite the (semi-)clandestine nature of various campaigns of regime terrorism, observable indicators exist for determining when such campaigns are taking place. These include outflow of refugees, the existence of torture, the occurrence of political murder and massacres, the presence of death squads, concentration camps, and disappearances. Reliable data on these phenomena are hard to come by, but just as an illustration of the magnitudes of victimization, here is a list from the UN Working Group on Disappearances in 2006, showing the number of cases of unsolved disappearances:[15]

Iraq	16,000
Sri Lanka	5,700
Argentina	3,400
Guatemala	2,900
Peru	2,400
El Salvador	2,300

George A. Lopez and Michael S. Stohl contend that engagement in regime terrorism can take place at three levels:[16]

1 The state can engage in a direct and systematic campaign, perpetrated by the armed forces and/or state security apparatuses with the intent to repress and terrify sectors of the population.
2 Terror can also be executed using extra-normal legal powers such as martial law, states of emergency, etc.
3 Finally, a state can covertly employ its own domestic security forces.

According to Stohl, within their own societies regimes use systematic state violence and terror (1) as an extension of oppression and repression systems; (2) as a method for the consolidation of power; (3) as a reaction to 'reformist-minded' political, social or economic organizations and their policy demands (challengers to the prevailing system); and (4) as a reaction to an insurgent challenge to the state.[17] The repertoire of repressive tactics of governments is broad and includes, in ascending order of severity and illegality, the following acts:

1 entry and search of homes without a warrant;
2 destruction of private property, e.g. dynamiting houses of suspect persons;
3 suppression of papers and other media;
4 suppression of political parties;
5 physical attacks on opposition party rallies;
6 beatings and physical assaults on individual opponents;
7 excessive use of force during arrests;
8 baton charges by security forces against unarmed and non-provoking demonstrators;
9 arbitrary arrests and incarceration;
10 threats and reprisals against the families of political opponents;
11 forced exile or domestic house arrest;
12 torture and mutilations;
13 political assassinations by death squads or vigilante groups provided with information by the security forces about the whereabouts of the opponent;

14   execution of prisoners without trial or after a fake show trial;
15   disappearances – secret individual abductions followed by torture and murder;
16   pogroms against opposition groups by mobs led by paid provocateurs;
17   premeditated massacres of opposition groups at funerals, mass meetings, etc.;
18   extermination of persons in slave labour camps by means of ration and sleep control, while working them to death;
19   death marches under the pretext of evacuation and deportation programmes;
20   mass terror for the purpose of 'ethnic cleansing'.[18]

Not all acts of repression are illegal, nor are they all terroristic. Deterrence can be achieved by draconian punishment that, like terrorism, can send a message to others who consider challenging state power. However, when exemplary punishment is not only excessive but also exercised against innocent people, it becomes terroristic in nature. Views as to what constitutes legitimate proportionality of punishment might, however, differ in wartime and peacetime, and on opposite sides of the conflict divide.

Domestic terrorism in peacetime

The classical theory of state terrorism was formulated in the early 1970s by Dallin and Breslauer[19], who were addressing the prolific use of state terrorism by totalitarian (read communist) regimes. They hold that regimes ensure public compliance with government directives by virtue of a variety of sanctions. These instruments are as follows:

- normative sanctions, which assume a monopoly on legitimacy and a right to the loyalty of citizens;
- material power, which is a mix of positive incentives such as access to public and private positions, state resources, and civil services;
- coercive power, which includes an inventory of negative or punitive sanctions.

Dallin and Breslauer contend that when communist regimes come to power, they lack normative and material resources. They are, consequently, forced to rely on negative sanctions (often including the use of regime terror) as a means for maintaining control of the state in order to keep rival political organizations, or antagonistic factions within the government, under control. An example is the great purges of communist cadres in the 1930s in the Soviet Union. The following is a list of the number of victims of Stalin's Great Terror in 1937–1938, as estimated respectively by Conquest and Nove:[20]

- arrests: 7 million (Conquest, 1990);
- executions (mostly shot): 1 million (Conquest, 1990); 681,692 (Nove, 1993);
- camp deaths 2 million (Conquest, 1990);
- camp population (1938): 8 million (Conquest, 1990); 3,593,000 (Nove, 1993).

Note that Nove's figure for the camp population covers both gulag camps and NKVD prisons, camps and colonies.

The political scientist Ted R. Gurr assumes that state terrorism reflects, in its essence, a conflict between elites and non-elites.[21] He defines the state as a 'bureaucratically institutionalized pattern of authority whose rulers claim to exercise sovereign (ultimate) control over the inhabitants of territory, and who demonstrate an enduring capacity to enforce that claim'.[22] State claims of sovereignty are either derived from a sense of popular legitimacy, or enforced by positive and negative inducements in the absence of such legitimacy. Terrorism is one such negative inducement in a state's repertoire of control. Echoing Lopez and Stohl's articulation of levels of involvement in regime terror, Gurr maintains that internal state terror in peacetime is facilitated by a perversion of the existing legal and security structures. While the term 'terrorism' implies a lack of legitimacy in regime behaviour, Gurr puts forward criteria for the intent and efficacy of internal state terror. First, the violence must have been intended to actualize a threat and to speak to a broader audience. Second, consistency is necessary to induce fear in the population; thus, an individual act of violence must fit within broader patterns of behaviour. Third, the violence must take place with the state's explicit or implicit approval. Gurr also proposes a proportionality principle whereby the reaction to non-elite challenges should be proportional to the threat posed by those groups. Gurr holds that there are two types of internal state terrorism: situation-specific and institutionalized. Situation-specific terrorism is a response to a specific threat present during a limited temporal span. Institutionalized terrorism, on the other hand, implies a systematic adoption of terror as a mechanism for maintaining state control. The former may be initiated through the imposition of short-term legal emergency measures such as the introduction of martial law. The latter is typically promulgated by the advent of new agencies whose task it is to manage regime terrorism. Gurr proposed a series of hypotheses regarding the breeding grounds that encourage regimes to have recourse to terrorist tactics:[23]

1   The greater the political threat posed by challengers, the greater the likelihood that a regime will respond with violence.
2   The greater the latent support for revolutionary challengers in a population, the greater the likelihood that a regime will respond with terrorism.
3   Regimes are more likely to use terrorism against politically marginal groups than against opposition groups that have influence on or supporters among the elite.
4   Weak regimes are more likely to use violence in response to challenges than strong regimes.
5   Elites who have secured and maintained their positions by violent means are likely to choose violent responses to future challenges.
6   Successful situational uses of state terror in polarized societies are likely to lead to institutionalized terror and to the pre-emptive use of terror to maintain political control.
7   The initial decision of a challenged elite to use state terror is usually modelled on others' successful use of state terror.
8   Democratic principles and institutions inhibit political elites from using state violence in general and terror specifically.
9   The greater the heterogeneity and stratification in a society, the greater the likelihood that a regime will use violence as a principal means of social control.
10 Minority elites in highly stratified societies are likely to use terror routinely as an instrument of rule.
11 Regimes facing external threats are likely to use violence against domestic opponents.
12 Regimes involved in proxy big-power conflicts are likely to use the most extreme forms of violence against challengers, including state terrorism.
13 Peripheral status in the world system increases the likelihood that regimes that rule by violence can do so with impunity.

Gurr offers one of the most comprehensive approaches to understanding why, how and when regimes turn to internal repression as a mode of governance. He divides structural conditions conducive to terror into four categories, reflecting in turn the challengers, the regime and prevailing ideology, the social structure, and the international system.[24] First and foremost in the decision-making calculus of those holding state power looms the nature of the non-elite challenge to the regime. At the most basic level, elites must perceive a threat to the status quo. The existence of challengers alone is not sufficient to prompt such fear, as not all political opposition movements provoke trepidation among rulers. Pursuant to this, the greater the threat posed by the challengers, the greater the likelihood that their presence will provoke violence. Typically this would entail a fairly large opposition whose stated goal is the overthrow of the current elites. The presence of latent support for the opposition within the broader population exacerbates this hostility. Regimes will often opt for violent reactions to non-elite challengers if those challengers themselves use violence as a means for obtaining political power. Challengers emanating from marginal elements of society are much more likely to be resisted by elite violence.

The nature of the opposition is only part of the equation; the nature of the regime and its political ideology also play a role in the likelihood of resorting to state terrorism. First, weak regimes are more likely to resort to violence than strong ones. Second, a history of state violence is likely to result in a return to violent tactics in the future. Third, a successful use of situational violence will often lay the foundations for an institutionalized campaign later on. Fourth, like insurgents, states typically learn by observation and thus model their domestic campaigns on successful violence by other regimes. Finally, Gurr observes that the presence of democratic institutions and principles inhibits (though does not preclude) the use of state terrorism. The prevalence of state terror is also a reflection of the dominant social structures in place in a state. State terrorism is more likely in heterogeneous or highly stratified societies. Violence might be especially severe if it is perpetrated by a minority regime that is attempting to maintain its position of privilege. Gurr believes this relationship is a result of social distance, which retards empathy and makes the choice to resort to violence easier on the regime.

Gurr does not assume that states operate in a vacuum. On the contrary, the nature of the international environment plays a part in determining when a state resorts to internal violence. For example, Gurr notes a correlation between the use of internal violence and the presence of external threats. Moreover, the choice to resort to violence is often easier in peripheral countries, where the leadership is less likely to provoke international reproach. Finally, client regimes of major powers often become caught up in hegemonic conflict as the powers confront each other via proxy wars inevitably involving domestic violence.

While the comprehensiveness of Gurr's approach sacrifices a degree of parsimony in order to address the complexities of state decision making with respect to internal terror, he offers one of the most useful and generalizable insights into the subject.

State repression and terrorism is, to some extent, quantifiable and measurable. Michael S. Stohl and Mark Gibney *et al.* offer a useful means for rating the severity of internal repression.[25] They use a scale of five levels:

- *Level 1.* Countries under the secure rule of law. People are not imprisoned for their view, and torture is rare or exceptional. Political murders are extremely rare.
- *Level 2.* There is a limited amount of imprisonment for non-violent political activity. However, few persons are affected; torture and beatings are exceptional. Political murder is rare.
- *Level 3.* There is extensive political imprisonment, or a recent history of such imprisonment. Executions or other political murders and brutality may be common. Unlimited detention, with or without a trial, for political reasons is accepted.
- *Level 4.* Civil and political rights violations have expanded to large numbers of the population. Murder, disappearances and torture are a common part of life. In spite of its generality, on this level terror affects primarily those who interest themselves in politics or ideas.
- *Level 5.* Terror has expanded to the whole population. The leaders of these societies place no limits on the means or thoroughness with which they pursue personal or ideological goals.[26]

Mark Gibney maintains a database coding information from the yearbooks of Amnesty International and the US Department of State's Country Reports on Human Rights Practices, and places all countries, year after year, in one of these five categories. This has led to interesting findings such as the observation that the level of state repression in all but the 30 relatively rich OECD countries has worsened in the post-Cold War period, 1991–2006, compared to the period 1977–1990. The average score for the post-9/11 years 2001–2006 has been 3 on the five-point scale – a level never reached for more than three consecutive years (1980–1982) in the previous period. Figure 4.1 shows the average political terror scores for 1976–2006 for non-DECD countries.

These averages, however, hide important regional differences. For three regions – East Asia and the Pacific, Latin America and the Caribbean region, and Europe and Central Asia, the average political terror scale declines for the post-1990 period compared to the pre-Cold War period. For three other regions, however – South Asia, sub-Saharan Africa, and the Middle East and North Africa – human insecurity increases quite dramatically. Somewhat counter-intuitively, the decline in security is larger in South Asia than it is in Africa or the Middle East.

Before one is inclined to attribute these differences to political culture, it is worthwhile to look at the income levels of the non-OECD countries. From this, it clearly emerges that the higher the income, the lower the use of terrorism and repression by regimes (Figure 4.2). On the basis of this finding, one is inclined to conclude that when there is more distributable income, the fight for scarce resources does not take such a bloody turn. The worldwide recession that started in 2008, combined with the stepping up of counter-terrorism and counter-insurgency in a great number of countries, has probably made repression worse for larger sections of the population.

State sponsorship of terrorism

Theories dealing with state sponsorship of international terrorism were popular during the Cold War period, when war-by-proxies was one of the tactics employed by the rival camps. There are three schools of thought, each denoting a particular more or less ideological take on state sponsorship – specifically, which of the hegemonic powers bore the main responsibility. One school held the view that the Soviet Union was responsible for a sizeable portion of international terrorism, but not for all, or even most, of it. A second school held that 'all roads lead to Moscow', fully blaming the masters in the Kremlin for international terrorism. A third school affirmed (not incorrectly) that some Western governments were also implicated in the backing of insurgent groups using terrorist tactics (e.g. the United States in the case of the Nicaraguan Contras). Serving as a patron of non-state terrorists, however, is not simply a privilege of superpowers and former colonial powers. Since

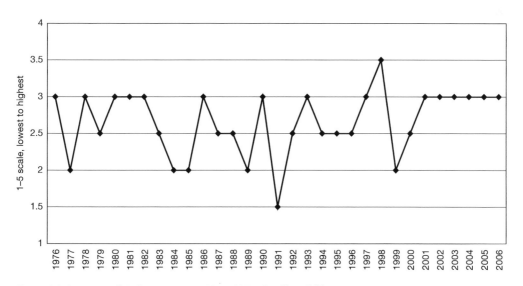

Figure 4.1 Average political terror scores, 1976–2006, for all available non-OECD countries.

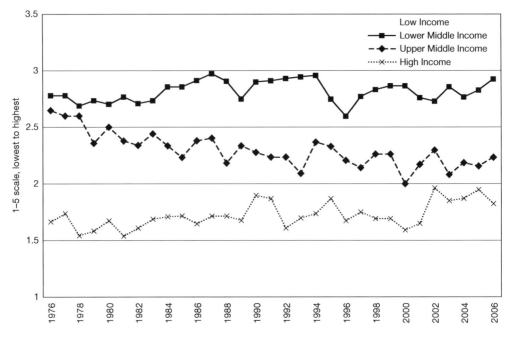

Figure 4.2 Average political terror scores, 1976–2006, for non-OECD countries by income level.

supporting client groups abroad is a cheap alternative to conventional conflict waging, terrorism-by-proxy has been utilized by a number of states for a variety of reasons, the most basic being 'my enemy's enemy is my friend'.

Despite the fact that the ability to attract a state sponsor often makes or breaks insurgent terrorists, little non-ideologically driven research on state-sponsored terrorism has been conducted. The outstanding exception is *Deadly Connections: States That Sponsor Terrorism*, by Daniel Byman.[27] Byman typologizes state sponsorship of insurgent movements on several levels: by type of state sponsor, by the type of support given, and by the motivation for support. He divides state sponsors of international terror into strong, weak, lukewarm, antagonistic, passive and unwilling sponsors:[28]

- Strong sponsors adamantly favour the cause of the insurgents and make available a sizeable portion of state resources to further their ends.
- Weak state sponsors are committed to the cause but lack the necessary resources to provide meaningful aid to the insurgents.
- Lukewarm patrons serve as advocates for insurgents but ultimately prove reluctant to mobilize resources to help in the conflict.
- Antagonistic supporters of terrorists wish to use a group to further the state's own aims, and as a result try to control its activities, often to the detriment of the sponsored organization.
- Passive supporters do not actively provide aid to insurgents, but do help by turning a blind eye to insurgent activities.
- Unwilling sponsors may wish to destroy the insurgents, but are too weak to take on the terrorists and reluctantly allow their territory and resources to be exploited by them.

Of these, only the first four can be considered active supporters. Byman observes that the motivation for providing support can be as varied as the degree of support given.[29] Broadly speaking, a state may be driven to come to the aid of a foreign insurgent movement by strategic concerns, ideology, and/or domestic politics. Strategic concerns include efforts to destabilize neighbours, attempts to project power beyond what the state is conventionally capable of, efforts to provoke regime change abroad, and a desire to have a hand in shaping the opposition to hostile regimes. Ideological concerns are less tangible, but nonetheless important. Typically, states may be swayed to support terrorists either as a vehicle for exporting their own political system, or as a means of enhancing the sponsor's international position. Domestic concerns may also persuade a state to sponsor outside insurgencies. Broad support to aid ethnic kin, or to help co-religionists, often plays a hand in fuelling such conflicts. However, a state may also support an internationally operating terrorist group in exchange for support in dealing with domestic opposition.

The motivation for the sponsorship often dictates the type of support given to insurgent movements. The most common is training and operational support. Money, arms and logistical aid are also valuable resources states can make available to armed client groups. Diplomatic backing can be important, although it is often less crucial to the terrorist group's survival. Sometimes, organizational assistance and ideological direction are sought from state sponsors. The single most important form of sponsorship, however, is the provision of sanctuary, from which insurgents can organize operations with impunity.[30] When determining whether and what type of aid to provide, a primary concern for state sponsors is the threat of escalation.[31] If the threat is strong that a sponsor will be drawn into a conflict on behalf of a violent non-state terrorist actor, then the motivations for support must be very salient (or the efforts for 'plausible denial' very successful). Further, the degree to which a state is inclined to help a terrorist group also depends on the extent to which a state is willing to be linked to insurgent activities. States like Pakistan, Iran, Syria and Sudan are, or have been, in the recent past, linked to the support of terrorist groups acting against neighbouring countries. In the past, Cuba, North Korea and Libya were also listed as 'rogue states'. Venezuela has apparently discontinued its support for the Colombian FARC, following embarrassing disclosures in 2008 that made 'plausible denial' no longer credible. Byman's conceptualization of state-sponsored terrorism is, in our view, a long-overdue new perspective on what was, until recently, a more political than analytical take on state sponsorship of terrorism.

Terrorism in war

While state terrorism as a whole has been under-studied,[32] the role of terrorism in civil and international war is even more neglected. Partly, this is due to the fact that, figuratively speaking, the terrorist 'trees' tend to be overlooked in the 'forest' (and fog) of war. Many of the crimes committed in warfare are much greater than terrorist acts tend to be. Yet certain practices of war, like ethnic cleansing and the creation of refugee flows, are often linked to terrorist tactics. Recently, systematic rape to terrorize and demoralize civilian populations has been added to the repertoire of terrorist tactics, especially in sub-Saharan Africa. However, terrorist tactics like the massacre of prisoners of war, the taking and killing of hostages, or the bombing of civilian populations have a long history. Many such acts are grave breaches of the rules of warfare – that is, war crimes, or even crimes against humanity. Such acts of terrorism often overlap with tactics outlawed by international humanitarian law, as codified in the Hague and Geneva Conventions and their Protocols, and, more recently, in the Rome Statute (1998), which established the International Criminal Court in The Hague. The main thrust of the international laws of warfare is, however, still geared towards interstate war, while such warfare has become far less frequent than intra-state warfare, with insurgents battling the state. Recently, there has been a trend towards warlords fighting not just each other but the civilian population, with the state sometimes fully or partly absent (as in Somalia and the Democratic Republic of the Congo). Certain features of air warfare, including the use of unmanned drones, often used in counter-terrorist operations, while not deliberately directed against civilians, have caused terror among civilians. For a rural population gathering in a market place, a bomb suddenly falling from the sky from an altitude of 12 kilometres is little different in its terrifying effects from an improvised bomb placed under one of the market stands: there is an apparent lack of discrimination, there are civilian casualties, and while in one case civilians might be classified as 'collateral damage' and in the other deliberately targeted, in either case innocent lives are shattered and survivors traumatized. Contemporary low-intensity warfare has often been characterized by a confluence of tactics and countermeasures: guerrilla ambushes, hit-and-run operations, acts of arson and sabotage, terrorist bombings, kidnappings for ransom or blackmail, rioting by sympathizers and protesters of one side or the other, political demonstrations, industrial strikes, parliamentary actions, individual assassinations, abductions and illegal renditions, raids and mass arrests, massacres, concentration camps and disappearances. The logic of such deadly cocktails of active and reactive violence is difficult to capture with any single theory. Yet the role of terrorism in warfare remains a major lacuna in our knowledge. An important recent contribution has been the study of Andreas Feldman and Victor Hinojosa on terrorism in Colombia, a country that in the period 1970-2004 recorded the highest incidence of terrorism in the world – 5,432 incidents, according to the Global Terrorism Database.[33] Feldman and Hinojosa argue that

> terrorism in Colombia constitutes a specific strategy that can be clearly distinguished from other manifestations of violence. Armed parties, particularly guerrilla and paramilitary groups, have turned terrorism into a pivotal element of their repertoires of action. These parties have not only increased their reliance on this strategy, but have also expanded the range of this practice and introduced new, more refined forms of terrorism, including de-territorialized terrorism. Moreover, the parties have specialized in particular forms of terrorism that suit their general objectives. While paramilitary groups rely mostly on massacres and forced disappearances, guerrillas concentrate on agitational terrorism including kidnappings and indiscriminate bombings.[34]

Feldman and Hinojosa manage to differentiate between governmental or state terrorism and non-governmental terrorism. They use the term 'state terrorism' for 'acts perpetrated by state agents or by private groups on the order of or on behalf of a state that seeks to terrorize the population and propagate anxiety among citizens to curb political opposition'.[35] They manage also to differentiate terrorism from guerrilla warfare, following the definition of the latter from the *Encyclopedia of Guerrilla Warfare*, which describes it as 'a set of military tactics utilized by a minority group within a state or an indigenous population in order to oppose the government or foreign occupying forces'.[36] It is worth citing them at some length since confusion about the difference between terrorism and guerrilla warfare is still widespread:

> Guerrilla warfare is a very ancient form of warfare generally used by the weaker parties that must confront superior forces. Unlike terrorism that deliberately seeks to injure civilians violating the International Humanitarian Law (IHL) principle of distinction, guerrilla warfare involves harassing the enemy by avoiding direct confrontation in pitched battles and concentrating on 'slowly sapping the enemy's strength and morale through ambushes, minor skirmishes, lightening raids and withdrawals, cutting of communications and supply lines, and similar techniques'. Guerrillas normally set up small military units and seek to establish liberated zones that may be used to challenge the state militarily. In these enclaves, usually located in the countryside, these groups normally create a parallel state structure. Such acts do not constitute terrorism, provided the perpetrators are constrained by the laws of war and the targets of the violence are combatants. Indeed, the crucial distinction between terrorism and guerrilla warfare is the nature of the act itself, irrespective of the organization or individual that carries out the actions.[37]

Feldman and Hinojosa conclude, looking at the non-state (but in some cases state-linked) activities of paramilitaries and guerrilleros:

Paramilitary groups have concentrated on massacres and disappearances and used them to drive peasants away from strategic areas they seek to control. These groups resort to terrorism to endorse the political *status quo*. Guerrillas, for their part, engage in agitational terrorism, including bombings and kidnappings, which seek to undermine the legitimacy and credibility of the state and also to convey the message that the state is incapable of providing security for its citizens. Many of the violent actions carried out by these groups, especially massacres, assassinations, and forced displacement, deliberately seek to instil fear in the civilian population. Additionally, some actions intended to help the organization obtain funds to wage war, such as the widespread practice of kidnapping, while not intentionally intended to spread terror, end up having the same effect. We also posit that waves of terror tend to correlate with period of intensified armed conflict . . . and that they materialize in strategic areas that parties seek to control militarily. . . . Civilian immunity, the cornerstone principle of IHL, is wilfully violated time and again by parties who cynically argue that infractions are the unfortunate although inevitable result of warfare in the Colombian context. A careful examination, however, shows that terrorism constitutes a calculated and deliberate strategy that parties undertake to maximize their goals in the general war effort.[38]

This is not new. Even governments fighting for a good cause – like opposing Nazism in the Second World War – have used terrorist tactics. The Allies fighting fascism and national socialism conducted bombing operations through much of the Second World War, killing an estimated 370,000 civilians in Germany.[39] A particularly drastic example was the bombing of Dresden in mid-February 1945, which cost up to 25,000, mostly civilian, lives. The British wartime leader, Winston Churchill, wrote in a secret memorandum drafted for General Ismay and the Chiefs of Staff Committee:

> It seems to me that the moment has come when the question of bombing of German cities simply for the sake of increasing the terror, though under other pretexts, should be reviewed. Otherwise we shall come into control of an utterly ruined land. . . . I feel the need for more precise concentration upon military objectives . . . rather than on mere acts of terror and wanton destruction, however impressive.[40]

Insurgent terrorism

Insurgent terrorism has captured the attention of policy makers, the media and researchers much more than wartime terrorism or peacetime domestic state terrorism. The theories in Terrorism Studies addressing insurgent terrorism cover a wide diversity of actors and actions. Terrorism is often seen by some of them (as well as by some terrorists themselves) as a tactic employed in attempts to trigger or maintain an insurgency.[41] However, insurgent terrorism itself can take many forms. Stepanova,[42] as we saw in the previous, chapter, on typologies, classifies insurgent terrorism according to whether it is global or local and whether or not the campaign of terror is part of a broader political conflict. On this basis, one could distinguish three broad strands of insurgent terrorism. There is what could be termed *stand-alone, peacetime terrorism*, which is often nothing but armed propaganda and agitation for recruitment and mobilization. Then there is *embedded terrorism* – that is, terrorism enmeshed with (other forms of irregular) warfare. Beyond that there is *global terrorism*, as enacted by movements with universal ambitions, of which Al-Qaeda can be seen as a prototype.

Since there is no general theory of terrorism, one has to content oneself with theories that cover one (sub-)type or other of the phenomenon. While Feldman and Hinojosa have advanced our theoretical understanding of terrorism by guerrilla and paramilitary forces that are often linked to the military, if not the civilian government, theoretical advances regarding the use of terrorism by states in inter-state warfare are still lacking. The problem, however, is one that deserves more study.[43]

For the purpose of this overview of theories of terrorism, we have divided the subsequent section into four sub-sections, according to the level of analysis used in research:

1   The first sub-section will deal with theories of terrorism utilizing the agent (or individual) level of analysis, including psychological theories, rational choice theories, theories of terror propounded by the insurgents themselves, and others.
2   The second sub-section will deal with the organizational level of analysis, analyzing the effects of group dynamics and goals on terror.
3   The third sub-section looks at studies utilizing the systemic level of analysis. These structural theories of terrorism include the 'root cause' debates, analysing economic, political and cultural feeders of insurgent violence.
4   Finally, we will close with an overview of dyadic studies of terrorism, including theories of counter-terrorism.

Insurgent terrorism: agent level of analysis

The agent level of analysis, focusing on the terrorist actor, has been among the more problematic areas in the study of terrorism, as it has often utilized ill-founded theories of terrorism based on individual personality and even physiognomic traits allegedly typical of terrorist criminals.[44] In part, studies of this nature were an outgrowth of a perhaps natural desire to view terrorists as abnormal. In addition, they often allowed states to de-legitimize the goals and aspirations of militant rebels by labelling them madmen. While terrorist groups have their share of psychologically unbalanced individuals, like other populations, it would be detrimental for any terrorist group to admit even borderline cases into its ranks, for reasons of security. However, life in the underground, with the threat of persecution, from both within and without, can create psychological stress which affects the behaviour of previously normal individuals. To the extent that members of terrorist groups use, or are given, mind-altering drugs to 'fire them up' before attacks, their behaviour can also become erratic, especially when embarking on high-risk and suicide missions. In the following, we will review some psychological theories, rational choice theories, the theories of terrorist practitioners, and the extant literature on violent radicalization.

Psychological theories of terrorism

Jeff Victoroff stated that the major deficiencies in the canon of psychological theories of terrorism arose from the fact that much of the research has been based on theoretical speculation or merely anecdotal empirical evidence.[45] Yet Victoroff and other specialists maintain that terrorism can result from identifiable (and malleable) social and psychological factors.[46] The focus of some current psychological research is on why individuals join terrorist organizations, why they leave such organizations and what the effects of membership in a clandestine organization are on the individual member.

John Horgan divides the application of psychology to the terrorism studies into two main categories: that dealing with individual psychology, and that dealing with how individuals are affected by organizational membership.[47] He echoes the concerns of many other psychologists and dismisses the popular notion that terrorists exhibit abnormal psychological traits. In point of fact, detailed studies of terrorists have shown that most of them are normal in a clinical sense[48] (although their atrocities are clearly not normal in a moral sense). Drawing distinctions between the violence of terrorists and the apolitical violence of psychopaths, Horgan shows that the lifestyle of a professional terrorist is not conducive to aberrant personalities. First, terrorist violence is generally undertaken in pursuit of collective goals, not the fulfilment of personal fantasies (except in the case of lone-wolf terrorists). Furthermore, membership in a terrorist organization requires extreme loyalty and commitment – rare qualities among those suffering from, say, extreme narcissism. From an operational point of view, Horgan observes that extreme personalities make individuals stand out in the public eye. As a result, secret organizations will actively avoid recruiting such people. His assertions are supported by Donatella Della Porta's study of female Italian terrorists, which illustrates the pro-social qualities of membership in the violent organizations she studied.[49] Horgan finds that at least three abnormal psychological theories continue to be erroneously applied to terrorists:[50]

1   The frustration–aggression theory. According to this theory, aggression is a response to the blockage of goal attainment. Terrorism, then, is an individual response to the lack of alternative modes of political expression. However, Horgan points out that such theories cannot account for the process by which blockage leads to terrorism, nor can they account for variations in individual outcomes, as only a few frustrated people turn to terroristic aggression. Horgan further notes that many frustration–aggression theorists make methodological errors when mixing up levels of analysis (individual or group).

2   Second, narcissism and narcissism–aggression theories understand violence as the result of enhanced ego concerns. As pointed out before, however, these sorts of personality disorders are not conducive to successful survival in an underground organization where the ego of the individual member is sacrificed to group survival.

3   Finally, Horgan finds that psychodynamic accounts for political violence continue to be employed, based on the assumption that violence is the result of latent desires going back to early childhood experiences. All this is not well supported by the available empirical evidence.

Andrew Silke, corroborating some of the findings of Horgan, points out that the vast number of studies that claim to provide evidence for psychotic personalities come from writers using only second-hand research, not personal interviews conducted by the researcher with individual terrorists in face-to-face situations.[51] Silke maintains that membership in a terrorist organization is the result of certain processes that share common factors[52] and have can be modelled by psychologists. Broadly speaking, a majority of violent extremists tend to come from the more risk-acceptant demographic cohort of young males between the ages of 18 and 25. Social identification with worthwhile others and marginalization are often salient features, with many terrorists identifying with groups (either their own or an adopted one) experiencing some kind of marginalization. Furthermore, Silke observes a process of vengeance seeking at work in the process of individual radicalization. Vengeance in this sense is an extreme manifestation of a primate's natural instinct for justice. The desire for vengeance is tied to feelings of self-worth and can act as a deterrent against further injustice. Silke notes, however, that this sense of injustice does not necessarily have to be personal, but can be vicarious as well, echoing Schmid's identification theory of insurgent terrorism (1984)[53] as well as more recent findings by organizational and structural theorists which will be expounded upon later. Individual radicalization may also be tied to the desire for status and personal rewards. For this to be a persuasive motivation, the group in question must carry the potential for a certain measure of respect among the constituency it claims to fight and speak for. In extremely polarized communities (as well as in prisons), individuals might seek membership in underground organizations as a means of protection from rival groups. If the environment is such that a myriad of different groups are vying for power, individual choice may be abrogated by press-ganging and conscription.

Horgan broadens the scope of psychological inquiry in Terrorism Studies beyond examining the reasons why individuals join violent organizations by focusing also on why individuals are exiting violent groups.[54] He divides the psychological study of terrorism into three stages: becoming a member of a terrorist group, remaining in the underground organization, and leaving terrorism behind by exiting the group.[55] The process of becoming a terrorist is, according to Horgan, a diverse one and is almost always the result of a gradual (rather than sudden) socialization into violence. Remaining a member of an outlawed organization requires psychological strength, loyalty, obedience and discipline. Groups tend to manage cohesion among their members by enforcing conformity. The process by which individuals leave an organization involves two phases: psychological disengagement and physical disengagement. Psychological disengagement occurs when members begin to mentally question their commitment to organizational membership. This often occurs as a result of the considerable pressures of life in the underground. Membership in outlawed communities tends to replace normal social processes such as dating, marriage, child rearing, etc. with organizational security concerns. As members become older, some eventually seek to reconnect to family-seeking processes. Additionally, the reality of life in the underground lacks glamour and rarely reflects the goals and aspirations that originally led members to join. The resulting disillusionment is often exacerbated by the prevalence of groupthink in radical organizations. The more detached members of underground organizations become from reality, the more some members are likely to question and rebel against organizational goals. Psychological disengagement may or may not be followed by physical disengagement, which in turn refers to the process by which individuals actually leave a terrorist organization. It can take place through a variety of processes and may or may not entail the revocation of support for the group's goals. It is usually correlated, according to Horgan, with one of the following processes: arrest, specialization in a non-violent role, the eviction of the individual from the organization, or simply a change in priorities on the part of the wavering individual.[56]

Psychologists have also made promising advances in the field of analysing the effects of terrorism on victims of terrorism. Especially since 9/11, there has been a renewed focus on victimological theories. Muldoon's studies look at the impact of low-intensity conflicts (LIC) on societies at large.[57] She finds that psychological effects of prolonged campaigns of violence are diffuse, but in some cases severe. Civilian deaths in LIC have a different effect on individuals from those that occur in conventional military campaigns because low levels of violence over prolonged periods tend to mask the true death toll.[58] In addition, the population at large tends to internalize violence and develop coping mechanisms, among them high levels of social categorization, often reinforced through political affiliation.[59] Nevertheless, prolonged unconventional campaigns take a high toll on community mental health. Ninety-two per cent of those polled by Muldoon reported some degree of mental disturbances.[60] The most common of these were anxiety, depression, phobias and irritability. Children in particular were observed to suffer acute anxiety attacks, nightmares and enuresis. Oddly enough, Muldoon found another angle on Horgan's dismissal of abnormal psychology in terrorism studies and established that there is no evidence that LIC results in higher levels of psychopathology. In point of fact, some types of aberrant behaviour, such as suicides, seem to go down after attacks.[61] Muldoon also analysed the various coping mechanisms individuals use to deal with large-scale violence. Three primary coping strategies seem to be the most effective. First, she discerns that a commitment to the cause tends to mitigate the psychological effects of violence. Second, distancing and denial also provide some inoculation against pervasive fear. And finally, Muldoon discovers that many individuals possess a high capacity for contextualizing violence into everyday routines, and thereby normalizing its effects on their lives.

A recent theory linked to terrorism is the terror management theory (TMT). In many ways, this is a theory of terror in name only, but in other ways it has some useful applications for the study of political violence. TMT takes as its core tenet the assumption that the purpose of fear is to ensure survival.[62] However, this fear is put in the context of intellectual abilities that allow humans to think and communicate in language, imagine potential futures, and engage in self-reflection and self-awareness. This means that we are instinctively programmed to avoid danger and stay alive. However, the tools we are given to further this end simultaneously provide us with the knowledge that we will one day die.[63] We also realize that death can happen at any time and can be quite gruesome. This combination of factors instils in human beings an ingrained sense of terror. In order to deal with this terror, humans contextualize their fear through the formulation of worldviews.[64] A worldview provides individuals with a framework for dealing with the world, as well as an instrument for coping with death. Worldviews give life meaning through cultural roles while allowing for the possibility of transcending death (literally or figuratively). For worldviews to be effective in the mitigation of terror, they must have consensual validation from extant communities. When we meet people whose cultural worldviews differ from our own, our faith is rattled and our ability to manage terror is undermined.

Further studies could obviously have implications for the study of radicalization, but Tom Pyszczynski uses TMT as a means for understanding the US response to 9/11 from a victimological perspective. Pyszczynski states that there are four converging hypotheses of TMT:[65]

- First, more self-esteem and faith in a cultural worldview makes the individual less susceptible to anxiety-related behaviour and thoughts of death.
- Second, reminding people of death leads to a wide variety of behaviour meant to reaffirm cultural worldviews.
- Third, boosting self-esteem lessens worldview fundamentalism.
- Fourth, convincing evidence of an after-life reduces anxiety and low self-esteem.

Pyszczynski claims that these statements, taken together, explain the US reaction to 9/11,[66] namely a heightened nationalism, a greater intolerance for dissent, an increase in hostility shown towards different people, a desire for vengeance, a need for heroes, and a desire to help. Controlled studies of TMT have been conducted by a variety of scholars, with promising results.

To close, researchers such as Andrew Silke, John Horgan and the Norwegian social anthropologist Tore Bjørgo appear to be taking agent-level analyses into new and promising directions. Others, such as Martha Crenshaw, however, have continued reservations about the applicability of psychological theories to terrorism studies. Crenshaw holds that such theories of terrorism are deficient, because the multitude of motivations behind terrorism. Since terrorism is rarely, if ever, the result of a single person, individual preferences and psychological predispositions do not, in her view, enter prominently into the equation.[67]

Theories of radicalization

Radicalization refers to a process of ideological socialization of (usually) young people towards effectuating fundamental political changes, usually through the use of violent tactics of conflict waging against the political enemies and their followers. Studies of radicalization approach the field of extremism and terrorism by focusing on the processes through which individuals become socialized into engaging in political violence without moral restraints. As the late Ehud Sprinzak stated, the study of terrorism is the study of 'human transformation, of a psycho–political passage in time from normal to extra–normal behaviour'.[68] Some theories of radicalization shift the locus of psychological studies away from individual aberrance and concentrate on the ways in which external influences transform otherwise normal individuals into potentially violent political activists. Thus, some theories of radicalization are only marginally agent based, preferring instead to look more broadly at the ways both institutions and structures affect agents in their individual decisions to engage in terrorist violence.

Seminal has been the late Ehud Sprinzak's concept of 'de-legitimization', which he saw at work when individuals move from conventional types of political activism towards more extreme forms. Part of the radicalization process is based on a process of de-legitimization. Terrorism is the pinnacle of this process, but it is not the first stage, nor is it necessarily the last. Sprinzak noted that terrorist groups are often radical splinter groups of existing more legitimate political groups or movements. What theories of radicalization in general, and Sprinzak's theory of de-legitimization in particular, try to illustrate is the movement, both psychologically and politically, from acceptable political activism to terrorism. Sprinzak found that radical groups, regardless of differences in motivations, share a common structural genealogy, a process of progressive radicalization as they emerge, in many cases, from already existing movements.[69] Yet the radicalization process itself can vary, depending upon the motivating factors behind political agitation. One of the trajectories in the process of de-legitimization is, according to Sprinzak, 'transformational de-legitimization' – a process followed by new political groups without ties to former movements. Typically, this takes the form of left-wing radicalism operating within democratic systems. In Sprinzak's observation, such groups represent the most extreme pathway to radicalization as the members of such groups are not predisposed to violence. He noted that transformational organizations are often composed of former advocates of the regime disillusioned with shortcomings in the democratic process. As the motivation for violence is inherently idealistic, the radicalization process is long and tortuous, and tends to go through distinct stages.

The first of these stages is the 'crisis of confidence'. In this phase of radicalization, former regime adherents become disillusioned with the seedier side of democratic political manoeuvrings. The rejection, however, is not geared towards the system as a whole at this point in time; rather, it focuses on those agents within it who are seen as manipulating the democratic process to the disadvantage of an 'other'. The initial reaction from these activists, then, is one of counter-culture but not militancy, though scuffles with law enforcement and other regime elements do occur in the context of the state's reaction to these challenges. A 'conflict of legitimacy' occurs when the activists begin to see the root of political problems not as being the fault of a few corrupted politicians, but rather as being inherent in a system devised to ensure the interests of a select few over an 'oppressed' majority. The end result of this realization is the perception that the system itself lacks legitimacy and must be changed. The movement, at this point catalysed by a sense of disappointment with the previous phase of activism, begins to break with the authorities by advocating an ideology that de-legitimizes the status quo.

This conflict is followed by a 'crisis of legitimacy', at which point the demonization of the system spreads to all those individuals associated with it. The resulting dehumanization creates the psychological preconditions for violence. Those radicals who have progressed to this point from the crisis of confidence begin to outwardly display a broader rejection of society through 'antinomian behaviour', effectively breaking down the barriers between political and personal illegality.[70] Political violence is the logical next step.

'Extensional de-legitimization', on the other hand, unlike 'transformational de-legitimization', requires no rigorous psychological process of radicalization, as it represents an 'extension' of pre-existing political antipathies. Most often, these take the form of ethno-nationalist or secessionist movements and/or movements rebelling against an oppressive authoritarian state system. In such circumstances, the crisis of confidence already exists, and organizational activism begins with the conflict of legitimacy. This phase occurs when the movement in question becomes impatient with too slow a pace of reform.[71] The impatience mounts and creates a crisis of legitimacy when the opposed government rebuffs continuous demands for reform, autonomy and/or independence. Political terrorism in such cases typically begins with the organization of 'self-defence' groups, whose violence is limited only by the rather flexible definition of the limits of what constitutes 'self-defence'.[72]

'Split de-legitimization' occurs, according to Sprinzak, when a group becomes radicalized in regard to potential opponents. In contrast to the universalistic groups described in the preceding two paragraphs, which direct their violence towards regimes, particularistic terrorist groups target other non-state groups – typically, rival communities.[73] Anti-regime sentiments are secondary to the primary focus on repressing the target community, and are typically a result of the perception that the regime is either protecting these communities or not being active enough in their repression. Accordingly, there are then two processes of de-legitimization.[74]

The primary de-legitimization occurs with respect to the target community. Since the 'other' is considered illegitimate a priori, this begins with the crisis of legitimacy.[75]

A secondary, or 'diluted', de-legitimization occurs with respect to the government.[76] This occurs when a sense of betrayal on the part of the radical group triggers a crisis of confidence with the state.

The terrorism of a particularistic group usually begins with an attempt to foment some form of cultural discrimination. If this fails, or if the group feels ignored by the government, then it will resort to violence. While anti-regime violence is rare among such groups, Sprinzak postulated that some militants-turned-terrorists will, over time, close the gap between the government and the target community.

Several researchers have built on Sprinzak or have been influenced by him. There are various step models. Among them is Moghadam's step model of radicalization, delineating six processes of violent radicalization.[77] In this work, Moghadam utilizes the metaphor of a six-storey building to represent each 'step' in the radicalization process. The ground floor represents a cognitive analysis of the structural circumstances in which the agent finds him- or herself. Here, the individual begins to interpret and ascribe causality to what he or she deems to be unjust circumstances. According to Moghadam, a majority of the population will find themselves on this 'foundational level'. On the first floor, one finds individuals who are actively seeking to remedy those circumstances they perceive to be unjust. In this stage, they explore various options to improving material or political circumstances. On the second floor, agents begin to place blame for injustice on out-groups. As Moghadam points out, this is often the cause of anti-American sentiment. The third floor involves a moral disengagement from society and a moral engagement within the nascent terrorist organization. Within this phase, values are constructed which rationalize the use of violence by the terrorists while simultaneously decrying the moral authority of the incumbent regime. On the fourth floor, members new to the organization are consolidated not only into the organizational structure of the group, but also (and perhaps more importantly) into its value structure. On the fifth, and final, floor, the organization allows the individual to circumvent his or her natural reluctance to engage in violence and engage in the 'terrorist act'.

While Moghadam's use of metaphor is illustrative and allows us to better comprehend the complex mental processes at work in the radicalization process, for empirical observations the more grounded theory of Silbner and Bhatt is useful. In their study, conducted for the New York Police Department, they envisage four steps:[78]

1 Pre-radicalization: the life situation before vulnerable individuals were exposed to and adopted jihadi-Salafi Islam as their own ideology. The majority of individuals involved in almost a dozen plots began as 'unremarkable', had 'ordinary' jobs, had lived 'ordinary' lives and had little, if any, criminal history.

2 Self-identification: the phase where individuals, influenced by both internal and external factors, begin to explore Salafi Islam, gradually gravitate away from their old identity and begin to associate themselves with like-minded individuals and adopt this ideology as their own. The catalyst for the 'religious seeking' is a cognitive opening, or crisis, which shakes one's certitude in previously held beliefs and opens an individual to be receptive to new worldviews. There can be many types of triggers: (a) economic (losing a job, blocked mobility); (b) social (alienation, discrimination, racism – real or perceived); (c) political (international conflicts involving Muslims); and (d) personal (a death in the close family).

3 Indoctrination: the phase in which an individual progressively intensifies his beliefs, wholly adopts jihadi-Salafi ideology, and concludes, without question, that the conditions and circumstances exist where action is required to support and further the cause. That action is militant jihad. This phase is typically facilitated and driven by a 'spiritual sanctioner'. While the initial self-identification process may be an individual act, as noted above, association with like-minded people is an important factor as the process deepens. By the indoctrination phase, this self-selecting group becomes increasingly important as radical views are encouraged and reinforced.

4 Jihadization: the phase in which members of the cluster accept their individual duty to participate in jihad and self-designate themselves as holy warriors or mujahideen. Ultimately,

the group will begin operational planning for the jihad or a terrorist attack. These 'acts in furtherance' will include planning, preparation and execution.

Silber and Bhatt noted, in nearly a dozen European and American cases of radicalization towards jihadism they studied, that while the first three phases of radicalization may take place gradually (over a period of two to three years), the jihadization component can be a very rapid process (taking weeks or a few months). In general, they found that there was no useful psychological profile to predict who will follow the entire trajectory of radicalization. However, they found that in spite of the differences in both circumstances and environment in each of the cases, there was a remarkable consistency in the behaviours and trajectory of each of the plots across all the stages. Such a consistency constitutes an element of theory and provides a potential tool for forecasting.[79]

A more academic approach has been suggested by Clark McCauley and Sophia Moskalenko. Their analysis of the radicalization process rests on functional and descriptive components. Functionally, radicalization entails 'increased preparation for and commitment to inter-group conflict'.[80] Descriptively, the authors state that 'radicalization means change in beliefs, feelings and behaviours in directions that increasingly justify inter-group violence and demand sacrifice in defence of the in-group'.[81] McCauley and Moskalenko utilize a pyramidal depiction of the radicalization process whereby successively smaller cadres of activists comprise elevated positions on a political pyramid. The base of the pyramid consists of the mass of supporters who conceive of themselves as being in conflict with an out-group. When this perception of conflict leads to the dehumanization of the out-group, hatred results, as well as polarization.[82] The middle range of the pyramid contains the radical groups. These organizations radicalize according to several processes:

1   First, there is the phenomenon of groupthink, whereby concentrations of like-minded actors tend to move towards extreme interpretations of reality.
2   Second, groups operating under isolation and threat tend to be suffering from closed information loops, compounding the negative effects of groupthink on decision making.
3   Third, the conflict with those holding state power helps to create a selection bias in group membership. When a group enters into conflict with the authorities, the majority of the more moderate members will tend to drop out, as the costs of dissident group membership become disproportionately high, given individual values. Those self-selecting to remain in an organization will invariably be the more radical members who place a higher value on the group's goals; they more readily accept violent action as a feasible pathway to fulfilling radical group objectives.
4   Finally, McCauley and Moskalenko observe that group competition tends to promote fractionalization, resulting in what Mia Bloom terms 'outbidding', or an escalation of violence in order to reaffirm organizational salience in situations of inter-group competition.[83]

Individual radicalization is spurred by personal grievances and experiences of the kind that encourage potential terrorists to associate with radical organizations. Radical group membership provides an additional escalatory effect on the individual – first, because such membership often provides a slippery slope to more offensive forms of political expression, and second, because the bonds of in-group identity promote radicalization, as most individuals tend to be recruited via close personal connections.[84] Each successive level of this pyramid represents both a more extreme form of political expression and a more exclusive cadre of active participants. The terrorist him- or herself represents only the extremist tip of a pyramid composed of like-minded, though less risk-seeking, activists and radicals.

A synthesis of current knowledge on radicalization can be found in a concise report of the European Commission's Expert Group on Violent Radicalisation, completed in May 2008. Its findings are based on common structural features of the radicalization process across jihadist as well as left- and right-wing movements. Defining radicalization as 'a socialization into extremism which manifests itself in terrorism',[85] the Expert Group identified the following common themes of violent radicalization:[86]

- All radicalization processes incubate in enabling environments wherein at risk individuals share a widely held sense of injustice. The exact nature of this perception of injustice varies with respect to the underlying motivation for violence (i.e. from secular extremism to *takfiri* jihadism), but the effects on the individual are surprisingly similar.
- The process of radicalization itself begins when these enabling environments intersect with personal 'trajectories', allowing the environmental causes of radicalism to resonate with the individual's personal experience.
- Terrorism itself is a minority-group phenomenon, not the work of a radicalized mass of people.

Echoing the pyramidal concept of McCauley and Moskalenko, the Expert Group concludes that violence is always perpetrated by a relatively small amalgam of radicalized individuals generally claiming to speak on behalf of a larger wronged community.

Much of the recent literature on the radicalization process is marked by its attempt to discern patterns for possible utilization in de-radicalization campaigns.[87] Thus, the relevant literature tends to focus on critical junctures in the radicalization process with the potential for intervention measures. It is perhaps for this reason that many of the more recent approaches lack the breadth and depth of earlier works such as Sprinzak's ground-breaking de-legitimization theory. Nevertheless, there is broad agreement on a number of points regarding the process of radicalization into violence. First, most researchers agree that terrorism and political violence are not phenomena unto themselves, but the outgrowth of a cycle of political activism. Second, most conclude that the terrorist's 'philosophy' is an aberrant extreme of more widely held beliefs. Finally, most research concludes that structural causes of discontent alone are insufficient for radicalization to take off. To make the leap from aggrieved individual to a fanatical terrorist, the enabling environment must resonate with the individual. Radical propaganda and the recruitment process often act as facilitators of this 'resonance'.

Rational choice theories

At first sight, there appears to be little rationality for a suicide bomber who is striving for a certain political goal to blow him- or herself up and thereby deprive him- or herself of being part of the hoped-for political results. Often, such individuals appear to be driven by feelings of revenge or painful humiliation rather than strategic calculations. The terrible deed that costs the lives of enemies can, however, provide the bomber with great emotional satisfaction. If he or she is a religious terrorist, there might be an expectation of rewards in paradise and possibly some earthly compensation for his or her family (in cases when a terrorist organization or its state sponsor offers rewards). However, there is something irrational about terrorist attacks that go beyond risk taking and involve certain death. Nevertheless, researchers have come up with expected utility and rational choice theories to explain terrorist behaviour.

Rational choice offers an economic evaluation of individual decision making. In its most reduced form, rational choice assumes that political outcomes are the result of individual rational calculus.[88] The inputs into this decision-making process are the universe of potential options, the assumed costs of the various potential options or choices, the likely benefit from given choices, and the probabilities of successfully pursuing various courses of action. The individual then makes the choice that appears to maximize expected outputs. What applies to the individual can, under certain circumstances, also be extended to the group. In the words of Dipak Gupta: 'When we consider the group as a single entity, we can assume that it behaves "rationally", that is, it aims at maximizing its own welfare.'[89]

A common misperception of those unschooled in rational choice theory is equating rationality in the economic sense with rationality in the humanities – implying the acquisition of truth through reasoned debate. Rather, rationality in the sense used here, is purely amoral.

From an economist's viewpoint, rationality is not determined on the basis of the desirability of an agent's objective or tactics. We consider terrorists to be rational actors who respond in an appropriate and predictable fashion to changes in their constraints as they optimize their objective while confronting an adversary who is trying to outwit and defeat them.[90]

Crenshaw analysed terrorism not primarily in expressive terms but in terms of instrumental violence. Instrumentalism assumes that terrorism is a rational strategy designed to bring about a shift in the political position of the government. It aims to modify political behaviour by manipulating the options of the opponent – in most cases the government. It is not a strategy intended to destroy (or indeed capable of destroying) military capabilities in a decisive way.[91] Terrorists themselves engage in the production of terror as a vehicle for political change for a number of reasons. While the value of the presumed outcome is thought to be extremely high, the production costs of terrorism are seen as low relative to those associated with alternative available political strategies. In their eyes, the status quo is simply intolerable, which raises the relative value of political change. Under certain circumstances, the probability of success of terrorist campaigns could be judged to be relatively high, as was the case during the decolonization period when one colonial power after the other withdrew from overseas territories, lacking the stomach to put up a major fight to keep what were in most cases peripheral possessions of declining economic importance.[92]

Rational choice theory, despite its plausible logic and parsimony, has some serious drawbacks. It assumes a fixed definition of rationality, when in fact there is none that is uncontroversial.[93] The resulting imprecision allows researchers to subsume a large number of behaviours under the rational choice label. This makes falsifying the claims of rational choice theory difficult. Additionally, rational choice has a problem in accounting for a number of human behaviours, including altruism (which may be applicable to extremist endeavours) and akrasia (seemingly non-rational decision-making based on abnormal moral reasoning, which may or may not have a bearing on certain types of violence, such as suicide terrorism). The broader discipline of International Relations has circumvented many of these pitfalls by assimilating rational choice into more nuanced theories of political action. Tellingly, the assumption of rationality underpins all mainstream theories of International Relations, including neo-realism and neo-liberalism, while the crux of the theory explains the origins of agent preference. In a similar vein, rational choice may prove of limited use on its own, but may be incorporated into other theories of terrorism.

Terrorist theories of terrorism

Theories of terrorism that are wrong would seem to be of little use in explaining terrorist behaviour – unless the terrorists themselves believe in them and, as a consequence, base their activities on them. Terrorists, or at least their leaders, are often intellectuals and as such are not averse to theorizing. A study of their writings is as important as a study of their behaviour in order to understand what makes them 'tick'. Brian M. Jenkins was right when he stated that 'unless we try to think like terrorists we are liable to miss the point'.[94]

Nearly every incarnation of militant movements espousing terror has published tracts on the presumed benefits of, and justifications for, this type of political violence. Among the first were Russian and European anarchists and socio-revolutionaries. They were later followed by the anti-colonial agitators. Twentieth-century Marxists such as Mao Zedong also wrote at length about the employment of various forms of political violence in revolutionary struggles. Some Marxists, while officially favouring mass action, also saw utility in terrorism, and one of them, Leon Trotsky, even wrote a book in defence of the Red Terror of the Bolshevik Revolution (which was, in reality, not so much a mass revolution as a *coup d'état* followed by massacres of political opponents, leading to a civil war).[95] He argued that '[t]he man who repudiates terrorism in principle, i.e. repudiates measures of suppression and intimidation towards determined and armed counterrevolution, must reject all idea of the political supremacy of the working class and its revolutionary dictatorship'. Trotsky also made a bold comparison between war and revolution:

The problem of revolution as of war consists in breaking the will of the foe, forcing him to capitulate and accept the conditions of the conqueror. . . . The question as to who is to rule . . . will be decided on either side, not by references to the paragraphs of the constitution, but by the employment of all forms of violence. . . . War, like revolution, is founded upon intimidation. A victorious war generally destroys only an insignificant part of the conquered army, intimidating the remainder and breaking their will. The revolution works the same way: it kills individuals and intimidates thousands.[96]

Currently, some Salafist ideologies (who borrowed from Leninism the idea of a vanguard) have become proponents of terrorism as asymmetric warfare against the 'near enemy' (Arab regimes) and the 'far enemy' (the United States and its allies). Despite the fact that insurgent terrorism has evolved in many ways (e.g. through the use of the internet), careful readings of the early theorists and practitioners of terrorism yield the insight that terrorism has not changed as much as some adherents of the 'new terrorism' school assume.

While there were individual theorists of terrorism like the German–American Karl Heinzen, author of *Murder and Liberty* (1850),[97] the first non-state group to truly articulate a coherent 'theory' of terrorism was Narodnaya Volya (People's Will). Its party programme of 1879 stated:

Terrorist activity, consisting in destroying the most harmful person in the government, in defending the party against espionage, in punishing the perpetrators of the notable cases of violence and arbitrariness on the part of the government and the administration, aims to undermine the prestige of the government's power, to demonstrate steadily the possibility of struggle against the government, to arouse in this manner the revolutionary spirit of the people and their confidence in the success of the cause, and finally, to give shape and direction to the forces fit and trained to carry on the fight.[98]

Narodnaya Volya persuasively argues for the utility of terrorism as a revolutionary tool, especially as 'propaganda of the deed'. Exemplary deeds of violence were meant to illustrate government weakness while creating a semblance of counter-power for the revolutionary group claiming responsibility, thereby forming a rallying point for others inclined to proceed from words to deeds in opposing a tsarist regime seemingly incapable of change. Morozov, writing in the 1880s on behalf of the People's Will, offers a slightly more in-depth analysis of the instrument of terror and in so doing illuminates a number of concepts that still comprise integral components of contemporary theories of terrorism:

[T]erroristic struggle has exactly this advantage that it can act unexpectedly and find means and ways which no one anticipates. All that the terroristic struggle really needs is a small number of people and large material means. This presents really a new form of struggle. It replaces by a series of individual political assassinations, which always hit their target, the massive revolutionary movements. . . . The movement punishes only those who are really responsible for the evil deed. Because of this the terroristic revolution is the only just form of revolution.[99]

Morozov's philosophy strives first and foremost to place terrorism within a broader revolutionary movement. Unlike successive practitioners of political violence, Morozov holds that terror is the primary vehicle for revolution. Partly in reaction to the failed Paris Commune, Morozov is the first to speak of terrorism as a form of collective jujitsu, using the strength of the state (namely the technology of state forces and the proliferation of assets to be viewed as targets) to the advantage of the revolutionary. The high costs in lives as a result of the disastrous War of the Barricades in Paris in the early 1870s gave Morozov cause to give preference to a conspiratorial revolutionary vanguard over mass mobilization. Rather than risk the brutal repression of a mass uprising, Morozov proposes to use the technology of modern militaries (the bomb and the pistol) as a panacea, obviating the need for mass mobilization. More succinctly, terror allows for selective violence to replace more extreme forms of revolutionary upheaval. Nevertheless, the appropriate application of force can serve both to undermine the power of the regime and to foment wider revolution by communicating political alternatives to the status quo. Morozov underlines that the success of the terrorist is largely reliant upon the ability of the group to project blame for violence onto the state. The 'selectivity' of Morozov's violence seeks this end. The concept of the 'just revolution' implies that terror is the inevitable result of tyranny. The terrorist, then, is simultaneously absolved for blame in the conduct of violence and elevated to the status of revolutionary hero in his or her role as the harbinger of a more just order.

While Morozov saw terrorism mainly as armed propaganda, other theorists saw terrorism as a form of irregular warfare, targeting also the enemy's armed forces. An example is General Grivas, who fought in the 1950s against the British occupation in Cyprus. He wrote:

> The truth is that our form of war, in which a few hundred fell in four years, was more selective than most, and I speak as one who has seen battlefields covered with dead. We did not strike, like the bomber, at random. We shot only British servicemen who would have killed us, if they could have fired first, and civilians who were traitors or intelligence agents. To shoot down your enemies in the streets may be unprecedented, but I was looking for results, not precedents. How did Napoleon win his victories? He took his opponents in the flank or in the rear; and what is right on the grand scale is not wrong when the scale is reduced and the odds are against you a hundred to one.[100]

The pattern of shifting blame sounds apologist in nature – and Grivas's campaign was not as discriminating as this particular text would lead the reader to believe – but it plays an integral role in terrorist campaigns, where ideology is used to maintain cohesion and facilitate recruitment in the absence of more formal modes of control and conscription. In terms of tactics, the need to perpetuate this illusion of innocence has profound implications for the employment of force. Ironically, the mismanagement of violence proved the eventual undoing of Grivas's EOKA. After successfully obtaining independence from British rule in 1960, the second campaign of EOKA-B was meant to unite Cyprus with the Greek mainland. The result was not a union, but a Turkish invasion producing 280,000 Cypriot refugees, and the division of the island into separate Turkish and Greek polities. Grivas was not the only terrorist whose strategy misfired. As Seth Jones (of the RAND Corporation) has pointed out, in a study surveying the rise and fall of 268 terrorist groups active between 1968 and 2006, only 10 per cent of them managed to achieve victory.[101] In other words, the failure rate of non-state terrorist groups is very high, partly because their strategic theory is inapplicable in most situations.

Another theorist was Carlos Marighela, the Brazilian communist. His work was influenced by the Cuban experience of Fidel Castro and Che Guevara, building on the voluntarist concept of a revolutionary *foco* – a spark that would ignite the revolution. In his 'Mini-manual of the Urban Guerrilla', Marighela states:

> There are two main ways in which revolutionary organizations can grow. One is through propaganda and ideology – by convincing people and arguing over documents and programmes. . . . The other way . . . is not through proselytism but by unleashing revolutionary action and calling for extreme violence and radical solutions. . . . The basic principle of revolutionary strategy in a context of permanent political crisis is to unleash, in urban and rural areas, a volume of revolutionary activity which will oblige the enemy to transform the country's political situation into a military one. The discontent will spread to all social groups and the military will be held exclusively responsible for all failure.[102]

Marighela opted for a strategy of using revolutionary violence as the catalyst for mass upheaval. Relabelling terrorism as urban guerrilla war, he echoed earlier practitioners of violence in his association of terror with propaganda of the deed. Marighela also adds another dimension to the theme of blame projection. His allegation that terrorist acts were not meant to upset the people was in actuality hypocritical, since he alleges later in the same text that one of the goals of violence is to provoke state repression against the people. It is by these means that the preconditions for revolution in the countryside will be met, he hoped. He was wrong, but never saw the full result of his miscalculation, as he was killed in 1969.

This dual function of terrorism, propaganda for the masses on one hand, and an increase of state repression intended to force the masses into participation on the other, found imitation in many other urban guerrilla campaigns. Horst Mahler, a theorist of the West German Red Army Faction, admitted, 'The strategy of the terrorist nuclei was aimed at provoking the overreaction of the state in the hope to stir the flames of hate against the state and to channel new recruits into the armed underground.'[103] In fact, the 'urban guerrilla' experience turned out to be quite different from that predicted by urban guerrilla theory. The 'overreaction' of the state, it transpired, should not have been taken for granted, and in those situations in which states did react disproportionately to insurgent challenges, they proved more likely to destroy the group in question than to mobilize involuntary mass support for the revolution. Nevertheless, the pressures of urban insurrection – the need for secrecy and the division of the group into small functional cells – moulded the textbook organizational style of terrorist groups. It has only begun to be challenged today by organizations such as Al-Qaeda, which apply a network concept and utilize elements of the leaderless resistance theorem.[104]

The rise of militant religious terrorism in the 1980s and 1990s has caused some students of terrorism to question whether or not more conventional notions of strategy still apply to contemporary faith-based movements like Salafist jihadists, Christian Identity militias, and esoteric cultic movements such as Aum Shinrikyo. Of particular concern to scholars of terrorism studies has been the apparent abandonment of constraints on violence previously observed in non-state terrorism. Bruce Hoffman remarks on the rationale behind the intense quality of religious terrorism:

> The reason that terrorist incidences perpetrated for religious motives result in so many more deaths may be found in the radically different value systems, mechanisms of legitimization and justifications, concepts of morality, and worldviews embraced by the religious terrorist and his secular counterpart.[105]

However, the thesis that Islamist terrorist groups tend to commit more high-casualty attacks has recently been modified by James Piazza. On the basis of empirical comparisons, he concluded that casualty rates of attacks vary widely across Islamist terrorist groups. He suggested that group organizational features and goal structures explain differing casualty rates better than does the overarching ideological type. Piazza found that strategic groups among them function similarly to secular national–liberation and regime-change movements, whereas 'abstract/universal groups' affiliated with the Al-Qaeda network do produce higher casualty rates.[106]

Early research into violent religious movements pointed to a lack of revolutionary strategy compared to more secular organizations. The inference was that the ritualistic violence of religiously motivated groups was part of a larger 'grand strategy'. Rather, religious violence was not thought of by researchers as revolutionary, but eschatological. As Bruce Hoffman states,

> Whereas secular terrorists regard violence either as a way of instigating the correction of a flaw in a system that is basically good or as the means to foment the creation of a new system, religious terrorists see themselves not as components of a system worth saving, but as 'outsiders' seeking fundamental changes in the existing order.[107]

More recent scholarship, however, has challenged this. Stout comments:

> The written works of a small but intellectually vigorous community of Salafi Jihadist thinkers in and associated with al Qaida provide proof that strategic thought exists within their terrorist movement. This strategic thought is grounded in the mainstream of world thought on revolutionary warfare.[108]

Contrary to the assertions of Hoffman (and Juergensmeyer), Stout holds that Islamist terrorists are in fact quite enamoured of revolutionary (Marxist) military theory. First, this is due to the fact that most Salafists base the rhetoric of international jihadism on Qutbism. Sayyid Qutb, in turn, was writing in the 1950s and 1960s, and while he was not a Marxist, communist theory and vocabulary nonetheless permeated revolutionary minds in the Third World at the time. Marxists wrote many of the works on revolutionary warfare in the twentieth century.[109] Lia and Hegghammer have noted that Salafist theorists have had little hesitation in importing non-Islamic doctrines in order to make the jihad more efficient from a political and military standpoint.[110] As a point of illustration, Abu Sayyaf (a Filipino group with Salafist underpinnings) even titled its handbook for the conduct of irregular warfare the 'Mini-manual for the Urban Mujahadeen', borrowing Carlos Marighela's use of 'mini-manual' and simply replacing 'guerrilla' with 'mujahadeen'.[111]

The analytical work of Brynjar Lia supports the notion that there are two camps in the current international Salafist movement: the fundamentalist purists and the more opportunist Jihadis.[112] While the purists are more concerned with doctrinal conformity, even to the point of fomenting schisms in the Salafist movement, the pragmatic opportunists among the jihadists have pursued military outcomes based on a more mundane logic of action.

Insurgent terrorism: institutional level of analysis

Political scientists have long observed that organizations significantly affect individual behaviour. Institutions aggregate interests, solve collective action problems and fall victim to principal-agent problems. Underground organizations and the environments in which they operate have also been the subject of a substantial amount of research. Organizational-level analysis allows the researcher to concentrate on issues of central concern to the discourse such as how institutions frame goals, mobilize resources, articulate strategies, recruit and maintain members, and (from a counter-terrorism perspective) what factors initiate institutional decline.

In the following, we will briefly outline major works in a number of theoretical approaches to studying terrorist organizations, including organizational process theory, the study of institutional motivations for insurgent violence, suicide terrorism, theories of asymmetrical conflict, communication theories of terrorism, and theories of social identity formation.

Organizational process theory

Of the canon of literature addressing the organizational level of terrorist groups, the works of two authors stand out in terms of the impact they have had on the discipline. The first is Martha Crenshaw's work on organizational process theory, and the second is David Rapoport's 'wave theory'.[113]

Framing the institutional debate in Terrorism Studies is undoubtedly Crenshaw's work on organizational process theory (OPT). Crenshaw defines organizational theories by way of comparison with agent-based instrumentalist theories. Counter-intuitively, she asserts that the end goal of any organization is not a priori the ends for which it was formed, but rather the maintenance of the organization itself.[114] Thus, some interests of the violent organization are inherently different from the disaggregated interests of the individuals who comprise the group. Crenshaw draws from a wider literature on principal–agent problems in the institutionalism discourse and applies their findings to terrorist organizations. She begins this analysis by defining similarities between violent activism and other forms of voluntary organizations.[115] First, terrorist groups have a defined structure and a systematic process by which decisions are made. Second, the organization's membership is divided according to function or role. Third, each organization has recognized leaders and authority. And finally, organizational goals are pursued collectively.

Political change, be it revolutionary or reformist in scope, represents a public good. Being non-excludable, it is subject to collective action problems. Institutional arrangements are therefore necessary to solve for the collectively undesirable outcomes resulting from individually rational free-riding on the part of agents. Violent organizations, according to Crenshaw, promulgate themselves by manipulation and aggregation of the divergent desires of their constituent members.[116] Leaders take on such roles out of a desire for prestige, a commodity inextricably linked to the standing of the organization. Members, however, react to incentive structures. Further, there are incentives to join as well as incentives for staying. These range from the desire to belong to a group, a quest to gain social status, the appeal of comradeship and adventure, and of course material benefits. In order to promote the prestige of the organization, the leadership manipulates incentives in order to prompt continued support. Broadly speaking, there are two types of incentives: structural and purposive. Structural incentives refer to environmental triggers for radicalism. Crenshaw is reticent about structural theories, however. She finds their explanatory power limited as structure is constant while the level of violence varies across time and geography. According to Crenshaw, then, it is the presence of the organization that accounts for terrorism.[117] Organizational behaviour can be explained through an analysis of the ways in which organizations manipulate purposive incentives. These can be the pursuit of a single goal, ideological incentives, or redemptive goals. Single goals, reflecting single-issue terrorism, being narrower in scope, are far more likely to achieve some measure of political success. Oddly enough, however, they have proven among the most resilient of radical groups as a result of the ease with which they have switched goals (moving, say, from environmental issues to animal rights issues, to human rights issues, etc.). Ideological incentives, on the other hand, generally involve a comprehensive rejection of the status quo. Membership in ideologically driven organizations requires a complex set of beliefs and implies a revolutionary goal. Redemptive motivations involve a belief in a fundamentally flawed system. Such movements are typically defined by eschatological or millenarian goals, and view political violence as an individual duty required for salvation, however esoterically defined.

Organizations are not static entities whose goals remain unchanged over time. By reducing organizational goals to the primary one of survival and longevity, Crenshaw accounts for a wide number of seemingly irrational behaviours observed in violent organizations. Crenshaw notes that with time, ideology loses salience as a dominant incentive for group membership, giving way to solidarity. Groups will often engage in spoiling activities designed to sabotage peace negotiations in order to perpetuate conflict, which, in turn, promulgates the continued salience of the organization. Moreover, groups will begin to emphasize material benefits (and concomitant criminal practices) over normative goals in order to maintain membership. Additionally, groups often shift their motivations over time in order to maintain relevance with sympathetic communities.[118]

There are, however, differences between terrorist organizations and other voluntary organizations.[119] The goals of a terrorist organization are much more ambitious than those of most conventional organizations. They often attempt, in some way, shape or form, to fundamentally redefine the status quo. As opposed to bona fide voluntary groups, terrorist organizations pursue their ends through illegal and violent means. Owing to the illegality of their actions, non-state terrorist groups are necessarily clandestine. Finally, most terrorist groups are extremely small in terms of membership and scope. This is a result of the clandestine nature of such groups, and the social marginality inherent in extremism itself.

The behaviour of a group is, in no small way, a result of the organizational choices it makes. When opting for an illegal mode of political protest and struggle, non-state terrorists by default organize in secret cadres. This necessitates a decentralized command-and-control structure, and such groups typically organize according to a functional compartmentalization of group members into cells. This results in a number of behaviours.[120] First, the leadership has a limited ability to tightly control organizational functions. The resulting independence of operational cells can lead to intra-organizational friction. Second, small groups, especially often substitute functional differentiation and complex structures for simpler organizational designs such as autonomous cells. While this enables a relatively small group of individuals to engage in political violence and, in some cases, avoid prosecution by the state, it makes it almost impossible to organize mass support. Such organizations often attempt to rectify their low profile in the community by escalating their violence.

In summation, Crenshaw states that organizational process theory sheds light both on how organizations view violence and on the processes by which organizations turn to violence as a strategy of political action. Not all terrorist groups view the utility of violence in the same way. Various organizational concerns determine the manner in which a given group employs violence.[121] The four primary concerns delineated by Crenshaw are:

1   how the organization views the resources available to it;
2   how the organization views opportunities;
3   how the organization views threats (these can be threats from state responses to those emanating from rival groups); and
4   how the organization chooses to react to its environment.

The choice to resort to violence is usually the result of one of two processes.[122] First, individuals often join an organization at its periphery, either through the covert organization's overt political arm, or through radical student movements, etc. Members move towards the clandestine core or centre over time. The process of radicalization for group members is therefore a gradual one requiring socialization into violence. Alternately, a pre-existing and formerly legal organization may opt for violence collectively. In such cases, the decision to engage in terrorism will be the result of intense debate, often resulting in a schism within the group.

Institutional motivations for terrorism

Walter Laqueur observed that sweeping theories of terrorism are impossible, as terrorism is far too heterogeneous a political phenomenon to be accounted for by a single general theory. Nevertheless, he maintained that a comparative analysis based on social scientific rigour is possible, provided it takes as point of departure a realistic typology of terrorist groups.[123] In response, the authors have detailed below numerous theories which differentiate terrorist organizations based on the motivation for violence within the extremist group. This section begins with an overview of Rapoport's 'wave theory', and then compliments this with critiques of the 'new terrorism' school, theories of ethnic terrorism, and Crenshaw's theory of revolutionary terror, respectively.

One of the more widely accepted delineations of terrorist movements by motivation for violence, and arguably one of the greatest contributions to the study of terrorism in the past two decades, is David Rapoport's 'wave theory'.[124] The theory was first conceived in terms of three historical waves of terrorism, but the current incarnation depicts four distinct waves, taking into account religious extremism. Rapoport's wave theory has proven useful not only because of its historical periodization of non-state terrorism, but also in its observation that the motivation for violence in each wave necessarily affected the nature and quality of the violence employed by groups in successive movements.

Rapoport's four waves span more than a century (Table 4.1) and include four broad political movements, each of which produced a plethora of related terrorist groups. He begins with nineteenth-century anarchism. The anarchists and social revolutionaries were supplanted by the post-First World War anti-colonial national liberation movements. Following the Second World

Table 4.1 Rapoport's 'four waves of terrorism'

Focus	Primary strategy	Target identity	Precipitant	Special characteristics
Anarchists, 1870–1920s	Elite assassinations, bank robberies	Primary European states	Failure/slowness of political reform	Developed basic terrorism strategies and rationales
Nationalists, 1920s–1960s	Guerrilla attacks on police and military	European empires	Post-1919 de-legitimization of empire	Increased international support (UN and diaspora)
New Left/Marxist, 1960s–1980s	Hijackings, kidnappings, assassination	Governments in general; increasing focus on USA	Viet Cong successes	Increased international training/cooperation/sponsorship
Religious, 1970s–2020s	Suicide bombings	USA, Israel, and secular regimes with Muslim populations	Iranian Revolution, Soviet invasion of Afghanistan	Casualty escalation. Decline in the number of terrorist groups

Source: Based on D.C. Rapoport, 'The Four Waves of Modern Terrorism'. In A.K. Cronin and J.M. Ludes (eds), *Attacking Terrorism: Elements of a Grand Strategy.* Washington, DC: Georgetown University Press, pp. 46–73; as summarized by K. Rasler and W.R. Thompson, 'Looking for Waves of Terrorism'. *Terrorism and Political Violence*, 21(1), 2009, p. 31.

War, these were gradually replaced by left-wing radical groups, mostly Western. More recently, international Islamist Salafist groups have become the most prominent of the right-wing/religious terrorists of the fourth wave. Rapoport does not imply that these represent discrete categories where one era consisted of one and only one form of terrorism. On the contrary, there was quite a degree of overlap from one wave to the next. However, a dominant movement, spurring in turn a proliferation of like-minded groups, defines each wave. Rapoport observed that very few organizations were able to outlive their epoch, each of which proved to last roughly a generation.

Each successive wave was prompted into being by a historic incident or a series of such incidents. Two factors inspired the first wave: the communication and technological revolution of the late nineteenth century, and the spread of a doctrine or culture of terrorism. The former included the proliferation of the telegraph, rotary press-produced cheap newspapers, and steamships and railways (which facilitated the spread of diasporas and expatriates, who played a major part in the internationalization of anarchism). In the second half of the nineteenth century, a distinct terrorist doctrine, based on the concept of 'propaganda of the deed', emerged. The more violent among the anarchists built their doctrine partly on the ancient tradition of tyrannicide, which was now made much easier thanks to the handgun and the invention of dynamite. They saw the modern-day equivalent of Greek tyrannicide as a substitute for the 'battles of the barricades' which nineteenth-century urban revolutionary crowds had used at a great cost in lives.[125] Pursuant to this end, early incarnations of anarchist groups were modelled along the lines of conspiratorial societies in the style of Blanqui and Buonarotti.[126] Anarchists attempted to compensate for their lack of mass mobilization potential by embracing the concept of 'propaganda of the deed'. The basic idea was simple: deeds speak louder than words. Voluntary revolutionary actions can, or so they hoped, act as catalyst for mass uprisings. Drawing partly on J.-J. Rousseau's notion of the 'revolutionary hero', the anarchists circumvented the need for institutional capacity building by promulgating a particular strategy of mass radicalization. Anarchist violence not only was geared towards the elimination of political enemies in government but also served as a means of demonstrating the precarious nature of a regime's control on society. The anarchist deed was meant to be exemplary, setting an example for others to follow. There was an element of self-sacrifice present. The refusal of many activists to flee after having committed an attack on a dignitary was also meant to refute the notion that anarchist violence was, in some manner, criminal. One of the lasting contributions of the anarchists to the annals of political violence was the creation of a 'science' of revolutionary warfare, achieved by combining armed strategy with propaganda for political agitation. While strategies and ideologies did change with successive movements, the basic crux of a revolution built around a core of a revolutionary vanguard did not.[127]

The second wave, according to Rapoport, was a result of the First World War and its concluding peace treaty of Versailles. In early 1918, partly as a response to the Bolshevik Revolution, the American president, Woodrow Wilson, had postulated a number of principles for post-war reordering of the world, including one of national self-determination. It was soon adopted by nationalists in European colonies. However, when it was originally formulated as part of Wilson's Fourteen Points, it was mainly meant as a political tool useful only for breaking up the empires of enemy countries. Accordingly, in the post-First World War peace treaties it was to be applied only to European territories, such as the Austrian-Hungarian Dual Monarchy. Non-European territories of defeated belligerents were instead meant to become League of Nations mandates. As a consequence, a number of powers, such as Germany, were forced to let go of overseas territories. The trend towards de-colonization was greatly accelerated by the outcome of the Second World War. In Palestine, Jewish underground organizations were among the first to talk the language of national liberation. Menachem Begin, leader of Irgun terrorist organization, was one of the first to refer to his members not as terrorists but as 'freedom fighters',[128] quickly setting an example for others, including the Palestine Liberation Organization (PLO), which of course opposes Zionism.

The nature of much of anti-colonial violence was decidedly different from that of the anarchists of the first wave. While the latter rejected the state, the national liberation fighters embraced the concept of a state of their own. Targeting was likewise different. Rather than pursuing campaigns of assassinations in line with previous movements, many of the anti-colonialists instead began targeting the security forces. Since the police were a major vehicle of colonial control, drawing them into a conflict for which they were ill-prepared prompted their replacement with more heavy-handed military and paramilitary units. Thus, the anti-colonialists were the first to successfully pursue terrorism as a strategic game, hoping to force the state (or occupying power) into utilizing counter-productive indiscriminate violence. The anti-colonialists also had an advantage over previous (and future) terrorist groups through the presence of large sympathetic local communities. This wellspring of support often enabled the second-wave terrorists to utilize guerrilla tactics along with terroristic violence in pursuit of their ends. Furthermore, the anti-colonialists were able to take advantage of the inherently international dimension of their conflict and use, for the first time, systematic campaigns intended to provoke the application of international pressure on opponent regimes.[129]

Invariably, most studies place the Vietnam War as the catalyst for the rise of Western left-wing terrorism (what Rapoport conceives of as the third wave). The American intervention in South-East Asia offered a potent mixture of signals to would-be radicals. First, it appeared to be a manifestation of 'Western (neo-)imperialism'. Second, the failure of the United States to subdue the insurgency in South Vietnam appeared to point to an internal weakness of Western imperialism. Third, and perhaps most importantly, it showed the potential efficacy of protracted resistance, as exemplified by the North Vietnamese-supported and -led Viet Cong rural rebels. Leftist terrorist groups and guerrilla movements began to emerge in developing countries, especially Latin America, but soon found sympathetic Marxist radicals in Europe (and to a lesser extent in the United States). These (mainly) student radicals often viewed themselves as something of a fifth column fighting for the interests of Southern emancipatory movements in the 'belly of the beast' – the 'imperialist' North. For many of them, after the fall of Saigon in 1975 the PLO replaced the Viet Cong as a model for revolutionary activism.

The third wave, like the two previous ones, placed its own mark on revolutionary violence. First, women were brought back in, having been largely absent in the second wave. Some of these women began to assume leadership roles, as they had in the first wave, especially among those from the nineteenth-century Russian intelligentsia involved in terrorism. Second, the operational environment of the third wave was such that violence was not usually perpetrated against military targets, as had been the case in the second wave, but took more the form of theatrically enacted spectacles focusing on symbolic targets and involving publicity-generating hijackings and hostage takings. Third, left-wing terrorists in a number of instances engaged in ordinary crimes, especially for fund-raising. Carlos ('the Jackal') and the Japanese Red Army under Ms Fusako Shigenobu, among others, found mercenary terrorism in the service of rogue-state sponsors to be a lucrative endeavour. The proliferation of potential state sponsors in the context of Cold War wars-by-proxy tended to exacerbate this phenomenon. Though many groups were able to take advantage of modern media as a means of gaining and maintaining a high profile, most eventually fell prey to the lack of popular backing that had already spelled the end of anarchist terrorism.

Rapoport suggests that the rise in Islamist violence, and the fourth wave of terror in general, can be traced to three defining events. Much of early Islamism was based on Shi'ah radicalism, which in turn was inspired by the Islamic revolution in Iran in 1979. Sunni militants had their galvanizing experience of success a few years after their Shi'ite counterparts when Soviet troops withdrew from Afghanistan towards the end of the 1980s. The arrival of a new Islamic century – al-Hijri 1400 (the year 1980 in the Gregorian calendar) added a millenarian element to both Shi'ah and Sunni radicalsm.

The nature and character of the fourth wave have caused a considerable amount of debate among scholars. However, there are a few empirical observations that deserve mention. To begin with, the fourth wave has been largely characterized by its most catastrophic strategy, suicide terrorism. This tactic, begun by Shi'ite groups in Lebanon, has spread to more than two dozen fourth-wave actors. Second, Rapoport, Hoffman and others note that while the number of active groups has dropped precipitously, the average size of the remaining groups has grown. Finally, organizational longevity has likewise increased among fourth-wave groups (usually, most terrorist groups do not survive beyond a year or two after being set up).

Not all aspects of the fourth wave are agreed upon, however. These debates usually centre upon the effect of religion on violent political movements. At one end of the spectrum are scholars who argue that the (re-)introduction of religion into political violence has fundamentally changed the nature of terrorism. At the other end are those who hold that religion simply acts as a collective action solution, and the ends of contemporary terrorism remain political change or reform in this world, not salvation in another world.

Magnus Ranstorp states that the rise of religious terror follows historically the rise of terror as a form of warfare.[130] However, Ranstorp maintains that a number of things differentiate religious radicals from more conventional terrorists. First, religious radicals feel themselves to be located at a critical juncture in history, an idea also expounded upon by Mark Juergensmeyer. These groups revolve around a spiritual guide, who may be separate from the leadership of the group itself (as in the case of Sheikh Yassin and the leadership of Hamas prior to his assassination by Israel). In addition, they are, more so than their secular predecessors, defined by an uncompromising attitude that Ranstorp believes is the inevitable result of having a Manichean belief that worldly events represent a struggle between good and evil.

Ranstorp disagrees, however, with Rapoport's characterization of the founding events of the fourth wave. He claims that Islamic radicalism actually evolved in certain phases, each of which was triggered by a distinct historical event.[131] Yet he is in agreement with Rapoport that the Iranian Revolution of 1979 provided a template for revolutionary Islam. In addition, it was with Iranian (and Saudi) assistance that Islamist violence was internationalized in the succeeding decades. Sunni radicals forged the networks necessary to garner international headlines during the jihad against the

Soviet intervention in Afghanistan. An event not mentioned by Rapoport, however, which Ranstorp finds to be central, is the Islamic Salvation Front's imminent election victory in Algeria in 1991. The subsequent nullification of the results helped to radicalize Islamic movements, especially in North Africa, and to disillusion their adherents with Western democratic principles. Writing in 1996, Ranstorp viewed the then current wave of spoiler terrorism as a direct result of the Palestinian–Israeli General Agreement on Principle, which he claimed undermined the Islamist goal of liberating Jerusalem. Given the now defunct status of this agreement, it is debatable how central this event would be viewed in the wider history of Islamist Radicalism.

Bruce Hoffman has also written at length regarding the 'new terrorism', and begins by drawing attention to the fact that Rapoport's wave theory speaks only to contemporary terror and that religion was, in actuality, an original motivation for non-state violence. It was in fact Rapoport's first wave in the nineteenth century[132] that secularized non-state terrorism. Hoffman argues that the rise in mass-casualty terror in the fourth wave is a result of the fact that religious terrorists see violence as a sacramental act, and that it is undertaken as the result of a theological imperative.[133] This results in a number of behaviours tending towards escalation in terms of lethality of attacks. First, the transcendent aspects of religious violence free radicals from the social and moral constraints faced by secular groups. Further, religious groups seek the elimination of a broadly defined enemy. Most terrorists have potential constituencies only, but religious radicals define that in-group more parochially. Finally, the 'new terrorism' school believes religious radicals are an extreme example of Crenshaw's redemptive groups. Religious extremists reject society wholesale and seek a radical path of spiritual revitalization.

Bruce Hoffman's work focuses on religious terrorism as part of a broader comparative analysis of contemporary terrorism. A narrower analysis of the new terrorism can be found in Mark Juergensmeyer's 'cosmic war' hypothesis. Juergensmeyer's hypothesis was driven by two trends in religious violence: a tendency towards mass-casualty violence, and an apparent lack of grand strategy in the employment of violence.[134] His answer to these puzzles was that the 'new terror' was an example of 'cosmic war', which in turn was an outgrowth of 'cosmic struggle'. According to Juergensmeyer, religion inherently deals with the struggle between order and disorder, the latter being intrinsically violent.[135] Religious violence is justified because it places terror in the context of the 'cosmic struggle' between order and disorder. Religion typically deals with conflict in the abstract. However, Juergensmeyer delineated five ways in which cosmic struggle can escalate to cosmic war, and thus actual violence.[136] First, the religious struggle alluded to must be perceived by the radical organization to be playing out in real time. Second, believers must be able to identify personally with the conflict, and are thus motivated to act on religious sanction. Third, since cosmic struggles cannot be won in real terms, believers must subscribe to the continuity of religious struggle in order to maintain commitment to the cause. Fourth, the extremists must perceive that the struggle has reached a point of crisis. Finally, the group must impute violence with a cosmic meaning. In short, Juergensmeyer conceives of religious violence as an abstracted Manichean struggle between good and evil, scripted by radical interpretations of theology. Thus, according to Juergensmeyer, violence is not strategic but dramatic, a piece of theatre playing to three audiences: victims, in-groups and a wider audience. Terrorism as drama can be either a performance event meant to make a symbolic statement, or a performative act that actually tries to change things. Since drama is about metaphor, and metaphor requires an interpretation, acts of terror mean different things to different audiences. Drama also requires stage, dramatic time and audiences.

Juergensmeyer's testing of his theory is plagued, however, by conceptual stretching that calls into question his findings. First, his case studies span Aum Shinrikyo, Al-Qaeda, Babar Khalsa and the Irish Republican Army (IRA). While the first is only nominally political (and thus it is debatable as to whether its activities quality as political violence), the last two might be only nominally religious, calling into question whether their actions can be ascribed to 'cosmic warfare'. Certainly those of the IRA cannot. Second, Juergensmeyer's contention that terrorism is performance rather than strategic seems to be based on the notion that prior instances of terror were not marked by symbolic violence. Given the asymmetric power between terrorists and their opponents, symbolic targets have often been a mainstay of violence. Further, many of the symbolic targets mentioned by Juergensmeyer – banks, centres of commerce, transport hubs – have always been prone to terrorist violence, and also serve the strategic end of disrupting the economic activity of target regimes.

Another researcher, the late Ehud Sprinzak, subdivided religious militancy into millenarian and post-millenarian (or messianic) camps. Sprinzak accounts for the variance in escalation to violence among radical religious movements by looking at particular attributes of each. Millenarian groups tend to focus on the redemptive qualities of eschatological events. Thus, redemption comes after divine intervention, often in the form of an apocalypse. The emphasis in such groups is therefore not on action but on correct living preceding judgement. Post-millenarian groups typically believe that divine intervention comes only after certain preconditions have been met. The radical Jewish movements analysed by Sprinzak often believe that the rebuilding of the Temple of Solomon will accomplish such ends. Regardless of the form of action required, messianic groups have, according to Sprinzak, grown impatient with the slow pace of redemption. They are therefore inclined to take 'historical shortcuts'.[137] As a result, they are far more prone to violence than their millenarian brethren.

Rapoport's wave theory represents a broad periodical classification of modern non-state terrorism. As noted earlier, it is perhaps the closest to a general theory of terrorism found in the current literature. Its breadth, however, comes with problems of specificity. By speaking of movements rather than individual groups, there are ambiguities to be found in its accounting for particular instances of political violence. For example, the same Marxist thought that drove the first wave informed much of the anti-colonial movements. And a strong argument could be made that the poster children for left-wing radicalism in the 1960s and 1970s (the Viet Cong and PLO, respectively) were in fact (also) anti-colonial,[138] rather than purely leftist. Perhaps the biggest shortcoming of Rapoport's wave theory is that it excludes non-state groups that managed to take state power – as in the case of the fascists and communists – and successfully engaged in large-scale state terrorism for long periods of time. Nevertheless, Rapoport's theory remains powerful in its ability to illustrate the relationship between motivations for violence and modes of violent activity. It has also has received empirical support in a statistical test relating to the last two waves, performed with ITERATE data.[139]

A much simpler periodization than Rapoport's four waves theory is provided by those who simply distinguish between an 'old terrorism' (ending at the latest on 9/11) and a 'new terrorism' that is religiously inspired. Authors adhering to this cleavage usually refer to up to a dozen alleged quantum changes since 11 September 2001:

1 attempts to acquire weapons of mass destruction;
2 religious fanaticism;
3 catastrophic terrorism;
4 border porosity;
5 global communication;
6 diaspora bridgeheads (portable conflicts);
7 kamikaze suicide terrorism;
8 expansion of range of targets (ICRC, UN);
9 links with organized crime;
10 new sources of financing;
11 failed and weak states as *de facto* safe havens;
12 new types of weapons (e.g. MANPADs).

However, many theorists call into question the stark division between religious terrorism and more secular political violence. Fawaz Gerges, for example, sees definitive organizational motivations behind the apparent lack of grand strategy in international Salafist movements. The substitution of localized revolution with anti-Western rhetoric and violence does not signal to Gerges a shift from conventional terrorism to 'cosmic war'. Rather, it is a strategy derived from the need to maintain organizational salience at a time when local conditions are not favourable for domestic revolt. It is not necessarily a signal that such movements are not revolutionary, merely that reality has dictated that they shift their respective *raison d'être* for the time being[140] – as would have been predicted by Crenshaw's organizational process theory. Contentions that radical religious organizations are as insensitive to constraints on violence as previous groups have proved false in a number of cases. The implosion of the Christian Identity movement in the United States following the public relations fiasco of the Oklahoma City bombing (in 1995) can be seen mirrored in the Indonesian backlash against the Bali bombings by Jemaah Islamiyah (in 2002), the Salafist reaction to GIA atrocities in Algeria (in the late 1990s), and perhaps even with Al-Qaeda, whose Iraqi subsidiary is currently on the ropes, largely as a result of its heavy-handed tactics. Brynjar Lia's work tracking the internal debates between al-Suri and al-Qatada illustrates that many in Salafist circles are keenly aware of their need to keep their violence within acceptable bounds. These debates are echoed even at the top echelons of the Al-Qaeda organization, as depicted in admonitions of Ayman al-Zawahiri to al-Zarqawi, the leader of Al-Qaeda in Iraq and architect of the more atrocious Al-Qaeda tactics such as videotaped beheadings and anti-Shi'ah violence.[141]

Ethnic terrorism

Ethnic conflict figured large in twentieth-century history, but ethnicity-based terrorism remains understudied despite the fact that it is often central to 'ethnic cleansing' – the expulsion of unwanted people with the help of atrocities that make people decide to flee their land. There are relatively few theories of ethnic terrorism. Here we will focus on two of them: Dan Byman's 'logic of ethnic terrorism' and Jeff Kaplan's 'fifth wave'.

Daniel Byman's work on the logic of ethnic violence is by far the most succinct new addition to the discourse at large. Beginning by way of differentiating ethnic terrorism from other forms of terrorism, Byman at once signals the uniqueness of ethnic terrorism, and the ways in which these exceptionalities affect the qualitative attributes of such violence.

The primary distinction between ethnic and other forms of political violence is that ethnic terrorism is geared towards forging an ethnic identity and serving as a facilitator of ethnic mobilization.[142] These ends are often accompanied by an advocacy of secession, or the elevation of one ethnic group to a privileged position within a state at the expense of other groups in the population. Since ethnic terrorist groups are by definition selective, they differ from other groups in that they limit membership to a specific sub-set of the population.[143] As a consequence, unlike many other groups, ethnic terrorists have a pre-existing receptive audience for the message underlined by their violence.[144] As noted previously, common approaches to ethnic terror often subsume their violence within studies of organizations with broader motivations such as religious movements. However, Byman maintains that ethnic terrorist groups are not strictly comparable with religious terrorists, though there is often overlap: whereas the latter are, in principle, universalist, the former are nationalistic and particularistic. Nor are such groups akin to social revolutionary organizations, as they do not attempt to reshape the whole of society. Rather, they serve the interests of a narrow section of the population (usually a minority, rarely a majority in a minority position).[145]

The effects of ethnic terrorism, according to Byman, are twofold.[146] First, ethnic terrorist groups seek to create a communal bloc in response to state retaliation. Second, as solidarity grows by virtue of the shared experience of persecution, so too does adhesion to 'the cause', as well as recruitment and financial support. The main strategy of ethnic terrorism is to sow fear among rival population groups.[147] This polarizes the political environment and marginalizes moderates. One of the main effects of such a strategy, however, is the fostering of a homogenization through the process of more or less 'voluntary emigration'. This, in turn, changes the demographic and political realities on the ground in favour of the demands posed by the ethnic group.[148] Where salient ethnic schisms do not pre-exist, the ethnic struggle is combined with a process of strengthening identity formation.[149] While there are typically a variety of potential claims on identity, those formulating ethnic identities reject competing claims. Byman notes that this is difficult, but, if successful, the organization responsible for ethnic polarization tends to exhibit a substantial staying power. This in turn helps to explain the longevity of ethnic groups when compared to some other types of organizations engaged in political violence. However, like other terrorists, ethnic extremists attempt to shift blame for violence to other parts of the community. Ethnic terrorism is always articulated by its leaders in terms of a cultural defence meted out as the result of marginalization: real, perceived, or merely possible at some future date.[150]

Some other theorists see problems with the disaggregation of ethnic terrorism from other forms of violence, upon which Byman bases his arguments. David Little, in particular, sees problems in differentiating ethnic conflict from religious conflict,[151] as ethnicity is inherently about genetic, linguistic and cultural peculiarities, with religion being a dominant component of the latter.[152] Little derives his concept of ethnicity from the Weberian premise that inherent to ethnicity is a comparative evaluation of the 'self' versus the 'other'. The idea of being a 'chosen people', or somehow relating culture to exceptionality, has, in Little's view, an intrinsic religious dimension to it.[153] Little bases such claims on an analysis of the Sri Lankan case. He finds that the notion of Sri Lanka as the land of Sinhala Buddhism was incompatible with the reality of a multi-ethnic state (including Tamils, Muslims and smaller minorities), resulting in the revival of Sinhala nationalism and ultimately the implementation of the Sinhala-only legislation in 1956, which sparked the 1984–2009 separatist Tamil insurgency.[154]

Slightly more contentious has been Jeffrey Kaplan's attempt to carry further David Rapoport's four waves theory. Kaplan posits that theorists have overlooked the emergence of a fifth wave.[155] This wave, according to Kaplan, is made up of groups that have broken off from more mainstream movements of the previous waves. These groups have as their defining characteristic an idealized, utopian vision of society, which motivates their radicalism. Kaplan holds that the defining event (accepting Rapoport's premise that all waves have one) was the rise of the Khmer Rouge in 1973, though it was not until the Ugandan Lord's Resistance Army (LRA), from 1987 to the present day, that the first true fifth-wave terrorist group was formed.

These movements are notorious for their extreme violence. Jeffrey Kaplan explores the reasons for this, listing 14 elements, including the following:

1   These groups are marked by a physical withdrawal into wilderness areas.
2   Groups pursue a radical quest for purity, though how they define this is relative.
3   In-group ideology is characterized by a belief in human perfectibility and a resulting radical utopianism. It is this belief that lays the groundwork for genocidal behaviour, as it results in a belief in the 'new man' (or woman). The old order is by default dehumanized, and this emphasis on the 'new' race enhances the role of women as both symbols of the new order and progenitors of the new man.
4   By virtue of their relative innocence, children tend to represent the 'vanguard of the new'.
5   Rape is a signature tactic of fifth-wave violence.
6   New recruits are initiated into the movement by an institutionalized process of rape and violence that not only inures them to violence itself but simultaneously cuts them off from the possibility of return to their civilization.
7   Fifth-wave movements are authoritarian, and leadership is centralized around charismatic rulers.
8   Most fifth-wave groups are deeply religious in nature and have millenarian doctrines as their theological cornerstones.

Kaplan concedes that ideal types of fifth-wave movements are hard to find, but suggests that the LRA in and around Uganda is the closest, with the genocidal Janjaweed in Sudan a distant second.

However, a number of problems exist with this conceptualization of the fifth wave. To begin with, it is based on a broad definition of terrorism. Many scholars could counter that most of these movements are in fact more complex than simple terrorist outfits, representing guerrilla groups, warlord militias or even governments (as in the case of the Khmer Rouge). Second, Kaplan's list is based upon a litany of characteristics drawn specifically from the worst attributes of a few armed movements operating in and after the Cold War. Kaplan admits that few if any actual movements fit his description in its entirety. Rather, he conceives of the fifth wave less as an actual historical phenomenon, as Rapoport does, and more of a conceptual ideal type that movements at a variety of historical junctures may or may not move towards. Thus, he is engaging in a different social scientific exercise altogether and should preferably not be linked to Rapoport's four waves. While the phenomena observed by Jeff Kaplan exist(ed) in sub-Saharan Africa (e.g. Sierra Leone, the Democratic Republic of Congo), we are dealing here with social formations that are more complex than stand-alone terrorist groups of the third wave, or embedded terrorist groups of the fourth wave. The widespread use of child soldiers, the mass rape of women in some of the more recent armed conflicts and the total lack of respect for neutral actors like the Red Cross and other humanitarian organizations in combat zones is a very worrisome feature of some post-Cold War conflict waging. Yet while it contains multiple acts of terrorism, terrorism itself is probably not the chief characteristic of such ultra-violent movements.

Revolutionary terrorism

A seminal, though oft-overlooked, theory of terrorist violence is Martha Crenshaw's theory of revolutionary terrorism, developed from her research on the Algerian independence struggle (1954–1962). By 'revolutionary terror', Crenshaw is referring to a brand of non-state insurgency wherein the goal of the organization is to seize control of the (colonial) state, and in so doing to promulgate widespread social and political change.[156] Though much of the post-9/11 discourse has focused on ritualistic or expressive aspects of the 'new terror' (as previously discussed), Crenshaw explained in her dissertation research that when the motivation for violence encompasses far-reaching goals, the tactics and quality of violence change as well. Accordingly, revolutionary terrorism must have the following properties:[157]

- Terrorism is part of a revolutionary strategy the end of which is the seizure of state power.
- Terrorism is manifested in socially unacceptable violence. It is more effective when the violence is unpredictable, but such unpredictability should not lead the researcher to misconstrue the violence as being random.
- The victims of terrorism are representative of a larger audience.
- The violence is intended to change a target group's behaviour by affecting its members psychologically.

Crenshaw's theory of revolutionary terrorism views political violence along T.P. Thornton's lines: as a process of violent action represented by a spectrum of activities that begins with terrorism, moves on to guerrilla warfare and subsequently expands into a civil war, with the end goal of the insurgent movement being to seize state power.[158] Crenshaw states that in the end, the group will utilize all three types of violence. The concept of revolutionary terrorism is elaborated upon by Price,[159] who details three targets of revolutionary violence;[160] victims, groups who identify with the victim, and the so-called 'resonant mass' represented by those who could be swayed by either the victim or the victimizer. Price provides greater detail in his analysis of revolutionary violence by dividing the opposed political system into three types, each with its own particular conflict of legitimacy:[161] the independent nation-state (a target of ideological violence), the colonial territory (a target of anti-colonial violence) and the internal colonial state (a target of ethnic terrorism). Terrorist tactics of revolutionary extremists vary as well, ranging from armed robbery to attacks on state military apparatus, to kidnappings, selective assassinations and indiscriminate attacks in public spaces.[162] With respect to the later strategy, however, Crenshaw cautions that terrorists must walk a fine line, as terrorism does not always produce terror. If the violence dulls or numbs a society to violence, the terrorists might provoke hostility rather than fear.[163] This tolerance results from two factors, which in turn prompts a move from 'fear of' to 'hostility towards' the terrorists:[164] the duration and magnitude of the campaign, and the inability of the organization to effectively communicate reasonable demands and realistic political alternatives.

Suicide terrorism

Despite the fact that a great deal of work on suicide terrorism has been done by psychologists using an agent-based approach, we will discuss suicide terrorism (or martyrdom operations, as some of its advocates call it) under the institutional level of analysis. The reason for this is twofold. First, most scholars concur that there is no evidence of major psychological deviance at the individual level of analysis. As an overview of relevant literature indicates, individual suicide bears little resemblance to the use of suicide as a tool of political terrorism. Meaningful insights psychologists have been able to offer have typically been in the realm of group rather than individual psychology, representing the ways in which human collectives can subject vulnerable individuals to pressure and offer them or their families incentives to throw away their lives while killing enemies. Second, most social scientists contend that organizations are nearly always responsible for individual acts of suicide, while individual acts of self-destruction combined with mass murder tend to be part of broader campaigns of violence. One early finding was that about 95 per cent of all suicide attacks were conducted by an organization as part of a concerted campaign. However, Ami Pedahzur cautions that this might be changing as transnational movements start to use it more than local domestic groups.[165]

Studies suggest that suicide terrorism began in earnest in the 1980s, with currently at least 32 groups spread out across 28 countries adopting this fearsome tactic.[166] Researchers have taken note of this phenomenon primarily as a consequence of its enhanced lethality (which tends to be markedly higher than in the case of merely placing a bomb on a site and then removing oneself from the crime scene or triggering the bomb by remote control). According to data gathered by Pedahzur and Perlinger, the average number of victims in a terrorist incident in which small arms are used is about three casualties (3.32). An attack using a remote-controlled bomb elevates the average number of victims to almost seven deaths and injured (6.92). When the perpetrator uses a suicide belt of explosives, however, this number increases significantly. If the suicide bomber is using an explosive-laden car or truck, the number goes up to almost 100 casualties (97.81) per attack.[167] In a way, the suicide bomber is the poor man's asymmetric equivalent of a guided missile or remotely controlled drone firing its rocket based on visual identification of the target. However, whereas those using drones and guided missiles, bound by humanitarian law, try to avoid civilian casualties, most contemporary suicide terrorists have no such qualms.

Scholars have found defining suicide terrorism difficult for many of the same reasons that make defining terrorism difficult. Assaf Moghadam has investigated a number of potential terms for use by scholars and concluded that 'suicide terrorism' is too narrow and pejorative. 'Homicide bombings', a potential alternative, is also too narrow. 'Martyrdom operations', terminology borrowed from the perpetrators themselves, Moghadam found too normative. In the end, he found 'suicide operations' to be the most value free of the available terms. Yet what qualifies as a suicide operation is still up for debate.[168] In its broadest sense, suicide operations could be used to refer to any lethal operation involving also the deliberate death of the assailant. A narrower reading, and one perhaps championed by the majority of relevant researchers, would refer only to those operations that make the death of the perpetrator a prerequisite for success. Still others believe that an even narrower reading is preferable. Israeli offers what is perhaps the most parochial label in the form of 'Islamikaze', which will be investigated in somewhat greater detail shortly.

Conceptualizing suicide terrorism only begins with the definitional debate. From this initial point of departure, a variety of theoretical approaches to the subject have emerged. Among those deemed most seminal are Gambetta's organizational studies approach, Atran's policy-oriented approach, Israeli's 'Islamikaze' thesis and the rational choice frameworks of Pape, Elster and Bloom.

Gambetta begins his work with the assumption that all suicide missions are perpetrated by organizations. From an academic perspective, then, organizational motivations for suicide campaigns should take precedence in security studies.[169] These motivations span a wide gamut, running from the impetus of religious radicals to the self-interest of secular states, as well, as much in between.[170] However, campaigns of suicide terrorism tend to share common denominators. First, Gambetta claims that all organizations that use suicide missions view such actions as one component in a broader strategic campaign of violence.[171] Second, the organizations that employ suicide missions typically either have very broad constituencies or lack any constituency whatsoever.[172] Third, Gambetta points to his observation that only the weaker side in a conflict utilizes suicide missions as proof that suicide missions are in fact rational and strategic.[173] Suicide missions are not, however, merely a means of last resort. Gambetta's studies show that sometimes such campaigns can be an effective strategy of organization building as these missions communicate to an appropriate audience the organization's fatalistic resolve to continue the struggle.[174] Finally, despite the fact that many secular organizations have utilized suicide missions, Gambetta found that 89.9 per cent of suicide missions directly target those of different religions from the perpetrators of the attack,[175] pointing to an even greater need for rationalizing such attacks within the organization.

Scott Atran focuses on the process of radicalization and socialization into suicide attacks, most notably the recruitment process of jihadists responsible for filling the ranks of *shaheeds* (martyrs). He also looks at the processes by which organizations manage to radicalize their members into suicide missions. In terms of recruitment, Atran makes several counter-intuitive observations. First, he finds that jihadi recruiters target that segment of the population, young Middle Eastern males, with the highest percentage of pro-American cultural values.[176] Second, Atran found that the profiles of jihadists are markedly different from those of other right-wing militants. Whereas the latter typically appeal to marginalized individuals who lack father figures, are unemployed, etc., the former are culled from largely middle-class, well-educated and tightly knit families. Atran surmises that the lack of personal marginalization and the lack of a cultural context of extreme violence point to the fact that the radicalization process into suicide terrorism is likewise different and follows the lines of Arendt's 'banality of evil'. Thus, suicide terror is less a product of personal animosity and more a result of a 'manipulation of contexts', engineered by organizations in order to manipulate agent choice (comparable to Stanley Milgram's electro-shock tests in the 1960s).[177] Atran's observations into this process offer a useful critique of agent-based analyses of suicide terrorism. According to the researcher, the majority of suicide terror work stating that one can explain individual behaviour by simply looking at personality traits suffers from the fundamental attribution error. In fact, Atran states that suicide attacks are the result of institutional manipulation, geared towards furthering organizational goals.[178]

Israeli's work on suicide terrorism echoes the findings of Atran, among others, and makes a case for conceiving of suicide terrorism as a phenomenon unto itself. Israeli disagrees with the term 'suicide' terror, however, since the agents responsible for these actions do not display any of the pathological behaviours of suicidal individuals.[179] In short, they are not suffering undue psychological distress and their actions are not done to avoid humiliation. Rather, what the discourse terms suicide terror is actually the result of socio-cultural impetuses, analogous to the Japanese Kamikaze who fought for their country towards the last days of the Second World War.[180] Far from suffering the feelings of extreme shame and isolation that drive suicidal behaviour in individuals, suicide terrorists, like the Kamikaze of the Second World War, fulfil a social-familial ideal, either by bringing honour to their households or by preparing the way to paradise for their kinsmen.[181] Further, suicidal individuals seek to maximize the damage they inflict upon themselves. In Kamikaze attacks, the individual seeks to maximize the damage done to his or her opponents while minimizing the damage done to him- or herself, conceived of as being, in effect, the organization or state.[182] Thus, Israeli differentiates between agent-based suicide and organizationally or culturally motivated suicide, and rejects the term 'suicide' altogether. Israeli adopts in its stead the term 'Islamikaze'. Drawing distinctions between suicidal actions and Islamikaze actions, Israeli provides a useful psychological critique of the discipline. He begins by delineating the steps of a clinical build-up to a suicidal mindset:[183]

1 A thought of killing oneself.
2 The presence of a plan, i.e. how to proceed, what are the precise steps to be taken, their sequence and timing, etc.
3 An energy level of the suicidal individual must exist, i.e. his capacity to carry out the plan.

All of these steps stand in stark contrast to the build-up of the Islamikaze ideology.[184]

1 . . . identify the enemy.
2 . . . strengthening the value of jihad as the religious duty of every Muslim against the enemy.
3 . . . instigating the Islamikaze to show personal valor, and self-sacrifice for the attainment of the prescribed goal.

While useful in terms of its provision of a straightforward and convincing comparison between suicidal behaviour and suicide terrorism, Israeli's thesis is troubled by its simultaneously general and parochial applicability. The term 'Islamikaze' itself emphasizes the relationship between insurgent and statist violence. At the agent level of analysis, this draws interesting parallels between the motivations for state-sanctioned suicide missions and those of suicide terrorists. However, the study is flawed on two levels. In the first instance, Israeli's comparison draws from two different levels of analysis. The suicidal individual is detailed at the agent level, and the Islamikaze is explored by virtue of institutional action (action is the result of an indoctrination process carried out by the sanctioning organization). Perhaps more importantly, however, Israeli's study obscures the differences in strategic rationale for suicide bombing between state agents and insurgents. States have historically employed suicide missions to some effect in military campaigns aimed at crippling the capabilities of rivals. Suicide terrorism, on the other hand, though definitely more lethal than conventional terror, nonetheless shares terrorism's inability to thwart an enemy by itself. Rather, suicide terrorism is a form of psychological war meant to further the ends of terrorist organizations through the imposition of fear in an opponent.

Few studies of suicide terrorism have gained the prominence of Pape's research into suicide terror as a function of strategic choice. Echoing other studies, Pape stipulates explicitly that suicide terror does not emanate from individual choice.[185] Further, it is not a function of religious indoctrination, nor is it a result of a psychological predisposition to such acts. In so doing, Pape takes the common tack in International Relations theories of applying rational choice theories to the institutional level of analysis. Rendering all agents functionally similar allows Pape to ignore the individual level of analysis. The agent may or may not be psychologically abnormal. It doesn't matter, since the strategy is planned by the organization, whose leadership is not.[186] Pape is addressing opponents to rational choice who charge that suicide terrorism represents akratic, or altruistic, actions, behaviour not well explained by rational choice predictions.[187] In order to address this challenge, Pape draws upon Schelling's 'rationality of the irrational' by stating that what is individually irrational is sometimes collectively rational.[188]

Pape conceives of suicide terrorism as the most destructive of three forms of terrorist violence.[189] The first and least destructive form of terrorism is '*demonstrative*' terror. Since demonstrative terror is meant to promulgate sympathy for the organization and its goals, it typically makes an attempt to avoid fatalities. *Destructive* terrorism represents a more aggressive incarnation of political violence and is geared towards mobilizing support and coercing opponents. *Suicide terrorism*, according to Pape, pursues coercion at the expense of popular support, which is lost not only because of the high death tolls associated with suicide terror (which arguably is the primary rationale for using the strategy) but also as a result of the contentious nature of suicide in religious or cultural scripts.

Pape delineates his study into five principal findings.[190] First, he concludes that suicide terrorism is strategic: it is usually conducted in waves or campaigns and it is used to pursue goals which have been articulated by organizations. Second, Pape maintains that suicide terrorism is designed to elicit concessions from democratic governments concerning issues related to national self-determination. Third, the use of suicide terrorism is rising because organizations observe that it is an effective tactic of rebellion. Fourth, Pape observed that moderate campaigns of suicide terrorism lead to moderate concessions from states. However, extreme campaigns are not likely to result in extreme concessions. Fifth, Pape's analysis of counter-terror solutions to suicide campaigns finds that military actions and concessions are not likely to thwart a suicide terror campaign. Rather, governments should focus their resources on limiting the ability of suicide missions to be successful.

Pape finds that, in its essence, suicide terrorism is an inversion of conventional strategic thought, since in international conflict the dominant state is traditionally the coercer. In order to coerce a rival, a state has one of two strategies: either to punish the other state, or to deny victory in such a way as to illustrate the futility of resistance. Since in suicide terror campaigns the coercer is the weaker party, denial is impossible, so the aggressor must seek a strategy geared towards punishment[191]. Suicide terror compounds the material punishment with stress, created by the promise of future violence. Thus, suicide attacks are only effective as part and parcel of broader campaigns[192]. They are credible in their threat of more attacks to come, and, by violating the norms of violence considered acceptable in armed conflict, suicide terror raises the target's expectations of future costs. In conclusion, Pape highlights three properties of suicide terrorism: it is always part of a consistent campaign; it is always directed towards achieving territorial independence, however defined; and it is used against democracies.[193] Pape is struck by the seeming success of suicide terror campaigns. Of 11 suicide terror campaigns since 1980, 6 ended in concession – indicating at least partial achievement of terrorist objectives.[194] Since states are successful at coercion only one-third of the time, a greater than 50 per cent success rate appears quite striking. Pape's findings and his data have been challenged by other scholars studying the phenomenon of suicide terrorism, and more recent data derived from the conflicts in Iraq and Afghanistan appear not to fit well with his hypotheses.

Another approach to suicide terrorism from the rational choice camp is John Elster's work on the motivation and beliefs underpinning suicide missions.[195] Elster takes a novel approach to the subject by disaggregating the key actors, individuals and organizations and looking at the interplay between them. Thus, it is not purely an organizational level of analysis. Elster believes this complication is necessary as suicide attacks are a result of the interaction between agents and the institutions sponsoring them. Additionally, each level has its own skill and constraint requirements.[196] Whereas agents need opportunities, skills and destructive technologies, organizations need opportunities (in the form of targets), funds, skills and volunteers. Different actors also have different motivations for violence.[197] Individuals have a fully instrumental appreciation for suicide bombing. They wish to kill as many as possible with their sacrifice. According to Elster, this wish could be motivated by either hatred or revenge. Elster contradicts the assumptions of some rationalists and states that religious imperatives and/or a desire for posthumous support for one's family typically helps make the decision, but only by alleviating key concerns such as 'Who will take care of my family when I'm gone?' However, it is never the primary motivation for an agent's decision to embark on a suicide mission. Organizational motivations, however, are not as narrow. Terrorist groups can see either an instrumental or an intrinsic benefit in suicide missions: it is instrumental if recruits are few and the organization needs to maximize effectiveness with scarce resources. On the other hand, suicide terror can have an intrinsic value for the organization as it demonstrates a resolve to continue the fight.

Elster's work is original and intuitively convincing. However, it does suffer from the more tautological inclinations of rational choice theory, at least at the agent level of analysis. By conflating desires for revenge and personal animosity with rational motivations for violence, the approach verges on having an overly broad definition of rationality, veering towards conceptual stretching.

Another influential work on suicide terrorism has been Mia Bloom's *Dying to Kill*, an empirical investigation of the subject. Bloom finds that suicide terrorism is mainly being driven by two elements: the failure of other forms of resistance previously employed by the group in question, and (more originally) the presence of intense inter-group competition. Bloom shows that Pape's assertion that terrorists lose support when conducting suicide operations is not always the case. Rather, suicide campaigns often develop in the latter stages of intense conflict in areas where groups have constituencies receptive to the targeting of civilians. Like those of Pape, Bloom's findings have been challenged, primarily on the grounds that inter-group rivalry as an explanatory factor has been overemphasized in her studies.

Theories of asymmetrical conflict

With a few notable exceptions, many theorists of terrorism neglect the relationship between terrorism and other forms of political violence. Nevertheless, one segment of the discourse focuses specifically on terrorism as a form of asymmetrical conflict, and in so doing draws parallels between terrorism and broader manifestations of violence. These theories can be generally disaggregated into one of two categories: those theories that look at terrorism as a tactic of asymmetric conflict, drawing from the military sciences (e.g. Liddell Hart's *Strategy: The Indirect Approach*) in order to understand tactics and strategies of terrorist organizations, and those theories that broaden the scope of the term 'asymmetry' in ways meant to elaborate the nature of the conflict between states and terrorist groups.

Of the former group, the largest contribution has come in the form of various analyses of organizational designs in terrorist groups, specifically the contemporary adoption of network-centric operational paradigms. Throwing this phenomenon into relief for the first time was the work of RAND researcher John Arquilla, author of the influential monograph *The Advent of Netwar*.[198] He later elaborated his thesis in subsequent volumes co-authored with RAND colleague David Ronfeldt.[199] The premise of the netwar doctrine is based in part on military science research into the Revolution in Military Affairs (RMA)[200] and on an emerging literature studying parallels between information-age business practices and modern incarnations of political violence.[201] Arquilla and Ronfeldt analysed the ways in which information revolution innovations were simultaneously changing the ways in which contemporary societies generate capital as well as wage war. As it relates to terrorism, netwar proponents contend that innovations in communication, transportation and weapons technologies have shifted advantage in conflict from hierarchical to networked organizations, the latter being defined as institutions whose command and control structures are flattened and decentralized as opposed to the vertical hierarchies of traditional political organizations such as states. These networked designs may take the form of chain networks, where individual nodes are connected linearly to other nodes of the organization, hub and spoke networks, where franchised cells collaborate with the core organization vis-à-vis a centralized command node, and the so-called full-matrix or all-channel network, wherein all nodes of a network are directly connected to all others (see Figure 3.11 in the previous chapter). According to netwar doctrine, these highly interconnected organizations have a number of operational advantages over hierarchically organized adversaries. First, they are able to share information more effectively across organizations, increasing the effectiveness of individual cells. Second, they are more resilient to attack than hierarchical organizations, as the destruction of all but the most critical cells will have little effect on remaining segments of the organization. And third, given their amorphous nature, distributed organizations are more adaptable and flexible than the rigid hierarchies of conventional armed forces, enabling them to institutionalize 'lessons learned' more quickly than their state foes.

While the netwar hypothesis has raised many interesting critiques of the statist reaction to the threat of terrorism, network theorists have in some instances a fundamentally flawed approach to the study of terrorist organizations. On methodological grounds, two issues come to the fore. First, there is little definitional debate regarding what precisely constitutes a 'network'. This allows researchers to use overly broad definitions of an organization, including in their analysis those elements of a movement with only tangential (indeed, sometimes only ideational) attachments to the organization being studied. It is impossible to accept a social scientific assessment of an entity (in this case a terrorist organization) without a clear idea of what constitutes that entity: that is, the core organization, external supporters, constituent communities, etc. Second, such studies overwhelmingly use as their case study the ill-understood and amorphous Al-Qaeda organization. This is problematic not only because of the atypical nature of Al-Qaeda (it is in many ways unlike any other terrorist organization, transnational or otherwise), but also because there is no clear consensus of what actually constitutes Al-Qaeda 'the organization'. This term has been used to refer to the high command in Pakistan (probably reduced to fewer than 100 core members) and those directly linked to them alone, or has been broadened to include allied organizations such as Al-Qaeda in Iraq, Al-Qaeda in the Islamic Maghreb, Jemmah Islamiyyah in South-East Asia and others, or even wider still, the *takfiri* Salafist-jihadist movement which takes as its brand name 'Al-Qaeda' despite the lack of any formal connection between local start-ups and the Bin Laden- and al-Zawahiri-led organization founded in 1988. Theorists have been able to support hyperbolic claims regarding the effectiveness of contemporary terrorist organizations largely by simultaneously referencing all three aspects of Al-Qaeda and assuming *a priori* that effective communication takes place between all relevant nodes. Since few if any broader studies of organization design have been conducted across a variety of cases, the claims of the netwar theorists are at present still unsubstantiated.

In terms of theory, netwar assumptions are problematic, as they tend to equate organizational success with levels of violence and/or organizational longevity. While these assessments address important facets, they do not address the key fact that terrorist organizations are political institutions and thus must procure political goods in order to maintain organizational salience. Historically, it has been the more hierarchical organizations such as Hamas, Hezbollah, the IRA, as well as a host of ethno-nationalist movements that have proven adept at providing the social and political goods associated with successful organizations. Highly distributed groups such as Al-Qaeda and the American Christian Identity community provide few if any political goods for constituent communities, either in the form of social welfare programmes or in terms of clear political victories in the organization's struggle against the state – reflected in obtaining tangible political or territorial concessions. The reason for this is twofold: decentralized command and control arrangements make it difficult for organizations to articulate a coherent political platform, while decentralized operational arrangements make coordinating sophisticated terrorist campaigns difficult.

The concept of 'leaderless resistance' is a distinct, but not altogether dissimilar, theory of terrorism that surfaced in the 1990s. The strategy was originally conceived of and propounded by American right-wing radical Louis Beam as a means of 'making a virtue out of weakness and political isolation'.[202] It called for the establishment of a radical movement composed of atomistic cells of like-minded activists rather than a distinct organization. Kaplan traces the origin of this strategy to the peculiar trajectory of the American radical right in the latter part of the twentieth century. Following several high-profile setbacks, including the assassination of George Lincoln Rockwell on 25 August 1967, much of the original cadre of national socialists disavowed violent activism in favour of legal modes of protest and propaganda.[203] Shortly thereafter, however, American Nazi movements begin to realize that ideals would never be palatable to a broad audience in the United States. The movement decomposed into a series of loose ad hoc groups. Faced with a political landscape hostile to his goals, and a movement largely decimated by internal decay and external pressure from law enforcement agencies, Louis Beam based his call for a strategy of 'leaderless resistance' on Colonel Ulius Amoss's work regarding the likely strategies of US resistance to a Soviet invasion in a Cold War context. While the leaderless resistance strategy failed to lift the American right-wing movement from obscurity, a number of single-issue left-wing groups such as the Earth Liberation Front and the Animal Liberation Front have used the concept to some effect in campaigns in both the United Kingdom and the United Statesto some effect in campaigns in both the United Kingdom and the United States.

Pursuant to the discussion on network-centric warfare, which spawned the discourse on both netwar and leaderless resistance, is the use of Kenney's organizational learning theory. It underscores the institutional similarities between narco-trafficking networks and international terrorist networks.[204] In brief, Kenney's theory analyses how organizations react to new information, store information and create routines that consistently produce good enough (note: not optimal) results.[205] Strategic advantage, according to Kenney, is accrued by those organizations best able to exemplify the traits of a 'learning organization'. Kenney states that an institution becomes a learning organization when it embeds institutional knowledge into its routine,[206] meaning that organizational activities are informed by storage of, and reflection on, organizational experience. The method of subsequent knowledge diffusion, however, depends upon the type of knowledge being dealt with.[207] Kenney breaks down organizational knowledge into two discrete categories: *techne* and *metis*. *Techne* represents abstract technical knowledge such as bomb making, document forging, etc. This sort of complex technical knowledge requires formal instruction and cannot be gleaned from books and distance-learning by internet alone. *Metis*, on the other hand, is experiential and intuitive knowledge such as targeting, law enforcement evasion and other modes of tradecraft. *Metis* comes from learning by doing. Becoming a learning organization requires a commitment to (or professional need for) innovation in day-to-day operations, as well as formal organizational processes for disseminating relevant information to various nodes in the organization. This contention of Kenney stands in contrast with what netwar theorists assume; he finds that loosely coupled networks lack connectivity and thus have a limited capacity for organizational learning.[208] Distributed networks, while potentially more resilient, have handicaps as they are not fully informed. At present, Kenney has only published the first book of a two-volume set investigating his theory. The completed volume reflects his study of narco-trafficking networks and has only marginally been tested with terrorist organizations. It remains to be seen, however, whether his theory is applicable beyond organized crime groups.

Among the most seminal studies on terrorism in recent years have been two small volumes by Marc Sageman.[209] Sageman begins with a methodological critique of current theories of terrorism and divides the approach according to three levels of analysis for terrorism studies:[210] a micro level, focusing on the individual; a macro level, focusing on the environment in which radicals operate; and a middle range, focusing on the nature of relationships within terrorist networks. The individual level of analysis is substandard, according to Sageman, as it cannot determine the scope of the problem.[211] As a result, it makes the false assumption that terrorists are fundamentally different from other segments of a given population, it neglects the structural factors faced by an organization, it assumes people understand what they are doing and why, and individual investigations contain no control cases.[212] Sageman likewise dismisses the macro or structural level of analysis because it assumes that people respond to structural imperatives similarly. Sageman maintains that they do not. Some of the work of Horgan suggests that organizational dynamics have a systematic effect on individual behaviour.[213] Some authors maintain that religion has little independent effect on radicalism. Sageman states as evidence that contemporary jihadis often have little if any religious training, echoing similar findings by the RAND organization in its studies of the links between Marxist doctrine and Viet Cong militants fighting inspiration during the Vietnam War.[214] Sageman, in turn, makes the case for the mid level of analysis, which he states focuses on the nature of relationships in terrorist networks.[215]

Of particular importance to investigators are the processes of interactions among disparate members of the organization. The processes Sageman delineates are radicalization, mobilization, motivation and separation.[216] The first of these, radicalization, is prompted by moral outrage caused by a major moral violation that prompts, in turn, a moral judgement. Sageman is quick to point out that this is not humiliation, as has been assumed by many studies, as such a reaction typically causes passivity and apathy rather than the rage associated with political violence. As it relates to the international Salafist networks studied by Sageman, this usually takes the form of a perceived 'war against Islam'. This is because moral outrage alone is insufficient to result in radicalism. Rather, the violation must be placed in the context of an ongoing conflict. Further, the radical agenda must resonate with personal experience. Many are exposed to radical beliefs. But for these to be internalized, they must resonate personally. It is for this reason, according to the researcher, that diasporas are so often fertile breeding grounds for radicalism, as their members find themselves marginalized (economically and/or culturally) in their host countries. Individuals, however, require opportunity structures to engage in political violence. This is achieved by the mobilization of at-risk individuals by underground networks. As it relates to Al-Qaeda (which Sageman defines rather loosely), there are two types of peer networks: face to face and virtual. Face-to-face networks typically occur vis-à-vis immigration patterns, radical student groups or radical mosques. Virtual mobilization, however, takes place by virtue of internet chat-rooms, the self-selection and anonymity of which typically serve the radicalization and mobilization process by creating the illusion of numbers.[217]

These uneven modes of mobilization in large part result in what is arguably Sageman's greatest theoretical contribution to terrorism studies: the delineation of global Islamism into three stages,[218] each with its peculiar characteristics, strengths, and limitations. The 'first wave' consists of the Afghan jihadis, those veterans of the war against the Soviets who received formal training in insurgency and benefited from an abundance of experience in the anti-Soviet jihadi campaign of the 1980s. The 'second wave' joined in the 1990s and was motivated by a broader spectrum of political events, namely the conflicts in Chechnya, Bosnia and Kashmir. Those in this second wave did not have the benefit of the Afghan jihad as a learning experience, but they did benefit from interactions with the first-wave jihadis in training camps located in North Africa and Central and South Asia. The 'third wave' is the first to have little to no contact with prior waves. This third wave represents the current manifestation of jihadi violence and can in turn be broken up into two distinct groups, the Middle Eastern radicals and the European radicals. Sageman's most controversial conclusions come from his study of this last group, which he states lacks the professionalism of prior waves. In so doing, Sageman largely discounts much of the discourse on the new terrorism and states that the current jihadi phenomenon is waning.

Homer-Dixon applies network analysis in a different manner, choosing instead the complex nature of modern societies as a subject for investigation.[219] He takes an opposite tack to most of the netwar school, and instead of focusing on the growth of capabilities in non-state groups, studies the growing vulnerabilities of modern states. Just as Arquilla and Ronfeldt apply network theory to terrorist organizations, Homer-Dixon views modernized states as networks of networks, a system of interconnected parts within a complex whole. These social, economic and political inter-connections serve to multiply the vulnerabilities of states through the production of 'feedback loops', or the propensity for disruptions in one aspect of a network to have echo effects across a number of interdependent nodes in the system. Thus, an attack on one system could have resounding effects across a number of other systems, effectively multiplying the destructive powers of non-state groups, which simultaneously are benefiting from technological advances in weapon systems.

As was stated previously, however, other researchers have broadened the notion of asymmetrical conflict and have drawn on a number of other attributes of conflict to address the relationship between states and insurgents. Stepanova explicitly defines terrorism as a form of asymmetrical conflict, yet states that there are three types of asymmetry.[220] The first asymmetry is that of power, and, according to Stepanova, it always favours the state. The second is an asymmetry of status, affording one party (almost always the state) a monopoly on legitimacy, not only at the domestic level but also internationally. Additionally, however, Stepanova takes note of a third type of asymmetry termed two-way asymmetries. Defined as vulnerabilities directly related to the strength of the dominant party, this asymmetry accrues to the advantage of the weaker side, because of ideological and structural disparities between terrorists and states.[221] These two-way asymmetries are fourfold. First, terrorists have an asymmetric ability to solve collective action problems.[222] This stems from a number of factors affecting the decision making of states fighting terrorist groups. Governments are overconfident and underestimate the need for interstate cooperation. Governments also often cannot agree on what constitutes a terrorist group. Finally, governments, specifically liberal democracies, usually make decisions based on electoral cycles and not on the long time horizons envisioned by Islamist terrorists. Second, Stepanova, echoing Homer-Dixon, points out that wealthy modern states represent an asymmetry of available targets. Third, states (at least, liberal democratic states) are restrained in their response to terrorist provocations, while terrorists appear to have no such restrictions. Fourth, terrorists have an asymmetry of knowledge regarding the states. Whereas governments often know very little about their non-state adversaries, terrorists are often very knowledgeable about the targeted state, its decision-making process, its human capital, its material weaknesses and its capabilities. Homer-Dixon's study is limited in its applicability because of his choosing to focus on state vulnerabilities rather than terrorist targeting, using as a point of illustration the North American rolling electricity blackouts of 2006, rather than an historical accounting of terrorist targeting of critical infrastructure. Thus, his study represents less of a risk analysis of modern society than a vulnerability assessment.

Among those mentioned in this section, Stepanova's work stands out in its holistic approach to asymmetric conflict, taking into account the relative advantages of both states and insurgents, expanding upon the unidimensional findings of Homer-Dixon while avoiding some of the hyperbole of Arquilla and Ronfeldt. It is therefore worth quoting Stepanova at some length:

> [T]he asymmetry dealt with here is a two-way asymmetry. One party to this asymmetrical confrontation is the state (and the international system in which states, despite the gradual erosion of some of other powers, remain key units). The state is faced with the toughest of its violent non-state anti-system opponents – the supranational, supra-state resurgent Islamist movement of the multilevel, hybrid network type. While the movement's ultimate utopian, universalist goals are unlikely to be realized, it can still spread havoc through its use of radical violent means, such as terrorism and especially mass-casualty terrorism. . . . This Research Report argues that these asymmetrical advantages of violent anti-system non-state actors employing terrorist means are their extremist ideologies and structures.[223]

Of all the authors mentioned above, Keohane applies the most esoteric use of asymmetry to the study of political violence in his analysis of theories of international relations in the wake of 11 September.[224] Terming such activity 'informal violence' in order to circumvent the definitional debate surrounding 'terrorism', Keohane uses the events of 11 September as an illustration of the shortcomings of mainstream international relations theories such as realism and liberalism, namely their relentless secularism, outdated concepts of geographic space and restricted notion of sovereignty.[225] According to Keohane, the significance of 11 September is that it proves that the information revolution has globalized informal violence in much the same way as the atomic revolution globalized state violence in the 1950s. This shrinking of geographic space brings the United States (or conceivably any superpower) into constant contact with hostile social forces at the same time as globalization itself creates friction between the United States, as hegemon, and those self-same forces. Thus, terrorism is empowered by globalization at the same time that it is a reaction against it. One of Keohane's more interesting contributions to Terrorism Studies is his contention that the threat of informal violence lies in the fact that it redefines the way theorists of international relations conceive of power. Conventional definitions conceptualize power as an 'asymmetry of interdependence', whereas informal violence exploits an asymmetry of vulnerability, stemming in turn from dual asymmetries of information and belief. In a similar vein to Stepanova's two-way asymmetries, asymmetry of information refers to the superior knowledge exercised by terrorists regarding their opponents than states exercise regarding terrorists. Asymmetries of belief, as described by Keohane, are slightly more abstract, and refer to the non-rational motivations behind terrorism, namely the theological imperatives of jihadist radicalism. Keohane does not state how these necessarily outweigh the rational desire for security emanating from states, however. In summation, Keohane notes that theorists of international relations have 'overemphasized states' and 'over-aggregated power', requiring a re-examination of international security in the information age which, according to the author will require an increasing emphasis on multilateral responses to insecurity rather than the unilateral application of traditional hard power.

Terrorism as communication

Terrorism can be conceptualized as a violent language of communication. Violence always demands attention – owing its life-threatening character – and impresses those at the receiving end as well as immediate and secondary witnesses. Communicative theories of terrorism focus on the persuasive and dissuasive effects of terminal violence or conditional violent intimidation of one group on various other witnessing audiences as well as the role of mass media in this signalling process. In *Violence as Communication: Insurgent Terrorism and the Western News Media*,[226] published originally in 1980, Schmid, the principal author of this volume, formulated a communication theory of terrorism, based on what the terrorists themselves had to say about terrorism as 'propaganda by the deed'.[227] He found that violence and propaganda have much in common. Violence often aims at behaviour modification by coercion. Propaganda aims at the same by persuasion. Terrorism can be seen as a combination of the two. Eugen Hadamovsky noted as early as 1933, in his book *Propaganda and National Power*, that '[p]ropaganda and violence are never contradictions. Use of violence can be part of propaganda'.[228] Terrorism, by using violence against one victim (group), seeks to intimidate, persuade and coerce others. The immediate victim is merely instrumental and victimization serves to achieve a calculated impact on a variety of audiences.[229]

Each act of terrorism is performed with an eye to sending a specific (set of) message(s) to impress or influence specific audiences in one way or another. The message to the adversary can be: this is only the beginning and we have plenty more prepared for you if you do not listen to us. The message to the constituency of the adversary can be: your government cannot protect you and you will be targeted again if you do not put pressure on your government to change its policies. The message to the victims and their families, in turn, can be: we have warned you before and you did not listen. That's why you have to pay the price. The message to those who identify with the victims because they share common characteristics can be: see what we can do, you had better change your ways or you will be next. The message to neutral audiences can be: you cannot be neutral: either you are with us or we are against you. The message to the terrorist's real or imagined constituency is likely to be: see what we can do for you, you had better join our ranks and increase your support for us. The message to sympathizers can be: we are the wave of the future, you had better support us or else. . . . The message to other terrorist groups might be: we are doing very well, why don't you either work for us or get out of the way? The message to members of the terrorist organization could be: we are capable of all that, let us do even more. Finally, the hidden message to the news media is likely to be: 'You had better report fully and accurately about what we do and why we do it. If you cooperate, we provide you with plenty more scoops. If not, some of your journalists will pay for it with their lives.' The relationship between terrorism and the media has been characterized by Brigitte Nacos, a journalist and a scholar herself, in these words: '[T]he news media and terrorists are not involved in a love story; they are strange bedfellows in a marriage of convenience'.[230]

One of the problems terrorists have is that different audiences have different needs, and one act of terrorism is unlikely to produce the desired message for all of them. Much depends on the selection of the target and the success of the terrorist attack itself. Even more depends on the momentum a series of attacks can generate during a terrorist campaign. Successful acts will attract new recruits, new sponsors and new sympathizers. Seen in this light, terrorism is a violent communication strategy whereby the violence creates news value, which in turn provides free publicity. That publicity might be largely unsympathetic, but bad publicity is still better than no publicity for an underground organization needing the cooperation of the mass media to draw attention to its existence. While a terrorist act might intimidate opponents and fill them with terror, the same act also serves to legitimize the terrorist cause among those who share the terrorist goals even if they do not fully approve of the methods chosen. Either way, the terrorist act propagates the movement's message to a wider audiences. With the arrival of the internet and its interactivity, terrorist groups (or their sympathizers and supporters) can fine-tune the message, and raise their profile by propaganda among sympathetic audiences. The speed with which the news of a terrorist atrocity spreads in society and across the globe is great, and millions can be reached in a matter of minutes, either indirectly, via the public and private media, or directly, through targeted messages on the internet. In a politically polarized environment, the terrorists, with their demands and deadlines (e.g. after a prominent kidnapping), can set the political agenda, can apply pressure on the government by releasing video footage of hostages pleading for their lives, and can win sympathy, respect and support from those who share their goals if not always approving of their methods. On the other hand, they can demoralize the public by showing people how impotent the government apparently is in fact against a clandestine enemy acting furtively from the underground. The news media, with their commercial news values, fall again and again for the propaganda of the terrorists, acting on well-established news selection principles such as 'If it bleeds, it leads' (meaning that violence is to be reported on the first page or as first item in the audio-visual media) or 'Good news is bad news and bad news is good news', meaning that negative stories sell more newspapers (or TV advertisements) than good, pro-social stories. As a public display of power over life and death, many acts of terrorism are high drama, making it almost irresistible for the media to report them. As one terrorist put it, 'We give the media what they need: newsworthy events. They cover us, explain our causes and this, unknowingly, legitimizes us.'[231] That legitimization bit might be wishful thinking, but in many ways the terrorists manage to hijack the news system again and again.

A communication theory of terrorism fits best the provocational terrorism of 'propaganda of the deed'. However, for other types of terrorism – terrorism as irregular warfare, terrorism as state repression, terrorism for criminal intimidation – its explanatory power becomes less. Nevertheless, since the publication of Schmid and de Graaf's *Violence as Communication* (1982), increasing use has been made of a communication theory approach to explain the rise of appeal of non-state terrorism, either as stand-alone terrorism in peacetime or as terrorism embedded in an ongoing low-intensity armed conflict. In either case, the media act as the global nervous system, and shocking violent news cynically produced by the terrorists greatly amplifies their power, as Bin Laden himself explained:

> Terror is the most dreaded weapon in [the] modern age and the Western media is mercilessly using it against its own people. It can add fear and helplessness in the psyche of the people of Europe and the United States. It means that what the enemies of the United States cannot do, its media is doing that.[232]

Already in 1996, Osama bin Laden had announced, 'God willing, you see our work on the news', viewing Western news media as his greatest allies. Despite the media's complicity in producing terror for the terrorists, a serious discussion about modifying our current news value system has yet to begin. A good starting point would be the introduction in public reporting of a distinction between bona fide news and malign pseudo-news, the latter being public performances that are staged for the purpose of forcing free access into the news system by means of violence (or the threat thereof) against civilians.

For a brief look at the importance of media and communication for Al-Qaeda, see Appendix 4.3 at the end of this chapter.

Social identity theory

Theories of social identity, as applied to terrorism studies, focus on the ways in which in-group identity formation influences an organization or social movement in the collective decision to resort to violence. At its most basic level, the process of identity formation requires that the in-group draw distinctions between themselves and others, highlighting the positive attributes of the in-group while simultaneously denoting the inferiority of out-group populations.[233] For identity formation to result in conflict, two processes need to occur: a formulation of group membership, and an articulation of cultural distance between groups, allowing for the dehumanization necessary to victimize out-groups. In each instance, the organization is a central tool for facilitating the trajectory towards collective violence.

Tajfel stipulates that group membership is determined by three components.[234] First, there is a cognitive component whereby the individual recognizes that he or she is part of a group. This is followed by an evaluative component wherein agents register that group membership has either a positive or a negative value. Finally, there is an emotional component where membership prompts either love or hate towards the in-group as well as rival populations. In the end, social identity is a result of these evaluations reinforced through the use of stereotypes.

Brannan *et al.* explain identity formation in the context of cultural difference, where emic (indigenous) attributes are contrasted with etic (outsider) points of view.[235] Group differentiation results from two factors:[236] social categorization (the process of increasing the similarities among members of the in-group while drawing distinctions between the in-group and the out-group, and social comparison (the process of defining a positive image of the in-group resulting in an in-group bias, and negative connotations for the out-group). The inevitable result of these processes is in-group favouritism and out-group discrimination.

Conflict, however, results not simply from in-group identity but from the differentiation of cultural attributes, resulting in social distance.[237] Hofstede puts forward five variables for characterizing national cultures.[238]

1   the significance of an individual group;
2   the differences in gender roles within the group;
3   the manner in which a group deals with inequality;
4   the degree of tolerance for the unknown held by members;
5   the trade-off between the long- and the short-term gratification of needs.

The additive component of these theories of social identity formation is that they articulate the psychological need for a rationalization for violence. Underscoring psychological theories of violence, social identity theorists concur that terrorists are not individually abnormal. Rather, they suffer from the same psychological aversions to violence as are found in the general population. Nevertheless, they are able to engage in violence via a process of redefining humanity, whereby the normal inhibitors of violence (empathy, sympathy, etc.) apply only to members of the in-group. If indeed identity formation is a key function of the radicalization process, then it merits meticulous research by students of (counter-)terrorism.

Insurgent terrorism: systemic level of analysis

Debates about terrorism at the systemic level of analysis invariably revolve around questions regarding the 'root causes' of terrorism. Oddly enough, structural feeders of violence have been harder to identify than casual observers might expect. Comparative studies experts and area study specialists have long held that structural attributes such as underdevelopment, autocratic political systems, the enabling environment of democratic political processes, and foreign intervention are responsible for creating the preconditions necessary for insurgent terrorism. However, broader studies controlling for a number of such relevant variables have found that terrorism flourishes in any number of environments and is perpetrated by a vast array of diverse agents by diverse means and for diverse ends. Indeed, the ranks of terrorist groups are filled with peoples of every class and ethnic background operating within and across a wide range of political environments. Nevertheless, a strong and diverse field of study has been developed around the investigation of systemic causes of insurgent violence. Fundamentally, the authors have discerned three primary categories of root causes plus a fourth which actually represents a fusion of the primary three. The primary classifications of structural feeders of violence are economic, political and cultural. However, the fourth category, globalization, carries with it economic, political and cultural attributes, yet nevertheless represents a phenomenon warranting separate consideration.

Economic theories of terrorism

Among the more popular theories of terrorism are those that try to link terrorism with economic underperformance, or marginalization. However, in fact the relationship between the two is far from obvious or direct. Gurr offered the first systematic analysis of the relationship between political violence and economic marginalization in his theory of 'relative deprivation'. Rather than illustrating a straightforward relationship between political violence and economic marginalization, Gurr's theory saw rebellion as a result of political frustration that in turn was derived from the gap between the perception of individual entitlement, and the reality of goal attainment.[239]

A number of external factors have the capacity to induce such discrepancies. Egypt's Islamist problem in the 1980s has been linked to the introduction of radically increased numbers of college graduates into a depressed labour market in the 1960s and 1970s, underscoring the fact that increasing educational attainment without a concomitant increase in employment opportunities can result in widespread discontent and potentially lead to terrorism – which has often been portrayed as a mode of fighting typical of the intelligentsia.[240] Alternately, situations in which two asymmetrically privileged groups coexist under the same national umbrella can lead to frustration on the part of either the 'aggrieved' or those who fear their privileged status might be in jeopardy. Tessier suggests that such an interplay between two such countervailing actors – the predominantly Hindu Tamils and Buddhist Sinhalese respectively – is to blame for the severity of the violence in the Sri Lankan context.[241]

Since the publication of Gurr's work, however, a number of notable small-*n* studies have challenged his findings. First, Berrebi's study of the biographies of 335 deceased Palestinian suicide bombers[242] discovered that only 16 per cent of the sample proved to have an income rated below the poverty line – while 31 per cent of Palestinians as a whole are classified as impoverished.[243] Further, Berrebi showed that of the sampled extremists, no fewer than 96 per cent had achieved a high school diploma, while a further 65 per cent had benefited from at least some form of higher education. This stands in stark contrast to the Palestinian population at large, only 51 per cent of whom have a high school education and only 15 per cent have some higher education.[244] Finally, Berrebi shows that unemployment itself was not a factor, as 94 per cent of the studied terrorists had employment, as opposed to only 69 per cent of the broader Palestinian population.[245] Counter-intuitively, Berrebi's evidence suggests that suicide bombers tend to be less deprived than the average Palestinian.[246] Krueger and Maleckova found similar patterns not only among Hezbollah members in Lebanon but also within the cadres of Israeli settlers who engaged in anti-Palestinian violence.[247] However, Li and Schaub's[248] criticism of the latter is applicable to the former as well. Since both works focus on groups operating in or against Israel, a generalization of their respective findings is questionable. Further, Li and Schaub postulate that the screening process for suicide terrorists could result in a selection bias that other forms of terrorist operations would not exhibit. Finally, these studies focus on the individual as a unit of analysis. When aggregated to a higher level, the findings may not hold.[249]

Rather than looking specifically at economic well-being as a static position of wealth attainment, some authors have rooted the origin of terrorism as a reaction to a lack of development, conceived of as a process. In other words, radicalism is less a reaction to a perceived state of underdevelopment than a result of a state's inability to achieve a reasonable rate of economic growth. Thus, non-state terrorism is not a result of poverty but a result of a lack of legitimacy on the part of the state – a symptom of government incompetence, corruption and/or ineffectiveness. This line of reasoning represents a substantial component of Li and Schaub's argument (explored in greater detail in the globalization section) regarding the impact of globalization on international terrorism.[250] Gerges, however, cautions against such a reductionist understanding of (specifically) Islamist sentiments and motivations by drawing attention to the case of Egypt, which, having achieved a substantial degree of economic reform by the mid-1990s, did not see support for the Egyptian Islamic Jihad and al-Jama'a wane.[251]

A prominent debate in contemporary Terrorism Studies has revolved around Sageman's contention that radicalization results not from relative but from 'vicarious deprivation'. Sageman thus effectively sidesteps the empirical debate surrounding the relationship between poverty and terrorism and states that it is neither an absolute nor a relative sense of impoverishment that drives terrorism and political violence, but, rather, an empathetic attachment with the dispossessed.[252] Sageman contends that this explains not only the lure for jihadism among the middle and professional classes, but also the prominence of Western left-wing radicals among the sons and daughters of middle- and upper-class parents. While Sageman's theory is plausible and even compelling, it still lacks broader social scientific testing. Operationalizing soft indicators such as measures of empathy proves more difficult than regressing simple events-based data against economic indicators. Suffice it to say the concept of vicarious deprivation, first introduced by Schmid in 1984,[253] still needs more rigorous testing.

Blomberg *et al.* utilize a more specific approach to the relationship between terrorism and economic standing in their analysis of internal threats to 'peaceful status quos'. In their analysis, such status quos are interrupted by violent organizations purporting to represent groups who want to increase either their share of material wealth or their agenda-setting power in the economic sphere.[254] This would qualify as a strict rational choice analysis of agent choice except for the fact that Blomberg *et al.* root the catalyst for such actions in negative external economic shocks.[255] Thus, endogenous attributes of terrorism, such as ideology, are merely rationalizations for aggressive rent-seeking behaviour, which in turn is made rational by negative externalities in the broader marketplace. To forward their point, Blomberg *et al.* break violence down into two forms, rebellion and terrorism. The former reflects a concerted effort to overthrow the government, and the latter represents a narrower form of violence performed by a small band whose purpose is to increase the economic voice of a group. Whether a given polity then suffers from terrorism or rebellion is, in Blomberg *et al.*'s view, a function of the relative strength of the state itself. Where the state is strong, one would expect to see terrorism, and where the state is weak, one would expect to find rebellion. This could explain why civil war is more often to be found in Africa and terrorism in Western liberal democracies. While this approach is interesting for its originality, it raises theoretical as well as methodological issues. Theoretically, by equating all desire for political influence with economic goals (since the former could lead to the acquisition of the latter), Blomberg's theory tends to be tautological. Using simple events data, researchers cannot disaggregate organizational motivations. Equally problematic is that Blomberg *et al.* use ITERATE data (which refer to international terrorism only, not domestic terrorism) as the basis for their analysis. This raises the question of how robust such findings may be, given that terrorism geared to promote agenda-setting power would most likely be targeting domestic political systems.

Political theories of terrorism: the democracy/authoritarian rule issue

Political theories of terrorism have traditionally revolved around questions regarding the enabling or motivational aspects of various regime types with respect to non-state violence. To put the matter succinctly, some theorists argue that certain attributes of democratic regimes make them more susceptible to terrorist violence, while others, notably those tied to policy circles, maintain that elements of authoritarian governance create grievances within radical populations (or even create the radical populations themselves), which in turn make terrorist activities more likely. Other avenues of investigation, while less visible in academic debates, have caused an equally large stir in policy circles. These studies focus on the relationship between 'state failure' and terrorism.

Gurr[256] was among the first to note that recourse to violence is more likely when individuals lack democratic avenues of goal attainment.[257] However, like the relationship between underdevelopment and terrorism, the effects of democratic systems on levels of terrorism and political violence have proved more amorphous than learned opinion would suggest. Schmid offered a theoretical framework for the inherent questions in this research, which can then be used to judge the empirical tests that have followed. He asserted that democracies have some strengths with which to avail themselves against the threat of terrorism. However, these advantages are largely offset by inherent vulnerabilities within not only democracies, but also the open market systems that often accompany them.[258] Among those attributes that democracies can count as strengths are free and fair elections, which reduces the need for political violence; an elite that is open to criticism and the concomitant recourse of public protest afforded to aggrieved communities; and independent judiciaries, with judges who often allow for the hearing of minority grievances even if elites are uninterested in or even hostile to such concerns.[259] In so far as the vulnerabilities of democracies are concerned, terrorists avail themselves of a freedom of movement not heard of in authoritarian states, a freedom of association that has proved conducive to the organization of underground societies, the proliferation of targets resulting from open societies, and the legal constraints imposed upon law enforcement in democratic regimes.[260] Additionally, Schmid also associated open markets with increased likelihood of terrorist operations. Among the attributes of capitalist economies are inequalities, which in turn fuel grievances, the diffusion of arms through a globalized arms industry, open borders that are ineffective barriers against smuggling operations (particularly in arms and people), and profit-based media that are drawn to violence, as it increases circulation and audiences.[261]

Eubank and Weinberg were the first to rigorously test the assumptions laid out by Schmid. To avoid the possibility of a selection bias in democratic countries that are more likely to allow terrorist violence to be reported than closed polities, Eubank and Weinberg opted to supplant events-based data with the presence or absence of terrorist organizations as a dependent variable.[262] Generally speaking, these authors found that one is 3.5 times more likely to encounter domestic terrorism in democratic than in non-democratic regimes.[263] Further, the following attributes of democratic systems were found to be highly correlated with terrorism: high civil rights indicators, the number of political parties, high levels of political protest, rapid economic growth, and high levels of wealth disparity[264] The first of these indicates that the relationship between terrorism and democratic governance largely revolves around the constraints imposed upon law enforcement by civil society. The second and third of these, the number of political parties and high levels of political protest, imply, one intuitively feels, that levels of political polarization and fragmentation are correlated with political violence. The fourth and fifth, rapid economic growth and high levels of wealth disparity, seem to undergird Schmid's assumptions regarding the radicalizing effects of open markets. Eubank and Weinberg are to be commended for bringing advanced statistical analysis into terrorism studies. However, their use of bivariate correlations does not adequately control for all relevant variables affecting the efficacy of terrorism, and thus leaves something to be desired in terms of robustness. Li conducted a more systematic evaluation of the links between terrorism and democracy, beginning with the assumption that empirical relations between terrorism and democracy did in fact exist (as had been ascertained by Eubank and Weinberg), but that these links had yet to be explored more rigorously.[265] Interestingly, Li finds that the presence or absence of democracy and an associated increase in terrorism is in fact a spurious correlation. In point of fact, it is institutional constraints on state action, which one often finds in democratic systems, that have a positive effect on levels of terrorist violence.[266] These facilitating institutional constraints are policy deadlock, which plays a hand in increasing the frustration of minority political movements, and the inability of law enforcement agencies to implement stringent counter-terror campaigns, as well as the fact that targeting civilians in democratic regimes is more effective for non-state terrorists as doing so tends to influence institutional behaviour more directly.[267] Theoretically, Li's careful analysis has yielded great insight into the nature of the relationship between regime type and non-state political violence. However, methodologically, there are significant shortcomings directly resulting from his use of ITERATE data in his research design. First, one must bring attention the selection bias inherent in this data set. Democracies are more likely to be more developed and as a result have more interests abroad. Thus, they are more likely to incur the ire of transnational terrorist movements. Second, autocratic systems would be more likely to incur the wrath of domestic groups. These would not be picked up by the ITERATE data. Finally, Li's analysis ignores the theoretical argument made by those who encourage democratization as a panacea against terror. This argument states that given democratic alternatives to air political grievances, individuals will be less tempted to engage in political violence. International terrorist organizations, however, are often playing to other than the domestic political system. As Schmid held, the proper functioning of a democratic system will inhibit domestic terrorism, while simultaneously leaving open democratic societies more open to threats from abroad.[268] Thus, a research design utilizing only ITERATE data does not adequately test the notion that democracy has a pacifying effect.

State failure, as a concept, has for better or worse been tied to the discourse on terrorism following the attribution of the 11 September attacks on the United States to Al-Qaeda, an organization that used the respective sanctuaries of Sudan and Afghanistan as staging areas for a series of terrorist actions against US interests, including the 9/11 attacks. The basic idea behind the state failure concept is that terrorist organizations take advantage not only of the geographic sanctuary provided by the near-collapse of effective governance, but also of the black markets that spring up to replace licit enterprises, giving terrorist organizations a convenient vehicle to both earn and transfer funds as needed. The robustness of this case, however, is inevitably tied not only to the definition of state failure but also to the selectivity of case studies. While caveats might be raised regarding the appropriateness of tying transnational terrorism to state failure, a more concrete correlation can be drawn between state disintegration and the rise of warlordism, a form of political violence distinct from terrorism, yet utilizing terrorism as a mainstay of political control.

One of the best definitions of state failure has been provided by Rotberg, who states that failed states are

> convulsed by internal violence and can no longer deliver positive political goals to their inhabitants. Their governments lose legitimacy, and the very nature of the particular nation state itself becomes illegitimate in the eyes and in the hearts of the growing plurality of its citizens.[269]

Rotberg is careful not to draw sharp distinctions between functioning and non-functioning governments, but instead suggests that there are gradations of state capacity to deliver political goods. These variations in turn differentiate between strong and weak states, and weak and failed states.[270] Furthermore, Rotberg establishes a hierarchy of political goods, with security being the most important. While other goods and services, such as the rule of law, the protection of private property, political participation, and the establishment and maintenance of critical infrastructure, are necessary for the proper functioning of a strong state, the provision of security is a precondition for all others.[271] Strong states are able to produce all of these goods, and weak states do so only unevenly. Failed states are unable to guarantee security, and the result is an erosion of all other services as well.[272] Some weak states perform poorly in all categories and subsequently fail. Others maintain strong security at the expense of all other goods.[273] Collapsed and failed states exhibit chronic insecurity, rule (in so far as rule is possible) by a parochial elite, and a symptomatic steep decline in GDP.[274]

Contrary to the claims of many scholars, Krasner[275] holds that state failure is actually quite a rare phenomenon, and one which terrorists have yet to exploit fully. According to Rotberg, only Somalia currently qualifies as a full-scale failed state. The arguments regarding the relationship between Al-Qaeda and Sudan and Afghanistan respectively do not hold according to even loose criteria for state failure. Both were experiencing severe internal conflict during the times in which they hosted Bin Laden, but the activities of Al-Qaeda therein almost always took place well within the bounds of the authority of Khartoum and Kabul, respectively. The only other potential example would be the use of Lebanon's Bekaa Valley by the PLO and associated organizations. However, even these activities took place under the auspices of Syria and with the blessing of Damascus. Thus, in all cases we are dealing with state-sponsored terrorism rather than organizations operating in the grey areas between governance and chaos. The argument that Afghanistan under the Taliban was more of a terrorist-sponsored state than a state sponsoring terrorism is a potential riposte to this criticism, but the importance of Al-Qaeda (with its fewer than 1,000 members before 9/11) for the Taliban has generally been overestimated.

Located somewhere in between state and guerrilla violence is warlordism, a form of political violence that has evolved hand in glove with the failure of state governance in some geographic spaces. Utilizing extreme terrorism as a matter of course, warlordism, according to Rich, represents the breakdown of formal modes of war and the introduction of informal and more complex modes of conflict.[276] This form of political violence is characterized by discipline and by a hierarchy localized around a single personality, who orders wanton and systematic violence as a vehicle for maintaining power. Under warlords, authority structures are of either an authoritarian/tribal or a hierarchic/gangster type. Warlords are different from revolutionaries in that they do not aim to supplant the state, in a Weberian sense. In some instances, they may actually avoid doing so, as they do not wish to inherit the civil service responsibilities inherent in such a role.[277] As Chan states, warlordism does not necessarily evolve as other forms of political violence do. It is not a conscious strategy of rebellion. Warlords fill a vacuum left by the state, and supplant state institutions with their own institutions and rituals, often out of realist necessity.[278] And yet, warlordism is more than organized criminal violence, as the ability to undertake illicit economic activity is in fact tied to the ability to exercise political control over specific territory. This political control is garnered through the systematic and copious use of terrorism.

Cultural theories of terrorism

Cultural theories of terrorism are, for obvious reasons, among the weakest of the structural theories of terrorism. Many revolve around what Mamdani refers to as the 'good Muslim–bad Muslim' debate,[279] which is actually less a theory than a meta-disciplinary critique of a series of counter-terror policies aimed at de-radicalization efforts pitting moderates and non-violent Salafists against jihadis. More interesting approaches look at the ways in which terrorist organizations assess and manipulate cultural processes in order to further their radical agenda. Walter Laqueur was the first to assume that culture played a hand in radicalism when he asserted that terrorism is always inherently populist, and by extension is an outgrowth of the cultural Zeitgeist of the moment.[280] This observation is valid; however, one might ask how some of the early nihilist and anarchist terrorists, who operated with little, if any, popular support, fit into this framework. Tololyan takes a more specific tack and conceives of terrorism as a social act produced by societies, with the terrorist him- or herself being socially constructed within a specific social context.[281] The researcher uses the case of Armenian terror and examines this phenomenon through the lens of 'projective narrative'.[282] These narratives use stories of the past to develop outlines for future action. This has the effect of elevating contemporary actions of 'transcendent collective values'. According to Tololyan, this approach addresses a shortcoming in political science in that it reduces all actions to political (read instrumental) acts.[283] This diminishes the complexity of social phenomena, and this reduction in turn lacks the concept of 'mediation', or past events which have become not merely political events but cultural narratives that have an element of morality attached to them. This line of reasoning may explain the longevity of certain groups that are able to tap into cultural narratives as a justification for violence. As the author states, 'Terrorism that has an authentically popular base is never a purely political phenomenon.'[284] How one assesses this assertion empirically is another question.

Globalization and terrorism

Disentangling globalization from other potential structural feeders of terrorism is difficult, as it has political, economic, and cultural features. Further, the nature of the effect of globalization on terrorism has proven difficult to pin down. Some argue that transnational terrorism is a reaction to globalization, others that local terrorism globalizes as the world does.[285] Thus, it is both a motivation for and an enabler of terror. It serves as a motivation for violence in so far as it promotes the cultural and economic interpenetration some scholars have cited as the main impetus behind the current wave of transnational violence.[286] It is an enabler of violence in that globalization not only allows for the movement of persons but also permits the global diffusion of potentially destructive technologies. Lia argues that terrorists are empowered by globalization in terms of geographic scope as well as destructive capabilities. Thus, while they are symptomatic of globalization, they are also important international actors, and thus affect globalization in their own right.[287] According to Lia, the future of globalization is central to the future of terrorism, as political violence is the result of both permissive and countervailing forces. To understand the future of terrorism, we must understand how future societal developments may affect these forces and, by extension, terrorism.[288] Lia broadens the scope of his study, however, as he maintains that these permissive and countervailing forces affect all forms of collective violence. Thus, it is of little use to look at terrorism in isolation from other forms of political activism, as they share the same underlying causality.[289] Lia ranks a series of causal relationships with respect to terrorism. Those variables that can be adversely affected by globalization are relative deprivation and inequality, the contagion theory, mass media and terrorism, rapid modernization, democratization, the ecology of terrorism,[290] hegemony, and economic and cultural globalization. Mass-casualty terrorism is also affected by globalization, as it is largely a function of social geometry, since massive violence is more likely when there is greater social distance between affected groups.[291] This is why homogeneous societies experience only rare terrorism. At present, globalization decreases physical distance but not social distance. Fawaz Gerges echoes the social geometry argument by stating that the internationalization of the jihad was necessary to re-energize the movement at a point at which it was beginning to weaken.[292]

Li and Schaub were the first to offer a thorough quantitative evaluation of the relationship between globalization and terrorism through an analysis of various national-level indicators (trade, foreign direct investment, and financial capital flows) and their effects on levels of transnational terrorism.[293] Like Lia, Li and Schaub differentiate between the countervailing theoretical arguments made with respect to terrorism and globalization. Theoretically, according to the authors, globalization acts as an enabler of terrorism, driving down the costs of terrorist campaigns relative to other forms of political action. Alternatively, however, globalization tends to promote the economic development necessary to deprive local radical organizations of their recruitment base.

The theory supporting the relationship between globalization and an increase in terrorism rests upon the assumption that terrorist activities depend on three factors: the relative costs of legal and illegal activity, the relative gains expected from legal as against illegal activity, and the resources available to the group in question.[294] Further, the authors assume that globalization results in three trends that adversely affect the aforementioned values: increased trade, resulting in increased smuggling; increased financial flows, resulting in more funding and laundering opportunities for terrorist networks; and increased foreign investment, resulting in a concentration of foreign targets, specifically making transnational incidents more likely.

In short, Li and Schaub postulate that groups operating in countries with relatively high levels of integration into the global economy will find terrorism more expedient than groups operating in more isolated locales. The findings, however, proved counter-intuitive, as Li and Schaub discerned no correlation between transnational terrorism and levels of economic globalization.[295] Further, as stated previously in this chapter, the authors did find a negative correlation between transnational terror and the level of economic development in a country. Thus, in so far as globalization enables development, the spread of global markets could have the indirect effect of lowering levels of international terrorism.

Li and Schaub's findings are intriguing, and their methodological astuteness enables them to control for a number of shortfalls that have plagued previous work. However, their theory tests only one aspect of the relationship between globalization and transnational terrorism – globalization as a technological enabler of violence. It takes for granted the motivation for political violence. Since their study does not speak to motivation, it stands to reason that domestic terrorism should be empowered as much as transnational groups. However, Li and Schaub use ITERATE data, which cover only transnational events. As Dugan, LaFree and Fogg have pointed out, ITERATE contains only a fraction of the events contained in global databases such as WITS or GTD, which include both domestic and international events.[296] Thus, it remains to be seen whether Li and Schaub's findings hold in an analysis using a more representative sample. Additionally, the research design utilized does not adequately address all theoretically relevant hypotheses regarding the relationship between terrorism and globalization. Neo-imperialist or cultural globalization arguments should utilize both domestic and transnational events data. What is also necessary is a dyadic level of analysis disaggregating indicators of economic globalization by country of origin, and focusing on transnational events directed against the 'encroaching' power. At present, such an examination has yet to be carried out.

The dyadic level of analysis: theories of counter-terrorism

Many, perhaps even most, theories of terrorism do not approach the phenomenon in terms of interactions between terrorists and their opponents. Yet as Crenshaw stated, the very nature of the conflict between the state and the insurgents is defined by the state's response, as it defines the nature and structure of the conflict, frames the realm of possible action and defines the issues at stake and the grounds for terminating the conflict.[297] Theories of counter-terrorism, on the other hand, tend to focus more on the interplay between action and counter-reaction, on the part of the state as well as of the challenging organization. Lum *et al.* have attempted to evaluate the state of the discipline in counter-terrorism studies utilizing a Campbell review process.[298] This review found that counter-terror theories could be delineated into four broad categories according to state strategy: preventive measures, detection-oriented measures, managerial measures and response-oriented measures. The review found a number of shortcomings. First, the largest single topic (18.9 per cent of all articles) is the threat of weapons of mass destruction (WMD), a strategy of terrorism that has proved exceedingly rare. The second largest volume of work did not address counter-terrorism per se but rather dealt with specific issues such as the Palestinian–Israeli conflict. Third, the literature reflected political responses to terrorism. And finally, sociological studies of terrorism were the fourth largest category, focusing on motivations for violence, root causes for radicalization, and the like. Ultimately, Lum *et al.* found few empirical evaluations of the legal aspect of terrorism, or of state responses to terrorism. Because of these short-comings, Lum *et al.* proposed an evidence-based strategy to appraise counter-terror policies and state responses to terrorism in general.

This section utilizes their framework to evaluate those theories of counter-terrorism that use state action as the unit of analysis, taking into account the strategic nature of the dyadic level of analysis.

Preventive counter-terrorism

Preventive counter-terrorism focuses on establishing obstacles between terrorists and their objectives. These obstacles can be in the form of defensive measures, law enforcement capabilities, legal reform, etc. Several authors, including Paul Bremer, hold that terrorism will never be completely stamped out. Therefore, the ends of counter-terrorism are to reduce terror to such levels that they no longer seriously divert attention away from other policy matters.[299] Accordingly, the end of preventive measures is invariably to raise the costs of terrorism relative to other modes of political expression and conflict waging. Thus, it focuses less on the destruction of the organization in question and more on complicating the strategy of terrorism *writ large*.

Among the best theories of preventive counter-terrorism are Martha Crenshaw's investigations of instrumental and organizational counter-terrorism. Instrumentalism, as previously discussed, is based on rational choice theory and takes as its crux for counter-terrorism the concept of 'substitution'.[300] Assuming that terrorism is a rational strategy geared towards maximizing an agent's expected utility, one also assumes that terrorism is but one of several potential avenues for political agitation. Substitution occurs when either the probability of successfully completing a terrorist act relative to other political acts becomes extremely low, or the costs of terrorism compared to other political strategies become relatively high. Thus, a radical is prompted to substitute his or her choice to pursue terrorism with a less destructive alternative with a higher success rate and/or a lower price tag.

There are two main types of counter-terrorism promulgated by instrumentalism: defence and deterrence.[301] Both of these strategies are geared specifically towards lowering the likelihood of successfully completing a terrorist attack. By defence, Crenshaw is referring to '[f]orcefully preventing an enemy from attaining physical objectives'.[302] Defensive measures can be either active or passive. Active measures include pre-emptive or preventive uses of force, differentiated by the time lag between the state action and the likely manifestation of the terrorist threat. A pre-emptive action is a move against an organization that is believed to be in the final stages of planning an attack. Preventive action is taken against organizations that are believed to pose a threat at some undetermined point in the future. Passive measures do not include the overt use of force, but rather actions that reduce the probability that a terrorist action will be successful. Such measures include target hardening and the imposition of border controls, etc. Deterrence as a strategy seeks to raise the costs of terrorism in an effort to promote substitution by less expensive forms of political protest. The two most common strategies of deterrence are denial and retaliation. The former is similar in practice to passive defence. However, it is not intended to make terrorism impossible, merely to raise the costs of terrorist strategies. Retaliation is more straightforward. Retaliatory acts can be either symmetrical or asymmetrical, but they must be weighed against the knowledge that provoking retaliation is a major strategy of terrorist violence.

A major problem with counter-terror policies that are aimed at substitution is that these can backfire on the counter-terror practitioner in one of two ways. Either they can prompt escalation as opposed to de-escalation, or they can result in transference instead of substitution.[303] If no other avenue is open to a terrorist organization, then it is likely that increasing the desperation of the terrorists will result in an escalation of violence, as there are no political alternatives. Transference occurs when a terrorist shifts tactics as opposed to strategies and opts for softer targets rather than alternative political activity.[304] In addition to tactical transference, it can also be temporal (wherein the organization lies low until such time as terrorism is more cost-effective), or geographic (a shift to locales where terrorism is more cost-effective). In order to reduce the chances of transference, governments must either make all modes of attack more difficult, or deplete the human, financial and material resources of the terrorist group.[305]

Organizational process theory moves away from the effects of state action on the rational calculus of individuals and concentrates on the ways in which state action can exacerbate internal turmoil within organizations. Crenshaw begins by positing that there are two reasons for organizational decline: exit and voice.[306] Exit occurs when individuals or small cadres either leave the violent struggle altogether or, more likely, either splinter into new organizations or join rival factions.[307] Voice refers to the internal process of vocalizing dissent.[308] Almost all organizations strongly discourage voice, as underground movements place a high premium on ideological conformity. In some of the more extreme ideological organizations, voicing opposition is all but impossible. Crenshaw explicitly states that the key vulnerability of violent organizations is the inability to attract and retain (new) members rather than the inability of a group to achieve political goals.[309] Thus, counter-terrorism should address the recruitment and retention rates of terrorist organizations. The two main avenues open to states in this respect would be affecting exit through amnesty programmes, proactively draining recruitment pools, and provoking schisms within and among clandestine organizations.

In a similar vein, Ross and Gurr argue that levels of terrorism are a result of group decisions. These decisions, in turn, reflect the socio-political environment in which the group operates. As a result, the decline or increase of terrorism is the result of common dynamics applicable to all groups, past, present and future. In short, terrorist groups die as their capabilities are eroded, either by state action or by the interaction of different intra-group factions.[310] The three major causes of organizational decline, according to Ross and Gurr, are pre-emption, deterrence and burnout.[311] Thus, while they focus on organizational decision making, they utilize the agent choice model Crenshaw applies to her instrumentalist approach. To this they add 'burnout', another term for exit that is sparked by factionalization, a growing risk aversion with the organization, a shift in organizational objectives from political action to predation, as well as a backlash against less than productive attacks.[312] Ross and Gurr are less specific, however, in their delineation of specific state strategies that may exacerbate these processes to the benefit of the counter-terrorist.

Managerial responses to terrorist violence

Managerial responses to terrorism include crisis management. However, these theories mostly deal with the practical aspects of public policy – that is, getting power grids back up after an attack, reopening transport terminals, treating victims, and the like. More interesting for a dyadic evaluation of terrorist versus counter-terrorist interactions are those theories dealing with political responses to terrorism. As Bremer states, rather than engaging terrorist organizations only directly, the strategic objective of counter-terrorism should be to make the political, economic and psychological environments in which terrorists operate more hostile to terrorist organizations.[313] His application of this far-reaching approach is, however, more narrow, as he demurs that the target of counter-terrorism then is not the terrorists themselves, but the 'community of nations and the overall strategic environment in which terrorists must act'.[314] Logically, then, the main crux of US counter-terror, once it shed its defensive posture left over from the 1970s, was to put pressure on governments that sponsor terrorism, and to erode the legitimacy of terrorism as a mode of political action.[315] This implies dealing with terrorists with judicial systems and treating the actors themselves as criminals. While Bremer's comments have theoretical weight, they are framed in such a way as to impute that the threat of terrorism is a state–centric issue, a stance that stands in contrast to a substantial body of scholarly research on terrorism.

Nevertheless, terrorist organizations are embedded in their relative environmental circumstance. The exogenous structures to which they are exposed both constrain and enable political violence. Finding mechanisms that strengthen the former and disable the latter is the subject of a wide body of literature on counter-terrorism. For instance, Karin von Hippel echoes calls for a structural approach to counter-terrorism. Like others, she holds that a multilateral, long-term response to terrorism is the best way to erode this type of violence in the long run.[316] Drawing from Weinberg's emphasis on the fact that terrorism is the result of long-term indoctrination and training, Von Hippel draws attention to the 'root causes' debate and claims – correctly – that counter-terrorist theorist have not appropriately addressed these.[317] She is, in the end, however, reluctant to propose a single course of state action, as all pertinent 'root causes' of terrorism either are only ambivalently supported by empirical research, or represent trends that are extremely difficult for state action to speak to. The first of these is poverty, whose direct relationship to terrorism, as the structural section of this chapter has already illustrated, is not supported by empirical research. The same can be said for the second – education. However, Von Hippel proposes that the content of education needs to be reformed, as the issue is not an increase in an average level of attainment. Assessing the impact of educational content on radicalization is, unfortunately, more difficult than straightforward analyses of grade-level attainment among radicals. There are a number of possible root causes of terrorism addressed by Von Hippel. Al-Qaeda in particular has proved astute at using grievances to gain footholds in foreign territories. Fundamentalist charities have also proved a boon to transnational terrorists, specifically jihadis exploiting the *zakat* system. Since *zakat* must be given discreetly, to avoid the humiliation of recipients, reform in this sector is made difficult. Cracking down on aid distribution, rather than charitable giving, however, is a useful avenue for reform and could bear many of the same fruits as end-user certificates have afforded the non-proliferation community. Further, addressing the social and economic marginalization of diasporas in Western countries could possibly reduce transnational recruitment.

Gompert and Gordon draw attention to the need to correctly frame state responses to violence in political terms. Stating that the 'global war' is the idea of the jihadists, the United States should try to diffuse this concept, not try to fight and win a war defined by its opponent, as this invariably plays into the jihadists' hands.[318] Instead, these authors suggest that the response should be defined as a global counter-insurgency. Insurgencies, according to Gompert and Gordon, have structural predictors, which are currently present in the Muslim world.[319] Effective counter-insurgency, then, should seek to address these structural predictors rather than just try to erode the material capabilities of the rebel organizations in question. These predictors are a lack of representative government, inept or corrupt government, insurgents committed to destroying regional governments, and a significant popular base of support for the insurgency. To undermine these factors, the authors suggest three counter-insurgency strategies.[320] The first of these is a carrot-and-stick approach based on a conditional distribution of civil services to local populations. The second is a 'hearts and minds' strategy based on a generous sharing of public services. Finally, Gompert and Gordon suggest 'transformation', by which they mean the creation of governance structures that undermine the rationale for insurgency. Many of such suggestions stumble, however, on the issue of sovereignty. While domestic governments have the ability to manipulate internal policy in such a way, outside powers can usually do so only by routeing aid and technical assistance through the very corrupt and inept powers that gave rise to the insurgency to begin with. Alternately, transformation can be effected by regime change or political pressure, both of which are easily construed as hegemonic arrogance, once again playing into the terrorists' hands.

It is useful to note, however, that the above-mentioned political responses are meant to speak to macro-level grievances rather than the (typically) more specific goals of terrorist groups. This is due to the fact that a response to root causes of violence should not be misconstrued as a call to engage terrorists in a quid pro quo that could be mistaken for concessions. As Crenshaw notes, the topic of concessions is a tricky one with potentially counter-productive results.[321] Not only could such activity represent a severe loss of face for the state, but it also signals to future terrorist groups that terrorism pays.[322] Further, the granting of concessions only after radicals resort to violence, can be counter-productive, as under these circumstances it not only undermines the authority of the state and hands the insurgents an easily recognizable victory, but also grants authority and legitimacy, if not to the terrorists themselves, then at least to their goals and aims.[323]

Crelinsten takes a markedly different approach in advocating political reactions to terrorism. His is a communication-driven theory of counter-terrorism.[324] He divides modes of political activism along an axis into deviance, dissent, crime and revolution, and assigns a corresponding mode of political control for each of these activities. The standard government responses range on the same axis from social control, to government, to criminal justice, to internal war, respectively.[325] If these modes of provocation and control can be arranged along two parallel structures, then communication can be said to take place up and down (with government institutions and political dissidents speaking to those directly above or below them), diagonally (police dealing with protesters as well as criminals), as well as horizontally (radicals dealing with rival groups).[326] If communication channels to the left are blocked by state action, activists might opt for movement to the right. Thus, state policies can potentially have an escalatory effect.[327] However, effectively blocking violent avenues can make dissidents move left across the spectrum to less destructive modes of political activism. The critical juncture, according to Crelinsten, lies between the activist choices of crime and revolution, and the concomitant state responses of criminal justice and internal war. This point is called the mobilization threshold. As radicals move to the right, they pass through political crime, insurgent terrorism and insurrection stages before moving into revolution. The state counters each individual stage with a movement rightward of its own, from political justice, to state terrorism, to counter-terrorism, and then to internal war.[328] The horizontal axis Crelinsten devised reminds one of the spectrum of political action Alex Schmid developed in the early 1980s – a revised version of which was presented earlier in this volume.

Response-oriented measures

Response-oriented measures taken by states are broadly, if somewhat misleadingly, referred to as retaliation. Brian Jenkins draws attention to the fact that how states view the insurgent problem determines the nature of the state response. Echoing the strategic concerns of a dyadic level of analysis, he stipulates that if the state does not understand how the insurgent views the conflict, then the state reaction can actually play into the terrorist's hands.[329] By way of illustration, Jenkins draws attention to the disconnect between US policy and Al-Qaeda's objectives. Accordingly, he states that the US approach to terrorism defines actors in terms of actions, not in terms of motives.[330] Al-Qaeda's violence and rhetoric, however, are geared towards formulating a transnational Islamist identity based on a Manichean clash-of-civilizations paradigm.[331] Jenkins holds that the failure to view the purpose of Al-Qaeda's strategy has meant that the United States unwittingly conceptualizes the war on terror in terms that mirror those of the jihadist terrorists. Further, there is a temporal disconnect between the two belligerents. Al-Qaeda does not view the conflict in the same finite temporal modes that the United States does. For the United States, the conflict began with 9/11 and will end at some point in time. For Al-Qaeda, it began long ago and continues to be ongoing, though the enemy will change faces.[332] Thus, the 'genius' of Al-Qaeda is that it utilizes a salient ideological message to mobilize those who are discontented with the current status quo (conceived of in macro terms).[333] US responses to Al-Qaeda that project American hegemony, such as the invasion of Iraq, inadvertently reinforce the message of Al-Qaeda. However, as the invasion of Afghanistan has shown, terrorist organizations must walk a fine line between inciting reactions that aid in organizational recruitment, and inciting reactions that result in the destruction of the organization. Al-Qaeda's leadership did not expect the strong US reaction to its provocation of 11 September 2001, and was arguably saved from destruction chiefly by the US invasion of Iraq.

Crenshaw states that an incumbent power (defined as the state) has three ways in which to view captured terrorists: as political criminals, as common criminals and as prisoners of war.[334] Each choice carries with it particular strategies of counter-terrorism ranging from political repression, to law enforcement, to paramilitary reactions. Crenshaw articulates that incumbent powers have two broad limitations with respect to counter-terror operations.[335] The first of these are limitations imposed by constituencies. Whereas terrorists generally have only potential constituents, states have a multitude of vested interests that could be affected by any number of counter-terror strategies. The second of these are limitations imposed on regimes regarding the ways in which they can employ force. Specifically, democratic regimes are constrained to socially acceptable forms of counter-terror activities. Ultimately, Crenshaw states that there are three broad determinants of the state's response.[336] First, institutional realities have to be taken into account, as the internal decision-making arrangements of the system have a profound impact on the state's choice of retaliatory measures. Second, a state must take into account international opinion, as this has the potential to create political and material support bases for terrorists. Finally, the military establishment has an impact on state responses –

specifically, the proximity of the military to centralized decision making, the institutional culture of the military establishment, and, of course, the material capabilities of the military have an effect on potential strategies of counter-terrorism. While the approach is inherently broad, Crenshaw offers a framework for evaluating counter-terror responses outside the narrow scope of Western responses to Salafist jihadism, and lays the groundwork for empirical evaluations of counter-terror strategies.

Perhaps no other form of terrorism challenges government counter-terrorism policies more than ethnic terrorism.[337] As was previously noted, when governments face ethno-nationalist sentiments the provocation of governmental overreaction is a central aim of the insurgent organization. Broad and blind retaliation fosters community identity among the targeted population on whose behalf the terrorists operate, or claim to operate. It also raises the visibility of the aggrieved community, marginalizes moderate political forces and often leads to uncontrolled vigilantism. As a result, traditional counter-terrorism is often futile, if not downright counter-productive.[338] If the terrorist group sees itself as instrumental to cultural survival, then attempts to delegitimize it through moral outrage alone fail. Conventional law enforcement often does not work since it must be public to be effective, but publicity often tends to serve the interests of the insurgents. Likewise, crackdowns play into the terrorist group's hands. Concessions as well as intransigence can create incentives for future violence. According to Daniel Byman, there are but three counter-terror options when dealing with ethno–nationalist movements:[339]

1   Governments can attempt to manipulate identities as well, such as through the promulgation of nationalism.
2   Governments can implement sweeping punishment across the ethnic community as a whole in an attempt to dissuade these groups from providing assistance to the terrorists.
3   Finally, governments can promote in-group policing.

The first of these options has proved very difficult, as governments have a limited ability to promote identity formation. The second of these options, as previously discussed, tends to radicalize communities and can also play into terrorist hands. The final method, in-group policing, is often the most adequate,[340] as it simultaneously places the onus of counter-terrorism on the ethnic community itself (thus deflecting blame from the government) while utilizing the presumed support network of the terrorist organization as the instrument of its defeat. Where this third strategy has been properly implemented, it has proved generally effective against ethnic terrorists.

A strategy of deterrence, through the threat of retaliation, is strongest when addressing organizations with extensive infrastructure and interests, which can be held to ransom. Thus, it is best utilized when addressing the problem of foreign state sponsorship of an insurgency. Whereas targeting the interests, personnel and material capabilities of terrorist organizations might prove difficult for states with asymmetric top-sight in regard to their non-state opponents, terrorist-group-sponsoring states represent target-rich environments for the application of both soft and hard power. Byman notes that the target state's counter-terror response needs to be geared to the specific motivation a sponsoring state has in aiding the group in question, but should also address the social, political and economic challenges faced by the belligerent state.[341] Byman's delineation of rationalizations for state sponsorship of terrorist groups has been listed in the section dealing with state terrorism. From this list, he has extrapolated a series of counter-terrorism measures geared towards offsetting any interest a rival regime may have in sponsoring terrorist organizations.[342] These include engaging the sponsor in a diplomatic manner; the extreme option of regime change; the punitive use of force, though on a smaller scale than regime change; the credible threat of force; economic sanctions; backing an insurgent organization against the sponsoring regime (if one is to be found); and diplomatic isolation. The more salient motivations for state sponsorship will require more extreme measures to offset, whereas economic or marginal rationalizations for insurgent sponsorship might be offset by more modest applications of soft power.

Conclusion

If we look at the theories that have been discussed in this chapter, one cannot fail to see (and deplore) the lack of common ground. Partly this is due to the absence of a generally accepted definition of terrorism and the conceptual stretching of 'terrorism' into many other forms of political violence and conflict waging. Partly it is also due to the fact that the scientific discussion of terrorism has been influenced strongly – and negatively – by the politicized discourse on terrorism. Despite much theorizing, there is no general theory of terrorism. If it existed, it would have to be a sub-theory of general theories of violence and conflict. Most theorizing not only fails to make that link, but is even negligent of the obvious link between non-state terrorism and governmental counter-actions. How scattered thinking on terrorism is comes out most clearly when one looks at the root cause debate – in a way, the heart of the theoretical discussion of terrorism. Here the wide variety of alleged root causes of terrorism illustrates how far apart academic and political observers of the phenomenon of terrorism still stand. However, this situation is not unique; the same applies to theories of crime and theories of war.

The reader will find two catalogues of alleged root causes of terrorism in two of the three appendices to this chapter. One is based on findings from the Club de Madrid conference in March 2005 – one of the largest ever gatherings of eminent academics and political leaders.[343] There were five workshops addressing the root causes of terrorism. They came up with nearly 50 (partly overlapping) causes of, and risk factors contributing to, terrorism.

A recent review of the literature by Brynjar Lia, an eminent Norwegian researcher, lists a similar number of causes or factors (46, while the Club of Madrid listed altogether 48 causal factors) in three categories. Most of these hypothetical causes and factors have never been tested empirically. Many of them are, in fact, not testable in their present formulations. They are brought together here to provide researchers with an inventory in the hope that more of them will be empirically tested.

Any reader of these two appendices might at this point well-nigh despair in the face of this multitude of possible explanations to the simple question 'why terrorism?'. Yet the situation is not altogether hopeless. One has to keep in mind that, as Tore Bjørgo, the editor of the volume *Root Causes of Terrorism: Myths, Reality and Ways Forward*,[344] noted:

> Because there are different types of terrorism with highly disparate foundations, there are very diverse types of causes and levels of causation. The notion that there is one single 'prime mover' behind terrorism is therefore not tenable. . . . What seems likely is that certain forms of terrorism are outcomes of certain combinations of factors: some of which may be more fundamental than others.[345]

Bjørgo, summarizing the findings of the contributors to his volume, distinguished between the following:

- *structural causes* (demographic imbalances, globalization, rapid modernization, transitional societies, increasing individualism with rootlessness and atomization, relative deprivation, class structure, etc.);
- *facilitator (or accelerator) causes*, such as the evolution of modern mass media, transportation, weapons technology, weak state control of territory, etc.;
- *motivational causes* – the actual grievances that people experienced at a personal level, motivating them to act;
- *triggering causes*, such as a political calamity, an outrageous act committed by the enemy, or some other events that call for revenge or action.[346]

This typology of causal factors is sound, and indicates that it is possible to bring some order in the often chaotic debate on the causes of (non-state) terrorism. Despite the shortcomings alluded to above, all in all, the theory formation in the field of Terrorism Studies has to a considerable degree matured since Schmid first summarized the state of theory formation in the 1980s.[347] Yet there is still a long way to go. What needs to be done to reach a better understanding of terrorism can be summarized in ten postulates regarding research quality desiderata:

1 more and better comparative case studies of terrorist organizations based on (anthropological) fieldwork in conflict zones;
2 more and better historical and longitudinal research into terrorist groups, their decision making and their life cycles in the nineteenth and twentieth century;
3 more and better research based on the internal and external communications of terrorist organizations and their supporting constituencies;
4 more and better research that is cultural and linguistically attuned to the objects of investigation;
5 more and better research that looks at the interaction between terrorist organizations and their governmental and vigilante opponents;
6 more and better research that looks at the similarities between criminal gangs, religious sects and terrorist groups;
7 more and better research into conflict parties that share the goals of terrorists but choose other methods of advancing their causes and comparing their relative success with that of terrorist groups;
8 more and better research into the theories of terrorists and counter-terrorists themselves and how these guide their (re)actions;
9 more and better research into the role of ideology, religion and media in inspiring and instigating terrorism;
10 more and better research integrating theories of terrorism with theories of violence, crime and (armed) conflict.

Notes

1 Alex P. Schmid, *Political Terrorism: A Research Guide to Concepts, Theories, Data Bases and Literature.* Amsterdam: North-Holland, 1984, pp. 160–244; reprinted unchanged in Alex P. Schmid, Albert J. Jongman *et al.*, *Political Terrorism: A New Guide to Actors, Concepts, Data Bases, Theories, and Literature.* Amsterdam: North-Holland, 1988, pp. 61–136.
2 Adapted from Earl Conteh-Morgan, *Collective Political Violence: An Introduction to the Theories and Cases of Violent Conflicts.* New York: Routledge, 2004, p. 8.
3 Heinrich-W. Krumwiede, 'Ursachen des Terrorismus'. In Peter Waldmann, 'Determinanten der Entstehung und Entwicklung terroristischer Organisationen: Forschungsstand und Untersuchungsergebnisse'. Manuscript, 2004, p. 70 (translated by A.S.).
4 Richard Jackson, Eamon Murphy and Scott Poynting (eds), *Contemporary State Terrorism: Theory and Practice.* London: Routledge, 2009, p. 2.
5 See, for example Friedrich and Brzezinski's work on the six pillars of totalitarian political control and Leonard Schapiro's work on the three-pronged system of state control. C. Friedrich and Z. Brzezinski, *Totalitarian Dictatorship and Autocracy.* Cambridge, MA: Harvard University Press, 1956; L. Schapiro, *Totalitarianism.* London: Macmillan, 1972.
6 Estimates from the Historical Clarification Commission (1999), cited at www.nsarcive.org/guatemala/logbook/index.htm (consulted 6 March 2009).
7 Daan Bronkhorst, *Encyclopedie van de menselijkheid.* Breda: De Geus, 2007, p. 66; Rosemary H. O'Kane, *Terrorism.* Harlow, UK: Pearson Education, 2007, p. 104.
8 Edward S. Herman and Gerry O'Sullivan, 'Terrorism' as Ideology and Cultural Industry', Alexander George (ed.), *Western State Terrorism.* New York: Routledge, 1991, pp. 41–42.
9 Ibid.
10 David Claridge, 'State Terrorism? Applying a Definitional Model', *Terrorism and Political Violence*, 8(3), 1996, p. 48.
11 Ibid., p. 50.
12 Ibid., pp. 52–53.

13 Alex P. Schmid, 'State Terrorism – a Thing of the Past?' Schapiro Lecture, London School of Economics, January 2008. Schmid's typology is based on, but expands and modifies, those of (i) Rosemary H.T. O'Kane, *Terrorism* Harlow: Pearson Education, 2007, p. 96; (ii) David Claridge, 'The Dynamics of the Terrorist State: A Comparative Analysis of the Effect of Policy Decisions and Structural Factors upon the Shape of State Terrorism'. PhD thesis, School of International Relations, University of St Andrews, 21 September 1998, p. iii; (iii) Daniel Byman, *Deadly Connections: States that Sponsor Terrorism*. Cambridge: Cambridge University Press, 2005, p. 11; (iv) Michael Stohl and George A. Lopez, 'Introduction'. In M.S. Stohl and G.A. Lopez (eds), *Terrible beyond Endurance? The Foreign Policy of State Terrorism*. Westport, CT: Greenwood Press, 1988, p. 4.

14 Michael S. Stohl, 'National Interests and State Terrorism in International Affairs', *Political Science*, 36(1), July 1984, p. 40.

15 Based on Daan Bronkhorst, *Encyclopedie van de Menselijkheid*, various places.

16 George A. Lopez and Michael S. Stohl, 'Problems of Concept and Measurement in the Study of Human Rights'. In Thomas B. Jabine and Richard P. Claude (eds), *Human Rights and Statistics: Getting the Record Straight*. Philadelphia: University of Pennsylvania Press, 1992, pp. 216–234.

17 Michael S. Stohl, 'The State as Terrorist: Purposes and Types'. *Democracy and Security*, 2, 2006, p. 7.

18 Adapted from Henry J. Chisholm, 'The Function of Terror and Violence in Revolution'. MA thesis, Georgetown University, Washington, DC, 1948, p. 29.

19 Alexander Dallin and George W. Breslauer, *Political Terror in Communist Systems*. Stanford, CA: Stanford University Press, 1970.

20 R. Conquest, *The Great Terror: A Reassessment*. London: Hutchinson, 1990; A. Nove, 'Victims of Stalinism: How Many?' In J.A. Getty and R.T. Manning (eds), *Stalinist Terror: New Perspectives*. Cambridge: Cambridge University Press, 1993, cited in Rosemary O'Kane, *Terrorism*. Harlow, UK: Pearson Education, 2007, pp. 78–79.

21 T.R. Gurr, 'The Political Origins of State Violence and Terror: A Theoretical Analysis'. In M. Stohl and G.A. Lopez (eds), *Government Violence and Repression: An Agenda for Research*. Westport, CT: Greenwood Press, 1986, *passim* (quoted from MS version).

22 Ibid., p. 2.

23 Adapted from T.R. Gurr, 'The Political Origins of State Violence and Terror', *passim* (quoted from MS version).

24 T.R. Gurr, 'The Political Origins of State Violence and Terrorism'.

25 M. Gibney and M. Dalton, 'The Political Terror Scale', *Policy Studies and Developing Nations*, 4, 1996, pp. 73–84.

26 Adapted from www.politicalterrorscale.org/about.html; based on Christopher Mitchell, Michael Stohl, David Carleton and Georg Lopez, 'State Terrorism. Issues of Concept and Measurement'. In M. Stohl and G. Lopez (eds), *State Terrorism: Agenda for Research*. Westport, CT: Greenwood Press, 1986, p. 39.

27 Daniel Byman, *Deadly Connections: States That Sponsor Terrorism*. New York: Cambridge University Press, 2005.

28 Ibid., p. 15.

29 Ibid., pp. 36–52.

30 Ibid., pp. 59–66.

31 Ibid., p. 51.

32 Cf. Richard Jackson, Eamon Murphy and Scott Poynting (eds), *Contemporary State Terrorism: Theory and Practice*. London: Routledge, 2010. However, the claim by Paul Rogers, in the introduction to their volume, that 'state terror is a common feature of state behaviour, across all regions of the world, from autocracies to democracies' (p. xi), is a gross exaggeration. There are many states, especially democracies in Northern Europe in the period since 1945, that make no use of such tactics.

33 Andreas E. Feldman and Victor J. Hinojosa, 'Terrorism in Colombia: Logic and Sources of a Multidimensional and Ubiquitous Phenomenon'. *Terrorism and Political Violence*, 21(1), 2009, pp. 42–61.

34 Ibid., p. 43.

35 Ibid., p. 44.

36 Ian F.W. Beckett, *Encyclopedia of Guerrilla Warfare*. Santa Barbara, CA: ABC-CLIO, 1999, p. ix.

37 A.E. Feldman and V.J. Hinojosa, 'Terrorism in Columbia', pp. 44–45, citing Timothy Wickham-Crowley, *Guerrillas and Revolution in Latin America*. Princeton, NJ: Princeton University Press, 1992, p. 3.

38 A.E. Feldman and V.J. Hinojosa, 'Terrorism in Columbia', pp. 55.

39 Rüdiger Overmans, *Deutsche militärische Verluste im Zweiten Weltkrieg*. Oldenburg, Germany, cited 2000; Wikipedia at http://en.wikipedia.org/wiki/German_casualties_in_World_War_II (accessed 9 June 2010).

40 W.S. Churchill to General Ismay for Chiefs of Staff Committee, draft 28 March 1945 (Prime Minister's Personal Top Secret Telegram Serial No. D. 83/5; facsimile repr. in: Wikipedia (German edition) under

'Luftangriff auf Dresden'. The version of the memorandum ultimately sent, on 1 April 1945, was far less explicit about the terror rationale of the air war.

41 Ariel Merari, 'Terrorism as a Strategy of Insurgency', *Terrorism and Political Violence*, 5(4), Winter 1993, p. 220.

42 Ekaterina Stepanova, *Terrorism in Asymmetrical Conflict: Ideological and Structural Aspects*. SIPRI Research Report no. 23. Oxford: Oxford University Press, 2008, pp. 9–11.

43 See Howard S. Levie, *Terrorism in War: The Law of War Crimes*. Dobbs Ferry, NY: Oceana, 1993, pp. i–ii.

44 For examples, see the critique of this type of literature by Walter Laqueur, 'Interpretations of Terror: Fact, Fiction, and Political Science'. *Journal of Contemporary History*, 12(1), January 1977, p. 2.

45 Jeff Victoroff, 'The Mind of the Terrorist: A Review and Critique of Psychological Approaches'. *Journal of Conflict Resolution*, 49(1), February 2005, p. 3.

46 Ibid.

47 John Horgan, 'The Search for the Terrorist Personality'. In Andrew Silke (ed.), *Terrorists, Victims, and Society: Psychological Perspectives on Terrorism and Its Consequences*. Chichester: John Wiley, 2003, pp. 4–5.

48 Ibid., pp. 6–7.

49 Donatella Della Porta. 'Recruitment Processes in Clandestine Political Organizations: Italian Left-Wing Terrorism'. *International Social Movement Research*, 1, 1988, pp. 155–169.

50 John Horgan, 'The Search for the Terrorist Personality', pp. 10–14.

51 Andrew Silke, 'Becoming a Terrorist'. In A. Silke (ed.), *Terrorists, Victims, and Society*, p. 31.

52 Ibid., pp. 35–47.

53 A.P. Schmid, 'Materials for an Identification Theory of Insurgent Terrorism'. In A.P. Schmid *et al.*, *Political Terrorism* (1998), pp. 92–97.

54 John Horgan. 'Leaving Terrorism Behind: An Individual Perspective'. In A. Silke (ed.), *Terrorists, Victims, and Society*, pp. 109–130.

55 Ibid., pp. 113–121.

56 Ibid., p. 122.

57 Orla Muldoon, 'The Psychological Impact of Protracted Campaigns of Political Violence on Societies'. In A. Silke (ed.), *Terrorists, Victims, and Society*, pp. 161–174.

58 Ibid., p. 162.

59 Ibid., p. 163.

60 Ibid., pp. 165–166.

61 Ibid., pp. 166–168.

62 Tom Pyszczynski, 'What Are We so Afraid of? A Terror Management Perspective on the Politics of Fear'. *Social Research*, 71(4), 2004, p. 829.

63 Ibid., p. 829.

64 Ibid., pp. 830–831.

65 Ibid., pp. 833–836.

66 Ibid., pp. 841–843.

67 M. Crenshaw, 'An Organizational Approach to the Analysis of Political Terrorism', *Orbis*, 29(3), Fall 1985, p. 472.

68 Ehud Sprinzak, 'The Process of Delegitimation: Towards a Linkage Theory of Political Terrorism'. *Terrorism and Political Violence*, 3(1), 1991, p. 59.

69 Ibid., pp. 51–52.

70 Ibid., p. 59.

71 Ibid., p. 60.

72 Ibid., p. 61.

73 Ehud Sprinzak, 'Right-Wing Terrorism in a Comparative Perspective: The Case of Split Delegitimization', *Terrorism and Political Violence*, 7(1), 1995, pp. 17–18.

74 Ibid., p. 20.

75 E. Sprinzak, 'An Organizational Approach to the Analysis of Political Tarrorism', p. 65.

76 E. Sprinzak, 'Right-Wing Terrorism in a Comparative Perspective', pp. 20–21.

77 F.M. Moghadam, 'The Staircase to Terrorism: A Psychological Explanation'. *American Psychologist*, 60(2), February–March 2005, pp. 161–169.

78 Mitchell D. Silber and Arvin Bhatt, 'Radicalization in the West: The Homegrown Threat'. New York: New York Police Department, August 2007. Available at: www.nyc.gov/html/nypd/pdf/dcpi/NYPD_Report-Radicalization_in_the_West.pdf (accessed 7 March 2009).

79 Ibid.

80 Clark McCauley and Sophia Moskalenko, 'Mechanisms of Political Radicalization: Pathways towards Terrorism'. *Terrorism and Political Violence*, 20, 2008, p. 416.

81 Ibid., pp. 416.
82 Ibid., pp. 426–427.
83 Ibid., pp. 422–426.
84 Ibid., pp. 418–422.
85 'Radicalisation Processes Leading to Acts of Terror'. A Concise Report prepared by the European Commission's Expert Group on Violent Radicalisation, Submitted to the European Commission on 15 May 2008, p. 7.
86 Ibid., pp. 9–11.
87 Cf. Froukje Demant, Marieke Slootman, Frank Buijs and Jean Tillie, *Decline and Disengagement: An Analysis of Processes of Deradicalisation*. Amsterdam: IMES, 2008.
88 Martha Crenshaw, 'Theories of Terrorism: Instrumental and Organizational Approaches'. In David Rapoport (ed.), *Inside Terrorist Organizations*. London: Frank Cass, 1988, p. 14.
89 Dipak Gupta, *Understanding Terrorism and Political Violence*. London: Routledge, 2008, p. 30.
90 Todd Sandler, Daniel Arce and Walter Enders, 'Transnational Terrorism'. Copenhagen: Consensus Challenge Paper, 6 March 2008, p. 11.
91 M. Crenshaw, 'Theories of Terrorism', p. 13.
92 Ibid., p. 14.
93 Jon Elster, 'Introduction'. In J. Elster (ed.), *Rational Choice*. Oxford: Basil Blackwell, 1986, pp. 1–33.
94 Brian M. Jenkins, 'Terrorism: A New Mode of Conflict'. In David Carlton and Carlo Schaerf (eds), *International Terrorism and World Security*. London: Croom Helm, 1975, p. 15.
95 L. Trotsky, *The Defence of Terrorism*. London: George Allen & Unwin, 1921.
96 L. Trotsky, *Terrorism and Communism*. Ann Arbor: University of Michigan Press, 1961, pp. 23, 51, 54–55, 58, 63, quoted in, Alexander Dallin and George W. Breslauer, *Political Terror in Communist Systems*. Stanford, CA: Stanford University Press, 1970, p. 11.
97 Daniel Bessner and Michael Stauch, 'Karl Heinzen and the Intellectual Origins of Modern Terror'. *Terrorism and Political Violence*, 22(2), 2010, pp. 143–176.
98 'Programma Ispolnitel'nogo Komiteta', cited in *The Encyclopaedia of the Social Sciences*, vol. 14. Macmillan: New York, 1936, p. 578.
99 Nicolas Morozov, 'Terrorist Struggle'; reprinted in F. Gross, *Violence in Politics: Terror and Political Assassination in Eastern Europe and Russia*. The Hague: Mouton, 1972, p. 106.
100 *The Memoirs of General Grivas*. New York: Praeger, 1964; quoted in Robert Taber, *The War of the Flea: Guerrilla Warfare, Theory and Practice*. London: Paladin, 1974, p. 106.
101 RAND Research Brief, *How Terrorist Groups End*. Santa Monica, CA: RAND, 2008 (www.rand.org).
102 Carlos Marighela, *For the Liberation of Brazil*. Harmondsworth, UK: Penguin Books, 1971, pp. 34–35.
103 Spiegel Gespräch, 'Wir müssen raus aus den Schützengrüben: Bundesminister Gerhart Baum und Ex-Terrorist Horst Mahler über das Phänomen terrorismus', *Der Spiegel*, 33(53), 31 December 1979, p. 47.
104 Marc Sageman, *Leaderless Jihad: Terror Networks in the Twenty-First Century*. Philadelphia: University of Pennsylvania Press, 2008.
105 B. Hoffman, *Inside Terrorism*. New York: Columbia University Press, 2006, pp. 88; James A. Piazza, 'Is Islamist Terrorism More Dangerous? An Empirical Study of Group Ideology, Organization, and Goal Structure', *Terrorism and Political Violence*, 21(1), 2009, p. 62.
106 J.A. Piazza, 'Is Islamist Terrorism More Dangerous', p. 63.
107 B. Hoffman, *Inside Terrorism*, p. 89.
108 M. Stout, 'In Search of Salafi Jihadist Strategic Thought: Mining the Words of the Terrorists'. Paper presented to the International Studies Association Convention, 29 March 2008, p. 1.
109 Ibid., p. 6.
110 B. Lia and T. Hegghammer, 'Jihadi Strategic Studies: The Alleged Al Qaida Study Preceding the Madrid Bombings', *Studies in Conflict and Terrorism*, 27(5), 2004, pp. 360–362.
111 M. Stout, 'In Search of Salafi Jihadist Strategic Thought', p. 7. The only difference between the two documents was, as Stout observed, the replacement of Marighela's Marxist rhetoric with jihadist jargon.
112 B. Lia, 'Abu Mus'ab al-Suri's Critique of Hard Line Salafists in the Jihadist Current', *CTC Sentinel*, 1(1), December 2007, p. 2.
113 M. Crenshaw, 'An Organizational Approach to the Analysis of Political Terrorism', pp. 465–487; David C. Rapoport. 'Modern Terror: The Four Waves'. In Audrey Cronin and J. Ludes (eds), *Attacking Terrorism: Elements of a Grand Strategy*. Washington, DC: Georgetown University Press, 2004, pp. 46–73.
114 M. Crenshaw, 'Theories of Terrorism', p. 18.
115 M. Crenshaw, 'An Organizational Approach to the Analysis of Political Terrorism', p. 466.
116 M. Crenshaw, 'Theories of Terrorism', p. 19.

117 These accounts are echoed by Charles Tilly, as violent institutions account for the opportunity structures necessary for the turn to political violence. Tilly, *The Politics of Collective Violence*. New York: Cambridge University Press, 2003.

118 M. Crenshaw, 'An Organizational Approach to the Analysis of Political Terrorism', p. 471.

119 Ibid., p. 466.

120 Ibid., pp. 467–468.

121 Ibid., p. 473.

122 Ibid., p. 477.

123 Walter Laqueur, 'Interpretations of Terror: Fact, Fiction, and Political Science', *Journal of Contemporary History*, 12(1), 1977, p. 13.

124 David C. Rapoport, 'The Four Waves of Modern Terrorism'. In Audrey K. Cronin and James M. Ludes (eds), *Attacking Terrorism: Elements of a Grand Strategy*. Washington, DC: Georgetown University Press, pp. 46–73.

125 Ze'ev Ivianski, 'The Terrorist Revolution: The Roots of Modern Terrorism'. In D.C. Rapoport (ed.), *Terrorism: Critical Concepts in Political Science*. London: Routledge, 2005, p. 82.

126 Ibid., pp. 74–75.

127 Ibid., p. 75.

128 The term 'freedom fighter' for terrorists was first introduced by Karl Heinzen in 1850 in his short treatise *Murder and Liberty*, originally written in German. D. Bessner and M. Stauch, 'Karl Heinzen and the Intellectual Origins of Modern Terror'. *Terrorism and Political Violence*, 22(2), 2010, where a new translation into English of the treatise is provided on pp. 153–167.

129 Rapoport noted that much anarchist writing was intended to speak to an international audience, especially those representative polities that might be provoked to action by sympathetic anarchists abroad. See D. Rapoport, 'The International World as Some Terrorists Have Seen It: A Look at a Century of Motives'. In D. Rapoport (ed.), *Inside Terrorist Organizations*. London: Frank Cass, 1988, pp. 32–58.

130 Magnus Ranstorp, 'Terrorism in the Name of Religion'. *Journal of International Affairs*, 50(1), 1996, pp. 2–5.

131 Ibid., pp. 6–7.

132 Bruce Hoffman, *Inside Terrorism*. New York: Columbia University Press, 1998, p. 83.

133 B. Hoffman, *Inside Terrorism*, pp. 94–95.

134 Mark Juergensmeyer, *Terror in the Mind of God: The Global Rise of Religious Violence*. Berkeley: University of California Press, 2000.

135 Mark Juergensmeyer, 'The Logic of Religious Violence'. In David C. Rapoport (ed.), *Inside Terrorist Organizations*. London: Frank Cass, 1988, p. 180.

136 Ibid., pp. 185–190.

137 Ehud Sprinzak, 'From Messianic Pioneering to Vigilante Terrorism: The Case of Gush Emunim Underground'. In D.C. Rapoport (ed.), *Inside Terrorist Organizations*, pp. 194–216.

138 In fact, RAND's work on US counter-insurgency in Vietnam clearly shows that captured Viet Cong more often than not knew next to nothing of Marxism. See Austin Long, 'On "Other War": Lessons from Five Decades of RAND Counterinsurgency Research'. Santa Monica, CA RAND, 2006, pp. 36–37.

139 Karin Rasler and William R. Thompson, 'Looking for Waves of Terrorism'. *Terrorism and Political Violence*, 21(1), 2009, p. 39.

140 Fawaz Gerges, *The Far Enemy: Why Jihad Went Global*. Cambridge: Cambridge University Press, 2005.

141 Letter from al-Zawahiri to al-Zarqawi, 9 July 2005. CSTPV Archive.

142 Daniel Byman, 'The Logic of Ethnic Terrorism'. *Studies in Conflict and Terrorism*, 21, 1998, p. 150.

143 Ibid., p. 151.

144 Ibid., p. 151.

145 Ibid., p. 151.

146 Ibid., p. 150.

147 Ibid., p. 159.

148 Ibid., p. 150.

149 Ibid., p. 154.

150 Ibid., pp. 156–157.

151 David Little, 'Religion and Ethnicity in the Sri Lankan Civil War'. In R. Rotberg (ed.), *Generating Peace in Sri Lanka: Civil War and Reconciliation*. Washington, DC.: Brookings Institution Press, 1999, pp. 41–55.

152 Ibid., p. 42.

153 Ibid.

154 Ibid., p. 42–49.

155 Jeffrey Kaplan, 'Terrorism's Fifth Wave: a Theory, a Conundrum, and a Dilemma'. *Perspectives on Terrorism*, 2(2). Available online at www.terrorismanalysts.com/pt/index.php?option=com_ rokzine&view=articl& id=27&itemid=54 (accessed 28 January 2007).

156 Martha Crenshaw, 'The Concept of Revolutionary Terrorism'. *Journal of Conflict Resolution*, 16(3), 1972, p. 384.

157 Ibid., p. 385.

158 Ibid., p. 387.

159 H. Edward Price, 'The Strategy and Tactics of Revolutionary Terrorism'. *Comparative Studies in Society and History*, 19(1), 1977, pp. 52–66.

160 Ibid., p. 52.

161 Ibid., p. 54.

162 Ibid., pp. 56–57.

163 M. Crenshaw, 'The Concept of Revolutionary Terrorism' p. 389.

164 Ibid.

165 Ami Pedahzur and Arie Perlinger; 'Introduction: Characteristics of Suicide Attacks'. In Ami Pedahzur (ed.), *Root Causes of Suicide Terrorism: The Globalization of Martyrdom*. London: Routledge, 2006, p. 2.

166 Ibid., p. 1.

167 Ibid., p. 2.

168 Assaf Moghadam, 'Defining Suicide Terrorism' In A. Pedahzur (ed.), *Root Causes of Suicide Terrorism*, pp. 13–24.

169 Diego Gambetta, 'Can We Make Sense of Suicide Missions?' In D. Gambetta (ed.), *Making Sense of Suicide Missions*. Oxford: Oxford University Press, 2006, p. 260.

170 Ibid.

171 Ibid.

172 Ibid.

173 Ibid.

174 Ibid., pp. 261–266.

175 Ibid., p. 288.

176 Scott Atran, 'Mishandling Suicide Terrorism'. *Washington Quarterly*, 27(3), 2004, p. 74.

177 Ibid., p. 80.

178 Ibid., pp. 80–81.

179 Raphael Israeli, 'Islamikaze and Their Significance'. *Terrorism and Political Violence*, 9(3), 1997, p. 97.

180 Ibid., p. 97.

181 Ibid., p. 106.

182 Ibid., pp. 106–107.

183 Ibid., p. 104.

184 Ibid., p. 108.

185 Robert Pape, 'The Strategic Logic of Suicide Terrorism'. *American Political Science Review*, 97(3), 2003, p. 343.

186 Ibid., p. 344.

187 J. Elster, *Rational Choice*.

188 R. Pape, 'The Strategic Logic of Suicide Terrorism', p. 344.

189 Ibid., p. 346.

190 Ibid., p. 344.

191 Ibid., p. 346.

192 Ibid., pp. 346–347.

193 Ibid., p. 347.

194 Ibid., p. 351.

195 Jon Elster, 'Motivations and Beliefs in Suicide Missions'. In Diego Gambetta (ed.), *Making Sense of Suicide Missions*. Oxford: Oxford University Press, 2006, pp. 233–258.

196 Ibid., p. 234.

197 Ibid., pp. 244–256.

198 John Arquilla, *The Advent of Netwar*. Santa Monica, CA: RAND, 1996.

199 John Arquilla and David Ronfeldt (eds) *in Athena's Camp: Preparing for Conflict in the Information Age*. Santa Monica, CA: RAND, 1997; John Arquilla and David Ronfeldt (eds), *Networks and Netwars: Terror, Crime, and Militancy in the Information Age*. Santa Monica, CA: RAND, 2001; also John Arquilla and David Ronfeldt, *Swarming and the Future of Conflict*. Santa Monica, CA: RAND, 2000.

200 For two excellent examples of such work, see Arthur Cebrowski and John Garstka, 'Network-Centric Warfare: Its Origin and Future'. *Proceedings of the Naval Institute*, January 1998; and David Jablonsky, 'The

Owl of Minerva Flies at Midnight: Doctrinal Change and Continuity and the Revolution in Military Affairs'. Carlisle, PA: U.S. Army War College Strategic Studies Institute, May 1994.

201 Two of the most notable works within this arena are Alvin Toffler and Heidi Toffler, *War and Anti-war: Making Sense of Today's Global Chaos*. New York: Warner Books, 1995. More in line with the application to Terrorism Studies is Peter Bergen, *Holy War, Inc: Inside the Secret World of Osama bin Laden*. New York: Free Press, 2001.

202 L. Beam, 'Leaderless Resistance'. *Seditionist*, no. 12, 1992; available at www.louisbeam.com/leaderless.htm; Jeffrey Kaplan, 'Leaderless Resistance'. *Terrorism and Political Violence*, 9(3), Autumn 1997, pp. 80–95.

203 J. Kaplan, 'Leaderless Resistance', p. 81.

204 Michael Kenney, *From Pablo to Osama: Trafficking and Terrorist Networks, Government Bureaucracies, and Competitive Adaptation*. University Park, PA: Penn State University Press, 2007.

205 Ibid., p. 3.

206 Ibid., p. 4.

207 Ibid., pp. 4–5.

208 Ibid., p. 5.

209 Marc Sageman, *Leaderless Jihad: Terror Networks in the 21st Century*. Philadelphia: University of Pennsylvania Press, 2008; Marc Sageman, *Understanding Terror Networks*. Philadelphia: University of Pennsylvania Press, 2004.

210 M. Sageman, *Leaderless Jihad*, p. 16.

211 Ibid., pp. 17–20.

212 In other words, individual psychological evaluations cannot tell us who might have become a terrorist but did not, and why.

213 J. Horgan, 'The Search for the Terrorist Personality'.

214 M. Sageman, *Leaderless Jihad*, p. 51.

215 Ibid., pp. 23–24.

216 Ibid., pp. 72–88.

217 Ibid., pp. 116–117.

218 Ibid., pp. 48–50.

219 Thomas Homer-Dixon, 'The Rise of Complex Terrorism'. *Foreign Policy*, January–February 2002. Available at: www.homerdixon.com/generalwriting.html.

220 Ekaterina Stepanova, *Terrorism in Asymmetrical Conflict. Ideological and Structural Aspects*. Oxford: University Press, 2008, pp. 17–20.

221 Todd Sandler *et al.*, 'Transnational Terrorism', pp. 22–24.

222 T. Sandler, *Global Collective Action*. Cambridge: Cambridge University Press, 2004.

223 E. Stepanova, *Terrorism in Asymmetrical Conflict*, pp. 152–153.

224 Robert Keohane, 'The Globalization of Informal Violence, Theories of World Politics, and the "Liberalism & Fear" '. *International Organization*, Spring 2002, pp. 29–43.

225 Ibid., pp. 29–30.

226 A.P. Schmid and J. de Graaf, *Violence as Communication: Insurgent Terrorism and the Western New Media*. London: Sage, 1982.

227 Peter Kropotkin, 'The Spirit of Revolt', cited in Ze'ev Iviansky, 'Individual Terror: Concept and Typology'. *Journal of Contemporary History*, 12, 1977, p. 45.

228 Quoted in Hannah Arendt, *The Origins of Totalitarianism*. New York: Harcourt Brace Jovanovich, 1971, p. 341.

229 Alex P. Schmid, 'Terrorism as Psychological Warfare'. *Democracy and Security*, 1, 2005, p. 138.

230 Brigitte Nacos, *Terrorism and Counterterrorism: Understanding Threats and Responses in the Post-9/11 World*, 3rd edn. Boston: Longman, 2010, p. 263.

231 Former terrorist active in the German Red Army Faction and Italian Brigate Rosse, quoted in G. Weimann and Conrad Winn, *The Theater of Terror: Mass Media and International Terrorism*. White Plains, NY: Longman, 1994, p. 61.

232 'Usama bin Laden says Al-Qaidah group had nothing to do with the 11 September attacks'. *Ummat* (Karachi), 28 September 2001 (www.robert-fisk.com/usama_interview_ummat.htm), p. 2; cit. Faisal Devji, *Landscapes of the Jihad: Militancy, Morality, Modernity*. London: Hurst, 2005, p. 160.

233 Avaro Rodriguez-Carballeira and Federico Javaloy. 'Psychosocial Analysis of the Collective Processes in the United States after September 11'. *Conflict Management and Peace Science*, 22(3), October 2005, p. 202.

234 David Brannan, Philip Esler and N.T. Anders Strindberg, 'Talking to Terrorists: Towards an Independent Analytical Framework for the Study of Violent Sub-state Activism'. *Studies in Conflict and Terrorism*, 24, 2001, p. 18.

235 Ibid., p. 5.
236 A. Rodriguez-Carballeira and F. Javaloy, 'Psychosocial Analysis of the Collective Processes in the United States after September 11', p. 202.
237 D. Brannan *et al.*, 'Talking to Terrorists', p. 16.
238 Ibid., p. 15.
239 Ted R. Gurr, *Why Men Rebel*. Princeton, NJ: Princeton University Press, 1970, p. 13.
240 Alam, in particular, states that it is discontent in politically active communities, such as among unemployed graduates, that has been a substantial contributing factor to radicalization in Egypt. Anwar Alam, 'The Sociology and Political Economy of "Islamic Terrorism" in Egypt'. *Terrorism and Political Violence*, 15(4), Winter 2003, pp. 114–142.
241 Scott Tessier, 'The Political Psychology of Ethnic Conflict in Sri Lanka'. *International Affairs Journal Quarterly*, 2(3), Spring 2006. Available online at: http://davisiaj.com/content/view/190/86/ (accessed 21 July 2008).
242 Claude Berrebi, 'Evidence about the Link between Education, Poverty, and Terrorism among Palestinians'. Manuscript, n.d., p. 23.
243 Ibid., p. 33.
244 Ibid., p. 32.
245 Ibid., p. 38.
246 Ibid., p. 40.
247 Alan Krueger and Jitka Maleckova, 'Education, Poverty and Terrorism: Is There a Causal Connection?' *Journal of Economic Perspectives*, 17(4), Fall 2003, pp. 119–144.
248 Quan Li and Drew Schaub, 'Economic Globalization and Transnational Terrorism: A Pooled Time-Series Analysis'. *Journal of Conflict Resolution*, 48(2), 2004, pp. 230–258.
249 Ibid., p. 237.
250 Ibid., pp. 230–258.
251 Fawaz A. Gerges, 'The Decline of Revolutionary Islam in Algeria and Egypt'. *Survival*, 4(1), 1999, pp. 113–125.
252 M. Sageman, *Leaderless Jihad*, p. 48.
253 A.P. Schmid, *Political Terrorism* (1984), p. 199, where he notes, 'The act of identification which enables us to empathize with others is also capable of leading to vicarious emotions, to anger and aggressiveness towards the apparent source of misery of the person or group we have love and compassion for.'
254 S. Brock Blomberg, Gregory D. Hess and Akila Weerapana, 'Economic Conditions and Terrorism'. *European Journal of Political Economy*, 20, 2004, pp. 463–478.
255 Ibid., p. 464.
256 T.R. Gurr, 'The Political Origins of State Violence and Terror', p. 317.
257 Ibid.
258 Alex P. Schmid, 'Terrorism and Democracy'. In A.P. Schmid and Ron Crelinsten (eds), *Western Responses to Terrorism*. London: Frank Cass, 1993, pp. 14–25.
259 Ibid., p. 17.
260 Ibid., pp. 18–19.
261 Ibid., pp. 20–21.
262 William Eubank and Leonard Weinberg, 'Does Democracy Encourage Terrorism?' *Terrorism and Political Violence*, 6(4), 1994, pp. 417–443.
263 Ibid., p. 426.
264 Ibid., pp. 429–432.
265 Quan Li, 'Does Democracy Promote or Reduce Transnational Terrorist Incidents?' *Journal of Conflict Resolution*, 49(2), 2005, pp. 278–297.
266 Ibid., p. 279.
267 Ibid., p. 283.
268 A.P. Schmid, 'Terrorism and Democracy', p. 17.
269 Robert I. Rotberg, 'Failed States, Collapsed States, Weak States: Causes and Indicators'. In R.I. Rotberg (ed.), *State Failure and State Weakness in a Time of Terror*. Washington, DC: Brookings Institution Press, 2003, p. 1.
270 Ibid., pp. 2–3.
271 Ibid., p. 3.
272 Ibid., p. 4.
273 Ibid., pp. 4–5.
274 Ibid., pp. 8–10.

275 Stephen Krasner and Carlos Pascual, 'Addressing State Failure'. *Foreign Affairs*, July–August, 2005.

276 Paul Rich, 'The Emergence and Significance of Warlords in International Relations'. In P. Rich (ed.), *Warlords in International Relations*. New York: St Martins Press, 1999, p. 5.

277 Ibid., pp. 5–12.

278 Stephen Chan, 'The Warlord and the Global Order'. In P. Rich (ed.), *Warlords in International Relations*, pp. 169–170.

279 Mahmood Mamdani, 'Good Muslim, Bad Muslim: A Political Perspective on Culture and Terrorism'. *American Anthropologist*, 104(3), 2002, pp. 766–775.

280 W. Laqueur, 'Interpretations of Terror', p. 14.

281 Khachig Tololyan, 'Cultural Narrative and the Motivation of the Terrorists'. In D. Rapoport (ed.), *Inside Terrorist Organisations*. London: Frank Cass, 1988, p. 217.

282 Ibid., p. 218.

283 Ibid., p. 219.

284 Ibid.

285 Brynjar Lia, *Globalization and the Future of Terrorism*. New York: Routledge, 2005, p. 2.

286 For an example of this line of reasoning, see Benjamin Barber, *Jihad vs. McWorld: Terrorism's Challenge to Democracy*. London: Corgi Books, 2003.

287 B. Lia, *Globalization and the Future of Terrorism*, p. 2.

288 Ibid., p. 5.

289 Ibid., p. 12.

290 A phrase used to denote the environment specific to terrorist groups such as the nature of state counter-terror capabilities as well as the prevalence of organized criminal elements who often aid terror groups.

291 B. Lia, *Globalization and the Future of Terrorism*, pp. 22–24.

292 Fawaz Gerges, *The Far Enemy*.

293 Quan Li and Drew Schaub, 'Economic Globalization and Transnational Terrorism', pp. 230–258.

294 Ibid., pp. 232–233.

295 Ibid., p. 232.

296 Laura Dugan, Gary LaFree and Heather Fogg, 'A First Look at Domestic and International Global Terrorism Events, 1970–1997'. Paper presented at Intelligence and Security Informatics Conference, Sain Diego, 23–24 May 2006.

297 Martha Crenshaw, 'The Image of Terrorism and the Government's Response to Terrorism'. In David C. Rapoport (ed.), *Terrorism: Critical Concepts in Political Science*. London: Routledge, 2006, p. 251.

298 Cynthia Lum, Leslie Kennedy and Alison Sherley, 'Strategies Related to the Prevention, Detention, Management and Response to Terrorism: A Campbell Systematic Review'. MS, 2003.

299 L. Paul Bremer, 'The West's Counter-terrorism Strategy'. In Alex P. Schmid and Ronald D. Crelinsten (eds), *Western Responses to Terrorism*. London: Frank Cass, 1993.

300 M. Crenshaw, 'Theories of Terrorism', p. 16.

301 Ibid.

302 Ibid.

303 Ibid.

304 T. Sandler *et al.*, 'Transnational Terrorism', p. 26.

305 Ibid.

306 M. Crenshaw, 'Theories of Terrorism', p. 22.

307 Ibid.

308 Ibid., p. 23.

309 M. Crenshaw, 'An Organizational Approach to the Analysis of Political Terrorism', p. 482.

310 Jeffrey Ian Ross and Ted Robert Gurr, 'Why Terrorism Subsides: A Comparative Study of Canada and the United States'. *Comparative Politics*, 21(4), 1989, pp. 405–426.

311 Ibid., pp. 407–409.

312 Ibid., p. 407.

313 L.P. Bremer, 'The West's Counter-terrorism Strategy'.

314 Ibid., p. 257.

315 Ibid., pp. 257–258.

316 Karin von Hippel. 'Responding to the Roots of Terror'. In Magnus Ranstrop (ed.), *Mapping Terrorism Research*. London: Routledge, 2007, pp. 94–105.

317 Ibid., pp. 95–102.

318 David Gompert and John Gordon, *War by Other Means: Building Complete and Balanced Capabilities for Counterinsurgency*. Santa Monica, CA: RAND, 2008, p. xxii.

319 Ibid., p. xxv.
320 Ibid., p. xxxix.
321 M. Crenshaw, 'The Image of Terrorism and the Government's Response to Terrorism', pp. 251–252.
322 T. Sandler *et al.*, 'Transnational Terrorism'.
323 M. Crenshaw, 'The Image of Terrorism and the Government's Response to Terrorism', p. 252.
324 Ronald Crelinsten, 'Analyzing Terrorism and Counter-terrorism: A Communication Model'. *Terrorism and Political Violence*, 14(2), 2002, pp. 77–122.
325 Ibid., p. 79.
326 Ibid., p. 81.
327 Ibid., pp. 81–82.
328 Ibid., p. 84.
329 Brian M. Jenkins, *Unconquerable Nation: Knowing Our Enemies, Strengthening Ourselves*. Santa Monica, CA: RAND, 2006.
330 Ibid., p. 53.
331 Ibid., p. 64.
332 Ibid., p. 68.
333 Ibid., p. 74.
334 M. Crenshaw, 'The Image of Terrorism and the Government's Response to Terrorism', p. 254.
335 Ibid., p. 252.
336 Ibid., p. 256.
337 D. Byman, 'The Logic of Ethnic Terrorism', p. 150.
338 Ibid., p. 162.
339 Ibid., p. 150.
340 Ibid., p. 163.
341 D. Byman, *Deadly Connections*, p. 273.
342 Ibid.
343 Cumbre Internacional sobre Democracia, Terrorismo y Seguridad, Madrid, 8–11 March 2005.
344 New York: Routledge, 2005.
345 Ibid., p. 3.
346 Ibid., pp. 3–4.
347 A.P. Schmid *et al.*, *Political Terrorism* (1988), chapter on theories, pp. 61–136.

Appendix 4.1

Psychological, Political, Economic, Religious and Cultural (Root) Causes of Terrorism, According to Scholars Gathered at the Club de Madrid Conference of 2005

In March 2005, more than 200 leading scholars and expert practitioners discussed the causes and underlying factors of terrorism at a conference in Madrid. They debated root causes in more than a dozen workshops addressing psychological, political, economic, religious and cultural factors potentially responsible for the emergence of terrorism. The following five lists summarize hypotheses suggested by participants. For more information about the International Summit on Democracy, Terrorism and Security, see http://english.safe-democracy.org/causes/.

First, according to the Club of Madrid Workshop,[1] the following are potential psychological causes of terrorism:

1 There is a multiplicity of individual motives: for some, it is to give a sense of power to the powerless; for others, revenge is a primary motivation; for still others, it is to gain a sense of significance.
2 The leader plays a crucial role in identifying the external enemy as the cause; he draws together alienated, frustrated individuals who would otherwise remain isolated and aggrieved.
3 A religious fundamentalist leader can use his authority to interpret religious scripture so as to justify extreme acts of violence.
4 A culture of martyrdom contributes to suicide terrorism.
5 Many Muslim immigrants and refugees in the diaspora suffer from an existential sense of loss, deprivation and alienation from the countries in which they live. Extreme ideologies can radicalize some of them and can facilitate re-entrance into the path of terrorism.

Second, the following are potential political causes of terrorism, according to Club of Madrid Workshop:[2]

1 Terrorism is rooted in political discontent.
2 Ideologies are associated with nationalism, revolution, religion, and defence of the status quo.

3 Contagion processes may operate cross-nationally and result in the spread of terrorism from the point of origin to locales with different conditions.

4 Globalization, for example, facilitates the spread of terrorism, but it is not a direct cause.

5 Historical contingencies and the perceptions and intentions of small, radicalized political conspiracies are most important in explaining terrorism.

6 Highly contentious polities and divided societies are likely to be associated with a greater risk of terrorism.

7 Among the different types of regimes, transitional or new democracies are the most fragile and more likely to experience terrorism because of either unresolved grievances or state weakness.

8 Causes of terrorism are international as well as domestic.

9 Some failed or failing states become hosts for radical conspiracies that both impede stabilization and export terrorism to other targets and audiences.

10 A state's susceptibility to terrorism is determined not just by how it treats its citizens at home but also by its actions abroad. When such actions lack international legitimacy and local populations perceive them as unjust, radical groups come to see terrorism as an appropriate response.

11 Disillusionment over the possibility of change through non-violence or through violence other than terrorism (e.g. guerrilla warfare) contribute to the choice of terrorism.

12 Nationalism has reappeared as a cause of terrorism.

13 The rise of intolerance, particularly on the right, could spawn new terrorist movements, at least in Europe.

14 Governmental success in promoting accommodation is likely to provoke terrorism from groups that continue to reject compromise and from factions that splinter off from the groups that accept dialogue.

The following are potential economic causes of terrorism, according to the same workshop:[3]

1 Terrorism is most likely to emerge in societies characterized by rapid modernization.

2 The increase in the proportional size of the young male population (a youth bulge) facing insecure employment prospects is a pervasive risk factor in developing societies. Low relative educational status and political participation of women are associated with higher levels of political violence and instability.

3 Structured inequalities within countries are breeding grounds for violent political movements in general and terrorism specifically. Structured inequalities across the interdependent global system have similar consequences.

4 Ethno-nationalist and revolutionary terrorist movements usually emerge in the context of larger political conflicts that are centred on the grievances of groups that see themselves as economically or politically marginalized.

5 Semi-repressive regimes contribute to the escalation of political conflicts to terrorism.

6 Some militant groups choose terror tactics in the expectation that governments will increase repression, leading to a shift in public support from the government to the terrorists' cause.

7 A specific hostile event that calls for revenge may result in a wave of terrorist attacks. Provocative government actions can cause a backlash that precipitates terrorism.

8 Diasporas may also promote terrorist tactics, especially when they see that non-violent political action is ineffective in dramatizing injustices and create imperatives for reform.

9 The presence of charismatic ideological leaders able to transform widespread grievances and frustrations into a political agenda for violent struggle is a decisive factor behind the emergence of a terrorist movement.

10 A collective or individual desire for revenge against acts of repression may be motive enough for terrorist activity.

11 The process of globalization has vastly increased incentives and opportunities for terrorism and makes it easier to organize, finance and sustain terrorist strategies.

12 Growing inequality may lead to terrorist acts by the perpetrators in the name of a more equitable distribution of wealth.

13 Globalization increases opportunities for militant and terrorist groups.

14 Education without opportunities for employment is an explosive combination; even more explosive is the expansion of traditional Islamic education that provides no skills for participation in modernizing societies but sanctions jihadist resistance to modernization and its agents.

The following are potential religious causes of terrorism:[4]

1 Political and economic grievances are primary causes or catalysts, and religion becomes a means to legitimate and mobilize.

2 Even though religion may not be the sole cause of terrorism, it can exacerbate the situation. Religion brings to a situation of conflict images of grand struggle and an abiding absolutism. Religion is often centred on themes that can be inherently polarizing – concepts of truth, notions of good, of absolutes and ultimate realities.

3 Religion can contribute to a culture of violence where violence becomes a 'defining issue' in the identity of activist groups.

4 Examples of religious terrorism can be found in all religious traditions. No one religious tradition holds a monopoly on violence, and all religious traditions can be used to justify acts of destruction and aggression.

5 Regarding its role in conflict, religion is seldom the problem, but the role of religion can be problematic.

Finally, the workshop put forward the following as potential cultural causes of terrorism:[5]

1 A culture of alienation and humiliation can act as a kind of growth medium in which the process of radicalization commences and virulent extremism comes to thrive.

2 Narratives and historical memories can give terrorists what they see as 'just cause' to engage in violence.

3 Alienation produced out of long-standing and deep cultural conflict constitutes an underlying condition for terrorism to flourish.

4 Local conflicts, as well as broader cultural ones between and within religious groups, or even between tribes and clans, set the stage for recruitment to terrorist groups.

5 The global jihadi movement has emerged out of 'deculturation'. It is not an expression of a given culture under siege, but a reflection of globalization and uprooting.

6 Forceful actions against external terrorist base areas may provoke potential internal actors into decisively changing their allegiances and moving to active violence in opposition to the West.

7 American and European prisons where Saudi charities now fund organizations that preach radical Islam are one source of recruits for violent extremist groups. Prisons are also a place where terrorist organizations recruit and make connections with organized criminals and other terrorist organizations.

8 Some groups which do not necessarily advocate or legitimize violence, such as Hizb-ut-Tahrir, a global Islamist organization, and Tablighi Jamaat, a revivalist group that aims to create better Muslims through 'spiritual jihad' (good deeds, contemplation and proselytizing), function as 'gateway organizations' to terrorist groups.

9 The perception that Western governments have been willing to play along with brutal dictators in the Middle East has increased the widespread resentment of the West.

10 Festering conflicts – and the state failure and weakness they induce – are important risk factors for terrorism.

Notes

1   Club de Madrid, *Addressing the Causes of Terrorism*. The Club of Madrid Series on Democracy and Terrorism. Madrid: International Summit on Democracy and Security, 8–11 March 2005, pp. 7–12.
2   Ibid., pp. 13–18.
3   Ibid., pp. 19–25.
4   Ibid., pp. 13–18.
5   Ibid., pp. 13–18.

Appendix 4.2

Insights and Hypotheses on Causes of Terrorism Identified on the Basis of a Survey of the Literature on Terrorism

Brynjar Lia

Why terrorism occurs is one of the most difficult questions facing terrorism researchers. Terrorists may be deprived and uneducated people, or affluent and well educated. Even if young males are usually highly over-represented in most terrorist organizations, one also finds terrorists among people of both sexes and of most ages. Terrorism occurs in rich as well as in poor countries; in the modern industrialized world and in less developed areas; during a process of transition and development, or prior to or after such a process; in former colonial states and in independent ones; and in established democracies as well as in less democratic regimes. This list could easily be extended, but it suffices as a demonstration of the wide diversity of conditions one needs to consider when trying to develop an understanding of the causes of terrorism. Obviously, this diversity makes it difficult to generalize about terrorism, since there are many 'terrorisms'. Different forms of terrorism also have different causes. We may distinguish between international and domestic terrorism; socio-revolutionary terrorism; and separatist terrorism. Socio-revolutionary terrorism spans different ideologies, including leftist, rightist and even religious trends. It is also important to recognize that what gives rise to terrorism may be different from what perpetuates terrorism over time.

When analysing the causes of terrorism, one is confronted with different levels of explanations. There are explanations at the individual and group levels, of a psychological or, more often, socio-psychological character, such as those that identify why individuals join a terrorist group, and why terrorist groups continue to resort to violence. Explanations at the societal or national level primarily attempt to identify non-spurious correlations between certain historical, cultural and socio-political characteristics of the larger society and the occurrence of terrorism. For example, the impact of modernization, democratization, economic inequality, etc. on terrorism falls into this category. Explanations at the world-system or international level seek to establish causal relationships between characteristics of the international state system and relations between states on the one hand, and the occurrence of international terrorism on the other.

The following are some psychological explanations of terrorism:[1]

1   There are a multitude of situations capable of provoking terrorism. What gives rise to terrorism may be different from what perpetuates terrorism over time.

2 The greater the political inequality of minority groups within a state, the more terrorism a state is likely to face (Lai).

3 Terrorism is most likely to occur under conditions of high levels of 'social distance' or 'social polarization' between perpetrators and victims, including a high degree of cultural and relational distance, inequality, and functional independence (Senechal de la Roche).

4 Suicide bombing is one result of hating one's sexual impulses (Baruch).

5 Both political and criminally motivated violence are overwhelmingly the work of young unmarried men (Buvinic and Morrison).

6 The choice of terrorism represents the outcome of a learning process from own experiences and the experiences of others (Crenshaw).

7 The failure to mobilize popular support for a radical political programme may trigger the decision to employ terrorism in order to engineer a violent confrontation with the authorities.

8 The decision to employ terrorism stems from the 'useful agenda-setting function' of international terrorist acts ('we force people to ask what is going on').

9 A sudden downturn in a dissident organization's fortunes may promote an underground organization to act in order to show its strength and potential.

10 Radical members of coalition groups will choose to resume and even escalate hostilities with a view to preventing a compromise between the moderate factions on both sides, and to undermine the government's confidence in ongoing negotiations (Stedman).

11 Terrorist groups and their enemy government often become locked in a cycle of attacks and counter-attacks, and the driving force is less the logic of deterrence and more their respective constituencies' demands that their victims must be avenged.

12 Periodic 'waves' of terrorism may be partly explained by the desire of terrorists to guarantee newsworthiness and consequently, media access (Weimann and Brosius).

13 Successful operations in one country are imitated by groups elsewhere.

The following are some societal explanations of terrorism:[2]

1 Modernization has dissolutional effects upon existing social norms and structures, through the rise of a society in which individuals find themselves alienated from social bonds, without any recognized structures of organization and influence, to the mobilization of frustration into terrorist activity.

2 Rapid economic modernization, measured in growth of real GDP, has a strong, significant impact on levels of ideological (as opposed to ethnic) terrorism in Western Europe (Engene).

3 There is a positive relationship between political deprivation of groups and the level of terrorism against the state, while economic measures of average individual deprivation in a state appear to have little effect (Lai).

4 Any connection between poverty, education and terrorism is indirect, complicated, and probably quite weak (Krueger and Maleckova).

5 The sheer number of terrorist and insurgent groups in countries with extreme poverty is overwhelming.

6 Despite claims to the contrary, the Palestinian–Israeli conflict also seems to confirm that poverty reinforces motivations for terrorism (Khashan).

7 Islamist terrorism in Egypt was not simply based on religious extremism. Rather, this movement grew out of the socio-economic conditions as well as the cultural and political tensions existing for the poorest of Egypt's poor (Nedoroscik).

8 The occurrence of terrorism in Western Europe is systematically related to low measures of freedom and democracy. This relationship is particularly strong for ideological (non-separatist) terrorism, but less so with regard to ethnic terrorism (Engene).

9   Ethnic terrorism in Western Europe is more likely in the less proportional democracies than in open, proportional systems, suggesting that the threshold for using violence depends on the existence of alternative channels of influence (Skjolberg).

10 Many developing countries today are ravaged by ethnic violence and terrorism after embarking on a transition process to market democracy. The causal link runs from the new free-market reforms, which allow ethnic minorities to accumulate disproportional wealth via political liberalization, permitting the spread of violent propaganda and the empowerment of the impoverished majorities, to the proliferation of ethnic violence (Chua).

11 Semi-authoritarian or semi-democratic countries, even without an ongoing democratization process, have the greatest risk of experiencing violent conflicts and terrorism (Ellingsen and Gleditsch).

12 Failed democracies that do not become consolidated authoritarian states are likely to experience tremendous amounts of terrorism (Lai).

13 Strong states capable of repressing terrorist and insurgent groups on their territory may do so only at the risk of transforming them into transnational terrorist organizations attacking targets abroad.

14 There is a strong association between ethnic diversity and ethnic terrorism in Western Europe (Engene).

15 Modern terrorism occurs because modern circumstances make terrorist methods exceptionally easy (Kegley).

16 Modern mass media is not the cause of terrorism per se, but it has considerable impact upon patterns of terrorism, once it has emerged. Important shifts in terrorism have coincided with the emergence and proliferation of new media technologies.

17 The presence of transnational organized crime groups creates a more permissive environment for transnational terrorism.

The following are some explanations linked to the international system:[3]

1   The global diffusion of certain political cultures and ideas, such as the concept of individuality, organization, and social action, provides local aggrieved parties with a conceptual model for rebellion and violent activism (Lizardo).

2   State sponsorship rarely explains the very occurrence of terrorism, with the important exception of state intelligence operatives perpetrating covert attacks abroad.

3   Serious foreign policy setbacks tend to increase the propensity for state-sponsored terrorism by authoritarian regimes (O'Brien).

4   Increased US dominance constrains the options for revisionist actors to alter the status quo through traditional means of influence, making terrorism a more attractive choice (Sobek and Braithwaite).

5   The projection of military power plants seeds of later terrorist reactions, as retaliation for previous American imperial actions (Bergesen and Liyzardo).

6   The contemporary wave of Islamist terrorism should be seen as an anti-colonial insurgency, rather than a religious backlash against modernity.

7   An international system dominated by hegemonic powers is likely to experience high levels of terrorism. A bipolar system is more likely to foster high, transnational anti-systemic terrorism.

8   Transnational terrorism thrives on armed conflicts. A central characteristic of terrorism is that terrorist acts often occur as part of a wider armed conflict.

9   Terrorism also occurs as part of widespread civil violence during intercommunal conflict.

10 Transnational terrorism reflects a civil war taking place between a government and its opposition movements, while foreign nationals and interests are targeted because of their assumed politico-military alliance with, or interventions on behalf of, the government in question (Doran).

11   If insurgent groups are unable to establish a domestic front, and are forced to flee, international terrorist attacks – whether on targets associated with the enemy regime or on its foreign allies – may often be the only possible way in which armed struggle can be pursued.

12   International attacks may also occur for agenda-setting purposes to past or ongoing wars.

13   The war in Vietnam appeared to contribute both directly and indirectly to the rise of radicalized leftist movements in the West, from which numerous terrorist groups emerged, many of which outlived the causes that had propelled them into action.

14   Participation in war intensifies social-political relations in a state, which in turn fosters radicalization of politics and the emergence of political violence groups. States participating in wars are likely to experience higher levels of terrorism (Lai).

15   States have facilitated international terrorism by fighting proxy wars through open or tacit support for insurgents and terrorist organizations operating in or against a foreign state (or states) (Byman).

16   One finds a relatively coinciding pattern of ebbs and flows of armed conflicts and international terrorism. Although terrorist tactics are used in one form or another during nearly all armed conflicts, only a minority of today's armed conflicts contribute *heavily* to international terrorism. When they do, factors such as direct foreign military presence or involvement (or in some cases lack of involvement) in the conflict appear to be critical, in addition to ideological and identity factors, such as the existence of politicized diasporas and refugee communities, and radical ideologies providing theoretical justifications for international attacks. Armed conflicts and terrorism are interlinked in multiple ways, and trends affecting the former will also impact on the latter.

Notes

1   Brynjar Lia, *Causes of Terrorism: An Expanded and Updated Review of the Literature*. Kjeller: Norwegian Defence Research Establishment, 2005, pp. 8–21.

2   Ibid., pp. 21–48.

3   Ibid., pp. 49–71.

Appendix 4.3

Al-Qaeda Communiqués by
Bin Laden and Al-Zawahiri:
A Chronology

Donald Holbrook

Terrorism consists of violence and propaganda, and the two should be viewed next to each other and analysed in their interaction. To illustrate the propaganda dimension, this appendix lists the communiqués of Osama bin Laden and Ayman al-Zawahiri, the leaders of the core of Al-Qaeda.[1]

> Many international media agencies corresponded with us requesting an interview with us. We believe this is a good opportunity to make Muslims aware of what is taking place over the land of the two Holy Mosques as well as of what is happening here in Afghanistan of establishing and strengthen the religion, and applying Shari'a. It is obvious that the media war in this century is one of the strongest methods; in fact, its ratio may reach 90% of the total preparation for the battles.
>
> *Osama bin Laden, undated letter to Mullah Umar, the leader of the Afghan Taliban*[2]

Recognizing the impact of propaganda and the importance of engaging with the media has been central to the strategy of the Al-Qaeda core leadership from the very beginning. Such messages seek to supplement, strengthen and justify the violent faith-based strategy. Appeals are made to the Muslim population (as a whole or within specific areas), who are urged to rise up against alleged oppression, secularism and immorality. Identified enemies are intimidated, threatened, but occasionally given conditions for the cessation of violence. Finally, Al-Qaeda distributes messages demanding support for the creation of a Shari'ah state, and justifies the violent tactics employed in reaching its goal, although it struggles to justify Muslim casualties.

Giving interviews to curious journalists was no longer an option in the wake of the 11 September attacks, prompting an increased emphasis on the indigenous message output. At first, some difficulties were encountered with distribution and the favoured method was sending material to satellite TV channels to achieve the desired global reach. Gradually, however, and with the help of internet forums and upload websites, the dedicated media wing, As-Sahab ('the clouds'), began distributing increasingly sophisticated videos online. The output leapt from 6 videos in 2002 to 97 five years later, although it has since abated.[3] Many other 'media production wings' have since emerged, attached to individual movements or the global militant Islamist cause in general.

The list that follows provides an overview of most of the Al-Qaeda messages by Osama bin Laden and Ayman al-Zawahiri. However, some of the earlier Zawahiri messages are more likely related to his capacity as 'Amir' of Egyptian Islamic Jihad, although the distinction is sometimes difficult to make. The decision to focus on Zawahiri and Bin Laden only was based on the way in which an analysis of their output provides a degree of continuity and thus the opportunity to grasp the extent of divergence over time. Several figures may have been just as, or even more, influential in terms of militant Islamist thinking.[4] Other individuals are also becoming increasingly prominent, especially Bagram escapee Abu Yahya al-Libi, whose statements are sought after on sympathetic internet forums.

The data collected are mostly from open sources and, given the increased use of the internet for distribution, increasingly easy to locate. For translations, publications such as the IntelCenter volumes have been a valuable source of material. In some cases, however, communiqués have been secured from more restricted sources, especially the Foreign Broadcast Information Service, now Open Source Center, which remains out of reach for most researchers outside the United States. One database that has been made publicly available is the Harmony Database component of larger Department of Defense-based databases, which provides researchers with interesting and valuable background data. Al-Qaeda output is also being monitored by various organizations, with the Nine-Eleven Finding Answers foundation being particularly prominent. Finally, the numerous books written about Al-Qaeda communiqués can often prove helpful. The overview includes several communiqués that were published in two particularly helpful volumes, *The Al-Qaeda Reader* and *Al-Qaeda in Its Own Words*.[5]

The timeline of the data reviewed is presented in the accompanying graph (Figure A4.3). It shows how Zawahiri has gradually taken over from Bin Laden in the dissemination of messages, providing detailed commentary on current events and justification of methods, while the shorter, less frequent, Bin Laden messages reiterate the basics. Tellingly, however, the graph also shows how a safe haven, direct access to reporters, and the opportunity to interact with them with impunity, resulted in considerable proliferation in the number of messages from Bin Laden in the 1990s. Relative freedom of operation in the Pakistani tribal areas, along with the benefits of technology, has seen output increase once more. Given the importance of such 'media operations' for the Al-Qaeda leadership, the need for researchers and the counterterrorism establishment to comprehend, monitor and counter this component of militant Islamism should be clear.

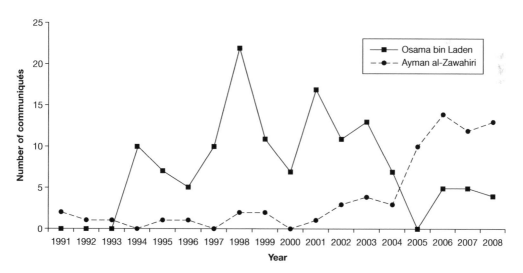

Figure A4.3 Frequency of communication releases by Al-Qaeda's leadership.

Date (dd/mm/yyyy)	AQ figure	Description	Source
00/01/1991	AAZ	'The Bitter Harvest: The Brotherhood in Sixty Years'	Raymond Ibrahim, (2007) *Al-Qaeda Reader*. Broadway Books, 2007 + G. Kepel and J.-P. Milelli (eds), *Al-Qaeda in Its Own Words*. Harvard U. Press, 2008.
00/01/1992	AAZ	'The Black Book: An Account of the Torture of Muslims in the Time of Husni Mubarak'	*Militant Ideology Atlas Research Compendium*, November 2006
00/01/1993	AAZ / Al-Jihad	'Advice to the Community to Reject the Fatwa of Sheikh Bin Baz Authorizing Parliamentary Representation: Published Under the Supervision of Ayman al-Zawahiri'	Kepel and Milelli (eds) (2008)
09/03/1994	OBL	'Osama bin Laden Denies "Terrorism" Link'. London *Al-Quds al-'Arabi* in Arabic 9 Mar 1994, p. 4	FBIS compilation 1994–2004 [*FBIS Report: Compilation of Osama bin Laden Statements 1994 – January 2004*]
12/04/1994	OBL	'Our Invitation to Give Advice and Reform'	CTC/Harmony [see www.ctc.usma. edu/harmony/harmony_docs.asp]
07/06/1994	OBL	'Saudi Arabia Supports the Communists in Yemen'	CTC/Harmony
11/07/1994	OBL	'The Banishment of Communism from the Arabian Peninsula: The Episode and the Proof'	CTC/Harmony
19/07/1994	OBL	'Quran Scholars in the Face of Despotism'	CTC/Harmony
08/08/1994	OBL	'Saudi Islamic Opposition Opens London Office'. London *Al-Quds al-'Arabi* in Arabic, 8 Aug. 1994, p. 1.	FBIS compilation 1994–2004
12/09/1994	OBL	'Saudi Arabia Unveils its War Against Islam and its Scholars'	CTC/Harmony
16/09/1994	OBL	'Urgent Letter to Security Officials'	CTC/Harmony
15/10/1994	OBL	'Higher Committee for Harm!!'	CTC-Harmony
29/12/1994	OBL	'Open Letter for Shaykh Bin Baz on the Invalidity of His Fatwa on Peace with the Jews'	CTC/Harmony
29/01/1995	OBL	'Second letter to Shaykh Abd Al Aziz Bin Baz from the Reform and Advice Foundation'	CTC/Harmony
12/02/1995	OBL	'Prince Salman and Ramadan Alms'	CTC/Harmony
09/03/1995	OBL	'Saudi Arabia Continues its War Against Islam and its Scholars'	CTC/Harmony
00/04/1995	AAZ	'Our Stance Towards Iran: Response to the Accusation of Cooperation Between the Salafi Jihadi Movement and Renegade Iran'	*Militant Ideology Atlas Research Compendium* November 2006

Date (dd/mm/yyyy)	AQ figure	Description	Source
06/05/1995	OBL	'Scholars are the Prophet's Successors'	CTC/Harmony
11/07/1995	OBL	'Prince Sultan and the Air Aviation Commissions'	CTC/Harmony
03/08/1995	OBL	'An Open Letter to King Fahd on the Occasion of the Recent Cabinet Reshuffle'	NEFA [+ see also other sources, e.g. Hegghammer (*FFI Rapport* 2002/01393)]
11/08/1995	OBL	'The Bosnia Tragedy and the Deception of the Servant of the Two Mosques'	CTC/Harmony
00/01/1996	AAZ	'Healing the Hearts of Believers: On Some Concepts of Jihad in the Islamabad Operation'	*Militant Ideology Atlas Research Compendium*, November 2006 + Chr. Hellmich 'Al-Qaeda – Terrorists, Hypocrites, Fundamentalists' in *Third World Quarterly* (2005) + Azzam Maha, Al-Qaeda: 'The Misunderstood Wahabi Connection . . .', RIIA *Briefing Paper* no. 1 (2003)
17/06/1996	OBL	'Osama bin Laden Reportedly Interviewed in London'. Cairo *Rose al-Yusuf* in Arabic on 17 June 1996 on pp. 25–27	FBIS compilation 1994–2004
10/07/1996	OBL	'Interview With Saudi Dissident Bin Laden'. London *Independent* in English, 10 July 1996, p. 14	FBIS compilation 1994–2005
02/09/1996	OBL	'Bin Laden Declares Jihad on Americans'. London AL-ISLAH in Arabic, 2 Sep. 1996. ['Message From Usama Bin-Muhammad Bin Laden to His Muslim Brothers in the Whole World and Especially in the Arabian Peninsula: Declaration of Jihad Against the Americans Occupying the Land of the Two Holy Mosques; Expel the Heretics From the Arabian Peninsula'	FBIS compilation 1994–2005 + www.kimsoft.com/2001/binladen war.htm
00/10/ 1996	OBL	'Mujahid Usamah Bin Laden Talks Exclusively to "*Nida'ul Islam*" About The New Powder Keg in The Middle East'	*Nida ul Islam* (iss. 16 October– November 1996) [islam.org.au]. See also Hegghammer (*FFI Rapport* 2002/01393)
27/11/1996	OBL	'Bin Laden interviewed on Jihad against the US'	FBIS compilation 1994–2004
20/02/1997	OBL	'Correspondent meets with opposition leader Bin Laden'	FBIS compilation 1994–2004
01/03/1997	OBL	'Peter Arnett interviews Osama bin Laden'	CNN
03/03/1997	OBL	'Bin Laden cited on Prince Sultan's US visit'	FBIS compilation 1994–2004

Date (dd/mm/yyyy)	AQ figure	Description	Source
15/03/1997	OBL	'Bin Laden charges US involvement in China bombings'	FBIS compilation 1994–2004
18/03/1997	OBL	'Pakistan interviews Osama bin Laden'	FBIS compilation 1994–2004
22/03/1997	OBL	'Muslim leader warns of a new assault on US forces'	FBIS compilation 1994–2004
16/04/1997	OBL	'The Saudi Regime and the Reputed Tragedies of the Pilgrims'	CTC/Harmony
06/06/1997	OBL	'Osama bin Laden dares US commandos to come to Afghanistan'	FBIS compilation 1994–2004
20/10/1997	OBL	'Osama bin Laden backs Harkatul Ansar against US'	FBIS compilation 1994–2004
27/11/1997	OBL	'Daily reports Osama bin Laden's threat against Americans'	FBIS compilation 1994–2004
17/01/1998	OBL	'Bin Laden claims foiling of UN's Afghan conspiracy'	FBIS compilation 1994–2004
16/02/1998	OBL	'Bin Laden condoles with al-Bashir on Salih's death'	FBIS compilation 1994–2004
23/02/1998	OBL & AAZ	Text of fatwa urging jihad against Americans	FBIS compilation 1994–2004 + Federation of American Scientists (FAS) + Walter Laqueur: *Voices of Terror.* Reed Press, 2004
23/03/1998	OBL	'Bin Laden urges "expulsion" of invaders'	FBIS compilation 1994–2004
31/03/1998	OBL	'Interview with Osama bin Laden reported'	FBIS compilation 1994–2004
15/04/1998	OBL	'Bin Laden warns against Richardson mission to Afghanistan'	FBIS compilation 1994–2004
07/05/1998	OBL	'Supporting the Fatwa of the Afghani Religious Scholars of Ejecting the American Forces from the Land of the Two Holy Mosques'	CTC/Harmony
14/05/1998	OBL	'Bin Laden backs Afghan fatwa on US forces'	FBIS compilation 1994–2004
18/05/1998	OBL	'Bin Laden sees US terrorism listing as good for Taliban'	FBIS compilation 1994–2004
19/05/1998	OBL	'World Islamic Front' statement urges jihad on America, Israel'	FBIS compilation 1994–2004
28/05/1998	OBL	'Bin Laden creates new front against US, Israel'	FBIS compilation 1994–2004
28/05/1998	OBL	'Bin Laden declares jihad against US troops'	FBIS compilation 1994–2004
00/05/1998	OBL	'Usama bin Laden answers questions from supporters	PBS Broadcasting
01/06/1998	OBL	Bin Laden congratulates Pakistan on nuclear weapons'	FBIS compilation 1994–2004
15/06/1998	OBL	Article on interview with Osama bin Laden	FBIS compilation 1994–2004
21/07/1998	OBL	'Bin Laden calls for "jihad" against Jews, Americans'	FBIS compilation 1994–2004

Date (dd/mm/yyyy)	AQ figure	Description	Source
23/08/1998	OBL	'Bin Laden warns Clinton "battle has not yet started"'	FBIS compilation 1994–2004
02/09/1998	OBL	'Bin Laden praises Pakistan for love of Islam'	FBIS compilation 1994–2004
12/09/1998	OBL	'Osama bin Laden sends message to anti-US conference'	FBIS compilation 1994–2004 + Hegghammer (*FFI Rapport* 2002/01393)
18/11/1998	OBL	'Bin Laden: expel Jews, Christians from holy places'	FBIS compilation 1994–2004
00/12/1998	AAZ	'Interview with Jamal Ismail'	Hegghammer (*FFI Rapport* 2002/01393)
24/12/1998	OBL	'Bin Laden denies role in bombing of US missions'	FBIS compilation 1994–2004
04/01/1999	OBL	'Associate Press carries excerpts from Bin Laden interviews'	FBIS compilation 1994–2004
06/01/1999	OBL	Journalist interviews Bin Laden	FBIS compilation 1994–2004
11/01/1999	OBL	*Time* magazine interviews Bin Laden	FBIS compilation 1994–2004 + *Time* magazine
13/01/1999	OBL	CBS releases interview with Bin Laden	FBIS compilation 1994–2004
14/01/1999	AAZ	'Muslim Egypt Between the Whips of the Torturers and the Administration of Traitors'	*Militant Ideology Atlas Research Compendium* November 2006
01/02/1999	OBL	*Esquire* interview with Bin Laden	FBIS compilation 1994–2004
20/02/1999	OBL	May 1998 interview with Bin Laden reported	FBIS compilation 1994–2004
19/04/1999	AAZ	'Letter to Abu Yasir'	Al-Qaeda's Secret Emails' *Al-Sharq al-Awsat* articles by Mohammed Al-Shafey, published 12/06/2005
08/06/1999	OBL	'Osama bin Laden pens a letter in support of Kashmir jihad'	FBIS compilation 1994–2004
10/06/1999	OBL	Al-Jazeera programme on Bin Laden	FBIS compilation 1994–2004
25/07/1999	OBL	'Bin Laden calls on Muslims to declare jihad on US'	FBIS compilation 1994–2004
12/09/1999	OBL	'OBL orders mujahidin to shoot US commandos "on sight"'	FBIS compilation 1994–2004
28/09/1999	OBL	'OBL denies providing military aid to Kashmiris'	FBIS compilation 1994–2004
09/01/2000	OBL	'Osama bin Laden denounces US-sponsored "world order"'	FBIS compilation 1994–2004
02/05/2000	OBL	'OBL sees holy war in "every street" of US'	FBIS compilation 1994–2004
22/06/2000	OBL	'Supporters of Shariah website publishes Bin Laden "speech"'	FBIS compilation 1994–2004
26/06/2000	OBL	'Osama bin Laden renews calls for jihad'	FBIS compilation 1994–2004
20/08/2000	OBL	Interview with *Ghazi* magazine	*Through our Enemies Eyes* by 'Anonymous' (2003)
21/09/2000	OBL	'Bin Laden, others, pledge "jihad" to release prisoners in US, Saudi jails'	FBIS compilation 1994–2004 + Hegghammer (*FFI Rapport* 2002/01393

Date (dd/mm/yyyy)	AQ figure	Description	Source
13/11/2000	OBL	Interview with *al-Ra'i al-'Amm*, a Kuwaiti newspaper	Hegghammer (*FFI Rapport* 2002/01393)
07/01/2001	OBL	'Daily prints Osama bin Laden "letter" calling for "Global Islamic State"'	FBIS compilation 1994–2004
03/03/2001	OBL	'Ausaf receives Bin Laden's poem on resolve to continue jihad'	FBIS compilation 1994–2004
07/03/2001	OBL	'Bin Laden implicitly praises USS *Cole* bombing at son's wedding'	FBIS compilation 1994–2004
01/04/2001	OBL	'Letter from Usama Bin Laden to the scholars of Deyubende in Peshawar in Pakistan'	Harmony Database/CTC + NEFA
03/04/2001	OBL	'Osama bin Laden regrets restrictions imposed by Taliban'	FBIS compilation 1994–2004
10/04/2001	OBL	'Bin Laden calls on Muslims to invest in Afghanistan, join jihad'	FBIS compilation 1994–2004
07/05/2001	OBL	'Transcript of Bin Laden's speech at his son's wedding'	FBIS compilation 1994–2004
17/05/2001	OBL	'Osama bin Laden would make life "miserable" for United States if Taleban allows'	FBIS compilation 1994–2004
27/06/2001	OBL	'OBL sends "message voice" to Palestinians, vows not to let them down'	FBIS compilation 1994–2004
16/09/2001	OBL	'Afghanistan: Bin Laden denies involvement in terrorist attacks in US'	FBIS compilation 1994–2004
20/09/2001	OBL	Al Jazeerah TV broadcasts Osama bin Laden's 1998 interview	FBIS compilation 1994–2004
24/09/2001	OBL	'Text of Bin Laden's letter to the Pakistani people, 24 Sept.'	FBIS compilation 1994–2004 + Hegghammer (*FFI Rapport* 2002/01393)
07/10/2001	OBL	'Al-Jazirah carries Bin Laden's address on US strikes'	FBIS compilation 1994–2004 + Hegghammer (*FFI Rapport* 2002/01393) + Ibrahim (2007)
03/11/2001	OBL	'Bin Laden condemns the UN, talks of Crusader-Zionist war against Muslims'.	Hegghammer (*FFI Rapport* 2002/01393)
10/11/2001	OBL	'Osama claims he has nukes: If US uses N-arms it will get same response' – Interview with Hamid Mir'	*The Dawn* + Hegghammer (*FFI Rapport* 2002/01393)
02/12/2001	AAZ	'Knights under the Prophet's Banner: Mediations on the Jihadist Movement'	FBIS Report of original article from *Al-Sharq Al-Awsat* also available from Islamist websites with new cover
13/12/2001	OBL	Al Jazeera airs video statement by Usama bin Laden	Al Jazeera + Archive.org / Islamist websites
27/12/2001	OBL	'Bin Laden speaks out against military operations in Afghanistan'	Hegghammer (*FFI Rapport* 2002/01393)

Appendix 4.3: Al-Qaeda Communiqués

Date (dd/mm/yyyy)	AQ figure	Description	Source
00/02/2002	OBL	Al Jazeerah TV website reports on 'row' with CNN over Bin Laden's tape	FBIS compilation 1994–2004
17/04/2002	OBL	MBC TV carries video of Bin Laden, aides supporting 911 attacks	FBIS compilation 1994–2004
18/04/2002	OBL	Al Jazeerah airs 'selected portions' of latest Al-Qa'ida tape in 11 Sept. attacks	FBIS compilation 1994–2004
19/05/2002	OBL	*Sunday Times* obtains film vowing revenge on UK, US, others. British-based Islamic news agency receives encrypted Bin Laden video	FBIS compilation 1994–2004
00/06/2002	OBL	'Al-Qaeda's Declaration in Response to the Saudi Ulema: "It's Best You Prostrate Yourselves in Secret". Purported OBL, or close affiliation'	Ibrahim (2007)
27/06/2002	OBL	'Website posts Bin Laden's statement on Saudi Crown prince Abdallah's initiative'	FBIS compilation 1994–2004
11/08/2002	Unkn.	'The "constitutional charter" of Al-Qaeda and the format of the pledge of allegiance to AQ'	CTC/Harmony, initially Defense Intelligence Agency
00/09/2002	AAZ	'The Interview of Dr Ayman al-Zawahiri'	ITSTIME + *IntelCenter: Words of Ayman al-Zawahiri* vol. 1 (2008)
06/10/2002	OBL	'A Message Addressed to the American People'	*IntelCenter: Words of Osama bin Laden* vol. 1 (2008) + FBIS
09/10/2002	AAZ	Message from Zawahiri which AP news agency received on a CD marked 'As-Sahab Foundation for Islamic Media'	Hegghammer (*FFI Rapport* 2005/1428)
14/10/2002	OBL	'Al-Qa'ida issues statement under Bin Laden's name on Afghan war anniversary'	FBIS compilation 1994–2004
26/10/2002	OBL	Islamist site publishes Bin Laden's 'Letter to the American People'	FBIS compilation 1994–2004 + Ibrahim (2007)
12/11/2002	OBL	'Osama bin Laden hails recent operations in Bali, Moscow, Jordan'	*IntelCenter: Words of Osama bin Laden* vol. 1 (2008) + FBIS compilation (p. 227) + Hegghammer (*FFI Rapport* 2005/1428)
28/11/2002	OBL	'Bin Laden urges "Arabian Peninsula" people to prepare for "all-out war"'	FBIS compilation 1994–2004
30/12/2002	AAZ	'Al Walaa wa al Baraa' (Loyalty and Enmity: An Inherited Doctrine and a Lost Reality' [Ibrahim's translation]), 'Loyalty and Separation: Changing an Article of Faith and Losing Sight of Reality' (Kepel and Milelli)	Ibrahim (2007) + Milelli (2008)

Date (dd/mm/yyyy)	AQ figure	Description	Source
19/01/2003	OBL	'Bin Laden message urges Islamic factions to unite, fight "external" enemy'	FBIS compilation 1994–2004
21/01/2003	OBL	Full text of interview held with Al-Qa'ida leader Osama bin Laden on 21 Oct. 2001	FBIS compilation 1994–2004 + Hegghammer (*FFI Rapport* 2005/1428)
01/02/2003	OBL	'On the obligation of Jihad for everyone, the weak foundations of America, the plot to annex Saudi Arabia and establish a Jewish superstate'	*IntelCenter: Words of Osama bin Laden* vol. 1
11/02/2003	OBL	'A Message to Our Brothers in Iraq'	*IntelCenter: Words of Osama bin Laden* vol. 1 + FBIS compilation, p. 247
00/03/2003	OBL	'Bin Laden's statement calls for revolt against Saudis, death to Americans, Jews'	FBIS compilation 1994–2004
09/04/2003	OBL	'Pakistan: Osama bin Laden urges Muslims to launch "suicide attacks" against US'	FBIS compilation 1994–2004
09/04/2003	OBL	Kashmiri daily reports OBL's message urging jihad against Pakistan, Arab States	FBIS compilation 1994–2004
21/05/2003	AAZ	Attack on Arab support for US war in Iraq. Call for attack on Norway *et al.*	Hegghammer (*FFI Rapport* 2005/1428)
29/05/2003	OBL	'Bin Laden threatens "terrible response" if death of 2 Saudi clerics is confirmed'	FBIS compilation 1994–2004
11/06/2003	OBL	Saudi sources: 'OBL denied involvement in Riyadh bombings in message to his mother'	FBIS compilation 1994–2004
03/08/2003	AAZ	Audiotape about Guantánamo prisoners	Hegghammer (*FFI Rapport* 2005/1428) + *IntelCenter Ayman Al-Zawahiri* vol. 1
10/09/2003	OBL & AAZ	Al Jazeerah Airs Bin Laden, Al-Zawahiri Tape on Anniversary of 11 Sept. Attacks	FBIS compilation 1994–2004
28/09/2003	AAZ	'Message to Muslims in Pakistan and Afghanistan'	Hegghammer (*FFI Rapport* 2005/1428)
18/10/2003	OBL	Al Jazeera carries Bin Laden's audio messages to Iraqis, Americans	FBIS compilation 1994–2004
18/10/2003	OBL	'Second letter to the Muslims of Iraq'	Kepel and Milelli: *Al-Qaeda in its Own Words* (2005, 2008) + see also FBIS
16/11/2003	OBL	Al Jazeera TV: Al-Qa'ida claims responsibility for Istanbul bombings	FBIS compilation 1994–2004
04/01/2004	OBL	Bin Laden warns of 'grand plots' against Arabs, criticizes Gulf rulers	FBIS compilation 1994–2004 + the *Observer*
24/02/2004	AAZ	'Zawahiri on the state of the union speech and the French headscarf ban'	Hegghammer (*FFI Rapport* 2005/1428)
08/03/2004	AAZ	Audiotape recognizing the two-year anniversary of the battle of Tora Bora	Hegghammer (*FFI Rapport* 2005/1428)

Date (dd/mm/yyyy)	AQ figure	Description	Source
25/03/2004	AAZ	Audiotape calling for Musharraf overthrow	Hegghammer (*FFI Rapport* 2005/1428)
14/04/2004	OBL	'Offer of peace treaty to Europeans'	Ibrahim (2007)
15/04/2004	OBL	'Peace offering to Europeans'	*IntelCenter: Words of Osama bin Laden* vol. 1
06/05/2004	OBL	'People of Iraq'	*IntelCenter: Words of Osama bin Laden* vol. 1
30/10/2004	OBL	'Message to Americans. On 9/11, how the idea (allegedly) was formed, and the policies of the two presidents Bush'	*IntelCenter: Words of Osama bin Laden* vol. 1 + also ITSTIME and MEMRI + *Al-Qaeda in its Own Words* (ed. Gilles Kepel and Jean-Pierre Milelli, trans. Pascale Ghazaleh).
16/12/2004	OBL	'Message concerning Saudi Arabia'	*IntelCenter: Words of Osama bin Laden* vol. 1 + Archive.org/Al-Hesbah
27/12/2004	OBL	'To the people of Iraq Muslims. On the Allawi regime, elections'	*IntelCenter: Words of Osama bin Laden* vol. 1 (2008)
11/02/2005	AAZ	'The Freeing of Humanity and Homelands under the Banner of the Quran'	Jihadunspun.com + forums.Islamicawakening.com
09/06/2005	AAZ	Zawahiri letter to Zarqawi	Director of National Intelligence
17/06/2005	AAZ	'On the need to rid the Muslim world of Crusaders and their supporters, implement Sharia. Need to unite Iraqis'	*IntelCenter: Words of Ayman al-Zawahiri* vol. 1
04/08/2005	AAZ	'Al-Qaeda Leader Ayman Al-Zawahiri Calls to Get Rid of Islamic Regimes'	MEMRI
15/11/2005	AAZ	'Wills of the Knights of the London Raid'	Ibrahim (2007)
06/12/2005	AAZ	'The Victory of the Islamic Religion in Iraq'	ITSTIME + *IntelCenter: Words of Ayman Al-Zawahiri* vol. 1
07/12/2005	AAZ	First interview with Ayman al-Zawahiri	Ibrahim (2007) + *IntelCenter: Words of Ayman Al-Zawahiri* vol. 1
10/12/2005	AAZ	'Obstacles to Jihad'	ITSTIME + *IntelCenter: Words of Ayman Al-Zawahiri* vol.1
19/01/2006	OBL	Bin Laden truce offer to the Americans	Ibrahim (2007) + IntelCenter + MEMRI + Archive.org/Islamist websites
20/01/2006	AAZ	'Zawahiri presents a poem from Maulawi Muhibbullah al-Kandahari'	Globalterroralert.com
30/01/2006	AAZ	'Bajawr Massacre and the Lies of the Crusaders' – Response to attempted attack on Zawahiri's location in the FATA (the village of Damdula, in Bajuar) which killed 18 people	Ibrahim (2007) + *IntelCenter: Words of Ayman Al-Zawahiri* vol. 1
04/03/2006	AAZ	'The Alternative is Da'wa and Jihad'	*IntelCenter: Words of Ayman Al-Zawahiri* vol. 1
12/04/2006	AAZ	'Four Years Since the Battle of Tora Bora – From Tora Bora to Iraq'	*IntelCenter: Words of Ayman Al-Zawahiri* vol. 1

Date (dd/mm/yyyy)	AQ figure	Description	Source
23/04/2006	OBL	'Oh People of Islam'	*IntelCenter: Words of Osama bin Laden* vol. 1 + Al-Jazeera + Archive.org/Islamist websites
28/04/2006	AAZ	'Letter to the People of Pakistan'	*IntelCenter Words of Ayman al-Zawahiri* vol. 1
23/05/2006	OBL	'A Testimony to the Truth'	*IntelCenter: Words of Osama Bin Laden* + Archive.org / Al-Hesbah
09/06/2006	AAZ	'Support for Palestinians'	*IntelCenter: Words of Ayman al-Zawahiri* vol. 1
21/06/2006	AAZ	'American Crimes in Kabul'	*IntelCenter: Words of Ayman al-Zawahiri* vol. 1
24/06/2006	AAZ	'Lamentation of Abu Musab Al-Zarqawi – 'Elegizing the Ummah's Martyr and Emir of the Martyrs Abu Musab al-Zarqawi, May Allah Have Mercy on Him'	ITSTIME + see also IntelCenter
27/06/2006	AAZ	'The Zionist Crusader's Aggression on Gaza and Lebanon'	*IntelCenter: Words of Ayman al-Zawahiri* vol. 1
29/06/2006	OBL	'Elegizing the Ummah's Martyr and Emir of the Martyrs, Abu Musab al-Zarqawi'	*IntelCenter: Words of Osama bin Laden* vol. 1
00/07/2006	OBL	'To the Ummah in General and to the Mujahideen in Iraq and Somalia in Particular'	*IntelCenter: Words of Osama bin Laden* vol. 1
02/09/2006	Zawahiri + Gadahn/ Amriki	'An Invitation to Islam'	As-Sahab/Al-Boraq.com
11/09/2006	AAZ	'Hot Issues with Shaykh Ayman Al-Zawahiri'	ITSTIME + see also IntelCenter
29/09/2006	AAZ	'Bush, the Vatican's Pope, Darfur and the Crusaders'	*IntelCenter: Words of Ayman al-Zawahiri* vol. 1
22/12/2006	AAZ	'Realities of the Conflict 'Between Islam and Unbelief'	*IntelCenter: Words of Ayman al-Zawahiri* vol. 1
30/12/2006	AAZ	'Congratulations on the Eid to the Ummah of Tawhid'	*IntelCenter: Words of Ayman al-Zawahiri* vol. 1 + Laura Mansfield
05/01/2007	AAZ	'Rise and Support our Brothers in Somalia'	*IntelCenter: Words of Ayman al-Zawahiri* vol. 1
22/01/2007	AAZ	'The Correct Equation'	You Tube + Laura Mansfield + *IntelCenter: Words of Ayman al-Zawahiri* vol.1
13/02/2007	AAZ	'Lessons, Examples and Great Events in the Year 1427'	*IntelCenter: Words of Ayman al-Zawahiri* vol. 1
11/03/2007	AAZ	'Palestine is the concern of all Muslims'	You Tube, forums, ITSTIME + see also *IntelCenter: Words of Ayman al-Zawahiri* vol. 1
05/05/2007	AAZ	'The Empire of Evil is About to End, And a New Dawn is About to Break Over Mankind'	ITSTIME + see also IntelCenter
23/05/2007	AAZ	Announces the death of Taliban leader Mullah Dadullah Akhund	ITSTIME + see also IntelCenter

Date (dd/mm/yyyy)	AQ figure	Description	Source
25/06/2007	AAZ	'Forty Years since the Fall of Jerusalem'	IntelCenter: Words of Ayman al-Zawahiri vol. 1
04/07/2007	AAZ	'The Advice of One Concerned'	IntelCenter: Words of Ayman al-Zawahiri vol. 1 + Archive.org
10/07/2007	AAZ	'Malicious Britain and its Indian Slaves'	IntelCenter: Words of Ayman al-Zawahiri vol. 1
11/07/2007	AAZ	'The Aggression Against Lal Masjid'	IntelCenter: Words of Ayman al-Zawahiri vol. 1
07/09/2007	OBL	'The Solution: A message from shaykh Osama bin Laden to the American people'	As-Sahab/You Tube/Al-Ekhlass/ NEFA also ITSTIME + IntelCenter
20/09/2007	OBL	'Come to Jihad: a Speech to the People of Pakistan'	NEFA foundation + see also IntelCenter
22/10/2007	OBL	'Message to the People of Iraq'	NEFA foundation + see also IntelCenter + Archive.org / Al-Hesbah
30/11/2007	OBL	'Message to the People of Europe'	Laura Mansfield/You Tube/ As-Sahab (Al-Ekhlaas forum)/ NEFA + see also IntelCenter + Archive.org
14/12/2007	AAZ	'Annapolis – The Betrayal'	NEFA foundation + see also IntelCenter
16/12/2007	AAZ	'A Review of Events' – As Sahab publishes fourth interview with Zawahiri	NEFA foundation, ITSTIME + see also IntelCenter
29/12/2007	OBL	'The Way to Frustrate the Conspiracies'	NEFA + IntelCenter
00/01/2008	AAZ	'Exoneration: A Letter Exonerating the Ummah of the Pen and the Sword from the Unjust Allegation of Feebleness and Weakness' or 'Exoneration: A treatise on the exoneration of the nation of the pen and sword of the denigrating charge of being irresolute . . .'	Open Source Center
27/02/2008	AAZ	'An Elegy to the Martyred Commander Abu al-Layth al-Libi'	NEFA Foundation + see also IntelCenter
06/03/2008	AAZ	'Letter to Abu Umar al-Baghdadi of the Islamic State of Iraq'	Foundation for Defence of Democracies – 12http://www. defenddemocracy.org/index.php? option=com_content&task=view& id=11782255&Itemid=353
19/03/2008	OBL	'May our Mothers be Bereaved of us if we Fail to Help our Prophet (Peace be upon Him)'	NEFA foundation, You Tube, LiveLink + see also IntelCenter
20/03/2008	OBL	'A way for the salvation of Palestine'	NEFA foundation, You Tube, forums + see also IntelCenter + Islamist forum
23/03/2008	AAZ	'A Call to Help Our People in Gaza'	NEFA foundation + see also IntelCenter

Date (dd/mm/yyyy)	AQ figure	Description	Source
02/04/2008	AAZ	'The Open Meeting with Sheikh Ayman al-Zawahiri, Part One'	*IntelCenter: Words of Ayman al-Zawahiri* vol. 1 + NEFA + Islamist websites / Archive.org
17/04/2008	AAZ	'Shaykh Ayman Al-Zawahiri – On the fifth anniversary of the invasion and torture of Iraq'	NEFA foundation, forums + see also IntelCenter
21/04/2008	AAZ	'The Open Meeting with Sheikh Ayman al-Zawahiri, Part Two'	*IntelCenter: Words of Ayman al-Zawahiri* vol. 1
16/05/2008	OBL	'Reasons of the struggle on the occasion of the 60th anniversary of the founding of the occupying state of Israel'	ITSTIME
18/05/2008	OBL	'A Message to the Muslim Nation'	Open Source Center + ITSTIME
04/06/2008	AAZ	'On the Anniversary of the Naksa . . . Break the Siege of Gaza'	Open Source Center
10/08/2008	AAZ	'A Message from Shaikh Ayman al-Zawahiri to Pakistan Army and the People of Pakistan'	NEFA + You Tube
24/08/2008	AAZ	'In Lamentation of a Group of Heroes'	NEFA
19/11/2008	AAZ	'The Exit of Bush and Arrival of Obama'	Archive.org / Islamist websites
21/11/2008	AAZ	'Al-Azhar: The Lions Den: Interview with Shaykh Ayman al-Zawahiri'	NEFA + Archive.org / Islamist websites
00/12/2008	AAZ	The Martyrdom of Heroes and Betrayal of our Rulers'	Global Islamic Media Front + see also NEFA
06/01/2009	AAZ	'The Massacre of Gaza and the Siege of the Traitors'	Archive.org / Islamist websites + NEFA
14/01/2009	OBL	'Call for Jihad to Stop the Gaza Assault'	Archive.org / Islamist websites + NEFA
13/02/2009	AAZ	'The Sacrifices of Gaza . . . And Conspiracies'	Global Islamic Media Front
22/02/2009	AAZ	From Kabul To Mogadishu'	Islamist websites
00/03/2009	AAZ	'The Crusade Sets Its Sights on the Sudan'	Islamist websites
14/03/2009	OBL	'Practical steps to liberate Palestine'	Islamist websites
19/03/2009	OBL	'Fight on, O Champions of Somalia'	Islamist websites
20/03/2009	AAZ	'Six years since the invasion of Iraq and thirty years since the signing of the Israeli Peace Accords'	Islamist websites
24/03/2009	AAZ	'The Crusade Sets its Sights on the Sudan'	Islamist websites
02/06/2009	AAZ	'The Floggers of Egypt and the Agents of America Welcome Obama'	Islamist websites
03/06/2009	OBL	Audio recording aired on Al Jazeera (subsequently distributed on Archive.org)	Reuters + Al Jazeera + Archive.org

Date (dd/mm/yyyy)	AQ figure	Description	Source
Unknown	AAZ	'Response to a Grave Uncertainty from Shaykh al-Albani Regarding Silence in the Face of Apostate Rulers'	Militant Ideology Atlas Research Compendium November 2006
Unknown	OBL	'Methodological Guidelines (1) According to the Guidelines of Bin Laden: We Proceed in the Way of Manhattan in Order to Defy America and Put an End to Their Controlling Evil'; (2); (3)	Militant Ideology Atlas Research Compendium November 2006
Unknown	AAZ	'The Forbidden Word'	Militant Ideology Atlas Research Compendium November 2006
Unknown	OBL	'Letter from OBL to Mullah Omar'	NEFA + DoD
Unknown	AAZ	Introduction in new journal – Characteristics of Jihad	CTC-Harmony
Unknown	AAZ	'Jihad, Martyrdom, and the Killing of Innocents' [Purported AAZ – Ibrahim claims it was 'overseen' by Zawahiri]	Ibrahim (2007)

Glossary

AAZ – Ayman al-Zawahiri
CTC – Combating Terrorism Center
DoD – Department of Defence
FBIS – Foreign Broadcast Information Service
FFI – Norwegian Defence Research Establishment
ITSTIME – Italian Team for Security, Terroristic Issues and Managing Emergencies
MEMRI – Middle East Media Research Institute
NEFA – Nine/Eleven Finding Answers
OBL – Osama bin Laden

Notes

1 For analyses of Al-Qaeda's internet presence, see Nico Prucha, 'Die Stimme des Dschihad' ('The Voice of Jihad'), *'Sawt al-gihad': al-Qa'idas erstes Online-Magazin*. Interdisziplinäere Schriftenreihe zur Islamwissenschaft, vol. 5. Hamburg: Verlag Dr Kovac, 2010: and Judith Tinnes, Internetnutzung islamistischer Terror- und Insurgentengruppen unter besonderer Berüecksichtigung medialer Geiselnahmen im Irak, Afghanistan, Pakistan und Saudi-Arabien', Phd thesis, Universitet des Saarlandes, Saarbrücken, 2010.
2 Harmony Database (AFGP-2002-600321), US Department of Defense.
3 Craig Whitlock, 'Al-Qaeda's Growing Online Offensive', *Washington Post*, 24 June 2008. Available at www.washingtonpost.com/wp-dyn/content/article/2008/06/23/AR2008062302135.html. See also: Christine Bartolf and Bernard I. Finel, 'Are we Winning? Measuring Progress in the Struggle Against al Qaeda and Associated Movements', *09 Report*, American Security Project, 2009.
4 The Combating Terrorism Center's *Militant Ideology Atlas* views these individuals as peripheral when it comes to assessing such influence; see William McCants *Militant Ideology Atlas*, West Point, NY: Combating Terrorism Center, November 2006.
5 Raymond Ibrahim, *The Al-Qaeda Reader*. Portland, OR; Broadway Books, 2007; Gilles Kepel and Jean-Pierre Milelli (eds), *Al-Qaeda in Its Own Words*. Cambridge, MA Belknap Press, 2008.

5

DATABASES ON TERRORISM

Neil G. Bowie and Alex P. Schmid

Introduction

When information becomes too overwhelming to grasp and handle, it has to be standardized and transformed into uniform units – that is, data which can be stored in databases that can be revisited and from which data can be retrieved in various combinations.[1] In the study of terrorism, databases are used in a number of ways:

- as extended memory for the analyst;
- to discover underlying patterns of terrorism;
- to facilitate trend analysis;
- to compare terrorist campaigns cross-nationally and over time;
- to generate probability estimates of future terrorist activities;
- to make statistical correlations with other phenomena that might be the causes, concomitants or consequences of terrorism;
- to evaluate the success of counter-terrorist policies.[2]

Most databases in the field of terrorism are held by governments to track terrorists and counter them. Access to such databases is generally restricted. Only through leaks and scandals, or after the fall of a regime, or after the archives open 30 or 50 years later to historians can the public and the research community obtain a glimpse of what kind of information and data were collected and combined and to what purpose and effect. Since public prosecutor Horst Herold began his experiments with *Rasterfahndung* (matrix searches) in the Federal Republic of Germany in the 1970s, the use and combination of data on such variables as travel movements, financial transactions, telephone communication exchanges and more have greatly expanded, especially after 9/11. Such population-wide data searches have been helpful in spotting a number of terrorists and preventing plots that might have killed many people. However, they have also eroded the privacy of millions of law-abiding citizens whose data are screened for potential telling signs and contacts with subversive activists.

Many of these databases take an event – the 'terrorist incident' – as unit of analysis. However, it might be more appropriate to take 'political violence – incident' as the unit of analysis and trace the frequency and severity of different types of political violence over time. Even more appropriate would be to take 'armed conflict' as the unit of analysis, as this would have brought in the opponents of the terrorists as well as their violent rivals. Ideally, 'political conflict' should be the chief unit of analysis, as this would also have brought into the picture, the role of non-violent extra-parliamentary groups, political parties in parliament, and allies of the conflict parties at home and abroad.

Many databases had their origin in simple chronologies, which were only later, when computers became more powerful, made searchable and interactive. Their coverage of events depended, in the early days, mainly on major national and international newspapers such as the *New York Times* or the *International Herald Tribune*. Countries without, or with few, foreign correspondents and/or domestic censorship tended to be under-reported. This situation has continued, for some countries (e.g. Myanmar, North Korea, the Congo) to this day.

Since the media are also the battleground for winning public opinion for one's cause, media records as building blocks for databases can suffer from a number of shortcomings, including:

- government censorship of media reports;
- disinformation or spin distributed by government agencies or special-interest lobbyists;
- media self-censorship;
- media inaccuracies due to the inclination to get a breaking story first rather than to get it right – mainly due to competitive pressures;
- blackmail of the media by terrorist groups in the form of death threats, kidnapping of reporters, etc.;
- false claims and disinformation from terrorist groups or their front organizations and websites.[3]

However, when media reports from multiple sources are compared to each other and coded, and when media-based information is later revisited and recoded in the light of newly available information, the degree of accuracy of event reports can be enhanced considerably. Open sources are the main sources on most events in the world – even for intelligence agencies.

Presentation of 20 databases

In the following, we present 20 databases, which are mostly in the public domain and for which we could gather some systematic information. In most cases, we managed to add some statistics and graphs that provide some insights into the nature of these data sets. Most of them are event data that take terrorist incidents as units of analysis. We also included in our discussion some databases that took other units of analysis – 'armed conflicts' or 'minorities at risk', for example.

Owing to the significant costs of maintaining major databases year after year, most of them are produced and held by governments or subsidized by government agencies. The United States is by far the most prolific producer of such databases. Since the definitions of terrorism utilized vary, the longitudinal (i.e. year-by-year) comparison of data is often difficult, even within a single database, as methodologies change over time. This is a troublesome feature but one that can only be solved by the fusion of data from various databases and a careful retroactive recoding of them. This is time-consuming and expensive, and very few attempts along these lines are made – an exception being a fusion project at START, a centre of excellence at the University of Maryland subsidized by the Department of Homeland Security.

Global Terrorism Database (GTD)

Name	Global Terrorism Database (GTD)
Parent host	National Consortium for the Study of Terrorism and Responses to Terrorism (START), University of Maryland
Website	www.start.umd.edu/gtd/
Email	infostart@start.umd.edu

Access	Free
Unit of analysis	Terrorist incident
Scope	Domestic and international terrorism
Period covered	1970–2007 and ongoing
Principal sources	Publicly available open-source material
Key variables	Incident date, region, country, state/province, city, perpetrator group name, tactic used in attack, nature of the target (see GTD website for other variables)

Introduction

The University of Maryland's National Consortium manages the Global Terrorism Database (GTD), publicly launched in 2007, for the Study of Terrorism and Responses to Terrorism (START). The GTD forms part of a new generation of web-based terrorism databases. It differs from some of its counterparts in that it records domestic, transnational and international incidents of terrorism. The database is open source and records processed and structured information on more than 80,000 terrorist attacks.

Historical background and database development

The original source data for the GTD came from data collected by Pinkerton Global Intelligence Service (PGIS) between 1970 and 1997. Serving the US private business sector, Pinkerton's original database was designed for risk analysis advice. Its aim was ambitious: to code every terrorist occurrence worldwide, over time. A variety of multilingual news sources were used. Pinkerton's definition of terrorism was broad: '[t]he threatened or actual use of illegal force and violence by a non-state actor to attain a political, economic, religious or social goal through fear, coercion or intimidation'.

In 2001, Pinkerton donated its entire data sets to START. Initially funded by the National Institute of Justice, START researchers refined, added to and coded the original Pinkerton data into a new database system, completing the task in December 2005. Additional funding in 2006 from the Department of Homeland Security (DHS) allowed the START team, in collaboration with the Center for Terrorism and Intelligence Studies (CETIS), to update the GTD to 2007. This process was completed by August 2008. In the spring of 2008, a new partner joined data collection efforts with START on the GTD. Researchers at the Institute for the Study of Violent Groups (ISVG) at the University of New Haven, Connecticut began contributing data for integration into the Global Terrorism Database.

An unusual feature of the early version of the GTD was that it was split into two data sets: GTD1 and GTD2. The rationale for the split was historical. The original Pinkerton data covering the period 1970–1997 had a limited set of around 45 variables. This data set was named GTD1. Using the original Pinkerton's generic incident cards, a web-based entry system was devised to code the 61,637 events (weighted 68,986) into a database system. Data verification was undertaken. Auto-fill fields were also generated to provide additional data where required. Key variables within GTD1 included group name, type of terrorist incident, date of incident, country, region, city and location. Other main entries included nature of target, identity of the target, e.g. corporation, nationality of target, weapons used, incident success and damage sustained. GTD1 also coded specific damage to US interests. Further variables detailed information on kidnappings, hostages, ransoms and hijackings. Despite extensive searches, the 1993 data for GTD1 were found to be missing; this was due to the loss of data in an office move by Pinkerton. START is retrospectively attempting to generate the 1993 data from other sources. With improved data collection methods and the addition of new types of data, the codified data from 1998 onwards were named GTD2. This second database was built and developed on behalf of START by CETIS. The eventual aim was to codify the GTD1 data set to be compliant with GTD2, thus providing a unitary longitudinal database of terrorist incidents from 1970 until the present day. In the autumn of 2008, the START team completed the synthesis of GTD1 and GTD2, the database subsequently simply being referred to as the Global Terrorism Database (GTD). The new GTD database contains over 120 variables, of which approximately 75 can be used for quantitative and statistical purposes.

Sources

Whereas GTD1 (1970–1997) used single open-source reports collected by Pinkerton, GTD2 and the newly synthesized GTD used an array of independent open-source material, or, where available, a single 'highly credible' source. These sources included books, electronic archives from news and media organizations, as well as legal documentation and journals. The source material for the 1998–2007 element of the GTD was collected by CETIS in association with START. Other material incorporated into the GTD includes data from the University of Ulster's Conflict Archive on the Internet (CAIN) and the National Abortion Federation, among others. START retains all source materials used in relation to a coded incident in an electronic format called a Reference Source Document. The GTD codebook, containing the database coding scheme and the criteria for the inclusion of a particular incident is available from the START website.

Definition

Both GTD1 and GTD2 worked under their own respective operational definitions. Pinkerton's definition of terrorism was adopted for GTD1. In addition to standard named terrorist groups, generic variables such as 'student protesters' and 'rebels' were also included in Pinkerton's broad definition of terrorism. GTD1 data required that incidents 'substantially concur' with the pre-defined criteria.

The GTD2 data set was not restricted to a set definition. The START team did, however, stipulate minimum criteria. 'Based on the original GTD1 definition, each incident included in the GTD2 had to be an *intentional act of violence or threat of violence by a non-state actor*' (GTD website). GTD2 avoided the contentious issue of a universally accepted definition of terrorism. The rigidity of any single definition of terrorism and its association with a particular data set has implications for the design, long-term content and empirical findings derived from the data. The resultant effect, that particular incidents are contained within one database and not others, compounded cross-comparison difficulties. Aware that a universally accepted definition of terrorism is still elusive, the designers of GTD2 took advantage of new web-based technology to allow users to configure the database to alternative definitions of terrorism – depending on the researcher's choices from three given criteria, of which two must be included. Within certain constraints, users are now able to filter out data that do not comply with their preferred definition of terrorism, taken from the GTD2 menu. In designing GTD2, researchers coded data covering a variety of definitions of terrorism, therefore offering selective definitions of terrorism within GTD2. This allowed researchers to work with definitions of terrorism appealing to a broader group of users. The criteria for inclusion in GTD2 were more rigorous: a minimum of two necessary criteria and two out of three sufficient criteria needed to be met prior to inclusion in the database. This facility is now available with the newly released unitary GTD. The criteria are:

- Criterion I: The act must be aimed at attaining a political, economic, religious or social goal.
- Criterion II: There must be evidence of an intention to coerce, intimidate or convey some other message to a larger audience (or audiences) than the immediate victims.
- Criterion III: The action must be outside the context of legitimate warfare activities – that is, the act must be outside the parameters permitted by international humanitarian law (particularly the admonition against deliberately targeting civilians or non-combatants).

The newly synthesized GTD was launched in the summer of 2009. The scope of the data within GTD is extensive. The GTD holds in excess of 27,000 bombings, 12,000 assassinations and 2,900 kidnappings. START engages over 75 data collectors with expertise in six language groups to build the GTD collections. Source material reviewed for the GTD is substantial. START researchers assessed over 3,500,000 news articles as well as 25,000 news sources for the GTD for 1998–2007.

The newly developed GTD website provides users with an extensive array of interactive functionalities. Users are able to search the database in a basic and an advanced format. The database can be queried using a browse facility, utilizing either keywords or the advanced search wizard. The resultant information is presented in a tabular format and displays key variables such as date, city country, perpetrator, fatalities and injuries. This is accompanied by narrative descriptions of incidents and, where relevant, graphical data. Users are able to print and email queried results. Further features include the GTD Data Rivers. This allows users to visualize key terrorist variables in the form of stack charts. In addition, the website provides a 'This Date in Terrorism' section and a rotating 'Features' web page on news, current research and developments at START.

To conclude, Figures 5.1–5.3 give some sample figures from GTD.

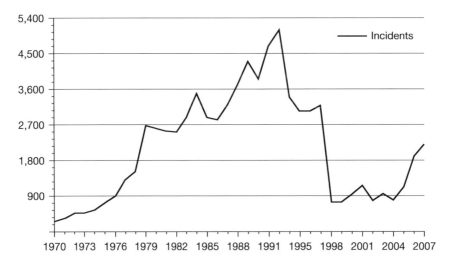

Figure 5.1 Number of incidents of terrorism worldwide, 1970–2007 (GTD).

Worldwide Incidents Tracking System (WITS)

Name	Worldwide Incidents Tracking System (WITS)
Parent host	United States National Counterterrorism Center (NCTC)
Website	http://wits.nctc.gov/
Email	N/A
Access	Free
Unit of analysis	Terrorist incident
Scope	Domestic and international terrorism
Period covered	2004–2009 and ongoing
Principal sources	Open-source material and unclassified data
Key variables	Incident date, region, country, state/province, city, event type, dead count, wounded count, perpetrator characteristics (see WITS website for other variables)

The Worldwide Incidents Tracking System (WITS) is a database of terrorist incidents operated by the United States National Counterterrorism Center (NCTC). The WITS database is presented in a web-based user interface. The database, publicly unveiled in 2005, contains terrorist incidents from 1 January 2004 to 31 March 2009 and is ongoing.

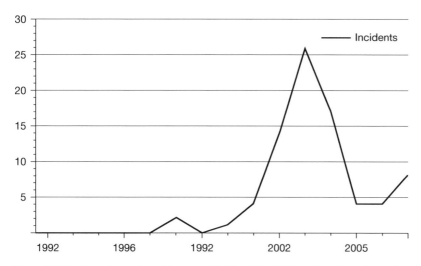

Figure 5.2 Number of terrorist incidents worldwide, 1992–2008, attributed to Al-Qaeda, according to GTD.

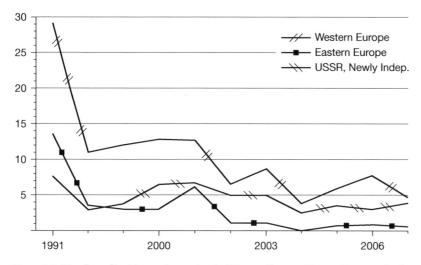

Figure 5.3 Number of incidents of terrorism in Western Europe, Eastern Europe, the former Soviet Union and the Newly Independent States (NIS) 1997–2007 (GTD).

Context and definition

The National Counterterrorism Center, under Section 2656f of Title 22 of the US Code, provides the United States Department of State with support in meeting the legal requirement to provide annual statistics on incidents of terrorism. These data are held within the US government's repository of terrorist incidents, called the Worldwide Incidents Tracking System (WITS) database.

The NCTC defines terrorism as follows: 'when groups or individuals acting on political motivation deliberately or recklessly attack civilians/non-combatants or their property and the attack does not fall into another special category of political violence, such as crime, rioting, or tribal violence'. It is on the basis of these criteria that terrorist incidents are deemed eligible for entry to the WITS database. As a result of methodological changes to the definition of terrorism, only the 2006 NCTC data onwards are directly comparable to the 2005 data. The 2004 data sets were coded on the basis of a narrower definition of terrorism.

Searching the WITS database

The WITS database offers both simple and advanced searches of terrorist incidents using basic and complex query menus. Searches can be executed using an interactive region/country map, by keywords or simple and more complex query commands. The map facility filters all countries relating to a specific region. The keyword facility allows researchers to ask for specific words: for example, 'British Airways', 'insurgent' or 'letter bomb'. Alternatively, wild card or fuzzy logic searches can be used within keywords where uncertainty over spelling occurs.

The Simple Search facility queries the WITS database for terrorist incidents by category. These include the date(s) of the incident(s), geographic region, country and characteristics of the perpetrator (for example, secular/political, anarchist or Hindu extremist). Other key fields include characteristics of victims and type of facility targeted. More complex combined searches can be undertaken. Some fields can be queried using exact or multiple values. For example, exact, minimum and maximum values can be placed within the hostage's field. Results are presented in a tabular report format. These data can be reordered on all fields, in either ascending or descending order. The data can be exported to spreadsheet for further analysis or transformed into PDF format.

The Advanced Search facility within WITS permits users to specify specific incident criteria from any of the pre-defined fields within the database. The system offers seven different methods for selecting search criteria. The database can be queried by incident control number (ICN), text, date ranges, number values pertaining to specific terrorist incidents, single selection (yes/no/either), multi-selection lists, e.g. arson/firebombing, and multi-selection pop-up screens offering extensive variables. Searches can be undertaken for terrorist incidents by 'event type'. These include such variables as armed attacks, bombings, arson and fire-bombings.

Included within the Advanced Search facility of the WITS database is the field 'defining characteristics'. The idea is to record, where possible, the issues that motivate individuals or groups to carry out a terrorist attack. From this, users are able to retrieve incidents conducted by similar types of groups or individuals, e.g. Sunni extremists. The database also allows users to query terrorist incidents based on victims. Groups or individuals victims can be identified in relation to their ethnic, religious and cultural identities. The system is even designed to identify victims who could have been targeted as a result of their religious, cultural or ethnic identities. Detailed information on numbers of individuals killed, wounded and kidnapped can be retrieved from the WITS database. Where events are ongoing, such as kidnappings and the release of hostages, or the status of critically injured changes, the database is updated.

The WITS database also classifies monetary damage as the result of an incident as light, moderate and heavy. All estimates are in US dollars.

In addition to query-driven data, the WITS website provides access to several publications produced by the NCTC. These include the annual 'NCTC Report on Terrorism' and 'A Chronology of Significant International Terrorism for 2004'. The database is also able to generate a series of pre-defined analytical reports. For example, the database will generate a report 'Number of Damaged Facilities by Targeting Characteristic', based on user input dates. The WITS database can then store, email or distribute the reports to other interested parties.

Methodology

The NCTC acknowledges that gathering data and coding incidents of terrorism is not an exact science. Incidents occurring in Afghanistan and Iraq have proven especially challenging in terms of the ability to collect complete data on all incidents. Added to this is the difficulty of differentiating between forms of violence, such as criminal acts and violent sectarian incidents. The NCTC highlights coding challenges, for example whether a particular incident can be defined as an act of terrorism or insurgency. In certain circumstances, the differences are both complex and subtle.

The WITS website publishes a series of basic 'counting rules' used in the compilation of the database. For an incident to be recorded, terrorists must have initiated and carried out an attack. Incidents such as hoaxes and failed or foiled attacks are not included within the database. The WITS data do not include genocidal acts.

The NCTC makes clear that the data derived from its WITS database of terrorist incidents need to be viewed in a much wider context than the narrower universe of data coded within the system. Among many challenges facing analysts is that data can often be vague or incomplete. The NCTC cautions against crude comparisons of annual aggregate data in efforts to test assumptions about the efficacy of counter-terrorism policies. For the NCTC, the general purpose of the database is to allow users to track terrorist incidents, and provide data and information on the location of the incident, its victims and the individuals or groups responsible for such acts. As a result, researchers may be able to discern trends in the nature of attacks.

The complete WITS data set can be downloaded to other application software including spreadsheet and database (Oracle). The exported 'Zip' files contain all terrorist incident data and related information. Also incorporated within the WITS website is a comprehensive and detailed online help facility, allowing users to familiarize themselves with the functionality of the WITS database. Accompanying this is a list of acronyms and an extensive glossary of definition of terms used within the database. For example, the glossary defines what 'Near Miss/Non Attack Incident' means, as used within the context of an incident. A detailed set of frequently asked questions (FAQs) explains the rationale and criteria behind some of the most common queries relating to the design and methodology of the WITS database.

WITS NextGen database

In the spring of 2010, the National Counterterrorism Center released a completely new interface for the WITS database called WITS NextGen. The WITS NextGen provides researchers with enhanced database functionality coupled with sophisticated reporting and visual presentation tools.

The WITS NextGen provides users with an extensive selection of pre-defined reports which can be generated by selecting an inclusive set of dates. Some of the many pre-defined reports include incidents (dead, wounded, hostage, total) grouped by country as well as country fatality ranges (e.g. 0, 2–4, 5–9, 10–19). Other available reports include the number of damaged facilities by targeted characteristic, number of victims by defining characteristic, and victim counts grouped by victim type and incident date. Results can then be presented by chart presentation, by a display of individual records, or in a summary format, available for export to spreadsheet. Aggregate totals are detailed within reports and throughout the database where pertinent. Reports can be generated from data derived from searches. Advanced functionality within the WITS NextGen database permits users to create sophisticated report generation of incidents using a series of metric criteria, groupings, 'drilldown' facilities and advanced query editing.

The WITS NextGen allows users to carry out keyword searches on specific incidents. To aid users, an incremental suggestion menu of place names, victim types, etc. appears, allowing users to choose from an extensive list. Searches can also be refined by date and numeric range. A history of current searches and current reports can also be viewed and saved. Users are also able to apply their own defined filter searches to all or various parts of the database. A further series of extensive tabbed filters provide detailed search criteria. These include event type, incident filters, location, victim, perpetrator and facility.

The methods by which users can visualize terrorist incident data within the WITS database have changed radically from the original WITS database. Users can view incidents in standard record format, by concept cloud, map, charts and report format. A detailed breakdown of individual incidents is available within the standard record format. In addition to the incident number (ICN) and narrative summary of the incident, an extensive array of variables relating to the incident is provided. Many of these variables are hyperlinked to other, related parts of the WITS NextGen database. The concept cloud (restricted to the attack tab in the database) presents users with an alphabetical list of words and phrases that have been used within the narrative summary of each terrorist attack. The more frequently a word or a phrase is used within the narrative summary of selected incidents, the larger the word (font size) will appear on screen, thus allowing users to quickly ascertain the frequency of words and phrases that may have some bearing on, link to, impact on or theme in their research. The Map function (restricted to the attack tab only) allows users to view terrorist attacks over a geographical area. This facility is available in both Google Map form and Google Earth (which requires a plug-in). Coloured clusters on the maps display single and multiple attacks and attack counts. With the new WITS NextGen system, users are able to create their own customized line charts, pie charts, 3D bar charts and stacked bar charts. In addition to viewing results by screen, data can be exported in .CSV, .XML and to Micosoft Excel format. The WITS NextGen website also provides a comprehensive and detailed user guide.

Figures 5.4–5.8 show some information from WITS.

ITERATE (International Terrorism: Attributes of Terrorist Events)

Name	ITERATE – International Terrorism: Attributes of Terrorist Events
Parent host	Vinyard Software Inc., Dunn Loring, VA
Website	www.vinyardsoftware.com
Email	info@vinyardsoftware.com
Access	Commercial purchase
Unit of analysis	Terrorist incident
Scope	International and transnational terrorism
Period covered	1968 onwards
Principal sources	Open-source material
Key variables	Date of incident, group initiating action, number of victims, total individuals wounded, terrorist logistical success

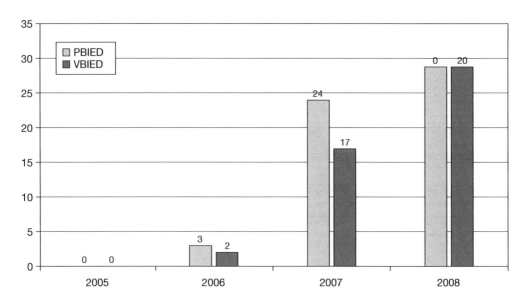

Figure 5.4 Trends in person-borne improvised explosive device (PBIED) vs. vehicle-borne improvised explosive device (VBIED) attacks for Pakistan, 2005–2008 (NCTC 2008 Report on Terrorism).

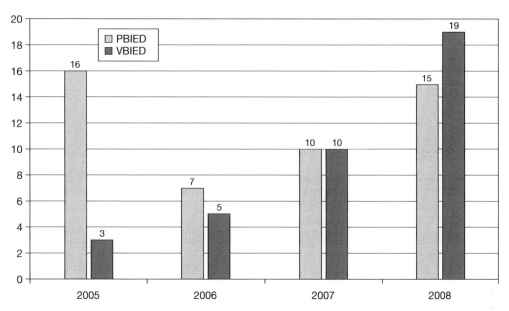

Figure 5.5 Trends in person-borne improvised explosive device (PBIED) vs. vehicle-borne improvised explosive device (VBIED) attacks for the rest of the world, 2005–2008 (NCTC 2008 Report on Terrorism).

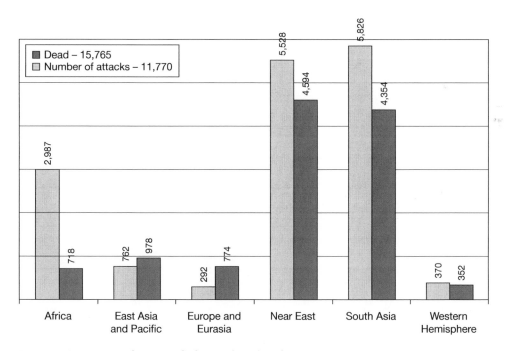

Figure 5.6 Comparison of terrorism fatalities and incidents by region (NCTC 2008 Report on Terrorism).

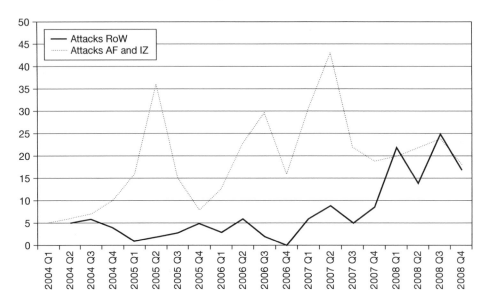

Figure 5.7 Comparison of high-fatality Sunni attacks in Iraq (IZ) and Afghanistan (AF) vs. the rest of the world (RoW), 2004–2008 (NCTC 2008 Report on Terrorism).

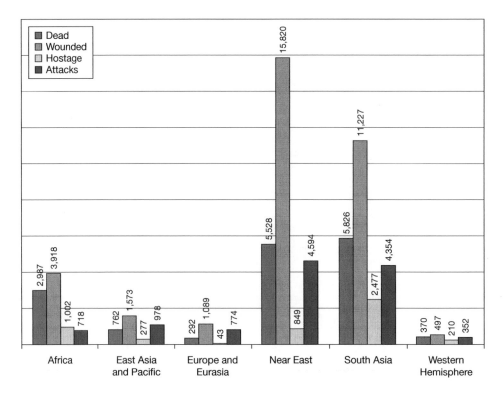

Figure 5.8 Comparison of terrorist attacks and victims by region (NCTC 2008 Report on Terrorism).

Introduction

The ITERATE (International Terrorism: Attributes of Terrorist Events) data set is one the longest-established chronologies on international and transnational terrorism. Produced in the United States, the data set files are available for purchase from Vinyard Software Inc., Dunn Loring, Virginia. Hardcopy versions of the chronologies have been published periodically by Ed Mickolus, Todd Sandler, Jean Murdock, Peter Flemming and Susan Simmons (Greenwood Press and Iowa State University Press).

The ITERATE data sets provide both quantitative and qualitative data and information for use by analysts and researchers within the terrorism and counter-terrorism fields. The data sets can also be used as indices in wider cognate areas of social, political, geopolitical and economic research.

Definition

The ITERATE project defines international/transnational terrorism as

> the use, or threat of use, of anxiety-inducing, extra-normal violence for political purposes by any individual or group, whether acting for or in opposition to established governmental authority, when such action is intended to influence the attitudes and behavior of a target group wider than the immediate victims and when, through the nationality or foreign ties of its perpetrators, its location, the nature of its institutional or human victims, or the mechanics of its resolution, its ramifications transcend national boundaries.

Format and source data

The ITERATE data sets record contemporary international terrorism incidents from 1968 up to present-day events. The ITERATE data sets are available in two formats: textual and numerical. The textual files, based on a chronology of international terrorism incidents from 1968 onwards, can be uploaded using Microsoft Word or WordPerfect. The numeric data sets (uploaded using Microsoft Excel) are coded into four related but separate computer files: COMMON, FATE, HOSTAGE and SKYJACK. The coded variables are derived from the data in ITERATE's textual chronologies of international terrorism. Codification of variables from the data sets' inception has been consistent. New attributes are coded with the emergence of new terrorist groups and events. The data sets are updated on a daily basis. The files can operate independently of each other or can be used in association with each other.

The source data used to compile the ITERATE data sets are eclectic. Information is drawn from government agencies, scholars, news media, information services and individuals. Chronologies and databases on international terrorism compiled by the FBI, the US Department of State, the CIA and the NCTC are all used by ITERATE staff to compile the data sets.

ITERATE derives information from extensive searches of the world's main news and media organizations, as well as information and research services. Some of the key media outlets used include Agence France-Presse (AFP), Reuters, Associated Press (AP), CNN, United Press International (UPI), Al Jazeera, the *New York Times, the Washington Post* and *Newsweek*. Other source information comes from academic publications and related documents.

In addition to established news media services, the ITERATE staff also compile source information from interviews with academics and government officials working within the terrorism and counter-terrorism field. Where possible, former hostages and individuals with direct experience of particular terrorist incidents have also been interviewed.

The ITERATE files

The files can be cross-referenced with each other on the basis of a unique incident code for each event. This permits researchers and analysts to link quantitative data to narrative information on terrorist incidents.

The vast majority of international terrorism incidents within the ITERATE data sets are contained within the COMMON file. The COMMON file codes the nature and type of incident, the terrorist group(s) involved, if known, and details relating to victims of incidents. This, the largest file, covers the period 1968-2007. The data set is continuous from 1968. At the beginning of 2010, the files held 13,087 cases relating to acts of international terrorism. The COMMON file contains 42 variables. The key variables include fatalities, victims wounded, immediate victims of an incident, nationalities of terrorists and terrorist groups, as well as the nationalities of victims. Victims' attachment to a sovereign state, an NGO or an IGO are also coded. Other variables include type of venue and the location of an act of international terrorism, for example territories, protectorates and states. Successes or failures of particular terrorist logistics are also catalogued.

The FATE file details the post-incident fate of the perpetrators, if established. This could include outcomes such as death, arrest (including numbers arrested), escape, prison term, extradition or asylum. The nationalities of individual terrorists are also recorded. Requests for extradition, the country requesting extradition and the outcome of the request are coded.

The HOSTAGE file details an array of 41 variables relating to hostage situations. This involves such incidents as hostage taking, kidnappings, skyjacking and the seizure of land-based transport systems (trains, buses, trucks, cars). The key variables include the nationalities of the individuals involved in the terrorist incident, the duration of the incident and its outcome. Behavioural aspects of terrorists are coded. These include demands for press or media attention, the release of certain prisoners, requests for political change and requests for ransoms, amounts and ransom sources. Other behavioural traits coded include terrorists' behaviour towards deadlines being met or passing, and their relationship towards hostages.

The SKYJACK file contains 27 variables related to terrorist hijackings and includes hijackings undertaken by non-terrorists. These data are also contained within the COMMON file. The key variables include the airlines and aircraft involved in a particular incident along with the incident location, the number of victims involved and any casualties. Negotiating success is recorded. The file also codes the type of weapons used in an incident and the duration of the incident. The flight plan and embarkation point for the hijacker, if known, can also be coded within the SKYJACK file.

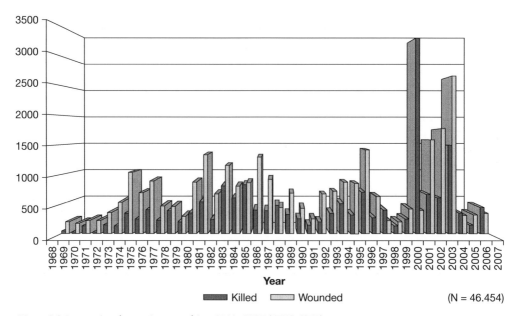

Figure 5.9 International terrorism casualties, 1968–2007 (ITERATE).

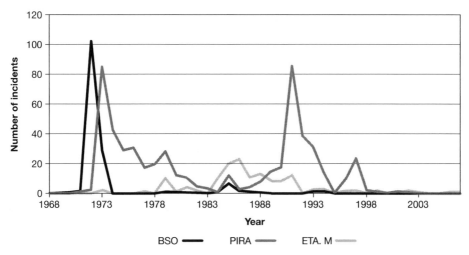

Figure 5.10 International terrorist activity of three major terrorist groups, 1968–2007 (ITERATE).
Note: BSO = Black September Organization; PIRA = Provisional Irish Republican Army;
ETA-M = Basque Liberation Movement – Militay Wing

Further variables within the SKYJACK file include intended flight destination, the desired destination of the hijackers, stopovers, and refuelling and actual end point. The logistical success of a particular hijacking incident is recorded and includes such variables as incident stopped by authorities, aborted by hijackers, and apparently completed as planned.

DOTS (Data on Terrorist Suspects)

A recently compiled data set, DOTS (Data on Terrorist Suspects), produced by Vinyard Software Inc., complements the ITERATE files by recording biographic details of every terrorist coded in the ITERATE chronologies on terrorism. Biographical data within the database include information on terrorist leaders, perpetrators, financial backers, detainees and defendants. The DOTS database covers the period 1968 up to the present. Vinyard Software Inc. has recently opened a website: www.vinyardsoftware.com.

Figures 5.9 and 5.10 show some illustrative graphs from ITERATE.

MIPT Terrorism Knowledge Base

Name	MIPT Terrorism Knowledge Base
Parent host	Oklahoma City National Memorial Institute for the Prevention of Terrorism (MIPT)
Website	www.mipt.org
Email	webmaster@mipt.org
Access	Access was free. The Terrorism Knowledge Base ceased operation in March 2008
Unit of analysis	Terrorist incident
Scope	Domestic and international terrorism
Period covered	1968–2008
Principal sources	Open-source material
Key variables	N/A

Introduction

The MIPT Terrorism Knowledge Base (TKB), launched in 2004, provided public access to a large collection of information on terrorist groups and their leaders, terrorist incidents and terrorist related court-case information. The TKB was free and completely internet-based. The knowledge base provided information on both domestic and international terrorism. The MIPT Terrorism Knowledge Base ceased operation on 31 March 2008. However, old MIPT files up to March 2008 can still be seen using the www.archive.org website.

Data for the TKB came from four key sources: the RAND Terrorism Chronology 1968–1997; the RAND-MIPT Terrorism Incident Database (1998–2008); the Terrorism Indictment Database at the Universities of Arkansas and Oklahoma; and DFI International, a research, analysis and consultancy organization. RAND verified all terrorist incidents entered in the TKB.

The TKB portal provided a fully integrated array of textual, graphical and multimedia terrorism data and information. In addition to providing core data on terrorist leaders, groups and incidents, the knowledge base provided contextualized in-depth background material on terrorist group histories, their affiliations, tactics employed and their geographic locations. The format also included biographical details, summaries, interactive maps and the ability for users to generate statistical data and dynamic graphs.

Definition
The TKB defined an act of terrorism as follows, in its glossary:

> Terrorism is violence, or the threat of violence, calculated to create an atmosphere of fear and alarm. These acts are designed to coerce others into actions they would not otherwise undertake, or refrain from actions they desired to take. All terrorist acts are crimes. Many would also be violation of the rules of war if a state of war existed. This violence or threat of violence is generally directed against civilian targets. The motives of all terrorists are political, and terrorist actions are generally carried out in a way that will achieve maximum publicity. Unlike other criminal acts, terrorists often claim credit for their acts. Finally, terrorist acts are intended to produce effects beyond the immediate physical damage of the cause, having long-term psychological repercussions on a particular target audience. The fear created by terrorists may be intended to cause people to exaggerate the strengths of the terrorist and the importance of the cause, to provoke governmental overreaction, to discourage dissent, or simply to intimidate and thereby enforce compliance with their demands.

Functionality and TKB maps
The TKB provided researchers with a wide range of search functions. Users were able to conduct basic searches by keywords or use an advanced search facility. Using drop-down menus, the advanced function allowed users to cross-query all elements of the knowledge base, including location, terrorist groups, leaders, terrorist incidents and any related legal cases. In addition, the TKB also contained an Image Archive of terrorist groups, leaders and attacks. This could be searched by keyword, name of individual or group name.

Another graphical feature of the TKB was TKB Maps. This allowed researchers access to a series of interactive maps giving satellite imagery of relevant geographic areas. Temporal and spatial map images could be generated indicating the location of group attacks, the volume of attacks and the type of targets attacked. Data could be filtered, and overlay functions also allowed users to display major infrastructure such as highways, pipelines and airports.

Knowledge base directory and TKB profiles
The Knowledge Base Directory of the TKB provided researchers with the ability to search for information using several variables, for example searches by terrorist group, their location and ideology. Other search functions permitted a breakdown of terrorist information by country, date or legal case, ideology, and tactic.

TKB profiles offered researchers an eclectic collection of terrorism-related information dating back to 1968. Drawing together information on a particular incident and related case data, the profiles function of the TKB provided a one-stop dossier for terrorism analysis.

The terrorist incident profile provided factual information relating to the terrorist group, dates, location, targets, tactics and statistical data on numbers injured and killed. Complementing this were the TKB's case profiles. This facility provided legal data and information pertaining to terrorism investigations undertaken by the FBI. This information collected by TKB analysts included indictment data and court documentation. Where available, details of charges, evidence presented within cases and sentencing results were made available. In more complicated court cases, cross-referencing of terrorist group connections was indicated. A further search tool gave access to detailed group, leader and membership profiles. This provided researchers with historical background on terrorist groups and their affiliates, as well as information on a terrorist group's philosophy and goals.

Analytical tools

Using web-based technologies, the TKB provided terrorism researchers with a series of flexible analytical tools that could generate a series of tables, charts and graphs derived from terrorism incident data and legal data based upon the indictment and prosecution of terrorists. Pre-defined statistical data on terrorism incidents could also be accessed. Its rivals and successors have so far not matched the user-friendliness of MIPT's database.

The Incident Analysis Wizard enabled a step-by-step process for users to generate a series of pie, line, bar and three-dimensional graphics based upon specific criteria, for example comparative terrorism trends over time or more detailed data and graphics on injury and fatality ranges.

The Statistical Incident Reports generated a series of interactive reports providing statistical data on terrorist incidents, including such variables as date of attack, target group, perpetrators, incident location and tactics employed. Statistical data taken from indictment data sets and outcome statistics of legal cases could also be compiled using TKB's software. The group comparison function of TKB was even able to compare and present on screen side-by-side statistical analysis of up to a dozen terrorist groups.

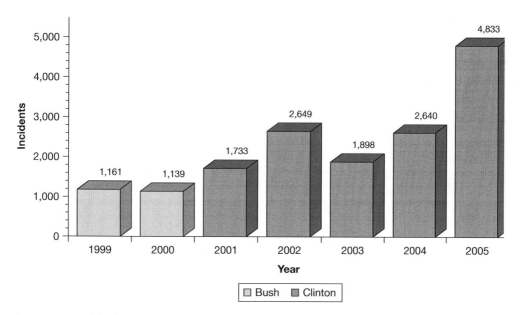

Figure 5.11 Worldwide terrorist incidents by year, 1999–2005 (MIPT Terrorism Knowledge Base).

Table 5.1 Top 20 countries in terms of terrorist fatalities per million people, 1968–2006

1 Iraq	439
2 Lebanon	329
3 Israel	229
4 West Bank	228
5 Colombia	32
6 Cyprus	32
7 Algeria	30
8 Angola	30
9 Afghanistan	29
10 Uganda	19
11 Chad	18
12 Jordan	15
13 Kuwait	14
14 Greece	14
15 Saudi Arabia	12
16 Mauritania	12
17 Somalia	11
18 Georgia	11
19 United States	11
20 Canada	10
Weighted average for 135 countries	14

Notes: Excluded from his list are five small countries: Barbados (261 per million), Gibraltar (107 per million), Djibouti (25 per million), Bahrain (18 per million) and East Timor (10 per million). It should be kept in mind that victims of domestic terrorism are counted by MIPT only from 1998 onwards.

Source: MIPT as processed by www.nationmaster.com/red/graph/ter_ter_act_196_fat_percap-1968–2006-fatalities-per-capita&b_printable=1 (accessed 27 June 2010).

Reference material

The MIPT Terrorism Knowledge Base provided links to a comprehensive collection of terrorism-related data and information held within the MIPT Library. In addition to hard-copy and 'PDF' documents, a large array of CD-ROMs, audio-visual material, proceedings, books and governmental documentation could be obtained via the TKB's website, including *Country Reports*, *Patterns of Global Terrorism*, the FBI's *Terrorism in the U.S.* and MIPT's *Terrorism Annuals*. Some of the TKB data have been transferred to the University of Maryland's Global Terrorism Database.

Figure 5.11 and Table 5.1 show some information obtained from the TKB.

RAND Worldwide Terrorism Incident Database (RWTID)

Name	RAND Worldwide Terrorism Incident Database (RWTID)
Parent host	The RAND Corporation, Santa Monica, CA
Website	www.rand.org/ise/projects/terrorismdatabase/
Email	www.rand.org/ise/projects/terrorismdatabase/about/contact.html
Access	Partly free, partly subscription based
Unit of analysis	Terrorist incident
Scope	Domestic and international terrorism
Period covered	1968–2008 and ongoing
Principal sources	Open-source material
Key variables	Search term, start date, end date, region, country, perpetrator, tactic, weapon, target

Introduction

The RAND Corporation is a non-profit institution with headquarters based in Santa Monica, California. The aim of RAND, which works closely with the US defence establishment, is to improve policy and decision making through research and analysis.

For nearly forty years the RAND Corporation has collected data on terrorism. This was initiated by two key events: the Japanese Red Army's massacre at Lod Airport, Israel, and the Black September terrorist attacks on the 1972 Munich Summer Olympic Games. As a result of these terrorist incidents, the RAND Corporation was asked by the US government's newly formed Cabinet Committee to Combat Terrorism to examine recent trends in terrorism. As part of this project the RAND Terrorism Chronology was established in 1972. Some card-index recording of international terrorism incidents is thought to have taken place at RAND before that.

The temporal period for the chronology dates from 1968 until the present day. Until its joint venture in 2004 with the Memorial Institute for the Prevention of Terrorism (MIPT), the RAND chronology dealt exclusively with international terrorism incidents from 1968–1997. From 2004 onwards, RAND–MIPT began to record both domestic and international terrorist incidents worldwide, covering the period 1998–2008.

The RAND Terrorism Chronology has developed and evolved over the years into what is now a terrorism database system. The core ownership and stewardship of the database have always remained with RAND. However, joint operational running of the chronology and database has periodically been shared with other institutions. What was originally for many years the RAND Terrorism Chronology became the RAND–St Andrews Chronology of International Terrorism from 1994 to 1998, when Bruce Hoffman became director of the Centre for the Study of Terrorism and Political Violence (CSTPV) at the University of St Andrews, Scotland. Then, after the return of Hoffman to the United States, the database became the RAND–MIPT Terrorism Incident Database from 2004 to 2008. With the cessation of the Memorial Institute for the Prevention of Terrorism (MIPT) Terrorism Knowledge Base® (TKB®) in 2008, the RAND component of the data reverted back to RAND. Incorporating the original RAND Terrorism Chronology and the RAND–MIPT Terrorism Incident Database, the new database is now known as the RAND Worldwide Terrorism Incident Database (RWTID), covering both domestic (in-country) and international (cross-border/transnational) terrorism.

Overview of RWTID

The RAND Worldwide Terrorism Incident Database (RWTID) now holds in excess of 36,000 terrorist incidents. Full access to the database is via a web subscription service established in January 2009. On its website, RAND defines terrorism for the purposes of the RWTID as:

> violence calculated to create an atmosphere of fear and alarm to coerce others into actions they would not otherwise undertake, or refrain from actions they desired to take. Acts of terrorism are generally directed against civilian targets. The motives of all terrorists are political, and terrorist actions are generally carried out in a way that will achieve maximum publicity.

On a functional level, the RWTID is operated by users selecting and filtering variables from a series of menus. The key variables the database can be queried on are start date, end date, region, country, perpetrator, tactic, weapon and target. Other filters allow users to query additional discrete variables: suicide attack, international incident, domestic incident, attacks claimed, coordinated, number of fatalities and number of injuries. The database can also be queried on keywords that could be contained within the narrative description of a particular incident.

The output for the RWTID comes in three formats: incidents lists, pie charts and chronological graphs. The incident lists contain core variables such as date of attack, location and perpetrator, if known. Accompanying this is a narrative description of the incident. The resultant data can also be exported into a spreadsheet format. The pie chart output allows users to generate charts based upon filtered variables from the database. This is presented in a graphical pie format with accompanying statistical data in a table format. For example, this could be the percentage of incidents undertaken by a terrorist group over a particular period of time, and a total count of incidents by each respective group. The chronological graphs come in two forms: cumulative graphs and incident frequency graphs. The cumulative graph is generated in a bar chart format and relates to the injuries or fatalities incurred in any particular incident(s) over a specified time period queried within the database. The incident frequency chronological graphs are generated on the basis of matches occurring from the users search criteria and display aggregate totals based upon a choice of three time intervals: days, months or years.

RAND's Voices of Jihad Database

The RAND Voices of Jihad Database project allows researchers access to a large array of interviews, speeches, statements and publications by jihadist leaders and their supporters. The information is sourced from publicly accessible websites, with the vast majority of material being available in English translation form.

The database covers a broad range of areas of what RAND identifies as 'jihadist ideology'. These include worldviews, for example on democracy or the role of women. Other areas include the justification of terror, grievances (against the West) as well as strategy and tactics.

Access to the material is via a simple query box. Users are then presented with links to original material and, dependent upon availability, full-text documents.

To conclude, Figures 5.12–5.14 show some sample figures from the RAND–MIPT database.

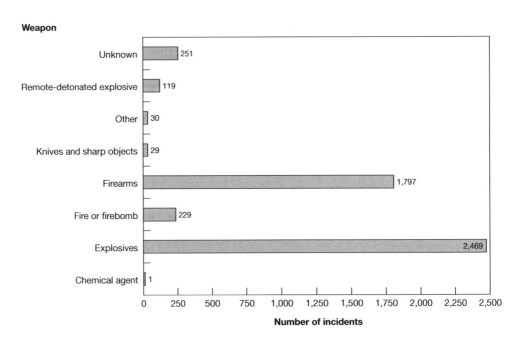

Figure 5.12 Terrorist incidents by weapon, as recorded in the RAND-MIPT Worldwide Terrorism Incident Database, 1 January 2005–31 December 2005 (*MIPT Terrorism Annual*, 2006).

Target

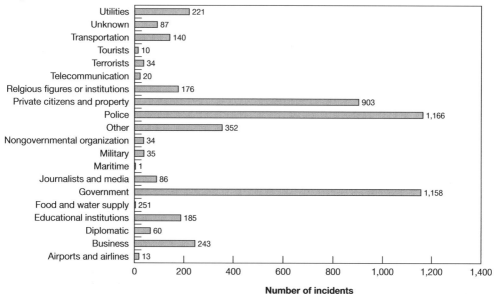

Figure 5.13 Terrorist incidents by target, as recorded in the RAND-MIPT Worldwide Terrorism Incident Database, 1 January 2005–31 December 2005 (*MIPT Terrorism Annual*, 2006).

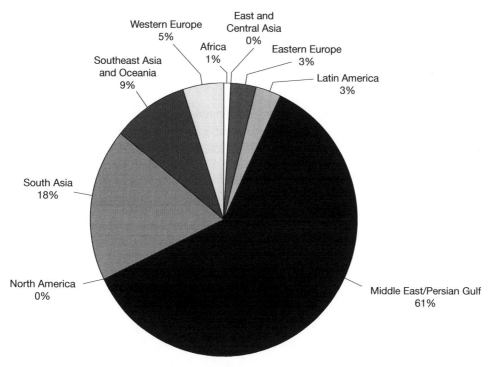

Figure 5.14 Domestic incidents of terrorism by region, as recorded in the RAND-MIPT Worldwide Terrorism Incident Database, 1 January 2005–31 December 2005 (*MIPT Terrorism Annual*, 2006).

Country Reports on Terrorism *(United States Department of State)*

Name	*Country Reports on Terrorism* – United States Department of State
Parent host	United States Department of State
Website	www.state.gov/s/ct/rls/crt/
Email	Via website: www.state.gov/s/ct/rls/crt/
Access	Free
Unit of analysis	Terrorist incident
Scope	Domestic and international terrorism
Period covered	First published 2004. Yearly report
Principal sources	Government sources, unclassified and open-source material
Key variables	Country-by-country overview

Introduction

The Country Reports on Terrorism were first published in 2004, replacing the annual *Patterns of Global Terrorism* publication. The US Secretary of State is legally required to present to Congress annually, by 30 April each year, the *Country Reports on Terrorism*. The report covers groups and countries as stipulated in legislation.

Historical background

The US government's publication of an annual report on international terrorism dates back to 1977. Published by the CIA, the first report was titled *International Terrorism in 1976*. In brief, the key aims of the report were to outline the scope and nature of international terrorism within a historical context and to discuss trends in international terrorism and their likely bearing upon the United States in the coming year. Numerous modifications to the publication occurred over the years. These ranged from changes of definitions of international terrorism, expanded narrative, addition of statistical appendices, to changes in statistical criteria. Other developments included the intro-duction of a chronology of significant terrorist incidents, the transfer of the publication to the State Department (1982), and a title change to *Patterns of Global Terrorism* (1984). Over the years, the annual report evolved into the US government's key publication on statistics, trends and developments in international terrorism.

The final *Patterns of Global Terrorism* was published in 2004. The reports' termination was the result of series of complex data integrity issues questioning the accuracy of the statistical data in *Patterns of Global Terrorism 2003*. As a result of academic questioning and media and political unease, the US State Department radically overhauled its annual report on international terrorism. Renamed *Country Reports on Terrorism*, the annual report is confined to narrative commentary. The statistical element on terrorism incidents is now produced by the National Counterterrorism Center (NCTC) and can be accessed via its website: www.nctc.gov.

Country Reports on Terrorism

The annual *Country Reports on Terrorism*, published by the US Department of State, provides a comprehensive assessment worldwide of terrorism incidents, commentary on terrorism-related issues, factual data and legal requirements.

The first chapter of the *Country Reports on Terrorism – 2007* is titled 'Strategic Assessment'. This offers a backdrop to the overall report. It discusses trends in terrorism for the particular year of publication, as well as highlighting continuing areas of concern. Chapter 2 provides an initial overview of the following geographic regions: Africa, East Asia and the Pacific, Europe, the Middle East and North Africa, South and Central Asia, and the Western Hemisphere. A detailed breakdown of developments within each country is provided. These include, for example, information on government action, counter-terrorism initiatives, new legislation, cooperation agreements, and terrorist trials and outcomes. Other information includes combatting terrorism finance, terrorist group activity and introduction of new technologies to counter acts of terrorism.

Chapter 3 of the *Country Reports on Terrorism* is dedicated to state sponsors of terrorism. The State Department currently cites four countries that meet its criteria: Cuba, Iran, Sudan and Syria. An overview of state-sponsored terrorism is given, accompanied by four key sanctions applied to the above states. In summary, these are: (1) the banning of arms-related exports and sales; (2) controls over the exports of dual-use items; (3) prohibition on economic assistance; and (4) imposition of miscellaneous financial and other restrictions. Detailed narrative explaining the respective countries' sponsorship of terrorism is provided.

Chapter 4 addresses the global challenges posed by weapons of mass destruction (WMD) and the danger that any of them might fall into the hands of non-state terrorists. An outline of how the United States approaches the issue of WDM on a diplomatic and strategic level is given. Several other areas are discussed. This includes the types of material that may be used by terrorists in WMD attacks, such as chemical, nuclear, biological and radiological substances and agents. The chapter also highlights concerns that either a state or the resources of a state might be used to conduct a WMD attack. Conversely, worries over emerging non-state facilitators acting knowingly or unknowingly as a channel for access to resources and expertise that could potentially lead to a WMD attack are also raised. Finally, a series of bilateral and multilateral partnerships with the United States aimed at combatting weapons of mass destruction are discussed.

Chapter 5 provides updated information on terrorist safe havens. This relates to the requirement by Congress that the *Country Reports on Terrorism* provides an update of information on what the US State Department identifies as terrorist safe havens or sanctuaries, as stipulated in the Intelligence Reform and Terrorist Prevention Act of 2004 (IRTPA), section 7120(b).

A list of what the State Department identifies as 'U.S. Government Designated Foreign Terrorist Organizations' (FTO) is provided in Chapter 6. An explanation of the terrorist group's names and aliases is given. In addition, a series of brief narratives provides a description of the groups, their activities, strength, location or area of operation, and any external aid received. The final chapter of the *Country Reports on Terrorism* sets out US legislative requirements relating to the report and key terms used. An annex attached to the report provides statistical information used in the compilation of the document. Discussion includes how, with support from the National Counterterrorism Center (NCTC), statistical

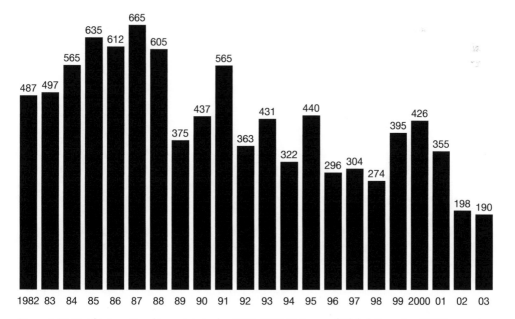

Figure 5.15 Total international terrorist attacks, 1982–2003 (Patterns of Global Terrorism 2003).

Table 5.2 Incidents of terrorism worldwide, 2005–2008

Incidents of Terrorism Worldwide	2005	2006	2007	2008
Attacks worldwide	11,157	14,545	14,506	11,770
Attacks resulting in death, injury, or kidnapping of at least 1 person	8,025	11,311	11,123	8,438
Attacks resulting in the death of at least one individual	5,127	7,428	7,255	5,067
Attacks resulting in the death of zero individual	6,030	7,117	7,251	6,703
Attacks resulting in the death of only one individual	2,880	4,139	3,994	2,889
Attacks resulting in the death of at least 10 individuals	226	293	353	235
Attacks resulting in the injury of at least one individual	3,842	5,796	6,256	4,888
Attacks resulting in the kidnapping of at least one individual	1,475	1,733	1,459	1,125
People killed, injured or kidnapped as a result of terrorism	74,280	74,709	71,608	54,747
People worldwide killed as a result of terrorism	14,560	20,468	22,508	15,765
People worldwide injured as a result of terrorism	24,875	38,386	44,118	34,124
People worldwide kidnapped as a result of terrorism	34,845	15,855	4,982	4,858

Source: Country Reports on Terrorism 2008: National Counterterrorism Center: Annex of Statistical Information

information for the reports is developed. Other areas covered include data interpretation, methodology and an academic perspective on the statistical data used in the reports.

Figure 5.15 and Table 5.2 show some information from *Patterns of Global Terrorism 2003* and *Country Reports on Terrorism 2008*, respectively.

Terrorism in Western Europe: Events Data (TWEED)

Name	Terrorism in Western Europe: Events Data (TWEED)
Parent host	Department of Comparative Politics, University of Bergen, Norway
Website	http://folk.uib.no/sspje/tweed.htm
E-mail	jan.engene@isp.uib.no
Access	Free
Unit of analysis	Terrorist incidents in Western Europe
Scope	Internal terrorism within 18 designated Western European countries
Period covered	1950–2008
Principal sources	*Keesing's Record of World Events*
Key variables	Date, month, year, country, type of agent, acting group

Introduction

Terrorism in Western Europe: Events Data (TWEED) was designed and compiled by Dr Jan Oskar Engene of the Department of Comparative Politics at the University of Bergen in Norway. The function of the data set is to allow researchers to analyse patterns of terrorism in Western Europe, whereby these are specifically related to historical and structural preconditions. The key unit of analysis within TWEED is the terrorism event, as well as any action undertaken against terrorists or terrorist groups.

The TWEED data set, covering the period 1950–2004, codes data and information on terrorism events covering 18 countries in Western Europe. The data set records only internal (domestic) terrorism events and does not include acts of international terrorism.

Definition

For the purposes of the TWEED data set, 'terrorism is understood theoretically as a form of violence that uses targets of violence in an indirect way in order to influence third parties, audiences' (http://folk.uib.no/sspje/tweed.htm). Given the theoretical and abstract nature of the definition for practical and operational running of the data set, the definitional criteria for an act of terrorism is used with reference to concrete terrorist events such as bombings, shootings, sieges, explosions, kidnap and armed attacks.

General

Only acts of internal terrorism are coded within TWEED, and only incidents carried out by individuals or groups originating from the designated 18 Western European countries are used within the data set. There are occasional exceptions when an agent from another West European country perpetrates an incident in one of the 18 countries.

The sole source used for the TWEED data set is *Keesing's Record of World Events* (formerly *Keesing's Contemporary Archives*). *Keesing's* longitudinal coverage of news events worldwide dates back to 1931. However, Dr Engene established 1950 as the start date for his data collection. In comparison, most other terrorism data sets have covered the temporal period 1968 onwards.

The TWEED data set records a total of 2,959 deaths attributed to terrorist agents. A total of 11,026 terrorist events are coded within the data set. The TWEED codebook (as PDF) and data set (SPSS) are both available for downloading from the TWEED website.

Figure 5.16 is taken from TWEED.

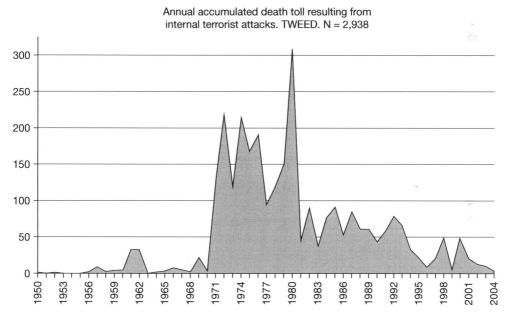

Annual accumulated death toll resulting from
internal terrorist attacks. TWEED. N = 2,938

Figure 5.16 Internal terrorism in Western Europe, 1950–2004 (TWEED at http://folk.uib.no/sspje/tweed.htm).

South Asia Terrorism Portal (SATP)

Name	South Asia Terrorism Portal (SATP)
Parent host	Institute for Conflict Management, New Delhi
Website	www.satp.org
Email	icm@satp.org
Access	Free
Unit of analysis	Terrorist incident
Scope	Domestic and international terrorism in the South Asia regions

Period covered	Varying years dependent upon country
Principal sources	Open–source material
Key variables	Date, incident

Introduction

The Institute for Conflict Management in New Delhi operates the South Asia Terrorism Portal (SATP), established in 2000. The institute is a registered non–profit, non–governmental organization. Geographically, the SATP covers Bangladesh, Bhutan, India, Nepal, Pakistan and Sri Lanka. In addition, the Select States of India are included: Assam, Jammu and Kashmir, Manipur, Mizoram, Nagaland, Punjab and Tripura.

The SATP is entirely web based. The portal provides a comprehensive mixture of detailed narrative, chronological listings, statistical data, graphs, maps and documentation on terrorist incidents and events in the South Asia regions. Information can be accessed via a series of hyperlinks or by using the search facility within the website.

The SATP is organized into a series of sections, as follows.

Assessment and Backgrounder

The Assessment section of the SATP provides a yearly in–depth review of the political climate within each country, and details terrorist events and activities over the year. Statistical data and tables from the SATP database are also included within the Assessments.

The Backgrounder section provides a historical context to political conflict and terrorism within regions and countries covered by the SATP. Detailed narrative is provided on the genesis of terrorist groups and the origins of particular conflicts. In addition, developments such as counter–terrorist operations, peace accords and negotiations between particular parties and their outcomes are discussed. The Backgrounder also includes statistical data on terrorism injuries and fatalities, and provides hyperlinks to in–depth information on particular terrorist groups and other related material.

Bibliography and Data Sheets

The website also provides a two–part bibliography listing books and articles for each country covered by the South Asian Terrorism Portal. Also, for each country, the SATP Data Sheets provide an eclectic mixture of data, including chronological listings of bomb blasts, terrorist attacks, fatality statistics, insurgency activities, assassinations, conflict maps and election results. The temporal period covered varies between each country and region. Data are sourced from local news reports.

Documents and Timelines

The Documents section provides terrorism researchers with primary source documentation relating to respective SATP countries and regions. These include legal documentation such as acts and ordinances, treaties, and regulations on terrorism–related matters. Additional papers are provided in the form of political speeches, statements and committee reports dealing with security, terrorism and conflict.

The Timeline provides a chronological format, broken down by day, month and year, detailing terrorist incidents, arrests of individuals, actions by police or security forces, trials and outcome of trials. The Timeline covers information for the past seven or eight years. Summary information on key historical terrorism and political events within each country is also provided. Dependent upon the country or region, this covers between the past 50 and the past 100 years.

Terrorist Group section

The Terrorist Group section provides a comprehensive list of terrorist groups associated with a particular SATP country or region. Further in–depth information is provided for some of the groups listed. This includes the origins of a particular terrorist group, its objectives and ideology, leadership, and group size and organisation. Where available, information is also provided on terrorist group funding, type of weaponry used in incidents, and details of specific terrorist attacks carried out by the group.

South Asia Intelligence Review (SAIR)

The *South Asia Intelligence Review* (SAIR) is a weekly publication produced by the SATP and provides a mixture of news and assessments on terrorism and counter-terrorism-related activities within the South Asia region. Further assessment and analysis on insurgencies and sub-conventional warfare are also provided. In addition, the SAIR also covers terrorism policy and response issues as well as social, political and economic topics related to the region. Advance copies of the *South Asia Intelligence Review* are available via email subscription.

The South Asia Terrorism Portal does not offer systematic aggregate annual data. A typical weekly assessment is as shown in Table 5.3.

Table 5.3 Weekly fatalities: major conflicts in South Asia, 9–15 March 2009

	Civilian	*Security force personnel*	*Terrorists insurgent*	*Total*
India				
Arunachal Pradesh	0	0	3	3
Assam	1	0	0	1
Jammu and Kashmir	1	0	8	9
Manipur	1	0	6	7
Left-wing extremism				
Bihar	5	0	1	6
Chhattisgarh	0	0	2	2
Jharkhand	1	0	3	4
Total (India)	9	0	23	32
Pakistan				
Balochistan	2	1	0	3
FATA	8	0	42	50
NWFP	14	0	37	51
Total (Pakistan)	24	1	79	104
Sri Lanka[a]	89	N/A	360	449

Note:

a The Ministry of Defence, Sri Lanka Government, has suspended release of casualty figures. Media access to areas of conflict is also denied, and no independent sources of data are now available. Civilian data are based on information published by the pro-LTTE website Tamil Net. Provisional data compiled from English-language media sources.

Source: South Asia Terrorism Portal, *Weekly Assessments and Briefings*, 7(36), 16 March 2009.

The International Policy Institute for Counter-Terrorism (ICT) – Terrorist Incident Database

Name	The International Policy Institute for Counter-Terrorism (ICT) – Terrorist Incident Database
Parent host	International Institute for Counter-Terrorism (ICT), Interdisciplinary Center (IDC), Herzliya, Israel
Website	www.ict.org.il/

Email	Via website
Access	Access status currently unknown
Unit of analysis	Terrorist incident
Scope	Primarily, but not exclusively, terrorist incidents in the Middle East
Period covered	1975–2008
Principal sources	Open-source material
Key variables	Organization, method used, target type, location, date range, casualties

Introduction

The Terrorist Incident Database is operated by the International Institute for Counter-Terrorism (ICT) at the Interdisciplinary Center (IDC), Herzliya, Israel. The ICT, an independent think tank, is a non-profit organization. The ICT provides specialist advice and expertise in a broad range of security-related fields, including terrorism and counter-terrorism, homeland security and intelligence analysis. The ICT's Terrorist Incident Database is an interactive web-based database focusing primarily, but not exclusively, on terrorism incidents in the Middle East.

The Terrorist Incident Database and terrorist organizations

The original Terrorist Incident Database dates back to 1975 and now contains in excess of 31,000 incidents. The database is divided into three key areas: Terrorist Organizations, International Terrorism and the Arab–Israeli Conflict.

The Terrorist Organizations section profiles over 50 terrorist organizations and their national affiliations. Links to each group provides in-depth information on a particular terrorist organization. This includes an explanation of the group's name, a historical background to the group's development, and details of its ideology and strategy. Detailed narrative on a terrorist group's organizational structure is also given, including leadership, hierarchy and the military arm (if one exists) associated with a particular group. If available, information on a terrorist group's financing and operations to counteract its funding is provided. The Terrorist Organizations section also displays terrorist group insignia and provides a chronological listing of terrorist attacks associated with each group. An extensive selection of primary and secondary source articles and documents relating to each individual terrorist group are also made available within this section of the database.

The Terror Attack Database permits researchers to query international terrorist incidents from 1986 onwards. The ICT updates the database monthly; however, the database is not exhaustive. Using a series of drop-down menus, the Terror Attack Database can be queried using a combination of up to six fields: Organization (name of terrorist organization), Method Used (tactics – e.g., bombing, chemical attack, hijacking, incendiary device), Target Type (e.g., embassy, school, airport), Location (worldwide), Date Range (1986 onwards) and Casualties (numbers).

The Arab–Israeli Conflict database allows researchers to search for incidents and casualties related specifically to the Middle East conflict. A combination of six drop-down fields can be searched: Type of Incident (e.g., terror attack, internecine violence, violent clash), Terrorist Organization Involved (restricted to Middle East groups within the menu), Method Used (tactic – letter bomb, suicide car bomb, mortar attack), Targeted (type of place or person targeted), Location (Gaza Strip, Israel, Palestine, West Bank, unknown), Date Range (1986–2006) and Casualties (numbers).

OSINT (Open Sources of Intelligence)

In recent years, the ICT has expanded its terrorism monitoring systems with the development of OSINT (Open Sources of Intelligence). Based upon open-source intelligence, the OSINT system is linked to ICT's Incidents and Activists Database. Interactively based, the OSINT system allows data to be linked relationally and cross-referenced. Holding in excess of 31,000 incidents, the database records both foiled and completed terrorist attacks as well as counter-terrorist operations. The system is also able to provide background narrative detail and follow-up information.

Figures 5.17 and 5.18 show some information from the Terrorist Incident Database.

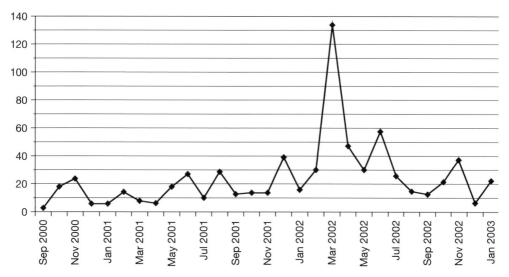

Figure 5.17 All Israeli fatalities, monthly, Palestinian–Israeli conflict, 2000–2003 (www.ict.org.il).

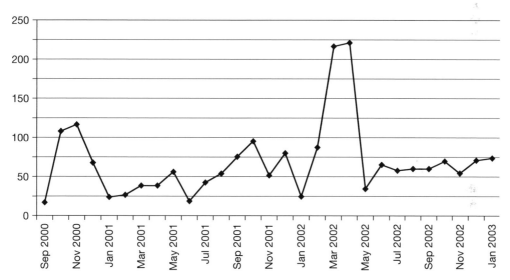

Figure 5.18 All Palestinian fatalities, monthly, Palestinian–Israeli conflict, 2000–2003 (www.ict.org.il).

The Political Terror Scale (PTS)

Name	Political Terror Scale (PTS)
Parent host	University of North Carolina at Asheville
Website	www.politicalterrorscale.org
Email	mgibney@unca.edu
Access	Free
Unit of analysis	Political violence and terror
Scope	Global
Period covered	1976–2007

| **Principal sources** | United States Department of State Country Reports on Human Rights Practices and Amnesty International's yearly reports |
| **Key variables** | Region, income level, OECD status, COW# scale (1–5) per year |

Introduction

The Political Terror Scale (PTS), originally developed at Purdue University in Indiana in the early 1980s, is a data set, updated annually, measuring yearly levels of political violence and terrorism by state actors. The PTS covers more than 180 countries with a temporal range 1976–2007. Since 1984, Mark Gibney, now based at the University of North Carolina at Asheville, has managed the PTS.

The data set

The Political Terror Scale uses as a measurement a scale of 1 to 5 to determine levels of political terrorism and repressive human rights practices occurring within countries within any one year. The terror scale was originally developed by the independent organization Freedom House. Although the PTS title implies a focus on political terrorism, it is essentially a data set on human rights violations by states. The term 'terror', as used by the PTS, 'refers to state-sanctioned killings, torture, disappearances and political imprisonment' (www. politicalterrorscale.org/faq.html). The data set records primarily levels of state-sanctioned violence. However, some forms of non-state violence are included, for example in civil war situations. The PTS emphasis is on the measurement of actual physical integrity violations rather than levels of general political repression within the state.

The following are the Political Terror Scale levels:

- Level 5: Terror has expanded to the whole population. The leaders of these societies place no limits on the means or thoroughness with which they pursue personal or ideological goals.
- Level 4: Civil and political rights violations have expanded to large numbers of the population. Murders, disappearances and torture are a common part of life. In spite of its generality, on this level terror affects those who interest themselves in politics or ideas.
- Level 3: There is extensive political imprisonment, or a recent history of such imprisonment. Execution or other political murders and brutality may be common. Unlimited detention, with or without a trial, for political views is accepted.
- Level 2: There is a limited amount of imprisonment for non-violent political activity. However, few persons are affected, and torture and beatings are exceptional. Political murder is rare.
- Level 1: These countries are under secure rule of law. People are not imprisoned for their views, and torture is rare or exceptional. Political murders are extremely rare (www.politicalterror scale.org/about.php).

Thus, the highest level of political terror (scale 5), ranges from terror that has reached the whole population of a country to the lowest (scale 1), where countries have secure rule of law, freedom of expression is permitted, and politically motivated murder and torture are extremely rare.

In addition to the scale rating of 1 to 5, the dynamics of the political terror scales are also based upon more subtle conceptual levels. The assumption is that the measurement of state use of violence can also be based on the trinity of scope, intensity and range. The first dimension, scope, indicates the actual type of violence that the state conducts. This could include killings, torture and imprisonment. The second dimension, intensity, relates to how often the state conducts a particular type of violence within a specified period; for the PTS this would be within any one year. The intensity variable also refers to the number of individuals targeted by the state. The third dimension, range, records the actual segment(s) of society encountering state violence.

The PTS uses two sources to compile the data set: the US State Department Country Reports on Human Rights Practices and Amnesty International's yearly report.

Both the Political Terror Scale ratings and countries data can be downloaded via the web in spreadsheet format. The PTS website provides users with an interactive map of geographic regions and country breakdown. This lists the PTS scores arrived from both coding Amnesty International and the US State Department annual reports. The scores derived from these two sources do not diverge as much as one would expect.

As an instrument to measure state use of terrorism rather than non-state use of such violence, this database is unique. However, it has its measurement problems, sometimes placing on the same level countries that have quite different levels of democracy and adherence to the rule of law.

Figures 5.19 and 5.20 show some information taken from the PTS.

The American Terrorism Study, 1980–2002

Name	The American Terrorism Study, 1980–2002
Parent host	Terrorism Research Center, Fulbright College, University of Arkansas
Website	http://trc.uark.edu/index.php/rschProjects/1 See also www.icpsr.umich.edu/cocoon/ NACJD/STUDY/04639.xml
Email	bls@uark.edu
Access	Free via the www.icpsr.umich.edu website. Certain identifying information within the dataset is restricted
Unit of analysis	Administrative records data
Scope	Indictments from federal 'domestic security/terrorism investigations' in the United States from 1980 to 2002
Period covered	January 1980–August 2002
Principal sources	United States District Court case records
Key variables	Demographic information, terrorist group information, prosecution and defence data. Count/case outcome and sentencing data

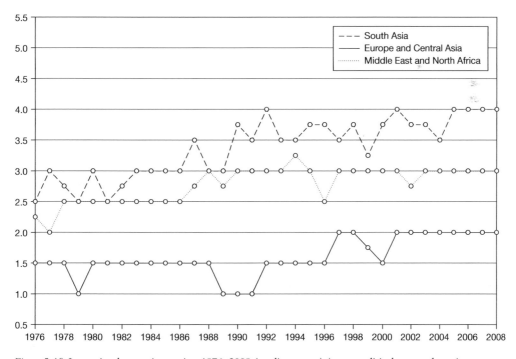

Figure 5.19 Increasing human insecurity, 1976–2008 (median scores) (www.politicalterrorscale.org).

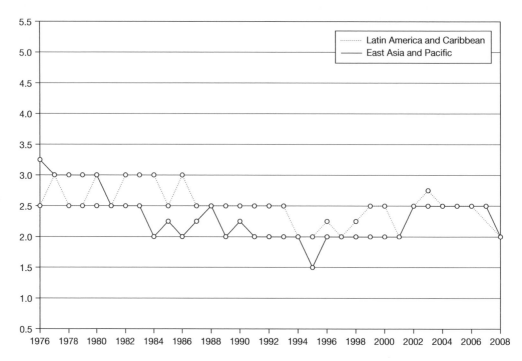

Figure 5.20 Decreasing human insecurity, 1976–2008 (median scores) (www.politicalterrorscale.org).

The American Terrorism Study (ATS) was established in 1989 by Brent L. Smith of the University of Arkansas and Kelly R. Damphouse of the University of Oklahoma. The origins of the project were driven by the paucity of data on acts of American terrorism. Source data for the study came from the Federal Bureau of Investigation's Terrorist Research and Analytical Center. In 1989, the Center released a list of individuals who had been indicted following investigation under the FBI's Counterterrorism Program. One of the key aims of the study was to establish an empirical database to permit researchers to evaluate criminological theories and government policy. The American Terrorism Study comprises two key constituent parts: a statistical database and a series of PDF files containing case documents. These include such items as indictments, judgement orders and sentencing memoranda.

From the list of persons who had been indicted in federal criminal courts, the results of official terrorism investigations, the research team was able to review each case. The review was undertaken at two venues: the federal district court (the actual location where the case was tried) and the federal regional records centre, which held archive records of the cases.

The American Terrorism Study consists of five data sets (Parts 1–5). Each dataset contains approximately 80 variables. The variables are categorized into four key areas: (1) demographic information; (2) information on the terrorist group of which the indictee is a member; (3) prosecution and defense data; and (4) count/case outcome and sentencing data (ICPSR).

The basic data set, Part 1 – Counts Data, contains data 'on every count for each indictee in each indictment'. Between 1980 and 2002, there were 7,306 counts. Part 2 – Indictees Data contains information on every indictee recorded between 1980 and 2002, 574 in total. Part 3 – Persons Data contains information on every person (510 in total) indicted by the federal government as a consequence of a terrorism investigation. Part 4 – Cases Data contains data on every criminal terrorism case that took place as a consequence of a federal terrorism investigation. The final data set, Part 5 – Group Data, 'provides one line of case data for each of the 85 groups that were tried in federal court for terrorism-related activity', according to the ICPSR. The FBI has made subsequent lists of data available to the principal investigators. The core ATS dataset is in the process of being merged with the geospatial and temporal projects datasets at the University of Arkansas.

The European Union Terrorism Situation and Trend Report (TE-SAT)

Name	The European Union Terrorism Situation and Trend Report (TE-SAT)
Parent host	Europol
Website	www.europol.europa.eu
Email	Via website
Access	Free
Unit of analysis	Terrorist incidents within the European Union
Scope	European Union
Period covered	2006–2008 and ongoing
Principal sources	Government figures and open-source material
Key variables	N/A

The European Union Terrorism Situation and Trend Report (TE-SAT) is published on an annual basis by Europol. Its origins derive from the terrorism events of 11 September 2001. The TE-SAT report is presented to the European Parliament on behalf of the Terrorism Working Party (TWP) of the Council of the European Union. The remit of TE-SAT is to make available basic factual data and information on terrorism within the European Union. The TE-SAT report is aimed at interested law enforcement officials, policy makers and the general public. It is a publicly available, unclassified publication, and can be accessed via the internet. Source information for the TE-SAT report is mostly provided and verified by recognized EU member state law enforcement officials. Additional

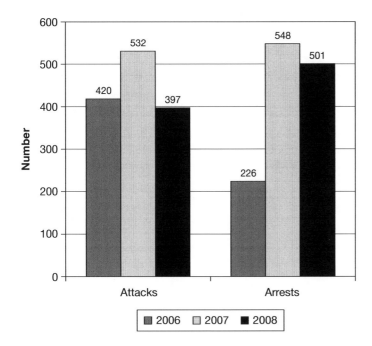

Figure 5.21 Number of failed, foiled or successful attacks and number of arrested suspects for separatist terrorism in member states, 2006–2008 (TE-SAT Report 2009).

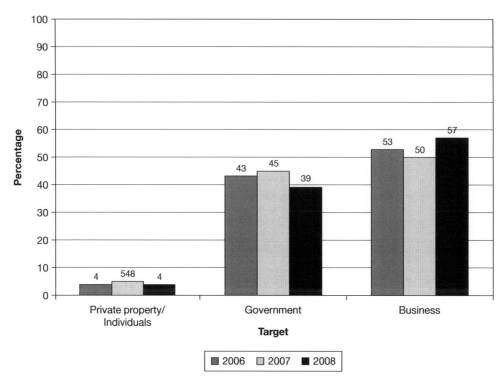

Figure 5.22 Left-wing and anarchist terrorist attacks by target, 2006–2008 (TE-SAT Report 2009).

open-source information is also used. As well as factual and statistical information, the TE-SAT report seeks to identify trends and developments in terrorism within the European Union. The most recent report (2010) covers terrorism data for the period 2006–2009.

The report is divided into a series of sections: methodology and data collection, a general overview of terrorism in the EU for 2008, Islamist terrorism, and ethno-nationalist and separatist terrorism. The remaining sections address left-wing and anarchist terrorism, right-wing terrorism, single-issue terrorism and terrorism trends in the European Union. Each section contains narrative commentary and analysis on terrorist attacks, arrested suspects and terrorist activities, as well as data, tables and graphics. Annexes defining terrorist offences, legal and definitional issues and basic statistical data for each EU member country are provided.

The Europol database suffers from the use of different definitions of what constitutes terrorism in different member states – despite the fact that there is a common EU framework definition. It also suffers from the fact that some countries provide a great deal of data (e.g. France and Spain) and many others far fewer (the United Kingdom).

Figures 5.21 and 5.22 show some information from a recent TE-SAT report.

Global Pathfinder

Name	Global Pathfinder
Parent host	International Centre for Political Violence and Terrorism Research (ICPVTR), S. Rajaratnam School of International Studies, Singapore
Website	www.pvtr.org
Email	iskelvinder@ntu.edu.sg

Access	Subscription
Unit of analysis	Terrorist incident
Scope	Terrorism globally, but special focus on terrorism and political violence within the Asia-Pacific region
Period covered	N/A
Principal sources	Primary documents and open-source material
Key variables	Profiles of terrorist groups, individuals, terrorist and counter-terrorist incident details, terror attack profiles

Global Pathfinder is a terrorism database operated by the International Centre for Political Violence and Terrorism Research (ICPVTR) within the S. Rajaratnam School of International Studies, Singapore. The Global Pathfinder database collects data on terrorism globally. However, it specializes in terrorism and political violence within the Asia-Pacific area, concentrating on South-East Asia, North Asia, South Asia, Central Asia and Oceania. Information within the database is open-source and proprietary. The database is a subscription-based service.

The Global Pathfinder database is divided into five key areas: (1) profiles of terrorist groups and individuals; (2) support data – terrorist and counter-terrorist incident details, terrorist attack profiles, information repository, news and sources; (3) counter-terrorism security – for example, agriculture and food, nuclear issues, and transportation; (4) strategic counter-terrorism – for example, ideology, informatics, legislation and terrorist financing; and (5) country of concern.

The database contains a broad range of documents. These include primary documents, terrorist training manuals, legal documents, interviews with terrorists and photographic material. Non-English jihadi website documents within the database are translated and analysed by specialists within the ICPVTR. The Global Pathfinder database can also generate reports, graphs and statistical tables.

The Institute for the Study of Violent Groups (ISVG) Database

Name	The Institute for the Study of Violent Groups (ISVG) Database
Parent host	Sam Houston State University, TX, in conjunction with the University of New Haven, West Haven, CT
Website	www.isvg.org
Email	isvg@shsu.edu
Access	Restricted
Unit of analysis	Extremism, terrorism and related transnational crime
Scope	Global
Period covered	2003 onwards. Currently logging data for previous 20 years
Principal sources	Open-source material
Key variables	N/A

The Institute for the Study of Violent Groups (ISVG) Database is based at Sam Houston State University, Huntsville, Texas, but is run in conjunction with the University of New Haven, West Haven, Connecticut. It is an open-source database (using more than 9,000 sources) recording information on extremism, terrorism and related transnational crime. Other data collected include information on terrorist tactics, logistical activities and counter-terrorist security operations.

The ISVG began its data collection in 2003. It currently logs data stretching back over 20 years. At present, the database is not fully accessible to the public; access is restricted to ISVG partners and US government-sponsored projects. The ISVG was planning to make available web-based access in some format from summer 2009 onwards.

The collection methodology is human-centric rather than machine-centric. The database is relational in design, providing a broad array of functionality. It contains up to 2,000 variables. It lists (as of May 2010) 2,471 groups and 27,576 individuals that are linked to terrorism and extremism. ISVG collects data on both violent incidents and non-violent ones (such as hostage releases). Its inventory of violent incidents covers 47,999 armed assaults, 4,759 cases of arson and 35,376 bombings, and also lists attempted chemical, biological, radiological and nuclear (CBRN) attacks (10 of the nuclear variety, 46 biological ones and 70 chemical). Individual incidents are coded as well as related tactical and operational information. Given the relational design of the ISVG Database, it can be used in conjunction with analysis and visualization software.

Figures 5.23 and 5.24 show some information taken from the ISVG Database.

The Monterey WMD Terrorism Database

Name	Monterey WMD Terrorism Database
Parent host	Monterey Institute of International Studies, Monterey, CA
Website	http://montrep.miis.edu/databases.html
Email	montrep@miis.edu
Access	Restricted
Unit of analysis	Sub-state actors who are involved in the acquisition, possession, threat and use of weapons of mass destruction (WMD)
Scope	Global
Period covered	1900 to present day
Principal sources	Open-source material
Key variables	N/A

The WMD Terrorism Database is operated by the Monterey Terrorism Research and Education Program (MonTREP) at the Monterey Institute of International Studies. The database records incidents by sub-state actors who are involved in the 'acquisition, possession, threat and use of

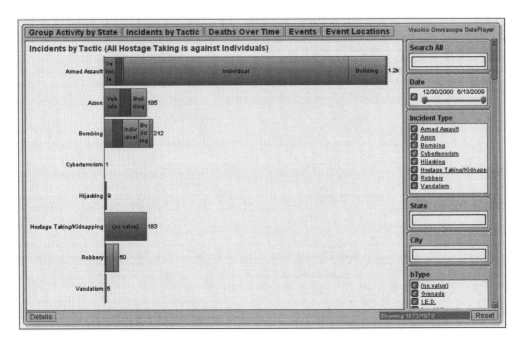

Figure 5.23 Sample ISVG Omniscope Dataplayer: incidents by tactics, Philippines, 30 December 2000–13 June 2009 (www.isvg.org).

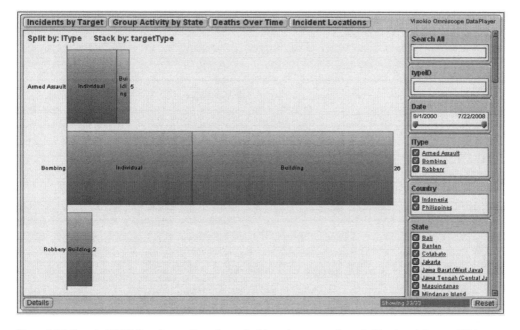

Figure 5.24 Sample ISVG Omniscope Dataplayer: incidents by targets, Jemaah Islamiya, 1 August 2000–22 July 2008 (www.isvg.org).

weapons of mass destruction' (www.mis.edu). In particular, these are incidents involving chemical, biological, radiological and nuclear (CBRN) materials. Incidents recorded date from 1900 to the present day. Sources used to compile the database derive from a large array of open-source materials. These include government documentation, media news services, unpublished material, academic journals and internet sites. Non-English source material is also used, including documentation in German, Arabic, Russian, Chinese and Korean. The Monterey WMD Terrorism Database holds in excess of 1,100 reported incidents. While access to the database is free, there are restrictions on the type of users permitted access, and registration is required. Use of the database is normally restricted to US federal, state and local government employees. In addition, current serving members of the US armed forces are also permitted access.

Armed Conflict Database: the International Institute for Strategic Studies (IISS)

Name	Armed Conflict Database
Parent host	International Institute for Strategic Studies (IISS), London
Website	www.iiss.org/publications–old/armed–conflict–database/
Email	Via website
Access	Subscription
Unit of analysis	Armed conflict
Scope	Global
Period covered	2000–2008
Principal sources	Open-source
Key variables	World map, country list, conflict list, non-state armed groups

The Armed Conflict Database (ACD) is a web-based interactive database providing access to information on armed conflicts worldwide. The ACD is maintained by the International Institute for Strategic Studies (IISS), based in London. It is a subscription-based service.

The ACD covers three areas of armed conflict: international, internal and terrorism conflict. The international conflict element of the database covers governments that are engaged in armed border and territorial conflicts over sovereignty. Internal armed conflict refers to conflict between a government and organized group(s). The territory in question, controlled either by government or by organized group(s), must be sufficient enough to sustain military operations.

One area the ACD compiles data on is terrorism. According to the IISS website, for the purposes of the database, 'Terrorism [is] attacks involving one or more factions in significant armed opposition to a state. The intensity in violence in such attacks varies. Violence directly attributable to organised crime is not included.'

The scope covered within the ACD's database ranges from information on internally displaced persons (IDPs), historical backgrounds to conflicts, the type of weapons used, to annual updates and a timeline on conflict. The database contains information on 70 armed conflicts. Data within the ACD dates back to 2000/2001. Annual and quarterly reports based on data from the Armed Conflict Database are produced by the IISS. The timelines are updated weekly.

Access to the Armed Conflict Database is via an interactive world map; users click on either a continent or a particular country. The Regional Map section of the ACD allows access to all current regional conflicts. Researchers can then navigate to a specific country's conflict pages. The conflict page provides a summary background to the conflict and factual information on the current status of the conflict. This includes the number of IDPs, numbers of refugees, fatalities and the type of weaponry used in the conflict. More specific sections of the database include political developments, military and security developments, humanitarian developments and historical backgrounds to each conflict. A Latest Timeline section provides regularly updated information on conflict developments. Users are also provided with links to related conflicts and official documents as well as IISS publications and materials.

The ACD also provides a search engine facility to retrieve data based on simple queries or more complex query operators, for example 'IRA AND Assassination'. Users of the ACD are also able

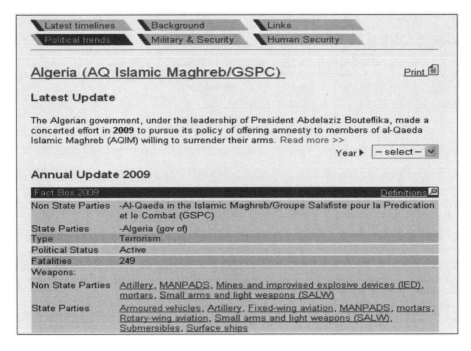

Figure 5.25 Algeria sample from Armed Conflict Database (The International Institute for Strategic Studies) (www.iiss.org).

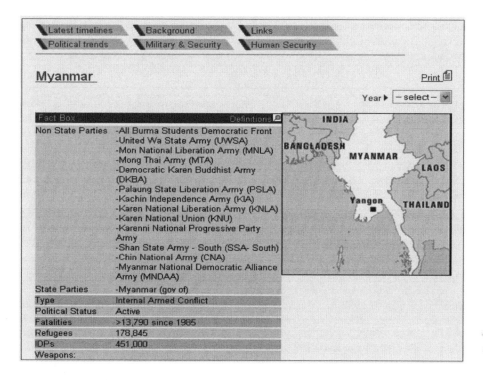

Figure 5.26 Myanmar sample from Armed Conflict Database (The International Institute for Strategic Studies) (www.iiss.org).

to access a series of tailored reports sourced from the database. In addition to general queries, the database can generate more specific queries on conflicts to be produced in report format. This also includes the correlation of reports from different years across regions and topics. The database can also query specific variables that can be presented in report format, including graphics such as pie, bar and line charts.

Figures 5.25 and 5.26 show examples for two particular countries taken from the ACD.

Iraq Body Count

Name	Iraq Body Count
Parent host	Iraq Body Count
Website	www.iraqbodycount.org/
Email	analyst@iraqbodycount.org
Access	Free. Archive data upon request
Unit of analysis	Solely civilian violent deaths from the post-invasion of Iraq 2003
Scope	Iraq
Period covered	2003 onwards
Principal sources	Open source material, official figures
Key variables	IBC incident number, type, deaths recorded, targeted or hit, place, date, sources

Introduction

The Iraq Body Count (IBC) was established in 2003. It is a web-based project that records solely civilian violent deaths following the invasion of Iraq, as a consequence of the 2003 military intervention by the United States. Deaths recorded within the Iraq Body Count include casualties resulting from the actions of US-led coalition forces. Deaths or crime attributable to paramilitary

331

actions and criminal activity are also included. The Iraq Body Count is a publicly accessible database. All deaths entered within the IBC database are factually recorded deaths. Volunteers operate the Iraq Body Count; they are drawn from a mixture of academic and activist backgrounds.

Overview

Material used to compile the Iraq Body Count database is sourced from an eclectic range of documents. Data are sourced from English-language media reports of deaths and bodies being found as a result of violent events. English translations of original non-English-language reports are also used where standards of translation are deemed to be proficient. The vast majority of incidents recorded in the database are obtained from reports by journalists with access to human sources. These include emergency service personnel, police, and survivors of incidents, eyewitnesses, and family members. The incidents are cross-checked for validity and to avoid duplication. In addition, supplementary data are also reviewed and extracted from non-governmental organizations, official figures, and hospital and morgue records. The data are used to provide running totals of civilian violent deaths. Two figures are provided: minimum deaths and maximum deaths.

Organization of the IBC data is divided into two key areas: first, a digital archive of original press and media source material; and second, a database with 18 key variables relating to recorded deaths. Access to the press and media archive, where deemed appropriate, is available to legitimate researchers. The database element of the Iraq Body Count is publicly available via the IBC website. The database provides users with two key sections: records of each recorded incident, and records of individual deaths as a result of violent events victimizing civilians. The database codes, where information is available, 12 key variables for each incident and 6 key variables relating to individual persons. Some of the key incident variables include date, time, place, target and maximum deaths. For each individual, the key variables are name, age and gender. Criteria for entry of incidents to the database require that at least two independent sources be cross-checked and verified. A recent events section provides very recent information on deaths (up to the past 48 hours) that still require full verification and validity checks prior to entry into the IBC database.

The database is dynamically searchable and provides data summaries, graphical data and tables as well as analyses of events. Data can be exported from the database in .CSV file format for uploading to a spreadsheet.

Figure 5.27 is an example taken from IBC data.

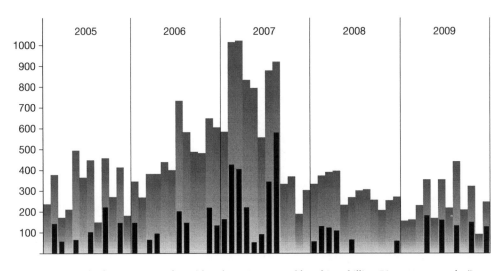

Figure 5.27 Deaths from non-state forces' bombings in Iraq and bombings killing 50 or more people (Iraq Body Count).

The IAEA Illicit Trafficking Database (ITDB)

Name	IAEA Illicit Trafficking Database (ITDB)
Parent host	International Atomic Energy Agency
Website	www-ns.iaea.org/security/itdb.htm
Email	Official.Mail@iaea.org
Access	Restricted
Unit of analysis	Illicit trafficking among states of nuclear and radioactive material and related unauthorized activities
Scope	Global
Period covered	1995 onwards
Principal sources	State-confirmed information and open-source material
Key variables	N/A

The Illicit Trafficking Database (ITDB) was established by the International Atomic Energy Agency (IAEA) in 1995. It records incidents involving the illicit trafficking in and between countries of nuclear and radioactive material and related unauthorized activities. The principal objective of the database is to allow for the exchange of authoritative information on the aforementioned activities. The ITDB has since developed into a broader information system generating statistical data for analysis, and the publication of quarterly and annual reports. The database is used by the IAEA in three key areas: the prevention of nuclear and radiological terrorism, as an alert system, and for the enhancement of nuclear security. Membership of the ITDB programme is based upon states voluntarily signing up. States signing up for the ITDB programme are required to nominate a single national Point of Contact (POC), who will liaise between the member state concerned and the IAEA. One hundred states had joined the ITDB programme as of 1 September 2008.

Incidents recorded within the ITDB include the theft, possession, loss, use, provision, transfer or disposal of radiological or nuclear materials. These incidents can occur within a state and across international borders. Failed and thwarted attempts at illicit trafficking of nuclear and radiological materials are also entered within the ITDB. Information used to compile the Illicit Trafficking Database comes from two main sources: state-confirmed information and open sources. Validation of open-source information on alleged incidents are always sought from the relevant state member(s). The ITDB contained 1,340 confirmed incidents as of 31 December 2007.

Figures 5.28 and 5.29 show information taken from the ITDB.

The Uppsala Conflict Data Program (UCDP)

Name	Uppsala Conflict Data Program (UCDP)
Parent host	Department of Peace and Conflict Research at Uppsala University, Sweden
Website	www.pcr.uu.se/research/UCDP/
Email	conflictdatabase@pcr.uu.se
Access	Free
Unit of analysis	Armed conflict
Scope	Global
Period covered	1946–2007
Principal sources	Open-source material
Key variables	Location, conflict parties, territory, year

Introduction

The Uppsala Conflict Data Program (UCDP) is based within the Department of Peace and Conflict Research at Uppsala University, Sweden. The programme holds an extensive collection of quantitative and qualitative data sets on armed violence, some dating back to 1946. Researchers can also use an interactive database on organized armed violence and related peacemaking efforts. All the

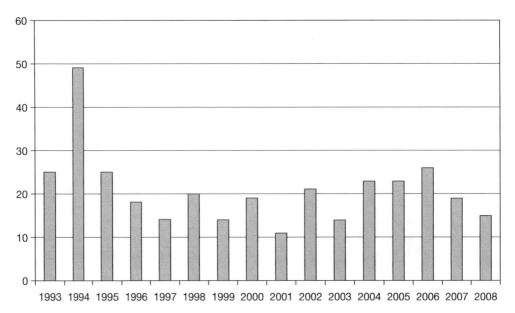

Figure 5.28 Confirmed incidents involving unauthorized possession of nuclear and radioactive materials and related criminal activities, 1993–2008 (www.ns-iaea.org).

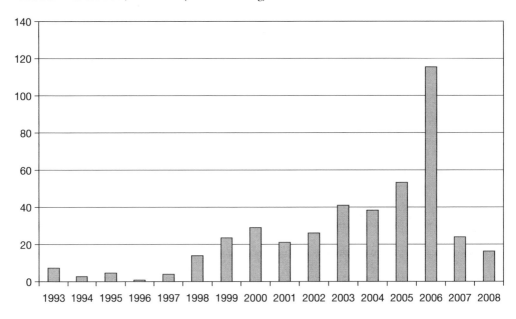

Figure 5.29 Incidents reported to the IAEA Illicit Trafficking Database involving theft or loss of nuclear and radioactive materials, 1993–2008 (www.ns-iaea.org).

data sets and the database are freely accessible via the UCDP website. A definitional list of the UCDP's conflict terminology explaining the key terms used within the data sets is available on the website.

The programme allows researchers interested in armed conflict to access relevant data sets that could be used in the analysis of the origins of conflict, its dynamics and resolution. Ongoing violent conflict data sets have been coded since the 1970s.

Definition

The UCDP working definition, as taken from the UCDP website, www.pcr.uu.se/research/ UCDP/index.htm, is as follows:

> An armed conflict is a contested incompatibility that concerns government and/or territory where the use of armed force between two parties, of which at least one is the government of a state, results in at least 25 battle-related deaths in one calendar year.

The UCDP-PRIO Armed Conflict data set

This project is jointly run by the UCDP and the Centre for the Study of Civil War at the International Peace Research Institute in Oslo (PRIO). The Armed Conflict data set has a global spatial domain and covers armed conflict where at least one actor in the conflict is the government of a state. It covers the period 1946–2007 and is updated on an annual basis. Key variables coded include location, year, incompatibility, opposition organization and intensity level. In addition, a dyadic data set edition of the UCDP/PRIO Armed Conflict Dataset covering 1946–2007 is produced and updated yearly.

The UCDP's Conflict Termination data set

The Conflict Termination data set records the start and the end dates for each armed conflict activity. The data set covers the period 1946–2007. Termination of a conflict is deemed to be non–activity for a minimum of a year. Non-activity refers to the criteria not being satisfied for incompatibility and levels of organization, and battle-related deaths numbering less than 25. Examples of data held within the data set include date of termination, length of conflict termination and the form of termination (e.g. victory, cease-fire or peaceful agreement). The UCDP Conflict Termination dataset can be used in conjunction with the UCDP/PRIO Armed Conflict dataset.

The UCDP's Peace Agreement data set

The UCDP Peace Agreement data set records every signed peace agreement initiated between warring parties in armed conflicts between 1989 and 2005. To be eligible for entry into the data set, a minimum of two opposing primary warring parties must have signed a peace agreement. Some of the data set's key variables include name of the peace agreement, date of signing, signatories, duration (of the peace agreement), third parties and provisions of accords.

The UCDP's Non-State Conflict data set

The UCDP Non-State Conflict data set records communal and armed conflict events between a minimum of two groups. The UCDP's website defines non-state conflict as 'the use of armed force between two organized armed groups, neither of which is the government of a state, which results in at least 25 battle-related deaths in a year'. The temporal domain for the dataset is 2002–2006. It is updated yearly.

The UCDP's One-Sided Violence data set

The UCDP One-Sided Violence data set collects data on civilians attacked purposely by a government actor of the state or formally organized groups. A minimum of 25 deaths need to be recorded to be eligible for entry into the data set. The temporal domain for the data set is 1989–2006. It is updated yearly.

Database

The UCDP website provides an interactive database, updated yearly, on organized armed violence and related peacemaking efforts. Using a series of interactive maps, researchers are able to search the database based on three separate criteria: war and minor conflict, non-state conflict and one-sided violence. Alternatively, all three criteria can be included for search purposes. The interactive map highlights the relevant countries and provides a further breakdown of conflict details based on geographic region and by country. The resultant information provides a detailed historical context on each country's conflicts, dating back to 1946. A large array of factual data are included within the database, for example start and end date of conflict, type of conflict, intensity and number of deaths. Further links within each country provide, where available, related narrative, statistical data and codebooks on minor armed conflicts and wars, non-state conflicts and one-sided violence. Where preventive efforts on conflicts have been undertaken and peace agreements reached, summaries and full-text agreements can be accessed from the database.

Graphs and publications

In addition to the data sets, the UCDP also makes available a series of predefined graphs charting data in active conflicts, active dyad levels, warring parties and peace agreement levels. The UCDP armed conflicts data sets are partly published in the *SIPRI Yearbook, States in Armed Conflict* and the

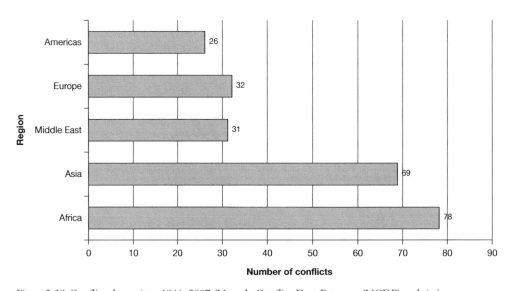

Figure 5.30 Conflicts by region, 1946–2007 (Uppsala Conflict Data Program (UCDP) website).

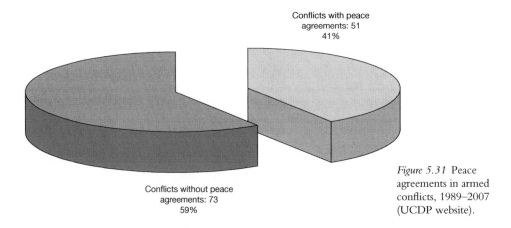

Figure 5.31 Peace agreements in armed conflicts, 1989–2007 (UCDP website).

Journal of Peace Research on an annual basis. Since 2005, the data sets have been published in the *Human Security Report*.

Figures 5.30 and 5.31 are examples from the UCDP.

The Minorities at Risk (MAR) project

Name	Minorities at Risk (MIR) project
Parent host	University of Maryland, College Park, MD
Website	www.cidcm.umd.edu/mar/
Email	minpro@cidcm.umd.edu
Access	Free
Unit of analysis	Conflicts between politically active communal groups worldwide whose current population is at least 500,000
Scope	Global
Period covered	1945–2003
Principal sources	Open-source material
Key variables	See *Minorities at Risk (MAR) Codebook Ver2/2009*, www.cidcm.umd.edu/mar/data/mar_codebook_Feb09.pdf

The Minorities at Risk (MAR) project is based at the University of Maryland, College Park. Ted Robert Gurr established the project in 1986. The MAR project examines conflicts of politically active communal groups worldwide whose current population is at least 500,000. Currently, the project holds data and information on more than 282 communal groups. The project has developed in a series of five separate phases. Phase I (1945–1989) covered 227 communal groups. Phase II (1990–1995) covered 275 communal groups. Phase III (1996–1998) also covered 275 groups. Phase IV (1998–2003) covered 287 groups. The Phase V data released so far cover the period 2004–2006.

The MAR project team monitors each conflict and analyses its status. One of the key aims of the MAR project is to provide researchers with standardized data, allowing for comparative studies and research across various conflicts. A key focus for the project, according to its website, is a data set 'that tracks groups on political, economic, and cultural dimensions'. Access to the MAR project is free and is available via an interactive website. Researchers are able to access a large array of information. This includes the Minorities at Risk Database, its codebook and a series of data sets and historical chronologies on conflict. External links to relevant websites are provided. In addition to core data, the project also provides access to summaries of group histories, risk assessments and a chronology for each group. Specialist data sets include data on ethno-political organizations in the Middle East and North Africa, and the Minorities at Risk Organizational Behavior (MAROB) data set.

Figure 5.32 is an example taken from the project.

Some conclusions

This survey covers only a small part of existing databases on terrorism and political violence or conflict – the part that is, to varying extents, in the public domain. Intelligence services maintain many more databases, but these are generally more specific to operational tasks.

Many of the databases discussed here (e.g. ITERATE, RAND) began by recording only acts of '*international* terrorism'. Only in the past ten years have domestic (internal, national, single country) incidents also been taken on board by major databases (e.g. by MIPT-RAND and GTD). This has been a late, and welcome, addition, since probably up to 85 per cent of all incidents are not cross-border/transnational or international. However, most existing terrorist event databases still show major shortcomings.

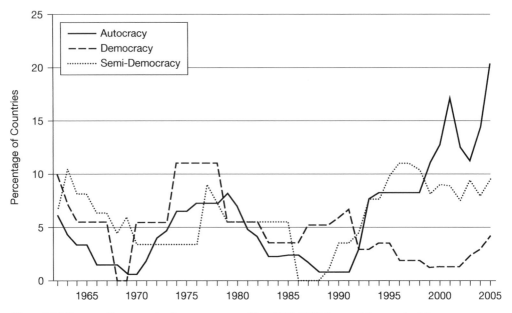

Figure 5.32 Post-conflict countries that revert to conflict, 1960–2007 (www.cidcm.umd.edu).

Seven major shortcomings of the databases discussed

1   *One-sidedness:* So far, there are no terrorism (as opposed to conflict) databases that systematically look at the activities of both or all sides of a conflict dyad. In particular, government (re)actions are excluded. What we have is a situation that is comparable to that of a reporter watching a tennis match and reporting only the activities of one of the players. Much terrorism is driven by revenge and tit-for-tat (re)actions and it is amazing that this has not led to databases that simultaneously record the activities of both, or all, sides. Only by looking at the interplay (and third-party interference) can one understand the next attack better. This is a big gap in our knowledge.

2   *Under-reporting of failed and foiled attacks and threats:* There is a second type of shortcoming. Most databases only record actual acts of terrorist violence and neglect to report failed and prevented or foiled attacks, or credible threats of attacks (other than obvious hoaxes). Some databases, such as the Europol one, record such attacks for some countries but not for others, depending on whether national authorities do or do not provide relevant data. Without knowing the ratio of foiled to successful attacks, it is impossible to judge how successful counter-terrorism measures are.

3   *Political violence other than terrorism is not reported, or is under-reported:* Even more serious is the neglect of monitoring of forms of political violence other than terrorism, of which there are many (e.g. sabotage; looting; rioting; mob violence; vigilante violence ('order without law'); Robin Hood-type banditry; warlordism; systematic rape; torture/mutilation/maiming; liquidation; disappearances (= kidnapping + torture/maiming + murder); pogroms; purges; mass deportations; massacres; ethnic cleansing; genocide). It would be very useful to know what other types of political (and non–political crimes) militant and terrorist groups commit and whether there is a progression or shift from one to another. We should have a comprehensive database that monitors the whole spectrum of political violence, not just terrorism, however broadly defined.

4 *Non-reporting of non- and not-violent activities of terrorists:* The fourth type of shortcoming of existing databases is the failure to monitor forms of not-violent and non-violent political activities committed by groups or movements that might or might not (also) engage in terrorism. Activities such as street demonstrations, blockades, boycotts, charity activities of NGOs and participation in elections as political parties or in support of political parties are outside the scope of existing terrorist databases. One study, *Political Parties and Terrorist Groups'* by L. Weinberg, A. Pedahzur and A. Perlinger (2nd edition, New York: Routledge, 2009), found, for instance, that 124 out of 399 terrorist groups had a political party as a front or were a splinter of a political party. Without looking at what political parties do (and fail to do), we arguably cannot fully understand terrorist groups. There is another unit of analysis that is neglected: social and political movements, revolutionary or reformist. Such movements produce both legal parties (and NGOs) and illegal underground organizations engaged in political violence and terrorism. A comprehensive understanding of terrorist campaigns and groups would require looking at this wider context as well.

5 *Absence of monitoring of non-political, criminal intimidation:* Almost uniformly, terrorism is defined in terms of (a specific form of) political violence. As a consequence, the use of terrorism by organized crime groups and the use of organized crime tactics by terrorist groups is a neglected area when it comes to database coverage. If 'intimidation' were taken as unit of analysis, the difference between the use or threat of force to obtain 'protection money' requested by mafia-type of organizations and 'revolutionary taxes' requested by some terrorist organizations would become largely insignificant. These two forms of bullying, leading to coercion and backed up by violence, are closely related. Since there is political crime, and since there are criminal politics and since organized crime groups not only strive for profits but also ally with political power holders and finance election campaigns in some countries, the distinctions between some forms and manifestations of crime and some types of politics (e.g. kleptocracies in Africa) are in need of being reviewed. There is a need for databases on the interface of politics, crime and terrorism. A disturbing number of intelligence and security services (as well as police forces) hunt and fish in these murky waters. Our knowledge about interactions between organized crime, security services and terrorism remains very limited.

6 *Absence of parallel systematic monitoring of terrorist communications:* A sixth major shortcoming is the absence of parallel monitoring of terrorist communications. Terrorism involves both a specific form of violence with few if any moral restraints, and the communication thereof to various audiences. While acts of violence in themselves are understood by some terrorist as 'the only language the West understands', terrorist violence tends to be preceded, accompanied and/or followed by various (other) types of communications: new threats, claims of responsibility for acts of terrorism, denials shifting the blame to others, videotapes of 'martyrs,' etc. To study the communication output of terrorists is as important as studying the acts of violence. The two – terrorist violence and communication or propaganda – should be monitored side by side, not separately. Counter-terrorism should focus as much on countering or neutralizing the communications and narratives of terrorist groups as on preventing and countering terrorist acts.

7 *Inadequate coverage of state or regime terrorism:* Of the 20 databases we surveyed, there is only one, the Political Terror Scale (PTS) that focuses on regime terrorism. It is based on an estimate of the scale of repression on a crude 1–5 scale using only two sources, not on the actual monitoring of incidents of state(sponsored) domestic terrorism. While it will never be possible to obtain a complete picture of illegal state repression that takes the form of terrorism – owing to secrecy, censorship and intimidation – the imbalance between our knowledge about non-state terrorism and state terrorism is great. In the Research Guide of 1988, Schmid complained that '[t]here is a conspicuous absence of literature that addresses itself to the much more serious problem of state terrorism'.[4] On the database front, this is still true. Human rights organizations such as Amnesty International and Human Rights Watch – understandably enough, from a

victimological point of view – mainly focus on qualitative evaluations. Yet academics should take up the challenge of creating databases in this area that go beyond the PTS. Many governments rule by fear, and while not all fear-based rule is state terrorism, and while those who oppose state power by insurgent terrorism would often make worse rulers than the present ones, the subject of state terrorism (with the partial exception of foreign state-sponsored terrorism) requires better coverage in databases.

Despite these shortcomings, the creation of databases has helped to reduce bias in the analysis of terrorism. Yet problems remain, especially that of terrorism in (civil) war situations, where it is difficult to tell acts of terrorism from acts of war and war crimes on the one hand and acts of (organized) crime on the other. This is particularly evident when it comes to monitoring conflict zones such as Iraq and Afghanistan.

In such war zones, academic research on the ground is almost impossible, and one has to rely on accounts by non-governmental organizations, the Red Cross and conflict parties, who are by definition partisan. In the military, there are of course also academics, and often there is a dialogue going on between government departments and academia. As more academics enter government agencies and engage in data collection, some shortcomings are likely to disappear over time. The call for more accurate metrics of terrorism and counter-terrorism has become louder in government in recent years. This is an opportunity but also a challenge for academia. The opportunity is to construct a more solid empirical database to 'speak truth to power'. The challenge is to speak with one authoritative voice, for, as two German researchers observed, 'As long as the world of violence portrayed by one data set differs from the worlds of violence described by other data sets, it is difficult to gain credibility outside the academic area.'[5] There is an additional problem: when academia fails to come up with its own credible and superior product, think tanks and government in-house research are likely to take its place – something that is already happening before our eyes.

Notes

1   Some authors use the terms 'data' and 'information' interchangeably. Others see 'data' as raw facts that are, through processing, turned into 'information'. In this chapter 'information' is understood as unprocessed facts and 'data' as processed facts.
2   Alex P. Schmid, 'Statistics on Terrorism: The Challenge of Measuring Trends in Global Terrorism', *Forum on Crime and Society*, 4(1–2), December 2004, pp. 49–50.
3   Adapted from Alex P. Schmid, ibid.
4   A.P. Schmid and A.J. Jongman, *Political Terrorism: A New Guide to Actors, Authors, Concepts, Data Bases, Theories, and Literature*. Amsterdam: North-Holland, 1988, p. 179.
5   Wolf-Dieter Eberwein and Swen Chojnacki, *Scientific Necessity and Political Utility: Data on Violent Conflicts*. Berlin, Social Science Research Centre Berlin, 2001, pp. 25–26.

6

INTRODUCTION TO THE WORLD DIRECTORY OF EXTREMIST, TERRORIST AND OTHER ORGANISATIONS ASSOCIATED WITH GUERRILLA WARFARE, POLITICAL VIOLENCE, PROTEST, ORGANISED CRIME AND CYBER-CRIME

Albert J. Jongman

Introduction

In the 1984 and 1988 editions of *Political Terrorism: A (New) Guide to Actors, Authors, Concepts, Database, Theories, and Literature* by A.P. Schmid and A.J. Jongman, a 'World Directory of Terrorist and Other Organisations associated with Guerrilla Warfare, Political Violence, and Protest' was included, listing 2,160 armed and militant groups. The present directory is an update. Because of space limitations, it was decided to include only the names of the more than 6,400 organisations listed here (in Appendix 7). In the Glossary to this handbook, the reader will find brief descriptions of some of the more prominent ones. For others, the reader will have to turn to the internet or to subscription-based data providers such as Jane's Terrorism and Insurgency Centre (JTIC) to find more information.

Much contemporary terrorism reflects a tactic employed by weak parties in asymmetric armed conflicts with one or several state actors. Many conflicts are of long duration and go through phases of varying intensity. Any printed directory, including the present one, is therefore bound to provide only a snapshot in the life cycles of non-state armed groups, and will, to some extent, already be outdated by the time it is published. Groups and organisations can quickly disappear, fracture, regroup or alter their names, become legal political parties, or cease to be designated as terrorist, insurgent or criminal entities. For these reasons, the list presented here is to a certain extent inflated, since different names of some organisations at different points in time in their life cycles appear as separate listings. Organisational splits, as well as fusions or alliances, pose problems for those trying to monitor these groups under a single name. To trace organisations that are often in existence for several decades, a genealogy tree with a timeline would offer the most appropriate representation. Here, the reader will only find a simple, 'flat' list. Most groups, however, are short-lived.

The current list includes extremist and terrorist groups, and criminal gangs, as well as organisations, movements and parties that have been associated with some forms of political protest and violence – and in some cases other illegal activities – during the period 1988–2009. In quite a number of cases, those listed not only applied violence themselves, but were also victims of violent activities.

Inclusion on this list does not necessarily mean that the organisation currently still uses (or suffers from) violence. Many organisations on the list have been repressed, are no longer active or have suspended the use of violence in favour of engagement and participation in the legitimate political process (with some groups going as far as to form legal parties). This indicates that the choice of certain violent tactics is often a temporary one, brought about by specific social, political, economic or religious conditions. Depending on the dynamics of a conflict and changes in the leadership of the opposing camp, leaders of organisations may decide to call a halt to violence – which, in turn, might split a violent organisation.[1]

In recent years, more research has focused on the nexus between terrorism and organised crime.[2] For instance, Interpol is currently investigating an air transportation route between Latin America and West Africa and its role in trafficking large quantities of cocaine. While drug trafficking is an activity typically associated with organised crime, in this particular case terrorist organisations are reportedly involved on both sides of this new Atlantic cocaine route. In Latin America, the Revolutionary Armed Forces of Colombia (FARC) is heavily involved in drug-trafficking activities, while in West Africa, Al-Qaeda-aligned organisations have shown an interest in trafficking cocaine from South America via Africa to Europe. It is feared that they will be using their profits to finance terrorist operations. In other regions, drug trafficking plays a major role in funding both armed conflicts and terrorist operations.[3] For this and other reasons, a number of organised criminal networks that are heavily involved in drug trafficking and other illegal activities are also included in the current 'World Directory'.

A new phenomenon that has arisen since the publication of our previous Research Guides is the emergence of cyber-crime and (still only potentially) cyber-terrorism.[4] New communication and internet technologies have made available a new set of tools that can be used in support of waging conflict. There are persons who have never been in physical contact with armed groups but nevertheless tried to perpetrate terrorist attacks in their name, purely by learning basic explosives-making skills from the internet. Nowadays there is hardly a significant terrorist (front) organisation that does not aspire to a virtual presence on the World Wide Web.[5] In recent years, we have seen that some terrorist organisations do not launch their terror campaigns before having organised a media branch capable of spreading their own information and propaganda about the goals, strategy and activities of the organisation – thereby circumventing to some extent private and public media outlets controlled by others.[6] The new technologies – based on camcorders, desk-top editing and internet transmission via sites such as YouTube have also led to new shock techniques (such as video-recorded beheadings) meant to dishearten opponents and empower supporters.

We have also seen that interstate conflicts are accompanied or preceded by cyber-warfare campaigns in efforts to weaken or paralyse the opponent's determination.[7] As states and societies become more dependent on internet-based knowledge and communication systems, they also experience new vulnerabilities. Some countries, including the United States, are already engaged in low-intensity cyber-conflicts characterised by aggressive efforts to collect intelligence on another country's critical military and civilian infrastructures, including electrical power grids, traffic control systems and financial market operations. Jihadist organisations, in turn, have called on their constituencies to collect information on Western oil, gas and nuclear energy infrastructures. Attempts at information espionage and warfare through the internet have led to calls to completely revise existing public information technology (IT) infrastructures in order to make them more resilient against attacks. In the light of such developments, the present directory also includes a number of hacking groups and intrusive spy networks that appear sometimes to have links to states and armed non-state actors.[8]

Many ongoing armed conflicts are asymmetric insurgencies, and there has been a significant proliferation of armed groups challenging the monopoly of (legitimate) violence held by states. In quite a number of cases, spontaneous or officially inspired militias have emerged with the aim of protecting civilian populations. In many cases, however, conflict dynamics have resulted in situations in which such paramilitary and vigilante militias also engage in terrorist tactics and war crimes. In some countries and conflicts, a real 'death culture' has developed, as exemplified by very inhumane and indiscriminate forms of violence, including rape and mutilations on a large scale that are terroristic in their effects.

In quite a number of states, indigenous peoples are subjected to discriminatory state policies and practices. In several countries, protest movements have emerged, and in a number of cases these protests have resulted in violent clashes with lethal consequences. In a number of countries, land distribution issues are a cause of violent conflict. The inclusion of such protest movements in our list does not necessarily mean that they have themselves engaged in terrorist violence. More often than not, they are the victims of violence, but sometimes they also defend themselves with legal and illegal tactics, or terrrorist groups claim to fight on their behalf.

In a number of cases, we have also listed anti-globalisation organisations. Some of these have been very active over the past decade and were involved in violent disturbances during major international summit meetings. Their listing does not necessarily mean that they are considered terrorist organisations in the sense of the Academic Consensus Definition developed in this volume. Most of them are genuine protest movements, albeit some of them violent, operating in the grey zone between legal and illegal activities. They have developed new protest and action methods to challenge governments. A few anti-globalisation organisations act as a kind of umbrella for a wide range of single-issue groups. In a number of cases, we decided to also list such single-issue groups separately. As with some other groups, they are often both victims and victimisers, often caught in spirals of tit-for-tat retribution.

In the more than 20 years since the publication of the previous Research Guides, there have been several conflicts that have resulted in the dissolution of federal states (notable the Soviet Union and Yugoslavia). This has led to the emergence of new independent states (such as Kosovo and East Timor). In this updated Handbook, relevant entries have been listed under the names of the new successor states. In the case of the Russian Federation, subheadings were made for several federal republics, especially in the Caucasus, which is still an active conflict zone.

In order to illustrate the geographical distribution, the changes in time and the variety of different organisations involved, the reader will find below overviews that compare the list of officially designated terrorist organisations by a number of countries and organisations (such as the United Nations, the European Union, the United States, the United Kingdom, Canada, Australia and the Russian Federation) alongside two other lists (from the International Institute for Strategic Studies (IISS) and IHS Jane's), and as well as with our own 1984 and 1988 Research Guide listings. The IISS publishes an annual survey of armed conflicts that contains a list of non-state groups involved in these. For each organisation, the date of establishment, the estimated strength, status, area of operations and aims are listed. The second listing is derived from Jane's Terrorism and Insurgency Centre (JTIC) – one of the few centres to collect information on the activities of terrorist organisations on a near real-time basis. Jane's also produces extensive profiles on active organisations, including chronologies of their attacks.

The IISS list contains 307 armed non-state actors (see Table 6.1), which is many times more than the number of US officially designated Foreign Terrorist Organisations (45, not counting some 60 other organisations on the US Terrorist Exclusion List). The Jane's Terrorism and Insurgency Centre (JTIC) list contained (in 2009) fewer entries (291) than the IISS list. The JTIC list focuses on insurgent as well as terrorist organisations, of which, however, quite a number have stopped their violent activities. In quite a number of cases, guerrilla and insurgent organisations are also using terrorist tactics. We have cast our net wider than the IISS and JTIC by including also groups involved in other types of political and non-political (gang) violence as well as sabotage (in the case of hackers). There are other lists that have also cast their net a bit wider, for example the US FAS-list of liberation movements, terrorist organisations, substance cartels, and other para-state entities. It contains 385 entries. The START list of the University of Maryland, based on the Global Terrorism Database (GTD), has a total of 865 entries. The Institute for the Study of Violent Groups (ISVG), described in Chapter 5 (p. 327), lists no fewer than 2,471 violent groups. The list in the present Handbook is, however, by far the most comprehensive, with about 3,900 entries (some organisations use several names, so the real number of organisations is lower).

Table 6.1 Comparison of the number of terrorist and extremist organisations in the comprehensive list of US-designated Foreign Terrorist Organisations (FTOs) with entries in the 1988 Research Guide (Schmid/Jongman) and the current edition of the Handbook as well as with Jane's 2009 Terrorism and Insurgency Centre (JTIC) Group Profiles and the 2008 International Institute for Strategic Studies (IISS) list of non-state actors involved in armed conflict

Country	Officially US-designated Foreign Terrorist Organisations (FTOs) as well as organisations from the Terrorism Exclusion List (TEL), 2009	Research Guide, 1988	Current edition of Handbook, 2011	JTIC 2009, group profiles	IISS, 2008, non-state actors
Afghanistan	2	39	83	4	7
Albania		3	9	1	3
Algeria	2	8	65	2	5
Angola		9	9	2	3
Argentina		17	9	0	0
Armenia		0	6	0	0
Australia		3	1	0	1
Austria		4	3	1	0
Azerbaijan		0	10	0	0
Bahamas		0	0	0	0
Bahrain		1	1	0	1
Bangladesh	1	16	168	5	12
Belarus		0	2	0	0
Belgium		22	3	2	0
Belize		2	0	0	0
Benin		1	1	0	0
Bolivia		10	12	2	0
Bosnia-Herzegovina		0	90	0	2
Brazil		37	18	0	0
Brunei		2	0	0	0
Bulgaria		2	5	0	1
Burma		36	71	15	14
Burundi		2	11	2	2
Cambodia		12	11	1	1
Cameroon		3	1	1	0
Canada		6	3	1	0
Cape Verde		1	0	0	0
C. African Republic		3	4	2	6
Chad		20	25	2	2
Chile		26	13	6	1
China		6	25	3	1
Colombia	3	33	160	8	6

Country	Officially US-designated Foreign Terrorist Organisations (FTOs) as well as organisations from the Terrorism Exclusion List (TEL), 2009	Research Guide, 1988	Current edition of Handbook, 2011	JTIC 2009, group profiles	IISS, 2008, non-state actors
Comoros		2	2	0	0
Congo, Br.		2	8	0	1
Congo, DR		13	57	9	13
Costa Rica		7	4	0	0
Croatia		0	7	0	0
Cuba		13	0	0	0
Cyprus		4	1	0	0
Czech Republic		0	0	0	0
Denmark		4	4	0	0
Djibouti		3	1	1	1
Dominica		1	0	0	0
Dominican Rep.		7	1	0	0
East Timor		0	23	0	0
Ecuador		5	15	3	3
Egypt	3	14	46	2	6
El Salvador		38	27	1	0
Eritrea		0	13	2	2
Ethiopia		36	11	4	1
Fiji		0	1	0	0
Finland		2	0	0	0
France		140	26	2	3
Gabon		3	0	0	0
Gambia		1	1	0	1
Georgia		0	12	3	3
Germany		110	36	1	1
Ghana		2	4	0	0
Greece	3	25	39	3	2
Grenada		4	0	0	0
Guatemala		55	18	1	0
Guinea		6	2	0	3
Guinea-Bissau		4	1	0	1
Guyana		3	0	0	
Haiti		9	12	0	1
Honduras		17	9	4	0
Hong Kong		0	4	0	0
Hungary		0	3	0	0
Iceland		1	0	0	0
India	1	54	263	18	48
Indonesia	1	23	67	8	6
Iran	1	62	36	6	7
Iraq	3	23	438	11	31
Israel	10	23	13	11	2
Italy	10	90	56	3	7
Ivory Coast		0	21	0	9
Jamaica		1	6	0	0
Japan	1	30	13	2	3

Country	Officially US-designated Foreign Terrorist Organisations (FTOs) as well as organisations from the Terrorism Exclusion List (TEL), 2009	Research Guide, 1988	Current edition of Handbook, 2011	JTIC 2009, group profiles	IISS, 2008, non-state actors
Jordan		6	21	0	2
Kazakhstan		0	4	0	0
Kenya		15	14	0	0
Korea, North		0	2	0	0
Korea, South		11	4	0	0
Kosovo		0	26	2	1
Kuwait		2	9	0	0
Kyrgyzstan		0	3	0	0
Laos		11	9	1	2
Latvia		0	0	0	0
Lebanon	3	107	62	7	3
Lesotho		4	0	0	0
Liberia		3	15	2	4
Libya	1	19	8	1	1
Luxembourg		2	0	0	0
Macau		0	3	0	0
Macedonia		0	23	2	2
Madagascar		3	0	0	0
Malawi		5	0	0	0
Malaysia		18	10	1	1
Mali		3	15	1	3
Mauritania		6	6	0	0
Mexico		24	77	3	2
Moldova		0	2	0	1
Montenegro		0	5	0	0
Morocco	1	6	23	1	4
Mozambique		8	1	0	0
Namibia		5	1	1	0
Nepal		5	22	2	2
Netherlands	1	36	24	0	0
New Zealand		0	1	0	0
Nicaragua		30	15	1	0
Niger		1	19	1	5
Nigeria		2	47	10	14
Norway		3	1	0	0
Pakistan	12	20	171	20	13
Panama		2	4	0	0
Paraguay		3	5	0	0
Peru	1	18	22	2	2
Philippines	2	60	48	10	7
Poland		6	1	0	0
Portugal		15	0	0	0
Qatar		0	4	0	0
Romania		1	0	0	0
Russian Fed.	2	8	157	3	13
Rwanda		0	18	2	2

Country	Officially US-designated Foreign Terrorist Organisations (FTOs) as well as organisations from the Terrorism Exclusion List (TEL), 2009	Research Guide, 1988	Current edition of Handbook, 2011	JTIC 2009, group profiles	IISS, 2008, non-state actors
Saudi Arabia	1	2	38	0	2
Senegal		1	6	1	1
Serbia		0	23	2	2
Seychelles		2	0	0	0
Sierra Leone		0	11	1	5
Singapore		1	1	0	0
Slovakia		0	0	0	0
Slovenia		0	0	0	0
Somalia	1	9	67	7	13
South Africa		28	88	1	2
Spain	2	36	18	3	2
Sri Lanka	1	14	23	2	1
Sudan		16	64	4	11
Suriname		14	11	0	0
Swaziland		0	0	0	0
Sweden		1	1	0	1
Switzerland		5	2	0	0
Syria		13	15	0	0
Taiwan		2	4	0	0
Tajikistan		0	6	1	0
Tanzania		2	6	0	0
Thailand		26	21	3	5
Togo		0	1	0	0
Trinidad and Tobago		0	3	0	0
Tunisia		5	10	1	1
Turkey	3	55	114	4	7
Turkmenistan		0	1	0	0
Uganda		25	34	3	3
Ukraine		0	3	0	0
United Kingdom (GB only)	6	27	29	11	12
United States		66	40	3	3
Uruguay		6	0	1	0
Uzbekistan	2	0	11	1	3
Vanuatu		1	0	0	0
Venezuela		7	25	0	0
Vietnam		9	5	1	0
Yemen	1	9	27	1	4
Yugoslavia		20	0	dissolved	
Zimbabwe		13	5	0	0
Territories					
Canary Islands		1	0		
French Guyana		1	0		
French Polynesia		2	0		
Guadeloupe		9	0		
Martinique		2	0		

Country	Officially US-designated Foreign Terrorist Organisations (FTOs) as well as organisations from the Terrorism Exclusion List (TEL), 2009	Research Guide, 1988	Current edition of Handbook, 2011	JTIC 2009, group profiles	IISS, 2008, non-state actors
New Caledonia		6	0		
Northern Ireland		33	33	See UK	
Palestine		58	119	12	12
Puerto Rico		8			
Western Sahara		12		See Morocco	
Worldwide			9		
Total	81	2,176	3,893	291	307

David Rapoport's 'wave theory' is frequently cited in the literature on terrorism. According to this theory, a fourth wave of terrorism started with the Iranian Revolution in 1979. While the third wave was mainly inspired by left-wing ideology, the fourth wave is mainly inspired by the Islamist ideology of a global jihad. As there is no sharp break between two waves – one fades out while the other rises – the listings in our previous Research Guides (1984 and 1988) and the current Handbook illustrate this shift. While the number of left-wing-inspired organisations has significantly decreased since the 1980s (e.g. France: from 140 to 26; Germany: from 110 to 36; Italy: from 90 to 56), the number of Islamist organisations has significantly risen. This rise is even more significant in the case of ongoing 'hot' armed conflicts. The most significant cases in point are Afghanistan (from 39 to 83); Bangladesh (from 16 to 168); Bosnia-Herzegovina (from 20 [in former Yugoslavia] to 90); Egypt (from 14 to 46); India (from 54 to 263); Indonesia (from 23 to 68); Iraq (from 23 to 438); Nigeria (from 2 to 47); Pakistan (from 20 to 171); Somalia (from 9 to 67); Sudan (from 16 to 64); Turkey (from 55 to 114); and Yemen (from 9 to 27).

The Maplecroft Company publishes an annual Terrorism Risk Index (TRI) ranking the countries most at risk from terrorist attacks.[9] Table 6.2 uses Maplecroft's ranking of the top ten countries most at risk in 2010 to provide the framework for a comparison of the number of Foreign Terrorist Organisations (FTOs), as officially designated by the United States, on the one hand and our own

Table 6.2 Number of US-designated Foreign Terrorist Organisations versus extremist or terrorist and other organisations listed in this Handbook

		US FTOs	List in this Handbook
1	Iraq	3	438
2	Afghanistan	2	83
3	Pakistan	12	171
4	Somalia	1	67
5	Lebanon	3	62
6	India	1	263
7	Algeria	2	65
8	Colombia	3	149
9	Thailand	0	21
10	Philippines	2	48
	Total	29	1,366

numbers of active or recently active violent groups. The comparison illustrates the mismatch between the number of (mostly international) terrorist organisations subjected to sanctions by the United States and the broader reality of terrorist and political violence indicated by the number of groups, movements, parties and organisations that are involved in (mostly intra-national) armed conflicts in these countries.

In the pages of the new Directory (Appendix 6.2), the reader will find our list of extremist, terrorist and other organisations associated with guerrilla warfare, political violence, protest, organised crime and cyber-crime. It is inevitable that such a long list will contain inaccuracies, as spelling, transcription and translation often pose a problem. The reader should use it with caution.

Before we reproduce the long list of more than 6,400 entries in Appendix 6.2, in Appendix 6.1 we give a short list of 120 terrorist and extremist groups blacklisted by the United Nations, the European Union and six major countries. The fact that there are more than 50 times as many violent, criminal and extremist groups 'out there' that are not officially blacklisted by two major international organisations and six major countries offers some food for thought about the real scope of international cooperation against terrorism.

Notes

1   There are various reasons why violence comes to a halt. G. Gvineria has identified eight of them: (i) substantial success; (ii) partial success; (iii) direct state action, including repression; (iv) disintegration through burnout; (v) loss of terrorist leaders; (vi) unsuccessful generational transition; (vii) loss of popular or external support; and (viii) the emergence of new alternatives for terrorism. See: Gaga Gvineria, ' How does terrorism end?' In Paul K. Davis and Kim Cragin (eds), *Social Science for Counterterrorism: Putting the Pieces Together.* Santa Monica, CA: RAND, 2009, pp. 257–298. See also Audrey Kurth Cronin, *Ending Terrorism: Lessons for Defeating al-Qaeda.* New York: Routledge, 2008.

2   'Al Qa'ida linked to rogue aviation network'. *Reuters,* 13 January 2010.

3   For ten case studies, see John Rollins, Liana Sun Wyler and Seth Rosen, *International Terrorism and Transnational Crime: Security Threats, US Policy, and Considerations for Congress.* R41004. Washington, DC: Congressional Research Service, 5 January 2010.

4   See Irving Lachow, 'Cyberterrorism: menace or myth?' In F.D. Kramer, S.H. Starr and L.K. Wentz (eds), *Cyberpower and National Security.* Washington, DC: National Defense University Press, 2009.

5   Cf. for instance Oliver Dengg, *Der Dschihad und das Mitmach-Netz. Wie 'virtuelle Dschihadisten' das Social Web benutzen.* Vienna: Landesverteidigungsakademie, 2010.

6   For a recent analysis of the jihadi distribution network, see D. Kimmage, 'Al-Qaeda Central and the Internet'. Counterterrorism Strategy Initiative Policy Paper. Washington, DC: New American Foundation, March 2010.

7   See J. Carr, *Inside Cyber Warfare: Mapping the Cyber Underworld.* Sebastopol, CA: O'Reilly, 2010.

8   For a more comprehensive listing, see Bruce Sterling, *The Hacker Crackdown: Law and Disorder on the Electronic Frontier.* New York: Bantam Books, 1992. For a more recent technical expose, see N. Dhanjani, B. Rios and B. Hardin, *Hacking: The Next Generation.* Sebastopol, CA: O'Reilly, 2009.

9   See webpage www.maplecroft.com.

Appendix 6.1

Officially Blacklisted Extremist or Terrorist (Support) Organisations

Benjamin J.E. Freedman

Introduction

For purposes of comparison, we present here the combined list of a number of countries' and two international organisations' (the United Nations' and European Union's) blacklisted terrorist and extremist (support) organisations. The United States' current list includes 45 foreign organisations which are designated as 'terrorist' (another 60 organisations and support groups or entities are on the Terrorist Exclusion List [TEL]). The United Nations' list, by contrast, contains 24 entities.[1] The United Kingdom has one of the most extensive lists, blacklisting 55 organisations. Canada has blacklisted 41 organisations, India 34,[2] the European Union 29, Australia 18 and Russia 16. It is instructive to compare these lists since there are notable omissions. Most significantly, Al-Qaeda is blacklisted by seven out of the eight countries or organisations compared below but is omitted from the European Union's list.

To a large degree, this comparative list of officially designated extremist or terrorist organisations and suspected support groups highlights the security interests, priorities and outlook of the designating countries and organisations. Each individual list reflects regional or, in some instances, global security concerns of the designating country or body. Several of the groups included on the Indian designation list, for instance, are Pakistani and operate within the immediate South Asian region. The United States' designation list, on the other hand, approaches the terrorist threat from a global, rather than regional, perspective. As such, the American list includes organisations deemed threatening to American security or personnel abroad, regardless of geographic location.[3]

Table A6.1, which compares lists from the European Union (EU), the United Nations (UN), the United Kingdom (UK), the United States (US), India (IND), Australia (AUS), Canada (CAN) and Australia (AUS) was compiled originally for the May 2010 issue of *Perspectives on Terrorism*, the electronic journal of the 'Terrorism Research Initiative'.

Table A6.1 120 officially designated extremist or terrorist organisations and suspected support groups: a comparison of UN, EU, US, UK, Russian, Canadian, Australian and Indian lists

Group name	AUS	CAN	EU	IND	RUS	UK	UN	US
1 Abu Nidal Organisation		✓	✓			✓		✓
2 Abu Sayyaf Group	✓	✓				✓	✓	✓
3 Achik National Volunteer Council (ANVC) in Meghalaya				✓				
4 Akhil Bharat Nepali Ekta Samaj (ABNES)				✓				
5 All Tripura Tiger Force (ATTF)				✓				
6 Al-Aqsa Martyrs Brigade		✓		✓				✓
7 Al Badr				✓				
8 Al Ghurabaa						✓		
9 Al Haramain					✓			
10 Al Ittihad Al Islamia (AIAI)		✓				✓	✓	
11 Al-Qaeda	✓	✓		✓	✓	✓	✓	✓
12 Al-Qaeda in the Arabian Peninsula (AQAP)							✓	✓
13 Al-Qaeda in Iraq (AQI)	✓						✓	✓
14 Al-Qaeda in the Islamic Maghreb (AQIM)/ Salafist Group for Call and Combat	✓	✓			✓	✓	✓	✓
15 Al-Shabaab	✓	✓				✓		✓
16 Al-Takfir and Al-Hijra			✓					
17 Al-Umar-Mujahideen				✓				
18 Ansar al-Islam	✓	✓				✓	✓	✓
19 Armed Islamic Group (GIA)		✓				✓	✓	✓
20 Asbat al-Ansar	✓	✓				✓	✓	✓
21 Aum Shinrikyo		✓	✓					✓
22 Babbar Khalsa		✓	✓			✓		
23 Babbar Khalsa International (BKI)		✓		✓				
24 Basque Fatherland and Liberty (ETA)		✓				✓		✓
25 Baluchistan Liberation Army (BLA)						✓		
26 Caucasus Emirate					✓			
27 Communist Party of India (Marxist-Leninist)				✓				
28 Communist Party of the Philippines/ New People's Army (CPP/NPA)			✓					✓
29 Congress of the Peoples of Ichkeria and Dagestan					✓			
30 Continuity Irish Republican Army/ Continuity Army Council						✓		✓
31 Cumann na mBan						✓		
32 Deendar Anjuman				✓				
33 Dukhtaran-e-Millat (DEM)				✓				
34 East Turkistan Islamic Movement (ETIM)							✓	
35 Egyptian Islamic Jihad (EIJ)		✓			✓	✓	✓	
36 Fianna na hEireann						✓		
37 Gama'a al-Islamiya (Islamic Group)		✓	✓		✓	✓		✓
38 Hamas/Izz al-Din al-Qassem Brigades	✓	✓	✓			✓		✓
39 Harakat ul-Jihad-i-Islami (HUJI)						✓		
40 Harakat ul-Jihad-i-Islami Bangladesh (HUJI-B)						✓		✓
41 Harakat ul-Mujahidin (HUM)	✓	✓		✓		✓	✓	✓
42 Hezb-e Islami Gulbuddin (HIG)		✓				✓		

Group name	AUS	CAN	EU	IND	RUS	UK	UN	US
43 Hizballah	✓	✓				✓		✓
44 Hizbul Mujahideen (HM)			✓	✓				
45 Hizb ut-Tahrir					✓			
46 Hofstadgroep			✓					
47 Hynniewtrep National Liberation Council (HNLC)				✓				
48 International Sikh Youth Federation (ISYF)		✓	✓	✓		✓		
49 Irish National Liberation Army (INLA)						✓		
50 Irish People's Liberation Organisation						✓		
51 Irish Republican Army (IRA)						✓		
52 Islamî Büyük Doğu Akıncılar Cephesı (IBDA-C) (Great Islamic Eastern Warriors Front)				✓				
53 Islamic Army of Aden	✓	✓				✓	✓	
54 Islamic Jihad Group/Islamic Jihad Union (IJU)					✓	✓	✓	✓
55 Islamic Movement of Uzbekistan (IMU)	✓	✓			✓	✓	✓	✓
56 Jaish-e-Mohammed (JEM)	✓	✓		✓		✓	✓	✓
57 Jamiat al-Islah al-Idzhtimai/Social Reform					✓			
58 Jamiat Ihya at-Turaz al-Islami (Revival of Islamic Heritage Society)						✓	✓	
59 Jamiat ul-Mujahideen				✓				
60 Jammat-ul Mujahideen Bangladesh (JMB)						✓		
61 Jammu and Kashmir Islamic Front				✓				
62 Jemaah Islamiya (JI)	✓	✓				✓	✓	✓
63 Jund al-Sham								
64 Kahane Chai (Kach)		✓	✓					✓
65 Kanglei Yaol Kanba Lup (KYKL)				✓				
66 Kangleipak Communist Party (KCP)				✓				
67 Kata'ib Hizballah								✓
68 Khalistan Commando Force (KCF)				✓				
69 Khalistan Zindabad Force (KZF)			✓					
70 Khuddam ul-Islam (KuI) and Jamaat ul-Furquan (JuF)						✓		
71 Kongra-Gel/Kurdistan Workers Party (PKK)	✓	✓	✓			✓		✓
72 Lashkar-e-Tayyiba (LT)	✓	✓		✓	✓	✓	✓	✓
73 Lashkar-e-Jhangvi	✓	✓					✓	✓
74 Liberation Tigers of Tamil Eelam (LTTE)		✓	✓	✓		✓		✓
75 Libyan Islamic Fighting Group (LIFG)						✓	✓	✓
76 Loyalist Volunteer Force (LVF)						✓		
77 Manipur People's Liberation Front (MPLF)				✓				
78 Maoist Communist Centre (MCC)				✓				
79 Moroccan Islamic Combatant Group (GICM)						✓	✓	✓
80 Mujahedin-e Khalq Organisation (MEK)		✓						✓
81 Muslim Brotherhood					✓			
82 National Democratic Front of Bodoland (NDFB)				✓				
83 National Liberation Army (ELN)		✓	✓					✓
84 National Liberation Front of Tripura (NLFT)				✓				
85 Orange Volunteers						✓		

Group name	AUS	CAN	EU	IND	RUS	UK	UN	US
86 Palestine Liberation Front (PLF)		✓	✓					✓
87 Palestinian Islamic Jihad (PIJ)	✓	✓	✓			✓		✓
88 People's Liberation Army (PLA)				✓				
89 People's Revolutionary Party of Kangleipak (PREPAK)				✓				
90 Popular Front for the Liberation of Palestine (PFLP)		✓	✓					✓
91 PFLP – General Command (PFLP-GC)		✓	✓					✓
92 Rajah Solaiman Movement (RSM)							✓	
93 Real IRA								✓
94 Red Hand Commando						✓		
95 Red Hand Defenders						✓		
96 Revolutionary Armed Forces of Colombia (FARC)		✓	✓					✓
97 Revolutionary Organisation 17 November						✓		✓
98 Revolutionary People's Front (RPF) in Manipur				✓				
99 Revolutionary People's Liberation Party/Front (DHKP/C)			✓			✓		✓
100 Revolutionary Struggle								✓
101 Saor Éire						✓		
102 Saved Sect/Saviour Sect						✓		
103 Shining Path (Sendero Luminoso, SL)		✓	✓					✓
104 Sipah-e Sahaba Pakistan (SSP)						✓		
105 Students Islamic Movement of India				✓				
106 Supreme Military Majlis ul-Shura of the United Mujahideen Forces of the Caucasus					✓			
107 Taliban					✓			
108 Tamil Nadu Liberation Army (TNLA)				✓				
109 Tamil National Retrieval Troops (TNRT)				✓				
110 Tehrik Nefaz-e Shari'at Muhammadi (TNSM)						✓		
111 Teyrbazen Azadiya Kurdistan (TAK)			✓			✓		
112 Tunisian Combatant Group							✓	
113 Ulster Defence Association (UDA)						✓		
114 Ulster Freedom Fighters (UFF)						✓		
115 Ulster Volunteer Force (UVF)						✓		
116 United Liberation Front of Assam (ULFA)				✓				
117 United National Liberation Front (UNLF)				✓				
118 United Self-Defense Forces of Colombia (AUC)		✓	✓					✓
119 Vanguards of Conquest (VOC)		✓						
120 World Tamil Movement		✓						

Notes

1 The full UN Al-Qaeda/Taliban Monitoring Group's consolidated list has some 300 names and includes 'individuals, groups, undertakings and entities associated with [Al-Qaeda, Osama bin Laden and the Taliban]'. For the purposes of this comparative list, however, UN-designated charities, banks, and generally non-violent support groups have been excluded. Only non-state armed groups are included, as this provides a clearer comparison with those terrorist organisations designated by individual nation-states.
2 Since May 2010, India has greatly expanded its list to almost 100 groups and organisations.

3   A note on spelling/transliteration and translation: The spellings, transliterations and translations used come from official governmental and intergovernmental lists, except for organisations from the Russian designation list, which were translated into English independently. Organisations are listed in absolute alphabetical order (e.g. by 'Al-' rather than 'Qaeda'), and every attempt has been made to list organisations by their most commonly known name, regardless of language. Where notable discrepancies in spelling and/or translation exist between lists, every effort has been made to include such variants alongside the organisation's most commonly known name.

Appendix 6.2

World Directory of Extremist, Terrorist and Other Organisations Associated with Guerrilla Warfare, Political Violence, Protest, Organised Crime and Cyber-crime

Albert J. Jongman

Afghanistan (83 entries)

AFI	Al-Furqan ul-Iran
AH	Al-Houda
AH	Afghan Hezbollah
AI	Defenders of Islam (Ansar al-Islam)
AJ	Azeri Group (Azeri Jamaat)
AJ	Holy War (Al-Jihad)
AQ	The Base (Al-Qaeda)
AQSB	Al-Qa'ida-al-Shahkhayn Brigade
AS	Defenders of the Prophet's Traditions (Ansar al-Sunna)
BEMF	Bara Ebn-e Malek Front
BG	Black Guard (OBL's security unit)
BH	Black Hand
CMU	Council of the Mujahedeen Union (= coalition of Mehsud, Nazir, Hafiz Gul Bahadur)
CP(M)A	Communist Party (Maoist) of Afghanistan
DII	Invitation to Islamic Unity (Da'wati-Ittehad-e-Islami)
FI	Islamic Warriors (Fedayeen-e-Islam)
G272	Group 272
HA	Freedom Party (Hezb-e-Azadi)
HGBG	Hafiz Gul Bahadar Group
HIG	Islamic Party – Gulbuddin Hekmatyar (Hezb-Islami-Gulbuddin)
HIK	Islamic Party – Younas Khalis (Hezb-Islami-Khalis)
HF	Hezb-ul-Furqan
HI	Islamic Movement (Harakat-e-Islami)
HIA	Islamic Party in Afghanistan (Hezb-e-Islami-e-Afghanistan)
HMIA	Islamic Revolutionary Movement of Afghanistan (Harakat Muqatila-e-Islami Afghanistan)
HWIA	Islamic Unity Party of Afghanistan (Hezb-e-Wahdat-e-Islami Afghanistan)
IEA	Islamic Emirate of Afghanistan
IIA	Islamic Union for the Liberation of Afghanistan (Ittehad-e Islami bara-ye Azadi-ye)
II/SNA	Ittihad-e-Islami/Shura-e-Nazar Alliance
IIF	International Islamic Front
IIFJJC	International Islamic Front for Jihad against Jews and Crusaders

JAA	Defenders of the Afghan People (Jamiat Ansar ul-Afghanistan)
JDI	Jamiat-e-Damar e-Islami
JDS	Salafi Taliban (Jama'at al-Dawa'ila al-Sunnah)
JI	Jawahar al-Islam (= alliance of AQ, TB and HIG)
JI	Islamic Society (Jamiat-i-Islami)
JJQS	Jama'at al Ja'wat al-Quran wal Sonat
JM	Army of Mohammed (Jaysh-e-Mohammed)
JM	Army of the Muslims (Jaysh-e-Muslimeen, Jaishol Moslimin)
JM	United Front (Jebh-i-Muttahed)
JM	Army of the Mahdi (Jaysh al-Mahdi) (mainly Turkish and Central Asians)
JMA	National Islamic Movement of Afghanistan (Junbisch-e-Melli Islami Afghanistan)
JSA	Jawanan Salahuddin Ayubi
JSM	Party of Young Mujahedeen (Jamiat ul-Shabab-ul-Muslimeen)
JSQFI	Wahhabi Army of the Call of Islamic Loyalists (Jaysh ul-Salfatullah dawat Qital Fidyani Islam)
JUI-F	Jamiat Ulema-e-Islam Fazal
JUI-H	Jamiat Ulema-e-Islam (Samiul Haq Group)
JUI-R	Jamiat Ulema-e-Islam (Fazlur Rahman Group)
KG	Khanan Group
LI	Lashkar-e Isar
LT	Lashkar-e-Taiba (aligned with AQ)
MAA	Muslims' Army Assembly
MIE	Mujahedeen of the Islamic Emirate (alternative name for Taliban)
MJ	Source of Holy War (Manba al-Jihad) (AQ affiliate)
MM	Mujahedeen Message
NI	Islamic Movement (Nahzat-e-Islami)
NI	Islamic Force (Niru-e-Islami)
O	The Oppressed
PJI	Guardians of Islamic Holy War (Pasdaran-e-Jihadi-e-Islami)
QJA	The Base for Holy War in Afghanistan (Qaidat al-Jihad in Afghanistan)
R	Razagars
RMA	Red Mujahedin Army
SAA	Salahudddin al-Ayoubi (new organisation for AQ/Taliban in Afghanistan)
SAMM	Secret Army of the Muslim Mujahedeen
SCIEA	Shura Council of the Emirate of Afghanistan
SM	Safai Mohammad
SM	The Majdi Corps (Sepah e-al-Mahdi)
SM	Sons of Martyrs
SM	Sword of Muslims (Saif-ul-Muslimeen/Saif-ul-Muslimeen Lashkar Jihad)
SN	Organisation for Victory (Sazeman-e-Nasr)
SN	Shura-e-Nazar (military council of the former Northern Alliance)
SP	Sepah Pasdaran (Iranian)
SS	Corps of the Companions of the Prophet Mohammed (Sepah Sahabeh)
SHL	Fast Moving Army (Suree-ul-Harkat Lashkar)
TBNM	Tora Bora Military Front (Tora Bora Nizami Mahaz)
TM	The Victorious Sect (Taifat ul-Mansura) (Turkish Jamaat)
TM	Student Movement (Taliban Movement)
TMHI	Tanzim-e-Mahsilaan-Hizb-e-Islami (HIG student organisation)
UFA	United Front for Afghanistan (Northern Alliance)
UP	Unity Party (Hezb-e-Wahdat)
UIFSA	United Islamic Front for Salvation of Afghanistan
313B	313 Brigade (special operations unit of AQ with participation of HMA, LJ, HJI, LT, JM)

Albania (9 entries)

ALUAG	Army for the Liberation and Union of Albanian Grounds
AM	Albanian Mafia
AM	Allah's Martyrs
BK	National Front (Balli Kombetar)
DS	Death Squad
FBKSH	Albanian National Unification
FI	Fire of Islam
IXT	Conveying Group (Tablighi Jama'at, Islamic Xhemat Tablik)
MAVI	Liberation Front for Northern Epirus (Metopo Apeleftherosis Voriou Ipirou)

Algeria (65 entries)

AB	Al-Ahouel Brigades
AIM	Armed Islamic Movement Mansouri Meliani
AK	Al-Ansar Brigades (Al-Ansar Katibat)
AKAL	Alliance for a Free Kabylia
AQIM	Al-Qaeda in the Land of Islamic Maghreb (Al-Qaeda fi Bilad al-Maghrib al-Islami)
AV	Afghan Veterans
BG	Belmokhtar Group (AQIM)
CD	Cabal of Death
CIADC	Coalition of the Village and Tribal Elders
D	al-Djazaraa
DB	Death Brigades
DD	Appeal and Struggle (Da'wa wal Djihad)
DDT	Conveying Group (Djama'at al-Da'wa wa al-Tabligh)
EB	Ethiopia Brigades
FIDA	Islamic Front for Armed Holy War (Front islamique pour le djihad armée)
FIS	Islamic Salvation Front (Front islamique du salut) (al-Jabha al-Islamiya li-l-Inqadh)
FLN	National Liberation Front (Front de libération nationale) (Jabhat at-Tahrir al-Wataniya)
FRF	Forum of Rebels for Freedom
FSF	Front of Socialist Forces
FSG	Free Salafist Group
GIA	Armed Islamic Group (Al Jama'a al-Islamiyah al-Musallahah, Groupe islamique armée)
GIA-GC	Armed Islamic Group – General Command
GSPC	Salafist Group for Predication and Combat (Groupe salafiste pour la prédiction et le combat) (Al Jama'ah al-Salafiyya li-al-Da'wa wa'l-Qital)
GSPC-L	Free Salafi Group for Call and Combat
HDS	Defenders of the Salafist Teachings (GIA-splinter) (previously al-Ahouel Brigades) (Dhamat Houmet Da'wa Salafia) (Humat ad-Da'wa as-Salafiya)
HIJM	Armed Algerian Islamic Movement (al-Haraka al-Islamiya al-Jaza'iriya al-Musallaha)
IRM	Islamic Revival Movement
JII	Islamic Salvation Army (Al-Jaysh al-Islami li-l-Inqadh, Armée islamique du salut)
JIMM	al-Jama'a al-Islamiya al-Maghrebiya al-Muqatila
JITJ	Islamic Group for Monotheism and Holy War (Jama'a al-Islamiya lil-Tawhid wal Jihad)
JSLJ	Salafi Group for Call and Holy War (Al-Jama'a Assalafiyah Lidda'wa Wal Jihad)
JSM	Fundamentalist Resistance Group (Al Jama'a assalafiyah al-Muqatilah)
JUM	Society of Algerian Muslim Scholars (Jam'iyat al-'Ulama al-Muslimin)
KS	Martyrs Brigades (Katibat al-Shuhada)
LDG	Legitimate Defense Groups
LIDD	Islamic League for Preaching and Holy War (Ligue islamique de la daawa et le djihad)

LYI	Committees for Ibadite Vigilance (Lijan al-Yaqsa al-Ibadiya)
MAK	Movement for the Autonomy of Kabylia
MAOL	Algerian Movement of Free Officers
MB	Al-Mulathamun Brigade (part of AQIM)
MEI	Movement of the Islamic State (Mouvement pour un état islamique)
MG	Macdat al-Gedamat (GSPC's recruitment apparatus)
MIA	Armed Islamic Movement (Mouvement islamique armée)
MIS	Movement for Islamic Society
MPS	Patriotic Salvation Movement (Mouvement patriotique de salut)
N	Ninjas
NB	Light Brigades (Katibat al-Nur)
NM	Nadim al-Magrebi
OJAL	Organisation of Free Young Algerians (Organisation des jeunes Algériens libres)
PD	Phalanx of Destruction
QJJ	The Base of Holy War in Algeria (Qa'idat al-Jihad fi al-Jaza'ir)
RCD	Collective Movement for Culture and Democracy
SCIAF	Supreme Council of the Islamic Armed Forces
SDG	Self-Defence Groups
SDM	Help and Support for Terrorist Networks (Shabakat Adda'm Walmousanadah)
SOSAR	Secret Organisation to Safeguard the Algerian Republic
TAY	Tahir bin Ammar al-Yusifi
TB	Terror Brigades
TH	Flight from Sin and Atonement (Takfir wal Hijra)
TIZB	Tarek Ibn Zaid Battalion (GSPC)
TQJBB	The Base Organisation of Holy War in the Land of the Berbers (Tanzim Qa'idat al-Jihad fi Bilad al-Berber)
UCHW	United Company of Holy War
VB	Volcano Branch (Seriat el-Bourkane)
2AC	2nd of April Commando

Angola (9 entries)

ELSC	Secret Army for the Liberation of Cabinda
FAC	Cabinda Armed Forces (Forces Armadas Cabindesas)
FDC	Cabinda Democratic Front (Frente Democrática de Cabinda)
FLEC	Front for the Liberation of the Enclave of Cabinda
FLEC-FAC	Front for the Liberation of the Enclave of Cabinda – Armed Forces of Cabina (Frente de Libertação do Enclave de Cabinda–Forces Armadas Cabinderas)
FLEC-P	FLEC-Platform
FLEC-R	Front for the Liberation of Cabina – Renewed (Frente de Libertação do Enclave de Cabina – Renovada)
FNLA	National Front for the Liberation of Angola (Frente Nacional de Libertação de Angola)
UNITA	Union for the Total Independence of Angola (União Nacional para a Independência Total de Angola)

Argentina (9 entries)

CGAIC	Che Guevara Anti-Imperialist Command
CGB	Che Guevara Brigade
CMP	Peronist Moralization Command (Comando de Moralización Peronista)
DSC	Dario Santillan Command
EPO	Eva Peron Organisation

MMNLC	Mariano Moreno National Liberation Command
MTP	All for the Country Movement (Movimiento Todos por la Patria)
PR	Pueblo Reagrupado
S	Spiders

Armenia (6 entries)

ANM	Armenian National Movement
ASALA	Armenian Secret Army for the Liberation of Armenia
DARF	Dachnak Armenian Revolutionary Federation (Dachnaktsoutsioun)
KPD	Karabakh People's Defense
NKDA	Nagorny-Karabakh Defense Army
UVY	Union of Volunteers Yerkrapah

Australia (1 entry)

| OS | L'Onerata Società (Italian mafia) |

Austria (3 entries)

CI	Cell for Internationalism
MFaHLS	Militant Forces against Huntingdon Life Sciences
RDR	Red Daughters of Rage

Azerbaijan (10 entries)

AFNK	Armed Forces of Nagorno-Karabakh
AMG	Azer Misirkhanov Group
APFP	Azerbaijan Popular Front Party
CIA	Caucasus Islamic Army
HT	Party of Liberation (Hezb ut-Tahrir)
IIPB	Islamic International Peacekeeping Brigade
J	Soldiers of Allah (Jeshullah)
JM	Warriors Group (Jama'at al-Muvahidun)
KC	Karabakh Committee
SFNK	Self-Defence Forces of Nagorno-Karabakh

Bahamas (0 entries)

Bahrein (1 entry)

| IFLB | Islamic Front for the Liberation of Bahrein |

Bangladesh (168 entries)

AA	Arakan Army
AD	Army of Allah (Allahr Dal) (JMB splinter)
AD	Amra Dhakabashi
AD	Amirate Din
AFK	Amanatul Forkan al-Khayeria
AHAB	Followers of the Traditions of the Prophet (Ahle-Hadith Andolan Bangladesh)

AHIP	Ahle Hadith (Insaf Party)
AHJS	Ahle Hadith Jubo Sangha
AI	Defenders of Islam (Ansar al-Islamia)
ALF	Arakan Liberation Front
ALP	Arakan Liberation Party
AM	Ansarul Muslemin
AMP	Arakan Mujahid Party
AP	Afgan Parisad
AP	Ayiamma Parisad
APA	Arakan People's Army
ARCF	Asif Reza Commando Force
ARF	Arakan Rohingya Force
ARIF	Arakani Rohingya Islamic Front
ARNO	Arakan Rohingya National Organisation
ATI	Anjumane Talamije Islamia
B	Basbid
BCL	Bangladesh Chhatra League (student wing)
BCM	Biplobi Chhatra Moitree
BI	Bangladesh Imam
BIF	Biswa Islami Front
BIRC	Bangladesh Islam Rokkya Committee
BKA	Bangladesh Khilafat Andolon
BML	Bangladesh Muslim League
BNP	Bangladesh Nationalist Party
BOA	Bangladesh Oikyo Andolon
BSBD	Bangladesh Anti-Terrorist Party (Bangladesh Santrash Birodhi Dal al-Qaeda)
BT	Bangladesh Taliban
CEKC-1971	Committee for the Elimination of the Killers and Collaborators of 1971
CF	Chhatra Front
DI	Dawatul Islam
DIK	Dawatul Islamia of Korea
DPA	Democratic Party of Arakan
EB	Ehoshad Bahini
F	Al-Ferdous
FEIS	Far East Islami Sangathan
H	Al-Haramain Islamic Foundation
H	Al-Hikma
H	Hokikot
HAO	Abu Omar Party (Hezb-e-Abu Omar)
HF-B	Hadith Foundation Bangladesh
HG	Hayatul-e-Gacha
HI	Islamic Movement (Al-Harakat al-Islamia)
HIS	Hizbulla Islami Somaj
HIZ	Holy War Islamic Movement (Harkat e-Islam al-Zihad)
HJI-B	Islamic Movement for Holy War Bangladesh (Harkat-ul-Jihadi-e-Islami-Bangladesh)
HKM-B	Holy Koran Mission Bangladesh
HM	Party of the Mahdi (Hezb al-Mahdi)
HTB	Liberation Party Bangladesh (Hezb-ut-Tahrir Bangladesh)
HT	Unity Party (Hezb-ut Tawhid)
HZ	Hikmatul Zihad
IBP	Islamic Solidarity Front (Islami Biplobi Parishad)
ICM	Islamic Constitution Movement

ICS	Islamic Student Front (Islami Chhatra Shibir) (Student front of JIB)
IDP	Islamic Democratic Party
IOJ	Islami Oikya Jote (political party)
IKNM	International Khtame Nabuyet Movement
ILTB	Islamic Liberation Tigers of Bangladesh
IM	Islamic Manch (Islamic Front)
IM	Ibtedatul al-Muslemin
IMB	Al-Islam Martyrs Brigade
IMPB	Islahul Muslemin Parishad Bangladesh
IPM	Islami Prochar Media
IS	Islami Samaj
ISA	Islamic Shashantabtra Andolon
ISPB	Al-Islami Sanghati Parishad Bangladesh
ITM	Iktadul Tulah l-Muslemin
IUA	Islamic Unity Alliance
IU	Ittifakul Ulema
IUM	Islamic Unity Movement
IWO	Islamic Invitation and Welfare Organisation (Al-Farooq)
JAH	Group of Followers of the Tradition (Jama'at-e-Ahle Hadith)
JAHA	Jamiatul Ahle Hadith Andolon
JCD	Jatiyatabadi Chhatra Dal (student wing)
JET	Jamiatul Ehia Turaj
JF	Welfare Group (Jama'at ul-Falah) (Jamyatul Falayia)
JH	Jangi Hakikat
JI	Jama'at-e-Islami
JIB	Jama'at-e-Islami Bangladesh (political party)
JIJ	Islamic Holy War Group (Jama'at al-Islamia al-Jihad)
JJ	People's Warrior Group (Jana Juddha)
JM	Army of Mustafa (Jaysh-e-Mustafa)
JM	Army of Mohammed (Jaysh Mohammad)
JM	Jama'at ul-Mudarassin
JMB	Jama'at ul Mufassirin Bangladesh
JMB	Warriors Group Bangladesh (Jama'at ul-Mujahideen Bangladesh)
JMB	Jamyate Mudarsin Bangladesh
JMJB	Reawakened Muslim Masses Bangladesh (Jagrata Muslim Janata Bangladesh)
JQ	Jadida al-Qaeda
JS	Jama'at-as-Sadat (Jumatul al-Sadat)
JT	Jamyote Talaba
JTA	Jama'at-e-Toleba-e-Arabia
JTJ	Monotheism and Holy War Group (Jama'at Al-Tawhid Wa al-Jihad)
JUI-B	Jama'at-e-Ulema-e-Islam Bangladesh
JYT	Jama'at-e-Yahia Trust (Jamayatul-e-Yahia-al-Turat)
K	Al-Khidmat
KB	Kotal Bahini
KB	Kotic Bahini
KD	Kalemar Dawat (Bhola)
KFS	Kital Fee Sabilillah
KMB	Khilafat Majlis Bangladesh
KNM	Khatm-e-Nabuyet Movement (Hifajate Khatame Nabuot)
LMF	Liberation Myanmar Force
LMK	Luzna Mokkwa al-Khayeria
MB	Muzam Bahini

MGS	Muslim Guerrilla Sangstha
MLFB	Muslim Liberation Front of Burma
MP	Warriors Party (Mujahid Party)
MIB	Al-Markaj ul Islami Bangladesh
MMBB	Muslim Mujahid Bahini Bangladesh
MMSC	Muslim Millah Saria Council
MRMOP	Muslim Rokkya Mujahidin Okkiyo Parishad
MT	Muzahidi Taiyab
MTKN	Mozlishe Tahafuje Khotome Nabuot
NRCP	New Revolutionary Communist Party
NUPA	National United Party of Arakan
PBCP	Purba Banglar Communist Party
PCJSS	Parbattya Chattagram Jana Sanghati Samiti (aka Santu Larma)
R	Al-Resalat
RAI	Rabeta al-Alam al-Islam
RIA	Rohingya Independent Army
RIF	Rohingya Independent Force
RIF	Rohingya Islamic Front
RIHS	Revival of Islamic Heritage Society
RPF	Rohingya Patriotic Front
RSO	Rohingya Solidarity Organisation
QFS	Qital Free Salilillah
PBCP	Purba Bangla Communist Party
PLA	People's Liberation Army
RPF	Revolutionary People's Front
SA	Sattabad Andolon
SB	Peace Force (Shanti Bahini)
SH	Shahadat-e-al-Hikma (Shahadat al Hiqma)
SMB	Al-Sayed Mujahid Bahini
SN	Shahadat-e-Nabuat
SNAB	Shahid Nasrullah Arafat Brigade (= JMB's high-risk operations group)
SP	Sarbahara Party
SP	Shotter Poth
SS	Corps of the Companions of the Prophet (Sepah-e-Sahaba)
SS	Suicide Squad
SSP	Shahaba Shainic Parishad
T	Al-Tanjib
T	Al-Turat
TB	Tanzim Bangladesh
TDB	Party of Abu Omar (Tamira ar-Din Bangladesh; Hezb e-Abu Omar) (Ta-Amir Uddin Bangladesh)
THPB	Tahfiz-e-Haramain Parishad Bangladesh (Tahliye Harmene Parishad)
TJ	Believers in the Oneness of Allah (Tawhidi Janata)
TJ	Talemaye Jama-et
TKN	Tahaf-fuz-e-Khatm-e-Nabuyet (Tanzine Khatame Nabuot)
TT	Tawhid Trust
U	Community of Believers (Al-Ummah)
UAB	Ulama Anjuman al-Bainat
UP	Ulema Parishad
UPDF	United People's Democratic Front
USAAM	United Student Association of Arakan Movement
WIF	Warot Islamic Front

WIF	World Islamic Front for Holy War
WIFKJ	Warot Islamic Front Kolema Jamaat
YM	Young Muslim
Z	Al-Jazeera/The Peninsula (Al-Zazira)
ZB	Holy War Bangladesh (Al-Zihad Bangladesh)

Belarus (2 entries)

| BNOA | Belarussian People's Liberation Army |
| NLA | National Liberation Army |

Belgium (3 entries)

APF	Arabian Peninsula Freeman
ARG	Armenian Resistance Group
BBET	Blood-Soil-Honour-Allegiance (Bloed-Bodem-Eer en Trouw)

Belize (0 entries)

Benin (1 entry)

| V | Vigilantes |

Bolivia (12 entries)

CM	Cocalero Movement
CNPZ	Nestor Paz Zamora Commission
CSUTCB	Bolivian Peasant Workers Central Union
DB	Daddy's Boys
EGTK	Tupac Katari Guerrilla Army
ELN-B	National Liberation Army of Bolivia
FAL-ZW	Zarate Wilka Armed Liberation Forces (Fuerzas Armadas de Liberación Zarate Wilka)
I	Inevitables, The
LC	La Paz Cartel
MAS	Movement toward Socialism
NACF	National Anti-Corruption Front
NLA	National Liberation Army (the second)

Bosnia-Herzegovina (90 entries)

A	Akrepi
A	Arkanovsci (Militia of Zeljko Raznjatovic [alias Arkan])
A	Avengers (paramilitary)
ABH	Armija Bosne i Hercegovine
AID	Research and Development Agency (Agencija za Istrazivanje i Dokumentaciju)
AIO	Active Islamic Youth (Aktivna Islamska Omladina)
AMI	Armed Militia of Islamists of Bosnia-Herzegovina
AS	Aid 'Sheve'
B	Rage (Besa)
B	Peony (Bozur)
BG	Butterfly Group

BH	Black Hand
BL	Black Legion
C	CIRKL
C	Chetnik Movement (Četnici)
CL	Black Swans (Crni Lebedi)
CRP	Čhetnički Ravnogorski Pokret
CV	Cutlucki Volci
DF	Democratic Forum
DSEB	Dusan the Mighty Forces (Dušan Silni Elite Battalion)
F	Faith
FB	Free Bosna (Slobodna Bosna)
FB	Frenki Boys (aka Red Berets)
FG	Fishhead Gang
FH	Fire Horses
FU	Fighters Union
G	Gazii
G	Groups (Grupa)
G	Guerrillas
GB	Green Berets (Zelene Beretke)
GPM	Gavrilo Princip Movement
H	Hamze
HIF	Al-Haramein Islamic Foundation
HM	Movement of Warriors (Harkatul ul-Mujahedin)
HT	Hamas Turabe
IA	Islamic Alliance (Islamska Liga)
IW	Islamic Warriors (Islamski Ratnici)
J	Janissaries (Janicari)
J	Joker (Jokeri)
JG	Jaguar Group
JNA	Yugoslav National Army
K	Mole (Krtici)
KK	Krashici Krajina
M	Brigade of Warriors (Al-Mudzahid) (Al-Mujahidin Brigade, Kateebat al-Mujahideen)
M	Muderiz
M	Maturice
MB	Muslim Brotherhood (Muslimansko Bratstvo)
MK	Militia of the Krajina
MOS	Muslim Youth Organisation (Muslimanski Omladinski Savjes)
MSU	Al-Mujahedin Special Unit
NG	Nighthawk Group (Soko)
O	Ostvenici (B-Serb paramilitary group)
OG	Oric Group
PDA	Party of Democratic Action (Stranka Demokratske Akcije)
P	Pharaohs (Faraoni)
PL	Patriotic League (Patriotska Liga)
PSU	Party of Serb Unity
Q	Quadrant
RP	The Return of the Prophet (Povratak Mesije)
RR	Red Rose (Crevena Ruza)
SDA	Muslim Party of Democratic Action
SG	Sahna Group
SG	Scorpion Group

SG	Serbian Guard
T	Tabut
T	Tajfa
T	Tiger (Tigrovi)
T	Tron (B–Serb paramilitary group)
TB	Ten of Bugojno
TDF	Territorial Defense Forces
TG	Taifun Group
TI	Taiba International
TWRA	Third World Relief Agency
U	Ustahsas (Ustashi)
UCS	Army of Liberation of Sandzak' (aka 'Albanian Brigade of Tuzi' or 'Army of Liberation of Plav and Gusinje', Korparmate Malesiya)
V	Wahhabis (Vehabije)
V	Knights (Vitezovi)
VRS	Vojska Republike Srpske
WA	White Angels
WE	White Eagles
WV	Wolves of Vukovar
YW	Yellow Wasps
Z	Zebras
Z	Zetra 1,2,3
ZL	Green Legion (Zelena Legija)
ZO	Zivinicki Axis (Zivinicki Osi)
ZS	Green Arrow (Zelena Strela)
3–9	3 from 9 (3 od 9)
7th BB	7th Banja Brigade

Brazil (18 entries)

AC	Acre Cartel
CV	Red Command (Comando Vermelho) (drug gang in Rio de Janeiro)
DS	Death Squad
ES	Espiritu Santo (death squad; Squad Le Cocq)
FF	Friends of Friends
IURD	Universal Church of the Kingdom of God (Igreja Universal Reino de Deus)
LOC	Peasant Workers' League (Liga Operaria Camponesa)
LOC	Peasant Fighting Organisation (Luta Organização Camponesa)
MCC	Corumbiara Peasant Movement
MI	Murder Inc. (death squad)
MLST	Movement for the Liberation of the Landless (MST offshoot)
MO	Golden Boys (Meninos de Ouro) (death squad)
MST	Landless Rural Workers' Movement (Movimiento Sem Terra)
PCC	Primeiro Comando da Capital
ROTA	Tobias de Aguiar Patrol (Rondas Ostensivas Tobias de Aguiar)
SNLFA	Socialist Forces of National Liberation (SFNLA)
T	Thundercats (death squad)
TC	Third Command

Brunei (0 entries)

Bulgaria (5 entries)

C777	Club 777 (organised crime group)
OMO-I	United Macedonian Organisation – Ilinden (Obedina Makedonska Organizatsiya 'Ilinden')
SIC	Sofia Insurance Company (organised crime group)
TG	TIM Group (organised crime group)
VIS	Loyalty, Investments, Security (organised crime group)

Burundi (11 entries)

CNND	National Council for the Defence of Democracy
FDD	Forces for the Defense of Democracy (Forces pour la défense de la démocratie)
FLN	National Liberation Front (Force nationale de libération)
FROLINA	National Liberation Front (Front pour la libération nationale)
I	Those who never close their eyes (Intagaheka)
KAZE-FDD	KAZE-Forces for the Defense of Democracy
PALIPEHUTU	Hutu People's Liberation Party (Parti pour la libération du peuple Hutu)
PARENA	Party for National Reconstruction (Parti pour le redressement national)
SD	The Undefeated (Sans défait)
SE	The Unstoppable Ones, The Infallibles (Sans échec)
U	Ubumwe

Cambodia (11 entries)

ANKI	National Army of Independent Kampuchea
CFF	Cambodian Freedom Fighters
CIA	Cambodian Islamic Association
CMDF	Cambodian Muslim Development Foundation
CPNLAF	Cambodia's People's National Liberation Armed Forces
CPK	Communist Party of Kampuchea
DNUM	Democratic National United Movement
FUNCINPEC	United Front for an Independent, Neutral, Peaceful and Cooperative Cambodia (Front uni national pour un Cambodge indépendant neutre, pacifique et coopérative)
KR	Red Khmer (Khmer Rouge; aka CPNLAF)
PA	Private Army of Hun Sen
PDK	Party of Democratic Kampuchea

Cameroon (1 entry)

SCNC	Southern Cameroon National Council

Canada (3 entries)

ALF	Animal Liberation Front
BCB	Big Circle Boys (motorcycle gang)
ELF	Earth Liberation Front

Cape Verde (0 entries)

Central African Republic (4 entries)

APRD	People's Army for the Restoration of Democracy (Armée populaire pour la restauration de la république)
GUDFU	Goula Union of Democratic Forces for Unity
KM	Karako Militia
PCJP	Patriotic Convention for Justice and Peace (Convergence des patriots centreafricains pour la justice et la paix)

Chad (25 entries)

ANR	National Resistance Alliance (Alliance nationale de la résistance)
CALD	Action Committee for Freedom and Democracy
CMAP	Coordination of Armed Political Opposition Movements (Coordination des mouvements armeés politiques de l'opposition)
CNAPD	National Committeee for Action for Peace and Democracy
CNRT	National Council for the Reconstruction of Chad (Conseil national de redressement du Tchad)
CPRM	Chadian People's Revolutionary Movement
CSNPD	National Reawakening Committee for Peace and Democracy (Comité de salut national pour la paix et la démocratie)
CSNPDT	Conseil de Salut National pour la Paix et la Démocratie au Tchad
DDS	Directorate of Documentation and Security (Direction de la documentation et la sécurité)
DRF	Democratic Revolutionary Front (Toubou)
FAIDT	Front for the Restoration of Democracy in Chad
FARF	Armed Forces for the Federal Republic (Forces armeés pour la république féderale)
FNTR	Renewed National Chadian Front
FROLINA	Chadian National Liberation Front
FROLINAT-FAP	Chadian National Liberation Front – People's Armed Force
FUC	United Front for Change
GSDNNC	Chadian National Nomadic Guard
JST	People's Front for Reform (Foulatiya) (Al-Jabha al-Sha'biya lil-Taqwim)
MDD	Movement for Development and Democracy
MDD-FANT	MDD National Armed Forces of Chad (MDD-Forces armeés nationales du Tchad)
MDJT	Movement for Democracy and Justice in Chad (Mouvement pour la démocratie et la justice au Tchad)
RFC	Rally of Forces for Change
SCUD	Platform for Change, Unity and Democracy (Socle pour le changement, l'unité et la démocratie)
UDF	Union of Democratic Forces
UFR	Union of Resistance Forces

Chile (13 entries)

ACC	Arnoldo Camu Command
ADFLC	Autonomous and Destructive Forces Leon Czolgosz
BDEPO	Banda Dinamitera Efrain Plaza Olmedo
CAM	Coordinadora Arauco Malleco
CCSPR	Chilean Committee of Support for the Peruvian Revolution
FNPL	Fatherland and Liberty Nationalist Front (Frente Nacionalista Patria y Libertad)
FPMR	Manuel Rodríguez Patriotic Front (Frente Patriótico Manuel Rodríguez)
FPMR-D	Manuel Rodríguez Patriotic Front Dissidents (Frente Patriótico Manuel Rodríguez – Dissidente)

HTC	Hernando Trizano Command
MAS-C	Movement toward Socialism – Chile
MIR	Movement of the Revolutionary Left (Movimiento de Izquierda Revolucionaria)
MJL	Lautaro Youth Movement (Movimiento Juvenil Lautaro)
UPAM	United Popular Action Movement

China (25 entries)

ACPAF	All China People's Autonomous Federation
BHSN	Black Hawk Safety Net (hackers' network)
CDP	China Democratic Party
CNC	Club of National Culture
CNM	Club for National Modernisation
DFSC	Democratic Front for the Salvation of China
ETIC	East Turkistan Information Center
ETIM	East Turkestan Islamic Movement
ETIP	East Turkestan Islamic Party
ETLO	Liberation Movement of East Turkestan (Sharqiy Türkistan Azatliq Tashkilati)
ETLT	East Turkistan Liberation Tigers
FG	Falun Gong (also Falun Dafa)
GDG	Green Dragon Gang
HA	Party of Allah (Hezh Allah)
HII	Party of Islamic Reform (Hezb al-Islah al Islami)
HIT	Islamic Party of Turkestan (Hezb al-Islami Li-Turkistan)
HUC	Hackers' Union of China (Red Hackers)
HuT	Party of Liberation (Hezb-ut-Tahrir)
MB	Muslim Brotherhood (Ikhwan Muslimeen)
NURF	National United Revolutionary Front
SHAT	Free Turkestan
TJ	Conveying Group (Tablighi Jamaat)
UHWO	Uighur Holy War Organisation
UNRFET	United National Revolutionary Front of East Turkestan
WUYC	World Uighur Youth Congress

Colombia (160 entries)

AA	Blue Eagles (Águilas Azules)
AC	Antioquia Clan
ACC	Peasant Self-Defence Groups of Casanare (Autodefensas Campesinas del Casanare)
ACCU	Peasant Self-Defence Groups of Córdoba and Urabá (Autodefensas Campesinas de Córdoba y Urabá)
ACDEGAM	Association of Cattlemen and Agricultural Producers of the Middle Magdalena
ACMV	Peasant Self-Defense Groups of Meta and Vichada
ACP	Armed Command of the People
ACUNV	Peasant Self-Defense Forces of the North of the Valley (Autodefensas Campesinas Unidas del Norte del Valle)
AD	Golden Eagles (Águilas Doradas)
AD/M-19	Democratic Alliance/M-19
AEKU	Anti-Extortion and Kidnapping Unit
AM	Aljibes Militiagroup
AN	Black Eagles (Águilas Negras)

ANC	Águilas Negras Catatumbo
AOC	Ariel Otero Command
AR	Red Eagles (Águilas Rojas)
AUC	United Self-Defense Groups of Colombia (Autodefensas Unidas de Colombia)
AUSAC	AUSAC (paramilitary organisation)
A19M	April 19 Movement
B	Los Blancos
B	Los Buitraguenos
BACRIM	criminal gangs (general description for dozens of criminal gangs) (bandas criminales)
BAG	Banda Alta Guajira
BAS	Antisubversive Bloc of the South (Bloc Antisubversivo del Sur)
BB	Banda Barraquilla
BB	Bloque del Busqueda
BB	Bombona Battalion
BBC	Banda Bajo Cauca
BBL	Banda Barranco Loba
BCN	Cacique Nutibara Bloc
BCP	Pipinta Indigenous Chief (Gang) (Banda Cacique Pipinta)
BHG	Banda Héroes de Granada
BJI	Banda Juago de Iberico
BJMC	Bloque Jose Maria Cordova
BLC	Bloque Llaneros del Casanare
BM	Bloque Metro
BMP	Banda Mosquera y Pizaro
BN	Bandera Negra (Black Gang)
BOC	Banda Oriente del Caldas
BPB	Banda Puble Bello
BRM	Banda Riohacha Maicao
BS	Banda Santander
BS	Black Serpent
BSC	Banda Sur del Cesar
BV	Banda Valledupar
C	Los Carranceros
C	Los Chamizos
C	Los Cheperos
C	Cobras
C	Combos
C	The Cleaners (Los Limpiadoros)
COLSINGUE	Colombia without Guerrillas (Colombia sin Guerrilla)
CONVIVIR	Civilian Rural Self-Defense Groups
CB	Castano Brothers
CB	Centauros Bloc (AUC Faction)
CC	Cali Cartel
CDS	Colina Death Squad
CF	Calima Front
CL	Colombia Libre
CQL	Commando Quíntin Lame
CRPAA	Colombian Revolutionary Popular Antiterrorist Army
CRS	Corriente de Renovación Socialista
CV	Citizen Vigilance
CW	Contrainsurgencia Wayuu
D	Disposables (Desechables)

DC	Dignity for Colombia
DLF	Domingo Lain Front (ELN front)
E	Extraditables (Los Extraditables)
E	The Hooded (Encapuchados)
ELN	National Liberation Army (Ejército de Liberación Nacional)
EP	Eastern Plains Paramilitary Self-Defense Group
EPDC	Eastern Plains Drug Cartel
EPL	People's Liberation Army (Ejército Popular de Liberación)
ERG	Guevarist Revolutionary Army (Ejército Revolucionario Guevarista)
ERP	Revolutionary People's Army (Ejército Revolucionario del Pueblo)
ERPAC	Popular Revolutionary Anti-Communist Army (Ejército Revolucionario Popular Anticomunista)
F	Ferchos (militia group)
FARC	Revolutionary Armed Forces of Colombia (Fuerzas Armadas Revolucionarias de Colombia)
FFG	Frente Francisco Garnica
FUNDECA	Paramilitary group in Sierra Nevada de Santa Marta
G	La Guajira Cartel
G	Gomelos (militia group)
G	Gorda (militia group)
GC	Green Commandos
GCSM	Gnostic Church Stella Maris
HC	Heroes de Castano
HP	Heroes of Palestine
HPL	Hope, Peace and Liberty (Esperanza, Paz y Libertad)
HRC	Human Rights Cartel
IFB	Integrated Forces of Bolivar
JBCG	Jaime Bateman Cayon Group
JEGA	Jorge Eliecer Gaitan Army
JI	Justiciero Implacable
JMBF	Jose María Becerra Front
L	Lina Group
LAPA	Latin American Patriotic Army
LL	Liberators of the Plains (Libertadores del Llano)
M	Males (Los Machos)
M	Los Masetos
M	The Twins (Los Mellizos)
M	Memos Militiagroup
MAO	Workers' Self-Defense Movement
MAS	Death to Kidnappers (Muerte a Secuestradores)
MB	Metro Bloc
MB	Mobile Brigade
MC	Medellín Cartel
MCG	Muerte a Comunistas y Guerrilleros
MMPSDM	Magdalena Medio Peasant Self-Defense Movement
MN	Black Hand (Mano Negro)
MORENA	National Restoration Movement (Movimiento de Restauración Nacional)
MPL	Movimiento Patria Libre
MRN	Death to Revolutionaries in North East Antioquia (Muerte a Revolucionarios del Nordeste Antioqueno)
M19	April 19 Movement

NBJ40	North Bloc of 'Jorge 40' (Jorge Tovar Pupo)
NVC	North Valley Cartel (Norte del Valle Cartel)
N100P	National 100 Percent
ONG	New Generation Organisation (Organización Nueva Generación)
ORP	People's Revolutionary Organisation
P	Los Paisas
P	Los Pecas
PAC	Popular Alternative Commands
PCC	First Commando of the Capital
PCC–ML	Communist Party of Colombia Marxist-Leninist
PEPES	Group of Those Persecuted by Pablo Escobar
PL	Pure Law
PLA	Popular Liberation Army
PLF	People's Liberation Forces
PM	People's Militias
PO	Fatherland and Order
PRA	Popular Revolutionary Army
R	The Tumbleweed (Los Rastrojos) (Northern Valley cartel's private army)
R	Rebirth (Renacer)
R	Romilocos Militiagroup
R	Rolos Militiagroup
RCP	Popular Peasant Patrols (Rondas Campesinas Populares)
RFF	Ricardo Franco Front
RGBF	Ramón Gilberto Barbosa Front
RT	Resistencia Tayrona
RUAN	Antonio Narino Urban Network
RVN	The Revenger without a Name
S	Hitmen (Sicarios)
SB	Search Bloc
SB	Southwest Bloc
SBCG	National Guerrilla Coordination Simón Bolívar
SDG	Self-Defense Group South Magdalena
SDG	Self-Defense Group San Fernando
SLU	Southern Liberators Unit (of USDF)
SPMV	Seguridad Privada Meta y Vichada
SV	Santander Vigilantes
T	Los Tangueros
T	La Terraza
T	The Dealers (Los Traquetos)
U	Los Uvos
UC–ELN	Camilist Union – National Liberation Army (Union Camilista – Ejército de Liberación Nacional)
UP	Patriotic Union
V	Cow Militia group (Vaca)
VSJ	Victors of Saint Jorge (Vencedores de San Jorge)
Y	Los Yeyos

Comoros (2 entries)

GIRMA	Group for the Recovery Initiative for the Anjouan Movement
NUDC	National Union for Democracy in the Comoros

Congo, Brazzaville (8 entries)

C	Cobras
C	Cocoyes (Koy Koy)
FAR	Resistance Self-Defence Forces
M	Mambas
MCDDI	Congolese Movement for Democracy and Integrated Development (Mouvement congolais pour la démocratie et le développement intégral)
N	Ninjas
NRMC	National Resistance Movement of Congo
Z	Zulus

Congo, Democratic Republic (57 entries)

ADFL	Alliance of Democratic Forces for the Liberation of Congo-Zaire
ARD	Alliance for Democratic Resistance (Alliance pour la résistance démocratique)
B	Bangalima
B	Bangerima
B	Banyarwanda
B	Banyamulenge
BK	Bundi dia Kongo
CDC	Congolese Democratic Coalition
CDR	Congolese Rally for Democracy
CDRZ	Democratic Revolution Committee for Zaire
CLA	Congolese Liberation Army
CNDP	National Congress for the Defense of People
CPP	People's Powers Committees
CRNL	Council of Resistance and National Liberation (Conseil de résistance et de libération national)
DPP	Division for Presidential Protection (Division de protection présidentielle) (private army of Jean-Pierre Bemba)
FAC	Congolese Armed Forces
FAP	Popular Self-Defence Forces
FAPC	Armed Forces of the Congolese People (Forces armées du peuple Congolais)
FARDC	Armed Forces of the Democratic Republic of Congo
FDLR	Democratic Forces for the Liberation of Rwanda (Forces démocratiques pour la libération du Rwanda)
FMM–FAP	Forces Mayi Mayi-Popular Self-Defense Forces (Forces d'autodeéfense populaires)
FNI	National Integrationist Front (Front des nationalistes et intégrationnistes)
FPC	Front Patriotique pour le Changement
FPJC	Popular Front for Justice in Congo
FRDC	People's Army in the Congo
FRF	Federal Republican Forces (Forces republicains at federalistes) (Banuamulenge Group)
FRPI	Patriotic Resistance Forces in Ituri (Forces résistance patriotique d'Ituri)
FSP	Front for Solidarity and Progress
GAS	Group for Action and Support of Jean-Pierre Bemba (Groupe d'action et de soutien à Jean-Pierre Bemba)
H	The Owls (Les Hiboux)
HU	Holy Union
K	Child Soldiers (Kadogos)
KT	Katanga Tigers (Front de libération nationale de Katanga)
LNR	Lummbirt National Resistance (Mayi-Mayi faction)
MAGRIVI	Hutu Militia Group

MLC	Congolese Liberation Movement (Mouvement de libération congolais)
MMI	Maji Maji Ingilima
MNC	Congolese National Movement
MNCL	Lumumba National Congolese Movement
N	Ngilima (Congolese force of different ethnic groups)
NRCD	National Resistance Council for Democracy
NRCK	National Resistance Council of Kivu
PPC	People's Power Committees
PRP	People's Revolutionary Party
PSDF	Popular Self-Defense Forces
PUSIC	Party for Unity, Security and Integrity of the Congo (Parti pour l'unité et la sauvegarde de l'intégrité du Congo)
RCD	Congolese Movement for Democracy
RCD-G	Congolese Rally for Democracy – Goma (Rassemblement congolais pour la démocratie – Goma)
RCD-ML-K	Congolese Collective Movement – Liberation Movement – Kisangani (Rassemblement congolais pour la démocratie – mouvement de libération)
RMLZ	Revolutionary Movement for the Liberation of Zaire
SDU	Self-Defence Units, People's Power Committees
UCP	Union of Congolese for Peace
UFERI	Party of the Union of Independent Republicans
UPC	Union of Congolese Patriots (Union des patriotes congolais)
URNL	Union of Republican Nationalists for Liberation
WL	White Legion

Costa Rica (4 entries)

BAP	Armed Wing of the People
CC	Commando Cobra
CMF	Commando María Félix
VGC	Viviana Gallardo Commando

Croatia (7 entries)

CDM	Croatian Defence Movement
CRF	Croatian Revolutionary Fraternities
HOS	Croatian Defense Forces (Hrvatska Oruzana Snaga)
HVO	Croatian Defence Council (Hrvatsko Vijece Obrane)
ITA	Istrian Terrorist Action
SUC	Special Units of Croatia
ZNG	Croatian National Guard (Zbor Narodne Garde)

Cuba (0 entries)

Cyprus (1 entry)

CNO	Cypriot Nationalist Organisation

Czech Republic (0 entries)

Denmark (4 entries)

ABSB	Abu Bakr al-Seddiq Brigades
AGEB	Action Group Extreme Beate
BHS	Blood and Honour Scandinavia
SHLM	Supporters of Horst Ludwig Meyer

Djibouti (1 entry)

FRUD	Front for the Restoration of National Unity and Democracy (Front pour la restauration de l'unité nationale et de la démocratie)

Dominica (0 entries)

Dominican Republic (1 entry)

RAP	Revolutionary Army of the People

East Timor (23 entries)

A	Alfa
A	Thorn (Aitarak)
BIM	Blood of Integration Militia
BMP	Red and White Iron (Besi Merah Putih)
CNRM	National Resistance Council of Maubere
CNRT	National Resistance Council of East Timor (Concelho Nacional Resistância de Timorese)
FALINTIL	Armed Forces of National Liberation of East Timor
FRETILIN	Revolutionary Front for an Independent East Timor (Frente Revolucionaria de Timor l'Este Independente)
GP	Gada Paksi
H	Lightning (Halilintar)
IFT	Indonesian Fighting Troops Militia
L	Laksaur Militia
M	Makikit
MAHIDI	Dead or Alive for Integration
N	Ninjas
NUF	National United Front
PFDI	Peace Force and Defender of Integration Militia
PPI	Command of the Pro-Integration Struggle
RB	Red Blood Militia
S	Saka
S	Sera
UFETA	United Front for East Timor Autonomy
WANRA	People's Resistance (Perlawan Rakyat)

Ecuador (15 entries)

ARL	Armed Revolutionary Left (Izquierda Revolucionaria Armada)
AVC	¡Alfaro Vive, Carajo! (Alfaro Lives, Dammit!)
CONAIE	Confederation of Indigenous Nationalities of Ecuador
EAPAF	Eloy Alfaro Popular Armed Forces

ERF	Ecuadorian Rebel Force
FARE-DP	Revolutionary Armed Forces of Ecuador – Defenders of the People
FDIP	Indigenous Defense Front for Pastaza Province
GCP	People's Combatants Groups (Grupos de Combatientes Populares)
MPD	Democratic People's Movement
NB	Neighborhood Brigades
PGG	Pirates of the Gulf Gang
PRM	People's Revolutionary Militias (Milicias Revolucionarias del Pueblo)
RCB	Ruminahui Communications Battalion
RS	Red Sun
WL	White Legion

Egypt (46 entries)

AGI	Islamic Group (Al-Gama'a al Islamiyya)
BMAA	Brigades of the Martyr Abdullah Azzam
EIJ	Egyptian Islamic Holy War (Jama'at al-Jihad bi-Misr)
EM	Egypt's Warriors (Egypt's Mujahideen)
ER	Egypt's Revolution
ERSG	Egyptian Revolutionary Socialist Group
GIJ	Group of International Justice
GS	Gang of Sons
GS	Green Shirts
IGBLN	Islamic Glory Brigades in the Land of the Nile
IJ	Islamic Holy War (Islamic Jihad)
IJG	International Justice Group
IM	Muslim Brotherhood (Al-Ikhwan al-Muslimun)
J	Holy War (Al-Jihad)
JAS	Group of Defenders of Islamic Law (Jama'at Ansar al-Sharia)
JIA	Global Islamic Community (al-Jam'a al-Islamiya al'Alamiya)
JIC	Jihadist Islamic Community (Al-Jama'a al-Islamiya al-Jihadiya)
JJ	Holy War Group (Jama'at al-Jihad)
JM	Community of Muslims (Jama'at al-Muslim)
JM	Group of Emigrants (Jama'at al-Muhajiroun)
JQI	Jaysh al-Quds al-Islami
KII	Brigades of Islamic Pride (Kata'ib al-'Izz al-Islamiya)
LP	Labor Party (outlawed)
ME	Mujahideen of Egypt
MF	Young Egypt (Misr al-Fatah)
NJ	New Holy War (New Jihad)
PIA	Palestinian Islamic Army
PNHW	Pioneers of the New Holy War
Q	Qutbiyyoun
QJBSAK	The Base Organsation of Holy War in the Levant and Egypt (Qaeda al-Jihad fi Bilad al-Sham wa Ardh al-Kinana)
QLN	The Base Organisation of Holy War in the Land of the Nile (Al-Qaeda in the Land of the Nile)
RAPA	Resistant Arab People's Alliance
S	Al-Shawqioun
SFP	Soldiers of the Friends of the Prophet
SG	Soldiers of God (Jund Allah)
SO	Shi'ite Organisation
TD	Withdrawal Movement (Al-Tableegh wal Daa'wa)

TE	Al-Thabeton in Egypt
TF	Vanguards of Conquest (Tala'eh al-Fatah)
TIB	Tawhid Islamic Brigades
TJ	Tanzim Muhammad Abd al-Salam Faraj (or Tanzim al-Jihad)
TJ	Monotheism and Holy War (Tawhid w'al Jihad)
TM	The Victorious Sect (Al-Ta'efa al-Mansoura)
TWH	Flight from Sin and Atonement (Takfir wal Hijra)
W	The Promise (al Wa'ad)
WIF	World Islamic Front

El Salvador (27 entries)

ABSB	Abu-Bakr al-Saddiq Brigades
AD	Angels of Death
ARENA	Nationalist Republican Alliance (Alianza Republicana Nacionalista)
BG	Benedicto Gang
BMA	Brigades of Martyr Atta Al-Qa'ida Organisation
BS	Black Shadow (Sombra Negra)
CERF	Clara Elizabeth Ramirez Front
C18	Calle 18
ERP	Revolutionary Army of the People (Ejército Revolucionario del Pueblo)
FAL	Armed Forces of Liberation (Fuerzas Armadas Liberaciones)
FARN	Armed Forces of National Resistance (Fuerzas Armadas de Resistencia Nacional)
FAS	Salvadorian Anti-Communist Front
FMLN	Farabundo Martí Liberation Front (Frente Farabundo Martí para la Liberación Nacional)
FPL	Popular Liberation Forces Farabundo Martí) (Fuerzas Populares de Liberación Farabundo Martí)
FRS	Salvadorean Revolutionary Front
GA	Guardian Angels
LP28F	February 28 Popular Leagues (Ligas Populares 28 de Febrero)
MS	Mara Salvatrucha (powerful transnational organized crime group)
N-ESA	New Salvadorean Anti-Communist Army
ORDEN	Democratic Nationalist Organisation (Organización Democrática Nacionalista)
P	Patriots (Los Patrióticos)
PCS	Salvadorean Communist Party (Partido Comunista Salvadoreno)
PLF	People's Liberation Forces (Ejército Popular de Liberación)
PRTC	Revolutionary Party of Central American Workers (Partido Revolucionario Trabajadores de la América Central)
RM	Rural Militia
RN	National Resistance (Resistencia Nacional)
UGB	White Fighting Union (Union Guerrero Blanco)

Eritrea (13 entries)

AENF	Alliance of Eritrean National Forces
AF	Warriors Army (Army of Fedayeen)
DFEN	Democratic Front of Eritrean Nationalities
DMLEK	Democratic Movement for the Liberation of the Eritrean Kunama
EDA	Eritrean Democratic Alliance
EDRMGS	Eritrean Democratic Resistance Movement Gash-Setit
EIF	Eritrean Islamic Front
EISF	Eritrean Islamic Salvation Front/ Movement

EJI	Eritrean Islamic Jihad (Harakat al-Khalas al-Islami)
ELF	Eritrean Liberation Front
EPLF	Eritrean People's Liberation Front
MBE	Warriors Brigades in Eritrea (Mujahedeen Brigades in Eritrea)
RSADO	Red Sea Afar Democratic Organisation

Ethiopia (11 entries)

AFD	Alliance for Freedom and Democracy
CUD	Coalition for Unity and Democracy
ENUF	Ethiopian National United Front
EPRA	Ethiopian People's Revolutionary Army
GPDC	Gambella People's Democratic Congress
OLF	Oromo Liberation Front
ONLA	Ogaden National Liberation Army
ONLF	Oromo National Liberation Front (Jabhadda Wadaniga Xoreynta Ogaadeenya)
PG	Palace Guard
TPLF	Tigray People's Liberation Front
UEDF	United Ethiopian Democratic Forces

Fiji (1 entry)

| CRWU | Counter Revolutionary Warfare Unit |

Finland (0 entries)

France (26 entries)

ACP	Army of the Corsican People
AC	Corsican Army (Armata Corsa)
ACN	A Cuncolta Naziunalista (political wing of FNLC)
ALN	National Liberation Army (Armata di Liberzione Naziunale)
ANC	Corsican Nationalist Alliance) (Accolta Naziunale Corsa)
AZF	Nitrogen Fertiliser (AZote Fertilisant)
CAV	Winegrowers' Action Committee (Comité d'Action Viticole)
CC	Clandestini Corsi
CRAF	Corsican Revolutionary Armed Forces
FLNC	National Liberation Front of Corsica (Front de libération nationale de la Corse)
FT	Francs Tireurs
G	Gazteriak
GB	Gracchus Babeuf
I	The Northerners (Iparretarrak)
I	Irrintzi (Basque war cry)
JAJI	Group of Defenders of Islamic Holy War (Jama'at Ansar al-Jihad al-Islamiyah)
MK	National Council of Resistance (Mujahedin-e-Khalq)
NFLK	National Front for the Liberation of Kurdistan
NRP	Nationalist Republican Movement
PNFE	French European Nationalist Party
RC	Corsican Resistance (Resistenza Corsa)
RG	Roubaix Gang
RU	Radical Unity

TAWG	Totally Anti-War Group (Groupe entièrement opposé à la guerre)
UGD	Union Defense Group (Group union défense)
V	Vitalunismo

Gabon (0 entries)

Gambia (1 entry)

| J22M | July 22nd Movement/Green Boys |

Georgia (12 entries)

AS	Abkhaz Separatists
BB	Bagramyan Battalion
FB	Forest Brothers
FSO	Free Swaneti Organisation (Abkhazia)
GM	Gali Militia
KC	Kutajsij Clan (organised crime group)
KP	Tenguiz Kitovani Partisans
M	Mkhedrioni
SC	Salvation Corps
SOS	South Ossetian Separatists
WL	White Legion
Z	Zviadists

Germany (36 entries)

AC	Autonomous Cells
AD	Autonomous Decorators
AFA	Anti-Fascist Action
AIC	Anti-Imperialist Cell
AIGLMAJ	Anti-Imperialist Group Liberty for Mumia Abu Jamal
ARN	Aktionsbüro Rhein-Neckar (neo-Nazi)
AU	Autonomous Union
B	Bandidos (motorcycle gang)
BB	Black Bloc
BHDD	Blood and Honour Division Germany (Blood and Honour Division Deutschland)
B81	Brigade 81 (motorcycle gang)
C	Chicanos (motorcycle gang)
CGR	Commando Global Resistance
FAU	Freie Arbeiterinnen Union
F24	Frontbahn 24 (neo-Nazi)
H	Main People Comradeship (Kameradschaft Hauptvolk)
HA	Hells Angels (motorcycle gang)
PKN	Guardians of the Seal of Prophethood (Pasban Khatm-e-Nabuyet)
KS	Comradeship South (Kameradschaft Süd)
L	Soldier (Landser)
MG	Meliani Group
MG	Militant Group
N	Nomads (motorcycle gang)
NM	National Movement

NM	Nonaligned Warriors (Nonaligned Mujahedin)
NWP	Nationaler Widerstand Pirna
RACG	Revolutionary Action Carlo Giuliani
RW	Robin Wood
S	Spectrum
SSS	Skinheads Sächsische Schweiz Aufbau Organisation
S27	Storm27 Comradeship (Sturm27 Kameradschaft)
S34	Storm34 Comradeship (Sturm34 Kameradschaft)
T	Monotheism (Al-Tawhid)
TH	Flight from Sin and Atonement (Al-Takfir wal Hijra)
UICA	Union of Islamic Communities and Associations
WJ	Viking Youth (Wiking Jugend)

Ghana (4 entries)

AQTN	Al-Qaeda Taliban Network
ASJ	Followers of the Traditions of the Prophet (Ahlu Sunnah wal Jama'ah)
CB	Chameleon Bombers (Accra Metropolitian Assembly Task Force)
SDT	Sanitation and Decongestion Tigers

Greece (39 entries)

AAT	Anarchic Attack Groups
ACRA	Autonomous Cells of Rebel Action
AF	Anarchist Faction
APS	Anti-Power Struggle
ARA	Autonomous Revolutionary Activity
ARGN	Anti-racist Guerrilla Nuclei
ASR	Anti-State Resistance
ASS	Anti-State Struggle
BSRG	Black Star Revolutionary Group
CA	Conscientious Arsonists
CN	Children of November
ELA	Revolutionary Popular Struggle
FS	Friendly Society (Philiki Eteria)
GD	Golden Dawn
GJ78	Group June 1978
GS	Greek Spring
GFF	Guerrilla Fighting Force
LED	Popular Revolutionary Action
LOK	Lochos Oreinon Katadromon (stay-behind network)
MA	Mavros Asteria
MAS	Fighting Guerrilla Formation (Machimos Antarcticos Sximatismos)
MAVI	Northern Epirus Liberation Front (Metopo Apeleftherosis Voriou Ipirou)
MKAG	Michaelis Kaltezar Anarchist Group
M98	May 1998
NC	November's Children
PR	Popular Resistance (Laiki Andistasi)
PRA	Popular Revolutionary Action
PW	Popular Will
RF	Revolutionary Front

RO17N	Revolutionary Organisation of November 17 (Epanastatiki Organosi Dekaefta Noemvri)
RC	Revolutionary Cells
RN	Revolutionary Nuclei (Epasnastatiki Pyrines)
RPS	Revolutionary People's Struggle
RS	Revolutionary Solidarity
RS	Rebelling Secte
RSG	Revolutionary Struggle Group (Epanastatikos Aghonas)
S	Scientology
SR	Social Resistance
1MO	1 May Organisation

Grenada (0 entries)

Guatemala (18 entries)

CACS	Commando Augusto Cesar Sandino
EGP	Guerrilla Army of the Poor (Ejército Guerrillero de los Pobres)
FAR	Rebel Armed Forces (Fuerzas Armadas Rebeldes)
IB	Islamic Brotherhood
JJ	Just Jaguar
J31PF	January 31 Popular Front
K	Kaibiles
MANO	White Hand (Movimiento de Acción Nacionalista Organizado)
MAR	Armed Insurgent Movement (Movimiento Armado Rebelde)
MCLPG	Marxist Communist Leninist Party of Guatemala
ORPA	Organisation of People under Arms (Organización del Pueblo en Armas)
P	Los Pasaco (crime syndicate)
PACs	Civil Defense Patrols
PGT	Guatemalan Party of the Workers (Partido Guatemalteco del Trabajo)
PUA	Anti-Communist Unification Party
RJ	All Equal (Runujel Junam)
RPAG	Rebirth of Peace Anti-Delinquency Group
URNG	Guatemalan National Revolutionary Union (Unidad Revolutionaria Nacional Guatemalteca)

Guinea (2 entries)

RFDG	Movement of the Democratic Forces of Guinea (Rassemblement des forces démocratiques de Guinée)
YV	Young Volunteers

Guinea-Bissau (1 entry)

MJ	Military Junta/Mané followers

Guyana (0 entries)

Haiti (12 entries)

A	Attachés
BN	Black Ninja

CA	Cannibal Army (Armée cannibale)
CL	Cité Lescot
FRAPH	Front for the Advancement and Progress of Haiti
GPR	Groups of Patriotic Resistance
MA	Motherless Army (Armada sans Mamman)
RA	Red Army
RARF	Revolutionary Artibonite Resistance Front
TM	National Security Volunteers (Tonton Macoutes)
UDPF	Union of Democratic and Patriotic Forces
UFNLH	United Front for the National Liberation of Haiti

Honduras (9 entries)

A7M	April 7 Martyrs
C	Los Chinchilla
DS	Death Squad
FMLN	Morazanist Front for the Liberation of Honduras (Frente Moranista para la Liberación Nacional)
FPR-LZ	Lorenzo Zelaya Popular Revolutionary Forces (Fuerzas Populares Revolucionarias Lorenzo Zelaya)
MLC	Cinchoneros Popular Liberation Movement (Movimiento de la Liberación Cinchoneros)
RUFM	Revolutionary United Front Movement
URF	University Reform Front
VN	Vigilantes of the Night

Hong Kong (4 entries)

SG	Snakehead Gang (triad = Chinese secret society involved in organised crime)
SYO	San Yee On (triad)
WOL	Wo On Lok (triad)
WSW	Wo Shing Wo (triad)

Hungary (3 entries)

ACM	Arrow Cross Movement
HNF	Hungarian National Front
HNFP	Hungarian National Freedom Party

Iceland (0 entries)

India (263 entries)

A	Ao Tribals
AB	Pride of India (Abhinav Bharat) (RSS breakaway)
ABN	Akhil Bharat Nepali
ABS	Akhil Bharatiya Sena
ACMF	Adivasi Cobra Militant Force
AGG	Arun Gawli Gang
AIAJC	All India Al Jihad Committee
AIATF	All India Anti-Terrorist Force
AIADMK	All Indian Dravidian Progressive Federation
AIBRB	All India Babri (Mosque) Rebuilding Committee

AIPRF	All India Peoples Resistance Front
AISSF	All India Sikh Students' Federation
AJSU	All Jarkhand Students Union
AK	Anil Kothari (aka Vinod Jain) (drug cartel)
AKA	Adivasi Kalayan Ashran
AMS	Adivasi Mukti Sangathan
AMSO	All Manipur Student Organisation (Manipur)
AMULFA	All Muslim United Liberation Front of Assam
ANG	Ashwin Naik Gang
ANVC	Achik National Volunteer Council (Megalaya)
AQJK	Al-Qaeda Jammu Kashmir
AS	Anoop Singh Gang
AS	Al-Arifeen Squad (Kashmir)
ARCF	Asif Reza Commando Force
ASG	Akhilesh Singh Gang (Bihar)
ASG	Ali Sena Group (Madhya Pradesh)
ASS	Adivasi Shanti Sangathan
AT	Allah Tigers
ATTF	All Tripura Tiger Force
AV	Aditha Vahini
AV	Anand Vahini
B	The Light (Al-Barq)
BA	Borok Army (armed wing of the NLTF)
BC	Black Commando (Kashmir)
BCF	Birsa Commando Force
BD	Bajrang Dal
BDN	Borda Dalam Naxal
BJP	Bharatiya Janata Party
BJP-TC	BJP – Trinamool Congress
BK	Babbar Khalsa
BKI	Babbar Khalsa International
BLFM	Bru Liberation Front of Mizoram
BLTF	Bodoland Liberation Tiger Forces (Assam)
BM	Al-Badr Mujahideen (Kashmir)
BNCT	Borok National Council of Tripura
BNLF	Bru National Liberation Front (Mizoram, Tripura)
BPCF	Black Panther Commando Force
BS	Brahmarshi Sena (Bhumihars) (Bihar)
BS	Bhahujan Samay
BSF	Bodo Security Force (Assam)
BTF	Bengali Tiger Force
C	Chakmas
C	Chhatisgarh
CM	Curry Mafia
CMS	Chasi Mulia Sangh
CPI (M)	Communist Party of India (Maoist)
CPI(ML-J)	Communist Party of India – Marxist Leninist-Janashakti
CPO	Chakesang Public Organisation
CPEB	Communist Party of East Bengal
CRG	Chhota Rajan Gang (Mumbai)
CSG	Chhota Shakeel Gang (Mumbai)
D	Untouchables (Dalits)

D	Deoband
DA	Deendar Anjuman
DC	D-Company (criminal organisation of Dawood Ibrahim)
DG	Dawood Ibrahim-Abu Salem Gang
DG	Dawood Gang (Chhota Shakeel Faction)
DHD	Dima Halim Daoga (Assam)
DK	Dhal Khalsa
DM	Dharmajagaran Manch
DM	Dalit Mahasabha
DM	Daughters of the Faith (Dukhtaran-e-Millat)
DMK	Dravida Munetra Kazhagam
DNSF	Dimasa National Security Force (Assam)
DP	Dalit Panthers
DR	Dashmesh 10th Regiment
DS	Dalit Sena
EILF	Arunachal Dragon Force (East India Liberation Front)
F	Al-Faran
G	Gorkha
GG	Gawli Gang
GG	Goga Gang
GKIG	Group Khalistan International GPSP
GNF	Garo National Front
GNLF	Gurkha National Liberation Front
GRD	Village Defense Force (Gram Raksha Dal)
GRMF	Gujarat Muslim Revenge Force (LeT offshoot)
GS	Gabga Sena (Rajputs and Bhumihars)
GT	Green Tigers (Andhra Pradesh)
IDF	Islamic Defense Force
H	Al-Hadid
H	Party of God (Hezbollah)
HA	Harkat ul-Ansar
HDS	Army of the Hindu religion (Hindu Dharam Sena) (RSS breakaway)
HG	Hariom Gang
HG	Hindu Garjana
HJI	Movement for Islamic Holy War (Harkat-al-Jihad-e-Islami)
HJM	Hindu Jagran Manch
HM	Hyrmiewtrep Movement
HM	Hezbul Monimeen (Kashmir)
HM	Hezb-ul-Mujahideen (Nasir-ul-Islam)
HNLC	Hynniewtrep National Liberation Council (Megalaya)
HPC-D	Hmar People's Convention – Democracy
HRF	Hmar Revolutionary Force (Mizoram)
IBRF	Indo-Burmese Revolutionary Front
IDF	Islamic Defence Force (Tamil Nadu)
IIM	Islami Inqilabi Mahaz
IM	Moslem Brotherhood (Ikhwan ul-Muslimoon)
IMMM	Indian Muslim Mohammadi Mujahideen
ISS	Islamic Followers Organisation (Islamic Sevak Sangh)
ISYF	International Sikh Youth Federation
J	Janashakti
JAH	Group of Followers of the Tradition (Jamaat Ahl-e Hadis)
JC	Holy War Committee (Jihad Committee)

JG	Jangara Gang
JI	Group of the Virtuous (Jamiyyathul Ishaniya)
JKLF	Jammu Kashmir Liberation Front
JKMS	Janwadi Kisan Mazdoor Samiti (Bihar)
JM	Group of Warriors (Jama'at ul-Mujahideen)
JMM	Jarkhand Liberation Front (Jarkhand Mukti Morcha)
JMM(S)	Jarkhand Mukti Morcha (S)
JP	Jungle Party (Bihar)
JSJG	Jasvinder Singh Jassa Gang
KA	Karvan-e-Azeemat
KBG	Kachcha-Barrian Gang
KCF	Khalistan Commando Force
KCP	Kangleipak Communist Party (Manipur)
KGBA	Karanpuran Ghati Bachao Andolan
KH	Karwan-e-Haider Militants
KI	Servants of Islam (Khuddam ul-Islam) (Kashmir)
KLA	Kuki Liberation Army
KLO	Kamtapur Liberation Organisation
KLF	Khalistan Liberation Front
KLNCLF	Karbi Longri North Cachar Liberation Front
KLS	Koi Labang Sangh
KLTT	Khalistan Liberation Tigers' Force
KM	Karwan-e-Mujahideen
KMSP	Kizan Mazdoor Sangrami Parishad (Bihar)
KNA	Khalistan National Army
KNA	Kuki National Army
KNV	Karbi National Volunteers (Assam)
KPF	Karbi People's Front (Assam)
KPG	Kishan Pahelwan Gang
KPP	Khamtapur People's Party
KRA	Kuki Revolutionary Army
KRRM	Kodagu Raiya Mukhti Morcha
KS	Kamatapur Sena
KS	Kunwar Sena (Rajputs)
KST	Kisan Security Tigers (Yadavs)
KT	Kuki Tribals
KYKL	Manipur Army for Independence (Manipur) (Kanglei Yawol Kanna Lup)
KZF	Khalistan Zindabad Force
LJ	Lashkar-e-Jabar
LK	Lashkar-e-Kahar
LK	Lashkar-e-Karbala (Kashmir)
LRG	Lala Ram Gang
LS	Lashkar-e-Sajjad
LS	Lorik Sena (Yadavs)
LYG	Laloo Yadav Gang (Bihar)
M	Al-Madina
MB	Madan Bhaiya Gang
MBT	Majlis Bachao Tehareek
MCC	Maoist Communist Center
MCC	Marxwadi Communist Party
MEELAL	United Forum for Safeguarding Manipuri Script and Language (Manipur) (Mayek Erol Evek Loinasillon Apunba Lup)

MG	Manchekar Gang
MI	Mahaz-e-Islami
MIM	Council of United Muslims (Majlis Ittehad Muslimeen)
MJC	United Holy War Council (Mutahida Jihad Council) (Kashmir)
MJF	Muslim Janbaz Force
MK	Mujahedin-e-Kashmir (Kashmir)
MM	Victorious Warriors (Mujahideen al-Mansooran)
MPA	United National Liberation Front (Manipur People's Army)
MPLF	Manipur People's Liberation Front (Manipur)
MPS	Madiga Porata Samithi
MULF	Muslim United Liberation Front
MULTA	Muslim United Liberation Tigers of Assam
N	Naxalites
NBA	Save the Narmada (Narmada Bachao Andolam)
NBG	Narender Balraj Gang
NCK	National Council of Khalistan
NDFB	National Democratic Front of Bodoland (Assam)
NDFB	National Democratic Front of Bongaion
NLFT	National Liberation Front of Tripura
NMS	Nari Mukti Samiti (Bihar)
NNC-F	Federal Naga National Council
NRF	National Revival Forum (Jashtroya Jagran Manch) (RSS breakaway)
NSCN	National Socialist Council of Nagalim (earlier: Nagaland)
NSCN(IM)	National Socialist Council of Nagaland – IM
NSCN-K	National Socialist Council of Nagaland-Khaplang
PDK	Periyar Dravidar Kazhagam
PDP	People's Democratic Party (Tamil Nadu)
PGA	People's Guerrilla Army
PLA	People's Liberation Army (Manipur)
PPG	Praja Pratighatna Group
PPSR	Peer Panchal Suran Regiment (Kashmir)
PREPAK	People's Revolutionary Party of Kangleipak
PULF	People's United Liberation Front (Assam)
PWG	People's War Group
QH	Al-Qaeda in India (Al-Qaeda fil Hind)
RAP	Rongpur Anchalik Parishad
RCF	Raza Commando Force
RJC	Common Revolutionary Command
RKM	Ranvir Kisan Mahasangh (armed wing of Ranvir Sena)
RNSF	Rabha National Security Force (Assam)
RPK	Revolutionary Party of Kanleipak (Manipur)
RRG	Rehman Radhey Gang
RS	Ranvir Sena (Ranvir Kisan Maha Sangh, Ranvir Mahila Sangh)
RSO	Rohingya Solidarity Organisation
RSP	Revolutionary Socialist Party
RSS	National Volunteer Corps (Rashtriya Swayamsevak Sangh)
RT	Red Tigers
SG	Shivastava Gang
SG	Siraya Gang
SIMI	Students' Islamic Movement of India (JeI's student wing)
SJ	Peace Mission (Salwa Judum) (anti-Maoist village defence movement)
SJMM	Sangarsh Jan Mukti Morcha (Jharkhand)

SJP	Samajwadi Janata Party (SJP)
SKF	Shadid Khalsa Force
SKM	Save Kashmir Movement
SMG	Suresh Manchekar Gang
SMF	Sanjukta Mukti Fouj
SLF	Suvarna Liberation Front (Bhumihars)
SP	Sangh Parivar
SRM	Sangh Rakshak Manch
SRS	Army of the God Rama (Sri Ram Sena) (RSS breakaway)
SS	Eternal Organisation (Sanatan Sanstha) (RSS breakaway)
SS	Shiv Sena (armed wing of the Shivaji Party)
SS	Sunlight Sena (Rajputs and others)
SULFA	Surrendered United Liberation Front of Assam
TC	Trinamul Congress
TIM	Organisation for the Improvement of Muslims (Tanzim Islahul Muslimeen) (Indian wing of the LeT)
TLOF	Tripura Liberation Organisation Front
TM	Warriors Movement (Tehrik-el-Mujahideen)
TMMK	Tamil Nadu Muslim Munnetra Kazagham (Tamil Nadu)
TNLA	Tamil National Liberation Army
TNRT	Tamil Nadu Retrieval Troops
TPC	Tritiya Prastuti Committee
TPDF	Tripura Peoples Democratic Front (Tripura)
TRS	Telangana Rashtriya Samithi
TSL	Tigers of Sikh Land
TTP	Student Movement Pakistan (Tehrik Taliban e-Pakistan)
TTVF	Tripura Tribal Volunteers Force
UBLF	United Bengali Liberation Front (Tripura)
UCM	United Committee of Manipur (Manipur)
UKD	Uttarakhand Kranti Dal
UKLF	United Kuki Liberation Front
ULFA	United Liberation Front of Assam
ULFBV	United Liberation Front of Barak Valley
UM	Community of Believers, Omar Warriors Al-Umma, al-Umar Mujahidin (Tamil Nadu, Kashmir)
UNLF	United National Liberation Front (Manipur)
UPDS	United People's Democratic Solidarity (Assam)
UPT	Uttar Pradesh Tribals
VDC	Village Defence Committees (Himachal Pradesh)
VDP	Village Defence Parties (Tripura)
VG	Verappan Gang
VHP	Vishwa Hindu Parishad
VKA	Vanvasi Kalyan Ashram (RSS outfit)
VRG	Village Resistance Groups (Bihar)
VVF	Village Voluntary Force (Bihar)
ZRA	Zomi Revolutionary Army (Manipur)
ZRF	Zomi Revolutionary Front

Indonesia (67 entries)

AASM	Angkatan Aceh Sumatra Merdeka
ACC	Anti-Communist Command
AGAM	Angkatan Gerakan Aceh Merdeka (military wing of the GAM)
AIPA	Alliance of the Indigenous People of the Archipelago
ASJF	Forum of the Followers of the Traditions of the Prophet (Ahlus Sunnah wal Jama'ah Forum)
ASNLF	Aceh/Sumatra National Liberation Front
BBF	Betawi Brotherhood Forum
BFM	Brigade Firaqul Maut
BKPM	Coordinating Body of the Mosque Youth (Badan Koordinasi Pemuda Mesjid)
CC	Commandos against Communism
CRF	Christian Red Force
DI	Abode of Islam (Darul Islam)
DIN	Nusantara Islamic State (Daulah Islamiyah Nusantara)
FKM	Maluku Sovereignty Forum
FPA	Forum for the Defense of Aceh (Forum Peneylamat Aceh)
FPK	Defenders of Trust Forum
FPI	Front for the Defense of Islam (Front Pembela Islam)
GAM	Movement of a Free Aceh (Gerakan Aceh Merdeka)
GPII	Indonesian Muslim Youth Movement (Gerakan Pemuda Islam Indonesia)
GPK	Gang of Public Order Disruptors (Gerombolan Pengacau Keamanon)
HTI	Liberation Party Indonesia (Hezb ut-Tahrir Indonesia)
IILF	Indonesian Islamic Liberation Front
IM	Muslim Brotherhood (Ikhwanul Muslimin)
IMJ	Muslim Brothers for Holy War (Ikhwanul Muslimun Jihad)
IMT	Ikhwanul Muslimun Tarbiyah (non-violent)
JI	Islamic Congregation (Jemaah Islamiya)
JMA	Jemaah Mujahidin Anshorullah
JTJ	Monotheism and Holy War Group (Jama'ah Tawhid wal Jihad)
KMM	Kumpulan Militan Malaysia
KOMPAK	Komite Aksi Penanggulangan Akibat Krisis
KPSI	Committee for Upholding Islamic Law (Komite Pengerak Syariat Islam)
LJ	Army of Holy War (Lashkar Jihad)
LJ	Army of Soldiers of Allah (Lashkar Jundullah)
LJM	Army of Jesus (Lashkar Jesus)
LM	Warriors Army (Laskar Mujahedin)
MDK	Mujahideen Division Khandaq
MH	Medan Hackers
MK	Kayamanya Warriors (Mujahidin Kayamanya)
MK	KOMPAK Warriors (Mujahedin KOMPAK)
MMI	Indonesian Warriors Council (Majlis Mujahedin Indonesia)
MSCSEA	Warriors Council for Southeast Asia (Mujahedin Shura Council for Southeast Asia)
MSF	Maluku Sovereignty Front
MYA	Muhamadi Yah Alliance
N	Ninjas (Aceh)
N	Ninjas (Java)
NAP	National Awakening Party
NII	Islamic State of Indonesia (Negara Islam Indonesia)
NN	Ngruki Network
NU	Nadhatul Ulama
OPM	Free Papua Movement (Organisasi Papua Merdeka)

PBM	Troops Who Dare to Die for Wahid (Pasukan Berani Mati)
PJKB	Javanese Sons of the Beloved People (Putra Jawa Kusama Bangsa)
PPME	Muslim Youth Association of Europe (Persatuan Pemuda Muslim se-Europa)
PTF	Papua Task Force (Irian Jaya)
PY	Pancacila Youth (Golkar thugs and enforcers)
QOJI	The Base Organisation of Holy War in Indonesia) (Al-Qaeda Organisation for Jihad in Indonesia)
RB	Ring Banten (DI splinter in West Java)
RM	League of Warriors (Rabitatul Mujahedeen)
RMS	South Maluku Republic (Republik Maluku Selatan)
RPII	Republik Persatuan Islam Indonesia
TM	The Victorious Sect (Thaifah Mansurah)
TQJUGKM	The Base Organisation of Holy War in the Malay Achipelago (Tandzim Qoedatul Jihad Untuk Gususan Kepulauan Melayu)
TRG	Tanah Runtuh Group
UDP	United Development Party
WI	Wahdaj Islamiah or Wahdah Islamiyah
YBS	Yellow Bamboo Sect

Iran (36 entries)

AH	Defenders of the Party of God (Ansar-e-Hezbollah)
AM	Army of the Mahdi (Ansar al-Mahdi)
AMK	Arbav Martyrs of Khuzestan
AS	Defenders of the Islamic Law (Ansar al-Sharia)
ASJ	Group of Followers of the Tradition (Ahl-e-Sunnah wal Jama'a) (split off from AI)
BH	Black Hand
BSGIA	Brigades of the Shahids of the Global Islamic Awakening
CRM	Circle of Revolutionary Movements
DM	Devotees for Martyrdom
DPKI	Democratic Party of Iranian Kurdistan (Hezb-e Dêmokratî Êran)
FI	Islamic Warriors (Fedayeen-e-Islam)
GAF	Generation of Arab Fury
GMMSAZ	Group of the Martyrs Mostafa Sadeki and Ali Zadeh
H	Charitable Society of the Mahdi (Hujjatiyyah)
ICA	Iranian Cyber Army
IFM	Iranian Freedom Movement
IJU	Islamic Jihad Union
JA	Soldiers of God (Jund Allah)
JMSPI	Jihadi Movement of the Sunni People in Iran
KOMALA	Revolutionary Organisation of Working People of Iranian Kurdistan
MB	Martyrs' Brigades (Kataeb al-Istishhadiyeen)
MHG	Mehdi Hashemi Gang
MK	The People's Mujahedin of Iran (Mujahedin-e-Khalq) (aka MEK)
MSS	Martyr Salah Shahadah
NCRI	National Council of Resitance Iran
NLA	National Liberation Army of Iran
NRA	National Religious Alliance
OG	Ossul Gerayan (The Fundamentalists)
PDF	People's Democratic Front
PEJAK	Party for a Free Life in Kurdistan
RC	Ramadan Command (Charargah Ramzan)
S	Shahin

SFLI	Students following the Line of the Imam
SIG	Sa'ida Imami Gang
SM	Mohammed Corps (Sepah–e–Mohammad)
YAG	Yahya Ayash Group

Iraq (438 entries)

A	Abagiah
A	Arizeh
A	The Return (Al-Awdah)
AA	Alif'Ayn
AA	Defenders of Allah (Ansar al-Allah)
AAH	League of the Righteous (Asaeb Ahl al-Haq)
AAI	League of the People of Iraq (Asaeb Ahl al-Iraqi)
AAS	Army of Ansar al-Sunna (Army of the Defenders of the Prophet's Tradition) (Jama'a Ansar al-Sunna Pi al-Iraq)
AASJ	Army of the Followers of the Traditions of the Prophet (Ansar Ahl al-Sunnah wal Jamaa)
AD	Defenders of al-Din (Ansar al-Din)
ADM	Assyrian Democratic Movement
AF	Conquering Army (Ansar Al-Fatihin)
AFGC	Armed Forces General Command (JM Brigade)
AHG	Ahmed Hassan Gang
AI	Defenders of Islam (Ansar al-Islam) (Pishtiwani Islam le Kurdistan)
AIG	Al-Ahbab Insurgent Group
AIJ	Iraqi Jihadi Leagues (Asaeb al-Iraq al-Jihadiyya)
AIM	Defenders of the Imam al-Mahdi (Ansar al-Imam al-Mahdi)
AIS	Al-Anbar Independent Scholars
AJ	Defenders of the Jihad (Ansar al-Jihad)
AJR	Army of Jund al-Rahman
ALF	Arab Liberation Front
ALTM	Army of the Lands of Those Who Are Mandated
AMD	Army of the Messenger's Descendents
ANG	Arab Nationalist Group
ANO	Abu Nidal Organisation
AQI	Al-Qaeda in Iraq
AQJ	Ansar Qa'idat al-Jihad
ARB	Arab Revolutionary Brigades
ARM	Arab Resistance Movement-Al-Rashid Brigades
AS	Defenders of Saddam (Ansar Saddam)
AS	Army of the Just (Ansar al-Siham)
ASBP	Arab Socialist Ba'ath Party
ASC	Anbar Salvation Council (tribal militia, Anbar province)
ASD	Al-Aqsa Support Division
ASI	Army of Supporters of Islam
ASK	Ansar al-Salam al-Kurdiyah
ASM	Supporters of the Sunni People (Ahl al-Sunnah al-Munasera)
ASO	Albu Sabah Organisation
AT	Al-Awaleen Tribe
ATSR	Ansar al-Tawhid wal-Sunna Regiments (part of ISI)
AZ	Defenders of Zawahiri (Ansar al-Zawahiri)
BC	Badr Corps
BJC	Basrah Jihad Companies (part of HCJL)

BLS	Brigades for Liberating the South (Baathist)
BM	Blood of the Moon
BO	Badr Organisation
BPG	Birds of Paradise (AQI suicide mission unit)
BR	Basic Regulation
BS	Black September
BSAFI	Battalion for Striking the American Forces in Iraq
BSCAAS	Brigades of the Shariah Committee of Ansar al-Sunnah
CIF	Coalition of Iraqi Freedom
CIR	Committee for Immediate Retribution
CMM	Constitutional Monarchy Movement
CP	Cells of the People
D	The Call (al-Da'wa)
DA	Defenders of the False Messiah (refers to al-Mahdi Army) (Ansar Al-Dajjal)
DB	Death Brigade
DCJL	Diyala Companies for Jihad and Liberation (part of HCJL)
DFG	Al-Da'wa Freedom Group
F	Al-Fadilah
F	Al-Fatihin
F	The Sword (Al-Fikar)
F	The Knight (Al-Fosran)
FA	Al-Fars Army (Baathist Kurdish)
FA	Al-Fatah Army
FA	The Free Fedayeen (Al-Fedayeen al-Ahrar)
FA	Al-Furqan Army (Ansar al-Furqan)
FC	Follow-up Committees
FDM	Free Democratic Movement
FLIP	Freedom Liberation of Iraq Pary
FM	Fedayeen Muhammad
FM	The Manifest Opener, or the Clear Conquest (Al-Fatih al-Mubeen)
FMT	Fatah Revolutionary Council (Fatah al-Majles al-Thawry)
FOM	Free Officers Movement
FRLC-B	Former Republican Loyalists Cell-Basrah
FS	Fedayeen of Saddam (suicide mission unit)
FSG	For the Sake of God
GCLI	Glory Companies for the Liberation of Iraq (Part of HCJL)
GFI	Group of Free Iraq
GTI	Islamic Monotheism Group (Gama'at al-Tawhid al-Islamiyya)
G60	Group of Sixty (secret group within Mahdi Army)
H	Hamas
HA	Hurras al-Aqid
HA	The Party of Return (Hezb al-Awda)
HDSC	Hezb al-Da'wa Security Committee
HDI	Movement of the Islamic Call (Al-Harakat al-Dawa al-Islamiya)
HDI	Party of the Islamic Call (Hezb al-Dawa al-Islamiya)
HDITI	Party of the Islamic Call Iraqi Organisation (Hezb al-Da'wa Islamiya Tanzim al-Iraq)
HF	Hamzah Faction
HFI	Islamic Party of the Virtuous (Hezb al-Fadhila al-Islami) (political wing of JAF)
HG	Al-Haswa Group (Jama'at al-Haswa)
HHI	Party of God Movement in Iraq (Al-Harakat Hezballah al-Iraq)
HI	Salvation Movement (Al-Harakat al-Inqadh)
HII	Iraqi Islamic Party (Hezb al-Islami al-'Iraqi)

HII	Islamic Movement of Iraq (Al-Harakat al-Iraq al-Islamiya)
HIIK	Islamic Movement for the Mujahedeen of Iraq (part of JCF) (Al-Harakat al-Islamiya Li Mujahidin al-Iraq)
HIK	Islamic Movement of Iraqi Kurdistan (Al-Harakat al-Islamiya fi Kurdistan)
HIS	Al-Harakat Al-Intifada Al-Shabaniya
HISS	Islamic Movement of the Lord of the Martyrs (Al-Harakat Islamiya Sayyid al-Shuhada)
HMAKR	Arab Resistance Movement-Al-Rashid Brigades (Al-Harakat al-Muqawama al-Arabiyah-Kata'ib al-Rashid)
HMI	Iraqi Mujahidin Movement (Al-Harakat Mujahidin Al-Iraq)
HMI	Islamic Resistance Movement (Part of PCIR) (Al-Harakat al-Muqawa al-Islamiya)
HNSM	Movement of the Elite Martyr of the Pulpit (Al-Harakat al-Nakhba-Shahid Al-Mihrab)
HR	Mesopotamia Party (Hezb al-Rafidayn)
HRB	Al-Harakat al-Rayat al-Baydiah
HS	Al-Harakat al-Saak
HSJ	Fundamentalist Jihadist Movement (Al-Harakat al-Salafiyah al-Jihadiyah)
HSS	Movement of the Lord of the Martyrs (Al-Harakat S'aid Ash-Shuhada)
HSUI	Iraqi Communist Party (Hezb al-Shuyu'i al-Ummali al-Iraqi)
HS15S	Movement of the 15th Shaban (Al-Harakat al-Sha'baniya 15 Sha'ban)
HT	Party of Liberation (Hezb al-Tahrir)
HT	Unity Movement (Al-Harakat al-Tawhid)
HTA	Thar Allah Party (military wing) (Hezb Thar Allah)
HTAI	Revenge of God Islamic Movement (Al-Harakat Thar'ar Allah al-Islamiya)
HTFI	Al-Harakat Thaw al-Fakar al-Islamiya
HT15S	Revolutionary Movement 15 Sha'ban (Al-Harakat Thuwaar 15 Sha'ban)
HUM	Muslim Scholars Association (Hiyat Ulama al-Muslamin)
HWI	Movement of the Islamic Accord (Al-Harakat al-Wifaq al-Islami)
HWII	Iraqi Islamic Union Hezbollah (Hezballah al-Wah'a al-Islamia fi-l-Iraq)
HWTI	National Revolutionaries Uprising Movement (Al-Harakat al-Wataneya Li-Thiwaar al-Intifada)
IAAG	Islamic Abu Abbas Group (Jama'at Abu Abbas Islamiya)
IAATJB	Imam Ali bin-Abi-Talib Jihad Brigade (Kata'ib Imam Ali bin-Ali-Talib Jihad)
IAC	Inter-Agency Committees
IAI	Islamic Action in Iraq (Jaysh al-Islami al-Iraqi)
ICF	Iraq Combatant Front (Baathist)
IF	Islamic Fury
IFGRO	Islamic Front for Guidance and Religious Orientation
IGK	Islamic Group of Kurdistan
IIFU	Iraqi Islamic Forces Union
IIRF	Islamic Iraqi Resistance Front (part of PCIR)
IIVNS	Islamic Iraqi Vanguards for National Salvation
IJP	Islamic Jihad Party (Hezb al-Jihadia al-Islamiya)
ILO	Islamic Labour Organisation
ILR	Iraqi Legitimate Resistance
IMC	Iraqi Military Council
INCC	Iraqi National Constituent Conference
INIR	Iraqi National Islamic Resistance
IOIPF	Iraqi Organisation of Islamic Patriotic Forces
IRLP	Iraqi Resistance and Liberation Group
IRM	Islamic Retaliation Movement
ISI	Islamic State of Iraq
ITF	Iraqi Turkoman Front
IUF	Islamic Unity Front
IUMK	Islamic Unity Movement of Kurdistan

J	Holy War (Al-Jihad)
JA	Al-Jihad wa-Alsalah
JA	Alkara Group (Jama'at Alkara)
JAMI	Iraqi Resistance Islamic Front (Al-Jabha al-Muqawa al-Islamiya al-Iraqi)
JAS	Army of the Followers of the Sunni Islam (Jaysh Ansar al-Sunnah) (part of PCIR)
JBC	Holy War–Baghdad Cell (Al-Jihad Baghdad Cell)
JCF	Jihad and Change Front (alliance)
JDO	Army of the Guardians (Jaysh Diyar al-Ousiya)
JDW	National Defense Battalions (Jaysh al-Difa' al-Watani)
JF	Organisation of the Virtuous (Jami'at Al-Fadilah)
JF	Jaysh al-Faruq
JF	Conquering Army (Jaysh al-Fatihin) (part of PCIR)
JFLAR	Jaysh al-Faris for Liberation of the Autonomous Region ((part of HCJL)
JH	Jaysh al-Hamzah (part of HCJL)
JH	Army of Truth (new name for Jaysh Mohammad) (Jaysh Al-Haqq)
JH	Hussein Army (Jaysh al-Hussein)
JH	Jaysh Hunayn (part of HCJL)
JI	Soldiers of Islam (Jund al-Islam)
JI	Army of Islam (Jaysh al-Islamiyah)
JI	Islamic Holy War (Al-Jihad al-Islami) (Sunni coalition) (part of ISI)
JIAH	Army of Imam Ahmed bin Hanbal (Jaysh Imam Ahmed bin Hanbal)
JII	Islamic Army in Iraq (Al-Jaysh al-Islami al-Iraqi) (Al-Jaysh al-Islami fi l'Iraq)
JII-KIW	Islamic Army in Iraq – Khalid Ibn al-Walid Brigade (Jaysh al-Islami al-Iraqi-Kata'ib Ibn al-Walid)
JIK	Soldiers of Islam in Kurdistan (Jund al-Islam fi Kurdistan)
JISK	Army of Islam al-Karrar Brigades (Jaysh al-Islam Saraya al-Karrar)
JJS	Group of Soldiers of the Prophet's Companions (Jama'at Jund al-Sahaba)
JJS	Jaysh Jumhuri Sari
JLQ	Jerusalem Liberation Army (Jaysh al-Tahrir al-Quds)
JM	Muhammed's Army, Army of Muhammed (Jaysh Mohammed)
JM	Direct or Straight Army (Jund al'Mostaqeem)
JM	Mahdi Army (Jaysh al-Mahdi)
JM	Army of the Warriors (Jaysh al-Mujahideen)
JM	Jaysh al-Murabitin
JM	Jaysh al-Mustafa
JMB	Mutassim Billah Group (Jama'at Mutassim Billah)
JMM	Death Group (Jama'at Majmoo'a a-Moat)
JMT	Second Army of Muhammed (Jaysh Muhammed al-Thani)
JOK	Omar bin Khattab Group (Jama'at Omar bin Khattab)
JR	Just Retribution
JR	Mesopotamia Group (Jama'at al-Rafidayn)
JR	Al-Rashideen Army (Jaysh al-Rashideen)
JR	Jaysh al-Risalah
JRF	Jihad and Reform Front (part of PCIR)
JRTN	Army of the Men of the al-Naqshbandia Order (Sufi) (Jaysh Rijal al-Tariqa al-Naqshbandia)
JS	Popular Army (Jaysh al-Sha'abi)
JS	Jaysh al-Sabrin
JS	Jaysh al-Saqr
JS	Soldiers of Heaven (Jund al-Samaa)
JS	Soldiers of the Companions of the Prophet Mohammed (Jund al-Sahaba)
JSG	Rayad Soot Group (Jama'at Rayad Soot)
JSM	Fundamentalist Warrior Group (Jama'at al-Salafiya al-Mujahedin)
JST	Group op the Second Sadr (Jama'at al-Sadr al-Thani)

JT	Takfir Group (Jama'at al-Takfir)
JT	Thulfiqar Army (Jaysh Tulfiqar)
JT	Al-Thib Group (Jama'at al-Thib)
JTI	Army of the Liberation of Iraq (Jaysh al-Tahrir al-Iraq)
JTJ	Monotheism and Holy War Group (Jama'at al-Tawhid wal Jihad) (Jama'at at-Tauhid wa-l-Jihad)
JTM	Army of the Victorious Sect (part of ISI) (Jaysh al-Taefa al-Mansura)
JWH	Jahafil Wa'ad al-Haq
JN	Al-Nusra Army (Jaysh al-Nusra)
JU	Al-Usrah Amy (Jaysh al-Usrah)
JUM	Umar Al-Mukhtar Group (Jama'at Umar al-Mukhtar)
KA	Al-Abbas Brigades (Kata'ib al-Abbas)
KA	Al-Aqsa Brigades (Kata'ib al-Aqsa)
KA	Brigades of Islamic Anger (part of ISI) (Kata'ib al-Ahwal)
KAA	Lions of Allah Brigades, Lions of God Brigades (Kata'ib Asad Allah)
KAAM	Abd al-Aziz al-Muqrin Brigades (Kata'ib Abd al-Aziz al-Muqrin)
KAAM	Victorious Lion of God Brigades (Kata'ib Asad-Allah al-Muntasir)
KAATJ	Ali bin Abu Taleb Holy War Brigades (Kata'ib Ali bin Abu Talib al-Jihad)
KABLS	Abu Bilal Al-Libi Martyrs Brigade (Kata'ib Abu Bilal al-Libi Shuhada)
KAFA	Abu al-Fadal al-Abas Brigades (Kata'ib Abu al-Fadal al-Abas)
KAHM	Abu Hafs al-Masri Brigades (Kata'ib Abu Hafs al-Masri)
KAHN	Abu Hanifah al-Numan Brigades (Kata'ib Abu Hanifah al-Numan)
KAI	League of Iraq Brigades (Kata'ib Asa'ab al-Iraq)
KAS	Black Flags Brigades (Kata'ib al-A'lam al-Sawda)
KAT	Brigades of the Defenders of Monotheism (part of ISI) (Katai'b Ansar al-Tawhid)
KAYM	Abu al-Yaman al-Madani Brigade (Kata'ib Abu al-Yaman al-Madani)
KB	Kurdistan Brigades (Kata'ib e-Kurdistan)
KBMS	Bara bin Malik Martyrdom Brigades (MSC Brigade for suicide operations) (Kata'ib al-Bara bin-Malik Shuhada)
KBW	Khalid-Bin-al-Walid Brigades (Kata'ib Bin al-Walid)
KCP	Kurdistan Communist Party
KDI	Shield of Islam Brigades (Kata'ib Dera Islamiya)
KDN	Dhi-al-Nurayn Brigades (Kata'ib Dhi al-Nurayn)
KDPI	Kurdistan Democratic Party of Iraq
KDR	Call and Stationed Brigades (Kata'ib al-Da'wah wal Ribat)
KF	Fallujah Brigades (Kata'ib al-Fallujah)
KF	Al-Faruq Brigades (Kata'ib al-Faruq) (unit for suicide missions)
KF	Al-Fursan Brigades (Kata'ib al-Fursan)
KFF	Kurdistan Freedom Forces
KFI	Islamic Conquest Brigades (militant wing Hamas of Iraq) (Kata'ib al-Fatihin al-Islamiya)
KFJ	Fallujah Jihad Companies (Kata'ib al-Fallujah Jihadia)
KFT	Fursan al-Tawhid Brigades (part of ISI) (Kata'ib Fursan al-Tawhid)
KG	Strangers Brigades (part of ISI) (Katai'b al-Ghuraba)
KG	Kamil Gang
KGI	Divine Wrath Brigades (Kata'ib al-Ghadab al-Ilahi)
KGI	Islamic Indignation Brigades (Kata'ib al-Ghazab al-Islami)
KH	Hezbollah Brigades (Kata'ib Hezbollah)
KH	Arrows of Righteousness Brigades, Arrows of Truth Brigades (Kata'ib al-Haq)
KHB	Al-Hasan al-Basri Brigades (Kata'ib al-Hasan al-Basri)
KI	Al-Ishrin Brigades (Kata'ib al-Ishrin)
KIA	Al-Kassim Islamic Association
KIH	Imam Hadi Brigades (Kata'ib Imam Hadi)
KIH	Imam al-Hussein Brigades (Kata'ib al-Imam al-Hussein)

KIK	Imam Kasim Brigades (Kata'ib Imam Kasim)
KIK	Ibn-al-Khattab Brigades (Kata'ib Ibn al-Khattab)
KIM	Imam al-Mujahedin Brigades (Kata'ib Imam al-Mujahedin)
KIU	Kurdistan Islamic Union
KIWBQ	Khalid Ibn al-Walid Brigades (Kata'ib Ibn al-Walid)
KJI	Islamic Holy War Brigades (Kata'ib al-Jihad al-Islamiyah)
KJMA	Holy War Brigades of Mohammed's Army (Kata'ib al-Jihad Jaysh Mohammed)
KJR	Soldiers of al-Rahman Brigades (Kata'ib Jund al-Rahman)
KK	Karbala Brigades (Kata'ib Karbala)
KK	Green Brigades of Mohammed (Kata'ib al-Khadra)
KKA	Brigades of Just Punishment (Kata'ib al-Kassas al-Adel)
KM	Warriors Brigades (Kata'ib al-Mujahedin)
KM	Pact of the Scented People (Khalf al-Mutayibeen)
KM	Al-Murabitin Brigades (Kata'ib al-Murabitin)
KMA	Brigades of Mohammed Abdullah (Kata'ib Mohammed Abdullah)
KMA	Mohammed Atta Brigades (Kata'ib Mohammed Atta)
KMF	Muhammed al-Fateh Brigades (Kata'ib Muhammed al-Fateh)
KMI	Mullah Ibrahim Brigades (part of ISI) (Kata'ib Mullah Ibrahim)
KMI	Islamic Resistance Brigades (Kata'ib al-Muqawa al-Islamiya)
KMJ	Muadh ibn Jabal Brigades (Kata'ib Muadh ibn Jabal)
KMM	Reconnaisance and Surveillance Brigades (Kata'ib al-Marsad wal Muraqaba)
KN	Al-Nu'man Brigades (Kata'ib Al-Nu'man)
KPC	Kurdistan People's Congress (KONGRA GEL)
KR	Al-Riyyal Brigade (Kata'ib al-Riyyal)
KS	Martyrs Brigades (Kata'ib Shuhada) (MSC unit for suicide missions)
KSAA	Martyrs Brigades of Ansar al-Sunna (Kata'ib Shuhada Ansar al-Sunna) (AS unit for suicide missions)
KSABS	Salafist Brigades of Abu Bakr al-Saddiq (Kata'ib Salafiya Abu Bakr al-Saddiq)
KSAQJJ	The Jihadi Brigades of Sheikh Abd al-Qadir al-Jilani (Sufi) (Kata'ib al-Sheikh Abd al-Qadir al-Jilanin al-Jihadia)
KSAY	Brigades of Martyr Ahmed Yasin (Kata'ib Shahid Ahmed Yasin)
KSD	Salah-al-Din Brigades (Kata'ib Salah-al-Din)
KSDA	Salah-al-Din al-Ayub Brigades-Military Wing (Sala al-Din al-Ayyubi Brigades) (Kata'ib Sala-Din al-Ayyubi)
KSDP	Kurdistan Socialist Democratic Party
KSH	Righteous Arrow Brigades (Kata'ib Siham al-Haq)
KSH	Swords of Righteousness Brigades (Kata'ib al-Saif al-Haq)
KSI	Iraqi Companions of the Prophet Mohammed Brigades (Kata'ib al-Sahada al-Iraqi)
KSI	Youth of Islam Brigades (Kata'ib al-Shabaab al-Islamiya)
KSI	Iraqi Martyrdom Brigades (Kata'ib Shuhada al-Iraqi)
KST	Al-Taff Martyrs Brigade (Kata'ib Shuhada al-Taff)
KT	Al-Taba'aeen Brigades (Kata'ib al-Taba'aeen)
KT	Liberation Brigades (Kata'ib al-Tahrir)
KT	al-Tamkin Brigades (Kata'ib al-Tamkin)
KT	Revenge Brigades (Kata'ib al-Thar)
KT	Empowerment Brigades (Kata'ib al-Tamkeen)
KTI	Thawrat al-Ishrin Brigades (Kata'ib Thawrat al-Ishrin)
KTLH	Latif Hussein Revolutionary Brigades (Baathist) (Kata'ib Thawra Latif Hussein)
KTM	Brigades of the Victorious Sect (Kata'ib al-Taifatul al-Mansura)
KTM	Unity of Muslims Brigades (Kata'ib al-Tawhid al-Muslimin)
KTN	Thul-Nawayn Brigades (Kata'ib Thul-Nuwayn)
KTP	Kurdistan Toilers Party

KUM	Umar al-Mukhtar Brigades (Kata'ib Umar al-Mukhtar)
KUM	Um al-Mu'munin Aisha Brigade (Kata'ib Um al-Mumunin)
KW	Khatt al-Wizzara/Wizrah
KWB	Brigades of the International Islamic Resistance (Kata'ib al-Wala'a wal Bara'a)
KWI	Waqas Islamic Brigade (Kata'ib al-Waqas al-Islamiya)
KZA	Al-Zubair Ebd al-Awwam Brigades (Kata'ib al-Zubair bin al-Awwam)
KZM	Earthquake Warriors Brigades (Kata'ib al-Zilzal al-Mujahidin)
LA	Security Committees (Lajnet al-Amniyeh)
LG	Lazem Group
LIA	Returnee Reception Committees (Lajnet Istiqbal al-A'idin)
LMNM	Committees to Fight Hostile Activity (Laynet Mukafahat al-Nashat al-Mu'adi)
M	Makhmudia
MAI	Islamic Action Organisation (Munadhamat al-'Amal al-Islami)
MB	Muslim Brotherhood (Al-Ikhwan al-Muslimun)
MCC	Warriors Central Command (Mujaheddin Central Command)
MCMI	Media Commission for the Mujahideen in Iraq
MCO	Movement for Continuing Organisation
MD	Warriors of Diyala (Mujahedeen of Diyala)
MF	Mujaheddin – The Faithful
MFA	Mohammed's First Army
MJR	Mesopotamian Jihad Regiments (part of High Command for Jihad and Liberation)
MMIRI	Movement of the Mujahideen of the Islamic Revolution in Iraq
MMM	Mujahadeen Movement of the Marshes
MMS	Militia of Muhammed Shibil
MP	Mesopotamia Party
MS	Fundamentalist Warriors (Mujahedeen al-Salafiyya)
MSMI	Mujahedeen Shura Council (Majlis Shura al-Mudjahidin fi al-Iraq) (four brigades: Fursan al-Tawhid, Knights of Monotheism, Millah Ibrahim, Religion of Ibrahim)
MTA	Munathamit Thar Allah
MTI	Warriors of Islamic Unity (Mujahedin Tawhid al-Islam)
MUC	Muslim Ulema Council
MW	Muntada al-Wilaya
MWI	Mujahedeen of Western Iraq
MWI	Al-Muqawama al-Wataniya al-Islamiya
MWI	Iraqi National Congress (al-Mu'tamar al-Watani al-Iraqi)
N	Renaissance (Nahda)
NA	National Agreement
NFIT	National Front for the Iraqi Tribes
NFLI	National Front for the Liberation of Iraq
NILF	National Iraqi Liberation Front
NIR-BMAY	National Islamic Resistance – Brigade of Mujahid Ahmed Yassin
NJR	al-Nur Jihadi Regiment
NLM	National Liberation Movement
NP	National Party
NRC	New Regional Command of the Ba'ath Party
NRF	National Rescue Front
NUR	National Unity for Reform
NWM	National Welfare Movement
OC	Officers against the Coalition
OLM	Office of the Lord of the Martyrs
OMS	Office of the Martyr Sadr
PBRF	Political Bureau of the Resistance Front

PCDK	Kurdish Democratic Resolution Party in Iraq
PCIR	Political Council for the Iraqi Resistance (alliance)
PDF	People's Defense Forces
PIB	Protectors of Islam Brigade
PIK	Peshtiwanawi Islam le Kurdistan
PJAK	Free Life Party of Kurdistan (Lajnet al-Mutaba'a)
PNFIL	People's National Front for Iraqi Liberation (part of HCJL)
PUK	Patriotic Union of Kurdistan (Yakêti Nistimani Kurdistan)
QAR	Darlings of the Prophet (Qwat al-Ahab al-Rasul)
QLC	Al-Qaeda Lion Cubs (unit for suicide missions)
QS	Army to Liberate Jerusalem (Al-Quds al-Sharif)
QS	Soran Unit (Quwat Soran)
QSH	Al-Qaeda of Saddam Hussein
QT	Emergency Unit (Quwat al-Taware)
RAA	Rebels of al-Anbar
RCC	Revolutionary Command Council
RFR	Ramadi Forgery Ring
RI	Religion of Ibrahim
RJF	Reformation and Jihad Front
RK	Regiments of Kurdistan (part of ISI)
RM	Rebels of the Mukhtar
RNI	Islamic Elite League (Ar-Rabita an-Nukhba al-Islamiya)
RPD	Regiment of the Promised Day
S	Eagle (Al-Saqar)
S	Al-Saydiya
SA	Batallion of the Companions of the Prophet Mohammed (Saraya al-Sahaba)
SA	God's Sword, Double-Edged Sword of God (Sayfallah, Seif Allah)
SAM	Second Army of Mohammed
SCIRI	Supreme Council for the Islamic Revolution in Iraq (al-Majlis al-A'lalil-Thawra al-Islamiya fil-'Iraq)
SCJL	Supreme Command for Jihad and Liberation (Baathist umbrella of 22 organisations)
SCLI	Supreme Council for the Liberation of Iraq
SDAM	Brigades for the Defense of the Holy Shrines (Saraya al-Difa an al-Atabat al-Muqaddasah)
SF	Warriors of Saddam (Saddam Fedayeen)
SF	Awakening Forces (Sahwa forces; tribal militias)
SG	Batallion of Strangers (Saraya al-Ghuraba)
SG	Revenge Batallion (Saraya al-Ghadab)
SI	Islamic Batallion (Saraya Islam)
SI	Fast Reaction Batallion (Saraya al-Igtiham) (QRF of the Mahdi Army)
SIIC	Supreme Islamic Iraqi Council (successor of SCIRI since May 2007)
SJB	Saddam Jihadic Base
SJII	Batallion of Islamic Holy War in Iraq (Saraya al-Jihad al-Islami Bil Irak)
SLH	Lions of Justice Batallion (Saraya Leith al-Haq)
SO	Snake Organisation
SSU	Second Soran Unit
SLC	Southern Liberation Companies (Part of HCJL)
SM	Fundamentalist Warriors (Salafiyah al-Mujahidin)
SM	Warriors Batallion (Saraya al-Mujahedin)
SM	The Right Path (Al-Sirat al-Mustaqim)
SMI	Creed of Abraham Brigade (Saraya Millat al-Ibrahim)
SPK	Socialist Party of Kurdistan
SS	Lightning Batallion (Saraya al-Sa'iqa)

SS	Lord of the Martyrs (Sayyid al-Shuhada)
SSAW	Sa'ad bin Abi Waqqas Battalion (Saraya Sa'ad bin Abi Waqqas)
SSJI	Jihadist Martyrs Battalion in Iraq (Saraya al-Shuhada al-Jihadiyah fi al-Iraq)
SSL	Sacred al-Sadr League
T	Al-Taleea'a
T	The Penitent (Al-Tawabeen)
T	Turkh
TAKG	Tamil al-Kuran Group
TH	Flight from Sin and Atonement (al-Takfir wa al-Hijrah)
THRC	Al-Taf al-Husayniyah Revolutionary Companies
TI	Islamic Vanguard (al-Talia al-Islamiya)
TID	Islamic Democratic Trend (At-Tayyar al-Islami ad-Democrati)
TJ	Monotheism and Holy War (Tawhid and Jihad)
TJI	Organisation of Holy War in Iraq (Tanzim al-Jihadia al-Iraq)
TOI	Talai Organisation of Iraq
TQJ	The Base Organisation of Holy War (Tanzim Qa'idat al-Jihad)
TQJBR	The Base Organisation of the Holy War in the Land of the Two Rivers (Tanzeem Qaedat al-Jihad Fee Bilad al-Rafidain) (Tanzim Qa'idat al-Jihad fi Bilad ar-Rafidain)
TSB	Al-Tawhid wal Sunnah Brigades
TTI	Iraqi Vanguard Organisation (Tanzim al-Talia al-Iraqi)
UIF	United Islamic Front
UIM	Islamic Lion Warriors (Usud al-Islam al-Mujahidin)
UMCI	United Mujahideen Command in Iraq
UOHM	United Organsiation of Halabjah Martyrs
UT	Lions of Monotheism (Usud al-Tawhid)
W	Al-Wahabeen
W	Iraqi National Accord (al-Wifaq)
WACB	We Are Coming Back
WB	Wolf Brigade
WF	White Flags
WIHI	Wahdat Istish-Hadiyin 'Iraqiyin
ZA	Zein al-Abedin
5BB	5 Black Battalion
11SO	11 September Organisation
11RAG	11th Revolutionary Ayloul Group
1920RG	1920 Revolutionary Brigades (Kata'ib Thawrat al-Ishrin) (part of JCF) (Kata'ib Thawrat al-Eishreen)
24	Twenty-Four

Israel (13 entries)

AN	Authart Nosh
AWG	Abu-Walid al-Ghamdi Brigade, Hamza Bin-Abd-al-Mutalib Company, Media Division, Occupied Palestine
CSH	Committee for the Security of the Highways
FPG	Free People of Galilee
GLB	Galilee Liberation Brigades
HY	Hilltop Youth (Noar Ha'Gvaot)
JL	Jewish Legion
JU	Jewish Underground (Haifa)
K	Kach
KC	Kahane Chai

RC	Revenge of the Children
RHB	Revenge of the Hebrew Babies
RM	Revava Movement (extreme right-wing)

Italy (56 entries)

AA	Conveying Group (Tabligh Eddawa Illalah)
AAN	Anticapitalist Attack Nuclei
AB	Angry Brigade
AC	Class Autonomy (Autonomia di classe)
AFPU	Anti-Fascist Proletarian Union (civil guard Toscane)
AI	Justice and Virtue (Al-Adl wal Ishan)
ASAP	Autonomia Sinistra Ante Parlementare
BH	Blood and Honour
BR-PCC	Red Brigades – Combatant Communist Party (Brigate Rosse/Partito Comunista Combattente)
BS	Black Spot (Macchianera)
C	Camorra (mafia in Campania)
CARC	Resistance Support Committees for Communism
CN	Cosa Nostra (mafia in/from Sicily)
CPN	Combatant Proletarian Nuclei
EO	Euro-Opposition (Europposizione)
F	Ferrara Clan
FAI	Informal Anarchist Federation (Federazione Anarchia Informale)
FAI/CCCCC	FAI/Cells against Capital, Prison, Prison Wardens and Prison Cells Cellula Contro Capitale, Carcere i suoi Carcerieri e le sue Celle)
FAI/FSCC	FAI/Fire and Similar Crafts Cooperative
FAI/IS	FAI/International Solidarity
FAI/20JB	FAI/20 July Brigade
FN	New Strength (Forza Nueva)
FNI	Italian National Front (Fronte Nazionale Italiano)
FRC	Revolutionary Front for Communism (Fronte Rivoluzionario per il Comunismo)
IBCA	Italy–Black Cuba Association (Associazione Italia Cuba Nera)
IS	International Solidarity
IU	Italian Unabomber
L	Laraspata Clan (mafia)
NCC	Combatant Communist Units (Nuclei Combatant Communist)
NOSH	Neptune Occupied Student House (Casa dello studente occupata Neptuno)
NTA-PCC	Anti-imperialist Territorial Nuclei (Nuclei Territoriali Anti-imperialista-Partito Comunista Combattente)
MGPRC	Mario Galesi Proletarian Resistance Cells
MO	Anti-Zionist Movement (Movimiento Antisionista)
MPO	Movimiento Politico Occidentale
N	Ndrangheta (mafia in Calabria)
PASP	Padanian Armed Separatist Phalanx
PB	Praetorian Brigade
PCG	Proletarian Combatant Group
PLF	Paedophile Liberation Front
PNC	Proletarian Nuclei for Communism (Nuclei Proletari per il Comunismo)
PRIU	Proletarian Revolutionary Initiative Units (Nuclei di Iniziativa Proletaria Rivoluzionaria)
RFC	Revolutionary Front for Communism
RL	Red Line (Linea Rossa)
RLB	Revolutionary Leninist Brigades

ROC	Revolutionary Offensive Cells
RPN	Revolutionary Proletarian Nucleus
RU	Revolutionary Unemployed
S	Strisciuglio (mafia clan, Bari)
SAM	Sardinian Autonomy Movement
SCU	United Sacred Crown (Sacra Corona Unita) (regional mafia group)
SSS	SSS (right-wing civil guard in Toscane)
TB	White Overalls (Tute Bianchi)
TP	Third Position (Terza Posizione)
T	Ein Tirol
UCC	Union of Combatant Communist
YB	Enough Already (Ya Basta!) (anti-globalists)

Ivory Coast (21 entries)

CN	Cosa Nostra Militia
COJEP	Pan-African Congress of Young Patriots (Congrès Panafrican des jeunes patriotes)
CPP	Convention of the Patriots for Peace (Convention des patriotes pour la paix)
FESCI	Student Federation of Côte d'Ivoire
FLGO	Front for the Liberation of the Great West (Front pour la libération du Grand Ouest)
FLN	National Liberation Front (Front national de libération)
FPI	Popular Ivorian Front
FSCO	Front for the Security of the Centre-West (Front pour la Sécurité du Centre-Ouest)
GPP	Group of Patriots for Peace (Groupe des patriotes pour la paix)
KM	Kamajors Militia
LF	Lima Force
MJP	Movement for Justice and Peace (Mouvement pour la justice et la paix)
MLGO	Movement for the Liberation of the Far West
MPCI	Patriotic Movement of Ivory Coast (Mouvement patriotique de Côte d'Ivoire)
MPIGO	Ivorian Popular Movement for the Great West (Mouvement populaire ivoirien du Grand Ouest)
NF	New Forces (Forces nouvelles)
PCC	P.C.Crise Militia
PCCM	P.C.Crise Marine Militia
RB	Red Brigade Militia
UPLTCI	Union of Patriots for the Total Liberation Côte d'Ivoire (Union des patriotes pour la libération totale de la Côte d'Ivoire)
YP	Young Patriots

Jamaica (6 entries)

KKK	Kool Kidz Krew
PLG	Park Lane Gang
RSG	Red Square Gang
SP	Shower Posse
TRG	Top Road Gang
Y	Yardies

Japan (13 entries)

| AIIB | Japanese Red Army/Anti-Imperialist Brigade |
| AS | Aum Supreme Truth (Aum Shinrikyo, aka Aleph) |

CH	Nucleus Faction or Middle Core Faction (Chukaku-Ha)
HSS	Ho-n-hana Sampagyo sect
JRA	Japanese Red Army (Nihun Sekign)
JVANI	Japan Volunteer Army for National Independence
K	Revolutionary Army (Kakumeigun)
K	Revolutionary Workers Federation (Kakurokyo)
KGCS	Kenkoku Giyugun Chosen Seibatsutai
KRA	Kansai Revolutionary Army (branch of Chukaku-Ha)
S	Sekiho Army, aka Blood Revenge Division of the People's Partisan Corps (Sekihotai, aka Nippon Minzoku Dokuritsu Giyyugun Betsudo Sekihotai)
SJS	Spiritual Justice School
YLOPYS	Youth League for the Overthrow of the Yalta and Potsdam Structure

Jordan (21 entries)

ACRP	Arab Communist Revolutionary Party
BI	Allegiance to the Imam (Bai'at al Imam)
HIT	Movement of Reform and Challenge (Harakat al-Islah wa-t-Tahaddi)
HTI	Parrty of Islamic Liberation (Hezb al-Tahrir al-Islami)
IM	Muslim Brotherhood (Ikhwan al-Muslimun)
JA	Jordanian Afghans
JAGU	Abu Ghaith al-Urduni Group (Jama'at Abu Ghaith al-Urduni)
JAI	Islamic Action Front (political arm of IM) (Jabhat al-'Amal al-Islami)
JS	Soldiers of the Levant (Jund al-Sham)
JM	Army of Muhammad (Jaysh Muhammed)
JTJ	Monotheism and Holy War Group (Jama'at al-Tawhid Wa'al Jihad)
KT	Unification Battalions (Kata'ib al-Tawhid)
MG	Mu'tah Group (Jama'at Mu'tah)
MSJIR	Movement for the Struggle of the Jordanian Islamic Resistance
QLCR	Al-Qaeda in the Land of the Crossed Rivers
QLE	Al-Qaeda in the Levant and Egypt
RF	Returnees from Fallujah
SNI	Shabab Al-Nafir al-Islami
SU	Honorables of Jordan (Shurafaa' al-Urdun)
VS	Victorious Sect (Al-Taa'efa al-Mansourah)
2000K	2000K Operations

Kazakhstan (4 entries)

IJG	Islamic Holy War Group (Jama'at Jihadia Islamiya)
IMK	Islamic Movement of Kazakhs
R	Rus
ZCAM	Group of Central Asian Warriors (Zhamaat of Central Asian Mujahedin)

Kenya (14 entries)

AA	Defenders of God (Ansar Allah)
FEM	February Eighteen Movement
FORD	Forum for the Restoration of Democracy
F18RA	February Eighteen Resistance Army
IPK	Islamic Party of Kenya

KPF	Kenya Patriotic Front
M	Mwakenya
M	Mungiki (Kikuyu)
MMC	Movement for Change (Muungano wa Magemzi)
NCEC	National Convention Executive Council
SLDF	Sabaot Land Defence Force (Sabaot, sub-tribe of Kalenjin)
SP	Noah's Ark Party (Safina Party)
SSV	Sungu Sungu Vigilantes
T	Taliban (Luo)

Korea, North (2 entries)

ANKD	Association of North Korean Defectors
CRONK	Committee for Reform and Openness of North Korea

Korea, South (4 entries)

QOSEA	Al-Qaeda Organisation in South and East Asia
BHM	Battalion of Hamud al-Masri
KMF	Korean Muslim Federation
YROO	Yellow–Red Overseas Organisation

Kosovo (26 entries)

AAK	Alliance for the Future of Kosovo
ABSMG	Abu Bakr Sadiq Mujahedin Group
AJD	Adem Jashari Division
AKSh	National Albanian Army (Armatë Kombetare Shqiptare)
ANUF	Albanian National Union Front
CRP	Chetnic Movement of the Flat Hill
DF	Delta Force
DPK	Democratic Party of Kosovo
FARK	Forces of the Republic of Kosovo
FBKSh	Front for the Albanian National Unification (Fronti për bashkimin kombëtar shqiptar)
FI	Fire of Islam
FNLA	Former National Liberation Army
FNUA	Front for National Unity of Albanians (military wing ANA)
G	Gjurma
JJK	Holy War Group Kosovo (Jama'at Jihad Kosovo)
L	Lightning (Munja)
LDK	Democratic League of Kosovo (Lidhya Demokratike e Kosevës)
LKCK	National Movement for the Liberation of Kosovo
SAJ	Specialnija Antiterroristicka Jedinica
TJ	Conveying Group (Tabligh Jammat)
TLU	Tzar Lazar Unit
TMK	Kosovo Protection Corps
UCK	Kosovo Liberation Army (Ushtria Clirimtare e Kosovës)
UCK	National Liberation Army (Ushtria Clirimtare Kombetare)
UCK-L	Kosovo Liberation Army–East
URK	New Army of Kosovo (Ushtrja e re te Kosovës)

Kuwait (9 entries)

D	Islamic Call (Al-Dawa)
HK	Hamas–Kuwait
HK	Hezbollah–Kuwait
HSI	Islamic Salafi Movement (Harakat Salafiya Islamiya)
JG	Al-Jahra Group
KUJ	Peninsula Lions Brigades (Kata'ib Usud al-Jazira)
MK	Kuwaiti Warriors (Mujahidin al-Kuwaiti)
SDAM	Brigades for the Defense of the Holy Shrines (Saraya al-Difa an al-Atabat al-Muqaddasah)
SFS	Sharia Falcons Squadrons

Kyrgyzstan (3 entries)

A	Akramiya movement (Hizb ut-Tahrir splinter)
MALK	Muslim Army for the Liberation of Kyrgyzstan
Y	Independence (Yegemen)

Laos (9 entries)

CIDL	Commitee for Independence and Democracy in Laos
CV	Sky Soldiers (Chao Va; God's Disciples)
ELOL	Ethnic Liberation Organisation of Laos
FDPGL	Free Democratic People's Government of Laos
FNR	Front for National Reconstruction
LNLM	Lao National Liberation Movement
SDC	Social Democrat Club
UGFDPL	Underground Government of the Free Democratic People of Laos
ULNLF	United Lao National Liberation Front

Latvia (0 entries)

Lebanon (62 entries)

A	Association of Islamic Charitable Projects (Al-Ahbash)
A	Amal Movement (Harakat Amal)
AA	Defenders of God (Ansar Allah)
AA	League of Supporters, League of Followers/Partisans (Asbat al-Ansar)
AN	Group of the Light (Asbat al-Nur)
ANM	Arab Nationalists' Movement
ARM	Arab Revolutionary Brigade-Foreign Section
AS	Followers of the Traditions of the Prophet (Ahl al-Sunna)
ASALA	Armenian Secret Army for the Liberation of Armenia
DG	Al-Dunniyah Group
FAL	Front for Arab Liberation
FF	Dawn Forces (Al-Fajr Forces; military wing of JI)
FF	Fighters for Freedom
FI	Fatah al-Islam
FL	Lebanese Forces Militia (Forces Libanaise Militia)
FPM	Free Patriot Movement
FU	Fatah Uprising

FUFS	Fighters for the Unity and Freedom of al-Sham
H	Party of God (Hezbollah)
HAMAS	Islamic Resistance Movement (Harakat al-Muqawama al-Islamiya)
HG	Habashi Group
HIM	Movement of Islamic Warriors (Al-Harakat al-Islamiya al-Mujahida)
HN	Victory Party (Hezb al-Nasr)
HT	Hezbollah–Toufayli Faction
HTI	Islamic Unification Movement (Harakat al-Tawhid al-Islami)
IM	Muslim Brotherhood (Al-Ikhwan al-Muslimun)
IR	Islamic Resistance
ISM	Islamic Struggle Movement
JI	Islamic Congregation (Al-Jemaah Islamiyah)
JI	Islamic Group (Jama'at al-Islamiya)
JI	Islamic Holy War (Jihad Islami)
JIM	Islamic Fighting Group (al-Jama'at al-Islamiyah al-Muqatilah)
JMAG	Jihad Movement for Aiding Gaza
JS	Soldiers of the Levant (Jund al-Sham)
KAA	Brigades of Abdallah Azzam (Kata'ib Abdallah Azzam)
KZJ	Brigades of Ziad al-Jarrah (Kata'ib Ziad al-Jarrah) (part of the KAA)
LLF	Lebanese Liberation Front
LNRF	Lebanese National Resistance Front
LP	Lebanese Platoon
LRB	Lebanese Resistance Brigades
MDR	Movement for Democratic Renewal
MIH	Islam without Borders Organisation (Majmou'at Islam bila Houdoud)
ML	Warriors of Lebanon (Mujahideen of Lebanon)
ML	Freedom Warriors (Mujahideen of Liberty)
MM	Giants Militia (Marada Militia; pro-Syrian, Faranjieh clan)
MM	Believers' Resistance (al-Muqawamah al-Mu'minah)
MSE	Diaspora Warriors in Europe (Mujahideen al-Shatat in Europe)
MWHS	Strugglers for the Unity and Freedom of Greater Syria (al-Munadilun min ajl Wihdat wa Hurriyat bilad al-Sham]
NI	Victory of Islam (Nasrat al-Islam)
NJS	Victory and Holy War in the Levant (Nasrat al-Jihad al-Sham)
ODPR	Organisation for the Defense of the Prisoners' Rights
OOE	Organisation for the Oppressed on Earth
QL	Al-Qaeda in Lebanon
RJO	Revolutionary Justice Organisation
S	Lightning (Al-Saiqa)
SLA	South Lebanese Army
SS	The Good Fundamentalist (Al-Salaf al-Saleh)
SSNP	Syrian Socialist Nationalist Party
TH	Flight from Sin and Atonement (Takfir wal Hijra)
TJ	Organisation of Holy War (Tanzim Jihad)
TM	Organisation of Warriors (Tanzim al-Mujahideen)
20thB SLA	20th Battalion of the South Lebanese Army

Lesotho (0 entries)

Liberia (15 entries)

AFL	Armed Forces of Liberia
C	Coalition
CRC	Central Revolutionary Council
LDF	Lofa Defense Force
LPC	Liberia Peace Council
LUDF	Liberian United Defense Forces
LURD	Liberians United for Reconciliation and Democracy
MODEL	Movement for Democracy in Liberia
MOJA	Movement for Justice in Africa
NB	Naked Brigade
NPLF	National Patriotic Front of Liberia
NPLF-W	National Patriotic Front of Liberia–Woewiyu
ULIMO	United Liberation Movement for Democracy
ULIMO-J	United Liberation Movement for Democracy–J
ULIMO-K	United Liberation Movement for Democracy–Krahn

Libya (8 entries)

ABL	Abu-Bakr al-Libi
HIS	Movement of Islamic Martyrs (Harakat al-Shuhada'a al-Islamiya)
IS	Idriss el-Senussi
KS	Martyrs Brigades (Kata'ib al-Shuhada)
KSM	Al-Mukhtar Suicide Brigades (Kata'ib Shahid al-Mukhtar)
LIFG	Libyan Islamic Fighting Group (Al-Jama'ah al-Islamiyyah al-Muqatilah bi-Libya)
LH	Libyan Hezbollah
SBM	Fighting Youth of Barqa (Shabibat Barqa al-Munadila)

Luxembourg (0 entries)

Macau (3 entries)

BC	Big Circle Gang (triad)
14 K	14 K (triad)
SF	Water Room (Soi Fong) (triad)

Macedonia (23 entries)

AB	Agim Bajrami
AIO	Active Islamic Youth
AK	Ahmed Kaqiku
AKHs	Albanian National Army
AM	Warriors Unit (Al-Mujahedin Unit)
BT	Black Tigers
DB	Debar Group
DG	Drenica Group
GW	Grey Wolves (Mujahedin)
IG	Islamic Group
KG	Kuka Group
M	Merhamet

MD	Macedonian Dawn
ML	Macedonian Lions (Lavovi)
MNF	Macedonian National Front
MP2000	Macedonian Paramilitary
MRO	Macedonian Revolutionary Organisation
NLA	National Liberation Army
RFNLAF	Real Former National Liberation Army Fighters
SU	Skanderbeg Unit
T	Tariqat
UCI	Republican Army of Ilirida (Ushtria Clirimtare Iliridas)
UCK (M)	Kosovo Liberation Army (Macedonia) (Ushtria Clirimtare e Kosovës)

Madagascar (0 entries)

Malawi (0 entries)

Malaysia (10 entries)

M	Brotherhood of Inner Power (Al Ma'unah)
DI	House of Islam (Darul Islam)
G13	Gang of 13
JI	Islamic Community (Jemaah Islamiyah)
KMM	Malaysian Militant Group (Kumpulan Mujahideen Malaysia, Kumpulan Militan Malaysia)
KMM2	Kumpulan Militan Malaysia Dua (aka Jemaah Islamiyah)
LHW	League of Holy Warriors (Rabitatul Mujahedeen) (Mujahedin Coalition)
MHA	Malaysian Hackers Association
RJ	Association of Comrades (Rufaqa Jama'at) (aligned with Tabligh; split from Arqam)
SN	Sri Nakharo

Mali (15 entries)

AIFEL	Arab Islamic Front of Edhalma Liberation
ARLA	Revolutionary Liberation Army of Azawad (Armée révolutionnaire de libération de l'Azawad)
DwT	Conveying Group (Da'wa wa Tabligh)
FFR	Front of the Reconstruction Forces (Front des forces de redressement)
FIAA	Islamic Arab Front of Azawad (Front Islamique Arabe de l'Azawad)
FPLA	Popular Liberation Front of Azawad (Front populaire de libération de l'Azawad)
GSPJM	Salafist Group for Predication and Jihad in Mali (Group salafiste pour le prédication et le jihad en Mali)
HTT	Education and Purification Movement (Harakat al-Tarbiah wa al-Tasfiah)
JT	Conveying Group (Jama'at al-Tabligh)
MEN	Movement for Hope in the North (Mouvement pour l'espoir du Nord)
MFUA	United Movement and Fronts of Azawad
MPA	Popular Movement of Azawad (Mouvement populaire de l'Azawad)
MPGK	Patriotic Movement of Ganda Koy (Mouvement patriotique Ganda Koy)
PN	Barefeet (Pieds Nus)
PTG	Al-Para Terrorist Group

Mauritania (6 entries)

AIMFC	Almoravid Defenders of Allah in the Land of Chenguitt (Ansar al-Islam al-Mourabitoune fi Bilad Cenguitt
FLAM	Liberation Front of the Africans in Mauritania (Front de libération des Africaines de Mauritanie)
FT	The Knights of Change (Foursan Taghyir)
GIPJM	Mauritanian Group for Preaching and Jihad in Mauritania (Groupe islamique pour la prédication et le jihad en Mauritanie)
JDT	Conveying Group (Jama'at al-Da'wa wa '-Tabligh)
MIM	Mauritanian Islamic Movement

Mexico (77 entries)

AB	Amezcua Brothers
AFO	Arellano Félix Organisation (Tijuana Cartel)
APPO	Oaxaca People's Assembly
BLC	Beltran Leyva Cartel
BMC	Barbaro Mexico Command
BO	Batallon Olimpico
BU–SD	Business United – The Squadron of Death
C	Chinchulines
C	Los Chombos
CC	Colima Cartel
CCI	Insurgent Peasant Commando (Comando Campesinas Insurgente)
CCRI-CG	Clandestine Indian Revolutionary Committee – General Command
CIAHLO	Clandestine Indigenous Army of the Highlands and Lowlands of Oaxaca
CJM23M	Comando Jamillista Morelense 23 de Mayo
CNLAF	Clandestine National Liberation Armed Forces
CRIC-LN	Revolutionary Indigenous Peasant National Liberation Command
CSA	Chilpancingo Subversive Army
EDC	Peasant Defense Army
EIRLN	National Indigenous Revolutionary Army
EIRS	Insurrection and Revolutionary Army of the South-East (Ejercito Insurgente Revolucionario del Sureste)
ELS	Liberation Army of the South
EP	Army of the Poor (Ejercito de los Pobros)
EPLMM	Jose Maria Morelos Popular Liberation Army
EPR	Revolutionary People's Army (Ejercito Revolucionario Popular)
ERPI	Revolutionary Army of the Insurgent People (Ejército Revolucionario Insurgente Popular)
ES	Army of the Sierra
EVLN	Villista Army of National Liberation
EZLN	Zapatista National Liberation Army (Ejercito Zapatista de Liberación Nacional)
FAC-MLN	Broad Front for the Creation of a National Liberation Movement
FALMG	Armed Front for the Liberation of the Marginalized People in Guerrero
FARP	People's Revolutionary Armed Forces (Fuerzas Armadas Revolucionarias del Pueblo)
FJP	Youth Front of the People (Frente Juventud del Pueblo)
FRECOMS	Revolutionary Front of Peasants and Workers (Frente Campesino Obrero Mexicana del Sureste)
GB	White Guards (Guardias Blancas)
GB	Grupo Beta
GC	Gulf Cartel
GGCJMMP	Group of Guerrilla Combatants of José María Morelos y Pavón
GH	Grupo Hank

GVEA	Genaro Vasquez Execution Army
INLC	Indigenous National Liberation Command
IRA	Insurgent Revolutionary Army
JADP	Justice Army of Defenseless People
JC	Juárez Cartel (or Vicente Carillo Fuentes Cartel)
JJC	28 de Junio Justiciero Command
JMC	Jaramilista Morelense Command
JMMNGCB	José María Morelos National Guerrilla Coordinating Board
L	La Línea (gang related to Juárez Cartel)
LAFMP	Liberation Armed Forces for Marginalized Peoples
MC	Millennium Cartel/Valencia Cartel
MM	Magonist Militias
MPLN	Popular Movement of National Liberation (Movimiento Popular de Liberación Nacional)
MULT	Triqui Movement for Unity and Struggle (Movimiento de Unificatión y Lucha Triqui)
MZSG	Zapatist Militia of the Sierra Gordo
NC	Los Negros Cartel
NDG	Northern Drug Gang
OC	Oaxaca Cartel
OCSS	Southern Sierra Peasant Organisation
OIPUH	Independent Organisation of the United Peoples of Huasteca
PJ	Peace and Justice (Paz y Justicia)
PMA	People's Majority Army
PRAF	People's Revolutionary Armed Forces
PROCUP	Clandestine Workers' Revolutionary Party, Union of the Poor (Partido Revolucionario Obrero Clandestino Union del Pueblo – Partido de los Pobros)
RACS	Revolutionary Armed Forces of the South
RIMZ	Revolutionary Indigenous Movement against the Zapatistas
RJRAM	Ruben Jaramillo Revolutionary Armed Movement
RWCUPP	Revolutionary Worker Clandestine Union of the People Party
SC	Sinaloa Cartel or Hector Palma, Joaquin Guzmán Cartel (Federation, Golden Triangle)
SLA	Southern Liberation Army
T	Shark (Tiburón)
T	The Torch
TAGIN	National Indigenous Guerrilla Triple Alliance
TC	Tijuana Cartel (or Arellano Félix Brothers Cartel)
UCI	Independent Peasant Union
Z	Zorros (Foxes)
Z	Los Zetas
ZC	Zambada Cartel

Moldova (2 entries)

MPF	Moldovan Popular Front
TS	Transnistrian Separatists

Montenegro (5 entries)

B	Clans (Bratstva)
FMO	Free Montenegro Organisation
MLM	Montenegrin Liberation Movement
MRARM	Movement for the Realisation of the Albanian Rights in Montenegro
UKMZ	Montenegrin National Army

Morocco (23 entries)

AI	Justice and Good Society (Al-Adl wal-Ishane)
AIM	Defenders of Islam in the Maghreb (Ansar al-Islam al-Maghribi)
AIMS	Ansar al-Islam in the Muslim Sahara, Land of the Veiled Ones
AM	Right Way (Assirat al-Moustaqim)
AQIM	Al-Qaeda Organisation in the Islamic Maghreb
AS	Followers of the Traditions of the Prophet (Ahl al-Sunna)
FA	Fath al-Andalous
GICM	Moroccan Islamic Fighting Group (al-Jama'ah al-Islamiyyah al-Mujahidah bi'l-Magrib; Groupe Islamique Combatant Marocain)
HASM	Islamic Resistance Movement in the Magreb (Harakat al-Islamiya al-Magrebiya al-Mukatila)
IA	Forward (Ila'l-Aman)
IGGAJM	Islamic Group for the Glorification of Allah and the Jihad in Morocco
IJG	Islamic Jihad Group
IYM	Islamic Youth Movement
JAEM	Group of Defenders of the Mahdi (Jama'at Ansar al-Mahdi)
JDT	Conveying Group (Jama'at al-Dawa Wal-Tabligh)
KAHM	Abu Hafs al-Masri Brigades (Kata'ib Abu Hafs al-Masri)
MA	Moroccan Afghans
POLISARIO	Polisario Front (Frente Popular para la Liberación de Saguía el-Hamra y Río de Oro)
SJ	Fundamentalists for Holy War (as-Salafiya al-Jihadiya)
SPLA	Sahrawi People's Liberation Army
TI	Unity and Reform (Tawhid al-Islah)
TH	Flight from Sin and Atonement (Takfir Wal Hijra)
TJIM	Monotheism and Islamic Holy War in Morocco (Tawheed wal-Jihad Islamic fi al-Maghrib)

Mozambique (1 entry)

MNRM	Mozambique National Resistance Movement

Myanmar (71 entries)

ABMU	All Burma Muslim Union
ABSDF	All Burma Students' Democratic Front
AIA/AIO	Arakan Independence Organisation/Army
ALA	Arakan Liberation Army
ALO	Arakan Liberation Organisation
ALP	Arakan Liberation Party
ANO	Arakan National Organisation
ANLP	Arakan National Liberation Party
ARIF	Arakan Rohingya Islamic Front
ARNO	Arakan Revolution National Organisation
BRF	Indo-Burma Revolutionary Front
CNF/A	Chin National Force/Army
CNLP	Chin National Liberation Party
CPA	Communist Party of Arakan
DAB	Democratic Alliance of Burma
DKBA	Democratic Karen Buddhist Army
DKBO	Democratic Kayin Buddhist Organisation
ENRC	Eastern Nagas Revolutionary Council
ESSA	Eastern Shan State Army

FTUB	Federation of Trade Unions of Burma
GA	God's Army
IBRF	Indo–Burma Revolutionary Front
ITM	Ittihad al-Tullab al-Muslimeen
KA	Karenni Army
KA	Kokang Army
KDA	Kachin Democratic Army
KIA	Kachin Independence Army
KIO	Kachin Independent Organisation
KMLF	Kawloothei Muslim Liberation Front
KNG	Kayen National Guard
KNLA	Karen National Liberation Army
KNLP	Kayan New Land Party
KNLRC	Kayan New Land Revolutionary Council
KNPLF	Karenni National People's Liberation Front
KSNLF	Karenni State Nationalities Liberation Front
KNPP	Karenni National Progressive Party
KNU	Karen National Union
KNU	Kayin National Union
KPLO	Karenni People's Liberation Organisation
LNO	Lahu National Organisation
LNUP	Lahu National United Party
MDUF	Myeik-Dawei United Front
MLOB	Muslim Liberation Organisation of Burma
MNDAA/P	Myanmar National Democratic Alliance Army/Party
MNDF	Mon National Democratic Front
MNLA	Mon National Liberation Army
MTA	Mong Tai Army
NCGUB	National Coalition Government of the Union of Burma
NDA	New Democratic Army
NDF	National Democratic Front
NLD	National League for Democracy
NLD-LA	National League for Democracy – Liberated Area
NMSP	New Mon State Party
NUFA	National United Front of Arakan
PNLA	Pao National Liberation Army
PNO	Pao National Organisation
PP21	People's Power 21st Century
PSLO	Palaung State Liberation Organisation/Army
RSO	Rohingya Solidarity Organisation
SPDC	State Peace and Development Council
SSLNO	Shan State Nationalities Liberation Organisation
SSNA	Shan State National Army
SSPA	Shan State Progress Army
SSRC	Shan State Restoration Council
SUA	Shan State Army
SURA	Shan United Revolutionary Army
TRC	Thailand Revolutionary Council
UWSA	United Wa State Army
VBSW	Vigorous Burmese Students Warriors
ZNF	Zomi National Front

Namibia (1 entry)

SWAPO	South-West Africa People's Organisation

Nepal (22 entries)

AK	All Nepal National Independent Students' Union – Revolutionary (Akhil Krantikari)
ANEC	All Nepal Ethnic Conference
ANNO	All Nepal Nationalities Organisation
CPN	Communist Party of Nepal
CPN-Masal	Nepalese Communist Party – Masal
CPN-M	Nepalese Communist Party – Maoist
CPN-ML	Nepalese Communist Party – Marxist-Leninist
CPN-UCM	Communist Party of Nepal – United Centre (Masal)
JSUN	Jamiah Siraj ul Uloom in Nepal
KLF	Karnali Liberation Front
KNLF	Kirat National Liberation Front
LLF	Limbuwan Liberation Front
NDA	National Defense Army (Hindu)
NLF	Newar Liberation Front
NLMN	Nationalities Liberation Movement of Nepal
NTLF	National Tamang Liberation Front
MLF	Magarat Liberation Front
SJM	United People's Front (Sanyukta Jana Morcha)
SOCM	Special Organisation Committee of Maoists
TLF	Tamu Liberation Front
TPNO	Tamang People's National Organisation
UPFN	United People's Front of Nepal (Bhattarai)

Netherlands (24 entries)

ANN	Action Front Nationalist Netherlands (Actiefront Nationalistisch Nederland)
BH	Blood and Honour
CRE	Communist Revolutionaries in Europe
DBF	Animal Liberation Front (Dierenbevrijdingsfront)
DM	Dutch Mafia (generic term)
DUC	Down Under Crew (computer hackers)
FKM	Front Kedaulatan Maluku
FvdI	Fable of the Illegal (Fabel van de Illegaal)
HG	Hofstad Group (Hofstadgroep)
LvT	Lions of Monotheism (Leeuwen van Tawheed)
LY	Lonsdale Youth (right-wing)
MEB	Mobile Unit for Biosecurity (Mobiele Eenheid voor Bioveiligheid)
MWC	Maluku War Child
NVB	Dutch People's Movement (Nederlandse Volksbeweging)
NVU	Dutch People's Union (Nederlandse Volksunie)
PAG	People against Genocide
PM	Polder Warriors (Poldermoedjahedien)
PP	Pigs in Peril
RH	Raging Hares (Razende Hazen)
RVF	Racial Volunteer Force (C-18 section of Blood and Honour)
SMR	South Maluku Republic

YG	York Gang
YM	Yugo Mafia (from former Yugoslavia)
XP	Xtreme Power (computer hackers)

New Zealand (1 entry)

911	September 11

Nicaragua (15 entries)

CPLM	Cinchoneros Popular Liberation Movement
FPI	Leftist Punitive Forces (Fuerzas Punitivas de Izquierda)
FROC	Workers and Peasants Revolutionary Front (Frente Revolucionario Obrero y Campesino)
FUAC	Andres Castro United Front
MADNA	National Armed Self-Defense Movement
MADOC	Armed Movement of Workers and Peasants
MISURASATA	Alliance of the Miskito, Sumu, Rama and the Sandinists
MNDSC	Movement for Dignity and National Sovereignty
NF380	Northern Front 380
NR	Nicaraguan Resistance (Resistencia Nicaragüense)
PFL	Punitive Forces of the Left
PNR	Party for Nicaraguan Resistance
R	Scrambled (Revueltos)
R380	Reconta 380
YATAMA	Yapti Tasba Masraka Nanih Aslatakanka

Niger (19 entries)

ABH	Association for the Banning of Heresy (Jam'iyat Izalat al-Bida)
AIGC	Association of Islamic Groups and Culture
ARLNN	Liberation Army of Northern Niger (Armée de libération du Nord Niger)
CAD	Self-Defense Committees (Comités d'autodéfense)
CRA	Coordination of Armed Resistance (Coordination de la résistance armée)
CVT	Tassara Vigilante Committee (Comité de vigilance de Tassara)
FARS	Revolutionary Armed Front of the Sahara (Front armée révolutionnaire du Sahara)
FDR	Democratic Front for Renewal (Front démocratique de renouveau)
FFL	Front of Liberation Forces (Front des forces de libération)
FLAA	Front for the Liberation of Air and Azouak (Front pour la libération de l'Air et de l'Azaouak)
FLT	Tamoust Liberation Front (Front de libération du Tamoust)
FPLS	Popular Front for the Liberation of the Sahara (Front populaire de libération du Sahara)
MJT	Tuareg Justice Movement (Mouvement de la justice Tourègue)
MNJ	Nigerian Justice Movement (Mouvement nigérien pour la justice)
MRLNN	Revolutionairy Movement for the Liberation of Northern Niger (Movement révolutionnaire de libération du Nord Niger)
MUR	Unified Revolutionary Moment (Movement unifié révolutionnaire)
NIA	Niger Islamic Association
ORA	Organisation of Armed Resistance (Organisation de la résistance armée)
UFRA	Union of Armed Resistance Forces (Forces armées révolutionnaires)

Nigeria (47 entries)

AB	ASMATA Boys
APC	Arewa People's Congress
ASJ	Group of Followers of the Tradition of the Prophet (Ahl al-Sunna wal Jamma)
AVS	Anambra Vigilante Service (aka Bakassi Boys)
BFF	Bakassi Freedom Fighters
BH	Boko Haram ('Western Education Is Sin'; Nigerian Taliban)
CMAND	Coalition for Militant Action in the Niger Delta
CRC	Common Revolutionary Council
EBA	Egbesu Boys of Africa
EE	Enough is Enough (Delta)
FNDIC	Federated Niger Delta Ijaw Communities
GOA	God's Oppressed Army
HG	Hisba/Hisbah Groups
I	Izala
ISIC	Independent Sharia Implementation Committee
ISTF	Internal Security Task Force
ISVS	Imo State Vigilante Service
IY	Iduwini Youths
IYC	Ijaw Youth Council
JHWT	Flight from Sin and Atonement Group (Jama'ah Hijra wa Takfir) (aka Northern Taliban)
JRC	Joint Revolutionary Council
JTMN	Jama'atu Ta'awunil Muslimeen Nigeria
MAD	Movement for the Advancement of Democracy
MASSOB	Movement for the Actualisation of a Sovereign State of Biafra
MB	Martyrs Brigade
MB	Mobile Force
MEND	Movement for the Emancipation of the Niger Delta
MOSOP	Movement for the Survival of the Ogoni People
NDC	National Democratic Coalition
NDPVF	Niger Delta People's Volunteer Force
NDV	Niger Delta Vigilante
NDVF	Niger Delta Volunteer Force
NPC	Northern People's Congress
O	Oha-na-Ese Ndi Igbo
OLN	Organisation for the Liberation of Nigeria
OLO	Ogoni Liberation Organisation
OPC	Oodua People's Congress
OVS	Onitsha Vigilante Services (formerly Bakassi Boys)
PLAN	People's Liberation Army of Nigeria
PNDRM	Pan Niger Delta Resistance Movement
RSISTF	Rivers State Internal Security Task Force
SETF	Sharia Enforcement Task Force (Zamfara)
SOMIFON	Southern Minorities Front of Nigeria
SP	Supernumerary Police
TS	Terror Squad, or Strike Force
UFLN	United Front for the Liberation of Nigeria
ZSVS	Zamfara State Vigilante Service

Norway (1 entry)

B	Bootboys (neo-Nazi)

Pakistan (171 entries)

A	Afridis
A	The Holy Men (Al-Arifeen)
AA	God is Great (Allah-o-Akbar)
AH	People of the Tradition (Ahl Al-Hadith)
AI	Defenders of Islam (Ansar-al-Islam)
AIC	Anti-India Crew
AJ	Azeri Group (Azeri Jama'at)
AMJ	Army of the Mahdi Jama'at
AMNAM	Movement for Enjoining Good and Forbidding Evil (Amr bil Maroof wa Nahi Anil Munkar)
APHC	All Parties Hurriyat Conference (umbrella organisation)
ARD	Alliance for the Restoration of Democracy
ARRSG	Abdul Rab Rasool Sayyaf Group
AS	Abu Saleem
ASJ	Followers of the Traditions of the Prophet (Ahl-e-Sunnat wal Jamat) (previously Sipah-e-Mohammad (Army of Mohammed, Pakistan))
ASS	Society of the Army of Companions of the Prophet (Anjuman Sepah-e-Sahaba)
AT	Ahl-e-Tashi (Shi'ah)
AT	Al-Akhtar Trust
B	The Lightning (Al-Barq)
BACK	Basic Association of Citizens of Karachi
BCCI/BN	BCCI/Black Network
BF	Al-Badr Foundation
BLA	Baluchistan Liberation Army
BLLF	Bonded Labor Liberation Front
BM	Al-Badr Warriors (Al-Badr Mujahedeen; Kashmiri)
BNF	Balawarian National Front
BNM	Balochistan National Movement
BPLF	Baluch People's Liberation Front
BS	Bhoomi Sena (Kurmis)
BSO	Baluch Students' Organisation
CIM	Chechen Islamic Movement
CT	Christian Taleban
DM	Daughters of the Communities (Dukhtaran e-Millat)
DUH	University of Education and Truth (Darul Uloom Haqqani)
ETIP	East Turkestan Islamic Party
F	Al-Faran
F	Al-Farooq
F	Conquest (Al-Fateh)
FH	Fedayeen al-Husayn (Shi'ite)
FI	Partisans of Islam (Fidayeen-e-Islam, Fedayan-e-Islam)
FI	Welfare of Humanity (Falah-e-Insaniyat) (previously JuD)
FM	Farzandan-e-Milat
HA	Movement of Defenders (Harakat al-Ansar)
HJI	Movement of Islamic Holy Warrirors (Harakat-al-Jehadi Islami)
HM	Movement of Holy Warriors (Harakat ul-Mujahedeen) (now IU)
HM	Party of Holy Warriors (Hezb-al-Mujahedeen)

HMA	International Movement of Holy Warriors (Harakat ul-Mujahedeen al-Alami)
HT	Party of Islamic Liberation (Hezb al-Tahrir)
HT	Al-Haq Tigers
I	Muslim Brotherhood (al-Ikhwan)
IBQ	Islambouli Brigades of al-Qa'ida
IGH	Islamic Group of Hackers (Al Sooraj Wing)
IJT	Islami Jamiat-e-Talaba
IP	Revenge of the People of Pakistan (Al-Intiqami al-Pakistani)
ISL	Islamic Students League
ISP	Islamic Students Pakistan (previously Lashkar-e-Janghvi)
ITP	Islami Tehrik e-Pakistan (formerly TJP)
IU	Insarul Ummah (new name of Harakat ul-Mujahideen)
J	The Almighty (Al-Jabbar)
J	Holy War (Al-Jihad)
J	Soldiers of God (Jund Allah, Jundullah Jandala)
JA	International Holy War (Al-Jihad al-Alami; external wing of LT)
JA	Group of the Defenders (Jama'at al-Ansar) (previously Harakat ul-Mujahedin)
JAHP –	Group of Followers of the Tradition Pakistan (Jama'at Ahle Hadith Pakistan)
JAM	Abdullah Mehsud Group (Jama'at Abdullah Mehsud)
JB	Bulgarian Group (Jama'at Bulgar) (group of foreign fighters in Waziristan)
JC	Holy War Council (Jihad Council)
JDP	Jama'at-ud-Daawa Pakistan (formerly LT, renamed Falah-e-Insaniyat)
JEM	Army of Mohammed (now KI) (Jaysh-e-Mohammed)
JF	Jund al-Fida
JF	Community of the Impoverished (Jama'at ul-Fuqra)
JF	Jama'at-ul-Furqan (Al-Qaeda-affiliated, previously JA)
JI	Islamic Group (Jama'at-e-Islami)
JJT	Monotheism and Holy War Group (Jamiat-i-Jihad wal Tawheed)
JKDFP	Jammu Kashmir Democratic Freedom Party
JKDLP	Jammu Kashmir Democratic Liberation Party
JKI	Jammu and Kashmir Ikhwan
JKIF	Jammu and Kashmir Islamic Front
JKNLA	Jammu Kashmir National Liberation Army
JLM	Lashkar-e-Jaysh-e-Mohammadiya
JM	Group of Warriors (Jama'at al-Mujahedeen)
JQJSA	Jaysh al-Qiba al-Jihadi al-Siri al-Alami
JSO	Jafferia Student Organisation (previously TJ)
JSQM	Long Live Sindh National Front (Jeay Sindh Qaumi Mahaz)
JSSF	Long Live Sindh Students Federation (Jeay Sindh Students Federation)
JT	Janghvi Tigers
JUI	Jama'at Ulema-e-Islami
JUP	Jama'at Ulema-e-Pakistan
KFM	Kashmir Freedom Movement
KIP	Servants of the Religion in Pakistan (Khaddam-al-Islam Pakistan) (previously JM)
KK	Karwan-e-Khalid
KN	Karwan-e-Nematullah
KNYF	Finality of the Prophethood Youth Force (Khatme e-Nabuyet Youth Force)
KSAA	Abdullah Azzam Martyrs Brigades (Kata'ib Shahid Abdullah Azzam)
LA	Warriors of Abdullah (Lashkar-e-Abdullah)
LI	Islamic Warriors (Lashkar-e-Islam)
LJ	Army of the Omnipotent Almighty (Lashkar-e-Jabbar)
LJ	Jhangvi Warriors (Lashkar-e-Jangvi)

LJ-LG	Lashkar-e-Jangvi (Lahori Group)
LJ-QG	Lashkar-e-Jangvi (Qari Group)
LK	Lashkar-e-Kahar (Lashkar-e-Qahar)
LO	Omar's Warriors (based on HJI and JA) (Lashkar-e-Omar/al-Qanoon)
LT	Lashkar-e-Toiba (The Army of the Pure, aka Lashkar-e-Tayyabba, Lashkar-e-Taiba, Lashkar-e-Tayyiba (now Jamaat-ud-Dawa)
M	Al-Mansuriya (Al-Mansurian)
MDI	Center for Call and Guidance (renamed Jamaatud Dawa) (Markaz-al-Dawat-Wal Irshad, Markaz Ud Daawa Wal Irshad)
MI	Mujahideen-e-Islam
MIP	Nation of Islam (Millat-e-Islamia Pakistan) (formerly SSP) (Sunni)
MK	Afghan Services Bureau (Maktab al-Khidamat, Maktab Khadamat al Mujahedin al-Arab)
MJAH	Center for the Group of Followers of the Tradition (Markazi Jamiat Ahle Hadith)
MLF	Mohmand Liberation Front
MMA	Mutahida Majlis-e-Amal
MJC	United Council of Holy War (Mutihadda Jihad Council)
MJK	Mujahedeen Jammu and Kashmir
MMI	Majlis-e-Murad-e-Islam
MQM	Mutahida Qaumi Movement
MQM-A	Mutahida Qaumi Movement – Afaq
MQM-H	Mutahida Qaumi Movement – Haqiqi
MR	Al-Medina Regiment (Kashmiri)
MUA	Muslim United Army
MUAS	Majlis-e-Ulema-e-Ahl-e-Sunnat
N	Al-Nawaz
N	Al-Nasireen (LT)
NMRPS	National Movement for the Restoration of Pakistani Sovereignty
OM	Al-Omar Warriors (Al-Omar Mujahedeen)
OSML	Organisation for Shi'ite Muslim Law
PAT	Pakistan Awami Tehrik
PFAR	Popular Front for Armed Resistance
PHC	Pakistan Hackerz Club
PI	Pasban-e-Islam (Sepah-e-Mohammed splinter)
PIC	Party of Islamic Clergy
PL	People's League
PML-N	Pakistan Muslim League – Nawaz Sharif Group
PPP(SB)	Pakistan People's Party (Shaheed Bhutto Group)
Q	The Law (Al-Qanun)
SIM	United Council of Holy Warriors (Shura Ittihad ul-Mujahideen; North Waziristan)
SKM	Save Kashmir Movement
SM	Defenders of the Messiah (Sepah-e-Mashiyah)
SM	Defenders of Muhammad (Sepah-e-Mohammed)
SS	Defenders of the Companions of the Prophet (now MIP) (Sepah-e-Suhaba)
SM	Sword of the Holy Warriors (Saif al-Mujahideen)
SPP	Sindhi Peoples Party
ST	Movement of the Sunni (Sunni Tehrik)
STPSF	Sindh Taraqqi Pasand Students Federation
SUC	Shia Ulema Council (previously Sepah-e-Mohammad) (Army of Mohammed, Pakistan))
TDS	Movement for the Defense of the Companions of the Prophet Mohammed (Tehrik-e-Difa-e-Sahaba)
TH	Righteousness Organisation (Tanzeem al-Haq)
THR	Movement for Defending the Honour of God (Tehrik-e-Hurmat-e-Rasool) (new name LT)

TI	Islamic Organisation (Tanzeem Islam)
TIUQ	Organisation of the Ulema of the Tribes
TJ	Conveying Group (Jama'at al-Tabligh)
TJ	Movement of the Shi'ah Twelvers Muslims (Tehrik-e-Jaferia) (now ITP)
TJ	Movement of Holy War (Tehrik-e-Jihad)
TJI	Revival of Islamic Holy War (Tajdid Jihad Islamiya)
TK	Students in Kashmir (Taliban-e-Kashmir)
TKAS	Movement of the Servants of the People of the Tradition (Tehrik-e-Khuddam-e-Ahl-e-Sunnat)
TMO	Movement of Mullah Omar (Tehrik-e-Mullah Omar)
TNBG	Thokar Niaz Baig Group
TNFJ	Tehrik-e Nifaz-e Fiqh-e-Jaafaria
TNRM	Front for the Protection of Prophet's Honour (Tahaffuz-e-Namoos-e-Risalat Mahaz)
TNSM	Movement for the Enforcement of Islamic Laws (Tehrik-e-Nifaz-e-Shariat-e-Muhammadi)
TQ	Tarjuman al-Qanun
TTM	Student Movement (Tehrik-e-Taliban)
TTP	Student Movement mainly in Pakistan (Tehrik-e-Taliban Pakistan)
TTP	Student Movement in Punjab (Tehrik-e-Taliban Punjab)
TTQA	Tehrik-e-Tahafuz Qibla Awal (LT)
UJC	United Jihad Council (umbrella organisation of 14 groups)
WFD	World Fantabulous Defacers (WFD)
Y	Yusufzais
ZI	Zarb-e-Islami
ZM	Zarb-e-Momin
313B	313 Brigades (special operations unit of AQ with participation of HMA, LJ, HJI, LT and JM)

Palestine (119 entries)

AA	Defenders of God (Ansar Allah)
AA	Partisans League (Asbat al-Ansar)
AA	al-Aqsa Association
AAB	Return Brigades (Al-Awda Brigades – aligned with Fatah)
ABIJ	Al-Aqsa Brigade of the Islamic Jihad
ADA	Al-Aqsa Dark Army (Al-Aqsa Sawad al Samra)
AF	Ansar Forces (military wing of the People's Party)
AI	Uprising (Al-Intifada)
AJ	Army of Holy War (Jaysh al-Jihad)
AJS	Al-Aqsa Popular Army (Al-Aqsa Jaysh Sha'bi)
AM	Army of Muhammed (Jaysh Mohammed)
AMB	Al-Aqsa Martyrs Brigade (military wing Fatah)
AMB-UC	Al-Aqsa Martyrs Brigade – Unified Command (dissident faction)
AMB-SAJU	Al-Aqsa Martyrs Brigade – the Shahid Ayman al-Jawdah Units (dissident faction)
AMJP	Armies of Monotheism and Holy War in Palestine (Jahafil al-Tawhid wal Jihad fi Filastin)
AMO	Abu Moussa Organisation
AMS	Abu Masoud Brigades (Kata'ib Abu Masoud)
AN	League of the Light (Asbat al-Nur)
ANO	Abu Nidal Organisation (Fatah Revolutionary Council) (Majlis al-Thawri al-Fatah)
ASY	Association of Sunni Youth
AU	Army of the Community of Believers (Ansar al-Ummah)
AW	Al-Amn al-Wiqa'i (security organ of Mohammed Dahlan)
A77	Asfah 77
BF	Badr Forces
BI	Allegiance to the Imam (Bai'at al-Imam)

BI	Brothers of Islam
BJC	Brigades of Justice and Clarity
BM	Brigades of the Mudjahedeen
BP	Black Panthers
DFLP	Democratic Front for the Liberation of Palestine (Jabhat al-Dimuqratiya lil-Tahrir Filistin)
DFLP/HF	Democratic Front for the Liberation of Palestine/Hawatmeh Faction (Al-Jabha al-Dimuqratiya li-Tahrir Filastin)
DFLP/ARF	Democratic Front for the Liberation of Palestine/Abd Rabbu Faction (Al-Jabha al-Dimuqratiya li-Tahrir Filastin)
DG	Dunniyah Group
F	Vanguard (Al-Fatah)
FAM	Al-Fatah-Abu Moussa (dissident faction)
FATAH	Movement for the Liberation of Palestine (Harakat al-Tahrir al-Filistini)
FB	Falcon Brigades
FBIS	Fatah Brigades of the Islamic Sword
FBL	Fatah-Black Leopards
FEF	Fatah Executive Force (Mohammed Dahlan militia)
FHH	The Knights of Justice and Rights (Al-Fursan al-Haq Wa al-Hadla)
FI	Uprising Vanguard (Fatah al-Intifadah)
FI	Islamic Vanguard (Fatah al-Islam) (Fatah splinter)
FIR	Islamic Vanguard Group in Palestine (Fatah al-Islam Group in the Land of Ribat)
FJO	Fighting Jewish Organisation
FNS	Front of National Salvation
FT	Vanguard Organisation (Fatah Tanzim)
F17	Force 17
GRPPTSR	Group of Redemption from the Party of Predication (Hamas) – The True Sons of Al-Rantissi
HAMAS	Islamic Resistance Movement (Harakat al-Muqawama al-Islamiya, Harkat el-Mukawama el Islamiya)
HBP	Hezbollah Brigades of Palestine
HCFINIO	High Committee Follow-up Intifada of Nationalist Islamic Organisations
HG	Hawari Group
HWJ	Holy Warriors of Jerusalem (Mujahideen of Beit al-Makdes)
IDQB	Izz-al-Deen al-Qassam Brigades (military branch of Hamas) (Aza-a-Din el Kassem Brigades)
IIB	International Islamic Brigade
IJ	Islamic Holy War (Islamic Jihad)
INRB	Islamic and National Resistance Brigades
INSP	Islamic National Salvation Party
IRLP	Islamic Revolution for the Liberation of Palestine
J	Soldiers of God (Jundullah)
J	Thunder (Jaljalat)
JAAHBM	Defenders of God in the Heart of Jerusalem (Jund Ansar Allah in the Heart of Beit al-Makdes)
JN	Group of the Light (Jama'at al-Nur)
JS	Soldiers of the Levant (Jund al-Sham)
JU	Army of the Community of Believers (Jaysh al-Ummah)
KAA	Abu Amar (Yasser Arafat) Brigades (Kata'ib Abu Amar) (split from Fatah)
KAI	Islamic Bloc (Al-Kutla al-Islamiya)
KIW	Ibn al-Walid Brigade (military wing of Arab Liberation Front) (Kata'ib Ibn al Walid)
KJM	Kata'ib al-Jihad al-Muqadis
KM	Death Brigades (Kata'ib al-Mawt)
KOK	Omar bin al-Khattab Brigades (Kata'ib Omar bin al-Khattab)
KSAA	Abdullah Azzam Martyrs Brigades (Kata'ib Shahid Abdullah Azzam) (part of Ma'asadat al-Mujahideen)

KSAAM	Abu-Ali Mustafa Martyrs Brigades (Kata'ib Shahid Abu Ali Mustafa) (military wing of PFLP)
KSAKH	Abdel Khader Husseini Martyrs Brigades (Kata'ib Shuhada Abdel Khader Husseini)
KSAR	Abu Rish Martyrs Brigades (Kata'ib Shahid Abu Rish)
KSJ	Jenin Martyrs Brigade (Kata'ib Shuhada Jenin)
KSOM	Omar al-Mukhtar Martyrs Brigades (Kata'ib Shahid Omar al-Mukhtar)
KTWJ	Monotheism and Holy War Brigades (Kata'ib Tawhid wal Jihad)
LARF	Lebanese Armed Military Faction
M	Al-Murabitoun (popular army of Hamas)
MM	Ma'sadat al-Mujahideen in Palestine
MB	Al-Mahamah Brigades (military wing of WIFLAM)
MCLSF	Mobility Company for the Liberation of Shebaa Farms
MKM	15 May Organisation (Munathamat Khamista'shar Mayo)
MY	Metzudat Yehuda
NH	Noblemen of Hamas
NRB	National Resistance Brigades (military wing of the DFLP)
NSDB	Al-Nasr Salah-al-Din Brigades (military wing of PRC) (An-Naser Salah ad-Din Brigades)
PAF	Popular Army and Front
PFLP	Popular Front for the Liberation of Palestine (Al-Jabhah al-Sha'biyyah li-Tahrir Filastin)
PFLP-GC	Popular Front for the Liberation of Palestine – General Command (Al-Jabhah al-Sha'biyyah li-Tahrir Filastin)
PFLP-SC	Popular Front for the Liberation of Palestine – Security Council (Al-Jabhah al-Sha'biyyah li-Tahrir Filastin)
PIJ	Palestinian Islamic Jihad-Shaqiqi Faction (Harakat al-Jihad al-Islami fi Filastin)
PIJ	Palestinian Islamic Jihad – Shalla Faction (Harakat al-Jihad al-Islami fi Filastin)
PLA	Palestine Liberation Army (Muna'mat al-Tahrir al-Filastiniyyat)
PLF	Palestinian Liberation Front – Abu Abbas Faction
PLF	Palestinian Liberation Front (Jabhat al-Tahrir al-Filastiniyyah)
PLF	Palestine Liberation Front – Abd al-Fatah Ghanim Faction
PLNA	Palestine National Liberation Army
PLO	Palestine Liberation Organisation (Munathamat al-Tahrir Filastiniyyat)
PPSF	Palestinian Popular Struggle Front (Jabhat al-Kifah al-Sha'bi al-Filastini)
PPSS	Palestinian Preventive Security Service
PRC	Popular Resistance Committees
PRFSS	Popular Resistance Force for Sabra and Shatila
PRCP	Palestine Revolutionary Communist Party
PSF	Preventive Security Force
QC	Jerusalem Committee (Al-Quds Committee)
QOBD	The Base Organisation of Holy War in the Border Districts
QOP	The Base Organisation of Holy War in Palestine (Al-Qaeda in the Land of Ribat)
S	Hussein Martyrs Brigades
SIR	Swords of Islamic Righteousness (Suf al-Haq Islamiya)
SQB	Jerusalem Brigades (military wing of Al-Jihad) (Saraya al-Quds)
SR	Storm Riders/Knights of the Tempest
SYA	Students of Yehiya Ayyash
T	Organisation (Tanzim)
TJBM	Monotheism and Holy War Group in Jerusalem (Tawhid and Jihad Group in Beit al-Maqdis)
13S	13th September

Panama (4 entries)

MLN29	November 29 National Liberation Movement (Movimento de Liberacion Nacional 29 de Noviembre)

OTCLAD	Omar Torrijos Commando for Latin American Dignity
SPF	Sovereign Panama Front
20DM	20th of December Movement

Paraguay (5 entries)

APP	Army of the Paraguayan People
FRPL	Lautaro Popular Rebel Forces
MAPU/L	United Popular Action Movement Lautaro Faction
MJL	Lautaro Youth Movement
PPL	Free Homeland Party (Partido Patria Libre)

Peru (22 entries)

CC	Christal Cartel
CCP	Farmers Confederation of Peru (Confederación Campesina del Peru)
CDP	Civilian Defense Patrols
CG	Colina Group
CR	Cacique Rivera Cartel
CRP	Revolutionary People's Commandos
E	Ethnocacerista
MAS-P	Movement toward Socialism – Peru
MIR	Movement of Revolutionary Left
MRTA	Tupac Amaru Revolutionary Movement (Movimiento Revolucionario Tupac Amaru)
PCP	Peruvian Communist Party (Partido Comunista del Peru)
PI/SR	Red Sun (Puka Inti, Sol Rojo)
PL	Puka Llacta
PUM	Mariatéquiste Unified Party
RC	Peasant Patrols (Rondas Campesinas)
RFC	Rodrigo Franco Command
RHR	People Who Kill Other People (Runa Huanuchiq Runa)
RMNP	Revolutionary Movement – New Peru
SL	Shining Path (Sendero Luminoso)
SR	Red Path (Sendero Rojo)
TLF	Tawanttinsuyo Liberation Front
TRC	Tio Rios Cartel

Philippines (48 entries)

ABB	Alex Boncayao Brigade
AJB	Abdurak Janjalani Brigade
AM	Ampatuan private militia (Maguindanao)
AS	Abu Sofia (kidnap for ransom gang)
ASG	Father of the Executioner, Bearer of the Sword (Abu Sayyaf Group, aka Harakat al-Islamiya)
ASG-UTG	Abu Sayyaf Group – Urban Terrorist Group
BI	New Rat (Bag-ong Ilaga)
BI	Return to Islam (Balik Islam)
BMA	Bangsa Moro Army
BMIAF	Bangsa Moro Islamic Armed Forces
BMLO	Bangsa Moro Liberation Organisation
CAA	Civilian Armed Auxiliary

CAFGUs	Citizen's Armed Forces Geographical Units
CPP	Communist Party of the Philippines
HI	Islamic Movement (Al-Harakatul al-Islamiyah)
I	Ilagas (see BI)
IPFA	Indigenous People's Federal Army
IWM	Islamic Worldwide Mission
JG	'Lost Command' (Jillang Gang)
JM	Army of the Mahdi (Jaysh al-Mahdi)
KBG	Kurateng Baleleng Gang
KM	Nationalist/Patriotic Youth (Kabataang Makabayan)
KPS	Soldiers of the Filipino People
KTF	Khalid Trinidad Force (Hukbong Khalid Trinidad)
MAC	Merardo Arce Command
MACC	Mindanao Allied Composite Christian Command
MCUC	Mindanao Christian Unified Command
MIAIP	Maehad Ibalaton al Arabi al Islami in the Philippines
MILF	Moro Islamic Liberation Front
MILF-LC	Moro Islamic Liberation Front – Lost Command
MIRG	Moro Islamic Reformist Group
MKOMPAC	Commission of Youth against Violence (Mujahideen KOMPAC)
MNLF	Moro National Liberation Front
LAI	Islamic Saturday Meeting (Likah Asept al-Islamiya)
LRC	Light Reaction Company
L9	Lucky 9
NCDA	New Christian Democratic Army
NDF	National Democratic Front of the Philippines
NPA	New People's Army
PKRG	Pentagon Kidnap for Ransom Group
RAM	Revolutionary National Alliance (Rebolusyonarong Alyansang Makabansa)
RHB	Communist Revolutionary Proletarian Army (Rebolusyonaryong Hukbong Bayan)
RSG	Red Scorpion Group
RSM	Rajah Solaiman Movement
TBK	Taong Bayan at Kawal
UDSS	Urban Death Squad Sabillah
UOB	Union of Overseas Bangsamoro
YOU	Young Officers Union

Poland (1 entry)

PM	Pruszków Mafia

Portugal (0 entries)

Qatar (4 entries)

BMJ	Brigade of the Media Jihad
JS	Soldiers of the Levant (Jund al Sham)
MQB	Mujahideen Qatar Brigades
QEO	Al-Qa'ida in the Emirates and Oman

Romania (0 entries)

Russia (109 entries)

A	Advet
A	Akopa
A	Arsmakowa
B	Bolschakowa
B	Bortsa
CA	Chusb–Allah
CM	Chechen Mafia
D	Derendjajewa
D	Derzhava
D	Djibu
D	Dolgoprudnenskaja
DC	Don Cossacks
DH	Dignity and Honour (veterans of KGB)
F	Frola
GDA	Great Don Army
GM	Grusinian Mafia
HTI	Islamic Party of Liberation (Hezb–ut–Tahrir al-Islami)
I	Ismailovskaya (powerful organised crime group)
IUAF	International Union of Armed Forces
J	Islamic Group (Jama'at or Dzhamaat)
K	Kadijewych
K	Katschanowa
K	Koschelewa
K	Krylowa
KG	Kazan Gang
KM	Krasnoyarsk Mafia
KRO	Congress of Russian Communities
LDP	Liberal Democratic Party
LEV	Law Enfocement Veterans
LG	Lithuanian Group
LW	Lonely Wolf
M	Mamedowa
M	Menjaly
M	Meschdunarodnaja
M	Mikerowa
MAIM	Movement against Illegal Immigration
MB	Miracle Boys
MBG	Movsar Bayayev Gang
MC	Mad Crowd
MG	Matsutskinskaya Group
MG	Most Group
MG	Muzlokandov's Gang
MO	Meschdunarodnaja OPG
MSSU	Military–Strong State Union (former military/intelligence officials)
MV	Mertvaya Voda
N	Naumowa
NBP	National Bolshevik Party

NDP	National Democratic Party
NE	Nogisnko–Elektrostalskaja
NKM	Vanguard of the Red Youth
NRA	New Revolutionary Alternative
NRAF	National Revolutionary Action Front
NRPR	National Republican Party of Russia
NSF	National Sports Foundation
NSU	National Socialist Union
O	Orlowa
P	Memory (Pamyat)
P	Podolskaja/Lalakina
P	Podolsk (organized crime syndicate)
P	Puschkinskaja
PARM	Peter Alexeev Resistance Movement
PSP-YF	People's Social Party – Youth Front
R	Revival
R	Rublewa
RANU	Russian All National Union
RBF	Russian Border Guard Force
RFAWI	Russian Fund for Invalids of the War in Afghanistan
RG	Red Guerillas
RK	Russian Knight
RLPB	Russian League for Professional Boxers
RM	Russian Mafia (generic)
RMCRSFSR	Revolutionary Military Council of the Russian Soviet Federative Socialist Republic
RNBP	Russian National Bolshevist Party
RNRC	Russian National Resistance Center
RNS	Russian National Union (Russky Natsionalny Sobor)
RNU	Russian National Unity
RP	Russian Party
RR	Russian Republic
RRP	Right Radical Party
S	Satanists
S	Saturn
S	Schelkowskaja
S	Schirokowa
S	Shield (Sjtsit)
S	Scythian (Skif)
S	Skinheads
S	Schmajenka
S	Solnzevskaya
S	Solntsevo Gang
S	Sportsmeny
SI	Sword of Islam
SPAS	Salvation
SS	Selenogradskaja–Schodsnenskaja
S88	Shultz 88
S88	Sieg 88 (right-wing extremists)
T	Tobolsk cell
TG	Tambovskaya Gang
UC	Union of Cossacks
UCG	Uralmash Crime Gang

UJ	Ulyanovsk Jamaat
UM	Uralmash Mafia
URW	Union of Revolutionary Writers
VvZ	Vori v Zakone
WPRA	Workers-Peasants Red Army
WS	Wahhabis Sect
W	Werchuschka
Z	Zentrowaja
Z	Zwetmet
Z	Zyganjata

Bashkortostan (4 entries)

BYL	Bashkir Youth League
FNGS	Followers of Bediuzzaman Nursi, Fetullah Gulen Nursi and Suleymanis
GW	Grey Wolves
MB	Muslim Brothers

Chechnya (15 entries)

B	Guerrillas (Boïeviki)
CPNC	Confederation of the Peoples of the North Caucasus
CV	Black Widows (Chyornyye Vdovy)
EC	Emirate of the Caucasus (Imarat Kavkaz)
IAK	Islamic Army of the Caucasus
IB	Islambuli Brigades (Liwa Haled al-Islambuli, Haled Islambuli Brigade, Islam Bouli Brigades)
GM	Followers of the Holy War (Gazotan-Murdash)
IIPB	Islamic International Peacekeeping Brigade
J	Islamic group (Jama'at or Dzhamaat)
K	Kadyrovstsy
MRPAWS	Movement of Radical Political Activities 'White Shadows'
MSB	Mujahideen Services Bureau
MSCM	Supreme Military Majlisul ul-Shura of United Mujahedin of the Caucasus
RSRSBCM	Riyadus-Salikhin Reconnaissance and Sabotage Battalion of Chechen Martyrs
SPIR	Special Purpose Islamic Regiment

Kartachai-Cherkessia (2 entries)

ICA	International Cherkess Association
JKC	Jama'at Karachai-Cherkessia

Dagestan (14 entries)

CPI&D	Congress of Peoples of Ichkeria and Dagestan
DLA	Dagestan Liberation Army
I	Righteous Mujahedeen of Dagestan (Istikama)
J	Paradise Group (Jama'at Dzhenet)
JA	Soldiers of God (Jund Allah)
JAD	Jihad Army of Dagestan
JC	Jama'at Chamilkala
JD	Jama'at Derbent

JG	Jama'at Gimny
JK	Jama'at Karaboudahkent
JS	Dagestan Jama'at 'Shariat' (Shariah Jama'at) (Jama'at al-Sharia)
JS	Jama'at Sergokala
KJ	Khasavyurt Jama'at
SA	Sword of God (Saif Allah)

Ingushetia (7 entries)

CFIS	Caucasus Front Ingush Sector
IJS	Ingush Jama'at Shariat
JA	Silence Group (Jama'at Amanat)
JG	Jama'at Galgaitche
JK	Jama'at Khalifate
JT	Jama'at Taliban
SOGS	Special Operations Group Sharia

Kabardino-Balkaria (2 entries)

JYMKB	Jama'at Yarmuk. Mujahedeen of Kabardino-Balkaria
MCKBY	Military Council of Kabardino-Balkaria Yarmuk

Ossetia (1 entry)

JKK	Power Brigades (Jama'at Kata'ib al-Khoul)

Tatarstan (3 entries)

BJ	Bulghar Jama'at
I	Ittifak
KC	Kazan Community

Rwanda (18 entries)

A	Fighters (Abatabazi)
A	Amasu
ALIR	Liberation Army of Rwanda (Armée de libération du Rwanda)
AS	Army of the Savior (Armée de Sauveur)
CDR	Coalition for the Defense of the Republic
FCD	Fighting Forces for Democracy and Human Rights in Rwanda (Forces combattant pour la démocratie et les droits de l'hommes au Rwanda)
FDLR	Democratic Forces for the Liberation of Rwanda (Forces démocratiques pour la libération du Rwanda)
FDR	Resistance Forces for Democracy (Forces de résistance pour la démocratie)
FPR	Rwanda Patriotic Front (Front patriotique rwandais)
FRI	Front of Internal Resistance
I	Those Who Stand Together (Interahamwe)
I	Inkontanyi
IM	Single-Minded Ones, Those Who Have the Same Goal (Impuza Mugambi)
LDU	Lightly Armed Civilian Local Defense Units
PALIR	Armed People of the Liberation of Rwanda (Peuple en armes pour la libération du Rwanda)

RDR	Rally for the Return of Democracy in Rwanda (Rassemblement pour le retour de la démocratie au Rwanda)
RPA	Rwanda Patriotic Army
ZN	Zero Network (Réseau Zéro)

Saudi Arabia (38 entries)

AA	Defenders of God (Ansar Allah)
ACH	Alliance of Clergymen of Hijaz
ARC	Advice and Reformation Committee (Hay'at al-Nasiha wal-Islah)
ASAP	Arab Socialist Action Party
BMAAH	Brigades of the Martyr Abdallah al-Hudhaifi (Sariyat ash-Shahid Abdallah al-Hudhaifi)
BMAAS	Brigade of the Martyr Abu Anas ash-Shami (Sariyat ash-Shahid Abu Anas ash-Shami)
BMNR	Brigade of the Martyr Nasir al-Rashid (Sariyat ash-Shahid Nasir al-Rashid)
BR	Blessed Relief
CDLR	Committee for the Defense of Legitimate Rights in Saudi Arabia
FOMP	Free Officers Movement of the Peninsula
HI	Reform Movement (Al-Harakat al-Islahiyya)
HS	Al-Haramayn al-Sharifayn (charity)
HT	Liberation Party (Hezb al-Tahrir)
IIRO	International Islamic Relief Organisation (charity)
IMC	Islamic Movement for Change
IR	Islamic Relief
IU	Islamic Union (al-Ittihad al-Islami)
JAP	Jihad in the Arabian Peninsula
JM	Jihadi Muwahhidin
JMC	Jaafar Marzuk Chueikhat
KF	Fallujah Brigades (Katibat al-Fallujah)
KH	Brigade of the Two Holy Mosques in the Arabian Peninsula (Kata'ib al-Haramayn)
KQ	Jerusalem Brigades (Katibat al-Quds)
KSOL	Brigades of Sheikh Osama bin Laden (Katibat Sheikh Osama bin Laden)
KM	Faith Brigades (Katibat al-Mu'min)
M	Mutaweeb
M	Mutawain
OIRAP	Organisation of Islamic Revolution in the Arab Peninsula
PGH	Party of God in Hijaz (Saudi Hezbollah)
Q	The Base (Al-Qaeda)
QAP	Al-Qaeda in the Arabian Peninsula
S	Fundamentalists (Salafyeen)
SF	SAR Foundation (Virginia, USA) (charity)
SKO	Sanabel al-Khayr Organisation (charity)
TG	Tigers of the Gulf
TQJJA	The Base Organisation of Holy War on the Arabian Peninsula (Tanzim Qa'idat al-Jihad fi Jazirat al-Arabiya)
TS	Victorious Sect (Al-Taa'efa al-Mansourah)
WAMY	World Assembly of Muslim Youth (charity)
WIL	World Islamic League

Senegal (6 entries)

A	Atika (Combatant – armed branch of the MFDC; see ARS)
ARS	Casamanche Resistance Army (Armée de résistance Casamance)
JI	Islamic Group (Jammatoul' Islamiya)
JIR	Jamaatu Ibadu Rahmane Islamic Society
MFDC	Movement of the Democratic Forces of Casamanche (Mouvement des forces démocratiques de la Casamance)
MWM	Men and Women Who Fight for the Truth (Moustarchindia wal Moustarchidati (aka Moustarchadines)

Serbia (23 entries)

BE	Black Eagles
BM	Belgrade Mafia
CR	The Black Hand (Crna Ruka)
F	Falcons
NH	New Hope (Novada Nada)
NSA	Nationalist Salvation Association (Savez Nazionalista Serbije)
NSR	National Serbian Renaissance
O	Obraz
RB	Red Berets (aka Frenki Boys; Special Operations Unit)
RR	Red Rose Muslim Organisation
S	Spider (Pauk)
SA	Serbian Army
SDG	Serb Voluntary Guard (Srpska Dobrovoljackagarda)
SDM	Serbian Defense Movement
SJF	Sveti Justin Filosof
SLA	Serbian Liberation Army
SNC	Serbian National Council
SPO	Serbian Patriotic Organisation
SRS	Serbian Radical Party
SSJ	Serbian Unity Party
SVG	Serb Voluntary Guard (aka Arkan Tigers)
UCPMB	Liberation Army of Presevo, Medvedja, and Bujanovac
ZG	Zemun Group (Zemunski)

Seychelles (0 entries)

Sierra Leone (11 entries)

AFRC	Armed Forces Revolutionary Council
CDF	Civil Defense Force
KM	Kamajor Militia
MDC	Movement for Democratic Change
NAFORD	National Front for the Restoration of Democracy
RSLMF	Revolutionary Sierra Leone Military Forces
RUF	Revolutionary Unified Front
RUF-I	Independent RUF
S	Sobels
TF	Tamaboro (juju) Fighters
WSB	West Side Boys

Singapore (1 entry)

JI   Islamic Congregation (Jemaah Islamiah)

Slovakia (0 entries)

Slovenia (0 entries)

Somalia (67 entries)

AAS	Asra Army of Somalia
ADS	Army of Difficulty in Somalia (Army of Adversity) (part of Shabaab) (Jaysh al-Asra fi Somal)
AIAI	Islamic Unity (Al-Ittihad al-Islamiyya)
ARPCT	Alliance for the Restoration of Peace and Counter-Terrorism
ARS	Alliance for the Re-liberation of Somalia (successor of IMI)
AS	Ansar al-Sunna
ASWJ	Followers of the Traditions of the Prophet (Ahlu Sunnah Wal Jama'ah)
ATI	Al-Tagammu al-Islami
ATA	Anti-Terrorism Alliance
BHM	Barre Hiiraale Militia
C	The Corporation (pirates)
DFSS	Democratic Front for the Salvation of Somalia
DI	Descendants of the Prophet Isma'il (Shabaab faction) (Duiriyatu Isma'il)
DSA	Digil Salvation Army
FSB	Friends of Somali Brigades
HI	Reform Movement (Harakat al-Islah)
HI	Islamic Party (coalition of four insurgent factions) (Hezbul al-Islam)
HJ	Movement of Holy War (Harakat ul-Jihad)
HMSBH	Popular Resistance Movement in the Land of the Two Migrations (Al-Harakat al-Maqawamah al-Sha'biyah fi al-Bilad al-Hijratayn)
HS	Youth Party (Hezb al-Shabaab)
HSM	Young Mujahideen Movement (Harakat al-Shabaab al-Mujahideen)
IMI	Islamic Courts Union (Ittihad al-Mahakim al-Islamiyyah)
ISS	Islamic State of the Central Regions of Somalia
IUS	Islamic Union of Fundamentalists (Islam Union Sellefia)
JHD	Jama'at Humat al-Din
JI	Islamic Front (Jabhat al-Islamiya)
JI	Islamic Group (Al-Jama'at al-Islamiya)
JIKS	Jama'at al-I'tisam bil Kitabi wa'l Sunna
JIS	Jama'at Ihya al-Sunna
JM	Group of Muslims (Jama'at al-Muslimuun)
JT	Conveying Group (Jama'at al-Tabligh)
JU	Army of Suffering (Jaysh al-Usrah)
JVA	Juba Valley Alliance
JWI	Jama'at al-Wifaq al-Islami
M	Mooryaan
MA	Anole Camp (Mu'askar Anole)
MB	Muslim Brotherhood (Al-Ikhwan al-Muslimun)
MI	Milati Ibrahim (Path of Ibrahim; Shabaab faction)
MRK	Ras Kamboni Camp (Mu'askar Ras Kamboni)
MUIS	Assembly of Islamic Scholars of Somalia (Majma Ulimadda Islaamka ee Soomaaliya)

N	Renaissance (Al-Nahdah)
NRFLS	National Resistance Front for the Liberation of Somalia
PM	Puntland Militias
RRA	Rahanweyn Resistance Army
SCIC	Supreme Council of Islamic Courts
SDA	Somali Democratic Alliance
SDM	Somali Democratic Movement
SIF	Somali Islamic Front (Jabhad al-Islamiya)
SJ	New Fundamentalists (Salafiya Jadiida)
SM	Al-Sunna al-Majam
SM	Somali Mujahidin
SNA	Somali National Alliance
SNF	Somali National Front
SNM	Somali National Movement
SPF	Somali Patriotic Front
SPM	Somali Patrotic Movement
SSDF	Somali Salvation and Democratic Front
SSF	Somali Salvation Front
TH	Flight from Sin and Atonement (Takfir wa'l Hijrah)
UIC	Union of Islamic Courts
USC	United Somali Congress
USC-MF	United Somali Congress – Ali Mahdi Faction
USC-PM	United Somali Congress – Patriotic Movement
UWSLF	United Western Somali Liberation Front
VP	Victory Pioneers Militia (Gullwadayaal)
WS	Wahdat al-Shabaab

South Africa (88 entries)

A	Amabutho (vigilantes)
AA	Ama Afrika (vigilantes)
AG	Americans Gang
AHS	Africa Hinterland Safari
AM	Afrikana Monarchiste
ANC	African National Congress (ruling party)
ANLA	Azanian National Liberation Army
APF	Afrikaner People's Front
APLA	Azanian People's Liberation Army
AS	Ama Sinyora Gang (vigilantes)
AV	Afrikaner Volksfront
AZAPO	Azanian People's Organisation
AZAYO	Azanian Youth Organisation
AWB	African Resistance Movement (Afrikaner Weerstands Beweging)
B	Farmer's Power (Boeremag)
BAT	Boer Attack Force (Boere Aanvalstroepe)
BC	Black Cats (vigilantes)
BK	Farmers Commandos (Boere Kommandos)
BRA	Boer Republican Army
BRM	Boer Resistance Movement
BV	White Security (Blanke Veiligheid)
BVB	Farmers Liberation Movement (Boeren vrijheids beweging)
BWB	White Resistance Movemnet (Blanke weerstands beweging)

BWB	Farmers Resistance Movement (Boereweerstands Beweging)
CCB	Civil Cooperation Bureau
CoG	Committee of Generals
CSAS	Congress of South African Students
C10	C-10 Unit
DAAD	Direct Action Against Drugs
DB	Dixie Boys Gang
DFN	Desai Family Network
FG	Fast Guns
FJJTS	Foundation of Jihad at the Junction of the Two Seas
FSF	Foundation for the Survival of Freedom
GF	G-Force (linked to PAGAD)
GFF	Gauteng Freedom Front
H	Hammer
HLG	Hard Livings Gang
IFP	Inkatha Freedom Party
IHB	Imam Haroon Brigades
ISU	Internal Stability Unit
IUC	Islamic Unity Convention
K	Kekanas (vigilantes)
K	Koevoet
KKK	Ku Klux Klan
M	Mbokodo (vigilantes)
M	Memesi (vigilantes)
MG	Mongrel Gang
MGO	Muslims against Global Oppression
MK	Spear of the Nation (Umkhonto We Sizwe, linked to the ANC)
MM	Colours of the Leopard (Mapogo-a-Mathamaga)
MP	Mabangalala Pagathis ('A'-team) (vigilantes)
MPAG	Mitchell's Plain American Gang
MUFC	Mandela United Football Club
NB	Naughty Boys Gang
NFC	National Consultative Forum
NW	National Warriors
OB	Orde Boerevolk (Order of Farmers Folks)
P	The Patriots
PAC	Pan African Congress
PAGAD	People against Gangsterism and Drugs
PBK	Pretoria Boere Kommandos
PF	Patriotic Front
Q	Al-Qibla (Direction Mecca)
S	Scorpions
SB	Sexy Boys (gang)
SDM	Self Defense Movement
SDU	Self Defence Units
SF	Stallard Foundation
TF	Third Force
TG	Toaster Gang (vigilantes)
TMG	Three Million Gang (vigilantes)
UNG	Umfela Ndawonge Group
UWUSA	United Workers Union of South Africa
V	People's Unity Committee (Volkseenheidscomité)

V	The People's Doctrine (Volksleer)
V	The People (Die Volk)
V	The Fist (Die Vuis)
VG	Varados Gang
VU	Vlakplaas Unit
W	White Clothes (Witdoeke) (vigilantes)
WAM	World Apartheid Movement
WVB	White Liberation Movement (Witte Vrijheidsbeweging)
WW	White Wolf (Wit Wolf)
Y	Ystergarde
Z-QI	Z-Squad Incorporated
32BB	32nd Buffalo Battalion

Spain (18 entries)

A	Anarchists
AHMB	Abu Hafs al-Masri Brigades
ANA	Abu Nayaf al-Afghani
ASF	Anti-System Front
CSCA	Commitee for Solidarity with the Arab Cause
DT	Conveying Group (Al-Da'awa wa al-Tabligh)
ETA	Basque Fatherland and Freedom (Euskadi ta Askatasuna)
GRAPO	First of October Antifascist Resistance Groups (Grupos de Resistencia Antifascista Primero de Octubre)
HAIKA	Raise Up (Haika)
J	Jarrai
KAS	Patriotic Socialist Coordinator (Koordinadora Abertzale Sozialista)
MM	Martyrs for Morocco (Martyrs pour le Maroc)
RP	Revolutionary Perspective
S	Segii
SB	Satan Brigades (Kata'ib Shaytan)
SCP-R	Spanish Communist Party – Reconstructed
TL	Free Land (Terra Lliure)
TTA	Organisation for the Liberation of Andalusia (Tanzim Tahrir al-Andalus)

Sri Lanka (23 entries)

BST	Black Sea Tigers
EG	Ellalan Group
EPRLF	Eelam People's Revolutionary Liberation Front
EROS	Eelam Revolutionary Organisation of Students
FB	Freedom Birds
HFZRLF	High Security Zone Residents' Liberation Force
IBT	Internet Black Tigers
JVP	Popular Liberation Front (Janetha Vimukhti Peramuna)
KF	Karuna Faction (dissident LTTE faction)
LTTE	Liberation Tigers of Tamil Eelam
MG	Mohan Group
MHG	Muslim Home Guards
MULF	Muslim United Liberation Front
NMAT	National Movement against Terrorism
PG	Pistol Gang

PLOTE	People's Liberation Organisation of Tamil Eelam
REO	Revolutionary Eelam Organisation
RG	Rasheek Group, Razeek Group
RPF	Rising People's Force
TELO	Tamil Eelam Liberation Organisation
TULF	Tamil United Liberation Front
WTA	World Tamil Organisation
WTM	World Tamil Movement

Sudan (64 entries)

AM	Army of Muhammad (Jaysh Mohammed)
AQBWN	Al-Qaeda (The Base) Organisation of Holy War in the Land between the Blue and White Niles
AQSA	Al-Qaeda in Sudan and Africa
AS	Fundamentalists (Al-Salafiyyun)
BC	Beja Congress – Armed Wing
BCF	Beja Congress Forces
BB	Blood Brigades
BM	Baggaras Militia
BM	Bechir Militia
DJMSFI	Darfur Jihad Movement for Stopping the Foreign Involvement
DJO	Darfur Holy War Organisation (Darfur Jihad Organisation)
DRFF	Democratic Revolutionary Force Front
EDF	Equatorial Defense Forces
EF	Eastern Front (coalition of BC, Free Lions Movement of Eastern Sudan, Justice and Equality Movement)
FLA	Falcons for the Liberation of Africa
FLM	Free Lions Movement of Eastern Sudan
FP	Forces for Peace (militia)
FWM	Free Will Movement
G19	G-19 (SLA splinter)
JAS	Jam'iya Ansar al-Sudaniya
JASM	Jama'at Ansar al-Sunnah al-Muhammadiyyah
JAT	Group of Defenders of Monotheism (Ansar al-Tawhid, Jama'a Ansar al-Tawhid)
JIKS	Jama'at al-I'tisam bil-Kitab wal-Sunnah
JKWSK	Jami'at al-Kitabah Wal-Sunnah al-Khayriyyah
JM	Janjaweed Militias
LC	Legitimate Command
LJS	Lions of Holy War in Sudan
JEM	Justice and Equality Movement (Al-Harakat al-Adl wa-l-Masawat as-Sudaniya)
M	Al-Musulman
MFU	Muslim Forces' Union (Itahaad Qiaa Muslimeen)
MM	Mawlid Militia
MM	Murahalin (Marhalin, Marllen, Murahaleen) militia (combination of SAF soldiers, retired SAF soldiers and tribal Islamic extremists)
NDA	National Democratic Alliance
NIF	National Islamic Front
NMRD	National Movement for Reform and Development
NRFD	National Redemption Front Darfur
NSB	New Sudan Brigade
PCSS	Popular Committees for Surveillance and Services
PDF	Popular Defense Forces

PFRD	Popular Force for Rights and Democracy
PFT	Popular Forces Troops
PRM	Patriotic Resistance Movement
SAF	Sudan Alliance Forces
SCP	Sudanese Communist Party
SFDA	Sudan Federal Democratic Alliance (At-Tahalif al-Federaliya ad-Dimuqrati as-Sudan)
SLA	Sudan Liberation Army (Al-Jaysh al-Tahrir as-Sudan)
SLM	Sudan Liberation Movement (Al-Harakat al-Tahrir as-Sudan)
SNMEM	Sudanese National Movement for the Eradication of Marginalisation
SPLA	Sudanese People's Liberation Army
SSDF	Southern Sudan Defense Force
SSIA	South Sudan Independent Army
SSIM/A	Southern Sudan Independence Movement
SSLM	Southern Sudan Liberation Movement
SSUA	Southern Sudan United Army (pro-government militia)
ST	Sufi Tijaniyyah sect
TH	Flight from Sin and Atonement (Takfir wal Hijra)
TM	Toposa Militia
UDSF	United Democratic Salvation Front
UFDD	Union of Forces for Democracy and Development
UFLD	United Front for the Liberation of Development
ULA	Ummah Liberation Army
UP	Umma Party (Military Wing)
URFWS	United Revolutionary Forces of West Sudan (merger of SLM & JEM)

Suriname (11 entries)

A	Angrula
DA	Dead or Alive
DUS	Democratic Union Suriname (Democratische Unie Suriname)
GLDP	General Liberation and Development Party
JC	Jungle Commando
MBNLM	Mandela Bush Negro Liberation Movement
NLU	National Liberation Union
RAF	Revolutionary Action Front
SK	Suri Cartel
SLF	Surinam Liberation Front
TA	Tucajana Amazonica

Swaziland (0 entries)

Sweden (1 entry)

GI	Global Intifada

Switzerland (2 entries)

FMAJ	Freedom for Mumia Abu Jamal
FRS	For a Revolutionary Perspective

Syria (15 entries)

G	Al-Gharra
CLGH	Committees for the Liberation of the Heights of Golan
FLG	Front for the Liberation of the Golan Heights
ITM	Islamic Tawheed Movement
JTJ	Monotheism and Holy War Group (Jama'at al-Tawhid wa al-Jihad)
MB	Muslim Brotherhood
MIL	Movement for Islamic Liberation
MNSR	Men of National Syrian Resistance
NI	Victory of Islam (Nasrat al-Islam)
Q	Al-Quds
RS	Foreigners in Syria (Rubaa al-Sham)
S	Lightning (Al-Saiqa)
SB	Al-Sadr Brigades
TJSJT	Organisation of the Soldiers of the Levant for Jihad and Monotheism (Tanzim Jund al-Sham lil-Jihad wal- Tawhid)
TM	Combatant Vanguard (al-Tali'ah al-Muqatilah)

Taiwan (4 entries)

BU	Bamboo Union (triad)
CW	Celestial Way (triad)
FST	Four Seas (triad)
HJA	Heavenly Justice Alliance (triad)

Tajikistan (6 entries)

FB	Faizali Brigade
IMT	Islamic Movement of Tajikistan
IRP	Islamic Renaissance Party
MB	Mahmoud Brigade
RSG	Rizvon Sadirov's Group
UTO	United Tajik Opposition (aka Baya't)

Tanzania (6 entries)

AA	Defenders of God (Ansar Allah)
BG	Blue Guard (youth wing of the Civic United Front)
BM	Black Mamba
S	Sungusungu (neighborhood and village anti-crime group)
UM	Association of Revival and Propagation of the Islamic Faith (Uamsho na Mihadhara)
WG	White Guard (youth wing of the Civic United Front)

Thailand (21 entries)

BERSATU	United Front for the Independence of Pattani
BRN	National Revolutionary Front (Barisan Revolusi Nasional)
BRN-C	National Revolutionary Front – Coordinate
CPM	Communist Party of Malaya
CPT	Communist Party of Thailand

GMIP	Pattani Islamic Mujahideen Movement (Gerakan Mujahidin Islam Pattani)
IPM	Islamic Warriors of Pattani State (Islam Pattani Mujahedeen)
JS	Community of Fundamentalists (Jemaah Salafiya)
MDG	Muslimin Dalowithaya Group
MP	Mujahedin Palakom
MSCSA	Mujahideen Shura Council in Southeast Asia
NEW PULO	New Pattani United Liberation Organisation
PC	People's Council
PLF	Pattani Liberation Front
PULO	Pattani United Liberation Organisation
RC	Revolutionary Council
RKK	Small Patrol Group (Ronda Kumpulan Kecil)
RM	Legion of the Fighters of God (Rabitat-ul-Mujahedin)
SW	Syaheed Warriors
SWV	South Warriors of Valaya
YLP	Young Liberators of Pattani

Togo (1 entry)

CR	Committee for Renewal

Trinidad and Tobago (3 entries)

JKM	Holy War against the Disbelievers and the Hypocrites (Jihad ul-Kuffari wal-Munafiqeen)
JM	Islamic group (Jama'at al-Muslimeen)
TIRM	Trinidad Islamic Resistance Movement

Tunisia (10 entries)

HII	Islamic Tendency Movement (Harakat al-Ittijah al-Islami)
HN	Renaissance Movement/Party (Harakat an-Nahda, Hezb Annadah)
HTI	Islamic Liberation Party (Hezb al-Tahrir al-Islami)
IALHS	Islamic Army for the Liberation of the Holy Sites
JAIG-UNB	Jihadist Army of Islam Group – Uqba bin Nafi' Brigade
PFTP	Partisans of Fundamentalism and the Tradition of the Prophet
SAIF	Soldiers of Assan Ibn al-Fourat
TFG	Tunisian Fighting (or Combat) Group (Groupe Combattant Tunisien, Jama'a Combattante Tunisienne)
TIF	Tunisian Islamic Front
ZG	Zarzis Group (aka Prophet Brigades)

Turkey (122 entries)

A	Aczmendi Sect
ACO	Agar-Ciller Organisation
AFIS	Anatolian Federal Islamic State
AGA	Atabeys Guerrilla Army (ultra-nationalist)
AKP	Justice and Development Party (Adelet ve Kalkinma Partisi)
ALPK	Army for the Liberation of the People of Kurdistan
AMGT	Avrupa Millî Görüş Teşkilatları
ARGK	People's Liberation Army of Kurdistan

ASALA	Armenian Secret Army for the Liberation of Armenia
ATIF	European Federation of Turkish Workers
AUHK	Activity Union of Haki Karaer
AULM	Activity Union of Lice Martyrs
AYRB	APO's Youth Revenge Brigades
B	Grey Wolves (Bozkurtlar)
BCB	Bolu Commando Brigade
BI	Allegiance to the Imam (Baya't al-Imam)
C	Ceysullah
CDA	Cehennemin Dibi Arkadaşlar
CDF	Civil Defence Force
CH	Holy War Movement (Cihat Hareketi)
CS	Caliphate's State (Association of Islamic Groups and Communities)
CWM	Communist Workers Movement
DEHAP	Democratic People's Party (successor to HADEP)
DEM-GENC	Democratic Youth Confederation (Demokratik Gençlik Konfederasyonu)
DGH	Duzce Group of Hezbullah
DHKP/C	Revolutionary People's Liberation Party/Front (Devrimci Halk Kurtuluş Partisi/Cephesi)
DIFD	Federation of Revolutionary Workers' Association
DK	Revolutionary Headquarters/Command (Devrimci Karargah)
DRS	Divine Rights Sect
DS	Revolutionary Left (Devrimci Sol)
E	Organisation (Ergenekon) (ultra-nationalist)
ERNK	National Liberation Front of Kurdistan
FAK	Kurdistan Freedom Guards (Fedaiye Azadiye Kurdistan)
FI	Fire of Islam
GPA	Guards of the President of APO
HADEP	People's Democratic Party (Halkın Demokrasi Partisi)
HPG	People's Defence Forces (Hêzên Parastina Gel)
HTI	Party of Islamic Liberation (Hezb-ut-Tahrir al-Islami)
IA	Islamic Action
IB	Union of Imams (İmamlar Birliği)
IBDA/C	Islamic Great Eastern Raiders Front (İslami Büyük Doğu Akıncıları Cephesi, aka Jama'at Ibdaj)
ICM	Islamic Community Movement
IGMG	Community of Islam National View Organisation
IM	Islamic Movement
IMP	Islamic Movement Process
IPT	Islamic Party of Turkistan
IRMK	Islamic Revolution Movement of Kurdistan
JAA	Jama'at Asadi Afandi
JAK	Jama'at Arab Kindi
JB	Jama'at Bughazichi
JI	Jama'at Iqtibas
JP	Jama'at Pinar
JR	Jama'at Risala
JS	Jama'at Saf
J16O	June 16 Organisation
K	Karagumrük
KADEK	Congress for Freedom and Democracy in Kurdistan
KDC	Kurdistan People's Congress
KH	Kurdish Hezbollah

KIUP	Kurdish Islamic Unity Party
KM	Kaplan Movement/Caliphate State (Islamist)
KOMALA	Revolutionary Organisation of the Toiling People of Kurdistan
KONGRA-GEL	People's Congress of Kurdistan
KOS-TAK	Kurdistan Freedom Hawks (Kurdistan Özgörlök Sahinleri/Teyrebazen Azadiya Kurdistan)
KPU	Kurdish Patriotic Union
KRB	Kurdish Revenge Brigade
KSP	Kurdish Socialist Party
MAHMB	Martyr Abul Hafız Misri Battalion
MCSG	Mahir Cayan Suicide Group
MHP	Turkish Nationalist Movement Party (mother party of the Grey Wolves in Europe) (Milliyetçi Hareket Partisi)
MG	Milli Görüs
MIT	Milli İstiharat Teskilatı
MKP	Maoist Communist Party
MLAPU	Marxist-Leninist Armed Propaganda Unit
MLKP	Marxist-Leninist Communist Party
MTIB	Milliyetçi Türk İşçileri Birliği (former umbrella organisation of Grey Wolves in Germany)
NA	Nizam-i-Alem (Islamist)
NKRT	Nationalist Kurdish Revenge Teams
OMIR	Organisation of the Mujahedeen of the Islamic Revolution
PKK	Kurdistan Workers' Party
PKK-V	Kurdistan Workers' Party – Vejine
PLAK	People's Liberation Army of Kurdistan
PRK-R	Liberation Party of Kurdistan-Rizgari (Partîya Rizharîya Kurdistan)
RBO	Revolutionary Barracks Organisation
RFA	Revenge Falcons of APO
RP	Refah Part (Refah Partisi)
SF	Sharia Fighters (Seriat Savascilari)
SF	Serhat Falcons
SL	Society of the Light
SP	Felicity Party (Saadet Partisi) (Islamist)
ST	Jerusalem Army (Selam Tevhid)
T	Muslim Youth (Tohum)
TECAK	Kurdistan Free Youth Movement
TH	Turkish Hezbollah
TIJ	Turkish Islamic Jihad
TIKKO	Turkish Workers' and Peasants' Liberation Army
TKEP/L	Communist Labour Party of Turkey/Leninist (Türkiye Komünist Emek Partisi/Leninist)
TKP/ML	Turkish Communist Party/Marxist Leninist (Türkiye Komunist Partisi/Marksist-Leninist-Turkiye Köylü Kurtuluş Ordusu)
TM	Victorious Sect (Al-Ta'ifah al-Mansurah)
TM	Turkish Mafia
TO	Türk Ocakları
TOCS	Turkish Organised Crime Syndicates:

- Ayanoğlu Organised Crime Syndicate
- Baybasin Organised Crime Syndicate
- Çatlı and/or Çakılı Organised Crime Syndicate(s)
- Heybetli Organised Crime Syndicate
- Karaduman Organised Crime Syndicate
- Musullulu Organised Crime Syndicate
- Reyhani Organised Crime Syndicate

	•	Senoğlu Organised Crime Syndicate
	•	Ulucan Organised Crime Syndicate
TORB		Turkish Ottoman Revenge Brigade
TPLF		Turkish People's Liberation Front
TQ		Turkish Al-Qaeda (El Kaide Turka)
TRB		Turkish Revenge Brigades
U		Idealists (Ülkücüler) (see Grey Wolves)
UH		Idealist Movement (Ülkücü Hareket)
VG		Vasat Group
VGS		Village Guard System (Kornculuk)
YAJK		Kurdistan Free Women's Union
YCK		Yekitar Ciwawen Kurdistan
YG		Charge Group (Yuruyus)

Turkmenistan (1 entry)

A	Unity National Movement (Agzybirlik)

Uganda (34 entries)

AA	Defenders of God (Ansar Allah)
AB	Arrow Boys (vigilantes)
ADA	Allied Democratic Army
ADF	Armed Democratic Forces
ARA	Anti Referendum Army
BNFA	Buganda National Federal Army
BSS	Buganda Salvation Army
CAMP	Citizens Army for Multiparty Politics
FEREA	Federal Republican Army
HSMB	Holy Spirit Mobile Forces
HSMF-2	Holy Spirit Mobile Forces-2
K	Karimojong
LDU	Local Defense Units
LRA	Lord's Resistance Army
LTU	Liberation Tigers of Uganda
MR10CG	Movement for the Restoration of the Ten Commandments of God
NALU	National Army for Liberation of Uganda
NDA	National Democratic Alliance
NDA	National Democratic Army
NFM	National Freedom Movement
NULU	National Union for the Liberation of Uganda
PRA	People's Redemption Army
ST	Conveying Group (Salaaf Tabliq, Tabliqs)
UDCA	Uganda Democratic Christian Army
UMSF	Uganda Muslims Salvation Front
UNFL	Uganda National Liberation Front
UNLF	United National Liberation Front
UNRF	Ugandan National Rescue Front II
UPDM/A	Uganda People's Democratic Movement/Army
UPF/PPF	Uganda Peoples Front/Popular Patriotic Front
USF/A	Uganda Salvation Front/Army
UYCF	Uganda Youth Crossing Fighters

WMLWC	World Message Last Warning Church
WNBF	West Nile Border Front

Ukraine (3 entries)

B	Brotherhood (Bratstvo)
UKM	Ukraine without Kuchma Movement
UNA-UNSO	Ukrainian National Asssembly – Ukrainian People's Self-Defense Organisation (paramilitary patriotic organisation aka Argo Squad, Viking Brigade)

United Kingdom (29 entries)

AHMB	Abu Hafs al-Masri Brigade
ALF	Animal Liberation Front
AS	Defenders of Islamic Law (Ansar al-Shari'ah)
ASG	Animal Support Group
ASJ	Followers of the Traditions of the Prophet (Ahl us-Sunnah wal Jamaah) (replaced al-Muhajiroun)
CW	Class War
C18	Combat 18
ELF	Earth Liberation Front
EVF	English Volunteer Force
E88	Englander 88
G	The Strangers (Al-Ghurabaa)
GR	Globalise Resistance (anti-globalists)
HRS	Hunt Retribution Squad
HSA	Hunt Saboteurs Association
I4UK	Islam4UK
JM	The Emigrants (Jama'at al-Muhajirun) (replaced by Islam4UK)
JM	Islamic Group (Jama'at al-Muslimin)
JOE	Jihad (Holy War) Organisation in Europe
MDM	May Day Monopoly
NRF	National Revolutionary Faction
PFL	People's Fuel Lobby
RCG	Revolutionary Communist Group
SHAC	Stop Huntingdon Animal Cruelty Group
SNLA	Scottish National Liberation Army
SOGQ	Secret Organisation Group of al-Qaeda
SS	The Saved Sect (al-Firqat un-Naajiyah)
TP	Third Position
UA	Urban Alliance
Y	The Yardies (Jamaican criminal gang)

Northern Ireland (33 entries)

C	Creepers
CAC	Continuity Army Council (Continuity Irish Republican Army)
CB	Women's League (Cumann na mBan)
CCD	Citizens against Crime and Drugs
CRF	Catholic Reaction Force
DAAD	Direct Action Against Drugs
FE	Warriors of Ireland (Fianna na hEireann)
FRU	Force Research Unit

INLA	Irish National Liberation Army
IPLO	Irish People's Liberation Organisation
IRLA	Irish Republican Liberation Army
IV	Irish Volunteers (Oglaigh na hEireann)
LVF	Loyalist Volunteer Force
NIFC	National Irish Freedom Committee
OIRA	Official Irish Republican Army
OV	Orange Volunteers
PAF	Protestant Action Force
PIRA	Provisional Irish Republican Army
PLA	People's Liberation Army
PRA	People's Republican Army
RAP	Royal Arch Purple
RBP	Royal Black Preceptory
RHC	Red Hand Commandos
RHD	Red Hand Defenders
RIRA	Real Irish Republican Army
SLV	South Londonderry Volunteers
SNH	Freedom of Ireland (Saoirse na hEireann)
UDA	Ulster Defense Association
UDF	Ulster Defence Force
UFF	Ulster Freedom Fighters
URM	Unified Republican Movement
UVF	Ulster Volunteer Force
32CSM	32 County Sovereignty Movement

United States (40 entries)

AF	American Front
AG	Army of God
ALF	Animal Liberation Front
AN	Aryan Nations
BB	Black Block
BURNO	Build Underground Resistance Not the Olympics (aka Burn the Olympics)
ELF	Earth Liberation Front
EMETIC	Evan Mecham Eco-Terrorist International Conspiracy
EPB	Boricua Popular Army (or Machete Wielders) (Ejercito Popular Boricua (or los Macheteros)
F	The Family (militia group)
F	The Opening (Al-Fatiha)
GKB	Gufield-Kutsenko Brigade (Russian organised crime group in New York)
HAMC	Hells Angels Motorcycle Club
HN	Hammerskin Nation (white supremacist)
ICP	Islamic Committee for Palestine or Islamic Concern Project
ITS	Islamic Thinkers Society (neo-Khawarij Muslim group)
JF	Community of the Impoverished (Jama'at al-Fuqra)
JIS	Jam'iyyat ul-Islam Is-Saheeh
KKK	Ku Klux Klan
M	Mongols
MA	Muslims of the Americas
M18	18th Street Gang
MS13	Mara Salvatrucha (Salvadorian crime syndicate)
NA	National Alliance

NAALF	North American Animal Liberation Front
NBG	New Breech Gang
NY	Nation of Yahweh (black supremacists)
O	The Outfit
OCBC	Oklahoma City Bombing Conspirators
PP	Phineas Priests (Christian identity group)
RCALB	Revolutionary Cells Animal Liberation Brigade
RT	Republic of Texas (independence movement)
S	The Vanguard (As-Sabiqun)
SACNA	Socialist Arab Coalition in North America
SWNC	Stormfront White Nationalist Community
U	Community of the Believers (Ummah)
UII	Up the IRS, Inc.
UVL	Unknown Vice Lords
VLN	Almighty Vice Lord Nation (street gang in Chicago)
WCC	World Church of the Creator (now the Creativity Movement) (white supremacists)

Uruguay (0 entries)

Uzbekistan (11 entries)

E	Al-Ekrimiyye
ERK	Freedom
HIT	Islamic Party of Turkestan (Hezb-al-Islami Turkestan)
HT	Party of Liberation (Hezb-ut-Tahrir)
IJGU	Islamic Jihad Group of Uzbekistan
IJU	Islamic Jihad Union (Islomiy Jihod Ittihodi)
IMT	Islamic Movement of Turkestan
IMU	Islamic Movement of Uzbekistan
JJI	Islamic Holy War Group (Jama'at al-Jihad al-Islami)
MWN	Ma Wara'un-Nahr (Division of the IJU)
TIJI	Movement of Islamic Holy War (Tehrik-e-Jihad-e-Islami) (umbrella organisation)

Vanuatu (0 entries)

Venezuela (25 entries)

AUV	United Self-Defense Forces of Venezuela (Las Autodefensas Unidas de Venezuela)
B	Brigadas (vigilante groups)
BCM	Bolivarian Continental Movement (replaced CCB)
BR	Bandera Roja
BGM	Bolivarian Guerrilla Movement
BLF	Bolivarian Liberation Forces (the first)
BLF	Bolivarian Liberation Forces (the second)
CB	Bolivarian Circles (Circulos Bolivarianos)
CCB	Bolivarian Continental Coordinator Coordinadora Continental Bolivariana; replaced by BCM)
CRLM	Carapaica Revolutionary Liberation Movement
E	Encapuchados
EG	Extermination Group
FUR	United Revolutionary Front

I	Los Invisibles (kidnap gang)
M	Los Mellizos
MMB	Military Movement Bolivar
PL	Pirates of the Llano
PLA	Popular Liberation Army (Ejercito del Pueblo en Armas)
R	Los Rapiditos (kidnap gang)
RF	Red Flag
TRM, J23	Tupamaro Revolutionary Movement, January 23
URF	United Revolutionary Front
V	Venceremos
YMES	Youth Movement Ezequiel Samora

Vietnam (5 entries)

FULRO	United Front for the Liberation of the Oppressed Races
FVM	Free Vietnamese Movement
FVRG	Free Vietnam Revolutionary Group
SSPL	Sacred Sword of the Patriots League
UBCV	Unified Buddhist Church of Vietnam

Yemen (27 entries)

AA	Al-Ayman Association
AAHB	Abu-Ali al-Harithi Brigade
AS	Al-Sururi (named after Surur Zain al-Abidin)
AS	Defenders of Islamic Law (Ansar al-Sharia'a)
AT	Defenders of Truth (Ansar al-Haq)
AWB	Al-Wahdah Brigades (Kata'ib al-Wahdah)
CC	Coordination Council
GOUB	General Organisation for Unification Brigades
H	Houthis (see Faithful Youth (SM))
HG	Hattat Group
HH	Hezb-al-Haqq (Zaidite)
HIY	Yemen Socialist Party (al-Hezb al-Ichtiraki al-Yamani)
IAA	Islamic Army of Aden-Abyan (Jaysh Adan-Abiyan al-Islami)
IJ	Islamic Holy War (Al-Jihad al-Islami)
MA	Mohammed's Army (Jaysh Mohammed)
MCA	General Popular Congress (al-Mutamar al-Cha'bi al-'Am)
QOLY	Al-Qaeda Organisation in the Land of Yemen
S	Salafists
SM	Faithful Youth (Al-Shabab al-Mu'minayn)
SM	Sadern Movement
SMM	Southern Mobility Movement (Al-Harak al-Janubi)
SQ	Sympathizers with al-Qaeda
TYI	Yemeni Congregation for Reform (Islah) (at-Tajammu' al-Yamani li-l-Islah)
WIJG	World Islamic Jihad Group
YIJ	Yemeni Islamic Holy War (Yemeni Islamic Jihad)
Z	Zaidite (Shi'ite sect)

Zimbabwe (5 entries)

MDC	Movement for Democratic Change
NLWVO	National Liberation War Veterans Organziation
ZANU	Zimbabwe African Nationalist Union
ZANU (PF)	Zimbabwean African Nationalist Union – Political Front
ZFM	Zimbabwe Freedom Movement

Worldwide/International (9 entries)

BB	Black Block
cDc	Cult of the Dead Cow (hackers group)
FBH	Federal Bureau of Hackers (hackers group)
IAACA	International Association for the Advancement of Criminal Activity (online criminals)
ICA	International Carder's Alliance (online criminals)
M	Mazafaka (online criminals)
QS	The Solid Base (Al-Qaeda al-Sulbah)
S	Shadowcrew (online criminals)
USG	Unix Security Guards (hackers group)

7

LIBRARY AND INTERNET RESOURCES FOR RESEARCH ON TERRORISM

Eric Price

Today, the younger generation of researchers is often more familiar with using the internet than with using a traditional library. While the internet is, in the field of communication, the greatest invention since the development of the printing press in 1439, it is also a dangerous one and cannot be a full substitute for a good academic library. We therefore asked a professional librarian who has worked for many years for the International Atomic Energy Agency (IAEA) in Vienna and who is familiar with both – internet and traditional library – to share some of his insights.

I don't need a library; I got Google.

A UN colleague, April 2002

Introduction

In this new millennium, there is a trend to rename an institution that we have known for centuries: the library. It is now often called an information bank, information resource centre or information knowledge management centre, yet in many ways it is still the same institution as the days of the Library of Alexandria in Egypt two thousand years ago. The formats have changed, just as have the practices, but the basics have not. Items, usually written ones, are located, collected, recorded, stored, and then made available to the user. A library holds documentary resources and librarians provide services to allow optimal use of these resources.[1] This is how librarians apply their specific knowledge management.

Data – information – knowledge

In order to acquire knowledge, one has to organize resources, as there is so much available. First, raw data have to be gathered and then processed into usable information. Information is related to meaning or intention. It is then applied to achieve knowledge, which is the capacity to understand, explain and deal with concepts, actions and intentions. The process is summarised in Figure 7.1. One needs a body of knowledge to interpret new data and combine them to information.[2] It may appear easy but in reality it is often not; in a complex world, it is no longer simple; at an academic level it is almost an art.[3]

Figure 7.1 The relationship between data, information and knowledge.

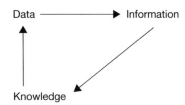

Since the invention of the World Wide Web at CERN in 1991, there has been the mis-understanding that the traditional library, as we know it, is no longer needed. For the average person's daily needs this may be true; but for academics, professionals and researchers, this is not so. On the surface, the 'open web' appears to encompass everything; in reality, only between 3 per cent and 7 per cent of what is actually available electronically is searchable on the World Wide Web. The rest is hidden in the 'Deep Web', where the indexing 'spiders' or 'crawlers' of search engines cannot reach. Access to such databases is often protected by ID (identification data) and password for reasons of privacy or control, or for commercial or other reasons.

Next to the 'Deep Web' there is the 'Dark Web', which is mainly used by the military and intelligence services. It is completely unreachable for any outsider as it is not linked to the internet but passes through secure, encrypted separate channels.

Everything, be it in printed or in electronic format, is subject to various laws, regulating access and intellectual property rights. In particular, this relates to the following:

- *Open access*. This type of literature has been defined by the Budapest Access Initiative in 2001; it is freely available on the public internet, permitting any user to read, download, copy, distribute, print, search or link articles, crawl them for indexing, pass them as data to software, or use them for any other useful purpose, without financial, legal or technical barriers.
- *Copyright and payment*. Open access to electronic journals, e-books, e-prints etc., will either let authors retain copyright of the material they have written, or ask authors to transfer copyright to the publisher. In either case, the copyright holder will have to consent to open access for published work. When publishers hold the copyright, they will consent to open access directly. When authors hold the copyright, they will ensure open access by signing a licence to the publisher authorizing open access.[4]

Those interested in studying terrorism and other forms of political violence seek to maximize their benefits from open-source Information (OSI). The terrorists are, after all, doing the same. The virtual world of the internet is where they try to size up each other. Governments in the Western world, through their democratic and liberal policies, have produced a wealth of unclassified or declassified information. A great deal of that is available free of charge and is not subject to any controls. Therefore, it can be used or misused by all, including, paradoxically, by those who want to shut down open societies.[5] However, in recent years, when it became apparent that terrorists and their supporters use a variety of features of the internet not only for recruiting but also for the preparation of attacks and the search of vulnerabilities in national critical infrastructures, certain types of hitherto open information have been removed from the internet by bodies such as the International Atomic Energy Agency (IAEA) and the United States Nuclear Regulatory Commission (USNRC).

A great deal of material on the World Wide Web is commercial, allowing only fee-based access. Other materials are protected by patent law and intellectual property (copyright) laws. While some of those materials can be located with the help of search engines such as Google, Yahoo or MSN, they cannot automatically be accessed without proper authorization and password. Yet despite such restrictions, the amount of information available freely and openly is staggering, and beyond the absorption capacity of any individual analyst, or even group of analysts. This is so for a variety of reasons, including the fact that information comes in hundreds of different languages. While some non-liberal governments, driven by ideology, religion or hunger to cling to power indefinitely, try to control access of their citizens to the World Wide Web, to make such controls effective is much harder than it used to be with the print media, where books could be physically seized, locked up and burned.

While censorship is generally bad, much of what passes on the internet as free information is propaganda in one form or another – which is almost as bad. Caution is therefore necessary, as the content provided by states, organizations or individuals (e.g. 'bloggers') can be driven by selfish or criminal motives, or a political agenda. The internet has become a battleground where users seek to establish credibility for themselves while trying to damage or destroy the credibility of their opponents. Increasingly, both sides to any conflict have been using the modern techniques of the largely uncontrolled web to spread disinformation and propaganda alongside credible information. On political issues, the critical user must therefore be able to distinguish the difference by relying on impartial sources (like those from the United Nations and associated organizations and many universities) and information provided by special interest groups and lobbyists for one particular cause or government or the other. For sites that merely provide information, one should at least take a look at the information in the 'About [us]' folder of the site. While it often professes to come from a 'non-profit' organization, a closer look and some background checking on other sites will often reveal that a government or political organization is supporting it and behind it. Academic sites will give the names of editorial staff and editorial board members; this is generally a reliable indicator of the quality of the material held in a database, indicating transparency and accountability of the staff of the database for its content.

Hence, users of the World Wide Web must be aware of some of its dangers and limitations. There are good electronic libraries on the web but they usually come at a price. An example of an affordable electronic library is Questia (www.questia.com), which describes itself as 'the first online library that provides 24/7 access to the world's largest online collection of books and journal articles in the humanities and social sciences, plus magazine and newspaper articles'. Comparing a fee-based site like Questia with the open-access materials on the web is an eye-opener, reminding the user what treasures a good library can hold. Let us have a look at how a traditional library is built and how it nowadays is linked to the internet.

Library research

Search catalogues

Through the internet it is often possible to access the catalogues of many libraries worldwide. Yet it is always wise to first check your own library's catalogue. Sometimes your library has a joint catalogue with other libraries; this is usually reflected in what is called a Federated Catalogue. It allows users to make a combined search, i.e. checking simultaneously the holdings of all connected libraries. If one wishes to go further in a specific search, one should go to the WorldCat at www.worldcat.org. This site connects you to collections and services of more than 10,000 libraries worldwide. It lists books, videos, articles and more; you can save your results, build a bibliography, and much more. A tip: Use the Advanced Search facility[6] and watch the video tutorial on YouTube (www.youtube.com) when compiling your bibliography.

It is also possible to access regional catalogues on the web; for certain topics, this may be a great advantage. Two useful collections are the following:

1   For the United Kingdom, consult www.uklibrariesplus.ac.uk/memaz.htm. This lists all the major libraries, and provides links to their catalogues and websites, as well as listing the contact and other information. It offers a better service to research postgraduates and members of academic staff.

2   For the United States, the address is http://catalog.loc.gov. The Library of Congress Catalogue holds without any doubt the biggest document collection in the world. It contains almost 150 million records (including more than 21 million catalogued books and much more in the form of manuscripts, cartographic materials, music, sound recordings, and visual materials). The catalogue also displays searching aids for users, such as cross-references and scope notes.

How to find books

Today, many books are offered to the reader both in paper format and in e-format (electronic format) as a file that can be downloaded from a server to a computer. However, this does not mean all books are available in e-format. Many old and valuable books, as well as standard works, will be found only in paper format and stored on shelves in the library. However, efforts are under way, for example by the Gutenberg Project (www.gutenberg.org) and Google (http://books.google.com/books) to make many of them available free of charge on the internet. Many newly published books are still only available in paper format, at least in the first year after publication.

To get a feel for a field, it is often useful to start with some subject-specific encyclopedias and dictionaries such as:

* *Encyclopedia of Modern Worldwide Extremists and Extremist Groups*, edited by Stephen E. Atkins (Westport CT: Greenwood, 2004). Describes around 290 terrorist groups, most since 1980.
* *Encyclopedia of Terrorism*, edited by Cindy C. Combs and Martin W. Slann 2nd revised edition (New York: Facts On File, 2007). Covers over 300 terrorist groups, from their activities to their methods and responses. Maps and chronology included. Emphasis is on the United States.
* *Encyclopedia of World Terrorism*, edited by Martha Crenshaw and John Pimlott (Armonk, NY: M.E. Sharpe, 1998–). Five volumes covering history, terrorist attacks, a bibliography of leaders and terrorist groups and counter-terrorism experts, as well as legal matters.
* *Talking Terrorism: A Dictionary of the Loaded Language of Political Violence*, by Philip Herbst (Westport, CT: Greenwood, 2003). This A–Z dictionary explains the (ab)use of terms, focusing on the biases of media and government in response to terrorist activity.
* *The McGraw-Hill Homeland Security Handbook*, edited by David G. Kamien (New York: McGraw-Hill, 2006), which focuses mainly on US counter-terrorism.

Knowledge from books (as opposed to the internet) has been underutilized, especially by counter-insurgency and counter-terrorism officials as well as intelligence analysts, because of the inconvenience of having to crawl through far more information than tight deadlines allow.[7] By using available e-books (e.g. through Sage or Elsevier), it is, however (thanks to powerful search engines) possible to efficiently exploit the contents of academic books and articles with the speed and ease which most digital users nowadays expect. This includes keyword searching, chapter-level descriptions and abstracts. Through these, contents of scholarly works can be mined in a manner not possible before. E-books may be procured as single titles or, increasingly, as part of a collection (e.g. through Informaworld, a one-stop site hosting journals, e-books, abstract databases and reference works published by Taylor & Francis (see www.informaworld.com)). Another website of interest for researchers in the field of terrorism is the one of the RAND Corporation, which has been doing research (mostly for the US government) on terrorism since the early 1970s: www.rand.org/publications/overview.html. It is possible either to purchase paper copies of books or to download the electronic version to be read in PDF (portable digital format).

Other good examples of electronic source publications on terrorism can be found with the Netherlands National Coordinator for Counterterrorism, e.g. *Jihads and the internet* (http://english.

nctb.nl/Images/Jihadis%20and%20the%20internet_tcm127-139397.pdf) or on the website of the United Nations (www.un.org), where one can find, *inter alia*, the UN Counter-Terrorism Online Handbook (www.un.org/terrorism/cthandbook/).

How to find relevant journals

Articles in journals are in some ways more important in a field than books. Books take longer to write and to publish, and some of the information is already dated by the time a volume is published. While not as fast as conference papers, articles in journals provide relatively up-to-date information, especially for the more scholarly user (as opposed to the intelligence analyst).

In recent years, journals have often been provided in both paper and electronic formats. Paper copies may be found available as 'reference only' in a library; they can be read and copied in the reading room but not taken away. Electronic journals are offered either cost-free (as in the case of *Perspectives on Terrorism* (see www. terrorismanalysts.com) or, at a price, with a subscription for single titles or as a package. The commercially produced journals can be obtained by accessing the journals either directly on the internet using IP (Internet Protocol) recognition or an ID and password. In many cases, publishers provide readers with the possibility of being alerted when a new issue of a journal, an article by a specific author or even an article on a specific (sub-)topic in the field one is interested in becomes available. Nevertheless, readers should not be surprised if there is a deviation from this practice. Many publishers and vendors have their own ideas about supplying; for example, a whole issue of a journal can be supplied via e-mail from the library, or a 'table of contents' with hyperlinks to the full text of the articles is offered. In all such cases, to ensure conformity with copyright regulations and responsibilities by the user, the library will request the completion of a commitment form by the user.

Some of the more prominent journals in the field are *Terrorism and Political Violence*, *Studies in Conflict and Terrorism*, *Behavioral Sciences of Terrorism and Political Aggression*, the *Journal of Conflict Studies*, the *Journal of Policing, Intelligence and Counter Terrorism*, *Critical Terrorism Studies* and *International Journal of Conflict and Violence*. Some open-access journals also covering terrorism topics are:

- *International Journal of Inclusive Democracy*, www.inclusivedemocracy.org/journal
- UNISCI Discussion Papers, www.ucm.es/info/unisci/UNISCI-Review.htm
- *ISYP Journal on Science and World Affairs*, www.scienceandworldaffairs.org
- ERCES online *Quarterly Review*, www.erces.com/journal/Journal.htm
- *Human Rights and Human Welfare*, www.du.edu/gsis/hrhw/
- *Journal of Crime, Conflict and Media Culture*, www.jc2m.co.uk.

For fuller lists of free journals with full-text, see:

- HighWire Press, http://highwire.stanford.edu/lists/freeart.dtl
- DOAJ – Directory of Open Access Journals, www.doaj.org/.

Commercial sources holding high-quality journal lists include:

- Ingenta, www.ingentaconnect.com/content/
- ProQuest, http://il.proquest.com/tls/jsp/list/tlsSearch.jsp
- Questia, www.questia.com.

How to find e-prints, reports and documents

The title of this sub-section refers to what are usually called 'non-conventional' items, as they are not sold in bookshops over the counter. Rather, they are collected through depository agreements and/or on subscription by academic and specialized libraries. Usually, exchanges are made between the libraries of different organizations as a result of long-standing bilateral or mutual agreements.

Such items usually form a separate collection and are identified by numbers assigned when published. Others will just have a title and author, and they will come with different names such as 'technical report', 'paper', 'discussion paper' and even 'non-paper'. Often they originate from a conference or a meeting, in which case they are generally termed 'proceedings'. Yet basically they are very similar and usually collected in the same place in a library.

Today, many of these items are generally made available cost-free on the web. This is where the internet search engines excel: hundreds of thousand of references and full-text files are to be found on the web. Although some organizations have removed sensitive items since 9/11, and separate password-protected databases have been created to retrieve them, it still remains unclear how permanent this fear of freedom of information will remain under the onslaught of those who want to close down open societies and use their instruments against them.

To be on the safe side, a library will sometimes download rather than just make links to a site that might be discontinued or hacked. Downloads can be found on an intranet section of the library, where they are stored in special topic folders of the LAN (local area network). Two examples of open-source locations of reports on terrorism (and many other subjects) are:

1   GAO (US Government Accountability Office), www.gao.gov/docsearch/featured/terrorism.html
2   RAND Corporation (a US think tank close to the government), www.rand.org/pubs/online/terrorism/index.html.

Readers will find further guidance by looking at the Directory of Open Access Repositories (Open DOAR) at www.opendoar.org. This is an authoritative directory of academic open-access depositories. It allows searches not only for repositories, but also into the contents of those depositories. It is the key resource for the Open Access Community.

Great resources for new knowledge are *doctoral theses*. These are available usually at the university where a PhD or other thesis has been accepted. Alternatively, theses can be found at a 'clearing house', which can be a national library or commercial undertaking. Here are some such depositories and portal to academic theses:

- Index to UK Theses is provided by the British Library at http://ethos.bl.uk. This site allows full-text access to more than 250,000 theses for free.
- ProQuest Digital Dissertations, http://proquest.umi.com/login. Over 2.3 million international dissertations and theses, from 1861 to the present. Titles published since 1997 allow 24-page previews.
- WorldCatDissertations, www.oclc.org. Details of over 8,000 international dissertations and theses.

Other collections

Each library creates its own collections. Libraries hold them in the form of DVDs, videos, films, microfiches, slides, pictures and, of course, printed documents. These can be obtained through various channels. Many organizations, including police and military but also other branches of government and non-governmental and intergovernmental ones, produce their own educational and training films. These are then exchanged with trusted partners. Sometimes these can also be accessed from university or research libraries. Although most such files are available only on the intranets of various organizations, here are some that are available to the general public:

- British Pathe's digital news archive, www.britishpathe.com
- Free Documentaries, with a rich collection on terrorism, http://freedocumentaries.org.

You should search also:

- YouTube, www.youtube.com
- Google Videos, http://video.google.com/videoadvancedsearch.

Internet research

The boundaries between real libraries that hold tangible printed documents and the virtual library of the internet, which holds electronic data and information that can be downloaded and printed out, are fuzzy, as the library's intranet and the internet blend into each other. The previous pages have already alluded to resources that are in fact both internal and external to the library.

How to find reliable news and trustworthy news services

Although a great deal of information is available in full text as 'open source', it is very often not complete. Many newspapers now publish a web version that is only a limited version of their paper edition. In the field of intelligence and terrorism, one of the most important – and expensive – collections is Jane's at www.janes.com/news. Jane's, which is UK based, gives an extract of an article – about 50 per cent, often less – for free and states that the complete article is only available to subscribers; in other cases, single items may be purchased.

To complete the topic, one should not overlook the special sites created to bring news only via the web. There is a blurred line between propaganda and news; some sites are part of the official broadcasting system of countries, and the news reflects as much public diplomacy as unbiased accounts of what is happening in the world. Much 'news' comes from various opaque organizations, or even individual media moguls with an idiosyncratic agenda. Great caution and care are needed as regards in believing and using such sources. They should always be cross-checked with reputable providers of news such as the BBC or Reuters. For example, in the years that followed the 9/11 terrorist attacks, there was ostensible collusion between much of the US press and the government. One instrument was the controlled leak of information to 'spin' news in a way that served certain policies. Even the best of the so-called free press is, when it comes to sensitive political and commercial issues, often only fully free for those who own it. The declaratory philosophy of liberal democracies was well expressed by President John F. Kennedy in the early 1960s.

> We are not afraid to entrust the American people with unpleasant facts, foreign ideas, alien philosophies, and competitive values. For a nation that is afraid to let its people judge the truth and falsehood in an open market is a nation that is afraid of its people

However, the reality has often fallen short of this ideal. Yet the situation is, in Western democracies, still much better than in most Islamic countries and most post-communist and communist countries, or many one-party states in developing countries. By cross-checking information across a range of sources from different countries and organizations at different ends of the political spectrum, it is usually possible to come close to a correct interpretation of what happened, something approximating 'the truth'. Unfortunately, investigative journalism is exceptional because it is expensive and there are not enough courageous journalists and whistleblowers around in government and the corporate world. Political or commercial pressures, with tight deadlines and too much work pressure producing superficial news, drive most journalism. While there are many bloggers on the internet engaged in 'citizen journalism', there is no formal quality control and accountability of their output. However, some mainstream weeklies, like *Der Spiegel* (Hamburg) or *The Economist* (London), have a reputation for accuracy also in their internet output.

To obtain a balanced judgement, major libraries usually take out several news service subscriptions from various vendors. They will also help their users in receiving these as well as helping users by pointing towards news sources that are available free of charge online. For all-round news, the pure subscription databases are the most reliable and the best. Among these are the following:

- Factiva (by Dow Jones), www.factiva.com
- Nexis (mainly for corporate and professional users), www.nexis.com
- World News Connection (WNC – a foreign news service from the US government), http://wnc.fedworld.gov
- ISI Web of Knowledge (provides access to the world's leading citation databases), www.isiweb ofknowledge.com.

Among the most popular library services are news desktop alerts. A user profile on a subject (such as 'terrorism') can be established and the library runs this through a database, with the selected results going directly to the user. These may become available as soon as they are released, or periodically at a given chosen time.

The traditional hard copy of newspapers, especially the major national dailies, is still offered by libraries and has its value but has now become less useful for news and research on terrorism. The competition from the internet, radio and television is very strong in this field. Here is a sample of open-source news services on terrorism:

- EMM News Briefs on Terrorist Attack (from the European Commission), http://press.jrc.it/ NewsBrief/alertedition/en/TerroristAttack.html
- ETH/International Relations and Security Network from the Polytechnic in Zurich, Switzerland), www.isn.ethz.ch/news/subs/
- Global Intelligence News Portal (by the 'father' of open-source intelligence), http://mprofaca. cro.net/profaca.html
- Homeland National Security Alert – US Homeland Security News, www.nationalterroralert. com.

Most library users will automatically go to an electronic version of their favourite newspaper (e.g. the *New York Times*) or broadcasting station (e.g. the BBC at www.bbc.co.uk). To get the best from any e-source, one should make sure that it provides automatic updating as provided by RSS (Really Simple Syndication)[8] or similar services such as Atom[9] (for more information on these feeds, see the Webfeed Directory[10]). Adding your 'Feeds' favourites to your browser makes it unnecessary to keep revisiting the site to check for updates. If there are 50 sites you visit regularly, doing so 'by hand' would take hours. When using RSS, you can see your results within minutes – which is a fantastic time-saver. It also saves you from revealing your e-mail address, which is often required by subscriptions.[11] Many websites now have such web feeds. A good example is the UK newspaper the *Independent*;[12] it offers well over 100 such feeds, including for crime, legal affairs, news and politics (www.independent.co.uk/news/rss).

How to find articles and make bibliographies

Once the researcher has selected topics of interest (like 'terrorism'), he or she will turn to search engines on the World Wide Web. It is advisable always to use the 'Advanced Search' function and Boolean logic options, like 'terrorism *and* internet', and use several other available options (e.g. time period, language) to narrow down what one is searching for. Otherwise, a researcher will get too many results, which cannot be properly dealt with and are often not required. It should be remembered too that these results are limited to full-text open sources. Many more references exist, but these are generally not available openly. As many 'hits' as one might get for a search, it should not forgotten that these list only items that are indexed – which is less than 10 per cent of what is available on the internet.

Most libraries subscribe to a variety of databases; some of them are made available to any in-house library user while others are available only to staff. This is very often due to financial constraints. It is best to use an internally available database that has access to full text or at least generates reliable references. Good libraries have subscriptions to:

- Factiva, www.factiva.com
- Illumina (ProQuest), http://www.csa.com
- ISI Web of Knowledge (by Thompson Reuters), www.isiwebofknowledge.com
- Lexis/Nexis, www.nexis.com
- World News Connect (WNC), http://wnc.fedworld.gov.

About the digital/electronic library

Today, some e-libraries are available completely on the World Wide Web. They are generally limited in number as well as content, as they have only their own material and materials not under copyright, but they usually have many links to other sources.

Then there are e-libraries, usually of higher education, which have a great deal of information. But full access is usually limited to onsite staff and students with an ID and password. A library's own publications may be offered for free, but the rest is not made available. An example is the e-library of the Centre for the Study of Terrorism and Political Violence at the University of St Andrews, which was set up and expanded by Alex P. Schmid and Joseph Easson (www. st-andrews.ac.uk/~wwwir/research/cstpv/aigaion/). Some items in CSTPV's Primary Document collection (originating from terrorist organizations) are password protected and kept on a separate server.

The most common form of e-library (electronic library) now available is on an intranet rather than the internet. Large organizations, in particular, place a great deal of information on their in-house net. Since not all staff require information on every subject connected to the issue area of the organization, there are different levels of access.

A e-library should have all its holdings or resources recorded in a catalogue, which is generally known as OPAC (Online Public Access Catalogue). The OPAC will also include links to items held not on a local LAN but derived from external sources. Ideally, all services available should be listed, including assistance on how to obtain material not held by the library itself. In addition to an inventory of databases available, there should also be links to the major sources available on the internet, combined with a brief descriptor of the source. Also, there should be links to relevant resource materials:

- legislation
- government agencies
- international organizations
- IGOs/NGOs
- publications
- research centres and think tanks
- archives, documentation and records centres
- abstracts and indexing of journal articles.

Such links should, for those interested in terrorism and political violence, also cover subject areas such as:

- international conflict
- law and legal matters
- border, migration and transport control
- religion and politics.

Exemplary in the field of terrorism research is the commercial e-library of Jane's (http://jtic. janes.com/). This very expensive prime database has a small sample of its resources freely available, as displayed in the top horizontal menu labelled 'public area'[13] and 'news'.[14] It includes topics such as:

- defence
- security
- public safety
- law enforcement
- transport.

Then there is the much larger 'client area' for those holding a subscription. The resources available are listed in a quick-access panel in Jane's 'production homepages'; these include:

- Terrorism and Insurgency Intelligence Centre
- Terrorism and Security Monitor
- Terrorism Watch Report
- World Insurgency & Terrorism.

At the Terrorism and Insurgency Intelligence Centre of Jane's, subscribers are able to access:

- Events Database
- Jane's News/Analysis
- Group Profiles (293 as of mid-2010)
- Country Briefs
- e-mail alerts.

Jane's also offers numerous other, related databanks, including:

- Defence Equipment Library
- Defence Magazine Library
- Market Intelligence Library
- Security Library
- Sentinel Security Assessment Library
- Special Reports Library
- Transport Library.

To get the best from Jane's, readers should consult the very useful Help page,[15] which covers the different ways searches can be conducted.[16]

Searching for databases and data banks

In Chapter 5, Bowie and Schmid presented 20 databases related to terrorism, political violence, armed conflict and similar topics. I can therefore be brief here. Open-source or commercial databases are usually part of a wider e-library where files are kept on various topics of terrorism. Information can be retrieved in various categories such as:

- cases
- countries or areas
- groups
- incidents
- leaders and members
- terrorist websites
- others, e.g. legal aspects.

Numerous websites have emerged providing a vast scope of issues covering open-source intelligence and terrorism such as the following:

- Terrorism Files, www.terrorismfiles.org
- RAND Database of Worldwide Terrorism Incidents, www.rand.org/nsrd/projects/terrorism-incidents
- The UN Terrorism Prevention Branch (Vienna), a specialized counter-terrorism legislation database at www.unodc.org/pdf/crime/terrorism/Brochure_GPT_April2005.pdf
- The Terrorism Research Center, an independent US research outfit that has been operating since 1996: www.terrorism.com.

The Terrorism Research Center provides free news alerts. In addition to links to the day's news on the home page, there are numerous sub-databases, including:

- country profiles
- group profiles
- terrorist attack archives
- counter terrorism profiles.

Terrorism poses legal problems, especially when it comes to international mutual legal assistance, extradition and rendition. In addition to the UNODC/TPB database mentioned above, there are the data contained in the world's largest library, the Library of Congress in Washington, DC (www.loc.gov/law/guide/terrorism.html).

Other worthwhile open-source sites include:

- The Peace Palace Library in The Hague (www.ppl.nl). It has one of the world's largest collections in the field of international law, public and private law, and foreign national law, as well as an extensive collection on international political and diplomatic history and the history of peace movements.
- The Internet Law Library – European Law (www.lectlaw.com/inll/1.htm). A compilation of links mainly on laws and treaties, law libraries, law books and publishers, covering all nations.

Some authors conceptualize acts of terrorism as peacetime equivalents of war crimes. From this perspective, it is also worth consulting Crimes of War (www.crimesofwar.org), an educational project on international humanitarian law promoting peaceful resolution of conflict and punishing those responsible for acts of terrorism. More specifically on terrorism is the Teaching Terror website of James Forest, a director of the Terrorism Research Initiative (TRI), at www.teachingterror.com/index.html. It is a research and information portal to support the study of terrorism and counter-terrorism for academics, students, policy makers, military and law enforcement professionals as well as others engaged in understanding, teaching and combatting terrorism.

Then there are the data banks available only through a subscription. The prime one is Lexis/Nexis (www.lexis.com), which advertises itself as 'the most expansive collection of online content available anywhere'. It is especially strong in the legal field. Like Jane's, it comes at a hefty price, but then quality, completeness and correctness have a price. Those with a small budget will have to make do with Questia (www.questia.com).

How best to use search engines

To get the best information, researchers should use the best search engines, being aware that there are certain ones with their specialities. Most professionals would agree that Google (http://google.com) is still the best for general purposes as it has easily the most web pages indexed. However, there are hundreds of other search engines, besides the obvious ones of Microsoft (www.bing.com) and Yahoo (www.yahoo.com). In order not to get inundated with too many hits, it is always advisable to use an Advanced Search option. This will enable you to limit your search very easily and therefore get the best results (for precise information how to do this, go, in the case of Google, to its Help Centre: Advanced Search Made Easy[17]).

Google also offers Topic-Specified Searches that you will find at the bottom of the Advanced Search page. Of importance here is Google Scholar, which searches for scholarly, academic papers; once again, it is best to go for the Advanced Scholar Search.[18] Also well worth searching is its News Archive by using the Advanced News Archive Search,[19] as there is very much material indexed, allowing you to get the best much faster; to find details and how to use it, go to 'about'.[20]

Language has always been an issue and a challenge, and with globalization its importance has grown. You should be aware that you can change the interface of your search engine, which may range from A (like Afrikaans) to Z (like Zulu) in the case of Google. You can also translate text and web pages, as well as visit the various Google sites in the country domains. Translation machines have became much better in recent years.

To give an example: to get the best from the Google database, click on 'advanced search'. Type in 'terrorism' in the first box and 'internet' in the second search box. This asks the database to look for occurrences of the word 'terrorism' and 'internet' in the body of all the materials it holds. Searched are author, title, abstract/summary and full text of every periodical, book, working paper, etc. it holds, and it shows the results of every instance of these two words appearing within the same document. Should there be too many items resulting from such a broad search, you can refine your search by various means:

- Enter your words in the title field only.
- Add other relevant words.
- Add synonyms (words with the same meaning).
- Use Boolean logic (operators between words, such as AND, OR and NOT).
- Restrict where to search by entering the words in the appropriate box. For example, click the box 'Journals' underneath the search boxes.

I would also recommended using Colossus (www.searchenginecolossus.com), which is an international directory of search engines. This World Wide Web road map allows surfers to efficiently gain access to the far reaches of the internet; it now has about 3,300 listings from 310 countries, regions, territories and other entities around the world. These 'territories' sometimes have an autonomous government, or are officially declared a 'nation' or 'union'; a good example of the latter is the European Union.[21] Unrecognized countries are also listed. The advantage of Colossus is that it indexes local search engines that index local sites much better. The local search engines may be in the local language as well as the main international languages. Some are even multilingual; see Hungary[22] as a good example. And remember that there are always alternative search engines that may suit your requirements better. For instance, http://AltSearchEngines.com is a website with much to be discovered, as it offers also reviews of the other search tools, hosted discussions between search engine representatives, and so on.[23]

Conclusion

Librarians these days come under various titles such as information manager, information officer, information scientist, information specialist or whatever. However, the ideal library expert on terrorism knowledge is hard to find in a non-specialized library.[24] A researcher on terrorism should make sure to contact the right person in the library; librarians specialize in their field of interest or educational knowledge. Network with that librarian. A librarian who is a specialist in one or several subject areas (e.g. on terrorism) will often go beyond what is expected in the line of duty. The best librarians see their profession as a vocation; in their hearts, they apply the Alexandrian principle in wanting to collect every relevant item. Some of them dream techno-dreams, as pioneered by H.G. Wells, the creation of a 'world brain' with a automated library available to generate the best information available.[25]

For example, it is not sufficient to know what is in the catalogue; a good librarian knows where relevant items can be found in his or her library, as well as elsewhere. Such knowledge comes also from participating in networking with others specializing on that librarian's or area of expertise. Such 'information experts' are priceless. Capturing their 'tacit knowledge' can produce quantum jumps in research. Tacit knowledge[26] includes realizing the significance of what one already has. That can only happen when librarians and users have bits and pieces of a question and answer, and only then when they get working on the problem together does this 'lost' or 'hidden' knowledge come to the surface and, as in a puzzle, things fall into place and the whole picture becomes visible. A good librarian can even become a partner in research, but extensive personal contact, confidence and trust must first be established before he or she goes out of his or her way to meet your research needs.

There is no denying that in the new millennium it has become common to turn to the internet and avoid the physical library. Smart librarians recognize this and become flexible and more user-oriented by combining all sorts of materials, collecting and storing, and making that available to the end-user in user-friendly ways.[27] The ambition of a professional librarian is to get the best material, with the correct information, in the fastest possible way to the serious researcher.

Notes

1 Ian H. Witten, *How to Build a Digital Library*. San Francisco: Morgan Kaufmann, 2003.
2 The relationship between 'data' and 'information' is conceptualized differently here as compared with in Chapter 5 on databases.
3 J.M. Matarazzo and S.D. Connolly, *Knowledge and Special Libraries*. Woburn, MA: Butterworth-Heinemann, 1999.
4 M.C. Sammons (ed.), *The Internet Writer's Handbook*. Boston: Allyn & Bacon, 1999.
5 R. Narasimha and A. Kumar, *Science and Technology to Counter Terrorism*. Washington, DC: National Academies Press, 2007.
6 www.worldcat.org/advancedsearch.
7 D. Nicholas, P. Huntington and I. Rowlands, 'E-books: How are Users Responding?' *Library + Information Update*, 6(11), 2007, pp. 29–31.
8 www.refeeds.com.
9 http://atomenabled.com.

10 http://en.wikipedia.org/wiki/RSS.

11 M. Belam, 'RSS Feeds: Managing the Mechanism'. *FUMSI*, March 2008, http://web.fumsi.com.

12 http://news.independent.co.uk.

13 www.janes.com.

14 www.janes.com/news/.

15 www.janes.com/help/index.html.

16 www.janes.com/help/index.html#arch.

17 www.google.com/intl/en/help/refinesearch.html.

18 http://scholar.google.com/advanced_scholar_search?.

19 http://news.google.com/archivesearch/advanced_search.

20 http://news.google.com/archivesearch/about.html.

21 www.searchenginecolossus.com/EuropeanUnion.html.

22 www.searchenginecolossus.com/Hungary.html.

23 M.E. Bates, 'Life beyond Google: Some of the Best of the Rest'. *FUMSI*, March 2008, http://web.fumsi.com.

24 M. Manley, *The Truth about Reference Librarians*. London: McFarland, 1996.

25 I.H. Witten, *How to Build a Digital Library*. San Francisco: Morgan Kaufmann, 2003.

26 R. Workman, *Capturing Tacit Knowledge: Managing Nuclear Knowledge*. Vienna: IAEA, 2005.

27 International Atomic Energy Agency, *IAEA Leadership Blueprint*. Vienna: IAEA, 2007.

8

THE LITERATURE
ON TERRORISM

Alex P. Schmid[1]

Terror is fear. Terrorism is inducing fear in another to advance one's position. . . .
Terrorism is also rule violation. . . . Terrorists are among the most egregious violators
of the minimal rules necessary for human stability. This explains not only the rage
they generate but also the advantages gained by those who grandly promise to punish
them.

J. Victoroff (2006)[2]

'Terrorism' has proved to be a highly problematic concept for expert analysis: analysts have
had difficulty establishing control over both the production of expertise and the conceptualization of terrorism as an object of knowledge. They have routinely been criticized
on both political grounds, with critiques from the left generally focusing on the exclusion
of state violence from conceptualizations of terrorism, while critiques from the right have
accused experts of 'sympathizing' with their research subjects. . . .

Terrorism research has also been marginalized within academia, where it has been subject
to a barrage of criticism from various corners, with some arguing that terrorism studies has
been insufficiently rigorous, failing to meet academic standards, while others have argued
that terrorism is a fundamentally biased concept, and therefore essentially unsuited for
academic analysis.

Lisa R. Stampnitzky (2008)[3]

Introduction

There have been several reviews of the literature on terrorism. To mention the main ones in
chronological order:

- In 1983, Edna F. Reid published her doctoral dissertation, 'The Analysis of Terrorism Literature;
  A Bibliometric and Content Analysis Study', at the University of Southern California in Los
  Angeles.
- In 1984, Alex P. Schmid published *Political Terrorism: A Research Guide to Concepts, Theories,
  Data Bases and Literature. With a Bibliography by the Author and a World Directory of 'Terrorist'
  Organizations by A.J. Jongman* (Amsterdam: North-Holland) (a revised, expanded and updated
  version was published in 1988 and reprinted in 2005).

- Also in 1984, Theresa Romano's dissertation 'Terrorism: An Analysis of the Literature' was published in New York at Fordham University's Department of Sociology, Criminology and Penology.
- In 1988, Reuben Miller discussed the literature on terrorism in a paper of that title in *Terrorism: An International Journal* (vol. 11, no. 1, pp. 63–87).
- In 1992, Martha Crenshaw wrote 'Current Research on Terrorism: The Academic Perspective' for *Studies in Conflict and Terrorism* (vol. 15, no. 1, 1992, pp. 1–11).
- Also in 1992, Bruce Hoffman wrote 'Current Research on Terrorism and Low-Intensity Conflict' for *Studies in Conflict and Terrorism* (vol. 15, no. 1, 1992, pp. 25–37).
- In 2001, Andrew Silke published 'The Devil You Know: Continuing Problems with Research on Terrorism' for *Terrorism and Political Violence* (vol. 13, no. 4, 2001, pp. 1–14).
- In 2004, Andrew Silke edited a volume entitled *Research on Terrorism: Trends, Achievements and Failures* (London: Frank Cass).
- In 2006, Magnus Ranstorp edited the volume *Mapping Terrorist Research: State of the Art, Gaps and Future Direction* (London: Routledge, 2006).
- In 2008, Lisa E. Stampnitzky completed her doctoral dissertation in sociology, 'Disciplining an Unruly Field: Terrorism Studies and the State, 1972–2001' (Berkeley: University of California).
- In 2008, E. Reid and H. Chen published 'Domain mapping of contemporary terrorism research', in H. Chen, E. Reid, J. Sinai, A. Silke and B. Ganor (eds), *Terrorism Informatics: Knowledge Management and Data Mining for Homeland Security* (New York: Springer, 2008), pp. 3–26.
- In 2009, Sam Raphael's dissertation 'Terrorism Studies, the United States and Terrorist Violence in the Global South (London: University of London, August 2009) was completed.

In the following, I shall recapitulate and discuss some of their findings and present some of my own, based on the responses to a questionnaire mailed out in 2006.

Pre-9/11 developments

Terrorism literature can be found mostly in the social sciences, especially political science, international relations, sociology, communication studies and law. It also draws from the military sciences but, strangely, hardly at all from criminology until recently.[4] Much of the scholarship in the field of Terrorism Studies has in recent decades followed cycles of (non-state) terrorism in world affairs, especially as perceived by the United States, the United Kingdom, Israel and some other, mainly Western, countries. As Edna Reid has pointed out, writing in the late 1990s,[5] the literature on terrorism in the last four decades of the twentieth century can be broken down into four periods, as follows.

A number of the seminal founding texts (e.g. those by Thornton and Walter[6]) were written in the 1960s. In part, they were a reflection of the armed conflicts the United States chose to get involved in in Vietnam and Latin America – insurgencies in which (urban) terrorism featured as one of several violent modes of confrontation.

By 1970, but especially after the (pro-)Palestinian attacks on the Munich Olympic Games and Israel's Lod Airport in 1972, the terrorism discourse 'took off'. Terrorism also became more frequent in the Northern Hemisphere (e.g. in Northern Ireland, Spain, Italy, Germany and France), and modest government funding was provided for research on international/transnational/urban terrorism by sub-state actors in a few countries. More academics (e.g. Rapoport, Wilkinson, Crenshaw, Bell[7]) and professionals with a military or intelligence background (e.g. Jenkins, Mickolus) began to specialize in terrorism. Rather than treating aspects of terrorism merely as sub-categories of political violence, armed conflict, guerrilla warfare or insurgency, they began to conceptualize it as something *sui generis*. The growing detachment of the study of terrorism from the study of other forms of violent political conflict was, in retrospect, an unfortunate development.[8] However, by the late 1970s Terrorism Studies as something like a distinct interdisciplinary field appeared to have taken shape, with its own conferences and journals.[9]

This research momentum stabilized in the first half of the 1980s as continued attention to leftist (and increasingly right-wing) terrorism maintained a level of interest in the subject. The decline of most radical left-wing groups in the West, as well as the decline and end of the Cold War, accompanied a relative decline in international Terrorism Studies from 1986 to 1990.

In the early 1990s, there was a further drop in the number of scholarly publications and professionals devoted to the field, and a number of scholars left the field for lack of funding. In 2000, Andrew Silke, reviewing the literature for the 1990s, concluded that there was a shortage of researchers with a continuing interest in terrorism, that most of them were based in the United States and most had a background in political science, although there was growing input from sociology, psychology and anthropology. Silke also found that research efforts were very much driven by issues of contemporary relevance, especially as these affected Western democracies in general and the United States in particular. He also noted that much research in the field was overly applied, with little focus on root causes, fundamental trends and patterns to terrorism that cross organizational, national and temporary divides.[10] Silke concluded:

> Prior to 9/11, the study of terrorism was carried out on the periphery of academia. The funding available for researchers was extremely limited and the number of researchers prepared to focus a substantial element of their career on the subject was paltry. In most cases it was harmful to an academic or research career to follow such interests and most of those who were genuinely interested in the subject found that they had to incorporate other issues into their work in order to remain professionally viable.[11]

Post-9/11 developments

Then came the Al-Qaeda attacks on New York and Washington on 11 September 2001. It was not just the intelligence community that was taken by surprise; academic researchers had also largely neglected to notice the rise of Al-Qaeda, which had been founded as early as 1988.[12] The vigorous reaction – many would say overreaction – to those attacks of 9/11 in the form of the declaration of a 'global war on terror' (GWOT) by the Bush administration not only facilitated a revival of Terrorism Studies but pushed the subject to the forefront of international and domestic security studies. Many writers who had hitherto focused on other subjects turned their attention to the issue of (non-state) terrorism. In the words of Louise Richardson,

> After September 11 an entirely new breed of terrorism experts emerged. These were people whose priority was counter-terrorism policy and American power. They were very knowledgeable about the workings of the US government and about military and security policy. Many had formerly worked on international security issues like nuclear proliferation or the conduct of the Cold War. Others had practical experience fighting, either overly or covertly, against terrorists, but very few had ever actually tried to understand terrorism. They found the terrorism studies community incurably soft on terrorism, ignorant of policy and blind to the threat of al-Qaeda.[13]

Many of these new 'experts' eagerly embraced the notion (proposed by Walter Laqueur and others) of a 'New Terrorism' that was qualitatively different from non-state terrorism before 1995 (when Aum Shinrikyo conducted a chemical attack in Tokyo) or before 2001 (Al-Qaeda's attack on the World Trade Center and the Pentagon). However, new empirical research did not increase proportionally with the production of new publications. Thus, much of the 'new' scholarship actually contained no study of primary documents from terrorist organizations in their original languages or interviews with ex-terrorists in prison, let alone field research in conflict zones. Instead, many newcomers to the field scavenged the work of others, sometimes combining some of their findings uncritically.[14] Much of it was superficial and crudely agenda-driven – politically by neo-conservatives, commercially by those close to a fast-growing homeland security counter-terrorism industry and individually by personal opportunism, responding to the availability of major government funding and the lure of being interviewed as an 'expert' by the news media. One author, reviewing part of the post-9/11 literature, went so far as to call it a collapse of objectivity.[15]

However, it would be unwarranted to generalize. There has been also been a surge in good research. To quote Karen Colvard, program director of the H.F. Guggenheim Foundation, which has sponsored research on violence for many years:

> After the attacks on the World Trade Center and Pentagon, I anticipated a deluge of proposals for research on terrorism, proposals that would ignore the findings of earlier work on the subject and reinvent the discipline in the fog of fear and anger that touched scholars as much as the average American citizen. That hasn't happened. We've seen good proposals to study political violence which have remained grounded in specific cases, taken perspectives free of moralizing, and analyzed the political and economic contexts of violent movements.[16]

Yet the avalanche of new publications (2,281 books between 2001 and 2008 alone, according to one count)[17] has created such a degree of overload that many of the more useful and insightful additions to Terrorism Studies are in danger of being snowed under. If one searches for books on terrorism with www.amazon.com, one finds more than 21,000 items (November 2010), academic and 'popular' (i.e. not peer reviewed). Lum, Kennedy and Sherley, surveying 14,006 articles on terrorism, noted that more than half of all articles ever published on terrorism (54 per cent) were published in 2002 and 2003.[18] The danger is, as Xavier Raufer, a French researcher, put it, that we risk drowning in a 'tide of misunderstood facts'.[19] How to tell what is solid research from secondary and epigonal products?

Major journals in the field of Terrorism Studies

Vital to accessing significant research are peer-reviewed professional journals – in particular, in the English language area, the two long-standing dedicated academic journals *Terrorism and Political Violence* (TPV) and *Studies in Conflict and Terrorism* (SCT; the product of a 1992 merger of the journal *Conflict* with *Terrorism: An International Journal*).[20] Founded in 1989 and 1992 respectively, TPV and SCT have served consistently as platforms for quality research in the field.[21] Recently, they have been joined by newcomers, some of which have yet to prove their worth. Examples include *Critical Studies in Terrorism*, established in 2008 and edited by Richard Jackson (Aberystwyth University); *Dynamics of Asymmetric Conflict*, published since 2008 and edited by Clark McCauley; the *Interdisciplinary Analyses of Terrorism and Political Aggression*, edited by Daniel Antonius *et al.*, which began publication in January 2010; and the *International Journal of Conflict and Violence*, established in 2007 and edited by Wilhelm Heitmeyer (University of Bielefeld) and others. In addition, most mainstream political science journals, such as *International Security*, the *American Political Science Review* and the *Journal of Conflict Resolution*, have also served as outlets for publications on the subject. These and scores of other journals have published thousands of articles, especially since 9/11.[22] The bibliography in this volume lists some 4,600 of the more important publications (articles and books) since the mid-1980s – including some of those of the respondents to the questionnaire. However, it is little more than a select sample in a recent flood of publications, many of them poorly researched and more ideological than empirical in their approach to the subject. They also often focus on what is high on the political agenda.

Major topics of recent research on terrorism

The major topics of recent research can be seen from the analysis of part of the literature made by Cynthia Lum, Leslie Kennedy and Alison Sherley, published in 2006. Reviewing 4,458 peer-reviewed articles on terrorism, they concluded that 96 per cent of these studies were 'think pieces'; only 3 per cent had an empirical basis and only 1 per cent were case studies'.[23] Lum, Kennedy and Sherley were mainly looking for evaluation research, particularly quantitative studies focusing on the effectiveness of counter-terrorist measures, and missed out on many good studies (e.g. all books) that did not fit their electronic research methodology.[24] Nevertheless, their study was a reminder that empirical research is still the exception in the field of Terrorism Studies (see Table 8.1).

Doing research on terrorism differs from standard social science research. Since we are dealing with underground organizations (or state secret police and paramilitary formations colluding with them), even basic data are often not in the public domain. To illustrate: for 9,000 of 14,000 terrorist incidents in 2006, no perpetrator groups could be identified from open sources, and for the remaining 5,000 incidents, 290 different subnational groups claimed credit for terrorist attacks, were accused of them or were confirmed perpetrators.[25] Sorting out authorship is, in such a situation, a Herculean task. Terrorism, despite the massive publicity it often generates, is often a 'war in the shadows'.[26] While most major successful terrorist attacks make it into the media, failed and foiled attacks less often do. Disinformation and distortions from both terrorists and their opponents are an additional problem for those working exclusively with open sources – which means the vast majority of academic researchers.[27] Doing investigative research in conflict zones with high levels of terrorism can be dangerous. Therefore, many academic researchers have often preferred to do their research on the basis of media news stories or reports released by governments – both often not very reliable

Table 8.1 Main topics of research on terrorism, according to a Campbell evaluation study (2005)

Subject matter	Peer-reviewed sources (n = 4,458)	Empirical only (n = 156)
Weapons of mass destruction (BCN)	18.1%	10.3%
Article on spec. issue (groups or incidents)	12.2%	5.1%
Political responses to terrorism (war, politics, IR)	9.5%	1.9%
Causes, motivations, psychology, trends of terrorism	8.7%	18.1%
Impact of terrorism (political, social, economic)	7.7%	5.2%
Non-political responses to terrorism (medical, social, etc.)	5.5%	3.9%
Victimology, coping mechanisms, psych. effects of terrorism	5.4%	25.8%
Other (nationalism, intell. issues, democracy, etc.)	5.4%	3.9%
Legal issues surrounding terrorism	5.2%	0.6%
Media and public attitudes towards terrorism	4.6%	18.7%
How to define terrorism	4.2%	1.3%
Non-conventional terrorism, cyber-terrorism and narco-terrorism	3.0%	0.6%
Religion and terrorism	2.6%	1.3%
State-sponsored terrorism	2.6%	1.3%
Law enforcement responses to terrorism (airport, police)	2.5%	0.6%
Research/science of studying terrorism	2.1%	0.6%
Domestic terrorism	0.6%	0.6%

sources. As a consequence, few of them create their own data and can formulate original conclusions on the basis of these. Evidence-based, rigorous empirical research, comparative in nature and covering prolonged campaigns of terrorism in context and taking into account the activities of opponents and rivals of terrorist groups, has been, and continues to be, more the exception than the rule.[28]

Since academics usually have no security clearances, much well-informed research has often been conducted by trusted (some would say 'embedded') researchers with security clearances at think tanks or within government agencies themselves. However, it is not impossible to do good research without access to classified information, as some investigative journalists like Ahmed Rashid or Jason Burke have proved. The question then becomes: against which standards should academic research on terrorism be judged – the products of classified research, good investigative journalism or regular academic research in non-problematic areas (e.g. the study of voting behaviour)? If it is the latter, then terrorism research is indeed often inferior – but then such a comparison is to some degree unfair.

Evaluating the literature on terrorism

Terrorism research has more often been criticized than praised, on both ideological and methodological grounds, by members of the terrorism research community themselves as well as outsiders. When it comes to ideology, among the earliest critics were Edward Herman and Gerry O'Sullivan, who published in the late 1980s *The 'Terrorism' Industry: The Experts and Institutions That Shape our View of Terror.*[29] They claimed – not without some justification – that much of the writing on terrorism was based on a number of dubious assumptions, namely:

1   The West is an innocent target and victim of terrorism. It stands for decency and the rule of law. . . . It follows that the United States (and, by association, its allies) does not engage in or support terrorism in any way, shape, or form.

2   The West only responds to other people's use of force. Argentina, for example, while engaging in 'deplorable' killings during the years from 1975 to 1983, was only responding to actions of others. . . .

3   In those cases where the West supports insurgents who use force, this is done 'on behalf of democracy against repressive regimes', as in the U.S. support of the Nicaraguan contras. Furthermore, insurgents supported by the West do not kill innocent civilians. . . .

4   Democracies are especially hated and . . . vulnerable to terrorists, and the aim of terrorists is 'to undermine institutions, to destroy popular faith in moderate government'. . . .

5   Underlying these varied efforts to undermine democracies is Soviet support. . . .[30]

This type of critique has recently been reiterated in even stronger terms by members of the Critical Terrorism Studies (CTS) School. They have accused 'orthodox terrorism scholars' (or 'terrorologists', as they also call them[31]) of, for instance, neglecting state terrorism. While it is true that state terrorism has received less attention from mainstream scholars, it has – often under a different name – received attention from human rights scholars. Some of them are also terrorism scholars.[32] Regarding alleged bias, Martha Crenshaw has made a valid point:

> Scholars in the area of political violence generally disagree as to whether their work should be practical and prescriptive or devoted to increasing knowledge for its own sake. It is difficult to avoid involvement in public issues, because something as simple as the choice of a research topic can lead to charges of bias. On theoretical grounds, narrowing one's scope to a specific form of political violence often makes sense. Yet, selectivity sometimes

is interpreted as an ideological statement. In the 1960s, scholars who analyzed insurrections or guerrilla warfare were accused of aiding and abetting government counterinsurgency efforts. Studies of oppositional terrorism are often criticized for the same reason.[33]

The criticism of the Critical Terrorism Studies school regarding 'orthodox terrorism scholars' is a mixture of justified and unjustified accusations. The justified ones can also be found within the ranks of mainstream scholars themselves and will be treated below. Some of the unjustified ones have already been countered in a series of publications by mainstream terrorism researchers.[34] However, to give the reader at least an idea of the nature of the CTS accusations, here is a passage from one of its principal advocates, Richard Jackson (of the University of Aberystwyth):

> [T]he field [of Terrorism Studies] has developed a debilitating set of characteristics that undermine its objectivity and independence and cause it to function politically as a tool of state power. For example, its problem-solving assumptions have led it to adopt a statist research agenda focused largely on devising effective counterterrorism policies. This has meant that a great deal of terrorism research has functioned politically to provide intellectual justification for state counterterrorism policy and the broader reproduction of state hegemony. It has also functioned to render invisible the much more serious problem of state terrorism, and in particular, the terror inherent to the violent forms of counter-terrorism. Terrorism studies has also uncritically adopted and reproduced statist assumptions and beliefs regarding the legitimacy of different forms of political violence, the nature of the terrorist threat, the particular groups considered to be 'terrorist' at a given moment, and the necessity for coercive forms of counterterrorism. Institutionally, so-called 'terrorism experts' have received funding for research from the state and have in turn provided policy-makers with practical advice. In the final analysis, given its research priorities and its uncritical reproduction of statist priorities and beliefs about sub-state political violence, terrorism studies appears to be academically moribund and politically biased.[35]

Furthermore, Jackson, in his criticism of 'orthodox terrorism studies', holds that it

> exhibits all the characteristics of a major stand-alone academic field, having its own: dedicated scholarly journals . . . graduate and post-graduate teaching and research pro-grammes at most major universities in America, Europe, and the Asia-Pacific; a growing number of dedicated research centres and think tanks; a coterie of widely recognised scholars and experts; regular academic conferences; and an accepted body of literature, including a number of widely cited core texts.[36]

Terrorism Studies: a stand-alone academic field?

Is this true – has Terrorism Studies become 'a major stand-alone academic field'? Let us pulse the opinions of some analysts who have studied writings on terrorism in depth. Avishag Gordon, a library information scientist from Israel who has been observing Terrorism Studies for a long time, wrote in 2007:

> Terrorism as a research field lacks constancy and the commitment of researchers to the field. This is one of the reasons that terrorism has not yet become an established and autonomous discipline in academia. . . . More than before, there are today in the terrorism research literature authors who publish occasionally and so contribute to the creation of a large periphery of irregular contributions to this field. At the same time, it is difficult to identify the group of continuant authors in this field, because of the large amount of discontinued research in this area.[37]

Earlier, in 2005, Gordon had concluded that 'the opportunity to create a new academic research subject area has so far been missed'.[38] Lisa Stampitzky, an American sociologist, noted in her 2008 dissertation on terrorism studies and the state:

> As I began to research the production of terrorism expertise, I found myself faced with a surprising finding. Rather than finding that terrorism experts were a powerful, influential group, I found instead a fragmented field, a group of experts unable to agree even upon how to define the object they were studying, and a recurring characterization of terrorism studies as a failure. The more I learned about this field of cultural production, the less it began to look like a proper 'field' at all. . . . Contra the assumptions of most theories of scientific/intellectual production, terrorism expertise is produced not in a bounded 'field' of its own, but in the boundary spaces between the fields of academia, journalism, and the political, military, and bureaucratic arms of the state.[39]

In a similar vein, information specialist Edna Reid also noted a certain lack of coherence (which one would expect from a single field). Writing in 2007, Reid and her colleague Chen concluded:

> The intellectual structure of contemporary terrorism research reveals the existence of several subfields of research such as international conflict, foreign policies, regional studies, and political violence. These subfields reflect the influences of several social science disciplines such as political science, international studies, and history, and substantiate the fact that terrorism research from the 1960s to early 2000s mainly attracted attention from a narrow section of the social science disciplines. This may be explained by the limited importance of studying terrorism as a research topic, the risk associated with terrorism, and the few resources . . . that were previously available for investigating the phenomenon prior to the September 11 attacks.[40]

However, the assumption that 'orthodox terrorism scholars' provide the ideology for repressive counter-terrorism, which is more or less explicit in much of the writings of Critical Terrorism Studies scholars, greatly overestimates the influence of those academics in the halls of government. It also does little justice to the great diversity of views within the terrorism research community. Like others before her, Lisa Stampnitzky found in 2008 that there were many one-time writers on terrorism. She found that '[o]f 1796 individuals presenting at conferences on terrorism between 1972 and 2001, 1505 (84%) made only one appearance' – which would confine the field to below 300 'regulars'.[41] However, since 9/11, hundreds of social scientists as well as members from other disciplines have entered the field of Terrorism Studies.

Identifying the research community in Terrorism Studies

The research community in Terrorism Studies consists of researchers who have devoted much of their academic career on the subject of terrorism. In the 1980s, I first tried – with the help of questionnaires – to establish who were the leading researchers in the field. Since then, others have attempted to do the same, using various methodologies. Recently, Sam Raphael compared four such efforts (including his own) and came up with a long list of 149 names and a short list of 47 core experts. Sixty-two per cent of the latter were already on my original list from the mid-1980s, which contained 35 names. Seventy per cent of the 47 authors identified by Raphael were on the Reid–Chen list of 42 key researchers in 2008;[42] 66 per cent were also on the list of editorial board members of the two leading journals (TPV and SCT), while 57 per cent were on the list of prolific authors Raphael identified. Seven scholars or experts out of the 47 central members of the Terrorism Studies research community identified by Sam Raphael made it to all four lists (see Table 8.2).

Table 8.2 The 47 'core members of the Terrorism Studies research community', according to Raphael

No.	Name (alphabetical)	Schmid/Jongman List (1988)	Reid/Chen List (2005)	Editor (5+ years)	Prolific author (4+ pieces)
1	Alexander, Yonah	yes	yes	yes	yes
2	Barkun, Michael			yes	yes
3	Bassiouni, Cherif	yes	yes		
4	Bell, J Bowyer	yes	yes	yes	yes
5	Carlton, David	yes	yes		
6	Chalk, Peter		yes	yes	yes
7	Cline, Ray S.	yes	yes	yes	
8	Clutterbuck, R.	yes		yes	yes
9	Cooper, H.	yes	yes		
10	Crelinsten, Ronald		yes	yes	yes
11	Crenshaw, Martha	yes	yes	yes	yes
12	Dobson, Chr.	yes	yes		
13	Evans, Ernest H.	yes	yes		
14	Ferracuti, Franco	yes		yes	
15	Freedman, L.Z.		yes	yes	
16	Friedlander, R.A.	yes	yes		
17	Gurr, T. R.	yes	yes	yes	
18	Hacker, F. J.	yes	yes		
19	Hoffman, Bruce		yes	yes	yes
20	Horgan, John		yes		yes
21	Jamieson, Alison			yes	yes
22	Jenkins, Brian M.	yes	yes	yes	yes
23	Kupperman, R.	yes		yes	
24	Laqueur, Walter	yes	yes	yes	
25	Livingstone, Neil	yes			yes
26	Merari, Ariel	yes	yes	yes	yes
27	Mickolus, E. V.	yes	yes		
28	Miller, Abraham H.	yes		yes	yes
29	Murphy, John F.			yes	yes
30	Paust, Jordan J.	yes	yes		
31	Pluchinsky, Dennis			yes	yes
32	Post, Jerrold M.		yes	yes	yes
33	Ranstorp, Magnus		yes	yes	yes
34	Rapoport, David C.		yes	yes	yes
35	Raufer, Xavier			yes	yes
36	Ronfeldt, David		yes		yes
37	Schmid, Alex	yes	yes	yes	yes
38	Schultz, Richard			yes	yes
39	Sloan, Stephan	yes	yes		
40	Smith, Michael L.R.			yes	yes
41	Sprinzak, Ehud			yes	yes
42	Sterling, Claire	yes	yes		
43	Stohl, Michael	yes	yes		
44	Wardlaw, Grant	yes	yes	yes	
45	Weinberg, Leonard			yes	yes
46	Wilkinson, Paul	yes	yes	yes	yes
47	Wolf, John B.	yes	yes		

Source: Sam Raphael, 'Terrorism Studies, the United States and Terrorist Violence in the Global South'. PhD thesis, University of London, August 2009, pp. 194–195.

Raphael also noted – though it is not quite clear how he established it – that most of these core members share a common understanding of their subject matter, claiming:

> [I]t can be said that terrorism is understood by most core experts in the field as: (1) violence (or the threat thereof); which is (2) instrumental, as opposed to aimless; and conducted for (3) political (i.e., non-personal) ends; in order to (4) influence an audience wider than the immediate target(s), generally through the creation of fear; achieved through (5) the deliberate and systematic violation of the established norms surrounding the use of force.[43]

Let us now compare Raphael's table with some results from a questionnaire I mailed out in 2006 to members of the research community. I requested researchers to identify the 20 leading authors.[44] Altogether, 234 names were suggested by the 91 respondents (including some self-mentionings!). Since many names were cited equally often by the respondents, these 234 names were ranked and fell into one of 45 ranks. It turned out that of the 47 core researchers identified by Raphael, 29 (61 per cent) were also among the 234 mentioned by my respondents.[45]. My own list includes in the first 10 ranks 17 names and in the second group (ranks 11–20) 63 names. Among these 80 top-20-ranked names, 17 (= 36 per cent) were also among the 47 researchers of Raphael's list.[46]

Sam Raphael also identified from his list of 47 core researchers those who had testified before the US Congress, or, in his words, 'who have provided intellectual services to the US Congress during 1980–2005 on the subject of terrorism from a position of "nominal independence" '.[47] The way he formulates it makes it sound like a reproach, the implication being that they were only 'nominally' but not really independent and impartial.

Terrorism Studies: politicized and biased?

Critics of experts in the field of Terrorism Studies have often accused academic experts, especially those with security clearances, of being 'politicized' and 'biased', implying that the production of neutral, objective and truthful knowledge about terrorism is prevented by state influence on academics. Since terrorism is generally seen as a form or sub-type of *political* violence, the maintenance of an impartial apolitical stance towards it by political scientists who are also civilian citizens and as such themselves potential objects of terrorist violence is admittedly not easy. As Lisa Stampnitzky has pointed out, the concept of terrorism is situated at the interface of scientific and political discourses:

> Rather than a purely political or a purely analytical concept, expert discourse on 'terrorism' must be understood as existing in an interstitial space between the realms of politics and science. This has had significant consequences for the sorts of expert discourses that tend to be produced and disseminated. Those who would address terrorism as a rational object, subject to scientific analysis and manipulation, produce a discourse which they are unable to control, and such attempts at scientific discourse are continually hybridized by the moral discourse of the public sphere, in which terrorism is conceived as a problem of evil and pathology.[48]

This raises the question whether impartial research on terrorism is possible at all. Even if the answer were negative, I would argue that academics should at least try to approach the ideal of impartiality. In 1988, I wrote:

> Ideally, the scientific literature of terrorism should be apolitical and amoral. The researcher should not take a 'top-down' perspective, looking at the phenomenon of terrorism through the eyes of the power holders; nor should the researcher look at terrorism from a

'revolutionary' or 'progressive' perspective, identifying with one just cause or another . . . he should not judge in-group and out-group by different standards. Moreover, the researcher should not confuse his roles. His role is not to 'fight' the terrorist fire; rather than a 'firefighter' he should be a 'student of combustion', to use a distinction introduced by T.R. Gurr. . . . Terrorist organizations must be studied within their political context, and the study of the terrorists' opponent and his (re-) actions are mandatory for the fuller understanding of the dynamics of terrorism. This sounds almost trivial, but the absence of such even-handedness is nevertheless the chief deficiency of the literature on terrorism.[49]

This even-handedness is still often missing in the literature on terrorism. Yet this is just one of the shortcomings of part (not all) of the literature. In the questionnaire I distributed in 2006 (to which I received 91 answers – however, not all respondents answered all the questions), I asked, among other questions, 'Where do you see the main (theoretical) shortcomings of the literature on terrorism?' Below are some of the answers and some brief comments on them. They are grouped in four clusters and presented as individual lists. Readers or researchers who engage in terrorism research might take these observations as checklist of pitfalls to be avoided and as recommendations to be kept in mind when designing and conducting their own research.

Thus, the following are a dozen charges of political biases or lack of balance or mistaken assumptions:

1 Too much 'political correctness' by terrorism academics (Sinai).
2 Current affairs focus, framing terrorism exclusively in terms of Al-Qaeda or Iraq (Scandinavian researcher).
3 Inconsistent and discriminatory character of approach to terrorism in different regions and by different groups (Sahni).
4 Overemphasis on certain geographical regions, and the neglect of others (Sahni).
5 Too much of a bias towards the Middle East (US researcher).
6 A notion that a solution to the Palestinian problem is the chief problem (US scholar).
7 Anglo-Saxon and Israeli dominance (content biased) (Asian scholar).
8 Principally led by the interests of dominant Western states, particularly the United States (Sahni).
9 Sentimentalism and internalization by liberal democratic theorists of the various justifications of terrorism. In this context, the uncritical extension of the theory of revolution – particularly Marxist and anti-colonialist paradigms – to contemporary terrorist movements (Sahni).
10 Highly politicized and tainted data banks (US-based scholar).
11 Contamination by political bias (Merari).
12 Many scholars are being misled by terrorism propaganda, writings and interviews and do not fully understand the real considerations and rationality of modern terrorism (especially global jihadi terrorism). The lack of understanding of their values, their way of thinking, their inspirations, etc. is causing a huge deficiency in the ability of scholars and decision makers to choose the best policies and practices to counter this phenomenon (Ganor).

These are broad and serious charges, and they certainly do not apply to *all* of the literature. They are also contradictory: are researchers biased in favour of certain terrorist writings or in favour of certain governments? The answer is that some lean in one direction and others in the other; yet many manage to be impartial. The charge that Anglo-Saxon and Israeli output dominates the literature, for instance, reflects partly a lack of knowledge of what is being written in languages other than English. Partly it also reflects the absence of sufficient research in certain regions. For instance, the editors of *Terrorism and Political Violence* (I have been on the editorial board since 1993 and co-editor between 2006 and 2009) were confronted with an abundance of submissions regarding the conflict in Northern Ireland while there was an absolute shortage of good-quality submissions from

Africa or on African terrorist groups such as the Lord's Resistance Army, despite editors encouraging authors in the region, or authors writing on the region, to make submissions. We also tried (with partial success) to add new members from non-Western countries to the editorial board.

As far as tainted data banks are concerned: for many years most events data banks focused on international terrorism only, which was definitely a shortcoming. Was it also a bias? Maintaining a data bank is costly in terms of time and manpower, and excluding domestic terrorism worldwide was also a choice that was partly the result of lack of funding. If bias is defined as a 'predisposition to exclude', or as 'unfair prejudice', that certainly exists in parts of the literature. Concern about Palestinian terrorism combined with disregard of Israeli (re)actions, some of them potentially also terrorist, some of them falling under other categories of political conduct of doubtful legality, would, for instance, indicate bias. One respondent, Ekaterina Stepanova, has indicated several forms of bias:

> Political bias of much of the literature, reflected, among other things, in:
> - Automatically extending the notion of 'terrorism' to apply to political opponents by both governments and opposition groups.
> - Deliberately 'confusing' terrorism with other forms of violence, including those not criminalized by international humanitarian law (such as rebel attacks against regular military and security forces in the context of ongoing armed conflict).
> - Radical changes in assessment of terrorists, depending on changing political context (e.g. rapid, almost 'overnight' transition from appraisal to demonization of Russian social-revolutionary terrorists of [the] 19th century in the post-Soviet literature of the 1990s). . . .
> - Some authors tend to cross the line between researching terrorism and 'popularizing' it and grossly exaggerating the real security threat it presents, thus . . . 'playing into the hands of terrorists'.

Shortcomings and gaps in the literature on terrorism

Some respondents noted various other shortcomings in the literature on terrorism, as the following list makes clear. It is a list of observations on the lack of basic tools, understanding and applicability in (some of) the literature on terrorism:

1 Too few researchers currently studying Islamist/jihadi terror understand the languages and cultural aspects. They therefore fail to understand cultural, religious and historical backgrounds and nuances (Whine).
2 In the absence of empirical data, much of the literature is purely speculative and relies on secondary sources, which are often unreliable (Merari).
3 Theory is hampered by inability to utilize much closed-source data (US researcher).
4 There is a disturbing lack of understanding of the ideological motivations and the mindset of the terrorist. Islamist terminology has received very little analysis and focus (M.J. Gohel).
5 There is an essential need to understand the terrorists' operational environment (to know their modus operandi and targeting patterns) (M.J. Gohel).
6 There is insufficient understanding of ground realities, and reliance on stock, politically correct, positions and paradigms (Sahni).
7 There is a lack of understanding of the strategic campaigns behind terrorism (Sloan).
8 There is not enough understanding of the technical and tactical aspects of terrorists (Davies).
9 Most authors lack practical, real-world experience in combatting terrorism (US government analyst).
10 The terrorism literature is not focused sufficiently on policy (R.V. Clarke).
11 It has little or no practical application (US defence analyst).

Again, such shortcomings exist among many but by no means all of the researchers. Lack of knowledge about many of the facets of terrorism is a widespread fact, especially among some of the more recent authors. But then, it is a broad field – too broad for any single researcher. Part of the solution is to create teams of researchers with different skills. Indeed, after 9/11 there has been an increase in collaborative projects.[50]

The literature on terrorism has also been criticized on narrower methodological grounds. Here are some of the (partly overlapping) charges and comments by respondents to our questionnaire concerning perceived methodological shortcomings found in (some of) the literature on terrorism:

1   There is a lack of methodological rigour (Moghadam).
2   There is a focus on a single discipline (mostly political science and psychology (US defence analyst).
3   There is too little connection to general theories and findings in social science (Merari).
4   There is a lack of a coherent integrated theory based on all social sciences and historical data (Augusteijn).
5   There is a lack of context (global and comparative) (Lutz and Lutz).
6   Failure to test existing theories with data is the principal shortcoming of the research (Horgan).
7   Few studies combine theoretical analysis with empirical research (Malthaner).
8   There is a lack of sufficient field research to generate insights (US-based scholar).
9   There is a large conceptual gap between insurgency and terrorism; generally, experts follow one or the other, despite overlap between the two types of groups (Dishman).
10 Formal modelling that offers no real analysis is to be found (US-based scholar).
11 The attempt by econometric academics to utilize quantitative methods has produced mediocre and inconsequential studies (Sinai).
12 Despite some improvements, the focus of part of the literature, particularly Western literature, is still *excessively on the individual-level* explanations at the expense of at least equal attention that should be paid to social group level . . . at national and inter (trans-) national/systemic level (Stepanova).

One US government respondent commented that

> [t]errorism theories could benefit from work and approaches in criminology, sociology, and comparative religion. I see a lot of work proclaiming terrorism different and unique, but I see a lot of similarities between it and criminal groups, fringe religious groups, and other subcultures/deviant groups. Perhaps more time should be spent incorporating the study of terrorism in other fields rather than trying to make terrorism a field of its own.

Good advice indeed.

Our respondents also pointed out existing gaps (lacunae) in our knowledge and suggested where further research is called for (research desiderata):[51]

1   There is very little empirical work of true relevance (Sinai).
2   There is little reliance on primary sources (US defence analyst).
3   Insufficient attention is paid even to available empirical data on terrorism; there is poor or little use of existing databases (Stepanova).
4   Database construction on counter-terrorism is underdeveloped (Chasdi).
5   Terrorist group-type typology construction is underdeveloped (Chasdi).
6   One of the main problems yet to be solved is how the efficiency of counter-terrorism should be measured (Ganor).
7   There is no persuasive theory on the causes of terrorism (Simon).

8   There is excessive emphasis on theory (Sahni).

9   A theory of terrorist campaigns is lacking (Sandlers).

10   A dynamic theory of recruitment is lacking (Sandlers).

11   There is a need for more study of strategic communications and information warfare (Forest).

12   There is very little information on the interaction between terrorism, counter-terrorism and public attitudes (US scholar).

13   There needs to be more work explaining the relationship between terrorism and other forms of violence (Flemming).

14   There needs to be more work explaining changes in patterns, frequency and intensity of terrorist incidents (Flemming).

15   There has been no effective or coordinated effort to contest and undermine the ideological underpinnings of terrorist movements (Sahni).

What to do with all these observations, especially when they contradict each other (e.g. excessive emphasis on theory versus lack of theory)? These reflect, in part, the 'contradictory and confusing reality' of the field of terrorism and its burgeoning literature.[52] I would also argue that such contradictions are, in fact, a sign that the field is alive with debates – and debates take us further.[53]

Conclusion

Despite many shortcomings, Terrorism Studies is not 'moribund', as Richard Jackson and other Critical Terrorism Studies writers claim.[54] There is a great deal of self-criticism within the field, and additional criticism from Critical Terrorism Studies (CTS) is welcome. However, for criticism to be heard, some common ground in terms of striving for impartiality and objectivity is also called for from Critical Terrorism Studies scholars. For many of the CTS scholars, 'objective social science . . . is a hegemonic project to sustain the status quo' while 'CTS is at heart an anti-hegemonic project'.[55] For Richard Jackson, 'terrorism is . . . a social fact rather than a brute fact' and 'does not exist outside of the definitions and practices which seek to enclose it, including those of the terrorism studies field'.[56] Victims of terrorism and their families will disagree that terrorism is only a 'political construction'. Behind many of the critical theorists who blame mainstream terrorism research for taking 'the world as it finds it', there is an agenda for changing the status quo and overthrowing existing power structures. There is, in itself, nothing wrong with wanting a new and better world order. It is badly needed. However, (Critical) Terrorism Studies is not the Archimedes lever with which to change the world.[57] Yet at the same time it is important, as Jackson stresses, to ask 'who is terrorism research for and how does terrorism knowledge support particular interests?'.[58] Yet that question should also be directed at non-state terrorists, their bomb makers and jihadist ideologues.

Looking back over four decades of terrorism research, one cannot fail to see that, next to much pretentious nonsense, a fairly solid body of consolidated knowledge has emerged. In fact, Terrorism Studies has never been in better shape than now. There are dozens of highly original researchers with great integrity in the field – academics like Crenshaw, Rapoport, Laqueur, Sageman, Lia, Ganor, Kepel, Waldmann, Stepanova – who would be rated first-class in any field. There are scores of others whose work is also of very good quality. Thanks to them and many others, Terrorism Studies – despite many shortcomings – has matured. The reader can find ample proof for this upbeat assessment among the 4,600 titles of the bibliography in this volume (Chapter 9).

Notes

1   With thanks to Bradley McAllister for drafting parts of the introduction.

2   Jeff Victoroff, 'Introduction: Managing Terror: The Devilish Traverse from a Theory to a Plan'. In Jeff Victoroff (ed.), *Tangled Roots: Social and Psychological Factors in the Genesis of Terrorism*. Amsterdam, IOS, 2006, p. 2.

3 Lisa R. Stampnitzky, 'Disciplining an Unruly Field: Terrorism Studies and the State, 1972–2001'. Phd thesis in sociology, University of California, Berkeley, Fall 2008. pp. 137–138.

4 Avishag Gordon, 'Homeland Security Literature in Relation to Terrorism Publications: The Source and the Response'. *Scientometrics*, 65(1), 2005, p. 63; Leslie W. Kennedy and Cynthia M. Lum, 'Developing a Foundation for Policy Relevant Terrorism? Research in Criminology'. MS, n.d., p. 2.

5 Edna Reid, 'Evolution of a Body of Knowledge: An Analysis of Terrorism Research'. *Information Processing and Management*, 33(1), 1997, pp. 91–106.

6 Thomas P. Thornton, 'Terror as a Weapon of Political Agitation'. In Harry Eckstein (ed.), *Internal War*. New York: Free Press, 1964, pp. 71–99; Eugene V. Walter, *Terror and Resistance: A Study of Political Violence with Case Studies of Some Primitive African Communities*. Oxford: Oxford University Press, 1969.

7 For a bibliography of pre-1988 publications, see the 5,831-item bibliography by A.P. Schmid in A.P. Schmid and A.J. Jongman, *Political Terrorism: A New Guide to Actors, Authors, Concepts, Data Bases, Theories, and Literature*. Amsterdam: North-Holland, 1988, pp. 237–484.

8 Martha Crenshaw commented in 1992: 'Most definitions of terrorism, however divided on other points, agree that it is a form of political violence. Unfortunately, this rare unanimity has only infrequently served as a foundation for research on political terrorism, which is typically isolated from the broader field. There are advantages to be gained from integrating research on terrorism into the analysis of political violence. The study of terrorism, which is widely recognized as theoretically impoverished, stands to gain in theoretical scope, precision, and cumulativeness of findings. Situating the study of terrorism in the broader field could point analysts towards problems of significance to a larger community of scholars. Moreover, the phenomenon of terrorism might serve as a useful test-case for general theories of violence, which are rarely applied to terrorism by their authors'. Crenshaw, 'Current Research on Terrorism: The Academic Perspective'. *Studies in Conflict and Terrorism*, 15(1), 1992, p. 1.

9 Sam Raphael, 'Terrorism Studies, the United States and Terrorist Violence in the Global South'. PhD thesis, University of London, August 2009, p. 36.

10 Andrew Silke, 'The Road Less Travelled: Trends in Terrorism Research 1990–1999'. Paper distributed at the International Conference on Countering Terrorism through Enhanced International Cooperation, Courmayeur, ISPAC, 22–24 September 2000, pp. 17–18; see also Andrew Silke (ed.), *Research on Terrorism: Trends, Achievements and Failures*. London: Frank Cass, 2004, which contains an updated version on pp. 186–213.

11 Andrew Silke, 'The Impact of 9/11 on Research on Terrorism'. In Magnus Ranstorp (ed.), *Mapping Terrorism Research: State of the Art, Gaps and Future Direction*. London: Routledge, 2006, pp. 89–90.

12 Andrew Silke wrote, '[T]he heavy attention paid to al Qaeda in the three years after 9/11 is in stark contrast to the very limited research attention the group received prior to 9/11. Only 2% of articles [in the two leading journals *Terrorism and Political Violence* (TPV) and *Studies in Conflict and Terrorism* (SCT)] with a group focus prior to 9/11 examined al-Qaeda. As a result, al-Qaeda did not even manage to make the top twenty list of terrorist groups which received the most research attention.' Ibid., p. 84.

13 Louise Richardson, *What Terrorists Want: Understanding the Terrorist Threat*. London: John Murray, 2006, p. 11.

14 For an example of such dubious research, see the review of Paul J. Smith's edited volume *Terrorism and Violence in Southeast Asia* in the 10 May 2005 edition of *Asia Times*, available online at www.atimes.com/atimes/Southeast_Asia/GE10Ae01.html (accessed 7 April 2008). In brief, the reviewer points out that many of the contributors cite each other as sources and Rohan Gunaratna as a primary source, who upon closer examination, often appeared to cite himself.

15 A. Shivani, 'The Collapse of Objectivity: Looking at Recent Books about Terrorism'. *Contemporary Review*, 289, Spring 2007, pp. 26–38.

16 K. Colvard, 'Trends in Violence Research after September 11'. *ISRA Bulletin*, 54(1), June 2003, p.2.

17 Andrew Silke, 'Contemporary terrorism studies: issues in research'. In R. Jackson, M. Breen Smyth and J. Gunning (eds), *Critical Terrorism Studies: A New Research Agenda*. London: Routledge, 2009, p. 34.

18 C. Lum, L.W. Kennedy and A. Sherley, *Strategies Related to the Prevention, Detection, Management and Response to Terrorism: A Campbell Systematic Review*, 2005, p. 5.

19 Quoted in John Horgan, 'Understanding Terrorism: Old Assumptions, New Assertions, and Challenges for Research'. In: J. Victoroff (ed.), *Tangled Roots*, p. 77.

20 *Terrorism and Political Violence* is currently edited by David Rapoport and Max Taylor (who succeeded Alex P. Schmid, who in turn became editor of *Perspectives on Terrorism*, the journal of the *Terrorism Research Initiative*). *Studies in Conflict and Terrorism* was founded by George K. Tanham and the current editor-in-chief is Bruce Hoffman, with Peter Chalk, Michael L.R. Smith and Ami Pedahzur as associate editors. Both journals are issued by Taylor & Francis. For details, see wwwtaylorandfrancis.com.

21 Between 1979 and 1999, there existed also the *TVI [Terrorism, Violence, Insurgency] Journal*, which, however, was less scholarly.

22 Avishag Gordon counted no fewer than 1,000 articles published on the subject of terrorism between 1988 and 1995. Gordon, 'The spread of terrorism publications: a database analysis'. *Terrorism and Political Violence*, 10(4), 1998, pp. 192–196; see also other publications from her such as 'Terrorism Dissertations and the Evolution of a Speciality: An Analysis of Meta-information'. *Terrorism and Political Violence*, 11(2), 1999, pp. 141–150; 'Terrorism and the Scholarly Communication System'. *Terrorism and Political Violence*, 13(4), 2001, pp. 116–124; 'The Peripheral Terrorism Literature: Bringing It Closer to the Core'. *Scientometrics*, 62(3), 2005, pp. 403–414; and 'Terrorism as an Academic Subject after 9/11: Searching the Internet Reveals a Stockholm Syndrome Trend'. *Studies in Conflict and Terrorism*, 28, 2005, pp. 45–59.

23 C. Lum *et al.*, *Strategies Related to the Prevention, Detection, Management and Response to Terrorism*: Part of it is reproduced as 'Are Counter-terrorism Strategies Effective? The result of the Campbell Systematic Review on counter-terrorism evaluation Research'. *Journal of Experimental Criminology*, 2(4), 2006, p. 492. The authors surveyed 14,006 publications but found that only 80 actually focused on evaluation. In the end, only 7 non-medical studies among these met their rigorous quantitative criteria as to how good evaluation studies should be conducted. Five out of the seven were based on the ITERATE dataset on international terrorism, which excludes the large majority of terrorist incidents since these are domestic (i.e. national) rather than transnational. The two remaining studies with an 'at least moderately strong research design' (Lum *et al.*, p. 30) used US Federal Aviation Administration data or, Spanish data on ETA. Cynthia Lum, Leslie W. Kennedy and Alison J. Sherley, 'The Effectiveness of Counter-terrorism Strategies: A Campbell Systematic Review'. Manassas, VA: George Mason University, MS, n.d., pp. 18–20.

24 Among the findings of the Campbell Systematic Review of Literature performed by Lum, Kennedy and Sherley are these:

- There is almost a complete absence of high-quality *scientific* evidence on counter-terrorism strategies.
- What evidence there is does not indicate consistently positive results: some counter-terrorism interventions show no evidence of reducing terrorism and may even *increase* the likelihood of terrorism and terrorism-related harm.
- Increasing the severity of punishment for hijackers does not appear to have a statistically discernible effect on reducing skyjacking incidents.
- Retaliatory attacks have significantly increased the number of terrorist attacks in the short run.
- The evidence base for policy making, strategic thinking and planning against terrorism is very weak; there is an urgent need to commission research and evaluation on counter-terrorism measures to determine whether these strategies work.

Cynthia Lum, Leslie W. Kennedy and Alison J. Sherley, 'The Effectiveness of Counter-terrorism strategies', p. 1 (summary).

25 U.S. National Counter-terrorism Center, as quoted in US Department of State, Country Reports on Terrorism and Patterns of Global Terrorism. Washington, DC: Office of the Coordinator for Counterterrorism, 2 March 2007, p. 7. Available at: www.state.gov/s/ct/rls/crt/2006/82739.htm (accessed 4 May 2007).

26 Robert Asprey, *War in the Shadows*. London: Little, Brown, 1994.

27 Joshua Sinai, 'New Trends in Terrorism Studies: Strengths and Weaknesses'. In M. Ranstorp (ed.), *Mapping Terrorism Research*, p. 33.

28 In 1988, when I surveyed the literature on terrorism, I had to conclude that '[t]here are probably few areas in the social science literature in which so much is written on the basis of so little research. Perhaps as much as 80 percent of the literature is not research-based in any rigorous sense.' A.P. Schmid and A.J. Jongman, *Political Terrorism*, p. 179. In the light of subsequent findings of Lum *et al.* (see Table 8.1), that appears to have been too low an estimate.

29 Earlier criticism can be found in T.R. Gurr, 'Empirical Research on Political Terrorism: The State of the Art and How It Might Be Improved' In Robert O. Slater and Michael Stohl (eds), *Current Perspectives on International Terrorism*. New York: St. Martin's Press, 1988, pp. 115–154.

30 Adapted from Edward Herman and Gerry O'Sullivan, *The 'Terrorism Industry'. The Experts and Institutions That Shape Our Views of Terror*. New York: Pantheon Books, 1989, pp. 37–38; see also Edward S. Herman, *The Real Terror Network: Terrorism in Fact and Propaganda*. Boston: South End Press, 1982.

31 For a biased survey of 277 alleged 'terrorologists', see http://spinprofiles.org/index.php?title=Category: Terrorologist&from=Rifkind%2C+Gabrielle.

32 Cf. A.P. Schmid, *Research on Gross Human Rights Violations*. Leiden: PIOOM, 1989.

33 M. Crenshaw, 'Current Research on Terrorism', p. 3.

34 Cf. D. Jones and M. Smith, 'We're All Terrorists Now: Critical – or Hypocritical – Studies on Terrorism?' *Studies in Conflict and Terrorism*, 32(4), 2009, pp. 292–302; Lee Jarvis, 'The Spaces and Faces of Critical Terrorism Studies'. *Security Dialogue*, 40(5), 2009, pp. 5–27; John Horgan and Michael J. Boyle, 'A Case against "Critical Terrorism Studies" '. *Critical Studies on Terrorism*, 1(1), April 2008, pp. 51–64.

35 Richard Jackson, 'Research for Counterterrorism: Terrorism Studies and the Reproduction of State Hegemony'. Paper prepared for International Studies Association (ISA) 47th Annual Convention, 28 February – 3 March 2007, Chicago, p. 1 (from Abstract). A few comments are in order:

- Much of the research on terrorism has taken place in the discipline of international relations – a discipline that studies the relationships between states. As long as there is no serious alternative to states in the international system, that framework has to be used. It is not the task of Terrorism Studies to replace the state system. This is not the same as 'the reproduction of state hegemony'.
- The implication raised that counter-terrorism is itself by definition a form of state terrorism is wrong. State repression of non-state armed groups is legitimate as long as the state adheres to the rule of law, and is proportional in its response in repressing those wishing to take state power by unconstitutional means, i.e. by force.
- What is wrong with problem-solving? Much of science tries to identify problems in society and offer solutions to better the situation. Should medicine study diseases without looking for cures? Should criminologists study crime without searching for ways to reduce victimization?
- The fact that 'terrorism experts' have received funding for research from the state is not unique; most academics get paid by the state without selling their autonomy and independence, and this also applies to researchers in the field of terrorism. In the United Kingdom, for instance, it was only after 9/11 that significant state funding became available through the UK research councils.
- Has a great deal of terrorism research functioned politically to provide intellectual justification for state counter-terrorism policy or to provide policy makers with practical advice? On the contrary: many bureaucrats complain how unhelpful academic research generally is in contributing to the control of terrorism. The allegation that the discourse of academic writing on terrorism justifies state practices of counter-terrorism greatly overestimates the influence of academics on policy makers.

36 R. Jackson, 'Knowledge, Power and Politics in the Study of Political Terrorism'. In R. Jackson, M. Breen Smyth and J. Gunning (eds), *Critical Terrorism Studies: A New Research Agenda*. London: Routledge, 2009, p. 66.

37 Avishag Gordon, 'Transient and Continuant Authors in a Research Field: The Case of Terrorism'. *Scientometrics*, 72(2), 2007, p. 217; see also: Avishag Gordon, 'The Effect of Database and Website Inconstancy on the Terrorism Field's Delineation'. *Studies in Conflict and Terrorism*, 27(2), 2004, pp. 79–88.

38 Avishag Gordon, 'Terrorism as an Academic Subject after 9/11: Searching the Internet Reveals a Stockholm Syndrome Trend'. *Studies in Conflict and Terrorism*, 28(1), 2005, p. 49.

39 L.E. Stampnitzky, 'Disciplining an Unruly Field', pp. 136–137.

40 Edna Reid and Hsinchun Chen, 'Mapping the Contemporary Terrorism Research Domain'. *International Journal of Human-Computer Studies*, 65, 2007, p. 53.

41 L. Stampnitzky, 'Disciplining an Unruly Field', p. 142.

42 Edna Reid and Hsinchun Chen, 'Domain Mapping of Contemporary Terrorism Research'. In H. Chen, E. Reid, J. Sinai, A. Silke and B. Ganor (eds), *Terrorism Informatics: Knowledge Management and Data Mining for Homeland Security*. New York: Springer, 2008, pp. 3–26; see also E. Reid and H. Chen, 'Mapping the Contemporary Terrorism Research Domain', p. 48, table 5. According to Reid and Chen, the leading 17 authors were, in declining order, P. Wilkinson, T.R. Gurr, W. Laqueur, Y. Alexander, J.B. Bell, M. Stohl, B. Hoffman, B.M. Jenkins, D. Ronfeldt, M. Crenshaw, J. Arquilla, E.F. Mickolus, R. Crelinsten, A.P. Schmid, G. Wardlaw, F. Hacker and D. C. Rapoport.

43 S. Raphael, 'Terrorism Studies, the United States and Terrorist Violence in the Global South', pp. 69–70.

44 The exact question was: 'If you had to point out the 20 leading authors on the subject of terrorism in declining order of importance – given your professional interest as stated at the beginning of this questionnaire – whom would you mention?'

45 Among our respondents, there were only five (11 per cent) who themselves belonged to the 47 core researchers identified by Sam Raphael.

46 The 17 researchers most often mentioned fell into ten ranks: in the first rank was Bruce Hoffman, followed in rank 2 by Martha Crenshaw, 3 by Alex Schmid, 4 by Walter Laqueur and then, as coequals on rank 5 (in terms of number of mentions), David Rapoport, Fernando Reinares, Marc Sageman, Mark Juergensmeyer, Mia Bloom, Peter Chalk, Reuven Paz, with Walter Reich on place 6, Brian Jenkins on place 7, Andrew Silke on place 8, Paul Wilkinson on place 9 and Giles Kepel and Jerrold Post on rank 10

(Schmid's high ranking is probably an artefact as more respondents knowing Schmid were likely to respond to the questionnaire). The list developed by E. Reid and H. Chen contained 42 key terrorism researchers (of whom 29 were from the United States, 4 from the United Kingdom and 1 from Ireland – leaving only 8 from non-Anglo-Saxon countries). The first 16 on the Reid-Chen list (established mainly on the basis of citation data) were, in this order: P. Wilkinson, T.R. Gurr, W. Laqueur, Y. Alexander, J.B. Bell, M. Stohl, B. Hoffman, B.M. Jenkins, D. Ronfeldt, M. Crenshaw, J. Arquila, E. Mickolus, R. Crelinsten, A.P. Schmid, G. Wardlaw, J.F. Hacker and D. Rapoport. E. Reid and H. Chen, 'Mapping the Contemporary Terrorism Research Domain', p. 7 (quoted from MS). It must be emphasized that these rankings should not be given too much weight. There are excellent researchers who either emerged only recently or were not fully recognized by our respondents, e.g. because they wrote in a language than English. A few who have really made a mark on the field but fall outside some of these shortlists (but are on the longer list of Schmid) are Ahmed Rashid, Brigitte Nacos, Christopher Hewitt, Max Taylor, Mohammed Hafez, Philip Heymann, Boaz Ganor, Daniel Pipes, Tore Bjørgo, Brynjar Lia, Louise Richardson, Scott Atran, Cherif Bassiouni, Donatella della Porta, Peter Waldmann, Ami Pedahzur, Matthew Levitt, Paul Pillar, Audrey K. Cronin, Charles Tilly, Daniel Byman, R.T. Naylor, Stephen Ulph, Adam Dolnik, Monty Marshall, J.I. Ross, Clark McCauley, Jarret Brachman and Adrian Guelke – and there are others. On the other hand, there are among those ranked among the top 20 in our list and others some authors who arguably are less influential or original than some of those ranked higher.

47 S. Raphael, 'Terrorism Studies, the United States and Terrorist Violence in the Global South', p. 56. – The 16 were, in alphabetical order, Yonah Alexander, J. Bowyer Bell, Peter Chalk, Ray Cline, Martha Crenshaw, Bruce Hoffman, Brian Jenkins, Robert Kupperman, Walter Laqueur, Neil Livingstone, Ariel Merari, John Murphy, Jerrold Post, Magnus Ranstorp, Claire Sterling and Paul Wilkinson.

48 L.E. Stampnitzky, 'Disciplining an Unruly Field', p. 3.

49 A.P. Schmid and A.J. Jongman, *Political Terrorism*, pp. 179–180.

50 A. Silke, 'The Impact of 9/11 on Research on Terrorism', 91.

51 For an extensive list of research desiderata, see A.P. Schmid and A.J. Jongman, 'Research Desiderata: An Update of a List Originally Prepared by the United Nations' Terrorism Prevention Branch'. In: M. Ranstorp (ed.), *Mapping Terrorism Research*, pp. 268–291.

52 Martha Crenshaw, 'The Debate over "New" vs. "Old" Terrorism'. MS, 2008, p. 30.

53 For a good example of debates within the terrorism research community, see Stuart Gottlieb (ed.), *Debating Terrorism and Counterterrorism; Conflicting Perspectives on Causes, Contexts, and Responses*. Washington, DC: Congressional Quarterly Press, 2010.

54 Richard Jackson, 'Research for Counterterrorism', p. 1 (from abstract).

55 Richard Jackson, Marie Breen Smyth and Jeroen Gunning (eds), *Critical Terrorism Studies: A New Research Agenda*. London: Routledge, 2009, pp. 106, 227.

56 Ibid., pp. 75–76.

57 'Give me a lever long enough and a fulcrum on which to place it, and I shall move the world', the Greek mathematician and engineer Archimedes has been quoted as saying. Richard Jackson had written in 2005 that 'it is crucial to our understanding of the "war on terrorism" to examine and explain how the discourse of counter-terrorism constructs the practice of counter-terrorism'. Jackson, *Writing the War on Terrorism: Language, Politics and Counterterrorism*. Manchester: Manchester University Press, 2005, p. 24. However, politicians and the military rarely sing from the song sheet of academics – although there are some notable exceptions.

58 Ibid., p. 224.

9

BIBLIOGRAPHY OF TERRORISM

Gillian Duncan and Alex P. Schmid

A. Bibliographies on terrorism and related forms of violence

Alexander, Y., *Terrorism: An International Resource File: 1970–1989 Bibliography*. Ann Arbor, MI: UMI, 1991

Babinka, A.M., *Terrorism: A Bibliography with Indexes*, 3rd edn. New York: Nova Science Publishers, 2005

Berry, L., Curtis, G. and Hudson, R., *Bibliography on Future Trends in Terrorism*. Congressional Research Service, 1988. Available at www.loc.gov/rr/frd/pdf-files/Future_trends.pdf (accessed 11 March 2009)

Bey, J.S., *Terrorism, A Selected Bibliography*. US Army War College Library, 2009. Available at www.dtic.mil/cgi-bin/gettrdoc?ad=ada403338&location=u2&doc=getrdoc.pdf (accessed 11 March 2009)

Forest, J.J.F., *Terrorism and Counterterrorism: An Annotated Bibliography*, vol. 1. Combating Terrorism Center at Westpoint, 2008. Available at: www.teachingterror.com/bibliography/ctc_bibliography_2004.pdf (accessed 11 March 2009)

Forest, J.J.F., Bengtson, T.A. Jr, Martinez, H.R., Gonzales, N. and Nee, B.C. *Terrorism and Counterterrorism: An Annotated Bibliography*, vol. 2. Combating Terrorism Center at Westpoint, 2008. Available at: www.teachingterror.com/bibliography/ctc_bibliography_2006.pdf (accessed 11 March 2009)

Freedman, L., *Terrorism and International Order: Bibliography*. London: Routledge, 1991

Green, S.W. and Douglas, J.E. (eds), *Information Sources of Political Science*. Santa Barbara, CA: ABC-CLIO, 2005

Janke, P., *Guerrilla and Terrorist Organisations: A World Directory and Bibliography*. Brighton: Harvester Press, 1983

Kira, H., *Terrorism: A Guide to Selected Resources*. Bloomington: Indiana University, 2004

Kushner, H.W., *Encyclopedia of Terrorism*. Thousand Oaks, CA: Sage, 2003

Lakos, A., *International Terrorism: A Bibliography*. Boulder, CO: Westview Press, 1986

Mickolus, E.F., *Terrorism, 1988–1991: A Chronology of Events and a Selectively Annotated Bibliography*. Westport, CT: Greenwood Press, 1993

Norton, A.R. and Greenberg, M.H., *International Terrorism: An Annotated Bibliography and Research Guide*. Boulder, CO: Westview Press, 1980

Ontiveros, S.R., *Global Terrorism: A Historical Bibliography*. Santa Barbara, CA: ABC-CLIO, 1986

Prunckun, H.W., *Shadow of Death: An Analytic Bibliography on Political Violence, Terrorism and Low-Intensity Conflict*. London: Scarecrow Press, 1995

Schmid, A.P. and Jongman, A.J., *Political Terrorism: A New Guide to Actors, Authors, Concepts, Data Bases, Theories and Literature*. New Brunswick, NJ: Transaction Books, 1988

B. Conceptual, definitory and typological aspects of terrorism

Baudrillard, J., *Der Geist des Terrorismus*. Vienna: Passagen Verlag, 2002

Butko, T., 'Terrorism Redefined', *Peace Review*, 19(1), January–March 2006, pp. 145–151

Carr, M., *The Infernal Machine: A History of Terrorism*. New York: New Press, 2007

Carus, S., *Defining 'Weapons of Mass Destruction'*. Washington, DC: National Defense University, Center for the Study of Weapons of Mass Destruction, 2008

Daase, C., 'Terrorismus – Begriffe, Theorien und Gegenstrategien. Ergebnisse und Probleme sozialwissenschaftlicher Forschung'. *Die Friedens-Warte*, 76, 2001, p. 1

Dabashi, H., *Post-Orientalism: Knowledge and Power in Time of Terror*. New Brunswick, NJ: Transaction, 2008

Dedeoglu, B., 'Bermuda Triangle: Comparing Official Definitions of Terrorist Activity'. *Terrorism and Political Violence*, 15(3), October 2003, pp. 81–110

Editors, The, Forum: 'On Terrorism: A Word with Ninety-Nine Meanings'. *World Policy Journal*, 24(1), Spring 2007, p. 39

Fletcher, G.P., 'The Indefinable Concept of Terrorism'. *Journal of International Criminal Justice*, 4(5), November 2006, pp. 894–911

Friedrichs, D., 'Transnational Crime and Global Criminology: Definitional, Typological, and Contextual Conundrums'. *Social Justice*, 34(2), 2007, pp. 4–18

Garrison, A., 'Defining Terrorism: Philosophy of the Bomb: Propaganda by Deed and Change through Fear and Violence'. *The Justice Professional*, 17(3), September 2004, pp. 259–279

Glynn, S., 'Deconstructing Terrorism'. *Philosophical Forum*, 36(1), March 2005, pp. 113–128

Gordon, A., 'The Peripheral Terrorism Literature: Bringing It Closer to the Core'. *Scientometrics*, 62(3), March 2005, pp. 403–414

Govier, T., *A Delicate Balance: What Philosophy Can Tell Us about Terrorism*. Boulder, CO: Westview Press, 2004

Grob-Fitzgibbon, B., 'What Is Terrorism? Redefining a Phenomenon in Times of War'. *Peace and Change*, 30(2), April 2005, pp. 231–246

Ibrahim, A., 'Conceptualisation of Guerrilla Warfare'. *Small Wars and Insurgencies*, 15(3), 2004, pp. 112–124

Ivie, R.L., 'Evil Enemy versus Agonistic Other: Rhetorical Constructions of Terrorism'. *Review of Education/Pedagogy/Cultural Studies*, 25(3), 2003, pp. 181–200

Jackson, B.A., 'Groups, Networks, or Movements: A Command and Control Driven Approach to Classifying Terrorist Organizations and Its Application to Al Qaeda'. *Studies in Conflict and Terrorism*, 29(3), April–May 2006, pp. 241–262

Jaggar, A.M., 'What Is Terrorism, Why Is It Wrong, and Could It Ever Be Morally Permissible?' *Journal of Social Philosophy*, 36(2), Summer 2005, pp. 202–217

Kaplan, J., 'The Fifth Wave: The New Tribalism?' *Terrorism and Political Violence*, 19(4), 2007, pp. 545–570

Keeley, R.V., 'Trying to Define Terrorism'. *Middle East Policy*, 9(1), March 2002, pp. 33–39

Kochler, H. (ed.), *Terrorism and National Liberation: Proceedings of the International Conference on the Question of Terrorism*. Frankfurt am Main: Lang, 1988

Meggle, G., 'Was ist Terrorismus?', in U. Kronfeld-Goharani (ed.), *Friedensbedrohung Terrorismus, Ursachen, Folgen und Gegenstrategien*. Münster: Lit-Verlag, 2005

Mishal, S. and Rosenthal, M., 'Al Qaeda as a Dune Organization: Toward a Typology of Islamic Terrorist Organizations'. *Studies in Conflict and Terrorism*, 28(4), July–August 2005, pp. 275–293

Mukhina, I., 'Islamic Terrorism and the Question of National Liberation or Problems of Contemporary Chechen Terrorism'. *Studies in Conflict and Terrorism*, 28(6), November–December 2005, pp. 515–532

Nadarajah, S. and Sriskandarajah, D., 'Liberation Struggle or Terrorism? The Politics of Naming the LTTE'. *Third World Quarterly*, 26(1), February 2005, pp. 87–100

Norris, P., Kern, M. and Just, M. (eds), *Framing Terrorism: The News Media, the Government and the Public*. London: Routledge, 2003

Novotny, D.D., 'What Is Terrorism?' *International Journal of Terrorism and Political Hotspots*, 1(1), 2004, pp. 1–9

Nuzzo, A., 'Reasons for Conflict: Political Implications of a Definition of Terrorism'. *Metaphilosophy*, 35(3), April 2004, pp. 330–344

Pease, K.K., 'De Facto Safe Haven after 9–11'. Honolulu: International Studies Association [ISA], March 2005

Roberts, N., 'Defining "Global Reach" Terrorism'. *Defence Studies*, 3(2), Summer 2003, pp. 1–19

Rochefort, D.A., 'US Definition of Terrorist States: A Rhetorical Analysis and Critique'. Honolulu: International Studies Association [ISA], March 2005

Roldán, F.S., Nestares, F.R., Paya, J.I.T. *et al.*, *2004/2005 Strategic Panorama*. Madrid: General Secretariat of Defence Policy, 2005

Ruby, C.L., 'The Definition of Terrorism'. *Analyses of Social Issues and Public Policy*, 2(1), December 2002, pp. 9–14

Schmid, A.P., 'Frameworks for Conceptualising Terrorism'. *Terrorism and Political Violence*, 16(2), April–June 2004, pp. 197–221

Schmid, A.P., 'Terrorism: The Definitional Problem'. *Case Western Reserve Journal of International Law*, 36(2–3), 2004, pp. 375–419

Senechal de la Roche, R., 'Toward a Scientific Theory of Terrorism'. *Sociological Theory*, 22(1), March 2004, pp. 1–4

Silke, A., 'The Devil You Know: Continuing Problems with Research on Terrorism'. *Terrorism and Political Violence*, 13(4), Winter 2001, pp. 1–14

Silke, A. (ed.), *Research on Terrorism: Trends, Achievements and Failures*. London: Frank Cass, 2004

Sorel, J.M., 'Some Questions about the Definition of Terrorism and the Fight against Its Financing'. *European Journal of International Law*, 14(2), April 2003, pp. 365–378

Sproat, P.A., 'Research Notes: Can the State Commit Acts of Terrorism? An Opinion and Some Qualitative Replies to a Questionnaire'. *Terrorism and Political Violence*, 9(4), 1997, pp. 117–150

Subedi, S.P., 'The UN Response to International Terrorism in the Aftermath of the Terrorist Attacks in America and the Problem of the Definition of Terrorism in International Law'. *International Law FORUM Du Droit International*, 4(3), 2002, pp. 159–169

Symeonidou-Kastanidou, E., 'Defining Terrorism'. *European Journal of Crime, Criminal Law and Criminal Justice*, 12(1), 2004, pp. 14–35

Tilly, C., 'Terror, Terrorism, Terrorists'. *Sociological Theory*, 22(1), March 2004, pp. 5–13

Waldron, J., 'Terrorism and the Uses of Terror'. *Journal of Ethics*, 8(1), March 2004, pp. 5–35

Weinberg, L. and Pedahzur, A., *Political Parties and Terrorist Groups*. New York: Routledge, 2003

C. General works on terrorism

Abrahms, M., 'Al Qaeda's Scorecard: A Progress Report on Al Qaeda's Objectives'. *Studies in Conflict and Terrorism*, 29(5), July–August 2006, pp. 509–529

Abrahms, M., 'Why Terrorism Does Not Work'. *International Security*, 13(2), Fall 2006, pp. 42–78

Bender, D. and Bruno, L., *Opposing Viewpoints, Terrorism*. St Paul, MN: Greenhaven Press, 1986

Bobbitt, P., *Terror and Consent: The Wars for the Twenty-First Century*. London: Allen Lane, 2008

Boff, L. and Schlupp, W.O., *Fundamentalismus und Terrorismus*. Göttingen: Vandenhoeck & Ruprecht, 2007

Chaliand, G.A., *The History of Terrorism: From Antiquity to Al Qaeda*. Berkeley: University of California Press, 2007

Combs, C. and Slann, M., *Encyclopedia of Terrorism*. New York: Checkmark Books, 2003

Costigan, S.S. and Gold, D. (eds), *Terrornomics*. Oxford: Ashgate, 2007

Crenshaw, M. (ed.), *Terrorism in Context*. University Park: Pennsylvania State University Press, 1995

Crenshaw, M. and Pimlott, J. (eds), *Encyclopedia of World Terrorism*, 5 vols. Armonk, NY: M.E. Sharpe, 1997

Cronin, I. (ed.), *Confronting Gael: A History of Terrorism*. New York: Thunders Mouth Press, 2002

Dietl, W., Hirschmann, K. and Tophoven, R., *Das Terrorismus-Lexikon: Täter, Opfer, Hintergründe*. Frankfurt am Main: Eichborn, 2006

Diken, B. and Laustsen, C.B., 'Becoming Abject: Rape as a Weapon of War'. *Body Society*, 11, March 2005, pp. 111–128

Dobson, C. and Payne, R., *Way Without End: The Terrorists: An Intelligence Dossier*. London: Sphere, 1987

Duncan, A., Opatowski, M. and Heisbourg, F., *Trouble Spots: The World Atlas of Strategic Information*. London: Sutton Publishing, 2001

Enders, W. and Sandler, T., *The Political Economy of Terrorism*. Cambridge: Cambridge University Press, 2006

Gehler, M. and Ortner, R. (eds), *Von Sarajewo zum 11. September: Einzelattentate und Massenterrorismus*. Vienna: Studien Verlag, 2007

Guelke, A., *Terrorism and Global Disorder*. Basingstoke, UK: I.B. Tauris, 2007

Gunaratna, R., *The Changing Face of Terrorism*. Singapore: Eastern University Press, 2004

Gupta, D., *Understanding Terrorism and Political Violence*. London: Routledge, 2008

Harmon, C.C., *Terrorism Today*. London: Routledge, 2007

Honderich, T., *After the Terror*. Oxford: Edinburgh University Press, 2003

Jamestown Foundation, *Unmasking Terror: A Global Review of Terrorist Activities*. Washington, DC: Brookings Institution, 2007

Jay, M., *Refractions of Violence*. London: Routledge, 2002

Kaschner, H., *Neues Risiko Terrorismus: Entgrenzung, Umgangsmöglichkeiten, Alternativen*. Wiesbaden: VS Verlag, 2008

Kemmesies, U.E., *Terrorismus-Extremismus: Der Zukunft auf der Spur*. Achim, Germany: Hermann Luchterhand, 2006

Klidev, A.V., *Terrorism Country by Country*. New York: Nova Science Publishers, 2005

Kronenwetter, M., *Terrorism: A Guide to Events and Documents*. London: Greenwood Press, 2004

Kushner, H.W. (ed.), *Essential Readings on Political Terrorism: Analyses of Problems and Prospects for the 21st Century*. Lincoln: University of Nebraska Press, 2002

Kushner, H.W., *Encyclopedia of Terrorism*. Thousand Oaks, CA: Sage, 2003

Laqueur, W., *The New Terrorism: Fanaticism and the Arms of Mass Destruction.* Oxford: Oxford University Press, 1999

Laqueur, W., *No End to War: Terrorism in the 21st Century.* New York: Continuum, 2004

Lacqueur, W. and Alexander Y., *Terrorism Reader: A Historical Anthology.* New York: Penguin, 1987

Leber, S., *Freiheit durch Gewalt? Zum Phaenomen des Terrorismus'. Vom Gedanken der Anarchie zur Propaganda der Tat.* Stuttgart: Verland Freies Geisterleben, 1987

Lee, N., Schlein, L. and Lavitas, M. (eds), *A Nation Challenged: A Visual History of 9/11 and Its Aftermath.* New York: Scholastic Non-Fiction, 2002

Linden, E.V. (ed.), *Focus on Terrorism,* vol. 1. New York: Nova Science Publishers, 2002

Linden, E.V. (ed.), *Handbook on Terrorism: A CD-ROM Presentation.* New York: Nova Science Publishers, 2006

Löckinger, G., 'Terminologie der Terrorismusbekämpfung: Eine Terminologiearbeit in den Sprachen englisch und deutsch'. Thesis, University of Vienna, 2004

Lutz, B. and Lutz, J.M., *Global Terrorism.* London: Routledge, 2007

Mahan, S. and Griset, P.L., *Terrorism in Perspective, 2nd edn.* Thousand Oaks, CA: Sage Publications, 2007

Maxwell, B. *Terrorism: A Documentary History.* London: CQ Press, 2003

Mickolus, E.F. and Simmons, S. L., *Terrorism, 1996–2001: A Chronology.* London: Greenwood Publishing, 2002

Mullins, W.C., *A Sourcebook of Domestic and International Terrorism: An Analysis of Issues, Organizations, Tactics and Responses,* 2nd edn. Springfield, IL: Charles C. Thomas, 1997

Nacos, B.L., *Terrorism and Counterterrorism.* London: Longman, 2007

Netzley, P.D., *Greenhaven Encyclopedia of Terrorism.* Garmington Hills, MI: Greenhaven Press, 2007

Neumann, P.R. and Smith, M.L.R., *The Strategy of Terrorism.* London: Routledge, 2007

O'Connor, D., 'The Political Uses of Lawlessness: Kruger, Warren and the Bechuanaland Field Force 1885'. *RUSI Journal,* 150(3), June 2005, pp. 68–72

Phillips, B. (ed.), *Understanding Terrorism: Building on the Sociological Imagination.* Boulder, CO: Paradigm, 2007

Polk, W.R., *Violent Politics: A History of Insurgency, Terrorism, and Guerrilla War, from the America Revolution to Iraq.* Glasgow: HarperCollins, 2007

Poole-Robb, S. and Bailey, A., *Risky Business: Corruption, Fraud, Terrorism and Other Threats to Global Business.* London: Merchant International Group, 2002

Rafhaeli, N., 'Financing of Terrorism: Sources, Methods and Channels'. *Terrorism and Political Violence,* 15(4), Winter 2003, pp. 59–82

Raman, B., 'Terrorism: The New Context'. *Strategic Analysis,* 25(9), December 2001, pp. 995–1001

Rapoport, D. (ed.), *Terrorism: Critical Concepts in Political Science,* 4 vols. New York: Routledge, 2005

Rasmussen, M.V., 'A Parallel Globalization of Terror': 9–11, Security and Globalization'. *Cooperation and Conflict,* 37, September 2002, pp. 323–349

Reinares, F. with Leyendecker, H., *Terrorismus Global. Aktionsfeld Europa.* Hamburg: Europäische Verlagsanstalt, 2005

Richardson, L., *What Terrorists Want: Understanding the Enemy, Containing the Threat.* London: John Murray, 2006

Robb, J., *Brave New War: The Next Stage of Terrorism and the End of Globalization.* Hoboken, NJ: John Wiley, 2007

Robertson, A.E., *Terrorism and Global Security.* London: Facts On File, 2007

Rosenthal, U. and Muller, E.R., *The Evil of Terrorism: Diagnosis and Countermeasures.* Springfield, IL: Charles C. Thomas, 2007

Rosie, G., *The Directory of International Terrorism.* Edinburgh: Mainstream Publishing, 1986

Ross, J.I., *Political Terrorism: An Interdisciplinary Approach.* New York: Peter Lang, 2006

Sageman, M., *Understanding Terror Networks.* Philadelphia: University of Pennsylvania Press, 2004

Sandler, T. and Enders, W., *The Political Economy of Terrorism.* Cambridge: Cambridge University Press, 2006

Seger Consulting Group. *Terror Tracker. 2005 Annual CD-ROM.* (Contains 51 Reports (Microsoft Word) in Database (Microsoft Access) with Information on 2384 Incidents during 2005), www.segercg.com (accessed 11 March 2009)

Shanty, F., Picquet, R. (eds) and Lalla, J. (doc. ed.), *Encyclopedia of World Terrorism: 1996–2002,* 2 vols. Armonk, NY: M.E. Sharpe, 2003

Sherman, D.J. and Nardin, T. (eds), *Terror, Culture, Politics: Rethinking 9/11.* Bloomington: Indiana University Press, 2006

Shughart, W., 'An Analytical History of Terrorism, 1945–2000'. *Public Choice,* 128(1–2), July 2006, pp. 7–39

Silverts, N., *Understanding Contemporary Terrorism and the Global Response.* London: UCL, 2007

Sinclair, A., *An Anatomy of Terror: A History of Terrorism.* London: Palgrave, 2005

Smith, P.J., *The Terrorism Ahead*. London: Eurospan, 2008

Sofsky, W., *Zeiten des Schreckens, Amok, Terror*. Frankfurt am Main: Krieg, 2002

Tan, A., *The New Terrorism: Anatomy, Trends, and Counter-strategies*. Singapore: Eastern University Press, 2002

Taylor, M. and Horgan, J. (eds), *Future of Terrorism*. London: Routledge, 2000

Thamm, B.G., *Terrorismus: Ein Handbuch über Täter und Opfer*. Hilden, Germany: VDP Verlag Deutsche Polizeiliteratur, 2002

Tilly, C., 'Terror as Strategy and Relational Process'. *International Journal of Comparative Sociology*, Vol. 46, April 2005, pp. 11–32

Von Knop, J. and Wowereit, K. (eds), *Countering Modern Terrorism: History, Current Issues and Future Threats*. 2e Internationale Sicherheitskonferenz. Bielefeld, Germany: W. Bertelsmann Verlag, 2005

Waldmann, P., *Terrorismus: Provokation der Macht*. Hamburg: Murmann Verlag, 2005

Weinberg, L., *Global Terrorism. A Beginner's Guide*. Oxford: Oneworld, 2005

Whittaker, D.J., *Terrorism Reader*. London: Routledge, 2007

Zulaika, J. and Douglass, W.A., *Terror and Taboo: The Follies, Fables, and Faces of Terrorism*. New York: Routledge, 1996

D. Regime terrorism and repression

Alexander, G., *Western State Terrorism*. Cambridge: Polity Press, 1991

Arendt, H., *Elemente und Ursprünge totaler Herrschaft: Antisemitismus, Imperialismus, Totalitarismus*, 6th edn. Munich: Piper, 1998

Armony, A.C., *Argentina, the United States and the Anti-communist Crusade in Central America, 1977–1984*. Athens, OH: Ohio University Press, 1997

Aussaresses, P., *The Battle of the Casbah, Counter-terrorism and Torture*. New York: Enigma Books, 2005

Byman, D., *Deadly Connections: States That Sponsor Terrorism*. Cambridge: Cambridge University Press, 2005

Carey, S.C., *Protest, Repression and Political Regimes*. London: Routledge, 2008

Catanzaro, R., *The Red Brigades and Left-Wing Terrorism in Italy*. London: Pinter, 1991

Chinnery, P.D., *Nazi Atrocities*. Bristol: Cerberus, 2005

Conteh-Morgan, E., *Collective Political Violence: An Introduction to the Theories and Causes of Violent Conflicts*. London: Routledge, 2004

Danner, M., *The Massacre at El Mozote: A Parable of the Cold War*. New York: Vintage, 1994

Dinges, J., *The Condor Years: How Pinochet and His Allies Brought Terror to Three Continents*. New York: The New Press, 2004

Dinges, J. and Landau, S., *Assassination on Embassy Row*. New York: Pantheon Books, 1980

Ensalaco, M., *Chile under Pinochet: Recovering The Truth*. Philadelphia: University of Pennsylvania Press, 2000

Gareau, F., *State Terrorism and the United States: From Counterinsurgency to the War on Terrorism*. Atlanta: Zed Books, 2004

Grandin, G., *The Last Colonial Massacre: Latin America in the Cold War*. Chicago: University of Chicago Press, 2004

Herbert, U. (ed.), *National Socialist Extermination Policies: Contemporary German Perspective and Controversias*, vol. 2. Oxford: Berghahn Books, 2000

Heryanto, A., *State Terrorism and Political Identity in Indonesia: Fatally Belonging*. London: Routledge, 2005

Kornbluh, P., *The Pinochet File: A Declassified Dossier on Atrocity and Accountability*. New York: The New Press, 2003

Kotek, J. and Rigoulot, P., *Das Jahrhundert der Lager: Gefangenschaft, Zwangsarbeit und Vernichtung*. Munich: Propyläen, 2001

Langguth, A.J., *Hidden Terrors: The Truth about US Police Operations in Latin America*. New York: Pantheon, 1978

McSherry, J.P., 'Tracking the Origins of a State Terror Network: Operation Condor'. *Latin American Perspectives*, vol. 29, January 2002, pp. 38–60

Maguire, P., *Facing Death in Cambodia*. New York: Columbia University Press, 2005

Mann, J., *How Our Leaders Explain Away Chinese Repression*. New York: Viking Adult, 2007

Menjívar, C. and Rodríguez, N. (eds), *When States Kill: Latin America, the U.S. and Technologies of Terror*. Austin: University of Texas Press, 2005

Müller, W.D. and Ueberschär, G.R., *Hitler's War in the East, 1941–1945: A Critical Assessment*. Oxford: Berghahn Books, 2005

O'Kane, R.H.T., *The Revolutionary Reign of Terror: The Role of Violence in Political Change*, Aldershot, UK: Edward Elgar, 1991

Overy, R., *The Dictators: Hitler's Germany, Stalin's Russia*. New York: W.W. Norton, 2005

Palmer H.J., *Hezbollah: The Changing Face of Terrorism*. London: I.B. Tauris, 2004

Palmer, M., *Breaking the Real Axis of Evil: How to Oust the World's Last Dictators by 2025*. Lanham, MD: Ronman & Littlefield, 2003

Perez, J., *The Spanish Inquisition: A History*. London: Profile Books, 2006

Power, S., 'How to Kill a Country: Turning a Breadbasket into a Basket Case in Ten Easy Steps – the Robert Mugabe Way'. *Atlantic Monthly*, December 2003

Priestland, D., *Stalinism and the Politics of Mobilization*. Oxford: Oxford University Press, 2007

Prunier, G., *Darfur: The Ambiguous Genocide*. Ithaca, NY: Cornell University Press, 2005

Quarrie, B., *The World's Secret Police*. London: Octopus Books, 1986

Rayfield, D., *Stalin and His Hangmen: The Tyrant and Those Who Killed for Him*. New York: Random House, 2005

Richter, M., 'A Family of Political Concepts: Tyranny, Despotism, Bonapartism, Caesarism, Dictatorship, 1750–1917'. *European Journal of Political Theory*, vol. 4, July 2005, pp. 221–248

Saxon, D., *To Save Her Life: Disappearance, Deliverance, and the United States in Guatemala*. Berkeley: University of California Press, 2008

Schmitz, D.F., *The United States and Right-Wing Dictatorships*. Cambridge: Cambridge University Press, 2006

Service, R., *Stalin: A Biography*. Cambridge, MA: Belknap, Harvard University Press, 2005

Stern, S.J., *Remembering Pinochet's Chile: On the Eve of London 1998*. Durham, NC: Duke University Press, 2004

Suny, R.G., 'Russian Terror/ism and Revisionist Historiography'. *Australian Journal of Politics and History*, 53(1), March 2007, pp. 5–19

Van De Voorde, C., 'Sri Lankan Terrorism: Assessing and Responding to the Threat of the Liberation Tigers of Tamil Eelam (LTTE)'. *Police Practice and Research*, 6(2), May 2005, pp. 181–199

Webber, F., 'Book Review: The Pinochet File: A Declassified Dossier on Atrocity and Accountability'. *Race Class*, Vol. 46, January 2005, pp. 85–89

Wilkinson, D., *Silence on the Mountain: Stories of Terror, Betrayal, and Forgetting in Guatemala*. Durham, NC: Duke University Press, 2004

E. Insurgent terrorism

Anderson, J.L., *Guerillas, Töten für eine bessere Welt*. Berlin: List 2005

Astrain, L.N., *The Basques: Their Struggle for Independence*. Cardiff: Welsh Academic Press, 1997

Aust, S., *Der Baader-Meinhof Complex*. Munich: Goldmann Taschenbuch, 1998

Bowyer-Bell, J., *IRA Tactics and Targets: An Analysis of Tactical Aspects of the Armed Struggle 1969–1989*. Dublin: Poolbeg Press, 1990

Byrne, H., *El Salvador's Civil War: A Study of Revolution*. Boulder, CO: Lynne Rienner, 1996

Clarke, R., *The Future of Terrorism*. Washington, DC: New American Foundation, 2005

Coll, S., *Ghost Wars: The Secret History of the CIA: Afghanistan and Bin Laden from the Soviet Invasion to September 10, 2001*. London: Penguin Books, 2005

Cronin, A.K., *Ending Terrorism*. London: Routledge, 2008

International Crisis Group, 'In Their Own Words: Reading the Iraqi Insurgency'. *Middle East Report* no. 50, Brussels: International Crisis Group, 15 February 2006

Khalil, L., 'Assessing al-Qaeda's Position in Iraq'. *Terrorism Focus*, 3(20), 23 May 2006. Available at: www.jamestown.org/programs/gta/single/?tx_ttnews[tt_news]=780&tx_ttnews[backPid]=239&no_cache=1 (accessed 13 March 2009)

Khalil, L. 'Who's Who in Ramadi among the Insurgent Groups?' *Terrorism Focus*, 3(24), 20 June 2006. Available at: www.jamestown.org/programs/gta/single/?tx_ttnews[tt_news]=810&tx_ttnews[backPid]=239&no_cache=1 (accessed 13 March 2009)

Kurz, A., *Fatah and the Politics of Violence: The Institutionalization of a Popular Struggle*. Eastbourne, UK: Sussex Academic Press, 2005

Kurz, A., 'Fatah's Electoral Defeat: The End of Inertia'. *Strategic Assessment*, 9(1), April 2006, pp. 12–18

Kydd, A.H. and Walter, B.F., 'The Strategies of Terrorism'. *International Security*, 31(1), Summer 2006, pp. 49–80

Marks, T.A., 'Urban Insurgency'. *Small Wars and Insurgencies*, 14 (3), 2003, pp. 100–157

Marks, T.A., 'Ideology of Insurgency: New Ethnic Focus or old Cold War Distortions?' *Small Wars and Insurgencies*, 15(1), 2004, pp. 107–128

Marks, T.A. and Palmer, D.S., 'Radical Maoist Insurgents and Terrorist Tactics: Comparing Peru and Nepal'. *Low Intensity Conflict and Law Enforcement*, 13 (2), 2005, pp. 91–116

Metz, S., 'Rethinking Insurgency'. *Strategic Studies Institute*, June 2007. Available at: www.strategicstudies institute.army.mil (accessed 13 March 2009)

Micholus, E.F. and Simmons, S.L., *Terrorism, 2002–2004: A Chronology*. Westport, CT: Greenwood Press, 2005

Miller, W.H., 'Insurgency Theory and the Conflict in Algeria: A Theoretical Analysis of the Civil War in Algeria'. *Terrorism and Political Violence*, 12(1), 2000, pp. 60–79

Norell, M., 'Ethno-Political Violence', Report for the Swedish Agency for Civil Emergency Planning, Stockholm (in Swedish), 1999

O'Neill, B.E., *Insurgency and Terrorism: From Revolution to Apocalypse*, 2nd edn, revised. Duelles, VA: Potomac Books, 2005

Parker, D. (ed.), *Revolutions and the Revolutionary Tradition in the West, 1560–1991*. London: Routledge, 2000

Phares, W., 'Future Terrorism: Mutant Jihads'. *Journal of International Security Affairs*, Fall 2006, pp. 97–102

Phillips, J., 'The Evolving Al-Qaeda Threat'. Testimony before the House Armed Services Committee, Subcommittee on Terrorism, Unconventional Threats, and Capabilities. February 16, 2006

Polk, W.R., *Violent Politics: A History of Insurgency, Terrorism and Guerrilla War: From the American Revolution to Iraq*, New York: Harper, 2007

Puchala, D.J., 'Of Pirates and Terrorists: What Experience and History Teach'. *Contemporary Security Policy*, 26 (1), April 2005, pp. 1–24

Rabasa, A., Chalk, P., Cragin, K., Daly, S.A., Gregg, H.S., Karasik, T.W., O'Brien, K.A. and Rosenau, W., *Beyond Al-Qaeda. Part 1: The Global Jihadist Movement*. Mg-429. Santa Monica, CA: RAND, 2006

Rabasa, A., Chalk, P., Cragin, K., Daly, S.A., Gregg, H.S., Karasik, T.W., O'Brien, K.A. and Rosenau, W., *Beyond Al-Qaeda. Part 2: The Outer Rings of the Terrorist Universe*. Mg-430. Santa Monica, CA: RAND, 2006

Shakibi, Z., *Revolutions and the Collapse of the Monarchy: Human Agency and the Making of Revolution in France, Russia, and Iran*. London: I.B. Tauris, 2007

Shultz, R.H. Jr and Dew, A.J., *Insurgents, Terrorists, and Militias: The Warriors of Contemporary Combat*. New York: Columbia University Press, 2006

Siqueira, K., 'Political and Militant Wings within Dissident Movements and Organizations'. *Journal of Conflict Resolution*, vol. 49, April 2005, pp. 218–236

Sprinzak, E., 'The Process of Delegitimization: Towards a Linkage Theory of Political Terrorism'. *Terrorism and Political Violence*, 3(1), 1991, pp. 61–81

Tilly, C., *Trust and Rule*. Cambridge: Cambridge University Press, 2005

Tul, D. and Mehler, M., 'The Hidden Costs of Power-Sharing: Reproducing Insurgent Violence in Africa'. *African Affairs*, 104(416), July 2005, pp. 375–398

Tumelty, P., 'An In-Depth Look at the London Bombers'. *Terrorism Monitor*, 3(15), 28 July 2005. Available at: www.jamestown.org/programs/gta/single/?tx_ttnews[tt_news]=535&tx_ttnews[backPid]=180&no_cache=1 (Accessed 13 March 2009)

Tumelty, P., 'New Developments Following the London Bombings'. *Terrorism Monitor*, 3(23), 16 December 2005, www.jamestown.org/programs/gta/single/?tx_ttnews[tt_news]=622&tx_ttnews[backPid]=180&no_cache=1 (Accessed 13 March 2009)

US Department of State. *Country Reports on Terrorism 2006*. Washington, DC: US Department of State, Office of the Coordinator for Counterterrorism, 2007

Vernitski, A., 'Russian Revolutionaries and English Sympathizers in 1890s London: The Case of Olive Garnett and Sergei Stepniak'. *Journal of European Studies*, vol. 35, September 2005, pp. 299–314

Waldmann, P., *Terrorismus und Bürgerkrieg: Der Staat in Bedrängnis*. Hamburg: Murmann Verlag, 2003

Yayla, A., *Terrorism as a Social Information Entity: A Model for Early Intervention*. Dissertation, University of North Texas, Denton. 2005

F. Vigilante terrorism

Graham, H.D. and Gurr, T.R. (eds), *Violence in America: Historical and Comparative Perspectives*. Beverly Hills, CA: Sage, 1979

Haysom, N., *Mabangalala: The Rise of Right-Wing Vigilantes in South Africa*. London: Catholic Institute for International Relations, 1986

Levitas, D., *The Terrorist Next Door: The Militia Movement and the Radical Right*. New York: Thomas Dunne Books/St Martin's Press, 2002

Peleg, S., 'They Shoot Prime Ministers Too, Don't They? Religious Violence in Israel: Premises, Dynamics, and Prospects'. *Studies in Conflict and Terrorism*, 20, July–September 1997, pp. 227–247

Rubin, M., *Into the Shadows: Radical Vigilantes in Khatami's Iran*. Washington, DC: Washington Institute for Near East Policy, 2001

Weisburd, D., *Jewish Settler Violence: Deviance as Social Reaction*. University Park: Pennsylvania State University Press, 1989

G. Other types of terrorism

Amster, R., 'Perspectives on Ecoterrorism: Catalysts, Conflations and Casualties'. *Contemporary Justice Review*, 9(3), September 2006, pp. 287–301

Benjamin, D. and Simon, S., *The Age of Sacred Terror: Radical Islam's War against America*. New York: Random House Trade, Reprint, 2003

Bergen, P., *The Osama Bin Laden I Know: An Oral History of Al Qaeda's Leader*. New York: B&T, 2006

Bloom, M., 'Suicide Terrorism'. *Political Science Quarterly*, 121(3), Fall 2006, pp. 503–504

Bloom, M., 'Female Suicide Bombers: A Global Trend'. *Daedalus*, Winter 2007, pp. 1–9

Brachman, J.M., *Global Jihadism*. London: Routledge, 2008

Brown, L.V., *Cyberterrorisn and Computer Attacks*, New York: Nova Science Publishers, 2006

Brym, R.J. and Araj, B., 'Suicide Bombing as Tragedy and Interaction: The Case of the Second Intifada'. *Social Forces*, 84(4), June 2006, pp. 1969–1986

Card, C., 'Recognizing Terrorism', *Journal of Ethics*, 11(1), March 2007, pp. 1–29

Chasdi, R.J., *Tapestry of Terror. A Portrait of Middle East Terrorism, 1994–1999*. Lanham, MD: Lexington Books, 2002

Chomsky, N., 'Terrorism, American Style'. *World Policy Journal*, 24 (1), Spring 2007, pp. 44–45

Colarik, A.M., *Cyber Terrorism: Political and Economic Implications*. Hershey, PA: Idea Group Publishing, 2006

Cremin, B., 'Extortion by Product Contamination: A Recipe for Disaster within the Food and Drink Industry'. *American Behavioral Scientist*, 44, February 2001, pp. 1042–1052

Croitoru, J., *Der Märtyrer als Waffe: Die historischen Wurzeln des Selbstmordattentats*. Munich: Hanser, 2003

Crutchley, T.M., Rodgers, J.B., Whiteside, H.P., Vanier, M. and Terndrup, T.E., 'Agroterror: Where Are We in the Ongoing War on Terrorism?' *Journal of Food Protection*, 70(3), March 2007, pp. 791–804

Devetak, R., 'The Gothic Scene of International Relations: Ghosts, Monsters, Terror and the Sublime after September 11'. *Review of International Studies*, 31(4), October 2005, pp. 621–643

Devji, F., *Landscapes of the Jihad: Militancy, Morality, Modernity*. Ithaca, NY: Cornell University Press, 2005

Duyvesteyn, I., 'How New Is the New Terrorism?' *Studies in Conflict and Terrorism*, 27(5), September–October 2004, pp. 439–454

Eagleton, T., *Holy Terror*. Oxford: Oxford University Press, 2005

Elsässer, J., *Wie der Dschihad nach Europa kam. Gotteskrieger und Geheimdienste auf dem Balkan*. St Pölten: Niederösterreichisches Pressehaus, 2005

Ganor, B. (ed.), *Post-modern Terrorism: Trends, Scenarios and Future Threat*. Herzliya, Israel: International Institute for Counter-Terrorism, 2005

Gilbert, P., *New Terror, New Wars*. Edinburgh: Edinburgh University Press, 2003

Graham, R., *Anarchism: A Documentary History of Libertarian Ideas*. Vol. 1: *From Anarchy to Anarchism (300 CE to 1939)*. Montreal: Black Rose Books, 2005

Greenberg, M.D., *Maritime Terrorism: Risk and Liability*. Santa Monica, CA: RAND, 2007

Gunn, M.J., 'Has the Threat of Mass-Casualty Terrorism Been Exaggerated?' *Defence Studies*, 3(2), Summer 2003, pp. 114–120

Gupta, D.K. and Mundra, K., 'Suicide Bombing as a Strategic Weapon: An Empirical Investigation of Hamas and Islamic Jihad'. *Terrorism and Political Violence*, 17(4), 2005, pp. 573–598

Hafez, M.M., *Suicide Bombers in Iraq: The Strategy and Ideology of Martyrdom*. Washington DC: United States Institute of Peace Press, 2007

Heine, P., *Terror in Allahs Namen: Extremistische Kräfte im Islam*. Freiburg: Herder, 2001

Hoffman, B., 'The Logic of Suicide Terrorism'. *Atlantic Monthly*, June 2003

Inbar, E. and Hillel, F., *Radical Islam and International Security*. London: Routledge, 2007

Israeli, R., *Islamikaze: Manifestations of Islamic Martyrology*. London: Frank Cass, 2003

IWPR Staff in Central Asia, 'Uzbekistan: Affluent Suicide Bombers'. *RCA* no. 278, 20, April 2004

Jones, D.M. (ed.), *Globalisation and the New Terror*. Cheltenham, UK: Edward Elgar, 2006

Josse, P., 'Leaderless Resistance and Ideological Inclusion: The Case of the Earth Liberation Front'. *Terrorism and Political Violence*, 193, Fall 2007, pp. 351–368

Kepel, G., *Jihad: The Trail of Political Islam*. London: Tauris, 2002

Kiernan, B., *Blood and Soil: A World History of Genocide and Extermination from Sparta to Darfur*. London: Yale University Press, 2007

Knights, M., 'Attack on Abqaiq Highlights Growing Focus on Oil Targets'. *Janes's Intelligence Review*, 18(5), May 2006, pp. 6–11

Leader, S.H. and Probst, P., 'The Earth Liberation Front and Environmental Terrorism'. *Terrorism and Political Violence*, 15(4), Winter 2003, pp. 37–58

Lentini, P. and Bakashmar, M. 'Jihadist Beheading: A Convergence of Technology, Theology and Teleology'. *Studies in Conflict and Terrorism*, 30(4), 207, pp. 303–326

Manenschijn, G., *Religie en haat: over religieus gemotiveerd terrorisme*. Kampen, Netherlands: Uitgeverij Ten Have, 2007

Manning, L., Baines, R.N. and Chadd, S.A., 'Deliberate Contamination of the Food Supply Chain'. *British Food Journal*, 107(4), 4 November 2005, pp. 225–245

Marten, K., 'Warlordism: Comparative Perspective'. *International Security*, 31(3), 2006–2007, pp. 41–73

Mayer, J.F., 'Cults, Violence and Religious Terrorism: An International Perspective'. *Studies in Conflict and Terrorism*, 24(5), September 2001, pp. 361–376

Michael, G., *The Enemy of My Enemy: The Alarming Convergence of Militant Islam and the Extreme Right*. Lawrence: University Press of Kansas, 2006

Mockaitis, T. R., *The 'New' Terrorism*. Westport, CT: Greenwood Press, 2006

Moghadam, A., 'Palestinian Suicide Terrorism in the Second Intifada: Motivations and Organizational Aspects'. *Studies in Conflict and terrorism*, 26(2), February–March 2003, pp. 65–92

Moghadam, A., 'Suicide Terrorism, Occupation, and the Globalization of Martyrdom: A Critique of "Dying to Win"'. *Studies in Conflict and Terrorism*, 29(8), December 2006, pp. 707–729

Nincic, D.J., 'The Challenge of Maritime Terrorism: Threat Identification, WMD and Regime Response'. *Journal of Strategic Studies*, 28(4), August 2005, pp. 619–644

Norell, M., 'New Terror'? (Ny Terror). In *Swedish Defence Research Agency User Report*, 'Follow-Up Study on the Terror Attacks – and their Consequences – on the World Trade Center and the Pentagon on September 11, 2001' (in Swedish), 2002

O'Day, A., *Roots of Modern Terrorism*. Aldershot, UK: Ashgate, 2008

O'Lear, S., 'Environmental Terrorism: A Critique'. *Geopolitics*, 8(3), October 2003, pp. 127–150

Orbach, I., 'Terror Suicide: How Is It Possible?' *Archives of Suicide Research*, 8(1), January–March 2004, pp. 115–130

Papachristos, A.V., 'Gang World'. *Foreign Policy*, March–April 2005, pp. 49–54

Pape, R.A., *Dying to Win: The Strategic Logic of Suicide Terrorism*. New York: Random House Trade Paperbacks, 2006

Pech, R.J., 'Inhibiting Imitative Terrorism through Memetic Engineering'. *Journal of Contingencies and Crisis Management*, 11(2), June 2003, pp. 61–66

Pech, R.J. and Slade, B.W., 'Imitative Terrorism: A Diagnostic Framework for Identifying Catalysts and Designing Interventions'. *Foresight*, 7(1), 2005, pp. 47–60

Pedazhur, A., *Suicide Terrorism*. Cambridge: Polity Press, 2005

Petros, G., *Art That Kills: A Panoramic Portait of Aesthetic Terrorism 1984–2001*. Houston, TX: Creation Books, 2007

Petrosino, C., 'Connecting the Past to the Future: Hate Crime in America'. *Journal of Contemporary Criminal Justice*, 15, February 1999, pp. 22–47

Plaxe, J., 'International Maritime Terror and Security'. *Journal of Counterterrorism and Homeland Security International*, 10(3), 2004, pp. 16–19

Post, J.M., Ruby, K.G. and Shaw, E.D., 'From Car Bombs to Logic Bombs: The Growing Threat from Information Terrorism'. *Terrorism and Political Violence*, 12(2), 2000, pp. 97–122

Quillen, C., 'A Historical Analysis of Mass Casualty Bombers'. *Studies in Conflict and Terrorism*, 5(5), September 2002, pp. 279–292

Ramasubramanian, R., 'Suicide Terrorism in Sri Lanka'. *IPCS Research Papers #5*. New Delhi: Institute of Peace and Conflict Studies, August 2004

Raymond, C.Z., 'The Threat of Maritime Terrorism in the Malacca Straits'. *Terrorism Monitor*, 4(3), 9 February 2006. Available at: www.jamestown.org/programs/gta/single/?tx_ttnews[tt_news]=670&tx_ttnews[back Pid]=181&no_cache=1 (accessed 16 March 2009)

Raymond, C.Z., 'Maritime Terrorism in Southeast Asia: A Risk Assessment'. *Terrorism and Political Violence*, 18(2), Summer 2006, pp. 239–257

Reuter, C., *My Life Is Weapon. A Modern History of Suicide Bombing*. Princeton, NJ: Princeton University Press, 2004

Richardson, M., *A Time Bomb for Global Trade: Maritime-Related Terrorism in an Age of Weapons of Mass Destruction*. Singapore: Institute for Southeast Asian Studies (ISEAS) Publications, 2004

Richardson, T.B., *Terror on the High Seas*. Westport, CT: Greenwood Press, 2007

Roberts, M., 'Suicide Missions as Witnessing: Expansions, Contrasts'. *Studies in Conflict and Terrorism*, 30(10), 2007, pp. 857–887

Rubin, C.B., 'Major Terrorist Events in the US and Their Outcomes: Initial Analysis and Observations'. *Journal of Homeland Security and Emergency Management*, 1(1), 2004. Available at: http://bepress.com/jhsem/vol1/iss1/2 (accessed 16 March 2009)

Rubin, M., 'Into the Shadows: Radical Vigilantes in Khatami's Iran'. Washington Institute for Near East Policy, *Policy Papers*, no. 56, 2001

Schoch, B., 'Der neue Terrorismus: Hintergründe und Handlungsfelder in arabischen Staaten'. In K. Hirschmann and C. Leggemann (eds), *Der Kampf gegen den Terrorismus: Strategien und Handlungserfordernisse in Deutschland*. Berlin: BWV, 2003

Schroedel, J. 'Review: Patricia Baird-Windle and Eleanor J. Bader, "Targets of Hatred: Anti-Abortion Terrorism". New York: Palgrave'. *Women's Studies*, 32(5), July–August 2003, pp. 677–679

Sedgwick, M., 'Al-Qaeda and the Nature of Religious Terrorism'. *Terrorism and Political Violence*, 16(4), October–December 2004, pp. 795–814

Speckhard, A., 'Defusing Human Bombs: Understanding Suicide Terrorism'. In J. Victoroff, (ed.), *Social and Psychological Factors in the Genesis of Terrorism*. Amsterdam: IOS Press, 2006

Speckhard, A. and Ahkmedova, K., 'The Making of a Martyr: Chechen Suicide Terrorism'. *Studies in Conflict and Terrorism*, 29(5), July–August 2006, pp. 429–492

Stohl, M., 'Cyber Terrorism: A Clear and Present Danger, the Sum of All Fears, Breaking Point or Patriot Games?' *Crime, Law and Social Change*, 46(4–5), December 2006, pp. 223–238

Taylor, B., 'Threat Assessment and Radical Environmentalism'. *Terrorism and Political Violence*, 15(4), Winter 2003, pp. 173–182

Taylor, R.W., Caeti, T.J., Kall Loper, D., Fritsch, E.J. and Liederbach, J., *Digital Crime and Digital Terrorism*. Upper Saddle River, NJ: Pearson/Prentice Hall, 2006

Tellidis, I., 'Preventing Terrorism? Conflict Resolution and Nationalist Violence in the Basque Country'. PhD thesis, St Andrews University, 2008 (unpublished)

Totten, S. and Bartrop, P.R., *Dictionary of Genocide*. Oxford: Greenwood Press, 2008

Ungerer, C. and Rogers, D., 'The Threat of Agroterrorism to Australia: A Preliminary Assessment'. *Studies in Conflict and Terrorism*, 29(2), March 2006, pp. 147–163

Vanderheiden, S., 'Eco-terrorism or Justified Resistance? Radical Environmentalism and the "War on Terror" '. *Politics and Society*, 33, September 2005, pp.425–447

Verton, D., *Black Ice: The Invisible Threat of Cyberterrorism*. London: McGraw-Hill/Osborne, 2003

Victor, B., *Army of Roses. Inside the World of Palestinian Women Suicide Bombers*. London: Robinson, 2004

Von Knop, J. and Frank, H. (eds), *Netz- und Computersicherheit: Sind wir auf einen Angriff auf unsere Informationssysteme und Informations-Infrastrukturen vorbereitet?* Düsseldorf: Heinrich Heine Universität, 2003

Vreja, L.O., 'Narcoterrorism in Southeastern Europe'. *Connections*, Spring 2005, pp. 91–102

Weimann, G., 'Cyberterrorism: How Real is the Threat'? Washington, DC: United States Institute of Peace. *Special Report 119*, December 2004

Weimann, G., 'Cyberterrorism: the Sum of all Fears?' *Studies in Conflict and Terrorism*, 28(2), March–April 2005, pp. 129–149

Zabel, S., *Der (ir)rationale Terrorismus: Selbstmordattentate aus ökonomischer und soziologischer Perspektive der Rational-Choice-Theorie*. Munich: GRIN Verlag, 2004

H. Terroristic activities, by region and country

H.1 Western Europe, general

Abbott, P.K., 'Terrorist Threat in the Tri-Border Area: Myth or Reality?' *Military Review*, September–October 2004, pp. 51–55

Abuza, Z., 'The Moro Islamic Liberation Front at 20: State of the Revolution'. *Studies in Conflict and Terrorism*, 28(6), November–December 2005, pp. 453–479

Del Valle, A., *Islamic Totalitarianism on the Attack against Democracies*. Paris: Syrtes, 2002

Europol, *Terrorist Activity in the European Union: Situation and Trends Report (Te-Sat), October 2003–17th October 2004*. The Hague: Europol, Dghii, file no. 100927, 2566–378, 2 December 2004

Europol, *EU Terrorism Situation and Trend Report 2007. Te-Sat 2007*. The Hague: Europol, 2007. Available at: www.europol.europa.eu (accessed 16 March 2009)

Ganser, D., *Gladio: NATO's Secret Armies. Operation Gladio and Terrorism in Western Europe*. London: Frank Cass, 2004

Leiken, R.S., *Europe's Mujahideen: Where Mass Immigration Meets Global Terrorism*. Washington, DC: Center for Immigration Studies, 2005. Available at: www.cis.org (accessed 16 March 2009)

Levitt, M. and Sawyer, J., 'Zarqawi's Jordanian Agenda'. *Terrorism Monitor*, 16 December 2004

Levitt, M., 'Islamic Extremism in Europe: Beyond Al-Qaeda: Hamas and Hezbollah in Europe'. Testimony before the House Committee on International Relations, Subcommittee on Europe and Emerging Threats, 27 April 2005

Martin, G., 'Sea Change: Perspective and the Modern Terrorist Environment'. In G. Ritzer (ed.), *Handbook of International Social Problems: A Comparative International Perspective*. Thousand Oaks, CA: Sage, 2003

Mekhennet, S., Sautter, C. and Hanfeld, M., *Die Kinder des Dschihad: Die neue Generation des Islamistischen Terror in Europa*. Munich: Piper, 2007

Pargeter, A., 'North African Immigrants in Europe and Political Violence'. *Studies in Conflict and Terrorism*, 29(8), December 2006, pp. 731–748

Phillips, M., *Londonistan*. New York: Encounter Books, 2006

Reeve, S., *One Day in September: The Story of the 1972 Munich Olympics Massacre: A Government Cover-Up and a Covert Revenge Mission*. London: Faber & Faber, 2001

Truby, J.D., *How Terrorists Kill: The Complete Terrorist Arsenal*. Boulder, CO: Paladin Press, 1978

Ulfkotte, U., *Heiliger Krieg in Europa: Wie die radikale Muslimbruderschaft unsere Gesellschaft bedroht*. Frankfurt am Main: Eichborn, 2007

Van Leeuwen, M., 'Ronselen in Europa voor de heilige oorlog'. *Justiële Verkenningen*, 31(2), March 2005, pp. 84–94

Vidino, L., *Al Qaeda In Europe: The New Battleground of International Jihad*. New York: Prometeus Books, 2006

H.1.1 German Federal Republic

Botzat, T., *Ein deutscher Herbst: Zustände 1977*, Frankfurtam, Main: Verlag Neue Kritik, 1997

Breloer, H., *Todesspiel: Von der Schleyer-Entführung bis Mogadischu: Eine documentarisch Erzählung*. Cologne: Kiepenheuer & Witsch, 1997

Chaussy, U., *Oktoberfest, ein Attentat*. Darmstadt: Luchterhand Literaturverlag, 1985

Hauser, D., *Baader und Herald: Beschreibung eines Kampfes*. Berlin: Alexander Verlag, 1997

Knobbe, M. and Schmitz, S., *Terrorjahr 1997: Wie die RAF Deutschland veränderte*. Munich: Heyne, 2007

Koenen, G., *Vesper, Ensslin, Baader. Urszenen des deutschen Terrors*. Frankfurt am Main: Fischer Taschenbuch Verlag, 2005

Kraushaar, W. (ed.), *Die RAF und die Linke: Terrorismus*, 2 vols. Hamburg: Hamburger Edition, 2006

Landgrebe, C., *'68 und die Folgen: Ein unvollständiges Lexikon*. Berlin: Argon-Verlaf, 1998

Malthaner, S. and Waldmann, P., 'Terrorism in Germany: Old and New Problems'. In M. van Leeuwen (ed.), *Confronting Terrorism*. The Hague: Kluwer Law International, 2003

Molloy, I., *Rolling Back Revolution: The Emergence of Low Intensity Conflict*. London: Pluto Press, 2001

Peters, B., *Tödlicher Irrtum: Die Geschichte der RAF*. Berlin: Argon-Verlag, 2005

Proll, A., *Hans und Grete: Bilder der RAF 1967–1977*. Berlin: Aufbau Verlag, 2004

Thamm, B.G., *Terrorbasis Deutschland: Die islamistische Gefahr in unserer Mitte*. Kreuzlingen and Munich: Heinrich Hugendubel Verlag, 2004

Tolmein, O., *Vom deutschen Herbst zum 11 September: Die RAF, der Terrorismus und der Staat*. Hamburg: Konkret Literatur Verlag, 2002

Uhlmann, J., 'L'Islamisme radicale et le djihadisme en Allemagne'. In J.-L. Marret, *Les fabricants de jihad*. Paris: Presse Universitaires France (PUF), 2004

Ulfkotte, U., *Der Krieg in unseren Städten: Wie radikale Islamisten Deutschland unterwandern*. Frankfurt am Main: Fischer Taschenbuch Verlag, 2004

Weisbrod, B., 'Fundamentalist Violence: Political Violence and Political Religion in Modern Conflict'. *International Social Science Journal*, 54(174), December 2002, pp. 499–508

H.1.2 France

Debat, A., 'Terror and the Fifth Republic'. *National Interest*, (82), Winter 2006, pp. 55–61

Touboul, D. 'GSPC: Al-Qaeda's Ally in the Sahel: A Threat to France?' *Islam in Africa Newsletter*, 2(1), January 2007

H.1.3 Ireland

Alexander, Y. and O'Day, A. (eds), *The Irish Terrorism Experience*. Aldershot, UK: Dartmouth, 1991

Alonso, R., *The IRA and the Armed Struggle*. London: Frank Cass, 2006

Arthur, P. and Jeffery, K., *Northern Ireland since 1968*. Oxford: Basil Blackwell, 1988

Bolton, R., *Death on the Rock and Other Stories*, London: W.H. Allen, 1990

Bruce, S., 'Terrorism and Politics: The Case of Northern Ireland's Loyalist Paramilitaries'. *Terrorism and Political Violence*, 13(2), Summer 2001, pp. 27–48

Clarke, L., *Broadening the Battlefield: The H-Blocks and the Rise of Sinn Féin*. Dublin: Gill & Macmillan, 1987

Doghartaigh, N.O., *From Civil Rights to Armalites: Derry and the Birth of the Irish Troubles*, 2nd edn. London: Palgrave, 2004

English, R., *Armed Struggle: The History of the IRA*. London: Pan, 2004

IMC, Eighteenth Report of the Independent Monitoring Commission. Presented to the Houses of Parliament by the Secretary of State for Northern Ireland in Accordance with the Northern Ireland (Monitoring Commission Etc.) Act 2003. London: The Stationery Office, May 2008

Moloney, E., *A Secret History of the IRA*. London: Penguin, 2002

Multhaupt, W.F., *Die Irisch-Republikanische Armee (IRA): Von der Guerilla-Freiheitsarmee zur modernen Untergrundorganisation*. Bonn: Hochschulschrift, 1988

Richards, A., 'Political Fronts of Terrorist Groups. A Comparative Study of Northern Ireland's Political Fronts, Their Evolution, Roles and Potential for Attaining Political Change'. PhD thesis, St Andrews University, 2003 (unpublished)

Roche, P.J. and Barton, B., *The Northern Ireland Question: Nationalism, Unionism, and Partition*. Aldershot, UK: Ashgate, 1999

Rowan, B., *Behind the Lines: The Story of the IRA and Loyalist Ceasefires*. Belfast: Blackstaff Press, 1995

Ryle Dwyer, T., *The Squad and the Intelligence Operations of Michael Collins*. Cork: Mercer, 2005

Stevenson, J., 'Exploiting Democracy: The IRA's Tactical Cease-Fire'. In E. Inbar, (ed.), *Democracies and Small Wars*. London: Routledge, 2003

Taylor, P., *Loyalists*. London: Bloomsbury, 2000

Tonge, J., *The New Northern Irish Politics?* Basingstoke, UK: Palgrave Macmillan, 2005

White, R., *Provisional Irish Republicans: An Oral and Interpretive History*. Westport, CT: Greenwood Press, 1993

White, R., 'The Provisional Irish Republican Army: An Assessment of Sectarianism'. *Terrorism and Political Violence*, 9, Spring 1997: pp. 20–55

White, R., 'The Irish Republican Army and Sectarianism: Moving beyond the Anecdote'. *Terrorism and Political Violence*, 9, Summer 1997, pp. 120–131

White, R., 'Don't Confuse Me with the Facts: More on the Irish Republican Army and Sectarianism'. *Terrorism and Political Violence*, 10, Winter 1998, pp. 166–191

Wood, I., *Crimes Of Loyalty: A History of the UDA*. Edinburgh: Edinburgh University Press, 2006

H.1.4 Italy

Curcio, R., *Mit offenem Blick: Ein Gespräch zur Geschichte der Roten Brigaden in Italien von Mario Scialoja*. Berlin: ID Verlag, 1997

Drake, R., *Apostles and Agitators: Italy's Marxist Revolutionary Tradition*. Cambridge, MA: Harvard University Press, 2003

Franceschini, A., *Pier Vittorio Buffa, Franco Giustolisi: Das Herz des Staates treffen*. Vienna: Europaische Verlagsanstalt, 1990

Ganser, D., 'The Ghost of Machiavelli: An Approach to Operation Gladio and Terrorism in Cold War Italy'. *Crime, Law and Social Change*, 45(2), March 2006, pp. 111–154

Grützmacher, C., *Islamistischer Terrorismus als Sicherheitsproblem in Asien: Kampf im Namen Allahs?* Hamburg: Kovac, 2008

Igel, R.A., *Politik zwischen Geheimdienst und Mafia*. Munich: Herbig, 1998

Igel, R., *Terrorjahre: Die dunkle Seite der CIA in Italien*. Munich: Herbig, 2006

Jamieson, A., *The Heart Attacked: Terrorism and Conflict in the Italian State*. London: Marion Boyars, 1989

Lanza, L., *Bomben und Geheimnisse: Geschichte des Massakers von der Piazza Fontana*. Hamburg: Nautilus, 1999

Olimpio, G. 'Italy and Islamic Militancy: From Logistics Base to Potential Target'. *Terrorism Monitor*, 3(18), 22 September 2005, pp. 4–6

Pisano, V.S., *The Dynamics and Subversion of Violence in Contemporary Italy*. Stanford, CA: Hoover Institution, 1987

Vidino, L., 'Is Italy Next in Line after London?' *Terrorism Monitor*, 3(18), 22 September 2005, pp. 1–3

H.1.5 Spain

Jiménez, J.O., *Policía, terrorismo y cambio político en España, 1976–1996*. Valencia: Universidad de Burgos, 2001

Lia, B. and Hegghammer, T., 'Jihadi Strategic Studies: The Alleged Al Qaeda Policy Study preceding the Madrid Bombings'. *Studies in Conflict and Terrorism*, 27, 2004, pp. 355–375

Mansvelt-Beck, J., *Territory and Terror: Conflicting Nationalisms in the Basque Country*. London: Routledge, 2005

Mees, L., 'Between Votes and Bullets: Conflicting Ethnic Identities in the Basque Country'. *Ethnic and Racial Studies*, 24(5), September 2001, pp. 798–827

Muñoz, A.A., *El terrorismo en España*. Barcelona: Planeta: Instituto de Estudios Económicos, 1982

Zulaika, J., *Basque Violence: Metaphor and Sacrament*. Reno: University of Nevada Press, 1988

H.1.6 The Netherlands

AIVD, *De gewelddadige jihad in Nederland: actuele trends in de Islamitisch-terroristische dreiging*. The Hague: Ministerie van Binnenlandse Zaken en Koninkrijksrelaties, 2006

AIVD, *Radicale dawa in verandering: de opkomst van Islamistisch neoradicalisme in Nederland*. The Hague: Ministerie van Binnenlandese Zaken en Koninkijksrelaties, 2007

Eikelenboom, S., *Niet bang om te sterven: dertig jaar terrorisme in Nederland*. Amsterdam: Nieuw Amsterdam Uitgevers, 2007

Figee, E. *et al.*, *Terrorisme en Nederland: een analyse van de dreiging*. 's-Hertogenbosch: Heinen, 2005

Groen, J. and Kranenberg, A., *Strijdsters van Allah: Radicale moslima's en het Hofstadnetwerk*. Amsterdam: Meulenhoff, 2006

Koenen, G., *Vesper, Ensslin, Baader: Urszenen des deutschen Terrors*. Frankfurt am Main: Fischer Taschenbuch Verlag, 2005

Meyer, T., *Am Ende der Gewalt? Der Deutsche Terrorismus: Protokoll eines Jahrzehnts*. Frankfurt am Main: Ullstein, 1980

Pekelder, J. and Boterman, F. (eds), *Politiek geweld in Duitsland: denkbeelden en debatten*. Amsterdam: Mets en Schilt Uitgevers, 2005

Smeets, H., *In Nederland gebleven: de geschiedenis van Molukkers 1951–2006*. Amsterdam: Bakker; Utrecht: Moluks Historisch Museum, 2006

Taarnby, M., *Jihad in Denmark: An Overview and Analysis of Jihadi Activity in Denmark (1990–2006)*. Copenhagen: DIIS Working Paper No. 2006/35

Thamm, B.G., *Terrorbasis Deutschland: Die Islamistische Gefahr in unserer Mitte*. Kreuzlingen and Munich: Heinrich Hugendubel Verlag, 2004

Tolmein, O., *Vom deutschen Herbst zum 11. September: Die RAF, der Terrorismus und der Staat*. Hamburg: Konkret Literatur, 2002

Verbij, A., *Tien rode jaren: links radicalisme in Nederland, 1970–1980*. Amsterdam: Ambo, 2005

Vermaat, E., *De Hofstadgroep: portret van een radikaal-Islamitisch netwerk*. Soesterberg, Netherlands: Uitgeverij Aspekt, 2005

Vermaat, E., *The Radicalization of Young Moroccans and Turks in the Netherlands*, 2007. Available at: www.militantislammonitor.org/article/ide/3243, (accessed 16 March 2009)

Vries, M. de, *Radicalisering gelokaliseerd: een wetenschappelijk onderzoek naar radicalisering in Nederland*. The Hague: SGBO, 2006

H.1.7 Other West European countries

Alexander, Y., Brenner, E.H. and S. Tutunoglu Krause, *Turkey: Terrorism, Civil Rights, and the European Union*. London: Routledge, 2008

Chalk, P., *West European Terrorism and Counter-terrorism: The Evolving Dynamic*. London: Macmillan, 1996

Doyle, N., *Terror Base UK: Inside a Secret War*. Edinburgh: Mainstream, 2006

EU SitCen, *SitCen Annual Report on International Terrorism 2005: Analysis and World Review of Terrorist Attacks and Significant Related Events in 2005*. Council of the European Union. EU Joint Situation Centre, 2006

Levitt, M., 'Islamic extremism in Europe: Beyond al-Qaeda: Hamas and Hezbollah In Europe'. Testimony before the House Committee on International Relations, Subcommittee on Europe and Emerging Threats. 27 April 2005

Norell, M., 'The Growing Threat of Islamic Militancy in Europe'. *Terrorism Monitor*, 3(8), 21 April 2005. Available at: www.jamestown.org/programs/gta/single/?tx_ttnews[tt_news]=296&tx_ttnews[backPid]=180&no_cache=1 (accessed 16 March 2009)

Paz, R., 'From Madrid to London: Al-Qaeda Exports the War in Iraq to Europe'. *Prism Occasional Papers*, 3(3), July 2005

Paz, R., 'Rakan Ben Williams: The Next Generation of Jihadi Terrorists in Europe'. *Prism Occasional Papers*, 3(8), November 2005

Pestana Barros, C. and Proença, I., 'Mixed Logit Estimation of Radical Islamic Terrorism in Europe and North America: A Comparative Study'. *Journal of Conflict Resolution*, 49, April 2005, pp. 298–314

Puistola, J. and Herrala, J., *Terrorism in Europe*. Chichester, UK: Bonnier Books, 2008

Steinberg, G., 'Terror – Europas internes Problem'., *Internationale Politik*, 11/2005, 2005, pp. 14–22

Taarnby, M., *Jihad in Denmark: An Overview and Analysis of Jihadi Activity in Denmark (1990–2006)*. Copenhagen: DIIS Working Paper no. 2006/35

Yildiz, K., *The Kurds in Turkey: EU Accession and Human Rights*. London: Pluto Press, 2005

H.2 Eastern Europe and Russia, general

H.2.1 Russia

Dunlop, J.B., 'The October 2002 Moscow Hostage-Taking Incident', Parts I–III, RFE-RL. *Organized Crime and Terrorism Watch*, 18 December 2003, 8 January 2004, 15 January 2004

Dunlop, J.B., *Beslan: Russia's 9/11?* American Committee for Peace in Chechnya and the Jamestown Foundation, October 2005

Henkin, Y., *Either We Win or We Perish! The History of the First Chechen War*. Tel Aviv: Maarachot, 2007

Kohlmann, E.F., *Al-Qaeda's Jihad in Europe: The Afghan–Bosnian Network*. Oxford: Berg, 2004

Kramer, M., 'Guerrilla Warfare, Counterinsurgency and Terrorism in the North Caucasus: The Military Dimension of the Russian–Chechen Conflict'. *Europe–Asia Studies*, 57(2), March 2005, pp. 209–290

Lynch, D., '"The Enemy Is at the Gate": Russia after Beslan'. *International Affairs*, 81(1), January 2005, pp. 141–162

Murphy, P., *The Wolves of Islam: Russia and the Faces of Chechen Terror*. New York: Brassey's US, 2004

Orr, M., *Russia's Wars with Chechnya, 1994–2003*. New York: Osprey, 2005

Politkovskaya, A., *Putin's Russia*. London: Harvill Press, 2004

Seth, R., *The Russian Terrorists: The Story of the Narodniki*. London: Barrie & Rockliff, 1996

Smith, S., *Allah's Mountains: The Battle for Chechnya*. London: Tauris Parke Paperbacks, 2005

Tishkov, V., *Chechnya: Life in a War-Torn Society*. Berkeley, CA: University of California Press, 2004

Van Zwol, C., *Gijzelaar van de Kaukasus: de ontvoering van Arjan Erkel*. Buffalo, NY: Prometheus, 2005

Vendina, O.I., Belozerov, V.S. and Gustafson, A., 'The Wars in Chechnya and Their Effects on Neighboring Regions'. *Eurasian Geography and Economics*, 48(2), March–April 2007, pp. 178–201

Vernitski, A., 'Russian Revolutionaries and English Sympathizers in 1890s London: The Case of Olive Garnett and Sergei Stepniak'. *Journal of European Studies*, 35, September 2005, pp. 299–314

H.2.2 Balkans, excluding Greece

Cline, L.E., 'From Öcalan to Al Qaeda: The Continuing Terrorist Threat in Turkey'. *Studies in Conflict and Terrorism*, 27(4), 2004, pp. 321–336

Innes, M.A., 'Terrorist Sanctuaries and Bosnia-Herzegovina: Challenging Conventional Assumptions'. *Studies in Conflict and Terrorism*, 28(4), 2005, pp. 295–305

International Crisis Group, 'Bin Laden and the Balkans: The Politics of Anti-terrorism'. Brussels: *ICG Balkans Report* no. 119, 9 November 2001

International Crisis Group, 'Iraq: Allaying Turkey's Fears over Kurdish Ambitions'. *Middle East Report* no. 35, 26 January 2005. Brussels: International Crisis Group

Kostovicova, D., *Kosovo: The Politics of Identity and Space*. London: Routledge, 2005

Lynch, D., *Engaging Eurasia's Separatist States: Unresolved Conflicts and De Facto States*. Washington, DC: United States Institute of Peace Press, 2004

Mincheva, L., 'The Decentralization Process in the Republic of Macedonia: Risk Assessment of the Regional Instability Factors Impacting on Macedonia's Inter-ethnic Peace'. In *The Decentralization Process in the Republic of Macedonia: Prospects for Ethnic Conflict Mitigation, Enhanced Representation, Institutional Efficiency and Accountability*. Sofia: IRIS, 2006

O'Shea, B., 'Kosovo: The Triumph of Ignorance'. *Studies in Conflict and Terrorism*, 28, 2005, pp. 61–65

Shay, S., *Islamic Terror and the Balkans*. Eddson, IL: Transaction, 2008

Tishkov, V., *Chechnya: Life in a War-Torn Society*. Berkeley, CA: University of California Press, 2004

Trenin, D., Malshenko, A. and Lieven, A., *Russia's Restless Frontier: The Chechnya Factor in Post-Soviet Russia*. Washington, DC: Carnegie Endowment for International Peace, 2004

Valiyev, A., 'Al-Qaeda in Azerbaijan: Myths and Realities'. *Terrorism Monitor*, 4(10), 18 May 2006. Available at: www.jamestown.org/programs/gta/single/?tx_ttnews[tt_news]=775&tx_ttnews[backPid]=181&no_cache=1 (accessed 16 March, 2009)

Valiyev, A., 'The Rise of Salafi Islam in Azerbaijan'. *Terrorism Monitor*, 3(13), 1 July 2005. Available at: www.jamestown.org/programs/gta/single/?tx_ttnews[tt_news]=518&tx_ttnews[backPid]=180&no_cache=1 (accessed 16 March 2009)

H.3 Middle East

Harari, H., *A View from the Eye of the Storm: Terror and Reason in the Middle East*. New York: Regan Books, 2005

Lennon, A.T.J. (ed.), *The Epicenter of Crisis: The New Middle East*. Cambridge, MA: MIT Press, 2008

Palmer Harik, J., *Hezbollah: The Changing Face of Terrorism*. London: I.B. Tauris, 2004

Rubin, B., 'The Real Roots of Arab Anti-Americanism'. *Foreign Affairs*, November–December, 2002, pp. 73–85

Smith, D., *The State of the Middle East: An Atlas of Conflict and Resolution*. Berkeley, CA: University of California Press, 2006

Tucker, S. and Roberts, P.M. (eds), *The Encyclopedia of the Arab–Israeli Conflict*. Santa Barbara, CA: ABC-CLIO, 2008

Youngs, R., *Europe and the Middle East: In the Shadow of September 11*. Boulder, CO: Lynne Rienner, 2006

H.3.1 Israel

Abedin, M., 'Post-Election Terrorist Trends in Iraq'. *Terrorism Monitor*, 3(5), 10 March 2005. Available at: www.jamestown.org/programs/gta/single/?tx_ttnews[tt_news]=313&tx_ttnews[backPid]=180&no_cache =1 (accessed 16 March 2009)

Abuza, Z., 'Balik Terrorism: The Return of the Abu Sayyaf'. *Strategic Studies*, 2005. Available at: www. strategicstudiesinstitute.army.mil/pubs/display.cfm?pubid=625 (accessed 16 March 2009)

Aharonovitz, G., 'Fences, Walls, and the Development of Cities: The Long-Term Effects of the Israeli–Palestinian Land Obstacle'. *Journal of Peace Research*, 43(1), January, pp. 55–65

Chehab, Z., *Iraq Ablaze: Inside the Insurgency*. London: I.B. Tauris, 2005

Heller, M.A., 'The Election of Abu Mazen and the Next Stage in Israeli–Palestinian Relations'. *Strategic Assessment*, 7(4), 2005, pp. 9–13

Heller, M.A., 'Hamas' Victory and Israel's Dilemma'. *Strategic Assessment*, 9(1), April 2006, pp. 1–4

ICT, 'The Israel Security Agency's 2006 Report Asserts that Hamas has taken over the Gaza Strip with the Support of Hezbollah and Iran'. Herzliya, Israel: ICT, 2007

Meital, Y., *Peace in Tatters: Israel, Palestine and the Middle East*. Boulder, CO: Lynne Rienner, 2006

Merari, A., 'Israel Facing Terrorism'. *Israel Affairs*, 11(1), January 2005, pp. 223–237

Nasr, K.B., *Arab and Israeli Terrorism: The Causes and Effects of Political Violence, 1936–1993*. Jefferson, NC: McFarland, 2007

Thomas, B., *How Israel Was Won: A Concise History of the Arab–Israeli Conflict (1900–1999)*. London: Lexington Books, 2004

H.3.2 Palestine

Agha, H. and Malley, R., 'The Lost Palestinians'. *New York Review of Books*, 52(10), 9 June 2005, pp. 20–24

Alexander, Y., *Palestinian Religious Terrorism: Hamas and Islamic Jihad*. Ardsley, NY: Transnational, 2002

Baumgarten, H., *Arafat, zwischen Kampf und Diplomatie*. Munich: Ullstein-Taschenbuch, 2002

Friesch, H., *The Islamic Dimension in Palestinian Politics*. Ramat Gan, Israel: Begin–Sadat Center for Strategic Studies, 2005

Ginat, R. and Bar-Noi, U., 'Tacit Support for Terrorism: The Rapprochement between the USSR and Palestinian Guerrilla Organizations following the 1967 War'. *Journal of Strategic Studies*, 30(2), 2007, pp. 255–284

Gunning, J., *Hamas in Politics: Democracy, Religion, Violence*. London: Hurst, 2008

Hafez, M., *Manufacturing Human Bombs: The Making of Palestinian Suicide Bombers*. Washington, DC: United States Institute of Peace Press, 2006

Herz, D., *Palestina, Gaza und Westbank: Geschichte, Politik, Kultur*. Munich: Beck, 2003

Inbari, P., *The Palestinians between Terrorism and Statehood*. Brighton: Sussex Academic Press, 1996

Intelligence and Terrorism Information Center, *Profile of the Hamas Movement*. Gellot, Israel: Center for Special Studies (CSS), 2006

Janardhan, N., 'Kuwait Wakes Up to the Face of Militant Islam'. *Terrorism Monitor*, 3(9), 6 May 2005

Jeapes, T., *SAS: Operation Storm: The Secret War in the Middle East*. Newbury, UK: Greenhill, 2005

John, W., 'Lashkar-E-Toiba: New Threats Posed by an Old Organization'. *Terrorism Monitor*, 3(4), 24 February 2005. Available at: www.jamestown.org/programs/gta/single/?tx_ttnews[tt_news]=314&tx_ttnews[back Pid]=180&no_cache=1 (accessed 16 March, 2009)

Jones, C. and Pedahzur, A. (eds), *Between Terrorism and Civil War: The Al-Aqsa Intifada*. New York: Routledge, 2004

Jones, S.G. and Riley, K.J., 'Law and Order in Palestine'. *Survival*, 46(4), 2004–2005, pp. 157–178

Jones, S.G., Wilson, J., Rathmell, A. and Riley, K.J., *Establishing Law and Order after Conflict*. Santa Monica, CA: RAND, 2005

Journalists of Reuters, *The Israeli–Palestinian Conflict: Crisis in the Middle East*. Englewood Cliffs, NJ: Reuters/Prentice Hall, 2002

Khalidi, R., *The Iron Cage: The Story of the Palestinian Struggle for Statehood*. Boston: Beacon Press, 2006

Kumaraswamy, P.R., 'The Cairo Dialogue and the Palestinian Power Struggle'. *International Studies*, 42, January 2005, pp. 43–59

Kurz, A., *Fatah and the Politics of Violence: The Institutionalization of a Popular Struggle*. Eastbourne, UK: Sussex Academic Press, 2005

Levitt, M. and Ross, D., *Hamas: Politics, Charity and Terrorism in the Service of Jihad*. London: Yale University Press, 2007

Makovsky, D., *A Defensible Fence: Fighting Terror and Enabling a Two-State Solution*. Washington, DC: Institute for Near East Policy, 2004

Mishal, S. and Sela, A., *The Palestinian Hamas: Vision, Violence and Coexistence*. New York: Columbia University Press, 2006

Rowley, C. and Taylor, J., 'The Israel and Palestine Land Settlement Problem: An Analytical History, 4000 B.C.E.–1948'. *Public Choice*, 128(Part 1), July 2006, pp. 41–75

Rowley, C. and Taylor, J. 'The Israel and Palestine Land Settlement Problem, 1948–2005: An Analytical History'. *Public Choice*, 128(Part 2), July 2006, pp. 77–90

H.3.3 Middle East, other countries

Abou Zahab, M. and Roy, O., *Islamist Networks: The Afghan–Pakistan Connection*. New York: Columbia University Press, 2004

Abuza, Z., 'Out of the Woodwork: Islamist Militants in Aceh'. *Terrorism Monitor*, 3(2), 27 January 2005. Available at: www.jamestown.org/programs/gta/single/?tx_ttnews[tt_news]=325&tx_ttnews[backPid]=180&no_cache=1 (accessed 16 March, 2009)

Abuza, Z., 'A Conspiracy of Silence: Who Is behind the Escalating Insurgency in Southern Thailand?' *Terrorism Monitor*, 3(9), 6 May 2005. Available at: www.jamestown.org/programs/gta/single/?tx_ttnews[tt_news]=470&tx_ttnews[backPid]=180&no_cache=1 (accessed 16 March, 2009)

Alam, A., 'The Sociology and Political Economy of "Islamic Terrorism" in Egypt'. *Terrorism and Political Violence*, 15(4), Winter 2003, pp. 114–142

Chasdi, R.J., 'The Lair and Layers of Al-Aqsa Uprising Terror: Some Preliminary Findings'. *Journal of Conflict Studies*, 24(2), Winter 2004, pp. 105–134

Chebatoris, M., 'Islamist Infiltration of the Moroccan Armed Forces'. *Terrorism Monitor*, 5(3), 15 February 2007. Available at: www.jamestown.org/programs/gta/single/?tx_ttnews[tt_news]=1016&tx_ttnews[backPid]=182&no_cache=1 (accessed 16 March 2009)

Cordesman, A.H., 'Iraq's Evolving Insurgency'. Washington DC: Center for Strategic and International Studies, 23 June 2005

Dietl, W. 'Pulverfass Pakistan'. *Terrorismus*, 6, December 2004

Dorronsoro, G., *Afghanistan: Revolution Unending, 1979–2003*. London: C. Hurst, 2004

Ewans, M., *Conflict in Afghanistan*. London: Routledge, 2005

Fishman, B. (ed.), *Bombers, Bank Accounts and Bleedout: Al-Qa'ida's Road in and out of Iraq*. Harmony Project. West Point, NY: Combating Terrorism Center, 2008

Gade, T., *Fatah Al-Islam in Lebanon: Between Global and Local Jihad*. Oslo: Norwegian Defence Research Establishment, 2007

Harik, J.P., *Hezbollah: The Changing Face of Terrorism*. Basingstoke, UK: I.B. Tauris, 2007

Hasatert, P.L., 'Operation Anaconda: Perception Meets Reality in the Hills of Afghanistan'. *Studies in Conflict and Terrorism*, 28(1), January–February 2005, pp. 11–20

Hashim, A.S., *Insurgency and Counterinsurgency in Iraq*. Ithaca, NY: Cornell University Press, 2005

Hasnat, S.F., 'Afghan Crisis: A Dilemma for Pakistan's Security and International Response'. *Perceptions*, 10(1), Spring 2005, pp. 35–52

Heazle, M. and Iyanatul, I., *Beyond the Iraq War*. Cheltanham, UK: Edward Elgar, 2006

Inbar, E. and Hillel, F., *Radical Islam and International Security*. London: Routledge, 2007

International Crisis Group, 'Hizbollah: Rebel without a Cause?' *Middle East Briefing* no. 7, Brussels: International Crisis Group, 30 July 2003

International Crisis Group, 'Dealing with Hamas'. *Middle East Report* no. 21, Brussels: International Crisis Group, 26 January 2004

International Crisis Group, 'Saudi Arabia Backgrounder: Who Are the Islamists'? *Middle East Report* no. 31, Brussels: International Crisis Group, 21 September 2004

International Crisis Group, 'After Arafat? Challenges and Prospects'. *Middle East Briefing* no. 16, Brussels: International Crisis Group, December 2004

International Crisis Group, 'Iran in Iraq: How Much Influence?' *Middle East Report* no. 38, 21 March 2005

International Crisis Group, *Jordan's 9/11: Dealing With Jihadi Islamism*. Brussels: International Crisis Group, 2005

International Crisis Group, 'Egypt's Sinai Question'. *Middle East/North Africa Report* no. 61. Brussels: International Crisis Group, 30 January 2007

Israeli, R., *War, Peace and Terror in the Middle East*. London: Frank Cass, 2003

Khodabandeh, M., 'The Disintegration of Mojahedin-E-Khalq in Post-Saddam Iraq'. *Terrorism Monitor*, 3(2), 27 January 2005. Available at: www.jamestown.org/programs/gta/single/?tx_ttnews[tt_news]=324&tx_ttnews[backPid]=180&no_cache=1 (accessed 16 March 2009)

Knights, M., 'Saudi Terrorist Cells Await the Return of Jihadists from Iraq'. *Jane's Intelligence Review*, 17(12), December 2005, pp. 12–15

Kramer, M., 'The Oracle of Hizbullah: Sayyid Muhammad Husayn Fadlallah'. In R.S. Appleby (ed.), *Spokesmen for the Despised: Fundamentalist Leaders of the Middle East*. Chicago: University of Chicago Press, 1997

Levitt, M., *No Good Terrorists: Middle Eastern Terrorist Groups, State Sponsors, and the War on Terror*. Washington, DC: Washington Institute for Near East Policy, 2002

Levitt, M., *Exposing Hamas: Funding Terror under the Cover of Charity*. London: Yale University Press, 2006

Levitt, M., *Hamas: Politics, Charity and Terrorism in the Service of Jihad*. London: Yale Univeristy Press, 2006

Levitt, M. and Sawyer, J., 'Zarqawi's Jordanian Agenda'. *Terrorism Monitor*, 16 December 2004

Norell, M., 'The Anatomy of Terror – HAMAS'. *IS* no. 2, Summer 1998 (in Swedish)

Norell, M. and Ranstorp, M., 'Terrorism in the Middle East; Hizb'allah, Hamas and Islamic Jihad.' In G. Jervas (ed.), *Swedish Defence Research Study on Terrorism*. Stockholm 1998

Obaid, N., *The Struggle for the Saudi Soul: Royalty, Islamic Militancy and Reform in the Kingdom*. Washington, DC: Center for Stategic and International Studies, 2006

Obaid, N. and Cordesman, A.H., 'Saudi Militants in Iraq: Assessment and Kingdom's Response'. Washington, DC: Center for Strategic and International Studies, 2005

Paz, R., 'Zarqawi's Strategy in Iraq: Is There a New Al-Qaeda'? *Prism Occasional Papers*, 3(5), August 2005

Romano, D., *The Kurdish Nationalist Movement: Opportunity, Mobilization, and Identity*. Cambridge: Cambridge University Press, 2006

Roul, A., 'Sipah-E-Sahaba: Formenting Sectarian Violence in Pakistan'. *Terrorism Monitor*, 3(2), 27 January 2005. Available at: www.jamestown.org/programs/gta/single/?tx_ttnews[tt_news]=323&tx_ttnews[backPid]=180&no_cache=1 (accessed 16 March, 2009)

Roul, A., 'Lashkar-E-Jangvi: Sectarian Violence in Pakistan and Ties to International Terrorism'. *Terrorism Monitor*, 3(11), 2 June 2005. Available at: www.jamestown.org/programs/gta/single/?tx_ttnews[tt_news]=497&tx_ttnews[backPid]=180&no_cache=1 (accessed 16 March, 2009)

Rubin, B. and Rubin, J.C. (eds), *Anti-American Terrorism and the Middle East. A Documentary Reader*. Oxford: Oxford University Press, 2004

Sharara, W. and Domont, F., *Le Hezbollah: un mouvement islamo-nationaliste*. Paris: Fayard, 2004

Shay, S., *The Axis of Evil: Iran, Hizballah and the Palestinian Terror*. New Brunswick, NJ: Transaction, 2005

Shay, S., *The Red Sea Terror Triangle: Sudan, Somalia, Yemen and Islamic Terror*. New Brunswick, NJ: Transaction, 2005

Teitelbaum, J., 'Holier than Thou: Saudi Arabia's Islamic Opposition'. *Washington Institute for Near East Policy. Policy Papers* no. 52, 2000

Tétreault, M.A., 'Terrorist Violence in Kuwait'. *Foreign Policy in Focus*, 23 February 2005

Tophoven, R., 'Zarqawis Netzwerk im Irak'. *Terrorismus*, no. 6, December 2004

H.4 Asia

Millward, J., 'Violent Separatism in Xinjiang: A Critical Assessment'. Washington, DC: East-West Center, *Policy Studies* no. 6, 2004

Selbourne, D., *The Losing Battle with Islam*. Amherst, NY: Prometheus Books, 2005

Thamm, B.G., *Jihad in Asia*. Munich: Deutscher Taschenbuch Verlag, 2007

Van de Voorde, C., 'Sri Lankan Terrorism: Assessing and Responding to the Threat of the Liberation Tigers of Tamil Eelam (LTTE)'. *Police Practice and Research*, 6(2), May 2005, pp. 181–199

Weitz, R. 'Storm Clouds over Central Asia: Revival of the Islamic Movement of Uzbekistan (IMU)?' *Studies in Conflict and Terrorism*, 27(6), November–December 2004, pp. 505–530

H.4.1 Indian subcontinent

Abbas, H., *Pakistan's Drift into Extremism: Allah, the Army and America's War on Terror*. Armonk, NY: M.E. Sharpe, 2004

Anak, A., 'Nabyu Perwita: Indonesia and the Muslim World'. *NIAS Reports* no. 50, December 2005

Chadah, V., *Low Intensity Conflicts in India*. New Delhi: Sage, 2005

Coppel, C., *Violent Conflicts in Indonesia: Analysis, Representation, Resolution*. London: RoutledgeCurzon, 2006

Gunaratna, R., Acharya, A. and Chua, S., *Conflict and Terrorism in Southern Thailand*. Singapore: Marshall Cavendish, 2005

Haleem, I., 'Micro Target, Macro Impact: The Resolution of the Kashmir Conflict as a Key to Shrinking Al-Qaeda's International Terrorist Network'. *Terrorism and Political Violence*, 16(1), Spring 2004, pp. 18–47

Haqqani, H., *Pakistan: Between Mosque and Military*. Washington, DC: Carnegie Endowment for International Peace, 2005

Howe, M., *Morocco: The Islamist Awakening and Other Challenges*. New York: Oxford University Press, 2005

International Crisis Group, *Terrorism in Indonesia: Noordin's Networks*. Brussels: International Crisis Group, 2006

Jalal, A., *Partisans of Allah: Jihad in South Asia*. Cambridge, MA: Harvard University Press, 2008

Lyon, P., *Conflict between India and Pakistan*. Santa Barbara, CA: ABC-CLIO, 2008

Momen, N. and Begum, M., 'Acts of Terrorism in Bangladesh: A General Assessment'. *International Journal of Terrorism and Political Hotspots*, 1(1), 2004, pp. 11–21

Mukherjee, J.R., *An Insider's Experience of Insurgency in India's North-East*. Delhi: Anthem Press, 2005

Singh, S.J., *Operation Black Thunder: An Eyewitness Account of Terrorism in Punjab*. Thousand Oaks, CA: Sage, 2002

Upadhyay, A., *India's Fragile Borderlands: The Dynamics of Terrorism in North East India*. London: I.B. Tauris, 2008

H.4.2 South-East Asia and China

Abuza, Z., 'Beyond Bali: A New Trend for Terrorism in Southeast Asia?' *Terrorism Monitor*, 3(19), 7 October 2005. Available at: www.jamestown.org/programs/gta/single/?tx_ttnews[tt_news]=568&tx_ttnews[back Pid]=180&no_cache=1 (accessed 16 March 2009)

Abuza, Z., *Militant Islam In Southeast Asia: Crucible of Terror*. Boulder, CO: Lynne Rienner, 2003

Adams, B. 'Nepal at the Precipice'. *Foreign Affairs*, 84(5), September–October 2005, pp. 121–134

China Eurasia Forum, *China Eurasia Forum Quarterly*, Special Issue on Terrorism, 4(2), May 2006

Conboy, K., *The Second Front: Inside Asia's Most Dangerous Terrorist Network*. Jakarta: Equinox Publishing, 2006

Hamilton-Hart, N., 'Terrorism in Southeast Asia: Expert Analysis, Myopia and Fantasy'. *Pacific Review*, 18(3), September 2005, pp. 303–325

HRIC, 'A Chronology of Unrest: Reported Cases of Uprisings in China over the Past 18 Months'. *Journal of Human Rights in China*, 1, 2005, pp. 20–23

Hutt, M. (ed.), *Himalayan 'People's War': Nepal's Maoist Rebellion*. Bloomington: Indiana University Press, 2004

International Crisis Group, 'Yemen: Coping with Terrorism and Violence in a Fragile State'. *Middle East Report* no. 8, January 2003. Brussels: International Crisis Group

International Crisis Group, *Southern Philippines Backgrounder: Terrorism and the Peace Process*. Singapore and Brussels: International Crisis Group, 2004

International Crisis Group, 'Islamic Terrorism in the Sahel: Fact or Fiction?' Brussels: International Crisis Group. *Africa Report* no. 92, 31 March 2005

International Crisis Group, 'Southern Thailand: Insurgency, not Jihad'. International Crisis Group, *Asia Report*, no. 98, 18 May 2005

International Crisis Group, *Counter-terrorism in Somalia: Losing Hearts and Minds?* Brussels: International Crisis Group, 2005

Khamidov, A., 'Hizb-Ut-Tahrir: An Enduring Challenge for Central Asia'. *AKI Crisis Today Dossier*. Available at: www.crisestoday.com (accessed 16 March 2009)

Knights, M., 'Internal Politics Complicate Counterterrorism in Yemen'. *Jane's Intelligence Review*, 18(2), February 2006, pp. 14–18

Koschade, S., 'A Social Network Analysis of Jemaah Islamiyah: The Applications to Counterterrorism and Intelligence'. *Studies in Conflict and Terrorism*, 29(6), September 2006, pp. 559–575

Kronstadt, K.A., 'International Terrorism in South Asia'. (Online) Library of Congress. Congressional Research Service, 3 November 2003. Available at: www.fas.org/irp/crs/RS21658.pdf (accessed 16 March 2009)

McCargo, D., *Tearing Apart the Land: Islam and Legitimacy in Southern Thailand*. Ithaca, NY: Cornell University Press, 2008

Mackerras, C., 'Xinjiang and the War against Terrorism'. In S. Shen (ed.), *China and Antiterrorism*. London: Nova Science Publishers, 2007

Miljard, M., *Jihad in Paradise: Islam and Politics in Southeast Asia*. Santa Barbara, CA: M.E. Sharpe, 2004

Mincheva, L., Gurr, T. and Marshall, M., 'Risks of Ethnopolitical Conflict in Central Asia in Year 2000: An Analysis of the Uzbek National Minorities in Tajikistan and Kyrgyzstan, and the Tajik and Kyrgyz National Minorities in Uzbekistan'. College Park: University of Maryland, 2000

Overton, S., 'The Yemeni Arms Trade: Still a Concern for Terrorism and Regional Security'. *Terrorism Monitor*, 3(9), 6 May 2005. Available at: www.jamestown.org/programs/gta/single/?tx_ttnews[tt_news]=471&tx_tt news[backPid]=180&no_cache=1 (accessed 16 March 2009)

Pavlova, E., 'From a Counter-society to a Counter-state Movement: Jemaay Islamiyah according to PUPJI'. *Studies in Conflict and Terrorism*, 30(9), 2007, pp. 777–800

Peterson, S. and Goedze, D., 'The Ties That Bind: Terrorist Diasporas in the Middle East and South Asia'. Honolulu: International Studies Association (ISA), March 2005

Rabasa, A.M., 'Political Islam in Southeast Asia: Moderates, Radicals and Terrorists'. *Adelphi Papers* no. 358, Oxford: Oxford University Press, 2004

Ranasinghe, J., 'Transforming the Norm: Conflict and Terrorism in South Asia'. Honolulu: International Studies Association (ISA), March 2005

Rashid, A., *Taliban: Militant Islam, Oil and Fundamentalism in Central Asia*, New Haven, CT: Yale Nota Bene, 2001

Ressa, M., *Seeds of Terror: An Eyewitness Account of Al-Qaeda's Newest Center of Operations in Southeast Asia*. New York: Free Press, 2003

Rüland, J., 'The Nature of Southeast Asian Security Challenges'. *Security Dialogue*, 36, December 2005, pp. 545–563

Singh, B., 'The Challenge of Militant Islam and Terrorism in Indonesia'. *Australian Journal of International Affairs*, 58(1), March 2004, pp. 47–68

Smith, P.J., *Terrorism and Violence in Southeast Asia: Transnational Challenges to States and Regional Stability*. Santa Barbara, CA: M.E. Sharpe, 2004

Swanström, N. and Björnehed, E., 'Conflict Resolution of Terrorist Conflicts in Southeast Asia'. *Terrorism and Political Violence*, 16(2), April–June 2004, pp. 328–349

Tan, A., *Handbook of Terrorism and Insurgency in Southeast Asia*. Cheltenham, UK: Edward Elgar, 2007

Tay, S.S.C., 'A More Insecure World: Conflicting Perspectives for Asia'. *Security Dialogue*, 36, September 2005, pp. 392–394

Tellis, A.J. and Wills, M. (eds), 'Confronting Terrorism in the Pursuit of Power. Strategic Asia 2004–05'. National Bureau of Asian Research. Available at: strategicasia.nbr.org (accessed 16 March, 2009)

Thapa, D. and Sijapati, B., *A Kingdom under Siege: Nepal's Maoist Insurgency, 1996 to 2004*. London: Zed Books, 2004

Thayer, C.A., 'International Conflict and Terrorism in Southeast Asia: Regional Responses and US Leadership'. Honolulu: International Studies Association (ISA), March 2005

Vicziany, M. (ed.), *Controlling Arms and Terror in the Asia Pacific*. Cheltenham, UK: Edward Elgar, 2007

Wehmeyer, M., *Vietnam Terrorism*. Victoria, Canada: Trafford Publishing, 2007

H.4.3 Japan

Katzenstein, P.J. and Tsujinaka, Y., *Defending the Japanese State: Structures, Norms and the Political Responses to Terrorism and Violent Social Protest in the 1970s and 1980s*. Ithaca, NY: East Asia Program, Cornell University, 1991

Selden, M. and So, A.Y., *War and State Terrorism: The United States, Japan, and the Asia-Pacific in the Long Twentieth Century*. Lanham, MD, Rowman & Littlefield, 2004

United States Congress, House Committee on International Relations, Subcommittee on Africa Global Human Rights and International Operations, *The Torture Victims Relief Act of 2005; supporting the Goals and Ideals of a National Weekend of Prayer and Reflection for Darfur, Sudan; and condemning the Democratic People's Republic of Korea for Abductions and Continued Captivity of Citizens of the Republic of Korea and Japan as acts of Terrorism and Gross Violations*: mark-up before the Subcommittee on Africa, Global Human Rights, and International Operations of the Committee on International Relations, House of Representatives, One Hundred Ninth Congress, first session, on H.R. 2017, H. Res. 333 and H. Con. Res. 168, June 23, 2005. Washington, DC: US GPO

H.5 Africa, general

McKay, S., 'Girls as "Weapons of Terror" in Northern Uganda and Sierra Leone Rebel Fighting Forces'. *Studies in Conflict and Terrorism*, 28, 2005, pp. 385–397

Mentan, T., *Dilemmas of Weak States: Africa and Transitional Terrorism in the Twenty-First Century*. Aldershot, UK: Ashgate, 2004

Rosenau, W., 'Al Qaeda Recruitment Trends in Kenya and Tanzania'. *Studies in Conflict and Terrorism*, 28(1), 2005, pp. 1–10

H.5.1 Northern Africa

Adekeye, A., 'Africa and America in an Age of Terror'. *Journal of Asian and African Studies*, 38, June 2003, pp. 175–191

Alexander, M. (ed.), *The Algerian War and the French Army (1954–62): Experiences, Images, Testimonies.* Basingstoke, UK: Palgrave Macmillan, 2002

Alonso, R., and Garcia, R.M., 'The Evolution of Jihadist Terrorism in Morocco'. *Terrorism and Political Violence,* 19(4), 2007, pp. 571–592

Carroll, D., *Albert Camus the Algerian: Colonialism, Terrorism, Justice.* New York: Columbia University Press, 2007

Gyves, C. and Wyckoff, C., 'Algerian Groupe Salafiste pour la Predication et le Combat (GSPC): An Operational Analysis'. *Strategic Insights,* 5(8), November 2006. Available at: www.ccc.nps.navy.mil/si/2006/Nov/gyves06.asp (accessed 17 March, 2009)

International Crisis Group, 'Islamism in North Africa I: The Legacies of History'. *Middle East and North Africa Briefing* no. 12, 20 April 2004. Brussels: International Crisis Group

International Crisis Group, 'Islamism in North Africa II: Egypt's Opportunity'. *Middle East and North Africa Briefing* no. 13, 20 April 2004. Brussels: International Crisis Group

International Crisis Group, 'Islamism, Violence and Reform in Algeria: Turning the Page'. *Middle East and North Africa Report* no. 29, 30 July 2004. Brussels: International Crisis Group

International Crisis Group, 'Understanding Islamism'. *Middle East/North Africa Report* no. 37, 2 March 2005. Brussels: International Crisis Group

Kemp, M.A., 'Re-readings of the Algerian War during the US "War on Terror": Between Recognition and Denial'. *Journal of European Studies,* 38, June 2008, pp. 157–175

McGregor, A., 'Bin Laden's African folly: Al-Qaeda in Darfur'. *Terrorism Monitor,* 4(10), 18 May 2006. Available at: www.jamestown.org/programs/gta/single/?tx_ttnews[tt_news]=772&tx_ttnews[backPid]=181&no_cache=1 (accessed 17 March, 2009)

Marret, J.-L., 'Al-Qaeda in Islamic Maghreb'. *Studies in Conflict and Terrorism,* 31(6), 2008, pp. 541–552

Pargeter, A., 'North African Immigrants in Europe and Political Violence'. *Studies in Conflict and Terrorism,* 29(8), December 2006, pp. 731–748

Roberts, H., *The Battlefield of Algeria, 1988–2002: Studies in Broken Policy.* London: Verso, 2003

Rotberg, R.I. (ed.), *Battling Terrorism in the Horn of Africa.* Cambridge, MA: World Peace Foundation; Washington, DC: Brookings Institution Press, 2005

Terdman, M., 'The Movement for the Emancipation of the Niger Delta (MEND): Al-Qaeda's Unlikely Ally in Nigeria'. *Islam in Africa Newsletter,* 2(1) January 2007

H.5.2 Sub-Saharan Africa

De Waal, A. (ed.), *Islamism and Its Enemies in the Horn of Africa.* London: Hurst, 2004

Gberie, L., *A Dirty War in West Africa: The RUF and the Destruction of Sierra Leone.* Bloomington: Indiana University Press, 2006

Keen, D., *Conflict and Collusion in Sierra Leone.* Oxford: James Currey, 2004

Omeje, K., 'Petrobusiness and Security Threats in the Niger Delta, Nigeria'. *Current Sociology,* 54, May 2006, pp. 477–499

Piombo, J., 'Terrorist Financing and Government Response in East Africa'. Honolulu: International Studies Association (ISA) March 2005

Rosenau, W., 'Al Qaida Recruitment Trends in Kenya and Tanzania'. *Studies in Conflict and Terrorism,* 28(1), 2005, pp. 1–10

Terdman, M., 'Al-Qaeda in Sudan: A Failure or Success?' *Islam in Africa Newsletter,* 2(1), January 2007

Terdman, M., 'Somalia Following the Defeat of the Union of Islamic Courts: Al-Qaeda's Next Front?' *Islam in Africa Newsletter,* 2(1), January 2007

Ukeje, C., 'Oil Communities and Political Violence: The Case of Ethnic Ijaws in Nigeria's Delta Region'. *Terrorism and Political Violence,* 13(4), 2001, pp. 15–37

Vinci, A., 'Existential Motivations in the Lord's Resistance Army's Continuing Conflict'. *Studies in Conflict and Terrorism,* 30(4), 2007, pp. 337–352

Vincy, A., 'The Strategic Use of Fear by the Lord's Resistance Army'. *Small Wars and Insurgencies,* 16(3), 2005, pp. 360–381

Vines, A., *Renamo: From Terrorism to Democracy in Mozambique?* London: James Currey, 1996

H.5.3 Southern Africa

Dialmy, A. 'Le terrorisme islamiste au Maroc'. *Social Compass,* 52, March 2005, pp. 67–82

Krause, V. and Otenyo, E.E., 'Terrorism and the Kenyan Public'. *Studies in Conflict and Terrorism,* 28(2), March–April 205, pp. 99–112

Kynoch, G., 'Crime, Conflict and Politics in Transition-Era South Africa'. *African Affairs,* 104(416), July 2005, pp. 493–514

H.6 Latin America, general

De Izcue, C.A., 'Peru's Shining Path and MRTA Analyzed with the Manwaring Paradigm'. *Low Intensity Conflict and Law Enforcement*, 12(2), 2004, pp. 52–66

Guedes da Costa, T., 'The Puzzle of the Iguazu Tri-Border Area: Many Questions and Few Answers Regarding Organised Crime and Terrorism Links'. *Global Crime*, 8(1), February 2007, pp. 26–39

Waldmann, P., 'Is There a Culture of Violence in Colombia?' *Terrorism and Political Violence*, 19(4), 2007, pp. 593–609

H.6.1 Argentina

Carbonari, C. and Instituto del Servicio Exterior de la Nación (Argentina), *Lavado de dinero, problema mundial: el régimen internacional contra el lavado de dinero y el financiamiento del terrorismo y su impacto en la República Argentina*. Buenos Aires: Grupo Editor Latinoamericano: ISEN, 2005

Corach, C. and Baizán, M., *La respuesta argentina frente al terrorismo*. Buenos Aires: FUPOMI Ediciones, 2002

Fayt, C.S., *Criminalidad del terrorismo sagrado: el atentado a la embajada de Israel en Argentina*. La Plata and Buenos Aires: Editorial Universitaria de la Plata, 2001

Goobar, W., *El tercer atentado: Argentina en la mira del terrorismo internacional*. Buenos Aires: Editorial Sudamericana, 1996

Marchak, M.P. and Marchak, W., *God's Assassins: State Terrorism in Argentina in the 1970s*. Montreal: McGill-Queen's University Press, 1999

United States Congress, House Committee on International Relations, *Terrorism in Latin America/AMIA Bombing in Argentina: Hearing before the Committee on International Relations*. House of Representatives, One Hundred Fourth Congress, First Session, September 28, 1995. Washington, DC: US GPO, 1996

Wright, T.C., *State Terrorism in Latin America: Chile, Argentina, and International Human Rights*. Lanham, MD: Rowman & Littlefield, 2007

H.6.2 Brazil

Evans, R.D., *Brazil: The Road back from Terrorism*. London: Institute for the Study of Conflict, 1974

H.6.3 Uruguay

Moss, R., *Uruguay: Terrorism versus Democracy*. London: Institute for the Study of Conflict, 1971

Rovira, A., *Subversión, terrorismo, guerra revolucionaria: la experiencia uruguaya: conferencia dictada el 17 de febrero de 1981 a una delegación de representantes de organizaciones norteamericanas interesadas en problemas de seguridad*. Montevideo, [s.n.], 1981

H.6.4 Other Latin American countries

Koc-Menard, S., 'Fragmented Sovereignty: Why Sendero Luminoso Consolidated in Some Regions of Peru but Not in Others'. *Studies in Conflict and Terrorism*, 30(2), 2007, pp. 173–206

Menzel, S.H., *Bullets versus Ballots: Political Violence and Revolutionary War in El Salvador, 1979–1991*. Miami: University of Miami Iberian Studies Institute, 1994

O'Ballance, E., *Sudan: Civil War and Terrorism, 1956–99*, Basingstoke, UK: Macmillan, 2000

Orozco Abad, I., *Combatientes, rebeldes y terroristas: guerra y derecho en Colombia*. Santa Fé de Bogotá: Instituto de Estudios Políticos y Relaciones Internacionales, Universidad Nacional: Temis, 1992

Radu, M., *Latin American Revolutionaries: Groups, Goals, Methods*. Washington, DC: Pergamon-Brassey's International Defense Publishers, 1990

Restrepo, J.A., Spagat, M. and Vargars, J.F., 'Special Data Feature: The Severity of the Colombian Conflict: Cross-Country Datasets versus New Micro-Data'. *Journal of Peace Research*, 43, January 2006, pp. 99–115

Simons, G., *Colombia: A Brutal History*. London: Palgrave, 2005

TNI, 'Colombia: Drugs and Security. On the Problems of Confusing Drug Policy and Security Policy'. *Drug Policy Briefing* no. 9, January 2005. Amsterdam: Transnational Institute

Zambelis, C., 'Al-Qaeda's Inroads into the Caribbean'. *Terrorism Monitor*, 3(20), 21 October 2005. Available at: www.jamestown.org/single/?no_cache=1&tx_ttnews[swords]=8fd5893941d69d0be3f378576261ae3e&tx_ttnews[exact_search]=Inroads&tx_ttnews[categories_1]=11&tx_ttnews[pointer]=1&tx_ttnews[tt_news]=591&tx_ttnews[backPid]=7&cHash=f91d467bd5 (accessed 17 March 2009)

Zambelis, C., 'Radical Islam in Latin America'. *Terrorism Monitor*, 3(23), 2 December 2005, pp. 9–12. Available at: www.jamestown.org/single/?no_cache=1&tx_ttnews[swords]=8fd5893941d69d0be3f378576261ae3e&tx_ttnews[exact_search]=Inroads&tx_ttnews[categories_1]=11&tx_ttnews[tt_news]=623&tx_ttnews[backPid]=7&cHash=22322b5b26 (accessed 17 March 2009)

Zambelis, C., 'Islamic Radicalism in Mexico: The Threat from South of the Border'. *Terrorism Monitor*, 4(11), 2 June 2006. Available at: www.jamestown.org/single/?no_cache=1&tx_ttnews[swords]=8fd5893941d 69d0be3f378576261ae3e&tx_ttnews[exact_search]=Mexico&tx_ttnews[categories_1]=11&tx_ttnews[tt_ news]=790&tx_ttnews[backPid]=7&cHash=c88a81a6cb (accessed 17 March 2009)

Zuhur, S., 'Syria: A Haven for Terrorists?' *Terrorism Monitor*, 3(16), 11 August 2005. Available at: www.james town.org/programs/gta/single/?tx_ttnews[tt_news]=549&tx_ttnews[backPid]=180&no_cache=1 (accessed 17 March 2009)

H.7 North America

Higgins, N.P., *Understanding the Chiapas Rebellion*. Austin: University of Texas Press, 2004

Wrighte, M.R., 'The Real Mexican Terrorists: A Group Profile of the Popular Revolutionary Army (EPR)'. *Studies in Conflict and Terrorism*, 25(4), July 2002, pp. 207–225

H.7.1 Canada

Thompson, J.C. and Turlej, J., 'Other People's Wars: A Review of Overseas Terrorism in Canada'. A Mackenzie Institute Occasional Paper, June 2003. Available at: www.mackenzieinstitute.com (accessed 17 March, 2009)

H.7.2 United States

Atkins, S.E., *The 9/11 Encyclopedia*. Oxford: Greenwood Press, 2008

Ayers, B., *Fugitive Days: A Memoir*. New York: Penguin, 2003

Berger, D., *Outlaws of America: The Weather Underground and the Politics of Solidarity*. Oakland, CA: AK Press, 2006

Berger, L., *Die USA und der islamistische Terrorismus: Herausforderungen im Nahen und Mittleren Osten*. Paderborn, Germany: Schöningh, 2007

Boyd, D., Dunn, L., Arnold, A., Ullrich, M., Scoures. J. and Fox, J., 'Why Have We Not Been Attacked Again? Competing and Complementary Hypotheses for Homeland Attack Frequency'. Science Applications International Corporation and Defense Threat Reduction Agency's Advanced Systems and Concepts Office. Report no. 2008 007, June 2008

Cooley, J.K., *Unholy Wars: Afghanistan, America and International Terrorism*. London: Pluto Press, 2002

Cox, M., 'Beyond the West: Terrors in Transatlantia'. *European Journal of International Relations*, 11, June 2005, pp. 203–233

Emerson, S., *Jihad Incorporated: A Guide to Militant Islam in the US*. New York: Prometheus, 2008

Fellman, M., *Twisting the Cross: Terrorism and the Shaping of America*. Berkeley, CA: University of California Press, 2007

Kushner, H., *Holy War on the Home Front. The Secret Islamic Network in the United States*. New York: Penguin, 2004

Lance, P., *1000 Years for Revenge: International Terrorism and the FBI, The Untold Story*. New York: Regan Books, HarperCollins, 2003

Lutz, B. and Lutz, J.M., *Terrorism in America*. New York: Palgrave Macmillan, 2007

Mickolus, E., 'Attack on the Pentagon, September 11, 2001'. In F. Shanty (ed.), *Encyclopedia of World Terrorism*. Armonk, NY: M.E. Sharpe, 2002

Mickolus, E., 'Attack on United Airlines Flight 93 in Pennsylvania'. In F. Shanty (ed.), *Encyclopedia of World Terrorism*, Armonk, NY: M.E. Sharpe, 2002

National Commission on Terrorist Attacks upon the United States. *The 911 Commission Report*. Waking Lion Press, 2007

Norell, M., 'Study of the Attacks on New York and Washington on September 11, 2001' (in Swedish). Swedish Defence Research Agency Report, September 2001

Petrosino, C., 'Connecting the Past to the Future: Hate Crime in America'. *Journal of Contemporary Criminal Justice*, 15, February 1999, pp. 22–47

Phares, W., *Future Jihad: Terrorist Strategies against America*. New York: Palgrave Macmillan, 2005

Pillar, P.R., *Terrorism and the US Foreign Policy*, Washington, DC: Brookings Educational Press, 2003

Ruthven, M.A., *Fury for God: The Islamic Attack on America*. New York: Granta, 2002

Stern, K.S., *A Force upon the plan: The American Militia Movement and the Politics of Hate*. New York: Simon & Schuster, 1996

Thompson, P., *The Terror Timeline: Year by Year, Day by Day, Minute by Minute: A Comprehensive Chronicle of the Road to 9/11 and America's Response*. Center for Cooperative Research, 2004

Wright, L., *The Looming Tower: Al-Qaeda and the Road to 9/11*. New York: Alfred A. Knopf, 2006
Wright, S.A., *Patriots, Politics, and the Oklahoma City Bombing*. Cambridge: University Press, 2007

I. International and transnational terrorism

Abrahms, M., 'Al Qaeda's Scorecard: A Progress Report on Al Qaeda's Objectives'. *Studies in Conflict and Terrorism*, 29, 2006, p. 516

Abu, K., *Bin Laden, Islam, and America's New 'War on Terrorism'*. New York: Seven Stories Press, 2002

Adams, J., *The Financing of Terror*. Sevenoaks, UK: New English Library, 1988

AIVD, *Van dawa tot jihad: de diverse dreigingen van de radicale Islam tegen de democratische rechtsorde*. The Hague: Ministerie van Binnenlandse Zaken en Koninkrijksrelaties, 2004

Alexiev, A., 'Wegschauen und verharmlosen: in Europa wird der islamistische Terror immer noch unterschätzt'. *Internationale Politik*, 60(9), September 2005, pp. 92–98

Allam, M., *Bin Laden in Italy: A Trip inside Radical Islam*. Milan: Mandadori, 2002

Andrew, C. (ed.), *The Mitrokhin Archive II: The KGB and the World*. London: Allen Lane, 2005

Andrew, C. and Mitrokhin, V., *The World Was Going Our Way: The KGB and the Battle for the Third World*. Jackson, TN: Basic Books, 2005

APF, 'Al-Zarqawi and the European Connection to Iraq'. London: Asia-Pacific Foundation. *APF Analysis-Terrorism-Transnational*, 16 June 2005

APF, 'The 7/7 London Bombings and the Wider Network'. Asia-Pacific Foundation. *APF Analysis-Terrorism-Transnational*, 20 July 2005

Archick, K., Rollins, J. and Woehrel, S., 'Islamist Extremism in Europe', *CRS Report for Congress*. RS22211, 29 July 2005

Aust, S., Cordt, S. *et al.*, *11 September, Geschichte eines modernen Krieges*. Munich: Deutsche Verlags-Anstalt: 2002

Ayoob, M., 'The Future of Political Islam: The Importance of External Variables'. *International Affairs*, 81(5), October 2005, pp. 951–962

Aysha, E. El-Din, 'September 11 and the Middle East: Failure of US "Soft Power": Globalisation contra Americanisation in the "New" US Century'. *International Relations*, 19, June 2005, pp. 193–210

Balencie, J.-M. and de la Grange, A., *Mondes rebelles: guerres civiles et violences politiques*. Paris: Editions Michalon, 1999

Bergen, P., *Holy War Inc.: Inside the Secret World of Osama bin Laden*. New York: Simon & Schuster, 2001

Boer, L., 'Vijf jaar na 9/11: groeiend inzicht in een veranderend al-Qaeda'. *Vrede en Veiligheid*, 35(4), 2006, pp. 504–512

Brisard, J.C. and Dasquie, G., *Die verbotene Wahrheit: Die Verstrickung der USA mit Osama bin Laden*. Zürich: Pendo, 2002

Burke, R.J., *International Terrorism and Threats to Security*. Cheltenham, UK: Edward Elgar, 2008

Chasdi, R.J., *Serenade of Suffering: A Portrait of Middle East Terrorism, 1968–1993*. Lanham, MD: Lexington Books, 1999

Chasdi, R.J., *Tapestry of Terror: A Portrait of Middle East Terrorism, 1994–1999*. Lanham, MD: Lexington Books, 2002

Coolsaet, R., *Al-Qa'ida: The Myth: The Root Causes of International Terrorism and How to Tackle Them*. Ghent, Belgium: Academia Press, 2005

CTC, *Al'Qa'ida's (Mis)adventures in the Horn of Africa*. West Point, NY: Combating Terrorism Center, 2007

Czempiel, E.-O., 'Der politische Terrorismus'. *Internationale Politik*, no. 7/2004, 2004, pp. 74–81

Dahlke, M., *Der Anshlag auf Olympia '72. Die politischen Reaktionen auf den internationalen Terrorismus in Deutschland*. Munich: Meidenbauer, 2006

de Silva, K.M. and May, R.J., *Internationalization of Ethnic Conflict*. London: Pinter, 1991

Devji, F., 'Al-Qaeda, Spectre of Globalisation'. *Soundings*. no. 32, March 2006, pp. 18–27

Dishman, C., 'Trends in Modern Terrorism', *Studies in Conflict and Terrorism*, 22(4), 1999, 357–362

Dobson, C., *War without End: The Terrorists: An Intelligence Dossier*. London: Sphere, 1987

Doran, M.S., 'Palestine, Iraq, and American Strategy'. *Foreign Affairs*, January–February, 2003, pp. 19–33

Dudziak, M.L., *September 11 in History: A Watershed Moment?* Durham, NC: Duke University Press, 2003

Emerson, S., *American Jihad: The Terrorists Living among Us*. New York: Free Press, 2002

Emerson, S., 'Money Laundering and Terror Financing Issues in the Middle East'. Testimony before the United States Senate, Committee of Banking, Housing, and Urban Affairs, 13, June 2005

Enders, W. and Sandler, T., 'Is Transnational Terrorism Becoming More Threatening? A Time-Series Investigation', *Journal of Conflict Resolution*, 44, 2000, pp. 307–332

Enders, W. and Sandler, T., 'Patterns of Transnational Terrorism, 1970–1999: Alternative Time-Series Estimates'. *International Studies Quarterly*, 46(2), June 2002, pp. 145–165

Enders, W. and Sandler, T., 'Distribution of Transnational Terrorism among Countries by Income Class and Geography after 9/11'. *International Studies Quarterly*, 50(2), June 2006, pp. 367–393

Errera, P., 'Three Circles of Threat'. *Survival*, 47(1), Spring 2005, pp.71–88

Esposito, J.L., *Unholy War: Terror in the Name of Islam*, New York: Oxford University Press, 2002

EU SitCen, *SitCen Annual Report on International Terrorism 2005*. Analysis and world review for terrorist attacks and significant related events in 2005. Council of the European Union. Brussels: EU Joint Situation Center, SN 2208/06, 2006

Eubanks, J. and Kohlmann, E. 'Trends in Anti-American Terrorism'. *Journal of Counterterrorism and Security International*, 5(4), pp. 22–24

Farah, D., *Blood From Stones. The Secret Financial Network of Terror*. New York: Broadway Books, 2004

Flabigan, S.T., 'Charity as Resistance: Connections between Charity, Contentious Politics and Terror'. *Studies in Conflict and Terrorism*, 29(7), 2006, pp. 641–655

Fouda, Y. and Fielding, N., *Masterminds of Terror: The Truth behind the Most Devastating Terrorist Attacks the World Has Ever Seen*. Edinburgh: Mainstream Publishing, 2003

Frank, H. and Hirschmann, K. (eds), *Die weltweite Gefahr: Terrorismus als internationale Herausforderung*. Berlin: Berliner Wissenschafts-Verlag, 2002

Friedman, N., *Terrorism, Afghanistan, and America's New Way of War*. Annapolis, MD: Naval Institute Press, 2003

Friedman, T.L., *Longitudes and Attitudes: Exploring the World after September 11*. New York: Farrar, Straus and Giroux, 2002

Galtung, J., *Pax Pacifica: Terrorism, the Pacific Hemisphere, Globalisation and Peace Studies*. London: Pluto Press, 2005

Ganser, D., *Gladio: NATO's Secret Armies. Operation Gladio and Terrorism in Western Europe*. London: Frank Cass, 2004

Gärtner, H. and Cuthbertson, I., 'European Security after September 11 and the War in Iraq'. Paper presented at the annual meeting of the International Studies Association (ISA), Canada, 2004 March 17

Geaves, R., Gabriel, T., Haddad, Y and Smith, J.I. (eds), *Islam and the West Post-September 11th*. Aldershot, UK: Ashgate, 2004

Gerecht, R.M., *The Islamic Paradox: Shi'ite Clerics, Sunni Fundamentalists and the Coming of Arab Democracy*. Washington, DC: AEI Press, 2004

Gerges, F.A., 'Islam and Muslims in the Mind of America'. *Annals of the American Academy of Political and Social Science*, 588, July 2003, pp. 73–89

Gerges, F.A., *The Far Enemy: Why Jihad Went Global*. Cambridge: Cambridge University Press, 2005

Gerolymatos, A., *Red Acropolis, Black Terror: The Greek Civil War and the Origins of Soviet American Rivalry, 1943–1949*. New York: Basic Books, 2004

Giessmann, H.J., Kuzniar, R. and Lachowski, Z., *International Security in a Time of Change: Threats, Concepts, Institutions*. Baden-Baden, Germany: Nomos Verlagsgesellschaft, 2004

Gold, D., *Hatred's Kingdom: How Saudi Arabia Supports the New Global Terrorism*. Washington, DC: Regnery, 2004

Gualo, R., *The Party of God: Radical Islam against the West*. Milan: Guerini, 1994

Guelke, A., *The Age of Terrorism and the International Political System*. London: I.B. Tauris, 1995

Gunaratna, R., *The Changing Face of Terrorism*. Singapore: Eastern University Press, 2004

Gunaratna, R., 'Global Terrorism Outlook 2005'. *UNISCI Discussion Papers*, January 2005

Haahr, K., 'New Reports Allege Foreign Fighters in Iraq Returning to Europe'. *Terrorism Focus*, 3(20), 23 May 2006

Halliday, F., *Two Hours That Shook the World: September 11, 2001: Causes and Consequences*. London: Saqi, 2002

Hamilton, D.S. (ed.), *Terrorism and International Relations*. Washington, DC: Brookings Education Press, 2008

Hammes, T., *Broken Eagle: How to Defeat a Superpower: Lessons of Fourth Generation Warfare*. Osceola, WI: Motorbooks, 2005

Haqqani, H., 'Islam's Medieval Outposts'. *Foreign Policy*, no. 133, November–December 2002

Harvey, F.P., *Smoke and Mirrors: Globalized Terrorism and the Illusion of Multilateral Security*. Toronto University of Toronto Press, 2004

Hiro, D., *War without End: The Rise of Islamist Terrorism and Global Response*. New York: Routledge, 2002

Hirschmann, K., 'The Changing Face of Terrorism'. *International Politics and Society*, no. 3, 2000

Hirst, P.Q., 'Another Century of Conflict? War and the International System in the 21st Century'. *International Relations*, 16, December 2002, pp. 327–342

Hirst, P.Q. and Thompson, G., 'The Future of Globalization'. *Cooperation and Conflict*, 37, September 2002, pp. 247–265

Hoffman, B., 'The Calculus of Terror'. *Atlantic Monthly*, 15 May 2003. Available at: www.theatlantic.com/doc/200305u/int2003-05-15 (accessed 17 March, 2009)

Honderich, E., *After the Terror*. Edinburgh: Edinburgh University Press, 2002

House Permanent Select Committee on Intelligence and the Senate Select Intelligence Committee, *Inquiry into the Terrorist Attacks of September 11*, 2001. Washington, DC, 2002

Hudson, R.A., *Castro's America Department: Coordinating Cuba's Support for Marxist-Leninist Violence in the Americas*. Washington, DC: Cuban American National Foundation, 1988

Hunt, E., 'Islamist Terrorism in Northwestern Africa. A "Thorn in the Neck" of the United States?' Washington Institute for Near East Policy, *Policy Focus*, February 2007

Hunt, M., 'Bleed to Bankruptcy: Economic Targetting Tactics in the Global Jihad'. *Jane's Intelligence Review*, 19(1), January 2007, pp. 14–17

Husayn, F., 'Al-Zarqawi: The Second Generation of Al-Qa'ida'. Serialized by *Al Quds al-Arabi*, May–July 2005

Jehl, D. and Johnston, D., 'In Detail: How Bin Laden Set Plan in Motion in '99'. *New York Times*, 17 June 2004

Jenkins, B.M., 'Redefining Enemy: The World Has Changed but Our Mindset Has Not'. *RAND Review*. Santa Monica CA, RAND Corporation, Spring 2004

Johns, D.M. (ed.), *Globalisation and the New Terror: The Asia Pacific Dimension*. Chaltenham, UK: Edward Elgar, 2004

Jordan, J. and Horsburgh, N., 'Mapping Jihadist Terrorism in Spain'. *Studies in Conflict and Terrorism*, 28(3), May–June 2005, pp. 169–191

Jordan, J. and Wesley, R., 'The Threat of Grassroots Jihadi Networks: A Case Study from Ceuta, Spain'. *Terrorism Monitor*, 5(3), 15 February 2007. Available at: www.jamestown.org/programs/gta/single/?tx_tt news[tt_news]=1013&tx_ttnews[backPid]=182&no_cache=1 (accessed 17 March 2009)

Kalis, M.A., 'A New Approach to International Terrorism'. *International Affairs Review*, 10(2), Summer–Autumn 2001, pp. 80–95

Kellner, D., 'September 11, Terrorism, and Blowback'. *Cultural Studies <=> Critical Methodologies*, 2, February 2002, pp. 27–39

Kippenberg, H.G. and Seidensticker, T. (eds), *Terror im Dienste Gottes*. Frankfurt am Main: Campus Verlag, 2004

Kohlmann, E.F., *Al-Qa'ida's Jihad in Europe: The Afghan–Bosnian Network*. Oxford: Berg, 2004

Kron, T. and Reddig, M., 'Analysen des transnationalen Terrorismus'. *Soziologische Perspektiven*. Wiesbaden:VS Verlag, 2007

Kurz, A., Merari, A., Kotzer, S. and Part, T., 'INTER 86: A Review of International Terrorism in 1986'. Jerusalem: Jerusalem Post, for Jaffee Center for Strategic Studies, 1987

Kurz, A. *et al.*, 'INTER 88: International Terrorism in 1988'. Jerusalem: Jerusalem Post, for Jaffee Center for Strategic Studies, 1989

Lahille, E., 'Terrorisme et politiques économiques: les Etats-Unis après le 11–9'. *Politique Etrangère*, 70(2), 2005, pp.387–399

Levy, B.H., *Who Killed Daniel Pearle?* Hoboken, NJ: Melville House, 2003

Lohlker, R., 'Islamismus und Globalisierung'. In Cl. Six *et al.* (eds), *Religiöser Fundamentalismus: Vom Kolonialismus zur Globalisierung* (Querschnitte 16)

Lutz, J.M. and Lutz, B.M., *Global Terrorism*. London: Routledge, 2004

Martin, G., 'Globalization and International Terrorism'. In G. Ritzer (ed.), *The Blackwell Companion to Globalization*. Oxford: Blackwell, 2007

Merari, A. 'Terrorism as a Strategy of Struggle: Past and Future'. *Terrorism and Political Violence*, 11(4), 1999, pp. 52–66

Mickolus, E., 'Trends in Transnational Terrorism'. In M. Livingston (ed)., *Terrorism in the Contemporary World*. Westport, CT: Greenwood Press, 1978

Mickolus, E., 'Chronology of Transnational Terrorist Attacks upon American Business People, 1968–1976'. *Terrorism: An International Journal*, 1(2), 1978, pp. 217–235; updated in Alexander, Y. and Kilmarx, R.A. (eds), *Political Terrorism and Business: The Threat and Response*. New York: Praeger, 1979

Mickolus, E., 'Transnational Terrorism'. In M. Stohl (ed.), *Uhe!Politics of Terrorism*. New York: Marcel Dekker, 1979. Updated for 2nd edn

Mickolus, E., *Transnational Terrorism: A Chronology of Events, 1968–1979*. Westport, CT: Greenwood Press, 1980

Mickolus, E. and Heyman, E. 'ITERATE: Monitoring Transnational Terrorism'. In Y. Alexander and J.M. Gleason, (eds), *Behavioral and Quantitative Perspectives on Terrorism.* New York: Pergamon, 1981

Mickolus, E., 'International Terrorism: Attributes of Terrorist Events, 1968–1977'. In *ITERATE 2 Data Codebook.* Ann Arbor, MI: Inter-University Consortium for Political and Social Research, 1982

Mickolus, E., 'Tracking the Growth and Prevalence of Terrorism'. In: G.S. Roukis and P.J. Montana (eds), *Managing Terrorism: Strategies for the Corporate Executive.* Westport, CT: Greenwood Press, 1983

Mickolus, E., 'Chronology of International Terrorist Attacks, November 1996–March 2002'. In F. Shanty (ed.), *Encyclopedia of World Terrorism.* Armonk, NY: M.E. Sharpe, 2002

Mickolus, E., Sandler, T. and Murdock, J., *International Terrorism in the 1980s: A Chronology*, vol. 1: 1980–1983. Ames, Iowa: Iowa State University Press, 1988

Mickolus, E., Sandler, T. and Murdock, J., *International Terrorism in the 1980s: A Chronology*, vol. 2: 1984–1987. Ames: Iowa State University Press, 1989

Mickolus E. and Simmons, S.L., *Terrorism, 2002–2004: A Chronology*, 3 vols. Westport, CT: Greenwood Press, 2005

Mickolus, E., and Simmons, S.L., *Terrorism, 2005–2007: A Chronology.* Westport, CT: Greenwood Press, 2008

Milbank, D.L. with Mickolus, E., 'International and Transnational Terrorism: Diagnosis and Prognosis' (available from Washington, DC: US Document Expediting Project, Library of Congress, PR 76 10030, April 1976)

Moghaddam, F.M., *From the Terrorists' Point of View: What They Experience and Why They Come to Destroy.* Westport, CT: Praeger Security International, 2006

Mullard, M. and Bankole, A.C. (eds), *Globalisation, Citizenship and the War on Terror.* Chaltenham, UK: Edward Elgar, 2007

Muray, P., *Chers Djihadistes.* Paris: Mille et une nuits, 2002

Nassar, J.R., *Globalization and Terrorism: The Migration of Dreams and Nightmares.* Lanham, MD: Rowman & Littlefield, 2005

NCTC, *A Chronology of Significant International Terrorism for 2004.* Washington, DC: National Counterterrorism Center, 2005

Norell, M., *Muslim Fundamentalism: A Real or Imagined Threat?* Swedish Military HQ, Stockholm 1994 (in Swedish)

Norell, M., 'Trends in the Middle East' and 'Trends in International Terrorism' ('Trender i Mellanöstern' och 'Trender i internationell terrorism'). Swedish Defence Research Memos for project 'FoRma', Stockholm, November 2005

Norton, A.R., *Hezbollah: A Short History.* Princeton, NJ: Princeton University Press, 2007

Norval, M., *Triumph of Disorder: Islamic Fundamentalism, The New Face of War.* Indian Wells, CA: McKenna, 2001

O'Donnell, P., *In Time of War: Hitler's Terrorist Attack on America.* New York: New Press, 2005

Palmer, M. and Palmer P., *At the Heart of Terror: Islam, Jihadists, and America's War on Terrorism.* Lanham, MD: Rowman & Littlefield, 2004

Peters, B., *Tödlicher Irrtum: Die Geschichte der RAF.* Berlin: Argon-Verlag, 2005

Phares, W., *Future Jihad: Terrorist Strategies against the West.* New York: Palgrave/St Martin's Press, 2006

Pillar, P.R., *Terrorism and U.S. Foreign Policy.* Washington, DC: Brookings Institution Press, 2001

Pluchinsky, D., 'The Evolution of the US Government's Annual Report on Terrorism: A Personal Commentary' [research note]. *Studies in Conflict and Terrorism*, 29(1), January–February 2006, pp. 91–98

Pohly, M. and Duran, K., *Osama bin Laden und der internationale Terrorismus.* Munich: Ullstein Taschenbuch Verlag, 2001

Quan Li and Schaub, D., 'Economic Globalization and Transnational Terrorism: A Pooled Time-Series Analysis'. *Journal of Conflict Resolution*, 48, April 2004, pp. 230–258

Quan Li, 'Does Democracy Promote or Reduce Transnational Terrorist Incidents?' *Journal of Conflict Resolution*, 49(2), April 2005, pp. 278–297

Rabasa, A., Chalk, P., Cragin, K., Daly, S.A., Gregg, H.S., Karasik, T.W., O'Brien, K.A. and Rosenau, W., *Beyond Al-Qaeda. Part 2: The Outer Rings of the Terrorist Universe.* MG-430. Santa Monica, CA: RAND, 2006

Rafhaeli, N., 'Financing of Terrorism: Sources, Methods and Channels'. *Terrorism and Political Violence*, 15(4), Winter 2003, pp. 59–82

Richardson, L., 'Terrorists as Transnational Actors'. *Terrorism and Political Violence*, 11(4), 1999, pp. 209–220

Riedel, B., 'Al Qaeda strikes back'. *Foreign Affairs*, 86(3), May–June 2007, pp. 24–40

Robb, J., *Brave New War: The Next Stage of Terrorism and the End of Globalization.* Hoboken, NJ: Wiley, 2007

Rosecrance, R.N. and Stein, A.A., *No More States? Globalization, National Self-Determination and Terrorism.* Lanham, MD: Rowman & Littlefield, 2006

Rosendorff, B.P. and Sandler, T., 'The Political Economy of Transnational Terrorism'. *Journal of Conflict Resolution*, 49(2), April 2005, pp. 171–182

Roy, O., *Globalized Islam: The Search for a New Ummah*. New York: Columbia University Press, 2004

Ruthven, M., *Fury for God: The Islamist Attack on America*. Cambridge: Granta, 2002

Sawyer, R. and Foster, M., 'The Resurgent and Persistent Threat of Al Qaeda'. *ANNALS of the American Academy of Political and Social Science*, July 2008

Schanzer, J., *Al-Qaeda's Armies: Middle East Affiliate Groups and the Next Generation of Terror*. Washington, DC: Washington Institute for Near East Policy, 2004

Schmid, A.P., 'Terrorism and Energy Security. Targeting Oil and Other Energy Sources and Infrastructure'. Oklahoma City: Memorial Institute for the Prevention of Terrorism, *MIPT Insight*, March 2007

Schneckener, W., *Transnationaler Terrorismus*. Frankfurt am Main: Suhrkamp, 2006

Schröm, O., *Al Qaida, Akteure, Strukturen, Attentate*. Berlin: Aufbau Verlag, 2005

Schwartz, S., *The Two Faces of Islam: Saudi Fundamentalism and Its Role in Terrorism*. New York: Doubleday, 2003

Schweitzer, Y. and Shay, S., *The Globalization of Terror: The Challenge of Al-Qaida and the Response of the International Community*. Eddson, IL: Transaction Press, 2003

Selth, A., *The Terrorist Threat to Diplomacy: An Australian Perspective*. Canberra: Strategic and Defence Studies Centre, Research School of Pacific Studies, Australian National University, 1986

Sendagorta, F., 'Jihad in Europe: The Wider Context'. *Survival*, 47(3), Autumn 2005, pp. 63–72

Shay, S., *The Endless Jihad: The Mujahidin, the Taliban and Bin Laden*. Eddson, IL: Transaction Press, 2002

Silverberg, M., *The Quartermasters of Terror: Saudi Arabia and the Global Islamic Jihad*. Lima, OH: Wyndham Hall Press, 2005

Steinhäusler, F., 'Strategic Terrorism: Threats and Risk Assessment'. In H. Gärtner and I.M. Cuthbertson (eds), *European Security and Transatlantic Relations after 9/11 and the Iraq War*. Basingstoke, UK: Palgrave Macmillan, 2005

Steinhäusler, F. and Bunn, G., 'Protecting Nuclear Material and Facilities: Is a New Approach Needed?' *Proc. 46th IAEA General Conference*, Scientific Forum, September 2002

Stock, J. and Herz, A., 'The Threat Environment Created by International Terrorism from the German Police Perspective'. *European Journal on Criminal Policy and Research*, 13(1–2), April 2007, pp. 85–108

Tarrow, S., *The New Transnational Activism*. Cambridge: Cambridge University Press, 2005

Taylor, P., *States of Terror: Democracy and Political Violence*. London: BBC Books, 1993

Thamm, B.G., *Al-Qaida: Das Netzwerk des Terrors*. Munich: Diederichs, 2005

Treverton, G.F., *Emerging Threats to National Security*. CT-234. Santa Monica, CA: RAND, February 2005

Treverton, G.F., *Making Sense of Transnational Threats*. Workshop Reports CF-200. Santa Monica, CA: RAND, 2005

United States, Department of State. *Patterns of Global Terrorism: 1991*. Washington, DC: US Department of State, 1992

United States, Department of State. *Patterns of Global Terrorism: 1992*. Washington, DC: US Department of State, 1993

United States, Department of State. *Patterns of Global Terrorism: 1994*. Washington, DC: US Department of State, 1995

Venzke, B. and Ibrahim, A. *The al-Qaeda Threat: An Analytical Guide to al-Qaeda's Tactics and Targets*. Alexandria, VA: Tempest, 2003

Vidino, L., *Al Qaedai in Europe: The New Battleground of International Jihad*. New York: Prometheus Books, 2005

Vinke, H., *Mit zweierlei Mass: Die deutsche Reaktion auf den Terror von rechts: eine Dokumentation*. Reinbek bei Hamburg: Rowohlt, 1981

Wallace, P., 'Lessons of Political Violence and International Terrorism'. In: *Conflict Resolution Strategies and Skills for South Asia*. Chandigarh: Institute for Development and Communications, November 2000

Wallace, P. and Barrier, N.G., 'International Dimensions of Sikh Political Violence'. In G. Singh (ed.), *Ethno-nationalism and Emerging World (Dis)Order*. New Delhi: Kanishka, 2002

Wenger, A., *International Relations: From the Cold War to the Globalized World*. Boulder, CO: Lynne Rienner, 2003

Whine, M., *Terrorist Incidents against Jewish Communities and Israeli Citizens Abroad, 1968–2003*. Israel website, International Policy Institute for Counterterrorism (ICT), 20 December 2003. Available at: www.ict.org.il/ (accessed 17 March, 2009)

Wiktorowicz, Q., *Radical Islam Rising: Muslim Extremism in the West*. Lanham, MD: Rowman & Littlefield, 2005

Williams, R., *Writing in the Dust: Reflections on 11th September and Its Aftermath*. London: Hodder & Stoughton, 2002

Wilson, N. and Thomson, G., 'The Epidemiology of International Terrorism Involving Fatal Outcomes in Developed Countries (1994–2003)'. *European Journal of Epidemiology*, 20(5), May 2005, pp. 375–381

Wolf, J.B., *Fear of Fear: A Survey of Terrorist Operations and Controls in Open Societies*. New York: Plenum Press, 1981

Zahab, M.A., *Islamic Networks: The Afghan–Pakistan Connection*. London: Hurst, 2004

Zimmermann, D., 'The Transformation of Terrorism: The "New Terrorism", impact scalability and the dynamic of reciprocal threat perception'. *Zürcher Beiträge zur Sicherheitspolitik und Konfliktforschubng*, no. 678. Zürich: Forschungsstelle für Sicherheitspolitik der ETH, 2003

Zimmermann, D., 'Tangled Skin or Gordian Knot? Iran and Syria as State-Supporters of Political Violence Movements in Lebanon and the Palestinian Territories'. *Zürcher Beiträge zur Sicherheitspolitik und Konfliktforschung*, no. 70. Zürich: Forschungstelle für Sicherheitspolitik der ETH, 2004

Žižek, S., *Welcome to the Desert of the Real! Five Essays on 11 September and Related Dates*. London: Verso, 2002

Zwikael, O., 'Al Qaeda's Operations: Project Management Analysis'. *Studies in Conflict and Terrorism*, 30(3), 2007, pp. 267–280

J. The terrorist personality and organization

Abedin, M., 'The Essence of Al Qaeda: An Interview with Saad al-Faqih'. *Spotlight on Terror*, 2(2), 5 February 2004

Adler, S., *Zwarte weduwen, het leven van drie Tsjetsjeense zussen tussen angst en vergelding*. Amsterdam: Pimento, 2005

Alexander, Y. and Swetnam, M.S., *Usama Bin Laden's Al-Qaida: Profile of a Terrorist Network*, Ardsley, NY: Transnational, 2001

Ali, F. and Dow, J., 'Women and Al Qaeda. Examining the Role and Contribution of Muslim Women in the Global Jihadi Movement'. Contribution to the IISS workshop on Female Suicide Bombers and Europe, 12 March 2007

Alimi, E.Y., 'Contextualizing Political Terrorism: A Collective Action Perspective or Understanding the Tanzim'. *Studies in Conflict and Terrorism*, 29(3), April–May 2006, pp. 263–283

al-Zayyatt, M., *The Road to Al-Qaeda: The Story of Bin Laden's Right-Hand Man*. London: Pluto Press, 2004

Anat, B., *The Path to Paradise. The Inner World of Suicide Bombers and Their Dispatchers*. Westport, CT: Praeger, 2007

Atwan, A.B., *The Secret History of al Qaeda*. London: Saqi Books, 2006

Ayman al-Zawahiri, *Fursan Taht Rayah Al-Nabi* (Knight under the Prophet's Banner). Casablanca, Morocco: Sar-al-Najaah Al-Jadeedah, 2001

Basaev, S., (Abdallah Shamil Abu Idris), *Book of a Mujahiddeen*. E-book, March 2004. Available at: www.scribd.com/doc/101788/Book-of-a-Mujahiddeen (accessed 17 March 2009)

Batal al-Shishani, 'M. Abu Mus'ab Al-Suri and the Third Generation of Salafi-Jihadists'. *Terrorism Monitor*, 3(16), 11 August 2005. Available at: www.jamestown.org/programs/gta/single/?tx_ttnews[tt_news]=547&tx_ttnews[backPid]=180&no_cache=1 (accessed 17 March, 2009)

Bayanouni, A., 'The Battle with Syria: An Interview with Muslim Brotherhood Leader Ali Bayanouni'. *Terrorism Monitor*, 3(16), 11 August 2005. Available at: www.jamestown.org/programs/gta/single/?tx_ttnews[tt_news]=551&tx_ttnews[backPid]=180&no_cache=1 (accessed 17 March, 2009)

Bergen, P., *Holy War Inc.: Inside the Secret World of Osama Bin Laden*. New York: Free Press, 2001

Bergen, P.L., *The Osama Bin Laden I Know: An Oral History of al Qaeda's Leader*. New York: Free Press, 2006

Bergen, P., 'Al Qaeda, The Organization: A Five-Year Forecast'. *ANNALS of the American Academy of Political and Social Science*, 618, July 2008, pp. 14–30

Bergen, P. and Reynolds, A., 'Blowback Revisited: Today's Insurgents in Iraq are Tomorrow's Terrorists'. *Foreign Affairs*, 84(6), November–December 2005, pp. 2–6

Bin Laden, O. and Lawrence, B.B., *Messages to the World: The Statements of Osama bin Laden*. London: Verso, 2005

Bjørgo, T. and Horgan, J., *Leaving Terrorism Behind*. London: Routledge, 2008

Blee, K.M., 'Women and Organized Racial Terrorism in the United States'. *Studies in Conflict and Terrorism*, 28, 2005, pp. 421–433

Bloom, M., 'Mother, Daughter, Sister, Bomber'. *Bulletin of the Atomic Scientists*, 61(76), November–December 2005, pp. 54–62

Bodansky, Y., *Bin Laden: The Man Who Declared War on America*. Rocklin, CA: Forum, 1999

Brisard, J.-C., *Zarqawi*. Cambridge: Polity Press, 2005

Brown, V., *Cracks in the Foundation: Leadership Schisms in al-Qa'ida from 1989–2006*. West Point, NY: Combating Terrorism Center, September 2007

Bunker, R.J. (ed.), *Networks, Terrorism and Global Insurgency*. London: Routledge, 2004

Burke, J., *Al-Qaeda: Casting a Shadow of Terror*. London: I.B. Tauris, 2003

Burke, J., *Al-Qaeda: The True Story of Radical Islam*. London: I.B. Tauris, 2005

Busool, A.N., *Muslim Women Warriors*. Chicago: Al Huda, 1995

Castaneda, J., *Che Guevara, Biographie von Jorge Castaneda*. Frankfurt am Main: Israel, 1997

Chan, A. and Garrick, J., 'Organization Theory in Turbulent Times: The Traces of Foucault's Ethics'. *Organization*, 9, November 2002, pp. 683–701

Chasdi, R.J., 'Middle East Terrorism, 1968–1993: An Empirical Analysis of Terrorist Group-Type Behavior'. *Journal of Conflict Studies*, 17(2), 1997, pp. 73–114

Collins, A., *My Jihad: The True Story of an American Mujahid's Amazing Journey from Usama bin Laden's Training Camp*. New Delhi: Manas Publications, 2006

Cook, D., 'Women Fighting in Jihad?' *Studies in Conflict and Terrorism*, 28, 2005, pp. 375–384

Corbin, J., *The Base: In Search of al-Qaeda, the Terror Network That Shook the World*. London: Simon & Schuster, 2002

Cragin, K. and Daly, S.A., *The Dynamic Terrorist Threat: An Assessment of Group Motivation and Capabilities in a Changing World*. MR-1782. Santa Monica, CA: RAND, 2004

Cruickshank, P. and Hage, A. M., 'Abu Musab Al-Suri: "Architect of the New al Qaeda"'. *Studies in Conflict and Terrorism*, 30(1), 2007, pp. 1–14

CTC, *Al-Qa'ida's Foreign Fighters in Iraq: A First Look at the Sinjar Records*. West Point, NY: Comabating Terrorism Center, 2007

CTC, *Harmony and Disharmony: Exploiting al-Qa'ida's Organizational Vulnerabilities*. Combating Terrorism Center, Department of Social Sciences, United States Military Academy, 14 February 2006

Cullison, A., 'Inside al-Qaeda's Hard Drive'. *The Atlantic*, 294(2), September 2004, pp. 55–72

Cunningham, K., 'True Confessions of an Eight-Year-Old Warrior'. *Qualitative Inquiry*, 10, October 2004, pp. 706–714

Degenhardt, H.W., *Revolutionary and Dissident Movements: An International Guide*, 2nd edn. London: Longman, 1988

DeMars, W.E., *NGOs and Transnational Networks: Wild Cards in World Politics*. London: Pluto Press, 2005

Denécé, E., *Al-Qaeda: les nouveaux réseaux de la terreur*. Paris, Ellipses, 2005

Dennis, A.J., *Osama bin Laden: A Psychological and Political Portrait*. Lima, OH: Wyndham Hall Press, 2002

Diani, M. and McAdam, D. (eds), *Social Movements and Networks: Relational Approaches to Collective Action*. Oxford: Oxford University Press, 2003

Dietl, W., *Carlos: das Ende eines Mythos*. Bergisch Gladbach, Germany: Goldmann, 1995

Enloe, C., *The Curious Feminist: Searching for Women in a New Age of Empire*. Berkeley, CA: University of California Press, 2005

Enzensberger, H.-M., *Schreckensmaenner: Versuch über den radikalen Verlierer*. Frankfurt am Main: Suhrkamp, 2006

Enzensberger, U., *Die Jahre der Commune I. Berlin 1967–1969*. Munich: Goldmann, 2006

Faber, M.J., 'Talking to Terrorists in Gaza', 16 February 2005. Paper for Club de Madrid Conference, March 2005

Feltrinelli, C., *Senior Service: Das Leben meines Vaters*. Munich: Hanser 2001

Ferber, A.L., 'Racial Warriors and Weekend Warriors: The Construction of Masculinity in Mythopoetic and White Supremacist Discourse'. *Men and Masculinities*, 3, July 2000, pp. 30–56

Fielding, N. and Fouda, Y., *Masterminds of Terror*. Hamburg: Europa Verlag, 2003

Follain, J., *Jackal: The Complete Story of the Legendary Terrorist, Carlos the Jackal*. New York: Arcade Publishing, 2000

Follath, E. and Mascolo, G. 'Der Clan des OBL'. *Der Spiegel*, 23, 2005, pp. 66–74

Gabriel, Y. (ed.), *Myths, Stories, and Organizations: Premodern Narratives for Our Times*. Oxford: Oxford University Press, 2004

Gambill, G., 'Abu Musab Al-Zarqawi: A Biographical Sketch'. *Terrorism Monitor*, 2(24), 16 December 2004. Available at: www.jamestown.org/programs/gta/single/?tx_ttnews[tt_news]=334&tx_ttnews[backPid]= 179&no_cache=1 (accessed 17 March 2009)

Gerges, F.A., *Journey of the Jihadist: Inside Muslim Militancy*. London: Harcourt Press, 2006

German, M., *Thinking Like a Terrorist: Insights of a Former FBI Undercover Agent*. Washington, DC: Potomac Books, 2007

Gerwehr, S. and Daly, S., 'Al-Qaida: terrorist selection and recruitment'. Santa Monica, CA: RAND, 2007. Chapter 5 in D. Kamien (ed.), *The McGraw-Hill Homeland Security Handbook*. New York: McGraw-Hill, 2006

Ghosh, A., 'Professor of Death: An Iraqi Insurgent Leader Reveals How He Trains and Equips Suicide Bombers and Sends Them on Their Lethal Missions'. *Time*, 24 October 2005, pp. 30–33

Gonzalez-Perez, M., 'Guerrilleras in Latin America: Domestic and International Roles'. *Journal of Peace Research*, 43, May 2006, pp. 313–329

Gonzalez-Perez, M., *Women and Terrorism*, London: Routledge, 2008

Gorman, S.P., *Networks, Security and Complexity*. Cheltenham, UK: Edward Elgar, 2005

Gowers, A. and Walker, A., *Arafat: Hinter dem Mythos*. Munich: DTV, 1994

Grau, L.W., 'Guerrillas, Terrorists, and Intelligence Analysis'. *Military Review*, July–August 2004, pp. 42–49

Gray, J., *Al Qaeda and What It Means to Be Modern*. London: Faber & Faber, 2003

Greenberg, K.J. (ed.), *Al Qaeda Now: Understanding Today's Terrorists*. Cambridge: Cambridge University Press, 2005

Groen, J. and Kranenberg, A., *Strijdsters van Allah: radicale moslima's en het Hofstadnetwerk*. Amsterdam: Meulenhoff, 2006

Guidère, M., *Les martyrs d'Al-Qaïda*. Nantes: Editions du temps, 2006

Gunaratna, R., *Inside Al Qaeda: Global Network of Terror*. New York: Berkley, 2003

Gupta, D.K., *Understanding Terrorism and Political Violence*. London: Routledge, 2008

Hellmich, Cr., 'Al-Qaeda: Terrorists, Hypocrites, Fundamentalists? The View from Within'. *Third World Quarterly*, 26(1), February 2005, pp. 39–54

Henry, T., 'Al-Qaeda's Resurgence'. *Atlantic Monthly*, June 2004

Hoffman, B., 'The Leadership Secrets of Osama bin Laden'. *Atlantic Monthly*, April 2003

Holmes, S., 'Al-Qaeda, September 11, 2001'. In D. Gambetta (ed.), *Making Sense of Suicide Missions*. Oxford Scholarship Online Monographs, March 2005

Huntington, S.P., 'Al-Qaeda: A Blueprint for International Terrorism in the Twenty-First Century'? *Defence Studies*, 4(2), Summer 2004, pp. 229–255

Husayn, F., *Al-Zarqawi: The Second Generation of al-Qa'ida*. Serialized by *Al Quds al-Arabi* (London), May–July 2005

Intelligence and Terrorism Information Center, *Profile of the Hamas Movement*. Center for Special Studies (CSS), 12 February 2006

Jackal, J.F., *Finally the Complete Story of the Legendary Terrorist Carlos the Jackal*. New York: Arcade, 2000

Jackson, B.A., 'Groups, Networks or Movements: A Command-and-Control-Driven Approach to Classifying Terrorist Organizations and Its Application to Al Qaeda'. *Studies in Conflict and Terrorism*, 29(3), April–May 2006, pp. 241–262

Jackson, B.A., Baker, J.C., Cragin, K., Parachini, J., Trujillo, H.R. and Chalk, P. *Aptitude for Destruction*, vol. 1: *Organizational Learning in Terrorist Groups and Its Implications for Combating Terrorism*. MG-331. Santa Monica, CA: RAND, 2005

Jackson, B.A., Baker, J.C., Cragin, K., Parachini, J., Trujillo, H.R. and Chalk, P., *Aptitude for Destruction*, vol 2: *Case Studies of Organizational Learning in Five Terrorist Groups*. MG-332. Santa Monica, CA: RAND, 2005

Jamali, A., 'Gulbuddin Hekmatyar: The Rise and Fall of an Afghan Warlord'. *Terrorism Monitor*, 3(2), 27 January 2005. Available at: www.jamestown.org/programs/gta/single/?tx_ttnews[tt_news]=322&tx_ttnews[back Pid]=180&no_cache=1 (accessed 18 March 2009)

Jandora, J.W., 'Osama bin Laden's Global Jihad: Myth and Movement'. *Military Review*, November–December 2006, pp. 41–50

Jenkins, B.M., 'Looking at al Qaeda from the Inside Out: An Annotated Briefing'. *DART Working Paper no. 03–4*, Arlington, VA: Hicks & Associates, 2003

Jihad Unspun, *The Osama bin Laden Collection*, vol. 1, 2006. (Collection of statements, interviews, articles, video releases, footage of AQ training camps, interactive photo archive)

Jones, D.M., Smith, M.L.R. and Weeding, M., 'Looking for the Pattern: Al Qaeda in Southeast Asia – the Genealogy of a Terror Network'. *Studies in Conflict and Terrorism*, 26(6), November–December 2003, pp. 443–457

Jones, S. and Libicki, M.C., *How Terrorist Groups End: Lessons for Countering al-Qa'ida*. Santa Monica, CA: RAND, 2008

Jongman, A.J. in collaboration with Schmid, A.P., 'World Directory of Terrorist and Other Organizations Associated with Guerrilla Warfare, Political Violence, and Protest'. In A.P. Schmid and A.J. Jongman, *Political Terrorism: A New Guide to Actors, Authors, Concepts, Data Bases, Theories, and Literature*. Amsterdam: North-Holland, 1988

Kapeliuk, A., *Yassir Arafat: Die Biographie*, Heidelberg: Palmyra, 2005

Kaplan, D.E. and Marshall, A., *The Cult at the End of the World: The Incredible Story of Aum*. London: Hutchinson, 1988

Kaplan, J., 'Leaderless Resistance'. *Terrorism and Political Violence*, 9(3), Fall 1997, pp. 80–96

Karmon, E., 'Al-Qa'ida and the War on Terror after the War in Iraq'. *MERIA Journal*, 10(1), March 2006

Katzman, K., 'Al Qaeda: Profile and Threat Assessment'. Washington, DC: *CRS Report for Congress*, RL33038, 17 August 2005

Kepel, G. and Millelli, J.-P. (eds), *Al-Qaida: Texte des Terrors*. Munich: Piper, 1996

Khatchadourian, R., 'Azzam the American: The Making of an Al Qaida Homegrown'. *New Yorker*, 22 January 2007

Khosrokhavar, F., *Quand Al-Qaïda parle: témoignages derrière les barreaux*. Paris: Grasset, 2006

Kimhi, S. and Even, S., 'Who Are the Palestinian Suicide Bombers'? *Memorandum* no. 73. Tel Aviv: JCSS, 2004

Kirby, A., 'The London Bombers as "Self-Starters": A Case Study in Indigenous Radicalization and the Mergence of Autonomous Cliques'. *Studies in Conflict and Terrorism*, 30, 2007, pp. 415–428

Klein, E., *Jihad: strijders en strijdsters voor Allah*. Amsterdam: Byblos, 2005

Knorr, C.K., 'Complex Global Microstructures: The New Terrorist Societies'. *Theory, Culture and Society*, 22, October 2005, pp. 213–234

Kohlmann, E.F., 'Lashkar-e-Taiba [LeT] (Pakistan/Kashmir) (aka "The Army of Medina", "The Army of the Righteous")'. Available at: www.globalterroralert.com, 2004 (accessed 10 March 2009)

Kohlmann, E.F., 'The Role of Islamic Charities in International Terrorist Recruitment and Financing'. DIIS Working Paper. Copenhagen: Danish Institute for International Studies, 2006/7

Kohlmann, E., *Al-Qaida's Jihad in Europe: The Afghan–Bosnian Network*. New York: Berg, 2004

Kopp., M., *Die Terrorjahre: Mein Leben an der Seite von Carlos*. Frankfurt am Main: DVA

Korteweg, R. and Ehrhardt, D., *Terrorist Black Holes: A Study into Terrorist Sanctuaries and Government Weaknesses*. The Hague: Clingendael Centre for Strategic Studies (CCSS), November 2005

Kramer, M., 'The Oracle of Hizbullah: Sayyid Muhammad Husayn Fadlallah'. In R.S. Appleby (ed.), *Spokesmen for the Despised: Fundamentalist Leaders of the Middle East*. Chicago: University of Chicago Press, 1997

Krebs, M., *Ulrike Meinhof: ein Leben im Widerspruch*. Reinbek bei Hamburg: Rowohlt, 1988

Kukis, M., *My Heart Became Attached: The Strange Journey of John Walker Lindh*. Washinghton, DC: Brassey's, 2003

Kurth, C.A., 'How al-Qaida Ends: The Decline and Demise of Terrorist Groups'. *International Security*, 31(1), Summer 2006, pp. 7–48

Laqueur, W. (ed.), *Voices of Terror: Manifestos, Writings and Manuals of Al Qaeda, Hamas, and Other Terrorists from around the World and throughout the Ages*. New York: Reed Press, 2004

Lawrence, B., *Messages to the World: The Statements of Osama bin Laden*. London: Verso, 2005

Leiken, R.S., 'Fair Game: Al-Qa'ida's New Soldiers'. *New Republic*, 26 April 2004

Lia, B., *Architect of Global Jihad: The Life of Al-Qa'ida Strategist Abu Mus'ab al-Suri*. London: C. Hurst, 2007

Library of Congress, *Global Overview of Narcotics-Funded Terrorist and Other Extremist Groups*. May 2002. Available at: www.loc.gov/rr/frd/pdf-files/NarcsFundedTerrs_Extrems.pdf (accessed 18 March 2009)

Lichbach, M.I., *The Rebel's Dilemma*. Ann Arbor: University of Michigan Press, 1998

Linden, E.V. (ed.), *Foreign Terrorist Organizations: History, Tactics and Connections*. Hauppage, NY: Nova Science Publishers, 2004

Louis, W.R., Taylor, D.M. and Douglas, R.L., 'Normative Influence and Rational Conflict Decisions: Group Norms and Cost–Benefit Analyses for Intergroup Behavior'. *Group Processes and Intergroup Relations*, 8, October 2005, pp. 355–374

Ly, P.E., 'The Charitable Activities of Terrorist Organizations'. *Public Choice*, 131(1–2), April 2007, pp. 177–195

McAllister, B., 'Al Qaeda and the Innovative Firm: Demythologizing the Network'. *Studies in Conflict and Terrorism*, 27(4), 2004, pp. 297–320

Malthaner, S. 'Terroristische Bewegungen und ihre Bezugsgruppen: Anvisierte Sympathisanten und tatsächliche Unterstützer'. In P. Waldmann (ed.), *Determinanten des Terrorismus*. Weilerswist, Germany: Velbrück, 2004

Mannes, A., *Profiles in Terror: The Guide to Middle East Terrorist Organizations*. Lanham, MD: Rowman & Littlefield, 2004

Mansfield, L., *The Al Qaeda 2006 Yearbook: A Complete Reference and Translation of al-Qa'ida Messages in 2006*. Morrisville, NC: Lulu, 2007

Martens, W.H.J., 'The Terrorist with Antisocial Personality Disorder'. *Journal of Forensic Psychology Practice*, 4(1), 5 April 2004, pp. 45–56

Meertens, R., Prins, Y.R.A. and Doosje, B., *In iedereen schuilt een terrorist: een sociaal-psychologische analyse van terroristische sektes en aanslagen*. Schiedam, Netherlands, Uitgeverij Scriptum, 2005

Miller, J., Stone, M. and Mitchell, C., *The Cell: Inside the 9/11 Plot, and Why the FBI and CIA Failed to Stop It*. New York: Hyperion, 2002

Moussaoiu, A.S., *Zacarias, My Brother: The Making of a Terrorist*. New York: Seven Stories Press, 2003

Münkler, H., 'Ältere und jüngere Formen des Terrorismus: Strategie und Organisationsstruktur'. In W. Weidenfeld (ed.), *Herausforderung Terrorismus: die Zukunft der Sicherheit*. Wiesbaden: VS Verlag, 2004

Murray, J. and Ward, R.H. (eds), Builta, J. A. (compiler), *Extremist Groups: An International Compilation of Terrorist Organizations, Violent Political Groups, and Issue-Oriented Militant Movements*. Chicago: Office of International Criminal Justice, 1996

Musharbash, Y., *Die neue al-Qa'ida: Innenansichten eines lernenden Terrornetzwerks*. Cologne: Kiepenheuer & Witsch, 2006

Muwaffaq, Z.A., *Usama bin Ladin without Mask*. Beirut: World Book Publishing, 2003

Napoleoni, L., 'Profile of a Killer'. *Foreign Policy*, November 2005, pp. 1–5

Napoleoni, L., *Insurgent Iraq: Al Zarqawi and the New Generation*. New York: Seven Stories Press, 2005

Nasiri, O., *Inside the Jihad: My Life with Al Qaeda: A Spy's Story*. New York: Basic Books, 2006

Nedoroscik, J.A., 'Extremist Groups in Egypt'. *Terrorism and Political Violence*, 14(2), Summer 2002, pp. 47–76

NEFA, 'Al-Qa'ida's Committee in Saudi Arabia: 2002–2003'. Occasional Paper, December 2005. Available from www.nefafoundation.org (accessed 10 March 2009)

Ness, C.N. (ed.), *Female Terrorism and Militancy*. London: Routledge, 2007

Nivat, A., 'The Black Widows: Chechen Women Join the Fight for Independence – and Allah'. *Studies in Conflict and Terrorism*, 28, 2005, pp. 413–419

Oliver, A.M. and Steinberg, P., *The Road to Martyrs' Square: A Journey into the World of the Suicide Bomber*. Oxford: Oxford University Press, 2005

Orr, T., *Egyptian Islamic Jihad*, New York: Rosen, 2003

Pedahzur, A., Perliger, A. and Weinberg, L. 'Altruism and Fatalism: The Characteristics of Palestinian Suicide Terrorists'. *Deviant Behavior*, 24(4), July–August 2003, pp. 405–423

Perliger, A. and Weinberg, L,. 'Jewish self-defence and terrorist groups prior to the establishment of the state of Israel: roots and traditions'. *Totalitarian Movements and Political Religions*, 4(3), December 2003, pp. 91–118

Perry, A., 'How Sri Lanka's Rebels Build a Suicide Bomber'. *Time*, 12 May 2006

Pincus, J.H., *Base Instincts: What Makes Killers Kill?* New York: W.W. Norton, 2001

Post, J., Merari, A. and Ganor, B., *The Mind of the Terrorist: The Psychology of Terrorism from the IRA to al-Qaeda*. Herzliya, Israel: ICT, 2008

Post, J.M., Ruby, K.G. and Shaw, E.D., 'The Radical Group in Context: Identification of Critical Elements in the Analysis of Risk for Terrorism by Radical Group Type'. *Studies in Conflict and Terrorism*, 25(2), April 2002, pp. 101–126

Post, J.M., Sprinzak, E. and Denny, L.M., 'The Terrorists in Their Own Words: Interviews with 35 Incarcerated Middle Eastern Terrorists'. *Terrorism and Political Violence*, 15(1), 2003, pp.171–184

Qutb, B., *Milestones*. New Delhi: Islamic Book Service, 2006

Rabasa, A., *Beyond al-Qaeda*. Part 1: *The Global Jihadist Movement*. Santa Monica, CA: RAND, 2006

Rana, M.A., *A to Z of Jehadi Organisations in Pakistan*. Lahore: Mashal, 2004

Randal, J.C., *Osama: The Making of a Terrorist*. New York: Vintage Books, 2005

Raphaeli, N., 'Ayman Muhammad Rabi' Al-Zawahiri: The Making of an Arch-terrorist'. *Terrorism and Political Violence*, 14(4), Winter 2002, pp. 1–22

Rapoport, D.C., *Inside Terrorist Organizations*. New York: Columbia University Press, 1988

Rauffer, X., ' "Al-Qaeda": A Different Diagnosis'. *Studies in Conflict and Terrorism*, 26(6), November–December 2003, pp. 391–398

Ressa, M., *Seeds of Terror: An Eyewitness Account of Al-Qaeda's Newest Center of Operations in Southeast Asia*. New York: Free Press, 2003

Reuter, C., *My Life Is Weapon: A Modern History of Suicide Bombing*. Princeton, NJ: Princeton University Press, 2004

Reuter, J., 'Chechnya's Suicide Bombers: Desperate, Devout, or Deceived?' American Committee for Peace in Chechnya, 16 September 2005

Riedel, B., *The Search for Al Qaeda: Its Leadership, Ideology, and Future*. Washington, DC: Brookings Institution Press, 2008

Roberts, M., 'Tamil Tiger "Martyrs": Regenerating Divine Potency?' *Studies in Conflict and Terrorism*, 28(6), 2005, pp. 493–514

Sageman, M., *Understanding Terror Networks*. Philadelphia: University of Pennsylvania Press 2004

Schbley, A.H., 'Toward a Common Profile of Religious Terrorism: Some Psychosocial Determinants of Christian and Islamic Terrorists'. *Police Practice and Research*, 7(4), September 2006, pp. 275–292

Scheuer, M., *Through Our Enemies' Eyes: Osama bin Laden, Radical Islam, and the Future of America*. Dulles, VA: Potomac Books, 2002

Seegmiller, B., 'Radicalized Margins: Eric Rudolph and Religious Violence'. *Terrorism and Political Violence*, 19(4), 2007, pp. 511–528

Shanty, F., 'Directory of Terrorist Groups and Organizations'. In *Encyclopedia of World Terrorism, 1996–2002*, vol. 4. Armonk, NY: M.E. Sharpe, 2003

Shapiro, J.N., 'The Greedy Terrorist: A Rational Choice Perspective on Terrorist Organizations' Inefficiencies and Vulnerabilities'. *Strategic Insights*, 4(1), 2005. Available at: www.ccc.nps.navy.mil/si/2005/Jan/shapiro Jan05.asp (accessed 18 March 2009)

Shay, S., *The Shahids: Islam and Suicide Attacks*. New Brunswick, NJ: Transaction, 2004

Sifaoui, M., *Inside Al Qaeda: How I Infiltrated the World's Deadliest Terrorist Organization*, Jackson, TN: Basic Books, 2004

Sprinzak, E., 'Rational Fanatics'. *Foreign Policy*, no. 120, September–October 2000

Steinberg, G., *Die Netzwerke des islamistischen Terrorismus: der nahe and der ferne Feind*. Munich: C.H. Beck Verlag, 2005

Suskind, R., 'The Unofficial Story of the Al Qaeda 14'. *Time*, 18 September 2006

Takeyh, R. and Gvosdev, N., 'Do Terrorist Networks Need a Home?' *Washington Quarterly*, Summer 2002, pp. 97–108

Taylor, M., *The Terrorist*. London: Brassey's Defence, 1988

Thompson, T., *Gangs: A Journey into the Heart of the British Underworld*. London: Hodder & Stoughton, 2004

Turner, M., 'The Management of Violence in a Conflict Organization: The Case of the Abu Sayyaf'. *Public Organization Review*, 3(4), 2003, pp. 387–401

Ulfkotte, U., *Propheten des Terrors*. Munich: Goldmann Verlag, 2001

Vaisman-Tzachor, R., 'Profiling Terrorists'. *Journal of Police Crisis Negotiations*, 7(1), 6 March 2007, pp. 27–61

Vermaat, E., *De Hofstadgroep: portret van een radikaal-Islamitisch netwerk*. Soesterberg, Netherlands: Uitgeverij Aspekt, 2005

Victoroff, J., 'The Mind of the Terrorist: A Review and Critique of Psychological Approaches'. *Journal of Conflict Resolution*, 49(1), February 2005, pp. 3–42

Vittori, J.M., 'Geschäftszweck: Terror: al-Qaida als multinationales Unternehmen'. *Internationale Politik*, 60(3), March 2005, pp. 48–55

Ward, R.H. (contributing editor) and Hill, S.D. (senior researcher), *Extremist Groups: An International Compilation of Terrorist Organizations, Violent Political Groups, and Issue-Oriented Militant Movements*, 2nd edn. Huntsville, TX: Office of International Criminal Justice and the Institute for the Study of Violent Groups, 2002

Weaver, M.A., 'Inventing al-Zarqawi: How a Video-Store Clerk and Small-Time Crook Became America's Nemesis in Iraq'. *Atlantic Quarterly*, July–August 2006, pp. 87–100

Weinberg, L., Pedahzur, A. and Perliger, A., *Political Parties and Terrorist Groups*, 2nd edn. London: Routledge, 2008

Weinhauer, K., Requate, J. and Haupt, H.G., *Terrorismus in der Bundesrepublik: Medien, Staat und Subkulturen in den 1970er Jahren*. Campus Verlag, 2006

Zedalis, D., 'Female Suicide Bombers'. Strategic Studies Institute, 2004. Available at: www.strategicstudies institute.army.mil/pubs/display.cfm?PubID=408 (accessed 18 March 2009)

Zirakzadeh, C.E., 'From Revolutionary Dreams to Organizational Fragmentation: Disputes over Violence within ETA and Sendero Luminoso'. *Terrorism and Political Violence*, 14(4), 2002, pp. 66–93

K. Victimological aspects

Albrecht, H., and Kilchling, M., 'Victims of Terrorism Policies: Should Victims of Terrorism Be Treated Differently?' *European Journal on Criminal Policy and Research*, 13(1–2), April 2007, pp. 13–31

Blackman, P.H., 'Coding the Deaths from the September 11 Terrorist Attacks'. *Homicide Studies*, 6, November 2002, pp. 361–368

Blackman, P.H., 'Response to "Classification of Deaths Resulting from Terrorism"'. *Homicide Studies*, 7, February 2003, pp. 92–95

Blackwell, D., 'Psychotherapy, Politics and Trauma: Working with Survivors of Torture and Organized Violence'. *Group Analysis*, 38, June 2005, pp. 307–323

Bogen, K.T. and Jones, E.D., 'Risks of Mortality and Morbidity from Worldwide Terrorism: 1968–2004'. *Risk Analysis*, 26(1), February 2006, pp. 45–59

Butler, A.S., Panzer, A.M. and Goldfrank L.R. (eds), 'Preparing for the Psychological Consequences of Terrorism: A Public Health Strategy'. Committee on Responding to the Psychological Consequences of Terrorism Board on Neuroscience and Behavioral Health. Washington, DC: National Academies Press, 2003

Charkow, B.W., Book Review: 'Mass Trauma and Violence: Helping Families and Children Cope'. *Family Journal*, 13, January 2005, pp. 107–109

Cole, A.M., *The Cult of True Victimhood: From the War on Welfare to the War on Terror*. Stanford, CA: Stanford University Press, 2007

Danieli, Y., Brom, D. and Sills, J. (eds), *The Trauma of Terrorism: Sharing Knowledge and Shared Care: An International Handbook*. Binghamton, NY: Haworth Maltreatment and Trauma Press, 2005

de Jong, J. (ed.), *Trauma, War, and Violence: Public Mental Health In Socio-cultural Context*. New York: Kluwer Academic/Plenum Publishers, 2002

Dixon, L. and Kaganoff Stern, R., 'Compensation for Lessons from the 9/11 Attacks'. Santa Monica, CA: RAND, 2005. Available at: www.rand.org/publications/MG/MG264 (accessed 18 March, 2009)

Doucet, G. (ed.), 'Terrorism, Victims and International Criminal Responsibility'. Paris: SOS Attendants, 2003

Eisinger, P., 'The American City in the Age of Terror: A Preliminary Assessment of the Effects of September 11'. *Urban Affairs Review*, 40, September 2004, pp. 115–130

Feinberg, K.R., 'What Is Life Worth? The Unprecedented Effort to Compensate the Victims of 9/11'. New York: PublicAffairs, 2005

Flouri, E., 'Post-Traumatic Stress Disorder (PTSD): What We Have Learned and What We Still Have Not Found Out'. *Journal of Interpersonal Violence*, 20, April 2005, pp. 373–379

Furer, L.R., *Checkpoint Syndrome*. Tel Aviv: Gewanim, 2003

Goodman, J.H., 'Coping with Trauma and Hardship among Unaccompanied Refugee Youths from Sudan'. *Qualitative Health Research*, 14, November 2004 pp. 1177–1196

Graves, K.D., Schmidt, J.E. and Andrykowski, M.A., 'Writing about September 11, 2001: Exploration of Emotional Intelligence and the Social Environment'. *Journal of Language and Social Psychology*, 24, September 2005, pp. 285–299

Henderson, M., *The Forgiveness Factor: Stories of Hope in a World of Conflict*. London: Grosvenor Books, 1996

Higgins, K. and McElrath, K., 'The Troubles with Peace: The Cease-Fires and Their Impact on Drug Use among Youth in Northern Ireland'. *Youth Society*, 32, September 2000, pp. 29–59

Hirsch, S., *In the Moment of Greatest Calamity: Terrorism, Grief, and a Victim's Quest for Justice*. Princeton, NJ: Princeton University Press, 2006

Hoffman, B., *The Victims of Terrorism; An Assessment of Their Influence and Growing Role in Policy, Legislation, and the Private Sector*. Santa Monica, CA: RAND, 2007

Khaled, N., 'Psychological effects of terrorism in Algeria'. *Journal of Aggression, Maltreatment and Trauma*, 9(1–2), 15 March 2005, pp. 201–212

Lascher, J.R. and Powers, E.L., 'September 11 Victims, Random Events, and the Ethics of Compensation'. *American Behavioral Scientist*, 48, November 2004, pp. 281–294

Levine, L.J., Whalen, C.K., Henker, B. and Jamner, L.D., 'Looking Back on September 11, 2001: Appraised Impact and Memory for Emotions in Adolescents and Adults'. *Journal of Adolescent Research*, 20, July 2005, pp. 497–523

Levy, B.H., *Who Killed Daniel Pearle?* Hoboken, NJ: Melville House, 2003

McKittrick, D., *Lost Lives: The Stories of the Men, Women and Children Who Died through the Northern Ireland Troubles*. Edinburgh: Mainstream, 1999

Malagreca, M.A., 'I Want Justice: A Performance about Impunity in Argentina'. *Qualitative Inquiry*, 11, August 2005, pp. 570–575

Marik, P.E. and Bowles, S., 'Management of Patients Exposed to Biological and Chemical Warfare Agents'. *Journal of Intensive Care Medicine*, 17, July 2002, pp. 147–161

Martí, M., Parrón, M., Baudraxler, F., Royo, A., Gómez León, N. and Álvarez-Sala, R., 'Blast injuries from Madrid Terrorist Bombing Attacks on March 11, 2004'. *Emergency Radiology*, 13(3), December 2006, pp. 113–122

Milivojevic, L., 'Importance of Projective Identification Influence on Countertransference in a Traumatized Group'. *Group Analysis*, 38, June 2005, pp. 237–248

Miller, L., 'Family therapy of terroristic trauma: psychological syndromes and treatment strategies'. *American Journal of Family Therapy*, 31(4), July–August 2003, pp. 257–280

Myers-Walls, J.A., 'Children as Victims of War and Terrorism'. *Journal of Aggression, Maltreatment and Trauma*, 8(1–2), May 2004, pp. 41–62

Pasquali, E.A., 'Humor: An Antidote for Terrorism'. *Journal of Holistic Nursing*, 21, December, 2003, pp. 398–414

Pat-Horenczyk, R., 'Post-traumatic Distress in Israeli Adolescents Exposed to Ongoing Terrorism: Selected Findings from School-Based Screenings in Jerusalem and Nearby Settlements'. *Journal of Aggression, Maltreatment and Trauma*, 9(3–4), March 2005, pp. 335–347

Pearle, M., *A Mighty Heart: The Brave Life and Death of My Husband Danny Pearle*. New York: Scribner, 2003

Peleg, K., Aharonson-Daniel, L., Stein, M. and Shapira, S.P., 'Patterns of Injury in Hospitalized Terrorist Victims'. *American Journal of Emergency Medicine*, 21, 2003, pp. 258–262

Pérez, A. and Bahamon, A., 'Coping Strategies in Prolonged Kidnappings'. *Terrorism and Political Violence*, 11(3), 1999, pp. 97–106

Peters, K., Richards, P. and Vlassenroot, K., 'What Happens to Youth during and after Wars? A Preliminary Review of Literature on Africa and an Assessment of the Debate'. RAWOO Working Paper, October 2003

Plante, T.G. and Canchola, E.L., 'The Association between Strength of Religious Faith and Coping with American Terrorism regarding the Events of September 11, 2001'. *Pastoral Psychology*, 52(3), January 2004, pp. 269–278

Quan Li and Ming Wen, 'The Immediate and Lingering Effects of Armed Conflict on Adult Mortality: A Time-Series Cross-national Analysis'. *Journal of Peace Research*, 42, July 2005, pp. 471–492

Raphael, B., Dunsmore, J. and Wooding, S., 'Terror and Trauma in Bali: Australia's Mental Health Disaster Response'. *Journal of Aggression, Maltreatment and Trauma*, 9(1–2), 15 March 2005, pp. 245–256

Shapira, S.C., Adatto-Levi, R., Avitzour, M., Rivkind, A.I., Gertsenshtein, I. and Mintz, Y., 'Mortality in Terrorist Attacks: A Unique Modal of Temporal Death Distribution', *World Journal of Surgery*, 30, 2006, pp. 1–8

Shapira, S.C. and Cole, L.A., 'Terror Medicine: Birth of a Discipline'. *Journal of Homeland Security Emergency Management*, 3(2), article 9, 2006

Shapira, S.C. and Mor-Yosef, S., 'Terror Politics and Medicine: The Role of Leadership'. *Studies in Conflicts and Terrorism*, 27, 2004, pp. 65–71

Shapira, S.C. and Shemer, J., 'Medical Management of Terrorist Attacks'. *Israel Medical Association Journal*, 4, 2002, pp. 489–492

Shapira, S.C., Shemer, J. and Oren, M., 'Hospital Management of a Bioterror Event'. *Israel Medical Association Journal*, 4(7), 2002, 493–494

Shapo, M.S., *Compensation for Victims of Terrorism*. Dobbs Ferry, NY: Oceana, 2005

Sharif, I., *The Success of Political Terrorist Events: An Analysis of Terrorist Tactics and Victim Characteristics, 1968–1977*. Lanham, MD: University Press of America, 1996

Sheffy, N., Mintz, Y., Rivkind, A.I. and Shapira, S.C., 'Terror Related Injuries: A Comparison of Gunshot Wounds versus Secondary-Fragments-Induced Injuries from explosives'. *Journal of the American College of Surgeons*, 203(3), 2006, pp. 297–303

Sheppard, B., Rubin, G.J., Wardman, J.K. and Wessely, S., 'Viewpoint: Terrorism and Dispelling the Myth of a Panic Prone Public'. *Journal of Public Health Policy*, 27(3), 2006, pp. 219–245

Siemens, A.A., *Für die RAF was es das System, für mich der Vater: Die andere Geschichte des deutschen Terrorismus*. Munich: Piper Verlag, 2007

Silke, A. (ed.), *Terrorists, Victims and Society: Psychological Perspectives on Terrorism and its Consequences*. Chichester, UK: Wiley, 2003

Somer, E., Buchbinder, E., Peled-Avram, M. and Ben-Yizhack, Y., 'The Stress and Coping of Israeli Emergency Room Social Workers following Terrorist Attacks'. *Qualitative Health Research*, 14, October 2004, pp. 1077–1093

SOS Attenats, *Terrorisme, victimes et responsabilité pénale internationale*. Paris: SOS Attenats, 2003

SOS Attentats, *Le livre noir*. Paris: SOS Attentats, 2002

Stadler, N., 'Terror, Corpse Symbolism, and Taboo Violation: The "Haredi Disaster Victim Identification Team in Israel" (*Zaka*)'. *Journal of the Royal Anthropological Institute*, 12(4), December 2006, pp. 837–858

Thielman, S.B., 'Observations on the Impact on Kenyans of the August 7, 1998 Bombing of the United States Embassy in Nairobi'. *Journal of Aggression, Maltreatment and Trauma*, 9(1–2), 15 March 2005, pp. 233–240

Tota, A.L., 'Ethnographying Public Memory: The Commemorative Genre for the Victims of Terrorism in Italy'. *Qualitative Research*, 4, August 2004, pp. 131–159

Trappler, B., *Modern Terrorism and Psychological Trauma*. New York: Gordian Knots, 2007

Tsang, S., *Intelligence and Human Rights in an Era of Global Terrorism*. Westport, CT: Greenwood Press, 2006

Urlic, I., 'Trauma and Reparation, Mourning and Forgiveness: The Healing Potential of the Group'. *Group Analysis*, 37, December 2004, pp. 453–471

Ursano, R.J., Fullerton, C.S. and Norwood, A. (eds), *Terrorism and Disaster: Individual and Community Mental Health Interventions*. Cambridge: Cambridge University Press, 2003

van Zwol, C., *Gijzelaar van de Kaukasus: de ontvoering van Arjan Erkel*. New York: Prometheus, 2005

Weine, S.M., *Testimony after Catastrophe: Narrating the Traumas of Political Violence*. Evanston, IL: Northwestern University Press, 2006

Williams, G., *13 Days of Terror: Held Hostage by Al-Qaeda Linked Extremists: A True Story*. Far Hills, NJ: New Horizons Press, 2003

Wimbush, S., Davies, G. and Lockey, D., 'The Presentation and Management of Victims of Chemical and Biological Agents: A Survey of Knowledge of UK Clinicians'. *Resuscitation*, 58(3), September 2003, pp. 289–292

L. Terrorism from a psychological perspective

Agosin, M., *Surviving beyond Fear: Women, Children and Human Rights in Latin America*. Fredonia, NY: White Pine Press, 1993

Ai, A.L., Cascio, T., Santangelo, L.K. and Evans-Campbell, T., 'Hope, Meaning, and Growth following the September 11, 2001, Terrorist Attacks'. *Journal of Interpersonal Violence*, 20, May 2005, pp. 523–548

Akhmedova, K. and Speckhard, A., 'A Multi-causal Analysis of the Genesis of Suicide Terrorism: The Chechen Case'. In J. Victoroff (ed.), *Social and Psychological Factors in the Genesis of Terrorism*. Amsterdam: IOS Press, 2006

Alexander, D.A. and Klein, S., 'The Psychological Aspects of Terrorism: From Denial to Hyperbole'. *Journal of the Royal Society of Medicine*, 98(12), December 2005, pp. 557–562

Arnold, D., Calhoun, L.G., Tedeschi, R. and Cann, A., 'Vicarious Posttraumatic Growth'. *Psychotherapy: Journal of Humanistic Psychology*, 45, April 2005, pp. 239–263

Arnold, T.E., *The Violence Formula: Why People Lend Sympathy and Support to Terrorism*. Lexington, MA: Lexington Books, 1988

Asquith, N., 'In Terrorem: "With their Tanks and Their Bombs, and Their Bombs and Their Guns, in Your Head" '. *Journal of Sociology*, 40, December 2004, pp. 400–416

Atran, S., 'The Moral Logic and Growth of Suicide Terrorism'. *Washington Quarterly*, 29(2), Spring 2006, pp. 127–147

Atran, S., Merari, A. and Wientjes, C., 'Suicide Terrorism: The Strategic Threat and Countermeasures'. Joint Report of the NATO Security through Science Programme in Brussels and the Research and Technology Organization in Brussels and Paris, 2004

Auchter, T., Büttner, C., Schultz-Venrath, U. and Wirth, H.-J. (eds), *Der 11. September: Psychoanalytische, psychosoziale und psychohistorische Analysen von Terror und Trauma*. Gieβan, Germany: Psychosozial-Verlag, 2003

Bevans, K., Cerbone, A.B. and Overstreet, S., 'Advances and Future Directions in the Study of Children's Neurobiological Responses to Trauma and Violence Exposure', *Journal of Interpersonal Violence*, 20, April 2005, pp. 418–425

Bjorgo, T. and Horgan, J., *Leaving Terrorism Behind: Individual and Collective Disengagement*. London: Routledge, 2008

Bongar, B. (ed.), *Psychology of Terrorism*. Oxford: Oxford University Press, 2007

Borell, K., 'Terrorism and Everyday Life in Beirut, 2005: Mental Reconstruction, Precaution and Normalization'. *Acta Sociologica*, 51, March 2008, 55–70

Bourke, J., *Fear: A Cultural History*. Emeryville, CA: Shoemaker, 2006

Chakrabarti, A., 'The Moral Psychology of Revenge'. *Journal of Human Values*, 11, April 2005, pp. 31–36

Christie, D.J., Wagner, R.V. and Du Nann Winter, D., *Peace, Conflict, and Violence: Peace Psychology for the 21st Century*. New York: Prentice Hall, 2001

Conradt, G., *Starbuck. Holger Meins: Ein Porträt als Zeitbild (Gebundene Ausgabe)*. Berlin: Espresso Verlag, 2001

Dekel, R., 'Motherhood in a Time of Terror: Subjective Experiences and Responses of Israeli Mothers'. *Affilia*, 19, February 2004, pp. 24–38

Dillenburger, K., Fargas, M. and Akhonzada, R., 'Long-Term Effects of Political Violence: Narrative Inquiry across a 20-Year Period'. *Qualitative Heath Research*, 18(10), October 2008, pp. 1312–1322

Dillinger, J., *Terrorismus: Wissen was stimmt*. Freiburg, Germany: Herder, 2008

Fitzduff, M. and Stout, C.E. (eds), *The Psychology of Resolving Global Conflicts: From War to Peace*. Vol. 1: *Nature vs. Nurture*; vol. 2: *Group and Social Factors*; vol. 3: *Interventions*. Westport, CT: Praeger, 2005

Friedland, N. and Merari, A., 'The Psychological Impact of Terrorism: A Double-Edged Sword'. *Political Psychology*, 6, 1985, pp. 591–603

Gambetta, D., *Making Sense of Suicide Missions*. Oxford: Oxford University Press, 2005

Graziano, F., *Divine Violence: Spectacle, Psychosexuality and Radical Christianity in the Argentine 'Dirty War'*. Boulder, CO: Westview Press, 1992

Healy, A.F., Hoffman, J.M., Beer, F.A. and Bourne, L.E.Jr, 'Terrorists and Democrats: Individual Reactions to International Attacks'. *Political Psychology*, 23(3), September 2002, pp. 439–467

Henriksen, R., 'Warriors in Combat: What Makes People Actively Fight in Combat?' *Journal of Strategic Studies*, 30(2), 2007, pp. 187–223

Horgan, J., *The Psychology of Terrorism*. London: Frank Cass, 2005

Intriligator, M.D. and Dagobert, L.B., 'The Potential Contribution of Psychology to Nuclear War Issues'. *American Psychologist*, 43, April 1988, pp. 318–321

Janssen, H.W.J. and Kertsholt, J.H., 'De psychologie van terroristische groeperingen: kenmerken en processen'. Soesterberg, Netherlands: TNO-DV3 2005-B 002. *TNO Defence, Security and Safety*, 2005

Jasinski, J.L., 'Trauma and Violence Research: Taking Stock in the 21st Century'. *Journal of Interpersonal Violence*, 20, April 2005, pp. 412–417

Jorish, A., *Beacon of Hatred: Inside Hizballah's Al-Manar Television*. Washington, DC: Washington Institute for Near East Policy, 2004

Kruglanski, A.W. and Fishman, S., 'The Psychology of Terrorism: "Syndrome" versus "Tool" Perspectives'. *Terrorism and Political Violence*, 18(2), Summer 2006, pp. 193–215

Landau, M.J., Solomon, S., Greenberg, J., Cohen, F., Pyszczynski, T., Arndt, J., Miller, C.H., Ogilvie, D.M. and Cook, A., 'Deliver Us from Evil: The Effects of Mortality Salience and Reminders of 9/11 on Support for President George W. Bush'. *Personality and Social Psychology Bulletin*, 30, September 2004, pp. 1136–1150

Lester, D., Yang, B., Lindsay, M., 'Suicide Bombers: Are Psychological Profiles Possible?' *Studies in Conflict and Terrorism*, 27(4), 2004, pp. 283–296

Leudar, I., Marsland, V. and Nekvapil, J., 'On Membership Categorization: "Us", "Them" and "Doing Violence" in Political Discourse'. *Discourse Society*, 15, May 2004, pp. 243–266

Low, S.M., Taplin, D.H. and Lamb, M., 'Battery Park City: An Ethnographic Field Study of the Community Impact of 9/11'. *Urban Affairs Review*, 40, May 2005, pp. 655–682

Lowrance, S., 'Identity, Grievances, and Political Action: Recent Evidence from the Palestinian Community in Israel'. *International Political Science Review*, 27, April 2006, pp. 167–190

MacIntosh, H.B. and Whiffen, V.E., 'Twenty Years of Progress in the Study of Trauma'. *Journal of Interpersonal Violence*, 20, April 2005, pp. 488–492

Maeseele, P.A., Verleye, G., Stevens, I. and Speckhard, A., 'Psychosocial Resilience in the Face of a Mediated Terrorist Threat'. *Media, War and Conflict*, 1(1), 2008, pp. 50–69

Michavila, N., *War, Terrorism and Elections: Electoral Impact of the Islamist Terror Attacks in Madrid*. Madrid: Real Instituto Elcano de Estudios Internacionales y Estratégicos, 2005

Moghaddam, F.M. and Marsella, A.J., *Understanding Terrorism: Psychosocial Roots, Consequences and Interventions*. Washington, DC: American Psychological Association, 2004

Oates, S., 'Framing Fear: Findings from a Study of Election News and Terrorist Threat in Russia' [Research Note]. *Europe-Asia Studies*, 58(2), March 2006, pp. 281–290

Oliverio, A. and Lauderdale, P., 'Terrorism as Deviance or Social Control: Suggestions for Future Research'. *International Journal of Comparative Sociology*, 46, April 2005, pp. 53–169

Post, J.M., 'The Psychology of WMD Terrorism'. *International Studies Review*, 7(1), March 2005, pp. 148–151

Post, J.M., 'When Hatred Is Bred in the Bone: Psycho-cultural Foundations of Contemporary Terrorism'. *Political Psychology*, 26(4), August 2005, pp. 615–636

Post, J.M., *Leaders and Their Followers in a Dangerous World: The Psychology of Political Behavior*. Ithaca, NY: Cornell University Press, 2005

Renkema, L.J., Stapel, D.A., Maringer, M. and Van Yperen, N.W., 'Terror Management and Stereotyping: Why Do People Stereotype When Mortality Is Salient?', *Personality and Social Psychology Bulletin*, 34, April 2008, pp. 553–564

Robin, C., *Fear: The History of a Political Idea*. Oxford: Oxford University Press, 2004

Robins, R.S. and Post, J.M., *Political Paranoia: The Psycho-politics of Hatred*. New Haven, CT: Yale University Press, 1997

Rodriguez-Carballeira, A. and Javaloy, F., 'Psychosocial Analysis of the Collective Processes in the United States after September 11'. *Conflict Management and Peace Science*, 22(3), Fall 2005, pp. 201–216

Schechter, L.R., 'From 9/11 to Hurricane Katrina: Helping Others and Oneself Cope Following Disasters'. *Traumatology*, 14, October 2008

Schlenger, W.E., 'Psychological Impact of the September 11, 2001 Terrorist Attacks: Summary of Empirical Findings in Adults'. *Journal of Aggression, Maltreatment and Trauma*, 9(1–2), 15 March 2005, pp. 97–108

Schmidbauer, W., *Der Mensch als Bombe: Eine Psychologie des neuen Terrorismus*. Reinbek bei Hamburg: Rowohlt, 2003

Shamir, J. and Shikaki, K., 'Self-Serving Perceptions of Terrorism among Israelis and Palestinians'. *Political Psychology*, 23(3), September 2002, pp. 537–557

Silke, A., *Terrorists, Victims and Society: Psychological Perspectives on Terrorism and Its Consequences*. Chichester, UK: Wiley

Silke, A., 'The Role of Suicide in Politics, Conflict and Terrorism'. *Terrorism and Political Violence*, 18(1), Spring 2006, pp. 35–46

Smelser, N.J., *The Faces of Terrorism: Social and Psychological Dimensions*. Princeton, NJ: Princeton University Press, 2007

Speckhard, A., *Sacred Terror: Insights into the Psychology of Religiously Motivated Terrorism: Christianity, Islam and Judaism between Constructive Activism and Destructive Fanaticism*. Antwerp: USCIA, 2006

Sternberg, R.J. and Weis, K., *Hate: Its Nature and Its Role in Terrorism, Massacres and Genocide*. London: Yale University Press, 2007

Stith Butler, A., Panzer, A.M. and Goldfrank, L.R. (eds), *Preparing for the Psychological Consequences of Terrorism: A Public Health Strategy*. Committee on Responding to the Psychological Consequences of Terrorism. Washington, DC: National Academies Press, 2003

Stout, C.E. (ed.), *The Psychology of Terrorism*, vol. 1: *A Public Understanding*. Westport, CT: Praeger, 2002

Stout, C.E. (ed.), *The Psychology of Terrorism*, vol. 2: *Clinical Aspects and Responses*. Westport, CT: Praeger, 2002

Stout, C.E. (ed.), *The Psychology of Terrorism*, vol. 3: *Theoretical Understandings and Perspectives*. Westport, CT: Praeger, 2002

Stout, C.E. (ed.), *The Psychology of Terrorism*, vol. 4: *Programs and Practices in Response and Prevention*. Westport, CT: Praeger, 2002

Stout, C.E., *Psychology of Terrorism. Condensed Edition. Coping with the Continued Threat*. Westport, CT: Praeger, 2004

Swanstrom, T., 'Are Fear and Urbanism at War?' *Urban Affairs Review*, 38, September 2002, pp. 135–140

Taylor, M., *The Fanatics: A Behavioural Approach to Political Violence*. London: Brassey's, 1991

Taylor, M. and Horgan, J., 'The Psychological and Behavioural Bases of Islamic Fundamentalism'. *Terrorism and Political Violence*, 13(4), 2001, pp. 37–72

Toland, J., *Hitler*. Ware, UK: Wordsworth, 1997

Tota, A.L., 'Terrorism and Collective Memories: Comparing Bologna, Naples and Madrid 11 March'. *International Journal of Comparative Sociology*, 46, April 2005, pp. 55–78

Ullman, C., *The Transformed Self: The Psychology of Religious Conversion*. New York: Plenum Press, 1989

Van Swaaningen, R., 'Public Safety and the Management of Fear'. *Theoretical Criminology*, 9, August 2005, pp. 289–305

Victoroff, J. (ed.), *Tangled Roots: Social and Psychological Factors in the Genesis of Terrorism*. Amsterdam: IOS Press, 2006

Victoroff, J., 'The Mind of the Terrorist: A Review and Critique of Psychological Approaches'. *Journal of Conflict Resolution*, 49(1), February 2005, pp. 3–42

Victoroff, J., *Psychology of Terrorism: Key Readings*. London: Psychology Press, 2007

Victoroff, J. and Kruglanski, A.W. (eds), *Psychology of Terrorism*. London: Routledge, 2008

Von Busekist, A., 'Uses and Misuses of the Concept of Identity'. *Security Dialogue*, 35, March 2004, pp. 81–98

Weimann, G., 'The Theater of Terror: The Psychology of Terrorism and the Mass Media'. *Journal of Aggression, Maltreatment and Trauma*, 9(3–4), 16 March 2005, pp. 379–390

Welch, M., *Scapegoats of September 11th: Hate Crimes and State Crimes in the War on Terror*. New Brunswick, NJ: Rutgers University Press, 2006

Wertz, F.J., 'An Experience of International Terrorism: Reflections on the Meanings of September 11th'. *Journal of Phenomenological Psychology*, 33(1), 2002, pp. 59–71

Wessely, S., 'Don't Panic! Short and Long Term Psychological Reactions to the New Terrorism: The Role of Information and the Authorities'. *Journal of Mental Health*, 14(1), February 2005, pp. 1–6

Yechiam, E., Barron, G. and Erev, I., 'The Role of Personal Experience in Contributing to Different Patterns of Response to Rare Terrorist Attacks'. *Journal of Conflict Resolution*, 49(3), June 2005, pp. 430–439

Young, R., 'Psychoanalysis, Terrorism and Fundamentalism'. *Psychodynamic Practice*, 9(3), August 2003, pp. 307–324

M. Terrorism from a criminological perspective

Anderson, T.S., 'Transnational Terror and Organized Crime: Blurring the Lines'. *SAIS Review*, 24(1), Winter 2004, pp. 50–52

Arena, M.P., 'Hizballah's Global Criminal Operations'. *Global Crime*, 7(3–4), August 2006, pp. 454–470

Bakonyi, J. and Jakobeit, C., 'Internationale Kriminalität/Internationaler Terrorismus'. In H. Schmidt and W. Wellmann (eds), *Handbuch zur deutschen Außenpolitik*. Wiesbaden: VS-Verlag, 2007

Barak, G., 'A Reciprocal Approach to Peacemaking Criminology: Between Adversarialism and Mutualism'. *Theoretical Criminology*, 9, May 2005, pp. 131–152

Barna, C., 'International Terrorism and Transnational Organized Crime'. *Romanian Journal of International Affairs*, 10(1–2), 2005, pp. 138–152

Brodeur, J.P., Book review: 'The Lesser Evil: Political Ethics in an Age of Terror'. *Theoretical Criminology*, 9, May 2005, pp. 227–230

Brodeur, J.P. and Shearing, C., 'Configuring Security and Justice'. *European Journal of Criminology*, 2, October 2005, pp. 379–406

Bunker, R.J., 'Defining Criminal States'. *Global Crime*, 7(3–4), August 2008, pp. 365–376

Ceballos, M.R., 'The Evolution of Armed Conflict in Medellín: An Analysis of the Major Actors'. *Latin American Perspectives*, 28, January 2001, pp. 110–131

Clarke, R.V. and Newman, G.R., *Outsmarting the Terrorists*. Westport, CT: Praeger Security International, 2006

Clutterbuck, R.L., *Terrorism, Drugs, and Crime in Europe after 1992*. London: Routledge, 1990

Cornell, S.E., 'Narcotics and Armed Conflict: Interaction and Implications'. *Studies in Conflict and Terrorism*, 30(3), 2007, pp. 207–228

Cornell, S.E., 'The Interaction of Narcotics and Conflict'. *Journal of Peace Research*, 42, November 2005, pp. 751–760

Curtis, G. and Karacan, T., *The Nexus among Terrorists, Narcotic Traffickers, Weapons Proliferators, and Organized Crime Networks in Western Europe*. Washington, DC: Library of Congress, 2002

de Lint, W. and Virta, S., 'Security in Ambiguity: Towards a Radical Security Politics'. *Theoretical Criminology*, 8, November 2004, pp. 465–489

Deflem, M., Book review: 'Reading Terrorism and Terrorists'. *Theoretical Criminology*, 9, May 2005, pp. 231–236

Dishman, C., 'Terrorism, Crime, and Transformation'. *Studies in Conflict and Terrorism*, 24(1), January 2001, pp. 43–58

Dishman, C., 'The Leaderless Nexus: When Crime and Terror Converge'. *Studies in Conflict and Terrorism*, 28(3), May–June 2005, pp. 237–252

Dolan, C.J., 'United States' Narco-terrorism Policy: A Contingency Approach to the Convergence of the Wars on Drugs and against Terrorism'. *Review of Policy Research*, 22(4), July 2005, pp. 451–471

Ehrenfeld, R., *Funding Evil: How Terrorism Is Financed – and How to Stop It*. Chicago: Bonus Books, 2004

Ehrenfeld, R., *Narco-terrorism*. New York: Basic Books, 1990

Farah, D., *Blood from Stones: The Secret Financial Network of Terror*. Broadway Books, 2004

Fekete, L., 'Europe: "Speech Crime" and Deportation'. *Race and Class*, 47, January 2006, pp. 82–92

Fijnaut, C., *Changes in Society, Crime, and Criminal Justice in Europe: A Challenge for Criminological Education and Research*. Cambridge, MA: Kluwer Law International, 1995

Galleotti, M., ' "Brotherhoods" and "Associates": Chechen Networks of Crime and Resistance'. *Low Intensity Conflict and Law Enforcement*, 11(2–3), 2002, pp. 340–352

Gheordunescu, M., 'Terrorism and Organised Crime: The Romanian Perspective'. *Terrorism and Political Violence*, 11(4), 1999, pp. 24–30

Goredema, C., *Organised Crime and Terrorism: Observations from Southern Africa*. Pretoria: Institute for Security Studies [ISA], March 2005

Hagedorn, J.M., *Gangs in the Global City: Alternatives to Traditional Criminology*. Champaign: University of Illinois Press, 2007

Hamm, M.S., 'Apocalyptic Violence: The Seduction of Terrorist Subcultures'. *Theoretical Criminology*, 8, August 2004, pp. 323–339

Hamm, M.S., Book review: 'After September 11'. *Theoretical Criminology*, 9, May 2005, pp. 237–250

Hamm, M.S., *Terrorism as Crime: From Oklahoma City to Al-Qaeda and Beyond*. New York: New York University Press, 2007

Holmes, L. (ed.), *Terrorism, Organised Crime and Corruption*. Cheltenham UK: Edward Elgar, 2007

Hudson, R., *Terrorist and Organized Crime Groups in the Tri-Border Area (TBA) of South America*. Washington, DC: Federal Research Division, Library of Congress, July 2003. Available at: www.loc.gov/rr/frd/terrorism.html (accessed 19 March 2009)

Jamieson, A. (ed.), *Terrorism and Drug Trafficking in the 1990s*. Aldershot, UK: Dartmouth, 1994

Johnson, D.D.P. and Tierney, D., *Failing to Win: Perceptions of Victory and Defeat In International Politics*. Cambridge, MA: Harvard University Press, 2006

Kane, J. and Wall, A., *Identifying Links between White-Collar Crime and Terrorism*. US Department of Justice, NCJRS, 209520, April 2005

Kaplan, D.E., *How Jihadist Groups Are Using Organized Crime-Tactics and Profits to Finance Attacks on Targets around the Globe*. US News and World Report, 5 December 2005

Kenney, M., 'Drug Traffickers, Terrorist Networks, and Ill-Fated Government Strategies'. In E. Krahmann (ed.), *New Threats and New Actors in International Security*. New York: Palgrave Macmillan, 2005

Killias, M., 'The Opening and Closing of Breaches: A Theory on Crime Waves, Law Creation and Crime Prevention'. *European Journal of Criminology*, 3, January 2006, pp. 11–31

Leonard, I.M. and Leonard, C.C., 'The Historiography of American Violence'. *Homicide Studies*, 7, May 2003, pp. 99–153

Library of Congress, *Global Overview of Narcotics-Funded Terrorist and Other Extremist Groups*. May 2002

Makarenko, T., 'The Crime–Terror Continuum: Tracing the Interplay between Transnational Organised Crime and Terrorism'. *Global Crime*, 6(1), 2004, pp. 129–145

Miljard, B.J. and Collins, R.O., *Alms for Jihad: Charity and Terrorism in the Islamic World*. Cambridge: Cambridge University Press, 2007

Mincheva, L. and Gurr, T., 'Unholy Alliances: How Transnational Terrorists and Crime Make Common Cause'. In W.R. Thomson and R. Reuveny (eds), *Coping with Contemporary Terrorism: Origins, Escalation and Responses*. Albany, NY: SUNY Press, 2008

Mythen, G. and Walklate, S., 'Criminology and Terrorism'. *British Journal of Criminology*, 46(3), May 2006, pp. 379–398

Passas, N., 'Cross-border Crime and the Interface between Legal and Illegal Actors'. *Security Journal*, 16(1), 2003, pp. 19–37

Passas, N., 'Indicators of Hawala Operations and Abuse'. *Journal of Money Laundering Control*, 8(2), 2004, pp. 168–172

Passas, N., 'Law Enforcement Challenges in Hawala-Related Investigations'. *Journal of Financial Crime*, 12(2), 2004, pp. 112–119

Passas, N., *Informal Value Transfer Systems and Criminal Organizations: A Study into So-Called Underground Banking Networks*. The Hague: Ministry of Justice, WODC, 1999. Available at: www.wodc.nl (accessed 20 March 2009)

Perry, B., *Hate and Bias Crime*. London: Routledge, 2003

Picarelli, J.T., 'The Turbulent Nexus of Transnational Organised Crime and Terrorism: A Theory of Malevolent International Relations'. *Global Crime*, 7(1), February 2006, pp. 1–24

Roth, M.P. and Sever, M., 'The Kurdish Workers Party (PKK) as Criminal Syndicate: Funding Terrorism through Organized Crime, a Case Study'. *Studies in Conflict and Terrorism*, 30(10), 2007, pp. 901–920

Scanlan, G., 'The Enterprise of Crime and Terror. The Implication for Good Business: Looking to the Future: Old and New Threats'. *Journal of Financial Crime*, 13(2), 2006, pp. 164–176

Schmid, A.P. (ed.), Special Issue on Terrorism. *Forum on Crime and Society*, 4(1&2) Vienna: United Nations Office on Drugs and Crime, December 2004

Schmid, A.P., 'The Links between Transnational Organized Crime and Terrorist Crimes'. *Transnational Organized Crime*, 2(4), Winter 1996, pp. 40–82

Shanty, F.G. (ed.), *Organized Crime: From Trafficking to Terrorism*. Santa Barbara, CA: ABC-CLIO, 2007

Shelley L.I. and Picarelli, J.T., 'Methods Not Motives: Implications of the Convergence of International Organized Crime and Terrorism'. *Police Practice and Research*, 3(4), January 2002, pp. 305–318

Shelly, L.I., 'Trafficking in Nuclear Materials: Criminals and Terrorists'. *Global Crime*, 7(3–4), August 2006, pp. 544–560

Sheppard, B., *The Psychology of Strategic Terrorism*. London: Routledge, 2008

Shoemaker, D.J., *Theories of Delinquence: An Examination of Explanations of Delinquent Behavior*. New York: Oxford University Press, 1996

Siresloudi, M., 'Waren die terroristischen Anschlagskampagnen als Folgen des Dritten Golfkrieges vorherzusehen?' In B. Kilian, C. Tobergte and S. Wunder (eds), *Nach dem Dritten Golfkrieg: Sicherheitspolitische Analysen zu Verlauf und Folgen des Golfkrieges*. Berlin: Berliner Wissenschaftsverlag, 2004

Spearin, C., 'Terrorism and Transnational Crime: State-Led Probition Regimes and the Challenge of Dismantling Illicit State Networks'. In E. Krahman (ed.), *New Threats and New Actors in International Society*. London: Palgrave Macmillan, 2005

Stepanova, E., *The Role of Illicit Drug Business in the Political Economy of Conflicts and Terrorism*. Moscow: Institute of World Economy and International Relations (IMEMO), 2005

Sullivan, J.P., 'Terrorism, Crime and Private Armies'. *Low Intensity Conflict and Law Enforcement*, 11(2–3), 2002, pp. 239–253

Thamm, B.G. and Freiberg, K., *Mafia Global: Organisiertes Verbrechen auf dem Sprung in das 21. Jahrhundert*. Hilden, Germany: Verlag Deutsche Polizeiliteratur, 1998

Thoumi, F.E., 'Illegal Drugs in Colombia: From Illegal Economic Boom to Social Crisis'. *Annals of the American Academy of Political and Social Science*, 582, July 2002, pp. 102–116

Urbina, M.G. and Kreitzer, S., 'The Practical Utility and Ramifications of RICO: Thirty-Two Years after Its Implementation'. *Criminal Justice Policy Review*, 15, September 2004, pp. 294–323

Van de Bunt, H., Siegel, D. and Zaitch, D. (eds), *Transnational Organized Crime: Current Developments*. Dordrecht, Netherlands: Kluwer, 2003

Van der Veen, H.T., 'Drugshandel en politiek geweld'. *Justiële Verkenningen*, 31(2), March 2005, pp. 95–109

van Scherpenberg, J., *Combating the Terrorist–Criminal Nexus*. Contribution to the project 'German and American Perspectives on the New Strategic Landscape: Sustaining the Coalition Against International Terrorism' of the American Institute of Contemporary German Studies. Washington, DC: AICGS, 2002

N. Terrorism from a military perspective

Adamec, L.W. and Woronoff, J., *Dictionary of Afghan Wars, Revolutions, and Insurgencies*. Lanham, MD: Scarecrow Press, 2005

Alley, R., *Internal Conflict and the International Community: Wars without End?* Aldershot, UK: Ashgate, 2004

Arnson, C.J. and Zartman, I.W., *Rethinking the Economics of War: The Intersection of Need, Creed and Greed*. Washington, DC: Johns Hopkins University Press, 2005

Arquilla, J. and Ronfeldt, D.F., *Networks and Netwars: The Future of Terror, Crime, and Militancy*. Santa Barbara, CA: RAND, 2002

Arreguin-Toft, I., 'How the Weak Win Wars: A Theory of Asymmetric Conflict'. *International Security*, 26(1), 2001, pp. 83–128

Art, R.H. and Waltz, K.N. (eds), *The Use of Force: Military Power and International Politics*. Lanham, MD: Rowman & Littlefield, 2004

Beck, U., *Der kosmopolitische Blick oder: Krieg ist Frieden*. Frankfurt am Main: Suhrkamp, 2004

Beck, U., 'War Is Peace: On Post-National War'. *Security Dialogue*, 36, March 2005, pp. 5–26

Beckett, I.F.W., *The Encyclopedia of Guerrilla Warfare*. New York: Facts On File, 2001

Bellflower, J.W., '4th Generation Warfare'. *Small Wars Journal*, no. 4, February 2006. Available at: http://smallwarsjournal.com/documents/swjmag/v4/bellflower.htm (accessed 20 March 2009)

Berkowitz, B.D., *The New Face of War: How War Will Be Fought in the 21st Century*. New York: Free Press, 2003

Besançon, M.L., 'Relative Resources: Inequality in Ethnic Wars, Revolutions, and Genocides'. *Journal of Peace Research*, 42, July 2005, pp. 393–415

Bethke, E.J., *Just War against Terror: The Burden of American Power in a Violent World*. New York: Basic Books, 2003

Bosworth-Davies, R., 'Money Laundering'. *Journal of Money Laundering Control*, 10(1), 2007, pp.47–65

Bowyer Bell, J., *A Time of Terror: How Democratic Societies Respond to Revolutionary Violence*. New York: Basic Books, 1978

Bowyer Bell, J., *The Dynamics of the Armed Struggle*. London: Frank Cass, 1998

Boyle, M.J., 'The War on Terror in American Grand Strategy'. *International Affairs*, March 2008, pp. 191–219

Braudy, L., *From Chivalry to Terrorism: War and the Changing Nature of Masculinity*. New York: Vintage Books, 2005

Brzoska, M., ' "New Wars" Discourse in Germany'. *Journal of Peace Research*, 41, January 2004, pp. 107–117

Buchanan, B.J., *Gunpowder, Explosives and the State: A Technological History*. Aldershot, UK: Ashgate, 2008

Bunker, R.J. (ed.), *Non-state Threats and Future Wars*. London: Routledge, 2002

Buzan, B., 'Will the Global War on Terrorism be the New Cold War?' *International Affairs*, 82(6), 2006, pp. 1101–1118

Carr, C., *The Lessons of Terror: A History of Warfare against Civilians: Why It Has always Failed, and Why It Will Fail Again*. New York: Random House, 2002

Chan, S., *Out of Evil: New International Politics and Old Doctrines of War*. London: I.B. Tauris, 2005

Chapman, J. (rapporteur), *Assessing the Military Threats of the Future*. Brussels: New Defence Agenda, Monthly Roundtable, April 2004

Chapman, J. (rapporteur), *Strategic Priorities for Protecting Europe's Infrastructure against Terrorism*. Brussels: New Defence Agenda, June 2005

Chizek, J.G., Elsea, J., Best, R.A. Jr and Bolkcom, C., *Military Transformation: Current Issues in Intelligence, Surveillance and Reconnaissance*. Hauppauge, NY: Nova Science Publishers, 2004

Clark, [General] W.K., *Winning Modern Wars: Iraq, Terrorism and the American Empire*. New York: Public Affairs, 2003

Clarke, J.L., Takacks, I., Klose, G.J. *et al.*, 'The Role of the Armed Forces in Homeland Security' [special issue]. *Connections*, 4(3), Fall 2005, pp. 1–133

Cordesman, A.H., *The War after the War*. Washington, DC: CSIS, June 2004

Cordesman, A.H. and Moravitz, J., *The Israeli–Palestinian War: Escalating to Nowhere*. Santa Barbara, CA: Praeger Security International, 2005

Cornish, P., *The Conflict in Iraq, 2003*. New York: Palgrave Macmillan, 2004

Covington, C., Williams, P., Arundale, J., and Knox, J. (eds), *Terrorism and War: Unconscious Dynamics of Political Violence*. London: Karnac Books, 2002

Cragin, K., Chalk, P., Daly, S. and Jackson, B.A., *Sharing the Dragon's Teeth: Terrorist Groups and the Exchange of New Technologies*. Santa Monica, CA: RAND, 2007

Cragin, K. and Hoffman, B., *Arms Trafficking and Colombia*. Santa Monica, CA: RAND, 2003

Craig, C., *Glimmer of a New Leviathan: Total War in the Realism of Niebuhr, Morgenthau and Waltz*. New York: Columbia University, 2007

Davids, D.E. and Pereira, A.W. (eds), *Irregular Armed Forces and Their Role in Politics and State Formation*. Cambridge: Cambridge University Press, 2003

Delpech, T., *Savage Century: Back to Barbarism*. Washington, DC: Carnegie Endowment for International Peace, 2007

Diamond, H. and Kitson, S. (eds), *Vichy, Resistance; Liberation: New Perspectives on Wartime France*. Oxford: Berg, 2005

Downes, A.B., *Targeting Civilians in War*. Ithaca, NY: Cornell University Press, 2008

Dumbrell, J. and Ryan, D. (eds), *Vietnam in Iraq: Tactics, Lessons, Legacies*. London: Routledge, 2006

Eckert, A.E. and Mofidi, M., ' "Unlawful Combatants" or "Prisoners of War": The Law and Politics of Labels'. *Cornell International Law Journal*, 36(59), 2003, pp. 59–92

Elsea, J., 'Terrorism and the Law of War: Trying Terrorists as War Criminals before Military Commissions'. In E.V. Linden (ed.), *Focus on Terrorism*, vol. 8. Hauppauge, NY: Nova Science Publishers, 2007

Evans, G., 'When Is It Right to Fight?' *Survival*, 46(3), 2004, pp. 59–81

Evans, M. (ed.), *Just War Theory: A Reappraisal*. Edinburgh: Edinburgh University Press, 2005

Ewans, M., *Conflict in Afghanistan: Studies in Asymmetric Warfare*. London: Routledge, 2005

Finlan, A., *Special Forces, Terrorism and Strategy: Warfare by Other Means*. London: Routledge, 2007

Fishel, K.L., 'Challenging the Hegemon: Al Qaeda's Elevation of Asymmetric Insurgent Warfare onto the Global Arena'. *Low Intensity Conflict and Law Enforcement*, 11(2–3), 2002, pp. 285–298

Fitzgerald, A.L., *Terrorism and National Security*. Santa Barbara, CA: Nova Science Publishers, 2006

Fox, J., 'Trends in Low Intensity Ethnic Conflict in Democratic States in the Post-Cold War Era: A Large Study'. In E. Inbar (ed.), *Democracies and Small Wars*. London: Routledge, 2003, pp. 54–71

Fox, J., *Religion, Civilization, and Civil War: 1945 through the New Millennium*. Lanham, MD: Lexington, 2005

Freedman, L., *Deterrence*. Cambridge: Polity Press, 2004

Freedman, L., *The Transformation of Strategic Affairs*. New York: Routledge for the International Institute for Strategic Studies, 2006

Freudenberg, D., *Theorie des Irregulären: Partisanen, Guerrillas und Terroristen im modernen Kleinkrieg*. Wiesbaden: VS-Verlag, 2008

Frey, B.A., 'Small Arms and Light Weapons: The Tools Used to Violate Human Rights'. *Disarmament Forum*, no. 3, 2004, pp. 37–46

Gardner, H. (ed.), *NATO and the European Union: New World, New Europe, New Threats*. Aldershot, UK: Ashgate, 2004

Gray, C.S., *Another Bloody Century: Future Warfare*. London: Weidenfeld & Nicolson, 2005

Gray, J.M., 'Understanding the "War on Terrorism": Responses to 11 September 2001'. *Journal of Peace Research*, 43(1), January 2006, pp. 23–36

Grenfell, D. and James, P., *Rethinking Insecurity, War and Violence*. London: Routledge, 2008

Heerle, W.P. (ed.), *Terrorism and the Military: International Legal Implications*. The Hague: T.M.C. Asser Press, 2003

Held, V., 'Terrorism and War'. *Journal of Ethics*, 8(1), March 2004, pp. 59–75

Jayasekara, S., "Threats Posed by Aviation Assets of Terrorist Groups and Proto-States", in the bi-annual report of the Council for Asian Terrorism Research, in collaboration with the Institute for Defense Analyses (IDA), Alexandria, VA, February 2006

Jones, H., *Death of a Generation: How the Assassinations of Diem and JFK Prolonged the Vietnam War*. Oxford: Oxford University Press, 2003

Kaldor, M., *Neue und alte Kriege: Organisierte Gewalt in Zeitalter der Globalisierung*. Frankfurt am Main: Suhrkamp, 2000

Kalyvas, S., 'The Paradox of Terrorism in Civil War'. *Journal of Ethics*, 8(1), March 2004, pp. 97–138

Karoubi, M.T., *Just or Unjust War? International Law and Unilateral Use of Armed Force by States at the Turn of the 20th Century*. Aldershot, UK: Ashgate, 2004

Kassimeris, G. (ed.), *The Barbarisation of Warfare*. London: Hurst, 2006

Kennedy, D., *Of Law and War*. Princeton, NJ: Princeton University Press, 2006

King, J., 'The New Warfare and Cooperative International Security'. *Foresight*, 6(4), 2004, pp. 212–217

Kummel, G. (ed.), *Asymmetrische Konflikte und Terrorismusbekämpfung: Prototypen zukünftiger Kriege*. Baden-Baden, Germany: Nomos 2003

Lang, A.F. and Beattie, A.R., *War, Torture and Terrorism*. London: Routledge, 2008

Lapham, L.H., *Theater of War*. New York: New Press, 2002

Lewer, N. and Davison, N., 'Non-lethal Technologies: An Overview'. Geneva: UNIDIR. Disarmament Forum 1, 2005, pp. 37–52

Long, A., *On 'Other War': Lessons from Five Decades of RAND Counterinsurgency Research*. Santa Monica, CA: RAND, 2006

Luttwak, E.N., 'Dead End: Counterinsurgency Warfare as Military Malpractice'. *Harper's Magazine*, February 2007. Available at: www.harpers.org/archive/2007/02/0081384 (accessed 27 March 2009)

Lutz, B.J. and Lutz, J.M., 'Terrorism as Economic Warfare'. *Global Economic Journal*, 6(2), 2006, pp. 1–22

McLendon, J.W., 'Information Warfare: Impacts and Concerns'. In E.V. Linden (ed.), *Focus on Terrorism*, vol. 5. Santa Barbara, CA: Nova Science Publishers, 2002

Maguire, D.C., *The Horrors We Bless: Rethinking the Just-War Legacy*. Minneapolis: Fortress Press, 2007

Malik, S.K., *The Quranic Concept of War*. Lahore, Pakistan: Associated Printers, 1979

Maoz, Z. and Gat, A., *War in a Changing World*. Ann Arbor: University of Michigan Press, 2001

Mater, N., *Voices from the Front: Turkish Soldiers on the War with the Kurdish Guerrillas*. Basingstoke, UK: Palgrave Macmillan, 2005

May, L., *War Crimes and Just War*. Cambridge: Cambridge University Press, 2007

Mohamedou, M.M., *Understanding Al Qaeda: The Transformation of War*. London: Pluto, 2007

Münkler, H., *Die neuen Kriege*. Reinbek bei Hamburg: Rowohlt Verlag, 2003

Orr, M., *Russia's Wars with Chechnya, 1994–2003*. Colchester, UK: Osprey Publishing, 2007

Peters, R., *Beyond Baghdad: Postmodern War and Peace*. Mechanicsburg, PA: Stackpole Books, 2003

Phythian, M., *The Business of Arms*. London: Routledge, 2005

Rogers, P., *Why We're Losing the War on Terror*. Cambridge: Polity Press, 2008

Rooney, D., *Guerrilla: Insurgents, Rebels and Terrorists from Sun Tzu to Bin Laden*. London: Brassey's, 2004

Rothstein, H.S., *Afghanistan and the Troubled Future of Unconventional Warfare*. Annapolis, MD: Naval Institute Press, 2006

Rukavishnikov, V., 'The Russian Perception of the American "War on Terror" '. Working Paper no. 27, Copenhagen Peace Research Institute, 2002

Ruloff, D., *Wie Kriege beginnen: Ursachen und Formen*. Munich: Verlag C.H. Beck, 2004

Russell, R., *Weapons Proliferation and War in the Greater Middle East*. London: Routledge, 2005

Sageman, M., 'Does Osama Still Call the Shots? Debating the Containment of al Qaeda's Leadership: The Reality of Grass-Roots Terrorism'. *Foreign Affairs*, 87, July–August, 2008, pp. 163–166

Sakwa, R., 'Chechnya: A Just War Fought Unjustly?' *Contextualizing Secession*, July 2003, pp. 156–187

Sanin, F.G., 'Telling the Difference: Guerrillas and Paramilitaries in the Colombian War'. *Politics and Society*, 36, March 2008, pp. 3–34

Sassòli, M., 'Terrorism and War'. *Journal of International Criminal Justice*, 4(5), 1 November 2006, pp. 959–981

Schbley, A., 'Defining Religious Terrorism: A Causal and Anthological Profile'. *Studies in Conflict and Terrorism*, 26(2), March–April 2003, pp. 105–134

Schmid, A.P., 'Terrorism as Psychological Warfare'. Paper given at the International Summit on Democracy, Terrorism and Security, Madrid, 8–11 March 2005

Schmid, A.P. and Jongman, A.J., 'Database Section: Violent Conflicts and Human Rights Violations in the Mid-1990s'. *Terrorism and Political Violence*, 9(4), 1997, pp. 166–193

Schröfl, J. and Pankratz, T. (eds), *Asymmetrische Kriegführung: Ein neues Phänomen der internationalen Politik*. Baden-Baden, Germany: Nomos, 2004

Sharif, I., *The Success of Political Terrorist Events: An Analysis of Terrorist Tactics and Victim Characteristics, 1968–1977*. Lanham, MD: University Press of America, 1996

Shaw, M., 'Risk-Transfer Militarism, Small Massacres and the Historic Legitimacy of War'. *International Relations*, 16(3), 2002, pp. 343–360

Shaw, M., *War and Genocide: Organized Killing in Modern Society*. Stafford, BC: Polity, 2003

Shervington, M.W., 'A Hundred Years of Irregular Warfare'. *Small Wars Journal*, no. 4, February 2006. Available at: http://smallwarsjournal.com/documents/swjmag/v4/shervington.htm (accessed 27 March 2009)

Shoham, D., 'Image vs. Reality of Iranian Chemical and Biological Weapons'. *International Journal of Intelligence and Counterintelligence*, 18(1), Spring 2005, pp. 89–141

Shultz, R.H., Jr and Dew, A.J., *Insurgents, Terrorists, and Militias: The Warriors of Contemporary Combat*. New York: Columbia University Press, 2006

Shultz, R.H., Farah, D. and Lochard, I. V., 'Armed Groups: A Tier-One Security Priority'. *INSS Occasional Paper 57*. USAF Institute for National Security Studies, USAF Academy, Colorado Springs, CO, September 2004

Siebelt, P., *De vierde wereldoorlog: het pad van Marx naar Allah*. Soesterberg, Netherlands: Uitgeverij Aspekt, 2005

Singer, J., *The Confederate Dirty War: Arson, Bombings, Assassination and Plots for Chemical and Germ Attacks on the Union*. Jefferson, NC: McFarland, 2004

Singer, P.W., *Children at War*. New York: Pantheon, 2005

SIPRI, *SIPRI Yearbook 2004: Armaments, Disarmament and International Security*. Oxford: Oxford University Press, 2004

Small Arms Survey 2005. Oxford: Oxford University Press, 2005

Smit, W. (ed.), *Just War and Terrorism: The End of the Just War Concept?* Leuven, Belgium: Peeters, 2005

Smith, [General Sir], R., *The Utility of Force: The Art of War in the Modern World*. London: Allen Lane, 2005

Soeters, S., *Het ontstaan en verloop van burgeroorlogen, ethnische twisten en terrorisme*. Amsterdam: Boom, 2004

Sprecher, C. and DeRouen, K. Jr, 'Israeli Military Actions and Internalization–Externalization Processes'. *Journal of Conflict Resolution*, 46, April 2002, pp. 244–259

Steinhäusler, F. and Edwards, F. (eds), *NATO and Terrorism: Catastrophic Terrorism and First Responders: Threats and Mitigation*. Berlin: Springer, 2005

Stevenson, J., 'Terrorism and Deterrence'. *Survival*, 46(4), Winter 2004–2005, pp. 179–185

Stubblefield, G. and Halberstadt, H., *Inside the US Navy Seals*. Osceola, WI: Motorbooks International, 1995

Swami, P., *India, Pakistan and the Secret Jihad: The Covert War in Kashmir, 1947–2004*. London: Routledge, 2007

TRADOC DCSINT, *Handbook No. 1: A Military Guide to Terrorism in the Twenty-First Century*. US Army Training and Doctrine Command, Deputy Chief of Staff for Intelligence, Assistant Deputy Chief of Staff for Intelligence-Threats. Version 3.0, 15 August 2005

TRADOC DCSINT, *Handbook Supplement 1.01: Terror Operations: Case Studies in Terrorism*. 2005

TRADOC DCSINT, *Handbook Supplement 1.02: Cyber Operations and Cyber Terrorism*. 2005

TRADOC DCSINT, *Handbook Supplement 1.03: Suicide Bombing*. 2005

TRADOC DCSINT, *Handbook Supplement 1.04: Defense Support Top Civil Authorities (DSCA) with a Focus on WMD/E Consequence Management and Emergency Response by Military Forces*. 2005

Trager, R.F. and Zagorcheva, D.P., 'Deterring Terrorism: It Can De Done'. *International Security*, 30(3), Winter 2005–2006, pp. 87–123

US Army TRADOC, *TRADOC G2 Handbook No. 1, A Military Guide to Terrorism in the Twenty-First Century*. Fort Leavenworth, KS: US Army Training and Doctrine Command, 2007

US Army TRADOC, *TRADOC G2 Handbook No, 1.04: Terrorism and WMD in the Contemporary Operational Environment*. Fort Leavenworth, KS: US Army Training and Doctrine Command, 2007

US Army TRADOC, *TRADOC G2 Handbook No. 1.01: Terror Operations: Case Studies In Terrorism*. Fort Leavenworth, KS: US Army Training and Doctrine Command, 2007

US Army TRADOC, *TRADOC G2, Handbook No. 1.02: Cyber Operations and Cyber Terrorism*. Fort Leavenworth, KS: US Army Training and Doctrine Command, 2007

US Army TRADOC, *TRADOC G2, Handbook No. 1.03: Suicide Bombing in the COE*. Fort Leavenworth, KS: US Army Training and Doctrine Command, 2007

Valeriano, N.D. and Bohannan, C.T.R., *Counter-Guerrilla Operations: The Philippine Experience*. Westport, CT: Praeger Security International, 2006

Van Creveld, M., *The Transformation of War*. New York: Free Press, 1991

Vayrynen, R., *The Waning of Major War*. London, Frank Cass, 2005

Vinci, A., *Armed Groups and the Balance of Power*. London: Routledge, 2008

Weismann, F. (ed.), *In the Shadow of 'Just Wars'*. London: Hurst, 2004

Zuhur, S., *Saudi Arabia: Islamic Threat, Political Reform, and the Global War on Terror*. Carlisle, PA: Strategic Studies Institute, March 2005. Available at: www.strategicstudiesinstitute.army.mil/pdffiles/PUB598.pdf (accessed 27 March, 2009)

O. Juridical aspects of terrorism

Adiri, J., *Counter Terror Warfare: The Judicidial Front: Confronting the 'Democratic Dilemma' of Counter Terror Warfare: The Evolution of the 'Probably Scope'*. Herzilya, Israel: International Policy Institute for Counter Terrorism, Interdisciplinary Center, July 2005

Alexander, Y. and Brennar, E.H. (eds), *Terrorism and the Law*. Ardsley, NY: Transnational Publishers, 2001

Apter, D.E., *The Legitimization of Violence*. New York: New York University Press, 1997

Arnaud, A.J., *Legal Culture and Everyday Life: Inauguration Ceremony, 24 May 1989*. Oñati, Gipuzkoa, Euskadi, Spain: Oñati International Institute for the Sociology of Law, 1989

Arnold, R., *The ICC as a New Instrument For Repressing Terrorism*. Ardsley, NY: Transnational Publishers, 2004

Arnold, R., 'The Prosecution of Terrorism as a Crime against Humanity'. *Zeitschrift für auslandisches öffentliches Recht und Volkerrecht*, 64(4), 2005, pp. 979–1000

Artz, D., 'The "Lockerbie Trial Families Project" Web-Site: Victim Assistance Goes Online'. *Syracuse Journal of International Law and Commerce*, 29, 2001, 121–134

Artz, D., 'The Lockerbie "Extradition by Analogy" Agreement: "Exceptional Measure" or Template for Transnational Criminal Justice?' *American University International Law Review*, 18, 2002, 163–236

Artz, D., 'Can Law Halt the Violence? Palestinian Suicide Bombings and Israeli "Targeted Assassinations" under International Humanitarian Law'. *ILSA Journal of International and Comparative Law*, 11(2), 2005, pp. 357–364

Bekou, O. and Cryer, R. (eds), *The International Criminal Court*. Aldershot, UK: Ashgate, 2005

Bellamy, A.J., 'Is the War on Terror Just?' *International Relations*, 19, September 2005, pp. 275–296

Bianchi, A. (ed.), *Enforcing International Law Norms against Terrorism*. Oxford: Hart, 2004

Bothe, M., 'Terrorism and the Legality of Pre-emptive Force'. *European Journal of International Law*, no. 14, 2003, pp. 227–240

Brough, M.W., Lango, J.W. and Van der Linden, H. (eds), *Rethinking the Just War Tradition*. New York: State University of New York Press, 2007

Bufacchi, V. and Arrigo, J.M., 'Torture, Terrorism and the States: A Refutation of the Ticking-Bomb Argument'. *Journal of Applied Philosophy*, 23(3), August 2006, pp. 355–373

Cassese, A., 'The Multifaceted Criminal Notion of Terrorism in Intenational Law'. *Journal of Internaitonal Criminal Justice*, 4(5), 1 November 2006, pp. 933–958

Cassese, A. and Greenleaves, S.J.K., *Terrorism, Politics and Law: The Achille Lauro Affair*. Cambridge: Polity Press, 1989

Chasdi, R.J., 'Terrorism: Stratagems for Remediation from an International Law Perspective'. *Shofar: An Interdisciplinary Journal of Jewish Studies*, 12(4), 2004, pp. 59–86

Cherif, B.M., 'Evolving Approaches to Jihad: From Self-Defense to Revolutionary and Regime-Change Political Violence'. *Chicago Journal of International Law*, 8(1), Summer 2007, pp. 119–146

Chan, M. and Artz, D., 'Walking While Muslim'. *Law and Contemporary Problems*, 68, 2005, 215–254

Clark, R.S., *The United Nations Crime Prevention and Criminal Justice Program: Formulation of Standards and Efforts at Their Implementation*. Philadelphia: University of Pennsylvania Press, 1994

Clark, R.S. and Sann, M., *The Prosecution of International Crimes*. New Brunswick, NJ: Transaction, 1996

De Koster, P., *Terrorism: Special Investigation Techniques*. Strasbourg: Council of Europe, 2005

Dressen, W., *Politische Prozesse ohne Verteidigung?* Berlin: K. Wagenbach, 1976

Emerson, S. and Duffy, B., *The Fall of Pan Am 103: Inside the Lockerbie Investigation*. New York: Putnam, 1990

Evans, M. (ed.), *Just War Theory: A Reappraisal*. Edinburgh: Edinburgh University Press, 2005

Falk, R., 'Recovering Normative Consciousness'. *International Relations*, 19, March 2005, pp. 79–90

Federman, C., 'Who Has the Body? The Paths to Habeas Corpus Reform'. *Prison Journal*, 84, September 2004, pp. 317–339

Finn, J.E., *Constitutions in Crisis: Political Violence and the Rule of Law*. Oxford: Oxford University Press, 1991

Fiss, O., 'The War against Terrorism and the Rule of Law'. *Oxford Journal of Legal Studies*, 26(2), Summer 2006, pp. 235–256

Fleck, D. and Bothe, M., *The Handbook of Humanitarian Law in Armed Conflicts*. New York: Oxford University Press, 1999

Frankenvrij, M.S.H., 'De Koran getoetst aan de Westerse beschaving en rechtsorde'. *Liberaal Reveil*, 2007, 1, pp. 32–45

Frey, R.G. and Morris, C.W. (eds), *Violence, Terrorism, and Justice*. Cambridge: Cambridge University Press, 1991

Galicki, Z., 'International Law and Terrorism'. *American Behavioral Scientist*, 48, February 2005, pp. 743–757

Garland, D., 'Capital Punishment and American Culture'. *Punishment Society*, 7, October 2005, pp. 347–376

Gartenstein-Ross, D., 'Note: A Critique of the Terrorism Exception to the Foreign Soveriign Immunities Act'. New York University *Journal of International Law and Politics*, 34(4), 2002, 887–947

Garzón, B., *A World without Fear*. Barcelona: Plaza & Janés, 2005

Gearty, C., '11 September 2001, Counterterrorism, and the Human Rights Act'. *Journal of Law and Society*, 32(1), March 2005, pp. 18–33

Gilbert, G., 'Terrorism and International Law'. *International and Comparative Law Quarterly*, 53(3), July 2004, pp. 537–548

Goldsmith, J., *The Terror Presidency: Law and Judgment inside the Bush Administration*. New York: W.W. Norton, 2007

Golove, D. and Holmes, S., 'Terrorism and Accountability: Why Checks and Balances Apply Even in "The War on Terrorism" '. *NYU Review of Law and Security*, no. 2, April 2004. Available at: www.lawandsecurity.org/publications/quarterly/spring04.pdf (accessed 27 March 2009)

Gomien, D., *Short Guide to the European Convention on Human Rights*. Strasbourg: Council of Europe, 1991

Goodin, R., *What's Wrong with Terrorism?* Cambridge: Polity Press, 2006

Grabosky, P.N. and Australian Institute of Criminology, *Wayward Governance: Illegality and Its Control in the Public Sector*. Canberra: Australian Institute of Criminology, 1989

Great Britain. Parliament. House of Lords. Select Committee on the European Union. *Counter Terrorism: The European Arrest Warrant*. London: Stationery Office Books, 2001

Greer, S.C., *Supergrasses: A Study in Anti-Terrorist Law Enforcement In Northern Ireland*. Oxford: Clarendon Press, 1995

Heere, W.P. (ed.), *From Government to Governance: The Growing Impact of Non-State Actors on the International and European Legal System. Proceedings of the Sixth Hague Joint Conference held in The Hague, the Netherlands, 3–5 July 2003*. The Hague: T.M.C. Asser Press

Hensel, H.M. (ed.), *The Law of Armed Conflict: Constraints on the Contemporary Use of Military Force*. Aldershot, UK: Ashgate, 2007

Higgins, R. and Flory, M., *Terrorism and International Law*. London: Routledge, 1997

Hmoud, M., 'Negotiating the Draft Comprehensive Convention on International Terrorism'. *Journal of International Criminal Justice*, 4(5), 1 November 2006, pp. 1031–1043

Huysmans, J., 'International Politics of Insecurity: Normativity, Inwardness and the Exception'. *Security Dialogue*, 37, March 2006, pp. 11–29

Indecki, K., 'Polish Substantive Penal Law against Terrorism'. *American Behavioral Scientist*, 48, February 2005, pp. 710–742

International Committee of the Red Cross, *International Law Concerning the Conduct of Hostilities: Collection of Hague Conventions and Some Other Treaties*. Geneva: International Committee of the Red Cross, 1989

International Crisis Group, 'Thailand's Emergency Decree: No Solution'. *Asia Report* no. 105, Brussels: International Crisis Group, 18 November 2005

International Monetary Fund, Legal Department, *Suppressing the Financing of Terrorism: A Handbook for Legislative Drafting*. Washington, DC: IMF, 2003

Jefferson, A.M., 'Book Review: Global Governance and the Quest for Justice. Volume 4: Human Rights.' *Punishment and Society*, 7, October 2005, pp. 490–493

Jeffery, R., 'Beyond Banality: Ethical Responses to Evil in Post-September 11 International Relations'. *International Affairs*, 81(1), January 2005, pp. 175–186

Joyner, C.C., 'The United Nations and Terrorism: Rethinking Legal Tensions between National Security, Human Rights, and Civil Liberties'. *International Studies Perspectives*, 5(3), August 2004, pp. 240–257

Kassimiris, G., 'Last Act in a Violent Drama? The Trial of Greece's Revolutionary Organization 17 November'. *Terrorism and Political Violence*, 1891), Spring 2006, pp. 137–157

Kilcommins, S. and Vaughan, B., *Terrorism, Rights and the Rule of Law: Negotiating Justice in Ireland*. Cullompton, UK: Willan, 2007

King, L.E. and Ray, J.M., 'Developing Transnational Law Enforcement Cooperation: The FBI Training Initiatives'. *Journal of Contemporary Criminal Justice*, 16, November 2000, pp. 386–408

Kochi, T., 'The Partisan: Carl Schmitt and Terrorism'. *Law and Critique*, 17(3), November 2006, pp. 267–295

Landau-Tasseron, E., *'Non-combatants' in Muslim Legal Thought*. Washington, DC: Hudson Institute Publications, 2006

Lazarus, W., 'Extradition as a Method of Combating International Terrorism: A U.S. Perspective', PhD thesis, University of St Andrews, 2002 (unpublished)

Leach, E.R., *Custom, Law, and Terrorist Violence*. Edinburgh: Edinburgh University Press, 1977

Lee, S.P. (ed.), *Intervention, Terrorism, and Torture: Contemporary Challenges to Just War Theory*. Dordrecht, Natherlands: Springer, 2007

Levi, H.S., *Terrorism in War: The Law of War Crimes*. New York: Dobbs Ferry, 1993

Levin, B. and Amster, S.E., 'An Analysis of the Legal Issues Relating to the Prevention of Nuclear and Radiological Terrorism'. *American Behavioral Scientist*, 46, February 2003, pp. 845–856

Lietzau, W.K., 'Old Laws, New Wars: Jus Ad Bellum in an Age of Terrorism'. *Max Planck Yearbook of United Nations Law*, 8(1), 2004, pp. 383–455

Limone, S., 'The Chemical and Biological Weapons Conventions'. *Strategic Assessment*, 7(1), May 2004, pp. 30–35

Lord Carlile of Berriew QC, *Report on the Operation in 2004 of The Terrorism Act 2000*. London: Home Office Publications, 2005. Available at: http://security.homeoffice.gov.uk/news-publications/publication-search/terrorism-act-2000/response_terroract1.pdf?view=Standard&pubID=480254 (accessed 1 April 2009)

Lowe, V., ' "Clear and Present Danger": Responses to Terrorism'. *International and Comparative Law Quarterly*, 54(1), January 2005, pp. 185–196

Lutz, B.J., Lutz, J.M. and Ulmschneider, G., 'British Trials of Irish Nationalist Defendants: The Quality of Justice Strained'. *Studies in Conflict and Terrorism*, 25(4), 2002, pp. 227–244

Lutz, B.J., Ulmschneider, G. and Lutz, J.M., 'The Trial of the Guildford Four: Government Error or Government Persecution'. *Terrorism and Political Violence*, 14(4), Winter 2002, pp. 113–130

Maggs, G.E., *Terrorism and the Law: Cases and Materials*. Eagan, MN: West Publishing, 2005

Mani, R., 'In Pursuit of an Antidote: The Response to September 11 and the Rule of Law'. *Conflict, Security and Development*, 3(1), April 2003. Available at: http://english.safe-democracy.org/documents/CCSD_3_1_06lores.pdf (accessed 1 April 2009)

Martinez, J.S., 'Towards an International Judicial System'. *Stanford Law Review*, 56, 2003, 429–460

Mathur, S., 'Surviving the Dragnet: "Special Interest" Detainees in the US after 9/11'. *Race and Class*, 47, January 2006, pp. 31–46

Mazandaran, P.A., 'An International Legal Response to an International Problem: Prosecuting International Terrorists'. *International Criminal Law Review*, 6(4), 2006, pp. 503–548

Michaelsen, C., 'Antiterrorism Legislation in Australia: A Proportionate Response to the Terrorist Threat?' *Studies in Conflict and Terrorism*, 28(4), 2005, pp. 321–339

Mulinen, F.D., *Handbook on the Law of War for Armed Forces*. Geneva: International Committee of the Red Cross, 2003

Müller, A.C., 'Legal Issues Arising from the Armed Conflict in Afghanistan'. *Non-State Actors and International Law*, 4(3), 2004, pp. 239–276

Müllerson, R., 'Jus ad bellum: plus ça change (le monde) plus c'est la même chose (le droit)?' *Journal of Conflict and Security Law*, 7(2), October 2002, pp. 149–190

Murphy, J.F., *Punishing International Terrorists: The Legal Framework for Policy Initiatives*, Totowa, NJ: Rowman & Allanheld, 1985

Myers, J.C., 'The Quranic Concept of War'. *Parameters*, Winter 2006–2007, pp. 108–127

National Council for Civil Liberties, *The Prevention of Terrorism Acts 1974 and 1976: A Report on the Operation of the Law*. London: The Council, 1976

Neuman, G.L., 'Humanitarian Law and Counterterrorist Force'. *European Journal of International Law*, 14(2), April 2003, pp. 283–298

Odera Oruka, H., *Punishment and Terrorism in Africa: Problems in the Philosophy and Practice of Punishment*. Nairobi: Kenya Literature Bureau, 1985

O'Neill, O., 'The Dark Side of Human Rights'. *International Affairs*, 81(2), March 2005, pp. 427–439

Papa, E.R., *Il processo alle Brigate rosse: Brigate rosse e difesa d'uffi: documenti: (Torino, 17 maggio 1976–23 giugno 1978)*. Turin: G. Giappichelli, 1979

Pastouna, J., *Guantánamo Bay: Gefangen im rechtsfreien Raum*. Hamburg: Europäische Verlagsanstalt, 2005

Pawlik, M., *Der Terrorist und sein Recht: Zur rechtstheoretischen Einordnung des modernen Terrorismus*. Munich: Beck Juristischen Verlag, 2008

Pejic, J., 'Terrorist Acts and Groups: A Role for International Law?' In J. Crawford and V. Lowe (eds), *British YearBook of International Law*, 75, 2004, pp. 71–100

Pejic, J., 'Procedural Principles and Safeguards on Internment/Administrative Detention in Armed Conflict and Other Situations of Violence'. *International Review of the Red Cross*, 87(858), June 2005, pp. 375–391

Perkovich, G., 'Giving Justice Its Due'. *Foreign Affairs*, 84(4), July–August 2005, pp. 79–93

Politi, M., and Nesi, G. (eds), *The International Criminal Court and the Crime of Aggression*. Aldershot, UK: Ashgate, 2004

Pratt, A.N., '9/11 and Future Terrorism: Same Nature, Different Face in IIHL.' In *Terrorism and International Law: Challenges and Responses*. San Remo, Italy: George C. Marshall Center, September 2002

Ramraj, V.V., Hor, M. and Roach, K., *Global Anti-terrorism Law and Policy*. Cambridge, Cambridge University Press, 2005

Reed, C. and Ryall, D., *The Price of Peace: Just War in the Twenty-First Century*. Cambridge: Cambridge University Press, 2007

Satkalmi, R., 'Material Support: The United States vs. the Lackawanna Six.' *Studies in Conflict and Terrorism*, 28(3), May–June 2005, pp. 193–199

Saul, B., 'International Terrorism as a European Crime: The Policy Rationale for Criminalization'. *European Journal of Crime, Criminal Law and Criminal Justice*, 11(4), 2003, pp. 323–349

Saul, B., 'The Legal Response of the League of Nations to Terrorism'. *Journal of International Criminal Justice*, 4(1), March 2006, pp. 78–102

Scharf, M.P., *Terrorism on Trial*. Durham, NC. Carolina Academic Press, 2007

Schmid, A.P., 'Terrorism and Human Rights: A Perspective from the United Nations'. *Terrorism and Political Violence*, 17(1–2), Winter 2005, pp. 25–35

Schmitt, M.N., 'The Legality of Operation Iraqi Freedom under International Law'. *Journal of Military Ethics*, 3(2), June 2004, pp. 82–104

Schwartz-Barcott, T.P., *War, Terror and Peace in the Qur'an and in Islam: Insights for Military and Government Leaders*. Mechanicsburg, PA: Stackpole Books, 2004

Slim, H., 'Why Protect Civilians? Innocence, Immunity and Enmity in War'. *International Affairs*, 79(3), May 2003, pp. 481–501

Slim, H., *Killing Civilians: Method, Madness, and Morality in War*. New York: Columbia University Press, 2008

Smith, A., 'Balancing Liberty and Security? A Legal Analysis of United Kingdom Anti-terrorist Legislation'. *European Journal on Criminal Policy and Research*, 13(1–2), April 2007, pp. 73–83

Sterba, J.P. (ed.), *Terrorism and International Justice*. Oxford: Oxford University Press, 2003

Stiles, K.W., 'The Power of Procedure and the Procedures of the Powerful: Anti-Terror Law in the United Nations'. *Journal of Peace Research*, 43(1), January 2005, pp. 37–54

Stiles, K.W. and Thayne, A., 'Compliance with International Law: International Law on Terrorism at the United Nations'. *Cooperation and Conflict*, 41, June 2006, pp. 153–176

Stromseth, J., Wippman, D. and Brooks, R., *Can Might Make Rights? Building the Rule of Law after Military Interventions*. Cambridge: Cambridge University Press, 2006

United Nations Office of the High Commissioner for Human Rights, *Digest of Jurisprudence of the UN and Regional Organizations on the Protection of Human Rights while Countering Terrorism*. 2003. Available at: www.unhchr.ch/html/menu6/2/digest.doc (accessed 1 April 2009)

United Nations, Office on Drugs and Crime, *Compendium of Useful Technical Assistance Tools and Legal Instruments to Prevent Terrorism and other Related Forms of Crime*. www.unodc.org in cooperation with www.icclr.law.ubc.ca (CD-ROM)

Van Krieken, P.J. (ed.), *Terrorism and the International Legal Order: With Special Reference to the UN, the EU and Cross-border Aspects*. The Hague: T.M.C. Asser, 2002

Vercher, A., *Terrorism in Europe: An International Comparative Legal Analysis*. Oxford: Clarendon Press, 1992

Verhoeven, S., 'Juridische slachtoffers van de oorlog tegen het terrorisme: de conventies van genève'. *Vrede en Veiligheid*, 34(1), 2005, pp. 38–57

Vladeck, S.I., Note: 'The Detention Power'. *Yale Law and Policy Review*, 22, 2004, p. 153

Von Schorlemer, S., 'Human Rights: Substantive and Institutional Implications of the War against Terrorism'. *European Journal of International Law*, 14(2), April 2003, pp. 265–282

Walker, C., *The Prevention of Terrorism in British Law*. Manchester: Manchester University Press, 1992

Walker, C., *Blackstone's Guide to the Anti-terrorism Legislation*. Oxford: Oxford University Press, 2002

Walker, C., 'The Treatment of Foreign Terror Suspects'. *Modern Law Review*, 70(3), May 2007, pp. 427–457

Wilke, C., 'War vs. Justice: Terrorism Cases, Enemy Combatants, and Political Justice in US Courts'. *Politics and Society*, 33, December 2005 pp. 637–669

Wittes, B., *Law and the Long War: The Future of Justice in the Age of Terror*. London: Penguin Books, 2008

Zajadlo, J., 'Legality and Legitimization of Humanitarian Intervention: New Challenges in the Age of the War on Terrorism'. *American Behavioral Scientist*, 48, February 2005, pp. 653–670

Zawati, H., *Is Jihad a Just War? War, Peace and Human Rights under Islamic and Public International Law*. Lewiston, NY: Edwin Mellen Press, 2001

P. Mass communication aspects of terrorism

Aboul-Enein, Y.H., 'Osama bin Laden Interview, June 1999: Entering the Mind of the Adversary'. *Military Review*, September–October 2004, pp. 109–112

Abou-Taam, M. and Bigalke, R., *Die Reden des Osama bin Laden: Analysiert und kommentiert*. Munich: Heinrich Hugendubel Verlag, 2006

Abrams, M., 'Al Qaeda's Miscommunication War: The Terrorism Paradox'. *Terrorism and Political Violence*, 17(4), 2005, pp. 529–549

Achugar, M., 'The Events and Actors of 11 September 2001 as Seen from Uruguay: Analysis of Daily Newspaper Editorials'. *Discourse Society*, 15, May 2004, pp. 291–320

Alali, A.O., *Terrorism and the News Media: A Selected, Annotated Bibliography*. Jefferson, NC: McFarland, 1994

Alali, A.O. and Eke, K.K., *Media Coverage of Terrorism: Methods of Diffusion*. UMI Books on Demand, 2002. Available at: www.umi.com/hp/Support/BOD/ (accessed 1 April 2009)

Alexander, Y. and Picard, R.G., *In the Camera's Eye: News Coverage of Terrorist Events*. Washington, DC: Brassey's, 1991

Alexander, Y. and Swetnam M.S. (eds), *Cyber Terrorism and Information Warfare: Threats and Responses*. Ardsley, NY: Transnational, 2001

Altheide, D.L., 'The Mass Media, Crime and Terrorism'. *Journal of International Criminal Justice*, 4(5), November 2006, pp. 982–997

Archetti, C., 'Constructivism and the Media: Exploring Meaning Construction in the War on Terrorism'. Honolulu: International Studies Association (ISA), March 2005

Armistead, L. (ed.), *Information Operations: Warfare and the Hard Reality of Soft Power*. Washington, DC: Brassey's, 2004

Arquilla, J. and Ronfeldt, D., *Preparing for Conflict in the Information Age*. Santa Monica, CA: RAND, USA, 1997

Arsenault, A. and Castells, M., 'Conquering the Minds, Conquering Iraq: The Social Production of Misinformation in the United States – a Case Study'. *Information, Communication and Society*, 9(3), June 2006, pp. 284–307

Ballard, J.D., Hornik, J.G. and McKenzie, D., 'Technological Facilitation of Terrorism: Definitional, Legal and Policy Issues'. *American Behavioral Scientist*, 45, February 2002, pp. 989–1016

Beck, U., 'The Silence of Words: On Terror and War'. *Security Dialogue*, 34(3), 2003, pp. 255–267

Bennett, S.E., Rhine, S.L. and Flickinger, R.S., 'The Things They Cared About: Change and Continuity in Americans' Attention to Different News Stories', 1989–2002'. *Harvard International Journal of Press/Politics*, 9, January 2004, pp. 75–99

Benschop, A., 'CyberJihad International: waarom terroristen van internet houden'. *Maatschappij- en Gedragswetenschappen Media Studies*, 16 March 2005

Ben-Yehuda, N., 'Terror, Media, and Moral Boundaries'. *International Journal of Comparative Sociology*, 46, April 2005, pp. 33–53

Bernays, E.L. and Miller, M.C., *Propaganda*. Brooklyn, NY: Ig Publishing, 2005

Bhatia, M. (ed.), Special Issue: 'The Politics of Naming: Rebels, Terrorists, Criminals, Bandits and Subversives'. *Third World Quarterly*, 26(1), 2005, pp. 5–22

Billig, M. and MacMillan, K., 'Metaphor, Idiom and Ideology: The Search for "No Smoking Guns" across Time'. *Discourse Society*, 16, July 2005, pp. 459–480

Bird, J., 'The Mote in God's Eye: 9/11, Then and Now'. *Journal of Visual Culture*, 2, April 2003, pp. 83–97

Bjola, C., 'Legitimating the Use of Force in International Politics: A Communicative Action Perspective'. *European Journal of International Relations*, 11, June 2005, pp. 266–303

Blancard, C.M., 'Al Qaeda: Statements and Evolving Ideology'. Washington, DC: Congress, RL32759, updated 20 June 2005

Blas Winett, L. and Lawrence, R.G., 'The Rest of the Story: Public Health, the News, and the 2001 Anthrax Attacks'. *Harvard International Journal of Press/Politics*, 10, July 2005, pp. 3–25

Boggs, C. and Pollard, T., 'Hollywood and the Spectacle of Terrorism'. *New Political Science*, 28(3), September 2006, pp. 335–351

Brachman, J., 'High-Tech Terror: Al Qaeda's Use of New Technology', *Fletcher Forum of World Affairs*, no. 20, 2006, pp. 149–164

Bratich, J.Z., '"Trust No One" (on the internet): The CIA-Crack-Contra Conspiracy Theory and Professional Journalism'. *Television and New Media*, 5, May 2004, pp. 109–139

Braun, N., *Terrorismus und Freiheitskampf. Gewalt, Propaganda und politische Strategie im irischen Bürgerkrieg 1922–1923*. Munich: Oldenbourg, 2003

Bueno de Mesquita, E. and Dickson, E.S., 'The Propaganda of the Deed: Terrorism, Counterterrorism and Mobilization'. *American Journal of Political Science*, 51(2), April 2007, pp. 364–381

Burger, P., *Kino der Angst: Terror, Krieg und Staatskunst aus Hollywood*. Düsseldorf: Schmetterling Verlag, 2005

Calabrese, A., 'Casus Belli: U.S. Media and the Justification of the Iraq War'. *Television and New Media*, 6, May 2005, pp. 153–175

Carment, D.A., 'Framework for Understanding Terrorist Use of the Internet'. *CCISS-ITAC Trends in Terrorism*, vol. 2006–2. Available at: www.carleton.ca/cifp/app/serve.php/1121.pdf

Centre of Excellence Defence Against Terrorism (ed.), *The Media: The Terrorists' Battlefield*. Amsterdam: IOS Press, 2007

Chaliand, G., *Terrorism: From Popular Struggle to Media Spectacle*. Atlantic Highlands, NJ: Saqi Books, 1987

Clifford, R., *The Marketing of Rebellion: Insurgents, Media, and International Activism*. Cambridge: Cambridge University Press, 2005

Cohen, A.A., Adoni, H. and Bantz, C.R., *Social Conflict and Television News*. Newbury Park, CA: Sage, 1990

Cohen, E.L. and Willis, C., 'One Nation under Radio: Digital and Public Memory after September 11'. *New Media and Society*, 6, October 2004, pp. 591–610

Cohen, Y., 'Broadcast News Diffusion in Crisis-Ridden Democracies: Israel and the Rabin Assassination'. *Harvard International Journal of Press/Politics*, 7, July 2002, pp. 14–33

Coll, S. and Galsser, S., 'Terrorists Turn to the Web as Base of Operations'. *Washington Post*, 7 August 2005

Collins, J. and Glover, R. (eds), *Collateral Language: A User's Guide to America's New War*. New York: New York University Press, 2002

Conway, M., 'Terrorism and Internet Governance: Core Issues'. *UNIDIR, Disarmament Forum no. 3*, 2007, pp. 35–44

Coufal, K.L., 'Applying Mediationalist Theory to Communication about Terrorism and War'. *Communication Disorders Quarterly*, 23(2), March 2002, pp. 84–86

Council of Europe, *'Apologie du Terrorisme' and 'Incitement to Terrorism'*. Strasbourg: Council of Europe, 2004

Cowan, T., 'Terrorism as Theatre: Analysis and Policy Implications'. *Public Choice*, 128(1–2), July 2006, pp. 233–244

Cram, I., 'Regulating the Media: Some Neglected Freedom of Expression Issues in the United Kingdom's Counter-terrorism Strategy'. *Terrorism and Political Violence*, 18(2), Summer 2006, pp. 335–355

Crelinsten, R.D., 'Analysing Terrorism and Counter-terrorism: A Communication Model'. *Terrorism and Political Violence*, 14(2), 2002, pp. 77–122

Crilly, K., 'Information Warfare, New Battlefields: Terrorists, Propaganda and the Internet'. *Aslib Proceedings: New Information Perspectives*, 53(7), 2001, pp. 250–264

Cromer, G., *A War of Words: Political Violence and Public Debate in Israel*. London: Frank Cass, 2004

Cronin, B., 'Information Warfare: Peering inside Pandora's Postmodern Box', *Library Review*, 50(6), 2001, pp. 279–295

Cukier, K.N., 'Who Will Control the Internet?' *Foreign Affairs*, 84(6), November–December 2005, pp. 71–73

Debrix, F., *Tabloid Terror: War, Culture and Geopolitics*. London: Routledge, 2008

Der Derian, J. 'Imaging Terror: Logos, Pathos and Ethos'. *Third World Quarterly*, 26(1), February 2005, pp. 23–37

De Young, K., 'Letter Gives Glimpse of Al-Qaeda's Leadership'. *Washington Post*, 2 October 2006

Dickey, B.J., 'In Pursuit of Justice: Audio and Video Recordings – Weapons of Terrorism'. *Forensic Examiner*, 16(1), 22 March 2007

Dimitrova, D.V., Kaid, L., Williams, A.P., Kaye D. and Trammell, K.D., 'War on the Web: The Immediate News Framing of Gulf War II'. *Harvard International Journal of Press/Politics*, 10, January 2005, pp. 22–44

Dingley, J. and Kirk-Smith, M., 'Symbolism and Sacrifice in Terrorism'. *Small Wars and Insurgencies*, 13(1), 2002, pp. 102–128

Donohue, L.K., 'Terrorist Speech and the Future of Free Expression'. *Cardozo Law Review*, 27(1), 2005, pp. 233–241

Donsbach, W., 'Psychology of News Decisions: Factors behind Journalists' Professional Behavior'. *Journalism*, 5, May 2004, pp. 131–157

Dor, D., *Intifafa Hits the Headlines: How the Israeli Press Misreported the Outbreak of the Second Palestinian Uprising*. Bloomington: Indiana University Press, 2005

Downes-Le Guin, T., *The Impact of Terrorism on Public Opinion, 1988 to 1989*. Santa Monica, CA: RAND, 1993

Dunn, E.W., Moore, M. and Nosek, B.A., 'The War of the Words: How Linguistic Differences in Reporting Shape Perceptions of Terrorism'. *Analyses of Social Issues and Public Policy*, 5(1), December 2005, pp. 67–86

Dutta-Bergman, M.J., 'Interpersonal Communication after 9/11 via Telephone and Internet: A Theory of Channel Complementarity'. *New Media Society*, 6, October 2004, pp. 659–673

Ehrlich, M.C., 'Shattered Glass, Movies, and the Free Press Myth'. *Journal of Communication Inquiry*, 29, April 2005, pp. 103–118

Engelbert, P. and Hummel, R., 'Let's Stick Together: Understanding Africa's Secessionist Deficit'. *African Affairs*, 104(416), July 2005, pp. 399–428

Fahmy, S., 'Emerging Alternatives or Traditional News Gates: Which News Sources Were Used to Picture the 9/11 Attack and the Afghan War?' *Gazette*, 67, October 2005, pp. 381–398

Farber, D. (ed.), *What They Think of Us: International Perceptions of the United States since 9/11*. Princeton, NJ: Princeton University Press, 2007

Farmanfarmaian, R., 'The Media and the War on Terrorism: Where Does the Truth Lie?' *Cambridge Review of International Affairs*, 15(1), April 2002, pp. 159–163

Feinstein, A., *Journalists under Fire: The Psychological Hazards of Covering War*. Baltimore: Johns Hopkins University Press, 2006

Fekete, L., 'Europe: "Speech Crime" and Deportation'. *Race and Class*, 47, January 2006, pp. 82–92

Felix, J. (ed.), *Die Postmoderne im Kino: Ein Reader*, Marburg: Schuren, 2002

Field, D., 'Literary Responses to Political Violence'. *Cambridge Quarterly*, 33(1), 2004, pp. 78–80

Foltz, C.B., 'Cyberterrorism, Computer Crime, and Reality'. *Information Management and Computer Security*, 12(2), 2004, pp. 154–166

Fried, A., 'Terrorism as a Context of Coverage before the Iraq War'. *Harvard International Journal of Press/Politics*, 10(3), July 2005, pp. 125–132

Gallaher, M.P., Link, A.N. and Rowe, B.R., *Cyber Security: Economic Strategies and Public Policy Alternatives*. Cheltanham, UK: Edward Elgar, 2008

Ganor, B., 'Terrorism as a Strategy of Psychological Welfare'. *Journal of Aggression, Maltreatment and Trauma*, 9(1–2), 2005, pp. 33–43

Gibbs van Brunschot, E.E. and Sherley, A.J. 'Communicating Threat: The Canadian State and Terrorism'. *Sociological Quarterly*, 46(4), September 2005, pp. 645–669

Gilbert, A., Hirschkorn, P., Murphy, M., Walensky, R. and Stephens, P. (eds), *Covering Catastrophe: Broadcast Journalists Report September 11*. Chicago: Bonus Books, 2002

Gillespie, M., 'Transnational Television Audiences after September 11'. *Journal of Ethnic and Migration Studies*, 32(6), August 2006, pp. 903–921

Glaab, S., *Medien und Terrorismus: Auf den Spuren einer symbiotischen Beziehung*. Berlin: Berliner Wissenschaft Verlag, 2007

Goldsmith, B.E., Y. Horiuchi and T. Inoguchi, 'American Foreign Policy and Global Opinion: Who Supported the War in Afghanistan?' *Journal of Conflict Resolution*, 49(3), June 2005, pp. 408–429

Gordon, A., 'Terrorism on the Internet: Discovering the Unsought'. *Terrorism and Political Violence*, 9(4), Winter 1997, pp. 159–165

Graham, P., Keenan, T. and Dowd, A.M., 'A Call to Arms at the End of History: A Discourse-Historical Analysis of George W. Bush's Declaration of War on Terror'. *Discourse Society*, 15, May 2004, pp. 199–221

Graves, K.D., Schmidt, J.E. and Andrykowski, M.A., 'Writing about September 11, 2001: Exploration of Emotional Intelligence and the Social Environment'. *Journal of Language and Social Psychology*, 24, September 2005, pp. 285–299

Greenberg, B.S., *Communication and Terrorism: Public and Media Responses to 9/11*. Cresskill, NJ: Hampton Press, 2002

Griffin, M., 'Picturing America's "War on Terrorism" in Afghanistan and Iraq: Photographic Motifs as News Frames'. *Journalism*, 5, November 2004, pp. 381–402

Grigorian, A. and Kaufman, S.J., 'Hate Narratives and Ethnic Conflict'. *International Security*, 31(4), Spring 2007, pp. 180–191

Grinyaev, S., 'The Mass Media and Terrorism: A Russian View'. *European Security*, 12(2), June 2003, pp. 85–88

Gurabardhi, Z., Gutteling, J.M. and Kuttschreuter, M., 'The Development of Risk Communication: An Empirical Analysis of the Literature in the Field'. *Science Communication*, 25, June 2004, pp. 323–349

Hafez, M.M., 'Martyrdom Mythologies in Iraq: How Jihadists Frame Suicide Terrorism in Videos and Biographies'. *Terrorism and Political Violence*, 19(1), 2007, pp. 95–115

Hammitt, H., 'Less Safe: The Dismantling of Public Information Systems after 9/11'. *Social Science Computer Review*, 23, November 2005, pp. 429–438

Hess, S. and Kalb, M., *The Media and the War on Terrorism*. Washington, DC: Brookings Institution, 2003

Hoffman, B., 'The Use of the Internet by Islamist Extremists'. Testimony presented to the House Permanent Select Committee on Intelligence, May 2006. Santa Barbara, CA: RAND, 2006

Hoffman, B. and McCormick, G.H., 'Terrorism, Signaling and Suicide Attack'. *Studies in Conflict and Terrorism*, 27(4), 2004, pp. 243–281

Holsti, O.R., *To See Ourselves as Others see Us: How Publics Abroad View the United States after 9/11*. Ann Arbor: University of Michigan Press, 2008

Horsman, S., 'Themes in Official Discourses on Terrorism in Central Asia'. *Third World Quarterly*, 26(1), February 2005, pp. 199–213

Hoyt, L., Book review: 'The Political Mapping of Cyberspace'. *Journal of Planning Education and Research*, 24, March 2005, pp. 348–349

Isikoff, M. and Corn, D., *Hubris: The Inside Story of Spin, Scandal and the Selling of the Iraq War*. New York: Crown, 2006

Jackson, R., *Writing the War on Terrorism: Language, Politics and Counter-terrorism*. Manchester: Manchester University Press, 2005

Jones, D.M. and Smith, M.L.R., 'Greetings from the Cybercaliphate: Some Notes on Homeland Insecurity'. *International Affairs*, 81(5), October 2005, pp. 925–950

Jones, D.M. and Smith, M.L.R., 'The Commentariat and Discourse Failure: Language and Atrocity in Cool Britannia'. *International Affairs*, 82(6), November 2006, pp. 1077–1100

Jordan, J., Torres, M.R. and Horsburgh, N., 'The Intelligence Services' Struggle against Al Qaeda Propaganda'. *International Journal of Intelligence and Counterintelligence*, 18(1), Spring 2005, pp. 31–49

Jorish, A., *Beacon of Hatred: Inside Hizballah's Al-Manar Television*. Washington, DC: Washington Institute for Near East Policy, 2004

Joscelyn, T., 'Spinning Zarqawi: What Three al Qaeda Terrorists Had to Say about Zarqawi's and al Qaeda's Cooperation with Saddam'. *Weekly Standard*, 15 June 2006

Justice, J.W., 'Of Guns and Ballots: Attitudes towards Unconventional and Destructive Political Participation among Sinn Féin and Herri Batasuna Supporters'. *Nationalism and Ethnic Politics*, 11(3), Autumn 2005, pp. 295–320

Kacowicz, A.M., 'Rashomon in The Middle East: Clashing Narratives, Images, and Frames in the Israeli–Palestinian Conflict'. *Cooperation and Conflict*, 40, September 2005, pp. 343–360

Kahn, R. and Kellner, D., 'New Media and Internet Activism: From the "Battle of Seattle" to Blogging'. *New Media Society*, 6, February 2004, pp. 87–95

Kalb, M., *The Israeli–Hezbollah War of 2006: The Media as a Weapon in Asymmetrical Conflict*. Joan Shorenstein Center on the Press, Politics and Public Policy. Research Paper Series no. R-29. Harvard University, John F. Kennedy School of Government, February 2007

Katsy, D.V., *The US War against Terrorism and Perceptions of Russian Society*. Honolulu: International Studies Association (ISA), March 2005

Katz, F.E., *Immediacy: How Our World Confronts Us and How We Confront Our World*. Baltimore: Discern Books, 2003

Kaylan, M., 'Losing the Propaganda Wars'. *World Policy Journal*, 23(4), Winter 2006/2007, pp. 19–26

Kellner, D., '9/11, Spectacles of Terror, and Media Manipulation'. *Critical Discourse Studies*, 1(1), April 2004, pp. 41–64

Kellner, D., 'Media Propaganda and Spectacle in the War on Iraq: A Critique of U.S. Broadcasting Networks'. *Cultural Studies <=> Critical Methodologies*, 4, August 2004, pp. 329–338

Kepel, G., *Jihad; The Trail of Political Islam*. London: I.B. Tauris, 2002

Kepel, G., *The War for Muslim Minds: Islam and the West*. Cambridge, MA: Harvard University Press, 2005

Kepel, G. and Milelli, J.-P. (eds), *Al-Qaida: Texte des terrors*. Munich: Piper, 2006

Kimmage, D. and Ridolfo, K., *Iraqi Insurgent Media: The War of Images and Ideas*. Prague: Radio Free Europe/Radio Liberty, 2007

Kimmage, D., *The Al-Qaeda Media Nexus*. An RFE/RL Special Report, March 2008. Available at: www.rferl.org/content/article/1079736.html (accessed 6 April 2009)

Kneschke, R., *Medien als Waffe: Zum Verhältnis von Medien und Terrorismus nach dem Irak-Krieg 2003*. Norderstedt, Germany: GRIN Verlag, 2004

Knightley, P., *The First Casualty: The War Correspondent as Hero and Myth-Maker from the Crimea to Iraq*. Baltimore: Johns Hopkins University Press, 2004

Knowlton, B., 'Global Image of the US is Worsening, Survey Finds'. *New York Times*, 14 June 2006

Kohlmann, E.F., 'The Real Online Terrorist Threat'. *Foreign Affairs*, 85(5), September–October 2006, pp. 115–124

Kohlmann, E.F., *State of the Sunni Insurgency in Iraq: August 2007*. NEFA Foundation, 2007. Available at: http://nefafoundation.org/index.html (accessed 6 April 2009)

Krueger, B.S., 'Government Surveillance and Political Participation on the Internet'. *Social Science Computer Review*, 23, November 2005, pp. 439–452

Kutais, B.G., *Internet Policies and Issues*, vol. 5. New York: Nova Science Publishers, 2003

Kuypers, J.A., *Bush's War: Media Bias and Justifications for War in a Terrorist Age*. Lanham, MD: Rowman & Littlefield, 2006

Lagos, M., 'Terrorism and the Image of the United States in Latin America'. *International Journal of Public Opinion Research*, 15(1), March 2003, pp. 95–101

Landau, M.J., Solomon, S., Greenberg, J., Cohen, F., Pyszczynski, T., Arndt, J., Miller, C.H., Ogilvie, D.M. and Cook, A., 'Deliver Us from Evil: The Effects of Mortality Salience and Reminders of 9/11 on Support for President George W. Bush'. *Personality and Social Psychology Bulletin*, 30, September 2004, pp. 1136–1150

Lawrence, B., *Messages to the World: The Statements of Osama bin Laden*, New York: B&T, 2005

Lech, J.J. and Colarik, A.M. (eds), *Cyber Warfare and Cyber Terrorism*. Hershey, PA: Information Science Reference, 2008

Leeman, R.W., *The Rhetoric of Terrorism and Counterterrorism*. New York: Greenwood Press, 1991

Levin, B., 'Cyberhate: A Legal and Historical Analysis of Extremists' Use of Computer Networks in America'. *American Behavioral Scientist*, 45, February 2002, pp. 958–988

Lewis, C.W., 'The Terror That Failed: Public Opinion in the Aftermath of the Bombing in Oklahoma City'. *Public Administration Review*, 60(3), May–June 2000, pp. 201–210

Lewis, J., 'Television, Public Opinion and the War in Iraq: The Case of Britain'. *International Journal of Public Opinion Research*, 16(3), 2004, pp. 295–310

Lewis, J., *Language Wars: The Role of Media and Culture in Global Terror and Political Violence*. London: Pluto Press, 2005

Lia, B., 'Al-Qaeda Online: Understanding Jihadist Internet Infrastructure'. *Jane's Intelligence Review*, 18(1), 1 January 2006, pp. 14–19

Lia, B., 'Jihadi Web Media Production: Characteristics, Trends, and Future Implications'. Paper presented at the 'Check the Web' Conference on 'Monitoring, Research and Analysis of Jihadist Activities on the Internet – Ways to Deal with the Issue, Berlin, 26–27 February 2007

Livingston, S., *The Terrorism Spectacle*, Boulder, CO: Westview Press, 1994

Lohlker, R., 'Cyberjihad: Das Internet als Feld der Agitation'. *Orient*, 43(4), 2002, pp. 507–536

Lord, C. and Barnett, F. (eds), *Political Warfare and Psychological Operations*. Washington, DC: National Defense University Press, 1989

Lorenz, M.N. (ed.), *Narrative des Entsetzens: Künstlerische, mediale und intellektuelle Deutungen des 11. September 2001*. Würzburg: Verlag Köningshausen & Neumann, 2004

Lynch, M., 'Al-Qaeda's Media Strategies'. *National Interest*, no. 83, Spring 2006, pp. 50–56

Maguire, T.E.R., Website review: 'Islamist Websites', *Global Media and Communication*, 1, April 2005, pp. 121–123

Maluf, R., Book review: 'US and the Others: Global Media on "The War on Terror" '. *European Journal of Communication*, 20, March 2005, pp. 131–133

Maluf, R., 'The FP Memorandum: Urgent: How to Sell America'. *Foreign Policy*, July–August 2005, pp. 74–79

McDonald, I.R. and Lawrence, R.G., 'Filling the 24/7 News Hole: Television News Coverage Following September 11'. *American Behavioral Scientist*, 48, November 2004, pp. 327–340

McLaren, P. and Martin, G., 'The Legend of the Bush Gang: Imperialism, War, and Propaganda'. *Cultural Studies <=> Critical Methodologies*, 4, August 2004, pp. 281–303

McMillan, N., 'Beyond Representation: Cultural Understandings of the September 11 Attacks'. *Australian and New Zealand Journal of Criminology*, 37(3), 10 August 2004, pp. 380–400

Matheson, D., 'Weblogs and the Epistemology of the News: Some Trends in Online Journalism'. *New Media and Society*, 6, August 2004, pp. 443–468

Mazza, C. and Strandgaard P.J., 'From Press to E-Media? The Transformation of an Organizational Field'. *Organization Studies*, 25, July 2004, pp. 875–896

MEMRI, 'The Enemy Within: Where Are the Islamist/Jihadist Websites Hosted, and What Can Be Done about It?' *Inquiry and Analysis Series* no. 374, 19 July 2007

Michavila, N., *War, Terrorism and Elections: Electoral Impact of the Islamist Terror Attacks in Madrid*. Madrid: Real Instituto Elcano de Estudios Internacionales y Estratégicos, 2005

Mickolus, E., 'Deadly Logic: Will Hostile Computer Code Become the Terrorism of the 1990s?' Paper prepared for the Seminar on Countering Terrorism, sponsored by the Washington, DC, Chapter of the Terrorist Activities Subcommittee of the American Society for Industrial Security, 13 June 1990

Mitnick, K. and Simon, W., *The Art of Intrusion: The Real Stories behind the Exploits of Hackers, Intruders and Deceivers*. Hoboken, NJ: Wiley, 2005

Mogensen, K., 'Television Journalism during Terror Attacks'. *Media, War and Conflict*, 1(1), 2008, pp. 31–49

Montgomery, M., 'The Discourse of War after 9/11'. *Language and Literature*, 14, May 2005, pp. 149–180

Moss, D., 'Does It Matter What the Terrorists Meant?' *Psychoanalytic Dialogues*, 12(3), 17 June 2002, pp. 421–431

Münkler, H., 'Terrorismus als Kommunikationsstrategie: Die Botschaft des 11. September'. *Internationale Politik*, 12, 2001, pp. 11–18

Muravchik, J., *Covering the Intifada. How the Media Reported the Palestinian Uprising*. Washington, DC: Washington Institute for Near East Policy, 2003

Nacos, B.L., 'The Terrorist Calculus behind 9–11: A Model for Future Terrorism?' *Studies in Conflict and Terrorism*, 26(1), January–February 2003, pp. 1–16

Nacos, B.L., 'Terrorism as Breaking News: Attack on America'. *Political Science Quarterly*, 118(1), Spring 2003, pp. 23–52

Nacos, B.L., 'The Portrayal of Female Terrorists In the Media: Similar Framing Patterns in the News Coverage of Women in Politics and in Terrorism'. *Studies in Conflict and Terrorism*, 28(5), September–October 2005, pp. 435–451

Nacos, B.L., *Mass-Mediated Terrorism: The Central Role of The Media in Terrorism and Counterterrorism*. Lanham, MD: Rowman & Littlefield, 2007

Nakra, P., 'Info-terrorism in the Age of the Internet: Challenges and Initiatives'. *Journal of Competitive Intelligence and Management*, 1(2), April 2003, pp. 1–12

Nicander, L. and Ranstorp, M. (eds) *Terrorism in the Information Age: New Frontiers?* Stockholm: National Defence College, 2004

Nossek, H. and Berkowitz, D., 'Telling "Our" Story through News of Terrorism'. *Journalism Studies*, 7(5), October 2006, pp. 691–707

O'Day, A. (ed.), *Cyberterrorism*. Aldershot, UK: Ashgate, 2004

Paletz, D.L., and Schmid, A.P. (eds), *Terrorism and the Media: How Researchers, Terrorists, Government, Press, Public and Victims View and Use the Media*. Newbury Park, CA: Sage, 1992

Parfit, T. and Egorova, Y. (eds), *Jews, Muslims and Mass Media*. London: Routledge, 2003

Paul, C. and Kim, J.J., *Reporters on the Battlefield: The Embedded Press System In Historical Context*. Santa Monica, CA: RAND, 2005

Pearle, M.A., *Mighty Heart: The Brave Life and Death of My Husband Danny Pearle*. New York: Scribner, 2003

Peleg, S., 'One's Terrorist Is Another's Blockbuster: Political Terrorism in American vs. European Films'. *New England Journal of Political Science*, 1(1), Summer 2003, pp. 81–108

Pew Global Attitudes Project, *Global Opinion Trends 2002–2007: A Rising Tide Lifts Mood in the Developing World: 47-Nation Pew Global Attitudes Survey*. Washington, DC: Pew Research Center, 24 July 2007

Pew Research Center for the People and the Press, Council on Foreign Relations, *America's Place in the World 2005: Opinion Leaders Turn Cautious, Public Looks Homeward*. Washington, DC: Pew Research Center, 17 November 2005

Pollack, K., 'Weapons of Misperception: How the Road to War with Iraq Was Paved with Misleading and Manipulated Intelligence'. *Atlantic*, 13 January 2004

Post, M., Ruby, K.G. and Shaw, E.D., 'From Car Bombs to Logic Bombs: The Growing Threat of Information Terrorism'. *Terrorism and Political Violence*, 12(2), 2000, pp. 97–122

Qin, J., Zhou, Y., Reid, E., Lai, G. and Chen, H., 'Analyzing Terror Campaigns on the Internet: Technical Sophistication, Content Richness, and Web Interactivity'. *International Journal of Human–Computer Studies*, 65(1), 2007, pp. 71–84

Rajiva, L., *The Language of Empire: Abu Ghraib and the American Media*. New York: Monthly Review Press, 2007

Raman, B., 'From Internet to Islamnet: Net-Centric Counterterrorism'. *South Asia Analysis Group*, no. 1584, 22 October 2005

Ranstorp, M., 'The Virtual Sanctuary of Al-Qaeda and Terrorism in an Age of Globalisation'. In J. Eriksson and G. Giacomello (eds), *International Relations and Security in the Digital Age*. London: Routledge, 2007

Ravault, R.J., 'Is There a Bin Laden in the Audience? Considering the Events of September 11 as a Possible Boomerang Effect of the Globalization of US Mass Communication'. *Prometheus*, 20(3), September 2002, pp. 295–300

Reynalds, J., *War of the Web. Fighting the Online Jihad*. Los Angeles, CA: World Ahead Publishing, 2007

Rogan, H., *Jihadism Online: A Study of How Al-Qaida and Radical Islamist Groups Use the Internet for Terrorist Purposes*. Kjaller, Norway: Norwegian Defence Research Establishment, FFI/Rapport-2006/00915

Rollins, J. and Wilson, C., 'Terrorist Capabilities for Cyberattack: Overview and Policy Issues'. *CRS Report for Congress*, RL33123, 20 October 2005

Rötzer, F., 'Das terroristische Wettrüsten'. In G. Palm and F. Rötzer (eds), *Medien, Terror, Krieg: Zum neuen Kriegsparadigma des 21. Jahrhunderts*. Hanover: Heise, 2002

Russell, J., 'Mujahedeen, Mafia, Madmen: Russian Perceptions of Chechens during the Wars in Chechnya, 1994–96 and 1999–2001'. *Journal of Communist Studies and Transition Politics*, 18(1), March 2002, pp. 73–96

Ryan, M., 'Framing the War against Terrorism: US Newspaper Editorials and Military Action in Afghanistan'. *Gazette*, 66, October 2004, pp. 363–382

Sawyer, J., *Terrorism, Press Freedom, and Democracy: A Nuanced Relationship*. Honolulu: International Studies Association (ISA), March 2005

Schaefer, T., 'When Terrorism Hits Home: Domestic Newspaper Coverage of the 1998 and 2002 Terror Attacks In Kenya'. *Studies in Conflict and Terrorism*, 29(6), September 2006, pp. 577–589

Schechter, D., Schatz, R. and Cronkite, W., *Media Wars: News at a Time of Terror*. Lanham, MD: Rowman & Littlefield, 2003

Schicha, C. and Brosda, C. *Medien und Terrorismus: Reaktionen auf den 11. September 2001*. Berlin: LIT Verlag, 2003

Schlesinger, P., *Media, State, and Nation: Political Violence and Collective Identities*. Newbury Park, CA: Sage, 1991

Schmid, A.P. and de Graaf, J., *Violence as Communication: Insurgent Terrorism and the Western News Media*. London: Sage, 1982

Shinar, D., 'Media Diplomacy and "Peace Talk": The Middle East and Northern Ireland'. *Gazette*, 62, April 2000, pp. 83–97

Shirazi, M., *Psychological Warfare and Propaganda: Concepts and Applications*. Secretariat of the First Conference on the Role of Propaganda and War. Geneva: *International Risk Governance Council* (IRGC) Command Staff College, Office of the Leader's Representative, 2002

Silberstein, S., *War of Words: Language, Politics and 9/11*. London: Routledge, 2004

Simon, S. 'Terrorists and Media'. *Spokesman*, Autumn 1995, pp. 45–53

Slisli, F., 'The Western Media and the Algerian Crisis'. *Race and Class*, 41, January 2000, pp. 43–57

Slocum, J.D. (ed.), *Terrorism, Media, Liberation*. New Brunswick, NJ: Rutgers University Press, 2005

Slone, M., 'Responses to Media Coverage of Terrorism'. *Journal of Conflict Resolution*, 44, August 2000, pp. 508–522

Spencer, A.T., 'Basque Nationalism and the Spiral of Silence: An Analysis of Public Perceptions of ETA in Spain and France'. *International Communication Gazette*, 70, April 2008, pp. 137–153

Srivastava, N., 'Interview with the Italian Film Director, Gillo Pontecorvo'. *Cineaste*, 25(2), 2000. pp. 24–25

Stanton, J.J., 'Terror in Cyberspace: Terrorists Will Exploit and Widen the Gap between Governing Structures and the Public'. *American Behavioral Scientist*, 45, February 2002, pp. 1017–1032

Stein, G.J., 'Information War: Cyber-netwar'. In E. V. Linden (ed.), *Focus on Terrorism*, vol. 5. Hauppauge, NY: Nova Science Publishers, 2002

Stenvall, M., 'An Actor or an Undefined Threat? The Role of Terrorism in the Discourse of International News Agencies'. *Journal of Language and Politics*, 2(2), 2003, pp. 361–404

Suedfeld, P. and Leighton, D.C., 'Early Communications in the War against Terrorism: An Integrative Complexity Analysis'. *Political Psychology*, 23(3), September 2002, pp. 585–599

Tatham, S., *Losing Arab Hearts and Minds: The Coalition, Al-Jazeera and Muslim Public Opinion.* London: Hurst, 2006

Taylor, P.A., 'From Hackers to Hacktivists: Speed Bumps on the Global Superhighway?' *New Media Society*, 7, October 2005, pp. 625–646

Taylor, P.M., 'Can the Information War on Terror Be Won? A Polemical Essay'. *Media, War and Conflict*, 1(1), 2008, pp. 118–124

Telhami, S., *Reflections of Hearts and Minds, Media, Opinion and Identity in the Arab World.* Washington, DC: Brookings Institution Press, 2006

Thomas, D., 'Globalizzazione del jihad ed attivismo on-line'. *AKI Crises Today Dossier*, 22 June 2006

Thomas, J., 'The Moral Ambiguity of Social Control in Cyberspace: A Retro-assessment of the "Golden Age" of Hacking'. *New Media and Society*, 7, October 2005, pp. 599–624

Thomas, T.L., 'Al Qaeda and the Internet: The Danger of "Cyberplanning" '. *Parameters*, Spring 2003, pp. 112–123

Thompson, V., 'Open-Source Spying'. *New York Times Magazine*, 3 December 2006

Todorov, A. and Mandisodza, A.N., 'Public Opinion on Foreign Policy'. *Public Opinion Quarterly*, 68(3), 2004, pp. 323–348

Tota, A.L., 'Terrorism and Collective Memories: Comparing Bologna, Naples and Madrid 11 March'. *International Journal of Comparative Sociology*, 46, April 2005, pp. 55–78

Towle, P., '11 September 2001 and the Media'. *Small Wars and Insurgencies*, 14(1), 2003, pp. 151–166

Tuman, J.S., *Communicating Terror: The Rhetorical Dimensions of Terrorism.* Thousand Oaks, CA: Sage, 2003

Vague, T., *Televisionaries: The Red Army Faction Story 1963–1993.* Edinburgh: AK Press, 1994

Valeri, L. and Knights, M., 'Affecting Trust: Terrorism, Internet and Offensive Information Warfare'. *Terrorism and Political Violence*, 12(1), 2000, pp. 15–36

Vennix, R., 'Wetsvoorstel verheerlijken van terrorisme: niet effectief en niet nodig'. *NJCM-Bulletin*, 30(8), December 2005, pp. 1085–1090

Verton, D., *Black Ice: The Invisible Threat of Cyberterrorism.* London: McGraw-Hill/Osborne, 2003

Weimann, G., *www.terror.net: How Modern Terrorists Use the Internet.* Special Report 116. Washington, DC: US Institute of Peace, March 2004

Weimann, G., *Cyberterrorism: How Real Is the Threat?* Special Report 119. Washington, DC: United States Institute of Peace, December 2004

Weimann, G., 'Cyberterrorism: The Sum of All Fears?' *Studies in Conflict and Terrorism*, 28(2), March–April 2005, pp. 129–149

Weimann, G., 'Review: B.L. Nacos, Mass-Mediated Terrorism'. *Studies in Conflict and Terrorism*, 28(6), November–December 2005, pp. 567–571

Weimann, G., *Terror on the Internet: The New Arena, the New Challenges.* Washington, DC: United States Institute of Peace Press, 2006

Weimann, G., 'Virtual Disputes: The Use of the Internet for Terrorist Debates'. *Studies in Conflict and Terrorism*, 29 (7), 2006, pp. 623–639

Wenden, A.L., 'The Politics of Representation: A Critical Discourse Analysis of an Aljazeera Special Report'. *International Journal of Peace Studies*, 10(2), Autumn–Winter 2005, pp. 89–112

Whine, M., 'Cyberspace: A New Medium for Communication, Command, and Control by Extremists', *Studies in Conflict and Terrorism*, 22(3), 1999, pp. 231–245

Whine, M., 'Islamist Organizations on the Internet'. *Terrorism and Political Violence*, 11(1), 1999, pp. 123–132

Wilkinson, P, 'The Media and Terrorism: A Reassessment'. *Terrorism and Political Violence*, 9(2), 1997, pp. 51–64

Willcox, D.R., *Propaganda, the Press and Conflict.* London: Routledge, 2005

Williams, N.J., *Matrix Warfare: The New Face of Competition and Conflict in the 21st Century.* Quantico, VA: Center for Emerging Threats and Opportunities, 2004

Windrich, E., 'The Laboratory of Hate: The Role of Clandestine Radio in the Angolan War'. *International Journal of Cultural Studies*, 3, August 2000, pp. 206–218

Winfield, B.H., Friedman, B. and Trisnadi, V., 'History as the Metaphor through Which the Current World Is Viewed: British and American Newspapers' Uses of History following the 11 September 2001 Terrorist Attacks'. *Journalism Studies*, 3(2), May 2002, pp. 289–300

Winston, T., *The Use of the Internet for Terrorist Purposes: An Exploration of the Intelligence Challenges in Tracking, Tracing and Investigating Terrorist Fund-Raising and Fund Transfer Activities using the Internet.* Honolulu: International Studies Association (ISA), March 2005

Wright, D.K., 'Examining How the 11th September, 2001 Terrorist Attacks Precipitated a Paradigm Shift Advancing Communications and Public Relations into a More Significant Role in Corporate America'. *Journal of Communication Management*, 6(3), 2002, pp. 280–292

Wright, J., *Terrorist Propaganda: The Red Army Faction and the Provisional IRA, 1968–86*. London: Macmillan, 1991

Yehoshua, Y., 'Islamist Websites as an Integral Part of Jihad: A General Overview'. *MEMRI*, no. 328, 21 February 2007

Zhang, J., 'Beyond Anti-terrorism: Metaphors as Message Strategy of Post-September 11 US Public Diplomacy'. *Public Relations Review*, 33(1), 2007, pp. 31–39

Zielinska, I., Book review: 'Criminal Visions: Media Representations of Crime and Justice'. *Crime, Media, Culture*, 1, August 2005, pp. 229–232

Zuhur, S., 'Precision in the Global War on Terror: Inciting Muslims through the War of Ideas'. Carlisle, PA: Strategic Studies Institute, April 2008. Available at: www.strategicstudiesinstitute.army.mil/pubs/display. cfm?pubID=843 (accessed 14 April 2009)

Q. The aetiology of terrorism

Acemoglu, D. and Robinson, J.A., *Economic Origins of Dictatorship and Democracy: Economic and Political Origins*. Cambridge: Cambridge University Press, 2006

Algar, H., *The Roots of the Islamic Revolution*. London: Open Press, 1983

Amir Rana, M., *The Seeds of Terrorism*. London: New Millennium, 2005

Ashour, O., 'Security, Oil and International Politics: The Causes of the Russo-Chechen Conflicts'. *Studies in Conflict and Terrorism*, 27, 2004, pp. 127–143

Bahua, F., 'Toward the Jungle: An Examination of the Many Injustices in Chinese Society That Drive People to Acts of Desperation'. *Journal of Human Rights in China*, 1, 2005, pp. 1–19

Bakker, E., 'Zin en onzin van de zoektocht naar oorzaken van terrorisme'. *Internationale Spectator*, 58(11), November 2004, pp. 542–547

Barash, D.P., *Understanding Violence*. Boston: Allyn & Bacon, 2001

Barrett, M.J., 'The Sources of Terrorist Conduct'. *Strategic Insights*, 3(2), December 2004. Available at: www.ccc.nps.navy.mil/si/2004/dec/barrettDec04.asp (accessed 7 April 2009)

Bjorgo, T. (ed.), *Root Causes of Terrorism: Myths, Reality and Ways Forward*. London: Routledge, 2005

Brass, P.R., *The Production of Hindu–Muslim Violence in Contemporary India*. Seattle: University of Washington Press, 2003

Burdman, D., 'Education, Indoctrination, and Incitement: Palestinian Children on Their Way to Martyrdom'. *Terrorism and Political Violence*, 15(1), 2003, pp. 96–124

Burgoon, B., 'On Welfare and Terror: Social Welfare Policies and Political-Economic Roots of Terrorism'. *Journal of Conflict Resolution*, 50, April 2006, pp. 176–203

Burton, A.M., *Revolutionary Violence: The Theories*. London: Cooper, 1977

Callaway, R.L., *Causes of Terrorism: The Case of Northern Ireland*. Honolulu: International Studies Association (ISA), March 2005

Callaway, R.L. and Harrelson-Stephens, J., 'Toward a Theory of Terrorism: Human Security as a Determinant of Terrorism'. *Studies in Conflict and Terrorism*, 29(8), December 2006, pp. 773–796

Calvi, M., Ceci, A., Sessa, A. and Vasaturo, G., *Le date del terrore: la genesi del terrorismo italiano e il microclima dell'eversione: 1945–2003*. Rome: Luca Sosella Editore, 2003

Carter, J., *The Blood of Abraham: Insights into the Middle East*. Fayetteville: University of Arkansas Press, 1993

Chenoweth, E., *Terrorism and Instability: A Structural Study of the Origins of Terror*. Honolulu: International Studies Association (ISA), March 2005

Christie, K., *Ethnic Conflict, Tribal Politics: A Global Perspective*. Richmond, UK: Curzon Press, 1998

Club de Madrid, 'Addressing The Causes of Terrorism'. I, 'Confronting Terrorism', II, 'Towards a Democratic Response', III, 'The International Summit on Democracy', *Terrorism and Security*, 8–11 March 2005

Coll, S., *Ghost Wars: The Secret History of the CIA, Afghanistan, and Bin Laden, from the Soviet Invasion to September 10, 2001*. London: Penguin Books, 2004

Coulomb, F., *Economic Theories of Peace and War*. London: Routledge, 2004

Crenshaw, M., 'The Causes of Terrorism'. *Comparative Politics*, 13(4), 1981, pp. 379–399

Crocker, C.A., 'Emerging Failing States'. *Foreign Affairs*, September–October 2003, pp. 32–44

Crosston, M., *Shadow Separatism: Implications for Democratic Consolidation*. Aldershot, UK: Ashgate, 2004

Czwarno, M., 'Misjudging Islamic Terrorism: The Academic Community's Failure to Predict 9/11'. *Studies in Conflict and Terrorism*, 29(7), 2006, pp. 657–678

De la Corte, L., Sabucedo, J.M. and de Miguel, J.M., 'Three Hypotheses about the Causes of Political Violence and Their Psychosocial Assumptions'. *Estudios de Psicologia*, 20(3), November 2006, pp. 251–270

Dreyfuss, R., *Devil's Game: How the US Helped Unleash Fundamentalist Islam*. New York: Metropolitan Books, 2005

Eckert, R., 'Deprivation, Kultur oder Konflikt? Entstehungsbedingungen von Terrorismus'. *Leviathan*, 33(1), 2005, 124–133

Ehrlich, P.R. and Liu, J., 'Some Roots of Terrorism'. *Population and Environment*, 24(2), November 2002, pp. 183–192

Elliott, A., 'Where Boys Grow Up to Be Jihadis'. *New York Times*, 25 November 2007

Ellis, S., 'The Old Roots of Africa's New Wars'. *Militaire Spectator*, 173(1), 2004, pp. 25–33

Elsässer, J., *Wie der Schihad nach Europa kam: Gotteskrieger und Geheimdienste auf dem Balkan*. Vienna: NP Buchverlag, 2005

Enders, W. and Sandler, T., 'Distribution of Transnational Terrorism among Countries by Income Class and Geography after 9/11'. *International Studies Quarterly*, 50(2), June 2006, pp. 367–393

Englander, E.K., *Understanding Violence*, 3rd edn. Mahwah, NJ: Lawrence Erlbaum, 2007

Evans, A., 'Understanding Madrasahs: How Threatening Are They?' *Foreign Policy*, 85(1), January–February 2006, pp. 9–16

Ewald, U. and Turković, K., *Large-Scale Victimisation as a Potential Source of Terrorist Activities: Importance of Regaining Security in Post-conflict Societies*. Amsterdam: IOS Press, 2006

Falkenrath, R.A., 'The 9/11 Commission Report: A Review Essay'. *International Security*, 29(3), Winter 2004–2005, pp. 170–190

Fawn, R. and Hinnebush, R. (eds), *The Iraq War: Causes and Consequences*. Boulder, CO: Lynne Rienner, 2006

Fontan, V., 'Polarization between Occupier and Occupied in Post-Saddam Iraq: Colonial Humiliation and the Formation of Political Violence'. *Terrorism and Political Violence*, 18(2), Summer 2006, pp. 217–238

Fontan, V., 'Understanding Islamic Terrorism: Humiliation Awareness and the Role of Nonviolence'. In S. Ram and R. Summy (eds), *Nonviolence: An Alternative for Defeating Global Terror(ism)*. Hauppauge, NY: Nova Science Publishers, 2007

Forest, J.F. (ed.), *The Making of a Terrorist: Recruitment, Training and Root Causes*, 3 vol. Westport, CT: Praeger Security International, 2005

Forsberg, O.J., *Terrorism and Nationalism: Theory, Causes and Causers*. Saarbrücken: VDM Verlag Dr. Müller, 2007

Fox, J.A. and Levin, J., 'Mass Murder: An Analysis of Extreme Violence'. *Journal of Applied Psychoanalytic Studies*, 5(1), January 2003, pp. 47–64

Fox, J., 'The Increasing Role of Religion in State Failure: 1960 to 2004'. *Terrorism and Political Violence*, 19(3), Fall 2007, pp. 395–414

Fox, J. and Sandler, S. (guest editors), special Issue: 'Religion and World Conflict'. *Terrorism and Political Violence*, 17(3), 2005

Fox, J. and Squires, J., 'Threats to Primal Identities: A Comparison of Nationalism and Religion as Impacts on Ethnic Protest and Rebellion'. *Terrorism and Political Violence*, 13(1), 2001, pp. 88–102

Franks, J., *Rethinking The Roots of Terrorism*. Basingstoke, UK: Palgrave Macmillan, 2006

Friedman, T.L., 'The Humiliation Factor'. *New York Times*, 9 November 2003

Gerges, F.A., *The Far Enemy: Why Jihad Went Global*. Cambridge: Cambridge University Press, 2005

Gheith, A., 'Why We Fight America'. *MEMRI* no. 388, 12 June 2002

Girogi, P.P., 'The Origins of Violence: New Ideas and New Explanations Affecting Responses to Terrorism'. In S. Ram and R. Summy (eds), *Nonviolence: An Alternative for Defeating Global Terror(ism)*. Hauppauge, NY: Nova Science Publishers, 2007

Gurr, T.R., 'Economic Factors'. In L. Richardson (ed.), *The Roots of Terrorism*. London: Routledge, 2006, pp. 85–102

Gurr, T.R., 'The Political Origins of State Violence and Terror'. In M. Stohl and G.A. Lopez (eds), *Government Violence and Repression: An Agenda for Research*. Westport, CN: Greenwood Press, 1986, pp. 45–71

Gurr, T.R., *Why Men Rebel*. Woodrow Wilson School of Public and International Affairs, Center of International Studies. Princeton, NJ: Princeton University Press, 1970

Hafez, M.M., 'Explaining the Origins of Islamic Resurgence: Islamic Revivalism in Egypt and Indonesia'. *Journal of Social, Political and Economic Studies*, 22(3), Fall 1997, pp. 275–324

Hafez, M.M., *Why Muslims Rebel: Repression and Resistance in the Islamic World*. Boulder, CO: Lynne Rienner, 2003

Hafez, M.M., 'From Marginalization to Massacres: Explaining GIA Violence in Algeria'. In Q. Wiktorowicz (ed.), *Islamic Activism: A Social Movement Theory Approach*. Bloomington: Indiana University Press, 2004

Hafez, M.M., 'Dying to Be Martyrs: The Symbolic Dimension of Suicide Terrorism', In A. Pedahzur (ed.), *Root Causes of Suicide Terrorism: The Globalization of Martyrdom*. New York: Routledge, 2006

Hafez, M.M., 'Rationality, Culture, and Structure in the Making of Suicide Bombers: A Preliminary Theoretical Synthesis and Illustrative Case Study', *Studies in Conflict and Terrorism*, 29(2), March–April 2006, pp. 165–185

Hafez, M.M., *Manufacturing Human Bombs: The Making of Palestinian Suicide Bombers*. Washington, DC: United States Institute of Peace, 2006

Halliday, F., *Two Hours That Shook the World: September 11, 2001: Causes and Consequences*. London: Saqi Books, 2002

Heitmeyer, W. and Hagan, J. (eds), *Internationales Handbuch der Gewaltforschung*. Wiesbaden: Westdeutscher Verlag, 2002

Heyman, E. and Mickolus, E., 'Imitation by Terrorists: Quantitative Approaches to the Study of Diffusion Patterns in Transnational Terrorism'. In Y. Alexander and J.M. Gleason (eds), *Behavioral and Quantitative Perspectives on Terrorism*. New York: Pergamon, 1981, pp. 175–228

Heyman, E. and Mickolus, E., 'Observations on "Why Violence Spreads" '. *International Studies Quarterly*, 24(2), June 1980, pp. 299–305

Holbein, J.R., *The 9/11 Commission: Proceedings and Analysis*. Dobbs Ferry, NY: Oceana, 2005

Houghton, D.P., 'Explaining the Origins of the Iran Hostage Crisis: A Cognitive Perspective'. *Terrorism and Political Violence*, 18(2), Summer 2006, pp. 259–279

House Permanent Select Committee on Intelligence and the Senate Select Intelligence Committee, *Inquiry into the Terrorist Attacks of September 11, 2001*. Washington, DC: GPO, 2003

Hudson, R., *The Other (Veiled) Face of Suicide Bombing: Who Becomes a Shahida and Why?* Washington, DC: Federal Research Division, Library of Congress, November 2005

Hudson, R., *Who Becomes a Terrorist and Why*. Guilford, CT: Lyons Press, 2002

Huq, A., 'Faith Is Not Destiny: Three Inquiries into Jihadism and Its Sources'. *World Policy Journal*, 23(3), Fall 2006, pp. 99–106

Kean, T.H. and Hamilton, L.H., *Without Precedent: The Inside Story of the 9/11 Commission*. New York: Knopf, 2006

Kennett, R., 'The Social Theory of Globalization and Terrorism'. *Journal of Police Crisis Negotiations*, 6(2), 15 June 2006, pp. 49–63

Kepel, G., *Der Prophet und der Pharao: Das Beispiel Ägypten: Die Entwicklung des muslimischen Extremismus*. Munich: Piper, 1995

Khalilzad, Z. and Lesser, I.O. (eds), *Sources of Conflict in the 21st Century: Regional Futures and the US Strategy*. MR897-AF. Santa Monica, CA: RAND, Project Airforce, 1998

Kinzer, S., *All the Shah's Men: An American Coup and the Roots of Middle East Terror*. Hoboken, NJ: Wiley, 2003

Kitschelt, H., *State Failure, Globalization, and Regime Conflict: Origins of Contemporary International Terrorism in the Middle East*. Bonn: Friedrich Ebert Stiftung, International Policy Analysis Unit, 2003

Klare, M., *Blood and Oil: How America's Thirst for Petrol Is Killing Us*. London: Penguin Books, 2005

Knight, C., Murphy, M. and Mousseau, M., 'The Sources of Terrorism'. *International Terrorism*, 28(2), Fall 2003, pp. 192–198

Konzelmann, G., *Dschihad und die Wurzeln eines Weltkonflikts*. Munich: Ullstein Taschenbuch, 2003

Krueger, A.B., *What Makes a Terrorist? Economics and the Roots of Terrorism*. Lionel Robbins Lectures. Princeton, NJ: Princeton University Press, 2007

Krueger, A. and Maleckova, J., *Education, Poverty, Political Violence and Terrorism: Is There a Causal Connection?* Woodrow Wilson School, Princeton University, May 2002; also in *Journal of Economic Perspectives*, 17(4), November 2003, pp. 119–144

Krumwiede, H.-W., 'Ursachen des Terrorismus.' In P. Waldmann (ed.), *Determinanten des Terrorismus*. Weilerswist, Germany: Velbrück, 2005

Lacina, B., 'Explaining the Severity of Civil Wars'. *Journal of Conflict Resolution*, 50, April 2006, pp. 276–289

Lambert, S.P., *The Sources of Islamic Revolutionary Conduct*. Washington, DC: Joint Military Intelligence College, Centre for Strategic Intelligence Research with the Cooperation and Support of the Institute for National Security Studies (INSS), USAF Academy, Colorado Springs, April 2005

Lamy, S., English, R., Smith, S. *et al.*, 'Hegemony and Its Discontents: A Symposium'. *International Studies Review*, 7(4), December 2005, pp. 525–628

Latino, R.J. and Latino, K., *Root Cause Analysis (RCA): Improving Performance for Bottom-Line Results* (2nd edn.). Boca Raton, FL: CRC Press, 2002

Lindsey, H., *Everlasting Hatred: The Roots of Jihad*. Lake Elsinore, CA: Oracle House Publishing, 2005

Lutz, J.M. and Lutz, B.J. *Terrorism: Origins and Evolution*. New York: Palgrave, 2005

Marsella, A.J. and Moghaddam, F.M., 'The Origins and Nature of Terrorism: Foundations and Issues'. *Journal of Aggression, Maltreatment and Trauma*, 9(1–2), March 2005, pp. 19–31

Meertens, R., Doosje, B. and Prins, Y., *In iedereen schuilt een terrorist: een sociaal-psychologische analyse van terroristische sekten en aanslagen*. Schiedam, Netherlands: Scriptum, 2006

Meir-Levi, D., *The Nazi Roots of Palestinian Nationalism and Islamic Jihad*. Los Angeles: David Horowitz Freedom Center, 2007

Mekhennet, S., Sautter, C. and Hanfeld, M., *Die Kinder des Dschihad: Die neue Generation des islamistischen Terrors in Europa*. Munich: Piper, 2006

Mincheva, L., 'What Accounts for Cross-border Terrorism: A View from the Balkans and Central Africa', Research paper submitted for T.R. Gurr, *The Roots of Terrorism*, vol. 1. London: Routledge, 2006

Moghadam, A., 'The Roots of Suicide Terrorism: A Multi-causal Approach'. In A. Pedahzur (ed.), *Root Causes of Suicide Terrorism: The Globalization of Martyrdom*. London: Routledge, 2006

Moghadam, A., *The Roots of Terrorism*. Philadelphia: Chelsea House, 2006

Moghaddam, F.M. and Marsella, A.J., *Understanding Terrorism: Psychosocial Roots, Consequences and Interventions*. Washington, DC: American Psychological Association, 2004

Morgan, M.J. 'The Origins of New Terrorism'. *Parameters*, Spring 2004, pp. 29–43

Morgan, R., *The Demon Lover: The Routes of Terrorism*. London: Piatkuas, 2001

Naimark, N.M., *Terrorists and Social Democrats: The Russian Revolutionary*. Cambridge, MA: Harvard University Press, 1983

Newman, E., 'Exploring the "Root Causes" of Terrorism'. *Studies in Conflict and Terrorism*, 29(8), December 2006, pp. 749–772

Oberschall, A., 'Explaining Terrorism: The Contribution of Collective Action Theory'. *Sociological Theory*, 22(1), March 2004, pp. 26–37

O'Day, A. (ed.), *Dimensions of Terrorism*. Aldershot, UK: Ashgate, 2004

Oliver, A.M. and Steinberg, P., *The Road to Martyrs' Square: A Journey into the World of the Suicide Bomber*. Oxford: Oxford University Press, 2005

Oliveti, V., *Terror's Source: The Ideology of Wahhabi-Salafism and Its Consequences*. Birmingham: Amadeus Books, 2002

Piazza, J.A., 'Rooted in Poverty? Terrorism, Poor Economic Development and Social Cleavages'. *Terrorism and Political Violence*, 18(1), Spring 2006, pp. 159–177

Pintak, L., *Seeds of Hate: How America's Flawed Middle East Policy Ignited the Jihad*. London: Pluto, 2003

Quan Li, 'Does Democracy Promote or Reduce Transnational Terrorist Incidents?' *Journal of Conflict Resolution*, 49, April 2005, pp. 278–297

Quan Li and Schaub, D., 'Economic Globalization and Transnational Terrorism: A Pooled Time-Series Analysis'. *Journal of Conflict Resolution*, 48, April 2004, pp. 230–258

Ray, E. and Schaap, W.H. (eds), *Covert Action: The Roots of Terrorism*. Melbourne: Ocean Press, 2003

Reich, W. (ed.), *Origins of Terrorism: Psychologies, Ideologies, Theologies, States of Mind*. Washington, DC: Woodrow Wilson Center Press, 1998

Reuter, C., *Selbstmordattentäter: Warum Menschen zu lebenden Bomben werden*. Munich: Bertelsmann, 2003

Richardson, L., *What Terrorists Want: Understanding the Enemy, Containing the Threat*. London: Random House, 2006

Rotberg, R.I., *State Failure and State Weakness in a Time of Terror*. Cambridge, MA: World Peace Foundation, 2003

Rotenberg, M., *The Truce of Terror: Psycho-religious Fundamentalism: Roots and Remedies*. Jerusalem: Rubin Mass House, 2001

Rubbelke, D., 'Differing Motivations for Terrorism'. *Defence and Peace Economics*, 16(1), February 2005, pp. 19–27

Rubin, B., 'The Real Roots of Arab Anti-Americanism'. *Foreign Affairs*, November–December 2002, pp. 73–85

Scheffler, T., 'Islamischer Fundamentalismus und Gewalt'. In U. Kronfeld-Goharani (ed.), *Friedensbedrohung Terrorismus: Ursachen, Folgen und Gegenstrategien*. Münster: Lit-Verlag, 2005

Schmid, A. 'Root Causes of Terrorism: Some Conceptual Notes, a Set of Indicators, and a Model'. *Democracy and Security*, 1, 2005, pp. 127–136

Schneider, F. and Hofer, B., *Ursachen und Wirkungen des weltweiten Terrorismus: Eine Analyse der gesellschaftlichen und ökonomischen Auswirkungen und neue Ansätze zum Umgang mit dem Terror*. Wiesbaden: VS Velag, 2007

Schweitzer, G. and Schweizer, C.D., *A Fearless Enemy: The Origins of Modern Terrorism*. Jackson, TN: Perseus Books, 2002

Sedgwick, M., 'Inspiration and the Origins of Global Waves of Terrorism'. *Studies in Conflict and Terrorism*, 30(2), 2007, pp. 97–112

Serafini, A., 'Terrorism: A Cultural Phenomenon'. *Connections*, Spring 2005, pp. 61–74

Shanty, F., 'Introduction: Why America Was Attacked'. In *Encyclopedia of World Terrorism, 1996–2002*, vol. 4. Armonk, NY: M.E. Sharpe, 2003, pp. 3–11

Shoebat, W., *Why I Left Jihad: The Root of Terrorism and the Return of Radical Islam*. Newtown, PA: Top Executive Media, 2005

Shore, Z., *Breeding Bin Ladens: America, Islam, and the Future of Europe*. Baltimore: Johns Hopkins University Press, 2006

Slootman, M. and Tillie, J., *Processen van radicalisering: waarom sommige Amsterdamse Moslims radicaal worden*. Amsterdam: IMES, 2006

Soeters, J., *Ethnic Conflict and Terrorism: The Origins and Dynamics of Civil Wars*, London: Routledge, 2005

Speckhard, A. and Akhmedova, K., 'The New Chechen Jihad: Militant Wahhabism as a Radical Movement and a Source of Suicide Terrorism in Post-war Chechen Society'. *Democracy and Security*, 21, January–June 2006, pp. 103–155

Sprinzak, E., 'The Process of Delegitimization: Towards a Linkage Theory of Political Terrorism', *Terrorism and Political Violence*, 3(1), 1991, pp. 61–81

Staub, E., *The Roots of Evil: The Origins of Genocide and Other Group Violence*. Cambridge: Cambridge University Press, 1992

Stern, J., *Terror in the Name of God: Why Religious Militants Kill*. New York: Ecco, 2003

Taarnby, M., *Recruitment of Islamist Terrorists in Europe: Trends and Perspectives*. Research Report funded by the Danish Ministry of Justice, 14 January 2005

Testas, A., 'Economic Causes of Algeria's Political Violence'. *Terrorism and Political Violence*, 13(3), 2001, pp. 127–144

Testas, A., 'Determinants of Terrorism in the Muslim World: An Empirical Cross-Sectional Analysis'. *Terrorism and Political Violence*, 16(2), 2004, pp. 253–273

Thayer, B.A., *Darwin and International Relations: On the Evolutionary Origins of War and Ethnic Conflict*. Lexington: University Press of Kentucky, 2004

Toft, M.D., *The Geography of Ethnic Violence*. Princeton, NJ: Princeton University Press, 2003

Trento, J.J., *Prelude to Terror: The Rogue CIA and the Legacy of America's Private Intelligence Network*. New York: Carroll & Graff, 2005

Tunç, H., 'What Was It All About After All? The Causes of the Iraq War'. *Contemporary Security Policy*, 26(2), August 2005, pp. 335–355

Urdal, H., 'A Clash of Generations? Youth Bulges and Political Violence'. *International Studies Quarterly*, 50(3), September 2006, pp. 607–629

van der Valk, A. 'Racism, a Threat to Global Peace'. *International Journal of Peace Studies*, 8(2), 2003, pp. 45–66

Vertigans, S., *Islamic Roots and Resurgence in Turkey: Understanding and Explaining the Muslim Resurgence*. New York: Praeger, 2007

Victoroff, J. (ed.), *Social and Psychological Factors in the Genesis of Terrorism*. Amsterdam: IOS Press, 2006

Volkan, V.D., *Bloodlines: From Ethnic Pride to Ethnic Terrorism*. New York: Farrar, Straus & Giroux, 1997

Von Hippel, K., 'The Roots of Terrorism: Probing the Myths'. *Political Quarterly*, 73 (Supplement 1), August 2002, pp. 25–39

Vranckx, R., *Geesten van het avondland: de roots van het moslimterrorisme*. Amsterdam: Meulenhoff, 2006

Vries, M. de, *Radicalisering gelokaliseerd: een wetenschappelijk onderzoek naar radicalisering in Nederland*. The Hague, SGBO, 2006

Waldmann, P., *Determinanten des Terrorismus*. Weilerswist, Germany: Velbrück, 2005

Weinberg, L., 'Turning to Terror'. *Comparative Politics*, 23(4), 1991, pp. 423–438

White, R., 'Political Violence by the Non-aggrieved: Explaining the Political Participation of Those with No Apparent Grievances'. In D. Della Porta (ed.), *International Social Movement Research: Participation in Clandestine Political Organizations*. Greenwich, CT: JAI Press, 1992

Wieviorka, M., *The Making of Terrorism*. Chicago: University of Chicago Press, 1993

WODC, *Radicalisering en jihad: justitiële verkenningen* 2005/2. The Hague: WODC, 2005 (contributions by R. Coolsaet, O. Roy, R. de Wijk, P. Mascini, M. Verhoeven, M. van Leeuwen and H.T. van der Veen)

Woodworth, P., 'Why Do They Kill? The Basque Conflict in Spain'. *World Policy Journal*, 18(1), 2001. Available at: www.allbusiness.com/public-administration/national-security-international/896365–1.html (accessed 14 April 2009)

Zimmerman, J., 'Sayyid Qutb's Influence on the 11 September Attacks'. *Terrorism and Political Violence*, 16(2), April–June 2004, pp. 222–252

R. Ideologies and doctrines of violence and violent liberation

Abraham, A.J., *Islamic Fundamentalism and the Doctrine of Jihad*. Lima, OH: Wyndham Hall Press, 2002

Abu Bakr, N., *The Management of Savagery: The Most Critical Stage through Which the Umma Will Pass*, trans. W. McCants. Cambridge, MA: John M. Olin Institute for Strategic Studies, 23 May 2006

Akbar, M.J., *The Shade of Swords: Jihad and the Conflict between Islam and Christianity*. London: Routledge, 2002

Ali, S.H., 'Islamic Education and Conflict: Understanding the Madrassahs of Pakistan'. Paper presented at the US Institute of Peace, 24 June 2005

Al-Saeed, R., *Al-Irhaab Al-Mutaslam* (Islamized Terrorism). Cairo: Akhbar El-Yom, 2004

Artz, D., 'The Role of Compulsion in Islamic Conversion: *Jihad, Dhimma* and *Ridda*'. *Buffalo Human Rights Law Review*, 8(15)

Attawheedy, Abu Mohamed (pseudonym of Belal Saadallah Khazaal) (compiler), *Provision on the Rules of Jihad: Short Judicial Rulings and Organizational Instructions for Fighters and Mujahideen against Infidels.* Placed on jihadist website, September 2003–May 2004: www.jihadwatch.org (accessed 25 October 2010)

Ayoob, M., *The Many Faces of Islam: Religion and Politics in the Muslim World.* London: Eurospan, 2007

Azzam, M., *Al-Qa'ida: The Misunderstood Wahhabi Connection and the Ideology of Violence.* London: Royal Institute of International Affairs, February 2003

Azzam, M., 'Islamism Revisited'. *International Affairs*, 82(6), 2006, pp. 1119–1132

Babbin, J.L., *In the Words of Our Enemies.* Washington, DC: Regnery, 2007

Badran, M., *Women and Radicalization.* DIIS Working Paper 2006. Copenhagen: Danish Institute for International Studies

Baran, Z. (ed.), *Understanding Sufism and Its Potential Role in US Policy.* Nixon Center Conference Report, March 2004. Available at: www.nixoncenter.org/Monographs/HizbutahrirIslamsPoliticalInsurgency.pdf (accessed 14 April 2009)

Baran, Z. (ed.), *The Challenge of Hizb Ut-Tahrir: Deciphering and Combating Radical Islamist Ideology.* Washington, DC: Nixon Center, September 2004. Available at: www.nixoncenter.org/Program%20Briefs/PB%202004/confrephiztahrir.pdf (accessed 14 April, 2009)

Baran, Z., *Hizb Ut-Tahrir: Islam's Political Insurgency.* Washington, DC: Nixon Center, 2004

Bergen, P., 'The Madrassa Scapegoat'. *Washington Quarterly*, 29(2), Spring 2006, pp. 117–125

Bergesen, A.J., *The Sayyid Qutb Reader.* London: Routledge, 2007

Blancard, C.M., *Al-Qa'ida: Statements and Evolving Ideology.* Washington, DC: Congress, RL32759, updated 26 January 2005

Bratkowski, S., 'Killing and Terror: The Cultural Tradition'. *American Behavioral Scientist*, 48(6), February 2005, pp. 764–782

Brooker, P., 'Terrorism and Counternarratives: Don Delillo and the New York Imaginary'. *New Formations*, no. 57, Winter 2005–2006, pp. 10–25

Bukay, D. (ed.), *Muhammed's Monsters: A Comprehensive Guide to Radical Islam for Western Audiences.* Manchester: New Leaf Press, 2004

Burleigh, M., *Sacred Causes: The Clase of Religion and Politics: From the Great War to the War on Terror.* London: HarperCollins, 2007

Catherwood, C., *Religion and Terrorism.* Oxford: Blackwell, 2007

Chapman, R.D., Book reviews, 'The View from the Mosque'. *Journal of Intelligence and Counterintelligence*, 18(4), Winter 2005–2006, pp. 734–744

Charters, D.A., *Something Old, Something New . . .? Understanding the 'Revolutionary' Nature of Jihadism.* Honolulu: International Studies Association (ISA), March 2005

Cook, D., *Understanding Jihad.* Berkeley: University of California Press, 2005

Coolsaet, R., 'Het islamitische terrorisme: percepties wieden en kweekvijvers dreggen'. *Justiële Verkenningen*, 31(2), March 2005, pp. 9–27

Coolsaet, R., *Jihadi Terrorism and the Radicalisation Challenge in Europe.* Aldershot, UK: Ashgate, 2008

Crick, B., 'Justifications of Violence'. *Political Quarterly*, 77(4), October–December 2006, pp. 433–438

Crossette, B., 'When Violence Is an End in Itself'. *World Policy Journal*, 24(1), Spring 2007, pp. 57–58

CSIS, *Currents and Crosscurrents of Radical Islamism.* Washington, DC: Center for Strategic and International Studies, April 2006

Dalrymple, W., 'Inside the Madrasas'. *New York Review of Books*, 1 December 2005, pp. 16–20

Debrix, F., 'Discouses of War, Geographies of Abjection: Reading Contemporary American Ideologies of Terror'. *Third World Quarterly*, 26(7), 2005, pp. 1157–1172

Dein, S. and Littlewood, R., 'Apocalyptic Suicide: From a Pathological to an Eschatological Interpretation'. *International Journal of Social Psychiatry*, 51, September 2005, pp. 198–210

Delong-Bas, N.J., *Wahhabi Islam: From Revival and Reform to Global Jihad.* Oxford: Oxford University Press, 2004

Devji, F., *Landscapes of the Jihad: Militancy, Morality Modernity.* Ithaca, NY: Cornell University Press, 2005

Duran, K., 'Jihadism in Europe'. *Journal of Counterterrorism and Security International*, Fall 2000, pp. 12–15

Eagleton, T., *Holy Terror.* Oxford: Oxford University Press, 2005

Ernst, C.W., *Following Muhammad: Rethinking Islam in the Contemporary World.* Chapel Hill: University of North Carolina Press, 2004

Esposito, J.L., *What Everyone Needs to Know about Islam.* Oxford: Oxford University Press, 2002

Esposito, J.L., *Unholy War: Terror in the Name of Islam.* Oxford: Oxford University Press, 2003

Evans, A., 'Understanding Madrasahs: How Threatening Are They?' *Foreign Policy*, 85(1), January–February 2006, pp. 9–16

Farah, D., *The Little Explored Offshore Empire of the International Muslim Brotherhood*. Alexandria, VA: International Assessment and Strategy Center, 18 April 2006. Available at: www.strategycenter.net/printVersion/print_pub.asp?pubID=102 (accessed 7 April 2009)

Fox, J. and Sandler, S. (eds), *Religion in World Conflict*. London: Routledge, 2007

Freedom House (Center for Religious Freedom), *Radical Islam's Rules: The Worldwide Spread of Extreme Shari'a Law*. Lanham MD: Rowman & Littlefield, 2005

Fuller, G.E., *The Future of Political Islam*. Basingstoke, UK: Palgrave, 2003

Gibbs, S., 'Islam and Islamic Extremism: An Existential Analysis'. *Journal of Humanistic Psychology*, 45, April 2005, pp. 156–203

Gritti, R. and Allam, M., *Islam, Italy: Who the Muslims Are That Live among Us and What They Think*. Milan: Guerini, 2001

Habeck, M., *Knowing the Enemy: Jihadist Ideology and the War on Terror*. London: Yale University Press, 2006

Hasan, N., *Laskar Jihad: Islam, Militancy, and the Quest for Identity in Post-New Order Indonesia*. Ithaca, NY: Cornell University, 2006

Hassan, M., 'Key Considerations in Counter-ideological Work against Terrorist Ideology'. *Studies in Conflict and Terrorism*, 29(6), September 2006, pp. 531–558

Haynes, J., 'Al Qaeda: Ideology and Action'. *Critical Review of International Social and Political Philosophy*, 8(2), June 2005, pp. 177–191

Hazim, H., 'Perpetual Jihad: Striving for a Caliphate'. *Global Crime*, 7(3–4), August 2006, pp. 428–445

Herf, J., Steinberg, G., Musharbash, Y. *et al.*, 'Terror: der neue Totalitarismus [Spezial]'. *Internationale Politik*, 60(11), November 2005, pp. 6–65

Hirschfeld, U., *Terrorism, Jihad, and Sacred Vengeance*. Gieben, Germany: Psychosozial Verlag 2004

Hirschmann, K., 'Internationaler Terrorismus gestern und heute: Entwicklungen, Ausrichtungen, Ziele'. In H. Frank and K. Hirschmann (eds), *Die weltweite Gefahr: Terrorismus als internationale Herausforderung*. Berlin: Berlin-Verlag, 2002

Hubband, M., *Warriors of the Prophet: The Struggle for Islam*, Boulder, CO: Westview Press, 1998

Hughes, M. and Johnson, G. (eds), *Fanaticism and Conflict in the Modern Age*. London: Frank Cass, 2004

Iannaccone, L. and Berman, E., 'Religious Extremism: The Good, the Bad, and the Deadly'. *Public Choice*, 128(1–2), July 2006, pp. 109–129

Israeli, R., 'A Manual of Islamic Fundamentalist Terrorism'. *Terrorism and Political Violence*, Winter 2002, pp. 23–40

Juergensmeyer, M., *Terror in the Mind of God: The Global Rise of Religious Violence*. Berkeley: University of California Press, 2000

Juergensmeyer, M., *Religion in Global Civil Society*. Oxford: Oxford University Press, 2005

Kamrava, M., *The New Voices of Islam*. London: I.B. Tauris, 2006

Kastfelt, N., *Role of Religion in African Civil Wars*. New York: Palgrave Macmillan, 2005

Kepel, G., *Das Schwarzbuch de Dschihad: Aufstieg und Niedergang des Islamismus*. Munich: Piper Verlag, 2002

Kepel, G., *Jihad: The Trail of Political Islam*. Cambridge, MA: Harvard University Press, 2002

Kepel, G., *Die neuen Kreuzzüge: Die arabische Welt und die Zukunft des Westens*. Munich: Piper, 2004

Kepel, G., *Fitna*. Paris: Gallimard, 2004

Kepel, G. and Milelli, J.P. (eds), *Al Qaeda in Its Own Words*. Cambridge, MA: Harvard University Press, 2008

Khan, S., 'Islamic Fundamentalism in the Asia-Pacific Region: Failures of Civil Societies or Backlash against the US Hegemony'. In E.V. Linden (ed.), *Terrorism in Focus*, vol. 9. Hauppauge, NY: Nova Science Publishers

Khosrokhavar, F., *Quand Al-Qaïda parle*. Paris: Grasset & Fasquelle, 2006

Klausen, J., *The Islamic Challenge: Politics and Religion in Western Europe*. Oxford: Oxford University Press, 2005

Labi, N., 'Jihad 0.2'. *The Atlantic Quarterly*, July–August, 2006, pp. 102–108

Lacorne, D. and Judt, T., *With Us or against Us: Studies in Global Anti-Americanism*. London: Palgrave, 2005

Lambert, S.P., *The Sources of Islamic Revolutionary Conduct*. Washington, DC: Joint Military Intelligence College, Center for Strategic Intelligence Research with the Cooperation and Support of the Institute for National Security Studies (INSS), USAF Academy, Colorado Springs, April 2005

Lane, J.E. and Redissi, H., *Religion and Politics: Islam and Muslim Civilisation*. Aldershot, UK: Ashgate, 2004

Larson, J.P., *Understanding Religious Violence: Thinking outside the Box on Terrorism*. Aldershort, UK: Ashgate, 2004

Lewis, B., *The Crisis in Islam: Holy War and Unholy Terror*. New York: Modern Library, 2003

Lincoln, B., *Holy Terrors: Thinking about Religion after September 11*. Chicago: University of Chicago Press, 2003

Lindsey, H., *Everlasting Hatred: The Roots of Jihad*. Lake Elsinore, CA: Oracle House Publishing, 2002

Lohlker, R., 'Die neue GihId-Theologie'. *Wiener Zeitschrift für die Kunde des Morgenlandes*, 96, 2006, pp. 211–240

McAuley, D., 'The Ideology of Osama bin Laden: Nation, Tribe and World Economy'. *Journal of Political Ideologies*, 10(3), October 2005, pp. 269–287

Maddy-Weitzman, B. and Inbar, E., *Religious Radicalism in the Greater Middle East*. London: Portland, 1997

Malik, S.K., *The Quranic Concept of War*. Lahore, Pakistan: Associated Printers, 1979

Mamdani, M., 'Whither Political Islam? Understanding the Modern Jihad'. *Foreign Affairs*, January–February, 2005, pp. 148–155

Mandaville, P., *Global Political Islam*, London: Routledge, 2007

Mascini, P. and Verhoeven, M., *Literatuurstudie naar de facilitering van de gewelddadige jihad*. The Hague: WODC, *Cahiers* 2005–3, 2005

Mazarr, M.J., *Unmodern Man in the Modern World: Radical Islam, Terrorism and the War on Modernity*. Cambridge: Cambridge University Press, 2007

Mitchell, R.P., *The Society of Muslim Brothers*. Oxford: Oxford University Press, 1993

Moaddel, M., *Islamic Modernism, Nationalism, and Fundamentalism*. Chicago: University of Chicago Press, 2005

Moubayed, S., 'The History of Political and Militant Islam In Syria'. *Terrorism Monitor*, 3(16), 11 August 2005. Available at: www.jamestown.org/programs/gta/single/?tx_ttnews[tt_news]=550&tx_ttnews[backPid]= 180&no_cache=1 (accessed 15 April, 2009)

Mukhina, I., 'Islamic Terrorism and the Question of National Liberation or Problems of Contemporary Chechen Terrorism'. *Studies in Conflict and Terrorism*, 28(6), 2005, pp. 515–532

Müller, R. (ed.), *Islamismus und terroristische Gewalt*. Reihe Orientalistik, Band 8. Würzburg: Ergon Verlag, 2004

Murphy, J.F. Jr., *Sword of Islam: Muslim Extremism from the Arab Conquest to the Attack on America*. Amhurst, NY: Prometheus Books, 2002

Myers, J.C., 'The Quranic Concept of War'. *Parameters*, Winter 2006–2007, pp. 108–127

Napoleoni, L., 'Modern Jihad: The Islamist Crusade'. *SAIS Review*, Summer–Fall, 2003, pp. 53–66

NCTB, *Radicalisation in Broader Perspective*. The Hague: National Coordinator for Counterterrorism, 2007

Nesser, P., 'Jihadism in Western Europe after the Invasion of Iraq: Tracing Motivational Influences from the Iraq War on Jihadist Terrorism in Western Europe'. *Studies in Conflict and Terrorism*, 29(4), June 2006, pp. 323–342

Novikov, E., 'The World Muslim League: Agent of Wahhabi Propagation in Europe'. *Terrorism Monitor*, 3(9), 6 May 2005

O'Ballance, E., *Islamic Fundamentalist Terrorism, 1979–95: The Iranian Connection*. Basingstoke, UK: Macmillan, 1997

O'Boyle, G., 'Theories of Justification and Political Violence: Examples from four Groups'. *Terrorism and Political Violence*, 14(2), Summer 2002, pp. 23–46

Open Source Center (OSC), *Compilation of Usama bin Laden Statements, 1994–January 2004*. ISC Report GMP20040209000243, 9 February 2004

Pacini, A., *The Muslim Brothers and the Debate on Political Islam*. Turin: Giovanni Agnelli Foundation Publications, 1996

Palmer, M. and Palmer, P., *At the Heart of Terror: Islam, Jihadists and America's War on Terrorism*. Lanham, MD: Rowman & Littlefield, 2004

Peters, R., *Jihad in Classical and Modern Islam*. Princeton, NJ: Markus Wiener, 1996

Phares, W., *Future Jihad: Terrorist Strategies against America*. New York: Palgrave Macmillan, 2005

Raddatz, H.P., *Von Allah zum Terror? Der Djihad und die Deformierung des Westens*. Munich: Herbig Verlag, 2002

Rashid, A., *Taliban: Militant Islam, Oil and Fundamentalism in Central Asia*. London: Yale University Press, 2001

Rashid, A., *Jihad: The Rise of Militant Islam in Central Asia*. London: Yale University Press, 2002

Rotenberg, M., *The Truce of Terror: Psycho-religious Fundamentalism: Roots and Remedies*. Jerusalem: Rubin Mass House, 2001

Roy, O., *Globalized Islam: The Search for a New Ummah*. New York: Columbia University Press, 2005

Ruthven, M., *Fundamentalism: The Search for Meaning*. Oxford: Oxford University Press, 2004

Ryan, K.J., *Radical Eye for the Infidel Guy: Inside the Strange World of Militant Islam*. New York: Prometheus Books, 2007

Sabucedo, J.M., Barreto, I., Borja, H., de la Corte, L. and Durán, M., 'Legitimising Violence and Its Context: Textual Analysis of the FARC-EP Discourse'. *Estudios de Psicología*, 27(3), November 2006, pp. 279–291

Sanchez, I.R., *L'Islam révolutionnaire*. Paris: Editions du Rocher, 2003

Schbley, A., 'Religious Terrorism, the Media, and International Islamization Terrorism: Justifying the Unjustifiable'. *Studies in Conflict and Terrorism*, 27(3), May–June 2004, pp. 207–233

Schluchter, W., *Fundamentalismus, Terrorismus, Krieg*. Weilerswist, Germany: Velbrück, 2003

Shepard, W.E., *Sayyid Qutb and Islamic Activism: A Translation and Critical Analysis of 'Social Justice in Islam'*. Leiden: Brill, 1996

Sheridan, G., 'Jihad Archipelago'. *National Interest*, no. 78, Winter 2004–2005, pp. 73–80

Shipp, G., *Militant Jihad: The Mentality of Muslim Terrorists*. Bishop Auckland, UK: Covenant Publishing, 2004

Sidel, J.T., *Riots, Pogroms, Jihad: Religious Violence in Indonesia*. Ithaca, NY: Cornell University Press, 2006

Silber, M.D. and Bhatt, A., *Radicalization in the West: The Homegrown Threat*. New York: NYPD Intelligence Division, August 2007

Sookhdeo, P., *Understanding Islamic Terrorism: The Islamic Doctrine of War*. McLean, VA: Isaac Publishing, 2004

Speckhard, A. and Akhmedova, K., *The New Chechen Jihad: Militant Wahhabism as a Radical Movement and a Source of Suicide Terrorism in Post-War Chechen Society*. London: Routledge, 2006

Spencer, R. (ed.), *The Myth of Islamic Tolerance: Islamic Law and Non-Muslims*. New York: Prometheus, 2005

Spencer, R., *Onward Muslim Soldiers: How Jihad Threatens America and the West*. Washington, DC: Regenery, 2003

Spencer, R., *The Politically Incorrect Guide to Islam and the Crusades*. Washington, DC: Regenery, 2005

Stern, J., *Terror in the Name of God: Why Religious Militants Kill*. New York: Ecco, 2003

Taheri, A., *Morden für Allah: Terrorismus im Auftrag der Mullahs*. Munich: Droemer Knaur, 1993

Tessore, D., *Der heilige Krieg im Christentum and Islam*. Düsseldorf: Patmos, 2004

Tétreault, M.A. and Denemark, R.A. (eds) *Gods, Guns and Globalization: Religious Radicalism and International Political Economy*. Boulder CO: Lynne Rienner, 2004

Tibi, B, *Islamischer Fundamentalismus, moderne Wissenschaft und Technologie*. Frankfurt am Main: Suhrkamp, 1992

Tibi, B., *The Challenge of Fundamentalism: Political Islam and the New World Disorder*. Berkeley, CA: University of California Press, 2004

Toft, M.D., 'Getting Religion? The Puzzling Case of Islam and Civil War'. *International Security*, 41(4), Spring 2007, pp. 97–131

Trifkovic, S., *The Sword of the Prophet: Islam. History, Theology, Impact on the World*. Salisbury, MA: Regina Orthodox Press, 2002

Ulfkotte, U., *Propheten des Terrors*. Munich: Goldmann Verlag, 2001

Vedino, L., *Islam, Islamism and Jihadism in Italy: Current Trends in Islamist Ideology*. Washington, DC: Hudson Institute, 2008

Vedino, L., 'The Muslim Brotherhood's Conquest of Europe'. *Middle East Quarterly*, 12(1), Winter 2005, 25–34

Venkatraman, A., 'Religious Basis for Islamic Terrorism: The Quran and Its Interpretations'. *Studies in Conflict and Terrorism*, 30(3), 2007, pp. 229–248

Viorst, M., *In the Shadow of the Prophet: The Struggle for the Soul of Islam*. Boulder, CO: Westview Press, 2001

Warburg, G., *Islam, Sectarianism and Politics in Sudan since the Mahdiyya*. London: C. Hurst, 2003

Ward, K., *Is Religion Dangerous?* Grand Rapids, MI: Eerdmans, 2007

Weaver, M.A., *A Portrait of Egypt: A Journey through the World of Militant Islam*. New York: Farrar, Straus & Giroux, 1999

Weinberg, L. and Pedazhur, A. (eds), *Religious Fundamentalism and Political Extremism*. London: Frank Cass, 2004

Weinberg, L., Pedazhur, A. and Hirsch-Hoefler, S., 'The Challenges of Conceptualizing Terrorism'. *Terrorism and Political Violence*, 16(4), October–December 2004, pp. 777–794

Wessels, M., *De extremistische variant van de Islam*. The Hague: Teldersstichting, 2001

Wessels, M., *De radicaal-islamitische ideologie van de Hofstadgroep: de inhoud en de bronnen*. The Hague: Teldersstichting, 2006

Whine, M., *Is Hizb ut-Tahrir Changing Strategy or Tactics?* Center for Eurasian Policy Occasional Research Paper Series 1 (Hizb ut-Tahrir), no. 1. Washington, DC: Hudson Institute August 2006

White, J.R., 'Political Eschatology: A Theology of Antigovernmental Extremism'. *American Behavioral Scientist*, 44, February 2001, pp. 937–956

Wiktorowicz, Q., *The Management of Islamic Activism: Salafis, the Muslim Brotherhood, and State Power in Jordan*. New York: State University of New York Press, 2001

Wiktorowicz, Q., 'The New Global Threat: Transnational Salafis and Jihad'. *Middle East Policy*, 8(4), December 2001, pp. 18–38

Wiktorowicz, Q., 'Framing Jihad: Intramovement Framing Contests and Al-Qaeda's Struggle for Sacred Authority'. *International Review of Social History*, 49, 2004, pp. 159–177

Wiktorowicz, Q., 'A Genealogy of Radical islam'. *Studies in Conflict and Terrorism*, 28(2), March–April 2005, pp. 75–97

Wiktorowicz, Q. and Kaltenhaler, K., 'The Rationality of Radical Islam'. In D.J. Caraley and K.L. Morales (eds), *Terrorist Attacks and Nuclear Proliferation: Strategies for Overlapping Dangers*. New York: Academy of Political Science, 2007

Wiktorowicz, Q. and Kaltner, J., 'Killing in the Name of Islam: Al-Qa'ida's Justification for September 11'. *Middle East Policy*, 10(2), Summer 2003, pp. 76–92

S. Countermeasures against terrorism

S.1 General

Aaron, D.L., Beauchesne, A.M., Buswell, F.G., Nelson, C.R., Riley, K.J. and Zimmer, B., *The Post 9/11 Partnership: Transatlantic Cooperation against Terror.* Washington, DC: Atlantic Council of the United States, 2004

Ablah, E., Wetta-Hall, R., Molgaard, C.A., Fredrickson, D.D., Grube, C.D., Skalacki, M.K., Wolfe, D.J. and Cook, D.J., 'Evaluation of Interdisciplinary Terrorism Preparedness Programmes: A Pilot Forum Group Study'. *Journal of Allied Health*, 35(4), Winter 2006, pp. 189–197

Abou el Fadl, K.M., *The Great Theft: Wrestling Islam from the Extremists.* San Francisco: Harper, 2005

ACIA, *Counterterrorism in a European and International Perspective: Interim Report on the Prohibition of Torture.* The Hague: Advisory Council on International Affairs, December 2005

Adam, H. and Moodley, K., *Seeking Mandela. Peacemaking between Israelis and Palestinians.* Philadelphia: Temple University Press, 2006

Agha, H., Feldman, S., Khalidi, A. and Schiff, Z., *Track-II Diplomacy: Lessons from the Middle East.* Cambridge, MA: MIT Press, 2005

Ahmed, A. and Forst, B. (eds), *After Terror: Promoting Dialogue among Civilizations.* Cambridge: Polity Press, 2005

Ahmed, S., 'No Size Fits All: Lessons in Making Peace and Rebuilding States'. *Foreign Affairs*, January–February 2005, pp. 162–169

Akerboom, E.S.M., *Counterterrorism in the Netherlands.* Zoetermear, Netherlands: AIVD, 2004. Available at: www.fas.org/irp/world/netherlands/ct.pdf (accessed 15 April 2009)

Akhlaque, H., 'Information Technology and Surveillance: Implications for Public Administration in a New World Order'. *Social Science Computer Review*, 23, November 2005, pp. 480–485

Aksu, M., Beperking van de vrijheid van meningsuiting (10 EVRM) met een beroep op terrorismebetrijding. *NCJM-Bulletin*, 30(4), June 2005, pp. 384–397

Al-Azmeh, A., *Making Governance Work against Radicalisation.* DIS Working Paper 2006/4. Copenhagen: Danish Institute for International Studies, 2006

Albini, J.L., 'Dealing with the Modern Terrorist: The Need for Changes in Strategies and Tactics in the New War on Terrorism'. *Criminal Justice Policy Review*, 12, December 2001, pp. 255–281

Albrecht, H. and Schlumberger, O., 'Waiting for Godot: Regime Change without Democratization in the Middle East'. *International Political Science Review/ Revue Internationale de Science Politique*, 25, October 2004, pp. 371–392

Aldis, A.C. and Herd, G.P. (eds), *The Ideological War on Terror: Worldwide Strategies for Counter-terrorism.* London: Routledge, 2006

Alexander, D.C., *Business Confronts Terrorism.* Madison: University of Wisconsin Press, 2003

Alexander, Y. (ed.), *Counterterrorism Strategies: Successes and Failures of Six Nations.* Dulles, VA: Potomac Books, 2006

Alexander, Y. and Woolsey, R.J., *Combating Terrorism: Strategies of Ten Countries,* Ann Arbor: University of Michigan Press, 2002

Allin, D.H. and Simon, S., 'America's Predicament'. *Survival*, 46(4), Winter 2004–2005, pp. 7–30

Allison, G. and Kokoshin, A., 'US–Russian Alliance against Megaterrorism', *Boston Globe*, 16 November 2001

Amoore, L. and de Goede, M. (eds), *Risk and the War on Terror.* London: Routledge, 2008

Anderson, R.H. and Brackney, R., *Understanding the Insider Threat: Proceedings of a March 2004 Workshop.* Santa Monica, CA: RAND, 2005

Anderson, W.J.L., *Disrupting Threat Finances: Utilization of Financial Information to Disrupt Terrorist Organizations in the Twenty-First Century.* Fort Leavenworth, KS: School of Advanced Military Studies, United States Army Command and General Staff College, 2007

Anon. [Michael Scheuer]. *Imperial Hubris: Why the West Is Losing the War on Terror.* New York: Brassey's, 2004

Arasly, J., 'Terrorism and Civil Aviation Security: Problems and Trends'. *Connections*, Spring 2005, pp. 75–89

Arkin, W., *Code Names: Deciphering US Military Plans, Programs and Operations in the 9/11 World.* Hanover: Steerforth Press, 2005

Art, R.J. and Richardson, L., 'Countering Terrorist Movements in India: Kashmir and Khalistan'. In *Democracy and Counterterrorism: Lessons from the Past.* Washington, DC: United States Institute Peace Press, 2006

Art, R.J. and Richardson, L. (eds), *Democracy and Counterterrorism: Lessons from the Past*. Washington, DC: United States Institute of Peace Press, 2007

Ashcroft, J., *Never Again: Securing America and Restoring Justice*. New York: Center Street, 2006

Austin, A., Fischer, M. and Ropers, N. (eds), *Transforming Ethnopolitical Conflict: The Berghof Handbook*. Wiesbaden: Verlag für Sozialwissenschaften, 2004

Australian Government, *Combating Terrorism in the Transport Sector: Economic Costs and Benefits*. Department of Foreign Affairs and Trade, Economic Analytical Unit, 2004

Aviv, J., *The Complete Terrorism Survival Guide: How to Travel, Work and Live in Safety*. Huntingdon, NY: Juris Publishing, 2003

Aydinli, E., 'From Finances to Transnational Mobility: Searching for the Global Jihadists' Achilles Heel'. *Terrorism and Political Violence*, 18(2), Summer 2006, pp. 301–313

Aylwin-Foster, N., 'Changing the Army for Counterinsurgency Operations'. *Military Review*, November–December 2005, pp. 2–15

Baer, R., *See No Evil: The True Story of a Ground Soldier in the CIA's War on Terrorism*. New York: Crown, 2002

Baer, R., 'Wanted: Spies Unlike Us'. *Foreign Policy*, no. 147, March–April 2005, pp. 66–71

Baer, R., 'Getting the CIA Back in the Game'. *Foreign Policy*, March–April 2005, pp. 66–70

Baker, J.C. and United States National Geospatial-Intelligence Agency, *Mapping the Risks: Assessing Homeland Security Implications of Publicly Available Geospatial Information*. Santa Monica, CA: RAND, 2004

Bakker, E., 'The Cracks in EU Anti-Terrorism Co-operation That Invite Attack'. *Europe's World*, 1, Autumn 2005, pp. 128–133

Bakker, E., 'Bestrijding van terrorisme-financiering: succes en falen in beleid'. *Atlantisch Perspectief*, 30(3), 2006, pp. 11–17

Bamford, J., *NSA: Die Anatomie des mächtigsten Geheimdienstes der Welt*. Munich: Bertelsmann, 2001

Banlaoi, R.C., *War on Terrorism in Southeast Asia*. Manila: Rex Book Store, 2004

Bapat, N.A., 'Insurgency and the Opening of Peace Process'. *Journal of Peace Research*, 42, November 2005, pp. 699–717

Bapat, N.A., 'State Bargaining with Transnational Groups'. *International Studies Quarterly*, 50(1), March 2006, pp. 213–229

Baran, Z., 'Fighting the War of Ideas'. *Foreign Affairs*, 84(6), November–December 2005, pp. 68–78

Barrenada, I., 'Alliance of Civilizations, Spanish Public Diplomacy and Cosmopolitian Proposal'. *Mediterranean Politics*, 11(1), March 2006, pp. 99–104

Basile, M., 'Going to the Source: Why Al Qaeda's Financial Network Is Likely to Withstand the Current War on Terrorist Financing'. *Studies in Conflict and Terrorism*, 27, 2004, pp. 169–185

Batabyal, A., 'ASEAN's Quest for Security: A Theoretical Explanation'. *International Studies*, 41, October 2004, pp. 349–369

Baud, J., *Le renseignement et la lutte contre le terrorisme: stratégies et perspectives Internationales*. Panazol, France: LaVauzelle, 2005

Baylis, J., *Contemporary Strategy*. New York: Holmes & Meier, 1987

Becker, T., *Terrorism and the State: Rethinking the Rules of State Responsibility*. Oxford: Hart, 2006

Beliaev, I.P. and Marks, J.D., *Common Ground on Terrorism: Soviet–American Cooperation against the Politics of Terror*. New York: W.W. Norton, 1991

Benjamin, D., *Terrorism and International Organizations*. Washington, DC: United Nations Foundation, 2004

Bercovitch, J. and Rubin, J.Z., *Mediation in International Relations: Multiple Approaches to Conflict Management*. New York: St Martin's Press, 1992

Bergen, P., 'The War on Terrorism: The Worst and the Best Books of 2003'. *Studies in Conflict and Terrorism*, 26, 2004, pp. 235–241

Bernstein, P.L., *Against the Gods: The Remarkable Story of Risk*. New York: John Wiley, 1996

Beyer, J.L., *Spanish Anti-Terrorism Policy and the Integration of National Minorities*. Honolulu: International Studies Association (ISA), March 2005

Biersteker, T.J. and Excker, S.E., *Countering the Financing of Terrorism*. London: Routledge, 2008

Bigo, D., *Policing Insecurity Today: Defense and Internal Security*, New York: Palgrave Macmillan, 2007

Birkland, T.A., 'Learning and Policy Improvement after Disaster: The Case of Aviation Security'. *American Behavioral Scientist*, 48, November 2004, pp. 341–364

Bohning, D., *The Castro Obsession: US Covert Operations against Cuba, 1959–1965*. Dulles, VA: Potomac Books, 2005

Bolechów, B., 'The United States of America vis-à-vis Terrorism: The Super Power's Weaknesses and Mistakes'. *American Behavioral Scientist*, 48, February 2005, pp. 783–794

Bolt, P.J., Coletta, D.V. and Shackelford C.G. Jr (eds), *American Defense Policy*. Baltimore: Johns Hopkins University Press, 2005

Bolz, F. Jr, Dudonis, K.J. and Schulz, D.P., *The Counterterrorism Handbook: Tactics, Procedures and Techniques* 3rd edn, Boca Raton, FL: CRC Press, 2005

Bonini, C. and D'Avanzo, G., *Il mercato della paura* 'The Market of Fear: The War on Islamic Terrorism: Investigation into the Italian Deception'. Turin: Einaudi, 2006

Bornstein, A.S., 'Borders and the Utility of Violence: State Effects on the "Superexploitation" of West Bank Palestinians'. *Critique of Anthropology*, 22, June 2002, pp. 201–220

Boulder, J. and Weiss, T.G. (eds), *Terrorism and the UN: Before and after September 11.* Bloomington: Indiana University Press, 2004

Boutwell, J. and Klare, M.T., *Light Weapons and Civil Conflict: Controlling the Tools of Violence*. Lanham, MD: Rowman & Littlefield, 1999

Bowman, R.L., *Is the Philippines Profiting from the War on Terrorism?* Honolulu: International Studies Association (ISA), March 2005

Bowyer Bell, J., *The Dynamics of Armed Struggle*. London: Frank Cass, 1998

Boyd-Judson, L., 'Strategic Moral Diplomacy: Mandela, Qaddafi, and the Lockerbie Negotiations'. *Foreign Policy Analysis*, 1(1), March 2005, pp. 73–97

Boyne, R., 'Cosmopolis and Risk: A Conversation with Ulrich Beck'. *Theory, Culture and Society*, 18, August 2001, pp. 47–63

Boyne, S., *Law vs. War: Competing Approaches to Fighting Terrorism*. Carlisle, PA: Strategic Studies Institute, July 2005

Brachman, J.M. and McCants, W.F., *Stealing Al-Qa'ida's Playbook*. CTC Report, February 2006

Brash, W., *America's Unpatriotic Acts. The Federal Government's Violation of Constitutional and Civil Rights*. New York: Peter Lang, 2005

Briggs, R. (ed.), *The Unlikely Counter-terrorists*. London: Foreign Policy Centre, 2002. Available at: http://fpc. org.uk/fsblob/45.pdf (accessed 15 April 2009)

Briggs, R. and Edwards, C., *The Business of Resilience: Corporate Security for the 21st Century*. London: Demos, 2006

Brimley, S., 'Tentacles of Jihad: Targeting Transnational Networks'. *Parameters*, Summer 2006, pp. 30–46

Brink, C.H., *Measuring Political Risk to Foreign Investment*. Aldershot, UK: Ashgate, 2004

Brown, A.P., 'The Immobile Mass: Movement Restrictions in the West Bank'. *Social and Legal Studies*, 13, December 2004, pp. 501–521

Brown, C. and Waltzer, H., 'Organized Interest Advertorials: Responding to the 9/11 Terrorist Attack and Other National Traumas'. *Harvard International Journal of Press/Politics*, 9, October 2004, pp. 25–48

Brown, M.E., Coté, O.R. Jr, Lynn-Jones, S.M. and Mille, S.E. (eds), *New Global Dangers; Changing Dimensions of International Security*. Cambridge, MA: MIT Press, 2004

Brownlee, J. *et al.*, 'Democratization in the Arab World?' *Journal of Democracy*, October 2002, pp. 5–68

Bruggeman, W., 'The ICC as an Important Partner in Enhancing Global Justice'. Paper presented at the Madrid Conference 'Confronting Terrorism', March 2005

Brzezinski, M., *Fortress America: On the Front Lines of Homeland Security: An Inside Look at the Coming Surveillance State*. St Albans, UK: Bantam, 2004

Brzezinski, M., *The Choice: Global Domination or Global Leadership*. New York: Basic Books, 2005

Bubandt, N., 'Vernacular Security: The Politics of Feeling Safe in Global, National and Local Worlds'. *Security Dialogue*, 36, September 2005, pp. 275–296

Buckley, M. and Fawn, R., *Global Responses to Terrorism: 9/11, Afghanistan and Beyond*. London: Routledge, 2003

Bueno de Mesquita, E., 'The Terrorist Endgame: A Model with Moral Hazard and Learning'. *Journal of Conflict Resolution*, 49, April 2005, pp. 237–258

Bueno de Mesquita, E., 'Conciliation, Counterterrorism, and Patterns of Terrorist Violence'. *International Organization*, 59(1), Winter 2005, pp. 145–176

Bundeswehr Military Intelligence Center, Regional Analysis Group Branch 1, *Intelligence Background Information: Radiological Dispersal Devices*. ZNBw-SpDst. AutrNr 0632–04, 2004

Burda, A.M. and Sigg, T., 'Pharmacy Preparedness for Incidents Involving Nuclear, Biological, or Chemical Weapons'. *Journal of Pharmacy Practice*, 17, August 2004, pp. 251–265

Bures, O., 'EU Counterterrorism Policy: A Paper Tiger?' *Terrorism and Political Violence*, 18(1), Spring 2006, pp. 57–78

Burgess, J.P. and Piper, R., 'Special Section: The Report of the High-Level Panel on Threats, Challenges and Change: Editors' Introduction'. *Security Dialogue*, 36, September 2005, pp. 361–363

Byman, D., 'Should Hezbollah Be Next?' *Foreign Affairs*, November–December 2003, pp. 54–66

Byman, D., 'Confronting Syrian-Backed Terrorism'. *Washington Quarterly*, 28(3), Summer 2005, pp. 99–113

Byman, D., *Deadly Connections: States That Sponsor Terrorism*. Cambridge: Cambridge University Press, 2005

Byman, D., 'Do Targeted Killings Work?' *Foreign Affairs*, March–April 2006, pp. 95–111

Byman, D.L., 'Friends Like These: Counterinsurgency and the War on Terrorism'. *International Security*, 31(2), Fall 2006, pp. 79–115

Byman, D., 'US Counter-terrorism Options: A Taxonomy'. *Survival*, 49(3), Autumn 2007, pp. 121–150

Byman, D., *The Five Front War: The Better Way to Fight Global Jihad*. Hoboken, NJ, John Wiley, 2008

Byman, D., Scheuer, M., Lieven, A. *et al.*, 'Symposium: Iraq, Afghanistan and the War on "Terror" '. *Middle East Policy*, 12(1), Spring 2005, pp. 1–24

Call, C.T. (ed.), *Constructing Justice and Security after War*. Washington, DC: United States Institute of Peace Press, 2006

Campbell, T., Chavali, M. and Reese, K. (eds), *Meeting the Homeland Security Challenge. Maritime and Other Critical Dimensions*. Washington, DC: Institute for Foreign Policy Analysis, 2002

Campos, J.H., II, *The State and Terrorism: National Security and the Mobilization of Power*. Aldershot, UK: Ashgate, 2007

Candreva, P.J. and Jones, L.R., 'Congressional Control over Defense and Delegation of Authority in the Case of the Defense Emergency Response Fund'. *Armed Forces and Society*, 32(1), October 2005, pp. 105–122

Cantori, L.J. and Norton, A.R. (eds), 'Evaluating the Bush Menu for Change In the Middle East'. *Middle East Policy*, 12(1), Spring 2005, pp. 97–121

Capoccia, G., *Defending Democracy: Reactions to Extremism in Interwar Europe*. Baltimore: Johns Hopkins University Press, 2005

Carens, J.H., 'The Integration of Immigrants'. *Journal of Moral Philosophy*, 2, April 2005, pp. 29–46

Carment, D., 'Democracy and Ethnic Conflict: Advancing Peace in Deeply Divided Societies'. *Journal of Peace Research*, 42, May 2005, pp. 359–360

Carnegie Commission on Preventing Deadly Conflict, *Preventing Deadly Conflict: Final Report*. Washington, DC: The Commission, 1997

Carothers, T. (ed.), *Promoting the Rule of Law Abroad: In Search of Knowledge*. Washington, DC: Carnegie Endowment for International Peace, 2006

Carpenter, T.G., *Smart Power: Toward a Prudent Foreign Policy for America*. Washington, DC: CATO Institute, 2008

Carter, A., 'How to Counter WMD'. *Foreign Affairs*, 83(5), September–October 2004, pp. 72–85

Carter, R.G. (ed.), *Contemporary Cases of U.S. Foreign Policy: From Terrorism to Trade*. Washington, DC: CQ Press, 2004

Celmer, M.A., *Terrorism, U.S. Strategy, and Reagan Policies*. New York: Greenwood Press, 1987

Chalk, P., *West European Terrorism and Counter-terrorism: The Evolving Dynamic*. New York: St Martin's Press, 1996

Chalk, P., 'North and West Africa: The Global War on Terror and Regional Collaboration'. *Terrorism Monitor*, 3(15), 28 July 2005, pp. 9–11

Chalk, P. and Rosenau, W., *Confronting the Enemy Within: Security Intelligence, the Police and Counterterrorism in Four Democracies*. MG-100-RC. Santa Monica, CA: RAND, 2004

Chandler, D. (ed.), *Protecting the Bosnian Peace: Lessons from a Decade of National Building*. London: Routledge, 2004

Chandler, M. and Gunaratna, R., *Countering Terrorism: Can We Meet the Threat of Global Violence?* London: Reaktion Books, 2007

Charney, C. and Akatan, N., *A New Beginning: Strategies for a More Fruitful Dialogue with the Muslim World*. New York: Council on Foreign Relations, 2005

Charny, I.W., *Fighting Suicide Bombing: A Worldwide Campaign for Life*. Westport, CT: Praeger Security International, 2007

Chatham House, *Security, Terrorism and the UK*. ISP/NNS Briefing Paper 05/01, 2005

Cheldelin, S., Druckman, D. and Fast, L. (eds), *Conflict: From Analysis to Intervention*. London: Continuum, 2003

Chickering, A., Coleman, I., Haley, P.E. and Vargas–Baron, E., *Strategic Foreign Assistance: Civil Society in International Security*. Stanford, CA: Hoover Institution, 2006

Chomsky, N. and Achcar, G., *Perilous Power: The Middle East and U.S. Foreign Policy: Dialogues on Terror, Democracy, War and Justice*. Boulder, CO: Paradigm, 2006

Chow, J.T., 'ASEAN Counterterrorism Cooperation since 9/11'. *Asian Survey*, 15(2), March–April 2005, pp. 302–321

Cirincione, J., Mathews, J.T. and Percovich, G., *WMD in Iraq: Evidence and Implications*. Washington, DC: Carnegie Endowment for International Peace, 2004

Cirincione, J., Wolfsthal, J.B. and Rajkumar, M., *Deadly Arsenals: Tracking Weapons of Mass Destruction*. Washington, DC: Carnegie Endowment for International Peace, 2002

Clark, R.P., *Negotiating with ETA: Obstacles to Peace in the Basque Country, 1975–1988*, Reno: University of Nevada Press, 1990

Clark, W.K., *Winning Modern Wars: Iraq, Terrorism and the American Empire*. New York: Public Affairs, 2004

Clarke, R.A., *Against All Enemies: Inside America's War on Terror*. New York: Free Press, 2004

Clarke, R.A., *Defeating the Jihadists: A Blueprint for Action*. Washington, DC: Century Foundation, 2004

Clarke, R.V. and Newman, G.R., *Outsmarting the Terrorists*. Westport, CT: Praeger, 2006

Cline, L.E., 'Special Operations and the Intelligence System'. *International Journal of Intelligence and Counterintelligence*, 18(4), Winter 2005–2006, pp. 575–592

Clough, C., 'Quid Pro Quo: The Challenges of International Strategic Intelligence Cooperation'. *International Journal of Intelligence and Counterintelligence*, 17(4), Winter 2004–2005, pp. 601–613

Clutterbuck, R., *Kidnap, Hijack and Extortion: The Response*. Basingstoke, UK: Macmillan, 1987

Cochlan, N., *Saddest Country: On Assignment in Colombia*. McGill-Queen's University Press, 2004

Cole, L., *The Anthrax Letters: A Medical Detective Story*. Washington, DC: Henry (Joseph) Press, 2003

Committee of Experts on Terrorism (CODEXTER), *Profiles on Counter-terrorist Capacity*. Strasbourg: Council of Europe, October 2004

Congressional Research Service, *Combating Terrorism: Are There Lessons Learned from Foreign Experiences?* Congressional Research Service, 18 January 2002

Coolsaet, R., *Between Al-Andalus and a Failing Integration: Europe's Pursuit of a Long-Term Counterterrorism Strategy in the Post-Al-Qaeda Era*. Egmont Paper 5. Brussels: Royal Institute for International Relations, May 2005

Cooper, N., 'Picking Out the Pieces of the Liberal Peaces: Representations of Conflict Economies and the Implications of Policy'. *Security Dialogue*, 36, December 2005, pp. 463–478

Cordesman, A.H., *International Cooperation in Counter-terrorism: Making the Myth a Reality*. Washington, DC: Center for Strategic and International Studies (CSIS), 2005

Cordesman, A.H. and Obaid, N., *Saudi Petroleum Security: Challenges and Responses*. Washington, DC: Center for Strategic and International Studies, 30 November 2004

Cordesman, A.H. and Obaid, N., *Saudi Counter Terrorism Efforts: The Changing Paramilitary and Domestic Security Apparatus*. Washington, DC: Center for Strategic and International Studies, 2 February, 2005

Cortright, D. and Lopez, G.A., *Economic Sanctions: Panacea or Peacebuilding in a Post-Cold War World?* Boulder, CO: Westview Press, 1995

Cortright, D. and Lopez, G.A. (eds), *Uniting against Terror: Cooperative Nonmilitary Responses to the Global Terrorist Threat*. Cambridge, MA: MIT Press, 2007

Council of Europe, *The Fight against Terrorism: Council of Europe Standards*, 3rd edn. Strasbourg: Council of Europe Publishing, Palais de l'Europe, 2005

Council of the European Union, *EU Plan of Action on Combating Terrorism*. Brussels, 11 June 2004

Council of the European Union, *EU Plan of Action on Combating Terrorism – Update*. Brussels, 10 June 2005

Covey, J., Dziedzic, M. and Hawley, L. (eds), *The Quest for Viable Peace: International Intervention and Strategies for Conflict Transformation*. US Institute for Peace Press, 2005

Cox, R., 'Law and Terrorism: US and British Responses Compared'. *Jane's Intelligence Review*, 17(10), October 2005, pp. 16–19

Cozzens, J.B., *Identifying Entry Points of Action in Counter Radicalisation: Countering Salafi-Jihadi Ideology through Development Initiatives: Strategic Openings*. DIIS Working Paper. Copenhagen: Danish Institute for International Studies, 2006

Cragin, K. and Gerwehr, S., *Dissuading Terror: Strategic Influence and the Struggle against Terrorism*. MG-184-RC. Santa Monica, CA: RAND, 2005

Crenshaw, M., *Terrorism and International Cooperation*. New York: Institute for East-West Security Studies. Boulder, CO: distributed by Westview Press, 1989

Crocker, C.A., Hampson, F.O. and Aall, P. (eds), *Taming Intractable Conflicts: Mediation in the Hardest Cases*. Washington, DC: United States Institute of Peace, 2004

Croft, S., *Culture, Crisis and America's War on Terror*. Cambridge: Cambridge University Press, 2006

Cronin, A.K. and Ludes, J.M. (eds), *Attacking Terrorism: Elements of a Grand Strategy*. Washington, DC: Georgetown University Press, 2004

CRS, *Border and Transportation Security: Possible New Directions and Policy Options*. Washington, DC: Congressional Research Service, 29 March 2005

Cunningham, K.J., 'Countering Female Terrorism'. *Studies in Conflict and Terrorism*, 30(2) 2007, pp. 113–130

Cunningham, M.K., 'Is the US Winning the War on Terrorism? An Assessment of the First Five Years'. Master's thesis, University of St Andraws, School of International Relations, August 2006

Curtis, P.M., *Maintaining Mission Critical Systems in a 24/7 Environment*. New York: Wiley-IEEE, 2007

Dahl, E.J., 'Warning of Terror: Explaining the Failure of Intelligence against Terrorism'. *Journal of Strategic Studies*, 28(1), February 2005, pp. 31–55

Dalacoura, K., '11 September 2001: A Critique'. *International Affairs*, 81(5), October 2005, pp. 963–980

Dankowitz, A., *Fighting Terrorism: Recommendations of Arab Reformists*. Washington, DC: Middle East Media and Research Institute (MEMRI), 28 July 2005

D'Arsy, M., O'Hanlon, M., Orszag, P., Shapiro, J. and Steinberg, J., *Protecting the Homeland 2006/2007*. Washington, DC: Brookings Institution, 2006

Das, D.K. and Kratcoski, P.C. (eds), *Meeting the Challenges of Global Terrorism: Prevention, Control and Recovery*. Lanham, MD: Lexington Books, 2003

Daun, A., 'Intelligence: Strukturen für die multilaterale Kooperation europäische Staaten'. *Integration*, 28(2), April 2005, pp. 136–149

Davidson, K., *Selected Web Sites on Homeland Security: The Serials Librarian*, 49(1–2), 14 September 2005, pp. 89–139

Davis, J., 'The Attribution of WMD Events'. April 2003. Available at: www.homelandsecurity.org/journal/articles/davis.html (accessed 15 April 2009)

Davis, L., Riley, K.J., Ridgeway, G., Pace, J. et.al., *When Terrorism Hits Home: How Prepared Are State and Local Law Enforcement?* Santa Monica, CA: RAND, 2005

Davis, P.K., *Deterrence and Influence in Counterterrorism: A Component in the War on Al Qaeda*. Santa Monica, CA: RAND, 2002

De Koster, P., *Terrorism: Special Investigation Techniques*. Strasbourg: Council of Europe, 2005

De Lange, R., 'Noodrecht en grondrechten'. *NCJM-Bulletin*, 30(5), July–August 2005, pp. 523–550

Dean, J., *Coping with the Possibility of Terrorist Use of WMD*. Background Paper no. 15 of the Weapons of Mass Destruction Commission, 2006

Deflem, M. and Maybin, L.C., 'Interpol and the Policing of International Terrorism: Developments and Dynamics since September 11'. In L.L. Snowden and B. Whitsel (eds), *Terrorism: Research, Readings and Realities*. Upper Saddle River, NJ, Prentice Hall, 2005, pp. 175–191

Delcour, B., 'Terrorism Prevention and Intervention'. In W.D. Eberwein and B. Badie (eds), *Sovereignty, Prevention and Intervention*. New York: Palgrave Macmillan, 2005

Denece, E., *The Secret War against Al-Qa'ida*. Paris: Ellipses Collection, Géopolitique, 2002

DeRosa, M., *Datamining and Data Analysis for Counterterrorism*. Washington, DC: CSIS, 2004

Dicter, A., *How To Win the War against Terrorism*. A Saban Center for Middle East Policy Symposium at the Brookings Institution, 22 September 2005

Dietl, W., *Die Agentin des Mossad: Operation Roter Prinz*. Düsseldorf: Econ Taschenbuch Verlag, 1993

Diettrich, M., *Facing the Global Terrorist Threat: A European Response*, Working Paper 14. Brussels: European Policy Centre, January 2005

Dingley, J., *Combating Terrorism in Northern Ireland*. London: Routledge, 2008

Dishman, C., 'Attacking Terrorist Financing'. *Bulletin of Atomic Scientists*, May–June 2004. Available at: www.encyclopedia.com/Bulletin+of+the+Atomic+Scientists/publications.aspx?pageNumber=1 (accessed 15 April 2009)

Dixon, L., Carroll, S.J., Lakdawalla, D., Reville, R. and Adamson, D.M., *Issues and Options for Government Intervention in the Market for Terrorism Insurance*. Santa Monica, CA: RAND, 2005

Dixon, P., *The Northern Ireland Peace Process: Choreography and Theatrical Politics*. London: Routledge, 2006

Dobbins, J., Crane, K., Jones, S., Rathmell, A. et al., *The RAND History of Nation-Building*, 2 vols. MG–304/1. Santa Monica, CA: RAND, 2005

Dobbins, J., Jones, S., Crane, K. et al., *The UN's Role in Nation-Building: From the Congo to Iraq*. MG–305. Santa Monica: RAND, 2005

Dobbins, J., Jones, S.G., Crane, K. and Cole, B., *The Beginner's Guide to Nation-Building*. Santa Monica, CA: RAND, 2007

Dodge, T., *Iraq's Future: The Aftermath of Regime Change*. Adelphi Papers. London: Routledge, 2005

Donaldson, R.H., *Russia, the United States, and the 'War on Terrorism'*. Honolulu: International Studies Association (ISA), March 2005

Donavan, L.A., 'Citizens as Intelligence Volunteers: The Impact of Value Structures'. *International Journal of Intelligence and Counterintelligence*, 18(2), Summer 2005, pp. 238–245

Dougherty, J.E., *Illegals: The Imminent Threat Posed by Our Unsecured U.S.–Mexico Border*. Nashville, TN: Thomas Nelson, 2004

Downer, A., 'Securing Australia's Interests: Australian Foreign Policy Priorities'. *Australian Journal of International Affairs*, 59(1), March 2005, pp. 7–12

Drew, E., 'Pinning the Blame' (review of 9/11 Commission Report). *New York Review of Books*, 23 September 2004, pp. 6–12

Duff, R.A., 'Notes on Punishment and Terrorism'. *American Behavioral Scientist*, 48, February 2005, pp. 758–763

Dunn, M.A. and Kristensen, K.S., *Security, the Homeland*. London: Routledge, 2007

Dunn, M., Wigerts, I., Wenger, A.M. and Metzger, J. (eds), *International CIIP Handbook 2004*. Zürich: Center for Security Studies at the ETH Zürich (Swiss Federal Institute of Technology), 2004

Duyvesteyn, I. and De Graaf, B. (eds), *Terroristen en hun bestrijders: vroeger en nu*. Amsterdam: Boom, 2007

Edwards, J.R. Jr, *Keeping Extremists Out: The History of Exclusion, and the Need for Its Revival*. Washington, DC: Center for Immigration Studies, 2005

Eilam, U., 'Technology in the Fight against Terrorism'. *Jaffee Center for Strategic Studies. Strategic Assessment*, 7(2), August 2004, pp. 39–44

Ellis, J.D. and Kiefer, G.D., *Combating Proliferation: Strategic Intelligence and Security Policy*. Baltimore: Johns Hopkins University Press, 2004

Emery, N., Werchan, J. and Mowles, D.G. Jr, 'Fighting Terrorism and Insurgency: Shaping the Information Environment'. *Military Review*, 85(1), January–February 2005, pp. 32–38

Enderlin, C., *Shattered Dreams: The Failure of The Peace Process in the Middle East, 1995–2002*. New York: Other Press, 2003

Enders, W. and Sandler, T., 'The Effectiveness of Anti-terrorism Policies: A Vector-Autoregression-Intervention Analysis'. *American Political Science Review*, 87(4), 1993, pp. 829–844

Enders, W., Sandler, T. and Cauley, J., 'UN Conventions, Technology, and Retaliation in the Fight against Terrorism: An Econometric Evaluation'. *Terrorism and Political Violence*, 2(1), 83–105, 1990

Erez, R., 'In Search of a Role: New European Efforts to Counter Nuclear Proliferation'. *Strategic Assessment*, 7(1), May 2004, pp. 15–21

EU Committee of Experts on Terrorism (CODEXTER), *Draft European Convention on the Prevention of Terrorism as Adopted in Second Reading by the CODEXTER at its 7th Meeting, Strasbourg, 7–11 February 2005*. CODEXTER (2004) 27 rev 6. Strasbourg, 14 February, 2005

EU, *Plan of Action on Combating Terrorism – Update*. Council of the European Union, 8211/05, ADD2, Brussels, 24 May 2005. Available at: www.statewatch.org/news/2005/may/eu-terr-action-plan-implementation.pdf (accessed 15 April 2009)

EU, *Prevention, Preparedness and Response to Terrorist Attacks*. October 2004. Available at: http://europa.eu/scadplus/leg/en/lvb/l33219.htm (accessed 15 April 2009)

EU, *Revised EU Plan of Action on Combating Terrorism*. June 2004. Available at: http://ue.eu.int/uedocs/cms Upload/EUplan16090.pdf (accessed 15 April 2009)

EU Counter Terrorism Strategy and Plans Handbook. Washington, DC: USA International Business Publications, 2008

Fair, C., *The Counterterror Coalitions: Cooperation with Pakistan and India*. Santa Monica, CA: RAND, 2005

Falk, R., 'The Communitarian Approach to International Relations and the Future of World Order'. *American Behavioral Scientist*, 48, August 2005, pp. 1577–1590

Falkenrath, R.A., 'Grading the War on Terrorism'. *Foreign Affairs*, 85(1), January–February 2006, pp. 122–128

Farer, T.J., *Confronting Global Terrorism: The Framework of a Liberal Grand Strategy*. Oxford: Oxford University Press, 2008

Faria, J.R., 'Terrorist Innovations and Anti-terrorist Policies'. *Terrorism and Political Violence*, 18(1), Spring 2006, pp. 47–56

Farley, J.D., *Toward a Mathematical Theory of Counterterrorism: Building the Perfect Terrorist Cell*. Carlisle, PA:. US Army War College, Center for Strategic Leadership, 2007

Fein, R.A. and Vossekuil, B., *Protective Intelligence and Threat Assessment Investigations*. US Department of Justice, Office of Justice Programs. Washington, DC: National Institute of Justice. July 1998

Feldman, N., *After Jihad: America and the Struggle for Islamic Democracy*. New York: Farrar, Straus & Giroux, 2003

Fessenden, H., 'The Limits of Intelligence Reform'. *Foreign Affairs*, 84(6), November–December 2005, pp. 106–121

Finlay, B. and Grotto, A., *The Race to Secure Russia's Loose Nukes: Progress since 9/11*. Washington, DC: Henry L. Stimson Center, Center for American Progress, September 2005

Fishman, B., 'Using the Mistakes of Al Qaeda's Franchises to Undermine Its Strategies', *Annals of the American Academy of Political and Social Science*, 618, July 2008, pp. 46–54

Folker, R.D., 'Intelligence Analysis in Theater Joint Intelligence Centers: An Experiment in Applying Structured Methods'. Occasional Paper no. 7. Washington, DC: Joint Military Intelligence College, January 2000

Foot, R., 'Human Rights and Counter-terrorism'. Adelphi Papers no. 363. Oxford: Oxford University Press, 2004

Forest, J. F. (ed.), *Homeland Security: Protecting America's Targets*, 3 vols. Westport, CT: Praeger Security International, 2006

Forsberg, R., Driscoll, W., Webb, G. and Dean, J., *Nonproliferation Primer: Preventing the Spread of Nuclear, Chemical, and Biological Weapons*. Cambridge, MA: Institute for Defense and Disarmament Studies 1999

Foxell, J.W. Jr, 'The U.S. War on Terrorism: Prospects for Success?' *American Foreign Policy Interests*, 25(3), June 2003, pp. 177–198

Fraher, A.L., ' "Flying the Friendly Skies": Why US Commercial Airline Pilots Want to Carry Guns'. *Human Relations*, 57, May 2004, pp. 573–595

Freedman, L. (ed.), *Superterrorism: Policy Responses*. Malden, MA: Blackwell, 2002

Frey, B., *Dealing with Terrorism: Stick or Carrot?* Cheltanham, UK: Edward Elgar, 2004

Friedman, B., 'Homeland Security'. *Foreign Policy*, 149, July–August 2005, pp. 22–28

Friedman, N., *Terrorism, Afghanistan and America's New Way of War*. Annapolis, MD: Naval Institute Press, 2003

Frum, D. and Perle, R., *An End to Evil: How to Win the War on Terror*. New York: Random House, 2003

Ganor, B., *The Counter-terrorism Puzzle: A Guide for Decision Makers*. New Brunswick, NJ: Transaction, 2005

GAO, *Terrorist Financing: US Agencies Should Systematically Assess Terrorists' Use of Alternative Financing Mechanisms*. GAO-04–163. Washington, DC: United States General Accounting Office, November 2003

GAO, *Infomation Sharing: The Federal Government Needs to Establish Policies and Processes for Sharing Terrorism-Related and Sensitive but Unclassified Information*. GAO-06–385. Washington, DC: United States Government Accountability Office, March 2006

Garfinkle, A. (ed.), *A Practical Guide to Winning the War on Terrorism*. Stanford, CA: Hoover Institution Press, 2004

Garson, G.D., 'Patriotic Information Systems: Evaluating Bush Administration Information Policy'. *Social Science Computer Review*, 23, November 2005, pp. 395–400

Gauss, F.G. III, 'Can Democracy Stop Terrorism?' *Foreign Affairs*, 84(5), September–October, 2005, pp. 62–76

Gazit, S., ' "Two Roads Diverged": Israel's Post-disengagement Strategic Options'. *Strategic Assessment*, 8(2), August 2005, pp. 1–5

George, J., *Die Rache is unser: Ein israelisches Geheimkommando im Einsatz*. Munich: Knaurs, 1984

Germani, L.S. and Kaarthikeyan, D.R. (eds), *Pathways out of Terrorism and Insurgency: The Dynamics of Terrorist Violence and Peace Processes*. Elgin, IL: New Dawn Press, 2005

Gershkoff, A. and Kushner, S., 'Shaping Public Opinion: The 9/11 Iraq Connection in the Bush Administration's Rhetoric'. *Perspectives on Politics*, 3(3), September 2005, pp. 525–537

Gerstein, D.M., *Securing America's Future: National Strategy in the Information Age*. New York: Praeger, 2005

Gertz, B., *Breakdown: How America's Intelligence Failures Led to September 11*. Washington, DC: Regnery, 2002

Geva, N. and Mosher, K.N., *Terrorism, Negative Emotions and Processing the Reliability of Information in Foreign Policy Decision Making*. Honolulu: International Studies Association (ISA) March 2005

Ghashghai, E., *Communications Networks to Support Integrated Intelligence, Surveillance, Reconnaissance, and Strike Operations*. Santa Monica, CA: RAND, 2005

Gilmour, R., *Dead Ground: Infiltrating the IRA*. London: Warner Books, 1999

Giraldo, J.K., *Terrorism Financing and State Responses: A Comparative Perspective*. Stanford, CA: Stanford University Press, 2007

Glassman, J., 'Winning the War of Ideas'. Washington, DC: Washington Institute for Near East Policy, 8 July 2008

Gleason, G., 'Collective Security and Non-State Actors in Eurasia'. *International Studies Perspectives*, 6(2), May 2005, pp. 274–284

Goede, M. de, 'De nederlandse "oorlog" tegen terrorismefinanciering in mondiaal perspectief'. *Vrede en Veiligheid: Tijdschrift voor Internationale Vraagstukken*, 35(2), 2006, pp. 118–136

Gompert, D.C., *Heads We Win: The Cognitive Side of Counterinsurgency (COIN)*. Santa Monica, CA: RAND, 2007

Graham, B. and Nussbaum, J., *Intelligence Matters: The CIA and FBI, Saudi Arabia, and the Failure of America's War on Terror*. London: Random House, 2004

Greene, R.W., *Confronting Catastrophe: A GIS Handbook*. Redlands, CA: ESRI Press, 2002

Greener-Barcham, B.K. and Barcham, B., 'Terrorism in the South Pacific? Thinking Critically about Approaches to Security in the Region'. *Australian Journal of International Affairs*, 60(1), March 2006, pp. 67–82

Gregoriou, G.N. (ed.), *Advances in Risk Management*. Basingstoke, UK: Palgrave Macmillan, 2007

Griffith, L., *The War on Terrorism and the Terror of God*. Grand Rapids, MI: William B. Eerdmans, 2002

Gross, E., *The Struggle of Democracy against Terrorism*. Charlottesville University of Virginia, 2007

Gruen, A., *Der Kampf um die Demokratie: Der Extremismus, die Gewalt und der Terror*. Stuttgart: Verlag Klett-Cotta, 2002

Guitta, O. and McNamara, S., *Homeland Security in a Global Context: An Overview of European–U.S. Cooperation*. Washington, DC: American Legislative Exchange Council, January 2006

Gunaratna, R., 'Responding to the Post 9/11 Structural and Operational Challenges of Global Jihad'. *Connections*, Spring 2005, pp. 9–42

Gunaratna, R. and Steven, G.C.S., *Counter-terrorism: A Reference Handbook*. Santa Barbara, CA: ABC-CLIO, 2005

Gunter, M.M., Jr, *Fighting the War on Terrorism with More Sustainable Development*. Honolulu: International Studies Association (ISA), March 2005

Gurmankin, A.D., Helweg-Larsen, M., Armstrong, K., Kimmel, S.E. and Volpp, K.G.M., 'Comparing the Standard Rating Scale and the Magnifier Scale for Assessing Risk Perceptions'. *Medical Decisions Making*, 25, September 2005, pp. 560–570

Haaland Kramer, H. and Yetiv, S. 'The UN Security Council's Response to Terrorism: Before and After September 11, 2001'. *Political Science Quarterly*, 122(3), Fall 2007, pp. 409–432

Hainmüller, J. and Lemnitzer, J.M., 'Why Do Europeans Fly Safer?: The Politics of Airport Security in Europe and the US'. *Terrorism and Political Violence*, 15(4), Winter 2003, pp. 1–36

Hale, W.C., 'Information versus Intelligence: Construction and Analysis of an Open Source Relational Database of Worldwide Extremist Activity'. *International Journal of Emergency Management*, 3(4), November 2006, pp. 280–297

Halibozek, E., Jones, A. and Kovacich, G.L., *The Corporate Security Professional's Handbook on Terrorism*. Oxford: Butterworth-Heinemann, 2007

Hall, H.V., *Terrorism: Strategies for Intervention*. New York: Haworth Press, 2003

Halliday, F., 'Beyond Armed Response: Terrorism and World Politics'. *World Today*, 61(5), May 2005, pp. 15–17

Hamilton, L., Hoffman, B. and Jenkins, B., *State of the Struggle: Report on the Battle against Global Terrorism*. Lanham, MD: Rowman & Littlefield, 2007

Hamzawy, A., 'The Key to Arab Reform: Moderate Islamists'. *Carnegie Endowment for International Peace, Policy Brief 40*, August 2005

Haniff Bin Hassan, M. and Pereire, K.G., 'An Ideological Response to Combating Terrorism: The Singapore Perspective'. *Small Wars and Insurgencies*, 17(4), 2006, pp. 458–477

Hansen, J., 'U.S. Intelligence Confronts the Future'. *International Journal of Intelligence and Counterintelligence*, 17(4), Winter 2004–2005, pp. 673–709

Harclerode, P., *Secret Soldiers: Special Forces in the War against Terrorism*. London: Orion, 2002

Harvey, F.P., *The Homeland Security Dilemma*. London: Routledge, 2008

Hastings, T.H., *Nonviolent Response to Terrorism*. Jefferson, NC: McFarland, 2004

Hayden, P., Lansford, T. and Watson, R.P. (eds), *America's War on Terror*. Aldershot, UK: Ashgate, 2003

Heng, Y.-K., 'Unravelling the "War" on Terrorism: A Risk-Management Exercise in War Clothing?' *Security Dialogue*, 33, June 2002, pp. 227–242

Hennessy, P., *The New Protective State: Government, Intelligence and Terrorism*. London: Continuum, 2007

Herren, E., *Tools for Countering Future Terrorism*. Herzliya, Israel: International Institute for Counter-Terrorism, 15 August 2005

Hess, M., 'A Partnership against Terrorism'. *Security Dialogue*, 34, December 2003, pp. 506–510

Heuser, B., 'The Cultural Revolution in Counter-insurgency'. *Journal of Strategic Studies*, 30(1), 2007, pp. 153–171

Heymann, P.B., *Terrorism and America: A Commonsense Strategy for a Democratic Society*. Cambridge, MA: MIT Press, 1998

Heymann, P.B., *Terrorism, Freedom and Security: Winning without War*. Cambridge, MA: MIT Press, 2004

Heymann, P.B. and Kayyem, J.N., *Protecting Liberty in an Age of Terror*. Cambridge, MA: MIT Press, 2005

Hicks, P., 'Correct Diagnosis, Wrong Prescription: The Human Rights Component of Security'. *Security Dialogue*, 36, September 2005, pp. 378–380

Hills, A., *The Future War in Cities: Rethinking a Liberal Dilemma*. London: Frank Cass, 2004

Hippler, J. (ed.), *Nation-building: Ein Schlüssel-konzept für friedliche Konfliktbearbeitung?* Bonn: Stiftung Entwicklung & Frieden, 2004

Hiro, D., *War Without End: The Rise of Islamist Terrorism and the Global Response*. London: Routledge, 2002

Hirschmann, K. and Leggemann, C. (eds), *Der Kampf gegen den Terrorismus: Strategien und Handlungserfordernisse in Deutschland*. Berlin: Berliner Wissenschafts Verlag, 2003

Hitz, F.P., 'The Myths and Current Reality of Espionage'. *International Journal of Intelligence and Counterintelligence*, 18(4), Winter 2005–2006, pp. 730–733

HM Government, *Countering International Terrorism: The United Kindom's Strategy*. London, July 2006. Available at: http://security.homeoffice.gov.uk/news-publications/publication-search/general/HO_Contest_strategy.pdf?view=Binary (accessed 17 April 2009)

Hobson, C., 'A Forward Strategy for Freedom in the Middle East: US Democracy Promotion and the "War on Terror"'. *Australian Journal of International Affairs*, 59(10), March 2005, pp. 39–53

Hoffman, B., *A Strategic Framework for Countering Terrorism and Insurgency*. Santa Monica, CA: RAND, 1992

Hoffman, B., *Responding to Terrorism across the Technological Spectrum*. Santa Monica, CA: RAND, 1994

Hoffman, B., *Combating Al Qaeda and the Militant Islamic Threat*. CT-255. Santa Monica, CA: RAND, 2006

Hoge, J.F. and Rose, G. (eds), *Understanding the War on Terror*. New York: W.W. Norton, 2005

Höglund, A.T., 'War on Terrorism: Feminist and Ethical Perspectives'. *Security Dialogue*, 34, June 2003, pp. 242–245

Holloway, D., *9/11 and the War on Terror*. Edinburgh: Edinburgh University Press, 2008

Hollywood, J., Snyder, D., Mckay, K. and Boon, J.E., Jr, *Out of the Ordinary: Finding Hidden Threats by Analyzing Unusual Behavior*. Santa Monica, CA: RAND, 2004

Hopmann, P.T., *The OSCE Response to 9/11*. Honolulu: International Studies Association (ISA), March 2005

House of Commons, *The Scientific Response to Terrorism*, vol. 1, 20 October 2003. Available at: www.publications.parliament.uk/pa/cm200203/cmselect/cmstech/415/415.pdf (accessed 17 April 2009)

Howard, L.M., *UN Peacekeeping in Civil Wars*. Cambridge: Cambridge University Press, 2007

Howard, R.D., Forest, J.F. and Moore, J. (eds), *Homeland Security and Terrorism: Readings and Interpretations*. New York: McGraw-Hill, 2005

Howard, R.D. and Sawyer, R.L., *Defeating Terrorism: Shaping the New Security Environment*. Guilford, CT: McGraw-Hill, 2004

Howe, D., *Planning Scenarios: Executive Summaries*. Washington, DC: Homeland Security Council, July 2004

Ho-Won, J., *Peacebuilding in Post-conflict Societies: Strategy and Process*. Boulder, CO: Lynne Rienner, 2005

Hughes Butts, K. and Reynolds, J.C. (eds), *The Struggle against Extremist Ideology: Addressing the Conditions That Foster Terrorism*. Carlisle, PA: Center for Strategic Leadership, 2005

Hulnick, A.S., *Keeping Us Safe: Secret Intelligence and Homeland Security*. Westport, CT: Praeger, 2004

Hulnick, A.S., 'Indicators and Warning for Homeland Security: Seeking a New Paradigm'. *International Journal of Intelligence and Counterintelligence*, 18(4), Winter 2005–2006, pp. 593–608

Hurrell, A.J., ' "There Are No Rules" (George W. Bush): International Order after September 11'. *International Relations*, 16, August 2002, pp. 185–204

Inozemtsev, V., 'Fighting Our Mind's Creation: Reason as a Forgotten Victim in the "War on Terror"'. *Militaire Spectator*, 174(6), 2005, pp. 278–287

International Crisis Group, 'Weakening Indonesia's Mujahidin Networks: Lessons from Maluku and Poso'. *Asia Report* no. 103. Brussels: International Crisis Group, 13 October 2005

International Monetary Fund, Legal Department, *Suppressing the Financing of Terrorism: A Handbook for Legislative Drafting*. Washington, DC: IMF, 2003

Jabri, V., 'War, Security and the Liberal State'. *Security Dialogue*, 37, March 2006, pp. 47–64

Jackson, J.H. with Mountcastle, R. and Charles, E., *The Counter-terrorist Handbook: The Essential Guide to Self-Protection in the 21st Century*. London: Michael O'Mara Books, 2005

Jacobson, M., *The West at War: U.S. and European Counterterrorism Efforts, post-September 11*. Washington, DC: Washington Institute for Near East Policy, 2006

Jenkins, B.M., *Unconquerable Nation: Knowing Our Enemy, Strengthening Ourselves*. Santa Monica, CA: RAND, 2006

Jenvald, J. and Morin, M., 'Simulation-Supported Live Training for Emergency Response in Hazardous Environments'. *Simulation Gaming*, 35, September 2004, pp. 363–377

Jermalavicius, T. (ed.), *Baltic Security and Defence Review*, vol. 8, *2006: NATO, European Security and the Baltic Sea Region*. Tartu, Estonia: Baltic Defence College, 2006

Jesse, N.G. and Williams, K.P., *Identity and Institutions: Conflict Reduction in Divided Societies*. Albany, NY: State University of New York Press, 2005

Johansen, R.C., 'Reviving Peacebuilding Tools Ravished by Terrorism, Unilateralism, and Weapons of Mass Destruction'. *International Journal of Peace Studies*, 9(2), Winter 2004, pp. 31–56

Jonas, G., *Die Rache is unser: Ein israelisches Geheimkommando im Einsatz*. Munich: Knaur, 1984

Jones, S.G., *The Rise of European Security Cooperation*. Cambridge: Cambridge University Press, 2007

Jones, T., *SAS: The First Secret Wars: The Unknown Years of Combat and Counter-insurgency*. London: I.B. Tauris, 2005

Jordá, J., Torres, M. and Horsburgh, N. 'The Intelligence Services' Struggle against Al-Qaeda Propaganda'. *International Journal of Intelligence and Counterintelligence*, 18(1), Spring 2005, pp. 31–49

Jürgensen, A., 'Terrorism, Civil Liberties, and Preventive Approaches to Technology: The Difficult Choices Western Societies Face in the War on Terrorism'. *Bulletin of Science, Technology and Society*, 24, February 2004, pp. 55–59

Kalyanaraman, S., 'The Indian Way of Counterinsurgency'. In E. Inbar (ed.), *Democracies and Small Wars*. London: Routledge, 2003, pp. 85–100

Kamien, D., *The McGraw-Hill Homeland Security Handbook: The Definitive Guide for Law Enforcement, and All Other Security Professionals*. New York: McGraw-Hill, 2005

Karagiannis, E. and McCauley, C., 'Hizb Ut-Tahrir Al-Islami: Evaluating the Threat Posed by a Radical Islamic Group That Remains Nonviolent'. *Terrorism and Political Violence*, 18(2), Summer 2006, pp. 315–334

Kargupta, H., Joshi, A., Sivakumar, K. and Yesha, Y. (eds), *Data Mining: Next Generation Challenges and Future Directions*. Cambridge, MA: MIT Press, 2004

Karmon, E., 'The Role of Intelligence in Counter-terrorism'. *Korean Journal of Defense Analysis*, 141, Spring 2002, pp. 119–139

Katona, P., Intriligator, M.D. and Sullivan, J.P. (eds), *Countering Terrorism and WMD*. London: Routledge, 2006

Katz, S. *The Hunt for the Engineer: The Inside Story of How Israel's Counterterrorist Forces Tracked and Killed the Hamas Master Bomber*. Guilford, CT: Lyon Press, 2002

Kaufman, E., Salem, W. and Verhoeven, J. (eds), *Bridging the Divide: Peacebuilding in the Israeli–Palestinian Conflict*. Boulder, CO: Lynne Rienner, 2005

Kaufman, S.J., 'Escaping the Symbolic Politics Trap: Reconciliation Initiatives and Conflict Resolution in Ethnic Wars'. *Journal of Peace Research*, 43, March 2006, pp. 201–218

Kayyam, J.N. and Pangi, R.L. (eds), *First to Arrive: The State and Local Response to Terrorism*. New York: Knopf, 2003

Keating, M., Le More, A. and Lowe, R. (eds), *Aid, Diplomacy and Facts on the Ground: The Case of Palestine*. London: Royal Institute of International Affairs, 2005

Keefe, P.R., *Chatter: Dispatches from the Secret World of Global Eavesdropping*. New York: Random House, 2005

Kemp, G. and Fry, D. (eds), *Keeping the Peace: Conflict Resolution and Peaceful Societies around the World*. London: Routledge, 2003

Kemp, R., 'Homeland Security: Best Practices in America'. *Public Works Management Policy*, 8, April 2004, pp. 271–277

Kennedy da Silva, E.N., 'Responding to International Terrorism: The Contribution of the United Nations'. PhD thesis, University of Queensland, May 2008 (unpublished)

Kenney, M., 'From Pablo to Osama: Counter-terrorism Lessons from the War on Drugs'. *Survival*, 45(3), 2003, pp. 187–206

Keohane, D., *The EU and Counter-terrorism*. Center for European Reform Working Paper, May 2005

Kephart, J., *Immigration Benefits and Terrorism: Moving beyond the 9/11 Staff Report on Terrorist Travel*. Washington, DC: Center for Immigration Studies, September 2005

Kessler, R., *The CIA at War: Inside the Secret Campaign against Terror*. New York: St Martin's Press, 2003

Kettl, D.F., 'Contingent Coordination: Practical and Theoretical Puzzles for Homeland Security'. *American Review of Public Administration*, 33, September 2003, pp. 253–277

Khalsa, S., *Forecasting Terrorism: Indicators and Proven Analytic Techniques*. Lanham, MD: Scarecrow Press, 2004

Kilcullen, D.J., 'Countering Global Insurgency'. *Journal of Strategic Studies*, 28(4), August 2005, pp. 597–617

Kilcullen, D.J., 'Subversion and Countersubversion in the Campaign against Terrorism in Europe'. *Studies in Conflict and Terrorism*, 30(8), August 2007, pp. 647–666

Klare, M. and Kornbluh, P., *Low Intensity Warfare, Counterinsurgency, Proinsurgency and Antiterrorism in the Eighties*. New York: Pantheon, 1998

Klein, A., *Die Rächer: Wie der israelische Geheimdienst die Olympia-Mörder von München jagte*. Munich: DVA, 2006

Koch, A., 'Counterterrorism Co-operation is Endangered by US Renditions'. *Jane's Intelligence Review*, 17(10), October 2005, pp. 20–23

Kolb, D.M., *When Talk Works: Profiles of Mediators*. San Francisco: Jossey-Bass, 1994

Kozlow, C. and Sullivan, J., *Jane's Facility Security Handbook*. Farmington Hills, MI: Gale Group, 2003

Krepinevich, A.F. Jr, 'How to Win in Iraq'. *Foreign Affairs*, 84(5), September–October 2005, pp. 87–104

Kumamoto, R.D., *International Terrorism and American Foreign Relations, 1945–1976*. Boston: Northeastern University Press, 1999

Kumar Singh, U., *The State, Democracy and Anti-terror Laws in India*. New Delhi: Sage, 2007

Kümmel, G. (ed.), *Asymmetrische Konflikte und Terrorismusbekämpfung: Prototypen zukünftiger Kriege*. Baden-Baden, Germany: Nomos, 2003

Kunczik, M., 'Public Relations in Kriegszeiten: Die Notwendigkeit von Lüge und Zensur'. In H.-P. Preußer (ed.), *Krieg in den Medien*. Amsterdamer Beiträge zur neueren Germanistik. Amsterdam: Rodopi, 2005

Kurth, J. (ed.), Special issue, 'America, Democratization and the Muslim World'. *Orbis*, 49(2), Spring 2005, pp. 195–322

Laborde, J.P. and DeFeo, M., 'Problems and Prospects of Implementing UN Action against Terrorism'. *Journal of International Criminal Justice*, 4(5), 1 November 2006, pp. 1087–1103

LaFree, G., Morris, N., Dugan, L. and Fahey, S., 'Identifying Global Terrorist Hot Spots'. In J. Victoroff (ed.), *The Psychology of Terrorism*. Amsterdam: IOS Press, 2006

Lahav, G., *Immigration and Politics in the New Europe: Reinventing Borders*. Cambridge: Cambridge University Press, 2004

Lahneman, W.J., 'Knowledge-Sharing in the Intelligence Community after 9/11'. *International Journal of Intelligence and Counterintelligence*, 17(4), Winter 2004–2005, pp. 614–633

Lai, B., 'Examining the Goals of US Foreign Assistance in the Post-Cold War Period, 1991–96'. *Journal of Peace Research*, 40, January 2003, pp. 103–128

Lansford, T., Pauly, R.J. Jr and Covarrubias, J. (eds), *To Protect and Defend: US Homeland Security Policy*. Aldershot, UK: Ashgate, 2006

Laurence, J. and Vaisse, J., *Integrating Islam: Political and Religious Challenges in Contemporary France*. Washington, DC: Brookings Institution, 2006

Le More, A., 'Killing with Kindness: Funding the Demise of a Palestinian State'. *International Affairs*, 81(5), October 2005, pp. 981–1000

Ledeen, M., *War against the Terror Masters: Why It Happened: Where We Are Now: How We'll Win*. New York: St Martin's Press, 2002

Lee Kuan Yew, 'The United States, Iraq and the War on Terror'. *Foreign Affairs*, 86(1), January–February, 2007, pp. 2–7

Lefevre, S., 'A Look at Intelligence Analysis'. *International Journal of Intelligence and Counterintelligence*, 17, 2004, pp. 231–264

Leffler, M.P., '9/11 and the Past and Future of American Foreign Policy'. *International Affairs*, 79(5), October 2003, pp. 1045–1064

Leiken, R.S., *Bearers of Global Jihad? Immigration and National Security after 9/11*. Washington, DC: Nixon Center, 2004

Leiken, R.S., *Europe's Mujahideen: Where Mass Immigration Meets Global Terrorism*. Washington, DC: Center for Immigration Studies, April 2005

Lennon, A.T.J. (ed.), *The Battle for Hearts and Minds: Using Soft Power to Undermine Terrorist Networks*. Cambridge, MA: MIT Press, 2003

Lerman, E., 'The Primacy of Regional Transformation: US Strategy in the Post-Engagement Era'. *Strategic Assessment*, 2(8), August 2005, pp. 17–21

Lesser, I.O., Hoffman, B., Arquilla, J., Ronfeldt, D., Zarini, M. and Jenkins, B.M., *Countering the New Terrorism*. Santa Monica, CA: Rand, 1999

Leurdijk, D.A. and Steeghs, G., *Decision-Making by the Security Council: Terrorist Acts Which Threaten International Peace and Security, 1989–2004: A Survey of Resolutions*. The Hague: Netherlands Institute of International Relations 'Clingendael', January 2005

Levitt, G.M. and Center for Strategic and International Studies (Washington, DC), *Democracies against Terror: The Western Response to State-Supported Terrorism*. New York: Praeger, 1988

Levitt, M., *Targeting Terror: US Policy toward Middle Eastern State Sponsors and Terrorist Organizations, post-September 11*. Washington, DC: Washington Institute for Near East Policy, 2002

Levitt, M., *No Good Terrorists: Middle Eastern Terrorist Groups, State Sponsors, and the War on Terror*. Washington, DC: Washington Institute for Near East Policy, 2002

Levitt, M., 'Untangling the Terror Web: Identifying and Counteracting the Phenomenon of Crossover between Terrorist Groups'. *SAIS Review*, 24(1), Winter–Spring 2004, pp. 33–48

Levy, B.S. and Sidel, V.W., *Terrorism and Public Health: A Balanced Approach to Strengthening Systems and Protecting People*. Oxford: Oxford University Press, 2003

Levy, Y., *Trial and Error: Israel's Route from War to De-escalation*. Albany, NY: State University of New York, 1997

Lewis, C.W., 'The Clash between Security and Liberty in the US Response to Terror'. *Public Administration Review*, 65(1), January–February 2005, pp. 18–30

Liotta, P.H., 'Through the Looking Glass: Creeping Vulnerabilities and the Reordering of Security'. *Security Dialogue*, 36, March, pp. 49–70

Little, R.G. and Weaver, E.A., 'Protection from Extreme Events: Using a Socio-technological Approach to Evaluate Policy Options'. *International Journal of Emergency Management*, 2(4), January 2006, pp. 263–274

Lord, C. and Barnett, F. (eds), *Political Warfare and Psychological Operations*. Washington, DC: National Defense University Press, 1989

Lubkemann, S.C., 'Migratory Coping in Wartime Mozambique: An Anthropology of Violence and Displacement in "Fragmented Wars" '. *Journal of Peace Research*, 42, July 2005, pp. 493–508

Lum, C., Kennedy, L.W. and Sherley, A.J., *The Effectiveness of Counter-terrorism Strategies*. Manassas, VA: George Mason University, 2006

Lutterbeck, D., *Switzerland and Cooperative Threat Reduction. Occasional Paper Series, no. 43*. Geneva: Centre for Security Policy (GCSP), September 2004

McCallie, [Ambassador] M.F., 'The Campaign against Terrorism: Finding the Right Mix of Foreign Policy Instruments'. In C.J.R. Martin (ed.), *Defeating Terrorism: Strategic Issues Analyses*. Carlisle, PA: Strategic Studies Institute, 2002

McCue, C., *Data Mining and Predictive Analysis: Intelligence Gathering and Crime Analysis*. Oxford: Butterworth-Heinemann, 2007

McCulloch, J. and Pickering, S., 'Suppressing the Financing of Terrorism'. *British Journal of Criminology*, 45(4), July 2005, pp. 470–486

MacFarlane, S.M. and Foong Khong, Y., *Human Security and the UN: A Critical History*. Bloomington: Indiana University Press, 2006

McInerney, T. and Vallely, P., *Endgame: The Blueprint in the War on Terror*. Washington, DC: Regnery, 2004

McIntyre, D.H. and Hancock W.I. (eds), *Business Continuity and Homeland Security*, vol. 1. Cheltenham, UK: Edward Elgar, 2008

McMillan, J. (ed.), *In the Same Light as Slavery: Building a Global Antiterrorist Consensus*. Washington, DC: Institute for National Strategic Studies, 2006

Major, J.S. (ed.), *Intelligence and the Nation's Security*, 2nd edn. Washington, DC: Joint Military Intelligence College, 2002

Makinda, S.M., 'Global Governance and Terrorism'. *Global Change, Peace and Security*, 15(1), 2003, pp. 43–58

Malici, A., 'Discord and Collaboration between Allies: Managing External Threats and Internal Cohesion in Franco-British Relations during the 9/11 Era'. *Journal of Conflict Resolution*, 49(1), February 2005, pp. 90–119

Malkasian, C., 'The Role of Perceptions and Political Reform in Counterinsurgency: The Case of Western Iraq, 2004–2005'. *Small Wars and Insurgencies*, 17(3), 2006, pp. 367–394

Malone, D.M., 'The High-Level Panel and the Security Council'. *Security Dialogue*, 36, September 2005, pp. 370–372

Maluf, R., 'The FP Memorandum. Urgent: How to Sell America'. *Foreign Policy*, July–August 2005, pp. 74–79

Maniscalco, P.M. and Christen, H.T., *Understanding Terrorism and Managing the Consequences*. Upper Saddle River, NJ: Prentice Hall, 2001

Marrin, S., 'Homeland Security and the Analysis of Foreign Intelligence'. *The Intelligencer: Journal of U.S. Intelligence Studies*, 13(2), Winter–Spring 2003, pp. 25–36

Marrin, S., 'Preventing Intelligence Failures by Learning from the Past'. *International Journal of Intelligence and Counterintelligence*, 17(4), Winter 2004–2005, pp. 655–672

Martinet, P., *La DGSE: service action, un agent sort de l'ombre* (The DGSE: Action Service, An Agent Comes Out of the Shadow). Paris: Editions Privé, 2005

Mason, A., 'Colombia's Democratic Security Agenda: Public Order in the Security Tripod'. *Security Dialogue*, 34(4), 2003, pp. 391–409

Mathieu, R., *La lutte contre les terrorismes, domaines de coopération au sein et entre les organisations sécuritaires en Europe*. Brussels: Defensiestudiecentrum, May 2005

Matthew, R. and Shambaugh, G., 'The Pendulum Effect: Explaining Shifts in the Democratic Response to Terrorism'. *Analyses of Social Issues and Public Policy*, 5(1), December 2005, pp. 223–233

Maxwell, B., *Homeland Security. A Documentary History*. Washington, DC: CQ Press, 2004

Melissen, J., *The New Public Diplomacy: Soft Power in International Relations*. Basingstoke, UK: Palgrave Macmillan, 2005

Mendelsohn, B., 'Sovereignty under Attack: The International Society Meets the Al Qaeda Network'. *Review of International Studies*, 31(1), January 2005, pp. 45–68

Merari, A., 'Deterring Fear'. *Harvard International Review*, 23(4), 2002, pp. 26–31

Mickolus, E.F., 'Multilateral Legal Efforts to Combat Terrorism: Diagnosis and Prognosis', *Ohio Northern University Law Review*, 6(1), 1979, pp. 13–51

Mickolus, E.F., 'How Do We Know We're Winning the War against Terrorists? Issues in Measurement'. *Studies in Conflict and Terrorism*, 25(3), 2002, pp. 151–160

Mickolus, E., Heyman, E.S., and Schlotter, J., 'Responding to Terrorism: Basic and Applied Research'. In S. Sloan and R. Schultz (eds), *Responding to the Terrorist Threat: Security and Crisis Management*. New York: Pergamon Press, 1980

Midford, P., *Japan, Germany, and the 'War on Terrorism': Culturalism, Defensive and Offensive Realism*. Honolulu: International Studies Association (ISA), March 2005

Mili, H., 'Securing the Northern Front: Canada and the War on Terror'. Part I. *Terrorism Monitor*, 3(14), 15 July 2005

Mili, H., 'Securing the Northern Front: Canada and the War on Terror', Part II. *Terrorism Monitor*, 3(15), 28 July 2005

Millar, A. and Rosand, E., *Allied against Terrorism: What's Needed to Strengthen Worldwide Commitment*. New York: Century Foundation Press, 2006

Miller, G.D., 'Confronting Terrorisms: Group Motivation and Successful State Policies'. *Terrorism and Political Violence*, 19(3), Fall 2007, pp. 331–350

Miller, J.A., 'Turning Open Source Data into Knowledge about Global Threat'. *Interaction Systems Incorporated Paper* (ISIP), no. 9, 6 May 2005

Ministerie van Binnenlandse Zaken, *Vierde voortgangsrapportage terrorismebestrijding*. The Hague: Ministerie van Binnenlandse Zaken en Koninkrijksrelaties, 7 June 2006

Ministerie van Justitie, Directie Algemene Justitiële Strategie, *Nota radicalisme en radicalisering*. 5358374/05/AJS/. The Hague, 19 August 2005

Miniter, R., *Shadow War: America's Secret Successes and Averted Disasters in the Ongoing War on Terror*. Washington, DC: Regnery, 2004

Mitchell, G.J., *Making Peace*. New York: Knopf, 1999

Miyaoka, T., 'Terrorist Crisis Management in Japan: Historical Development and Changing Response (1970–1997)'. *Terrorism and Political Violence*, 10(2), 1998, pp. 23–52

Mockaitis, T.R. and Rich, P.B., *Grand Strategy in the War against Terrorism*. London: Portland, 2003

Mohsin, M., 'The Twelfth SAARC Summit: Quest for Durable South Asian Cooperation'. *South Asian Survey*, 12, March 2005, pp. 35–46

Molier, G., 'De strijd tegen terrorisme en de mythe van de vooruitgang'. *Vrede en veiligheid*, 34(3), 2005, pp. 376–386

Möller, H. (ed.), *Der rote Holocaust und die Deutschen: Die Debatte um das 'Schwarzbuch des Kommunismus'*. Munich: Piper, 1999

Moolakkattu, S.J., 'The Concept and Practice of Conflict Prevention: A Critical Reappraisal'. *International Studies*, 42, January 2005, pp. 1–19

Moore, K.C., *Airport, Aircraft, and Airline Security*. Boston: Butterworth-Heinemann, 1991

Morag, N., 'Measuring Success in Coping with Terrorism: The Israeli Case'. *Studies in Conflict and Terrorism*, 28(4), July–August 2005, pp. 307–320

Moss, T., Roodman, D. and Standley, S., *The Global War on Terror and U.S. Development Assistance: USAID Allocation by Country, 1998–2005*. Washington, DC: Center for Global Development, July 2005

Mullard, M. and Cole, B.A. (eds), *Globalisation, Citizenship and the War on Terror*. Cheltenham, UK: Edward Elgar, 2007

Müller-Kraenner, S., *Energy Security*. London: Earthscan, 2008

Mulqueen, M., *United We Stand? EU Counterterrorism Initiatives Meet a Small Member State's Security Community*. Honolulu: International Studies Association, March 2005

Munday, P., Pakenham, M., Nicoll, A. *et al.*, *New European Approaches to Counterterrorism*. Reading, UK: Thales Research and Technology, 21 March 2006

Muni, S.D., 'Human Rights, State Sovereignty and Military Intervention: Reflections on a Critical Discourse'. *International Relations in a Globalising World*, 1, June 2005, pp. 99–114

Mylroie, L., 'The Need for Strategic Intelligence'. *Journal of Counterterrorism and Homeland Security International*, 10(3), 2004, pp. 28–33

Naftali, T., *Blind Spot: The Secret History of American Counterterrorism*. Jackson, TN: Basic Books, 2005

National Research Council, *Making the Nation Safer: The Role of Science and Technology in Countering Terrorism*. Washington, DC: National Academic Press, 2002

Nesi, G. (ed.), *International Cooperation in Counter-terrorism: The United Nations and Regional Organizations in the Fight against Terrorism*. Aldershot, UK: Ashgate, 2006

Noda, S., 'Container Shipping and Security Issues: The Carriers' Responsibility in the Fight against Terrorism'. *Maritime Economics and Logistics*, 6(2), June 2004, pp. 157–186

Nuñez-Neto, B. and Viña, S., 'Border Security: Barriers along the U.S. International Border'. CRS Report. *International Journal of Terrorism and Political Hotspots*, 1(2/3), 2004, pp. 205–232

Obaid, N. and Cordesman, A., *Saudi National Security Imperatives: Challenges and Developments*. Washington, DC: CSIS, 2005

Oceana Publications, *Terrorism: Documents of International and Local Control*. Dobbs Ferry, NY: Oceana Publications, 1979–2004

O'Donnell, P., *In Time of War: Hitler's Terrorist Attack on America*. New York: New Press, 2005

OECD, *The Financial War on Terrorism: A Guide by the Financial Action Task Force*. Paris: OECD, 2004

OECD, 'Terrorism Risk Insurance in OECD Countries: Summary of Conclusions and Policy Options: Policy Issues in Insurance no. 09'. *OECD Finance and Investment/Insurance and Pensions*, 2005 (9), April 2006, pp. 9–30

O'Hanlon, M.E., *Protecting the American Homeland: A Preliminary Analysis*. Washington, DC: Brookings Institution Press, 2002

Omand, D., 'Countering International Terrorism: The Use of Strategy'. *Survival*, 47(4), Winter 2005–2006, pp. 107–116

O'Neil, P.H., 'Complexity and Counterterrorism: Thinking about Biometrics'. *Studies in Conflict and Terrorism*, 28(6), 2005, pp. 547–566

O'Sullivan, M., *Shrewd Sanctions: Statecraft and State Sponsors of Terrorism*. Washington, DC: Brookings Institution, 2003

Pape, M.S., 'Constitutional Covert Operations: A Force Multiplier for Preemption'. *Military Review*, March–April 2004, pp. 52–59

Parfomak, P.W., *Vulnerability of Concentrated Critical Infrastructure: Background and Policy Options*. CRS Report for Congress RL33206, 21 December 2006

Patman, R.G., *Globalization, Civil Conflict and the National Security State*. London: Frank Cass, 2005

Patman, R., 'Globalisation, the New US Exceptionalism and the War on Terror'. *Third World Quarterly*, 27(6), September 2006, pp. 963–986

Pedazhur, A. and Ranstorp, M., 'A Tertiary Model for Countering Terrorism in Liberal Democracies: The Case of Israel'. *Terrorism and Political Violence*, 13(2), Summer 2001, pp. 1–26

Peers, S., 'EU Responses to Terrorism'. *International and Comparative Law Quarterly*, 52(1), January 2003, pp. 227–244

Pena, C. and Scheuer, M., *Winning the Un-War: A New Strategy for the War on Terrorism*. Dulles, VA: Potomac Books, 2007

Pentagon, *Measuring Stability and Security in Iraq*. House Conference Report 109–72 accompanying H.R. 1268, Emergency Supplementary Appropriations Act for Defense, the Global War on Terror, and Tsunami Relief, 2005, Public Law 109–13

Perle, R., *Combating Terrorism: The Challenge of Measuring Effectiveness*. CRS Report for Congress RL33160, Congressional Research Service, Library of Congess, 23 November 2005

Perliger, A. and Pedahzur, A., 'Coping with Suicide Attacks: Lessons from Israel'. *Public Money and Management*, 26(5), November 2006, pp. 281–286

Perliger, A., Pedahzur, A. and Zalmanovitch, Y., 'The Defensive Dimension of the Battle against Terrorism: An Analysis of Management of Terror Incidents in Jerusalem'. *Journal of Contingencies and Crisis Mangement*, 13(2), June 2005, pp. 79–91

Perrow, C., *The Next Catastrophe: Reducing Our Vulnerabilities to Natural, Industrial, and Terrorist Disasters*. Princeton, NJ: Princeton University Press, 2007

Perry, R.W., 'Emergency Operations Centres in an Era of Terrorism: Policy and Management Functions'. *Journal of Contingencies and Crisis Management*, 11(4), December 2003, pp. 151–159

Perry, R.W., 'Municipal Terrorism Management in the United States'. *Disaster Prevention and Management: An International Journal*, 12(3), 2003, pp. 190–202

Peters, R., *Beyond Terror: Strategy in a Changing World*. Mechanicsburg, PA: Stackpole Books, 2002

Peterson, M.B. (ed.), *Intelligence 2000: Revising the Basic Elements*. Sacramento, CA, and Lawrenceville, NJ: Law Enforcement Intelligence Unit (LEIU)/International Association of Law Enforcement Intelligence Analysts (IALEIA), 2000

Phythian, M., 'Still a Matter of Trust: Post-9/11 British Intelligence and Political Culture'. *International Journal of Intelligence and Counterintelligence*, 18(4), Winter 2005–2006, pp. 653–681

Pieth, M., 'Criminalizing the Financing of Terrorism'. *Journal of International Criminal Justice*, 4(5), November 2006, pp. 1074–1086

Pillar, P., *Terrorism and U.S. Foreign Policy*. Washington, DC: Brookings Institution Press, 2003

Pillar, P., 'Counterterrorism after Al Qaeda'. *Washington Quarterly*, 27(3), 2004, pp. 101–113

Pillar, P., 'Intelligence, Policy, and the War in Iraq'. *Foreign Affairs*, 85(2), March–April 2006, pp. 15–28

Posen, B.R., 'The Struggle against Terrorism: Grand Strategy, and Tactics'. *International Security*, 26(3), Winter 2001–2002, pp. 39–55

Posner, R.A., *Catastrophe: Risk and Response*. Oxford: Oxford University Press, 2004

Posner, R.A., *Countering Terrorism: Blurred Focus, Halting Steps*. Lanham, MD: Rowman & Littlefield, 2007

Powers, T., *Intelligence Wars: American Secret History from Hitler to Al-Qaeda*. New York: New York Review of Books, 2004

Press-Barnathan, G., 'The Changing Incentives for Security Regionalization: From 11/9 to 9/11'. *Cooperation and Conflict*, 40, September, 2005, pp. 281–304

Preston, E., 'The USA PATRIOT Act: New Adventures in American Extraterritoriality'. *Journal of Financial Crime*, 10(2), 2003, pp. 104–116

Primakov, E.M., *A World Challenged: Fighting Terrorism in the Twenty-First Century*. Washington, DC: Nixon Center and Brookings Institution Press, 2004

Probst, P.S., 'Measuring Success in Countering Terrorism: Problems and Pitfalls'. Paper presented at the IEEE Symposium on Intelligence and Security Informatics, Atlanta, 19–20 May 2005

Purcell, J.S. and Weintraub, J.D. (eds), *Topics in Terrorism: Toward a Transatlantic Consensus on the Nature of the Threat*. Washington, DC: Atlantic Council, 2004

Quandt, W.B., *Peace Process: American Diplomacy and the Arab–Israeli Conflict since 1967*. Washington, DC: Brookings Institution, 2005

Quénivet, N., 'You Are the Weakest Link and We Will Help You! The Comprehensive Strategy of the United Nations to Fight Terrorism'. *Journal of Conflict and Security Law*, 11(3), 2006, pp. 371–397

Rademaker, J.M.G. and den Hollander, C.J., *Intelligence Gathering: Looking for the Needle in the Haystack*. Brussels: NATO, 2006

Rami Mroz, J., 'Countering Violent Extremism: Videopower and Cyberspace'. East-West Institute. Policy Paper 1, 2008

Rasmussen, M.V., *The Risk Society at War: Terror, Technology and Strategy in the 21st Century*. Cambridge: Cambridge University Press, 2007

Rasser, M., 'The Dutch Response to Moluccan Terrorism, 1970–1978'. *Studies in Conflict and Terrorism*, 28(6), 2005, pp. 481–492

Rees, W., *Transatlantic Counter-terrorism Cooperation: The New Imperative*. London: Routledge, 2006

Rees, W. and Aldrich, R., 'Contending Cultures of Counterterrorism: Transatlantic Divergence or Convergence?' *International Affairs*, 81(5), October 2005, pp. 905–924

Reinares, F., *European Democracies against Terrorism: Governmental Policies and Intergovernmental Cooperation*. Aldershot, UK: Ashgate, 2000

Report of the Presidential Study Group. *Security, Reform, and Peace: The Three Pillars of US Strategy in The Middle East*. Washington, DC: Washington Institute for Near East Policy, 2005

Report on the Status of 9/11 Commission Recommendations, Part I: Homeland Security, Emergency Preparedness and Response. 9/11 Public Discourse Project, 14 September 2005

REU, *Bestrijding van terrorismefinanciering: halfjaarlijks verslag*. Brussels: Raad van de Europese Unie, 21 November 2005

REU, *Uitvoering van het actieplan inzake terrorismebestrijding*. Brussels: Raad van de Europese Unie, 29 November 2005

REU, *Terrorismebestrijdingsstrategie van de Europese Unie*. Brussels: Raad van de Europese Unie, 30 November 2005

Reuter, P. and Truman, E.M., *Chasing Dirty Money: The Fight against Anti-Money Laundering*. Washington, DC: Institute for International Economics, 2004

Richelson, J.T., *The Wizards of Langley: Inside the CIA's Directorate of Science and Technology*. Jackson, TN: Basic Books, 2001

Riedel, B., *The Search for al Qaeda: Its Leadership, Ideology, and Future*. Washington, DC: Brookings Institution, 2008

Rifkind, G., *Making Terrorism History*. London: Random House, 2007

Riley, K.J., Treverton, G.F., Wilson, J. and Davis, L.M., *State and Local Intelligence in the War on Terrorism*. MG-394-RC. Santa Monica: RAND, 2005

Romaniuk, P., *Global Counterterrorism*. London: Routledge, 2009

Rosand, E., 'The UN-Led Multilateral Institutional Response to Jihadist Terrorism: Is a Global Counterterrorism Body Needed?' *Journal of Conflict and Security Law*, 11(3), 2006, pp. 399–427

Rosenthal, U., 'September 11: Public Administration and the Study of Crises and Crisis Management'. *Administration Society*, 35, May 2003, pp. 129–143

Roshandel, J. and Chadha, S., *Jihad and International Security*. New York: Palgrave Macmillan, 2006

Rotberg, R.I. (ed.), *Battling Terrorism in the Horn of Africa*. Washington, DC: Brookings Institution, 2005

Rothkopf, D., *Running the World: The Inside Story of the National Security Council and the Architects of American Power*. New York: PublicAffairs, 2005

Rubin, B.M., *The Politics of Counterterrorism: The Ordeal of Democratic States*. Washington, DC: Johns Hopkins Foreign Policy Insitute, 1990

Rubin, C. and Olson, L.L., 'Countering Terrorism: Dimensions of Preparedness'. *Journal of Homeland Security and Emergency Management*, 1(2), 2004. Available at: http://bepress.com/jhsem/vol1/iss2/17 (accessed 21 April 2009)

Rudman, W.B., Clarke, R.A. and Metzl, J.F., *Emergency Responders: Drastically Underfunded, Dangerously Unprepared*. Independent Task Force Report. New York: Council on Foreign Relations, 2004

Rudner, M., 'Challenge and Response: Canada's Intelligence Community and the War on Terrorism'. *Canadian Foreign Policy*, 11(2), Winter 2004, pp. 1–24

Rudner, M., 'Hunters and Gatherers: The Intelligence Coalition against Islamic Terrrorism'. *International Journal of Intelligence and Counterintelligence*, 17, 2004, pp. 193–230

Rudner, M., 'Protecting North America's Energy Infrastructure against Terrorism'. *International Journal of Intelligence and Counterintelligence*, 19(3), Fall 2006, pp. 424–442

Rudner, M., 'Using Financial Intelligence against the Funding of Terorism'. *International Journal of Intelligence and Counterintelligence*, 19, 2006, pp. 32–58

Salij, J., 'The Significance of "Ineffective" Methods of Fighting Terrorism'. *American Behavioral Scientist*, 48, February 2005, pp. 700–709

Sandler, T., 'Fighting Terrorism: What Economics Can Tell Us'. *Challenge*, 45, May–June 2002, pp. 5–18

Savage, P., *The Safe Travel Book: A Guide for the International Traveler*. Lexington, MA: Lexington Books, 1988

Savitch, H.V., 'Does 9–11 Portend a New Paradigm for Cities?' *Urban Affairs Review*, 39, September 2003, pp. 103–127

Savitch, H.V., *Cities in a Time of Terror*. London: Eurospan, 2008

Scheuer, M., 'Assessing London and Sharm Al-Sheaikh: The Role of Internet Intelligence and Urban Warfare Training'. *Terrorism Focus*, 2(15), 5 August 2005

Schleifer, R., 'Democracies, Limited War and Psychological Operations'. In E. Inbar (ed.), *Democracies and Small Wars*. London: Routledge, 2003

Schleifer, R., 'Psychological Operations: A New Variation on an Age Old Art: Hezbollah versus Israel'. *Studies in Conflict and Terrorism*, 29(1), January–February 2006, pp. 1–19

Schmid, A.P., 'The Strategy of the United Nations in Preventing and Combating International Terrorism'. Paper prepared for the Istanbul Conference on Democracy and Global Security, 9–11 June 2005

Schmid, A.P. and Crelinsten, R.D. (eds), *Western Responses to Terrorism*. London: Frank Cass, 1993

Schmid, J., 'Ein Neuansatz in der Auseinandersetzung mit dem internationalen Terrorismus'. *Europäische Sicherheit*, December 2005, pp. 75–80

Schneier, B., *Beyond Fear: Thinking Sensibly about Security in an Uncertain World*. New York: Copernicus Books, 2003

Schröm, O., *Gefährliche Mission: Die Geschichte des erfolgreichsten deutschen Terrorfahnders*. Frankfurt am Main: Scherz Verlag, 2005

Schulhofer, S.J., *Rethinking the Patriot Act: Keeping America Safe and Free*. Washington, DC: Century Foundation, 2005

Schwartz, J.M., 'Misreading Islamist Terrorism: The "War against Terrorism" and Just-War Theory'. *Metaphilosophy*, 35(3), April 2004, pp. 273–302

Segell, G.M., 'Intelligence Methodologies Applicable to the Madrid Train Bombings, 2004'. *International Journal of Intelligence and Counterintelligence*, 18(2), Summer 2005, pp. 221–238

Seifert, J.W., *Data Mining and Homeland Security: An Overview*. CRS Report for Congress. RL31798, 7 June, 2005

Selliaas, A., *From Internationalization of Terrorism to the Internationalization of Anti-terrorism: The Role of the Summer Olympic Games*. Oslo: Norwegian Institute of International Affairs, 2005

Shapiro, I., *Containment: Rebuilding Strategy against Global Terror*. Princeton, NJ: Princeton University Press, 2007

Shapiro, J. and Suzan, B., 'The French Experience of Counter-terrorism'. *Survival*, 45(1), 2003, pp. 67–98

Shapiro, S., 'Intelligence Services and Political Transformation in the Middle East'. *International Journal of Intelligence and Counterintelligence*, 17(4), Winter 2004–2005, pp. 575–600

Sharansky, N., *The Case for Democracy: The Power of Freedom to Overcome Tyranny and Terror*. New York: PublicAffairs, 2004

Shaun, G., 'France and the War on Terrorism'. *Terrorism and Political Violence*, 15(1), March 2003, pp. 124–147

Simon, S. and Martini, J., 'Terrorism: Denying Al Qaeda Its Popular Support'. *Washington Quarterly*, 28(1), Winter 2004–2005, pp. 131–145

Simon, S. and Stevenson, J., 'Her Majesty's Secret Service'. *The National Interest*, No. 82, Winter 2005–2006, pp. 48–54

Singer, S., *Confronting Jihad: Israel's Struggle and the World after 9/11*. London: Simon & Schuster, 2007

Singh, S. and Singh, M., 'Explosives Detection Systems (EDS) for Aviation Security'. *Signal Processing*, 83(1), January 2003, pp. 31–55

Smith, A.L., 'The Politics of Negotiating the Terrorist Problem in Indonesia'. *Studies in Conflict and Terrorism*, 28(1), 2005, pp. 33–44

Spence, K., 'World Risk Society and War against Terror'. *Political Studies*, 53(2), 2005, pp. 284–302

Spencer, A., 'The Problems of Evaluating Counter-terrorism'. UNISCI Discussion Paper no. 12, Munich, October 2006, pp. 179–201

Stafford, G., Yu, L. and Kobina Armoo, A. 'Crisis Management and Recovery: How Washington, D.C., Hotels Responded to Terrorism'. *Cornell Hotel and Restaurant Administration Quarterly*, 43, October 2002, pp. 27–40

Stahnke, U., 'Pakistan: Die islamische Nuklearmacht und der der Kampf gegen den Terror' *Europäische Sicherheit*, 55(1), January 2006, pp. 28–33

Stanley Foundation, *Capturing the 21st Century Security Agenda: Prospects for Collective Response*. Muscatine, IA: Stanley Foundation, 2004

Stanton, B., *The Anti-terror Checklist: Preparing for the Unthinkable*. London: Harper, 2001

Steiner, B.H., *Collective Preventive Diplomacy: A Study in International Conflict Management*. Albany, NY: State University of New York Press, 2004

Stepanova, E., *Anti-terrorism and Peace-Building during and after Conflict*. Stockholm: Stockholm International Peace Research Institute, June 2003

Stepanova, E., 'War and Peace Building', *Washington Quarterly*, 27(4), Fall 2004, pp. 127–136

Stepanova, E., 'Russia's Approach to the Fight against Terrorism'. In J. Hedenskog, V. Konnander, B. Nygren, I. Oldberg and C. Pursiainen (eds), *Russia as a Great Power: Dimensions of Security under Putin*. London: Routledge, 2005

Stepanova, E., 'The Suppression of the Financing of Terrorism', *Mezhdunarodnyie Protsessy*, 3(2)(7), May–August 2005, pp. 66–73

Stephens, A.C. and Vaughan-Williams, N. (eds), *Terrorism and the Politics of Response*. London: Routledge, 2008

Steven, G.C.S. and Gunaratna, R., *Counterterrorism: A Reference Handbook*. Santa Barbara, CA: ABC-CLIO, 2004

Stevenson, J., 'Counter-terrorism: Containment and Beyond'. Adelphi Papers. London: International Institute for Strategic Studies

Stever, J.A., 'Adapting Intergovernmental Management to the New Age of Terrorism'. *Administration and Society*, 37, September 2005, pp. 379–403

Stohl, M., *Approaching Counter-terrorism: The Global War on Terror and the Problem of Metrics*. University Of California, Santa Barbara, June 2006

Stone, C., *Hunting Eric Rudolph*. New York: Berkley Books, 2005

Strategy Unit, *Investing in Prevention: A Prime Minister's Strategy Unit Report to the Government: An International Strategy to Manage Risks of Instability and Improve Crisis Response*. London: Strategy Unit, Admiralty Arch, February 2005

Stein, T., 'Preemption and Terrorism'. In H. Langholtz, B. Kondoch and A. Wells (eds), *International Peacekeeping: The Yearbook of International Peace Operations*, vol. 9. Leiden: Nijhoff, 2005

Suder, G., *Corporate Strategies under International Terrorism and Adversity*. Cheltenham, UK: Edward Elgar, 2006

Sullivan, J.P. and Bunker, R.J., 'Multilateral Counter-insurgency Networks'. *Low Intensity Conflict and Law Enforcement*, 11(2–3), 2002, pp. 353–368

Swienty, W.Ç., 'Bekämpfungsstrategien gegen den internationalen islamistischen Terrorismus'. *Terrorismus*, no. 6, December 2004

Szyliowicz, J.S., 'Aviation Security: Promise or Reality?' *Studies in Conflict and Terrorism*, 27(1), January–February 2004, pp. 47–63

Taarnby, M., 'Yemen's Committee for Dialogue: Can Jihadists Return to Society?' *Terrorism Monitor*, 3(14), 15 July 2005. Available at: www.jamestown.org/programs/gta/single/?tx_ttnews[tt_news]=527&tx_tt news[backPid]=180&no_cache=1 (accessed 21 April 2009)

Taspinar, O., *Fighting Radicalism with Human Development, Education and Growth in the Islamic World*. Washington, DC: Brookings Institution Press, 2005

Taylor, P.M., 'Can the Information War on Terror Be Won? A Polemical Essay'. *Media, War and Conflict*, 1, April 2008, pp. 118–124

Tenet, G., *At the Center of the Storm*. London: HarperCollins, 2007

Theidon, K., 'Justice in Transition: The Micropolitics of Reconciliation in Postwar Peru'. *Journal of Conflict Resolution*, 50, June 2006, pp. 433–457

Thomas, J., 'The Moral Ambiguity of Social Control in Cyberspace: A Retro-assessment of the "Golden Age" of Hacking'. *New Media and Society*, 7, October 2005, pp. 599–624

Thomas, T.S., *Beneath the Surface: Intelligence Preparation of the Battlespace for Counterterrorism*. Washington, DC: Joint Military Intelligence College, Center for Strategic Intelligence Research, November 2004

Thomas, W.C., *American Public Diplomacy in Thailand: Garnering Support for the Fight against Terrorism*. Honolulu: International Studies Association (ISA), March 2005

Tir, J., 'Dividing Countries to Promote Peace: Prospects for Long-Term Success of Partitions'. *Journal of Peace Research*, 42, September 2005, pp. 545–562

TNO, 'Dossier terrorisme: focus op terreurbestrijding: activiteiten in vele schakels van de veiligheidsketen'. *TNO Magazine*, The Hague, December 2005, pp. 13–20

Tsoukala, A., 'Democracy in the Light of Security: British and French Political Discourses on Domestic Counter-terrorism Policies'. *Political Studies*, 54(3), October 2006, pp. 607–627

Tucker, H.H., *Combating the Terrorists: Democratic Responses to Political Violence*. New York: Facts On File, 1988

Tudor, R., 'Romania Creates New Counterterrorism Unit'. *Jane's Intelligence Review*, 17(1), January 2005, pp. 18–21

UK Government, Joint Committee on Human Rights. Government Response to the Committee's Third Report of This Session: Counter-terrorism Policy and Human Rights: Terrorism Bill and Related Matters. Tenth Report of Session 2005–2006, February 2006. Available at: www.publications.parliament. uk/pa/jt200506/jtselect/jtrights/114/114.pdf (accessed 17 April 2009)

Ullman, H., 'Is the US Winning or Losing the Global War on Terror and How Do We Know?' *Australian Journal of International Affairs*, 60(1), March 2006, pp. 29–41

Ullman, H.K., *Finishing Business: Ten Steps to Defeat Global Terror*. Washington, DC: Center for Strategic and International Studies, 2004

UN Counter-terrorism Online Handbook. New York: United Nations, 2007. Available at: www.un.org/terrorism/ cthandbook/ (accessed 21 April 2009)

United Nations, *A More Secure World: Our Shared Responsibility: Report of the High-level U.N. Panel on Threats, Challenges and Change*. 2 December 2004

United Nations Office on Drugs and Crime (UNODC), *Delivering Counter-terrorism Assistance*, April 2005

United Nations Global Counter-terrorism Strategy and Plan of Action. *Resolution adopted by the General Assembly*. New York: United Nations, 2006 (A/RES/60/288, 60th Session, agenda items 46 and 120), 20 September 2006

United Nations General Assembly, *Uniting against Terrorism: Recommendations for a Global Counter-terrorism Strategy: Report of the Secretary-General*. New York: United Nations General Assembly, 2006

United Nations Office on Drugs and Crime (UNODC), *Combating International Terrorism: The Contribution of the United Nations*. New York: United Nations, 2003

United Nations Office on Drugs and Crime (UNODC), *2008 World Drug Report*. United Nations Publication, 2008

University of Arizona, Eller College of Management, Artificial Intelligence Lab, 'Terrorism Knowledge Discovery Project: A Knowledge Discovery Approach to Addressing the Threats of Terrorism', August 2004. Available at: http://ai.eller.arizona.edu

University of Arizona, Eller College of Management, Artificial Intelligence Lab. The Dark Web Portal. 'Collecting and Analyzing the Presence of Domestic and International Terrorist Groups on the Web', August 2004

Urban, J., *Die Bekämpfung des Internationalen islamistischen Terrorismus*. Wiesbaden: VS-Verlag, 2006

Urban, M., *Big Boys' Rules: SAS and The Secret Struggle against the IRA*. London: Faber & Faber, 1992

US Government, *The National Security Strategy of the United States of America*. Washington, DC: White House, 2006

US–Russian Collaboration in Combating Radiological Terrorism. Washington, DC: National Academies Press, 2007

V&W, *De Nederlandse overheid en port and maritime security*. Ministerie van Verkeer en Waterstaat/DGG, 2 November 2004. Available at: www.minvenw/dgg/dgg/nl/sealgemeen.shtml

Van Amersfoort, R., Van Buuren, J., Kalkman, K. [*et al.*] *Onder druk: terrorismebestrijding in Nederland*. Breda, Netherlands: Papieren Tijger, 2006

Van den Heuvel K. (ed.), *A Just Response on Terrorism; Democracy and September 11, 2001*. New York: Thunder's Mouth Press/Nation Books, 2002

van Ham, P., 'War, Lies, and Videotape: Public Diplomacy and the USA's War on Terrorism'. *Security Dialogue*, 34, December 2003, pp. 427–444

Van Leeuwen, M. (ed.), *Confronting Terrorism: European Experiences, Threat Perceptions and Policies*. The Hague: Kluwer Law International 2003

Van Woensel, J., *Vrij van explosieven: de geschiedenis van het EOCKL en zijn voorgangers, 1944–2004*. Amsterdam: Boom, 2005

Vidino, L., 'A Preliminary Assessment of Counter-radicalization in the Netherlands'. *CTC Sentinel*, 1(9), 2008, pp. 12–14

Vines, A., 'Combating Light Weapons Proliferation in West Africa'. *International Affairs*, 81(2), March 2005, pp. 341–360

Von Hippel, K. (ed.), *Europe Confronts Terrorism*. Basingstoke, UK: Macmillan, 2005

Von Hippel, K., *Counter Radicalization Development Assistance*. DIIS Working Paper 2006/9. Copenhagen: Danish Institute for International Studies, 2006

Von Knop, J. and Frank, H. (eds), *Netz- und Computersicherheit: Sind wir auf einen Angriff auf unsere Informationssysteme und Informations-Infrastrukturen vorbereitet?* Düsseldorf: Heinrich Heine Universität, 2003

Von Knop, J. and Wowereit, J. (eds), *Countering Modern Terrorism: History, Current Issues and Future Threats.* Bielefeld, Germany: W. Bertelsmann, 2005

Von Tangen Page, M. and Hamill, O., *Security Sector Reform and Its Role in Challenging of Radicalism.* DIIS Working Paper 2006/10. Copenhagen: Danish Institute for International Studies, 2006

Voskuilen, T., 'Operation Messiah: Did Christianity Start as a Roman Psychological Counterinsurgency Operation?' *Small Wars and Insurgencies,* 16(2), 2005, pp. 192–215

Voss, C.T., 'Crisis Negotiation: A Counter-intuitive Method to Disrupt Terrorism'. *Studies in Conflict and Terrorism,* 27(5), September–October 2004, pp. 455–459

Walker, C., 'Clamping Down on Terrorism in the United Kingdom'. *Journal of International Criminal Justice,* 4(5), 1 November 2006, pp. 1137–1151

Walker, D.H., *Developing Metrics for the Global War on Terrorism.* Newport, RI: Naval War College, Joint Military Operations Department, 2005

Wallace, P., 'Alternatives to Ethnic Cleansing: Transfers of Population or Power Sharing'. In N.I. Xirotiris (ed.), *Ethnic Identities and Political Action in Post Cold War Europe.* Xanthi, Greece: International Demokritos Foundation Press, 2001

Wallace, P., 'Countering Terrorist Movements in India: Kashmir and Khalistan'. In R. Art and L. Richardson (eds), *Democracy and Counterterrorism Lessons from the Past,* Washington, DC: United States Institute of Peace, 2006

Wallace, P. and McDonnell, S., 'Deal with the Devil: Negotiating the Threat of Terrorism'. *University of Missouri Peace Studies Review,* 1(2), Spring 2005, pp. 9–17

Wallensteen, P. and Staibano, C. (eds), *International Sanctions: Between Deeds and Words.* London: Frank Cass, 2005

Warbrick, C., 'The European Response to Terrorism in an Age of Human Rights'. *European Journal of International Law,* 15(5), November 2004, pp. 989–1018

Ward, C.A., 'Building Capacity to Combat International Terrorism: The Role of the United Nations Security Council'. *Journal of Conflict and Security Law,* 8(2), October 2003, pp. 289–305

Warde, I., *The Financial War on Terror.* London: I.B. Tauris, 2004

Warde, I., *The Price of Fear: Al-Qaeda and the Truth behind the Financial War on Terror,* London: I.B. Tauris, 2007

Watkins, E., 'Yemen's Innovative Approach to the War on Terror'. *Terrorism Monitor,* 3(4), 24 February 2005. Available at: www.jamestown.org/programs/gta/single/?tx_ttnews[tt_news]=316&tx_ttnews[backPid]= 180&no_cache=1 (accessed 21 April 2009)

Wehr, A., 'Terrorismusbekämpfung in Europa'. *Analysis and Alternatives,* no. 7, 2002, pp. 863–870

Weinberg, L. (ed.), *Democratic Responses to Terrorism.* New York: Routledge, 2008

White, G.F., 'Free Trade as a Strategic Instrument in the War on Terror: The 2004 US–Moroccan Free Trade Agreement'. *Middle East Journal,* 59(4) Autumn 2005, pp. 597–616

Wijk, R., 'De. Terrorismebestrijding: een strategie van "hearts and minds" '. *Justiële Verkenningen,* 31(2), March 2005, pp. 47–62

Wilkenfeld, J., Young, K., Quinn, D. and Asal, V., *Mediating International Crises.* London: Routledge, 2005

Wilkinson, P., *The Problem of Terrorism in the Contemporary International System and the European Union's Response.* Strasbourg: European Parliament, 1996

Wilkinson, P., *International Terrorism: The Changing Threat and the EU's Response.* Paris: European Union Institute for Security Studies, October 2005

Wilkinson, P., *Terrorism versus Democracy: The Liberal State Response,* 2nd edn. London: Routledge, 2006

Wilkinson, P. (ed.), *Homeland Security in the UK: Future Preparedness for Terrorist Attack since 9/11.* London: Routledge, 2007

Willis, H. and Ortiz, D.S., *Evaluating the Security of the Global Containerized Supply Chain.* Santa Monica, CA: RAND, 2005

Willis, H.H., *Analyzing Terrorism Risk.* CT-252. Santa Monica, CA: RAND, 2005

Willis, H.H., Morral, A.R., Kelly, T.K. and Medby, J.J. *Estimating Terrorism Risk.* MG-388-RC. Santa Monica, CA: RAND, 2005

Wills, D.C., *The First War on Terrorism: Counter-terrorism Policy during the Reagan Administration* Lanham, MD: Rowman & Littlefield, 2003

Windsor, J.L., 'Promoting Democratization Can Combat Terrorism'. *Washington Quarterly,* Summer 2003, pp. 43–58

Winkler, C.K., *In the Name of Terrorism: Presidents on Political Violence in the Post-World War II Era.* New York: State University of New York Press, 2005

Winkler, I., *Spies among Us: How to Stop the Spies, Terrorists, Hackers and Criminals You Don't Even Know You Encounter Every Day*. New York: Wiley, 2005

Wismans, G. (ed.), *Crisisbeheersing belicht*. The Hague: Ministerie van Binnenlandse Zaken en Koninkrijksrelaties, Directie Crisisbeheersing, November 2005

Woessner, M.C. and Sims, B., 'Technological Innovation and the Application of the Fourth Amendment: Considering the Implications of Kyllo V: United States for Law Enforcement and Counterterrorism'. *Journal of Contemporary Criminal Justice*, 19, May 2003, pp. 224–238

Wolf, J.B., *Antiterrorist Initiatives*. New York: Plenum Press, 1989

Woo, B., 'A Growing Role for Regional Organisations in Fighting Global Terror'. *Helsinki Monitor*, 16(1), 2005, pp. 88–97

Wright, J., 'The Importance of Europe in the Global Campaign against Terrorism'. *Terrorism and Political Violence*, 18(2), Summer 2006, pp. 281–299

Yallop, D.A., *To the Ends of the Earth: The Hunt for the Jackal*. London: Jonathan Cape, 1993

Yallop, H.J., *Explosion Investigation*. Edinburgh: Scottish Academic Press, 1980

Yamashita, H., *Humanitarian Space and International Politics: The Creation of Safe Areas*. Aldershot, UK: Ashgate, 2004

Yoder, A. (ed.), *United Nations Cooperation against Terrorism*, New York: Crane, Russak, 1983

Yusaku, F., Yoshiura, N. and Ohta N., 'Creating a Worldwide Community Security Structure using Individually Maintained Home Computers: The E-JIKEI Network Project'. *Social Science Computer Review*, 23, May 2005, pp. 250–258

Zambelis, C., 'Crackdown against Islamist Opposition in Morocco Intensifies'. *Terrorism Focus*, 3(24), 20 June 2006

Zehfuss, M., 'Remembering to Forgive? The "War on Terror" in a "Dialogue" between German and US Intellectuals'. *International Relations*, 19, March 2005, pp. 91–102

Zimmermann, D., 'The European Union and Post-9/11 Counterterrorism: A Reappraisal'. *Studies in Conflict and Terrorism*, 29(2), March 2006, pp. 123–145

Zimmermann, D. and Wenger, A. (eds), *How States Fight Terrorism: Policy Dynamics in the West*. Boulder, CO: Lynne Rienner, 2006

S.2 Military

Addicott, J.F., 'The Role of Special Operations Forces in the War on Terror'. In E.V. Linden (ed.), *Focus on Terrorism*, vol 8. Hauppauge, NY: Nova Science Publishers, 2007

Amidror, Y., *Winning Counterinsurgency War: The Israeli Experience*. Jerusalem: Jerusalem Center for Public Affairs, 2008

Aspen Strategy Group Workshop, *Mapping the Jihadist Threat: The War on Terror since 9/11*. Aspen, CO, 5–10 August 2005

Byman, D., *The Five Front War: The Better Way to Fight Global Jihad*. Hoboken, NJ: John Wiley, 2008

Byman, D., 'Scoring the War on Terrorism'. *The National Interest*, Summer 2003, pp. 75–84

Charney, I.W., *Fighting Suicide Bombing: A Worldwide Campaign for Life*, Westport, CT: Praeger Security International, 2007

Chirot, D. and McCauley, C., *Why Not Kill Them All? The Logic and Prevention of Mass Political Murder*. Princeton, NJ: Princeton University Press, 2006

CoE, *The Fight against Terrorism*. Council of Europe standards, 4th edn. Strasbourg: CoE, 2007

Cole, L.A., *Terror: How Israel Has Coped and What America Can Learn*. Bloomington: Indiana University Press, 2007

De Nevers, R., 'NATO's International Security Role in the Terrorist Era'. *International Security*, 31(4), Spring 2007, pp. 34–66

Feichert, A., *US Military Operations in the Global War on Terrorism: Afghanistan, Africa, the Philippines, and Colombia*. CRS Report for Congress, RL32758, 4 February 2005

Feith, D., *The Best Defense: Inside the Pentagon at the Dawn of the War on Terrorism*. New York: Regan Books, 2007

Friedrichs, J., *Fighting Terrorism and Drugs: Europe and International Police Cooperation*. London: Routledge, 2007

Galula, D., *Counterinsurgency Warfare: Theory and Practice*. Westport, CT: Praeger Security International, 2006

Gardner, H., *American Global Strategy and the War on Terrorism*. Aldershot, UK: Ashgate, 2007

Glaessner, G.J. and Lorenz, A., *Europäisierung der innereren Sicherheit: Eine vergleichende Untersuchung am Beispiel von organisierter Kriminalität und Terrorismus*. Wiesbaden: VS Verlag, 2005

Gordon, M.R. and Trainor, B.E., *Cobra II: The Inside Story of Invasion and Occupation of Iraq*. New York: Pantheon, 2006

Gordon, P.H., 'Can the War on Terror Be Won? How to Fight the Right War'. *Foreign Affairs*, 86(6), November–December 2007, pp. 53–66

Jafa, Y.S., 'Defeating Terrorism: A Study of Operational Strategy and Tactics of Police Forces in Jammu and Kashmir'. *Police Practice and Research*, 6(2), May 2005, pp. 141–164

Kilcullen, D., 'Globalisation and the Development of Indonesian Counterinsurgency Tactics'. *Small Wars and Insurgencies*, 17(1), 2006, pp. 44–64

Kilcullen, D.J., 'Countering Global Insurgency'. *Journal of Strategic Studies*, 28(4), August 2005, pp. 597–617

Kretzmer, D., 'Targeted Killing of Suspected Terrorists: Extra-judicial Executions or Legitimate Means of Defence?' *European Journal of International Law*, 16(2), April 2005, pp. 171–212

Lambeth, B.S., *Air Power against Terror: America's Conduct of Operation Enduring Freedom*. MG-166-CENTAF. Santa Monica, CA: RAND, 2005

Lewer, N. and Davison, N., 'Non-lethal Technologies: An Overview'. Geneva: UNIDIR. *Disarmament Forum* 1, 2005, pp. 37–52

Mariani, C., *Terrorism Response Handbook for Police Officers in New York State*, 2nd edn. New York: Looseleaf Law Publications, 2004

Marks, T.A., 'India: State Response to Insurgency in Jammu and Kashmir: The Jammu Case'. *Low Intensity Conflict and Law Enforcement*, 12(3), 2004, pp. 122–143

Melson, C.D., 'Top Secret War: Rhodesian Special Operations'. *Small Wars and Insurgencies*, 16(1), 2005, pp. 57–82

Moorcraft, P., Winfield, G. and Chisholm, J. (eds), *Axis of Evil: The War on Terror*. Barnsley, UK: Pen and Sword Military, 2005

Mulcahy, A., 'The "Other" Lessons from Ireland? Policing, Political Violence and Policy Transfer'. *European Journal of Criminology*, 2, April 2005, pp. 185–209

Murray, J., 'Policing Terrorism: A Threat to Community Policing or Just a Shift in Priorities?' *Police Practice and Research*, 6(4), September 2005, pp. 347–361

Murray, W., *Strategic Challenges for Counterinsurgency and the Global War on Terrorism*. Carlisle, PA: Strategic Studies Institute, U.S. Army War College, 2006

Nance, M., *Terrorist Recognition Handbook: A Practitioner's Manual for Predicting and Identifying Terrorist Activities*, 2nd edn. Boca Raton, FL: CRC Press, 2008

O'Day, A. (ed.), *Cyberterrorism*. Aldershot, UK: Ashgate, 2004

Ozdag, U. and Aydinli, E., 'Winning a Low Intensity Conflict: Drawing Lessons from the Turkish Case'. In E. Inbar (ed.), *Democracies and Small Wars*. London: Routledge, 2003

Pottier, P., 'GCMA/GMI: A French Experience in Counterinsurgency during the French Indochina War'. *Small Wars and Insurgencies*, 16(2), 2005, pp. 125–146

Rashid, A., *Descent into Chaos: How the War against Islamic Extremism Is Being Lost in Pakistan, Afghanistan and Central Asia*. London, Allen Lane, 2008

Rees, W. and Aldrich, R.J., 'Contending Cultures of Counterterrorism: Transatlantic Divergence or Convergence?' *International Affairs*, 81(5), October 2005, pp. 905–923

Roberts, A., 'The "War on Terror" in Historical Perspective'. *Survival*, 47(2), Summer 2005, pp. 101–130

Satloff, R.B. (ed.), *The War on Terror: The Middle East Dimension*, Washington, DC: Washington Institute for Near East Policy, 2002

Scarborough, R., *Rumsfeld's War: The Untold Story of America's Anti-terrorist Commander*. Washington, DC: Regnery, 2004

Schroen, G.C., *An Insider's Account of How the CIA Spearheaded the War on Terror in Afghanistan*. London: Presidio, 2005

Silke, A., 'Success and Failure in Terrorist Investigations: Research and Lessons from Northern Ireland'. *Low Intensity Conflict and Law Enforcement*, 13(3), 2005, pp. 250–261

Silvers, R.B. and Epstein, B. (eds), *Striking Terror: America's New War*. New York: New York Review of Books, 2002

Simons, A. and Tucker, D., 'United States Special Operations Forces and the War on Terrorism'. *Small Wars and Insurgencies*, 14(1), 2003, pp. 77–91

Thornton, R., 'The British Army and the Origins of Its Minimum Force Philosophy'. *Small Wars and Insurgencies*, 15(1), 2004, pp. 83–106

Ucko, D., 'Countering Insurgents through Distributed Operations: Insights from Malaya 1948–1960'. *Journal of Strategic Studies*, 30(1), 2007, pp. 47–72

Yoo, J., *War by Other Means: An Insider's Account of the War on Terror*. New York: Atlantic Monthly Press, 2006

S.3 Legal

Abeyratne, R.I.R., *Aviation Security: Legal and Regulatory Aspects*. Aldershot, UK: Ashgate, 1998

Gurulé, J., *Unfunding Terror: The Legal Response to the Financing of Global Terrorism*. Cheltenham, UK: Edward Elgar, 2008

Olivier, C., 'Human Rights Law and the International Fight against Terrorism: How Do Security Council Resolutions Impact on States' Obligations under International Human Rights Law?' (Revisiting Security Council Resolution 1373). *Nordic Journal of International Law*, 73(4), 2004, pp. 399–419

United Nations. Office on Drugs and Crime. *Compendium of Useful Technical Assistance Tools and Legal Instruments to Prevent Terrorism and Other Related Forms of Crime*. Vienna: UNODC, 2005. Available at: www.unodc.org/documents/corruption/publications_compendium_e.pdf (accessed 21 April 2009)

S.4 Hostage-saving measures

Hayes, R.E., Kaminski, S.R. and Beres, S.M., *Negotiating the Non-negotiable: Dealing with Absolutist Terrorists: International Negotiation*, 8(3), 2003, pp. 451–467

Matusitz, J. and Breen, G.M., 'Negotiation Tactics in Organizations Applied to Hostage Negotiation'. *Journal of Security Education*, 2(1), 29 December 2006, pp. 55–73

Neumann, P.R., 'Negotiating with Terrorists'. *Foreign Affairs*, 86(1), January–February 2007, pp. 128–138

Pruitt, D.G., 'Negotiation with Terrorists'. *International Negotiation*, 11(2), 2006, pp. 371–394

Schneider, A.K. and Honeyman, C. (eds), *The Negotiator's Fieldbook: The Desk Reference for the Experienced Negotiator*. Washington, DC: American Bar Association, 2006

Van Hasselt, V.B., Baker, M.T., Romano, S.J., Sellers, A.H., Noesner, G.W. and Smith, S., 'Development and Validation of a Role-Play Test for Assessing Crisis (Hostage) Negotiation Skills'. *Criminal Justice and Behavior*, 32, June 2005, pp. 345–361

S.5 Protecting individuals against terrorism

Currance, P.L., *RAPID Medical Response to Weapons of Mass Destruction*. St Louis: Mosby, 2005

D'Arcy, O'Hanlon M., Orszag, P., Shapiro, J. and Steinberg, J., *Protecting the Homeland 2006/2007*. Washington, DC: Brookings Insitution, 2008

Flynn, S., *America the Vulnerable: How Our Government Is Failing to Protect Us from Terrorism*. New York: Harper Perennial, 2005

Lukov, V., 'Counter-terrorism Capability: Preventing Radiological Threats'. *Connections*, 4(2), Summer 2005, pp. 47–66

McCreery, T. and Bryden, W., 'Defence against Biological, Chemical and Radiological Attacks: The Technological Way Forward'. *Military Technology*, June 2006, pp. 13–21

Melnick, A., *Biological, Chemical, and Radiological Terrorism: Emergency Preparedness and Response for the Family Physician*. New York: Springer, 2007

Morkunas, G. and Klevinskas, G., 'National System for Prevention of Nuclear and Radiological Terrorism in Lithuania'. *International Journal of Nuclear Law*, 1(3), 21 August 2006, pp. 296–303

Pavlin, J., 'Medical Surveillance for Biological Terrorism Agents'. *Human and Ecological Risk Assessment*, 11(3), June 2005, pp. 525–537

Siegrist, D.W. and Graham, J.M. (eds), *Countering Biological Terrorism in the U.S.: An Understanding of Issues and Status*. Dobbs Ferry, NY: Oceana, 1999

US Government, *Guide to Surviving Terrorism*. New York: Barnes & Noble, 2003

Veneema, T., *Disaster Nursing and Emergency Preparedness for Chemical, Biological, and Radiological Terrorism*. New York: Springer, 2007

Wenger, A. and Wollenmann, R. (eds), *Bioterrorism: Confronting a Complex Threat*. Boulder, CO: Lynne Rienner, 2007

World Health Organization (WHO), *Public Health Response to Biological and Chemical Weapons*. Geneva: World Health Organization, 2004

S.6 Countermeasures against regime terrorism

Fulton, K. with Nally, J. and Gallagher, I., *Unsung Hero: How I Saved Dozens of Lives as a Secret Agent inside the IRA*. London: John Blake, 2006

Nardin, T. and Williams, M.S. (eds), *Humanitarian Intervention*. New York: New York University Press, 2006

Nincic, M., *Renegade Regimes: Confronting Deviant Behavior in World Politics*. New York: Columbia University Press, 2005

Seybolt, T.B., *Humanitarian Military Intervention: The Conditions for Success and Failure*. Oxford: Oxford University Press; Stockholm: SIPRI, 2007

Weiss, T.G., *Military–Civilian Interactions: Humanitarian Crises and the Responsibility to Protect*. Lanham, MD: Rowman & Littlefield, 2005

S.7 Critiques of state countermeasures against insurgent terrorism

Ackerman, B., *Before the Next Attack: Preserving Civil Liberties in an Age of Terrorism*. London: Yale University Presss, 2006

AIV, *Terrorismebestrijding in Europees en internationaal perspectief; interim-advies over het folterverbod*. The Hague: Adviesraad Internationale Vraagstukken, 16 December 2005

Amnesty International, *Guantànamo: Lives Torn Apart: The Impact of Indefinite Detention on Detainees and Their Families*. London: Amnesty, 2006

Arms Control Association, *Chronology of Bush Administration Claim That Iraq Attempted to Obtain Uranium from Niger (2001–2003)*. Arms Control Association Factsheet, Washington, DC, November 2005

Aust, S., *Mauss, ein Deutscher Agent*. Hamburg: Hoffmann & Campe, 1998

Aust, S., *Der Lockvogel: Die tödliche Geschichte eines V-Mannes zwischen Verfassungsschutz und Terrorismus*. Reinbek bei Hamburg: Rowohlt, 2002

Babington, A., *Military Intervention in Britain: From the Gordon Riots to the Gibraltar Incident*. London: Routledge, 1991

Bader, M., 'Extraordinary rendition: een omstreden wapen in terrorismebestrijding'. *Internationale Spectator*, 60(1), January 2006, pp. 14–19

Baev, P.K., 'Instrumentalizing Counterterrorism for Regime Consolidation in Putin's Russia'. *Studies in Conflict and Terrorism*, 27(4), 2004, pp. 337–352

Baev, P., 'Contre-terrorisme et islamisation du Caucase du Nord'. *Politique Etrangère*, no. 1, 2006, pp. 79–89

Bamford, J., *A Pretext for War: 9/11, Iraq and the Abuse of America's Intelligence Agencies*. New York: Doubleday, 2004

Bankus, B.C., 'We've Done This Before'. *Small Wars Journal*, no. 4, February 2006

Baran, Z., *Combating Al-Qaeda and the Militant Islamic Threat*. United States House of Representatives, Committee on Armed Services, Subcommittee on Terrorism, Unconventional Threats and Capabilities, 16 February 2006

Barber, B.R., 'Imperialism or Interdependence?' *Security Dialogue*, 35, June 2004, pp. 237–242

Beason, D., *The E-Bomb: How America's New Directed Energy Weapons Will Change the Way Future Wars Will Be Fought*. Cambridge, MA: Da Capo Press, 2005

Beattie, M. and Stevens, L.Y., 'Comment: An Open Debate on United States Citizens Designated as Enemy Combatants: Where Do We Go from Here?' *Maryland Law Review*, 62, 2003, 975–1027

Bebler, A., 'NATO and Transnational Terrorism'. *Perceptions*, 1994, Winter 2004–2005, pp. 159–175

Bellamy, A.J., 'Ethics and Intervention: The "Humanitarian Exception" and the Problem of Abuse in the Case of Iraq'. *Journal of Peace Research*, 41, March 2004, pp. 131–147

Bellamy, A.J., 'No Pain, No Gain: Torture and Ethics in the War on Terror'. *International Affairs*, 82(1), January 2006, pp. 121–148

Benedek, W. and Yotopoulos-Marangopoulos, A. (eds), *Anti-terrorist Measures and Human Rights*. Leiden: Martinus Nijhoff 2004

Bennett, J.T., *Homeland Security Scams*. New Brunswick, NJ: Transaction, 2006

Bennis, P., Leaver, E. and IPS Taskforce, 'The Iraq Quagmire: The Mounting Costs of War and the Case for Bringing Home the Troops'. A Study by the Institute for Policy Studies and Foreign Policy in Focus, Washington, DC, 31 August 2005

Bensahel, N., *The Counterterror Coalitions: Cooperation with Europe, NATO and the European Union*. Santa Monica, CA: RAND, 2003

Bensahel, N., 'A Coalition of Coalitions: International Cooperation against Terrorism'. *Studies in Conflict and Terrorism*, 29(1), January–February 2006, pp. 35–49

Bergen, P., 'The Long Hunt for Osama'. *The Atlantic*, October 2004, pp. 88–102

Berger, S.R., Scowcroft, B. and Nash, W.L. (eds), *In the Wake of War: Improving US Post-Conflict Capabilities*. New York: Council on Foreign Relations, 2005

Berkowitz, P. (ed.), *Terrorism, the Laws of War, and the Constitution*. Stanford, CA: Hoover Institution, 2005

Bigo, D. and Tsoukala, A., *Terror, Insecurity and Liberty*. London: Routledge, 2008

Blank, S., 'Rethinking the Concept of Asymmetric Threats in U.S. Strategy'. *Comparative Strategy*, 23(4–5), 2004, pp. 343–368

Blaufarb, D., *The Counterinsurgency Era: U.S. Doctrine and Performance, 1950 to the Present*. New York: Free Press, 1977

Bonsiore, E. and Eshel, D., 'Countering the IED Threat'. *Military Technology*, June 2006, pp. 108–121

Bortfeldt, W., *Deckname 'Kette': Der Verfassungsschutz und der Mord an Ulrich Schmucker*. Zürich: Luchterhand, 1992

Bowden, M., 'The Desert One Debacle', *The Atlantic Online*. Available at: www.theatlantic.com/doc/2006 05/iran-hostage (accessed 21 April 2009)

Brown, C., *Lost Liberties: Ashcroft and the Assault on Personal Freedom*. New York: New Press, 2003

Bryett, K. and Lewis, C., *Un-Peeling Tradition: Contemporary Policing*. South Melbourne: Macmillan Education Australia, 1994

B'Tselem, *Through No Fault of Their Own: Punitive House Demolitions during the Al-Aqsa Intifada*. Jerusalem: B'Tselem, 2005

Bunn, G., Steinhäusler, F. and Zaitseva, L., 'Strengthening Nuclear Security against Terrorists and Thieves Requires Better Training'. *Nonproliferation Review*, 8(3), 2001, pp. 137–149

Byman, D., 'Do Targeted Killings Work'? *Foreign Affairs*, March–April, 2006, pp. 95–111

Calzini, P., 'Vladimir Putin and the Chechen War'. *International Spectator*, 40(2), April–June 2005, pp. 19–28

Campbell, K. and Wertz, R., *Non-Military Strategies for Countering Islamist Terrorism: Lessons Learned from Past Counterinsurgencies*. Princeton Project on National Security, 2006

Carvin, S., *Acts and Pacts: Losing the Middle Ground in the Dispute of International Humanitarian Law in the War on Terror*. Honolulu: International Studies Association (ISA), March 2005

Cary, L.W., *Terrorism's Implications for Preemption and Legislation: A Futurist Perspective*. Carlisle, PA: US Army War College, 19 March 2004

Cassidy, R.M., 'Back to the Street without Joy: Counterinsurgency Lessons from Vietnam and Other Small Wars'. *Parameters*, 34(2), Summer 2004, pp. 73–83

Cassidy, R.M., 'Winning the War of the Flea: Lessons from Guerrilla Warfare'. *Military Review*, September–October 2004, pp. 41–46

Cassidy, R.M., *Counterinsurgency and the Global War on Terror: Military Culture and Irregular War*. New York: Praeger Security International, 2006

CFR, *The Law of War in the War on Terrorism: A Council of Foreign Relations Debate*. New York: Council on Foreign Relations, 14 April 2005

Chomsky, N. and Peck, J., *The Chomsky Reader*. New York: Pantheon Books, 1987

Christie, S. and Delle Chiaie S., *Portrait of a Black Terrorist*. Black Papers no. 1. London: Anarchy Magazine/Refract Publications, 1984

Cingatnelli, D.L. and Richards, D.L., 'Respect for Human Rights after the End of the Cold War'. *Journal of Peace Research*, 36, September 1999, pp. 511–534

Cirincione, J., *Repairing the Regime: Preventing the Spread of Weapons of Mass Destruction*. New York: Routledge, 2000

Clarke, R.A., *Against All Enemies: Inside America's War on Terror*. New York: Free Press, 2004

Clarke, R.A., *The Forgotten Homeland*. Washington DC: Century Foundation Press through Brookings Institution Press, 2006

Clements, K.P., 'Terrorism: Violent and Non-violent Responses'. In S. Ram and R. Summy (eds), *Nonviolence: An Alternative for Defeating Global Terror(ism)*. Hauppauge, NY: Nova Science Publishers, 2007

Clunan, A.L., Lavery, P.R. and Martin, S.B. (eds), *Terrorism, War, or Disease? Unraveling the Use of Biological Weapons*. Stanford, CA: Stanford University Press, 2008

Clutterbuck, L., 'Countering Irish Republican Terrorism in Britain: Its Origin as Police Function'. *Terrorism and Political Violence*, 18(1), Spring 2006, pp. 95–118

Cohen, E., Crane, C., Horvath, J. and Nagl, J., 'Principles, Imperatives, and Paradoxes of Counterinsurgency'. *Military Review*, 86(2). March–April 2006, pp. 49–53

Cole, D., *Terrorism and the Constitution: Sacrificing Civil Liberties in the Name of National Security*. New York: W.W. Norton, 2002

Cole, D. and Lobel, J., *Less Safe, Less Free: Why America Is Losing the War on Terror*. New York: New Press, 2007

Collacott, M., *Canada's Inadequate Response to Terrorism: The Need for Policy Reform*. Calgary: Fraser Institute, February 2006

Collins, A., *Contemporary Security Studies*. Oxford: Oxford University Press, 2007

Comfort, L.K., Ko, K. and Zagorecki, A., 'Coordination in Rapidly Evolving Disaster Response Systems: The Role of Information'. *American Behavioral Scientist*, 48, November 2004, pp. 295–313

Conference Proceedings, *Democracy, Peace, and the War on Terror: America and the Middle East, Post-September 11*. Washington DC: Washington Institute for Near East Policy, 2002

Cope, N., 'Intelligence Led Policing or Policing Led Intelligence? Integrating Volume Crime Analysis into Policing'. *British Journal of Criminology*, 44(2), 2004, pp. 188–203

Cordesman, A.H., *The War after The War: Strategic Lessons of Iraq and Afghanistan*. Washington, DC: Center for Strategic and International Studies, 2004

Cordesman, A.H., *Iraqi Security Forces: A Strategy for Success*. Washington, DC: CSIS, 2005

Cotton, J., 'The Proliferation Security Initiative and North Korea: Legality and Limitations of a Coalition Strategy'. *Security Dialogue*, 36, June 2005, pp. 193–211

Council of Europe, *Special Investigation Techniques in Relation to Serious Crimes Including Acts of Terrorism*. Recommendation (2005) 10 and explanatory memorandum. Brussels, 2005

Council of Europe, *Terrorism: Protection of Witnesses and Collaborators of Justice*. Brussels, 2006

Cowell, A., *The Terminal Spy*. New York: Doubleday, 2008

Crahan, M., Goering, J. and Weiss, T.G. (eds), *The Wars on Terrorism and Iraq: The US and the World*. London: Routledge, 2004

Cross, J.P., *'A Face Like a Chicken's Backside': An Unconventional Soldier in South East Asia, 1948–1971*. London: Greenhill Books; Mechanicsburg, PA: Stackpole Books, 1996

Crotty, W.J. (ed.), *The Politics of Terror: The US Response to 9/11*. Lebanon, PA: Northeastern University Press, 2003

Daalder, I.H., *America Unbound: The Bush Revolution in Foreign Policy*. Washington, DC: Brookings Institution, 2003

Danner, M., *Torture and Truth: America, Abu Ghraib, and the War on Terror*. New York: New York Review of Books, 2004

Davenport, C. (ed.), *Paths to State Repression*. Lanham, MD: Rowman & Littlefield, 2000

Davidson, R.A., *Reagan vs. Qaddafi: Response to International Terrorism?* Düsseldorf: Booklooker.com, 2002

Davies, N., *Ten-Thirty-Three: The Inside Story of Britain's Secret Killing Machine in Northern Ireland*. Edinburgh: Mainstream Publishing, 1999

Davis, J.K. and Perry, C.M., *Rethinking the War on Terror: Developing a Strategy to Counter Extremist Ideologies: A Workshop Report*. Cambridge, MA: Institute for Foreign Policy Analysis, 2007

Davis, L.M. and National Memorial Institute for the Prevention of Terrorism, *When Terrorism Hits Home: How Prepared Are State and Local Law Enforcement?* Santa Monica, CA: RAND, 2004

Davis, L., Mosher, D., Brennan, R., Greenberg, M., McMahon, K.S. and Yost, C., *Army Forces for Homeland Security*. Santa Monica, CA: RAND, 2005

De Weger, M.J. and Neuteboom, P.C.J., 'Samenwerking tussen politie en krijgsmacht: verschillende scenarios'. *Militaire Spectator*, 173(5), 2004, pp. 278–291

Debrix, F., *The United States and the 'War Machine': Re-imagining Security and Terror after September 11*. Honolulu: International Studies Association (ISA) March 2005

Debus, T., Kreide, R., Krennerich, M. and Mihr, A., *Zeitschrift für Menschenrechte: Menschenrechte und Terrorismus: Heft 2001/1*. Schwalbach am Taunus, Germany: Wochenschau Verlag, 2007

Deflem, M., 'Europol and the Policing of International Terrorism: Counter-terrorism in a Global Perspective'. *Justice Quarterly*, 23(3), September 2006, pp. 336–359

Delong, M., *Inside CENTCOM: The Unvarnished Truth about the War in Afghanistan and Iraq*. Washington, DC: Regnery, 2004

Dempsey, J.K., *Combat and Confidence: The Foreign Policy Attitudes of the U.S. Soldiers Engaged in the Global War on Terror*. Honolulu: International Studies Association (ISA) March 2005

Derksen, K., 'The Logistics of Actionable Intelligence Leading to 9/11'. *Studies in Conflict and Terrorism*, 28(3), May–June 2005, pp. 253–268

Derrer, D.S., *We Are All the Target: A Handbook of Terrorism Avoidance and Hostage Survival*. Annapolis, MD: Naval Institute Press, 1992

Diamond, L., 'What Went Wrong in Iraq?' *Foreign Affairs*, 83(5), September–October 2004, pp. 34–56

Donahue, L., *In the Name of National Security: US Counterterrorist Measures, 1960–2000*. Executive Session on Domestic Preparedness, BCSIA, JFK School of Government, Harvard University, August 2001

Doyle, M. and Sambanis, N., *Making War and Building Peace: United Nations Peace Operations*. Princeton, NJ: Princeton University Press, 2006, p. 400

Drakos, K. and Kutan, A.M., 'Regional Effects of Terrorism on Tourism in Three Mediterranean Countries'. *Journal of Conflict Resolution*, 47, October 2003, pp. 621–641

Durch, W.J. (ed.), *Twenty-First Century Peace Operations*. Washington, DC: United States Institute of Peace Press, 2006

Durch, W.J., *Who Should Keep the Peace? Providing Security for Twenty-First-Century Peace Operations*. Washington, DC: Henry L. Stimson Center, 2006

Durch, W.J. and Holt, V.K., *The Brahimi Report and the Future of Peace Operations*. Washington, DC: Henry L. Stimson Center, 2004

Duyvesteyn, I. and Angstrom, J., *Rethinking The Nature of War*. London: Frank Cass, 2004

Eckert, N., *Fatal Encounter: The Story of the Gibraltar Killings*. Dublin: Poolbeg, 1999

Edwards, A. and Hughes, G., 'Comparing the Governance of Safety in Europe: A Geo-historical Approach'. *Theoretical Criminology*, 9, August 2005, pp. 345–363

Eggert, W., *London – Die Lizenz zum Töten: Die Verstrickung der Geheimdienste in den Terrorismus*. Munich: Chronos-Medien Vertrieb, 2005

Einhorn, R.J. and Flournoy, M.A., *Protecting against the Spread of Nuclear, Biological, and Chemical Weapons*, vol. 1: *Agenda for Action*. Washington, DC: Center for Strategic and International Studies 2003

Ellersiek, C. and Beker, W., *Das Celler Loch: Geschichte einer Geheimdienstaffäere*. Hamburg: Galgenberg, 1987

Elshtain, J.B., *Just War against Terror: The Burden of American Power in a Violent World*. New York: Basic Books, 2003

Elworthy, S. and Rifkind, G., *Hearts and Minds: Human Security Approaches to Political Violence*. London: Demos, 2005

Eppright, C.T., 'Counterterrorism and Conventional Military Force: The Relationship between Political Effect and Utility'. *Studies in Conflict and Terrorism*, 20(4), 1997, pp. 333–344

Erickson, R.J., *Legitimate Use of Military Force against State-Sponsored International Terrorism*. Honolulu: University Press of the Pacific, 2002

Etzioni, A., *How Patriotic Is the PATRIOT Act? Freedom versus Security in the Age of Terrorism*. New York: Routledge, 2004

Etzioni, A., 'Response'. *American Behavioral Scientist*, 48, August 2005, pp. 1657–1665

Etzioni, A., *Security First: For a Muscular, Moral Foreign Policy*. New Haven, CT: Yale University Press, 2007

Evelegh, R., *Peace Keeping in a Democratic Society: The Lessons of Northern Ireland*. London: C. Hurst, 1978

Evron, Y., 'Disengagement and Israeli Deterrence'. *Strategic Assessment*, 8(2), August 2005, pp. 11–16

Fair, C., 'Military Operations in Urban Areas: The Indian Experience'. *India Review*, 2(1), January 2003

Falk, R., *The Great Terror War*. Moreton in Marsh, UK: Arris Books, 2004

Falkenrath, R.A., 'Grading the War on Terrorism'. *Foreign Affairs*, 85(1), January–February 2006, pp. 122–128

Fallows, J., 'Blind into Baghdad'. *The Atlantic*, January–February, 2004. Available at: www.theatlantic.com/doc/200401/fallows (accessed 22 April 2009)

Fallows, J., 'Bush's Lost Year'. *The Atlantic*, 294(3), October 2004, pp. 68–87

Fallows, J., 'Why Iraq Has No Army'. *The Atlantic*, 296(5), December 2005, pp. 60–77

Farer, T.J., Archibugi, D., Brown, C., Crawford, N.C., Weiss, T.G. and Wheeler, N.J., 'Roundtable: Humanitarian Intervention after 9/11'. *International Relations*, 19, June 2005, pp. 211–250

Faruqui, A., 'Viewpoints: Is the USA Fighting Terrorism with the Wrong Weapons?' *Security Dialogue*, 34, March 2003, pp. 121–123

Federal Bureau of Investigation (FBI), *Strategic Plan 2004–2009*. US Department of Justice, 2004. Available at: www.fbi.gov/publications/strategicplan/stategicplantext.htm (accessed 22 April 2009)

Feichert, A., *US Military Operations in the Global War on Terrorism: Afghanistan, Africa, the Philippines, and Colombia*. CRS Report for Congress, RL32758, February 4, 2005

Ferguson, C.D., *Preventing Catastrophic Nuclear Terrorism*. New York: Council on Foreign Relations, March 2006

Flynn, S.E., *America the Vulnerable: How Our Government Is Failing to Protect Us from Terrorism*. New York: HarperCollins, 2004

Flynn, S.E., 'The Neglected Home Front'. *Foreign Affairs*, 83(5), September–October 2004, pp. 20–33

Flynn, S.E., 'Port Security Is Still a House of Cards'. *Far Eastern Economic Review*, 169(1), January–February 2006, pp. 5–11

Foot, R., 'Collateral Damage: Human Rights Consequences of Counterterrorist Action in the Asia-Pacific'. *International Affairs*, 81(2), March 2005, pp. 411–426

Foot, R., 'Human Rights and Counterterrorism in Global Governance: Reputation and Resistance'. *Global Governance*, July–September 2005, pp. 291–310

Fouskas, V.K. and Gökay, B., *The New American Imperialism: Bush's War on Terror and Blood for Oil*. New York: Praeger, 2005

Fowler, M.C., *Amateur Soldiers, Global Wars: Insurgency and Modern Conflict*. New York: Praeger, 2005

Franke, V.C. (ed.), *Terrorism and Peacekeeping: New Security Challenges*. Westport, CT: Praeger, 2005

Freedman, L., 'War in Iraq: Selling the Threat'. *Survival*, 46(2), Summer 2004, pp. 7–50

Freeman, M., *Freedom or Security: The Consequences for Democracies using Emergency Powers to Fight Terror*. Westport, CT: Praeger, 2002

Freilich, C. ' "The Pentagon Revenge" or Strategic Transformation: The Bush Administration's New Security Strategy'. *Strategic Assessment*, 9(1), April 2006, pp. 19–23

Friedman, G., *America's Secret War: Inside the Hidden Worldwide Struggle between America and its Enemies*. New York: Random House, 2004

Galbraith, P.W., 'Iraq: The Bungled Transition'. *New York Review of Books*, 23 September 2004, pp. 70–74

Galbraith, P.W., *The End of Iraq: How American Incompetence Created a War without End*. New York: Simon & Schuster, 2007

Galula, D., *Pacification in Algeria, 1956–1958*. MG-478-RC. Santa Monica, CA: RAND, 2006

GAO, *Gun Control and Terrorism: FBI Could Better Manage Firearm-Related Background Checks Involving Terrorist Watch List Records*. GAO-05-127. Washington, DC: Government Accounting Office, January 2005

Garcia, M.J., *Renditions: Constraints Imposed by Laws on Torture*. CRS Report for Congress, 28 April, 2005

Garland, D., 'Book Review: Cruel and Unusual: Punishment and US Culture'. *Social Legal Studies*, 14, June 2005, pp. 299–302

Garrison, D., *Bracing for Armageddon: Why Civil Defense Never Worked*. Oxford: Oxford University Press, 2006

Geraghty, T., *Who Dares Wins: The Story of the SAS, 1950–1992*. London: Abacus, 2002

Giangreco, D.M. and Griswold, T., *Delta: America's Elite Counterterrorist Force*. Osceola, WI: Zenith Press, 2005

Gill, L., *The School of the Americas: Military Training and Political Violence in the Americas*. Durham, NC: Duke University Press, 2004

Giragosian, R., 'The US Military Engagement in Central Asia and the Southern Caucasus: An Overview'. *Journal of Slavic Military Studies*, 17, 2004, pp. 43–77

Glenn, R. and Kingston, G., *Urban Battle Command in the 21st Century*. MG-181. Santa Monica, CA: RAND, 2005

Goldstein, J.S., *The Real Price of War: How You Pay for the War on Terror*. New York: New York University Press, 2004

Goldstein, L.J., *Preventive Attack and Weapons of Mass Destruction: A Comparative Historical Analysis*. Stanford, CA: Stanford University Press, 2006

Golts, A., 'Military Reform in Russia and the Global War against Terrorism'. *Journal of Slavic Military Studies*, 17(1), March 2004, pp. 29–41

Graham, B. and Nussbaum, J., *Intelligence Matters: The CIA and FBI, Saudi Arabia, and the Failure of America's War on Terror*. New York: Random House, 2004

Gray, C.S., *The Sheriff: America's Defense of the New World Order*. Lexington: University Press of Kentucky, 2004

Gray, C.S., *Another Bloody Century: Future Warfare*. London: Weidenfeld & Nicolson, 2005

Gray, J.M., 'Understanding the "War on Terrorism": Responses to 11 September 2001'. *Journal of Peace Research*, 43(1), January 2006, pp. 23–36

Greenberg, K.J. (ed.), *The Torture Debate in America*. Cambridge: Cambridge University Press, 2006

Greenberg, K.J. and Dratel, J.L. (eds), *The Torture Papers: The Road to Abu Ghraib*. Cambridge: Cambridge University Press, 2005

Grey, S., *Das Schattenreich der CIA: Amerikas schmutziger Krieg gegen den Terror*. Munich: Deutsche Verlags-Anstalt, 2006

Griffith, J., Book review: 'Military Leadership: In Pursuit of Excellence (5th Ed.)'. *Armed Forces and Society*, 32, April 2006, pp. 475–477

Gurtov, M., *Superpower on Crusade: The Bush Doctrine in US Foreign Policy*. Boulder, CO: Lynne Rienner, 2006

Hafez, M.M. and Hatfield, J.M., 'Do Targeted Assassinations Work? A Multivariate Analysis of Israel's Controversial Tactic during Al-Aqsa Uprising'. *Studies in Conflict and Terrorism*, 29, June 2006, pp. 359–382

Hagman, D.J., *Tactical Surveillance: An Investigator's Guide to Conducting Surveillance Operations*. Erie, PA: Tactical Publications, 2004

Hammel, E.M., *The Root: The Marines in Beirut, August 1982 – February 1984*. Pacifica, CA: Pacifica Press, 1993

Harclerode, P., *Secret Soldiers: Special Forces in the War against Terrorism*. London: Cassell, 2001

Harris, [Sir] Arthur, *Bomber Offensive*. Barnsley, UK: Pen and Sword Books, 2005

Hastings, M., *Yoni, Hero of Entebbe*. New York: Dial Press/J. Wade, 1979

Hastings, T.H., *Nonviolent Response to Terrorism*. Jefferson, NC: McFarland, 2004

Hayden, P., Lansford, T. and Watson, R.P. (eds), *America's War on Terror*. Aldershot, UK: Ashgate, 2003

Hayes, B., *The Activities and Development of Europol: Towards an Accountable 'FBI' in Europe*. London: Statewatch, 2002

Heiken, G., Valentine, G.A., Brown, M., Rasmussen, S., George, D.C., Greene, R.K., Jones, E., Olsen, K. and Andersson, C., 'Modeling Cities: The Los Alamos Urban Security Initiative'. *Public Works Management Policy*, 4, January 2000, pp. 198–212

Heinz, W.S. and Arend, J.M., *The Internatinal Fight against Terrorism and the Protection of Human Rights: With Recommendations to the German Government and Parliament*. Berlin: German Institute for Human Rights, 2005

Helmer, D.I., *The Flipside of the COIN: Israel's Lebanese Incursion between 1982–2000*. Fort Leavenworth, KS: Combat Studies Institute Press, 2007

Heng, Y.-K., 'Unravelling the "War" on Terrorism: A Risk-Management Exercise in War Clothing' *Security Dialogue*, 33, June 2002, pp. 227–242

Henshall, I. and Morgan, R., *9/11 Revealed. Challenging the Facts behind the War on Terror*. London: Robinson, 2005

Herman, E.S. and O'Sullivan, G., *The 'Terrorism' Industry: The Experts and Institutions That Shape Our View of Terror*. New York: Pantheon Books, 1989

Hermann, K. and Koch, P., *Assault at Mogadishu*. London: Corgi, 1977

Herring, E. and Ranwala, G., *Iraq in Fragments: The Occupation and Its Legacy*. Ithaca, NY: Cornell University Press, 2006

Hersh, S.M., 'Annals of National Security up in the Air: Bush's Intransigence and the Coming Air War: Where Is the Iraq War Headed Next?' *New Yorker*, 5 December 2005, pp. 42–54

Hersh, S.M., *Chain of Command: The Road from 9/11 to Abu Ghraib*. New York: HarperCollins, 2004

Hersman, R.K.C. and Koca, T.M., 'Eliminating Adversary WMD: Lessons for Future Conflicts'. *Strategic Forum*, no. 211, October 2004. Washington, DC: National Defense University

Heymann, P.B., *Terrorism, Freedom, and Security: Winning without War*. Cambridge, MA: MIT Press, 2003

Higgs, R., *Resurgence of the Warfare State: The Crisis since 9/11*. Oakland, CA: The Independent Institute, 2005

Hillyard, P., *Suspect Community: People's Experience of the Prevention of Terrorism Acts in Britain*. London: Pluto Press in association with Liberty, 1993

Hinton, M.S., 'A Distant Reality: Democratic Policing in Argentina and Brazil'. *Criminal Justice*, 5, February 2005, pp. 75–100

Hocking, J. and Lewis, C. (eds), *Counter-terrorism and the Post-Democratic State*. Cheltenham, UK: Edward Elgar, 2007

Hoge, J.F. Jr and Rose, G. (eds), *Understanding the War on Terror*. London: W.W. Norton, 2005

Holmes, S., *The Matador's Cape: America's Reckless Response to Terror*. New York: Cambridge Univerity Press, 2007

Holzgrefe, J.L. and Keohane, R.O., *Humanitarian Intervention: Ethical, Legal, and Political Dilemmas*. Cambridge: Cambridge University Press, 2003

Horn, B., de Taillon, J.P. and Last, D. (eds), *Force of Choice: Perspectives on Special Operations*. Montreal: McGill-Queen's University Press, 2005

Howard, R.D., 'Thinking Creatively in the War on Terrorism: Leveraging NATO and the Partnership for Peace Consortium'. *Connections*, Spring 2005, pp. 1–8

Hudson, H., ' "Doing" Security as Though Humans Matter: A Feminist Perspective on Gender and the Politics of Human Security'. *Security Dialogue*, 36, June 2005, pp. 155–174

Hudson, R., 'Dealing with International Hostage-Taking: Alternatives to Reactive Counterterrorist Assaults'. *Terrorism: An International Journal*, 12, 1989, pp. 321–78

Hugen, D. and Musser, S., *Can the War on Terrorism Be Won?* Farmington Hills, MI: Greenhaven Press, 2007

Human Rights Watch, *The United States 'Disappeared'. The CIA's Long-Term 'Ghost Detainees'*. A Human Rights Watch Briefing Paper. Washington, DC: Human Rights Watch, October 2004

Human Rights Watch, 'Witness to Abuse: Human Rights Abuses under the Material Witness Law since September 11'. *Human Rights Watch*, 17(2). Washington, DC, June 2005

Hunt, K. (ed.), *Gendering the War on Terror*. Aldershot, UK: Ashgate, 2007

ICT, *Countering Suicide Terrorism*. Herzliya, Israel: International Institute for Counter-Terrorism, 2002

Ignatieff, M. (ed.), *American Exceptionalism and Human Rights*. Princeton, NJ: Princeton University Press, 2005

Ingram, M. and Harkin, G., *Stakeknife: Britain's Secret Armies in Ireland*. Dublin: O'Brien, 2004

Isikoff, M. and Corn, D., *Hubris: The Inside Story of Spin, Scandal and the Selling of the Iraq War*. New York: Crown, 2006

Jacobs, B. (ed.), Special issue, 'Urban Vulnerability: Public Management in a Changing World'. *Journal of Contingencies and Crisis Management*, 13(2), June 2005, pp. 39–100

Jafa, Y.S., 'Defeating Terrorism: A Study of Operational Strategy and Tactics of Police Forces in Jammu and Kashmir'. *Police Practice and Research*, 6(2), May 2005, pp. 141–164

Jansen, P.T., 'The Consequences of Israel's Counter Terrorism Policy'. PhD thesis, University of St Andrews, 2008 (unpublished)

Jenkins, B.M., *Numbered Lives: Some Statistical Observations from 77 International Hostage Episodes*. Santa Monica, CA: RAND, 1977

Jenkins, B.M., *Embassies under Siege: A Review of 48 Embassy Takeovers, 1971–1980*. Santa Monica, CA: RAND, 1981

Jenkins, B.M., *Terrorism and Personal Protection*. Boston: Butterworth, 1985

Jenkins, B.M., *Countering Al Qaeda: An Appreciation of the Situation and Suggestions for Strategy*. Santa Monica, CA: RAND, 2002

Johnson, C., *Blowback: The Costs and Consequences of American Empire*. London: Time Warner, Paperback 2002

Johnson, T.H. and Russell, J.A., 'A Hard Day's Night: The United States and the Global War on Terrorism'. *Comparative Strategy*, 24(2), April–June 2005, pp. 127–151

Jones, T., 'Bioterrorism Preparedness: What Progress Has Congress Made since September 2001?' *Policy, Politics, and Nursing Practice*, 3, August 2002, pp. 217–219

Kahana, E., 'Analyzing Israel's Intelligence Failures'. *International Journal of Intelligence and Counterintelligence*, 18(2), Summer 2005, pp. 262–27

Kam, E., 'Curbing the Iranian Nuclear Threat: The Military Option'. *Strategic Assessment*, 7(3), December 2004, pp. 1–8

Kam, E., 'The Recent American Intelligence Failures'. *Strategic Assessment*, 7(4), March 2005, pp. 21–28

Kaplan, R.D., *Imperial Grunts: The American Military on the Ground*. New York: Random House, 2005

Karoubi, M.T., *Just or Unjust War? International Law and Unilateral Use of Armed Force by States at the Turn of the 20th Century*. Aldershot, UK: Ashgate, 2004

Kasmi, A.S., *La police algérienne: une institution pas comme les autres*. [Algiers]: Editions ANEP, 2002

Kassimeris, G., *Playing Politics with Terrorism: A User's Guide*. New York: Columbia University Press, 2007

Kay, S., 'NATO's Open Door: Geostrategic Priorities and the Impact of the European Union'. *Security Dialogue*, 32, June 2001, pp. 201–215

Keller, W.W. and Mitchell, G.R. (eds), *Hitting First: Preventive Force in U.S. Security Strategy*. Pittsburgh: University of Pittsburgh Press, 2006

Kellman, B., *Bioviolence: Preventing Biological Terror and Crime*. Cambridge: Cambridge University Press, 2007

Kellner, D., *From 9/11 to Terror War: The Dangers of the Bush Legacy*. Lanham, MD: Rowman & Littlefield, 2003

Knights, M., *Troubled Waters: Future US Security Assistance in the Gulf*. Washington, DC: Washington Institute for Near East Policy, 2006

Kolko, G., *The Age of War: The United States Confronts the World*. Boulder, CO: Lynne Rienner, 2006

Konishi, W., *The Case for Deterrence in the Anti-terror Campaign*, 2002. Available at: www.weltpolitik.net/Sachgebiete/Internationale%20Sicherheitspolitik/Problembereiche%20und%20L%C3%B6sungsans%C3%A4tze/Terrorismus/Analysen/The%20Case%20for%20Deterrence%20in%20the%20Anti-terror%20Campaign.html (accessed 22 April 2009)

Konst, J.A., 'Beveiliging van militaire objecten bij defensie'. *Militaire Spectator*, 173(10), 2004, pp. 503–509

Koopman, J., *McCoy's Marines: Darkside to Baghdad*. St Paul, MN: Zenith Press, 2005

Kramer, M., 'The Perils of Counterinsurgency: Russia's War in Chechnya'. *International Security*, 29(3), Winter 2004–2005, pp. 5–63

Krishan, K. (ed.), *National Security Guard Led Training Pamphlet*. New Delhi, 1987

Krishan, K., 'Chasing Shadows: Sub-conventional Warfare – Doctrinal Issues'. *PINNACLE – The ARTRAC Journal*, 4(1). Shimla, India: Army Training Command, April 2005

Kundnani, A., 'Wired for War: Military Technology and the Politics of Fear'. *Race and Class*, 46, July 2004, pp. 116–125

Kunreuther, H. and Heal, G., 'Interdependent Security'. *Journal of Risk and Uncertainty*, 26(2–3), 2003, pp. 231–249

Kutnjak Ivković, S. and O'connor Shelley, T., 'The Bosnian Police and Police Integrity: A Continuing Story'. *European Journal of Criminology*, 2(4), October 2005, pp. 428–464

Ladd, J.D., Melton, H.K. and Mason, P., *Clandestine Warfare: Weapons and Equipment of the SOE and OSS*. London: Blandford Press, 1988

Lambeth, B.S., *Air Power against Terror: America's Conduct of Operation Enduring Freedom*. MG-166-CENTAF, Santa Monica, CA: RAND, 2005

Langguth, A.J., *Hidden Terrors: The Truth about U.S. Police Operations in Latin America*. New York: Pantheon, 1978

Lanza, L., *Bomben und Geheimnisse: Geschichte des Massakers von der Plazza Fontana*. Hamburg: Nautilus, 1999

Larsen, H., 'The EU: A Global Military Actor?' *Cooperation and Conflict*, 37, September 2002, pp. 283–302

Leander, A., 'The Market for Force and Public Security: The Destabilizing Consequences of Private Military Companies'. *Journal of Peace Research*, 42, September 2005, pp. 605–622

Lebovic, J.H., 'Uniting for Peace? Democracies and United Nations Peace Operations after the Cold War'. *Journal of Conflict Resolution*, 48, December, 2004, pp. 910–936

Leebaert, D., *To Dare and to Conquer: Special Operations and the Destiny of Nations from Achilles to Al Qaeda*. New York: Little, Brown, 2006

Levi, M.A., 'Deterring Nuclear Terrorism'. *Issues in Science and Technology*, Spring 2004, pp. 53–74

Lieber, R.J., *The American Era: Power and Strategy for The 21st Century*. Cambridge University Press, 2005

Lieberfeld, D., 'Theories of Conflict and the Iraq War'. *International Journal of Peace Studies*, 10(2), Autumn–Winter, 2005, pp. 1–21

Lindstrom, G. and Schmitt, B. (eds), 'One Year On: Lessons from Iraq'. *Chaillot Paper* 68. Paris: European Union Institute for Security Studies, March 2004

Liotta, P.H., 'Boomerang Effect: The Convergence of National and Human Security'. *Security Dialogue*, 33, December 2002, pp. 473–488

Liotta, P.H., 'Converging Interests and Agendas: The Boomerang Returns'. *Security Dialogue*, 33, December 2002, pp. 495–498

Lloyd, R.M (ed.), *A Nation at War: Reconciling Ends and Means*. Proceedings of the Naval War College Intersessional Conference. Newport, RI, 7–8 March 2005. Newport, RI: Naval War College, 2005

Loof, J.P., 'Hoe Osama bin Laden het Verenigd Koninkrijk een noodtoestand bezorgde: enkele aspecten van het spanningsveld tussen terrorismebestrijding en mensenrechtenbescherming'. *NJCM-Bulletin*, 30(1), January 2005, pp. 8–24

Loof, J.P., Grinsven, M.P.J.M., Groenhart, N.W. [*et al.*], 'Rode draad: mensenrechten en terrorismebestrijding'. *NCJM-Bulletin*, 30(2), February–March 2005, pp. 137–158

Lopez, A.M., Comello, J.J. and Cleckner, W.H., 'Machines, the Military and Strategic Thought'. *Military Review*, September–October 2004, pp. 71–77

Lustick, I.S., *Trapped in the War on Terror*. Philadelphia: University of Pennsylvania Press, 2006

Luttwak, E.N., 'Iraq: The Logic of Disengagement'. *Foreign Affairs*, 84(1), January–February 2005, pp. 26–36

Lynk, M., 'Down by Law: The High Court of Israel, International Law, and the Separation Wall'. *Journal of Palestine Studies*, 35(1), Autumn 2005, pp. 6–24

Lyon, D., *Surveillance after September 11*. Cambridge: Polity Press, 2003

McClellan, S., *What Happened: Inside the Bush White House and Washington's Culture of Deception*. New York: Public Affairs, 2008

McCreery, T. and Bryden, W., 'Defence against Biological, Chemical and Radiological Attacks: The Technological Way Forward'. *Military Technology*. June 2006, pp. 13–21

McKelvey, T., *Inside America's Policy of Secret Interrogation and Torture in the Terror War*. New York: Carroll & Graf, 2007

Macmaster, N. 'Torture: From Algiers to Abu Ghraib'. *Race and Class*, 46, October 2004, pp. 1–21

MacWillson, A.C., *Hostage-Taking Terrorism: Incident-Response Strategy*. New York: St Martin's Press, 1992

Maguire, E.R. and King, W.R., 'Trends in the Policing Industry'. *Annals of the American Academy of Political and Social Science*, 593, May 2004, pp. 15–41

Makovsky, D., *A Defensible Fence: Fighting Terror and Enabling a Two-State Solution*. Washington, DC: Institute for Near East Policy, 2004

Malkin, M., *Invasion: How America Still Welcomes Terrorists, Criminals, and Other Foreign Menaces to Our Shores*. Washington, DC: Regnery, 2004

Mandel, R., *Security, Strategy and the Quest for Bloodless War*. Boulder, CO: Lynne Rienner, 2004

Margulies, J., *Guantánamo and the Abuse of Presidential Power*. New York: Simon & Schuster, 2006

Mariano O.D., 'Community Planning for Bioterrorism'. *Home Health Care Management and Practice*, 13, August 2001, pp. 409–410

Marks, T.A., 'At the Frontlines of the GWOT: State Response to Terrorism in Sri Lanka'. *Journal of Counterterrorism and Homeland Security International*, 10(3), 2004, pp. 34–35

Martin, J.E. (ed.), *Defeating Terrorism: Strategic Issue Analyses*. Carlisle, PA: US Army War College, Strategic Studies Institute, January 2002

Marty, D., *Alleged Secret Detention Centres in Council of Europe Member States: Roadmap for the PACE Inquiry*. Council of Europe, 645a(2005), 25 November 2005

Matveeva, A., *Macedonia: Guns, Policing and Ethnic Division*. Saferworld and Bonn International Center for Conversion. London: Boon, 2003

Meggle, G. (ed.), *Ethics of Terrorism and Counter-terrorism*. Frankfurt am Main: Ontos, 2005

Merritt, G. (ed.), *Countering Bioterrorism: Science, Technology and Oversight*. A report of the second meeting of the New Defence Agenda's Bioterrorism Reporting Group, 2004

Merritt, G. (ed.), *Next Generation Threat Reduction: Bioterrorism's Challenges and Solutions*. A report of the third meeting of the New Defence Agenda's Bioterrorism Reporting Group. Brussels: New Defence Agenda, January 2005

Merrit, G. (ed.), *Countering Bioterrorism: How Can Europe and the US Work Together?* A report of the fourth meeting of the New Defence Agenda's Bioterrorism reporting Group co-organised with the Chemical and Biological Arms Control Institute (CBACI), April 2005

Mestrovic, S.G., *The Trials of Abu Ghraib: An Expert Witness Account of Military Shame and Honor*. Boulder, CO: Paradigm, 2006

Michaelsen, C., 'Antiterrorism Legislation in Australia: A Proportionate Response to the Terrorist Threat?' *Studies in Conflict and Terrorism*, 28(4), July–August 2005, pp. 321–339

Mickolus, E., 'Negotiating for Hostages: A Policy Dilemma'. *Orbis*, 19(4), Winter 1976, pp. 1309–1325. Reprinted in J.D. Elliott and L. Gibson (eds), *Contemporary Terrorism: Selected Readings*. Gaithersburg, MD: International Association of Chiefs of Police, 1978, pp. 207–221

Miles, S.H., *Oath Betrayed: Torture, Medical Complicity and the war on Terror*. New York: Random House, 2006

Miller, C., *Blood Money: Wasted Billions, Lost Lives, and Corporate Greed in Iraq*. London: Little, Brown, 1981

Mincheva, L., 'The African Union as Peacemaker: Challenges before the EU Policy toward Africa'. In K. Nikolov (ed.), *More Than a Dwarf? FORNET Essays on Europe's Foreign, Security and Defense*. Sofia: BECSA, 2005

Miro, S. and Kaufman, S.G., 'Anthrax in New Jersey: A Health Education Experience in Bioterrorism Response and Preparedness'. *Health Promotion Practice*, 6, October 2005, pp. 430–436

MIVD, *Jaarverslag MIVD 2005*. The Hague: Militaire Inlichtingen- en Veiligheidsdienst, March 2006

Mockaitis, T.R., 'Winning Hearts and Minds: The Unlearned Lesson of Counterinsurgency'. *Militaire Spectator*, 174(6), 2005, pp. 252–261

Mockaitis, T.R. and Rich, P.B. (eds), *Grand Strategy in the war against Terrorism*. London: Frank Cass, 2004

Morgan, M.J., 'American Empire and the American Military'. *Armed Forces and Society*, 32, January 2006, pp. 202–218

Morgan, T., *My Battle of Algiers: A Memoir*. New York: HarperCollins, 2006

Mueller, J., 'Simplicity and Spook: Terrorism and the Dynamics of Threat Exaggeration'. *International Studies Perspectives*, May 2005, pp. 208–234

Mueller, J.E., *Overblown: How Politicians and the Terrorism Industry Inflate National Security Threats, and Why We Believe Them*. New York: Free Press, 2006

Mueller, J., 'Is There Still a Terrorist Threat?' *Foreign Affairs*, 85(5), October 2006, pp. 2–8

Muellerson, R., 'Being Tough on Terrorism or Respecting Human Rights: A False Dilemma of Authoritarian and Liberal Responses'. *American Behavioral Scientist*, 48(12), August 2005, pp. 1626–1656

Mulcahy, A., 'The "Other" Lessons from Ireland? Policing, Political Violence and Policy Transfer'. *European Journal of Criminology*, 2, April 2005, pp. 185–209

Muller, E.R., Starink, D. and de Jong, J.M. (eds), *Krijgsmacht: studies over de organisatie en het optreden*. Alphen aan de Rijn: Kluwer, 2004

Müller, H., *Amerika schlägt zurück: Die Weltordnung nach dem 11. September*. Frankfurt am Main: Fisher Taschenbuch Verlag, 2003

Müller, L., *Gladio – das Erbe des Kalten Krieges: Der Nato-Geheimbund und sein Deutscher Vorläeufer*. Hamburg: Rowohlt, 1991

Munoz-Rojas, D. and Frésard, J.J., 'The Roots of Behaviour in War: Understanding and Preventing IHL Violations'. *International Review of the Red Cross*, 86(853), March 2004, pp. 189–206

Murphy, M.C. and Wilds, M.R., 'X-Rated X-Ray Invades Privacy Rights'. *Criminal Justice Policy Review*, 12, December 2001, pp. 333–343

Murphy, S.D., 'International Law, the United States, and the Non-Military "War" against Terrorism'. *European Journal of International Law*, 14(2), April 2003, pp. 347–364

Murray, N., Book review: 'Guantánamo: The War on Human Rights', 'Guantánamo: What the World Should Know'. *Race and Class*, 47, July 2005, pp. 92–95

Naert, F., 'De binding van NAVO- en EU-strijdkrachten aan mensenrechten bij operaties tegen terrorisme'. *NCJM-Bulletin*, 30(7), November 2005, pp. 909–919

Nagl, J., *Learning to Eat Soup with a Knife: Counterinsurgency Lessons from Malaya and Vietnam*. Chicago: University of Chicago Press, 2005

Nardin, T. and Williams, M.S. (eds), *Humanitarian Intervention*. New York: New York University Press, 2006

National Commission on Terrorist Attacks upon the United States, Kean, T.H. *et al.*, *The 9/11 Commission Report: Final Report of the National Commission on Terrorist Attacks upon the United States*. Washington, DC: National Commission on Terrorist Attacks upon the United States. Washington, DC: GPO, 2004

Naylor, R.T., *Satanic Purses: Money, Myth, and Misinformation in the War on Terror*. Montreal: McGill-Queen's University Press, 2006

Nelles, W., 'American Public Diplomacy as Pseudo-education: A Problematic National Security and Counter-terrorism Instrument'. *International Politics*, 41(1), March 2004, pp. 65–93

Neumann, P.R. and Smith, M.L.R., 'Missing the Plot? Intelligence and Discourse Failure'. *Orbis*, 49(1), Winter 2005, pp. 95–107

Norell, M., 'The Role of the Military and Intelligence in Combating Terrorism'. *Romanian Journal of International Affairs*, 8(4), 2002

Norell, M., 'National Counter-terrorism Policy: The Case of Sweden'. Paper presented at International Expert Conference on National Counter-terrorism Policy, Zürich, 24–26, March 2004

Norell, M., *Swedish National Counter Terrorism Policy after 'Nine-Eleven': Problems and Challenges*. Swedish Defence Research Agency User Report, April 2005

Oakley, R.B. and Hammes, T.X., 'Securing Afghanistan: Entering a Make-or-Break Phase?' *Strategic Forum*, no. 205, March 2004. Washington, DC: National Defense University

O'Connell, M.E., *International Law and the Use of Force: Cases and Materials*. New York: Foundation Press, 2004

O'Day, A. (ed.), *War on Terrorism*. Aldershot, UK: Ashgate, 2004

O'Hanlon, M.E., *Defense Strategy for the Post-Saddam Era*. Washington, DC: Brookings Institution, 2005

Oppenheimer, A., 'NBC Defence: How Countermeasures Work'. *NATO's Nations*, 1, 2004, pp. 27–32

ORG, *Alternatives to the War on Terror*. London: Oxford Research Group, 2007

Oxford Research Group, *Learning from Fallujah: Lessons Identified 2003–2005*. London: Oxford Research Group, 2005

Packer, G., *The Assassin's Gate: America in Iraq*. New York: Farrar, Straus & Giroux, 2005

Parker, C.F. and Stern, E.K., 'Bolt from the Blue or Avoidable Failure? Revisiting September 11 and the Origins of Strategic Surprise'. *Foreign Policy Analysis*, 1(3), November 2005, pp. 301–331

Pastouna, J., *Guantanamo Bay: Gefangen im rechtsfreien Raum*. Hamburg: Europäische Verlagsanstalt, 2005

Patterson, E., and Casale, T., 'Targeting Terror: The Ethical and Practical Implications of Targeted Killings'. *International Journal of Intelligence and Counterintelligence*, 18(4), Winter 2005–2006, pp. 638–652

Pauly, R.J. Jr and Lansford, T., *Strategic Preemption: US Foreign Policy and the Second Iraq War*. Aldershot, UK: Ashgate, 2004

Paust, J.J., 'Postscript: Antiterrorism Military Commissions: The Ad Hoc DOD Rules of Procedure'. *Michigan Journal of International Law*, 23, 2002, p. 677

Payne, R.A., and Samhat, N.H., *Has the War on Terror Undermined Global Democracy?* Honolulu: International Studies Association (ISA), March 2005

Payne, K.B., Zaborski, J., McInnis, K.J. *et al.*, 'Reassessing Deterrence' [special section]. *Washington Quarterly*, 28(3), Summer 2005, pp. 135–199

Peña, C.V., *Winning the Un-War: A New Strategy for the War on Terrorism*. Dulles, VA: Potomac Books, 2006

Pena, C.V., 'A Smaller Military to Fight the War on Terror'. *Orbis*, 50(2), Spring 2006, pp. 289–306

Petro, J.B., 'Intelligence Support to the Life Science Community: Mitigating Threats from Bioterrorism'. *Studies in Intelligence*, 2007. Available at: https://www.cia.gov/library/center-for-the-study-of-intelligence/csi-publications/csi-studies/studies/vol48no3/article06.html (accessed 22 April 2009)

Pfarrar, C., *Warrior Soul: The Memoir of a Navy Seal*. New York: Presidio, 2005

Pillar, P., 'Metaphors and Mantras: A Comment on Shultz' and Vogt's Discussion of Terrorism, Intelligence, and War'. *Terrorism and Political Violence*, 15(2), June 2003, pp. 139–151

Pintak, L., *Seeds of Hate: How America's Flawed Middle East Policy Ignited the Jihad*. London: Pluto, 2003

Poponete, C.R., Book review: 'America's Military Today: The Challenge of Militarism'. *Armed Forces and Society*, 6(32), April 2006, pp. 480–482

Posner, R.A., *Countering Terrorism: Blurred Focus, Halting Steps*. Lanham, MD: Rowman & Littlefield, 2006

Prados, J. and Dee, I.R., *Safe for Democracy: The Secret Wars of the CIA*. Chicago: Ivan Dee, 2006

Prantl, H., *Der Terrorist als Gesetzgeber: Wie man mit Angst Politik macht*. Munich: Droemer Knaur, 2008

Presbey, G. (ed.), *Philosophical Perspectives on the 'War on Terrorism'*. Amsterdam: Editions Rodopi, 2007

Pushies, F.J. and Bryant, R., *U.S. Army Special Forces*. St Paul, MN: Motorbooks International, 2001

Ranstorp, M. and Wilkinson, P. (eds), Special issue: 'Terrorism and Human Rights'. *Terrorism and Political Violence*, 17(1–2), Winter 2005

Rashid, A., *Descent into Chaos: The United States and the Failure of Nation Building in Pakistan, Afghanistan and Central Asia*. New York: Viking Adult, 2008

Reck, M.G.J., 'The Necessity for Psychological Operations to Support Special Operations Forces during Unconventional Warfare'. *Small Wars Journal*, no. 4, February 2006

Record, J., *Bounding the Global War on Terrorism*. Carlisle, PA: US Army War College, 2003

Record, J., *Dark Victory: America's Second War with Iraq*. Annapolis, MD: Naval Institute Press, 2004

Reischl, G., *Unter Kontrolle: Die fatalen Folgen der staatlichen Überwachung für Wirschaft und Gesellschaft*. Frankfurt am Main: Redline Verlag, 2002

Renshon, J., *Why Leaders Choose War: The Psychology of Prevention*. New York: Praeger, 2006

Ricks, T.E., *Fiasco: The American Military Adventure in Iraq*. New York: Penguin Books, 2006

Rieff, D., *At the Point of a Gun: Democratic Dreams and Armed Intervention*. New York: Simon & Schuster, 2005

Rinehart, J.F., *The Cycle of Conflict Model and the US Global War on Terrorism: Conditions, Contexts, Processes, and Consequences*. Honolulu: International Studies Association (ISA), March 2005

Risen, J., *State of War: The Secret History of the CIA and the Bush Administration*. New York: Free Press, 2005

Roberts, A., 'The "War on Terror" in Historical Perspective.' *Survival*, 47(2), Summer 2005, pp. 101–130

Roberts, H., *The Battlefield: Algeria, 1988–2002: Studies in a Broken Polity*. London: Verso, 2003

Robinson, L., *Masters of Chaos: The Secret History of the Special Forces*. Jackson, TN: Public Affairs Books, 2004

Rogers, P., *Iraq and the War on Terror: Twelve Months of Insurgency 2004/2005*. London: Oxford Research Group, November 2005

Rogers, P., *Iraq and the War on Terror*. London: I.B. Tauris, 2007

Rogers, P., *Why We're Losing the War on Terror*. Cambridge: Polity Press, 2008

Rose, D., *Guantanamo: The War on Human Rights*. New York: New Press, 2005

Rosen, G. (ed.), *The Right War? The Conservative Debate on Iraq*. Cambridge: Cambridge University Press, 2005

Rosendorff, B.P. and Sandler, T., 'Too Much of a Good Thing? The Proactive Response Dilemma'. *Journal of Conflict Resolution*, 48, October 2004, pp. 657–671

Satloff, R.B. (ed.), *The War on Terror: The Middle East Dimension*. Washington, DC: Washington Institute for Near East Policy, 2002

Scheuer, M., 'How Not to Catch a Terrorist'. *The Atlantic*, December 2004, pp. 50–52

Scheuer, M., 'Al-Qaeda Doctrine: The Eventual Need for Semi-conventional Forces'. *Terrorism Focus*, 3(20), 23 May 2006

Scheuer, M., *Marching toward Hell: America and Islam after Iraq*. New York: Free Press, 2008

Schmitt, M., *Alger, été 1957: une victoire sur le terrorisme*. Paris: Harmattan, 2002

Scholl-Latour, P., *Kampf dem Terror – Kampf dem Islam? Chronik eines unbegrenzten Krieges*. Berlin: Ullstein, 2004

Scraton, P. (ed.), *Beyond September 11th: An Anthology of Dissent*. London: Pluto Press, 2002

Sebastian, L.C., 'Indonesian State Responses to September 11, the Bali Bombings and the War in Iraq: Sowing the Seeds for an Accommodationist Islamic Framework', *Cambridge Review of International Affairs*, 16(3), October 2003, pp. 429–446

Secretary of State for Foreign and Commonwealth Affairs, *Foreign Policy Aspects of the War against Terrorism. Session 2003–2004. Second Report from the Foreign Affairs Committee*. Presented to the Parliament by the Secretary of State for Foreign and Commonwealth Affairs, by Command of Her Majesty, March 2004

Shapira, S.C. and Mor-Yosef, S., 'Applying Lessons from Medical Management of Conventional Terror to Responding to Weapons of Mass Destruction Terror: The Experience of a Tertiary University Hospital'. *Studies in Conflict and Terrorism*, 26(5), September 2003, pp. 379–385

Shapiro, J. and Byman, D., 'Bridging the Transatlantic Counterterrorism Gap'. *Washington Quarterly*, 29(4), Autumn 2006, pp. 33–50

Shaw, M., *The New Western Way of War: Risk-Transfer and, its Crisis in Iraq*. Cambridge: Polity Press, 2005

Shields, P., 'When the "Information Revolution" and the US Security State Collide: Money Laundering and the Proliferation of Surveillance'. *New Media and Society*, 7, August 2005, pp. 483–512

Siboni, G., 'The Military Battle against Terrorism: Direct Contact vs. Standoff'. *Strategic Assessment*, 9(1), April 2006, pp. 42–47

Sidell, F.R., Patrick, W.C., and Dashiell, T.R., *Jane's Chem-Bio Handbook*, 2nd edn. Alexandria, VA: Jane's Information Group, 2002

Siegel, M., *False Alarm: The Truth about the Epidemic of Fear*. Hoboken, NJ: John Wiley, 2005

Siegrist, D.W. and Graham, J.M. (eds), *Countering Biological Terrorism in the U.S.: An Understanding of Issues and Status*. Dobbs Ferry, NY: Oceana, 1999

Silkenat, J.R., *The Imperial Presidency and the Consequences of 9/11: Lawyers React to the Global War on Terrorism*, 2 vols. Santa Barbara, CA: Praeger Security International, 2007

Silvers, R.B. and Epstein, B. (eds), *Striking Terror: America's New War*. New York: New York Review of Books, 2002

Simon, J.D., 'Biological Terrorism: Preparing to Meet the Threat', *Journal of the American Medical Association*, 6, August 1997, pp. 428–430

Singer, P.W., *Corporate Warriors: The Rise of the Privatized Military Industry*. Ithaca, NY: Cornell University Press, 2004

Skålnes, L.S., *The War on Terror, Intelligence, and US Unilateralism: Why 9/11 Made No Difference*. Honolulu: International Studies Association (ISA), March 2005

Slater, J., 'Tragic Choices in the War on Terrorism: Should We Try to Regulate and Control Torture?' *Political Science Quarterly*, 121(2), Summer 2006, pp. 191–215

Sloan, S., *Beating International Terrorism: An Action Strategy for Preemption and Punishment, with a New Prologue*, 2nd edn. Maxwell Air Force Base, AL: Air University Press. Available at: www.au.af.mil/au/aul/aupress/ Books/Sloan/Sloan.pdf (accessed 22 April 2009)

Smith, G.A., 'President Bush's Enthymeme of Evil: The Amalgamation of 9/11, Iraq, and Moral Values'. *American Behavioral Scientist*, 49, September 2005, pp. 32–47

Smith, M., 'Intelligence-Sharing Failures Hamper War on Terrorism'. *Jane's Intelligence Review*, 17(7), July 2005, pp. 20–24

Smithson, A.E., 'A Call for Tighter Policing Tools for Biological Weapons'. *BICC Bulletin*, no. 35, April 2005

Soros, G., *The Bubble of American Supremacy: Correcting The Misuse of American Power*. New York: PublicAffairs, 2003

Soros, G., *The Age of Fallibility: Consequences of the War on Terror*. New York: PublicAffairs, 2006

Stanley, T., 'Australian Anti-terror Raids: A Serious Plot Thwarted'. *Terrorism Monitor*, 3(23), 2 December 2005, pp. 1–4

Stares, P.B. and Yacoubian, M., 'Rethinking the "War on Terror": New Approaches to Conflict Prevention and Management in the Post-9/11 World'. In C.A. Crocker, F.O. Hampson and P. Aall (eds), *Leashing the Dogs of War: Conflict Management in a Divided World*. Washington, DC: United States Institute of Peace, 2007

Steinhäusler, F., 'Guarding Nuclear Reactors and Material from Terrorists and Thieves', *Arms Control Today*, 31(8), 2001, pp. 8–12

Steinhäusler, F., 'Chernobyl and Goiânia: Lessons for Responding to Radiological Terrorism'. *Health Physics*, 89(5), 2005, pp. 566–574

Stephens, A.C. and Vaughan-Williams, N., *Terrorism and the Politics of Response*. London, Routledge, 2008

Tago, A., 'Determinants of Multilateralism in US Use of Force: State of Economy, Election Cycle, and Divided Government'. *Journal of Peace Research*, 42(5), September 2005, pp. 585–604

Taillon, J.P. de B., *The Evolution of Special Forces in Counter-terrorism: The British and American Experiences*. Westport, CT: Praeger, 2000

Talentino, A.K., *Military Intervention after the Cold War: The Evolution of Theory and Practice*. Columbus: Ohio State University Press, 2005

Talmor, R., *Demolition and Sealing of Houses as a Punitive Measure in the West Bank and the Gaza Strip during the Intifada*. Jerusalem: B'Tselem, the Israel Information Center for Human Rights in the Occupied Territories, 1989

Taylor, M. and Black, W., 'In Search of Reason: Libraries and the USA PATRIOT Act'. *Journal of Librarianship and Information Science*, 36, June 2004, pp. 51–54

Terry, J.P., *The Regulation of International Coercion: Legal Authorities and Political Constraints*. Newport, RI: Naval War College, October 2005

Testrake, J., *Triumph over Terror on Flight 847*. Eastbourne, UK: Kingsway, 1988

Thakur, R., *The United Nations, Peace and Security: From Collective Security to the Responsibility to Protect*. Cambridge: Cambridge University Press, 2006

Thomas, T.L., 'The War in Iraq: An Assessment of Lessons Learned by Russian Military Specialists through 31 July 2003'. *Journal of Slavic Military Studies*, 17, 2004, pp. 153–180

Thompson, L., *The Rescuers: The World's Top Anti-terrorist Units*. Boulder, CO: Paladin Press, 1986

Thompson, L., *Secret Techniques of the Elite Forces*. Mechanicsburg, PA: Stackpole Books, 2005

Thornton, R., 'Getting It Wrong: The Crucial Mistakes Made in the Early Stages of the British Army's Deployment to Northern Ireland (August 1969 to March 1972)'. *Journal of Strategic Studies*, 30(1), 2007, pp. 73–107

Tophoven, R., *GSG 9: Kommando gegen Terrorismus*. Koblenz: Wehr und Wissen, 1977

Torture Papers, The: The Legal Road to Abu Ghraib. Cambridge: Cambridge University Press, 2005

Towle, P., *Pilots and Rebels: The Use of Aircraft in Unconventional Warfare, 1918–1988*. London: Brassey's, 1989

Trager, R.F. and Zagorcheva, D.P., 'Deterring Terrorism: It Can be Done'. *International Security*, 30(3), Winter 2005–2006, pp. 87–123

Tsang, S. (ed.), *Intelligence and Human Rights in the Era of Global Terrorism*. Stanford, CA: Stanford University Press, 2008

Tucker, D. and Lamb, C.J., 'Restructuring Special Operations Forces for Emerging Threats'. *Strategic Forum*, no. 219, January 2006

Turner, M.A., *Why Secret Intelligence Fails*. Dulles, VA: Potomac Books, 2004

Uesseler, R., *Krieg als Dienstleistung: Private Militärfirmen zerstören die Demokratie*. Berlin: Ch. Links Verlag, 2006

Ulfstein, G., 'Terrorism and the Use of Force'. *Security Dialogue*, 34, June 2003, pp. 153–167

United States Congress, Senate Committee on Governmental Affairs, *Vulnerability of the Nation's Electric Systems to Multi-site Terrorist Attack*. Hearing before the Committee on Governmental Affairs, United States Senate, One Hundred First Congress, second session, 28 June 1990. Washington: GPO, 1990

United States Navy Department, *Combating Terrorism*. Quantico, VA: U.S. Marine Corps, 1990

US Department of Justice, *A Review of the FBI's Handling of Intelligence Information Related to the September 11 Attacks*. Office of the Inspector General, November 2004

US Government Guide to Surviving Terrorism. New York: Barnes & Noble, 2003

Van Creveld, M., *Defending Israel: A Controversial Plan toward Peace*. New York: St Martin's Press, 2004

van Ham, P., 'War, Lies, and Videotape: Public Diplomacy and the USA's War on Terrorism'. *Security Dialogue*, 34, December 2003, pp. 427–444

Veegens, K., 'Het Straatsburgse recht op vrijheid en veiligheid en Nederlandse verdenkingscriteria voor "terrorismeverdachten" ' *NCJM-Bulletin*, 31(2), March 2006, pp. 182–204

Velenzuela, A.A. and Rosello, V.M., 'The War on Drugs and Terrorism: El Salvador and Colombia'. *Military Review*, March–April 2004, pp. 28–35

Vervaele, J.A.E., 'The Anti-terrorist Legislation in the US: Inter Arma Silent Leges?' *European Journal of Crime, Criminal Law and Criminal Justice*, 13(2), 2005, pp. 201–254

Von Bülow, A., *Im Namen des Staates: CIA, BND und die kriminellen Machenschaften der Geheimdienste*. Munich: Piper 2000

Wallace, P., 'Political Instability and the military in India'. In L. Parmar (ed.), *Armed Forces and the International Diversities*. Jaipur, India: Pointer, 2001, 1–33

Wallis, R., *Combating Air Terrorism*. Washington, DC: Brassey's, 1993

Weiss, T.G., Crahan, M.E. and Goering, J. (eds), *Wars on Terrorism and Iraq: Human Rights, Unilateralism, and U.S. Foreign Policy*. New York: Routledge, 2004

Welch, M., 'Trampling Human Rights in the War on Terror: Implications to the Sociology of Denial'. *Critical Criminology*, 12(1), 2003, pp. 1–20

Weldon, C., *Countdown to Terror: The Top-Secret Information That Could Prevent the Next Terrorist Attack on America and How the CIA Has Ignored It*. Washington, DC: Regnery, 2005

West, B., *No True Glory: Fallujah and the Struggle in Iraq – A Frontline Account*. New York: Presidio, 2005

Wheeler, N., 'Dying for "Enduring Freedom": Accepting Responsibility for Civilian Casualties in the War against Terrorism'. *International Relations*, 16, August 2002, pp. 205–225

White, R., 'Repression and the Liberal State'. *Journal of Conflict Resolution*, 39, 1995, pp. 330–352

Williams, B.G., 'Target Dostum: The Campaign against Northern Alliance Warlords'. *Terrorism Monitor*, 3(20), 21 October 2005. Available at: www.jamestown.org/programs/gta/single/?tx_ttnews[tt_news]=592&tx_tt news[backPid]=180&no_cache=1 (accessed 22 April 2009)

Wilson, R.A. (ed.), *Human Rights in the 'War on Terror'*. Cambridge: Cambridge University Press, 2005

Wolfendale, J., 'Terrorism, Security, and the Threat of Counterterrorism'. *Studies in Conflict and Terrorism*, October–November 2006, pp. 753–770

Woodward, A., 'Banning Biological Weapons'. *African Security Review*, 14(1), 2005. Available at: www.iss.co.za/pubs/ASR/14No1/FWoodward.htm (accessed 22 April 2009)

Woodward, B., *Plan of Attack*. New York: Simon & Schuster, 2004

Woodward, B., *State of Denial*. New York: Simon & Schuster, 2006

Woodworth, P., *Dirty Wars, Clean Hands: ETA, the GAL, and the Spanish Democracy*. Cork, Ireland: Cork University Press, 2001

World Health Organization (WHO), *Public Health Response to Biological and Chemical Weapons: WHO Guidance*. Geneva: World Health Organization, 2004

Xianting Li, Jianrong Yang and Wei Sun, 'Strategy to Optimise Building Ventilation to Aid Rescue of Hostages Held by Terrorists'. *Indoor and Built Environment*, 14, February 2005, pp. 39–50

Yamashita, H., *Fighting Terrorism and Fighting Displacement: Two Approaches to 'Elastic' Sovereignty*. Honolulu: International Studies Association (ISA), March 2005

Yoo, J., *The Powers of War and Peace: The Constitution and Foreign Affairs after 9/11*. Chicago: University of Chicago Press, 2005

Yoo, J., *War by Other Means: An Insider's Account of the War on Terror*. New York: Atlantic Monthly Press, 2006

Young, P., *Licensed to Kill: Hired Guns in the War on Terror*. New York: Crown Publishers, 2006

Zegart, A.B., 'September 11 and the Adaptation Failure of US Intelligence Agencies'. *International Security*, 29(4), Spring 2005, pp. 78–111

Zegart, A.B., 'An Empirical Analysis of Failed Intelligence Reforms before September 11'. *Political Science Quarterly*, 121(1), 2006, pp. 33–60

Zimmermann, D., 'Between Minimum Force and Maximum Violence: Combating Political Violence Movements with Third-Force Options'. *Connections*, Spring 2005, pp. 43–60

Zuijdam, F., 'Voor recht en vrijheid: George W. Bush en de strijd tegen het terrorisme'. *Militaire Spectator*, 174(7–8), 2005, pp. 316–327

Zussman, A. and Zussman, N., 'Assassinations: Evaluating the Effectiveness of an Israeli Counterterrorism Policy using Stock Market Data'. *Journal of Economic Perspectives*, 20(2), Spring 2006, pp. 193–206

T. Special forms of terrorism

T.1 Assassination

Blondiau, H., *Tod auf Bestellung: Politischer Mord im 20. Jahrhundert*. Munich: Ullstein, 2000

Goldfarb, A. and Litvinenko, M., *Death of a Dissident: The Poisoning of Alexander Litvinenko and the Return of the KGB*. New York: Free Press, 2007

Goldman, F., *The Art of Political Murder: Who Killed the Bishop?* New York: Grove Press, 2007

Iqbal, Z. and Zorn, C., 'The Political Consequences of Assassination'. *Journal of Conflict Resolution*, 52, June 2008, pp. 385–400

Jones, H., *Death of a Generation: How the Assassinations of Diem and JFK Prolonged the Vietnam War*. Oxford: Oxford University Press, 2003

Kellerhoff, S.F., *Attentäter: Mit einer Kugel die Welt verändern*. Cologne: Böhlau, 2005

Korn, D.A., *Assassination in Khartoum*. Bloomington: Indiana University Press, 1993

Külbel, J. K., *Mordakte Hariri: Underdrückte Spuren im Libanon*. Berlin: Karl Homilius Verlag, 2008

Laucella, L., *Assassination: The Politics of Murder*. Los Angeles: Lowell House, 1998

O'Brian, K.A., 'The Use of Assassination as a Tool of State Policy: South Africa's Counter-Revolutionary Strategy, 1979–1992' (Part I). *Terrorism and Political Violence*, 10(2), 1998, pp. 53–85

O'Brian, K.A., 'The Use of Assassination as a Tool of State Policy: South Africa's Counter-revolutionary Strategy, 1979–1992' (Part II). *Terrorism and Political Violence*, 13(2), 2001, pp. 107–142

Talmadge, C., 'Detering a Nuclear 9/11'. *Washington Quarterly*, 30(2), 2007, pp. 21–34

Thomas, W., 'Norms and Security: The Case of International Assassination'. *International Security*, 25(1), Summer 2000, pp. 105–133

T.2 Bombing

Artz, D., 'Pan Am Flight 103', *Dictionary of American History*, 3rd edn. Farmington Hills MI: Gale, 2002

Brodie, T.G., *Bombs and Bombings: A Handbook to Protection, Security, Detection, Disposal and Investigation for Industry, Police and Fire Departments*, 3rd edn. Springfield IL: Charles C. Thomas, 2005

Davis, M., *Buda's Wagon: A Brief History of the Car Bomb*. London: Verso, 2007

NEFA, *Bojinka II: The Transatlantic Liquid Bomb Plot*. Report no. 15 in a NEFA series, 'Target: America'. April 2008

NEFA, *KSMs Transatlantic Shoe Bomb Plot*. Report no. 11 in a NEFA series, September 2007

T.3 Hijacking and hostage taking

Alexander, Y. and Sochor, E., *Aerial Piracy and Aviation Security*. Dordrecht: Martinus Nijhoff, 1990

Bron, R.P. and de Hoog, D., 'Civiele luchtvaart en terroristische incidenten: historische ontwikkelingen en toekomstige trends'. *Justitiële Verkenningen*, 33(5), 2007, pp. 21–37

Harrison, J., *International Aviation and Terrorism*. London: Routledge, 2009

Jenkins, B., *Aviation Terrorism and Security*. London: Frank Cass, 2007

McDermott, T., *Perfect Soldiers: The Hijackers: Who They Were, Why They Did It*. London: HarperCollins, 2005

Matar, K.I. and Thabit, R.W., *Lockerbie and Libya: A Study in International Relations*. Jefferson, NC: McFarland, 2004

Merari, A., 'Attacks on Civil Aviation: Trends and Lessons'. *Terrorism and Political Violence*, 10(3), 1998, pp. 9–26

Moysey, S.P., 'The Balcombe Street and Iranian Embassy Sieges: A Comparative Examination of Two Hostage Negotiation Events'. *Journal of Police Crisis Negotiations*, 4(1), 23 February 2004, pp. 67–96

Phillips, T., *Beslan: The Tragedy of School No. 1*. London: Granta Books, 2007

Seidenstat, P., 'Terrorism, Airport Security, and the Private Sector'. *Review of Policy Research*, 21(3), May 2004, pp. 275–291

Silke, A., 'When Sums Go Bad: Mathematical Models and Hostage Situations'. *Terrorism and Political Violence*, 13(2), Summer 2001, pp. 49–66

Strentz, T., *Psychological Aspects of Crisis Negotiation*. London: Taylor & Francis, 2006

Wilkinson, P. and Jenkins, B.M. (eds), Special Issue: 'Aviation Terrorism and Security'. *Terrorism and Political Violence*, 10(3), 1998

T.4 Kidnapping

Abad Castelos, M., *La toma de rehenes como manifestación del terrorismo y el derecho internacional: obligaciones estatales previas, coetáneas y posteriores a la comisión del delito*. Madrid: Ministerio del Interior, Secretaría General Técnica, 1997

Amara, E. and Pieczenik, S.R., *Nous avons tué Aldo Moro*. Paris: Robin, 2006

Antokol, N. and Nudell, M., *No One a Neutral: Political Hostage-Taking in the Modern World*. Medina, OH: Alpha Publications of Ohio, 1990

Baliani, M., *Corpo di stato: il delitto Moro*. Milano: Rizzoli, 2003

Bejarano, J.A., *Colombia: inseguridad, violencia y desempeño económico en las áreas rurales*. Bogotá: Fondo Financiero de Proyectos de Desarrollo: Universidad Externado de Colombia, 1997

Bolz, F., Dudonis, K.J. and Schulz, D.P., *The Counterterrorism Handbook: Tactics, Procedures, and Techniques*. Boca Raton, FL: CRC Press, 2005

Bonfigli, S. and Sce, J., *Il delitto infinito: ultime notizie sul sequestro Moro*. Milan: Kaos, 2002

Cento Bull, A. and Giorgio, A., *Speaking Out and Silencing: Culture, Society and Politics in Italy in the 1970s*. London: Legenda, 2006

Child, G., *Over the Edge: The True Story of Four American Climbers' Kidnap and Escape in the Mountains of Central Asia*. New York: Villard Books, 2002

Clarke, R.V.G. and Felson M., *Routine Activity and Rational Choice*. New Brunswick, NJ: Transaction, 2004

Collin, R. and Freedman, G.L., *Winter of Fire: The Abduction of General Dozier and the Downfall of the Red Brigades*. New York: Dutton

Economist, The, 'Plots and Super-Plots: Claims Osama Bin Laden Was behind Kidnappings in Yemen'. 9 January 1999

Economist, The, 'Hizbullah Basks in Its Glory: Israeli Soldiers Abducted at Israel–Lebanon Border'. 14 October 2000

Katz, S.M., *Targeting Terror: Counterterrorist Raids*. Minneapolis: Lerner Publications, 2005

Meyr, E., 'Israel, Hamas May Clash over Kidnapping'. *Jane's Intelligence Review*, 12 (February 2000), pp. 28–30

Mortenson, G. and Relin, D.O., *Three Cups of Tea: One Man's Mission to Fight Terrorism and Build Nations – One School at a Time*. New York: Viking, 2006

Murphy, P.J., *The Wolves of Islam: Russia and the Faces of Chechen Terror*. Washington, DC: Brassey's, 2004

Quin, M., *Kidnapped in Yemen: One Woman's Amazing Escape from Captivity*. Guilford, CT: Lyons Press, 2005

Resos, D.C., *Hard Target: Protecting Yourself from Terrorists and Kidnappers*. Manila: Transform Nation News, 2003

Sciascia, L., Robb, P. and Rabinovitch, S., *The Moro Affair; and, The Mystery of Majorana*. New York: New York Review of Books, 2004

Ulloa Bornemann, A., *Surviving Mexico's Dirty War: A Political Prisoner's Memoir*, ed. A. Schmidt and A.C. de Schmidt. Philadelphia: Temple University Press, 2006

United States Congress, House Committee on the Judiciary, Subcommittee on Crime, Terrorism and Homeland Security, *Child Abduction Prevention Act and the Child Obscenity and Pornography Prevention Act of 2003: hearing before the Subcommittee on Crime, Terrorism, and Homeland Security of the Committee on the Judiciary, House of Representatives*, One Hundred Eighth Congress, first session, on H.R. 1104 and H.R. 1161, March 11, 2003. Washington, DC

T.5 Nuclear terrorism

Acton, J.M., Rogers, M.B. and Zimmerman, P.D., 'Beyond the Dirty Bomb: Re-thinking Radiological Terror'. *Survival*, 49(3), Autumn 2007, pp. 151–168

Albright, D. and Hinderstein, C., 'Unraveling the A.Q. Khan and Future Proliferation Networks'. *Washington Quarterly*, 29(2), Spring 2005, pp. 111–128

Alexander, Y. and Hoening, M., *The New Iranian Leadership: Ahmadinejad, Terrorism, Nuclear Ambition and the Middle East*. Westport, CT: Praeger, 2008

Allison, G., *Nuclear Terrorism: The Ultimate Preventable Catastrophe*. New York: Times Books, 2004

Allison, G. (ed.), 'Confronting the Specter of Nuclear Terrorism'. *Annals of the American Academy of Political and Social Science*, 607, September 2006

Allison, G., *Nuclear Terrorism: The Risks and Consequences of the Ultimate Disaster*. London: Constable, 2006

Allison, G.T., Coté, O.R., Jr, Falkenrath, *Avoiding Nuclear Anarchy: Containing the Threat of Loose Russian Nuclear Weapons and Fissile Material*. Cambridge, MA: MIT Press, 1995

Allison, G. and Kokoshin, A., 'The New Containment: An Alliance against Nuclear Terrorism'. *The National Interest*, Fall 2002

Asculai, E., 'Rethinking the Nuclear Non-proliferation Regime'. Tel Aviv: Jaffee Center for Strategic Studies, *Memorandum* no. 70, June 2004

Atran S., 'A Failure of Imagination'. *Studies in Conflict and Terrorism*, 29(3), April–May 2006, pp. 285–300

Basrur, R.M. and Steinhäusler, F., 'Nuclear and Radiological Terrorism Threats for India: Risk Potential and Countermeasures'. *Journal of Physical Security*, 1(1), 2004

Bosch, O. and van Ham P. (eds), *Global Non-proliferation and Counter-terrorism: The Impact of UNSCR 1540*. The Hague: Clingendael, 2007

Brackett, D.W., *Holy Terror: Armageddon in Tokyo*. New York: Weatherhill, 1996

Braun, C., Steinhäusler, F. and Zaitseva, L., 'International Terrorists' Threat to Nuclear Facilities'. Paper presented at American Nuclear Society meeting, Washington, DC, 19 November 2002

Brookes, P., *A Devil's Triangle: Terrorism, WMD and Rogue States*. Washington, DC: Heritage Foundation, 2005

Bunn, G. and Braun, C., 'Terrorism Potential for Research Reactors Compared with Power Reactors: Nuclear Weapons, "Dirty Bombs," and Truck Bombs'. *American Behavioral Scientist*, 46, February 2003, pp. 714–726

Bunn, G. and Chyba, C.F. (eds), *US Nuclear Weapons Policy: Confronting Today's Threats*. Washington, DC: Brookings Institution, 2006

Bunn, M. and Wier, A., *Securing the Bomb: An Agenda for Action: Project on Managing the Atom*. Belfer Center for Science and International Affairs, John F. Kennedy School of Government, Harvard University. Commissioned by the Nuclear Threat Initiative, May 2004

Bunn, M. and Wier, A., 'The Seven Myths of Nuclear Terrorism'. *Current History*, April 2005, pp. 153–161

Bunn, M. and Wier, A., *Securing the Bomb 2005: The New Global Imperatives: Project on Managing the Atom*. Belfer Center for Science and International Affairs, John F. Kennedy School of Government, Harvard University. Commissioned by the Nuclear Threat Initiative, May 2005

Bunn, G., Braun, C. and Steinhäusler, F., 'Nuclear Terrorism Potential: Research Reactors vs. Power Reactors'. Paper presented at the EU High-Level Scientific International Conference on Physical Protection: Strengthening Global Practices for Protecting Nuclear Material, Salzburg, Austria, September 2002

Bunn, G., Steinhäusler, F. and Zaitseva, L., 'Could Terrorists or Thieves Get Weapons Usable Material from Research Reactors and Facilities?' Paper presented at the 43rd Institute of Nuclear Materials Management Conference, Orlando, FL, June 2002

Bunn, G., Braun, C., Glaser, A., Lyman, E. and Steinhäusler, F., 'Research Reactor Vulnerability to Sabotage by Terrorists'. *Science and Global Security*, September–December 2003

Bunn, G., Rinne, R. and Steinhäusler, F., 'Strengthening Global Physical Protection Practices: Gaining Better Information on National Practices for Protection of Nuclear Material'. Paper presented at the IAEA International Conference on Security of Material: Measures to Prevent, Intercept and Respond to Illicit Uses of Nuclear Material and Radioactive Sources, Stockholm, 7–11 May 2001

Cameron, G., *Nuclear Terrorism: A Threat Assessment for the 21st Century*. New York: Macmillan, 1999

Caraley, D.J. and Morales Kando, L. (eds), *Terrorist Attacks and Nuclear Proliferation: Strategies for Overlapping Dangers*. New York: Academy of Political Science, 2007

Choi, Jin-Tai, *Aviation Terrorism: Historical Survey, Perspectives, and Responses*. Basingstoke, UK: Macmillan, 1994

Cirincione, J., *Bomb Scare: The History and Future of Nuclear Weapons*. New York: Columbia Press, 2007

Dugan, L., LaFree, G. and Piquero, A.R., 'Testing a Rational Choice Model of Airline Hijackings'. *Criminology*, no. 43, 2005, pp. 1031–1065

Emerson, S., *The Fall of Pan Am 103*. London: Futura, 1990

Ferguson, C.D., *Preventing Catastrophic Nuclear Terrorism*. New York: Council on Foreign Relations, 2006

Flibbert, A., 'After Saddam: Regional Insecurity, Weapons of Mass Destruction, and Proliferation Pressures in Postwar Iraq'. In D.J. Caraley and K.L. Morales (eds), *Terrorist Attacks and Nuclear Proliferation: Strategies for Overlapping Dangers*. New York: Academy of Political Science, 2007

Frantz, D. and Collins, C., *The Nuclear Jihadist: The True Story of the Man Who Sold the World's Most Dangerous Secrets and How We Could Have Stopped Him*. New York: Twelve, 2007

Gero, D., *Flights of Terror: Aerial Hijack and Sabotage since 1930*. Sparkford, UK: Patrick Stephens, 1997

Gressang, D., 'Audience and Message: Assessing Terrorist WMD Potential'. *Terrorism and Political Violence*, 13(3), Autumn 2001, pp. 83–106

Heal, G. and Kunreuther, H., 'IDS Models of Airline Security'. *Journal of Conflict Resolution*, 49, April 2005, pp. 201–217

Houghton, D.P., 'Explaining the Origins of the Iran Hostage Crisis: A Cognitive Perspective'. *Terrorism and Political Violence*, 18(2), Summer 2006, pp. 259–279

Howard, R.D., *Weapons of Mass Destruction and Terrorism*. Maidenhead: McGraw-Hill/Dushkin, 2007

Howard, R.D. and Forest, J.J.F. (eds), *Terrorism and Weapons of Mass Destruction*. Maidenhead, UK: McGraw-Hill, 2007

Jiwa, S., *The Death of Air India Flight 182*. London: W.H. Allen, 1986

Kingshott, B.F., 'An Assessment of the Terrorist Threat to Use a Nuclear or Radiological Device in an Attack'. *International Journal of Nuclear Law*, 1(2), 11 July 2006, pp. 141–161

Langewiesche, W., *The Atomic Bazaar*. New York: Farrar, Straus & Giroux, 2007

Levi, M., *On Nuclear Terrorism*. Cambridge, MA: Harvard University Press, 2007

Maerli, M.B., Schaper, A. and Barnaby, F., 'The Characteristics of Nuclear Terrorist Weapons'. *American Behavioral Scientist*, 46, February 2003, pp. 727–744

Malloy, S.L., *Atomic Tragedy: Henry L. Stimson and the Decision to Use the Bomb against Japan*. Ithaca, NY: Cornell University Press, 2008

Medalia, J., 'Nuclear Terrorism'. In: E.V. Linden, (ed.), *Focus on Terrorism*, vol. 4. Hauppauge, NY: Nova Science Publishers, 2002

O'Neil, A., 'Terrorist Use of Weapons of Mass Destruction: How Serious Is the Threat?' *Australian Journal of International Affairs*, 57(1), April 2003, pp. 99–112

Parachini, J.V., 'Comparing Motives and Outcomes of Mass Casualty Terrorism Involving Conventional and Unconventional Weapons'. *Studies in Conflict and Terrorism*, 24(5), September 2001, pp. 389–406

Parachini, J.V., Mosher, D.E., Baker, J.C., Crane, K., Chase, M.S. and Daugherty, M., *Diversion of Nuclear, Biological and Chemical Weapons Expertise from the Former Soviet Union*. DB-457-DOE. Santa Monica, CA: RAND, 2005

Piksaikin, V., Pshakin, G. and Roshchenko, V., 'Review of Methods and Instruments for Determining Undeclared Nuclear Materials and Activities'. *Science and Global Security*, 14(1), January–April 2006, pp. 49–72

Quillen, C., 'Terrorism with Weapons of Mass Destruction: The Congressional Response'. *Terorism and Political Violence*, 13(1), Spring 2001, pp. 47–65

Rensselaer, L., 'Nuclear Smuggling and International Terrorism: Issues and Options for US Policy'. In E.V. Linden, (ed.), *Focus on Terrorism*, vol. 6. Hauppauge, NY: Nova Science Publishers, 2003

Riedel, P., *Terrorismus und die Verwendung von Massenvernichtungswaffen: Risikoanalyse und Gegenstrategie*. Bonn: Bouvier, 2008

Russell, P.A. and Preston, F.W., 'Airline Security after the Event: Unintended Consequences and Illusions'. *American Behavioral Scientist*, 47, July 2004, pp. 1419–1427

Schaper, A., 'Nuklearterrorismus: Neue Bedrohungsszenarien', *Spektrum der Wissenschaft*, March 2003, 2003, p. 32

Schaper, A., 'Nuklearterrorismus als neue Herausforderung an die Rüstungskontrolle'. In G. Neuneck and C. Mölling (eds), *Die Zukunft der Rüstungskontrolle*. Baden-Baden, Germany: Nomos 2005

Schaper, A., 'The Technical Challenges of Nuclear and Radiological Terrorism'. In J.J.F. Forest (ed.), *Teaching Terror: Strategic and Tactical Learning in the Terrorist World*. Lanham, MD: Rowman & Littlefield, 2006

Schaper, A., Maerli, M. and Barnaby, F., 'The Characteristics of Nuclear Terrorist Weapons'. *American Behavioral Scientist*, 46(6), 2003, pp. 727–744

Schmid, A.P., 'Terrorism and the Use of Weapons of Mass Destruction: From Where the Risk?' *Terrorism and Political Violence*, 11(4), 1999, pp. 106–132

Schwarz, M. and Erdmann, H., *Atomterror. Schurken, Staaten, Terroristen: Die neue nukleare Bedrohung*. Munich: Droemer Knaur, 2004

Snowden, L.L., 'How Likely Are Terrorists to Use a Nuclear Strategy?' *American Behavioral Scientist*, 46, February 2003, pp. 699–713

Spyer, J., 'The Al Qaeda Network and Weapons of Mass Destruction'. *Middle East Review of International Affairs*, 8(3), September 2004, pp. 29–45

Steinhäusler, F., 'Upgrading Airport Security'. *Aviation Security International*, 8(6), 2002, pp. 18–22

Steinhausler, F., 'What It Takes to Become a Nuclear Terrorist'. *American Behavioral Scientist*, 46, February 2003, pp. 782–795

Tarvainen, T., 'Al-Qaeda and WMD: A Primer'. *Terrorism Monitor*, 3(11), 2 June 2005. Available at: www.jamestown.org/programs/gta/single/?tx_ttnews[tt_news]=498&tx_ttnews[backPid]=180&no_cache =1 (accessed 30 April 2009)

Van Hasselt, V.B., Baker, M.T., Romano, S.J., Sellers, A.H., Noesner, G.W. and Smith, S. 'Development and Validation of a Role-Play Test for Assessing Crisis (Hostage) Negotiation Skills'. *Criminal Justice and Behavior*, 32, June 2005, pp. 345–361

Wells, T., *444 Days: The Hostages Remember*. New York: Harcourt Brace Jovanovich, 1985

Wenger, A. and Wollenmann, R. (eds), *Bioterrorism: Confronting a Complex Threat*. Boulder, CO: Lynne Rienner, 2007

Wilkinson, P. and Jenkins, B.M., *Aviation Terrorism and Security*. London: Frank Cass, 1999

Wolfsthal, J.B. and Collina, T.Z., 'Nuclear Terrorism and Warhead Control in Russia'. *Survival*, 44(2), 2002, pp. 71–83

Zaitseva, L. and Hand, K., 'Nuclear Smuggling Chains: Suppliers, Intermediaries, and End-Users'. *American Behavioral Scientist*, 46, February 2003, pp. 822–844

T.6 Other forms of terrorism

Ackerman, G., 'WMD Terrorism Research: Whereto from Here?' Discussion paper for Conference on Non-state Actors, Terrorism and Weapons of Mass Destruction, CIDCM, University of Maryland, College Park, 15 October 2004

Ackerman, G.A. and Moran, K.S., 'Bioterrorism and Threat Assessment'. Background paper for the Weapons of Mass Destruction Commission, 2006

Alexander, Y. and Hoenig, M. (eds), *Super Terrorism: Biological, Chemical, and Nuclear*. Ardsley, NY: Transnational, 2001

Bakker, E., 'CBRN-terrorisme: niet een kwestie van of, maar van wanneer'. In G. Wismans, (ed.), *Crisisbeheersing*. The Hague: Ministerie van Binnenlandse Zaken en Koninkrijksrelaties, Directie Crisisbeheersing, November 2005, pp. 85–91

Ballard, J.D. and Mullendore, K., 'Weapons of Mass Victimization, Radioactive Waste Shipments, and Environmental Laws: Policy Making and First Responders'. *American Behavioral Scientist*, 46, February 2003, pp. 766–781

Barber, B.R., *Jihad vs. McWorld*. New York: Ballantine Books, 1996

Barnaby, F., *The New Terrorism: A 21st Century Biological, Chemical and Nuclear Threat*. London: Oxford Research Group, 2001

Barnaby, F., *Waiting for Terror: How Realistic Is the Biological, Chemical and Nuclear Threat?* London: Oxford Research Group, October 2001

Barnaby, W., *De biologische oorlogsvoering*. Rijswijk, Netherlands: Uitgeverij Elmar BV, 2002

Barnaby, W., *The Plague Makers: The Secret World of Biological Warfare*. New York: Continuum, 2002

Barnaby, F., *Dirty Bombs and Primitive Nuclear Weapons*. London: Oxford Research Group, June 2005

Barnaby, F., *The Future of Terror*. London: Granta, 2007

Barrett, C.L., Eubank, S.G. and Smith, J.P., 'If Smallpox Strikes Portland'. *Scientific American*, 292(3), 2005, pp. 42–49

Behrens, C. and Holt, M., *Nuclear Power Plants: Vulnerability to Terrorist Attack*. CRS Report for Congress, RS21131, 4 February 2005

Benschop, A., *Kroniek van een aangekondigde politieke moord: jihad in Nederland*. Utrecht; Forum, 19 October 2005

Blondiau, H., *Tod auf Bestellung: Politischer Mord im 20. Jahrhundert* Munich: Ullstein, 2000

Brackett, D.W., *Holy Terror: Armageddon in Tokyo*. New York: Weatherhill, 1996

Cameron, G., *Nuclear Terrorism: A Threat Assessment for the 21st Century*. New York: St Martin's Press, 1999

Campbell, K.M., Einhorn, R. and Reiss, M. (eds), *The Nuclear Tipping Point: Why States Reconsider Their Nuclear Choices*. Washington, DC: Brookings Institution Press, 2004

Chalk, P., *Hitting America's Soft Underbelly: The Potential Threat of Deliberate Biological Attacks against the U.S. Agricultural and Food Industry*. MG-135-OSD. Santa Monica, CA: RAND, 2004

Chari, P.R. and Rajain, A. (eds), *Biological Weapons: Issues and Threats*. London: Marshall Cavendish Academic, 2004

Chittister, C.G. and Haimes, Y.Y., 'Risks of Terrorism to Information Technology and to Critical Interdependent Infrastructures'. *Journal of Homeland Security and Emergency Management*, 1(4), 2004. Available at: http://bepress.com/jhsem/vol1/iss4/402 (accessed 30 April 2009)

Chubin, S., *Iran's Nuclear Ambitions*. Stanford, CA: Carnegie Endowment for International Peace, August 2006

Chyba, C.F. and Greninger, A.L., 'Biotechnology and Bioterrorism: An Unprecedented World'. *Survival*, 46(2), Summer 2004, pp. 143–162

Colin, T.J. (ed.), 'Nuclear Proliferation and Terrorism: Can "Rogue" States and Terrorists Acquire Nuclear Weapons?' *CQ Researcher*, 14(13), 2 April 2004, pp. 297–320

Cordesman, A.H., *The Challenge of Biological Terrorism*. Washington, DC: Center for Strategic and International Studies, 2005

Corera, G., *Shopping for Bombs: Nuclear Proliferation, Global Insecurity and the Rise and Fall of the A.Q. Khan Network*. Oxford: Oxford University Press, 2006

Cornish, P., 'The CBRN System: Assessing the Threat of Terrorist Use of Chemical, Biological, Radiological and Nuclear Weapons in the UK'. *International Affairs*, 8 February 2007

Cornish, P., 'Chemical Biological, Radiological and Nuclear Terrorism: Tomorrow's Threat'. *Internaitonal Affairs*, 1 March 2007

Daly, S.A., Parachini, J.V. and Rosenau, W., *Aum Shinrikyo, Al Qaeda and the Kinshasa Reactor. Implications of Three Case Studies for Combating Nuclear Terrorism.* DB-458-AF. Santa Monica, CA: RAND, 2005

Dando, M., *Bioterrorism: What Is the Real Threat?* Science and Technology Report no. 3, March 2005

Dando, M., 'The Bioterrorist Cookbook'. *Bulletin of the Atomic Scientists*, 61(6), November–December 2005, pp. 34–39

Dilger, F. and Halstead, R., 'The Next Species of Trouble: Spent Nuclear Fuel Transportation in the United States, 2010–2048'. *American Behavioral Scientist*, 46, February 2003, pp. 796–811

Dishman, C., 'Understanding Perspectives on WMD and Why They are Important'. *Studies in Conflict and Terrorism*, 24(4), July 2001, pp. 303–313

Dunn, L.A., *Can Al Qaeda Be Deterred from Using Nuclear Weapons?* Occasional Paper 3, Center for the Study of Weapons of Mass Destruction, July 2005

Fängmark, I. and Norlander, L., *Indicators of State and Non-state Offensive Chemical and Biological Programmes.* Background Paper no. 30, for the Weapons of Mass Destruction Commission

Ferguson, N., 'The Next War of the World'. *Foreign Affairs*, 85(5), September–October 2006, pp. 61–74

Ferguson, C.D. and Potter, W.C., *Improvised Nuclear Devices and Nuclear Terrorism.* Background Paper no. 2 for the Weapons of Mass Destruction Commission, 2006

Ferguson, C.D., Potter, W.C., Sands, A., Spector, L.S. and Wehling, F.L., *The Four Faces of Nuclear Terrorism.* Monterey, CA: Monterey Institute, Center for Nonproliferation Studies, 2004

Flory, P.C.W., Opayne, K., Podvig, P., Arbatov, A., Lieber, K.A. and Press, D.G., 'Nuclear Exchange'. *Foreign Affairs*, 85(5), September–October 2006, pp. 149–157

Friedman, D., 'Preventing the Proliferation of Biological Weapons: Situation Overview and Recommendations for Israel'. *Strategic Assessment*, 7(3), December 2004, pp. 24–29

Friesen, S., *Machiavellian Opportunism: The Evolving CBRN Terrorism Environment.* CRTI-IRTC, CRTI-R-2003–004, September 2005

Frost, R.M., *Nuclear Terrorism after 9/11.* London: Routledge, 2005

GAO, *Anthrax Detection: Agencies Need to Validate Sampling Activities in Order to Increase Confidence in Negative Results.* GAO-05–21, Washington, DC, March 2005

Garwin, R.L., *Nuclear and Biological Megaterrorism.* 27th Session of the International Seminars on Planetary Emergencies, August 21, 2002. Available at: www.fas.org/rlg/020821-terrorism.htm. (accessed 30 April 2009)

Ghosh, T.K., Preslas, M.A., Viswanath, D.S., Loyalka, S.K. and Mitchell, R.H., *Science and Technology of Terrorism and Counterterrorism.* New York: Marcel Dekker, 2002

Gilmore, J.S. III, *The Fifth Annual Report to the President and the Congress of the Advisory Panel to Assess Domestic Response Capabilities for Terrorism Involving Weapons of Mass Destruction. V. Forging America's New Normalcy.* 13 December 2003

Glaser, A. and von Hippel, F.N., 'Global Cleanout: Reducing the Threat of HEU-Fueled Nuclear Terrorism'. *Arms Control Today*, 36(1), January–February 2006, pp. 18–23

Gorka, S. and Sullivan, R., 'Biological Toxins: A Bioweapon Threat in the 21st Century'. *Security Dialogue*, 33, June 2002, pp. 141–156

Guillemin, J., *Biological Weapons: From the Invention of State-Sponsored Programs to Contemporary Bioterrorism.* New York: Colombia University Press, 2004

Gurr, N. and Cole, B. (eds), *The New Face of Terrorism: Threats from Weapons of Mass Destruction.* London: I.B. Tauris, 2008

Hartnett, S.J. and Stengrim, L.A., 'The Whole Operation of Deception: Reconstructing President Bush's Rhetoric of Weapons of Mass Destruction'. *Cultural Studies/Critical Methodologies*, 4, May 2004, pp. 152–197

Heiduk, F., 'Maritimer Terrorismus in Südostasien und die Regional Maritime Security Initiative'. *SWP Diskussionspapier*, July 2004

Heinrich, J., 'Bioterrorism: Review of Public Health Preparedness Programs'. In V.B. Mellehovitch, (ed.), *Bioterrorism and Public Health.* Hauppauge, NY: Nova Science Publishers, 2004

Henry L. Stimson Center, *Ataxia: The Chemical and Biological Terrorism Threat and the US Response.* Washington, DC, 2005

Herron, K.G. and Jenkins-Smith, H.C., *Critical Masses and Critical Choices: Evolving Public Opinion on Nuclear Weapons, Terrorism, and Security.* Pittsburgh University of Pittsburgh Press, 2000

Hoffman, B., 'CBRN Terrorism post-9/11'. In R.D. Howard and J. Forest, (eds), *Terrorism and Weapons of Mass Destruction.* Maidenhead, UK: McGraw-Hill, 2007

Houghton, B.K., *Gearing Up and Getting There: Improving Local Response to Chemical Terrorism.* Santa Monica, CA: RAND, 2004

Howard, R.D. and Forest, J.J.F. (eds) *Terrorism and Weapons of Mass Destruction.* Maidenhead, UK: McGraw-Hill, 2007

Intriligator, M. and Toukan, A., 'Terrorists' Use of WMD'. In P. Katona, M.D. Intriligator and J.P. Sullivan (eds), *Countering Terrorism and WMD: Creating a Global Anti-terrorism Network*. London: Routledge, 2006

Jones, D., 'Structures of Bio-terrorism Preparedness in the UK and the US: Responses to 9/11 and the Anthrax Attacks'. *British Journal of Politics and International Relations*, 7(3), August 2005, pp. 340–352

Kam, E., *From Terror to Nuclear Bombs: The Significance of the Iranian Threat*. Tel Aviv: JCSS, Ministry of Defense Publishing House, 2004

Kaplan, J. and Toukan, A., 'Terrorists' Use of Weapons of Mass Destruction'. In: P. Katona, M.D. Intriligator and J.P. Sullivan (eds), *Countering Terrorism and WMD: Creating a Global Counter-terrorism Network*. London: Routledge, 2006

Karam, P., 'Radiological terrorism'. *Human and Ecological Risk Assessment*, 11(3), June 2005, pp. 501–523

Karpin, M., *The Bomb in the Basement: How Israel Went Nuclear and What That Means for the World*. New York: Simon & Schuster, 2006

Katona, P., Intriligator, M.D. and Sullivan, J.P. (eds), *Countering Terrorism and WMD: Creating a Global Anti-terrorism Network*. London: Routledge, 2006

Kelam, B., 'Criminalization and Control of WMD Proliferation: The Security Council Acts'. *Non-Proliferation Review*, 11(2), Summer 2004, pp. 142–161

Khan, S.A., 'Nuclear South Asia: Resolving or Protracting the Protracted Conflict'. *International Relations*, 15, June 2001, pp. 61–77

Koch, E.R., *Atomwaffen für al-Qa'ida: Dr. No und das Netzwerk des Terrors*. Berlin: Aufbau Verlag, 2005

Kosal, M., 'Terrorism Targeting Industrial Chemical Facilities: Strategic Motivations and the Implications for U.S. Security'. *Studies in Conflict and Terrorism*, 29(7), October–November 2006, pp. 719–751

Kuhr, S. and Hauer, J.M., 'The Threat of Biological Terrorism in the New Millennium'. *American Behavioral Scientist*, 44, February 2001, pp. 1032–1041

Kupatadze, A., 'Radiological Smuggling and Uncontrolled Territories: The Case of Georgia'. *Global Crime*, 8(1), February 2007, pp. 40–57

Kurz, A., 'Non-conventional Terrorism: Availability and Motivation'. *Strategic Assessment*, 7(4), March 2005, pp. 29–35

Langbein, K., Skalnik, C. and Smolek, I., *Bioterror*. Stuttgart: DVA, 2002

Langewiesche, W., 'How to Get a Nuclear Bomb'. *The Atlantic*, 298(5), December 2006, pp. 80–99

Larson, B.M.D., Nerlich, B. and Wallis, P., 'Metaphors and Biorisks: The War on Infectious Diseases and Invasive Species'. *Science Communication*, 26, March 2005, pp. 243–268

Lederberg, J., *Biological Weapons: Limiting the Threat*. Cambridge, MA: MIT Press, 1999

Lehrman, T.D., 'Rethinking Interdiction. The Future of the Proliferation Security Initiative'. *Nonproliferation Review*, Summer 2004, pp. 1–45

Leitenberg, M., *The Problem of Biological Weapons*. Stockholm: Elanders Gotab, the Swedish National Defence College, 2004

Leitenberg, M., 'Assessing the Biological Weapons and Bioterrorism Threat'. Paper prepared for international conference 'Meeting the Challenges of Bioterrorism: Assessing the Threat and Designing Biodefense Strategies', Frutigen, Switzerland, 22–23 April 2005

Lennon, A.T.J. (eds), *Contemporary Nuclear Debates: Missile Defense, Arms Control, and the Arms Races in the Twentieth Century*. Cambridge, MA: MIT Press, 2002

Levi, M.A. and O'Hanlon, E., *The Future of Arms Control*. Washington, DC: Brookings Institution Press, 2005

Lindstrom, G., *Protecting the European Homeland: The CBR Dimension*. Chaillot Paper 69. Paris: European Union Institute for Security Studies, 2004

Loeppky, R., 'Biomania and the US Foreign Policy'. *Millennium*, 34(1), 2005, pp. 85–113

McMillan, J., 'Apocalyptic Terrorism: The Case for Preventive Action'. *Strategic Forum* no. 212, November 2005. Washington, DC: National Defense University

McNamara, R.S., 'Apocalypse Soon'. *Foreign Policy*, May–June 2005, pp. 29–35

Maerli, M.B., Schaper, A. and Barnaby, F., 'The Characteristics of Nuclear Terrorist Weapons'. *American Behavioral Scientist*, 46, February 2003, pp. 727–744

Mangold, T. and Goldberg, J., *Plague Wars: A True Story of Biological Warfare*. New York: St Martin's Press, 2000

Medalia, J., *Nuclear Terrorism: A Brief Review of Threats and Responses*. RL32595 Washington, DC: CRS Report for Congress, 22 September 2004

Meyer, B., 'Demokratische Terrorismusbekämpfung im Spannungsfeld von Freiheit und Sicherheit'. In J. von Knop and H. Frank (eds), *Netz- und Computersicherheit: Sind wir auf einen Angriff auf unsere Informationssysteme und Informations-Infrastrukturen vorbereitet?* Bielefeld, Germany: Bertelsmann, 2004

Miasnikov, E., *Threat of Terrorism using Unmanned Aerial Vehicles: Technical Aspects*. Moscow: Center for Arms Control, Energy and Environmental Studies, Moscow Institute for Physics and Technology, 2005

Michael, M., 'When Everything Changes, Everything Does Change: Nuclear Power after September 11th'. *Bulletin of Science, Technology and Society*, 21, December 2001, pp. 501–506

Moltz, J.C., Orlov, V.A. and Stulberg, A.N. (eds), *Preventing Nuclear Meltdown: Managing Decentralization of Russia's Nuclear Complex*. Aldershot, UK: Ashgate, 2004

Njuguna, J.T., 'Evaluating the Threat of Biological Weapons in Eastern Africa'. *Africa Security Review*, 14(1), 2005, pp. 13–21

Norton, A.R. and Greenberg, M.H. (eds), *Studies in Nuclear Terrorism*. Boston: G.K. Hall 1979

NRC, *Terrorism and the Chemical Infrastructure: Protecting People and Reducing Vulnerabilities. Committee on Assessing Vulnerabilities Related to the Nation's Chemical Infrastructure*. Washington, DC: National Academies Press, 2006

O'Day, A. (ed.), *Weapons of Mass Destruction and Terrorism*. Aldershot, UK: Ashgate, 2004

Pita, R., 'Assessing Al-Qaeida's Chemical Threat'. *International Journal of Intelligence and Counterintelligence*, 20(3), Fall 2007, pp. 480–511

Pogorely, M., 'Prospects for Russian–US Cooperation in Preventing WMD Proliferation'. *Journal of Slavic Military Studies*, 17, 2004, pp. 79–98

Preslar, D., 'Biological Weapons Control and Disease Surveillance'. *African Security Review*, 14(1), 2005, pp. 123–128

Quillen, C., 'Three Explanations for Al-Qaeida's Lack of a CBRN Attack'. *Terrorism Monitor*, 5(3), 15 February 2007. Available at: www.jamestown.org/programs/gta/single/?tx_ttnews[tt_news]=1015&tx_ttnews[backPid]=182&no_cache=1 (accessed 30 April 2009)

Rapoport, D.C., 'Terrorism and Weapons of the Apocalypse'. *National Security Studies Quarterly*, 5(3), 1999, pp. 52–55

Roberts, B. (ed.), *Terrorism with Chemical and Biological Weapons: Calibrating Risks and Response*. Alexandria, VA: Chemical and Biological Arms Control Institute, 1997

Rogers, K. and Kingslay, M.G. (eds), *Calculated Risks: Highly Radioactive Waste and Homeland Security*. Aldershot, UK: Ashgate, 2007

Rollins, J. and Wilson, C., *Terrorist Capabilities for Cyberattack: Overview and Policy Issues*. CRS Report for Congress, RL33123, 20 October 2005

Rosen, S.P., 'After Proliferation'. *Foreign Affairs*, 85(5), September–October 2006, pp. 9–14

Sarasin, P., *Anthrax: Bioterror as Fact and Fantasy*. Cambridge, MA: Harvard University Press, 2006

Scheuer, M., 'New York Subway Plot and Al-Qaeida's WMD Strategy'. *Terrorism Focus*, 3(24), 20 June 2006

Schierow, L.J., *Chemical Facility Security*. CRS Report for Congress, RL31530, 29 July 2005

Sedlacek, D., *Maritimer Terror und Piraterie auf hoher See*. Bremerhaven: Wirtschaftsverlag, 2006

Sellström, A. and Nordquist, A., *Comparison of State vs. Non-state Actors in the Development of Biological Weapons*. Background paper no. 16 for the Weapons of Mass Destruction Commission, 2006

Shaffer, M.B., 'The Missile Threat to Civil Aviation'. *Terrorism and Political Violence*, 10(3), 1998, pp. 70–82

Shanty, F., 'Threats Involving Chemical and Biological Agents'. In *Encyclopedia of World Terrorism, 1996–2002*, vol. 4. Armonk, NY: M.E. Sharpe, February 2003

Shea, S.A. and Gottron, F., *Small-Scale Terrorist Attacks using Chemical and Biological Agents: An Assessment Framework and Preliminary Comparisons*. CRS Report for Congress, 20 May 2004

Simon, J.D., *Terrorists and the Potential Use of Biological Weapons: A Discussion of Possibilities*. R–3771–AFMIC. Santa Monica, CA: RAND December 1989

Simon, J.D., 'Nuclear, Biological, and Chemical Terrorism: Understanding the Threat and Designing Responses'. *International Journal of Emergency Mental Health*, Spring 1999, pp. 81–89

Simon, J.D., 'Lone Operators and Weapons of Mass Destruction'. In B., Roberts (ed.), *Hype or Reality: The 'New Terrorism' and Mass Casualty Attacks*. Alexandria, VA: Chemical and Biological Arms Control Institute, 2000

Simon, J.D., 'The Alphabet Bomber'. In J.B. Tucker (ed.), *Toxic Terror: Assessing Terrorist Use of Chemical and Biological Weapons*. Cambridge, MA: MIT Press, 2000

Sinai, J., 'Forecasting Terrorist Groups' Warfare: "Conventional" to CBRN'. In H. Chen, F. Wang, C.C. Yang, D. Zeng, M. Chau and K. Chang (eds), *Intelligence and Security Informatics*. Berlin: Springer, May 2005

Smolinski, M.S., Hamburg, M.A. and Lederberg, J. (eds), *Microbial Threats to Health-Emergence: Detection and Response: Committee on Emerging Microbial Threats to Health in the 21st Century*. Washington, DC: National Academies Press, 2003

Snowden, L.L., 'How Likely Are Terrorists to Use a Nuclear Strategy?' *American Behavioral Scientist*, 46, February 2003, pp. 699–713

Sprinzak, E., 'The Great Superterrorism Scare'. *Foreign Policy*, Fall 1998, pp. 110–124

Spyer, J., 'The Al Qaeida Network and Weapons of Mass Destruction'. *Middle East Review of International Affairs*, 8(3), September 2004, pp. 29–45

Steinhäusler, F., 'What It Takes to Become a Nuclear Terrorist'. *American Behavioral Scientist*, 46, February 2003, pp. 782–795

Steinhäusler, F. and Zaitseva, L., 'Illicit Trafficking in Nuclear and Other Radioactive Materials, with a Focus on Nuclear and Radiological Terrorism'. Paper quiery at the International Conference on Trafficking: Networks and Logistics of Transnational Crime and International Terrorism Courmayeur, Mont Blanc, Italy, ISPAC, 6–8 December, 2002

Steinhäusler, F., Braun, C., Bunn, G. and Zaitseva, L., 'Terrorist Threats to Civilian Nuclear Installations: A Comparative Assessment between Europe and the US'. Paper quiery at 43rd INMM Annual Meeting, Orlando, FL, July 2002

Steinhäusler, F., Bremer-Maerli, M. and Zaitseva, L., 'Assessment of the Threat from Diverted Radioactive Material and Orphan Sources: An International Comparison'. IAEA Paper quiery at the International Conference on Security of Material: Measures to Prevent, Intercept and Respond to Illicit Uses of Nuclear Material and Radioactive Sources, Stockholm, 7–11 May 2001

Stern, J., *The Ultimate Terrorists*. Cambridge, MA: Harvard University Press, 1999

Stevens, N. and Gottron, F., 'Anthrax in the Mail'. In A.P. Rogers, (ed.), *Bioterrorism Reader*. Hauppauge, NY: Nova Science Publishers, 2003

Steyn, B., 'Understanding the Implications of UN Security Council Resolution 1540'. *African Security Review*, 14(1), 2005, pp. 85–91

Strassberg, B.A., 'A Pandemic of Terror and Terror of a Pandemic: American Cultural Responses to HIV/AIDS and Bioterrorism'. *Zygon*, 39(2), June 2004, pp. 435–463

Strongin, R.J. and Redhead, C.S., 'Bioterrorism: Public Health Preparedness'. In A.P. Rogers, *Bioterrorism Reader*. Hauppauge, NY: Nova Science Publishers, 2003

Tanter, R., *Rogue Regimes: Terrorism and Proliferation*. New York: St Martin's Griffin, 1999

Taylor, E.R., *Lethal Mists: An Introduction to the Natural and Military Sciences of Chemical, Biological Warfare and Terrorism*. Hauppauge, NY: Nova Science Publishers, 2001

Thakur, R., 'Envisioning Nuclear Futures'. *Security Dialogue*, 31, March 2000, pp. 25–40

Tigner, B. and Henderson, J. (rapporteurs), *Brainstorming Meeting Report of the New Defence Agenda's Bioterrorism Reporting Group*. Brussels: New Defence Agenda, 2004

Tophoven, R. and Hirschmann, K., 'NBC-Terrorismus: Nichts ist unmöglich?' *Terrorismus*, no. 6, December 2004

Trofimov, Y., *The Siege of Mecca*. New York: Doubleday, 2007

Tucker, D., 'What Is New about the New Terrorism and How Dangerous Is It?' *Terrorism and Political Violence*, 13(3), Fall 2001, pp. 1–14

Tucker, J.B., *War of Nerves: Chemical Warfare from World War I to Al-Qaeda*. New York: Pantheon Books, 2006

US Senate, Committee on Health, Education, Labor and Pensions, Subcommittee on Bioterrorism and Public Health Preparedness. *Meeting the Bioterrorism Challenge*, 11 May 2005. (Testimonies of John Deutsch, Harvey V. Fineberg, Shelley Hearne, Guenael Rodier, Craig Venter)

Utgoff, V.A. (ed.), *The Coming Crisis: Nuclear Proliferation, US Interests and World Order*. Cambridge, MA: MIT Press, 2000

Venter, A.J., *Allah's Bomb: The Islamic Quest for Nuclear Weapons*. Guilford, CT: Lyons, 2007

Vignard, K. (eds), 'Science, Technology and the CWB Regimes'. *Disarmament Forum*, no. 1, pp. 1–2. Geneva: UNIDIR

Vignard, K. (ed.), 'CTBT: Passing the Test'. *Disarmament Forum*, no. 2, pp. 1–2. Geneva: UNIDIR, 2006

Vignard, K. (ed.), 'Toward a Stronger BTWC'. *Disarmament Forum*, no. 3, pp. 1–2. Geneva: UNIDIR, 2006

Walker, C., 'Biological Attack, Terrorism and the Law'. *Terrorism and Political Violence*, 17(1–2), Winter 2005, pp. 175–200

Walker, W., 'Weapons of Mass Destruction and International Order'. Adelphi Paper 370. London: International Institute for Strategic Studies

Warden, H.N. IV, 'Overcoming Challenges to the Proliferation Security Initiative'. Naval Postgraduate School, Monterey, CA, September 2004

Weapons of Mass Destruction Commission. *Weapons of Terror: Freeing the World of Nuclear, Biological and Chemical Arms*, 2006. Available at: www.wmdcommission.org (accessed 30 April 2009)

Wenger, A. and Wollenmann, R. (eds), *Bioterrorism: Confronting a Complex Threat*. Boulder, CD: Lynne Rienner, 2007

Wesley, R., 'Al-Qaeida's WMD Strategy prior to the U.S. Intervention in Afghanistan'. *Terrorism Monitor*, 3(19), 7 October 2005

Wesley, R., 'Al-Qaeida's WMD Strategy after the U.S. Intervention in Afghanistan'. *Terrorism Monitor*, 3(20), 21 October 2005

Wiener, S.W. and Hoffman, R.S., 'Nerve Agents: A Comprehensive Review'. *Journal of Intensive Care Medicine*, 19, January 2004, pp. 22–37

Williams, S.J., 'Bioattack or Panic Attack? Critical Reflections on the Ill-Logic of Bioterrorism and Biowarfare in Late/Postmodernity'. *Social Theory and Health*, 2(1), February 2004, pp. 67–93

Winfield, G., 'Nuclear Spring'. *Military Technology*, no. 5, 2004, pp. 55–65

WMDC, *Weapons of Terror: Freeing the World of Nuclear, Biological and Chemical Arms*. Stockholm: Weapons of Mass Destruction Commission, 2006

Woolf, A.F. (ed.), *Ninn-Lugar Cooperative Threat Reduction Programs*. Hauppauge, NY: Nova Science Publishers, 2004

Yarsike Ball, D. and Gerber, T.P., 'Russian Scientists and Rogue States: Does Western Assistance Reduce the Proliferation Threat?' *International Security*, 29(4), Spring 2005, pp. 50–77

Zaitseva, L. and Hand, K., 'Nuclear Smuggling Chains: Suppliers, Intermediaries, and End-Users'. *American Behavioral Scientist*, 46, February 2003, pp. 822–844

Zaitseva, L. and Steinhäusler, F., 'Illicit Trafficking of Weapons-Usable Nuclear Material: Facts and Uncertainties'. *Physics and Society Newsletter*, 33(1), (2004), pp. 5–8

Zaitseva, L. and Steinhäusler, F., 'Illicit Trafficking Trends in Russia and Eastern Europe'. In *Illicit Trafficking and Criminal Use of CBRN Materials and Weapons: An Analysis of the New Members of the European Union and Their Neighbouring Countries*. UNICRI/EUROPOL/SECI Report, September 2005

Zaric, G.S., Brevata, D.M., Cleophas, J.-E. *et al.*, 'Modelling the Logistics of Respnse to Anthrax Bioterrorism'. *Medical Decision Making*, 58, June 2008, pp. 378–401

U. Varia and related studies

Adams, J., 'The Strange Demise of East German State Security'. *International Journal of Intelligence and Counterintelligence*, 18(1), Spring 2005, pp. 1–22

Adams, N., *Terrorism and Oil*. Tulsa, OK: PennWell, 2003

Aldrich, R.J. and Hopkins, M.F., *Intelligence, Defence, and Diplomacy: British Policy in the Post-War World*. London: Portland, 1994

Ali, T.M. and Matthews, R.O. (eds), *Durable Peace: Challenges for Peacebuilding in Africa*. Toronto: University of Toronto Press, 2004

Allott, P., *The Health of Nations: Society and Law beyond the State*. Cambridge: Cambridge University Press, 2002

Al-Rasheed, M., *Contesting the Saudi State: Islamic Voices from a New Generation*. Cambridge: Cambridge University Press, 2007

Amstutz, M.R., *The Healing of Nations: The Promise and Limits of Political Forgiveness*. Lanham, MD: Rowman & Littlefield, 2004

Anderson, F. and Cayton, A., *The Dominion of War: Empire and Conflict in America, 1500–2000*. London: Atlantic, 2005

Andrews, C. and Wassili, M., *Das Schwarzbuch des KGB*, Bd. 1: *Moskaus Kampf gegen den Westen*, Berlin 1999

Angenendt, S., Cooper, B., Süssmuth, R. *et al.*, 'Migration und Sicherheit' (thematic issue) *Internationale Politik*, 61(3), March 2006, pp. 6–49

Ansari, H., *The Infidel Within: Muslims in Britain since 1800*. London: Hurst, 2004

Anu-Nimer, M., Khoury, A.I. and Welty, E., *Unity in Diversity: Interfaith Dialogue in the Middle East*. United States Institute of Peace Press, 2007

Apostolov, M., *The Christian–Muslim Frontier: A Zone of Contact, Conflict or Co-operation*. London: Routledge, 2003

Armstrong, J.S., *Principles of Forecasting: A Handbook for Researchers and Practicioners*. New York: Kluwer, 2001

Arndt, O., *Demonen: Zur Mythologie der Inneren Sicherheit*. Hamburg: Edition Nautilus, 2005

Artz, D., 'Jihad for Hearts and Minds: Proselytizing in the Qur'an and the First Three Centuries of Islam'. In J. Witte Jr and R.C. Martin (eds), *Sharing the Book: Religious Perspectives on the Rights and Wrongs of Proselytism*. New York: Orbis Books, 1999

Asal, V., and Rethemeyer, R.K., 'Researching Terrorist Networks'. *Journal of Security Education*, 1(4), 20 October 2006, pp. 65–74

Aslan, R., *No God but God: The Origins, Evolution and Future of Islam*. London: Random House, 2005

Aysegul, A., 'The Tragic Vision of Politics: Ethics, Interests and Orders'. *Journal of Peace Research*, vol. 42, May 2005, p. 361

Baker, J., Lachman, B., Frellinger, D., O'Connell, K., Hou, A., Tseng, M., Orietsky, D. and Yost, C., *Mapping the Risks: Assessing the Homeland Implications of Publicly Available Geospatial Information*. MG-142-NGA. Santa Monica, CA: RAND, 2004

Bakier, H.H., 'A Profile of Al-Qaeda's New Leader in Iraq: Abu Ayyub Al-Masri'. *Terrorism Focus*, 3(24), 20 June 2006. Available at: www.jamestown.org/programs/gta/single/?tx_ttnews[tt_news]=812&tx_ttnews [backPid]=239&no_cache=1 (accessed 20 April 2009)

Bamford, J., *A Pretext for War: 9/11, Iraq and the Abuse of America's Intelligence Agencies*. New York: Doubleday, 2004

Banks, A.S., Muller, T.C. and Overstreet, W.R. (eds), *Political Handbook of the World 2007*. Washington, DC: CQ Press, 2007

Barakat, S., *Reconstructing War-Torn Societies: Afghanistan*. New York: Palgrave Macmillan, 2004

Barany, Z. and Moser, R.G. (eds), *Ethnic Politics after Communism*. Ithaca, NY: Cornell University Press, 2005

Barenblatt, D., *The Secret Genocide of Axis Japan's Germ Warfare Operation*. London: HarperCollins, 2004

Barger, D., *Toward a Revolution in Intelligence Affairs*. Santa Monica, CA: RAND, 2005

Baudrillard, J., *The Spirit of Terrorism and Other Essays*. London: Verso, 2003

Bawer, B., *While Europe Slept: How Radical Islam Is Destroying the West from Within*. New York: Doubleday, 2006

Belfield, R., *Terminate with Extreme Prejudice: An Expose of the Assassination Game, Its Killers and Their Paymasters*. London: Constable & Robinson, 2005

Belkin, A., *United We Stand? Divide-and-Conquer Politics and the Logic of International Hostility*. New York: University of New York Press, 2005

Belkin, A.R., 'US–Russian Relations and the Global Counter-terrorist Campaign'. *Journal of Slavic Military Studies*, 17, 2004, pp. 13–28

Bellamy, A.J. and Williams, P. (eds), *Peace Operations and Global Order*. London: Routledge, 2005

Bennett, S.E., *American's Attitudes about Foreign Affairs: How Much Change since 9/11 and the Iraq War*. Honolulu: International Studies Association (ISA), March 2005

Bercovitch, J., *Regional Guide to International Conflict and Management from 1945 to 2003*. Washington, DC: CQ Press, 2004

Biddle, S., 'Seeing Baghdad, Thinking Saigon'. *Foreign Affairs*, 85(2), March–April 2006, pp. 2–145

Black, I. and Morris, B., *Mossad, Shin Bet, Aman: Die Geschichte der israelischen Geheimdienste*. Heidelberg: Palmyra, 1994

Blomberg, S.B., Hess, G.D. and Orphanides, A., 'The Macroeconomic Consequences of Terrorism'. *Journal of Monetary Economics*, 51(5), 2004, 1007–1032

Bloom, C., *Violent London: 2000 Years of Riots, Rebels and Revolts*. London: Sidgwick & Jackson, 2004

Boone, J.V., *A Brief History of Cryptology*. New York: Presidio, 2005

Boot, M., *War Made New: Technology, Warfare, and the Course of History, 1500 to Today*. New York: Gotham Books, 2006

Booth, K. (ed.), *Critical Security Studies and World Politics*. Boulder, CO: Lynne Rienner, 2004

Booth, K. and Dunne, T. (eds), *Worlds in Collision: Terror and the Future of Global Order*. Basingstoke, UK: Palgrave, 2002

Born, H., Johnson, L.K. and Leigh, I., *Who's Watching the Spies? Establishing Intelligence Service Accountability*. Dulles, VA: Potomac Books, 2005

Borradori, G., *Philosophy in a Time of Terror: Dialogues with Jürgen Habermas and Jacques Derrida*. Chicago: University of Chicago Press, 2003

Boulden, J. and Weiss, T.G. (eds), *Terrorism and the UN: Before and after September 11*. Bloomington: Indiana University Press, 2004

Boyle, F.A., *Destroying World Order: U.S. Imperialism in The Middle East before and after September 11*. Atlanta, GA: Clarity Press, 2004

Brown, C. and Ainley, K., *Understanding International Relations*. New York: Palgrave Macmillan, 2005

Brown, J.F., *Surge to Freedom: The End of Communist Rule in Eastern Europe*. Durham, NC: Duke University Press, 1991

Buddenberg, D. and Burd, W.A. (eds), *Afghanistan's Drug Industry: Structure, Functioning, Dynamics, and Implications for Counternarcotics Policy*. United Nations Office on Crime and Drugs and World Bank, 2006

Bugajski, J., *Cold Peace: Russia's New Imperialism*. Praeger, Westport, CT: 2004

Bulloch, J. and Morris, H., *Saddam's War: The Origins of the Kuwait Conflict and the International Response*. London: Faber & Faber, 1991

Buruma, I. and Margalit, A., *Occidentalism: The West in the Eyes of Its Enemies*. New York: Penguin Books, 2004

Byman, D., 'The Decision to Begin Talks with Terrorists: Lessons for Policymakers'. *Studies in Conflict and Terrorism*, 29(5), July–August 2006 pp. 403–414

Callinicos, A., *The New Mandarins of American Power: The Bush Administration's Plans for the World*. Cambridge: Polity Press 2003

Campbell, C., *Fenian Fire: The British Government Plot to Assassinate Queen Victoria*. London: HarperCollins, 2002

Carment, D. and Schnabel, A., *Conflict Prevention: Path to Peace or Grand Illusion?* Tokyo: United Nations University Press, 2003

Cesari, J., *When Islam and Democracy Meet: Muslims in Europe and the United States*. New York: Palgrave Macmillan, 2006

Chasek, P.S., 'Power Politics, Diplomacy and Role Playing: Stimulating the UN Security Council's Response to Terrorism'. *International Studies Perspectives*, 6(1), February 2005, pp. 1–19

Chenoy, A.M., 'A Plea for Engendering Human Security'. *International Studies*, 42, April 2005, pp. 167–179

Cherkashin, V. with Feifer, G., *Spy Handler: Memoirs of a KGB Officer: The True Story of the Man Who Recruited Robert Hansen and Aldrich James*. New York: Basic Books, 2005

Chernykh, I., 'Conditions for Securitization of International Terrorism in Central Asia'. *Connections*, Spring 2005, pp. 131–142

Chesterman, S., *You, the People: The United Nations, Transitional Administration and State-Building*. Oxford: Oxford University Press, 2004

Chesterman, S., Ignatieff, M. and Thakur, R. (eds), *Making States Work: State Failure and the Crisis of Governance*. Tokyo United Nations University Press, 2005

Chomsky, N., *Deterring Democracy*. London: Vintage, 1992

Chomsky, N., *Hegemony or Survival: America's Quest for Global Dominance*. New York: Metropolitan Books, 2003

Chua, A., *World on Fire: How Exporting Free Market Democracy Breeds Ethnic Hatred and Global Instability*. New York: Doubleday, 2002

Cofman Wittes, T. (ed.), *How Israelis and Palestinians Negotiate: A Cross-cultural Analysis of the Oslo Peace Process*. Washington, DC: US Institute of Peacee Press, 2005

Cohen-Tanugi, L., *An Alliance at Risk: The United States and Europe since September 11*. Baltimore: Johns Hopkins University Press, 2003

Colombani, J.-M., *Tous Américains? Le monde après le 11 Septembre 2001*. Paris: Fayard, 2002

Copeland, T., *Fool Me Twice: Intelligence Failure and Mass Casualty Terrorism*. Leiden: Martinus Nijhoff, 2007

Cortright, D., *Gandhi and Beyond: Nonviolence for an Age of Terrorism*. Boulder, CO: Paradigm, 2006

Cox, M. and Stokes, D. (eds), *US Foreign Policy*. Oxford: Oxford University Press, 2008

Crawford, J.R., *The Creation of States in Internatonal Law*. Oxford: Oxford University Press, 2007

Crile, G., *Charlie Wilson's War: The Extraordinary Story of the Largest Covert Operation in History*. New York: Atlantic Monthly Press, 2003

Crockatt, R., *America Embattled: September 11, Anti-Americanism, and the Global Order*. London: Routledge, 2003

Crocker, C.A., Hampson, F.O. and Aall, P. (eds), *Grasping the Nettle: Analyzing Cases of Intractable Conflict*. Washington, DC: United States Institute of Peace, 2005

Cross, S., 'Russia's Relationship with the United States/NATO in the US-Led Global War on Terrorism'. *Journal of Slavic Military Studies*, 19(2), June 2006, pp. 175–192

Cullather, N., *Secret History: The CIA's Classified Account of Its Operations in Guatemala, 1952–1954*. Stanford, CA: Stanford University Press, 2006

Curtis, M., 'Britain's Real Foreign Policy and the Failure of British Academia'. *International Relations*, 18, September 2004, pp. 275–287

Darby, J., *The Effects of Violence on Peace Processes*. Washington, DC: United States Institute of Peace Press, 2001

Davies, P.H.J., *MI6 and the Machinery of Spying*. London: Frank Cass, 2004

De Groot, G.J., *The Bomb: A Life*. Cambridge, MA: Harvard University Press, 2005

De Rivera, J., 'Assessing the Basis for a Culture of Peace in Contemporary Societies'. *Journal of Peace Research*, 41, September 2004, pp. 531–548

Dennis, A.J., *The Rise of the Islamic Empire and the Threat to the West*. Lima, OH, Wyndham Hall Press, 2001

Der Derian, J., *Antidiplomacy: Spies, Terror, Speed, and War*. Cambridge, MA: Blackwell, 1992

Diamond, J., *Guns, Germs and Steel: The Fates of Human Societies*. London: W.W. Norton, 2003

Diamond, J., *Collapse: How Societies Choose to Fail or Survive*. London: Allan Lane, 2005

Diamond, L. and Morlino, L. (eds), *Assessing the Quality of Democracy*. Balitmore: Johns Hopkins University Press, 2005

Dillon, M., *The Enemy Within*. New York: Doubleday, 1994

Dolnik, A., *Understanding Terrorist Innovation*. London: Routledge, 2007

Donnelly, J., *International Human Rights*. Boulder, CO: Westview Press, 2007

Doran, M.S., 'The Saudi Paradox'. *Foreign Affairs*, January–February, 84(1), 2004. Available at: www.all academic.com//meta/p_mla_apa_research_citation/0/7/2/8/5/pages72852/p72852-1.php (accessed 30 April 2009)

Dorff, R.H., 'Failed States after 9/11: What Did We Know and What Have We Learned?' *International Studies Perspectives*, 6(1), February 2005, pp. 20–34

Dorronsoro, G., *Afghanistan: Revolution Unending, 1979–2003*. New York: C. Hurst, 2005

Drakos, K. and Kutan, A.M., 'Regional Effects of Terrorism on Tourism: Evidence from Three Mediterranean Countries'. *Journal of Conflict Resolution*, 47, 2003, pp. 621–641

Dryzek, J.S., 'Transnational Democracy in an Insecure World'. *International Political Science Review/Revue internationale de science politique*, 27, April 2006, pp. 101–119

Dunmire, P.L., 'Preempting the Future: Rhetoric and Ideology of the Future in Political Discourse'. *Discourse Society*, 16, July 2005, pp. 481–513

Eisinger, P., 'The American City in the Age of Terror: A Preliminary Assessment of the Effects of September 11'. *Urban Affairs Review*. 40, September 2004, pp. 115–130

Elsayed, N.M., Atkins, J.L. and Gorbunov, N.V., *Explosion and Blast-Related Injuries: Effects of Explosion and Blast from Military Operations and Acts of Terrorism*. Amsterdam: Elsevier, 2008

Enders, W. and Sandler, T., *The Political Economy of Terrorism*. Cambridge: Cambridge University Press, 2006

Eppler, E., *Vom Gewaltmonopol zum Gewaltmarkt?* Frankfurt am Main: Suhrkamp, 2002

Eriksson, J., 'Observers or Advocates: On the Political Role of Security Analysts'. *Cooperation and Conflict*, 34, September 1999, pp. 311–330

Erlande, M.B., *Terrorist Financing*. Hauppauge, NY: Nova Science Publishers, 2006

Esposito, J.L. (editor in Chief), *The Oxford Dictionary of Islam*. Oxford: Oxford University Press, 2003

Esposito, J.L. and Mogahed, D., *Who Speaks for Islam? What a Billion Muslims Really Think*. London: Gallup Press, 2007

European Centre for Conflict Prevention, International Fellowship of Reconciliation *et al.*, *People Building Peace: 35 Inspiring Stories from around the World*. Utrecht: European Centre for Conflict Prevention, 1999

Falk, R., *The Declining World Order*. London: Routledge, 2004

Fallows, J., 'Bush's Lost Year'. *The Atlantic*, October 2004, pp. 68–84

Farber, D.R., *What They Think of Us: International Perceptions of the United States since 9/11*. Princeton, NJ: Princeton University Press, 2007

Feldman, R., 'Fund Transfers – African Terrorists Blend Old and New: Hawala and Satellite Telecommunications'. *Small Wars and Insurgencies*, 17(3), 2006, pp. 356–366

Firestone, R., *Jihad: The Origin of Holy War in Islam*. Oxford: Oxford University Press, 1999

Fischbach, M., *The Peace Process and Palestinian Refugee Claims*. Washington, DC: United States Institute of Peace Press, 2006

Fischer, M. and Schmelze, B. (eds), Transforming War Economies: Dilemmas and Strategies'. *Berghof Handbook Dialogue*, Series 3, 2005. Available at: www.berghof-handbook.net (accessed 30 April 2009)

Fisk, R., *The Great War for Civilisation: The Conquest of the Middle East*. New York: Vintage Books, 2007

Fletcher, N.B. Jr, 'The Rule of Law, Human Rights and Proportionality as Components of the War against Terrorism: Is the US Judiciary in Self-Imposed Exile?' *Journal of Money Laundering Control*, 7(3), 2004, pp. 218–253

Florini, A., *The Coming Democracy: New Rules for Running a New World*. Washington, DC: Brookings Institution, 2005

Foot, R., *Human Rights and Counter-terrorism in America's Asia Policy*. Oxford: Oxford University Press for the International Institute for Strategic Studies, 2004

Forest, J.F. and Sousa, M.V., *Oil and Terrorism in the New Gulf: Framing U.S. Energy and Security Policies for the Gulf of Guinea*, Lanham, MD: Lexington Press, 2006

Forsythe, D.P., *Human Rights and Peace: International and National Dimensions*. Lincoln: University of Nebraska Press, 1993

Fortna, V.P., *Peace Time: Cease-Fire Agreements and the Durability of Peace*. Princeton, NJ: Princeton University Press, 2004

Fox, J., 'Religion and State Failure: An Examination of the Extent and Magnitude of Religious Conflict from 1950 to 1996'. *International Political Science Review/Revue internationale de science politique*, vol. 25, January 2004, pp. 55–76

Fox, J., *Religion, Civilization, and Civil War: 1945 through the New Millennium*. Lanham, MD: Lexington Books, 2005

Frey, M., *Geschichte des Vietnamkriegs: Die Tragöedie in Asien und das Ende des amerikanischen Traums*. Munich: C.H. Beck, 1999

Friedman, T.L., *The World Is Flat: A Brief History of the Twenty-First Century*. New York: Farrar, Straus & Giroux, 2007

Frost, M., *Towards a Normative Theory of International Relations: A Critical Analysis of the Philosophical and Methodological Assumptions in the Discipline with Proposals towards a Substantive Normative Theory*. Cambridge: Cambridge University Press, 1986

Fukuyama, F., *State-Building: Governance and World Order in the 21st Century*. Ithaca, NY: Cornell University Press, 2004

Fuller, G.E., *The Future of Political Islam*. Basingstoke, UK: Palgrave, 2003

Gabriel, B., *Because They Hate: A Survivor of Islamic Terror Warns America*. New York: St Martin's Press, 2006

Gabriel, R., *Empires at War: A Chronological Encyclopedia from Sumer to the Fall of Byzantium*, 3 vols. New York: Greenwood Press, 2004

Gabrile, M.A. and Rendel von Resch, C., *Islam und Terrorismus: Was der Koran wirklich über Christentum, Gewalt und die Ziele des Djihad lehrt*. Gräfeling, Germany: Taschenbuch, 2004

Gal-Or, N., *Tolerating Terrorism in the West: An International Survey*. London: Routledge, 1991

Ganguly, R. (ed.), *A Dictionary of Ethnic Conflict*. London: Routledge, 2005

Ganser, D., *NATO's Secret Armies, Operation Gladio and Terrorism in Western Europe*. London: Frank Cass, 2005

Geaves, R., *Islam and the West Post 9/11*. Aldershot, UK: Ashgate, 2004

Gerges, F.A., 'Islam and Muslims in the Mind of America'. *Annals of the American Academy of Political and Social Science*, 588, July 2003, pp. 73–89

Gibbs, S., 'Islam and Islamic Extremism: An Existential Analysis'. *Journal of Humanistic Psychology*, 45, April 2005, pp. 156–203

Glain, S., *Mullahs, Merchants, and Militants: The Economic Collapse of the Arab World*. New York: St Martin's Press, 2004

Glasius, M. and Kaldor, M. (eds), *A Human Security Doctrine for Europe: Project, Principles, Practicalities*. London: Routledge, 2005

Glassé, C., *The Concise Encyclopaedia of Islam*. London: Stacey International, 1989

Glendon, M.A., *Rights Talk: The Impoverishment of Political Discourse*. New York: Free Press, 1991

Glenn, J.C. and Gordon, T.J., *2005 State of the Future*. Washington, DC: American Council for the United Nations University, 2005

Glenny, M., *McMafia: A Journey through the Global Criminal Underworld*. New York: Alfred A. Knopf, 2008

Godson, R. (ed.), *Counterintelligence*. Washington, DC: National Strategy Information Center; New Brunswick, NJ: Transaction Books, 1980

Gold, D., *The Fight for Jerusalem: Radical Islam, the West, and the Future of the Holy City*. Washington, DC: Regnery, 2007

Gompert, D.C., Green, J.D., Neu, C.R., Robinson, G., Shine, K. and Simon, S., *Building a Successful Palestinian State*. Santa Monica, CA: RAND, 2004

Gopin, M., *Holy War, Holy Peace: How Religion Can Bring Peace to the Middle East*. Oxford: Oxford University Press, 2002

Gordon, A., 'Computerized Databases and Terrorism: An Examination of Multidisciplinary Coverage'. *Terrorism and Political Violence*, 7(4), 1995, pp. 171–177

Gordon, A., 'Terrorism and the Science Technology and Medicine Databases: New Concepts and Terminology', *Terrorism and Political Violence*, 8(1), 1996, pp.167–173

Gordon, A., 'The Spread of Terrorism Publications: A Data Base Analysis'. *Terrorism and Political Violence*, 10(4), 1998, pp. 192–196

Gordon, A., 'Terrorism Dissertations and the Evolution of a Specialty: An Analysis of Meta-information'. *Terrorism and Political Violence*, 11(2), 1999, pp. 141–150

Gordon, A., 'Terrorism and the Scholarly Communication System'. *Terrorism and Political Violence*, 13/4, 2001, pp. 116–124

Gordon, A., 'The Effect of Database and Website Inconstancy on the Terrorism Field's Delineation'. *Studies in Conflict and Terrorism*, 27(2), 2004, pp. 79–88

Gordon, A., 'Terrorism and Knowledge Growth: A Database and Internet Analysis'. In A. Silke (ed.), *Terrorism Research: Trends, Achievements and Failures*. London: Frank Cass, 2004

Gordon, A., 'Terrorism as an Academic Subject after 9/11: Searching the Internet Reveals a Stockholm Syndrome Trend'. *Studies in Conflict and Terrorism*, 28(1), January–February 2005, pp. 45–59

Gordon, A., 'Homeland Security Literature in Relation to Terrorism Publications: The Source and the Response'. *Scientometrics*, 65(1), October 2005, pp. 55–65

Gordon, A., 'The Peripheral Terrorism Literature: Bringing It Closer to the Core'. *Scientometrics*, 62(3), 2005, pp. 403–414

Gordon, A., ' "Purity of Arms", "Preemptive War", and "Selective Targeting": General, Conceptual and Legal Analyses'. *Studies in Conflict and Terrorism*, 29, 2006

Gordon, M.R. and Trainor, B.E., *Cobra II: The Inside Story of the Invasion and Occupation of Iraq*. New York: Pantheon, 2006

Goulden, J.C., *The Death Merchant: The Rise and Fall of Edwin P. Wilson*. New York: Bantam, 1985

Gow, J.J., 'A Revolution in International Affairs?' *Security Dialogue*, 31, September 2000, pp. 293–306

Gressang, D. and Baxter, J.A., 'Crawling into the Terrorist's Head: Coordination and Cooperation across Levels of Government'. *Defense Intelligence Journal*, 14(1), 2005, 121–140

Griffiths, M., *Realism, Idealism, and International Politics: A Reinterpretation*. London: Routledge, 1992

Gross, M.L., 'Killing Civilians Intentionally: Double Effect, Reprisal, and Necessity in the Middle East'. In D.J. Caraley and L. Morales Kando, (eds), *Terrorist Attacks and Nuclear Proliferation: Strategies for Overlapping Dangers*. New York: Academy of Political Science, 2007

Guéhenno, J.-M., *The End of the Nation-State*. Minneapolis: University of Minnesota Press, 1995

Gupta, D.K., *Path to Collective Madness: A Study in Social Order and Political Pathology*. Westport, CT: Praeger, 2001

Haass, R.N., *The Opportunity: America's Moment to Alter History's Course*. New York: Public Affairs, 2005

Habermas, J., *De gespaltene Westen: Kleine politische Schriften*. Frankfurt am Main: Suhrkamp, 2004

Halper, S.A. and Clarke, J., *America Alone: The Neo-Conservatives and the Global Order*. Cambridge: Cambridge University Press, 2005

Halperin, M.H. and Scheffer, D.J. with Small, P.L., *Self-Determination in the New World Order*. Washington, DC: Carnegie Endowment for International Peace, 1992

Hamilton, D.S. (ed.), *Terrorism and International Relations*. Washington, DC: Center for Transatlantic Relations, 2006

Hampson, F.O. and Malone, D. (eds), *From Reaction to Conflict Prevention: Opportunities for the UN System*. Boulder, CO: Lynne Rienner, 2002

Hannum, H., *Guide to International Human Rights Practice*. Ardsley, NY: Transnational Publishers, 2004

Hanson, R., 'Designing Real Terrorism Futures'. *Public Choice*, 128(1–2), July 2006, pp. 257–274

Haqqani, H., *Pakistan: Between Mosque and Military*. Washington, DC: Carnegie Endowment for International Peace, 2005

Harbom, L. and Wallensteen, P., 'Armed Conflict and its International Dimensions, 1946–2004'. *Journal of Peace Research*, 42, September 2005, pp. 623–635

Harff, B. and Gurr, T.R., *Ethnic Conflict in World Politics*. Boulder, CO: Westview Press, 2004

Harris, L., *Civilization and Its Enemies: The Next Stage of History*. New York: Free Press, 2004

Harrison, E., *The Post-Cold War International System*. London: Routledge, 2004

Harvey, D., *The New Imperialist*. Oxford: Oxford University Press, 2005

Hastedt, G., *Estimating Intentions in an Age of Terrorism: Garthoff Revisited*. Honolulu: International Studies Association (ISA), March 2005

Hefner, R.W. and Qasim Zaman, M. (eds), *Schooling Islam: The Culture of Politics of Modern Muslim Education*. Princeton, NJ: Princeton University Press, 2007

Held, D., *Models of Democracy*. Stanford, CA: Stanford University Press, 1987

Herod, A. and Wright, M.W. (eds), *Geographies of Power: Placing Scale*. Malden, MA: Blackwell, 2002

Herzog, M., 'Can Hamas Be Tamed?' *Foreign Affairs*, 85(2), March–April 2006, pp. 83–94

Hill, J., 'Chinese Reactions to the September 11th Attack'. In S. Shen (ed.), *China and Antiterrorism*. Hauppauge, NY: Nova Science Publishers, 2007

Hirsi Ali, A., *Ayaan Verzameld: essays en toespraken*. Amsterdam: Augustus, 2006

Hoffman, P.J., *Sword and Salve: Confronting New Wars and Humanitarian Crises*. Lanham, MD: Rowman & Littlefield, 2006

Hoffman, S., *Chaos and Violence*. Lanham, MD: Rowman & Littlefield, 2006

Holert, T. and Terkesidis, M., *Entsichert: Krieg als Massenkultur im 21. Jahrhundert*. Cologne: Kiepenheuer & Witsch, 2003

Houen, A., *Terrorism and Modern Literature: From Joseph Conrad to Ciaran Carson*. Oxford: Oxford University Press, 2002

Hough, P., *Understanding Global Security*. London: Routledge, 2004

Huband, M., *Brutal Truths, Fragile Myths: Power Politics and Western Adventurism in the Arab World*. New York: Basic Books, 2004

Human Security Centre, *Deadly Connections: The War/Disease Nexus*. Workshop Report, Vancouver, 22–23 March 2004

Human Security Centre, *Human Security Report 2005: War and Peace in the 21st Century*. Oxford: Oxford University Press, November 2005

Hunter, S. (ed.), *Strategic Developments in Eurasia after 11 September*. London: Frank Cass, 2004

Hunter, S.T. with Malik, H. (eds), *Islam and Human Rights: Advancing a U.S.–Musim Dialogue*. Washington, DC: Center for Strategic and International Studies, 2005

ICC, *Hall of Shame: The World's 10 Worst Persecutors of Christians*. Washington, DC: International Christian Concern, 2008

Ignatieff, M., *The Lesser Evil: Political Ethics in an Age of Terror*. Edinburgh: Edinburgh University Press, 2004

IISS, *Strategic Survey 2004/5: An Evaluation and Forecast of World Affairs*. London: Routledge, 2005

IISS, *The Military Balance 2005–2006*. London: Routledge, October 2005

Indyk, M., 'A Trusteeship for Palestine?' *Foreign Affairs*, May–June 2003, pp. 51–66

Irfani, S., *Iran's Islamic Revolution: Popular Liberation or Religious Dictatorship?* Lahore: Vanguard Books, 1983

Isherwood, L., 'Incarnation in Times of Terror: Christian Theology and the Challenge of September 11th'. *Feminist Theology*, 14, September 2005, pp. 69–81

Israeli, R., *Muslim Minorities in Modern States: The Challenge of Assimilation*. New Brunswick, NJ: Transaction, 2008

Jabar, F.A., *Postconflict Iraq: A Race for Stability, Reconstruction, and Legitimacy*. Special Report 120. Washington: DC: United States Institute of Peace, May 2004

Jackson, B.A., Baker, J.C., Cragin, K., Parachini, J., Trujillo, H.R. and Chalk, P., *Aptitude for Destruction*, vol 1: *Organizational Learning in Terrorist Groups and Its Implications for Combating Terrorism*. MG-331. Santa Monica, CA: RAND 2005

Jackson, B.A., Baker, J.C., Cragin, K., Parachini, J., Trujillo, H.R. and Chalk, P., *Aptitude for Destruction*, vol. 2: *Case Studies of Organizational Learning in Five Terrorist Groups*. MG-332. Santa Monica, CA: RAND, 2005

Jacoby, W., *The Enlargement of the European Union and NATO: Ordering from the Menu in Central Europe*. Cambridge: Cambridge University Press, 2006

Jamal, A. and Maira, S., 'Muslim Americans, Islam, and the "War on Terrorism" at Home and Abroad' [review article]. *Middle East Journal*, 5992, Spring 2005, pp. 303–309

Jensen, C.J. III, 'Beyond the Tea Leaves: Futures Research and Terrorism'. *American Behavioral Scientist*, 44, February 2001, pp. 914–936

Jensen, N.M. and Young, D.J., 'A Violent Future? Political Risk Insurance Markets and Violence Forecasts'. *Journal of Conflict Resolution*, 52, August 2008, pp. 527–547

Jewett, R., *Captain America and the Crusade against Evil: The Dilemma of Zealous Nationalism*. Grand Rapids, MI: W.B. Eerdmans, 2003

Jickling, M. and Jackson, W.D., 'The Impact of the World Trade Center Attack on the Financial System'. In E.V. Linden (ed.), *Focus on Terrorism*, vol. 4. Hauppauge, NY: Nova Science Publishers, 2002

Johnson, C., *Blowback: The Costs and Consequences of American Empire*. New York: Metropolitan Books, 2004

Johnson, C., *The Sorrows of Empire: Militarism, Secrecy, and the End of the Republic*. New York: Metropolitan Books, 2004

Jonas, G., *Vengeance: A True Story*. London: Pan in association with Collins, 1985

Junne, G. and Verkoren, W., *Postconflict Development: Meeting New Challenges*. Boulder, CO: Lynne Rienner, 2004

Kagan, R., *Dangerous Nation*. New York: Alfred A. Knopf, 2006

Kahana, E., *Historical Dictionary of Israeli Intelligence*. Lanham, MD: Scarecrow Press, 2006 Available at: http://tinyurl.com/zf6r4 (accessed 20 April 2009)

Kahn, D., 'The Rise of Intelligence'. *Foreign Affairs*, 85(5), September–October 2006, pp. 125–135

Kalicni, J.H. and Goldwyn, D.L., *Energy and Security: Toward a New Foreign Policy Strategy*. Baltimore: Johns Hopkins University Press, 2005

Kam, E., 'Marching Johnny Home: Evacuating the American Forces from Iraq'. *Strategic Assessment*, 8(4), February 2006, pp. 13–20

Kaplan, J., 'Absolute Rescue: Absolutism, Defensive Action and the Resort to Force'. *Terrorism and Political Violence*, 7(3), Autumn 1995, pp. 128–163

Kaplan, J., 'Islamophobia in America? September 11 and Islamophobic Hate Crime'. *Terrorism and Political Violence*, 18(1), Spring 2006, pp. 1–33

Karsh, E., *Islamic Imperialism: A History*. New Haven, CT: Yale University Press, 2006

Kay, S., 'Globalization, Power, and Security'. *Security Dialogue*, 35, March 2004, pp. 9–25

Kearney, R., 'Terror, Philosophy and the Sublime: Some Philosophical Reflections on 11 September'. *Philosophy and Social Criticism*, 29, January 2003, pp. 23–51

Kemp, G. and Fry, D. (eds), *Keeping the Peace: Conflict Resolution and Peaceful Societies around the World*. New York: Routledge, 2003

Kemp, W.A., 'The Business of Ethnic Conflict'. *Security Dialogue*, 35, March 2004, pp. 43–59

Kendall, S.L., *A Unified General Framework of Insurgency using a Living Systems Approach*. Monterey, CA: Naval Postgraduate School, June 2008

Kennedy, P.M., *Preparing for the Twenty-First Century*. New York: Random House, 1993

Kenyon, L.S., *Dangerous Sanctuaries: Refugee Camps, Civil War and the Dilemmas of Humanitarian Aid*. Ithaca, NY: Cornell University Press, 2005

Keohane, R.O., *Power and Governance in a Partially Globalized World*. London; Routledge, 2002

Kepel, G., *The War for Muslim Minds: Islam and the West*. Cambridge, MA: Belknap Press of Harvard University Press, 2004

Keppley Mahmood, C., 'Terrorism, Myth, and the Power of Ethnographic Praxis'. *Journal of Contemporary Ethnography*, 30, October 2001, pp. 520–545

Kiernan, V.G., *The Lords of Human Kind: European Attitudes to Other Cultures in the Imperial Age*. London: Serif, 1995

King, I. and Mason, W., *Peace at Any Price: How the World Failed Kosovo*. Ithaca, NY: Cornell University Press, 2006

King, N., 'Security, Disease, Commerce: Ideologies of Postcolonial Global Health'. *Social Studies of Science*, 32, December 2002, pp. 763–789

Klare, M.T., *Resource Wars: The New Landscape of Global Conflict*. New York Metropolitan Books, 2001

Klaus, E. and Kassel, S., 'The Veil as a Means of Legitimization: An Analysis of the Interconnectedness of Gender, Media and War'. *Journalism*, 6, August 2005, pp. 335–355

Klausen, J., *The Islamic Challenge: Politics and Religion in Western Europe*. Oxford: Oxford University Press, 2005

Knezo, G.J., *Counter Terrorism: Impacts on Research, Development and Higher Education*. Hauppauge, NY: Nova Science Publishers, 2002

Knight, M. and Özerdem, A., 'Guns, Camps and Cash: Disarmament, Demobilization and Reinsertion of Former Combatants in Transitions from War to Peace'. *Journal of Peace Research*, 41(4), July 2004, pp.499–516

Koch, M. and Gartner, S.S., 'Casualties and Constituencies: Democratic Accountability, Electoral Institutions, and Costly Conflicts'. *Journal of Conflict Resolution*, 49, December 2005, pp. 874–894

Kolodziej, E.A., *Security and International Relations*. Cambridge: Cambridge University Press, 2005

Kotzé, D., 'Implications of the Democracy–Development Relationship for Conflict Resolution'. *African Journal on Conflict Resolution*, 5(1), 2005, pp. 61–90

Kramer, M., *Ivory Towers on Sand: The Failure of Middle Eastern Studies in America*. Washington, DC: Washington Institute for Near East Policy, 2001

Kressel, N.J., *Mass Hate: The Global Rise of Genocide and Terror*. Boulder, CO: Westview Press, 2002

Kupchan, C.A., 'Independence for Kosovo'. *Foreign Affairs*, November–December 2005, pp. 14–21

Kurtenbach, S. and Lock, P. (eds), *Kriege als (Über)Lebenswelten: Schattenglobalisierung, Kriegsökonomien und Inseln der Zivilität*. Bonn: Stiftung Entwicklung und Frieden, 2004

Kurth, J. (ed.), Special issue, 'America, Democratization and the Muslim World'. *Orbis*, 49(2), Spring 2005, pp. 195–322

Lacina, B., 'From Side Show to Centre Stage: Civil Conflict after the Cold War'. *Security Dialogue*, 35, June 2004, pp. 191–205

LaFree, G. and Dugan, L., 'How Does Studying Terrorism Compare to Studying Crime?' In M. DeFlem (ed.), *Criminology and Terrorism*. Elsevier, 2004, pp. 53–74

Lahav, G., 'Public Opinion toward Immigration in the European Union: Does It Matter?' *Comparative Political Studies*, 37, December 2004, pp. 1151–1183

Lammers, C.J., *Vreemde overheersing: bezetten en bezetting in sociologisch perspectief*. Amsterdam: Bert Bakker, 2005

Lansford, T. and Watson, R.P., *Debating the War on Terrorism*. Dubuque, IA: Kendall/Hunt, 2003

Laqueur, W., *The Changing Face of Antisemitism: From Ancient Times to the Present Days*. Oxford: Oxford University Press, 2006

Lawrence, B., *The Qu'ran: A Biography*. New York: Atlantic Monthly Press, 2007

Le Billon, P. (ed.), *The Geopolitics of 'Resource Wars'*. London: Frank Cass, 2004

Lebel, U. (ed.), *Civil–Military Relations in Israel: Communicating Security*. London: Routledge, 2005

LeBor, A., 'Complicity with Evil': The United Nations in the Age of Modern Genocide*. New Haven, CT: Yale University Press, 2006

Leonard, M. (ed.), *Re-ordering the World*. London: Foreign Policy Centre, 2002

Levene, M. and Roberts, P. (eds), *The Massacre in History*. New York: Berghahn Books, 2005

Lewis, B., *The Crisis of Islam: Holy War and Unholy Terror*. New York: Modern Library, 2003

Liang-Fenton, D. (ed.), *Implementing U.S. Human Rights Policy: Agendas, Policies and Practices*. Washington, DC: US Institute of Peace Press, 2004

Lockman, Z., *Contending Visions of the Middle East: The History and Politics of Orientalism*. Cambridge: Cambridge University Press, 2004

Lomborg, B. (ed.), *How to Spend $50 Billion to Make the World a Better Place*. Cambridge: Cambridge University Press, 2006

Lomsky-Feder, E. and Ben Ari, E. (eds), *The Military and Militarism in Israeli Society*. Albany, NY: SUNY Press, 2000

Lopez, G.A. and Stohl, M., *International Relations: Contemporary Theory and Practice*. Washington, DC: CQ Press, 1989

Loveman, B. (ed.), *Strategy for Empire: US Regional Security Policy in Post-Cold War Era*. Providence RI: Brown Univeristy: Scholarly Resources, 2004

Lucassen, L., *The Immigrant Threat: The Integration of Old and New Migrants in Western Europe since 1850: Common Threads in the Long-Term Integration Experience of Migrants, Past and Present*. Champaign: University of Illinois Press, 2005

Lustick, I.S., *Trapped in the War on Terror*. Philadelphia: University of Pennsylvania Press, 2006

McGowan, P.J., 'Coups and Conflict in West Africa, 1955–2004: Part II, Empirical Findings'. *Armed Forces and Society*, 32, January 2006, pp. 234–253

McKee, G., *Time Bomb*. London: Bloomsbury, 1988

McLaren, P., 'The Dialectics of Terrorism: A Marxist Response to September 11 (Part Two: Unveiling the Past, Evading the Present'. *Cultural Studies <=> Critical Methodologies*, 3, February 2003, pp. 103–132

McLaren, P. and Martin, G., 'The Legend of the Bush Gang: Imperialism, War, and Propaganda'. *Cultural Studies <=> Critical Methodologies*, 4, August 2004, pp. 281–303

Makdisi, U. and Silverstein, P.A. (eds), *Memory and Violence in the Middle East and North Africa*. Bloomington: Indiana University Press, 2006

Malone, D.M. (ed.), *The UN Security Council: From the Cold War to the 21st Century*. Boulder, CO: Lynne Rienner, 2004

Mandelbaum, M., *The Case for Goliath: How America Acts as the World's Government in the 21st Century*. New York: PublicAffairs Books, 2005

Mann, J., *Rise of the Vulcans: The History of Bush's War Cabinet*. New York: Viking, 2004

Marshall, M.G. and Gurr, T.R., *Peace and Conflict 2005*. College Park, MD: Center for International Development and Conflict Management, 2005

Martel, W.C., *Victory in War: Foundations of Modern Military Policy*. Cambridge: Cambridge University Press, 2007

Martin, D., *Does Christianity Cause War?* Oxford: Oxford University Press, 2004

Matar, K.I. and Thabit, R.W., *Lockerbie and Libya: A Study in International Relations*. Jefferson, NC: McFarland, 2004

Matheson, M.J., *Council Unbound: The Growth of UN Decisionmaking on Conflict and Postconflict Issues after the Cold War*. Washington, DC: United States Institute of Peace Press, 2006

Mattox, H.E., *A Chronology of United States–Iraqi Relations, 1920–2006*, London: Eurospan, 2008

May, E.R. and Zelikow, P.D., *Dealing with Dictators: Dilemmas of US Diplomacy and Intelligence Analysis, 1945–1990*. Cambridge, MA: MIT Press, 2005

Mendus, S., *Toleration and the Limits of Liberalism*. Atlantic Highlands, NJ: Humanities Press International, 1989

Merkley, P.C., *American Presidents, Religion, and Israel: The Heirs of Cyrus*. Westport, CT: Praeger, 2004

Mertus, J. and Helsing, J.W. (eds), *Human Rights and Conflict: Exploring the Links between Rights, Laws and Peacebuilding*. Washington, DC: United States Institute of Peace, 2006

Meyer, C., *DC Confidential: The Controversial Memoirs of Britain's Ambassador to the U.S. at the Time of 9/11 and the Iraq War*. London: Weidenfeld & Nicolson, 2005

Michel-Kerjan, E. and Pedell, B., 'How Does the Corporate World Cope with Mega-terrorism? Puzzling Evidence from Terrorism Insurance Markets'. *Journal of Applied Corporate Finance*, 18(4), Fall 2006, pp. 61–75

Mickolus, E., *ITERATE: International Terrorism: Attributes of Terrorist Events, Data Codebook*. Ann Arbor, MT: Inter-University Consortium for Political and Social Research, 1976

Mickolus, E., 'An Events Data Base for Studying Transnational Terrorism'. In R.J. Heuer (ed.), *Quantitative Approaches to Political Intelligence: The CIA Experience*. Boulder, CO: Westview Press, 1978, pp. 127–163

Miler, S.E., 'Terrifying Thoughts: Power, Order, and Terror after 9/11' (review essay). *Global Governance*, 11(2), April–June 2005, pp. 247–271

Miljard Burr, J. and Collins, R.O., *Alms for Jihad. Charity and Terrorism in the Islamic World*. Cambridge: Cambridge University Press, 2007

Milliken, J., *State Failure, Collapse and Reconstruction*. Oxford: Blackwell, 2003

Mirza, M., Senthilkumaran, A. and Ja'far, Z., *Living Apart Together: British Muslims and the Paradox of Multiculturalism*. London: Policy Exchange, 2007

Mockaitis, T.R., 'Conclusion: The Future of Terrorism Studies'. *Small Wars and Insurgencies*, 14(1), 2003, pp. 207–212

Mohammed bin Saud Al-Bishr (ed.), *Saudis and Terrorism: An International Vision*. Riyadh: Ghaina Publishing House, 2005

Mostafa, M.M. and al-Hamdi, M.T., 'Political Islam, Clash of Civilizations, US Dominance and Arab Support of Attacks on America: A Test of a Hierarchical Model'. *Studies in Conflict and Terrorism*, 30 (8), August 2007, pp. 723–736

Munger, M., 'Preference Modification vs. Incentive Manipulation as Tools of Terrorist Recruitment: The Role of Culture'. *Public Choice*, 128(1–2), July 2006, pp. 131–146

Munjoz, H., *Democracy Rising: Assessing the Global Challenges*. Boulder, CO: Lynne Rienner, 2005

Münkler, H., *Die neuen Kriege*. Reinbek bei Hamburg: Rowohlt Verlag, 2003

Münkler, H. (ed.), *Der Partisan: Theorie, Strategie, Gestalt*. Opladen, Germany: Westdeutscher Verlag, 1990

Mylroie, L., *Bush vs. the Beltway: How the CIA and the State Department Tried to Stop the War on Terror*. New York: Regan Books, HarperCollins, 2003

Nasir, S.A., 'Al-Zawahari's Pakistani Ally: Profile of Maulana Faqir Mohammed'. *Terrorism Monitor*, 4(3), 9 February 2006, pp. 1–3

Nasr, V., *The Shia Revival: How Conflicts within Islam Will Shape the Future*. New York: W.W. Norton, 2006

Neumayer, E., 'The Impact of Political Violence on Tourism: Dynamic Cross-national Estimation'. *Journal of Conflict Resolution*, 48, April 2004, pp. 259–281

Newhouse, J., *Imperial America: The Bush Assault on the World Order*. New York: Knopf, 2003

Newman, E. and Richmond, O.P., *The United Nations and Human Security*. New York: Palgrave, 2001

Nisbet, E.C., Nisbet, M.C., Scheufele, D.A. and Shanahan, J.E., 'Public Diplomacy, Television News, and Muslim Opinion'. *Harvard International Journal of Press/Politics*, 9, April 2004, pp. 11–37

Nordstrom, C., *Fieldwork under Fire: Contemporary Studies of Violence and Survival*. Berkeley: University of California Press, 1995

Norell M., 'Terror as a Threat'. In *Threat Perceptions in the Swedish Defence Establishment*. Joint Study between the National Defence College and the Swedish Defence Research Agency, Stockholm 1998 (in Swedish)

Nye, J.S. Jr, *Soft Power: The Means to Success in World Politics*. New York: PublicAffairs, 2004

O'Day, A. (ed.), *Weapons of Mass Destruction and Terrorism*. Aldershot, UK: Ashgate, 2004

O'Hagan, J., 'Beyond the Clash of Civilizations?' (review article). *Australian Journal of International Affairs*, 59(3), September 2005, pp. 383–400

Olivas–Luján, M.R., Harzing, A.W. and McCoy, S., 'September 11, 2001: Two Quasi-experiments on the Influence of Threats on Cultural Values and Cosmopolitanism'. *International Journal of Cross Cultural Management*, 4, August 2004, pp. 211–228

Oliverio, A. and Lauderdale, P., 'Terrorism as Deviance or Social Control: Suggestions for Future Research'. *International Journal of Comparative Sociology*, 46, April 2005, pp. 53–169

O'Loughlin, J., 'The War on Terrorism, Academic Publication Norms, and Replication'. *The Professional Geographer*, 57(4), November 2005, pp. 588–591

O'Neill, O., 'The Dark Side of Human Rights'. *International Affairs*, 81(2), March 2005, pp. 427–439

Orr, J. and Klaic, D. (eds), *Terrorism and Modern Drama*. Edinburgh: Edinburgh University Press, 1990

Orr, R.C. (ed.), *Winning the Peace: An American Strategy for Post-conflict Reconstruction*. Washington, DC: Center for Strategic and International Studies, 2004

Osborne, R., *Literature and Terrorism*. London: Pluto Press, 2007

Pappe, I., *The Ethnic Cleansing of Palestine*. Oxford: Oneworld Publications, 2006

Paris, R., *At War's End: Building Peace after Civil Conflict*. Cambridge: Cambridge University Press, 2004

Parker, D. (ed.), *Revolutions and the Revolutionary Tradition in the West, 1560–1991*. London: Routledge, 2000

Parsons, N.C., *The Politics of the Palestinian Authority: From Oslo to Al-Aqsa*. London: Routledge, 2005

Pauly, R.J. Jr, *Islam in Europe: Integration or Marginalization?* Aldershot, UK: Ashgate, 2004

Pekelder, J., *Sympathie voor de RAF: de Rote Armee Fraktion in Nederland, 1970–1980*. Amsterdam: Jan Mets, 2007

Peleg, S., 'One's Terrorist Is Another's Blockbuster: Political Terrorism in American vs. European Films'. *New England Journal of Political Science*, 1(1), Summer 2003, pp. 81–108

Pelletière, S., *America's Oil Wars*. Westport, CT: Praeger, 2004

Pelton, R.Y., *The World's Most Dangerous Places*, 5th edn. New York: Tembo LLC, 2003

Posner, G., *Secrets of the Kingdom: The Inside Story of the Saudi Connection*. New York: Random House, 2005

Primor, A., *Terror als Vorwand*. Düsseldorf: Droste Verlag, 2004

Putra, I.N.D. and Hitchcock, M. 'The Bali Bombs and the Tourism Development Cycle'. *Progress in Development Studies*, 6(2), March 2006, pp. 157–166

Quan Li, 'Does Democracy Promote or Reduce Transnational Terrorist Incidents?' *Journal of Conflict Resolution*, 49, April 2005, pp. 278–297

Quandt, W.B., *Peace Process: American Diplomacy and the Arab–Israeli Conflict since 1967*. Washington, DC: Brookings Institution, 2005

Rabasa, A.M., Benard, C., Chalk, P., Fair, C.C., Karasik, T., Lal, R., Lesser, I. and Thaler, D., *The Muslim World after 9/11*. Santa Monica, CA: RAND, 2004

Radack, J.A., 'United States Citizens Detained as "Enemy Combatants": The Right to Counsel as a Matter of Ethics'. *William & Mary Bill of Rights Journal*, 12, 2003, pp. 221–241

Ram, S., 'Understanding the Indirect Strategy of Terrorism: Insights from Nonviolent Action Research'. In S. Ram and R. Summy (eds), *Nonviolence: An Alternative for Defeating Global Terror(ism)*. Hauppauge, NY: Nova Science Publishers, 2007

Ramadan, T., *Western Muslims and the future of Islam*. New York: Oxford University Press, 2004

RAND Palestinian State Study Team, *Building a Successful Palestinian State*. MG-146. Santa Monica, CA: RAND, 2005

RAND Palestinian State Study Team, *Helping a Palestinian State Succeed: Key Findings*. MG-146/1. Santa Monica, CA: RAND, 2005

Rapoport, D.C. and Weinberg, L. (eds), special issue: 'The Democratic Experience and Political Violence'. *Terrorism and Political Violence*, 12(3–4), 2000

Ravi, N., 'Looking beyond Flawed Journalism: How National Interests, Patriotism, and Cultural Values Shaped the Coverage of the Iraq War'. *Harvard International Journal of Press/Politics*, 10, January 2005, pp. 45–62

Reid, E.F. and Hsinchun Chen, 'Mapping The Contemporary Terrorism Research Domain'. *International Journal of Human–Computer Studies*, 65(1), 2007, pp. 42–56

Reid, J., 'Architecture, Al-Qaeda, and the World Trade Center: Rethinking Relations between War, Modernity, and City Spaces after 9/11'. *Space and Culture*, 7, November 2004, pp. 396–408

Reid, J., 'The Biopolitics of the War on Terror: A Critique of the "Return of Imperialism" Thesis in International Relations'. *Third World Quarterly*, 26(2), 2005, pp. 237–252

Richardson, J., *War, Science and Terrorism: From Laboratory to Open Conflict*. London: Routledge, 2002

Rivlin, P. and Even, S., 'Political Stability in Arab States: Economic Causes and Consequences'. Tel Aviv: Jaffee Center for Strategic Studies, *Memorandum* no. 74, December 2004

Roeder, P.G. and Rothchild, D.S., *Sustainable Peace: Power and Democracy after Civil Wars*. Ithaca, NY: Cornell University Press, 2005

Romano, D., *The Kurdish Nationalist Movement: Opportunity, Mobilization and Identity*. Cambridge: Cambridge University Press, 2006

Rootes, C. (ed.), *Environmental Protest in Western Europe*. Oxford: Oxford University Press, 2007

Rosecrance, R.N. and Stein, A.A., *No More States? Globalization, National-Self-determination and Terrorism*. Lanham, MD: Rowman & Littlefield, 2006

Rotberg, R.I., *State Failure and State Weakness in a Time of Terror*. Washington, DC: World Peace Foundation/Brookings Institution Press, 2003

Ruohomaeki, O. (ed.), *Development in an Insecure World: New Threats to Human Security and Their Implications for Development Policy*. Helsinki: Ministry for Foreign Affairs of Finland, 2005

Sahm, A., Sapper, M., and Weichsel, V. (eds), *Die Zukunft des Friedens: Eine Bilanz der Friedens-und Konfliktforschung*. Wiesbaden: Westdeutsche Verlag, 2002

Sampson, A., *The Arms Bazaar: From Lebanon To Lockheed*. New York: Viking Press, 1977

Sandole, D.J.D. and Van der Merwe H., *Conflict Resolution Theory and Practice: Integration and Application*. Manchester: Manchester University Press, 1993

Scheerer, S., *Die Zukunft des Terrorismus: Drei Szenarien*. Lüneburg, Germany: Klampen Verlag, 2002

Schmid, A.P. and Berends, E., *Soviet Military Interventions since 1945: with a Summary in Russian*. New Brunswick, NJ: Transaction Books, 1985

Schneckener, U. and Wolff, S. (eds), *Managing and Settling Ethnic Conflicts: Perspectives on Successes and Failures in Europe, Africa and Asia*. London: Hurst, 2004

School of Peace Culture, Alert Unit *Alert 2004: Report on Conflicts, Human Rights and Peace Building*. Barcelona: Icaria editorial; Escola de Cultura de Pau, UAB, 2004

Schulteis, G., *Waging Peace: A Special Operations Team's Battle to Rebuild Iraq*. New York: Gotham, 2005

Schwartz-Barcott, T.P., *War, Terror and Peace in the Qur'an and in Islam: Insights for Military and Government Leaders*. Carlisle, PA: Army War College Foundation Press, 2004

Schweikart, L., *America's Victories: Why the U.S. Wins Wars and Will Win the War on Terror*. New York: Sentinel, 2006

Scott, L.V. and Jackson, P. (eds), *Understanding Intelligence in the Twenty-First Century*. London: Frank Cass, 2004

Scruton, R., *The West and the Rest: Globalization and the Terrorist Threat*. Wilmington, ISI DE: Books, 2002

Seliktar, O., *Politics, Paradigms, and Intelligence Failures: Why So Few Predicted the Collapse of the Soviet Union*. Armonk, NY: M.E. Sharpe, 2004

Senate Select Committee on Intelligence, *Report on the U.S. Intelligence Community's Prewar Intelligence Assessments on Iraq*. Washington, 2004

Shahid Alam, M., *Challenging the New Orientalism: Dissenting Essays on the 'War against Islam'*. Cambridge, MA: Harvard University Press, 2007

Shanty, F., 'Anti-Muslim Sentiments and Violence'. In *Encyclopedia of World Terrorism, 1996–2002*, vol. 4. Armonk, NY: M.E. Sharpe, February 2003, pp. 105–107

Shenon, P., *The Commission: The Uncensored History of 9/11 Investigation*. New York: Twelve/Hachette, 2008

Sikand, Y., *Bastions of the Believers: Madrasas and Islamic Education in India*. New Delhi: Penguin India, 2005

Silberman, I., Higgins, E.T. and Dweck, C.S., 'Religion and World Change: Violence and Terrorism versus Peace'. *Journal of Social Issues*, 61(4), December 2005, pp. 761–784

Silke, A., 'The Devil You Know: Continuing Problems with Research on Terrorism'. *Terrorism and Political Violence*, 13(4) Winter 2001, pp. 1–14

Simon, J., 'Partnership for Peace: Charting a Course for a New Era'. *Strategic Forum*, no. 2006, March 2004. Washington, DC: National Defense University

Simonsen, J., Kinacioglu, M., Ruperrez, J. *et al.*, 'Special Issue on the United Nations'. *Perceptions*, 10(2), Summer 2005

Sims, J.E. and Gerber, B., *Transforming U.S. Intelligence*. Washington, DC: Georgetown University Press, 2005

Sinai, J., *How the Social and Behavioral Sciences Can Contribute to Understanding and Countering Terrorism*. Honolulu: International Studies Association (ISA) March 2005

Sinai, J., 'Combating Terrorism Insurgency Resolution Software: A Research Note'. In Chen, H., Wang, F., Yang, C.C., Zeng, D., Chan, M. and Chang, K. (eds), *Intelligence and Security Informatics*. Berlin: Springer, May 2006

Siresloudi, M., 'Early Detection of Terrorist Campaigns'. In A.P. Schmid, (ed.), *Forum on Crime and Society. Special Issue on Terrorism*. New York: United Nations, 2004

Siresloudi, M., 'How to Predict the Unpredictable: On Early Warning of Future Terrorist Campaigns'. *Defense and Security Analysis*, 21, 2005, pp. 341–363

Slaughter, A.M., *A New World Order*. Princeton, NJ: Princeton University Press, 2004

Sloboda, J., Elworthy, S., Hilder, P. and Rifkind, G., *Iraqi Liberation? Towards an Integrated Strategy*. London: Oxford Research Group, December 2005

Smith, A.G., 'From Words to Action: Exploring the Relationship between a Group's Value References and Its Likelihood of Engaging in Terrorism'. *Studies in Conflict and Terrorism*, 27(5), September–October 2004, pp. 409–437

Smith, B.L. and Damphouse, K.R., *Pre-Incident Indicators of Terrorist Incidents: The Identification of Behavioral, Geographic and Temporal Patterns of Preparatory Conduct*. Rockville, MD: National Criminal Justice Reference Service, May 2006

Smith, D., *The State of the Middle East: An Atlas of Conflict and Resolution*. Berkeley, CA: University of California Press, 2006

Smith, D. *et al.*, *The State of the World Atlas*. London: Penguin Books, 1999

Smith, G.A., 'President Bush's Enthymeme of Evil: The Amalgamation of 9/11, Iraq, and Moral Values'. *American Behavioral Scientist*, 49, September, 2005, pp. 32–47

Smith, S., Hadfield, A. and Dunne, T. (eds), *Foreign Policy: Theories, Actors and Cases*. Oxford: Oxford University Press, 2007

Smucker, P., *Al Qaeda's Great Escape: The Military and the Media on Terror's Trail*. New York: Brassey's, 2004

Sniderman, P.M. and Hagendoorn, L., *When Ways of Life Collide: Multiculturalism and Its Discontents in the Netherlands*. Princeton, NJ: Princeton University Press, 2007

Snyder, J., 'One World, Rival Theories'. *Foreign Policy*, November–December 2004, pp. 53–62

Solaün, M., *U.S. Intervention and Regime Change in Nicaragua*. Lincoln: University of Nebraska Press, 2005

Steen, J., Liesch, P.W., Knight, G.A. and Czinkota, M.R., 'The Contagion of International Terrorism and Its Effects on the Firm in an Interconnected World'. *Public Money and Management*, 26(5), November 2006, pp. 305–312

Steinhoff, U., *On the Ethics of War and Terrorism*. Oxford: Oxford University Press, 2007

Stempel, J.D., 'The Impact of Religion on Intelligence'. *International Journal of Intelligence and Counterintelligence*, 18(2), Summer 2005, pp. 280–295

Sternberg, E., 'Research Directions in Terrorism, Disaster, and Urban Security: An Introduction'. *Journal of Security Education*, 1(4), 20 October 2006, pp. 61–64

Strathern, A., Stewart, P.J. and Whitehead, N.L. (eds), *Terror and Violence: Imagination and the Unimaginable*. London: Pluto Press, 2006

Strauss, D.S., *The Complete Idiot's Guide to World Conflicts*. Indianapolis, IN: Alpha, 2002

Sturkey, D., *The Limits of American Power*. Chaltanham, UK: Edward Elgar, 2007

Suisman, D., Simon, S., Robinson, G., Anthony, C.R. and Schoenbaum, M., *The Arc: A Formal Structure for a Palestinian State*. MG-327. Santa Monica, CA: RAND, 2005

Sullivan, M.P., *Cuba and the State Sponsors of Terrorism List*. CRS Report for Congress, RL32251, 12 May 2005

Talbott, S. and Chanda, N. (eds), *The Age of Terror: America and the World after September 11*. Oxford: Perseus Press, 2001

Tarzi, S.M., 'Coercive Diplomacy and an "Irrational" Regime: Understanding the American Confrontation with the Taliban'. *International Studies*, 42, January 2005, pp. 21–41

TCF, *In from the Cold: The Strategic Contribution of Intelligence*. Report of the Twentieth Century Fund Task Force on the Future of US Intelligence. New York: Twentieth Century Fund, 1996

Telhami, S., *The Stakes: America and the Middle East: The Consequences of Power and the Choice for Peace*. Boulder, CO: Westview Press, 2002

Tellis, A.J., Szayna, T.S. and Winnefeld, J.A., *Anticipating Ethnic Conflict*. Santa Monica, CA: RAND, 1997

Thayer, B.A., *Darwin and International Relations: On the Evolutionary Origins of War and Ethnic Conflict*. Lexington: University Press of Kentucky, 2004

Tibi, B., *Islamische Zuwanderung: Die gescheiterte Integration*. Munich: DVA, 2002

Todd, E., *After the Empire: The Breakdown of the American Order*. New York: Colombia University Press, 2004

Toft, M.D., *The Geography of Ethnic Violence*. Princeton, NJ: Princeton University Press, 2003

Trento, J.J., *Prelude to Terror: The Rogue CIA and the Legacy of America's Private Intelligence Network*. New York: Carroll & Graff, 2005

Treverton, G.F., Gregg, H.S., Gibran, D. and Yost, C., *Exploring Religious Conflict*. CF-211. Santa Monica, CA: RAND, 2005

Trifkovic, S., *The Sword of the Prophet: Islam, History, Theology, Impact on the World*. Salisbury, MA: Regina Orthodox Press, 2002

Tujan, A., Gaughran, A. and Mollett, H., 'Development and the "Global War on Terror" '. *Race and Class*, 46, July 2004, pp. 53–74

Turman, J., *Spoils of War: The Human Cost of America's Arms Trade*. New York: Free Press, 2005

Tyerman, C., *Fighting for Christendom: Holy War and the Crusades*. Oxford: Oxford University Press, 2004

Tyerman, C., *God's War: A New History of the Crusades*. London: Allen Lane, 2006

United Nations, *In Larger Freedom: Towards Development, Security and Human Rights for All*. Report of the Secretary-General, A/59/2005, 21 March 2005

University of Arizona, Eller College of Management, Artificial Intelligence Lab, *The Dark Web Portal: Collecting and Analyzing the Presence of Domestic and International Terrorist Groups on the Web*. August 2004

U.S. Commission on National Security in the 21st Century [chaired by former US Senators Gary Hart and Warren Rudman] (1999) *New World Coming: American Security in the 21st Century*. September 1999

Van Biezen, I., 'Terrorism and Democratic Legitimicy: Conflicting Interpretations of the Spanish Elections'. *Mediterranean Politics*, 10(1), March 2005, pp. 99–108

Vanhanen, T., 'Domestic Ethnic Conflict and Ethnic Nepotism: A Comparative Analysis'. *Journal of Peace Research*, 36, January 1999, pp. 55–73

Vignard, K. (ed.), 'Human Rights, Human Security and Disarmament'. *Disarmament Forum*, no. 3, 2004

Viorst, M., *In the Shadow of the Prophet: The Struggle for the Soul of Islam*. Boulder, CO: Westview Press, 2001

Volgy, T.J., Kanthak, K., Frazier, D. et al., *Resistance to Hegemony within the Core: Domestic Politics, Terrorism, and Policy Divergence within the G7*. Pittsburgh: Ridgeway Center for International Security Studies at the University of Pittsburgh, 2005

Volmann, W.T., *Rising Up and Rising Down: Some Thoughts on Violence, Freedom and Urgent Means*. London: HarperCollins, 2005

Volpi, F. (ed.), *Transnational Islam and Regional Security*. London: Routledge, 2008

Walker, R.J.B., 'Lines of Insecurity: International, Imperial, Exceptional'. *Security Dialogue*, 37, March 2006, pp. 65–82

Walton, C.D., 'The West and Its Antagonists: Culture, Globalization, and the War on Terrorism'. *Comparative Strategy*, 23, 2004, pp. 303–312

Wark, W.K., *Twenty-First Century Intelligence*. London: Routledge, 2004

Weede, E., 'On Political Violence and Its Avoidance'. *Acta Politica*, 39(2), July 2004, pp. 152–178

Weinberg, L., 'Elections and Violence'. In D. Rapoport and L. Weinberg (eds), *The Democratric Experience and Political Violence*. London: Frank Cass, 2001

Weiner, T., *Legacy of Ashes: The History of the CIA*. New York: Doubleday, 2007

Weiss, W.M., *Islam*. Hauppauge, NY: Barron's, 2000

Westad, O.A., *The Global Cold War: Third World Intervention and the Making of Our Times*. Cambridge: Cambridge University Press, 2006

Wiebes, C., *Intelligence and the War in Bosnia, 1992–1995*. Münster: Lit Verlag, 2003

Wiebes, C. and Aid, M.M., *Secrets of Signals [Intelligence] during The Cold War and Beyond*. London: Frank Cass, 2001

Wiemken, U., 'Betrachtungen zum Risikobegriff'. *Europäische Sicherheit*, December 2004, pp. 8–12

Wiener, S.W. and Hoffman, R.S., 'Nerve Agents: A Comprehensive Review'. *Journal of Intensive Care Medicine*, 19, January 2004, pp. 22–37

Wijk, R. de and Toxopeus, R., 'Hoe binnen- en buitenlandse veiligheid verweven zijn'. *Internationale Spectator*, 59(7–8), July–August 2005, pp. 421–425

Wilkinson, P., *International Relations: A Very Short Introduction*. Oxford: Oxford University Press, 2007

Williams, P.D., *Security Studies: An Introduction*. London: Routledge, 2008

Willis, H.H., Morral, A.R., Kelly, T.K. and Medby, J.J., *Estimating Terrorism Risk*. Santa Monica, CA: RAND, 2005

Wilshire, B.W., *Get 'Em All! Kill 'Em! Genocide, Terrorism, Righteous Communities*. Lanham, MD: Lexington Books, 2005

Wimmer, A., Goldstone, R., Horowitz, D.L., Joras, U. and Schetter, C., *Facing Ethnic Conflicts: Toward a New Realism*. Lanham, MD: Rowman & Littlefield, 2004

WINEP, *Security Reform and Peace: The Three Pillars of U.S. Strategy in the Middle East: Report of the Presidential Study Group*. Washington, DC: Washington Institute for Near East Policy, 2005

Winter, J., *Dreams of Peace and Freedom: Utopian Movements in the Twentieth Century*. Westport, CT: Yale University Press, 2006

Woo, G., 'Quantitative Terrorism Risk Assessment'. *Journal of Risk Finance*, 4(1), 2002, pp. 7–14

Wozniak, J.F., 'Toward a Theoretical Model of Peacemaking Criminology: An Essay in Honor of Richard Quinney'. *Crime Delinquency*, 48, April 2002, pp. 204–231

Yadgar, Y., 'A Myth of Peace: "The Vision of the New Middle East" and Its Transformations in the Israeli Political and Public Spheres'. *Journal of Peace Research*, 43, May 2006, pp. 297–312

Yetiv, S.A., *Crude Awakenings: Global Oil Security and American Foreign Policy*. Ithaca, NY: Cornell University Press, 2004

Zartman, I.W., *Cowardly Lions: Missed Opportunities to Prevent Deadly Conflict and State Collapse*. Boulder, CO: Lynne Rienner, 2005

Zisk Marten, K., *Enforcing the Peace: Learning from the Imperial Past*. New York: Colombia University Press, 2004

10

GLOSSARY AND ABBREVIATIONS OF TERMS AND CONCEPTS RELATING TO TERRORISM AND COUNTER-TERRORISM

Alex P. Schmid

AAA Alianza Anticommunista Argentina/Argentinan Anti-Communist Alliance, aka Triple A. Vigilante death squads created by the Isabel Peron government, active in Argentina between 1974 and 1976, linked to police and collaborating with the military. It was a precursor to the 'dirty war' of the Argentinean military.

AAIA Aden Abyan Islamic Army/Jaysh Adan-Abiyan al-Islami, aka Islamic Army of Aden (IAA), Army of Mohammed and the Jaish Adan Al Islami, Jaysh Adan, Muhammed's Army. It is a Salafist group that emerged in 1998, supporting Al-Qaeda and opposing the Yemeni government.

AAMB Al-Aqsa Martyrs Brigades (Palestine).

AANLA All Adivasi National Liberation Army (India).

ABB Alex Boncayao Brigade, aka Revolutionary Proletarian Army, Alex Boncayao Brigade, Red Scorpion Group. Hit squad of Communist Party of the Philippines' New People's Army, established in 1984. Later also fighting the NPA. The Brigade signed a truce with the government's armed forces in 2000.

Abdul Rahim al-Nasheri Full name Abdul Rahim Mohammed Hussein Abd al-Nasheri. Al-Nasheri was a senior leader of Al-Qaeda and head of Al-Qaeda operations on the Arabian Peninsula. He was also the mastermind behind the botched suicide attack against the USS *The Sullivans* in January 2000 and the successful suicide attack against the USS *Cole* in October 2000. He also organised the suicide attack on the tanker *Limburg* in October 2002. His interest in maritime strikes earned him the nickname 'Prince of the Sea'. In November 2002, he was arrested on Yemeni territory and handed over to US authorities. He is currently detained at an unknown location. In September 2004, he was sentenced to death *in absentia* by a Yemeni court for his role in the USS *Cole* attack.

ABSDF All Burma Students' Democratic Front. Founded in 1988 by Burmese students living abroad who opposed the military dictatorship of Myanmar. Some terrorist attacks committed in its name are reportedly more likely the work of agents provocateurs of the regime.

Abu Al-rish Brigades Aka Ahmed Abu al-Rish Brigades, Fatah Hawks, al-Reish Brigades (Gaza). A splinter group of Al-Fatah which has been active since 1993 moving towards Hamas.

Abu Hafs al-Masari Brigade Name of the group claiming responsibility for March 2004 Madrid train bombings; the same group also claimed responsibility for the 7 July 2005 London transport system bombings. Associated with Al-Qaeda.

Abu Nidal Organisation See ANO.

Abu Sayyaf Group See ASG.

ACF Adivasi Cobra Force, aka Adivasi Cobra Militant Force (Assam, India). Group based on ethnic Santhals in Assam, formed in 1996 in response to ethnic cleansing by the rival Bodo ethnic group. It signed a ceasefire with the Indian government in 2001.

Achille Lauro Italian cruise liner hijacked by four members of a faction of the Palestine Liberation Front (PLF) on 7 October 1985 in the port of Port Said, Egypt. Ninety-seven passengers were held hostage, and one of them, US citizen Leon Klinghoffer, was killed. After protracted negotiations with Italian, Egyptian and Syrian authorities, the four hijackers agreed to end their action and to leave the ship two days later. A boat took them aboard in Egyptian waters near Port Said. It later emerged that their original intention might have been to attack Ashdod, Israel, which would have been the next port of call after Port Said.

Active cadre Those members of an insurgent group who are directly involved in carrying out attacks.

Active measure Operations to influence policies of other states and organisations, including disinformation, forgery, blackmail and the use of front organisations.

Activist A member of a political movement who goes beyond subscribing to the goals of a programme, taking active steps to implement it.

AD Action Directe/Direct Action, aka GBGPGS. Small left-wing French group active 1979–1989, originating from elements of GARI (Revolutionary Action Group) and the Maoist NAPAP (New Arms for Popular Autonomy), attacking both national French and international (NATO) targets, cooperating with German RAF.

Aden-Abyan Islamic Army Yemen-based group, linked to Al-Qaeda, responsible for suicide attack on the USS *Cole* in October 2000 in the port of Aden.

ADF Allied Democratic Forces (Uganda, Congo).

ADM Atomic demolition munitions. These are suitcase- or backpack-format, man-portable, low-yield nuclear devices weighing less than 75 pounds (about 34 kilos). They were developed by the United States and Soviet Union during the Cold War for sabotage operations behind enemy lines. The United States developed about 300 special atomic demolition munitions (SADM) 'backpacks', apparently based on its W-54 warhead. The Soviet Union reportedly developed two types of suitcase bombs.

ADS Anti Democratic Struggle (Greece).

AES Arms and explosives search.

AFGC Armed Forces Revolutionary Council. A Sierra Leon-based military regime, including RUF warlords and, post-1997, the West Side Boys.

Afghanis The name used for international, mainly Arab, veterans from the Afghan liberation struggle against Soviet occupation, 1978–1989, as well as those who later received training and ideological indoctrination by Osama bin Laden and others.

Agent provocateur Literally, 'provoking agent': person infiltrated into the adversary camp to provoke compromising actions, including terrorist attacks, so that the blame can be placed with the adversary and the incident can serve as a pretext for retaliation or intervention.

Aggression In common parlance, an unprovoked act of violence. In social science, 'aggression' is a motivational construct (conceived as either 'impulse', 'drive' or 'attitude') which may, together with other motivations, give rise to 'aggressive behaviours'. Some 'aggressive behaviours' fall under the label 'violent behaviours', involving harming and destruction. Much violent behaviour, especially in politics, is not aggressively motivated but is purposely calculated, instrumental acts. In other words, there can be aggression without violence, just as there can be violence without aggression. In the field of international relations, the General Assembly of the United Nations defined aggression in 1974 as the 'use of force by a state against the sovereignty, territorial integrity or political independence of another state, or in any manner inconsistent with the "Charter of the United Nations"'.

Agitational terror The use of terrorist methods to start an insurgency.

Agro-terrorism A term created to describe terrorist attacks on food supply chain; like cyber-terrorism, it is more a theoretical than a practical reality.

AI Ansar al-Islam/Followers of Islam. A Kurdish Sunni Islamist group formed in December 2001 to fight against other, more secular Kurdish groups such as the Patriotic Union of Kurdistan.

AIAI Al-Ittihad al-Islami/Islamic Union (Somalia). Islamist group formed in the late 1980s that strives for Islamic states in both Somalia and Ethiopia's Ogaden region; also active in Kenya, where it assisted Al-Qaeda in the attack on the US embassy in August 1988.

AIIB Anti-Imperialist International Brigade, aka Japanese Red Army (JRA). It was active in Europe and the Middle East between 1986 and 1988.

Air marshal Armed security guard travelling incognito with airline passengers and trained to neutralise hijackers in mid-air.

AIS Armée Islamique du Salut/Islamic Salvation Army, aka Front Islamique du Salut. Algerian Islamic insurgent group created by the FIS in July 1994 to avoid further defection of members to the GIA in the fight against the Algerian regime, which had cancelled elections in January 1992 that the FIS was poised to win. The AIS ceased activities in 1997.

AIS Automated identification system. Mandatory since December 2004, AIS is a maritime security device enabling ports and maritime law enforcement agencies to track vessels in coastal waters, and a maritime safety device meant to assist ship masters to prevent collisions in congested waters. As an open system, AIS information can (or could?) be received or monitored by anybody with an AIS receiver – including pirates and terrorists.

AIZ Antiimperialistische Zellen/Anti-Imperialist Cells (German Federal Republic). Amateur successor group to RAF, formed in 1994, active until 1996.

AJ Al-Jihat, aka Egyptian al-Jihad, New Jihad, Egyptian Islamic Jihad, Jihad Group. Islamist group active since 1979 in Egypt and abroad, responsible for assassination of the Egyptian president Anwar Sadat in 1981. Split into two factions, one led by Ayman al-Zawahiri and the other (also called Vanguards of Conquest) by Ahmad Husayn Agiza.

AJAI Al Jama'a Al Islamia. The Egyptian terrorist group responsible for the 1993 attack on the World Trade Center.

AK-KKK American Knights of the Ku Klux Klan. Racist US group active in the 1990s.

AK-47 Abbreviation for an automatic high-velocity Soviet rifle developed by Mikhail Kalashnikov in the 1940s.

ALA Armée pour la Libération Nationale/National Liberation Army. The guerrilla arm of the Algerian FLN (1954–1962).

ALA Armenian Liberation Army, aka JCAG (q.v.).

Al-Aarifeen Aka Al-Arifeen Squad. Kashmiri separatist group that emerged in 2002 and, according to some sources, is a front for Lashkar-e-Taiba.

Al-Aqsa Brigade Aka al-Aqsa. Palestinian group, linked to Al-Fatah, active in the West Bank, Gaza and inside Israel.

Al-Asifa Literally, 'the storm'. Name used for the armed wing of the Fatah movement, active since the mid-1960s.

Al-Badhr Al-Badhr Mujahidin (Pakistan). Name of the group originally created by Pakistan's ISI, involved in the genocide in Bangladesh in 1971. In the 1980s, a group called Al-Badr, supported by the ISI, fought the Soviets in Afghanistan under Gulbuddin Hekmatyar. In 1999, an Al-Nasireen (q.v.) group calling itself Al Badr crossed the Line of Control into Indian Kashmir and fought Indian forces until the ceasefire in July 2000.

Al-Bara Malek Brigades Suicide bomb group operating in Iraq and Jordan since 2005; linked to the Al-Zarqawi network.

Al-Barq 'The lightning'. Kashmiri separatist group active since 1978, linked until 2000 to the Jammu and Kashmir People's Conference Party. Then it joined the Kashmir Freedom Force. It trains foreign Islamic militants in its camps.

Al-Dawa Hizb al Dawa al Islamiyya/Islamic Call Party. Shi'ite Iraqi group opposed to Ba'ath rule founded in the late 1960s and backed by Ayatollah Khomeini's regime in Iran.

Aleph Successor to AUM (q.v.).

Alert A state of readiness to repel anticipated harmful action. Several alert levels are distinguished. In the United Kingdom there are five: (1) low – meaning an attack is unlikely; (2) moderate – an attack is possible, but not likely; (3) substantial – an attack is a strong possibility; (4) severe – an attack is highly likely; (5) critical – an attack is expected imminently. The US advisory system, created after 11 September 2001, also consists of five levels: 'low', or green; 'guarded', or blue; 'elevated', or yellow; 'high', or orange; and 'severe', or red.

Alex Boncayao Brigade (ABB) Philippine group led by Felimon Lagman, linked to the Communist Party (NPA) and later to the Revolutionary Proletarian Army (RPA); held responsible for a series of assassinations since 1984.

ALF Arab Liberation Front. This Palestinian group was founded in 1969 by Iraqi Ba'ath Party members; a proxy of the Iraqi government, active until 1986; later supporting families of Palestinian suicide bombers.

ALF Animal Liberation Front. Name used for militant and sometimes violent groups defending animal rights.

Al-Fatah Reverted acronym for Harekat al-Tahrir al-Wataniyyeh al-Filastiniyyeh, aka Al-Asifa, Conquest, Palestinian National Liberation Movement. A secular organisation founded in Kuwait in 1957, led from 1964 until 2004 by Yasser Arafat. Became the main military arm of the PLO after 1967; based in Jordan and later Lebanon, the West Bank and Gaza. In 1993, in the Oslo Accords, it renounced the use of violence, but the Al-Aqua (Martyr) Brigades and the Fatah-Tanzim acted in the second Intifada as its violent arm, engaging in suicide attacks. A group with same name also exists in Jammu and Kashmir, seeking accession of this state to Pakistan.

Al-Gama'a al-Islamiyya Islamic group founded in the 1970s, numbering more than 1,000 members in 2001, active in south Egypt, with links with Al-Qaeda. Sheikh Abdul Raman, involved in the 1993 World Trade Center bombing, is considered its spiritual leader.

ALIR Army for the Liberation of Rwanda, aka Democratic Front for the Liberation of Rwanda (FDLR), ex-FAR (Armed Forces of Rwanda), Interahamwe. It was formed by former Hutu genociders in 1994.

Al-Islambouli Brigades of Al-Qaeda Aka Islambouli Brigade of Martyrs, Platoon of Martyr Khaled Islambouli, al-Islambouli Brigades, al-Qaeda Organisation (Pakistan). Group reportedly led by Muhammad Shawqi al-Islambouli (brother of the murderer of Egyptian president Anwar Sadat in 1981), who served Bin Laden in Peshawar in the 1980s; active since 1995 in Pakistan.

Al-Jamal's al-Islamiyah al-Umatilla al Libya Libyan Islamic Fighting Group. The group was founded in 1995.

Al-Jihad AJ (q.v.). Egyptian Islamist group led by Ayman Zawahiri; merged with Al-Qaeda in the late 1990s.

All Burma Students' Democratic Front See ABSDF.

Alliance of Eritrean Forces Coalition of armed groups formed in 1999, numbering 3,000, aiming to overthrow the Eritrean government.

Allied Democratic Front Uganda allied democratic army. Group numbering 500 (2001) established in 1996, seeking to introduce a regime based on Shari'ah law in Uganda.

Al-Mansoorain (India) Name assumed by a Pakistan-backed Kashmir and Jammu separatist group that emerged in 2003; probably a front for Lashkar-e-Taiba (LeT).

Al-Muhajiroun Exiled Islamic group founded in 1983 by Syrian Sheik Omar Bakri Mohammed, who, after his expulsion from Saudi Arabia, preached at Finsbury Park mosque in London before his expulsion from the United Kingdom. Banned in the UK in 2005.

Al-Muqatile Libyan group founded by Afghani veterans linked to Al-Qaeda.

ALN Armée de Libération Nationale/National Liberation Army. This is the armed wing of the Algerian National Liberation Front (FLN), which wrested independence from France between 1954 and 1962.

ALN Armata di Liberazione Naziunale/Army of National Liberation (France). A Corsican separatist group active between 1970 and 2002.

Al-Nasireen Kashmir-based group.

Al-Nawaz Pakistani group.

ALQ Armée de Libération Québecois/Liberation Army of Quebec.

Al-Qaeda (Arabic for 'the base'), aka Al-Qaida, Qa'idat al-Jihad, the Islamic Army, the World Islamic Front for Jihad against Jews and Crusaders, the Islamic Army for the Liberation of the Holy Places, the Group for the Preservation of the Holy Sites, the Islamic Salvation Foundation, the Osama bin Laden Organisation/Network. Salafist jihad network of Sunni Arab and Muslim militants, some of whom fought the Soviet Union in Afghanistan, with followers from many countries. The original 'Afghan Arabs' were organised by Osama bin Laden, his Palestinian mentor Abdullah Azzam and Abu Ubaydah al-Banshiri around 1988. Several thousand volunteers are said to have been trained by Al-Qaeda and later surfaced in wars, insurgencies and resistance movements in Algeria, Armenia (Nagorno-Karabakh), Bosnia-Herzegovina, Chechnya, Egypt, Kashmir, Lebanon and the Philippines. Al-Qaeda merged with the Egyptian Islamic Jihad of Al-Zawahiri in 1998, and is held responsible for more than 50 attacks (and more than 800 if those of its affiliates and self-starters acting under the Al-Qaeda banner are counted), including the attacks on two US embassies in East Africa in 1998 and on the World Trade Center and the Pentagon in the United States on 11 September 2001. It opposes both the 'near enemy' (un-Islamic regimes and apostate rulers) and the 'far enemy' (the United States and its allies). It supports, by training and the dispatch of fighters, groups wanting to establish their own state in Palestine, Chechnya, Dagestan and Mindanao, and groups opposing repressive regimes said to exist in Kosovo, India, Russia and Indonesia. Its primary goal is to neutralise the US and Western presence in the Arab peninsula, the Gulf and Iraq and to capture Jerusalem. Its maximalist goal is to establish a pan-Islamic caliphate throughout the Muslim world, from Morocco to the Philippines. It is estimated that its core membership consists of a few hundred in Pakistan and a few dozen in Afghanistan (2010) with many more followers in dozens of other countries, e.g. Yemen. The original network of Al-Qaeda, which had trained thousands of Mujahedin since the 1980s, was severely disrupted after the US intervention (Operation Enduring Freedom) in Afghanistan. Al-Qaeda became, to some extent, also a brand label adopted by self-starting cells with little or no links to the original Al-Qaeda. One of its 'trade marks' is simultaneous attacks aiming to create mass casualties among its multiple enemies. According to a fatwa of 28 February 1998 of the World Islamic Front for Jihad it is 'the duty of all Muslims to kill US citizens – civilians or military – and their allies everywhere'.

Al-Qaeda Organisation in the Land of the Two Rivers Tanzim Qa'idat al-Jihad fi Bilad al-Rafidayn, aka Monotheism and Holy Struggle, Organisation of Jihad's Base in the Country of the Two Rivers, Tawhid and Jihad, Al-Qaeda in Iraq, Al-Zarqawi network. The organisation was formed in 2004 by Abu Musab Zarqawi, consisting of foreign terrorists, indigenous Sunni Iraqis and members of the Kurdish Islamist group Ansar al-Islam. In addition to opposing the Coalition forces, the group tries to provoke civil war between Shi'ah and Sunnis, and has also staged attacks in Jordan. Following the 'surge' of American troops in 2007 and the 'Awakening' of Iraqi indigenous forces originally opposed to the American presence, Al-Qaeda in Iraq had lost most of its influence by 2010.

Al-Qanoon Literally, 'the law'. A Pakistani group that emerged in 2002.

Al-Sabbah, Hassan ibn Founder of the eleventh-century sect of the Assassins in the Near East.

Al-Sai'qa 'The thunderbolt', aka Eagles of the Palestinian Revolution. Palestinian group founded in 1968 and linked to, and probably controlled by, the Syrian army and Ba'ath Party; also operating under the name 'Eagles of the Palestinian Revolution'. It was active until the mid-1980s; part of the PLO.

Al-Tahrir Al-Islami Aka Hizb al Tahrir al Islami/Islamic Liberation Party. This was an Egyptian fundamentalist group emerging from the Muslim Brotherhood, founded by Sheikh Takieddin Nabhani in exile in Jordan.

Al-Takfir and Al-Hijra Literally, 'excommunication and exile'. Extremist Islamist sect dedicated to the restoration of the caliphate. Members include Ayman al-Zawahiri.

Al-Tawhid Islamic group linked to al-Zarqawi and the Al-Qaeda network.

Amal Afwaj al Muqawama al Lubnaniya/Lebanese Resistance Detachments; *amal* also means 'hope' in Arabic, aka Movement of Hope. Military arm of the Lebanese Movement of the Disinherited, a Shi'ite party formed in 1975, first supported by Iran and later by Syria.

Ambush Surprise attack at a prepared location against a moving adversary, usually with secret escape routes.

Amir/Emir Arab for 'lord', chief, a figure of power in Islam; title also used for the chief of Islamist groups.

Amir-ul-Momineen Commander of the Faithful. Title assumed by Mullah Mohammed Omar, leader of the Afghan Taliban.

Amnesty Literally, 'oblivion'. Act of state to pardon political or criminal offenders, cancelling or reducing the length of a prison term, or suspending prosecution, often in order to achieve reconciliation; sometimes linked to conditions.

AMR Al Madina Regiment; India, Kashmir, linked to LeT (q.v.).

AN Avanguardia Nazionale. Italian right-wing group reportedly founded in 1959 by Stefano Delle Chiaie, part of the 'Black Orchestra' of other right-wing groups in Western Europe; merged in 1973, after a failed *coup d'état* in 1970, with the 'Black Order'.

AN Aryan Nations. White right-wing racist group founded by Richard Butler in the 1970s; part of the Christian Identity movement in the United States.

ANA Albanian National Army. Former Yugoslav Republic (FYR) of Macedonia-based group formed in 2002, allegedly striving for a unification of Albanians in the Balkans, but criminal in nature.

ANAL Ammonium nitrate and aluminium (improvised explosive device).

Ananda Marga Path of Eternal Bliss, aka the Ananda Marga Yoga Society, the Universal Army, Black Order. Violent Hindu group founded by Prabhat Ranjan Sarkar in 1955, banned in 1975, active at home and abroad (especially in Australia) until the late 1970s.

Anarchism Literally, 'non-rule'. Political movement rejecting political authority and advocating the replacement of the state by a federally structured organisation of commune- and syndicate-based society founded on voluntary cooperation and free association of emancipated individuals for mutual benefit. While many anarchists were reformists preaching non-violence, others in the late nineteenth century and later used knives, guns and bombs to attack representatives of the state and the bourgeoisie, and thereby contributed to the emergence of modern non-state terrorism. The concept of 'propaganda of the deed' (q.v.) was also one of their contributions to terrorism.

Anarchy In international relations theory, the absence of a (strong) supra-state ruling body to regulate and enforce state compliance with international norms.

ANC African National Congress. South African black political party founded in 1912, non-violent until 1961. It created the armed wing Umkhonto we Sizwe/Spear of the Nation. Except for a number of attacks in the 1980s, ANC did not engage in widespread terrorism. It became the governing party under Nelson Mandela when apartheid ended in 1994.

ANFO Ammonium nitrate and fuel oil: the primary ingredient in most fertilisers, although the amount of ammonium nitrate (AN) in fertilisers has been reduced in recent years. AN is mixed with motor oil or diesel fuel to make ANFO, one of the simplest improvised explosive devices.

Among the high explosives, ANFO has one of the lowest detonation velocities, approximately 1,097 metres/second (3,600 feet/second). ANFO requires a very powerful initiator to begin detonation. The mixture of AN and diesel fuel is used as a blasting device in car and truck bombs, as in 1993 at the World Trade Center or, in 1995, outside the Oklahoma City Federal Building.

Angry Brigade Left-wing/anarchist militant British student group, active 1968–1971.

Animal Liberation Front (ALF) Single-issue group within a broader animal liberation movement that emerged in the mid-1970s, especially in the United Kingdom and in the United States, engaging in vandalism, sabotage, intimidation and occasionally terrorism.

Anni di Piombo Italian; literally, 'years of the bullet'. Period in Italian politics (1969–1981) when left- and right-wing armed groups' violence was most intense.

ANNIE Ammonium nitrate and nitrobenzene.

ANO Abu Nidal Organisation, aka Fatah Revolutionary Council (FRC), Black June/Black September, Arab Revolutionary Brigades, Revolutionary Organisation of Socialist Muslims. ANO is the name given to various groups commanded by Sabri al-Banna (*nom de guerre*: Abu Nidal), who split from Al-Fatah in 1974 and was killed in August 2002 in Baghdad, presumably by Saddam Hussein.

ANS Aktionsfront Nationale Sozialisten/National Socialist Action Front. German right-wing party founded by Mike Kühnen in 1977, banned in 1983.

ANS Ammonium nitrate and sugar.

Ansar al-Islam Literally, 'followers of Islam'. An Islamist group founded in 2001 in northern Iraq, reportedly affiliated to, and funded and trained by, Al-Qaeda, fighting Coalition forces and advocating an Islamic state in all of Iraq.

Ansar Allah Followers of Allah (Lebanon). A group linked to Hezbollah, responsible for the July 1994 attack against the Argentinan Israeli Mutual Aid Association. It is currently reportedly led by the Syrian-backed former Hezbollah secretary-general Sobhi Tufaili.

Ansar al-Sunnah Army Followers of the Tradition Army (Iraq). This Sunni Jihadist group has been active since 2003 against Coalition forces and their local allies.

Ansbat al-Ansar Lebanese-based Al-Qaeda affiliate.

Anthrax Caused by *Bacillus anthracis*. A blood-poisoning disease of cattle and sheep caused by a bacillus that affects people through inhalation and can be lethal (anthrax pulmonary). Used as a military weapon in the twentieth century. Used in letters in autumn 2001 in the United States presumably by US Army microbiologist Bruce E. Ivins killing five persons.

Anti-abortion groups Single-issue groups, often religiously motivated, attacking clinics and doctors performing abortions.

Anti-American Arab Liberation Front Name used to claim responsibility for bombing of La Belle discotheque in Berlin on 5 April 1986, for which Libya was held responsible by the United States.

Anti-Globalisation Movement Broad and mixed array of groups opposing worldwide free market trends; some of them are violent; a few of them also employ terrorist tactics.

Anti-Semitism Dislike of and/or hatred towards Jews, based on religious, economic or racial grounds; widespread in certain periods of European history, especially under Nazism.

Anti-terrorism Preventive and defensive measures against terrorism such as target hardening and enhanced patrolling. The term is sometimes used next to 'counter-terrorism', a term that is broader, including also active and offensive (both pre-emptive and retaliatory) measures to suppress terrorism.

ANYOLP Arab National Youth Organisation for the Liberation of Palestine, aka Arab Nationalist Youth for the Liberation of Palestine (ANYLP), Seventh Suicide Squad (Libya). Short-lived group created by the Libyan regime in 1973, targeting American and Israeli aviation.

APDF Al-Ahwaz Arab People's Democratic Front, aka Al-Ahwaz Arab Popular Democratic Front, Arab People's Democratic Front. This is a separatist group that emerged in 2005, striving for the independence of Khuzestam, an oil-rich region in Iran inhabited by Arabs.

APEC Asia-Pacific Economic Cooperation.

APG Asia-Pacific Group on Money Laundering.

Appeasement Literally, 'pacifying' (an opponent). Originally the word was used to characterise British policy towards the expansionist policy of Nazism, which only emboldened Hitler to grab more territory. The term is now used for any likely-to-fail policy of accommodation vis-à-vis an aggressive opponent. Yielding to the demands of an unreasonable opponent in order to avoid open conflict at any price tends to invite repetition of demands ('salami tactics')

AQ Al-Qaeda (q.v.).

AQAP Al-Qaeda in the Arabian Peninsula (Saudi Arabia). This group emerged in 2004.

AQB Al-Qassam Brigades (Palestine).

AQI Al-Qaeda in Iraq.

AQM Al-Quds Brigades (Palestine).

ARA Armenian Revolutionary Army. It was a nationalist group calling for an independent Armenian state on Turkish territory. It emerged in 1970 and was active until 1985; it had an overlapping membership with the JCAG.

ARA Aryan Resistance Army. This was a neo-Nazi group active in the US Midwest between 1994 and 1996.

Arab Liberation Front PLO faction formed by Iraq's Ba'ath Party, numbering some 300 members by 2001.

Arab Revolutionary Brigade One of the names used by the Abu Nidal Organisation (see ANO).

Arab Struggle Movement for the Liberation of Ahvaz (Iran) Separatist group in the oil-rich province of Ahvaz whose members feel discriminated against by the Iranian government; emerged in 2006.

Arabian Sea (Western) part of the northern Indian Ocean situated between the western coast of South Asia (India, Pakistan, Iran) and East Africa.

Arabs People from Arab-speaking countries centred on Saudi Arabia and stretching into North Africa, including, in particular, Syria, Lebanon, Jordan, Egypt, Libya and Sudan; most of them of Islamic faith.

ARB Armée Révolutionaire Bretonne/Breton Revolutionary Army. Armed group formed in 1998, fighting for the independence of Brittany from France.

ARC Action pour la Renaissance de la Corse/Corsican Renaissance Action.

ARENA Alianza Republicana Nacional/National Republican Alliance, aka Anti Communist Front. This is a right-wing Salvadorean political party, some members of which were linked to death squad activities in the 1980s; founded in 1982 by Maj. Roberto D'Aubuisson.

Argentinian Anti-Communist Alliance See AAA.

ARGK Arteshen Rizgariya Gelli Kurdistan/People's Liberation Army of Kurdistan, aka Kurdistan National Liberty Army, People's Defence Force. This group was formed in 1984 as the military wing of the PKK (q.v.). It killed many of the over 30,000 civilians who died from political violence in Turkey in the 1980s.

Armageddon Biblical reference to the place where the final, decisive battle between the forces of good and evil will be fought before Judgement Day.

Armalite Assault rifle, used by both terrorists and security forces.

Armed attack An offensive act of violence carried out by (or on behalf of) an organised armed group or military and police forces with the object of weakening or destroying an opponent.

Armed conflict Originally, combat between forces both possessing weapons of war. The term is now used more broadly for various types of violent confrontations between state and/or non-state actors (private, illegal, unsanctioned, non-recognised, or criminal), sometimes preceded by failure to solve conflict by peaceful or non-violent means. While interstate armed conflicts have become exceptional, clashes between armed non-state actors or between state and non-state actors have increased since the end of the Cold War in many parts of the world.

Armed forces Legal military uniformed troops of recognised states.

Armed Islamic Front for the Jihad Armed wing of the Algerian Islamic Salvation Front (FIS, q.v.). It was mainly active between 1992 and 1999.

Armed Islamic Group See GIA.

Armenian Secret Army for the Liberation of Armenia (ASALA) Marxist group founded in the mid-1970s which attacks Turkish targets at home and abroad in protest of the Turkish denial of what ASALA and others regard as the genocide of up to 1.5 million Armenians between 1915 and 1922. ASALA was divided into ASALA-M, an extreme and ASALA-RM, a more moderate wing, and was active until 1997.

Armistice A suspension of military operations by agreement between the opposing belligerent parties (ICRC).

Arms embargo Multilateral agreement to prohibit export of weapons and ammunition to regions of tension or war.

Army Organised, hierarchically structured combat force, usually serving a state and its people for the defence of its own territory. Private 'armies' are held by warlords and guerrilla and terrorist groups, sometimes manned by child soldiers.

Army for the Liberation of Rwanda (ALIR) Congo-based Hutu armed force consisting of members of the former Rwandan armed forces, Interahamwe militias and others opposed to the post-1994 Tutu-dominated government in Rwanda.

Army of God Christian fundamentalist group which has attacked abortion clinics in the United States since 1982.

Arson Malicious and deliberate setting of fire to cause property loss or to endanger lives, e.g. with an incendiary device.

Aryan Nazi race typology category referring to Nordic white non-Jewish people.

Aryan Nations (AN) Aka Church of Aryan Nations, Church of Jesus Christ – Theological Arm. A US neo-Nazi group founded in the 1970s by Richard Butler. Has a sizeable membership in US prisons.

Aryan Republican Army (ARA) US-based white supremacist group known principally for its bank robberies in the 1990s in the Midwest.

AS Al-Shahaab (Somalia), Islamist insurgency groups linked to Al-Qaeda.

ASALA See Armenian Secret Army for the Liberation of Armenia.

Asbat al-Ansar Literally, 'League of the Followers': aka Partisans' League. Sunni-based Lebanese Palestinian group (*c.* 300 strong), emerging around 1990; suspected of links with Al-Qaeda. It was based in 'Ayn al-Hilwah refugee camp near Sidon in southern Lebanon.

ASEAN Association of South East Asian Nations. A regional organisation.

ASG Abu Sayyaf Group (Arabic for 'Bearer of the Sword'). This group, formed in 1991 and based in the southern part of the Philippines, especially Mindanao and the Sulu Islands, was formed by Abdurajak Abubakar Janjalani after his return from Afghanistan. The name was chosen to honour Janjalani's teacher, Abu Sayyaf. After the death of Abdurajak Janjalani in a shoot-out with Philippine police units on 18 December 1998, the group splintered. The largest faction is led by Khaddafy Janjalani, the younger brother of Abdurajak Janjalani. The ASG operates in a grey area between terrorism and organised crime. ASG members are known to cooperate with factions of the much larger Moro Islamic Liberation Front (MILF, q.v.).

Askaris South African government-backed death squad which targeted ANC members during the apartheid period.

Aspergillus flavus Fungus that produces the toxin aflatoxin, which causes cancer. This was produced on a large scale by Saddam Hussein.

Assassination Deliberate and usually premeditated, selective murder by stealth or surprise of a specified high-ranking or prominent person in a leadership position within a community; it can be politically or religiously motivated and is not necessarily terroristic (e.g. tyrannicide would only scare other tyrants). Motives include revenge, punishment, disruption of political process (e.g. peacemaking) and removal of a rival. The victim of such political murder is usually not physically in captivity or under the legal jurisdiction of the perpetrator or his superiors. Assassination is also one of the oldest terrorist tactics and was first developed by Ismaili fedayeen in the late eleventh century ('Hashsishhin' – those under the influence of hashish, according to one etymological interpretation) as a serial tactic for sowing terror. Assassination is only 'terroristic' if the victim is not the primary target but the act serves to generate shock and fear among a wider public. In practice, the distinction is often difficult to make. Series of assassinations tend to be terroristic, even when they are in themselves discriminate.

Assassins A radical Shi'ite Ismaili brotherhood/sect, commanded by Hasan-Dan-Sabah, the 'Old Man in the Mountains', who waged a campaign of murder against 'servants of the unrighteous' in Persia and Syria in the twelfth and thirteenth centuries.

Assault Attack on (a group of) persons, often with ad hoc weapons (sticks, bricks, stones), usually resulting in injury but sometimes leading to death. Also used for attacks with (machine) guns.

Asset Resource, instrument at the disposal of an organisation.

ASU Active Service Unit (cell of the Irish Republican Army (see IRA).

Asymmetric warfare Indirect strategy of insurgents who target a militarily superior adversary outside any battlefield, often with disregard for the rules of warfare, using unconventional weapons and tactics, including terrorism. For example, a suicide terrorist bomber would be the substitute for lack of an air force.

ATA (US) Anti-Terrorism Assistance. Technical support programme to enhance counter-terrorist capabilities of allies of the United States in the war on terrorism.

ATMM Akhil Terai Mukti Morcha-Abinash, Nepal.

Atomic bomb The most powerful explosive weapon, generating a blast, heat and radiation. Two main types are used, fission bombs (uranium or plutonium based) and fusion bombs (hydrogen based). It takes about 7 kg of plutonium (Pu), 10 kg of plutonium oxide (PuO_2), 25 kg of metallic uranium (U-235), 35 kg of highly enriched uranium oxide (UO_2) or somewhere around 200 kg of intermediately enriched uranium oxide (UO_2) to build a crude atomic bomb. U-233 is also a possible basis for an atomic bomb. In a uranium-235 fission bomb, two subcritical masses are shot towards each other with conventional explosives, whereby neutrons trigger a chain reaction, releasing energy. In a plutonium bomb a subcritical mass of plutonium-239 is packed with a mantle of explosives that condense a heavy layer of inert tamping metal which passes the impulse on to the plutonium core, which in turn becomes critical and enters a series of chain reactions whereby a beryllium layer reflects the neutrons. Thermonuclear fusion bombs produce more energy. A fusion of the hydrogen isotopes deuterium and tritium is brought about with an atomic bomb as initial energiser. In fact, the hydrogen bomb is a fission–fusion–fission bomb. The lethality of nuclear explosives is awesome. If a 20-kiloton nuclear fission weapon exploded on Wall Street at noon on a business day it could, in the estimate of T. Taylor, kill about one million people. Hydrogen bombs are many times more powerful.

Atomic demolition munitions See ADMs.

Atrocity Violent behaviour and its outcome which violate human norms, creating a shock and arousing a sense of horror among direct or indirect witnesses.

ATTF All Tripura Tiger Force, aka 'All Tripura Tribal Force' (India, Tripura). Group formed in 1990, opposing Bengali-speaking immigrants and clashing with the rival NLFT.

ATU Action Against Terrorism Unit. This is a small coordination body of the OSCE.

AU African Union – a regional organisation of more than 50 states with headquarters in Addis Ababa.

AUC Autodefensas Unidas de Colombia/United Self-Defence Forces of Colombia. Right-wing paramilitary organisation (*c.* 8,000 fighters) consolidated in 1997 from existing paramilitary self-defence groups and supported by large landowners and drug lords, led by Carlos Castanos; broke up into several groups in 2003; heavily involved in illicit narcotic drug production and trafficking. Until 1989, it was supported indirectly by the Colombian military. More than 26,000 members disarmed by 2006.

AUM Aum Shinrikyo, aka Aum Supreme Truth, Aleph: 'Supreme Truth', aka Aum and later Aleph. Japanese millenarian cult founded in the mid-1980s by Shoko Asahara, which aimed to 'take over Japan and then the world'; it attempted to buy and construct weapons of mass destruction and launched a sarin attack in March 1995 in the Tokyo subway; numbered 1,500 to 2,000 by 2001.

Authoritarianism Rule 'from above', usually by a traditional elite or military usurper, in disregard of popular consent, often backed up by repression, including gross human rights violations.

AVC ¡Alfaro Vive, Carajo! 'Alfaro Lives, Damnit!'. A left-wing group founded in the late 1970s in Ecuador; except for one faction, it ceased activities after a peace agreement with the government.

Avengers of the Martyrs Government-backed death squad active in Chile after the 1973 *coup d'état* by General Pinochet.

Ayatollah (Senior) Shi'ah Muslim cleric.

Baader–Meinhof Group Aka Red Army Faction/Rote Armee Fraction. German left-wing group which emerged after 1968, led by Andreas Baader, Gudrun Ensslin and Ulrike Meinhof until their suicides in 1977; disbanded in 1998.

Ba'athism *Ba'ath* is Arabic for 'renaissance'. This was a secular Arab nationalist, socialist movement, founded in 1945. It was the ruling party in Syria and in Iraq under Saddam Hussein.

Bab el-Mandeb Arabic for 'Gate of Tears'. Refers to the strait connecting the Red Sea with the Arabian Sea.

Babbar Khalsa Sikh group, based in Amritsar's Golden Temple complex, fighting for an independent Sikh homeland (Khalistan) in the late 1970s and 1980s.

Bacteria Single-cell organisms such as those that cause anthrax, tularaemia, plague, cholera and Q-fever, which can be used in biological warfare.

Bacteriological terrorism See Biological terrorism.

Balance of terror Situation of mutually assured destruction between the United States and Soviat Union during the Cold War, based on nuclear weapons and second-strike capabilities of rivals; this 'pax atomica' (atomic peace) is credited by some with having prevented war between the superpowers.

Bandera Roja Red Flag (Venezuela). Marxist group formed around 1970; some of its members joined the Chávez government after 1998, others opposed it.

Bandit Rebel without a political cause who resorts to robbery, kidnapping or guerrilla-type ambushes and hit-and-run attacks and hides out in inhospitable areas.

Banditry A form of economic parasitism undertaken by ambushes and raids, practised by warlords and criminal gangs.

Barometric bomb Explosive device linked to an altitude meter, triggering an explosion above a certain height. Used by terrorists for mid-air explosions.

Barricade-siege situation When terrorists and hostages are trapped in a building, surrounded by security forces.

Base Camp for training; headquarters from which to initiate activity.

Basque Fatherland and Liberty Euskadi Ta Askatasuna; see ETA.

Battalion 3–16 Government-backed Honduran death squad active in the 1980s.

Battalion of the Martyr Abdullah Azzam Aka Al-Qaeda in the Levant and Egypt, Al-Qaida in Syria and Egypt, Martyr Abdallah Azzam Brigades, Al-Qai-dah organisation – The Land of Al-Sham and Al-Kananah, Tanzim al-Qaida fi Balad ash-Sham wa Ard al-Kinanah. This group is responsible for attacks in tourist centres in the Sinai since 2004.

Battle Concentrated and time-wise and territorially limited combat of military forces of states or guerrilla movements during warfare.

Bay of Bengal (Eastern) part of the northern Indian Ocean situated between the east coast of South Asia (India, Bangladesh, Myanmar) and the western shores of Indonesia (Sumatra).

Beja Congress Established in 1993 and numbering about 500 (2001) fighters, the group claims to control the area around Garoura and Hamshkoraib in eastern Sudan and wants to establish an autonomous Beja state.

Bersatu (Malay for 'united'), aka Ber Satu, Payong Organisation, United Front for the Independence of Pattani (Thailand). A separatist group formed in 1991.

Bhagwan Shree Rajneesh Cult Sect that used food poisoning with salmonella bacteria in 1984 in the Pacific north-west of the United States.

BIMCO Baltic and International Maritime Council. In its own view, it is 'the world's largest shipping organisation'.

Binary weapon Chemical weapon where the last stage of the production process is moved from the factory to the warhead, where the mixing of two, generally non-toxic, precursor substances takes place in flight just before deployment, creating a toxic product. Advantages are that manufacture, storage and transport are much safer for personnel handling binary chemical weapons such as sarin (BG-2), soman (GD-2) and VX (VX-2).

Biological agents Micro-organisms that can cause diseases and death such as pulmonary anthrax, brucellosis, cholera, pneumonic plague, tularaemia, Q-fever, smallpox, arboreal encephalitis, east or west Nile viruses, viral haemorrhagic fever, Ebola, Marburg disease, botulism toxin, saxitoxin, staphylococcal enterotoxin B, ricin, mycotoxins, trichothecine mycotoxin (aka T-2 or 'yellow rain'), glanders, melioidosis, psittacosis typhus, epsion toxin of *Clostridium perfringens*, salmonella, *E. coli*, shigella.

Biological terrorism Use of bacterial and viral and related agents to kill and harm in order to create fear, panic and feelings of helplessness.

Biological warfare Use of weaponised bacteria, viruses, toxins or rickettsiae as a weapon of war and terror.

Biological weapons Among the about 60 known biological micro-organisms suitable for incapacitating an opponent in acts of biological warfare are bacteria, viruses, fungi, rickettsiae and protozoa. They tend to be more lethal than toxic chemical materials but less lethal than nuclear weapons (10 grams of anthrax is said to have the same lethality as 1,000 kilograms of sarin, under optimal dispersion conditions). They are based on biologically produced toxins or pathogenic infectious organisms causing flu-like illnesses, often leading to death after an incubation period of a few days. Small quantities, if properly dispersed at night (or micro-encapsulated to prevent oxygen, dryness or light disabling the substance), can cause several tens of thousands of victims. A more advanced biological weapon is judged to be able to kill or injure hundreds of thousands of people. Detection and the containment of epidemic contagion are major problems owing to the delayed onset of clear symptoms. Biological agents can also be used against animals and crops. They are generally not effectively transmitted by water. Vectors are animals or aerosols.

Bioregulators A new class of weapons that can damage the nervous system, alter moods, trigger psychological changes and even kill, and cannot be traced by pathologists. A Soviet programme called Flute worked on germs and other agents that could be used mainly for political assassinations, according to Kanatjan Alibekov (Ken Alibek), a Soviet defector.

Birmingham Six Group of Irishmen convicted on the basis of fabricated evidence for bombing two pubs in Birmingham in 1974; released in 1991.

BKA Bundeskriminalamt/Federal Office of Criminal Investigations in Germany.

BKI Babbar Khalsa International. Sikh separatist group formed in 1978; suspected by India to be linked to Pakistan's ISI.

BKO Babbar Khalsa Organisation. This is a Canada-based Sikh group seeking an independent Sikh state, Khalistan (Land of the Pure); suspected of involvement in blowing up an Air India passenger plane in 1985.

BLA Baloch Liberation Army, aka Baluchistan Liberation Army. Group formed in 2003; opposes exploitation by Pakistan.

BLA Black Liberation Army (USA). Founded in 1971.

Black Brigades Shi'ite group active in the 1980s in Kuwait and Iraq, linked to Dawa al Islami.

Black Hand Society Nationalist Serbian group linked to the Serbian military; formed in 1908 (1911, according to other sources); responsible for the assassination of Archduke Ferdinand in 1914 which triggered the First World War.

Black Hebrew Israelites African racial supremacist cult active in Florida in the 1980s.

Black Hundreds Anti-Semitic organisation responsible for pogroms against Jews in tsarist Russia.

Black June One of the many *noms de guerre* of the ANO (q.v.), named after the Phalangists' massacre of Palestinians in the Tal az Zatar refugee camp in Lebanon. Its 1982 assassination attempt on the Israeli ambassador to the United Kingdom, Shlomo Argov, triggered the Israeli invasion of Lebanon.

Black Liberation Army US left-wing group, active from the 1960s to the early 1980s, linked to the Black Panther Party.

Black Order Ordine Nero. Neo-fascist Italian group led by Pierluigi Concutelli, held responsible for the 1974 Munich–Bologna train bombing and the 1980 Bologna railway station bombing.

Black Panthers Aka Black Panther Party for Self-Defense. A US militant black left-wing nationalist revolutionary group founded in 1966 by Huey Newton and Bobby Seale, and active until 1972.

Black Panthers The group which, during the first Intifada, was held responsible for killing Palestinians collaborating with Israel.

Black powder The oldest known explosive. Roger Bacon (1220–1292, England) is generally credited with its (re)invention in Europe. However, black powder was known in China in the tenth century, and similar substances were known in ancient Greece. Berthold Schwarz (fourteenth century, Germany) used black powder as a propelling agent. Black powder is a mixture of potassium or sodium nitrate, sulphur and charcoal or carbon. The detonation velocity of black powder is quite low, about 400 metres/second. It is very unstable and is often accidentally ignited. Black powder, having been used as a propellant in firearms for many years, is often called gunpowder. However, modern smokeless gunpowder consists mostly of nitrocellulose (gun cotton).

Black Tiger/Black Sea Tigers Suicide squads of the LTTE; the former committed land attacks, the latter attacks by sea, usually in 'wolf-pack fashion' (several boats used for one concerted attack). The first known operation of the Black Sea Tigers took place on 10 July 1990, when three Black Sea Tigers – Major Kantharuban, Captain Collins and Captain Vinoth – badly damaged the Sri Lankan navy ship *Edithara*.

Black Widows Name given to female Chechen suicide bombers who emerged in 2000.

Blister agents Chemical agent that burns the skin, producing large water blisters that heal slowly and may become infected; cause damage to the eyes, blood cells and respiratory tract. The best-known is mustard gas (bis(2-chloroethyl) sulphide) or Yperite). Another is Lewisite (2-chlorovinyl dichloroarsine), which is often used in combination with mustard gas.

Blood agents Absorbed by breathing, such agents prevent the synthesis of molecules used by the body as energy sources so that vital organs cease to function within 15 minutes. Examples are hydrogen cyanide and pathogenic chloride.

Blood gas Agent that blocks absorption of oxygen in the lungs; a fast-acting surprise weapon.

Bloody Sunday Clash between Irish demonstrators and British paratroopers in Londonderry/Derry on 30 January 1972, in which 13 unarmed protesters and bystanders were killed by the British armed forces.

BLT Bodo Liberation Tigers, aka Boto Liberation Tiger Force, Terrorist Group of Assam. This group was formed in 1986 in Assam, India.

BND Bundesnachrichtendienst/(German) Federal Intelligence Service.

B-NICE Acronym for biological, nuclear, incendiary, chemical and explosive, used for identifying five main categories of terrorist single-phase incidents.

BNCT Borok National Council of Tripura (India). Separatist group formed in 2000.

Bomb A detonating mix of chemicals releasing gas and energy very rapidly, usually stored in a container (e.g. pipe bomb) – the classical terrorist weapon.

Bombing The detonation of an overt or clandestinely placed explosive device aboard an aircraft or on the ground. The device is usually meant to damage or destroy facilities or kill people. The most common tactic employed by terrorism (sometimes labelled: 'the philosophy of the bomb').

Booby trap Concealed explosive device triggered by touch or by stepping on it.

Botulinum toxin A bacterial toxin that can be weaponised; Aum Shinrikyo attempted but apparently failed to produce it.

BR Brigate Rosse/Red Brigades, aka Armed Communist Combatants, Italian Red Brigade, Red Regiments. Italian left-wing group formed in 1969 and most active in the 1970s, when it kidnapped and killed former Italian prime minister Aldo Moro. The group split in 1984 into the Communist Combatant Party (BR-PCC) and the Union of Combatant Communists (BR-UCC); most of its activities ended in the late 1980s after a series of arrests. Two tiny splinter groups survive: BR/PCC and BR/UCC.

BR/PCC Brigate Rosse, Partito Comunista Combattante, (New) Red Brigades, Communist Combatant Party (Italy). This group was formed in 1984.

BR/UCC Red Brigades, Union of Combatant Communists. The successor to BR.

Brigand Freebooter who lives by plunder, kidnapping for ransom, robbery, theft or piracy.

Brigata XX Luglio 20th July Brigade. This was an Italian anti-globalisation group active in 2002.

Brigate Rosse per la Costruzione del Partito Comunista Combattente Red Brigades for the Construction of the Fighting Communist Party, Italy.

BRN Barisan Revolusi Nasional Melayu Pattani, National Revolutionary Front (Thailand, Malaysia). Group formed in 1963 seeking to unite southern Thailand and northern Malaysia.

Brucella suis* and *Brucella melitensis Biological warfare agent developed by the United States, causing brucellosis (undulant fever).

BSO Black September Organisation. Group created by Al-Fatah (q.v.) to avenge the repression of the PLO in Jordan in September 1970, led by Salah Khalaf, aka Abu Iyad. This Lebanese-based group, most active between 1971 and 1974, was also responsible for the attack on the 1972 Olympic Games in Munich.

BTX Type A botulinal toxin. A biological neurotoxin agent of extreme lethality. It is won from the *Clostridium botulinum* bacterium and the most lethal poison in nature. BTX is produced by a living organism; its use does not depend on infecting the victim with the living organism, but is based on the indigestion or inhalation of the chemical substance BTX.

Burqa Whole-body cloth worn by some Muslim women; enforced by some fundamentalist groups such as the Taliban and Lashkar-e-Jabbar.

BW Biological weapon.

BWC Biological weapons convention.

BZ (QNB) Quinuclidinol benzillate. An incapacitating psychotomimetic agent developed in the 1950s. This psycho-chemical hallucinogen substance affects the nervous system, causing visual and aural false perceptions and a sense of unreality.

C-4 Composite-4. A US military plastic explosive equivalent to Semtex.

Cadre Core of trained and motivated professionals or militants.

Caesium-137 Radioisotope suitable for RDD (q.v.).

CAL Comandos Armadas de Liberación (Puerto Rico). Founded in 1968.

Caliph Literally, 'Prince of the Faithful'; title of the religious leader used by successors of Mohammed.

Caliphate Dominion of the caliph. It is a goal of Salafi jihadist terrorists linked to Al-Qaeda to recreate a caliphate theocracy based on total observance of Koranic Shari'ah laws.

CALN Commandos Armadas por la Liberación Nacional/Armed Commandos for National Liberation. Puerto Rican separatist group formed in 1969; later joined FALN (q.v.).

Camp X-ray US detention centre for Al-Qaeda and Taliban 'enemy combatants' in Guantánamo, Cuba.

Campaign Series of terrorist acts meant to create momentum and pressure to bring about desired political outcome, e.g. the cessation of peace talks.

Capital punishment Execution of a person by hanging, electrocution, lethal injection, guillotining or shooting in the name of the state, following a conviction by a competent court acting within the rule of national law.

Capitulation The agreed surrender of arms and/or cessation of combat by the weaker party following armed conflict.

Carlos *Nom de guerre* of Venezuelan terrorist Ilyich Ramírez Sanchez, 'Carlos the Jackal'. Worked *inter alia* for the PFLP, e.g. when it attacked the OPEC headquarters in Vienna in December 1975, and later became a terrorist entrepreneur, running, since 1983, the Organisation for the Armed Arab Struggle. He was eventually caught in Sudan in 1994 and imprisoned in France.

Carnivore Internet communication surveillance system developed for the US Federal Bureau of Investigations, also called DCS-1000.

Carrot-and-stick approach The combined application of incentives (carrots) and negative sanctions (stick) to encourage/compel/coerce a conflict party to alter its stance.

Case officer Senior operational investigator who tries to solve a crime case, e.g. a kidnapping.

Casualty Person incapacitated in or by armed conflict, including dead, wounded, missing, captured soldiers as well as civilians.

Catastrophic terrorism High-fatality terrorism; according to some authors, terrorism has moved from discriminate attacks with relatively few casualties to the infliction of mass fatalities since the late 1990s.

Catechism of the Revolutionist Key text in the development of modern terrorism, authored in 1869 by the 22-year-old Russian nihilist Sergey G. Nechaev.

CBP US Bureau of Customs and Border Protection.

CBRN Chemical, biological, radiological, nuclear [weapons].

CBW Chemical and biological weapons.

CCC Cellules Communistes Combattantes/Communist Fighting Cells, aka Collectif des Prisonniers des Cellules Communistes Combattantes/Collective of Prisoners of the Communist Fighting Cells. This small Belgian left-wing group was active in 1984–86, led by Pierre Carrette, attacking US and NATO targets.

CCCCC Cellula Contro Capitale, Carcere i suoi Carcerieri e le sue Celle/Cell Against Capital, Prison, Prison Warders and Prison Cells (Italy). This anarchist group was active in 2002 against Spain.

CCTV Closed-circuit television.

CDCJ European Committee on Legal Cooperation.

CDDH Steering Committee on Human Rights; EU body.

CDF Civilian Defence Force (Sierra Leone). Community defence movement that degenerated into warlordism (q.v.) after 1997.

CDPC European Committee on Crime Problems.

Ceasefire Temporary suspension of fighting (armistice) sometimes combined with limited troop withdrawal from front-line positions.

Cell Quasi-autonomous units of militants, agents or criminals, usually between three and ten people, which engage in clandestine illegal activities as part of a compartmentalised, secret underground organisation with which it maintains only controlled contacts, based on the need to know or act, in order to minimise vulnerability and reduce the consequences of defection and infiltration.

CEPOL European Police College.

CERF Frente Clara Elizabeth Ramírez. Left-wing Salvadorean group forming part of FMLN, active in the 1980s.

CFF Cholana Kangtoap Serei Cheat Kampouchea, aka Cambodian Freedom Fighters. Founded in 1998; based in California.

CFSP European Common Foreign and Security Policy.

CGSB Coordinadora Guerrillera Simón Bolívar/Simón Bolívar Guerrilla Coordinating Board. Established in 1987 in Colombia as an umbrella for FARC, M-19, ELN, EPL, PRT and the Quintín Lame Command. It was dissolved in 1990.

Che Nickname of Ernesto Guevara (1928–1967), an Argentinian revolutionary who fought with Fidel Castro in Cuba and later left for Bolivia, where he tried in vain to foment a peasant uprising.

Chechen separatists Generic name for secular and Islamic Chechen guerrilla and terrorist fighters, striving for separatism or autonomy from the Russian Federation.

Cheka Acronym of the Bolshevik security police, which engaged in Red Terror (q.v.); later evolved into the KGB.

Chemical agent Substance capable of incapacitating, injuring or killing people, such as irritating agents, choking agents, blood agents, blister agents or nerve agents.

Chemical explosive Chemically unstable material that can produce a detonation by means of a very rapid self-propagating transformation of the material into more stable substances. Shock, noise and heat accompany the transformation and the formation of gases. Explosive mixtures usually consist of a combustible and an oxidiser. A distinction is made between *low explosives*, which are said to deflagrate (burn) rather than to detonate (explode), and *high explosives*, which shatter and destroy owing to detonation velocities ranging from 1 to 9 kilometres (and more) per second. High explosives must, as a rule, be initiated by the shock of a blasting cap, in contrast to low explosives.

Chemical terrorism Use of poisonous substances (gas, liquid or solid) to incapacitate or kill human beings in order to sow terror.

Chemical warfare Use of chemical agents in war; initially used in the First World War.

Chemical weapons (CW) There are several types of munitions and other delivery systems that contain substances intended to injure or kill or incapacitate personnel or to deny access or use of area, facilities and materials. There is a distinction between *harassing agents, incapacitating agents* and *casualty or lethal agents*. The latter are highly toxic man-made substances that are dispersed in liquid or gas form. They include (1) choking agents like chlorine (Cl) and phosgene (CG); (2) blood gases such as hydrogen cyanide (AC, HCN) and cyanogen chloride (CK); (3) vesicants or blister agents such as sulphur mustard gas (H, HD, HS, T) or nitrogen mustard gas (HN1, HN2, HN3) and Lewisite (L) which cause burns and (lung) tissue damage; and (4) nerve agents such as VX (TX60), GB (sarin) and GA (tabun). Except with indoor use, where thousands of fatalities can result from a single attack, large quantities (thousands of kilos) are needed to produce high numbers of fatalities; with outdoor use, fatalities are likely to be in the hundreds. The effect of chemical weapons manifests itself within hours, rather than days, as with biological weapons. Effects include coughing, difficulty in breathing, increased sweating, nausea, vomiting, cramps, diarrhoea, muscular twitching and death by suffocation. Some of the milder ones are used for riot control, e.g. chloroacetophenone (CN) or *o*-chloro-benzylidene malnonitrile (CS).

Chikunggunya virus A biological agent.

Chlorine A choking agent.

Choking agents Attack the respiratory tract, making the membranes swell so that the lungs fill with fluid whereby the victim drowns; survivors suffer chronic breathing problems. Lethal choking agents include carbon chloride or phosgene, trichloromethyl chloroformate or diphosgene, chloropicrin or trichloronitromethane.

Cholera Disease caused by the bacterium *Vibrio comma*.

Christian identity Racist, right-wing ideological belief in Aryan Supremacy, opposed to non-whites and Jews (calling them 'mud people'), and considering the United States to be the 'promised land'.

Chukaku-Ha Middle Core, aka Nucleus Faction. Marxist Japanese group opposed to the monarchy, US military presence on Japanese soil and Narita airport construction. This group was active mainly from the mid-1960s to mid-1980s; allegedly also a front organisation of the Kansai Revolutionary Army.

CI Critical infrastructure.

CIA Central Intelligence Agency. US federal agency established in 1947; involved *inter alia* in anti-terrorist intelligence operations and active measures.

CIRA Continuity Irish Republican Army, aka Continuity Army Council. A Northern Ireland Catholic small splinter group of PIRA that rejects the ceasefire and Good Friday Agreement of 1998.

CIS Commonwealth of Independent States. The association of former Soviet Union member states.

Civil protection Measures to prevent or reduce harm to civilian population in the event of a man-made or natural emergency or disaster.

Civil war Open armed conflict within one country, initially subject to a usually legal authority, fought by two or more organised parties for control of the government, territory, population or economic resources. Civil wars occur usually in contexts of internal repression, attempts at coups and revolution and in the wake of interstate war and intervention. They are often accompanied by organised crime, warlordism and terrorism (P. Baev). They also have a tendency to come back: nearly 50 per cent of countries that have emerged out of civil wars fall back into armed conflict within five years.

The variation of domestic conflict is considerable and there are few 'pure' types, with most civil wars involving more than one element of the following:

- secessionist civil war;
- revolutionary guerrilla war;
- conflicts between the military and civilian authorities (including police versus military);
- criminal gang wars, among themselves and against the state;
- terrorist campaigns;
- religious sects and fundamentalist movements trying to desecularise the state;
- genocidal campaigns against, and ethnic cleansing of, minorities;
- conflict between the state and (sectors of) society;
- conflicts between two peoples or nations for control of one territory;
- conflicts between factions of parties or armed forces;
- conflicts between religious groups, ethnic communal groups, linguistic groups, tribes and clans;
- wars between nomadic peoples and sedentary people;
- clashes between immigrants and natives.

For the last four categories, delineation from social unrest is sometimes difficult. Some analysts take 1,000 fatalities per year as the criterion for inclusion under the term '(civil) war'.

Civilian Term used for a person who is not involved in military service in wartime or is not a member of an organised armed group or party in a conflict. In the context of armed conflict, non-combatant civilians bearing no arms, either overtly or covertly, enjoy – in theory if not in practice – immunity from acts of war. Humanitarian law was created in order to: (1) protect both combatants and non-combatants from unnecessary suffering; (2) safeguard certain fundamental human rights of persons who fall into the hands of the enemy, particularly prisoners of war, and the wounded and the sick, as well as civilians. UN General Assembly resolution 2444 (19 December 1968) stipulated that it is prohibited to launch attacks against the civilian population as such and that a distinction must be made at all times between persons taking part in the hostilities and members of the civilian population to the effect that the latter be spared as much as possible. For terrorist groups, civilians are preferred targets because they are 'soft targets', and attacking them creates more terror than when an armed group is ambushed.

CJCC Church of Jesus Christ Christian. White racist group linked to Aryan Nations (USA).

Clandestini Corsi Clandestine Corsican. A group that emerged in 1999; opposed to North African immigration into Corsica.

Cleveland Disaster The first industrial LNG accident, at the Cleveland LNG terminal on 20 October 1944. One of the four LNG storage tanks of the facility leaked; the LNG vapour cloud wafted into the streets of Cleveland and seeped into the sewer system without anybody noticing. The vapour was ignited by a spark and detonated. As a result of the fireball and the overpressure, houses in two streets were damaged and burst into flames. This started a catastrophic chain reaction: the other tanks began to melt, exploding in fireballs hotter than the sun; more liquid gas ran down the streets, seeped into the sewer system and the basements of houses, and house after house exploded. All in all, a square mile of buildings was destroyed. Since most of the inhabitants were out at work and the children at school, the death toll was 'only' 131 people; it could have been considerably worse.

Clostridium botulinum A food-poisoning bacterium that causes botulism; there are seven varieties, of which type A is the deadliest.

Clostridium perfringens Biological agent.

Clostridium tetani Biological agent.

Club of Berne Informal meeting group of the 25 EU heads of security, plus Norway and Switzerland.

CMAT Consequence Management Advisory Team.

CN (chloracetophenone) A non-persistent irritant used in civilian tear gas for harassment.

CNI Critical National Infrastructure. Term used by the UK government to describe key sectors and services that support the economic, political and social life of the United Kingdom, the loss of which would be critical to the public and/or the government.

CNPZ Comisión de Nestor Paz Zamora/Nestor Paz Zamora Commission. Bolivian Guevarist group active in the early 1990s, named after a student guerrilla leader (brother of the then president of Bolivia) who died in 1970.

Cobalt-60 Radioisotope suitable for RDD (q.v.).

Cobra Emergency committee of the UK government to deal with terrorist emergencies.

CODEXTER Committee of Experts on Terrorism. This European body is responsible for coordinating counter-terrorist activities of the Council of Europe in the legal field.

COE Council of Europe.

COINTELPRO Counter-intelligence programme of the FBI during the Nixon presidency, aimed at militant subversive elements and parts of the civil rights movement.

Cold War Characterisation of the rivalry, competition, tensions and conflict between communist and Western governments in the period from 1945–1947 to 1991 which usually fell short of a shooting war, such as in Korea, 1950–1953. The 'Third World' was seen as an area where the global balance of power between the communist and the capitalist blocs could be changed in one's own favour. This led to overt and covert interventions and proxy wars as the 'balance of terror', based on thermonuclear weapons, prevented a direct confrontation between the United States and the Soviet Union.

COLINA National Liberation Commando. This Brazilian Marxist militant group was active in Minas Gerais between 1967 and the early 1970s.

Collateral damage Term from the laws of war referring to civilian casualties as an unintended side effect of military operations. Terrorists, on the other hand, intentionally target civilians, generally avoiding clashes with security forces.

Colletotrichum coffeanum var. virulans Pathogenic fungus.

Colonel Karuna Faction Aka Karuna Faction, Tamil National Front. Splinter group from LTTE, led by Colonel Karuyna (aka Vinayagamoorthi Muralithran), who took 6,000 of the Tamil Tigers' 15,000 fighters with him in 2004. More moderate than the Tigers, the Colonel Karuna Faction was seeking autonomy only, rather than independence, for the Tamils of Sri Lanka.

Combatant Soldier of a regular army or member of an irregular force taking part in battle, under the terms of the international laws of war.

COMINT Communications Intelligence.

Commando operation Surprise armed raids into enemy territory to seize or destroy targets, conducted by special forces or guerrilla and terrorist teams.

Communiqué Many terrorist groups, especially left-wing ones, in the nineteenth and twentieth centuries usually accompanied their acts of violence with (often long) written statements explaining the rationale for their deeds. While full of propaganda, these documents provide a glimpse into the mindset of the terrorists.

Communism Egalitarian anti-capitalist ideology based on collective ownership of goods (as opposed to private property) and, in theory (though not in practice), rule by the working class (as opposed to by the bourgeoisie), led by an avant-garde communist party that aims to introduce a classless society. With the seizure of power by the Bolsheviks in Russia in 1917, communist reality began to overtake the ideology and ideals of nineteenth-century theorists and produced a totalitarian one-party dictatorship with power concentrated in a centrally controlled state, which ruled by terror and propaganda until the death of Stalin in 1953.

Communist Party of the Philippines New People's Army (see CPP/NPA).

Compellance Forcing an adversary to do something against his will, e.g. by threatening punishment to spur action.

Composition B High explosive, 60:40:1 mixture of RDX, TNT and wax.

Composition C RDX-based high explosive that can be shaped by hand. It contains 88.3 per cent RDX and 11.7 per cent non-explosive oily plasticiser. It is very stable and powerful.

Concentration camp Establishment for the large-scale imprisonment of political opponents, ethnic and other groups behind barbed wire, first introduced in the Boer War by the British rulers of South Africa. Most widely used by Nazi and communist regimes for repression and extermination, often in combination with forced labour.

Concessionary options Anti-terrorist response measures in hostage situations based on fulfilling (some of the) terrorists' demands to resolve the crisis (e.g. free escape in return for release of hostages).

Conciliatory responses Anti-terrorist measures addressing the underlying conditions of terrorist violence to resolve (hostage) crisis.

Confiscation Seizure of assets by the state based on legal procedures.

Conflict A confrontation between individuals or groups caused by opposite or incompatible ends or means. There are dozens of partly overlapping, partly conflicting definitions. One can, for instance, view conflict as an antagonistic situation or adversarial process between at least two individual or collective actors over means or ends such as resources, power, status, values, goals, relations or interests. The range of outcomes includes victory, defeat, domination, surrender, neutralisation, conversion, coercion, injury or destruction and elimination of the opposite party or, alternatively, the solution, settlement or transformation of the conflict issue. In military terminology, conflict is also used to describe a situation between war and peace.

Conflict, ethnic, typology of Weiner (1992; cited in Van Goor, 1994: 26) proposed the following eight types of ethnic conflict:

1 *Irredentism*: a form of nationalism which claims that a group living outside the borders of a state actually belongs to that state and ought to be brought within the state's borders by means of annexation of the territory in which it lives. The claim may focus on the related group or on the territory itself. Two types of irredentism are possible. First, the group outside the state may form a minority in the territory claimed for annexation. Second, the group may form a minority in two territories. In Weiner's opinion, the driving force of irredentism may be an ideology, a political movement or government policy.

2 *Separatism*: a group's desire to separate itself from the state to which it belongs.

3 *Autonomy*: the desire of a group concentrated in a particular territory of a state to acquire greater influence over the government of that territory. The desire for autonomy is often seen as the first step towards separatism.

4 The demands of *interest groups*: here Weiner is referring to groups that are spread throughout the country, but whose members have common interests in the educational, religious or economic fields. Such groups often strive for education in their own language, religious freedom and an end to discrimination.

5 *Ethnic corporatism*: the demand of an ethnic group to be recognised as such and to obtain certain rights on the basis of this recognition, such as the right to a proportionate share in the country's government.

6 *Nativism*: The demand of a group that regards itself as more indigenous for greater political, cultural or economic authority than other groups in the running of the state. People who do not belong to the original population are excluded as far as possible. These groups adhere to slogans such as 'X-land for the X-landers'.

7 *Hegemonic demands*: the demand of one group for the right to dominate others, based on cultural or racial arguments often accompanied by an appeal for the survival of the state.

8 *Fundamentalism*: the assertion by fundamentalist groups that some former golden age will return provided the community reverts to its fundamental religious values. Everyone living within the state is obliged to accept and profess these old values. Fundamentalism can assume various forms, not all of them very radical, including what Weiner refers to as religious reformism and religious nationalism.

Conflict management Efforts to contain the spread of hostilities, reduce the level of confrontation and offer solutions to parties involved in a particular confrontation.

Conflict prevention A broad concept that refers to anticipation and aversion of escalation and violence in social, political and international conflicts (Nicolaides, 1996: 27; Jongman, 1997: 91–92). It covers:

- *Primary prevention* (minimising the chance of occurrence of violent conflict): proactive measures to prevent the emergence of conflict formation between parties; and prophylactic measures to prevent the likely outbreak of a conflict between parties.
- *Secondary prevention* (containment and mitigation): active measures to prevent the vertical escalation of existing conflicts; reactive measures to limit the horizontal escalation of already ongoing conflict to other areas; and palliative measures to mitigate the consequences of an outbreak of conflict.
- *Tertiary prevention* (preventing the recurrence of armed conflict). Revalidation measures to prevent the recurrence or post-conflict renewal of the conflict cycle.

Conflict resolution Efforts to reduce antagonism and increase cooperation and mutual problem solving between adversaries, usually with the help of third parties. The term covers a number of academic and activist – and to a lesser extent military and diplomatic – approaches to conflict termination and transformation. The term generally implies a 'real' or 'true' solution to the underlying conflict in a constructive and non-violent way, based on a redefinition of the contestants' relationship, rather than a violent, destructive 'solution' (as in genocide) or a mere settlement that 'freezes' the current power distribution between opponents who might still harbour revenge in their hearts.

Since conflict is often about conquering, or maintaining or defending positions of power, conflict resolution must address the issue why those with more power would be willing to share power with those with less power. The more powerful party often has less interest in power sharing and, by implication, more of an interest in continuing a conflicting relationship or, alternatively, solving it by force rather than by peaceful means. To bring both, or all, sides into a constructive mode rather than a destructive one is the major challenge of conflict resolution. Often a third party is necessary to achieve this, a party that can counterbalance the power asymmetry between the contestants and guide them to a transformed situation that is in the enlightened long-term self-interest of all parties.

There are many definitions of 'conflict resolution'. Most refer to an outcome or distribution of benefits acceptable to all sides. While they all focus on the facilitation of a solution, they place, however, different emphasis on non-competitive, cooperative, non-adversarial, non-confrontational, non-zero-sum (positive sum), win–win and consensus decision-making processes and outcomes. Such desirable outcomes can be the result of joint problem-solving workshops, negotiation, mediation and arbitration. The concept of conflict resolution has various meanings in the legal literature, the domestic conflict literature and that on international relations as it is used for two-party personal relationships, labour–management issues, business negotiation, victim–offender reconciliation, inter-group conflicts and international conflicts.

Conflict, rules for waging Conflicts are supposed to be waged according to rules (rules of engagement, laws of war, codes of conduct). These are incorporated in various documents such as the 1907 Hague Convention respecting the laws and customs of war on land, and the 1949 Geneva Convention relating to the protection of civilian persons in time of war. Often, conflict parties resort to means of control and coercion that are outlawed: they resort to the use of illicit weapons or tactics, including war crimes, grave breaches (q.v.), crimes against humanity, ethnic cleansing and other forms of 'dirty war' (e.g. the use of starvation as a method of warfare against civilian persons).

The following are some of the basic principles of civilised conduct of war are (International Committee of the Red Cross, 1987):

- Civilian persons may not be attacked, unless they participate directly in hostilities.
- Civilian persons, prisoners of war and captured military and religious personnel must be respected and treated humanely.
- Wounded and shipwrecked shall be cared for as required by their state of health.
- The taking of hostages is prohibited.
- Spies may be used but they do not have the right to prisoner-of-war status.
- Enemy civilian persons may not be compelled to give information.
- Military necessity may be invoked only in so far as and to the extent that the law of war permits.
- Weapons and means of combat shall be chosen and used so as to avoid any harm to civilian persons and damage to civilian objects which are not necessary to fulfil the mission given.
- It is prohibited to use civilian persons or inhabited areas to shield military units, movements and positions.
- The military character of the objective or target shall be verified by reconnaissance and target identification.

Congo-Crimean haemorrhagic fever virus Biological agent.

Conotoxin Biological agent.

Consequence management Disaster response; emergency measures to alleviate damage, loss, hardship and suffering following (terrorist) incident.

Contagion Spread of disease by some form of contact; the term is also used for copycat crimes triggered by (successful) exemplary terrorist attacks.

Container revolution Started in the 1950s, and consequently ports are under pressure to grow larger and larger to accommodate ever bigger container ships. As a side effect, the container revolution drove out of business many old harbours unable to grow any further. Nowadays, there are a couple of 'mega-ports' such as Hong Kong, Singapore, Long Beach–Los Angeles and Rotterdam, and a multitude of smaller feeder ports serving them – the so-called 'hubs and spokes' model of maritime (container) trade. Currently, there are a total of 15 million containers worldwide, being transported by several thousand smaller and bigger container ships, and making roughly 230 million port calls annually. Some fear that containers filled with nuclear or biological agents are used by terrorists.

CONTEST UK strategy against terrorism document.

Contingency planning Advance planning and preparing for emergencies, disasters and crises that demand a rapid response.

Contras From contrarevolucionarios/counter-revolutionaries. Their formation was backed first by the Argentinean military and then the American CIA. Formed mainly from the former National Guard of dictator A. Somoza (overthrown in 1979), based in Honduras and Costa Rica, trained by Argentina and by the US government in early 1980s to overthrow the elected revolutionary Nicaraguan Sandinista government. It was demobilised in 1990 after electoral defeat of the Sandinistas.

Controller Case officer/handler who 'runs' agent or terrorist.

Convention Treaty regulating behaviour between states in certain issue areas, where one-state solutions are inadequate and mutual interest in addressing an issue exists, e.g. hijacking.

Convulsants Substances that make muscles contract.

Cooperativa Artigiana Fuoco ed Affini – Occasionalmente Spettacolare Cooperative of Handmade Fire and Similar [Items] – Occasionally Spectacular (Italy). Anarchist group formed in 1999.

COREPER Committee of Permanent Representatives, of EU member states.

COSI Committee on Internal Security. European standing committee proposed in the abortive EU Constitution.

COSPOL Comprehensive Operational Strategic Planning for the Police. European policy document produced in 2005.

COTER Committee on Terrorism. This is a working group of the European Union dealing with terrorism.

Counter-insurgency Doctrine for fighting insurgents, in particular guerrilla forces, based on winning the 'hearts and minds' of the population so as to deprive insurgents of their support base and gain intelligence on them. For that purpose, selective political, economic and social reforms, civil actions and psychological operations are implemented to support military operations. Simultaneously, and sometimes predominantly, efforts are made to defeat insurgents by using some of their own tactics. From secure bases, larger and larger parts of the country are to be 'pacified', encroaching on the territorial bases of the insurgents.

Counter-intelligence Monitoring, neutralising and, if possible, utilising activities of foreign intelligence services in one's own country by recruiting agents within foreign intelligence services and by uncovering suspected espionage.

Counter-proliferation Activities to prevent, impede and reverse the spread of sophisticated weapons as well as precursors and instruments for building them, especially in the area of CBRN and missile technology.

Counter-revolution Efforts to undo the outcome of a social revolution and restore the *status quo ante* with the help of armed force and foreign allies.

Counter-sabotage Measures to prevent and obstruct sabotage operations.

Counter-terrorism A proactive effort to prevent, deter and combat politically motivated violence directed at civilian and non-combatant targets by the use of a broad spectrum of response measures – law enforcement, political, psychological, social, economic and (para)military.

Countervalue targeting strategy Targeting population and industrial centres (rather than military infrastructures and forces), as a Cold War strategy of superpowers.

Coup d'état literally 'blow to the state'; *Putsch* in German. The sudden and forcible but sometimes bloodless seizure of institutions of the state, usually by (a small part of) the armed forces and without much popular participation. Overthrows are most likely in periods of crises.

Covenant, the Sword, and the Arm of the Lord, The See CSA.

Covert operation Secret police, military or intelligence activities of states against foreign (and sometimes domestic) adversaries, involving illegal tactics and plausible denial if uncovered.

Covert surveillance Clandestine observance of suspect persons or potentially targeted objects.

Coxiella burnetii Bacterium; a biological agent experimented with by AUM.

CPDL Christian-Patriots Defense League. US survivalist group led by John Robert Harrell.

CPI-Maoist Communist Party of India – Maoist, aka Naxalites (India). This party emerged in September 2004 from a merger of the Maoist Communist Center (MCC) and the People's War Group.

CPN-M Communist Party of Nepal – Maoist. This group numbered more than 10,000, and waged the 'People's War' from 1996 to replace the constitutional monarchy with a Maoist republic. The group engaged in a ceasefire in 2006 and became a ruling party in 2008.

CPP Communist Party of the Philippines, aka New People's Army (NPA). Founded in 1969 by Jose Maria Sison, numbering *c.* 10,000 members.

CPP-ML Communist Party of the Philippines, Marxist-Leninist. This is the parent organisation of the New People's Army founded in 1969.

Crime Intentional act of commission (more rarely: omission) against people or property, prohibited and punishable by the state under penal law owing to its socially harmful, immoral, dangerous or undesirable character. The concept of crime varies greatly across time and cultural space as the laws vary and as what is and is not considered moral varies. An act of omission (or inaction) that results in preventable harm can also constitute a crime (such as failure to help someone in a life-threatening situation). The state has the prerogative to proscribe an act that is deemed harmful and make it a crime. The state also assumes the right to punish the offender. Some offences are so serious that they are considered morally wrong in all civilised societies. In particular, this applies to murder, the premeditated, unprovoked killing of a human being. In murder cases, legal systems tend to consider not only the act criminal but also the mindset of the perpetrator. Violations of rules of combat in war can fall under war crimes.

Crimes against humanity A legal category introduced at the Nuremberg trials, which covers murder, extermination, enslavement, deportation and other inhumane acts committed against any civilian population before or during the war, as well as persecutions on political, racial or religious grounds in execution of, or in connection with, any crime within the jurisdiction of the [Nuremberg] Tribunal, whether or not the crime is in violation of the domestic law of the country where it is perpetrated. Leaders, organisers, instigators or conspiracy to commit any of the foregoing crimes are responsible for all acts performed by any person who executes such a plan. Crimes against humanity fall under the jurisdiction of the International Criminal Court in The Hague. If acts of terrorism are (1) part of a widespread or systematic attack on civilians, and (2) the perpetrators are aware or cognisant of the fact that their criminal acts are part of a general or systematic pattern of conduct, then they might also fall under the category 'crime against humanity'. Typical crimes against humanity to create terror in such a context would be murder, extermination, torture, systematic rape, mutilation and similar inhumane acts.

Criminal justice model An approach to countering terrorism that relies primarily on the use of police and courts to deal with terrorism, as opposed to a military warfare model.

Criminal law Part of the law that defines criminal offences, regulates arrest, charging, trial and punishment of persons suspected of criminal conduct.

Crisis There is considerable confusion and overlap about the relationship between crisis and conflict; the terms 'conflict management' and 'crisis management' are often used interchangeably. Some see crisis from a structural, systemic perspective as the grey zone between peace and war or between conflict and war and therefore interpret it as a stage of conflict (war-in-sight crisis). Others, who follow the decision-making approach, focus more on the rapid sequences of interactive decision making among the conflict parties that are producing instability with potentially large consequences (Evans and Newham, 1992: 58–59). In the latter view, political crises are often characterised by:

- short action/reaction time;
- incomplete information for taking far-reaching and possibly irreversible decisions;
- a high risk of advent of violence or loss of lives;
- a high price for doing nothing;
- danger of losing control of the situation.

In the structural approach, crises tend to be seen as 'sudden eruptions of unexpected events caused by previous conflict' (Billing, 1992: 92). A more system-related approach (Maoz, 1982: 16) sees the main features of an (international) crisis as:

- acute and rapid changes in the variety and intensity of interaction patterns among states;
- decreased systemic stability;
- increased probability of violence in the system; and
- short duration.

Crisis management A set of law enforcement and other measures to regain control of a harmful situation by establishing the extent of damage and initiating damage control and mitigation measures, which combines the activities of several specialised agencies. In terrorist situations, it involves the isolation of the scene of crime and counter-terrorist and victim relief operations.

Critical infrastructure Essential elements for the functioning of societies, such as transport, telecommunications, energy, banking, postal services, water systems, pipelines, health services and electricity networks.

Critical mass The minimum quantity of enriched plutonium or uranium needed to support a chain reaction for a nuclear fission bomb.

Croatian Freedom Fighters Part of the Croatian national independence movement; also active in the 1970s and 1980s in the United States.

Cruise missile Low-flying rocket-propelled smart bomb using a sophisticated satellite-supported guidance system to attack the enemy below the radar screen.

CS gas Propanedinitrile ((2-chlorophenyl) methylene). Tear gas used for riot and crowd control.

CSA The Covenant, the Sword, and the Arm of the Lord. White US supremacist Christian Identity survivalist apocalyptic and anti-Semitic group, opposed to the alleged 'Zionist Occupation Government' (ZOG), formed in 1978 by James Ellison; based in Arkansas and linked to the Aryan Nations organisation; it intended to poison urban water supplies with potassium cyanide; active 1978–1985.

CSG Counterterrorism Security Group. The crisis team of US counter-terrorism agencies.

CSI Container security initiative. An international effort to monitor 15 million containers and their 230 million annual port calls against terrorist attacks or their use as floating bombs. Launched in

2002 in the wake of 9/11 by the US Bureau of Customs and Border Protection (CBP) as a means to increase the security of cargo containers shipped to US ports by pre-screening suspicious containers in their ports of departure.

CSIS Canadian Security Intelligence Service.

CSNPD Committee of National Vigour for Peace and Democracy, aka 02/92. Paramilitary group formed in southern Chad in the early 1990s.

CSPPA Comité de soutien avec les prisonniers politiques et arabes et du Moyen-Orient/ Committee of Solidarity with Arab and Middle East Political Prisoners. Name assumed by the Iranian-backed Hezbollah group, which bombed public places in Paris in the mid-1980s.

CT Counter-terrorism.

CTC Counter-Terrorism Committee of the UN Security Council. Established in September 2001.

CTC Counterterrorist Center. The CIA's arm to implement counter-terrorist operation programmes.

CTD Counterterrorism Division, section of the US Federal Bureau of Investigation (FBI).

CTG Counter Terrorism Group. This body comprises members of the EU security services. Formed in September 2001.

C-TPAT Customs–Trade Partnership Against Terrorism. A voluntary initiative to improve the supply chain security, launched in November 2001 by the US Bureau of Customs and Border Protection (CBP).

CTS Counter-terrorist search.

CW Chemical weapons/warfare.

CWIED Command-wire improvised explosive device.

CX Phosgene oxime, a toxic industrial chemical stored by the Soviet Union for chemical warfare.

Cyanide chloride Blocks the oxygen intake of the blood.

Cyber-terrorism Attacks against information, data and computer infrastructures, systems and programs aimed at damaging an adversary's society or government computers, networks and information storage systems in order to produce, indirectly, civilian casualties. The term is often used loosely for a variety of internet-based crime (hacking, spreading of computer viruses) which mostly comprises cases of criminal sabotage and has nothing to do with terrorism. Cyber-terrorism has so far been more of a theoretical possibility than an actual occurrence.

Cyclohexylmethylphosphonofluoridate (GF) A Low-volatility nerve gas that kills through skin contact or inhalation. GF is dispersed as gas or aerosol.

Cyclonite Type of high-velocity explosive.

Cyclo-sarin A nerve agent.

Dagestan Liberation Army Islamist separatist group associated with the September 1999 apartment bombings in Moscow.

Dal Khalsa Army of the Pure. Sikh group founded in 1978, seeking independence from India's Punjab.

Dar al-Ahad Countries that have peace treaties with Muslims and therefore ought not to be attacked.

Dar al-Harb 'House of War'. Countries ruled by other than Islamic regimes. According to some scholars, a country where Muslims can practise their faith is not Dar al-Harb.

Dar al-Islam 'House of Islam'. Muslim countries (as opposed to Dar al-Harb, 'House of War' countries ruled by non-Islamic regimes). Because of the absence of a contemporary caliphate, the definition of Dar al-Islam is problematic.

Dashmesh Regiment Tenth Regiment. Group named after the tenth Sikh guru, Gobind Singh, who started the Sikh warrior tradition. A Sikh armed group fighting for a Sikh state, Khalistan, which claimed responsibility for downing the Air India jetliner in 1985 en route from Toronto to London.

DCI Director of Central Intelligence, head of the CIA (USA).

DEA (US) Drug Enforcement Agency. Law enforcement agency engaged in controlling illicit narcotic trafficking and use.

Death list The publication or 'leaking' of names of individuals to be killed in a insurgency or counter-insurgency, which serves as an instrument of terror.

Death squad Usually (but not exclusively) a right-wing clandestine military or paramilitary vigilante group, controlled, sponsored or tolerated by (often) a military government, and engaged in intimidation and violence, including extra-judicial executions, torture, rape and disappearances of (often) left-wing political activists and suspected guerrilla supporters; often consists of off-duty policemen and members of the armed forces of a state. First known in Brazil as Esquadrãos de Morte in the 1960s, they spread to other Latin American countries and beyond.

Death threat A usually anonymous threat (by phone, letter or in the form of a published 'death list') with the aim of terrorising the person(s) targeted in order to prevent them from pursuing activities that are perceived as contrary to the interests of the authors of the threat.

Decommissioning The process of disarmament. An example would be in the context of Northern Ireland after the 1998 peace accord.

Decryption Process of making readable/understandable information and signals that were encrypted for security purposes by enemy or rival.

Defensive Action UK single-issue group.

Defensive Action US anti-abortion single-issue group, involved in murder.

Defoliant A toxic chemical substance that causes plants to shed their leaves prematurely or unnaturally. Used on a large scale to remove jungle cover in South-East Asia by the United States – Agent Orange.

Delta Force 1st Special Forces Operational Detachment – Delta, aka Combat Applications Group (CAG). US army secret operations unit numbering some 2,500 men at headquarters in Fort Bragg, established in 1977; modelled after the British SAS and used in counter-terrorist operations such as the failed Operation Eagle Claw in April 1980 to rescue US embassy staff taken hostage in Tehran.

Demand In the context of a terrorist campaign, or in the case of hostage taking or kidnapping terrorists formulate (often outrageous) demands, sometimes accompanied with deadlines, promising to desist from killing or cease a campaign if demands are met. Demands are sometimes secret and sometimes not sincere, and giving in to them in order to save lives opens the door to new demands, so the official line of governments is often not to bargain with terrorists at all.

Democide Term that encompasses various forms of mass killings by governments, e.g. genocide, politicide, massacres of generally unarmed civilians.

Democracy Literally, in Greek, 'rule by the people/the many' (as opposed to rule by one (autocracy) or few (oligarchy)). A political system based on free elections (one person – one vote, one vote – one value), majority or coalition rule, respect for minority rights, rule of law (rather than arbitrary rule), system of checks and balances between executive, legislative and judicative branches of government. In practice, democracies show considerable differences in terms of representatives, but they offer at the very least an opportunity to replace unpopular rulers without recourse to force. Democracy is a system of government that derives its legitimacy from the consent of the governed. Democratic societies have institutionalised procedures for periodically choosing representatives among contenders for public office. In a representative democracy, the voters periodically elect representatives who are responsible for making political decisions. A characteristic of all democracies is that they have a high regard for the right of the individual to choose between alternatives, which presupposes civil liberties such as freedom of speech and assembly. Democracy thrives when at least some of the following conditions are met:

- diffusion of power;
- restraints on government power;

- tolerance of dissent;
- access to information;
- absence of major cleavages;
- advanced economic development.

Democracy involves accountability of rulers to their subjects through the introduction of checks on the arbitrary use of power, agreed rules and procedures, and a separation of powers between the executive, parliament and the judiciary. Contemporary democracies are characterised by universal franchise, competitive elections, equality before the law, rule of law and, in most cases, the existence of a formal constitution. While the basic principle of democracy is that the majority decides, there must be due regard for the rights of minorities.

Dengue fever virus A biological agent that has been investigated by the United States for its suitability for biological warfare.

Deobandism Indian school of Islamic law, founded in 1867 in reaction to British rule. This was a fundamentalist Islamic reform movement, which emerged in nineteenth-century India from the Sunni Hanafi legal school. Deobandism is named after the Indian town where the movement began. Its anti-colonial and anti-modernist stance appealed to the Taliban in the 1990s in Afghanistan. Taught in madrassas in Pakistan where Taliban students were educated. Lately, the Deobandi movement has distanced itself from indiscriminate terrorism.

Department of Homeland Security (DHS) A new US government department created after 9/11, combining a large number of previously separate government agencies.

Desparecidos Literally, 'disappeared'. A tactic of state terrorism using a combination of kidnapping, torture, rape and/or mutilation of individuals deemed dangerous by the regime, followed by their murder and disposal of the body at a secret location. This tactic was practised widely in Latin America in the 1970s, especially in Argentina and Chile.

Deterrence A strategy to persuade an adversary that offensive action would be costly or unsuccessful, usually by a threat of inflicting great damage and harm on the opposite leadership, population or infrastructure. This threat-based dissuasive method of conflict escalation prevention acts on the political will of an opponent in an attempt to dissuade him from engaging in aggression or continuing further aggression. Conflict management is sometimes achieved by strategies of mutual deterrence. The balance-of-power system of conflict management is based on it. Deterrence is derived from the possession of credible power instruments to inflict high or even unacceptable damage on an opponent, thereby presumably restraining the latter from exploiting opportunities and pursuing expansionist intentions. Deterrence is meant to create a negative outcome in a cost–benefit calculation and is achieved by a combination of political determination, military capabilities and strategic skills. Deterrence theory is, however, based on a number of assumptions, such as that one state does not misperceive the balance of power or that the vulnerability of the stronger state is limited despite the existence of cheap weapons of mass destruction (Lutz, 1980: 16–23; Wolf, 1991, cit. Treverton and Bennett, 1997: 13; Evans and Newnham, 1992: 52).

Deuterophoma tracheiphilia (syn. *Phoma tracheipl. hila*). A pathogenic plant fungus.

Dev Sol See DHKP/C.

Dev Yol 'Revolutionary Road'. Armed group that split in 1975 from the TPLA (q.v.).

DFLP Democratic Front for the Liberation of Palestine/al-Jabha al-Dimuqratiyya li-Tahrir Filastin. Marxist splinter group from the PFLP, established in 1969 and supported by Syria; carried out operations against Israel and was led by Naif Hawatmeh; numbers some 500 members.

DHD Dima Halam Daoga (India, Assam). DHD was formed in 1996 as an ethnic liberation group in north-eastern India.

DHKP/C Devrimci Halk Kurtuluş Partisi/Cephesi/Revolutionary People's Liberation Army, aka Dev(rimci) Sol (Karatas Faction), RPLP/F, Revolutionary Left, Revolutionary People's

Liberation Party/Front. Group active in Turkey, a Marxist splinter faction of the Turkish People's Liberation Party Front, formed in 1978.

DHS Department of Homeland Security (q.v.).

DIA Defense Intelligence Agency. The intelligence arm of the US Department of Defense.

Diaspora Emigrant/refugee/expatriate community abroad that maintains links with its homeland. Can provide cover for, *inter alia*, terrorist sleepers.

Dictatorship Unchecked and arbitrary rule by a single individual or a 'junta', standing above the law and relying, if at all, on popular elections only pro forma. Legitimacy might, to the extent it exists, be derived from claims of divine will and charismatic leadership.

Dimethyl methylphosphonate (DMMP) Dual-use precursor substance, usable for sarin production.

DIN ('Avenge Israeli Blood'): Jewish militants who planned in April 1946 to kill German prisoners of war in revenge for the Holocaust.

DINA Dirección de Intelligencia Nacional/National Intelligence Directorate. Chilean secret police established in 1974 (renamed in 1978 as Central Nacional de Informaciones/National Information Center). Engaged in death squad activities, torture and mass detention under General Pinochet; also operated abroad against Chilean dissidents.

Dioxin (TCDD – 2,3,7,8-tetrachlorodibenzoparadioxin). This is a by-product of Silvex herbicides production; more toxic than plutonium.

Diphenylchloroarsine A non-persistent harassing agent.

Diplomacy Activity by states to promote and defend their interests abroad, usually by means of peaceful negotiations; sometimes in combination with persuasive incentives and coercive disincentives (gunboat diplomacy).

Direct action A political initiative by large groups of people, taken sometimes inside, sometimes outside the legal and constitutional framework, ranging from non-violent protests, boycotts, sit-ins, labour strikes to seizure of buildings, and sometimes even acts of terrorism. Originally linked to militant worker actions.

Direct Action Action Directe (see AD).

Dirty bomb Term used for a radiological dispersal device (RDD), a package of radioactive material disseminated with the help of a conventional explosion. A dirty bomb is often erroneously confused with weapons of mass destruction.

Dirty war Term denoting campaign of state terror by the Argentinian military dictatorship between 1976 and 1983, resulting in the 'disappearance' (kidnapping, followed by torture, murder and secret disposal of bodies) of up to 30,000 people suspected to be enemies of the regime.

Disappearance From the Spanish *desaparecido*. A government practice developed especially in Guatemala (after 1966), Chile (after 1973) and Argentina (after 1976) of the undocumented abduction of individuals, often followed by torture and murder, with burial of the body at a secret location. The uncertainty about the fate of the victim places great psychic stress on their relatives and friends.

Disarmament Reduction and/or removal of weapons or weapon systems, usually following successful negotiations or military conflict.

Disinformation Dissemination of false or misleading information through the press and audiovisual media with the purpose of manipulating (sectors of) the public.

Dissuasion A strategy to make it unattractive for an opponent to engage in harmful behaviour, combining elements of diplomacy and deterrence.

DKBA Democratic Karen Buddhist Army. Established in 1994 and numbering some 2,000 members, it seeks independence for the Karen minority.

DOD Department of Defense (USA), aka the Pentagon.

Domestic terrorism Local, national terrorism, as opposed to international or global terrorism.

Doukhobors Russian Orthodox Christian sect in Canada, including 'Sons of Freedom', a militant group responsible for terrorist bombings between 1960 and 1985.

DRFLA Democratic Revolutionary Front for the Liberation of Arabistan.

DS Bureau of Diplomatic Security. This is the security service of the US diplomatic service.

Dual–use technologies Instruments and materials that can be used for peaceful purposes as well as for war.

Due process A legal principle that no person shall be arrested or imprisoned or deprived of his or her liberty, outlawed or banished except according to the prevailing law.

Dynamite A high explosive patented in 1867 by Alfred Nobel, based on a mixture of nitroglycerine (discovered in 1846 in Italy) and wood pulp plus sodium nitrate to stabilise the explosive. It is used as a secondary explosive requiring a detonator as primary explosive. Dynamites are made from liquid nitroglycerine (NG), oxidisers and a binder material or from a mixture of ethylene glycol denitrate (EGDN), a small amount of nitroglycerine with oxidisers and a binder material. There are many other formulas.

EAG Eurasian Group.

Ear Slang for clandestine informant.

Earth First Environmental single-issue group in the United States, founded in 1980 and engaging in a range of tactics (arson, sabotage).

Earth Liberation Front (ELF) Environmentalist single-issue group active in the United States since the late 1990s; involved in arson but falls short of eco-terrorism; linked to the Animal Liberation Front. Also, radical UK-based environmental protection group, founded in 1992. The ELF is also active in Canada.

Eavesdropping Covert electronic surveillance of private conversations of persons or planting equipment for this purpose.

EAW European arrest warrant.

Ebola virus A biological agent. This is a Marburg-like virus that Aum Shinrikyo tried to acquire in 1991 when cult leader Shoko Asahara led an expedition to Zaire. According to Ken Alibek, Russian bio-weapon researchers may have created a recombinant Ebola-smallpox, grafting a DNA copy of the disease-causing parts of Ebola into smallpox, thereby combining the haemorrhages caused by Ebola with the high contagiousness of smallpox.

EC European Commission.

Echelon Global electronic wiretap system maintained by the US National Security Agency, which is able to intercept large quantities of electromagnetic communications from phones, satellites and radio.

ECJ European Court of Justice.

ECM Electronic countermeasures.

ECOMOG West African multilateral military force, established by ECOWAS.

Economic sanctions Usually collective efforts to curtail trade with a state, e.g. for sponsoring or sheltering terrorist groups; used against Libya and the Taliban in Afghanistan by the United Nations.

Eco-terrorism Term used by some national authorities to refer to activities of single-issue groups engaged in acts of sabotage and violence (against property, rarely human beings) used for environmentally or ecologically unfriendly purposes, usually falling short of proper terrorism. An alternative definitional focus has been suggested by Daniel Schwartz, who posits that the term 'eco-terrorism' 'should be reserved for incidents in which the environment itself is disrupted or threatened by the perpetrator as a symbol that elicits trepidation in the larger population over the ecological consequences of the act'.

ECOWAS Economic Community of West African States.

EDS Explosive detection systems. These instruments are used to detect bombs and other explosive devices through X-ray screening, etc.

EGP Ejército Guerrillero de los Pobres/Guerrilla Army of the Poor (Guatemala). Established in 1972 and active until the peace accords of 1996.

EGTK Tupac Katari Guerrilla Army. Indigenous Bolivian armed group active in the early 1990s.

EIJ Egyptian Islamic Jihad, aka Al-Jihad, Al-Jihad al-Islami, Jihad Group, New Jihad Group, Qaeda al-Jihad, Talaa'al-Fateh/Vanguards of Conquest. The EIJ emerged in the late 1970s and was responsible for the assassination of Egyptian president Anwar Sadat in 1981. It merged with Al-Qaeda in June 2001.

EIJM Eritrean Islamic Jihad Movement/Harakat al Jihad al Islami al Eritrea, aka Eritrean Islamic Jihad (EIJ), Eritrean Islamic Reform Movement, Islamic Salvation Movement (Harakat al Khalas al Islam), Abu Sihel Movement. Established in 1980, opposed to the ruling People's Front for Democracy and Justice (PFDJ) government (see EPLF); reportedly affiliated to Al-Qaeda.

EIM Eritrean Islamic Movement. The group was formed in 1989, allegedly by the Sudanese ruling party.

Einsatzgruppen (German for 'task groups'). Nazi special forces which implemented policies of mass extermination in occupied territories during the Second World War.

Ejército de Liberación Nacional National Liberation Movement. Term used by groups in Bolivia and Colombia.

Ejército Popular de Liberación People's Liberation Army. The name of a Colombian group.

Ejército Revolucionario del Pueblo People's Revolutionary Army. The name of a group in El Salvador.

EJPI Ejército Justiciero del Pueblo/Justice Army of Defenseless People, aka Avenging Army of Defenseless People (Mexico, Guerrero). The EJPI was active between 1996 and 1998.

ELA Epanastatikos Laikos Agonas/Revolutionary Popular Struggle, aka Revolutionary People's Struggle, National Front. This small Greek left-wing group was originally set up to oppose the military dictatorship and US influence in Greece from 1973; active 1975–1994.

ELF See Earth Liberation Front.

ELF Eritrean (People's) Liberation Front. Formed in 1960 and gained independence in 1993.

ELINT Electronic intelligence.

ELN Ejército de Liberación Nacional. The ELN was a Communist Bolivian insurgent group established by Ernesto 'Che' Guevara in late 1966.

ELN Ejército de Liberación Nacional/National Liberation Army. The second largest Marxist rebel group in Colombia, founded in 1964; numbers about 3,000 fighters and active mainly in the north, north-east and south-west of Colombia.

Embargo Prohibition of commerce with another state by government order.

Emergency laws Special stern laws that come into force on the declaration of a state of emergency due to internal crisis or external threat; usually contain provisions for the exercise of legislative powers by the head of state or a special body.

Emergency management Procedures to deal with natural or man-made disasters, including terrorism; related to preparation, mitigation, response and recovery measures.

Emergency responder Professional and volunteer forces (fire-fighting, medicine, law enforcement, etc.) called to the scene of a disaster to assist victims.

Encryption Translation of (plain-) text into cipher text that can only be read or understood by persons who hold the code key.

Endotheline A blood vessel-contracting natural substance discovered in 1988 in Japan; easy to synthesise. This is considered to be one of the biggest threats to conventions against chemical and biological weapons.

'Enduring Freedom' Code name for the US operation against the Taliban in Afghanistan, which began on 7 October 2001.

Enforcement terrorism Violence directed against a group's own ranks and constituency in order to force them to support, or at least not to betray, the group that claims to represent their interests.

Enhanced radiation and reduced blast (ERRB) weapon A fission–fusion neutron bomb that produces less blast than a normal hydrogen bomb.

Entebbe raid Successful Israeli hostage rescue operation at Entebbe (Uganda) airport in 1976, where hijacking victims, mostly Jews, were held by German terrorists.

Enterohaemorrhagic *Escherichia coli 0157* A biological agent.

Entrepreneurial terrorism Term used (infrequently) to denote either mercenary terrorism, criminal extortion terrorism or certain forms of single-issue terrorism.

Environmental groups Activists concerned about the decline of the human habitat due to pollution; only a few environmental groups engage in tactics that involve terrorism.

EO Explosives officer.

EO Executive Outcomes. This is a private South African security firm active in Sierra Leone 1992–1997.

EOD Explosive ordnance disposal.

EOKA Ethniki Organosis Kyprion Agoniston/National Organisation of Cypriot Fighters. The national liberation movement of Cyprus, which managed to expel the British from the island after three years of struggle (1955–1958). When unification ('Enosis') with Greece was blocked by the British, a second campaign of violence was initiated from 1971 to 1974 by its founder, General George Grivas (EOKA-B), against Turkish Cypriots and the United States, which led to a Turkish invasion in 1974 and *de facto* partition of the island. In 1978, EOKA was dissolved.

EOP Emergency operation plan. A disaster management document that specifies lines of authority, assignment of organisational responsibilities, protection measures, resource management and sequence of action to mitigate the consequences of a disaster during the response and recovery phase.

EPA Ejército del Pueblo en Armas/Army of the People under Arms (Venezuela). Formed in 2002, a paramilitary group supporting the Chávez regime.

Epanastatiko Laikos Agonas Revolutionary Popular Struggle, a Greek group.

EPB Ejército Popular de Boricua/Popular Army of Boricua, aka Macheteros (Puerto Rico). The EPB was formed in 1978 to obtain the independence of Puerto Rico from the United States.

EPCTF European Police Chiefs Task Force.

EPL Ejército Popular de Liberación/Popular Liberation Army. Rural armed Marxist-Leninist group active since 1967, fighting Colombia's oligarchy and US influence.

EPLF Eritrean People's Liberation Front, aka People's Front for Democracy and Justice. Eritrean separatist movement founded in the early 1960s; gained independence in 1994.

EPR Ejército Popular Revolucionario/Popular Revolutionary Army. Based in Guerrero, Mexico, formed in 1996 and linked to the Democratic Popular Revolutionary Party/Partido Democrático Popular Revolucionario (PDPR).

EPRDF Ethiopian People's Revolutionary Democratic Front. Formed around 1963.

ERCA Red Army for the Liberation of Catalonia/Ejército Rojo Catalan de Liberación. This Marxist–nationalist Catalan group was active in the 1980s and aimed to unite Catalans on both sides of the Spanish–French border in a Catalan state.

ERP Ejército Revolucionario del Pueblo/Revolutionary People's Army. Argentinian Trotskyite group founded in 1969 by Roberto Santucho; said to be acting as the military arm of the Ligas Populares 28 de Febrero (LP-28). Largely destroyed by the Argentinian military by 1977.

ERPA Ethiopian People's Revolutionary Army. Marxist guerrilla group opposed to the Military Administrative Council (PMAC) of Ethiopia in the 1970s.

ERT Emergency response team.

ESA Ejército Secreto Anticomunista/Secret Anticommunist Army. Consisted of state-sponsored death squads in Guatemala, active from 1977 onwards.

ESDC European Security and Defence College. Established in 2005 as a network of national military and police training institutes.

Espionage The activity of obtaining secret information about (attack) plans, war preparations, capabilities and resources of adversary; sometimes also takes the form of industrial espionage.

Esquadrones de la muerte See Death squad.

ESS European Security Strategy.

ESSAMLG Eastern and Southern Africa Anti-Money-Laundering Group.

ETA Euzkadi Ta Askatasuna/'Basque Fatherland and Liberty', aka Tierra Vasca y Libertad; affiliates include K.a.s., Xaki, Ekin, Jarrai-Haika-Segi, Gestoras pro-amnistia, Askatasuna, Batasuna, Herri Batasuna, Euskal Herritarrok. Marxist separatist group mainly active in Spain's Basque northeast, founded in the late 1950s and most active after the death of General Franco; sought to create a state of its own in parts of Spain (Vizcaya, Guipuzcoa, Alava, Navarra) and, to a lesser extent, union with the Basque regions of France (Basse-Navarre, Labourd, Soule). ETA was responsible for more than 800 killings between 1969 and 2010. It has used Herri Batasuna (aka Euskal Herritarrok) as a front organisation.

ETD Explosive trace detectors.

Ethnic cleansing Expulsion from a territory of an 'alien' population or sub-groups by massacres, rape or torture which cause other members of target group to leave their homes for fear for their lives. Ethnic cleansing is often perpetrated by paramilitary forces and sometimes borders on genocide, which aims at total elimination rather than spatial displacement. While deportation involves the forceful expulsion of people from their place of residence, ethnic cleansing seeks to achieve the same result by exemplary atrocities (arbitrary killings, rape, mutilation, torture) that create terror, panic and flight. If successful, this form of political crime produces results similar to ethnocide and/or genocide, while fatality levels are much lower.

Ethnic conflict See Conflict, ethnic, typology of

Ethnic group Part of the population of one or more states that share a cultural identity. Such ethnic communities have usually a number of the following characteristics: (1) a common proper name; (2) myths of common ancestry; (3) historical memories; (4) one or more distinct elements of culture, such as language or festivities; (5) an association with a given territory; and (6) a sense of social solidarity. Ethnic groups are usually a minority group within a state. There are more than 5,000 ethnic groups in the world. Some of them strive to form states. There are, however, only 12 ethnically homogeneous states. Another 25 states have a single ethnic group constituting 90 per cent of the population. In yet another 25 states, one ethnic group totals 75 per cent of the population. In 31 states, the dominant ethnic group accounts for between 50 per cent and 74 per cent of the population. There are 39 major states where no single ethnic group accounts for half of the population.

Ethnicity A sense of shared cultural identity derived from (imagined or real) common ancestry, traditions, customs, language or behavioural patterns.

Ethnocide A term sometimes used interchangeably with genocide, especially when indigenous peoples are exterminated. Sometimes it is also used to refer to the destruction of the culture of a people rather than their physical destruction.

ETIM East(ern) Turkistan Islamist Movement (China, Xinjiang-Uygur region). A separatist group formed in 1990; linked to Al-Qaeda, according to the Chinese government.

ETLO East(ern) Turkistan Liberation Organisation/Sharq azat Turkistan. The ETLO emerged in 2002, dedicated to the creation of an Islamic state in Xinjiang.

EU European Union. An organisation of 25 European states.

EUROGENDFOR European Gendarmerie Force. A paramilitary force for crisis management.

EUROJUST European judicial coordination body, established in 2002.

EUROPOL European Police Organisation. Multinational law enforcement agency seated in The Hague.

Evacuation Fast removal of people from a building or transport vehicle following a warning of imminent danger.

EW Electronic warfare.

EW Early warning.

Explosive Solid or liquid chemical substance capable of rapidly producing both hot gas and energy on a self-sustaining basis when triggered to do so, e.g. by shock or ignition. The gas pressure of an explosive bomb, which is sometimes spiked with shrapnel, is often lethal.

Extortion Criminal tactic of blackmailing individuals and businesses to pay 'protection money' or 'revolutionary taxes' to mafia-type organised crime groups and terrorist organisations. Non-compliance can result in arson, kidnapping of children or shooting.

Extraditables Spanish term. Those members of the Medellín drug cartel around Pablo Escobar Gaviria and José Rodríguez Gacha to be extradited (to the United States). In 1989, they organised a campaign of terrorism against the Colombian government to prevent their extradition.

Extradition Removal of a foreign person (sometimes also a citizen) from one state and transfer to another state where he or she is suspected of, or sought for, a serious crime, usually based on a bi- or multilateral international judicial agreement that regulates the conditions for handing over a suspected or convicted offender. Exceptions made for 'political crimes' have been curtailed and abolished for terrorist crimes by many states.

Extra-judicial execution Killing of political opponents or suspected offenders by armed forces, law enforcement officials or groups enjoying the tacit support of government agencies (e.g. death squads). The executions take place without any preceding judicial process. The term covers both summary and arbitrary executions.

Extremism In the context of democratic societies, a form of political expression (usually on the far left or the far right of the political spectrum) that is not acceptable to the more moderate mainstream of political life. Extremist groups and parties tend to be anti-constitutional, anti-democratic, anti-pluralistic, fanatical, intolerant, non-compromising, single-minded, authoritarian and adhering to an ends-justify-means philosophy, wanting to realise their goals by any means, including the use of political violence against opponents. Extremists on the political left or right and those of a religious-fundamentalist orientation favour violence over persuasion, uniformity over diversity, unity over pluralism and orders over dialogue. Since they also reject the rule of law and democracy, democracies cannot be tolerant against the intolerant, and face the dilemma of whether or not to prohibit such groups (risking that they will go underground and turn terrorist). Roger Scruton (1996: 186) identified three meanings of the term 'extremism':

1 taking a political idea to its limits, regardless of 'unfortunate' repercussions, impracticabilities, arguments, and feelings to the contrary, and with the intention not only to confront but also to eliminate opposition;
2 intolerance towards all views other than one's own;
3 adoption of means to political ends that disregard accepted standards of conduct, in particular which show disregard for the life, liberty and human rights of others.

According to the late Frank Buijs, all forms of extremism have five characteristics in common: (1) a feeling of acute threat and a tendency to exaggerate the enemy; (2) a rejection of the existing world order; (3) the counterbalance of a utopia (a good and harmonious world); (4) a chosen population group that can achieve this utopia under the leadership of a front line of steadfast individuals, directed by a leader of noble spirit; and (5) in order to overcome the forces of Evil and purify the world, the Good must employ violence and establish a dictatorship. (Buijs *et al.*, 2007).

Religious extremism is a variant of radicalism that shares its basic points of departure but differs in the specific assignment of an active role which the true believer is meant to play. According to Buijs (2002: 62),

> extremism turns the striving for the desired ideal society into the highest goal (utopism), absolutises the contradiction between the forces of good and evil (Manichaeism) and propagates a specific reading of the jihad, namely that it is the duty of all Muslims to use all possible means to fight evil and to realise the good society. Extremism is characterised by the idea that there is an irreconcilable contradiction between the true believers and the apostate rulers, which needs to be solved by means of armed struggle

which will destroy the heretics and bring the fighters to a pure belief. . . . Extremists and radicals share views about the utopia they strive for, but differ in opinion on the way to it. Radicals can turn extremists and extremists can turn radicals.

EYAL A group opposing the Israeli–Palestinian peace process in the 1990s, linked to the assassination of the Israeli prime minister Yitzhak Rabin.

EZLN Ejército Zapatista de Liberación Nacional/Zapatista Army of National Liberation (Chiapas, Mexico). The EZLN was formed in 1983 by Subcomandante Marcos, numbering more than 5,000 members. It staged an uprising in 1994 and entered mainstream politics in 2005.

FAA Federal Aviation Administration (United States).

Facility attack Bombing, arson and mortar or rocket attack on a specific building, object or installation for destruction, occupation, robbery or damage.

FACT Federation of Associations of Canadian Tamils, aka World Tamil Movement (WTM), World Tamil Association (WTA); linked to the LTTE.

Faction Section or group within a larger political movement or party.

FAI Federazione Anarchia Informale/Unofficial Anarchist Federation (Italy). Conglomerate of anarchist groups that emerged in 2003.

FAL Frente Argentino de Liberación/Argentine Liberation Front.

FAL Fuerzas Armadas de Liberación/Armed Liberation Forces; part of the Salvadorean FMLN.

FALN Fuerzas Armadas de Liberación Nacional (Puertorriqueña)/(Puerto Rican) Armed Forces of National Liberation. Puerto Rican group fighting for independence from the United States through bombing campaigns between 1974 and 1983 against US targets.

FALN Fuerzas Armadas de Liberación Nacional (Venezuela). Founded in 1974.

False-flag operation Deceptive action to incriminate falsely an adversary.

FAP Fuerzas Armadas Peronistas/Peronist Armed Forces (Argentina). The FAP was established in 1967 as a left-wing terrorist splinter of the Peronist Youth movement (Juventud Peronista).

FAP Forces d'Auto-Défense Populaires, aka Mai-Mai, May-May, Mayi-Mayi (DR Congo). FAP was formed in 1993 and consists of nationalist militias opposing Rwandan and Ugandan interventions but, more recently, also the Congolese armed forces.

FAR Fuerzas Armadas Revolucionarias/Revolutionary Armed Forces. A left-wing Argentinian group.

FAR Rebel Armed Forces. Left-wing guerrilla organisation established in December 1962 in Guatemala; joined the URNG (q.v.) in 1982.

FARC Fuerzas Armadas Revolucionarias de Colombia, Ejército del Pueblo/Revolutionary Armed Forces of Colombia, People's Army. Marxist guerrilla army founded in 1958 (1964 according to some accounts) by Manuel Marulanda Vélez ('Tirofijo') and Rigoberto Losada. It numbered some 12,000 fighters of whom up to 7,000 were child soldiers in 2004. FARC is financed mainly from drug production and trafficking as well as kidnappings and extortion, and also engages in terrorist operations. At one time, it enjoyed a temporary safe haven in 'Farclandia', an area of Colombia as large as Switzerland. By 2010, FARC was only a shadow of its former self.

FARC Fronti Armi Rivolutionnaire Corse/Corsican Revolutionary Armed Forces, aka Corsican Revolutionary Armed Front. FARC was formed in 1992 in protest against the French presence on Corsica.

FARL Factions Armées Revolutionnaires Libanaises/Lebanese Armed Revolutionary Faction. A Lebanese Marxist group that split from the PFLP-SOG (Special Operations Groups) after the death of its leader, Wadi Haddad (1979). FARL was active until the mid-1980s.

FARN Fuerzas Armadas de Resistencia Nacional/Armed Forces of National Resistance. A Marxist guerrilla faction established in 1975 in El Salvador by ERP dissidents; joined the FMLN in 1982, which in 1991 became a political party.

FARN Fuerzas Armadas Revolucionarias Nicaragüenses/Revolutionary Armed Forces. FARN is the official name of the Contras (q.v.).

Fascism An ideology of violent, nationalist, militarist, state-centred, corporatist, authoritarian, elitist, antirational, anti-communist, anti-liberal, paramilitary and sometimes racist movements based on a single right-wing party and charismatic leadership, which emerged after the First World War in Italy and elsewhere in Europe, especially Germany (National Socialism) and, in less extreme form, Spain (Falange).

Fatah See Al-Fatah.

Fatah Revolutionary Council See FRC and ANO.

FATF Financial Action Task Force. An international unit maintained by 31 countries which monitors money laundering and terrorist financing. There are regional sub-units, in particular CFATF (Caribbean FATF), GAFISUD (FATF of South America against Money Laundering) and MENAFATF (Middle East and North Africa FATF).

Fatwa An Islamic legal edict or judgement of an Islamic scholar/jurist (*ulama*) based on analysis of the holy texts of Islam, issued by an Islamic authority in response to a question by a lay Muslim on a specific issue. Osama bin Laden issued a fatwa against the United States and Israel despite the fact that he was no authoritative Islamic scholar (*alem*).

FBI Federal Bureau of Investigation. The branch of the US Department of Justice concerned with internal security, espionage, organised crime and terrorism. Since 1981, the FBI has had a Terrorist Research and Analytical Center (TRAC); it also has a Hostage Response Team (HURT).

FBL Fuerzas Bolivarianas de Liberación/Bolivarian Liberation Forces (Venezuela); formed in 1992.

FCO Fighting Communist Organisation. Term applied to several European left-wing terrorist groups such as the BR, CCC and RAF.

FDD Forces pour la Défence de la Démocratie; the armed wing of National Council for the Defence of Democracy in Burundi. The FDD has been active since 1994 in the Democratic Republic of Congo, west Tanzania and Burundi. It numbers 10,000 fighters.

FDLR Democratic Forces for the Liberation of Rwanda.

Fear An individual and collective human emotion as well as a psychological response triggered by perceptions of (life-threatening) danger, resulting in flight, defence, (counter-)attack or paralysis and irrational behaviour.

Fedayeen Derived from the Arab *fidai*, literally 'martyr'. A term used by different guerrilla and terrorist groups, including those Palestinians displaced in 1948 who attempted to fight the Israel Defense Forces in the 1950s and beyond with commando-type operations.

Fedayeen-e-Khalq-e-Iran People's Fedayeen of Iran. This communist Iranian group had been active since 1963 but was suppressed in 1981 by the Islamic Revolutionary Guard.

Fedayeen-i-Islam Shi'ite group founded in 1944, active in Iran and Iraq.

Federal Emergency Management Agency (FEMA) US government disaster response agency created in 1979.

FEMA Federal Emergency Management Agency (United States).

Fenian Brotherhood A republican movement of the nineteenth century that sought to liberate Ireland from Britain. The precursor to the IRA.

Fertiliser truck bomb A vehicle filled with large quantities of commercially available ammonium nitrate, detonated by conventional explosives.

FIDA Front Islamique du Djihad Armé, Anti-Fascist Resistance Group. See GRAPO.

Fiqh Islamic jurisprudence as interpreted by *fuqaha*, canonical specialists of Islam.

FIS Front Islamique du Salut/al-Jabha al-Islamiyyah li-Inqadh/Islamic Salvation Front (Algeria). This Islamist movement was founded on 10 March 1989 by Abbasi Madani. It was banned and repressed in 1991 because in the first round of parliamentary elections it was leading in 188 of 231 contests.

Fission bomb Nuclear weapon whereby uranium (U-233 or U-235) or plutonium (Pu-239) is split by neutron bombardment, triggering huge energy release in a chain reaction.

Fitna Arabic for 'communal discord', sedition. Such a 'war at the heart of Islam' is a practice that is regarded as highly undesirable, to be denied. The split between Sunnis and Shi'ah which occurred under the fourth caliph, Ali (the cousin and son-in-law of the prophet Muhammad), is sometimes seen as such.

Five C's See CCCCC.

FLB Front de Libération de la Bretagne/Breton Liberation Front. Founded in the 1980s.

FLEC Frente de Liberação do Enclave de Cabinda/Front for the Liberation of the Enclave of Cabina. This was a composite group fighting from 1963 onwards for independence of the oil-rich Cabina region from Portugal and later Angola.

FLLF Front for the Liberation of Lebanon from Foreigners. Formed in 1977 by right-wing Christian Phalangists, who opposed the Palestinian and Syrian presence in Lebanon; active until 1983.

FLN Front de Libération Nationale. Today's Algerian ruling party, which fought and won against French colonial rule in 1954–62.

FLNA National Front for the Liberation of Angola.

FLNC/FNLC Fronte di Liberazione Naziunale di Corsica/Front National pour la Liberation de la Corse/Corsican National Liberation Front. Separatist Corsican group established in 1976.

FLNKS Front de Libération Nationale Kanake Socialiste/Kanak Socialist National Liberation Front. A group fighting during the 1980s and 1990s for the independence of New Caledonia from France and sovereignty for the indigenous people, who make up less than half the population of the French territories in the South Pacific.

Floating bomb The scenario of maritime terrorists kidnapping an LNG tanker and turning it into a floating bomb – a veritable 'weapon of mass destruction' – is one of the nightmares of maritime security specialists. However, it is questionable whether such a scenario could ever happen; most specialists believe that in 99 out of 100 cases, the liquefied gas would not even burn, let alone explode in a catastrophic blast.

FLQ Front de Libération du Québec/Quebec Liberation Front. A left-wing nationalist and separatist French-Canadian Marxist group seeking secession of Quebec from Canada, active between 1963 and 1972. The group resurfaced in 1995 as the Quebec National Liberation Movement.

FMFLN Farabundo Martí Front for National Liberation. Salvadorean left-wing guerrilla alliance of five groups, formed in 1979. In the 1990s, it became a parliamentary party.

FMLH Frente Morazanista para la Liberación de Honduras/Morazanist Front for the Liberation of Honduras. The FMLH was formed in the late 1980s. The group is unrelated to the Morazanist Patriotic Front; it is linked to the Communist Party of Honduras.

FMLN–FDR Frente Farabundo Martí para la Liberación Nacional, Frente Democrático Revolucionario/Farabundo Martí National Liberation Front, Democratic Revolutionary Front. Salvadorean guerrilla umbrella organisation established in 1979, including the FPL (Fuerzas Populares de Liberación/Popular Liberation Forces, Ejército Revolucionario del Pueblo/Revolutionary People's Army (ERP), Fuerzas Armadas de la Resistencia Nacional/Armed Forces of National Resistance (FARN) and Partido Revolucionario de los Trabajadores Centroamericanos/Revolutionary Party of Central American Workers (PRTC).

FNL Forces of National Liberation (Burundi).

FOAM-X An explosive that can be put in an aerosol can and pass for shaving cream.

Foco theory Voluntarist idea developed by Che Guevara and Fidel Castro, who held that it is not necessary to wait for the objective conditions for a insurgency to be ripe; a small group of determined armed insurgents could act as a focal point ('*foco*') for discontents to rally around them once they have given the example.

Force The use of physical power to remove a person/object from a place against resistance; also used as a synonym for violence when applied by lawful authorities. Except in cases of self-defence, the use of force is generally held to be a prerogative of the state.

Force is an ambiguous concept sometimes equated with, and sometimes contrasted to, violence. Force as the application of physical coercion is sometimes considered legitimate if it is used to deter, to contain or to reduce violence and disorder, and if it is sanctioned by the proper authority and not disproportionate to its challenge. Justified violence can, from this perspective, transform into legitimate 'force', while unrestrained 'force' can degenerate into violence. The Carnegie Commission (1997: xxv–xxvi) recommended that three broad principles should govern the decision to use forceful measures:

- Any threat or use of force must be governed by universally accepted principles, as the UN Charter requires. Decisions to use force must not be arbitrary, or operate as the coercive and selectively used weapon of the strong against the weak.
- The threat or use of force should not be regarded only as a last resort in desperate circumstances. Governments must be attentive to opportunities when clear demonstrations of resolve and determination can establish clear limits to unacceptable behaviour.
- States – particularly the major powers – must accept that the threat or use of force, if it does become necessary, must be part of an integrated, usually multilateral strategy, and used in conjunction with political and economic instruments.

Force 17 Bodyguard of former Fatah chief Yasser Arafat and his closest colleagues, led by Khalil al Wazir until Israel killed him in 1988; also responsible for terrorist activities against Israel. Became part of Arafat's presidential security force in 1994.

Force 777 Egyptian counter-terrorist elite unit.

Force protection condition Security programme for US military personnel and their families; ranging from low- to high-threat conditions Alpha, Bravo, Charlie to Delta.

Fourth–Generation Warfare (4GW) A concept related to asymmetric warfare, in which there is no clear separation between war and peacetime and zones, states are not the only players and the traditional rules of warfare are pushed aside by one or both parties to a conflict.

FP-25 Forças Populares do 25 Abril/Popular Forces of 25 April, aka Armed Revolutionary Organisation and Autonomous Revolutionary Groups. Marxist Portuguese armed revolutionary group named after the military coup that overthrew the Salazar dictatorship in 1974. It was active from 1980 to 1986, targeting business, military and NATO representatives.

FPC Fronte Patriotu Corsu/Corsican Patriotic Front. The FPC was founded in 1999.

FPI Front Pembela Islam/Front for the Defenders of Islam, aka Islamic Defenders Front (Indonesia). The FPI was formed in the late 1990s, comprising several thousand members who are dedicated to the strict application of Shari'ah law and opposed to Western influences.

FPL-FM Farabundo Martí Popular Forces of Liberation. Guerrilla/terrorist group active in El Salvador from 1970, named after a former Communist Party secretary-general who was killed in 1932.

FPM Frente Patriótico Morazanista/Morazanist Patriotic Front, aka Morazanista Liberation Front, Morazanista Patriotic Front, Morazano National Liberation Front. This Honduran left-wing group was active from the late 1980s until the mid-1990s. It opposed the US and Contra military presence in Honduras during subversion of the Sandinista government of Nicaragua.

FPMR Frente Patriótico Manuel Rodríguez/Manuel Rodríguez Patriotic Front. Dissident armed wing of the Chilean Communist Party, active against the Pinochet dictatorship; founded in 1983 and active until 1994.

Francia Front d'Action Nouvelle Contre l'Indépendence et l'Autonomie/National Action Front Against Independence and Autonomy. This was a vigilante group targeting FNLC (q.v., under FLNC) in the late 1970s.

Francisella tularensis (*Pasteurella tularensis*) Bacterium causing an infectious rabbit disease, used by Japan in the Second World War; developed into a biological weapon by the United States.

FRAP Armed urban Marxist group active in El Salvador in the 1970s.

FRAP Fuerzas Revolucionarias Armadas del Pueblo (Mexico). Active 1970–73.

FRC Fatah Revolutionary Council. Terrorist group founded in 1974 by Sabri Khalil al Banna, aka Abu Nidal (aka ANO).

FRC Fronte Rivoluzionario del Comunismo (Italy). The FRC emerged in 1996.

Free Aceh Movement See GAM.

Freedom Absence of external constraints on individual or group; liberty to shape one's own life and ability to choose among different courses of action. A distinction is often made between *freedom to* (the possibility to act according to one's own will without any limitations imposed by or on behalf of others) and *freedom from* (a guarantee not to be arbitrarily deprived of one's personal integrity, such as in unlawful arrest, detention, deportation or slavery).

Freedom Birds Suthanthirap Paravaikal, aka Birds of Freedom. This was the female wing of LTTE fighters.

Freedom fighter Term used by some guerrilla fighters, terrorists and their sympathisers to justify (some of) their violence. Since it refers to a 'noble' goal – freedom – adherents of an ends-justifying-means philosophy deny that freedom fighters can be terrorists. The attempt to avoid the stigma of terrorism on account of the political ends pursued by freedom fighters is a major element that makes it difficult to achieve a universal definition of terrorism. Freedom is a goal, while terrorism is a means, the use of which denies freedom to victims, and since most of the direct victims of terrorism are not oppressors of those seeking freedom, the use of deliberate attacks against civilians (as opposed to attacks against security forces) should not be permitted in the name of a liberation struggle. A terrorist can be a freedom fighter and a freedom fighter a terrorist; the terms do not exclude each other.

Freezing Blocking or restraining of (usually financial) assets by competent authorities owing to suspicion that these were acquired illegally or serve an unlawful purpose.

FRELIMO Front for the Liberation of Mozambique.

Front An above-ground, apparently legal party, business or organisation used to conceal terrorist, criminal or espionage activity (e.g. a travel agency, or journalistic accreditation).

FRONTEX External border security agency of the European Union's 27 member states.

FRP-LZ Fuerzas Revolucionarias Populares Zeleya/Lorenzo Zeleya Popular Revolutionary Forces (Honduras).

FRUD Front pour la Restauration de l'Unité et de la Démocratie/Front for the Restoration of Unity and Democracy (Djibouti). A group representing the Afar people of Djibouti, formed in 1991; based in northern Djibouti and Ethiopia.

FSB Federal Security Service (Russia). The FSB was the successor to the KGB.

FSLN Frente Sandinista de Liberación Nacional/Sandinist National Front for the Liberation of Nicaragua, aka 'Sandinistas'. Marxist-Leninist insurgent group founded in 1960 which overthrew Anastasio Somoza's dictatorship and ruled Nicaragua from July 1979 to April 1990; was harassed by the US-backed Contras. After electoral defeat, some 'Sandinistas' returned to the use of political violence.

FTAT Foreign Terrorist Asset Tracking Center. US agency tracking, seizing or freezing supposed terrorist assets worldwide.

FTO Foreign Terrorist Organization. Denomination used by US government.

FUAC Frente Unido Andres Castro/Andrés Castro United Front (Nicaragua). This was a group of former Sandinista military officers, which attacked the government from 1995 onwards.

Fuerzas Armadas de Liberación Nacional (FALN) National Armed Liberation Forces, active in Colombia.

FULK Front Uni de Libération Kanak/Kanak United Liberation Front (New Caledonia).

Fundamentalism An ideology or movement of religious-political 'true believers' who claim to be in possession of unchallengeable truths derived from revealed divine and/or sacred texts and consider themselves superior to others, who, in turn, are often characterised as infidels or heretics. They strive to reorder state and society according to timeless 'fundamental' truths of a holy script that is taken literally (though often used only selectively). Extremists among fundamentalists tend to be non-compromising and resort to violence, including acts of terrorism, to further their cause. The intolerant, anti-pluralist, anti-secular orientation of fundamentalists (who exist not only in Islam but also among Christians, Jews, and Hindus) and the willingness of the extremists among them, possessed by doctrinal certainty, to kill and die for their cause causes frictions and clashes with host societies. Fundamentalism can be seen as a reaction to anomic tendencies in society, a reaction to the accelerating individualisation and pluralisation of modernising societies. Radical and extremist fundamentalist Muslims form, like the more secular, liberal modernists, a minority vis-à-vis the mainstream conservative traditionalist Islam. They view almost all rulers of Islamic societies as falling short of implementing the Islamic laws and therefore deserving to be overthrown. In addition, radical fundamentalists postulate that true Muslims have not only the right but the duty to bring about change by all possible means. There are, however, fundamentalists who are neither radical nor extremist – devout Muslims who take the holy scripts literally and see them as authentic and revealed. Oliver Roy, an authority on radical Islam, sees a neo-fundamentalist trend in modern Islam and finds the original term 'fundamentalism' no longer useful.

Fusion bomb Hydrogen bomb in which atoms 'melt' into each other rather than split to produce energy. Most hydrogen bombs are fission–fusion bombs or fission–fusion–fission bombs. The X-rays of the fission atom bomb act as triggers for the hydrogen bomb.

FUZ Frente Urbano Zapatista/Zapata Armed Front (Mexico).

G-8 Group of seven leading industrial nations (Canada, France, Germany, Italy, Japan, the United Kingdom and the United States), plus Russia.

GA Tabun; phosphoramidocyanidic acid, dimethyl-, ethyl ester. The first nerve gas, discovered in 1936.

GAC General Army Convention. This is the decision-making body of the Irish Republican Army (see IRA).

GAI Al Gama'a al-Islamiyya/ (Egyptian) Islamic Group, aka Al-Gamat al-Islamiya, Islamic Group (IG), Jamaat al-Islamiyya. Egyptian-based group whose spiritual leader is Sheikh Umar Abd al-Rahman (in prison for his role in the attack on the World Trade Center in 1993); held responsible for the 1995 assassination attempt on President Mubarak in Ethiopia and an attack on tourists in Luxor in 1997. The militant faction of GAI affiliated with Al-Qaeda in 1988.

GAL Grupos Antiterroristas de Liberación/Anti-Terrorist Liberation Group. Spanish security forces-backed death squad directed against ETA, also active in southern France between 1983 and the late 1980s.

GAM Gerakin Aceh Merdeka/Free Aceh Movement. Armed insurgency group based in Aceh on the northern tip of Sumatra, Indonesia, in the process of transforming itself into a regional political party. GAM was formed on 24 December 1976 as a guerrilla force to fight for the independence of resource-rich Aceh from Indonesia. In July 2005, GAM ceased hostilities after successful peace talks with the Indonesian government, and on 27 December 2005, GAM disbanded its military wing. The peace process in Aceh is monitored by an Aceh Monitoring Mission consisting of ASEAN and EU observers.

Gama'a al-Islamiyya (IG) Aka Al-Gama'a al-Islamiyya (IG). This Islamic association was the name of several Islamic movements in Egypt during the 1970s and 1980s. The Egyptian IG was responsible for the failed assassination attempt on the Egyptian president Hosni Mubarak. IG is affiliated to Al-Qaeda.

GB Sarin; phosphonofluoridic acid, methyl-, 1-methylethyl ester. GB is a colourless, odourless nerve gas discovered in 1939. A single breath of air containing sarin vapour is enough to kill a person.

GBR Grupo Bandero Roja/Red Banner Group (Venezuela).

GCHQ Government Communications Headquarters (UK). GCHQ is responsible for the British SIGINT collection, established in 1952.

GD Soman; phosphonofluoridic acid, methyl, 1,2,2-trimethylpropyl ester [R-(R*,R*)]. A nerve agent that can be weaponised, discovered in 1944.

Genetically engineered organisms The genetic targeting of only certain ethnic groups is considered a possibility, by bacteria or viruses treated in specific ways that could affect the genetic structure of human cells or activate a standard germ. Owing to the delayed action of genetic targeting, it is judged to be difficult to establish causality and recognise an attack as such. Genetic warfare is a fearful prospect.

Genetically modified micro-organisms Or genetic elements that contain nucleic acid sequences associated with pathogenicity.

Geneva Conventions Humanitarian rules of warfare, laid down in four conventions. The first Geneva Convention (1864) refers to the condition of wounded and sick armed forces in the field. The second Geneva Convention (1906) extended the first one in connection with the Hague Conventions of 1899 to the sea (naval forces). The third Geneva Convention (1929) introduced a new provision stating that its terms refer not only to the citizens of state-signatories, but to all people irrespective of their citizenship, covering military and civilians. The fourth Geneva Convention (1949) focused on the protection of civilian and military persons in times of war and established strict standards for civilian protection in areas covered by war and in occupied territories. In 1977, two additional protocols to the 1949 convention were adopted, relating to the protection of victims of international armed conflicts and to the protection of victims of non-international conflicts.

Genocide Premeditated, purposive, centrally planned group annihilation through mass killings for ethnic, religious or other purposes; a crime against humanity. The term covers one-sided, systematic large-scale extermination policies targeting specific unarmed groups of people by reason of their membership of a human collective (based on race, religion, class, etc.) as defined by the perpetrator (usually a criminal regime). The UN Genocide Convention of 9 December 1948 uses the term 'genocide' for 'any of the following acts committed with the intent to destroy, in whole or in part, a national, ethnic, racial or religious group, as such:

- killing members of the group;
- causing serious bodily or mental harm to members of the group;
- deliberately inflicting on the group conditions of life calculated to bring about its physical destruction in whole or in part;
- imposing measures intended to prevent births within the group; and
- forcibly transferring children of the group to another group.

Since the Genocide Convention does not cover lethal mass violence against unarmed people for political reasons, the term 'politicide' has been coined to cover that eventuality. Less often used are the terms 'democide' and 'ethnocide'.

GEO Grupo Especial de Operaciones/Special Operations Group. This is the Spanish national police counter-terrorist unit, used *inter alia* for hostage liberation.

Gestapo Geheime Staatspolizei/secret state police. Under National Socialism (1933–45), a repressive organ used to discover, infiltrate and destroy opposition to Hitler's regime of terror.

GHQ General Headquarters Staff. These staff are a unit of the Irish Republican Army (see IRA).

GI Gama'a al-Islamiyya/Islamic Group (q.v.).

GIA Group Islamique Armée/Armed Islamic Group. Terrorist group, especially active since 1992 in Algeria after an electoral victory of the Islamic Salvation Front (FIS) was annulled. A splinter group of FIS, founded by Afghan veterans, they number hundreds to thousands of fighters. According to the Algerian government, the GIA was supported by Iran and Sudan; it was also active in France, where it was supported by some expatriates. When President Abdelaziz Bouteflika's Peace and Reconciliation Charter was implemented in 2006, some gave up the struggle while others reportedly joined the GSPC.

GICM Moroccan Islamist Combatant Group. Al-Qaeda-affiliated group formed by former Afghan veterans in the 1990s as a splinter of Shabiba Islamiya.

GIGN Groupe d'Intervention de la Gendarmerie Nationale/Intervention Group of Military Police. The GIGN is a small French gendarmerie elite paramilitary unit used against terrorists at home and abroad.

Gilmore Commission US government advisory panel on the risk of terrorists using weapons of mass destruction.

Global Salafi Jihad (GSJ) Term coined by Marc Sageman to refer to violent fundamentalist attacks on the United States, Israel and the West in general by a fundamentalist movement of which Al-Qaeda is the most visible part.

Globalisation The process of growing integration of economies across regions through intensification of capital movements, trade, services, transportation and communication across borders, with concomitant political, social and cultural spin-offs. Globalisation is critically viewed by some as an uneven process and/or favouring Americanisation or Westernisation of non-Western cultures.

Glock-17 Austrian-manufactured plastic pistol with few metal parts, which makes detection by magnetometers difficult.

GMT Multidisciplinary Group on International Action Against Terrorism. Committee of governmental experts from the 46 member states of the Council of Europe, established in 2001.

God's Army Christian fundamentalist splinter group of the Karen National Union, formed in 1997 to resist the military dictatorship of Myanmar; active in Myanmar/Burma until 2001.

Good Friday Agreement Treaty accepted by popular vote on 10 April 1998 in Northern Ireland and the Irish Republic, meant to put an end to sectarian violence.

GPC Grupo de Combatientes Populares/Group of Popular Combatants (Ecuador). GPC is the armed wing of the Ecuadorian Marxist-Leninist Communist Party, formed in 1994.

GRAPO Grupo de Resistencia Antifascista, Primero de Octubre/First of October Anti-Fascist Group. Small Spanish communist group formed in 1975.

Grave breaches of the law of war These are considered to be war crimes to be repressed by legal sanctions. They include, according to the International Committee of the Red Cross in 1987:

- wilful killing, torturing or inhuman treatment;
- causing great suffering or serious injury to body or health;
- inhuman and degrading practices involving outrages upon personal dignity;
- taking of hostages;
- unlawful confinement;
- unlawful deportation or transfer of all or parts of the population of the occupied territory within or outside this territory;
- transfer by the occupying power of parts of its own civilian population into the territory it occupies;
- depriving of the rights of fair and regular trial;
- unjustifiable delay in the repatriation of prisoners of war or civilian persons;
- compelling to serve in the forces of an enemy party.

Great Satan Label used in the 1980s by Iran's Ayatollah Khomeini for the United States.

Great Terror Period under Stalinism from 1935 to 1938, which included purge of the Communist Party and Red Army by means of show trials, extra-judicial executions and labour concentration camps (gulag).

Grey Wolves Bozkurtlar (Turkey). Anti-Communist youth group linked to the Nationalist Action Party (NAP/MHP – Milliyetçi Hareket Partisi). Led by Col. Alparslan Türkes. A paramilitary secret organisation, formed in the early 1970s, the goal of which is to (re)create a Great Turkish Empire.

Grid computer-based search (German: *Rasterfahndung*). This is a method of systematic screening of personal data (banking, telecommunications, utilities, etc.) to discover persons that meet a certain (terrorist) profile.

Gross human rights violations The most severe human rights violations, related to the physical integrity of individual human beings: the right to life. They include political killings (extra-judicial executions), disappearances and torture. The term also covers arbitrary arrests that lead to prolonged detention without trial.

Ground Zero Site of the former World Trade Center in New York.

GSG-9 Grenzschutzguppe 9/9th Border Guard Group. German counter-terrorist special force established after the 1972 disaster at the Olympic Games in Munich.

GSJ Global Salafi Jihad (q.v.).

GSPC Groupe Salafiste pour la Prédication et le Combat/Salafist Group for Call and Combat. A splinter group from the GIA, founded in 1996, affiliated with Al-Qaeda, fighting from Mali, Mauritania, Niger and Algeria, with a presence in Western Europe.

Guardians of the Islamic Revolution Shi'ite group responsible for murdering exiled opponents of the Iranian cleric regime in the 1980s.

Guerrilla Spanish for 'small war'; a term applied to irregular mobile warfare by numerically inferior lightly armed small-size forces (guerrillas) but with potentially strong popular backing against colonial powers, foreign occupation forces or a domestic oppressor. Tactics include ambushing of security forces, 'hit-and-run' attacks and sabotaging infrastructures and supply lines of the government or occupation force in a protracted war of attrition, sapping the political will and capabilities of the opponent. Guerrilla forces usually control some territory or sectors of the population, from which they draw support. Sometimes guerrilla warfare is used in combination with acts of (urban) terrorism. The term is applied both to offensive operations by insurgents and to acts of resistance against occupation by partisans.

Guerrilla warfare Involves one or several of the following tactics: partisan warfare behind enemy lines, hit-and-run operations, sabotage, ambushes, urban terrorism. While purporting to move among the people like a fish in the water, guerrilla fighters often recruit new fighters by kidnapping and coercion, making ample use of child soldiers. Violations of laws of war and criminal activities are not uncommon and often prevent guerrilla groups from gaining the moral high ground which could induce the people (or the minority group they purport to represent) to side with them rather than with the sitting regime (Parkinson, 1979: 149–152).

Guildford Four Like the Birmingham Six, these people were convicted of a PIRA-attributed bombing in Guildford, UK, in 1974 on the basis of flawed evidence and released many years later on appeal.

Gunpowder A mixture of potassium nitrate (saltpetre), carbon (charcoal) and sulphur; the classic explosive until the nineteenth century.

Gush Emunim Bloc of the Faithful. A fundamentalist Jewish group seeking a Greater Israel that would correspond to the biblical kingdom of Israel.

GWOT Global War on Terrorism. US abbreviation used by the Bush administration after 9/11 for its counter-terrorist operations in the framework of a broad international coalition against terrorism.

Habeas corpus Literally, 'may you have the body'. This is the name of a British Act of Parliament (1679) for the prevention of arbitrary arrest. The act demands that the arrested person be presented to a judge within a certain time (usually within 48 hours) so that he can determine the lawfulness of the arrest. It prohibits detention of persons without a court warrant and guarantees that each case will be heard in an appropriate court. The act broadened the principles of civil rights protection contained in Magna Carta (1215) and the Petition of Rights (1628). Nowadays, habeas corpus is used as a writ directed to the person detaining another, requiring him to produce the prisoner or person detained with the day and cause of his or her arrest and detention. The validity of the detention has to be determined by a judicial authority, and if the detention is not lawful, the person has to be released. It is a legal measure against illegal confinement, and central to the rule of law.

Hactivist Computer hacker with political agenda who attacks adversaries' websites.

Hadith Recorded stories on the life of the prophet Muhammad.

Hague Convention Second in a series of international conventions and protocols meant to enhance aviation security against terrorists. Opened for signature in 1970 in The Hague, this anti-hijacking legal instrument had received some 180 ratifications by 2006.

Hamas/HMS Harakat al-Muqawammah al-Islamiyya/Islamic Resistance Movement (including its armed wing, Izz al-Din al-Qassam Brigades). Hamas was founded on 14 December 1987 at the beginning of the first Intifada as the Palestinian branch of the Muslim Brotherhood in Gaza and on the West Bank. Hamas, currently led by Khaled Mashaal (Damascus), seeks to remove the Israeli state from Palestine, putting in its place an Islamist state. Sheikh Ahmad Yasdin, its founder and spiritual leader, was assassinated by the IDF in March 2004. Hamas has more than 1,000 active members and hundreds of thousands of supporters and sympathisers. It won the parliamentary elections in 2006 and Ismail Haniyeh became prime minister of the Palestinian political entity. After 2006, it purged Gaza of Fatah followers and established a rule that tolerates no serious opposition.

Hanafi Muslim Movement US-based Islamic group responsible for taking hostages in 1977 in Washington, DC.

Hantaan virus A biological agent.

Harakut ul-Jihad-I-Islami (HUJI) (Kashmir/Pakistan). HUJI was founded in the late 1990s.

Harakut ul-Mujahidin/Movement of Holy Warriors See also HUM. Pakistan/Kashmir-based Sunni militant group founded in 1993 and banned in 2002 in Pakistan. Affiliated to Al-Qaeda.

Harb (dar al) War zone; area inhabited by infidels against whom it is, in some Islamist interpretations, legal to wage jihad (as opposed to dar al-Islam, the land of Islam, where Shari'ah law is applied).

Hard targets Objects with active and passive security systems against intrusion, sabotage and attack; as opposed to 'soft targets', which lack them.

Harkat-ul-Ansar Originally Hizb-ul-Mujahedin. Sunni organisation founded in 1980 in Pakistan to support Afghan mujahedin against Soviet occupation; also active in Kashmir.

Hate crime Attack on a person because of his or her ethnic origin, sexual orientation, religious outfit or other marker of difference.

Hawala Informal money-transfer system using trusted brokers (hawaladars) rather than official banks, leaving little or no paper or electronic trail and therefore open to terrorist abuse; also known under different names like Hindi.

Hawari Group Named after Col. Hawari, aka Abdullah Abdulhamid Labib. Special operations group of Al-Fatah engaged in terrorist bombings in, *inter alia*, Italy and Switzerland, especially in the second half of the 1980s.

Hazmat Hazardous materials.

HB Herri Batasuna, aka Batasuna. This is the political front of the Basque ETA.

H-Bomb see Hydrogen bomb.

HD Mustard gas, mustard sulphur; (1,1′-thiobis(2-chloroethane)). A blister agent.

Hegemony In international politics, the predominance of one power over others, based on (a combination of) military, economic, cultural, technological and other resources. In domestic politics, the ability of a class or other formation to maintain its dominance without direct recourse to violence or repression.

Hel Hizb-e-Islami (Afghanistan).

Herbicide A chemical agent that is toxic to plants and crops, also used as a defoliant.

HEU Highly enriched uranium: uranium that contains more than 20 per cent (as opposed to the naturally occurring level of 0.7 per cent) of U–235 isotopes. 'Weapons-grade' uranium is enriched to at least 90 per cent, while a workable improvised nuclear device (IND) is assumed to contain 80 per cent or more of U–235. Weapons-grade plutonium consists of about 94 per cent of the isotope Pu–239.

Hezbollah Aka Islamic Jihad, Islamic Jihad for the Liberation of Palestine, Organisation of the Oppressed on Earth, Party of Allah (God), Revolutionary Justice Organisation, Islamic Resistance. Led by Hassan Nasrallah, Hezbollah is dedicated to the destruction of Israel and turning Lebanon into an Islamic state. The sizeable Shi'ah Lebanese Hezbollah group (several thousand fighters) split from the Shi'ite Amal Party in 1982, following the Israeli invasion of Lebanon, and is supported by Syria and even more so by Iran. The group was involved in numerous acts of suicide terrorism and hostage taking against Westerners, *inter alia*, in the 1980s. In March 2004, the group announced that it had joined forces with Hamas. It holds seats in the Lebanese parliament and is represented in government. In July/August 2006, it provoked a full-scale war with Israel in Lebanon. Hezbollah has conducted terrorist attacks abroad, including in Argentina, Sweden, the United Kingdom and Thailand. By 2010, it had become the strongest force in Lebanon, thanks to Iran's finamncial and military support. The name 'Hezbollah' is also used by groups in Iran, Saudi Arabia, Turkey and India.

HG Hauthi Group (Yemen).

HIG Hizb-i-Islami Gulbuddin, Islamic Party. Afghan group commanded by Hikmatyar. The HIG is affiliated to Al-Qaeda.

Hijacking Taking temporary control of a vehicle (most often an aircraft) by threat or force against the will of the pilot, either for escape and transport or for coercive bargaining to compel authorities to do or abstain from doing certain things (e.g. prisoner release). Hijacking for escape only is criminal but usually not terroristic.

Hikmatul Zihad Wisdom of Jihad, aka Hikmat-ul-Jihad (Bangladesh). The group emerged in 2004 with an unsuccessful assassination attempt on the leader of the Awami League, Sheikh Hasina.

Hirabah Arabic term for terrorism; that which is prohibited; an unholy 'war on society' involving crimes against humanity and war crimes.

Hit Slang word for an attack on or the murder of an individual belonging to an adversary camp.

Hit man (Mercenary) killer who murders individuals for an organised crime syndicate, terrorist group or secret service.

Hizb Arabic for (political) party, e.g. Hizb al-Shaitan (Party of Satan).

Hizballah See Hezbollah.

Hizb-i-Islami Islamic Party, a.k.a. Hizbul-i-Islami (Afghanistan). Founded by the warlord Gulbuddin Hekmatyar in the mid-1970s, this insurgent group first fought the Daud regime, then the Soviet invaders with Pakistani and US support.

Hizb-i-Islami Gulbuddin A faction of Hizb-i-Islami. It emerged in 1977 and fought the Soviet invaders; it was later linked to the Taliban and Al-Qaeda, fighting the United States and the Afghan Transitional Administration.

HLAAR High-level armed assault and robbery. Also known as major criminal hijack (MCHJ) (q.v.).

HLH Terror Triangle The Hong Kong–Luzon–Hainan Triangle. Part of the South China Sea and a hot spot of piracy in the 1990s, and still regarded as dangerous waters.

HM Hizb ul-Mujahideen (Kashmir, India), aka HM of the Jamaat-e-Islami. The military wing of Jamaat-i-Islami, Pakistan's largest Islamic political party. It was formed in 1989 and is reportedly linked to the ISI. Active in Afghanistan in the early 1990s and, above all, in Kashmir, which the HM wants to merge with Pakistan.

HME Homemade explosive.

HNLC Hynniewtrep National Liberation Council (India (Meghalaya)).

Hoax Bogus bomb or other threat to scare people and/or cause the evacuation of a place.

Hofstad Group Dutch-based takfiri group justifying violence against infidels (*kuffar*) and apostate in Muslims; formed in 2002–2003 in Amsterdam and responsible for the execution of the Dutch movie producer Theo van Gogh.

Holocaust Term used to describe the genocide of up to six million Jewish persons murdered by the Nazi regime during the Second World War.

Holy Spirit Mobile Force Cult group founded by Alice Lakwena, who instigated its members to fight against the Ugandan Army in 1987; thousands of cult members died, believing wrongly that the holy oil on their bodies protected them from bullets. The remnants were reorganised into the Lord's Resistance Army, which was still active in 2006.

Homeland Security Term denoting US domestic security measures after 9/11.

Homeland Security Advisory System (HSAS) US government alert system warning the public of the level of risk of an impending terrorist attack: Red = Severe, Orange = High, Yellow = Elevated, Blue = General, Green = Low.

Homicide Non-premeditated killing of a human being.

Hostage Person held in the power of the adversary (voluntarily or, more often, by force), in order to obtain specific concessions (release of prisoners, cancellation of military operations, ransom, etc.) from the opposite party to the conflict or from particular individuals (e.g. terrorists).

Hostage taking Detention of a person at a known location usually against his or her will to coerce a third party to perform a certain act or desist from a certain act upon penalty of death for the victim in the event of non-compliance. Acts of hostage taking are prohibited by the International Convention against the Taking of Hostages (1979); under the laws of war they are a war crime.

Hostilities Actual fighting aimed at the incapacitation or destruction of the adversary in violent and armed stages of conflict. It is the key characteristic distinguishing a dispute from a conflict. There is no consensus about the minimum number of fatalities that distinguishes a 'violent political conflict' from a low- and high-intensity conflict. Some analysts define war or serious hostilities as entailing at least 1,000 casualties. This definition of hostilities does not include lesser violent incidents such as a border skirmish with a relative handful of casualties or a *coup d'état* change of regime that includes some casualties.

HPG People's Defence Forces (Turkey). The armed wing of Kongra-Gel, the People's Congress of Kurdistan, led by Abdullah Öcalan until his arrest in 1999. The HPG resumed fighting in 2004, after a ceasefire. It numbers up to 5,000 fighters.

HRT Hostage Rescue Team (FBI, United States).

HSAS Homeland Security Advisory System (q.v.).

HTI Hizb al-Tahrir al-Islami, the Islamic Liberation Party.

HUA Harkat-ul-Ansar, renamed Harakat ul-Mujaheddin. HUA is an Islamist fundamentalist group that based in Pakistan aims to unite Indian Kashmir with Pakistan; founded in 1993.

Hudna Arabic for 'truce', ceasefire.

HUJI Harakat ul-Hihad-I-Islami/Movement of Islamic Holy War (Pakistan).

HUJI-B Harkat-ul Jihad al-Islami/Movement of Islamic Jihad (Bangladesh). The group was formed in 1992 to establish an Islamist regime in Bangladesh. It is reportedly linked to Al-Qaeda.

HUKS Hukbong Bayan Laban Sa Hapon/People's Anti-Japanese Resistance Army, aka Hukbalahap. The group was active between 1842 and 1954 in the Philippines against the Japanese and later the Americans.

HUM Harakat ul-Mujahedeen, aka Islamic Freedom Fighters' Group, Jamiat-ul-Ansar. This is a pro-Pakistani group active in Afghanistan and in Jammu and Kashmir, established in 1985 and numbering several hundred members; it is reportedly linked to Pakistan's ISI and to Al-Qaeda.

Human rights Concept derived from the doctrine of natural rights, which holds that all members of society, based on the fact that they are human beings (moral persons), possess fundamental rights beyond those described in national laws. Human rights are meant to protect those attributes that are essential to a life in dignity as a human being. A number of fundamental rights are generally considered to be inherent, natural and inalienable, and may not be violated by the state. Core human rights are freedom from arbitrary arrest and imprisonment, and freedom from torture, cruel and unusual punishment, unfair trials and invasion of privacy. Rights to food, shelter, health care and education, freedom of thought, speech, assembly, religion, press, movement and participation in government are also core rights. Altogether, there are more than 75 human rights. However, their enforcement necessitates the cooperation of sovereign states and the international community, based on political will and the allocation of resources.

Humanitarian law The laws of war as codified in the Geneva Conventions of 1864, 1906, 1929 and 1949, as well as the two additional protocols of 1977 to the fourth Geneva Convention.

HUMINT Human intelligence. Information obtained directly from individual persons through clandestine acquisition (spying), debriefing of foreigners and travellers, and liaison with other intelligence services and embassy reports, as opposed to intelligence gained by technical means (SIGINT).

Hydrogen bomb (H-bomb) A thermonuclear weapon deriving its power from the fusion reaction of lithium, deuterium and/or tritium, usually triggered by an atomic bomb.

IAA Islamic Army of Aden (Yemen), founded in 1998.

IAEA International Atomic Energy Agency, based in Vienna.

IAI Islamic Army in Iraq/al-Jaish al-Islami fi al-Iraq. Islamic group active since 2004, targeting (kidnapping) Westerners and Iraqis, linked to Abu Musab al-Zarqawi and Ansar al-Sunnah.

IBDA-C İslami Büyük Doğu Akıncıları Cephesi/Great Eastern Islamic Raiders' Front/Great Islamic Eastern Warriors Front, aka Front Islamique des Combattants du Grand Orient. IBDA-C was a Turkish Islamist group established in the 1970s that opposed secular tendencies in Turkish society; targeting also Jewish and Western representatives and facilities in Turkey. It is affiliated with Al-Qaeda.

ICC International Criminal Court in The Hague. It has not been granted jurisdiction over terrorist acts. However, to the extent that terrorist acts are crimes against humanity, the court does have jurisdiction over them, at least in theory.

ICS Incident Command System (q.v.).

ICS Islami Chhatra Shibir (Bangladesh). Militant student group linked to Jamaat-e-Islami, founded in 1941.

Ideological terrorism Term usually denoting left- and right-wing indiscriminate political violence against non-combatant civilians.

Ideology In political affairs, ideology stands for all systems of ideas that tell people how the social world is (supposed to be) functioning, what their place in it is and what is expected of them. Ideologies are patterns of beliefs and expressions that people use to interpret and evaluate the world in a way designed to shape, mobilise, direct, organise and justify certain modes and courses of action. They are often a set of dogmatic ideas associated with a system of values about how communities should be structured and how its members should behave. Major political ideological doctrines are nationalism, liberalism, fascism, communism and anarchism. Ideologies are often a secular substitute for lack of a religious orientation, offering an interpretation of social reality, a way to a better future and a model of the Good Society with a prescription how this could be brought about. In practice, ideologies often serve as mobilising instruments for those in power or those aspiring to state power.

IDF Israel Defense Forces, or armed forces of Israel.

IDQ Izz al-Din al-Qassam Brigades (q.v.).

IEA International Energy Agency.

IED Improvised explosive device: mines and bombs constructed from commercially available chemicals (e.g. agricultural fertilisers), as opposed to more powerful military and research department explosives (RDX).

IEDD Improvised explosive device disposal.

IFLO Islamic Front for the Liberation of Oromo. A separatist group seeking independence from Ethiopia.

IG Al Gama'at al-Islamaya/Islamic Group (Middle East).

IIF International Islamic Front for Jihad against Jews and Crusaders. A name used by Bin Laden/Al-Qaeda.

IIPB Islamic International Peacekeeping Brigade (Chechnya). One of the major Chechen groups founded in 1998 by Shamil Basayev and financed by Al-Qaeda associates in the Gulf region.

IIPF Islamic International Peacekeeping Brigade.

IIRO International Islamic Relief Organisation.

IJU Islamic Jihad Union, aka Islamic Jihad Group (Uzbekistan). The IJU is a splinter group of the IMU, active in 2004 against American, Israeli and Uzbek targets.

IK Iparretarrak (France). Basque autonomous movement, formed in 1973 in part of the Basque region on French territory.

Ikhwan Muslimun Muslim Brotherhood. A semi-secret fundamentalist movement/society founded in 1928 in Egypt.

ILA Iraqi Liberation Army/Jaish al-Tahrir al-Iraqi. Kurdish separatist group emerged in 1980, operating in Iraq, Lebanon and Turkey.

Imam The person who leads prayers in a mosque; (junior) Muslim cleric.

IMB International Maritime Bureau.

IMB International Muslim Brotherhood.

IMINT Imagery intelligence.

IMLIN International Money Laundering Brotherhood.

Imperialism A political slogan, analytical concept and historical period in European history. Historically, it refers to the UK, French, Spanish, Portuguese, Dutch, Belgian, Italian and German projection of military power beyond the borders of these countries in order to take possession of the territory of other countries or penetrate them for economic or military reasons, as in the decades preceding the First World War, when European powers sought to obtain or strengthen their rule over colonies. After decolonisation, the term was used to describe policies of political and economic domination without formal territorial control of penetrated client states.

Improvised nuclear device (IND) A low-budget, low-tech 'home-made' fission explosive or radiological dispersal device.

IMRO Inner Macedonian Revolutionary Organisation. A nationalist terrorist group fighting for Macedonian independence against the Ottoman Empire; founded in 1893, sponsored by Bulgaria and later by Hungary and Italy; active until the Second World War.

IMT Islamic Movement of Turkistan. A fundamentalist movement founded in 2001.

IMU Islamic Movement of Uzbekistan.

IMU–IPT Islamic Movement of Uzbekistan/Islamic Party of Turkistan. Founded in 1996 (1998?), the IMU-IPT aims to create an Islamic state covering Uzbekistan, Kyrgyzstan, Tajikistan, Kazakhstan, Turkmenistan and Xinxiang (China). The movement was active between 1999 and

2001, when its leader, Juma Namangiani, was killed in Afghanistan. It is supported by the Taliban and Al-Qaeda.

Incapacitants Chemical substances that temporarily produce physiological or psychological debilitation, rendering a person incapable of performing or functioning normally. Such incapacitating agents include bradykinin, psychotropic substances, cannabis, cannabis derivates (tetrahydrocannabinol, amino-cannabinoids), phencyclidine and derivatives (hallucinogen), chlorpromazine (anti-psychotic), fentanyl (narcotic), QNB derivates (hallucinogens), enkephalins (body-made morphine), morphine, etonitaze (painkiller), benzodiazepine derivates (convulsants), heroin.

Incident An occurrence, man-made or natural, that requires intervention for harm reduction, damage control or consequence management.

Incident Command System (ICS) Integrated, pre-planned, on-scene response system for handling emergencies, allowing seamless communication, cooperation and coordination between agencies with different task assignments.

IND Improvised nuclear device (q.v.).

Independent Republic of Armenia Group that attacked Turkish targets until about 1983.

Industrial agent Chemical agent used in industry, agriculture or other civilian sectors with dual-use capacity for chemical terrorism (e.g. herbicides and pesticides).

Infiltration Clandestine entry of enemy territory or organisation for the purpose of intelligence gathering, sabotage or assassination (the opposite is exfiltration).

Influenza Flu, a viral infection of the respiratory tracts, comes in three variants (A, B, C). Type A influenza caused the Spanish flu epidemic in 1918, which killed 20 million people – more than the fatalities of the previous four years of war – in a few months.

INGO International non-governmental organisation.

Ingush Jama'at Shariat Caucasian Islamic separatist group in Ingushetia led by Amir Khabibulla that emerged in 2005 to fight 'Russian colonists'.

INLA Irish National Liberation Army. A small Marxist-Leninist splinter group of the Official IRA based in Dublin, active since 10 December 1974 and founded by Seamus Costello; reorganised in the late 1980s, it fought for the expulsion of the British from Northern Ireland until 1998, when it declared a ceasefire.

Insecticides Various types are close to weaponised nerve gas in their chemical structure.

Insurgency An armed uprising, revolt or rebellion by a political group or party against domestic or foreign ruling regime in order to subvert it, overthrow it, expel it, and break away from it, or simply to enhance the group's bargaining position for subsequent political compromise. Acts of terrorism are a frequent occurrence in many insurgencies.

Intelligence (1) The product (collected, processed, analysed, interpreted and evaluated) of (usually secret) information gathering concerning domestic and foreign actual and potential situations which is designed to be operationally useful by decision makers to deal with adversaries (political, military, economic, ideological, criminal or terrorist actors). It is partly gained from open sources and partly from confidential or secret sources by either technical (e.g. satellite imaging) or human (e.g. espionage) methods of acquisition. (2) An intelligence organisation, usually of the state, that engages in clandestine information gathering, analysis and dissemination to policy makers, and also conducts covert operations in support of national security policy.

Intelligence agency A state (rarely: commercial) organisation gathering open information and secret intelligence on the capabilities and intentions of (potential) (military) adversaries and competitors in order to protect (state) security interests from foreign and/or domestic threats.

Interahamwe Army for the Liberation of Rwanda (ALIR). The armed wing of the Party for the Liberation of Rwanda; established around 1994 and numbering 2,000+ (2001), seeking to regain Hutu control of Rwanda after its expulsion following the genocide of 1994; active in the Democratic Republic of Congo and Rwanda.

Interception Acquiring electromagnetic signals and other messages between third parties for purposes of intelligence gathering.

Internal war Intra-state or domestic armed conflict. According to Eckstein (1972: 9), 'any resort to violence within a political order to change its constitution, rulers or policies'. With the growth of foreign diasporas (exiled people, emigrants, refugees) which take an active interest in the politics 'back home' and with the use of local and diaspora actors as proxies by neighbouring and other states, few civil wars are truly domestic.

International armed conflict Interstate wars; the term is sometimes also used for wars of national liberation and self-determination (Protocol I, 1977 to the fourth Geneva Convention).

International community Term referring to the collection of states, most of which are part of the United Nations with its 192 members. It is sometimes mistakenly used in the sense of 'international society' or 'world society', which, in a narrow sense of the term, does not (yet) exist.

International crime According to Cassese (2003: 129), 'Terrorist acts amount to *international crimes* when, first, they are not limited in their effects to one State solely, but *transcend national boundaries* as far as the persons implicated, the means employed, and the violence involved are concerned: and, secondly, they are carried out with the support, the toleration, or the acquiescence of the State where the terrorist organisation is located or of a foreign State.'

International law The body of customary rules and treaty-based agreements between states and other entities (e.g. international organisations) that regulate mutual relationships and treatment of each other's citizens and officials.

International terrorism A definitional construct developed by B.M. Jenkins and US colleagues, which refers to 'those acts in which the terrorists crossed national frontiers to carry out attacks, or attacked foreign targets at home such as embassies or international lines of commerce as in airline hijackings' (Jenkins, 1999: vi). For a while, this concept competed with the term 'transnational terrorism' (in analogy with transnational organised crime) but it has since become dominant, and is often considered a synonym of terrorism, despite the fact that up to 90 per cent of terrorist acts are confined to the territory of one state.

The term is often used loosely in analogy to 'international communism' and sometimes also served in propaganda terms as a successor enemy construct. Its relationship to 'transnational terrorism' and 'global terrorism' is therefore not always clear. Terrorist groups operating outside their countries are often termed 'international terrorists'. Acts of international terrorism cover attacks against foreign governments or international organisations, or representatives thereof, as well as attacks against any national of a foreign country because s/he is a national of a foreign country.

International war A form of armed conflict involving at least two recognised independent states or coalitions of states, whether or not hostilities have been preceded by a formal declaration of war.

Internment Forced detention, encampment or imprisonment of dissident nationals or dangerous foreigners, applied sometimes to terrorist suspects.

INTERPOL International Criminal Police Organisation. INTERPOL has its headquarters in Lyon, France.

Interrogation The questioning of someone who is suspected of criminal, illegal, subversive and/or terrorist behaviour or anyone who presumably has knowledge relevant to that, with the aim of extracting information. In a number of countries, interrogations are conducted by teams applying various forms of psychological, mental or physical pressure, including torture.

Intervention Term referring to various forms of interference by one or several states into affairs that are within the jurisdiction of another state, in pursuance of their own or, less frequently, humanitarian interests. Uninvited military interventions are banned by the UN Charter (art. 2, para. 7).

Interventions are, when uninvited, often coercive, compulsive or manipulative, open or clandestine temporary external interference in the internal affairs of a state – diplomatic, economic or, above all, military – in order to modify either the other state's domestic decision-making or its foreign relationships. In the meaning of sending military forces across international borders, it partly overlaps with war and aggression, and is outlawed in Art. 2.7 of the United Nations Charter. Yet sometimes intervention is executed on the basis of an invitation by (sectors of) a government or an opposition or a third party, such as a regional security organisation or the United Nations. Since intervention infringes on a state's sovereignty, non-intervention is the professed norm in international law. Tillema found that between 1945 and 1985 there were 296 conflicts but no fewer than 591 overt military interventions in the international system (cited in Van Goor, 1994: 6).

When interference in the form of 'military assistance' is added to this, the number increases to thousands of episodes. Hoffman (1993: 88) defined intervention as '[a] move by a state or an international organization to involve itself in the domestic affairs of another state, whether the state consents or not'. There are various intervention types. Glasl (1997: 148–149) distinguishes between:

- Preventive interventions before the outbreak of a conflict.
- Curative intervention aimed at the solution, limitation, control or regulation of an existing conflict.
- De-escalating intervention, which aims at reducing tension and must be based on insight into the factors and mechanisms that led to escalation in the first place.
- Escalating interventions: it can be in the interest of a permanent conflict resolution to escalate a 'cold' conflict (one in which the parties avoid both contact and confrontation).

In situations of state crimes, justifiable grounds for intervention exist. According to Haas (1993: 81), an emerging global consensus about the permissibility of multilateral coercive actions covers the following situations:

- to prevent and punish aggression by one state against another;
- in a civil war, to reimpose peace terms on one party that has reneged, provided the terms had originally resulted from UN peacemaking;
- to enforce violations of international agreements banning the possession, manufacture, or trade of weapons of mass destruction;
- to enforce agreements banning or limiting trade in conventional arms, including trade in dual-use and forbidden technologies;
- to prevent an event certified by experts as an immediate impending ecological catastrophe;
- to prevent genocide;
- to protect an established democratic polity from anti-democratic armed challenges, but not to protect a dubious or fictitious one; and
- to prevent and alleviate famine and mass epidemics.

Intervention, military The entering of a country by armed forces of a foreign power against the wishes of the government in power. It can be (but rarely is) humanitarian in nature if the purpose is to protect civilians and if it is sanctioned by the international community.

Intervention, overt military Kinsella and Tillema (1995: 311) defined overt military interventions as 'combat-ready military operations openly undertaken by a state's regular forces within a foreign territory. [The term] includes operations by conventional ground combat units, commando and other small unit raids, aerial attacks, ground-based artillery and rocket attacks, and naval bombardment'. Many contemporary interventions are covert, or conducted by proxies, with 'plausible denial' propaganda strategies surrounding them for damage control in case of discovery or failure.

Intifada Arabic for 'shaking off'. Name given to a low-violence Palestinian uprising between 1987 and 1991; a second insurrection, the 'Al-Aqsa Intifada', which was much more violent and involved suicide attacks, started in 2000.

Intiharioun Suicide (volunteer) who engages in a kamikaze mission.

Intimidation A threat, either verbal, written or through exemplary acts, that expresses intent to inflict (further) harm to a subject his or her relatives or friends. In addition to individualised intimidation directed against a specific person, there is collective intimidation of a selected group of people (e.g. witnesses in court).

Invasion An armed attack on the territory of another state.

Iodine–131 A radioisotope suitable for RDD.

IPK Islamic Party of Kenya. A group reportedly linked to the government of Sudan, active in the 1990s.

IRA Irish Republican Army. An association of radical Irish nationalists seeking secession from the United Kingdom formed in 1913. It succeeded in liberating all but six of the counties of Ireland between 1916 and 1922. After the civil war of 1921–1923, the Official IRA favoured, on the whole, bringing about a unified, socialist Ireland by peaceful means. Yet intermittently, some of its adherents used terrorist methods to unite Northern Ireland with the Irish Free State (and, after 1949, the Irish Republic). In the 1970s, many nationalist Catholics from the IRA joined the more militant PIRA (q.v.), which was formed as a faction in 1969 and soon assumed the name of the official IRA. The latter discontinued the armed struggle in 1972.

IRA Izquierda Revolucionaria Armada/Armed Revolutionary Left (Ecuador). First emerged in February 2004.

Iran–Contra Affair Illegal activity by the US National Security Council of the Reagan administration in the 1980s whereby profits from secret arms sales to Iran were channelled to Nicaraguan counter-revolutionaries, partly in order to free Western hostages in Lebanon with the help of the Shi'ah authorities in Tehran.

Iraultza Basque Armed Revolutionary Workers' Organisation. Iraultza was a Marxist group active mainly in the 1980s, targeting Spanish and American interests.

IRB Irish Republican Brotherhood. Emerged from the Fenian Brotherhood and prepared the 1916 Easter Rising in Dublin; the precursor to the IRA.

IRGC Islamic (or Iranian) Revolutionary Guards Corps. Paramilitary and later official force created by Ayatollah Khomeini in Iran in May 1979 to protect the Iranian Revolution and repress opposition at home and abroad, including by terrorism.

Irgun Zvai Leumi (IZI) 'National military organisation'. The IZI was a terrorist group active between 1937 and 1948, when it joined the Israel Defense Forces. It was led by Menachem Begin after the death of its founder, David Raziel. It was, *inter alia*, responsible for blowing up the King David Hotel in 1946 (which housed the British military intelligence headquarters; 91 were killed, 45 injured) and the massacre of more than 200 Arabs in the village of Deir Yassin in 1948. The latter led to an exodus of Palestinians and to the first Arab–Israeli war.

Irhab Arabic for 'terrorism'.

Irhabiyoun Arabic for 'terrorists'; also 'irhabis' or 'irhabists'. Those identified by this term tend to use a number of euphemisms like 'jihadis', 'jihadists', 'mujahideen' and 'shahideen', which have more positive connotations.

Irredentism From the Italian for 'unrecovered'. (1) The ideological basis of political movements seeking to (re)gain by force lost or claimed territory from a neighbouring state where the same language, religion or ethnic group prevails; or (2) alternatively, a national minority of one state seeking (re)union with the majority in a neighbouring state.

Irregular war(fare) Asymmetric warfare by a weaker party using ambushes, raids, stealth, harassment and deception to compensate for military inferiority.

ISAF International Security Assistance Force in Afghanistan, established in December 2001.

ISI Inter-Services Intelligence. The chief external Pakistani military security service, held responsible for financing foreign guerrilla and terrorist groups, especially in Afghanistan, Kashmir and the north-east of India.

Islamic Refers to adherence to the belief of Islam.

Islamic Amal Splinter group of Amal (q.v.), opposed to the secular rule of Nabih Berri.

Islamic Army for the Liberation of the Holy Places The name of a group identical with, or affiliated with, Al-Qaeda, which claimed responsibility for the bombings of US embassies in East Africa on 7 August 1998.

Islamic Army of Yemen A group affiliated to Al-Qaeda.

Islamic Front for the Liberation of Bahrain A Shi'ite group striving for a repetition of the revolution in Iraq.

Islamic fundamentalism A radical movement which believes that the original Islamic laws are key to the solution of socio-economic and political problems. It preaches jihad to purge Muslim countries of un-Islamic laws, institutions and rulers, and foreign powers that back them. The movement has an *islahi* (reformist) wing that is linked to the Muslim Brotherhood (q.v.) and a *salafi* (puritan) wing that preaches the use of violence to bring about a revolution after the failure of both nationalism and socialism in Arab and Muslim countries.

Islamic Group Egyptian Al-Qaeda affiliate.

Islamic Jihad Al-Jihad Al-Ismali/Islamic Holy War. A term used by various groups in Palestine (Islamic Jihad of Palestine), Lebanon (Hezbollah) and Egypt (Munazzamat al Jihad). The Egyptian IJ, founded in 1979, merged with Al-Qaeda in 1998.

Islamic Jihad Aka Al-Jihad, Egyptian Islamic Jihad, Jihad Group, Vanguards of Conquest. Founded in 1979, active around Cairo and abroad, numbering some thousands by 2001.

Islamic Movement for Change Composite group based in Saudi Arabia and Syria, active in 1995–1996 against US targets.

Islamic Tendency Movement An Islamic renaissance movement in Tunisia opposing the regimes of President Habib Bourguiba (1956–1987) and his successor, Zine El Abidine Ben Ali.

Islamism A radical extremist political ideology within Islam striving to transform society both socially and politically in the image of what is believed to be the original 'pure' Islam, based on the Koran and the Sunna – the sayings and deeds of the Prophet. Classical (i.e. early-twentieth-century) Islamism is fundamentalist: that is, the holy texts are interpreted and applied literally. Classical Islamism is also exclusive in the sense that other points of view are dismissed, as the believer possesses the absolute truth. Finally, classical Islamism is integralist: that is, all questions of private and public live are judged to be answered by Islam. Islamism in itself is not necessarily violent, but terrorism is a tactic used by some Islamist groups. As a religious–political ideology, Islamism seeks to reunite the Islamic nations in an Islamic state ruled by Shari'ah law. According to Oliver Roy (2004), Islamism is different from fundamentalism with regard to the issues of political action, Shari'ah and women (whose participation in social and political life is not rejected).

Islamist Refers to adherence to an Islamic fundamentalist ideology; often applied to members of groups advocating armed struggle against non-believers and heretics (jihad).

Ismaili A branch of Shi'ah Islam currently led by the Aga Khan; historically associated at one point in the twelfth century with the legendary sect of the Assassins.

ISPS International Ships and Port Security Code. This is a mandatory security code of the International Maritime Organization (IMO) for ports and ships, including contingency arrangements, computer systems, surveillance equipment and manual patrols. ISPS, which came into force on 1 July 2004, contains detailed security-related requirements for governments, port authorities and shipping companies, including the appointment of security officers, conducting risk assessments, devising security plans and enhancing the overall security through technical devices of both ships and ports.

ISYF International Sikh Youth Federation.

ISYU International Sikh Youth Union, aka People's Resistance Movement of Iran (PRMI).

IT Information technology.

Ijtihad The effort of interpreting Islamic sacred texts.

IYC Ijaw Youth Council (Nigeria).

IZL Irgun Zvai Leúmi/National Military Organisation, aka Etzel. This was a Jewish terrorist group active in Palestine from 1931. When Israel declared statehood unilaterally in 1948, its members were incorporated into the official Israel Defense Forces.

Izz al-Din al-Qassam Brigades Aka Al-Qassam. The military wing of Hamas, established around 1987, numbering 500 members by 2001.

J Jundullah (Iran).

Jaish Arabic for 'army'. Often used as part of the name of terrorist groups which pretend to, and aspire to, be armies.

Jaish Al-Taifa Al-Mansoura Army of the Victorious Community, aka Jaiech al-Taifa al-Mansoura, Victorious Army Group, Victorious Army Sect (Iraq). Sunni group formed in 2003 opposing US intervention, allegedly affiliated with Al-Qaeda and the Abu Musab al-Zarqawi Jihad network. The group joined the Mujahideen Shura Council, an umbrella organisation of the resistance against the US-led intervention in January 2006.

Jamaa Arabic for group, association, company.

Jama'at Al-Tawhid Wa'al-Jihad (Iraq) Al-Zarqawi network (see JTJ).

Jamaat al-Fuqra Community of the Impoverished. Pakistan-based Islamic group active since the 1970s, with a presence in the United States.

Jamaat-e-Islami (JI) Pro-Pakistani party in Kashmir, established by Sayyid A'la Mawdudi (1903–1979), a leading advocate of Salafi jihadism.

Jama'at-i-Tulaba Student wing of the JI, advocating Iranian-type revolution for Kashmir; has attacked Hindu civilians and Indian police stations.

Jama'at Jund al-Sahaba Soldiers of the Prophets Companions (Iraq). Sunni extremist group targeting Shi'ites and US troops.

Jamiat ul-Ansar A group formerly called Harakat ul-Mujahidin (HUM).

Jammu and Kashmir Contested territory between Pakistan and India claimed by Pakistan but integrated with the Republic of India in 1957 after Maharajah Sire Hari Singh had announced the accession of Kashmir to India ten years earlier. One district of Kashmir, Ladakh, was occupied by China in 1962.

Jammu and Kashmir Islamic Front A separatist group fighting Indian rule of Jammu and Kashmir since 1995, allegedly formed by Pakistan's foreign intelligence arm, ISI.

Jammu and Kashmir Liberation Front Movement fighting Indian rule in Jammu and Kashmir.

Japanese B encephalitis virus A biological agent causing brain of inflammation.

JCAG Justice Commandos for the Armenian Genocide. A nationalistic group founded in 1975 in Lebanon which sought to establish an Armenian state. The JCAG reportedly continued activities after 1983 under the name Armenian Revolutionary Army (ARA). It ceased activities in 1983.

JCT Jama'a Combattante Tunisienne/Tunisian Combatant Group, aka Groupe Combattant Tunisien, Tunisian Combat Group, Tunisian Islamic Fighting Group. The JCT was formed around 2000, linked to Al-Qaeda.

JDL Jewish Defense League. Originally a New York-based vigilante group founded in 1968 by Rabbi Meir Kahane, who led the JDL until 1985, targeting anti-Jewish and anti-Israeli state and non-state actors, including representatives of the PLO and the Soviet Union.

JEM/JeM Jaish-e-Mohammed/Army of Mohammed, aka Army of the Prophet Mohammed, National Movement for the Restoration of Pakistani Sovereignty and Army of the Prophet, Tehrik Ul-Furqaan. A Pakistani-based group established in 2000 by Masood Azhar, reportedly supported by the ISI, seeking to unite Kashmir with Pakistan. This Al-Qaeda-affiliated group was alleged to be behind the 2001 attack on the Indian parliament in New Delhi. The group was banned in December 2001 by President Pervez Musharraf.

Jemaah Islamiya Group/Organisation (JI) Al-Qaeda affiliate in Indonesia and South-East Asia.

Jenin Martyrs' Brigade (West Bank, Gaza) The name used by Hamas supporters for a suicide attack in 2003 against an Israeli bus.

JI Jemaah Islamiyah. Founded in the early 1990s; fighting for an Islamic state (named either Nusantara or Malaysia Raya – 'Greater Malaysia') based on the Shari'ah, to include the deep south of Thailand, Malaysia, Indonesia, Singapore, Brunei Darussalam and the southern parts of the Philippines. JI was led by Riduan bin Isomoddin (better known as Hambali), who was captured in 2003. Members of JI were responsible for both (2002 and 2005) Bali blasts and the bombings in Jakarta of the Marriott Hotel and the Australian embassy, among other activities such as fanning racial hatred between indigenous Muslims and ethnic Chinese Christians on Java or between Javanese Muslim immigrants and autochthonous tribal groups on Kalimantan – all under the banner of jihad.

Jihad Literally, 'to strive', 'to struggle', 'to exert oneself'. It refers to 'striving in the path of Allah' (*jihad fi sabil Allah*) (Leemhuis, 1991: 54). 'Jihad' is often translated as 'holy war'. It referred, in the period 750–1258, mainly to 'missionary warfare' directed against non-Muslim 'infidels', either to convert them or to subdue them as *dhimmis* (non-Muslims living under Muslim rule) (Zimmerman, 2007: 279).The meaning of the term is controversial. There are several forms of 'jihad': the term 'greater jihad' (*jihad al-Akbar*) is sometimes used to refer to a Muslim individual's struggle to do what is right and good according to Islam (jihad of the heart – the struggle against one's own instincts, sinful inclinations and temptations); there is also the 'jihad of the tongue' (*jihad al-lissan* or *da'awah* – speaking on behalf of the good and forbidding evil) and the *jihad al-kabir* – the spiritual/intellectual quest to spread knowledge of divine revelation through Allah's prophets and to carry out *ijtihad* – consultative efforts throughout the *ummah*. The understanding of jihad as 'spiritual struggle', however, is only weakly supported by the Hadith. There is only one reference to it in a less authoritative report, while there are 199 references to jihad as warfare in the so-called Bukhari hadidths. (Zimmerman, 2007: 280). Far more common, however, than this interpretation of jihad as non-violent spiritual struggle is the use of the term for warlike activities; in this sense, jihad is used to refer to the collective or individual armed struggle and the propagation of Islam against infidels (*kufr*). This is also referred to as jihad of the sword (*jihad as-sayf*). Traditionally, this term was used to describe military struggle against non-Muslims – not necessarily for purely religious reasons, but either defensively to protect or free Muslims from oppression or, more commonly, as offensive jihad for conquest to establish Islam in other countries. David Cook, in *Understanding Jihad*, has pointed out that the jihad references in the Koran were used as justification for 1,000 years of Islamic expansion from the seventh to the seventeenth centuries throughout the Middle East, North Africa, Central Asia, Europe and India (cited by Zimmerman, 2007: 281). While these conquests are usually portrayed by their apologists as benign and benefiting the conquered, this view is not shared by many of their victims, who did not see them as liberators.

Some contemporary Sunni proponents of jihad attempt to elevate offensive jihad to the sixth pillar (*arkan*) of Islamic obligations. In Shi'ite Islam, the idea of offensive jihad has, in theory, been shelved until the return of the twelfth imam (who disappeared in 874) from his occultation (concealment) (Zimmerman, 2007: 285). The revival of the jihad doctrine in the 1980s was to an important extent the work of the Palestinian university professor Abdullah Azzam, who, from 1984, published the Arabic magazine *Al Jihad* in Pakistan. In his booklet 'Defending the Land of the Muslims Is Each Man's Most Important Duty', he proclaimed that jihad became an individual obligation (rather than a collective one) and that every Muslim had to participate in it morally or financially. His vision went beyond Afghanistan: 'This duty shall not lapse with victory in Afghanistan, and the jihad will remain an individual obligation until all other lands which formerly were Muslim come back to us and Islam reigns within them once again. Before us lie Palestine, Bukhara, Lebanon, Chad, Eritrea, Somalia, the Philippines, Burma, South Yemen, Tashkent, Andalusia' (quoted in Keppel, 2002: 146–147).

Azzam had been Bin Laden's teacher at the Abd-al-Aziz University of Jeddah and became his spiritual mentor in Afghanistan until 1988, when he broke with him, one year before he was assassinated. Osama bin Laden, in turn, released a Declaration of Jihad against the Americans Occupying the Land of the Two Holy Places on 23 August 1996, which referred to Azzam as one of the authorities on which this 11-page declaration was based (Keppel, 2002: 317).

Bin Laden's mentor divided the worldwide jihad into three categories (Fighel, 2001):

1   within Muslim countries, with the goal of reinstating rule by Shari'ah;
2   in countries with Muslim minorities, situated on the 'fault lines' with other cultures, e.g. the Balkans, Chechnya, Kashmir;
3   the international cultural struggle, in which Islam takes on Western – especially American – civilisation.

Abdullah Azzam and Bin Laden have given the concept a very belligerent interpretation – a call to arms, a mandatory obligation for each individual Muslim to take up the sword to fight on all fronts: to overthrow their own governments, intervene in countries where Muslims are engaged in civil war and take up arms against the superpower America and its Western allies.

Jihad Pegah Aka Jihad Base. A Kurdish Islamic group active in 2005 in northern Iraq, affiliated to Al-Qaeda and opposed to the secular Kurdish government of the PUK and KDP.

Jihadi Militant person engaged in-religious campaign against internal and external enemies of his or her interpretation of Islam.

Jihadism Violent Salafist Islamism based on the notion that Islam is under threat and must be defended by the sword against unbelievers (*kafir*), who are considered inferior. The ultimate goal is the universal expansion of Islam.

JJTM-G Janatantrik Terai Mukit Morcha-G (India (Jarkhand)).

JJTM-J Janatantrik Terai Mukti Morcha-Jwala Singh (India (Jarkhand)).

JLT Jharkhand Liberation Tigers (India (Jarkhand)).

JMB Jamatul Mujadein Bangladesh. Islamist group targeting secularists and Hindus; formed in the late 1990s and responsible for 400 simultaneous explosions on 17 August 2005 in Bangladesh.

Joint War Committee (JWC) The JWC, which represents London-based marine insurance companies, is constituted of members of the Lloyd's Market Association (LMA) and the International Underwriting Association (IUA). It issues the 'JWC Hull War, Strikes, Terrorism and Related Perils Listed Areas' list, which assesses the insurance risks of certain regions and waterways as a professional service to the insurance market.

JRA Japanese Red Army/Nippon Sekigun. A small (30–40 members) left-wing international terrorist group formed in 1970 as a breakaway of the Japanese Communist League – Red Army Faction and headed by a woman, Fusako Shigenobu. It aimed for the overthrow of the Japanese monarchy and world revolution. The group was mainly active abroad as the Anti-Imperialist International Brigade (AIIB) and at one time was supported by Syria. The JRA worked with PFLP. It was disbanded in 2000 by Fusako Shigenobu, the year she was arrested.

JSD National Socialist Party. Maoist group formed in the 1960s in Bangladesh, led by Major J. A. Jahil. It had two armed wings: the People's Revolutionary Army and the Rohingya Solidarity Organisation (RSO).

JTAC Joint Terrorism Analysis Centre (UK). The JTAC was created in June 2003 as Britain's main centre for the analysis and assessment of international terrorism.

JTJ Jama'at Al-Tawhid Wa'al-Jihad/Tawhid and Jihad, aka Monotheism and Holy Struggle, Tanzim Qa'idat al-Jihad fi Bilad al-Rafidyan, Unification and Jihad, Al-Qaeda in Iraq, al-Rawhid, al-Zarqawi network. Group led by the late al-Zarqawi, opposing US intervention in Iraq.

JUA Jamiat ul-Ansar, aka Harakat ul-Mujahidin.

JUD Jamaat ud-Dawa, aka Lashkar-e-Tayyiba (LT) and Army of the Righteous (Pakistan).

Judicial murder From German *Justizmord*. A death sentence handed down to an innocent person by a non-independent court on the basis of false testimony and/or fabricated evidence for political reasons.

JUM Jamiat ul-Mujahedin (Kashmir, India). An irredentist group trying to integrate Kashmir and Jammu into Pakistan; formed in 1990 as a breakaway from Hizb ul-Mujahideen (HM), active in Kashmir, also employing Pakistani jihadists.

June Second Movement Bewegung zweiter Juni. German left-wing group formed after the death of a student in Berlin on 2 June 1967; became linked to the RAF (q.v.).

Junin virus A biological agent.

Junta Spanish for 'council'. A clique of the military that comes to power by a *coup d'état*, sometimes in response to a real or exaggerated threat to the state.

Jurisdiction The range and sphere of legal authority for addressing an occurrence (a crime or disaster).

Jus ad bellum (Latin) law to (conduct) war. It refers to a theory that stipulates when it is justified to go to war. Key elements are: (1) war has to be declared by a lawful authority; (2) there has to be a just cause; and (3) war needs to be conducted with the intention to restore a peaceful order.

Jus in bello (Latin) law applicable to warfare; the theory that lays down principles of just conduct during warfare. Key elements are: (1) the proportionality of the means utilised; and (2) the immunity of non-combatants.

Justice A yardstick by which to judge the behaviour of persons and institutions, especially with regard to the legitimacy of rule and division of goods, including elements such as equal treatment, impartiality and lack of arbitrariness. 'The morally justifiable apportionment of rewards or punishments, each person being given what he or she is "due" ' (Heywood, 1997: 407).

Justice Commandos of the Armenian Genocide Group active from the 1970s to avenge Ottoman genocide during and after the First World War against Armenians.

Justice Department The name assumed by British and Canadian animal liberation groups active since 1993.

JVP 'People's Liberation Front'. A left-wing anti-Tamil party in Sri Lanka active since the 1970s.

Kach Hebrew for 'Thus'. Right-wing extremist Jewish group founded in 1971 by Rabbi Meir Kahane (1932–1990), which aimed to restore the biblical Jewish kingdom. Kach was outlawed in 1994 after a massacre in a mosque in Hebron by a Kahane supporter.

KADEK Kurdistan Freedom and Democracy Congress, aka Kongra-Gel (KGK) and Freedom and Democracy Congress of Kurdistan; linked to the PKK (Turkey).

Kafir Arabic for 'Infidel'. A term used by fundamentalists to describe non-Muslims, against whom war is supposed to be an Islamic duty.

Kahane Chai (Kach) Hebrew for 'Kahane lives'. A successor group to Kach, formed in 1990 by the founder's son, Binyamin Kahane; a Jewish extremist group that aims to restore the Biblical Jewish kingdom, expelling Arabs from land claimed for Israel.

Kamikaze A term denoting Japanese suicide pilots at the end of the Second World War who tried to crash by the hundreds their explosive-filled planes into US warships in the Pacific.

KCP Kangleipak Communist Party (India (Manipur))

KDP Kurdish Democratic Party/Partiya Demokrata Kurdistanê. Founded in 1946 by Mustafa Barzani, it seeks autonomy or independence from Iraq, and is partly funded by Iran. A rival of the PUK until 1998; they now jointly form the Kurdish regional government.

KFOR Kosovo Force (NATO).

KGB Komitet Gosudarstvennoe Bezopasnosti/Committee for State Security. Internal and external security forces of the Soviet Union.

KGK Kongra-Gel, formerly the Kurdistan Workers' Party (PKK), KADEK.

Khmer Rouge Red Khmer, aka Khmer Communist Party/Party of Democratic Kampuchea. Genocidal Communist Party, formed in 1951, led by Pol Pot, which exercised a reign of terror in Cambodia between 1975 and 1978, costing 1.5 million or more lives. Out of power for more than a dozen years, the Khmer Rouge was still active in the 1990s against the government of Cambodia.

KIA Kachin Independence Army. This is the armed wing of the Kachin Independence Organisation, founded in 1961, numbering 8,000 members by 2001; active until the ceasefire in north Myanmar.

Kidnapping The unlawful and usually covert seizure and abduction of one or several (often specific) person(s). This is usually followed by detention at a secret location, and then by a series of demands for blackmail or ransom. Unlike in a hostage taking, the location of the victims is not known. When kidnapping is for ransom only, it need not be terroristic. When used to force the release of prisoners, or to bring about some other political objective, it is considered terroristic.

Killing Deprivation of life by manslaughter or premeditated murder without any due process.

KKK Ku Klux Klan. Extremist hooded white racist group founded in 1866 in Tennessee after the American Civil War was lost by the slaveholding white South. The KKK objected to the emancipation of black Americans and engaged in acts of intimidation through the burning of crosses and lynching of black citizens for more than a century thereafter, changing its membership and organisation several times. The KKK, now only a shadow of its past self, is also anti-Semitic, anti-homosexual and anti-Catholic.

KKKK Knights of the Ku Klux Klan. One of the larger American racist clan groups.

KLA Kosovo Liberation Army/Ushtria Çlirimtare e Kosovës/UCK. Irredentist group formed in 1992 originally striving to unite ethnic Albanians of the Balkans into 'Greater Albania'. It became, after 1995, a liberation movement of the Serbian province of Kosovo, attacking both Serbian police and civilians, seeking to secede from Yugoslavia and 'cleanse' the province of Serbs. During NATO's war against Yugoslavia, its strength increased to 12,000–20,000 men.

KLA Khalistan Libertation Army (India (Manipur)).

KLNLF Karbi Longri North Cachar Hills Liberation Front (India (Assam)).

KMM Kumpulan Mujahedeen Malaysia. Founded in 1995.

KMT Kuomintang. Chinese Nationalist Party, defeated by Mao Zedong and exiled to Taiwan and Burma since the late 1940s.

KNA/KNF Kuki National; Army/Karbi People's Front (India (Manipur)).

Kneecapping The crippling of a person by shooting off the kneecap for intimidation and revenge. Frequently practised by the PIRA and BR.

KNLA Karen National Liberation Army. Has sought, since 1947, to establish a Karen state in Myanmar; it numbers 4,000 and is active on the Thai border.

KNU Karen National Union (Myanmar/Burma). The KNU was formed in 1959, struggling for independence of Karen province, numbering some 4,000 fighters in 2004.

KOMOLA Kurdistan Organisation of the Communist Party of Iran. Active since 1967, numbering 200 members in 2001.

Kopassus Indonesian army special forces, which engaged in state terrorism in East Timor and elsewhere.

KRMM Kodagu Raiya Mukhta Morcha (India (Manipur)).

KSM Khalid Shaikh Mohammed. Al-Qaeda's mastermind of the 9/11 attacks on the World Trade Center and the Pentagon. Captured on 1 March 2003 in Rawalpindi/Pakistan by members of the Pakistani Inter-Services Intelligence (ISI), possibly in cooperation with the FBI, and immediately transferred to US custody.

Kufr Also *kafir* or *kaffir*; Arabic for 'heretic'.

Kuki Revolutionary Army In north-eastern India. A tribal Christian Assam-based group fighting for an independent Kukiland straddling India and Myanmar, formed in 1999.

Kurdistan One of the largest nations in the world (*c.* 25–30 million) not in possession of a state, split up mainly between Iraq, Iran, Turkey and Syria.

Kurdistan Freedom Hawks See TAK.

Kurdistan Workers' Party See PKK.

Kyasanur Forest virus A biological agent.

KYKL Kanglei Yawol Kanna Lup/Organisation to Save the Revolutionary Movement in Manipur, aka Kanglei Yaol Kanba Lup/Organisation to Save the Revolutionary Movement of Manipur (India). Formed in 1994 and funded through extortion, this vigilante group of ethnic Meteis is one of a dozen insurgent groups in Manipur.

LAEF In India (Meghalaya).

Laissez-faire Literally, 'let go' or tolerate. A policy of some democratic governments with regard to the media response to terrorism, which places no restrictions on the media coverage of terrorism, however serious the threat of violence.

Lashkar Urdu for 'battalion'; also used for 'army'.

Lashkar-e-Islam Army of Islam linked to LeT (Pakistan).

Lashkar-e-Jhangvi (LeJ) Aka Lashkar i Janghvi (LJ), Army of Jhangvi. Al-Qaeda-affiliated Sunni Deobandi group formed in 1996 and linked to the Taliban. Attacks Shi'ahs in Pakistan as well as Iranians; also operates in India.

Lashkar-e-Omar Army of Omar, aka Al-Qanoon (Pakistan). A coalition of fundamentalist, Taliban-type groups consisting of Lashkar-e-Jhangvi (LeJ), Harkat-ul-Jihad-i-Islami (HuJI) and Jaish-e-Mohammed and others, formed in October 2001; held responsible for the attack on the US consulate in Karachi in June 2002 and the murder of US journalist Daniel Pearl. Linked to Al-Qaeda.

Lashkar-e-Tayyiba (LT) Aka Lashkar-e-Toiba, Army of the Pure, Army of the Righteous, Soldiers of the Pure. Kashmir-based Islamist terrorist group numbering several thousand members in eastern Kashmir and Pakistan, led by Abdul Wahid Kashmiri and founded in 1989. Its political wing is Jamaat ud Daawa, aka Markaz-ud-Dawa-wal-Irshad (MDI). Reportedly funded from 1994 onwards by Inter-Services Intelligence (ISI) for attacking Hindus, training of Muslims in other parts of India, and promoting the merger of Kashmir with Pakistan. Affiliated to Al-Qaeda. Banned by President Pervez Musharraf in January 2002. Suspected of being behind the train bombings in Mumbai on 11 July 2006 and the November 2008 attacks in Mumbai.

Laskar Jihad Army of Jihad, aka Holy War Warriors (Indonesia). A Salafist nationalist paramilitary group. After training in Java, possibly by Al-Qaeda, in 2000, it entered, up to 10,000 strong, the predominantly Christian Moluccan Islands and killed thousands, destroying whole villages and engaging in ethnic cleansing and forced conversions for two years, allegedly supported by the Indonesian military. In 2005, Laskar Jihad was reportedly operating in West Papua and on the Solomon Islands.

Lassa fever virus A biological agent, causing a very contagious disease; a potential biological agent sought by AUM in Congo.

Lautaro Youth Movement A faction of the Chilean United Popular Action Movement (Movimiento de Acción Popular Unitaria); active since the 1980s.

Law Binding and usually enforceable rules for a political community; established by tradition or formally enacted by a political authority (e.g. parliament) and backed up by the power of the state, or introduced through international treaties.

Law enforcement Public agencies (police, gendarmerie, etc.) entrusted with the prevention, detection and investigation of crime and the arrest of alleged offenders.

Laws of war The body of prescriptions on the conduct of combat and the protection of victims of combat contained in the Hague Conventions, the Geneva Conventions and the other international treaties that belligerents are to respect for humanitarian reasons. These rules – which are often disregarded in practice – contain such rules for behaviour in military action as the following:

Combat rules:
- fight only combatants;
- attack only military targets;
- spare civilian persons and objects;
- restrict destruction to what your mission requires.

Enemy combatants who surrender:
- spare them;
- disarm them;
- treat them humanely and protect them;
- hand them over to your superior or the nearest medical personnel.

Civilian persons:
- respect them;
- treat those in your power humanely;
- protect them against ill-treatment; vengeance and taking hostages are prohibited;
- respect their property; do not damage or steal it.

(Source: ICRC, Summary for Commanders, 1987: 1)

LDI Lajnat Al-Daawa Al-Islamiya/Islamic Cell Committee (Kuwait).

Leaderless resistance An organisational construct developed by Louis Beam in 1994 on the basis of the experience of right-wing militia groups in the United States, to prevent infiltration by state agents. It relies on 'lone wolf'-type individual initiatives to act for a common cause with minimal or no conspiratory contacts between like-minded militants.

Left A term referring to the position of political parties on the left–centre–right spectrum; ranges from social liberal parties to social democratic, socialist, communist and extremist parties. Key professed values usually encompass equality, progress, reform, a decent standard of living for the common person, and international solidarity with the poor and unjustly treated.

Left-wing terrorism The use of generally indiscriminate and unlawful violence against civilians and non-combatants by political forces adhering to Marxist, Leninist, Stalinist, Maoist or other left-wing theory or practice, seeking to undermine or obtain state power by acts of targeted violence against representatives of the state and the capitalist economic system.

LEHI Lohame Herut Israel/Fighters for the Freedom of Israel, aka the Stern Gang. A Jewish terrorist group that split from Irgun (q.v.), also known as Stern Gang, active against the British and Palestinians between 1940 and 1948.

LeJ/LJ Lashkar-e-Jhangvi. See under Lashkar-e-Omar.

Leninism The Russian variant of Marxism, named after Vladimir Lenin, a Russian intellectual who became the first leader of the Soviet Union, 1917–24. Officially, Leninism relied on mass action to obtain state power; however, Lenin also advocated terrorism, especially during the Russian Civil War.

LESLP London Emergency Services Liaison Panel.

LeT/LET Lashkar e Tayyiba, Army of the Pure, aka Pashan-e-Ahle Hadis. This is a Pakistan- and Jammu- and Kashmir-based group founded in 1992, numbering 300 members seeking accession of Jammu and Kashmir to Pakistan. Banned by Pakistan in January 2002 as a terrorist organisation.

Liberation Army Fifth Battalion The name of the Islamist group responsible for the first World Trade Center bombing, of 26 February 1993.

Liberation movement Term used for anti-colonial and anti-(neo-)imperialist political movements that used non-violent campaigns, guerrilla warfare and/or terrorist acts to achieve independence and self-determination.

Liberation theology A dissident Latin American Catholic Church movement in the 1960s and beyond that tried to combine Christian solidarity with Marxist revolutionary ideology.

Liberation Tigers of Tamil Eelam See LTTE.

Liberation war An anti-colonial war recognised by international law.

Libyan Islamic Fighting Group Al-Qaeda-affiliated group.

LIJ Lashkar i Jhangvi (Pakistan). In LIJ was founded in 1996.

Limburg French supertanker (VLCC of 300,000 dwt) attacked by a two-man suicide squad on a speedboat on 6 October 2002 while loading crude oil in the Yemeni port of Minah al-Dabah. The explosion tore a gaping hole in the double hull of the ship, resulting in a raging fire and an oil spill. Several sailors were injured during the attack, and a sailor drowned when the ship was evacuated. The *Limburg* survived the attack and was subsequently sold and renamed.

Liquidation Murder of individuals or groups of people for political reasons, usually by execution. The term is also used for targeted killings by criminal gangs of rival gangs or suspected traitors.

LJ Lashkar i Jhangvi, Army of Jhangvi (Pakistan).

LLF Linbuwan Liberation Front (Nepal)

LNG Liquefied natural gas. Natural gas (commonly 95–97 per cent methane, with the remainder a combination of ethane, propane and other heavy gases) that has been cooled to its liquid state at atmospheric pressure, i.e. $-260\,°F$ ($-162.2\,°C$) and 14.7 psia.

LNRF Lebanese National Resistance Front, aka Jammoul. LNRF was linked to the Lebanese Communist Party, formed in reaction to Israeli intervention of 1982 in Lebanon. Attacks in its name against IDF were carried out by various left-wing and Palestinian groups.

LOAC Law of armed conflict. Legal rules that determine which military conduct is lawful and what constitutes a war crime.

LoC Line of control. The provisional borderline between India and Pakistan in Jammu and Kashmir.

Lohame Herut Israel/Fighters for the Freedom of Israel (Stern Gang) Founded in 1940.

Lone-wolf terrorist Unaffiliated individual engaging in (a series of) attacks; often for idiosyncratic rather than political reasons.

Lord's Resistance Army See LRA.

Los Macheteros (Puerto Rico) Founded in 1976.

Low-intensity conflict (LIC) Form of fighting that falls short of full-scale war (as contrasted to high-intensity conflict). It often involves acts of sabotage, violent demonstrations, arson, assassinations, bombings and protracted urban and guerrilla warfare. The term is also used to refer to certain (para)military operations, such as (1) foreign internal defence: counter-insurgency, encompassing those actions taken by states to assist friendly governments resisting insurgent threats; (2) 'pro-insurgency': the sponsorship and support of anti-government insurgencies in other countries; (3) peacetime contingency operations: short-term military activities, rescue missions, show-of-force operations, punitive strikes; (4) counter-terrorist action: the defensive and offensive measures taken by armed forces to prevent or counter international terrorism; (5) anti-drug trafficking operations: the use of military resources to attack and destroy overseas sources of illegal narcotic drugs, and to curb the flow of drugs into a country; (6) peacekeeping operations: the use of force (usually under regional or UN auspices) to police ceasefire agreements or to establish a buffer between hostile armies.

Low-level armed robbery (LLAR) A type of piracy, also called maritime robbery/burglary. Maritime robbery is usually conducted in territorial waters close to the coast or in a harbour area if harbour security is lax. This form of piracy is usually rather opportunistic, with no connection to organised crime, and it constitutes the bulk of all piratical acts. According to the United Nations definition, these acts would not even qualify as piracy.

Loyalist Protestant Irish supporter of union with Great Britain, 'loyal' to the British monarchy; some Loyalists were involved in paramilitary violence against Catholics in Northern Ireland.

LPG Liquefied petrol gas, a by-product of oil refining. It is also known as butane/propane gas.

LRA Lord's Resistance Army. A Christian fundamentalist armed group that operates partly out of southern Sudan, the Congo and Uganda and seeks to create a great Nile Republic in northern Uganda; established in 1992 and numbering more than 3,000, most of them abducted child soldiers. The group emerged from the Holy Spirit Mobile Force and is currently led by Josef Kony. The LRA has been responsible for kidnapping thousands of children and using them as child soldiers and sex slaves. It has terrorised and driven away hundreds of thousands of people in the Gulu and Kitgum districts. Supported by Sudan until 2002; it declared a ceasefire in 2006.

LRF London Resilience Forum.

LRIT Long-range identification and tracking. LRIT will be made mandatory as a new safety regulation of the International Maritime Organization's Maritime Safety Committee for all passenger ships, vessels of 300 gross tonnage and upwards and mobile offshore drilling units. Like AIS, LRIT systems provide information on data such as ship's identity, location, and time and date of its last transmitted position. Unlike AIS, LRIT systems are capable of tracking vessels anywhere in the world and, also unlike AIS, LRIT is a closed system, providing information only to recipients entitled to receive such information.

LRT London Resilience Team.

LSD Lysergic acid diethylamide. A psychedelic drug, a hallucinogen, used as an incapacitating agent.

LT Lashkar-e-Tayyiba, Army of the Righteous, aka Jamaat ud-Dawa (JUD). Active in/from Pakistan.

LTTE Liberation Tigers of Tamil Eelam, aka Tamil Tigers, also operating as the World Tamil Movement/World Tamil Association, Ellalan Force, Sangilian Force, Federation of Associations of Canadian Tamils (FACT). Powerful (8,000 members by 2006) and sophisticated Sri Lankan Tamil separatist guerrilla and terrorist organisation founded in 1976 and led by Vellupillai Prabakharan. Armed struggle started in 1983 and ceased, for a while, after 11 September 2001. The LTTE pioneered suicide attacks with its Black Tiger and Black Sea Tigers. Its naval–wing activities were resumed in 2005 and intensified in 2006. The LTTE was decisively beaten by May 2009 by the Sri Lankan armed forces in a ruthless extermination campaign that spared few of those thousands of civilians who were used as human shields by the LTTE in the final weeks of the showdown.

LVF Loyalist Volunteer Force. Protestant paramilitary group in Northern Ireland that split from UVF after the latter declared a ceasefire. The LVF took part in the peace process after 1998 Good Friday Accords.

LWE Left-wing extremists in India, esp. in Andhra Pradesh.

M–19 Movimiento 19 de April/19th April Movement. This populist left–wing Colombian terrorist and drug-trafficking group was founded by adherents of Rojas Pinilla, who lost presidential elections on 19 May 1970. It was active until the 1990s.

Macheteros 'Machete wielders'; nickname of the Ejército Borican Popular/Popular Army of Borica. This was a Puerto Rican group fighting for independence from the United States during the 1970s and early 1980s.

MACP Military aid to civil power (UK).

Madrassa Arabic for 'school'; plural: *madaris*: A free or low–cost religious school in a Muslim country where Islamic law and religion are taught. Some madrassas are considered hotbeds of radicalism and suicide terrorism by some observers.

MAGO Muslims Against Global Oppression, aka Qibla and PAGAD (People Against Gangsterism and Drugs), Muslims Against Illegitimate Leaders (MAIL). Based in South Africa; emerged in 1998 from PAGAD (q.v.).

Maiming Infliction of permanent injury, incapacitation or disfigurement (e.g. 'kneecapping', hacking off hands, castration) on a person, but short of loss of life, to punish a victim or intimidate others.

Majlis al-Shura Islamic consultation council which deliberates over major decisions.

Major criminal hijack (MCHJ) A type of piracy in which the target ship gets hijacked and converted for the purpose of illegal trading and maritime fraud. The crew is detained to be marooned or killed at a later stage, the cargo being offloaded and sold somewhere, and the ship re-registered with fraudulent papers. MCHJ is also known as high-level armed assault and robbery (HLAAR).

MAK Mekhtab al Khidemant (Afghanistan).

MANPADS Man-portable air defence systems. Shoulder-fired, man-portable surface-to-air missiles, of which some 500,000 have been produced. Some are on the black market; some in the hands of terrorists.

Maoism Marxist ideological variant promoted by the Chinese communist dictator Mao Zedong. In Mao's stage theory of insurgency, terrorism plays a prominent role.

Marburg virus A potential germ weapon (variant U). A virus developed but not weaponised by the Soviet Union in the 1980s.

Maritime Asia Consists of the maritime Indian Ocean and Asia-Pacific regions: the Arabian Sea, Bay of Bengal, Strait of Malacca, Java Sea, South China Sea and East China Sea.

Maritime choke point A narrow waterway or strait, the closure of which would interrupt seaborne trade. Examples are the Strait of Gibraltar, the Strait of Hormuz and the Strait of Malacca.

Maritime terrorism Attacks against off- and onshore vessels and facilities, including, ships and ports, or involving ships (e.g. LPG tankers) for the purpose of intimidation, coercion, blackmail, ransom and/or propaganda. This special variant of terrorism could be defined as: (1) a plotted or executed attack against a ship, port facility or offshore facility; or (2) an attempt to further political motives by utilising elements in the maritime environment to execute an act of terrorism. This definition highlights the fact that some elements in the maritime environment, i.e. ships, could be both targets of maritime terrorism and instruments of maritime terrorism – just imagine an oil tanker scuttled in a narrow strait or blown up in a major port. Again, this definition should not be seen as excluding somewhat more pedestrian acts committed with the intent to finance a wider terrorist or guerrilla struggle. Such acts, like kidnapping sailors and their ships for ransom, occur quite frequently in the Strait of Malacca and off the coast of Somalia, thus establishing a 'grey area' where piracy committed for private ends by organised pirate groups overlaps with piracy committed for political reasons by maritime terrorist groups.

Martial law The term refers to various situations such as (1) rule by domestic military forces over a province or whole country, also called a state of siege, when the armed forces take over the administration of a territory and judicial functions, suspending many civil rights; or (2) the military command in occupied territory, also called a military government, allied to military and civilian persons.

Marxism A political philosophy developed by German philosopher Karl Marx (1818–1883) and Friedrich Engels (1820–1895) which is based on the assumption that the political, social and cultural life of a society is determined by the structures governing economic relationships. Marx sought to develop a theory of revolution to bring about the abolition of private property and the creation of a classless society based on the mobilisation of the proletarian working class. Marx wrote the *Communist Manifesto* in 1848, which proved influential and led to the creation of communist parties, which in a number of countries managed to take state power, without, however, bringing about more just and egalitarian societies than existed under other economic systems. The disintegration of the Soviet Union and most other communist states, and the disclosures about the reality of 'communist' rule, discredited the communist project worldwide. Marx himself was opposed to terrorism; many of his followers were not.

MAS Muerte a los Sequestradores/Death to the Kidnappers. A right-wing paramilitary organisation founded in 1981 by Colombian cocaine kingpins.

Massacre Deliberate slaughter of a group of unarmed civilians and disarmed prisoners of war, often combined with special cruelty and carried out by special (para) military personnel.

Mau Mau A national liberation movement founded in 1950. This was a violent Kenyan secret society that terrorised white settlers and fellow Africans loyal to them between 1952 and 1956. Despite massive and brutal British countermeasures, its suspected leader, Jomo Kenyatta, later became Kenya's president.

Maximiliano Hernández Martínez Anti-Communist Brigade Salvadorean right-wing state-sponsored death squad emerging in the late 1970s and reportedly steered by Roberto D'Aubuisson, subsequent founder of the ARENA party.

May 1 Left-wing Greek group reportedly linked to ELA (q.v.).

May 15 Organisation Palestinian splinter group from the Popular Front for the Liberation of Palestine-Special Operations Group (PFLP-SOG), led by Muhammad al-Umari, aka Abu Ibrahim, the 'bomb man', based in Iraq and active 1979–1985, responsible for the 1982 mid-air bombing between Hong Kong and Honolulu.

MB Muslim Brotherhood/Al-Ikhwan Al-Moselmoon. Organisation founded in 1928 in Egypt with branches in other Arab countries; partly banned during its history.

MCC Maoist Communist Centre, aka Dakshin Desh (1969–1975) Maoist Communist Centre of India (MCCI), Maoist Coordination Committee (MCC), Naxalites. The MCC merged in 2004 with the People's War Group, forming the Communist Party of India – Maoist (CPI-Maoist).

MCHJ Major criminal hijack; see Piracy.

MCR Communist Revolutionary Movement. A Brazilian group of militants active in the 1970s.

MDD Movement for Democracy and Development (Chad). Guerrilla group led by former president Hissène Habré; partly based in Nigeria and Niger.

MDJT Mouvement pour la démocratie et la justice au Tchad/Movement for Democracy and Justice in Chad. A group formed in 1998 and supported by Libya; less active after its leader, Youssouf Togoimi, died, in September 2002.

MEK Aka MKO, Mujahedin-e-Khalk Organisation, aka Mujahideen-e Khalq Organisation (MKO)/People's Mojahedeen of Iran, National Liberation Army of Iran (NLA), People's Mujahidin of Iran (PMOI), National Council of Resistance (NRC), National Council of Resistance of Iran (NCRI). Iranian armed group opposing theocratic regime, based in Iraq; founded in 1963.

MEND Movement for the Emancipation of the Niger (Nigeria). Ijaw-based group known for its oil pipeline sabotage, bombings, kidnapping and extortion in the Niger Delta. The group had succeeded in reducing Nigerian oil production by 25 per cent by the spring of 2006.

Mercenary A usually well-paid soldier of fortune, recruited locally or abroad, to participate in armed conflicts not as part of his own government's army but as a 'hired gun' by a government or private company.

Messianism A term applied to a religious movements led by a supposed messenger of God (a Messiah) or believing in a saviour who brings adherents to the Promised Land.

Metal detector An electromagnetic screening instrument to locate hidden knives and guns at security checkpoints (e.g. airports), operated by screeners.

MFDC Mouvement des Forces Démocratiques de Casamance/Movement of Democratic Forces of Casamance. The group numbers between 2,000 and 3,000 and was established in 1982 to seek independence from Senegal; engaged in peace talks with the government since 2000.

MG Machine gun.

MI5 British domestic intelligence and security service, founded in 1906; widely considered the best in Europe.

MI6 British secret foreign intelligence service.

MIA Mouvement Islamique Armé (Algeria).

Micro–organisms Bacteria, viruses, rickettsia, fungi and protozoa are categories of organisms used in biological warfare.

MILF Moro Islamic Liberation Front. A separatist movement numbering some 10,000, based in Mindanao (the Philippines), formed in 1978 when it split from the Moro National Liberation Front. It signed a peace treaty on 7 August 2001 with the Philippine government which its military wing, the Bangsa Moro Islamic Liberation Front, did not accept.

Military intervention The entering of a country by the armed forces of a foreign power against the wishes of the government in power, affecting the territorial integrity and political independence of a country. There is a sliding scale of both pro- and anti-regime interventions, involving many forms of military assistance to one or several parties (e.g. arms donations, arms sales, cash donations for arms acquisition, supply of mercenaries, training of local forces in a donor country, training of local forces in friendly third countries, supplying specialist forces for peacetime operations, supplying defence equipment, building defence-related infrastructure, providing satellite reconnaissance or other intelligence to local conflict parties, maintaining military equipment) or military intervention (e.g. peacetime stationing of troops as a deterrent against third parties, providing bodyguards and palace guards to local rulers, stationing military missions at the headquarters of local armed forces for planning military operations, combat participation of foreign special forces (e.g. pilots), 'volunteers' serving in combat, 'regular' troops engaged in combat).

Military warfare model An approach to countering terrorism that favours a hard-handed, forceful approach to terrorism, as opposed to a minimal-force, police-based criminal justice model approach.

Militia A part-time, local armed group of citizens gathered for (usually) defensive purposes, usually in times of emergency.

Millenarianism Belief in a future thousand-year age of bliss; any doctrine based on a promise of the lasting overcoming of existing misery, or the doctrine of a group adhering to such a religious belief.

Millennium bombing plot An ambitious pre-9/11 plan by Al-Qaeda to attack Los Angeles Airport and other US facilities/interests in early 2000.

Minutemen A right-wing survivalist US group, founded in 1961 by Robert de Pugh.

MIR Movimiento de la Izquierda Revolucionaria/Movement of the Revolutionary Left. Founded in 1965 and supported by Cuba, this Chilean insurgent group became, after the coup by General Pinochet in 1973, a resistance movement against the dictatorship. However, it engaged in terrorist attacks even after the Pinochet regime.

MIR Movimiento de la Izquierda Revolucionaria. This is the name of groups active in Venezuela and Peru in the mid-1960s.

MIRA Movimiento Independentista Revolucionario Armado/Armed Revolutionary Independence Movement ((Puerto Rico). MIRA was founded in 1967 and trained in Cuba.

Mitigation Reduction of the harmful consequences of event by adequate consequence management following a disaster or a terrorist attack.

MKO Mujahedin-e Khalq Organisation, aka MEK (q.v.).

MLAAR Medium-level armed assault and robbery. A type of piracy in which the attack is violent and the crew of the ship detained or locked up. The perpetrators usually take the content of the ship's safe, the property of the crew and, maybe, some high-value goods if these can be easily transported.

MLAPU Marxist-Leninist Armed Propaganda Unit. A Marxist Turkish group active between 1973 and 1980.

MLC Mouvement de Libération Conglolais/Movement for the Liberation of the Congolese People. A movement numbering 18,000 (2001), active in northern Congo.

MLF Moro Liberation Front, aka Moro National Liberation Front (MNLF). A Muslim group based on southern Philippine islands calling for Islamic self-rule; formerly supported by Qaddafi from Libya. MLF was formed in the late 1960s as a loose framework combining various Islamic groups fighting in the southern Philippines (mainly Mindanao) for an independent 'Bangsamoro' ('Moro Land'). The MNLF was organised by Abul Khayr Alonto and Jallaludin Santos, and chaired by Nur Misuari. In 1987, the MNLF gave up its fight for independence in favour of an offer from the government of Corazon Aquino to establish an autonomous province. The four-province Autonomous Region for Muslim Mindanao (ARMM), with its own governor and unicameral legislature, was officially inaugurated on 6 November 1990, with Nur Misuari as governor and the (mainstream of) MNLF as a political party. However, various MNLF factions carry on fighting since they do not recognise the peace accord.

MLN Movimiento de Liberación Nacional – Uruguayan left-wing group better known as the Tupamaros (q.v.).

MLN National Liberation Movement, aka 'Party of Organised Violence' (Guatemala). A right-wing group emerging from an invasion force that took state power in 1954 under Carlos Castillo Armas.

MLNF Basque National Liberation Movement.

MLPC/MPL Chinchoneros Popular Liberation Movement. An armed Honduran communist group established in 1978; linked to the Sandinistas in Nicaragua and opposed to US influence. The URP (Revolutionary People's Party) was its political wing.

MMT Madeshi Mukti Tigers (Nepal).

MNJ Niger Movement for Justice (Niger).

MNLA Mon National Liberation Army. The MNLA is the armed wing of the New Mon State Party, active since its foundation in 1958 along the Thai border of Myanmar, numbering 1,000. It observed a ceasefire in 2001.

MNLF Moro National Liberation Front, aka Moro Liberation Front (MLF, q.v.). Muslim separatist guerrilla army based in the southern Philippines (Mindanao and Sulu) and founded in 1972.

MNR Mozambique National Resistance – the predecessor organisation to the Mozambican RENAMO movement.

Modus operandi Method of operation; style of handling things.

Mohamed Boudia Commando Founded in 1973 by 'Carlos' (q.v.).

Molly Maguires Irish secret society of coal miners in Pennsylvania, active in the second half of the nineteenth century.

Molotov cocktail A hand-thrown gasoline-filled glass bottle with a burning cotton rag inserted as a wick, which ignites on impact. First used by the Russian resistance against German occupation in the Second World War. Molotov cocktails of gasoline, diesel, kerosene, ethyl or methyl alcohol or turpentine are widely used.

Momentum weapon Uses the kinetic energy of a very heavy and large object in motion, such as a very large crude carrier (VLCC), e.g. to attack port facilities and ships.

Monitoring In the context of conflict situations and crises, monitoring refers to the standardised collection and organisation of information based on regular and continuous observation of, and reporting on, controversial events in a given region or zone.

Montoneros Movimiento Peronista Montonero/Peronist Montonero Movement. An Argentinian armed party with up to 20,000 members at its height, founded around 1970 by supporters of exiled the Juan Domingo Perón, who had ruled Argentina from 1946 to 1955. They obtained a $60-million ransom for kidnapping sons of Argentina's wealthiest family. After Perón's return in 1973, the relationship with him and his successor, Isabel Perón, turned sour. They were crushed by the military dictatorship that followed her.

Montreal Convention (1971) A treaty that requires state parties to prosecute or extradite anyone who commits acts of sabotage against airports or aircraft on the ground, and empowers the International Civil Aviation Organization (ICAO) to suspend air travel to states that fail to comply.

MOOTW Military operations other than war. The use of armed forces in support of diplomatic efforts in peacetime or in conflict and post-conflict situations. Demurenko and Nikitin (1997: 113–114) give the following types:

- various peacekeeping operations;
- international police operations, e.g. eradicating international criminal groups, combatting terrorism, piracy, illegal arms and drugs trade, and guarding strategically important facilities, such as atomic power plants; and
- legal interventions.

'Operations other than war' also covers the use of armed forces to clean up after large-scale disasters, natural or man-made, and types of rescue and humanitarian action.

Moro Islamic Reformist Group A group active in the southern Philippines since 1978, numbering 900. It split from the MNLF and seeks an independent Islamic state in the South.

Moroccan Islamic Combatant Group (GICM) Affiliated to Al-Qaeda.

Mossad H. Mossad Merkazi le-Modiin U-letafkidim Meyuhadim/Institute for Intelligence and Security. Israel's external intelligence service, founded in 1951.

Movement A social, political, religious, ecological, ethnic, cultural or gender-related collective extra-parliamentary action group with a lower degree of organisation and institutionalisation than a party, seeking to realise political reforms or changes.

Movsar Baryayev Gang (Russia, Chechnya). An Islamist group composed of members of the Special Purpose Islamic Regiment (SPIL) and the International Islamic Brigade (IIB). Responsible for Moscow theatre hostage taking on 23 October 2002.

MPL Movimiento Popular de Liberación (Cinchonero). This is the armed wing of the Honduran People's Revolutionary Union, named after the nineteenth-century peasant leader Serapio Cinchonero Romero; a left-wing group active in the 1980s.

MPLA Movement for the Liberation of Angola.

MQM-H Muttahida Qami Movement, aka Mohajir Quami Movement, Real Mohajir Qami Movement, United National Front (Pakistan). MQM-H is active in Sindh province and its capital Karachi. Formed in 1992 – according to some observers by Pakistan's security forces and intelligence services – to attack a rival group (MQM-A) of Mohajir Muslim immigrants from India after the 1947 partition of the subcontinent.

MR-8 Movimiento Revolucionario do 8 Octubre/8 October Revolutionary Movement. A Brazilian Marxist-Leninist group taking its name from the day Che Guevara was killed. It ceased to exist in the early 1970s.

MRP Milicias Revolucionarias del Pueblo/People's Revolutionary Militias (Ecuador). An anti-globalisation group that emerged in 2002.

MRPF Frente Patriótico Manuel Rodríguez/Manuel Rodríguez Patriotic Front. An armed left-wing group that opposed the dictatorship of General Pinochet in Chile.

MRTA Movimento Revolucionario Tupac Amaru/Revolutionary Movement Tupac Amaru. Founded in 1983 in Peru and based on Marxism; best known for occupation of the Japanese embassy between 17 December 1996 and 22 April 1997.

MS/MS-13 Mara Salvatrucas. A multinational Salvadorean criminal gang formed in the 1980s in Los Angeles; active in the United States, Canada, El Salvador, Guatemala and Honduras (estimated membership: 50,000); also engages in terror-like attacks.

MTA Mong Thai Army. Established in 1964 to protect the Shan people, it numbers 3,000 fighters; it began observing a ceasefire in 2001.

Mufsiduun Islamic term for evildoers, sinners and corrupters whose criminality will incur God's wrath; ultimate condemnation on the Day of Judgement.

Muharibuun Arabic for ruthless transgressors guilty of heinous crimes and mortal sins such as engaging in *irhab* (q.v.) and *hirabah* (q.v.).

Mujahedeen/Mujahidin Arabic for 'those who wage a jihad'. The name was originally given to local fighters and armed Arab volunteers, in particular in Afghanistan fighting Soviet occupation between 1979 and 1989. Since then extended to other 'holy warriors' and 'freedom fighters'.

Mujahedeen Brigades Palestinian group operating in Gaza.

Mujahideen Army Jaish al-Mujahideen (Iraq). A Sunni insurgent group.

Mujahidin Shura Council (Iraq): An umbrella organisation of Iraqi jihadist groups, including Al-Qaeda Organisation in the Land of the Two Rivers.

Mukharabat Secret service of Saddam Hussein in Iraq prior to 2003.

Mullah An Islamic scholar; (senior) Muslim cleric.

Munafiquun Arabic for hypocrites as regards Islam, who pretend to follow the Qur'an but who actually violate basic rules, mandates and prohibitions.

Munazzamat Al Jihad Aka Tanzim al Jihad and Jihad. A Sunni fundamentalist group inspired by the writings of Sayyid Qutb, who was an activist Egyptian Muslim leader from the Muslim Brotherhood; responsible for killing the Egyptian president Anwar Sadat in 1981.

Murder Unlawful, premeditated, malicious or spontaneous killing of a human being by another; also, any killing done while committing some other felony, such as rape or robbery. Killing of a person without due process of law and in situations other than self-defence or a just war conducted within the framework of humanitarian law is a very serious crime.

Murtadd Arabic for apostasy (abandonment of belief).

Muslim Brotherhood Majallar al-Ikhwan al-Musalamin. A Sunni movement founded in Egypt in 1928 by Hassan al-Banna, promoting a more fundamentalist and militant Islam. In 1957, Colonel Nasser jailed 20,000 of its members. It arranged the murder of the Egyptian premier in 1948 and also made an attempt on the life of Gamal Abdel Nasser in 1954. The Muslim Brotherhood has branches in many Muslim countries, including Iraq, Jordan and Palestine; in some countries, it is tolerated or legal.

Mustard gas A First World War weapon that causes skin blisters and lung burns. It is a colourless, odourless liquid that kills slowly, if at all. There are several types: sulphur mustard (HD), sesqui mustard (Q). Saddam Hussein had stockpiled 500 tons of mustard and nerve agents.

N Naxalites (q.v.)

N 17 Revolutionary Organisation of 17 November/Dekati Evdomi Noemvri (Greece).

NA Northern Alliance (an anti-Taliban Tajik group); conquered Kabul in the wake of the US intervention in Afghanistan in late 2001.

NAR Nuclei Armati Rivoluzionari/Armed Revolutionary Nucleus. This was a right-wing group active in Italy between 1977 and 1981.

NAR New Armenian Resistance. An Armeniam exile group active between 1977 and 1983 in Europe.

Narco-terrorism A concept introduced in 1983 by Peruvian president Belaunde Terry to characterise the atrocious nature of attacks by drug traffickers on security forces. Since then, used with various meanings: (1) drug criminals using terrorist methods; (2) cooperation between drug traffickers and terrorist groups; (3) terrorist organisations financing themselves partly by illicit narcotic drug production and trafficking; and (4) as a propagandistic tool to de-legitimise armed groups fighting for political goals.

Narodnaya Volya People's Will. This was a Russian revolutionary student group, active between 1878 and 1881, which developed one of the first theories of modern terrorism. The group opposed the killing of innocent civilians or the use of terrorism in democratic societies.

Nation A group of people linked to a (historical) territory who through common sacrifices in the past and the willingness to undergo sufferings again if necessary stay together. They regard themselves as a natural political community. Sometimes a nation is coextensive with a state, but there are nations without states (e.g. Kurds) and nations with two states (e.g. North and South Korea), and multinational states (e.g. India). Where the territory of a nation coincides with that of a state, it is a nation-state. Most states are not homogeneous nation-states but host minorities of different ethnic, cultural, religious and linguistic identities, and attempts to create homogeneity have usually led to tragic results (population exchange, deportation, ethnic cleansing, genocide, civil war). Nation, like 'people', is a term not defined in international law.

National Democratic Front of Bodoland See NDFB.

National Liberation Army See ELN.

National Liberation Front of Tripura See NLFT.

National liberation movement A term referring to anti-colonial or anti-imperialist groups working towards national independence from foreign occupation or dominance through non-violent resistance, sabotage, guerrilla warfare, terrorism or a combination thereof.

National Socialism A variety of fascist ideology that dominated the German state between 1933 and 1945; a criminal regime based on militarism, racism, anti-communism, opposition to parliamentarian democracy, anti-Semitism, totalitarianism, imperialism and genocide.

Nationalism A sentiment of loyalty towards a nation which is shared by people. In addition, and politically more explosively, the term is also used for an ideology that claims that a nation (defined in a variety of ways, often involving shared historical experience, common language, culture, religion, history or geographic location) should have, and be coextensive with, a state, based on the principle of (or right to) self-determination.

Nationalist (-separatist) terrorism Use of indiscriminate violence against non-combatant civilians in the pursuit of (re)gaining statehood for a minority group ethnically or religiously distinct from other sectors of the population of a state.

NATO North Atlantic Treaty Organization. A Western military alliance originally established against the Soviet Union.

Naxalites A left-wing, student-based Indian group striving for a Chinese-style 'cultural revolution' and championing the cause of peasants; named after the West Bengal village of Naxabarai, where it incited a short-lived revolt of oppressed peasants in 1967. Its 'Red Army' took over some 100 villages in 1985–1986. By 2010, it had become a major security threat in some rural parts of India.

NAYLP National Arab Youth for the Liberation of Palestine.

Nazi Abbreviation for National Sozialisten/National Socialists, the German nationalist, anti-Semitic, anti-Bolshevik fascist party founded in 1919 and led by Adolf Hitler (1889–1945), who ruled the country from 1933 to 1945 by totalitarian methods, including state terror.

NBC Nuclear, biological, chemical (weapons).

NCDD National Council for the Defence of Democracy (Burundi). A Hutu paramilitary group formed in early 1994.

NCK National Council of Khalistan. A Sikh organisation led by Balbir Singh Sandu. Established in 1972 to bring about an independent Sikh state; banned in 1982 after perpetrating terrorist acts.

NCTC National Counterterrorism Center (United States).

NDA Nepal Defense Army. Hindu group threatening Christians.

NDFB National Democratic Front of Bodoland, aka Bodo Security Force (BSF) (India, north-east). A separatist group (*c.* 1, 500 members) formed in 1988.

NELA Neos Epanastatikos Laikos Agonas/New Revolutionary Popular Struggle (Greece).

Neo-Nazi Descriptor for white racist, right-wing, anti-Semitic groups in Germany, the United States and other countries seeking to revive elements of Hitler's National Socialist regime after the defeat of Nazism in the Second World War.

Nerve agents Highly toxic and potentially lethal chemical agents that affect the human nervous system by inhibiting the enzyme that aids the transmission of nerve impulses. They cause blurred vision, crying, nausea, vomiting, urinary incontinence, respiratory distress and reduced mental capability by attacking the nerve system. Symptoms are convulsion, coma and death by suffocation as the respiratory muscles become paralysed. There are two types: G–agents, which are non-persistent and cause death by inhalation; and V–agents, which are persistent and are absorbed through the skin. Examples of nerve agents are tabun (GA), sarin (GB), soman (GD) and VX.

Nerve gas Probably the most widely stocked chemical agents; liquid, gas or aerosol toxins belonging to the group of organo–phosphorus compounds which are absorbed by the skin or through the lungs, usually within 20–30 minutes. The nerve agent becomes bound to an enzyme, acetylcholinesterase, inhibiting vital nervous-system activities in human beings. Death through suffocation is the result.

NEST (US) Nuclear Emergency Search Team. A rapid response force trained to search for, identify and disarm lost, stolen or improvised nuclear weapons anywhere in the United States.

Network A form of non-hierarchical, communication-based organisation that allows for local initiative, is marked by flexibility and has the ability to repair damage to its structure.

Neutralise To make someone no longer an active party to a conflict; usually a euphemism for killing.

New People's Army See NPA.

New PULO New Pattani United Liberation Organisation, aka Bersatu (together with 'old' PULO) (Thailand). New PULO was formed in 1995 to struggle for autonomy from Thailand.

New Sudan Brigade The eastern branch of the SPLA (q.v.), numbering 2,000 fighters (2001).

New Terrorism A term coined to characterise attributes of terrorism post-9/11, especially the high casualty aspect.

NFL National Liberation Front (Aden). Jabhat al Tahrir al Quamia, founded in 1963. It managed to force, in 1968, a British withdrawal from Aden following a rural and then urban terrorist campaign.

NGO Non-governmental organisation.

Nihilism The ideology of some nineteenth-century Russian opponents of the tsarist regime influenced by the idea that if 'God is dead' (Nietzsche), everything may be allowed. Some Russian adherents of nihilism claimed that everything that stood in the way of revolution was immoral and everything that helped to bring it about was moral. A cult of destruction of the social, political and cultural order without a clear vision of what would follow the abolition of old structures characterised some nihilist terrorists.

Ninth of July Organisation A group of ASALA members that targeted Switzerland in 1981.

NIPR Nuclei di Iniziativa Proletaria Rivoluzionaria/Revolutionary Proletarian Initiative Nuclei (Italy). The NIPR, a Marxist-Leninist group, emerged in 2000.

Nitroglycerine A highly explosive and unstable oily liquid. In the early 1860s, Alfred Nobel discovered that it could be combined with Kieselguhr to make the much more stable explosive known as dynamite. Dynamite is exploded by means of a blasting cap made of black powder.

NKVD Narodny Kommisariat Vnutrennikh Del, People's Commissariat of Internal Affairs. The name of Russian secret police under Stalin, preceded by the GPU and succeeded by the KGB. The chief instrument of the Great Terror (1935–1938).

NLA National Liberation Army. The name of several groups, e.g. in the Former Yugoslav Republic of Macedonia, where the NLA, established in 2001, asserts the Albanian minority's rights.

NLFT National Liberation Front of Tripura (India, north-east); formed in 1989.

NO New Order. Right-wing Greek organisation directed against the Left and established under the military dictatorship (1964–1973); recognised as a political party in 1974.

Nom de guerre Literally, 'war name'; alias, a false identity used by members of secret underground organisations to make detection by authorities more difficult. The name chosen is often grandiloquent to impress rivals and enemies (e.g. Stalin, from 'steel').

Non-combatant A person who is not equipped or able to engage in armed conflict, carrying no arms; the term also covers persons who have laid down their arms and those placed *hors de combat* by wounds, sickness or detention.

Non-combatant immunity The principle in the laws of war (*jus in bello*) that military force should not be used against unarmed civilians. The violation of this principle constitutes a war crime.

Non-proliferation The policy of restricting the spread of weapons of mass destruction and their delivery systems. It is often used to refer to the principle of keeping the number of nuclear powers small, based on a treaty concluded between the United States, Soviet Union, United Kingdom and France in 1970. More recently, the proliferation of know-how and CBRN technology to rogue states and terrorist non-state actors has become a source of international concern.

NORAID Irish Northern Aid Committee. A fund-raising organisation in the United States founded in 1970, ostensibly to help the Catholic victims of political violence in Northern Ireland but also used to procure money and arms for the Provisional IRA.

November 17 Epanastaiki Organosi 17 Noemvri/Dekati Evdomi Noemvri, Revolutionary Organisation 17 November. Greek anti-American, anti-NATO terrorist group named after the day when a Greek student was killed in 1973 during demonstrations in Athens; active since 1974.

NPA New People's Army. The NPA is the armed wing of the Communist Party of the Philippines. It was founded in 1969, led by Jose Maria Sison, aka Armando Liwanag, aka Joma. The NPA is active in rural Luzon, Visayas and Mindanao, numbering some 16,000.

NPC Nuclei Proletari per il Comunismo, aka Proletarian Combatant Groups (Italy). The NPC emerged in 2003.

NPD National Democratic Party. A German right-wing party established in 1964, in whose name numerous acts of terrorism were claimed.

NPFL National Patriotic Front of Liberia. Formed in 1984 by Charles Taylor and trained by Libya; after victory in the civil war (1990–1995), incorporated into the government and military.

NRB National Resistance Brigades (Palestine).

NSA National Security Agency. US eavesdropping organisation established in 1952; intercepts radio signals as well as numerous other signals from electromagnetic fields (SIGINT).

NSCN-IM National Socialist Council of Nagaland-Isak-Muivah (India, Nagaland). Christian/Maoist separatist group formed in 1988.

NSCN-K National Socialist Council of Nagaland – Khaplang (India (Nagaland)).

NSCM-U In India (Nagaland).

NSDAP Nationalsozialistische Deutsche Arbeiterpartei/National Socialist German Workers Party. The NSDAP was the anti-Semitic, anti-Bolshevik, nationalist right-wing party of which Adolf Hitler became leader in 1921.

NSS National Security Strategy (United States).

NSWPP National Socialist White People's Party (United States).

NTA Nuclei Territoriali Antimperialisti/Anti-Imperialist Territorial Nuclei for the Construction of the Fighting Communist Party (Italy). A small left-wing group in the footsteps of BR; uses the same logo.

Nuclear terrorism The use, or credible threat of use, of destructive force against non-combatant or civilian groups of people for the purposes of propaganda, coercion (blackmail or extortion) or intimidation of a target audience, whereby the perpetrator:

- has managed or threatens to trigger a fission (or fission/fusion) of nuclear material (HEU, Pu);
- is credibly held to be in possession of weapons-grade/usable nuclear material or a nuclear weapon with intent to use it; or
- is attacking or sabotaging facilities containing harmful nuclear materials or is targeting them in transport or at storage sites in order to produce an explosion or other release of such substances or;
- disperses in water, soil or air harmful radioactive substances by explosion or diffusion.

Nuclear weapons The most powerful weapons available, based on nuclear fission, fusion or a combination thereof. Nuclear weapons come in three types:

1 radiological weapons: where radioactive material is dispersed by conventional explosions but does not itself explode; fatalities low but increasing over time;
2 fission weapons: triggered by conventional explosives or a laser beam, a chain reaction releasing energy (radiation, heat, a shockwave); fatalities in the range of 100,000 from a single explosion in an urban area;
3 fusion weapons: triggered by a fission process leading to a powerful thermonuclear explosion; fatalities in the millions.

Nuclear warhead The part of a weapon containing the fissile materials. Many types of nuclear devices have been developed. The United States manufactured, between 1945 and 1985, some 60,000 nuclear warheads in 71 types for 116 weapon systems (Norris *et al.*, 1989: 82).
Nuclei Armati Comunista Armed Units for Communism (Italy).
Nuclei Territoriali Antimperialisti Anti-Imperialist Territorial Units (Italy).
NUMAST National Union for Marine, Aviation and Shipping Transport Officers. An influential British trade union.
NWLF New World Liberation Front (United States).

OAS Organisation de l'Armée Secrète/Secret Army Organisation. An organisation of French settlers and military officers in Algeria that resisted the French handover of Algeria to the FLN, first by attempting a *coup d'état* in April 1961 and then by acts of terrorism in Algeria and France until the mid-1960.
OAS Organization of American States, aka Regional Organization of the Western Hemisphere.
OBL Osama bin Laden, the charismatic leader of Al-Qaeda. He is of Saudi origin, heir to a fortune from his father, a Yemeni immigrant who created a construction business empire under the patronage of the House of Saud. He assisted the anti-Soviet resistance in Afghanistan in the 1980s and co-founded Al-Qaeda ('the base') in 1988. He left Afghanistan in 1991 and returned there, from Sudan, in 1996. OBL was involved in assassination and terrorism plots from the mid-1990s, including the attacks on the World Trade Center and the Pentagon on 11 September 2001, which killed 2,977 people (and 19 terrorists).
Occupation Military rule over the territory of another state or nation.
Odinism The ideology of small right-wing, racist, neo-Nazi, anti-Semitic groups in the United States and northern Europe, based on Teutonic mythology.
OEF Operation Enduring Freedom. The US intervention in Afghanistan, following the attacks of 11 September 2001 on New York and Washington, originally termed 'Operation Infinite Justice' but then renamed to remove religious connotations that might have offended Muslims.
OFAC Office of Foreign Assets Control (United States).
OIC Organisation of the Islamic Conference.
OIRA Official Irish Republican Army. An Irish resistance organisation founded in 1913 to create a state independent of Great Britain.
Oklahoma bombing A major domestic terrorist attack (killing 168 people) on a US federal government building on 19 April 1995 by Timothy McVeigh, who sought revenge for the death of members of the Branch Davidian cult in Waco, Texas.
OLF Oromo Liberation Front. Separatist ethnic group established in 1973, numbering 200+ (2001), which seeks to liberate the Oromo people and overthrow the Ethiopian government, allegedly with the support of Eritrea and Somalia.
Omega 7 Cuban exile terrorist group based in Florida, founded in 1974 by Eduardo Arocena. It targeted individuals and groups considered to be sympathetic to Fidel Castro's regime in Cuba. The group was active, also in drug trafficking, until the early 1980s.

ONLF Ogaden National Liberation Front. The ONLF has sought since 1984, to establish the rights of the Ogaden population in Ethiopia.

OPCON Operational control – command authority.

OPCW Organisation for the Prohibition of Chemical Weapons. The Hague-based international organisation designed to control chemical weapons.

Operation A military action on a tactical level, limited in space and time. An operation is a specific, often covert, armed activity at the edge of, or behind, enemy lines.

Operation Anaconda A US–UK military operation against the Taliban and Al-Qaeda in eastern Afghanistan in 2001.

Operation Condor Cooperation between the security services of six Andean countries to neutralise not just guerrilla fighters and terrorists but also mere political dissidents in the 1970s.

Operation Desert Storm The US-led invasion of Kuwait in 1991, aiming to expel Shi'ites from Iraq.

Operation Eagle Claw The name of the failed US military attempt to extract 53 hostages from the US embassy in Tehran on 24 April 1980.

Operation El Dorado Canyon The name of the bombing of Libyan targets on 14 April 1986 in retaliation for the La Belle bombing in Berlin.

Operation Enduring Freedom Originally 'Operation Infinite Justice'. The code name of the US response in Afghanistan to the 11 September 2001 attacks; it led to the ousting of the Taliban regime and the destruction of Al-Qaeda bases and the arrest of some members of both groups.

Operation Thunderbolt The code name of the Israeli hostage rescue operation in Entebbe, Uganda, in 1976.

Oplan Bojinka An ambitious early plan by Al-Qaeda simultaneously to attack and destroy 11 US airliners over the Pacific on 21/22 January 1995. The plan, which was discovered by the Philippine police on 6 January 1995, was connected to the attempt to assassinate Pope John Paul II during his visit to Manila on 15 January 1995. The masterminds behind these plans were Khalid Sheikh Mohammed and Ramzi Yousef. A repetition of the plot, over the Atlantic with planes leaving from the United Kingdom, was made public by British authorities on 10 August 2006.

OPM Organisasi Papua Mer(e)deka/Free Papua Movement. The OPM has struggled since 1962 for independence from Indonesia through its military wing, the Liberation Army of the Free Papua Movement (TPN).

Oppression A situation where social and economic privileges are denied to whole classes of people, regardless of whether they oppose the authorities.

Orange, Agent A toxic defoliant containing dioxin, of which some 64 million litres was dropped by the United States on Vietnam. The Vietnamese authorities claimed that half a million people died or contracted serious illnesses over the years because of the spraying.

Orange Volunteers (OV) A small Loyalist Protestant group in Northern Ireland; maybe linked to the UVF or UDA. OV are opposed to the political settlement with Catholic nationalists, attacking Irish Catholics after the 1998 Good Friday Agreement.

Orden Organización Democrática Nacional/National Democratic Organisation. The name of a Salvadorean rural militia, founded in 1968 by General José Alberto Medrano, which turned into a death squad before it was disbanded in 1979.

Order, The Aka The Silent Brotherhood, White American Bastion. A US white neo-Nazi supremacist group founded in 1982 by Robert Jay Matthews, named after a group in a novel (*The Turner Diaries*). It purported to fight the 'Zionist Occupation Government' (ZOG) until the arrest of most of its members in 1985. It was succeeded by Order II, aka 'Bruder Schweigen'/Brother Silence Strike Force II.

Ordine Nuovo New Order. An Italian right-wing group held responsible for the bombing campaign that started in December 1969 in Milan.

Organisation of the Oppressed of the Earth The name of the Lebanese Hezbollah group which hijacked TWA Flight 847 in 1985.

Organised crime Generic name referring to structured groups of three or more persons engaging professionally in high-profit crimes such as drug trafficking, trafficking in human beings and arms, illegal gambling operations, loan-sharking and smuggling, using intimidation, corruption and violence for extortion and compliance.

Orly Group An Armenian splinter group of the Armenian Secret Army for the Liberation of Armenia (q.v.). The group was active in France in the early 1980s.

OSCE Organisation for Security and Co-operation in Europe. The OSCE is a regional organisation of 56 countries, including the United States, Canada, European states, the Russian Federation and Soviet successor states. Its counter-terrorism activities are coordinated by ATU, the Action Against Terrorism Unit.

OSINT Open-source collection from the internet, media, government and academic publications and civil society (NGOs), etc.

Ottoman Empire A Turkish Islamic empire that extended from North Africa through the Middle East and the Balkans. It collapsed during and after the First World War and was replaced by successor states in 1923.

OV See Orange Volunteers.

OVPR Organisation of Volunteers for the Puerto Rican Revolution. An armed pro-independence group active since 1979 in Puerto Rico against US targets.

PA Palestinian Authority.

PAGAD People Against Gangsterism and Drugs, aka Muslims Against Global Oppression (MAGO), Muslims Against Illegitimate Leaders (MAIL). Originally a Muslim vigilante anti-crime group active in the Cape Town area of South Africa since 1995; it became increasingly political and Islamist.

PAL Permissive action links. A warhead locking security mechanism in nuclear weapons intended to prevent unauthorised use, e.g. by terrorists. Such blocking mechanisms can include altitude meters for air-dropped bombs and velocity meters for nuclear artillery. Only when certain parameters are met can a nuclear explosion occur.

Palestinian Islamic Jihad See PIJ.

Palestinian Revolution Forces General Command (West Bank, Gaza) Active between 1985 and 1987.

PALIKA Parti de Libération Kanak/Kanak Liberation Party (New Caledonia).

Palipehutu Parti pour la Libération du People Hutu/Party for the Liberation of the Hutu People. This is the armed wing of Forces Nationales de Libération, established in 1980, numbering 2,000–3,000 and active in the Tanzanian border area and Burundi.

Paramilitary Refers to armed civilian vigilante groups with various types and degrees of links with official security forces.

Parathion Commercially available potent toxic insecticide.

Partisan war Irregular war waged by volunteer units on a territory occupied by an invader or on the area of one's own state against a ruling regime for the purpose of expelling the occupier, changing the government, gaining independence or avoiding repression.

Party, political An institution that (1) seeks to influence a state, often by attempting to occupy positions in government, and (2) usually consists of more than a single interest in the society and so, to some degree, attempts to 'aggregate interests' (Weinberg and Pedahzur, 2003: 5).

Pashtun The largest ethnic group in Afghanistan (*c.* 40 per cent).

PATRIOT Act Acronym for 'Providing Appropriate Tools Required to Intercept and Obstruct Terrorism' Act. A US law passed in October 2001 following the 9/11 attacks. A broad-ranging set of counter-terrorist measures that provides the government with unprecedented powers to prevent and combat terrorism.

Patriot Movement US identity movement opposed to the government in Washington, DC, and prone to conspiracy theories; some of its members are organised in armed survivalist militias.

PBCP-ML Purbo Banglar Communist Party (Bangladesh). Maoist group; split into Red Flag and Janajuddho factions in 2002.

PBSB East Bangladesh Proletarian Party. An armed group led by Siraj Sikder, fighting the government between 1971 and the late 1970s.

PCBR Revolutionary Communist Party of Brazil. A Maoist splinter party engaged in rural armed struggle and urban terrorism between 1967 and 1973.

PCC-ML Communist Party of Colombia – Marxist-Leninist. A Maoist and Castroist party linked to the EPL, a guerrilla group it set up.

PCES Communist Party of El Salvador. Pro-Moscow group that went underground in 1979 to engage in armed struggle.

PCJSS Parbatya Chattagram Jana Sanghati Samiti/Chittagong Hill Tracts United People's Party. An independence movement founded in 1972.

PDD-39 US presidential directive, issued in 1995, to prevent and counter terrorist acts, including CBNR incidents.

PDFLP Democratic Front for the Liberation of Palestine.

Peace A political condition other than one of organised armed conflict (war), and often distinguished from a situation of non-war (= neither war nor peace) (Evans and Newnham, 1992: 250). Positive definitions of peace are based on four concepts (Banks, 1987; cited in Burgess and Burgess, 1997: 230–231):

1 peace as harmony (stressing the absence of conflict);
2 peace as order (stressing stability and 'peace through strength');
3 peace as justice (stressing the absence of domination and poverty); and
4 peace as conflict management (stressing peace as a process for obtaining interests and needs, rather than as an end in itself).

Most definitions use elements of more than one of these four interpretations.

Peace Conquerors The name of environmental groups active since the mid-1980s in Australia, Belgium and Germany.

Penetration Clandestine infiltration of adversary structure.

Pentagon Literally, object with five sides. The seat of the US Department of Defense; attacked by Al-Qaeda on 11 September 2001 with hijacked aircraft, causing 189 deaths.

Pentiti 'Repentant'. Italian name for those who repent their past misdeeds and membership of criminal organisations; it follows 1981 legislation encouraging defection from terrorist groups. Many imprisoned members of the Red Brigades received a reduced sentence in return for repentance for their crimes.

Pentolite A mix of TNT and PETN, used in IEDs.

People A term which, like 'nation', is not defined in international law; it refers to a community (sometimes a nation) that shares a common history, language and cultural traits; is often considered to be the (nominal) sovereign in democracies.

People's War Maoist doctrine of insurgency, based on protracted guerrilla warfare and terrorist tactics.

Pepes People Persecuted by Pablo Escobar. This is a Colombian paramilitary group responsible for some 50 killings of the Medellín drug lord's entourage and family.

Peshmerga Generic term for a Kurdish guerrilla fighter.

PETN Pentaerythritol tetranitrate. An explosive used for IEDs.

PFAR Fascist Party of Revolutionary Action. A French group claiming responsibility for a court bombing in Paris in May 1980.

PFLI People's Liberation Front of India (Maoist), active in Jharkhand.

PFLP Popular Front for the Liberation of Palestine, aka al-Jabha ash-Sha'abiya li-Tahir Falastin. The PFLP is a Pan-Arabist Marxist-Leninist group founded in 1967 by George Habash (nicknamed 'al-Hakim'), cooperating with West European terrorists and engaging in hijackings in the late 1960s. A rival of Al-Fatah, the PFLP has been held co-responsible for triggering Jordan's repression of Palestinian fedayeen and Lebanese civil war. Since 2001, it has had its headquarters in Ramallah and is headed by Ahmed Sadat; it numbers 100+ members.

PFLP-GC Popular Front for the Liberation of Palestine – General Command. A Syrian-backed group founded by Ahmed Jibril in 1968; it operates from Syria and Lebanon.

PFLP-SC Popular Front for the Liberation of Palestine – Special Command. A Syria- and Lebanon-based Marxist group formed in 1979.

PFLP-SOG PFLP – Special Operations Group.

PFSP Port facility security plans.

PGT Guatemalan Labour Party. Founded in 1949 as the Communist Party of Guatemala and banned in 1954 after a CIA-sponsored coup. The group was engaged in armed struggle in 1961; its members joined the FAR and URNG after the murder of its leaders.

Phalangists A Maronite Christian paramilitary militia in Lebanon established in imitation of Spanish and Italian paramilitary political parties in the 1930s. The group was supported by Syria and later by Israel and the United States in the civil war (1975–1991).

Phosgene Carbonyl chloride, $COCl_2$. A colourless, poisonous choking agent (gas) used in warfare before more potent agents were discovered.

Physical protection Measures to secure (nuclear) materials against theft and sabotage.

Physical security Measures for the protection of civilian and military personnel (including VIPs), facilities and materials against intrusion, sabotage and damage. The measures include barriers, detection devices, alarm systems.

PIJ Palestinian Islamic Jihad. A Syrian and Gaza-based extremist Palestinian group established in the 1970s by Fathi Shaqaqi.

PIJ Palestinian Islamic Jihad/Harakat al-Jihad al-Islami Fi Filastin (West Bank, Gaza, Syria). A Sunni armed group founded in the late 1970s in Egypt as a splinter of the Muslim Brotherhood.

Pilocarpine A poison used by secret services.

Pipe bomb Improvised explosive device consisting of a metallic pipe filled with explosives and (sometimes) shrapnel, sealed on both ends.

PIRA Provisional (Wing), Irish Republican Army; slang 'Provos'. A paramilitary cell-structured terrorist nationalist organisation based in Northern Ireland, founded in 1969 and, by 1972, successor to the more Marxist Official IRA. It strove for reunification of the six northern Irish counties with the South from 1969 on; its front organisation, Sinn Féin, became, after the Good Friday Agreement of 1998, part of the governing political coalition in Northern Ireland.

Piracy An act of boarding or attempting to board any ship with the intent to commit theft or any other crime and with the intent or capability to use force in the furtherance of that act (IMB). According to the United Nations' Law of the Sea definition, piracy can be defined as 'any illegal acts of violence or detention, or any act of depredation, committed for private ends by the crew or the passengers of a private ship or a private aircraft and directed (i) on the high seas, against another ship or aircraft, or against persons and property on board of such ship or aircraft; (ii) against a ship, aircraft, persons or property in a place outside the jurisdiction of any State'. The definition of the International Maritime Bureau (IMB) is much broader: maritime piracy is 'an act of boarding or attempting to board any ship with the intent to commit theft or any other crime and with the intent or capability to use force in the furtherance of the act'. Sub-types of piracy are low-level armed robbery (LLAR), medium-level armed assault and robbery (MLAAR), and high-level armed assault and robbery (HLAAR), also called major criminal hijack (MCHJ).

PJAK Party for a Free Life in Kurdistan (Turkey/Iran)

PKK Partiya Karkarên Kurdistan/Kurdistan Workers' Party, aka Kurdistan Freedom and

Democracy Congress (KADEK), People's Congress of Kurdistan/Kongra-Gel. An originally Marxist terrorist/guerrilla/organised crime organisation opposing Turkish rule and seeking Kurdish autonomy for south-east Turkey, founded on 27 November 1978 and led by Abdullah Öcalan, who, subsequent to his capture in 1999, started a 'peace initiative'. However, by 2010 the PKK was again engaged in major fighting with Turkey's security forces, which attacked its bases in Iraq.

PKO Peacekeeping operation. A PKO is usually undertaken by a regional or international organisation, such as ECOMOG or the United Nations.

PL Prima Linea/Front Line Group. A left-wing group active in Italy between 1976 and 1982.

PLA Palestine Liberation Army.

PLA People's Liberation Army (India, Manipur). Established in 1978. Its political wing is the Revolutionary People's Front (RPF).

Plague A highly contagious disease, the causal agent of which can be weaponised.

Plant Agent infiltrated by opposition forces.

Plastic explosive Putty-like material that can be shaped for better hiding, e.g. Semtex.

PLF Palestine Liberation Front. A group founded in 1961 by Ahmed Jibril (who also founded the PFLP – General Command) and later led by Abu Abbas.

PLO Palestine Liberation Organization. A national liberation umbrella organisation founded in 1964 by the Arab League in Cairo, encompassing various Palestinian armed groups and chaired from 1969 until his death in 2004 by Yasser Arafat. Since 2005, it has been led by Mohmood Abbas.

Plutonium–239 A highly carcinogenic alpha-ray emitter obtained by bombarding U-238 isotope with neutrons; it is the best fission explosive nuclear material. A nuclear explosive device is said to require 3–8 kg, although the significant quantities standard should, according to some experts, be lowered to as little as 1 kg of plutonium (however, such a bomb would require super-compression techniques beyond the reach of most states). The bomb dropped on Nagasaki contained 6.1 kg. There is some 1,200 tons of plutonium on our planet, of which some 230 tons has been produced for military purposes. Plutonium is about ten times as toxic as nerve gas. When inhaled, the smallest particles cause cancer: 12,000 micrograms (millionths of a gram) inhaled causes death within 60 days. For weapon production, plutonium has to be at least 93 per cent enriched. Plutonium technology for bomb construction is judged to be more difficult than uranium-focused techniques.

PMC Private military company. A PMC is an enterprise that provides military experts (including mercenaries) to governments and private corporations for training, logistical support, equipment procurement, intelligence gathering and defensive or offensive operations.

PMOI People's Mujahidin of Iran, aka National Liberation Army of Iran (NLA), Mujahidin-e Khalq Organisation (MEK), National Council of Resistance (NCR), National Council of Resistance of Iran (NCRI), Muslim Iranian Students' Society. Based in Iraq.

PNC Palestinian National Council. The PNC is the legislative decision-making body of the PLO (q.v.), and elects the 15-member PLO Executive Committee.

Pogrom Ostensibly spontaneous violent actions directed against religious, national or ethnic minorities, often organised by the police of a repressive government and/or right-wing groups. The concept emerged in 1881 after an attempt on the life of Tsar Alexander II, when, in the face of rumours spread by the police that the attempt on his life had been the work of Jews, pogroms occurred in the Jewish sections of many Russian cities, involving also the plundering of Jewish stores.

Police Uniformed personnel to maintain law and order, usually armed, who serve to protect the public and government officials against crime.

Police state A form of government whereby the police apparatus acts as a private army of the ruling elite, using the justice system as a political weapon and exercising control over citizens by arbitrary arrests and torture to intimidate the populace.

POLISARIO Frente Popular para la Liberación de Saguía el-Hamra y del Río de Oro/Front for the Liberation of Territories annexed by Morocco following Spanish decolonisation in 1975. The armed wing of the Saharawi People's Liberation Army, numbering 3,000–6,000 members by 2001. It accepted the Basker peace plan in 2003, but Moroccan obstructionism prevents a referendum on independence or integration with Morocco.

Political front Legal arm of a guerrilla, terrorist or vigilante organisation; often a political party which portrays itself as more moderate, saying that it shares (some of) the goals of the terrorist group but does not agree with (all of) its methods.

Political killing Unlawful and deliberate killings of persons for their political beliefs or activities, religion, ethnic origin, language or other group characteristic, carried out by order of government agencies or with their complicity by (vigilante) groups. The term covers killings in which there is evidence of government instigation, absence of due process of law or of political motivation by government or by opposition forces. It also covers 'summary executions' and is used for assassinations and terroristic murders.

Political offence A term used, especially in the nineteenth century, in treaties on asylum and extradition. Persons accused of non-violent offences (e.g. fighting for democracy and constitutional government) were often not extradited by liberal states to illiberal regimes. Acts of terrorism, war crimes and crimes against humanity are generally not considered political offences, and perpetrators of such acts are therefore subject to extradition.

Political risk assessment (PRA) Evaluation procedures first introduced in the 1960s by multinational corporations fearing nationalisation and other forms of financial loss in unstable Third World countries due to non-market factors such as macro-economic and social policies, or to revolution, civil war, terrorism, etc. Information for PRA is gained from observational data, individual expert-generated data and expert-group-assessed data (either Delphi or non-Delphi). Both theory-based structured methods and intuitive, unstructured methods are used (Jeuken, 1996: 12, 45, 47).

Political terrorism Use or threat of often indiscriminate and unlawful violence by individuals or groups against civilians and non-combatants for non-criminal and non-idiosyncratic purposes, aiming to attack or preserve political order in a state by acts of intimidation, coercion and demonstrative violence.

Political violence Certain instrumental forms of violence that are neither criminally motivated nor flowing from the state of mental health of a person or group of persons perpetrating it are often referred to as 'political' when performed for collective rather than individual purposes. Such violence, which challenges the state's claim to a monopoly of force/violence in the area under its jurisdiction, is outlawed as common or political crime, whether it seeks to replace the sitting regime or the social and political system as a whole.

Politicide Mass killing that is targeted at a political class rather than an ethnic, linguistic or religious group.

Politics Activity linked to obtaining, maintaining, expanding and changing state or government power and organising the common good (welfare, security and other community interests) of a society. In a democracy, it is a process through which citizens organise and change rules governing them, based on negotiating compromises between parties with conflicting interests, involving coalition building and mass mobilisation to realise goals or defend acquired privileges and positions. When referring to terrorism, 'political' is used to differentiate it from merely criminal violence aimed at obtaining a material benefit. However, 'political terrorism' belongs to the category of 'criminal politics', rather than to the realm of mainstream 'politics', the realm of (organised) 'crime' or the category of 'political crime'.

Popular Front for the Liberation of Palestine See PFLP.

Popular Front for the Liberation of Palestine – General Command See PFLP-GC.

Popular Organisation for the Liberation of the Golan A group that emerged in August 2006 after the alleged 'success' of Hezbollah's resistance to Israel in Lebanon.

Popular Resistance Front A left-wing Argentinian group led by Enrique Haroldo Gorriarán Merlo, a former commander of the ERP; active in the 1980s.

Posse Comitatus 'Power for the county'. This is a US anti-federal government, right-wing, racist group with thousands of members, formed in 1969 by H.L. Beach and W.P. Gale, with a social base among impoverished farmers in the Midwest of the United States.

Post–modern terrorism Refers to the theory that a 'new terrorism' emerged after the Cold War, with an expanding set of actors and the use of weapons of mass destruction, no longer aiming primarily to obtain publicity and recognition for a cause but striving to create mass casualties.

Power Power can be conceived as the capacity to shape interaction by threat power, economic power or, alternatively, by integrative power (based on such relationships as legitimacy, respect, affection, love, community, and identity) (Boulding, 1989). In political life, power refers to the ability to achieve a preferred outcome despite opposition. It can be exercised through inducement, persuasion, exhortation and promise of rewards, exchange of favours, threats of punishment, intimidation, coercion and manipulation of political discourse by media control, or sheer force.

Power can, *inter alia*, be based on military or police force, economic resources, technological superiority, political organisation, cultural dominance, social solidarity, institutional control, demographic preponderance or religious belief.

Power relates to conflict in those power differentials between individuals, groups and states that create different interests (an interest to reduce, maintain or increase the power gap). According to Dahrendorf, the resulting domination conflicts can only be regulated, not resolved, because the structural basis of conflict is never eliminated. As social change takes place, the relative power position of social actors is altered and new incompatibilities (but also harmonies) can arise between individuals, groups, nations and states. The result is either cooperation, conflict or an issue-based limited confrontation in a framework of peaceful coexistence.

Conflict-prone domination–submission relationships exist in many fields (old v. young, rich v. poor, male v. female, citizens v. immigrants, etc.). Within states, democratic procedures and equality before the law are used to regulate such conflicts. In the international arena, fewer regulating mechanisms exist. According to Morgenthau, the father of 'realism' in international relations, powerful nations try to stay that way and weaker nations try to become more powerful through alliances, armaments, etc. The result of this game of domination and resistance is a constant international power struggle (see his book *Politics among Nations*, 1948). Political conflicts are contests of power whereby the quarrelling parties attempt to mobilise their coercive resources, their economic resources, their organisational resources, their information resources, their status-linked resources, and their moral capital resource (authority), while trying to undermine those of the antagonist(s) (Sederberg, 1989: 8).

Power politics An approach to politics that regards the pursuit of power as the principal human or national goal.

PRE Popular Resistance Committees (West Bank/Gaza). Formed in 2000; maintains an armed wing, the Salah al-Din Battalions/Brigades.

Precursor chemical materials Substances that, following chemical processing, form building blocks for the construction of chemical weapons. Examples are thiodiglycol, phosphorus oxychloride, dimethyl methylphosphanate, methylphosphonyl difluoride (DF), methylphosphonyl dichloride (DC), dimethyl phosphite (DMP), phosphorus trichloride, trimethyl phosphite (TMP), thionyl chloride, 3-hydroxy-1-methylpiperidine, *N,N*-diisopropyl-(beta)-aminoethyl chloride, *N,N*-diisopropyl-(beta)-aminoethane thiol, 3-quinuclidinol, potassium fluoride, 2-chloroethanol, dimethylamine, diethyl ethylphosphonate, diethyl *N,N*-dimethylosphoramidate, diethyl phosphite, dimethylamine hydrochloride, ethylphosphinyl dichloride, ethylphosphinyl difluoride, hydrogen fluoride, methyl benzilate, methylphosphinyl dichloride, *N,N*-diisopropyl-(beta)-aminoethanol, pinacolyl alcohol, *O*-ethyl-2-diisopropylaminoethyl methylphosphonite (QL), triethyl phosphite, arsenic trichloride, benzilic acid, diethylmethylphosphonite, dimethyl ethylphosphonate, ethyl phosphinyl difluoride, 3-quinuclidone, phosphorus pentachloride, pinacolone, potassium cyanide, potassium bifluoride, ammonium bifluoride, sodium bifluoride, sodium fluoride, sodium cyanide, triethanolamine, phosphorus pentasulphide, diisopropylamine, diethylaminoethanol, sodium sulphide, sulphur monochloride, sulphur dichloride, tri-ethanolamine hydrochloride, *N,N*-diisopropyl-2-aminoethyl chloride hydrochloride.

Pre-emptive attack/pre-emption A short-term proactive offensive against an adversary before he can fully gather his forces; anticipatory self-defence in a situation of perceived threat.

PREPAK People's Revolutionary Party of Kangleipak (India).

Prevention The taking of long-term proactive measures to remove the causes of an undesirable development or to obstruct the occurrence of an unwanted situation; social and technical engineering to reduce individual or collective harm or damage by inhibiting, dissuading or deterring potential offenders, also by creating environments where criminal activity is made more difficult (situational crime prevention).

Preventive diplomacy Measures taken by governments, international organisations and non-governmental organisations in the fields of diplomacy, politics, economics as well as the military to reduce chances of conflict escalation, limit the level of violence in conflict and prevent its spread into neighbouring regions.

Preventive war Military offensive that attempts to pre-empt any gain an adversary might achieve from a future attack, or from blackmail based on its growing military might. A preventive war usually aims to destroy key elements of the war-making capabilities of the opponent. Military strategists see considerable advantages in first strikes:

* Surprise.
* The initiative is in one's own hand.
* The combat zone is on enemy territory.
* Own population exposure to enemy attacks is reduced because enemy military forces are weakened after the first strike.
* Part of the enemy forces are destroyed before war begins.
* The enemy might be so stunned that his morale collapses (Lutz).

Prince of the Sea See Abdul Rahim al-Nasheri.

Privateer A private ship (or its captain) that was authorised by a government by a 'Letter of Marque' to attack and seize cargo from another country's ships. Privateers were outlawed by European powers in the 'Declaration of Paris' of 1856, and by other powers, including the United States, in the Hague Conventions of 1899 and 1907.

Product adulteration Covert application of a toxic or other harmful substance to food or drink or medicine, often in supermarkets with shelf access to shoppers, used for extortion of money from the proprietor or for publicity.

Profiling A method of scanning groups of people for suspects of crime or terrorism, based on often doubtful and sometimes controversial selection criteria.

Proletariat Marxist term referring to the working class which does not own means of production.

Proliferation The spread of advanced weapon systems (especially rockets and weapons of mass destruction), associated know-how and technologies as well as experts to other states or non-state actors.

Propaganda One-sided and manipulative dissemination of information, mixing (half-)truths and lies in an effort to influence the behaviour of targeted audiences by persuasive communications that are meant to make an audience accept a certain definition of the situation or stimulate certain behaviour or politics. Propaganda is formulated so as to appeal to the emotions of groups of people in order to reinforce (less often to change) public opinions, stimulate political action or secure continued rule. Propaganda reduces complex phenomena to simple clichés, creating dichotomies of black and white, them and us, good and evil. Often the real purpose of a propaganda statement is different from its apparent purpose.

Propaganda of the deed A concept developed in the 1870s, based on the idea that daring and violent 'exemplary deeds' with high symbolic and news value could serve as a mobilising device for bringing the 'spirit of revolt' to 'the people' and could popularise the techniques used, and demands made, by perpetrators of such armed propaganda.

Propaganda techniques (commercial) There are some parallels between political and commercial propaganda. In order to obtain attitudinal and behavioural results in selected target audiences, commercial propaganda appeals to values and attitudes already present. They include:

- glittering generalities: a technique of surrounding a candidate, product or policy with symbol-loaded positive words that evoke a favourable response;
- name calling: a method used in negative propaganda in order to attach an unfavourable label to something that the propagandist opposes;
- transfer: a method of winning approval for something by associating it with something else that is known to be viewed favourably;
- testimonial: a technique of using famous or respected people to make public statements favouring or opposing something;
- plain folks: a method of identifying the propagandist's ideas or product with 'ordinary' people;
- card stacking: an argument in which the facts (or falsehoods) are arranged in such a way that only one conclusion seems to be logically flowing from it;
- bandwagon: a method that tries to build support for a particular viewpoint or product by creating the impression that 'everyone else is already doing/thinking it' and that it is time to join the alleged majority.

Protest Non-violent or violent form of political expression, usually involving demonstrations, rallies, marches, sit-ins, strikes, etc., to draw public attention to some grievance and exert political pressure.

Provo A member of the Provisional IRA. See PIRA.

PRTC Workers' Revolutionary Party of Central America. The PRTC was a Trotskyite group active between the late 1970s and 1990s in Honduras, Guatemala, El Salvador and Mexico.

PSC Private security company. PSCs are legally established enterprises providing services that include either guarding, protecting or defending assets, and/or counselling and training clients to develop their own security measures. Unlike PMCs, PSCs do not engage in any offensive exercise of force by military means.

PSF (Palestinian) Popular Struggle Front/Jabhat al-Kifah al-Sha'bi (Lebanon). A Syrian-based breakaway Palestinian group from the PLO between 1974 and 1991, led by Dr Samir Ghosheh; it was part of the Rejectionist Front objecting to a deal with Israel.

PSI Proliferation security initiative. The PSI was established in May 2003 as an attempt to interdict shipments of weapons of mass destruction (WMD) and missile-related technologies and equipment by stopping and searching suspicious ships and planes.

PSLA Palaung State Liberation Army. Armed force of the Ta'ang people in Myanmar, forced by the military to disarm in 2005.

PSNI Police Service of Northern Ireland.

Psychotomimetic agent A chemical agent (e.g. BZ) that damages the central nervous system and causes symptoms resembling some psychotic disorders.

PSYOP Psychological operations. A method of delivering loaded messages to enemy audiences ('you are fighting a losing battle'), the home audience (demonising the enemy) and third parties (convincing them of injustices done by the enemy) for purposes of winning a hot or cold war. Covert propaganda activities are used in wartime (sometimes also in peacetime) against enemy forces and/or populations, third parties and sometimes also against a country's own population. PSYOP can serve offensive and defensive purposes aimed at affecting the attitudes and behaviour of targeted audiences regarding political and military matters. Techniques include defamation of the opponent through the dissemination of (usually) biased information, subversion of the morale of opposing forces through exaggeration of one's own strength or spread of rumours on the corruptness of the leadership of the opponent, as well as false-flag operations to shift blame onto the adversary. The general goal is to win sympathy for one's own cause while bedevilling the opponent's, especially with third parties whose attitude and behaviour are deemed relevant in the conflict at hand.

PUK Patriotic Union of Kurdistan/Yaketi Nishtimani Kurdistan (Iraq). Established in 1975, it supported the US invasion of Iraq in 2003. Its leader, Jalal Talabani, became president of Iraq in 2005.

PULF People's United Liberation Front (India). Formed in 1995 and reportedly supported by Pakistan's Inter-Services Intelligence (ISI).

PULO Pattani United Liberation Organisation Group fighting for independence from Thailand for Muslim-Malayan Pattani; established in 1968. This group is active in the deep south of Thailand – that is, in the provinces of Pattani and Yala, where the majority of the population is of Malayan origin and professes Islam, unlike the vast majority of ethnic Thais, who are Buddhists. The PULO has splintered into several small factions, fighting either for an autonomous Muslim-Malay province of Pattani within Thailand or for secession from Thailand and accession to Malaysia.

PUP Progressive Unionist Party; political form of the UVF (q.v.).

PVCP Permanent vehicle checkpoint.

PWG People's War Group, aka People's War, Naxalites, People's Guerrilla Army, Communist Party of India–Marxist-Leninist (India). Formed in 1980 and merged in 2004 with the Maoist Communist Center to form the Communist Party of India–Maoist (CPI-Maoist).

Qaeda see Al-Qaeda.

Qassam Home-made rockets developed by Palestinians, who fire them from Gaza into Israel.

QRF Quick reaction force.

Quebec Liberation Front See FLQ.

Racial killing Murder by state agents, private persons or vigilante (death squad) groups (e.g. KKK lynchings) where the target is selected on the grounds of ethnic origin in general or colour of skin in particular.

Racism Hostility towards people with different ethnic features such as skin and hair colour, physique and facial traits, often combined with feelings of superiority. As a theory, racialism represents a non-egalitarian, pseudo-scientific doctrine advocating organisation of (international) society along biological markers. Despite the fact that there is no genetic base to justify racism (all human beings originate from Africa and are part of the same species), discrimination against and marginalisation, oppression, enslavement, persecution, ethnic cleansing and elimination of members of other races has been widely practised in history, including during nineteenth-century colonialism and twentieth-century fascism and in apartheid politics. Racists sometimes also tend to target people of different religious and sexual orientation.

Radicalisation Individual but usually group process of ideological socialisation of young people (sometimes recent converts) towards the use of violent tactics of conflict waging, sometimes including self-destruction in the process of harming political opponents (as in suicide bombings). The process often begins with a feeling of displacement (e.g. from migration), a feeling of relative deprivation (e.g. in relation to the host society) and a feeling of alienation and existential doubts. There is often a need for meaning, for belonging to a (subculture) community and for purity (hence conversions) in the vulnerable individual or (small) group (Buijs *et al.*, 2007). The radicalisation process can be short or long, depending on how many ties to the existing order the radicalising individual has. It can have several layers (population groups, generations, cliques of spiritual sympathisers) and take several forms (socio-cultural, religious or ideological, and political). Buijs *et al.* (2007) distinguish between three general development stages: (1) the breach of confidence phase, where trust in the existing order is undermined and a conflict erupts between a disenchanted group and specific authority figures in relation to a specific policy; (2) a conflict of legitimacy phase, where no longer specific policies but the political system itself is questioned and an alternative ideological system is developed; and finally, an extremist stage of the legitimacy crisis is reached, where the criticism focuses on individuals, who are dehumanised.

Radicalism Advocacy of, and commitment to, thoroughgoing change and restructuring of political and social institutions; an attitude associated mostly with left- and right-wing but at times also with centrist ideologies (reactionary conservativism and ultra-liberalism), wishing to do away with traditional and procedural restrictions that support the status quo to implement a desired political programme or policy. Fascism has sometimes been considered an example of right-wing radicalism, and communism an example of leftist radicalism. As an ideology of international relations, radicalism denies the legitimacy of established norms, laws and procedures of international politics and economics and favours a revolutionary, violent overthrow of the international system to establish a more just world order. Radicals are sometimes distinguished from extremists in terms of their lesser willingness to use violence to bring about drastic political change. Terrorism, as violence without moral restraint, is generally associated with extremism.

Religious radicalism refers to a religious-political movement that is driven by the conviction:

- that religion is marginalised in modern society on the level of politics, the societal institutions and norms and values, which inevitably will lead to the demise of society;
- that many civil rulers facilitate this marginalisation, and that therefore mistrust and resistance against them and their socio-political order is justified;
- that most religious authorities acquiesce in the decline of the central place of religion in society and thereby betray the fundaments of religion;
- that the fundaments of religion need to be restored by a return to the traditional religious norms and values and a literal reading of the holy scripture;
- that one's own religion is superior and should in fact form the basis for society and the state, and should be the yardstick for politics;
- that the true believer must play an active role in the realisation of the desired society.

According to Buijs (2002: 61–62), radicalism utilises various strategies: political-reformist actions, cultural struggle, and strengthening of the community of believers by means of creating basic provisions, missionary work and militant activism. Violence against persons, however, is in general not one of the means utilised.

'Islamic radicalism' is (according to Buijs *et al.* 2007) based on the conviction that (1) in modern society, Islam is being marginalised and threatened with annihilation; (2) many civic leaders are collaborating towards this, so that distrust and opposition against them and their socio-political order is justified; (3) most religious leaders acquiesce in the loss of religion's central place in society and are therefore traitors to the underlying principles of the faith; (4) the underlying principles of the faith must be restored by a reversion to traditional religious standards and values and a literal reading of the Qur'an; (5) one's own religion is superior and must in fact form the basis for society and the state, as well as being the touchstone for politics; and (6) the true believer must play an active role in achieving the desired society, so that intervention is a matter of the utmost urgency.

Some radical Islamists justify their militant activities by referring to the Qur'an (Sura 8, verse

40) in which Muhammad calls on believers to fight infidels until 'all belief is directed towards Allah'. They see themselves at war with the enemies of Islam, who include their own governments and Muslims who have left the correct path of the faith. For them, jihad justifies violence to prepare the path to the desired end state (Bauer, 1999: 38). Islamic radicalism in its most extreme form accepts that all means justify the end of bringing about the ideal society. Furthermore, it is based on belief in the uniqueness and superiority of the true believers, and a specific interpretation of jihad promulgated, making it an individual duty for all Muslims to deploy all imaginable resources in bringing about the desired end state (Buijs *et al.* 2007).

Radiological agent Nuclear or radioactive substance which can be used for a RDD, such as americium-241, americium-243, californium-252, caesium-137, curium, iodine-131, neptunium-237, plutonium-238, plutonium-239, plutonium-241, plutonium-242, thorium, tritium, uranium-233 and uranium-235.

RAF Rote Armee Fraktion/Red Army Faction, aka Baader-Meinhof Gang/Group. Small German left-wing terrorist group responsible for more than 50 attacks between 1972 and the early 1990s; it received some support from Middle Eastern terrorist groups and the East German government. The group declared a ceasefire in April 1992 and disbanded in March 1998.

Rangers US airborne elite troops trained to fight behind enemy lines.

Ransom Money demanded or extorted for the safe return of a kidnapped person.

RATF Revolutionary Armed Task Force, aka United Freedom Fighters, Revolutionary Fighting Group, Red Guerrilla Resistance and Armed Resistance Unit. The RATF is a left-wing group founded in the United States in the late 1970s from remnants of the Weather Underground (q.v.) and the Black Liberation Army (BLA). Most members had been arrested by 1986.

RAW Research and Analysis Wing. Indian intelligence agency.

RCD Rassemblement Congolais pour la Démocratie – Mouvement de Libération/Congolese Rally for Democracy – Liberation Movement. Has been active since 1999, numbering 2,000–3,000.

RCD-GOMA Rassemblement Congolais pour la Démocratie – Goma/Congolese Rally for Democracy – Goma. RCD-GOMA was established in 1998.

RCIED Radio-controlled improvised explosive device.

RDD Radiological dispersal device, aka 'dirty bomb'. A combination of conventional explosives or other dispersal agent to scatter radioactive debris (e.g. spent fuel rods) for area contamination and denial. Depending on concentration, radiation damage might take weeks if not months or years to produce large numbers of fatalities. According to one estimate (Krieger, 1977), the release of 4.4 pounds (2kg) of plutonium oxide in powder form in a population centre could produce a 100 per cent probability of bone and lung cancer for every person within a distance of 1,800 feet (550 m) downwind of the release point and a 1 per cent risk as far as 40 miles (64 km) downwind. The amount and type of radioactive material used also determine damage and fatality. The effect appears to be mainly psychological, making it a potentially useful terrorist tool rather than a militarily useful weapon. However, the radiation overdose hazard to those constructing and delivering the weapon might weigh against its use (Ford, 1998).

RDX Explosive substance used in plastic bombs.

Reactionary An adherent of an ideology that wishes to establish the status of a bygone age; usually right-wing.

Rebellion Open intra-state resistance to the authority of a government, sometimes involving armed insurrection by civilians and/or (parts of) the security forces of a government against the ruling regime. Rebellions are usually aimed only at replacing the sitting rulers, not the political system itself (which would be revolutionary).

Recovery The post-attack phase in consequence management to support individuals and communities struck by man-made or natural disasters.

RED Radiation emission device. A tool to disperse radioactive materials in air, water, food, etc. See also RDD.

Red Army Faction See RAF.

Red Brigades Brigate Rosse (BR) (q.v.). An Italian left–wing terrorist group founded in 1969 and largely inactive since the early 1980s.

Red Hand Commandos An anti-Catholic splinter group of the Ulster Defence Association; active in the 1970s.

Red Mercury RM 20/20; $Hg_2Sb_2O_7$, mercury antinomy oxide. An apparently useless material, the subject of a smuggling hype in the early 1990s in Europe; claims that it can be used as an explosion booster have not been substantiated.

Red team In simulation exercises, the team of players that assumes the role of the enemy.

Red Terror A policy decreed on 5 September 1918 by the Bolshevik government in Russian after an assassination attempt on Lenin, to suppress opposition; it resulted in 10,000–15,000 extra-judicial executions of suspected and real political opponents of the Soviet government in just the first two months, setting a pattern of inhumane rule by terror not abandoned until Stalin's death in 1953.

Regime Term referring *inter alia* to the form of rule, such as in 'authoritarian regime', 'communist regime', 'democratic regime', or 'terror regime' (such as the *régime de terreur* of the Jacobins in France, 1793–1794).

Rehabilitation Restorative measures for groups and societies affected by disaster to secure the functioning of infrastructure and hospitals, so as to enable them to resume normal life after a catastrophe.

Reign of Terror Term denoting the most violent period of the French Revolution (30 August 1793 to 28 July 1794), when Jacobins under Robespierre arrested at least 300,000 regime opponents and executed 17,000 of them.

Religion Belief in something sacred or someone supernatural and immortal to which or whom human beings can relate through worship, sacrifice, priests, prayer, spiritual or mystical experience and from which or whom they can draw consolation, rewards and meaning for their lives.

Religious terrorism Indiscriminate and unlawful use of violence against non–combatant civilians justified by perpetrators in terms of a higher (divine) authority, Holy Scripture or performed for the alleged defence of a religious community or the creation or expansion of a theocratic regime; also, the indoctrination and mobilisation of members of sects and cults with the help of religious themes. The goal is sometimes a restoration of an ideal situation that allegedly existed in some golden past.

RENAMO Resistência Nacional Moçambicana/Mozambican National Resistance. Large (20,000 in the late 1980s) guerrilla and terrorist organisation formed in 1976 by the Rhodesian military and also supported later by South Africa in order to destabilise the Marxist FRELIMO government. RENAMO was transformed, after having killed at least 100,000 people in the 1980s, into a political organisation after the 1994 elections.

Repentance and Holy Fight An anti-Western Islamist Egyptian group founded in 1971 by Shukry Mustafa; repressed in 1977.

Repression Political control measures taken against political opponents or potential opponents. The term is often used for acts or a situation of subjugation effectuated by intimidation or physical violence; sometimes a government response to protest and violent movements involving harsh, indiscriminate measures against militants and those suspected of being part of the dissident or insurgent movement. When taken by a legitimate government while it is under attack by armed sections of the population, selective repression, based on the principle of proportionality, is legal. Repression involves both non–lethal and lethal coercive measures. Repression is not the exclusive prerogative of state actors; national liberation movements, resistance groups and terrorist actors also use it for internal disciplining. Repression often transgresses what is legally permitted, even under a state of emergency; however, not all repression is illegal or illegitimate. Selective repression, based on the principles of legality and proportionality, against destructive mob action does not constitute a 'crime of repression'. According to Hess, 'repressive crimes' are illegal acts 'committed to maintain, strengthen or – above all – defend privileged positions, in particular those of power and property' (1976: 1–22). The repertoire of repressive tactics of governments is broad and can also include terrorism.

Reprisals Responses to illegal acts committed against a state party that would be illegal themselves except for the fact that they were reactive.

Republican In the Irish context, the term is used for Catholic nationalists wishing to unite Northern Ireland and the Republic of Ireland, often by use of force.

Resistance A more-or-less organised movement, often in the underground, which opposes a government or occupying (foreign) power regarded as oppressive and unjust by (sectors) of the population. Resistance involves opposition to rule perceived as illegitimate or foreign, in the form of either passive (civil disobedience), selective (rejecting only part of the exercise of power) or active means; the latter include boycotts, sit-ins, strikes and, in extreme situations, attacks on the holders of state power and the violent removal of the ruler. Resistance by armed force to established authority has been justified by a number of authors when the latter is illegal, illegitimate, unjust, immoral, arbitrary, unsurpatory, despotic, or tyrannical, or is doing grave damage to the life and property of members of the community, or engages the state needlessly in foreign wars.

Response Disaster-related emergency measures to mitigate damage, save lives, and/or remove or dispel the source of harm.

Retaliation A punitive counter-attack for revenge and/or to deter future attacks.

Revolution An abrupt, wide-reaching, popular change of a country's rulers (Tilly, 1993). A revolution is the forcible transfer of power over a state, involving the mobilisation of large sectors of the population in the power struggle between challengers and defenders of the *status quo ante*. This would often happen in the wake of invasion or (defeat in) war. If successful, the result is not just a replacement of the ruling elite but a destruction of the old order (*ancien régime*) and the creation of a new political system.

Revolutionary Armed Forces of Colombia See FARC.

Revolutionary Catechism Title of a pamphlet written by the Russian nihilist theorist of terrorism Sergei Nechayev.

Revolutionary Cells Revolutionäre Zellen. Part-time terrorists active in Germany in the 1970s.

Revolutionary Nuclei Epanastatiki Pirines (Greece). Formed in 1974; possibly linked to the ELA.

Revolutionary Nuclei (RN) Italian left-wing group.

Revolutionary Organisation 17 November Greek group active since the 1970s.

Revolutionary Struggle Epanastatikis Aghonas (Greece); emerged in September 2003.

Revolutionary taxes Money extorted for one cause or another; often little more than the protection money demanded by organised crime for bogus protection services.

Revolutionary terrorism A type of political violence that involves generally indiscriminate and unlawful attacks against civilians and non-combatants and is meant to foster revolution or accompany revolutionary transformations of the entire political and social system.

RFF Ricardo Franco Front. A small left-wing group that split from the Colombian FARC in 1984 and killed 100 of its own dissidents in a purge in 1985.

RFJ Rewards for Justice. A US programme for obtaining information on wanted persons.

RGR Red Guerrilla Resistance. A New York-based anti-Israeli US left-wing group active in the mid-1980s.

RHB Rebolusyonaryong Hukbong Bayan (Philippines). The RHB was established in 1998 as the armed wing of the MLPP, the Marxist-Leninist Party of the Philippines.

RHD Red Hand Defenders. A small (20 members) Loyalist paramilitary group in Northern Ireland, opposed to the Good Friday Agreement of 1998, involved in attacks on Roman Catholics.

Ricin A poison derived from the beans of the castor-oil plant and developed as a toxic weapon during the Second World War. Ricin is a fast-working biological toxin (used by the communist Bulgarian secret service to kill several exiled opposition leaders) that decomposes rapidly, making it a hard-to-detect weapon for assassinations.

Rickettsiae A class of biological agents including the Japanese encephalitis virus and *Coxiella burnetii*, *Rickettsia quintana* (also known as *Rochalimea quintana*) and *Rickettsia prowasecki*.

Rift Valley fever virus A biological agent.

Right Term referring to political parties that are generally conservative and status quo–oriented, often preferring market liberalisation and limited state intervention in the economy. The political right includes Christian, conservative, neo–liberal, populist and extremist parties. Key values usually encompass nationalism, tradition, authority and order.

Right-wing terrorism Generally indiscriminate and unlawful use of violence against civilians and non-combatants for the purpose of defending or bringing about a conservative, pro–business regime; in extreme cases, a racist, fascist, militarist and/or undemocratic authoritarian regime.

Rigid raiders Semi-inflatable speedboats with a reinforced bottom.

Riot Violent protest demonstration or civil disturbance involving large numbers of people, often accompanied by looting and property damage. Such disruptions of public order are often sparked by a confrontation between different groups of demonstrators or between demonstrators and police or military forces.

Riot control agent A chemical substance used for crowd control, e.g. pepper spray or tear gas.

RIRA Real Irish Republican Army, aka Óglaigh na hÉireann, True IRA and New IRA. The RIRA is a splinter group of the PIRA that does not respect the 1998 Good Friday Agreement count some 100+ members. Held responsible for the Omagh bombing in August 1998 (29 people killed).

Risk The degree of danger associated with a given operation, course of action, or failure to act in a crisis situation. Since some high-risk operations promise high gains, strategists sometimes take a calculated risk. For forecasting, it makes sense to distinguish between levels of risks, for example:

- high risk
- high moderate risk
- moderate risk
- low moderate risk
- low risk.

For mathematical modelling purposes, risk is often expressed as the probability of an unwanted occurrence multiplied by the severity of its consequences.

Risk assessment Calculation and/or simulation of the degree of danger attached to a course of action for the purpose of uncertainty reduction. According to Gurr (1996: 137), 'risk assessment and early warning are distinct but complementary activities. Risk assessments are based on the systematic analysis of remote and intermediate conditions. Early warning requires near-real-time assessment of events that, in a high-risk environment, are likely to accelerate or trigger the rapid escalation of conflict'.

Riyad us-Saliheyn Martyrs' Brigade, aka Riyadh-as-Saliheen, Riyadus-Salikhin Reconnaissance and Sabotage Battalion of Chechen Martyrs. The group was led by the Chechen warlord and president Shamil Basayev until his death in July 2006 and used 'Black Widows' for suicide attacks.

RMS Republik Maluku Selatan/South Moluccan Republic. A Christian Indonesian separatist group that established a short-lived republic in 1950 on Ambon (Spice Islands). An exile group in the Netherlands has engaged in terrorist violence against-Indonesian and Dutch targets; since 1998, the group has been active in homeland to defend Christian Moluccans against, jihadists.

Rocio virus A biological agent.

Rodrigo Franco Command Death squad linked to the defence of the Peruvian American Popular Revolutionary Alliance (ARPA) against Shining Path attacks; mainly active in 1987 and 1988.

RO-N17 Revolutionary Organisation 17 November/Epanastatiki Organosi 17 Noembri, aka 17 November (N17) (Greece). RO-N17 was formed in 1975 and active until 2002.

RPF Revolutionary People's Front (India, Manipur). The RPF was established in 1979, fighting for independence.

RPG–7 Soviet-produced rocket-propelled grenade.

RPL Revolutionary Party of the Left. A Greek left-wing group active in the mid-1980s.

RS Revolutionary struggle.

RSM Rajah Solaiman Movement (Philippines). The RSM was established in 2002; it is linked to the ASG.

RSRSBCM Riyadus-Salikhin Reconnaissance + Sabotage Battalion of Chechen Martyrs.

RUC Royal Ulster Constabulary. The former name for the police force of Northern Ireland, predominantly Protestant and in the 1970s and 1980s viewed by Catholic militants as a British occupation force. Replaced by the Police Service of Northern Ireland in November 2001.

RUF Revolutionary United Front. A Sierra Leone rebel group numbering 8,000 (2001), including many child soldiers, established in 1988 (or 1991?) to oppose the corrupt regime of President Joseph Momoh. Since 1991, 'hijacked' by Foday Sankoh with the support of Charles Taylor of Liberia. The RUF is notorious for its tactic of hacking off people's hands. Following the November 2000 ceasefire in Abuja, the group, including many child soldiers, was supposed to disarm.

RUFP Revolutionary United Front Party (Sierra Leone).

Rule of law The notion that (1) people should be ruled not by the whims of individuals but by the objective determination of general laws; (2) that nobody should stand above the law, that ordinary citizens can find redress against the more powerful for any act that involves a breach of law; and (3) that nobody should fall outside the protection of the law.

Rules of engagement (ROE) In an armed conflict, force can be applied in different ways, with or without previous warning, with high- or low-intensity force application – from 'saturation bombing' to 'minimum necessary force', the latter being defined as 'the measured and appropriate application of violence or coercion, sufficient only to achieve a specific objective and confined in effect to the legitimate target intended' (British Army, 1997: chap. 4: 9). The use of lethal force is regulated in rules of engagement. ROE are, according to the same British Army manual, 'directives that delineate the circumstances and limitations under which force may be used. ROE will reflect legal and political restraints; however, they will always authorise self-defence and should never inhibit a commander's ability to take all necessary action to protect his force. While it is highly desirable that national contingents within the same force harmonise their ROE, national laws will invariably over-ride UN and Force ROE'.

RVX A nerve agent.

RZ Revolutionäre Zellen/Revolutionary Cells. A German left-wing group active since 1974 and into the 1990s; less violent than the RAF (q.v.).

SA-7 ('Grail') Sold by the thousands after the fall of the Soviet Union, the SA-7 'Grail' uses an optical sight and tracking device with an infrared-seeking mechanism to strike flying targets with great force. Its maximum effective range is approximately 6,125 metres and maximum effective altitude is approximately 12,900 feet (about 4,000 m). It is known to be in the stockpiles of terrorist and guerrilla groups.

SAARC South Asian Association for Regional Cooperation – a regional organisation.

Sabotage An act of deliberate and purposeful damaging or destroying of (transportation or production) machinery or a public or private object or facility to prevent further economic or military functioning, usually not involving direct loss of human lives.

Safeguards A system of monitoring, controlling and handling of nuclear materials to prevent, detect and respond to unauthorised possession or destruction of nuclear materials, as maintained by the International Atomic Energy Agency (IAEA).

Safe haven A sanctuary for a persecuted individual or group, including terrorists in another state, or a specific area not accessible to security forces.

Safe house A shelter where agents and fugitives can hide from government, with low probability of discovery.

Safety Freedom from danger, injury, damage or malfunctioning due to a set of precautionary measures taken to secure the object or situation.

Salafia Jihadia Wahhabi jihadist doctrine exported from Saudi Arabia since the 1990s.

Salafia Jihadia/Salafist Holy War (Morocco). An Islamist network established in the second half of the 1990s.

Salafism A fundamentalist ideological current or social movement closely linked to Wahhabism seeking to purge Islam of social and cultural outside influences and return to the orthodox Islam practised by 'pious ancestors', i.e. Muhammad and his immediate successors; adhering to a 'pure' interpretation of the Qur'an. Salafism can be apolitical, political or militant in the jihadi sense. It is the leading ideology of a transnational jihadi movement of which Al-Qaeda is the most prominent representative.

Salafist From *salaf*, meaning 'pious ancestor', 'forefather'. A strict orthodox follower of the supposedly 'pure' original Islam of the glorious period of the Prophet and the first four caliphs thereafter, as reflected in the Qur'an and the Sunni.

Salafist Group for Preaching and Combat See GSPC.

Salafiya Jihadia Jihad for Pure Islam. A Moroccan group held responsible for attacks in Casablanca in 2003.

SAM Surface-to-air missile.

Sanctions Punitive actions by one (group of) state(s) against another for previous objectionable behaviour.

Sandinistas See FSLN.

Santa Maria Name of the Portuguese cruise liner that was temporarily taken over in January 1961 off the Venezuelan port of La Guaira by a 25-man unit of the Portuguese National Independence Movement, led by Henrique Galvão, in protest against the Portuguese and Spanish regimes. During the event, the *Santa Maria*'s third watch officer was killed and one other person wounded. After protracted negotiations between the hijackers, Portugal and Brazil, the ship sailed to the Brazilian port of Recife, where the passengers were allowed to disembark. The hijackers were given political asylum by Brazil.

Saraya al-Shuhuada al-Jihadiya fi al-Iraq Squadrons of the Jihad for the Liberation of Iraq.

Sarin A chemical agent (nerve gas) used by Aum Shinrikyo in the Tokyo underground in 1995, killing 12 people and severely injuring more than 40 others.

SAS Special Air Service. The SAS is a regiment of the British Army established in the Second World War. It specialises in commando operations and irregular warfare; it is engaged in counter-terrorist operations at home and abroad.

SATCEN Satellite Centre. SATCEN is a body of the European Union; a provider of satellite imagery for security matters.

SAVAG National Security and Information Organisation. The Iranian secret police under Shah Reza Pahlavi, feared for its torture techniques and assassinations of dissidents abroad. The organisation was succeeded by VEVAK under the Khomeini regime.

Saxitoxin A poison allegedly used by the CIA, derived from shellfish.

Sayaret Israeli counter-terrorist unit of the IDF, founded in 1957.

Schengen The town in Luxembourg where some European member states signed the Schengen Convention in 1990, abolishing internal borders and replacing them with a Schengen Information System (SIS).

SCO Shanghai Cooperation Organisation – Regional Security organisation.

Scuba Self-contained underwater breathing apparatus.

SDS Students for a Democratic Society. A US student organisation active during the Vietnam War.

Sea Tigers Maritime arm of the LTTE, also called 'the navy of the LTTE'.

SEALS Sea Air Land Forces. US Navy special operations commando units trained for counter-terrorist operations; size about 2,200.

Search and destroy The military tactic of entering enemy territory to eliminate hostile forces.

Search and rescue The process of locating and recovering victims of a disaster and providing them with medical first aid and decontamination, and preparing them for transport to a hospital or morgue.

Secession Separation of population and territory from existing state to become an independent internationally recognised state, or to join a neighbouring state; often preceded by revolt and leading to civil war.

Second Soran Unit A military unit within the Islamic Movement of Kurdistan (later: Islamic Unity Movement), hosting Arab Afghanis. The Second Soran Unit has since joined the Tawhid Islamic Front.

Secret Organisation of Al Qaeda in Europe The name of an alleged group that claimed responsibility on an Islamist website for suicide bombings on the London transport system on 7 July 2005.

Secret police Non-uniformed clandestinely operating police forces used to deal with political opponents under non-democratic regimes by a variety of means, sometimes even involving selective assassinations, torture and the sowing of terror.

Sect A body of persons adhering to a particular religious cult.

Sectarian violence Term used in the Northern Ireland context for religious communal violence.

Sectarianism Strict adherence to a religious, ethnic or political ideology or religion.

Security A state of protection, freedom from danger and fear, guarantee of peaceful condition; an organisation that claims to provide these public goods. Security has several foci, the broadest being 'human security', as in human rights terminology, which speaks of 'the right to security of person' (Universal Declaration of Human Rights, 1948, Art. 3). There is also 'internal security' and 'national security', or, within alliance security communities, 'collective security', and in an even broader sense 'common security', involving several alliance systems.

There are, according to the Carnegie Commission (1997: xxxi), three main sources of insecurity today:

1 the threat posed by nuclear and other weapons of mass destruction;
2 the possibility of conventional confrontation between militaries; and
3 sources of internal violence, such as terrorism, organised crime, insurgency, and repressive regimes.

With regard to internal security within states, the Carnegie Commission identified four essential elements to internal stability:

1 a corpus of laws that is legitimately derived and widely promulgated and understood;
2 a consistent, visible, fair and active network of police authority to enforce laws;
3 an independent, equitable and accessible grievance redress system, including, above all, an impartial judicial system;
4 a penal system that is fair and prudent in meting out punishment.

Security survey A set of measures to establish, through on-site examination, the condition of an object or facility in terms of its defence against intrusion, sabotage and attack, resulting in a report on existing deficiencies and containing recommendations for required protective measures to reduce risk to an acceptable level.

Seizure of assets The taking control of funds and valuables belonging to a criminal or terrorist organisation.

Self-determination A claim by a group (nation, people) to establish a political order without outside (e.g. colonialist) interference, based on principles of freedom and (sometimes) equality. Since neither 'nation' nor 'people' is defined in international law, the determination of the 'self' is problematical, as are the rights of minorities vis-à-vis the main secessionist group. Many countries that gained self-determination by force or by the withdrawal of a colonial power still lack meaningful democratic rule by the people. Secessionist movements in former colonies claiming self-determination are generally denied the same right claimed in the past by those who gained self-determination from European colonial powers. In general, there are the following types of self-determination claims:

- anti-colonial self-determination: by a territorial population under colonial rule or alien domination seeking complete freedom or (a larger share of) political power;
- trans-state self-determination: a claim involving the concentrated grouping of a people in more than one existing state;
- self-determination of dispersed people: a claim by peoples (e.g. Gypsies) dispersed throughout one or more states.
- indigenous self-determination: a claim by indigenous communities, i.e. groups characterised by a distinct ethnicity and a long historical continuity as a pre-colonial or pre-invasion society;
- representative self-determination: a claim by a population of an existing state that seeks to change its political structure in favour of a more representative structure.

Semtex A powerful Czech-manufactured metallic, malleable, easy-to-cut, hard-to-detect plastic explosive discovered in 1966 by Stanislav Brebera in the Czech town of Semtin. Equivalent is the US-manufactured C-4 plastic explosive.

Separatism A belief, nurtured by the idea of self-determination, that a particular territory or ethnically distinct people should be allowed to secede from an existing state or community of which it forms a part to create a new independent political entity or to join another sovereign state. Separatist campaigns often lead to violence and terrorism, and frequently result in civil war.

Serious crime Illegal conduct constituting an offence punishable by deprivation of liberty for at least four years or a more serious penalty.

SHAC Stop Huntingdon Animal Cruelty. SHAC is a UK-based Animal Liberation Front campaign name.

Shaheed Also *shahideen*, or *shuada*; the Arabic word for martyr, used by sympathisers who died in a struggle considered to be sanctified. The term is also used for kamikaze suicide bombers who achieve *shahadat* (martyrdom).

Shari'ah Islamic law derived from the holy text (the Qur'an), the teaching of Muhammad (the Hadith) and jurisprudence of Islam, prescribing cultural, social and legal rules to which Muslims should submit.

Shi'ism The minority faction in Islam. Originally the supporters of Ali, the son-in-law of the prophet Muhammad, who refused to accept the caliph Muáwiyya. About 10 per cent of Muslims are Shi'ites; in Iran and Iraq they form a majority.

Shin Bet Israel's domestic security service.

Shining Path Sendero Luminoso; see SL.

Shoot to kill An instruction given to law enforcement officials or the military to use lethal force for the control of violent demonstrations.

Sicarii Dagger men of Zealots (q.v.) opposing Roman rule of Palestine; also targeted collaborating Jews (AD 66–70).

Siege Encirclement and containing of persons inside a structure and severing supplies.

SIGINT Signals intelligence; information gained from electronic terrestrial and satellite-based listening devices. Such technical collection of signals consists of intercepted communications

(COMINT), electronic intelligence (ELINT) and foreign instrumentation signals intelligence (FISINT).

SIMI Students Islamic Movement of India. SIMI are underground fundamentalist anti-Hindu and anti-Western organisation, established in 1977 and reportedly linked to Pakistan; committed to jihad and overthrow of the Indian government.

Single–issue terrorism Use of generally indiscriminate and unlawful violence against civilians and non-combatants when the agenda of the perpetrators is limited to one social, economic or political issue only, e.g. animal rights, anti-abortion or environmental issues. The borderline between protest, harassment, sabotage, arson, intimidation and terrorism is often fluid.

Sinn Féin Gaelic for 'We Ourselves'/'Ourselves Alone'. Irish political party founded in 1905 by Arthur Griffith. Later it became the political wing of the Irish Republican Army and was widely seen as a front organisation of the PIRA (q.v.).

SIS Schengen Information System. The SIS is a cross-border police information system in participating EU countries.

SIS Secret Intelligence Service (United States).

Skinheads White, mostly right-wing, youth protest movement whose members have shaved heads. It originated in the United Kingdom and United States but since the late 1980s is also to be found in Germany and Eastern Europe, often involved in racial and anti-Semitic violence and linked to neo-Nazi groups.

Skyjacking Hijacking of airliners, both for escape and for terrorist blackmail.

Sky marshal Armed guard who mingles unobtrusively on board passenger planes to deter and combat aerial hijackings.

SL Sendero Luminoso/Shining Path. Peruvian Maoist/Stalinist terrorist organisation, aka Revolutionary Student Front for the Shining Path of Mariátegui. Based mainly in the Upper Huallaga and Ene river valleys, an insurgent group formed in 1969 and led by former university philosophy professor Abimael Guzmán (Comrade Gonzalo) until his capture in September 1992; later headed by Óscar Ramírez Durand and Judith Ramos Cuadros. Its terror and the government counter-terror caused the deaths of some 70,000 people. After near-defeat it has experienced a recent revival; its strength in 2006 was estimated at around 500 (down from a previous 10,000).

SLA Sierra Leone Army. During the early 1990s, like its opposing RUF, it plundered and raped the civilian population.

SLA South Lebanon Army. Militia set up by Israel during the Lebanese civil war in the south of country.

SLA Symbionese Liberation Army. A very small California-based militant group mainly known for kidnapping Patricia Hearst (daughter of the media mogul William Hearst) in 1974.

Sleeper An infiltrated member of an armed group who leads a seemingly normal above-ground life in a host society until activated by a parent organisation to support or conduct sabotage or terrorist operations in or from his or her place of residence. Sometimes sleepers also provide safe houses, intelligence, arms, logistics, forged identity papers and money to operatives.

SLOC Sea line of communication (sometimes also rendered as sea lane of communication).

Smallpox Cowpox, a highly contagious, person-to-person-transmitted variola virus. While wild smallpox was eradicated worldwide in 1977, laboratory samples continue to exist and could be reactivated and used against younger generations not inoculated. There have been allegations that the Soviet Union experimented with laboratory supplies of smallpox virus for use as a bio-weapon.

SMP Sipah-e-Mohammed Pakistan (Soldiers of the Prophet Mohammed in Pakistan).

Sniper Marksman who uses a rifle with a telescope for long-distance killing, either for assassinations or for indiscriminate, random killings.

Social movement Unconventional, only partly organised group attempting to bring about or to prevent reformist or radical social change (Wood and Jackson, 1982).

Socialism A political doctrine, historically linked to the labour movement, situated between liberalism and communism, stressing equality, non-private ownership, social justice, reform and state intervention to improve the situation of disadvantaged classes of society. In Marxist theory, socialism was seen as an interim stage in the transition from capitalism to mature communism.

Society Social collective held together by common social practices and processes; members interact more with each other than with other people. A society usually possesses a territory, a distinct culture and an institutional structure. Its relationship with the state varies – originally, all societies were stateless. On the other hand, state formation has sometimes preceded the creation of societies, e.g. in post-colonial situations.

Soft target Largely unprotected, civilian infrastructure that is wide open to a surprise terrorist assault.

SOLAS Convention Safety of the Life on Sea Convention. First adopted on 17 June 1960, the convention came into force on 26 May 1965 and was amended in 1974. The most important international treaty concerning the safety of merchant ships and seafarers, the SOLAS Convention sets minimum standards for the construction, equipment and operations of commercial ships.

Soldier A uniformed, armed, usually male person, conscripted or voluntary, who is involved in a military service organisation.

Soldiers of Justice Group of Shi'ite Muslims from Saudi Arabia and Lebanon, formed by Iranian Islamic Revolutionary Guards dedicated to the overthrow of the Saudi monarchy.

Soman (GD) Pinacolyl methylphosphonofluoridate; the fastest-killing nerve gas, produced in 1944 for the first time at IG Farben by Otto Ambros. It kills through both inhalation and skin contact.

South Maluku Republic Short-lived (1950) state of Christian pro-Dutch local fighters. Conquered by Indonesia; gave rise to the exile resistance movement RMS.

Sparrow Squads Hit teams of the Communist New People's Army in the Philippines.

SPEAC Stop Primate Experiments at Cambridge. This was a UK campaign by Animal Liberation Front (ALF) members.

Special Forces Highly trained small US units engaged in counter-terrorism and unconventional warfare.

Special operations Clandestine, commando-type operations by highly trained military units behind enemy lines or on third-party territory involving reconnaissance, sabotage, arson, selective assassinations and false-flag operations.

Spetsnaz Soviet Special Forces trained for commando operations behind enemy lines.

Spillover Displacement of a phenomenon to other areas with better operating conditions, e.g. in the case of domestic conflict, into neighbouring countries.

SPIR Special Purpose Islamic Regiment. A Chechen group formed in 1996 and responsible for the 2002 attack on the Dubrovka theatre in Moscow.

SPLA Sudan People's Liberation Army. The armed wing of the Sudan People's Liberation Movement (SPLM), having been fighting since 1983 (1973 according to other sources) for a secular and democratic Sudan; numbering 20,000–30,000. The SPLA signed a peace agreement with the Sudanese government in 2005. The SPLA represents mainly Christians in southern Sudan opposed to Islamic rule as introduced in Sudan in 1983.

SSA/SSPA Shan State (Progress) Army. Since 1964, has fought for freedom and democracy for Shan state; numbers 3,000 fighters. Opposes military rulers of Myanmar.

SSIM Southern Sudan Independence Movement, aka Movement of Riak Machar, Southern Sudan Independence Army, Southern Sudan Independence Movement/Army (SSIM/A), Sudan People's Liberation Army United (SPLA United). The SSIM was established in 1991.

SSNP Syrian Social Nationalist Party. A right-wing Syrian-sponsored Lebanese party active since the 1930s for the creation of a 'Greater Syria'; responsible for the assassination of president-elect Bashir Gemayel in September 1982.

SSP Sipah-e-Sahab, aka Anjuman Sipah-e-Sahaba, Millat-e-Islamia/Pakistan, Guardians of the Friends of the Prophets, Soldiers of the Prophet's Companions. A Pakistani Deobandi Sunni paramilitary group formed in 1985; outlawed in 2002, it continued under its other name, Millat-e-Islamia.

State An association of a permanent population for the purpose of government, legally constituted, linked to a particular defined territory and recognised by other states. The state claims a monopoly of force and, in return, assumes various responsibilities such as the guarantee of public order and security. Where such a claim cannot be upheld, one speaks of a weak or failed state.

State-sponsored terrorism The use of generally indiscriminate and unlawful violence against civilians and non-combatants by agents of a foreign state to foster its foreign policy goals such as destabilisation of a neighbouring government and bringing about a regime change. The actual perpetrators can be local armed groups or international mercenary terrorists. The sponsoring, which is more often than not covert rather than overt, involves a variety of activities such as the arming and training of terrorists, and providing them with intelligence and logistical assistance, false documents, funding, sanctuary, safe houses and operational support.

State-supported international terrorism A concept overlapping with state-sponsored terrorism, it involves any of the following acts by a state:

- furnishing arms, explosives or other lethal substances to any individual, group or organisation that engages in acts of international terrorism;
- directing, providing training for or assisting any individual, group or organisation that plans or executes any act of international terrorism;
- providing financial support for any individual, group or organisation that plans or executes any act of international terrorism;
- providing diplomatic facilities which aid and abet the commission of any act of international terrorism;
- failing to permit the extradition or prosecution of any individual within its territory who has committed any act of international terrorism.

State terrorism The use of indiscriminate and unlawful violence against civilians and non-combatants by agents of the state in defence of political power, for purposes of party politics or in the framework of colonial policies and military occupation. The use of terror as a repressive governing instrument to enforce obedience of a frightened population or sections thereof is widespread among authoritarian and totalitarian regimes.

Steganography Coding technique of hiding written information (plain text, cipher text, images) in another digital picture which can be transmitted by the internet.

Stern Gang Aka Lehi. A breakaway group from Irgun (q.v.) founded by Abraham Stern in 1940; it was responsible for the assassination of Lord Moyne, a British Foreign Office minister. The Stern Gang was later led by Yitzhak Shamir, who became prime minister of Israel.

Stinger (FIM92A) Proven to be highly effective in the hands of muhajedeen guerrillas during their insurgency against the Soviets in Afghanistan, the Stinger is a man-portable, infrared-guided, shoulder-launched surface-to-air missile (SAM). Its maximum effective range is approximately 5,500 metres; its maximum effective altitude is approximately 15,750 feet (about 4,800 m). It can be used to target high-speed jets or helicopters.

Stockholm syndrome The psychological process of hostages becoming friendly with hostage takers; first observed in August 1973 during a siege at a Stockholm bank when two bank robbers and four hostages were surrounded by police.

Strait of Gibraltar Waterway that connects the Atlantic Ocean to the Mediterranean, 14 km wide at its narrowest point and 300 metres deep. One of the maritime choke points: since the Strait of Gibraltar is the Mediterranean's only direct connection to the Atlantic Ocean, a closure of this strait would have a serious impact on global trade.

Strait of Hormuz Waterway that connects the Persian Gulf to the Arabian Sea. Since this is the only waterway out of the Gulf, it forms a formidable maritime choke point: blocking this strait would have a serious impact on the world's oil supply. The name comes from the ancient port of Hormuz, situated on the Omani side of the strait.

Strait of Malacca One of the world's most important waterways, 800 km long and only 1.5 km wide at its narrowest point, which connects the Indian Ocean (Bay of Bengal) with the South China Sea; has led to the port of Singapore being one of the world's most important hub ports. It is also dubbed the 'iron highway' because of the dense traffic; two-thirds of the world's supply of liquefied natural gas and about 50 per cent of the world's crude oil, nearly all for the East Asian economies of China, Taiwan, Japan and South Korea, pass through this strait.

Strategy The science or art of utilising resources in conflict or some other competitive situation towards realisation of a goal, using a variety of tactics in planned sequence while also inducing the opponent or rivals to take ultimately self-defeating measures.

Strontium-90 Radioisotope suitable for RDD (q.v.).

SUA Convention The Convention for the Suppression of Unlawful Acts Against the Safety of Maritime Navigation of 1988 addresses unlawful acts such as ship seizure or violence on board that could result in physical injury or damage to the ship or cargo. Although the SUA Convention was developed with the *Achille Lauro* hijacking in mind, terrorism as such is not explicitly mentioned.

Subversion The activity of preparing the weakening or overthrow of an incumbent government by violence. Subversion can be a domestic activity or consist of the undermining of one state by another state by supporting disaffected local citizens financially, ideologically, logistically or operationally, with the help of infiltrators, agitators and terrorists (Holsti, 1988: 253, 259).

Suicide bomber Individual with explosives strapped to his (less often her) body which he or she explodes among target audience; the term can also refer to drivers of car and truck bombs who sacrifice themselves in bringing the explosives into the target zone.

Suicide bombing Man- (or car-) portable bomb, triggered by a carrier who perishes with the victims he or she has approached with the concealed explosive device.

Suicide terrorism The use of generally indiscriminate and unlawful violence against civilians and non-combatants with the help of a hidden explosive device attached to the body or car of a volunteer willing to kill him- or herself while destroying others in a targeted area for political and/or religious motives. Suicide terrorists tend to target democratic societies where the government is responsive to public concerns and might therefore be more inclined to make concessions to terrorist groups that use this tactic. First developed by Hezbollah in Lebanon in 1983, the tactic spread to more secular groups such as the LTTE in Sri Lanka.

Summary execution The killing of persons, usually suspected of a (political) crime, without fair trial by state or non-state actors.

Sunna A collection of accounts about the prophet Muhammad which provides guidance to Muslims.

Sunnism Literally, 'those who adhere to the trodden path'. This is the majority doctrine in Islam (85 per cent, as opposed to minority Shi'ites).

Super Ferry 14 Philippine modern roll-on, roll-off ferry, burned out and sunk in the Bay of Manila in the early hours of 27 February 2004 as a result of a bombing attack carried out by an ASG member, Redendo Cain Dellosa, who managed to smuggle a bomb on board before the ship left harbour; 116 people died in this disaster.

Supergrasses Turncoats in Northern Ireland who, when captured, would, in exchange for a reduced sentence, incriminate their own former group members at trials without juries.

Superterrorism A term that denotes the use of weapons of mass destruction by terrorists.

Supply chain security Relates to efforts to enhance the security of the supply chain, i.e. the transport and logistics system for cargo. It combines traditional practices of supply chain management with security requirements that are driven by threats such as terrorism, piracy and theft.

Surgical strike Swift and focused military action by airborne troops against a single target, with minimal collateral damage among civilians.

Surveillance Monitoring of individual, group or facility by human or technical observation or inspection in order to detect criminal or terrorist plans and preparations.

SWAPO South West Africa People's Organisation. Formed in 1960; took power in Namibia in 1989.

T Taliban (Afghanistan/Pakistan).

TA Terai Army (Nepal). Madhesi minority-based group in southern plains.

Tablighi Jamaat Literally, 'Propagators of the Faith'. Extreme Sunni Islamist secretive society established in 1927 in British India. Legal in the United States (50,000 followers) and United Kingdom, (3,000 followers). Considered by some intelligence experts to be an 'antechamber of terrorism' and 'a driving force of Islamic extremism and a major recruiting agency for terrorist causes worldwide' (*Sunday Telegraph* London, 20 August 2006, p. 20).

Tabun (GA) O-Ethyl dimethylamidophosphorylcyanide. Tabun (GA), the first nerve gas, was developed in 1936 by G. Schrader at IG Farben, Germany. It is easy to manufacture as the necessary chemicals are available on the open market.

TACON Tactical control; Limited command authority in operation.

Tactic A method of action to gain the upper hand in an engagement or fight. In the case of contemporary terrorism, the most frequent tactic is bombing, followed by armed assault, kidnapping, murder or assassination, arson, barricade/hostage taking and hijacking.

Tajiks The second largest ethnic group in Afghanistan, comprising 25 per cent of the population.

TAK Terybazen Azadiya Kurdistan/Kurdistan Freedom Hawks, aka Kurdish Vengeance Brigade, Kurdistan Freedom Falcons (Organisation). The TAK emerged in 2004, possibly as a splinter of the PKK.

Takfir Excommunication; Arabic for accusing another Muslim of heresy. Wahhabi and other fundamentalist *takfiri* (those accusing others of deserting the "true" faith) hold that those denounced as unbelievers can be killed.

Takfir Wa al-Hijra Literally, 'Rejection of Sins and Exodus', aka Martyrs for Morocco. A multinational ultra-fundamentalist pan-Islamic religious sect, established in the early 1970s or early 1980s, following the example of an Egyptian group of that name active in the 1960s.

Takfiri Salafi extremists who view violent jihad as a personal duty for all Muslims and see themselves as entitled to kill allegedly heretic Muslims who do not observe all the rules of the Qur'an and the Sunna, as well as infidels.

Taliban/The Students Afghan (mainly Pashtun) students raised in Pakistani Islamic schools, supported by the ISI and trained by Pakistani Frontier Constabulary; since 1994, led by Mullah Mohammad Omar. The Taliban took power in 95 per cent of Afghanistan in 1996, but were recognised as the legitimate government only by Saudi Arabia, Pakistan and the United Arab Emirates. After 1996, the Taliban hosted Bin Laden and Al-Qaeda, and were driven into the underground and into exile by the Northern Alliance and the United States following the attack of Al-Qaeda on the United States on 11 September 2001. The Taliban regime oppressed women and banned music and television with its religious police, while being unable to develop the Afghan economy. In 2006, Taliban fighters, reportedly supported by Pakistan's ISI, managed to regain partial control over parts of south-eastern Afghanistan, fighting NATO troops.

Tamil Tigers See LTTE. A major guerrilla and terrorist group fighting for the secession of north-east Sri Lanka from the Buddhist south. After peace talks in 2001 came to nothing, full-scale fighting resumed in the summer of 2006. The LTTE were defeated in May 2009.

Tanzeem From *askari tanzeemat*. Pakistani militant (and often jihadist) organizations, such as the Kashmir-oriented Deobandi tanzeems Jaish-e-Mohammad, Harkat-ul-Ansar/Harkat-ul-

Mujahidin. The term also covers groups like Lashkar-e-Taiba, Al–Badr and Hizbul Mujahidin and sectarian groups like the anti-Shi'ah Lashkar-e-Jhangvi and Sipah-e-Sahaba Pakistan.

Tanzim Arabic for 'organisation'. A Palestinian group in Gaza and the West Bank opposed to Arafat's exile government in Tunisia; formed in 1993 and led by Marwan Barghouti (currently jailed in Israel).

Tanzim al-Jihad Holy War Organisation. An Egyptian fundamentalist group responsible for the assassination of President Anwar Sadat in 1981; the name is also used by a PLO-linked group fighting for the liberation of Palestine by means of suicide attacks.

Tanzim Qa'idat Al-Jihad fi Bilad al Rafidayn See JTJ.

Taqqiya Arabic for 'deception'. This is the strategy of using ruses to convince opponents of peaceful intent to lull them into false sense of security. Such dissimulation is sometimes exercised by Muslims in a non-Islamic environment as a measure of precaution.

Target Non-state terrorist groups tend to focus on soft civilian targets and iconic objects, but their attacks are also directed at police and government offices, business facilities and public utilities (including water supplies), oil and gas installations, electric pylons, schools, post offices, railway stations, hospitals, shopping centres, churches and transportation infrastructure (including aircrafts, trains, buses, underground trains, ships and ferries). Other targets include diplomatic representatives or embassies, tourists, sport arenas, abortion clinics, communication facilities, international and non-governmental organisations, food and water supplies, media and journalists, venues for special events, and events that attract large crowds, as well as maritime and military installations. The choice of targets is partly opportunistic, partly based on the strategic or tactical consideration behind the attack: propaganda to rally new recruits, coercion to exercise leverage over the opponents or damage to inflict economic loss on the opponent or simply revenge for a loss suffered from the opponent. In terms of frequency of incidents, private citizens and property are the main target, followed by government, business, diplomatic, police, transportation, religious institutions, transportation, and utilities, according to MIPT figures.

Targeted assassination The use of snipers, precision-guided munitions, bombings, and drone- and helicopter-based attacks against persons suspected of involvement in the preparation of terrorist crimes.

Target hardening Enhancing the physical protection of persons and objects (e.g. embassies) through access controls, alarm systems, surveillance cameras, barriers, improved policing, etc.

Tawhid Arabic for 'monotheism'. The term is sometimes used to express the religious character of a terrorist group, as in Abu Musab al-Zarqawi's Tawhid and Jihad.

Tawhid Islamic Brigades (Egypt, Sinai).

TCG Tunisian Combatant Group, aka Tunisian Islamic Fighting Group, Jama'a Combattante Tunisienne. Founded in 2000.

Tear gas CN: chloroacetophenone; CR: dibenz [b,f][1,4] oxazepine; CS: orthochlorobenzylidene malonitrile. Tear gas causes pain in the eyes, a flow of tears and difficulty in keeping eyes open. Used for crowd and riot control.

TECHINT Technical intelligence.

Tehrik-e-Jihad Armed group that advocates self-determination for Kashmir; established in 1997.

TEL Terrorist exclusion list. A US government list developed by the State Department which lists organisations that either commit or incite terrorist acts and activities related to terrorism.

TEPP Commercially available, potent insecticide, almost as toxic as some military chemical warfare agents.

Terodotoxin A biological poison agent.

Terra Lliure 'Free Land'. Left-wing Catalan nationalist-separatist (from Spain) group striving for a Greater Catalonia (including the Balearics and the French province of Roussillon) during the 1970s and 1980s; it renounced terrorism in 1991.

Terror State of mind induced by intense fear resulting from witnessing (often) arbitrary acts of atrocity against civilians and non-combatants (public executions, mutilation, wanton destruction, mass rape and murder, etc.) that are intended to intimidate, shock and traumatise victims and witnesses; the latter show strong emotional reactions, often fearing they might be the next victims of such ostentatious violence. Some of them submit to the source of terror in an attempt to survive; others are paralysed by fear and, in their despair, helpless and incapable of rational behaviour; others flee in panic; and yet others try to fight back, sometimes using counter-terror against the source of terror or those suspected of supporting it. The word 'terror' is sometimes used for 'state terrorism' by authors who reserve the term 'terrorism' for indiscriminate non-state violence.

Terrorism Politically loaded and contested concept of which several hundred definitions exist but about which international consensus in the United Nations is still (November 2010) elusive, mainly because of the reservations of Arab and Muslim countries. In terrorist struggles, the media – and more recently the internet – play an important role, magnifying the threat and carrying it to wider audiences ('1 per cent bang – 99 per cent publicity'). Responsibility for a terrorist atrocity is sometimes claimed, while on other occasions, especially with right-wing and state terrorism, the perpetrators wish to remain anonymous. Terrorism is usually a tactic of a minority (either in power or trying to achieve power) that lacks the patience, willingness, public support or capability to utilise morally more acceptable instruments to exert political influence. It sometimes serves to provoke an overreaction from the opponent. When used by government, it serves to discourage open dissent, allowing a regime to perpetuate its rule without visible opposition. Terrorist violence is often random, indiscriminate, while at other times it is focused and symbolic. It is sometimes intended to shift public opinion towards support for authoritarian solutions by the state (by false-flag attacks by secret services). In other instances, it is meant to awaken public opinion to some grievance or situation (such as showing the 'fascist face' behind the 'liberal mask' of a regime). In itself, terrorism can rarely bring about a change of the political power constellation. However, it may bring about a revolutionary (or counter-revolutionary) situation and also inspire others to go and do likewise.

Terrorist Person (usually a young male, less often a female) using (or threatening to use), alone or as part of a cell or group, interpersonal violence, generally against non-combatants and civilians in order to intimidate, impress or coerce third parties (e.g. a government, segment of society, international organisation), usually as part of a strategy of conflict waging for mostly political ends. Terrorist practitioners usually avoid the term 'terrorist' and prefer words with more positive connotations such as freedom fighter, urban guerrilla, resistance fighter, mudjahedeen, etc. Many of their crimes would be war crimes if a state of war existed (e.g. deliberate attacks against civilians, the taking of hostages, etc.).

Terrorist act One can draw a distinction between single-phase acts (shooting, (suicide) bombing, maiming, mutilating, raping, decapitating, arson, etc.) and dual-phase attacks (kidnapping, hostage taking, hijacking, etc.). They serve purposes like sending a message of fear to people other than the direct victims. Such violence might also serve purposes of provocation, revenge, retaliation, attention seeking, blackmail and coercion.

Terrorist group Non-state terrorists often operate in small cells, although sometimes a group consists of only one large cell. Rarely do terrorist groups exceed a few hundred members, and groups numbering thousands of members are very exceptional. They generally lack mass support and act from the underground. Their members are often well educated and sometimes militarily trained.

Teryl The most common military booster for explosions.

Texas City disaster This disaster virtually destroyed the harbour of Texas City near Galveston, Texas, in 1947. In the morning of 16 April, a cargo vessel loaded with ammonium nitrate, the *Grandcamp,* caught fire and detonated, resulting in burning debris raining down on the town and a miniature tidal wave sweeping through the harbour. Since the raging fires could not be extinguished (most of Texas City's fire-fighters died when the *Grandcamp* exploded), another vessel loaded with ammonium nitrate and sulphur, the *High Flyer*, detonated the next morning, also destroying a third ship, *William B. Keene*. In this disaster, nearly 600 people died, and more than 2,000 were injured – of a total population of 16,000.

Thanatophil ideology An ideological perspective in which death is idealised and depicted as a desired goal, bringing many sensual rewards in the afterlife. This ideology is characteristic of suicide terrorism.

Theocracy Literally, 'rule by God'. An absolutist form of government of which the rulers – often a group of self-appointed clerics – claim to be direct agents of the authority of the deity whereby religious laws are also made a source of political obligations for people.

Thermonuclear bomb Hydrogen fusion weapon with a typical yield of 0.5 megatons (500 million tons of TNT). Both the United States and Russia have many weapons in the 9- to 20-megaton range. The highest-yield weapon ever exploded was a Russian one of 58 megatons (the equivalent of almost 5,000 Hiroshima-sized bombs).

Third position An ideology that postulates convergence between extremist left- and extremist right-wing groups on themes such as anti-Semitism and anti-government.

THKO Türkiye Halk Kurtuluş Ordusu/Turkish People's Liberation Army (TPLA) – established in 1971.

Threat Coercive statement (or otherwise visible gesture or signal) announcing or indicating impending harm, punishment and/or use of violence. Occasionally, it is a prelude to further conflict escalation when it elicits counter-threats and reaction. Threats are often conditional and then serve the purpose of blackmail, deterrence, extortion, intimidation and submission.

Threat analysis An ongoing review of terrorist movements, resources, capabilities, intentions and targeting patterns based on all-source information gathering and analysis.

THREATCON Threat condition. The US system of announcing terrorist threat levels on a 1–5 scale (Normal, Alpha, Bravo, Charlie and Delta) for US force protection.

Tigers Term used for members of the Tamil Tigers (see LTTE).

TIP Terrorist Interdiction Program (United States).

Tit-for-tat A process by which two or more parties reciprocate one another's actions, often in a negative way ('getting even' type of revenge actions).

TKEP Türkiye Komünist Emek Partisi/Leninist/Turkish Communist Labour Party/Leninist – established in 1990.

TKP/ML-TIKKO Türkiye Komünist Partisi/Marksist-Leninist/Türkiye İşçi Köylü Kurtuluş Ordusu/Turkish Communist Party/Marxist, aka Maoist Komünist Partisi/Maoist Communist Party, People's Liberation Army, Turkish Communist Party/Marxist-Leninist, Turkish Workers' and Peasants Liberation Army. Established in 1972.

TNT Trinitrotoluene. A high-velocity commercial explosive used for rock blasting; abused by terrorists.

Tonton Macoutes Creole for 'Uncle Knapsack'; aka Boogeymen, National Security Volunteers. Evolved from the presidential bodyguard and turned into paramilitary vigilante groups created as 'Volunteers for National Security' in 1957 by Haitian dictator Francois Duvalier ('Papa Doc') to stifle military and civilian opposition to his rule; officially dismantled in 1985 when Jean-Claude Duvalier ('Baby Doc') was deposed. Tonton Macoute terrorists resurfaced again in opposition to Jean-Bertrand Aristide.

Tora Bora Mountain cave complex in Afghanistan used by Al-Qaeda in 2001.

Torture The deliberate and illegal application of severe physical and/or mental pain (electrical discharges, beatings, burnings, immersion, hanging, stretching, mutilation, etc.) to a person held in captivity for purposes of obtaining information, confession of crime, punishment or intimidation of third parties.

Totalitarianism Term used for an ideology-driven system of government based on the 'totality of the state', whereby those holding state power attempt to control both the public and the private lives of their subjects as well as the economy in a dictatorial manner by means of a personality cult and mass ceremonies, media control and propaganda, single-party rule, militarisation of society and terroristic policing. Torture, liquidation and concentration camps face those who dare to oppose them. The concept has been used to describe both communist and fascist regimes. However, the degree of state control implied by the concept has been rarely achieved.

Toxic Poisonous; if ingested, causing injury to the physiological mechanisms of an organism by chemical means.

Toxin weapons Non-contagious biological weapons that disseminate generally odourless, tasteless and invisible poisonous substances produced by living organisms.

Toxins Poisons derived from plants, animals and microbes which cause diseases and can be lethal. Examples include botulinum toxins, *Clostridium perfringens* toxins, conotoxin, ricin, saxitoxin, shiga toxin, *Staphylococcus aureus* toxins, tetrodoxins, verotoxins and microcystin (cyanginosin).

TPC Tritiya Prastuti Committee (India). Third Preparatory Committee, splinter of CPI-Maoist.

TPLA Turkish People's Liberation Army. Left-wing Soviet-sponsored Turkish revolutionary group founded in 1968. In 1975, a faction called Dev Yol (the Revolutionary Road) split from it.

TPLF Tigray People's Liberation Front, established in 1975 to oppose the Mengistu dictatorship. Currently dominating the ruling Ethiopian People's Revolutionary Democratic Front (EPRDF).

TPLF Turkish People's Liberation Front. The armed wing of the Turkish People's Liberation Party, active in the 1970s until the Turkish military took state power in 1980.

TPLF Türkiye Halk Kurtuluş Partisi-Cephesi/Turkish People's Liberation Front, aka Turkish People's Liberation Party-Front (TPLP-F). Emerged in 1971 from the left-wing revolutionary youth movement Dev Genç.

TR Tuareg Rebels (Niger/Mali).

Transnational terrorism Term used for cross-border terrorism that is not state-controlled or state-sponsored but operating in more than one country.

Trevi Group A group of anti-terrorist police officials from the European Community, established in the mid-1970s in Rome (where the Trevi fountain is located) to coordinate anti-terrorist and other security-related efforts.

Troubles, the Euphemism used to describe the sectarian violence between militant Protestant Loyalists and Catholic Republicans in Northern Ireland between 1968 and 1998.

TULF Tamil United Liberation Front. A separatist organisation active in Sri Lanka since the 1980s as a political party; its youth organisation in 1972 founded the new Tamil Tigers (q.v.), which in 1976 became the Liberation Tigers of Tamil Eelam (LTTE).

Tunisian Combat Group See JCT.

Tupac Amaru Revolutionary Movement Movimiento Revolucionario Tupac Amaru (MRTA). A left-wing urban-based revolutionary group formed in 1983 in Peru, numbering 1,000–2,000 members in the early 1990s. The group declined after its Japanese embassy takeover in 1996.

Tupamaros Nickname (based on Tupac Amaru, an eighteenth-century Indio leader) of the Movimiento de Liberacion Nacional (MLN)/Movement for National Liberation; a Uruguayan urban terrorist group founded in 1963 by Raúl Sendic Antonaccio. It enjoyed a Robin Hood image in the late 1960s. It was largely repressed in 1973 by the military. Tupamaros became a legal party after the end of military dictatorship in 1985.

Turkish Hezbollah Sunni group active since the early 1980s, first allied with, then opposed to, the PKK.

Turkish Islamic Jihad Active since 1991; believed to be supported by Iran.

Turner Diaries, The Anti-Semitic novel depicting a future race war in the United States, written by US neo-Nazi William Pierce in 1978; influential among right-wing white Aryan Nation members.

Turn(ing) Bringing a captured or identified agent of the adversary to spy or act against his or her (former) master.

Typology of terrorist groups The spectrum of groups and conflict parties (inc. state actors) using tactics of terrorism is wide, ranging, if motivation is taken as the criterion, from anarchists, anti-globalisation groups, communists (Marxist, Leninist, Trotskyist, Maoist) and social revolutionary groups, to environmental (eco-terrorist) groups, leftist groups, nationalist (inc. chauvinist and irredentist), separatist, racist (inc. fascist and national socialist), religious (inc. Salafist jihadist, millenarian) and right-wing groups (both conservative and reactionary). In terms of location, distinctions have been made between domestic (national), transnational, international and global terrorism, but the differences between these are often vague. Other typological divides take the state as criterion and distinguish between state (or regime) terrorism, state-sponsored terrorism (usually abroad) and non-state terrorism. It is also possible to distinguish terrorism on the basis of methods used: bio-terrorism, chemical terrorism, cyber-terrorism, nuclear terrorism, radio-logical terrorism, or suicide terrorism. Other typological categories feature terms such as single-issue terrorism or narco-terrorism.

Tyrannicide Assassination of a non-democratic leader held to be tyrannical; an often morally justified political crime.

Tyranny Rule by a selfish individual who utilises arbitrary violence to keep control over society.

UAV Unmanned aerial vehicles. Remotely controlled, fixed-wing drones used for territorial surveillance and rocket attacks.

UÇPMB Liberation Army of Preševo, Medveđja and Bujanovac. Group established in 2000, numbering some 800 members, active in the Preševo Valley and linked to Kosovo Albanians.

UDA Ulster Defence Association. A formerly legal Protestant Loyalist paramilitary vigilante organisation established in 1971 in Northern Ireland to defend the status quo. It is large, with some 30,000–60,000 members. The group was outlawed in 1992 after a history of kidnappings and murder. It ended its armed campaign in 2007.

UDCA Uganda Democratic Christian Army. Established in 1990 by Joseph Kony; reformed in 1994 as the LRA (q.v.).

UDF Ulster Defence Force. A Protestant group in Northern Ireland.

UDHR Universal Declaration of Human Rights. A document elaborated by the United Nations and accepted by the General Assembly in 1948.

UFF Ulster Freedom Fighters. A violent Protestant Loyalist group that split in 1973 from the UDA; it supported the 1998 Good Friday Agreement. Founded in 1974; inactive after the 1980s.

UFF United Freedom Front (United States).

UGB Union de Guerreros Blancos/White Warriors' Union. Right-wing Salvadorean death squad founded in 1976 by Roberto D'Aubuisson, who later founded the Republican National Alliance Party (ARENA), which absorbed the UGB.

UGFDPL Underground Government of the Free Democratic People of Laos, aka Free Democratic People's Government of Laos, Free Democratic Government Committee of the Lao People. The UGFDPL emerged in the early 2000s.

Uigur Separatist Movement Established in 1990 in north-west China to seek to create a separate East Turkistan state.

UKLF United Kuki Liberation Front (India, Manipur). Active since the late 1990s.

ULCC Ultra-large crude carrier. An oil tanker of over 300,000 dead weight tons (dwt).

ULFA United Liberation Front of Assam (India). A separatist insurgent group in the north-eastern province of Assam, India; established in 1979

ULFBV United Liberation Front of the Barak Valley (India (Assam)).

Ultimatum A demand in a crisis situation that is portrayed as non-negotiable and combined with a deadline, after the passing of which hurting behaviour is threatened.

UMF (Nepal). United Madhesi Front; an alliance of four parties.

Umkhonto We Sizwe (MK) 'Spear of the Nation'. The armed wing of the African National Congress (ANC), which engaged mainly in sabotage between 1961 and 1977, progressing to guerrilla and also terrorist attacks thereafter.

Ummah Arab for 'community'. Refers to the community of the faithful in Islam; also translated as World Islamic Community or Islamic Nation.

Unabomber The term used to describe the Harvard-educated lone-wolf terrorist Ted Kaczynski, who killed people in universities (therefore the 'Un') and in airlines ('A') – hence Universities and Airline Bombings, UNABOMB – with parcel bombs in the United States and was only apprehended in 1996 when his own brother turned him in after the FBI had searched for him in vain for seventeen years.

UNAMSIL United Nations Forces in Sierra Leone.

UNCLOS United Nations Convention on the Law of the Sea, 1982. UNCLOS includes, among many other provisions, definitions on piracy.

Unconventional warfare The term refers to a broad spectrum of military and paramilitary operations conducted in disputed conflict zones, including sabotage, assassination, booby traps, and the use of pseudo-gangs, terrorism and guerrilla tactics by special forces.

Undercover operative Covert agent who infiltrates an adversary cell or structure.

Underground Clandestine organisation, criminal, resistance or terrorist, operating undercover and/or at night against a superior enemy.

UNGA United Nations General Assembly.

Unified Unit of Jihad (Algeria) Aka United Company of Jihad. Established in the early 1990s; probably linked to the FIS.

UNIFIL United Nations Interim Force in Lebanon.

UNITA União Nacional para a Independência Total do Angola/National Union for the Total Independence of Angola, aka Armed Forces for the Liberation of Angola. UNITA was founded in 1966 by Jonas Savimbi to fight Portuguese colonialism. After independence was gained in 1975, it continued partly with US help, its struggle against the Marxist government of the Popular Movement for Liberation of Angola (MPLA) until Jonas Savimbi was killed, in February 2002.

United Nations International organisation of more than 190 states, created in 1945 to provide peace and security after the Second World War. It managed to reduce interstate conflict but was less successful in dealing with domestic conflicts.

United Self-Defence Forces of Colombia See AUC.

UNLF United National Liberation Front (India, Manipur). Founded in 1964.

UNMIK United Nations Mission in Kosovo.

UNMIL United Nations Mission in Liberia.

UNMISET United Nations Mission of Support on East Timor.

UNOCI United Nations Operation in Côte d'Ivoire.

UNODC United Nations Office on Drugs and Crime.

UNOSOM United Nations Operation in Somalia.

UNSC United Nations Security Council.

UPDF United People's Democratic Front (Bangladesh, Chittagong Hill Tracts).

UPDS United People's Democratic Solidarity (India, eastern Assam).

Uranium-233 A fissile, weapon-usable isotope of uranium derived from the element thorium-232. Uranium-233 is a fissionable material. Only 10-20 kilograms is required for a nuclear device. It is less common than U-235 for making nuclear explosives.

Uranium-235 A highly enriched isotope of the element uranium; a fissile material used for nuclear explosions; used in Hiroshima in 1945.

Urban guerrilla The term derives from a doctrine developed by Abraham Guillen, the Mexican author of *Philosophy of the Urban Guerrilla* (1973). It was used by terrorists to legitimise armed attacks involving civilian targets. The term was introduced by Carlos Marighela, a Brazilian communist, in his *Mini-Manual of the Urban Guerrilla* (1969). The Tupamaros in Uruguay popularised the concept, which was later also imitated in Western Europe by young student militants. In practice, it involved assassinations, kidnappings and armed assaults in urban settings in order to provoke mass repression, which in turn was supposed to make more people join the rebels.

URFB United Revolutionary Front of Bhutan.

URNG Guatemalan National Revolutionary Union/Unidad Revolucionaria National Guatemalteca. URNG is a Guatemalan umbrella organisation including the Guerrilla Army of the Poor (EGP – Ejército Guerrillero de los Pobres), the Rebel Armed Forces (FAR – Fuerzas Armadas Rebeldes) and the Revolutionary Organisation of the People in Arms (ORPA – Organización Revolucionaria del Pueblo en Armas).

USS *Cole* Arleigh Burke-class destroyer, attacked on 16 October 2000 by two Al-Qaeda suicide terrorists on board a small, explosives-laden boat. Seventeen US sailors were killed and more than 30 injured.

USS *The Sullivans* Arleigh Burke-class destroyer unsuccessfully targeted by Al-Qaeda suicide terrorists in January 2000 as part of the 'millennium bombing plot'. Since the boat chosen for the attack was overloaded with explosives, it sank as soon as it was launched. However, the tactice was successfully repeated in October 2000 in the USS *Cole* attack.

USSS United States Secret Service.

Ustashi A Croatian nationalist group active in the Second World War and before the independence of Croatia.

UVBT Under-vehicle booby trap.

UVF Ulster Volunteer Force. A Protestant Loyalist militia in Northern Ireland, and re-established in 1966 originally founded in 1912 to oppose the IRA. Held responsible for much of the anti-Catholic violence. It disarmed in May 2007.

UWSA United Wa State Army. Established in 1989, it numbers 30,000 members and operates in the Wa Hills of Myanmar but observes a ceasefire with the military rulers.

UXO Unexploded explosive device.

V-agents Group of stable nerve agents that are about ten times more toxic than sarin.

VBIED Vehicle-borne improvised explosive device, i.e. a car or truck bomb.

VBSW Vigorous Burmese Student Warriors (VBSW). A resistance movement engaged in occupation of Myanmar's consulate in Bangkok in 1999.

VCP Vehicle check point.

Vectors of disease The delivery system of a biological weapon. Vectors can include birds, insects and other animals.

Vehicular bomb A car or truck filled with explosives.

Verotoxin A biological agent producing serotypes.

Vesicular stomatitis virus An animal pathogen.

Vibrio comma The biological agent that causes cholera.

Viet Cong Viet Nam Cong San/National Liberation Front of Vietnamese Communists. The Viet Cong was an insurgent organisation that fought for the unification of Vietnam against the US-backed South Vietnamese government in the 1960s.

Vigilante terrorism The use of illegal and often indiscriminate political violence against civilians and non-combatants by non-state (but often pro-state) self-appointed groups or organisations for the maintenance of the law, the status quo or the restoration of order without due process of law. In some countries, the activities of such vigilantes are supported by the army, police or the secret service, and sometimes some of the vigilante personnel consist of off-duty policemen. While the activities of vigilantes are illegal, their activities are often not prosecuted, either because the authorities are too weak to enforce the law or because they lack the political will

Vigilantism Activities of private citizens to defend the status quo in the absence of forceful government action by police or military against criminal or political violence or perceived threats to the dominant order. Using extra-legal means to defend the existing socio-political order, vigilante activities are often condoned and sometimes secretly supported by security forces, some of whom take part off-duty in vigilante acts, which can range from preventive measures to reprisals and proactive acts of terrorism.

Violence Usually unlawful use of force deliberately to inflict harm on people. The term is sometimes extended to destructive behaviour against objects, including sabotage. In the first case, it usually involves direct psychological hurting (as in rape) or physical harm to someone's bodily integrity (violation as in beating, torture, maiming and mutilation) and ultimately life itself (killing). It can be a result of an aggressive attitude (or impulse) or of instrumental behaviour meant to incapacitate human beings in order to achieve a variety of ends, such as enforcing (or avoiding) dominance. Some authors distinguish between violence to preserve the social order (often called force) and violence to destroy the social order. Some extend the meaning of the concept beyond physical violence to 'structural violence' or even 'cultural violence', which makes the term very imprecise. Adherents of political violence against the state sometimes portray their violence as a response to the 'structural violence' of 'the system' to justify their illegal use of force.

The concept of violence is contested, and definitions generally reflect moral and political motivations. The social science discourse and the political discourse on violence overlap. One of the problems is in distinguishing 'violence' from 'force' – which has an aura of legitimacy 'violence' lacks – and between other forms of coercive influence. There are also distinctions between direct and structural violence, and between physical and psychological violence – to name only two. Physical violence involves direct harm to someone's body or mind (violation as in torture, rape, mutilation, or beating) and ultimately to (killing) life itself, or the exerting of coercive influence on the opponent or third parties. Given the potential lethality and irreversibility of acts of violence, such damaging and injuring transgressions, which go beyond generally accepted limits of behaviour, require justification (e.g. self-defence) to avoid being considered immoral and/or criminal.

Violence, cultural A new term introduced by Galtung (1996: 196) that is almost as broad as his other term (structural violence): '[t]hose aspects of culture, the symbolic sphere of our existence – exemplified by religion and ideology, language and art, empirical science and formal science (logic, mathematics) – that can be used to justify, legitimise, or direct structural violence.'

Violence, psychological Indirect acts of negative influence that aim to affect or arouse fear or break the mental resistance of a target audience by indoctrination (brainwashing), misinformation, propaganda, blackmail or terror.

Violence, structural A broad concept introduced by Galtung that refers to concealed violence in unjust, unequal and unrepresentative social structures and to situations in which the 'actual somatic and mental realizations of human beings are below their potential realizations'. See Galtung (1990).

Virus Class of biological agents including viruses such as Ebola, dengue, Marburg and white pox.

VLCC Very large crude carrier. An oil tanker of up to 300,000 dead weight tons (dwt).

VMO Vlaams Militant Orde/Flemish Militant Order. Neo-Nazi paramilitary Belgian organisation founded in 1948, and from which in 1988 the VB (Vlaams Blok/Flemish Bloc) split to become the main xenophobic party in Belgium.

VMRO-MNM Vnatrešno-Makedonska Revolucionerna Organizacija/Internal Macedonian Revolutionary Organisation. The name VMRO refers to an anti-Ottoman group active in the late nineteenth century and in the interwar period. The VMRO-MNM (Macedonia for the Macedonians) wants to establish a greater Macedonia, consisting also of parts of Bulgaria and Greece, and opposes the idea of a Greater Albania.

Vomit gas Super tear gas, a Soviet favourite.

VPR Vanguardia Popular Revolucionaria/Popular Revolutionary Vanguard. A Brazilian Marxist armed group active between 1968 and 1970 in São Paulo and Rio de Janeiro.

VX (Phosphonothioic acid, methyl-,*S*-[2-[bis(1-methylethyl)amino]ethyl] *O*-ethyl ester). VX is an odourless, colourless liquid that disrupts the stimulus from nerve to muscle in the human body, causing convulsions, paralysis and death. This sticky liquid, which easily passes the human skin, was discovered in the United Kingdom in 1952 and produced industrially for military purposes in 1961 in the United States. The substance can remain for several weeks on terrain, equipment or material; it is mainly taken up through skin but also through inhalation as a gas or aerosol.

Waco siege Scene of a stand-off between the US government and the Branch Davidians in Texas in 1993 which ended, after the breakdown of negotiations, in tragedy: 75 people were killed.

Wahhabism Doctrine of the disciples of Mohammed ibn Abd al-Wahhab (1703-1792), a puritanical ideology that constitutes the official interpretation of Islam in Saudi Arabia and is closely related to fundamentalism. It is often considered largely synonymous with Salafism, but Salafis of non-Wahhabi groups often severely criticize Wahhabis. Wahhabism is one school of thought in modern Salafism. Wahhabi scholars operate through electronic media (the internet, satellite TV), printed brochures, etc. and a network of educational and religious institutions, centres and mosques. Wahhabism advocates a literal interpretation of the Qur'an and seeks to reduce human judgement in its favour. Fundamentalist Wahhabism, which strives for a return to the Islam of the pious ancestors (Muhammad and his immediate successors), is puritanical and radical, and overlaps with Salafism. The latter, however, strives for a universal caliphate while Wahhabism is satisfied with local rule. It believes in predestination and advocates a state that follows only religious law. Believers have to demonstrate total obedience to the authorities. The Saudi dynasty entered a pact with the Wahhabists in 1744 and financed, with oil revenues, the expansion of Wahhabism abroad.

WAR White Aryan Resistance (United States). Neo-Nazi supremacist group.

War 'Collective, direct, manifest, personal, intentional, organised, institutionalised, instrumental, sanctioned, and sometimes ritualised and regulated, violence' (Van der Dennen, 1995). It is most often used for a situation of armed conflict between centrally directed military forces (professional or conscripted) of states that engage in battles to bring about victory. Since the twentieth century, the range of combatants has expanded to political units other than states, and includes warlords, private military companies, mercenaries, child soldiers, mujahedeen and other irregular fighters. The theatre of armed conflict has also expanded, and civilians rather than regular fighters bear the brunt of war. The Clausewitz conceptualisation regards war as an instrument for a political goal, such as settling a conflict issue with a rival state. Clausewitz's (1962: 212) definition of war as 'the continuation of politics with an admixture of other means' is still the most influential one. To him, interstate war was a form of coercive diplomacy: 'War is an instrument of policy. . . . The conduct of war . . . is policy itself which takes up the sword in place of the pen' (ibid.). While many eighteenth-century Enlightenment thinkers saw war as a cruel aberration, as an interruption of politics, Clausewitz postulated that war was an instrument the state employs for political ends, and that it was part and parcel of international relations and politics (Van Creveld, 1991: 124). The 'Clausewitzean' 'trinitarian' war with its implied unity of purpose of government + people + army is, however, challenged. As Martin van Creveld put it, 'Where armed force is directed by social entities that are not states, against social organizations that are not armies, and people who are not soldiers in our sense of the term, trinitarian concepts break down' (1991: 72). Given the dominance of internal wars, the relevance of Clausewitz's approach is to some extent diminished.

Many definitions of war exist. Whereas some modern definitions set minimum levels of fatalities (usually 1,000) among uniformed combatants, others include civilian deaths. Some definitions require that at least one of the actors is regular government forces and that the struggle is controlled on at least one side by a central authority which engages in a planned strategy. Others insist that acts of war must show a certain continuity or that there must be some symmetry between the actors (e.g. both being states).

War by proxy During the Cold War, this was an indirect form of superpower and medium-power confrontation in which client states were armed and used offensively to expand zones of influence (e.g. Soviet use of Cuba). The practice continued into the 1990s.

War crime Combat-related conduct of hostilities prohibited by the laws or customs of war, e.g. deliberate attacks on civilian non-combatants, killing of hostages, murder or ill-treatment of prisoners of war, deportation to slave labour of civilian population. In times of war, terrorist acts against non-combatants or civilian objects are prohibited as war crimes. Acts or threats of violence, the primary purpose of which is to spread terror among the civilian population, are also prohibited in internal armed conflicts, according to the Additional Protocol of 1977 to the Geneva Convention.

Warlordism A type of predatory rule by the gun in weak and failed states, whereby the civilian population is terrorised. Warlords maintain marauding gangs, sometimes small armies, rule by savagery and engage in looting, pillage, ransom, extortion, the extracting of tributes, and displacement of people in order to take their possessions and other forms of economic exploitation, largely independent from the state.

Weapon Instrument or device designed to kill, injure or disable people, or to damage or destroy property. Weapons include bombs, firearms, handguns, knives, fire and biological, chemical and radiological and nuclear agents.

Weapons of Mass Destruction Nuclear weapons, especially those based on plutonium-239 or uranium-235. The term also refers to biological weapons (which so far have not been used as WMD) and chemical weapons (which have caused tens of thousands of deaths, especially in the First World War). Historically, only nuclear weapons have so far been weapons of mass destruction. However, mass destruction has often been brought about by conventional weapons applied massively. Radiological weapons are more weapons of mass disruption than mass destruction and have so far not been used on a serious scale.

Weathermen Aka Weather Underground Organization (WUO). Members of a militant left-wing faction of the US Students for a Democratic Society (SDS), active between 1960 and 1976; some of them went underground and a number of them were killed in March 1970 when their explosives accidentally detonated in a New York townhouse. The group dissolved in 1977.

Wehrsportgruppe Hoffmann Military Sports Group Hoffmann. This group was a German neo-Nazi group led by Karl-Heinz Hoffman, responsible *inter alia* for an attack on the Munich Oktoberfest in September 1980.

White Hand Mano Blanco. A government-controlled right-wing death squad in Guatemala, active since 1966.

White Patriot Army White supremacist Ku Klux Klan-linked group based in North Carolina, opposing the 'Zionist occupation government' of the United States.

White Terror Atrocity tactics attributed to the White Guards, the armed opponents of the Bolsheviks in the Russian civil war, 1918–1921, in parallel to the much more serious Red Terror of the Communist regime.

Wired Refers to a person or object that carries or contains a concealed listening (and/or viewing) device for surveillance.

WNBF West Nile Bank Front (DR Congo, Uganda). The WNBF was founded in the early 1990s by followers of Idi Amin, Uganda's former dictator.

World Islamic Front for the Jihad against Jews and Crusaders One of the names used by Al-Qaeda.

World Islamic Jihad Group Yemen; possibly linked to the AAIA.

WTC World Trade Center; business building complex in Manhattan with the Twin Towers. A first failed attempt to topple it was made on 26 February 1993 by exploding a car in the underground garage; it killed six people and was masterminded by Ramzi Ahmed Yousef. The second attempt, with two hijacked passenger aircraft on 11 September 2001, was successful, killing 2,752 people in the towers and on the ground, in addition to those on the planes.

Wrath of God Mivtzan Elohim. A military commando unit originally created by Israel to hunt down perpetrators of the massacre of Israeli athletes at the Munich Olympic Games in 1972.

WTA World Tamil Association, aka World Tamil Movement, Ellalan Force, Sangilian Force, Federation of Associations of Canadian Tamils (FACT); linked to the LTTE.

WTC World Trade Center. Destroyed by Al-Qaeda on 11 September 2001 by crashing two civilian airliners into the Twin Towers, after having survived an earlier bomb attack in 1993.

WTO World Trade Organization.

WUO Weather Underground Organization. A splinter of the Weathermen, a US student-based group that emerged in the early 1970s.

Xenophobia Fear, distrust, dislike and aversion vis-à-vis strangers, foreigners, immigrants and political asylum seekers as individuals or as a group, resulting often in ethnocentrism and nationalism, and sometimes leading to political violence, including acts of terrorism.

YCL Young Communist League (India/Nepal) (Maoist).

Yellow fever virus A biological agent developed by the United States as a biological weapon.

Yemen Islamic Jihad Affiliated to Al-Qaeda; implicated in the attack on USS *Cole*.

***Yersinia pestis* (*Pasteurella pestis*)** Plague bacterium causing the 'black death'; named after its discoverer, A. Yersin.

Yersinia pseudotuberculosis A biological agent.

YMM Young Mujahideen Movement (Somalia).

Zakat Almsgiving – an obligation that is one of the five Pillars of Islam. *Zakat* has allegedly been abused to finance the terrorist activities of Al-Qaeda.

ZAPU Zimbabwe African People's Union. Founded by Robert Mugabe, who became leader of Zimbabwe in 1980.

Zealots Aka Sicarii ('those wielding daggers'). A group of Jewish insurgents who opposed Roman rule of Judaea, AD 66–70, by assassinating Roman officials and Jewish collaborators as well as kidnapping for ransom. When cornered by a Roman army in the Masada fortress, they committed collective suicide to escape capture.

Zionism A Jewish movement, founded in the late nineteenth century, fuelled by anti-Semitism in Europe, to create a Jewish national homeland in Palestine by means of migration and a revival of the Hebrew language. It resulted in the unilateral declaration of the state of Israel in 1948 and the subsequent expulsion and flight of hundreds of thousands of Palestinians.

ZOG Zionist occupation government. The neo-Nazi term for the US government.

ZRA Zomi Revolutionary Army (India, north-east). Founded in 1997.

Sources and references

Anderson, Sean and Stephen Sloan. *Historical Dictionary of Terrorism*. Metuchen, NJ: Scarecrow Press, 1995.

Bar, Shmuel. 'The Religious Sources of Islamic Terrorism'. Herzliya, Ismal: Institute for Policy and Strategy, Interdisciplinary Center Herzliya. Paper, n.d.

Bauer, Kirsten. *Fundamentalismus*. Munich: Wilhelm Heyne Verlag, 1999, p. 38.

Billing, Peter. *Eskalation und Deeskalation internationaler Konflikte: Ein Konfliktmodel auf der Grundlage der empirischen Auswertung von 288 internationalen Konflikten seit 1945*. Frankfurt an Main: P. Lang, 1992.

Bloomfield, L.P. and Allen Moulton. *Managing International Conflict*. New York: St Martin's Press, 1997.

Boulding, Kenneth. *Three Faces of Power*. Newbury Park, PA: Sage, 1989.

Buijs, Frank J. *Democratie en terreur: de uitdaging van het islamistisch extremisme*. Amsterdam: Uitgeverij SWP, 2002.

Buijs, Frank, Demant, Froukje and Atjef Hamdy. *Home Grown Warriors: Radical and Democratic Muslims in the Netherlands*. Amsterdam: Amsterdam University Press, 2007.

Burgess, Heidi and Guy M. Burgess. *Encyclopedia of Conflict Resolution*. Santa Barbara, CA: ABC-CLIO, 1997.

Burke, Jason. *Al-Qaeda: The True Story of Radical Islam*. London: Penguin Books, 2004.

Burke, Robert. *Counter-terrorism for Emergency Responders*. Boca Raton, FL: Lewis, 2000.

Carnegie Commission on Preventing Deadly Conflict. *Preventing Deadly Conflict*. Final Report. New York: Carnegie Corporation, 1997.

Cassese, Antonio. *International Criminal Law*. Oxford: Oxford University Press, 2003.

Clausewitz, Carl von. *On War*. Princeton, NJ: Princeton University Press.

Cook, David. *Understanding Jihad*. Berkeley: University of California Press, 2005.

Crenshaw, Martha and John Pimlott (eds). *Encyclopedia of World Terrorism*. Armonk, NY: M.E. Sharpe, 1997.

Demurenko, Andrei and Alexander Nikitin. 'Basic Terminology and Concepts in International Peacekeeping Operations: An Analytical Review'. *Low Intensity Conflict and Law Enforcement*, 6(1) (Summer 1997).

Eckstein, Harry. 'On the Etiology of Internal Wars'. Originally published in 1965 in *History and Theory*, 4(2), pp. 133–162; reprinted in Ivo K. Feierabend, Rosalind L. Feierabend and Ted Robert Gurr. *Anger, Violence and Politics: Theories and Research*. Englewood Cliffs, NJ: Prentice Hall, 1972, pp. 9–30.

Elliott, Florence. *A Dictionary of Politics*. Harmondsworth, UK: Penguin, 1969.

Evans, Graham and Jeffrey Newnham. *The Dictionary of World Politics: A Reference Guide to Concepts, Ideas and Institutions*. London: Harvester Wheatsheaf, 1992.

Evers, D., M. Miller and T. Glover. *Pocket Partner*. Littleton, CO: Sequoia Publishing, 2003.

Fighel, Jonathan. 'Sheik Abdullah Azzam: Bin Laden's Spiritual Mentor' (27 September 2001), at www.ict.org.il/articles/articledet.cfm?articleid=388; cited in Patrick Sookhdeo. *Understanding Islamic Terrorism*. Pewsey, UK: Isaac Publishing, 2004, pp. 60–61.

Ford, James L. 'Radiological Dispersal Devices: Assessing the Transnational Threat'. *Strategic Forum*, no. 136, March 1998, pp. 1–6 at p. 3.

Galtung, Johan. 'Cultural Violence'. *Journal of Peace Research*, 27(3), August 1990, pp. 145–165.

Galtung, Johan. *Peace by Peaceful Means: Peace and Conflict, Development and Civilization*. London: Sage, 1996.

Glasl, Friedrich. 'Konfliktmanagement'. In Berthold Meyer (ed.), *Forman der Konfliktregelung*. Opladen, Germany: Leske + Budrich, 1997, pp. 145–65.

Goor, L.L.P. van. *Conflict and Development: The Causes of Conflict in Developing Countries*. The Hague: NIIR, Clingendael, 1994.

Guirard, Jim. 'Three Mini Glossaries to Fellow Word Warriors'. Alexandria, VA: TrueSpeak Institute, 2007.

Gurr, T.R. 'Early-Warning Systems: From Surveillance to Assessment to Action'. In Kevin M. Cahill (ed.). *Preventive Diplomacy. Stopping Wars Before They Start*. New York: Basic Books, 1996.

Haas, Ernst B. 'Beware the Slippery Slope: Notes toward the Definition of Justifiable Intervention'. In Laura W. Reed and Carl Kaysen (eds). *Emerging Norms of Justified Intervention*. Cambridge, MA: American Academy of Arts and Sciences, 1993, pp. 63–87.

Harris, Sam. *The End of Faith: Religion, Terror, and the Future of Reason*. London: The Free Press, 2006.

Henderson, Harry. *Global Terrorism: The Complete Reference Guide*. New York: Checkmark Books, 2001.

Hess, Henner. 'Repressives Verbrechen'. *Kriminologisches Journal*, 8(1), 1976.

Heywood, Andrew. *Politics*. London: Macmillan, 1997.

Hoffman, Stanley. 'Commentary on Ernst B. Haas' "Beware the Slippery Slope: Notes toward the Definition of Justifiable Intervention" '. In Laura W. Reed and Carl Kaysen (eds). *Emerging Norms of Justified Intervention*. Cambridge, MA: American Academy of Arts and Sciences, 1993, pp. 88–89.

Holsti, K.J. *International Politics: A Framework for Analysis*. Englewood Cliffs, NJ: Prentice Hall, 1977 and 1988.

International Institute for Strategic Studies. *The Military Balance, 2001–2002*. Oxford: Oxford University Press, 2001.

Jenkins, Brian Michael. 'Foreword'. In Ian O. Lesser, Bruce Hoffman, John Arquilla *et al. Countering the New Terrorism*. St Monica, CA: RAND, 1999.

Jeuken, G.D. 'Analyzing Corporate Political Risk: Towards Operational Relevance: An Integration of PRA and Scenario Techniques'. Master's thesis, Leiden, Department of Political Sciences, 1996.

Jongman, Albert J. 'Preventing Violent Conflict: Methods and Actors in the Field of Preventive Diplomacy'. In A.P. Schmid (ed.). *Violent Crime and Conflicts*. Milan: ISPAC, 1997, pp. 85–106.

Jongman, Albert J. and Alex P. Schmid. *Monitoring Human Rights: Manual for Assessing Country Performance*. Leiden: PIOOM Foundation, 1994.

Kegley, Charles Jr and Eugene R. Wittkopf. *World Politics: Trends and Transformation*, 7th edition. London: Macmillan, 1999.

Keppel, Gilles. *Jijhad: The Trail of Political Islam*. Cambridge, MA: Belknap Press, 2002.

Kinsella, David and Herbert K. Tillema. 'Arms and Aggression in the Middle East: Overt Military Interventions, 1948–1991'. *Journal of Conflict Resolution*, 39(2), June 1995, pp. 306–329.

Krieger, D.M. 'What Happens If . . .? Terrorists, Revolutionaries, and Nuclear Weapons'. *Annals of the American Academy of Political and Social Science*, 430, 1977, pp. 44–57.

Kuper, Adam and Jessica Kuper (eds). *The Social Science Encyclopaedia*. London: Routledge & Kegan Paul, 1985.

Kushner, Harvey W. *Encyclopedia of Terrorism*. Thousand Oaks, CA: Sage, 2003.

Leemhuis, Fred. 'De djihaad in de vroege Islam'. In Martin Gosman and Hans Bakker (eds). *Heilige oorlogen: een onderzoek naar historische en hedendaagse vormen van collectief religious geweld*. Kampen, Netherlands: Kok Agora, 1991, p. 54.

Löckinger, Georg. *Terrorismus, Terrorismusabwehr, Terrorismusbekämpfung*. Vienna: Landesverteidigungsakademie, 2006.

Lutz, Ernst. *Lexikon zur Sicherheitspolitik*. Munich: C.H. Beck Verlag, 1980.

Maoz, Zeev. *Paths to Conflict: International Dispute Initiation, 1816–1976*. Boulder, CO: Westview, 1982.

Marshall European Center for Security Studies. *Glossary of Terms*. Garmisch-Partenkirchen, Germany: Marshall Center, 2002, pp. 18–19.

Martin, Gus. *Understanding Terrorism: Challenges, Perspectives, and Issues*. Thousand Oaks, CA: Sage, 2003.

Mattox, Henry E. *Chronology of World Terrorism, 1901–2001*. Jefferson, NC: McFarland, 2004.

Medhurst, Paul. *Global Terrorism*. New York: UNITAR, 2000. Annex B: Glossary of Terms, pp. 175–80.

Memorial Institute for the Prevention of Terrorism. *Terrorism Knowledge Base*. Oklahoma City: MIPT, August 2006.

Morgenthau, Hans. *Politics among Nations: The Struggle for Power and Peace*. New York: Alfred A. Knopf, 1948.

Napoleoni, Loretta. *Modern Jihad: Tracing the Dollars Behind the Terror Networks*. London: Pluto Press, 2003.

Nicolaïdis, Kalypso. 'International Preventive Action: Developing a Strategic Framework'. In R. O. Rotberg (ed.). *Vigilance and Vengeance: NGOs Preventing Ethnic Conflict in Divided Societies*. Washington, DC: Brookings Institution Press, 1996.

Nohlen, Dieter *et al.* (eds). *Politische Theorien und politische Begriffe*, vols 1 and 7 of *Lexikon der Politik*. Munich: C.H. Beck, 1998.

Norris, Robert S., Thomas B. Cochran and William M. Arkin. 'History of the Nuclear Stockpile'. *Bulletin of the Atomic Scientists*, 1985, p. 106; cited in William D. Perdue. *Terrorism and the State: A Critique of Domination through Fear*. New York: Praeger, 1989, p. 82.

Parkinson, Roger. *Encyclopaedia of Modern War*. London: Paladin, 1979.

Peters, Ruud. 'Djihaad tussen wettig gezag en revolutie: de heilige oorlog in de hedendaagse Islam'. In: Martin Gosman and Hans Bakker (eds). *Heilige oorlogen*. Kampen, Netherlands: Kok Agora, 1991, pp. 178–179.

Richardson, Jacques G. 'Optimizing the Terrorist Dialogue: Overcoming Fear; Approach and Transaction; Expectations'. Authon la Plaine, Manuscript, 2007.

Roberts, Geoffrey K. *A Dictionary of Political Analysis*. London: Longman, 1971.

Robin, Corey. *Fear: The History of a Political Idea*. Oxford: Oxford University Press, 2004.

Roy, Oliver. *Globalized Islam: The Search for a New Ummah*. London: Hurst, 2004.

Schleifer, Ron. 'Psychological Operations: A New Variation on an Age Old Art: Hezbollah versus Israel'. *Studies in Conflict and Terrorism*, 29(1), 2006, pp. 1–19.

Schmid, Alex P. 'The Problems of Defining Terrorism'. In M. Crenshaw and J. Pimlott (eds). *Encyclopedia of World Terrorism*. Armonk, NY: M.E. Sharpe, vol. 1, 1997, pp. 12–22.

Schmid, Alex P. *Thesaurus and Glossary of Early Warning and Conflict Prevention Terms*. London: FEWER, 2000.

Schmid, Alex P. and Albert J. Jongman *et al. Political Terrorism: A New Guide to Actors, Authors, Concepts, Data Bases, Theories and Literature*. Amsterdam: North-Holland, 1988.

Scruton, Roger. *A Dictionary of Political Thought*, 2nd edition. London: Macmillan, 1996.

Sederberg, P.C. *Terrorist Myths*. Englewood Cliffs, NJ: Prentice Hall, 1989.

Sfeir, Antoine *et al. Dictionnaire mondial de l'Islamisme*. Paris: Plon, 2002.

Shafritz, Jay M., E.F. Gibbons Jr and Gregory E.J. Scott. *Almanac of Modern Terrorism*. New York: Facts On File, 1991.

Steven, Graeme C.S. and Rohan Gunaratna. *Counterterrorism: A Reference Handbook*. Santa Barbara, CA: ABC-CLIO, 2004.

Thackrah, John Richard. *Encyclopaedia of Terrorism and Political Violence*. London: Routledge & Kegan Paul, 1987.

Tilly, Charles. *European Revolutions, 1492–1992*. Oxford: Blackwell, 1993.

Treverton, Gregory F. and Bruce W. Bennett. *Integrating Counterproliferation into Defense Planning*. Santa Monica, CA: RAND, Issue Paper, 1997.

United Kingdom, Government, Intelligence and Security Committee. 'Report into the London Terrorism

Attacks on 7 July 2005' (chairman: Paul Murphy, MP), presented to Parliament by the Prime Minister, London, 2006 (Cm 6785).

Van Creveld, Martin. *The Transformation of War*. New York: Free Press, 1991.

Van der Dennen, J.M.G. *The Origins of War: The Evolution of a Male-Coalitional Reproductive Strategy*. Groningen: Origin Press, 1995.

Weinberg, Leonard and Amy Pedahzur. *Political Parties and Terrorist Groups*. London: Routledge, 2003.

Weiner, M. 'Peoples and States in a New Ethnic Order?' *Third World Quarterly*, 13(2), 1992, pp. 317–333.

Wilkinson, Paul. *Terrorism versus Democracy: The Liberal State Response*, 2nd edition. London: Routledge, 2006.

Williams, Clive. *Terrorism Explained: The Facts about Terrorism and Terrorist Groups*. Sydney: New Holland, 2004.

Wood, James L. and Maurice Jackson. *Social Movements: Development, Participation, and Dynamics*. Belmont, CA: Wadsworth, 1982.

Yallop, H.J. *Explosion Investigation*. Harrogate, UK: Forensic Science Society, 1980.

Zimmerman, John C. 'Jihad, Theory and Practice: a Review Essay'. *Terrorism and Political Violence*, 19(2), Summer 2007, pp. 279–287.

Acknowledgement

The author wishes to thank Dr Peter Lehr (CSTPV, University of St Andrews) for providing a number of entries referring to maritime matters.

INDEX

Note: Page numbers ending in 'f' refer to figures, ending in 'n' refer to notes, and ending in 't' refer to tables.